JUDICIAL REVIEW HANDBOOK

FIFTH EDITION

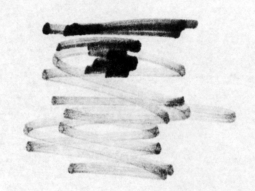

JUDICIAL REVIEW HANDBOOK

FIFTH EDITION

by

Michael Fordham QC

Blackstone Chambers, London
www.blackstonechambers.com

BA (Oxon) BCL (Oxon) LLM (Virginia)
Human Rights Lawyer of the Year 2005
Public Law Junior of the Year 2005
Bar Pro Bono Award 2006
Human Rights and Public Law Silk of the Year 2008
College Lecturer, Hertford College, Oxford
michaelfordham@blackstonechambers.com

Foreword by
The Rt Hon The Lord Woolf, former Lord Chief Justice

·HART·
PUBLISHING

OXFORD – PORTLAND OREGON
2008

Published in North America (US and Canada) by
Hart Publishing
c/o International Specialized Book Services
920 NE 58th Avenue, Suite 300
Portland, OR 97213-3786
USA
Tel: +1 503 287 3093 or toll-free: (1) 800 944 6190
Fax: +1 503 280 8832
E-mail: orders@isbs.com
Website: http://www.isbs.com

Hart Publishing Ltd, 16C Worcester Place, Oxford, OX1 2JW
Telephone: +44 (0)1865 517530 Fax: +44 (0)1865 510710
E-mail: mail@hartpub.co.uk
Website: http://www.hartpub.co.uk

British Library Cataloguing in Publication Data
Data Available

ISBN: 978-1-84113-824-4
Typesetting: Michael Fordham and Hope Services (Abingdon) Ltd
Editorial and Production Manager: Melanie Hamill
Proof-reading and Quote-Checking: Douglas McMahon, Ruth Turvey
Indexing: Chantal Hamill
Tabling: Deborah Harris

Printed and bound in Great Britain on acid-free paper by
TJ International Ltd, Padstow, Cornwall

Related Journal: *Judicial Review* (quarterly since 1996)
Editors: Michael Fordham and James Maurici
Consultant Editors: The Rt Hon Michael Beloff QC and Lord Woolf of Barnes

For Foxy

FOREWORD

by Lord Woolf, former Lord Chief Justice

Writing in January 1994 (First Edition): This 'Handbook' adopts an entirely novel approach to make available the vast volume of material which now constitutes the corpus of administrative law. It is an approach which I have found, having used a pre-publication version of the book, works extremely well in practice. Over the years administrative law, which is the law applied on applications for judicial review, has grown like Topsy. The application of the law involves, so far as this is possible, identifying from a mass of case law the underlying principles. This is just what the Handbook helps to achieve. It works by identifying the principles and then setting out the authorities which support those principles. The principles may have to be reconsidered as the case law develops but in their present form they provide an admirable base from which to start and the copious references by which they are supported provide an extremely important resource.

The Handbook is therefore a valuable addition to the literature which is available on judicial review. As its virtues become known I feel confident it will prove popular with everyone who is concerned with judicial review and in particular those who practise in the public law field, among whom I include the judiciary.

Its title includes the word 'Handbook'. While I understand the use of this word as part of the title and appreciate that practitioners will certainly find the book 'handy', I very much hope that the use of the word 'Handbook' will not give the impression that it deals with the subject superficially. This is very far from the case. The 'Handbook' skilfully absorbs a remarkable amount of learning. I hope that it has the extremely bright future it deserves.

Writing in March 1997 (Second Edition): I have the highest expectations of the second edition having frequently used the first edition.

Writing in September 2001 (Third Edition): I expressed the hope in 1994, that the Handbook would have the bright future it deserved. I am delighted that my hopes have been fulfilled. If we needed the first edition our needs are greater now for a third edition. In the intervening seven years the pace of the development of judicial review has continued to accelerate and the Human Rights Act has now acted as a catalyst.

During those seven years the Handbook has regularly come to my aid. I, like many other lawyers and jurists, have become addicted to it. It is our first port of call when we have an administrative law problem. So I am delighted that there is to be an up to the minute third edition. I am also delighted to be able to predict that it will be at least as successful and as valuable to those involved in public law as the two previous editions.

Writing in September 2004 (Fourth Edition): I am delighted to have this opportunity of welcoming the 4th edition of this most valuable Handbook.

One of the great strengths of judicial review is that it has been entirely created through the decisions of the courts over the years. As it has evolved so have the principles around which it is structured. The foundations are sound and courts continue to build upon them.

However, as a result the number of authoritative cases continues to grow. Not even the most able and experienced practitioners or judges can possibly keep abreast with the continuously increasing number of authorities. For both, the Handbook is a most valuable resource.

Certainly, in my work I find the Handbook extremely valuable and I am delighted that there is once again an up-to-date edition so I can again, having consulted it, know that there is no important decision which I have overlooked.

The Human Rights Act made the author's task even more difficult but he can be relied upon not to let standards slip. I am confident that this new edition will cause public lawyers, irrespective of the sphere in which they work, to share my enthusiasm for the Handbook.

FOREWORD TO THE FIFTH EDITION

I am delighted to welcome the 5th edition of this volume, which has become an institution for those who practise public law. Ever since the first edition, I have been a great admirer of the Handbook and its author. When I wrote the foreword for the first edition, I was very optimistic about its prospects and it gives me pleasure in regard to the Handbook to have had my judgements proved correct.

This edition has of necessity been the subject of significant and strategic pruning. The Handbook was in danger of being smothered by its own success. Such has been the growth of its contents, matching the growth of judicial review that there was a danger of its no longer being so convenient to use. However, unsurprisingly, Michael Fordham has recognised this danger and ensured that his pruning has eradicated it. As with the previous editions, the subject is still treated in sufficient depth; it retains the best of the past while including the most recent cases, with which practitioners, judges and academics have to keep abreast.

In the first edition, Michael Fordham made clear that as a practitioner of judicial review, he was a novice. That is far from the position today. He is now one of the most distinguished leaders in this field at the Bar, as has been acknowledged by his being declared Chambers UK's Human Rights and Public Law Silk of the Year 2008; an award which, from my own knowledge, he richly deserves. The selection of the cases included in the latest edition has, therefore, an authority which was absent from the first edition. It has the authority that comes from being compiled by an author of singular distinction.

Lord Woolf
House of Lords
October 13, 2008

PREFACE

Much can be achieved in public law through instinct, experience and familiarity with general principles which are broad, flexible and designed to accord with common sense. Nevertheless, the case-law—overwhelming in its volume and flow—is an indispensable source. It gives us authoritative exposition and working illustration. There is almost always a case which helps on the point you are considering. The challenge is to find it.

When I wrote the first edition of this Handbook, never—I confess—having actually done a judicial review case, I focused on the primary sources: the decided cases. My aim was to read as many as a I could and try to extract, classify and present illustrations and statements of principle. Into this fifth edition, that is still my approach. I keep the Handbook up to date using Lawtel and the law reports.

I have culled many of the case references from the previous edition, resisting the strong temptation to add and never subtract, trying to achieve a manageable size and density. Older references can always be found in previous editions. The Case Synopses, printed within previous editions, are no longer here but are instead freely available for reference at *www.judicialreviewhandbook.com.*

I found myself preparing this edition at the moment at which Lord Bingham has retired as our Senior Law Lord. It has proved to be a most opportune time to take stock. Lord Bingham's rulings and reasoning, overflowing with pithy insights, will guide practitioners and judges for decades to come. His is an immense and lasting contribution: a Binghamised public law.

My thanks to Richard Hart and the Hart Publishing team; my clerks at Blackstone Chambers; and my long-suffering family: Alison (foxy), Anna, Bradley and Lois. The idea that comforts me when I disappear to the attic—that I am not "working" but "doing my book"—is, to them, rightly a distinction without a difference.

Michael Fordham QC
Blackstone Chambers, London
www.blackstonechambers.com
michaelfordham@blackstonechambers.com
30th September 2008

TABLE OF CONTENTS

A. NATURE OF JUDICIAL REVIEW
keys to understanding what the Court is doing (P1–P25)

B. PARAMETERS OF JUDICIAL REVIEW

further dominant themes shaping the law and practice (P26–P44)

* Note: Some recent case references were added post-preparation of the Table of Cases.

JUDICIAL REVIEW HANDBOOK

a detailed guide to the law and practice

containing:
principles (P1 etc)
outline commentary (1.1 etc)
illustrations (1.1.1 etc)

cross-references:
<1.1> means "see para 1.1"

A. THE NATURE OF JUDICIAL REVIEW

keys to understanding what the Court is doing

<1.1> means "see para 1.1"

```
┌─────────────────────────────────────────────────────────────┐
│          P1 Practical steps. A judicial review case involves  │
│          a series of prescribed and case-managed steps.       │
└─────────────────────────────────────────────────────────────┘
```

1.1 Basic steps in a judicial review case

1.1 **Basic steps in a judicial review case**.[1] Judicial review proceedings generally involve a sequence of familiar practical steps, taken by the parties. Attention needs to be paid to the rules, especially Part 54 of the Civil Procedure Rules (CPR 54) and the Part 54 Practice Direction (CPR 54PD), the Administrative Court Office's *Notes for Guidance* (ACO:NFG) and the Judicial Review Pre-Action Protocol (JR:PAP) and Urgent Cases Procedure (JR:UCP). There is a vast amount of case-law giving guidance on the principles and approach to judicial review.

Key sources can be found at the end of this book:
64.1	Supreme Court Act 1981 s.31 **(SCA s.31)**
64.2	Civil Procedure Rules Part 54(I) **(CPR 54)**
64.3	Civil Procedure Rules Part 54 Practice Direction **(CPR 54PD)**
64.4	Administrative Court Office Notes for Guidance **(ACO:NFG)**
64.5	Judicial Review Pre Action Protocol **(JR:PAP)**
64.6	Judicial Review Urgent Cases Procedure **(JR:UCP)**
64.7	Human Rights Act 1998 **(HRA)**

1.1.1 **Potential claim.** Where someone is aggrieved about something done (or not done) by a public authority, they can obtain specialist legal advice (as may the public authority). In assessing the potential for judicial review it is helpful to consider: (1) whether there is a reviewable act or omission; (2) on what ground might it be challenged; (3) when would be the right time for such a challenge; (4) what judicial review would achieve; and (5) whether it can be achieved by other means. There may be no substitute for early, specialist legal advice. It is necessary for the claimant to act promptly.

1.1.2 **Letter before claim (LBC).** The potential claimant should generally write a letter before claim, preferably using the suggested format. This is the chance to persuade the public authority, and at what is effectively a no-cost-risk stage, to accommodate your concern rather than face being judicially reviewed. It is also an opportunity to outline the envisaged challenge, ask questions and request documents. The letter should be written very promptly, sent to the relevant public authority and those who would be an interested party in (ie. directly affected by) the judicial review proceedings. It is normal to specify 14 days for reply.

1.1.3 **Letter of response (LOR).** Having received the LBC, the defendant public authority has the chance to back down gracefully, usually without any exposure to the claimant's pre-action costs, and may agree to accommodate the claimant's grievance, whether (1) because the proposed claim is a strong one or (2) because good sense and pragmatism allow the position to be modified or revisited as requested. Otherwise, this is a good opportunity to seek to persuade the claimant's team that the proposed claim is unfounded, and to draw attention to any material, provision or authority which they may have overlooked.

1.1.4 **Claim bundle.** The claimant's team needs to draft a claim form (N461) and supporting grounds, having the dual-purpose of (1) an appetizer speedily to interest a busy permission

---

[1] As to practice and procedure, see James Findlay [2005] JR 27; Michael Fordham [2005] JR 90; John Halford [2006] JR 153; Andrew Lidbetter [2007] JR 99; Paul Brown [2006] JR 325.

judge and (2) a framework for a substantive hearing. The claim should face up to any discretionary hurdle (delay, alternative remedy etc) and fit within a paginated indexed bundle generally including a witness statement, documentary evidence and key legal materials. The claim must be lodged promptly or with good reason for delay. Include an essential reading list and any suggested directions. Double-sided copying is environmentally responsible and perfectly satisfactory (they do it that way in the House of Lords). There is a fee to pay on lodging and the bundle must be served on defendants and other directly affected parties.

1.1.5 **Acknowledgment of service (AOS).** The AOS is the opportunity for the defendant or interested party, served with the claim bundle, to respond with summary grounds which show the permission judge (1) that permission for judicial review should be refused (with assessed costs of preparing the AOS) or (2) what case-management directions should be given for the future conduct of the case. Entrenchment should be avoided and consideration should be given as to whether (a) to concede the claim or accommodate the complaint or (b) to agree to permission being given. The claimant may contact the Administrative Court Office to secure the opportunity to lodge a brief reply to the summary grounds.

1.1.6 **Permission.** A judge will look at the papers and decide whether to grant permission. If permission is adjourned into open court, or refused on the papers, the claimant can pursue the matter at an oral hearing. The oral permission-stage hearing may also deal with ancillary matters, including interim remedies, expedition, protective costs orders and case-management directions. If permission is refused after an oral hearing, the claimant may appeal to the Court of Appeal.

1.1.7 **Detailed response.** After the grant of permission for judicial review, the defendant and any interested party must lodge their detailed grounds of response and evidence in support. The claimant may lodge evidence in reply.

1.1.8 **Skeletons/bundles.** In the run up to the substantive hearing, the claimant must lodge a hearing bundle and a skeleton argument, to which the defendant and interested parties will reply with their own skeletons. The parties will also lodge bundles of the authorities relied on. As always, double-sided copying is environmentally responsible and perfectly satisfactory (they do it that way in the HL).

1.1.9 **Substantive hearing.** At the hearing, advocates for the parties will supplement their written skeletons by oral submissions made to a judge who will have pre-read some of the key papers. Judgment will be given, often at a later date, and the important questions of costs and permission to appeal to the Court of Appeal will then be dealt with.

1.1.10 **Appeal.** Appeal is to the Court of Appeal (in a civil case) and the parties need to comply with the rules in CPR 52. The appellant must begin by lodging an appellant's notice and bundle, together with a skeleton at the outset if permission to appeal was refused below. It is imperative that all skeletons and bundles are lodged in good time for the substantive appeal hearing. Appeals to the House of Lords are governed by the HL Practice Directions.

> **P2 Supervisory jurisdiction.** By judicial review the Administrative
> Court exercises a supervisory role over public bodies.

2.1 Supervising public authorities. Judicial review is a central control mechanism of administrative law (public law), by which the judiciary take the historic constitutional responsibility of protecting against abuses of power by public authorities. It is an important safeguard which promotes the public interest, assists public bodies to act lawfully and ensures that they are not above the law, and protects the rights and interests of those affected by the exercise of public authority power. This special supervisory jurisdiction is different from both (1) ordinary (adversarial) litigation between private parties and (2) an appeal (rehearing) on the merits. The question is not whether the judge disagrees with what the public body has done, but whether there is some recognisable public law wrong. The procedure has evolved, and the rules have been reformed and refined.

2.1.1 Supervision of public authorities. ACO:NFG <64.4> para 2.1.
(A) CONTROLLING ADMINISTRATIVE ACTION. *Council of Civil Service Unions v Minister for the Civil Service* [1985] AC 374, 408E (Lord Diplock: "Judicial review ... provides the means by which judicial control of administrative action is exercised"); *R (Beeson) v Dorset County Council* [2002] EWCA Civ 1812 [2003] UKHRR 353 at [17] ("The basis of judicial review rests in the free-standing principle that every action of a public body must be justified by law, and at common law the High Court is the arbiter of all claimed justifications"); *HM Government Consultation Paper: Access to Justice With Conditional Fees* (March 1998) ("the Government believes that the ability to challenge the acts or omissions of public authorities is a necessary check on the use of the power of the State, and a positive encouragement to maintain high standards in public administration by public bodies").
(B) RESTRAINING ABUSES. *R v Secretary of State for the Home Department, ex p Brind* [1991] 1 AC 696, 751B (Lord Templeman: "judicial review [is] a remedy invented by the judges to restrain the excess or abuse of power"); *R v Secretary of State for the Environment, ex p Greater London Council* 3rd April 1985 unrep. ("judicial review ... aims to provide a prompt remedy for an obvious injustice"); *R v Horseferry Road Magistrates' Court, ex p Bennett* [1994] 1 AC 42, 62B ("The great growth of administrative law during the latter half of this century has occurred because of the recognition by the judiciary and Parliament alike that it is the function of the High Court to ensure that executive action is exercised responsibly and as Parliament intended"); *R (International Transport Roth GmbH) v Secretary of State for the Home Department* [2002] EWCA Civ 158 [2003] QB 728 at [27] (under the HRA, "the court's role ... is as the guardian of human rights"); <12.1.4> (judicial review as a protection).
(C) SECURING OBEDIENCE TO LAW. *Sheffield City Council v Smart* [2002] EWCA Civ 4 [2002] HLR 639 at [20] (judicial review as "the means by which the exercise of power by any public authority is strictly limited to the scope and purposes of the power's grant, and subjected also to the common law's insistence on rationality and fairness", with the Human Rights Act 1998 as "a condition of the lawful exercise of power by every public authority");*R v Secretary of State for Transport, ex p London Borough of Richmond Upon Thames (No.3)* [1995] Env LR 409, 415 ("the purpose of judicial review is to ensure that government is conducted within the law"); *Mercury Energy Ltd v Electricity Corporation of New Zealand Ltd* [1994] 1 WLR 521,

526A ("Judicial review was a judicial invention to secure that decisions are made by the executive or by a public body according to law"); <12.1> (judicial review and the rule of law).

2.1.2 Judicial review as the domain of the High Court. *R v Secretary of State for the Home Department, ex p Malhi* [1991] 1 QB 194, 205C-D ("judicial review is and has always been a matter for the High Court and not for an inferior tribunal"); *Adan v Newham London Borough Council* [2001] EWCA Civ 1916 [2002] 1 WLR 2120; Supreme Court Act 1981 s.31 <64.1>; County Courts Act 1984 s.38(3)(a); Courts and Legal Services Act 1990 s.1(10).

2.1.3 The constitutional dimension.[2] *R (Baiai) v Secretary of State for the Home Department* [2008] UKHL 53 [2008] 3 WLR 549 at [25] (Lord Bingham: "the court cannot abdicate its function of deciding whether as a matter of law the [statutory] scheme, as promulgated and operated, violate[s] the ... [Convention] right"); *R v Ministry of Defence, ex p Smith* [1996] QB 517, 556D-E ("the court [has] the constitutional role and duty of ensuring that the rights of citizens are not abused by the unlawful exercise of executive power" and "must not shrink from its fundamental duty to 'do right to all manner of people'"); *R v Secretary of State for the Home Department, ex p Fire Brigades Union* [1995] 2 AC 513, 567D-568B ("The courts interpret the laws, and see that they are obeyed. This requires the courts on occasion to step into the territory which belongs to the executive, to verify not only that the powers asserted accord with the substantive law created by Parliament but also that the manner in which they are exercised conforms with the standards of fairness which Parliament must have intended... To avoid a vacuum in which the citizen would be left without protection against a misuse of executive powers the courts have had no option but to occupy the dead ground ... Absent a written constitution much sensitivity is required of the parliamentarian, administrator and judge if the delicate balance of the unwritten rules evolved ... is not to be disturbed, and all the recent advances undone"); <7.2.2> (the separation of powers as a constitutional principle).

2.1.4 Supervisory jurisdiction in a nutshell.[3] *Reid v Secretary of State for Scotland* [1999] 2 AC 512, 541F-542A (Lord Clyde: "Judicial review involves a challenge to the legal validity of the decision. It does not allow the court of review to examine the evidence with a view to forming its own view about the substantial merits of the case. It may be that the tribunal whose decision is being challenged has done something which it had no lawful authority to do. It may have abused or misused the authority which it had. It may have departed from the procedures which either by statute or at common law as a matter of fairness it ought to have observed. As regards the decision itself it may be found to be perverse, or irrational, or grossly disproportionate to what was required. Or the decision may be found to be erroneous in respect of a legal deficiency, as for example, through the absence of evidence, or of sufficient evidence, to support it, or through account being taken of irrelevant matter, or through a failure for any reason to take account of a relevant matter, or through some misconstruction of the terms of the statutory provision which the decision-maker is required to apply. But while the evidence may have to be explored in order to see if the decision is vitiated by such legal deficiencies it is perfectly clear that in a case of review, as distinct from an ordinary appeal, the court may not set about forming its own preferred view of the evidence"); *R (Q) v Secretary of State for the Home Department* [2003] EWCA Civ 364 [2004] QB 36 at [112] ("Starting from the received checklist of justiciable errors set out by Lord Diplock in [*GCHQ*] [1985] AC 374, the courts ...

---

[2] Nicholas Bamforth & Peter Leyland [2003] JR 157; Christopher Forsyth & Elizabeth Kong [2004] JR 17.

[3] Michael Fordham, 'Judicial Review Cheat Sheet' [2003] JR 131.

have developed an issue-sensitive scale of intervention to enable them to perform their constitutional function in an increasingly complex polity. They continue to abstain from merits review - in effect, retaking the decision on the facts - but in appropriate classes of case they will today look very closely at the process by which facts have been ascertained and at the logic of the inferences drawn from them. Beyond this, courts of judicial review have been competent since the decision in [*Anisminic*] [1969] 2 AC 147 to correct any error of law whether or not it goes to jurisdiction; and since the coming into effect of the Human Rights Act 1998, errors of law have included failures by the state to act compatibly with the Convention"); *R v Panel on Take-overs and Mergers, ex p Datafin Plc* [1987] QB 815, 842F-H ("an application for judicial review is not an appeal. The panel and not the court is the body charged with the duty of evaluating the evidence and finding the facts. The role of the court is wholly different. It is, in an appropriate case, to review the decision of the panel and to consider whether there has been `illegality', ... `irrationality', ... or `procedural impropriety'"); *In re Michael Nwafor* [1994] Imm AR 91, 93 (referring to the need for "some legal error cognisable in public law").

2.1.5 History and Reform.
(A) THE HISTORICAL CONTEXT. Sir Stephen Sedley, *The Common Law and the Constitution* in *The Making and Remaking of the British Constitution* (1997) p.19 ("it was in fact the Victorian judges ... who were responsible for first turning judicial review into a developed system for supervising the lower courts and official bodies to whom state power was being systematically delegated. It was in their judgments that you will first find the tests of lawful decision-making which Lord Greene MR later summarised in the *Wednesbury* case"); *R v Somerset County Council, ex p Dixon* [1998] Env LR 111, 119 ("there turns out to be little which was not considered and decided in the great flowering of English public law between the 1860s and the First World War").
(B) THE 1977/1981 REFORMS. *M v Home Office* [1994] 1 AC 377, 417f (describing "[t]he changes made in procedure introduced in 1977 by RSC Ord 53 for judicial review", "given statutory authority by primary legislation in s.31 of the Supreme Court Act 1981"); *R v Inland Revenue Commissioners, ex p National Federation of Self-Employed and Small Businesses Ltd* [1982] AC 617, 638E-F ("a single simplified procedure"), 657E-F (changes "designed to stop the technical procedural arguments which had too often arisen and thus marred the true administration of justice"); *O'Reilly v Mackman* [1983] 2 AC 237, 280B (old "procedural disadvantages" removed by the new Order 53 of the Rules of the Supreme Court in 1977); *Cocks v Thanet District Council* [1983] 2 AC 286, 294F (with "safeguards built into the Order 53 procedure which protect from harassment public authorities on whom Parliament has imposed a duty to make public law decisions").
(C) THE CPR REFORMS[4]. *R (Corner House Research) v Director of the Serious Fraud Office* [2008] EWHC 246 (Admin) at [5] (describing the CPR reforms); Woolf Report, *Access to Justice* (1996), chapter 18; the Bowman Review[5]. *Hashtroodi v Hancock* [2004] EWCA Civ 652 [2004] 1 WLR 3206 at [12] (CPR as a new era and self-contained code); *R (Mount Cook Land Ltd) v Westminster City Council* [2003] EWCA Civ 1346 [2004] 1 PLR 29 at [68] (CPR 54PD <64.3> as "an indication of the normal practice of the courts").

---

[4] As to the CPR changes, see Caroline Neenan [1999] JR 6; David Elvin & James Maurici [1999] JR 72 & 207, [2000] JR 164; Michael Fordham [1999] JR 93, [2002] JR 14; Trevor Griffiths [2000] JR 209; Sir Andrew Collins [2002] JR 1.

[5] See Stephen Cragg [1996] JR 236; LCD Press Notice [1999] JR 95; Bowman Letter to the LC [2000] JR 67; LCD Press Notice [2000] JR 70; Summary of Recommendations and Conclusions [2000] JR 72.

(D) OTHER KEY REPORTS.[6] See especially the Justice/All Souls Report, *Administrative Justice: Some Necessary Reforms* (1988); and the Law Commission Report No.226, *Administrative Law: Judicial Review and Statutory Appeals* (1994).

2.2 **Importance and range of subject-matter.**Judicial review is an important control ventilating a host of varied types of problem. The focus of cases may range from matters of grave public concern to those of acute personal interest; from general policy to individualised discretion; from social controversy to commercial self-interest; and anything in between.

2.2.1 **Importance of judicial review.** *R v Inland Revenue Commissioners, ex p National Federation of Self-Employed and Small Businesses Ltd* [1982] AC 617, 641C-D (Lord Diplock, referring to "progress towards a comprehensive system of administrative law" as "having been the greatest achievement of the English courts in my judicial lifetime"); *Woolwich Equitable Building Society v Inland Revenue Commissioners* [1993] AC 70, 173H (Lord Goff, referring as a legal landmark to the development of "our modern law of judicial review ... from its old, ineffectual, origins"); *Kleinwort Benson Ltd v Lincoln City Council* [1999] 2 AC 349, 378E (Lord Goff, referring as "perhaps the most remarkable" of "radical" judicial developments, "the decisions of this House in the middle of this century which led to the creation of our modern system of administrative law"); *Mahon v Air New Zealand Ltd* [1984] AC 808, 816G ("The extension of judicial control of the administrative process has provided over the last 30 years the most striking feature of the development of the common law in those countries of whose legal systems it provides the source"); *Roberts v Gwyrfai District Council* [1899] 2 Ch 608, 614 (Lindley MR: "I know of no duty of the Court which it is more important to observe, and no power of the Court which it is more important to enforce, than its power of keeping public bodies within their rights"); *R v Somerset County Council, ex p Fewings* [1995] 1 All ER 513, 515c-d ("judicial review is an area of the law which is increasingly, and rightly, exposed to a good deal of media publicity"); *Scott v National Trust for Places of Historic Interest or Natural Beauty* [1998] 2 All ER 705, 710j (judicial review as an "increasingly important jurisdiction"; *Access to Justice* (1996) p.250 ("the growth of public law and, in particular, judicial review has been one of the most significant developments in the English legal system in the last 25 years").

2.2.2 **Range of subject-matter: some examples.** *R (Pretty) v Director of Public Prosecutions* [2001] UKHL 61 [2002] 1 AC 800 (refusal to rule out prosecution for compassionate assisted suicide); *R v Inland Revenue Commissioners, ex p Woolwich Equitable Building Society* [1990] 1 WLR 1400 (judicial review to secure the return of £57m plus £6.7m interest from the Revenue); *R v Legal Aid Board, ex p Bruce* [1992] 1 WLR 694 (scope of legal aid); *R (European Roma Rights Centre) v Immigration Officer at Prague Airport* [2004] UKHL 55 [2005] 2 AC 1 (racial discrimination in immigration pre-clearance); *R (L (A Minor)) v Governors of J School* [2003] UKHL 9 [2003] 2 AC 633 (reinstatement of excluded pupil); *Belize Alliance of Conservation Non-Governmental Organisations v Department of the Environment* [2004] UKPC 6 [2004] Env LR 761 (environmental impact assessment duty)[7]; *R (Quintavalle) v Human Fertilisation and Embryology Authority* [2005] UKHL 28 [2005] 2 AC

---

[6] Matthew Holt (JUSTICE/All Souls Report) [2000] JR 56; James Maurici (Law Commission 226) [1996] JR 111; Stephen Grosz (JUSTICE/PLP Report) [1996] JR 147 & Barbara Hewson [1996] JR 152.

[7] On environmental judicial review, see Michael Beloff QC [2005] JR 93; Richard Harwood [2006] JR 356; Richard Macrory [2008] JR 115.

561 (lawfulness of tissue typing, selecting embryos for compatible stem cell material); *R v Brent London Borough Council, ex p Awua* [1996] 1 AC 55 (meaning of "settled" in housing law); *R (Ullah) v Secretary of State for the Home Department* [2004] UKHL 26 [2004] 2 AC 323 (immigration removals and HRA:ECHR rights); *Council of Civil Service Unions v Minister for the Civil Service* [1985] AC 374 (ban on unions at GCHQ); *R v Secretary of State for Trade, ex p Vardy* [1993] ICR 720 (unlawful pit closure decision-making); *R v Secretary of State for the Environment, ex p Nottinghamshire County Council* [1986] AC 240 (rate support grant); *R (Anderson) v Secretary of State for the Home Department* [2002] UKHL 46 [2003] 1 AC 837 (lifer tariff-setting); *Chief Constable of the North Wales Police v Evans* [1982] 1 WLR 1155 (dismissal of police officer); *R (Limbuela) v Secretary of State for the Home Department* [2005] UKHL 66 [2006] 1 AC 396 (approach to denial of welfare benefits to asylum-seekers); *R (Jackson) v Attorney General* [2005] UKHL 56 [2006] 1 AC 262 (validity of an Act of Parliament).

2.3 Terminology. The language of judicial review was altered under CPR 54. It is worth knowing the old terminology, to make sense of the older case-law.

2.3.1 The lexicon of judicial review.

under CPR 54 <64.2>	previously called
"the Administrative Court"	"the Crown Office List"
"claimant"	"applicant"
"defendant"	"respondent"
"disclosure"	"discovery"
"Form N461"	"Form 86A"
"mandatory order"	"mandamus"
"permission"	"leave"
"prohibiting order"	"prohibition"
"quashing order"	"certiorari"
"remedy"	"relief"
"request for reconsideration"	"Form 86B"

2.3.2 The change of terminology. See *Practice Direction (Administrative Court: Establishment)* [2000] 1 WLR 1654, 1654H-1655D.

2.3.3 Meaning of particular phrases. CPR 54.1(2)(a) ("claim for judicial review"); CPR 54.1(2)(e) ("the judicial review procedure"); CPR 54.1(2)(f) ("interested party"); CPR 54.1(2)(g) ("court") <64.2>.

2.4 The Administrative Court. The Administrative Court is part of the Queen's Bench Division of the High Court. Judges are drawn from a list of nominated judges, and the case-load is handled by the Administrative Court Office (ACO).

2.4.1 Administrative Court.[8] *Practice Direction (Administrative Court: Establishment)* [2000] 1 WLR 1654 (renaming the Crown Office List as "the Administrative Court", and the Crown Office as "the Administrative Court Office"), 1654H (announcing that "from among the High Court judges nominated to hear cases from the Crown Office List there should be appointed a

---

[8] Michael Fordham, `How to Make the Administrative Court a Better Place: Some Procedural Suggestions' [2006] JR 98.

lead nominated judge with overall responsibility for the speed, efficiency and economy with which the work of the Crown Office List is conducted")[9]; *Wandsworth London Borough Council v A* [2000] 1 WLR 1246, 1259C-D ("public law issues have been thought to require the attention of a specialised judiciary"); *R v Wicks* [1998] AC 92, 106C-D ("Challenges to the lawfulness of an order often raise complex and sophisticated issues, suited for decision by the specialist judges in the Divisional Court"); *O'Reilly v Mackman* [1983] 2 AC 237, 259D (referring to what "a division of the High Court which might well be called the Administrative Division. It is manned by judges specially versed in administrative law"); Lord Woolf (1989 Hamlyn Lecture), *Protection of the Public - a New Challenge*, p.117 ("I regard it as being of the greatest importance that there should exist among the judiciary a body of judges which has the necessary insight into the process of administration"). There is an Administrative Court Master.[10] *Practice Statement (Administrative Court: Annual Statement) 2001/2* [2002] 1 All ER 633; *Administrative Court: Annual Statement 2002/3* [2004] 1 All ER 322.

2.4.2 **Administrative Court Office (ACO).** See CPR 54PD <64.3> para 2.2 (ACO address for filing documents); ACO:NFG <64.4> para 19.1 (contacting the ACO); *Practice Statement (Administrative Court: Annual Statement)* [2002] 1 All ER 633, 636a-c (ACO contact details). ACO newsletters are reproduced in the journal *Judicial Review*.[11]

2.4.3 **Other features and players.** *Administrative Court: Annual Statement 2002/3* [2004] 1 All ER 322 at 325h (describing the Administrative Court Users' Group as "a useful forum for discussion between court users, the court staff and the nominated judges")[12]; Administrative Law Bar Association;[13] Government Legal Representatives;[14] other.[15]

---

[9] Mr Justice Collins, `The Role of the Lead Judge in the Administrative Court' [2005] JR 18; The Nominated Judges [1997] JR 252 (October 1997); [1999] JR 123 (May 1999); [2001] JR 132 (March 2001); [2003] JR 58 (March 2003); [2004] JR 305 (July 2004); [2007] JR 134 (January 2007).

[10] Katharine Hogg, `The Role of the Crown Office Master' [1999] JR 148.

[11] ACO Newsletters: 11.02 [2003] JR 1; 3.03 [2003] JR 116; 7.03 [2003] JR 181; 11.03 [2004] JR 1; 7.04 [2004] JR 237; 11.04 [2005] JR 1; 3.05 [2005] JR 196; 7.05 [2005] JR 273; 11.05 [2006] JR 148; 3.06 [2006] JR 251.

[12] Gavin Eynon, `The Crown Office Users' Association' [1999] JR 124.

[13] Jenni Richards [1996] JR 114.

[14] Stephen Richards, `The Role of the Treasury Devil' [1997] JR 244; Roland Phillips, `The Public Law Group at the Treasury Solicitor's Department' [2002] JR 53. Attorney-General's Panels of Counsel: see D.A.Hogg [1997] JR 170; Ross Cranston QC MP [1999] JR 272; Lord Williams QC [2001] JR 127; Lord Goldsmith QC [2003] JR 166; Anthony Inglese [2003] JR 204.

[15] Helena Cook (Public Law Project) [1996] JR 240; Vanessa Sims (Bar Pro Bono Unit) [1996] JR 246; Jamie Woolley (EarthRights) [1996] JR 129; Katherine Davis (Environmental Law Foundation) [1996] JR 255; David Thomas (CPAG) [1997] JR 49; John Wadham (Liberty) [1997] JR 178; Emma Playfair (INTERIGHTS) [1997] JR 247; Cambridge Centre for Public Law [1998] JR 110; Hamish Arnott

2.5 **Some special procedural aspects.**Alongside the rules which govern judicial review, a number of aspects of public law litigation are worth noting. They illustrate its special nature, virtues and flexibility.

2.5.1 **The Court's special function.** *R v Leeds County Court, ex p Morris* [1990] 1 QB 523, 530G & 531B (describing judicial review as "the unique and multi-purpose function of the Divisional Court of the High Court ... having wide powers to countermand the decisions of others no matter where those decisions emanate from, be it below the High Court or outside the courts altogether"); *R v Greater Manchester Coroner, ex p Tal* [1985] QB 67, 80G-H (describing the "supervisory jurisdiction"); *Estate of M Kingsley (dec'd) v Secretary of State for Transport* [1994] COD 358 (referring to the reviewing court as the guardian of the public interest); *R v Secretary of State for the Home Department, ex p Gashi* [1999] INLR 276, 308D-E (explaining that judicial review, in an asylum context, is not purely adversarial litigation; rather the court has an overriding obligation to promote a welfare consideration); *In re Waldron* [1986] QB 824, 840D ("Judicial review involves an *inquiry* into a decision ... not *an action against* the decision-maker"); *R v Greenwich London Borough Council, ex p Lovelace (No.2)* [1992] QB 155, 165H (judicial review court is "a court of first instance").

2.5.2 **Proceedings in the name of the Crown.** *R v Commissioners of Customs and Excise, ex p Kay and Co* [1996] STC 1500, 1517c-d ("It might be thought that ... the bringing of ... judicial review proceedings in the name of the Crown is no more than a formality. However, it reflects the fact that this court is dealing with what are essentially issues of public law"); *R v Traffic Commissioner for the North Western Traffic Area, ex p BRAKE* [1996] COD 248 (whereas private law proceedings involve claimant asserting rights, judicial review representing claimant invoking supervisory jurisdiction of the Court, through proceedings brought nominally by the Crown); *R (Ben-Abdelaziz) v Haringey London Borough Council* [2001] EWCA Civ 803 [2001] 1 WLR 1485 (although nominally in the name of the Crown, judicial review not "proceedings brought by or at the instigation of a public authority" for the purposes of HRA s.22(4) <64.7>).

2.5.3 **Control by the Court, not the parties.** <2.6> (strict case-management); CPR 54.5(2) and CPR 54.8(3) <64.2> (parties cannot extend time by agreement); <34.2.5> (jurisdiction is not conferred by parties' agreement/consent); *R v Secretary of State for the Home Department, ex p Bulger* [2001] EWHC Admin 119 [2001] 3 All ER 449 at [18] (court raising question of standing of its own motion); *R (O'Byrne) v Secretary of State for the Environment, Transport and the Regions* [2001] EWCA Civ 499 [2002] HLR 567 (CA) at [40] (appeal restored because of different basis for decision appearing to the Court after the close of argument); *Cachia v Faluyi* [2001] EWCA Civ 998 [2001] 1 WLR 1966 at [16] (permission to amend granted, to take HRA point, "since the court would in any event have been obliged to consider it pursuant to our duty under section 6(1) of the Act"); *R (Cowl) v Plymouth City Council* [2001] EWCA Civ 1935 [2002] 1 WLR 803 at [2] (court should use "ample powers under the CPR to ensure that the parties try to resolve the dispute with the minimum involvement of the courts"), [3] ("To achieve this objective the court may have to hold, on its own initiative, an inter partes hearing at which the parties can explain what steps they have taken to resolve the dispute without the involvement of the courts"); *R (Lord v Secretary of State for the Home Department*

(Prisoners' Legal Rights Group) [1999] JR 139; Karen Mackay (Legal Action Group) [2002] JR 57; Phil Michaels (FOE Rights and Justice Centre) [2006] JR 246.

[2003] EWHC 2073 (Admin) at [26] (court convening an "in camera" hearing of its own motion).

2.5.4 Judicial review: the need for cooperation and candour. <10.1> (judicial review as a cooperative enterprise).

2.5.5 Public interest litigation.[16] *R (Corner House Research) v Director of the Serious Fraud Office* [2008] EWHC 246 (Admin) at [18] ("judicial review claims ... are the more likely to be matters of genuine public concern than litigation between individuals"); *R v Lord Chancellor, ex p Child Poverty Action Group* [1999] 1 WLR 347, 353G (Dyson L, describing a "public interest challenge" as having the "essential characteristics ... that it raises public law issues which are of general importance, where the [claimant] has no private interest in the outcome of the case"); <22.2.10> (public interest intervention); *Public Law Project, Third Party Interventions in Judicial Review: An Action Research Study* (PLP, May 2001) chapter 2 ("public interest cases": "Cases which raise issues, beyond any personal interests of the parties in the matter, affecting identifiable sectors of the public or vulnerable groups; seeking to clarify or challenge important questions of law; involving serious matters of public policy or general public concern; and/or concerning systematic default or abuse by a public body"); <38.2.1> (liberal approach to standing); <38.2.7> (standing and the public interest).

2.5.6 Friendly actions. *R v Legal Aid Board, ex p Bruce* [1992] 1 WLR 694, 697H ("Litigation has throughout been conducted on what [counsel] described as a friendly basis, both parties co-operating with one another to obtain a decision as to what is the true position in law"); *In re Ashton* [1994] 1 AC 9, 19G (central issue non-contentious); *Chertsey Urban District Council v Mixnam's Properties Ltd* [1965] AC 735, 747D (a "friendly action"); *Royal College of Nursing of the United Kingdom v Department of Health and Social Security* [1981] AC 800, 830C-D (RCN "neutral" but simply seeking "clarification and guidance from the court"); *Bugg v DPP* [1993] QB 473, 490C-D ("friendly actions"); *Ainsbury v Millington* [1987] 1 WLR 379, 381C ("what are called `friendly actions'"), considered in *R v Holderness Borough Council, ex p James Robert Developments Ltd* [1993] 1 PLR 108, 118D.

2.5.7 Non-appearing/non-adversarial defendants. *London Borough of Islington v Camp* (1999) [2004] LGR 58, 66b ("in public law cases one of the parties ... will sometimes choose not to adopt an adversarial role before the court: for example, [defendant] magistrates may file evidence for the assistance of the court but are rarely represented at a hearing. In those circumstances the court has to rely on an interested party such as the prosecutor or on an amicus to present one side of the case; or it has to do its best in the absence of competing submissions"); *R (Secretary of State for Defence) v Pensions Appeal Tribunal* [2005] EWHC 1775 (Admin) (adjournment to allow PAT's arguments on important point to be advanced by Counsel or an amicus); *R (Oldham Metropolitan Borough Council) v Manchester Crown Court* [2005] EWHC 930 (Admin) at [21]-[22] (importance of judge's note of proceedings under review being supported by an affidavit); *R (Latif) v Social Security Commissioners* [2002] EWHC 2355 (Admin) at [12] ("save in exceptional circumstances, it is unlikely that the [social security] commissioner will wish to participate actively in the application for judicial review of his decision"); *R (B) v Dr Haddock* [2005] EWHC 921 (Admin) at [39] (in forced medication case, not usually necessary for second certifying practitioner to appear in judicial review); *R (Percy) v Corby Magistrates Court* [2008] EWHC 607 (Admin) (wrong of magistrates not to respond to letter before claim or claim form); <18.1.12> (costs and non-appearing decision-

---

[16] Professor John Griffith [1997] JR 195; Nigel Pleming QC [1998] JR 63.

makers).

2.5.8 "Self-challenges". *R (Carroll) v South Somerset District Council* [2008] EWHC 104 (Admin) (council's leader obtaining judicial review of planning permission grant which did not match decision-making resolution); *Oxfordshire County Council v Oxford City Council* [2006] UKHL 25 [2006] 2 AC 674 (CPR Part 8 application by registration authority for guidance on issues arising from town green registration inquiry); *R (Lord Chancellor) v Chief Land Registrar* [2005] EWHC 1706 (Admin) [2006] QB 795 at [14] (Lord Chancellor seeking declarations by judicial review, where legality of his scheme had been doubted by the Chief Land Registrar); *R v London Transport Executive, ex p Greater London Council* [1983] QB 484 (GLC obtaining by judicial review a declaration of legality of the direction it had issued to the LTE); *R v Bromley London Borough Council, ex p Lambeth London Borough Council* The Times 16th June 1984 (declaration as to legality of own subscriptions); *In re Rapier, decd* [1988] QB 26 (coroner obtaining judicial review and statutory review to quash own inquest verdict, given new evidence); *R (Meredith) v Merthyr Tydfil County Borough Council* [2002] EWHC 634 (Admin) at [8] ("the council is in substance, although not in form, both the claimant and the defendant in this action"); *R v Statutory Committee of the Pharmaceutical Society of Great Britain, ex p Pharmaceutical Society of Great Britain* [1981] 1 WLR 886 (judicial review of own committee's decision);*Agricultural, Horticultural & Forestry Industry Training Board v Aylesbury Mushrooms Ltd* [1972] 1 WLR 190 (Board seeking declarations as to lawfulness of Orders setting it up); *Local Authority v Health Authority* [2003] EWHC 2746 (Fam) [2004] Fam 96 (where dispute as to whether own report sufficiently anonymised to protect vulnerable children, authority applying to Family Division for order permitting publication); *Airedale NHS Trust v Bland* [1993] AC 789 (claim to establish whether proposed action lawful); *Ealing London Borough Council v Race Relations Board* [1972] AC 342 (declaration that own housing policy not racially discriminatory); *National Trust for Places of Historic Interest or Natural Beauty v Ashbrook* [1997] 4 All ER 76 (claim for declarations as to scope of own statutory powers);*London Borough of Islington v Camp* (1999) [2004] LGR 58 (council seeking declaration as to what it should do); *National Assembly for Wales v Cardiff City and County Council* [2005] EWHC 974 (QB) [2006] LGR 540 (public authorities' friendly claim form action obtaining declarations as to vires of agreements transferring assets).

2.5.9 Practical substance and judicial review. <4.1>.

2.5.10 Flexibility/anti-technicality/procedural ingenuity.
(A) GENERAL. *R (Zeqiri) v Secretary of State for the Home Department* [2002] UKHL 3 [2002] INLR 291 at [39] (treating Secretary of State's letter maintaining certificate as, in substance, a decision to issue a fresh one); <13.5.4(D)> (benevolent approach to decisions/reasons); <26.3.6> (delay rules not applied in a technical manner); <27.3> (procedural exclusivity: liberal approach).
(B) WRONG CHOICE OF PROCEDURE.*Chen v Government of Romania* [2007] EWHC 520 (Admin) [2008] 1 All ER 851 at [66] (by agreement, treating extradition appeal as judicial review and waiving all requirements); *PJG v Child Support Agency* [2006] EWHC 423 (Fam) [2006] 2 FLR 857 (where no appeal to family division and case stated out of time, claim treated as transferred to judicial review, time extended and claim granted); *R (Gillan) v Winchester Crown Court* [2007] EWHC 380 (Admin) [2007] 1 WLR 2214 at [15] (case stated excluded by statute, so permitting claim to proceed as judicial review); *R v Clerkenwell Metropolitan Stipendiary Magistrate, ex p Director of Public Prosecutions* [1984] QB 821, 836C-D (treating judicial review as case stated, out of time); *Cala Homes (South) Ltd v Chichester District Council* [1999] 4 PLR 77 (statutory application, erroneously commenced by Part 7 claim form, permitted to be transferred to the Admin Court); *Thurrock Borough Council v Secretary of*

State for the Environment, Transport and the Regions The Times 20th December 2000 (treating s.289 planning appeal as s.288 appeal); *R (Binyan Mohamed) v Secretary of State for Foreign and Commonwealth Affairs* [2008] EWHC 2048 (Admin) at [62] (judicial review allowed to be used, albeit that *Norwich Pharmacal* claim would normally be by ordinary claim form action).

(C) COURT OF APPEAL'S "ORIGINAL" JURISDICTION. *Chief Adjudication Officer v Foster* [1993] AC 754, 761C-D (CA judge acting as first instance judge to grant permission but refuse the substantive application, to enable the claimant "to invoke the original jurisdiction of the Court of Appeal to entertain an application for judicial review"), applied in *Johnson v Valks* [2000] 1 WLR 1502, 1508A; *R v Miall* [1992] QB 836 and *R v Lee* [1993] 1 WLR 103, 109B-C (CA reconstituting itself as a DC); *Lenehen v Secretary of State for the Home Department* [2002] EWHC 1599 (Admin) (DC reconstituting itself as CA (Criminal Division), so as to reduce a sentence, having dismissed a claim for judicial review regarding the release date calculation); *Bowman v Fels* [2005] EWCA Civ 226 [2005] 1 WLR 3083 at [16] (CA simply proceeding, noting that it could have used the device of a judicial review claim, with all the formalities, "in less than ten minutes"); *Secretary of State for the Home Department v Dahir* [1995] Imm AR 570, 574-576 (CA simply treating appeal from IAT as application for judicial review, without any need for procedural devices); *Farley v Child Support Agency* [2005] EWCA Civ 869 [2005] 3 FCR 343 (CA reconstituting case as judicial review, where had purported to allow an appeal by case stated, but where no jurisdiction); *R v Secretary of State for the Environment, Transport and the Regions, ex p Spath Holme* [2001] 2 AC 349, 354C (CA) at [2] (when deciding substantive judicial review, having granted permission on appeal, CA "exercising an original jurisdiction, but as the Court of Appeal and not as a Divisional Court").

(D) MODE OF REVIEWING REFUSAL TO STATE A CASE. *R (Donnachie) v Cardiff Magistrates Court* [2007] EWHC 1846 (Admin) [2007] 1 WLR 3085 at [6] (where wrong not to state a case, deal directly with the underlying issue on judicial review); *R (Griffin) v Richmond Magistrates Court* [2008] EWHC 84 (Admin) [2008] 1 WLR 1525 at [1], [36] (treat as the case stated appeal).

(E) COURT ACTING TO PERMIT ISSUES TO GO FURTHER. *R v Director of Public Prosecutions, ex p Camelot Group Plc* (1998) 10 Admin LR 93, 105E-F (although CA regarding judicial review as clearly inapt, granting permission and dismissing the substantive application, so that the arguments might go further); *R v Parliamentary Commissioner for Standards, ex p Al Fayed* [1998] 1 WLR 669 (given importance of issue, CA treating as substantive application, to leave open possible appeal to HL); *R v Oxfordshire County Council, ex p Sunningwell Parish Council* [2000] 1 AC 335, 349B-C (CA granting permission, but in light of CA authority which may have been wrongly decided, refusing substantive application and granting permission to appeal to HL); *Taylor v Lawrence* [2002] EWCA Civ 90 [2003] QB 528 at [76] (permission to appeal to CA granted to preserve right of appeal to the HL); *Westminster City Council v O'Reilly* [2003] EWCA Civ 1007 [2004] 1 WLR 195 at [20]-[21] (leaving open possibility of judicial review where High Court case stated decision final and unappealable); cf. *Gibson v United States of America* [2007] UKPC 52 [2007] 1 WLR 2367 (wrong to recharacterise habeas corpus decision as judicial review so as to permit jurisdiction on appeal, overruling *Cartwright v Superintendent of Her Majesty's Prison* [2004] UKPC 10 [2004] 1 WLR 902).

(F) RECONSTITUTING AS A COURT OF CRIMINAL APPEAL. *R v Crown Court at Manchester, ex p H* [2000] 1 WLR 760 (DC allowing judicial review of crown court judge's decision to discharge restriction order), 769H-770B (instead of remitting, "it is pragmatic in the present case to take a different course", namely reconstitution as Court of Appeal (Criminal Division), to make substitutionary order).

2.5.11 Dual listing.
(A) JUDGES CROSSING DIVISIONS. *R v Portsmouth Hospitals NHS Trust, ex p Glass* [1999] 2 FLR 905, 910A-B ("The court always has sufficient powers to make sure that if a party adopts the pro-active course then the right course can still be pursued and, if necessary, a judge from one Division can sit in the other Division to see that the matter is dealt with"); *Administrative Court: Annual Statement 2002/3* [2004] 1 All ER 322 at 322e (nominated judges "include judges of the Chancery and Family Divisions who act as additional judges of the Queen's Bench Division when dealing with Administrative Court cases").
(B) DUAL LISTING/ DUAL CAPACITY. *R v South Somerset District Council, ex p DJB (Group) Ltd* (1989) 1 Admin LR 11, 20B-21D ("There is no reason why arrangements cannot be made for both sets of proceedings to be heard together, where an application to this effect is made ... and a court considers that is the appropriate course"); *R v Serumaga* [2005] EWCA Crim 370 [2005] 1 WLR 3366 at [5] (3-judge court sitting as DC (judicial review) and CA (criminal appeal), where uncertainty as to correct mode); *R v Secretary of State for the Home Department, ex p Probyn* [1998] 1 WLR 809 (sitting as DC on judicial review and Court of Criminal Appeal as to appeal); *R v Council of Legal Education, ex p Eddis* (1995) 7 Admin LR 357 (judges sitting both as (a) DC on judicial review and (b) Visitors to the Inns of Court); *R (Secretary of State for the Home Department) v Immigration Appeal Tribunal* [2001] EWHC Admin 1067 [2002] INLR 116 at [8] (CA sitting as a DC to hear linked judicial review with immigration appeal).
(C) JUDICIAL REVIEW AND ORDINARY ACTION. *British Airways Board v Laker Airways Ltd* [1984] QB 142, 184F-185A (injunction and cross-judicial review); *R v Football Association Ltd, ex p Football League Ltd* [1993] 2 All ER 833 (judicial review and cross-originating summons); *West Glamorgan County Council v Rafferty* [1987] 1 WLR 457 (judicial review and possession defence); *R (Carvill) v Commissioners of Inland Revenue* [2002] EWHC 1488 (Ch) [2002] STC 1167 (judicial review and restitution claim).
(D) JUDICIAL REVIEW AND FAMILY/CHANCERY PROCEEDINGS. *Re R (Adult: Medical Treatment)* [1996] 2 FLR 99, 104D-E (judicial review and originating summons listed together by Family Division judge); *Re T* [1994] Imm AR 368 (Family Division residence proceedings and judicial review); *Soden v Burns* [1996] 3 All ER 967 (judge sitting simultaneously in Chancery Division (Companies Court proceedings) and Queen's Bench (judicial review)); *Scott v National Trust for Places of Historic Interest or Natural Beauty* [1998] 2 All ER 705 (originating summons and Chancery writ action heard with judicial review); *R (Thompson) v Fletcher (HM Inspector of Taxes)* [2002] EWHC 1447 (Ch) [2002] EWHC 1448 (Admin) [2002] STC 1149 (Revenue's case stated appeal and taxpayer's cross-claim for judicial review).
(E) JUDICIAL REVIEW AND HABEAS CORPUS. *R v Barking Havering and Brentwood Community Healthcare NHS Trust* [1999] 1 FLR 106, 117B (although habeas corpus not a remedy available in judicial review, where both pursued, they should be heard together using the same documents); *Attorney-General of Hong Kong v Ng Yuen Shiu* [1983] 2 AC 629; *R v Governor of Brixton Prison, ex p Walsh* [1985] AC 154; *In re Schmidt* [1995] 1 AC 339.
(F) JUDICIAL REVIEW AND APPEAL. *R (Revenue and Customs Commissioners) v Teesside Crown Court* [2007] EWHC 1183 (Admin) [2007] 4 All ER 925 at [48] (judicial review and case stated); *R (BBC) v Information Tribunal* [2007] EWHC 905 (Admin) [2007] 1 WLR 2583 (appeal, judicial review and cross-judicial review); *R (Bermingham) v Director of the Serious Fraud Office* [2006] EWHC 200 (Admin) [2007] QB 727 (judicial review and extradition appeal); *Re G (A Child)* [2008] EWCA Civ 86 at [13] (judicial review of pathway plan and appeal against interim care order).
(G) OTHER. *R (Walker) v Secretary of State for Communities and Local Government* [2008] EWHC 62 (Admin) (judicial review and statutory review); *R (Sutovic) v HM Coroner for Northern District of Greater London* [2006] EWHC 1095 (Admin) (judicial review and

statutory application for new inquest); *Rees v Crane* [1994] 2 AC 173 (judicial review and Constitutional motion); *R v Comptroller of Patents, Designs and Trade Marks, ex p Lenzing AG* [1997] EuLR 237 (judicial review and application to Patent Court); *R v Liverpool Magistrates' Court, ex p Ansen* [1998] 1 All ER 692 (judicial review and application relating to confiscation order); <21.2.3> (rolled-up hearing: permission and substantive application for judicial review).

2.5.12 **Approach to issue estoppel/res judicata/abuse of process.**[17] *R v Secretary of State for the Environment, ex p Hackney London Borough Council* [1984] 1 WLR 592, 602A-B and 606D (doubting whether issue estoppel has any place in judicial review); *R (Barber) v Secretary of State for Work and Pensions* [2002] EWHC 1915 (Admin) [2002] 2 FLR 1181 at [47] ("the question of issue ... estoppel does not and cannot arise in judicial review proceedings"); *R v Commissioners of Customs and Excise, ex p Kay and Co* [1996] STC 1500, 1516g-1517h ("great difficulties in the doctrine [of issue estoppel] applying in judicial review proceedings"); *R v Commissioners of Customs and Excise, ex p Building Society Ombudsman Co Ltd* [2000] STC 892 at [90] (touching on issue estoppel, and suggesting that broader principle in *Henderson v Henderson* (1843) 3 Hare 100, 115, preventing relitigation of points which should have been brought forward at an earlier hearing, might apply in judicial review); *R v Caradon District Council, ex p Knott* [2000] 3 PLR 1, 23B (issue estoppel preventing planning enforcement action); *R (Opoku) v Principal of Southwark College* [2002] EWHC 2092 (Admin) [2003] 1 All ER 272 at [9] (permission decision interlocutory so no res judicata, but may be abuse of process to make repeat application absent new material); *Thrasyvalou v Secretary of State for the Environment* [1990] 2 AC 273 (whether issue estoppel applies to adjudications in the field of public law); *Regalbourne Ltd v East Lindsey District Council* (1994) 6 Admin LR 102, 111C ("highly unlikely" that tribunal decision creating issue estoppel as to future years); *Dunlop v Woollahra Municipal Council* [1982] AC 158, 165D-H (declarations that planning resolutions invalid enabled tort action in which council `issue estopped' from denying invalidity); *R (Machi) v Legal Services Commission* [2001] EWHC Admin 580 at [24] (judicial review ruling of unlawfulness "would create an issue estoppel" in subsequent damages claim) (CA is [2001] EWCA Civ 2010 [2002] 1 WLR 983); *Secretary of State for Defence v Percy* [1999] 1 All ER 732, 742b-d (MoD bound to have regard to decision of competent court holding that its byelaws invalid, even though not a party to those proceedings); *Abdul Sheikh v Secretary of State for the Home Department* [2001] INLR 98 (abuse of process to challenge decision by habeas corpus when judicial review on same grounds previously refused for delay); *Nahar v Social Security Commissioners* [2002] EWCA Civ 859 (no issue estoppel from adjudicator determination arising on the facts); *R v Secretary of State for Trade and Industry, ex p Greenpeace* [2000] Env LR 221, 259 (claimant entitled to bring same challenge to subsequent round of decisions, albeit previous challenge to previous decisions dismissed for delay); *R v Managers of South Western Hospital, ex p M* [1993] QB 683, 693G-H (no issue estoppel problem since "no second set of proceedings"); *R v Life Assurance and Unit Trust Regulatory Organisation Ltd, ex p Tee* (1995) 7 Admin LR 289, 309D-310G, 314G (refusing to characterise as `an abuse of process', Mr Tee's pursuit of a point not relied upon in earlier proceedings (*ex p Ross* [1993] QB 17) where Mr Tee's company had been treated as the true claimant); *R v Secretary of State for Transport, ex p Richmond Upon Thames London Borough Council* [1995] Env LR 390, 395-396 (principle "that there should be an end to litigation ... has to be approached with caution in the public law field"); *Secretary of State for the Home Department v AF* [2008] EWCA Civ 117 (no issue estoppel in control

---

[17] This subparagraph in a previous edition was cited in *Human Fertilisation and Embryology Authority v Amicus Healthcare Ltd* [2005] EWHC 1092 (QB) at [31].

order proceedings).

2.6 Strict case-management. Public law cases frequently involve the Courts adhering to a strict approach to procedural control. Such an approach is supported by the culture signified by the Civil Procedure Rules. It is also explicable by reference to the enormous caseload under which the Courts operate.

2.6.1 **Procedural strictness in judicial review.**[18] *R v Secretary of State for Trade and Industry, ex p Greenpeace Ltd* [1998] Env LR 415, 424-425 (Laws J: "the judicial review court, being primarily concerned with the maintenance of the rule of law by the imposition of objective legal standards upon the conduct of public bodies, has to adapt a flexible but principled approach to its own jurisdiction. Its decisions will constrain the actions of elected government, sometimes bringing potential uncertainty and added cost to good administration. And from time to time its judgments may impose heavy burdens on third parties. This is a price which often has to be paid for the rule of law to be vindicated. But because of these deep consequences which touch the public interest, the court in its discretion - whether so directed by rules of court or not - will impose a strict discipline in proceedings before it. It is marked by an insistence that [claimants] identify the real substance of their complaint and then act promptly, so as to ensure that the proper business of government and the reasonable interests of third parties are not overborne or unjustly prejudiced by litigation brought in circumstances where the point in question could have been exposed and adjudicated without unacceptable damage. The rule of law is not threatened, but strengthened, by such a discipline. It invokes public confidence and engages the law in the practical world. And it is administered, of course, case by case... I think that these considerations apply with special force to proceedings brought by a public interest [claimant]").

2.6.2 **General case-management and the CPR.** See CPR 1.1 (overriding objective); CPR 1.4 (active case-management); *Arbuthnot Latham Bank Ltd v Trafalgar Holdings Ltd* [1998] 2 All ER 181, 191c-d (describing the development of "court controlled case management techniques").[19]

2.6.3 **Procedural strictness.** *Arbuthnot Latham Bank Ltd v Trafalgar Holdings Ltd* [1998] 2 All ER 181, 191e-j (delay to be "assessed not only from the point of view of the prejudice caused to the particular litigants whose case it is, but also in relation to the effect it can have on other litigants who are wishing to have their cases heard and the prejudice which is caused to the due administration of civil justice"); <P26> (delay); *R v Lancashire County Council, ex p Sellers and Petty* 10th April 1997 unrep. (further extension of time for evidence refused)[20]; *R v Sandwell Metropolitan Borough Council, ex p Lyn* [1994] COD 431 (granting extension of time for evidence and doubting "wholly exceptional" test referred to in *Practice Note: Judicial Review - Affidavit in Reply* [1989] 1 WLR 358); *R v General Council of the Bar, ex p Percival* [1991] 1 QB 212, 236A-B (importance of permission filter to deal with "excessive applications whether tactical or merely optimistic"); <P18> (costs); <4.6> (hypothetical/academic issues); <P36> (alternative remedy).

---

[18] Michael Fordham, `Practitioner Standards' [1996] JR 1.

[19] Jonathan Solly, `Managing "Big Issues" in the Crown Office List' [1999] JR 218.

[20] Gregory Jones [1998] JR 71.

2.6.4 **Managing the Administrative Court caseload: the 2008 steps.**[21] See *Statement by Collins J* (4.4.08) [2008] JR 162 (backlog addressed by substantial increase in judges sitting).

---

[21] Conrad Haley, `Action on Administrative Court Delays' [2008] JR 69; Richard Clayton QC, `New Arrangements for the Administrative Court' [2008] JR 164.

> **P3 Impact.** A successful claim does not necessarily guarantee a
> favourable ultimate outcome, nor a wider knock-on effect.

3.1 Remittal and repeatability
3.2 Sterile/counterproductive victories
3.3 Judicial review as a monetary springboard
3.4 Securing assurances/provoking comment
3.5 Wider impact/knock-on effect

3.1 Remittal and repeatability.A successful judicial review will typically result in a "remittal": sending the matter back to the decision-maker for reconsideration afresh. This may or may not produce a different outcome. It is a reality and limitation which must be understood by lawyers and explained to clients. Sometimes the Court's judgment means that a particular course of action is precluded, as when it has been held to be unreasonable or unlawful. Often, the decision-maker is left with a corrected process or approach but retaining overall freedom to decide.

3.1.1 **Quash and remit: the rules.** Supreme Court Act 1981 s.31(5) <64.1>; CPR 54.19 <64.2>.

3.1.2 **Remittal means appropriate body decides.** *R v London Borough of Sutton, ex p Partridge* (1996) 28 HLR 315 (council's review Board should reconsider housing benefit); *R v Criminal Injuries Compensation Board, ex p Johnson* [1994] PIQR 469 (although entitlement to compensation seeming clear, matter remitted); *General Medical Council v Spackman* [1943] AC 627, 647 ("The council ought to take up the inquiry again. I do not seek in any way to suggest or forecast how they will hold it. The discretion and responsibility for the procedure are theirs").

3.1.3 **Remittal to a differently-constituted decision-maker.** *R v Number 8 Area Committee of the Legal Aid Board, ex p Megarry* [1994] PIQR 476 (remittal for reconsideration by different area committee); *R v Solihull Metropolitan Borough Council Housing Benefits Review Board, ex p Simpson* (1994) 92 LGR 719, 730 (matter remitted for redetermination by a differently constituted board); *R (Secretary of State for the Home Department) v Mental Health Review Tribunal* [2004] EWHC 1029 (Admin) at [28] (remitting to a different MHRT); *R v Board of Visitors of Hull Prison, ex p St Germain (No.2)* [1979] 1 WLR 1401, 1412E-F ("the charges remain capable of being the subject of a fresh investigation before a differently constituted board"); cf. *R (London Fire & Emergency Planning Authority) v Board of Medical Referees* [2007] EWHC 2805 (Admin) (remittal to same Board).

3.1.4 **Defendant body may reach the same decision again.** *R (Ali) v Secretary of State for the Home Department* [2003] EWHC 899 (Admin) at [31] ("Of course, dependent upon reconsideration on sufficient and proper evidence, the Secretary of State may reach exactly the same decision"); *Attorney-General of Hong Kong v Ng Yuen Shiu* [1983] 2 AC 629, 639F (quashing order "entirely without prejudice to the making of a fresh removal order ... after a fair inquiry has been held at which the [claimant] has been given an opportunity to make such representations as he may see fit as to why he should not be removed"); *R v Secretary of State for Education, ex p Prior* [1994] ELR 231, 251A ("it is quite likely that he will reach the same decision again, albeit by a different route, but nothing is certain and in my judgment [the claimant] is entitled to a decision on his complaint which is not seriously flawed as a matter of law"); *R v Secretary of State for Education and Science, ex p Islam* (1993) 5 Admin LR 177, 188B (judicial review granted albeit "the Secretary of State may reach exactly the same decision"); *R v Hillingdon Health Authority, ex p Goodwin* [1984] ICR 800, 811E-F ("I do not know what the result will be... I accept that the authority would be entitled to come to the same decision as they did previously. Equally, I recognise that there could now be a different decision reached in the light of the proper approach"); *R v Somerset County Council, ex p Fewings* [1995] 1 WLR 1037, 1046H (Sir Thomas Bingham MR: "I leave open, but express no view on, the possibility that the same decision could have been reached on proper grounds").

3.1.5 **Court giving guidance as to reconsideration.** *R v Barnet London Borough Council, ex p Nilish Shah* [1983] 2 AC 309, 350G-351A (on remittal "it will be their duty to follow the guidance as to the law now given by your Lordships' House"); *R v Tower Hamlets London Borough Council, ex p Chetnik Developments Ltd* [1988] AC 858, 879A (mandatory order requiring "a fresh decision" with the House of Lords' guidance as to which reasons were permissible and which were not); *R v Director of Public Prosecutions, ex p C* (1995) 7 Admin LR 385, 393D-E (reconsideration "in the light of the judgment of this court, and ... of all that has happened since the original decision was made"); *R v Immigration Appeal Tribunal, ex p Singh* [1987] 1 WLR 1394, 1399E (remittal for determination "in the light of the views on the law expressed by this court"); *West Glamorgan County Council v Rafferty* [1987] 1 WLR 457, 478D-H (declaration inapt because council "must be left free, to deal with the situation as they think best having regard to their duty and powers"), 478F-H (wrong to pre-judge reasonableness of future decisions); *R v Dairy Produce Quota Tribunal, ex p PA Cooper & Sons* (1994) 6 Admin LR 540, 552A ("It is not for this court to pre-empt the jurisdiction of the Tribunal by making the declarations sought"); *R v Uxbridge Justices, ex p Heward-Mills* [1983] 1 WLR 56, 64D ("Nothing that I have said today must fetter the justices when the position is reconsidered in the light of the principles to which I have drawn attention"); <24.4.14(D)> (no fetter by mandatory order).

3.1.6 **Reconsideration: effect of different kinds of intervention.**
(A) PROCEDURAL UNFAIRNESS. *R v Lord Chancellor, ex p Law Society* (1994) 6 Admin LR 833 (DC), 866D (describing cases where "procedural irregularities will make it appropriate for a court to quash an existing decision and to declare that a further decision should only be reached after proper consultation has taken place"); *R v Secretary of State for the Home Department, ex p Benwell* [1985] QB 554, 574C-E (remitting the matter for a decision, to be reached ignoring previous tainted proceedings); *Cocks v Thanet District Council* [1983] 2 AC 286, 295D-F (court's decision does not "determine the issue" where the "decision is successfully impugned on ... [grounds] that the [claimant] was not fairly heard").
(B) UNLAWFULNESS. *R v Ealing District Health Authority, ex p Fox* [1993] 1 WLR 373, 387H-388A (declaration identifying error of law for reconsideration accordingly); *R v Criminal Injuries Compensation Board, ex p Ince* [1973] 1 WLR 1334, 1342H (decision quashed for error of law and remitted for reconsideration); *R v Chief Metropolitan Stipendiary Magistrate, ex p Secretary of State for the Home Department* [1988] 1 WLR 1204, 1219C (matter remitted with direction to commit if satisfied that conduct amounting to extradition crimes); *R v South East Hampshire Family Proceedings Court, ex p D* [1994] 1 WLR 611, 614A (matter remitted "for a decision to be made on the correct principle"); *Rajkumar v Lalla* 29th November 2001 unrep. (PC) at [23] ("there may be cases in which the result of a successful judicial review is that the legal considerations provide a unique admissible decision which the statutory authority could lawfully give in the circumstances").
(C) UNREASONABLENESS. *R (Bramall) v Law Society* [2005] EWHC 1570 (Admin) at [70]-[71] (finding was unreasonable and could not be repeated on reconsideration); *Cocks v Thanet District Council* [1983] 2 AC 286, 295D-F (describing "cases where the court's decision will effectively determine the issue, as for instance where on undisputed primary facts the court holds that no reasonable housing authority, correctly directing itself in law, could be satisfied");

Stovin v Wise [1996] AC 923, 953D-E (irrational failure to exercise statutory power amounting to public law duty to act); *West Glamorgan County Council v Rafferty* [1987] 1 WLR 457, 478C-479A (defendant free to deal as it thinks best, unless Court able to decide that a particular course perverse); *R v Cornwall County Council, ex p Cornwall & Isles of Scilly Guardians ad Litem & Reporting Officers Panel* [1992] 1 WLR 427, 436H-437C (although unreasonable decision matter nevertheless "referred back to the county council to reconsider"); *R v Secretary of State for Trade, ex p Vardy* [1993] ICR 720, 761D-E (decision irrational, court granting declaration as to the course required to be adopted); *R v Warwickshire County Council, ex p Powergen Plc* [1997] 3 PLR 62, 70B-D (court making clear that only one reasonable course open).

3.1.7 No remittal where only one proper course. *R v Preston Crown Court, ex p Lancashire County Council* [1995] COD 388 (compensation orders quashed with no remittal); *R v Nottingham Crown Court, ex p Toms* [1995] COD 389 (driving disqualification and fine quashed with no remittal); *R v Chief Constable of the Merseyside Police, ex p Merrill* [1989] 1 WLR 1077, 1088B-F (quash disciplinary proceedings, declining to remit, since prejudicial delay would "inevitably lead him to discontinue the inquiry"); *T v Secretary of State for the Home Department* [1995] 1 WLR 545 (CA), 559F-G (no need to remit immigration appeal to IAT where Court can decide it, given IAT's clear findings of fact); <4.2> (non-material flaw); <4.4> futility; <24.4.2> (substitutionary remedy: court retaking decision).

3.1.8 Partial quashing. <43.1.6>.

3.2 Sterile/counterproductive victories. Although many successful judicial review cases will lead to the claimant ultimately securing the desired outcome, many will not. The chance of reconsideration afresh can be well worth fighting for. But claimants need to understand that a victory in judicial review may sometimes leave their circumstances unchanged and, worse than that, can leave their position (or that of others) even worse than before.

3.2.1 No gain? *R v Secretary of State for Trade, ex p Vardy* [1993] ICR 720 (successful procedural challenge to pit closure decisions, but Government went on to close the pits anyway: see *R v British Coal Corporation, ex p Price (No.2)* [1993] COD 323 and 482); *R v Secretary of State for the Environment, ex p Brent London Borough Council* [1982] QB 593 (successful challenge but Minister duly reconsidered but reached substantially the same decision, which was upheld: see *R v Secretary of State for the Environment, ex p Hackney London Borough Council* [1984] 1 WLR 592); *Padfield v Minister of Agriculture Fisheries & Food* [1968] AC 997 (mandatory order secured requiring the Minister to reconsider, but in the event the Minister declined to follow the committee's advice); *R v London Borough of Lambeth, ex p Miah* (1995) 27 HLR 21, 28-29 (court concluding that the council purported to exercise a power which it did not have, but identifying two legal avenues which would be open to it).

3.2.2 Outcome reversed by legislation. *Daymond v Plymouth City Council* [1976] AC 609 was reversed by the Water Charges Act 1976: see *South West Water Authority v Rumble's* [1985] AC 609); *R (M) v Slough Borough Council* [2008] UKHL 52 [2008] 1 WLR 1808 at [19] (explaining that Asylum and Immigration Act 1996 was enacted to reverse the effect of the previous *JCWI* and *Kihara* cases).

3.2.3 Worse than before? *R v Richmond upon Thames London Borough Council, ex p McCarthy & Stone (Developments) Ltd* [1992] 2 AC 48 (HL explaining that local authority not entitled to make nominal charge for pre-planning advice, but entitled to withhold the advice altogether); *R v Hereford & Worcester Local Education Authority, ex p Jones* [1981] 1 WLR

768 (claimant establishing unlawfulness of "modest" charges towards daughters' violin and clarinet tuition, but CA pointing out that education authority perfectly entitled to discontinue the tuition altogether); Bouchard in *Taggart (ed.), Judicial Review of Administrative Action in the 1980s*, at p.184 (describing the consequences of *O'Brien v National Parole Board* (1984) 12 Admin LR 249, a judicial review establishing that parole hearings were unlawful unless involving the whole decision-making panel, as a result of which all hearings were scrapped); cf. *R v Parole Board, ex p Watson* [1996] 1 WLR 906 (CA dismissing a challenge which "could only work to the disadvantage of discretionary life prisoners recalled").

3.3 **Judicial review as a monetary springboard** A successful judicial review can be a step towards a monetary claim. Monetary remedies can be sought in the judicial review claim but may attract circumspection if they are the true focus of the claim. One way or the other, issues of liability and quantum are likely to be dealt with at a separate hearing.

3.3.1 **Tort claims following successful judicial review.** *Gulf Insurance Ltd v Central Bank of Trinidad and Tobago* [2005] UKPC 10 (having declared on judicial review that bank assets unlawfully transferred at an undervalue, PC ruling that bank entitled to damages for conversion); *Slough Estates Plc v Welwyn Hatfield District Council* [1996] 2 PLR 50 (developer awarded £48.5m damages in deceit, following successful judicial review proceedings); *In re McC (A Minor)* [1985] AC 528 (judicial review claim having resulted in detention order being quashed, leading to a successful tort claim against the magistrates for false imprisonment); *Rowling v Takaro Properties Ltd* [1988] AC 473 (claimant having obtained judicial review of decision by the New Zealand Minister of Finance refusing consent to a proposed share transfer, but PC overturning subsequent $300,000 damages award in negligence); *Calveley v Chief Constable of Merseyside* [1989] AC 1228 (failed tort claims, for breach of statutory duty, negligence and misfeasance, founded on the successful judicial review proceedings in *R v Chief Constable of the Merseyside Police, ex p Calveley* [1986] QB 424); *R v Governor of Brockhill Prison, ex p Evans (No.2)* [2001] 2 AC 19 (false imprisonment damages, judicial review claim having established correct prisoner release date).

3.3.2 **Restitution claims following successful judicial review.** *Woolwich Equitable Building Society v Inland Revenue Commissioners* [1993] AC 70 (restitution to allow recovery of money paid pursuant to an unlawful tax demand, following successful application for judicial review to quash the regulation on which the demand had been based: *R v Inland Revenue Commissioners, ex p Woolwich Equitable Building Society* [1990] 1 WLR 1400); *R v East Sussex County Council, ex p Ward* (2000) 3 CCLR 132 at [40] (restitution issues requiring separate proceedings, the unlawfulness of the agreement for payment having been established on judicial review); *Waikato Regional Airport Ltd v Attorney General* [2003] UKPC 50 (restitution granted in New Zealand judicial review proceedings, where airport levy unfairly imposed); <25.1.4> (restitution claim in judicial review).

3.3.3 *Francovich* **reparation following successful judicial review.** *Francovich* reparation claims <8.5.2> were included in judicial review proceedings such as *R v HM Treasury, ex p British Telecommunications Plc* [1996] QB 615; and *R v Ministry of Agriculture Fisheries and Food, ex p Hedley Lomas (Ireland) Ltd* [1997] QB 139. Cf. *R v Secretary of State for Employment, ex p Equal Opportunities Commission* [1995] 1 AC 1, 32B-D (*Francovich* issues appropriate for separate damages actions), applied in *R v Secretary of State for Employment, ex p Seymour-Smith* [1997] 1 WLR 473, 480E.

3.3.4 **Other monetary consequences of successful judicial review.** *Risk Management Partners Ltd v Brent London Borough Council* [2008] EWHC 1094 (Admin) [2008] LGR 429 (damages under Public Contract Regulations 2006, following successful judicial review claim); *McLaughlin v Governor of the Cayman Islands* [2007] UKPC 50 [2007] 1 WLR 2839 (salary and pension entitlements following from judicial review of procedurally invalid dismissal of public office-holder).

3.3.5 Caution where judicial review solely to underpin damages. <25.1.7>.

3.3.6 Public law wrong not sufficient for damages. <25.2>.

3.3.7 Whether judicial review exclusive means of establishing public law wrong. <27.3.10> (procedural exclusivity and public law condition precedent).

3.4 Securing assurances/provoking comment. Whatever the result of the case, a party may find reassurance or vindication in comments made to or by the Court.

3.4.1 Assurances. *R v West London Stipendiary Magistrate, ex p Simeon* [1983] 1 AC 234, 239D-E, 243F (confirmation that no prosecutions would take place); *R v Southwark Crown Court, ex p Mitchell* [1994] COD 15 (Crown undertaking to offer no evidence after quashed crown court decision); *R v Oldham Metropolitan Borough Council, ex p Garlick* [1993] AC 509, 520H (council undertaking to reconsider); *R v Secretary of State for the Home Department, ex p Abdi* [1996] 1 WLR 298, 302F (agreement to review the "cases on the merits"); *R v Social Fund Inspector, ex p Ali* (1994) 6 Admin LR 205, 223F-G (undertaking to "review the matter *de novo* in the light of this new evidence"); *R v Secretary of State for the Home Department, ex p Doody* [1994] 1 AC 531, 563B-C (Home Secretary giving undertaking that life prisoners were entitled to make representations as to their `tariff' periods); *R v Secretary of State for Trade, ex p Vardy* [1993] ICR 720, 761F-G (promised consultation and assurance of no irreversible step); *McInnes v Onslow-Fane* [1978] 1 WLR 1520, 1536G-H (offer of a hearing); *R v Secretary of State for the Home Department, ex p Fire Brigades Union* [1995] 2 AC 513, 548D-E (assurance that no claimant would be adversely affected by the changed scheme); *New Zealand Maori Council v Attorney-General of New Zealand* [1994] 1 AC 466, 473A (at court's invitation, Crown "scheme designed to protect the Maori language"), 485D-F (assurances regarding scheme giving legitimate expectation); *R (Zeqiri) v Secretary of State for the Home Department* [2002] UKHL 3 [2002] INLR 291 (no sufficiently clear representation that test case result would be generally applied).

3.4.2 Securing action. *R v Northavon District Council, ex p Smith* [1994] 2 AC 402, 413C-E ("under the threat of judicial review, the housing authority did, in fact, call off the eviction, and allowed the Smith family to remain in temporary accommodation"); *R v Council of Legal Education, ex p Eddis* (1995) 7 Admin LR 357, 370F-371E (describing CLE's change of position in the light of *Ex p Toms, Latimer & Nightingale* The Times 5th May 1994); *R v London Borough of Lambeth, ex p G* [1994] ELR 207, 212H-213C (concession during the hearing of the judicial review that, on the state of the evidence, willing to make an award); *R v Birmingham City Council, ex p A* [1997] 2 FLR 841, 846 ("the making of the application brought the matter to a head and ... concentrated the minds of the local authority upon the position, and to that extent it has had an effect").

3.4.3 Provoking comment.
(A) CLEARING THE CLAIMANT'S NAME. *Chief Constable of the North Wales Police v Evans* [1982] 1 WLR 1155, 1166B-C (comments "to make clear to the North Wales police force or indeed to any other police force he may now seek to join that [the claimant] emerges from this litigation with his reputation wholly untarnished"); *R v Life Assurance and Unit Trust*

Regulatory Organisation Ltd, ex p Tee (1995) 7 Admin LR 289, 303F (Lautro stating in open court that claimant cleared of damaging imputations).

(B) EXPECTED BEHAVIOUR. *R (Heffernan) v Sheffield City Council* [2004] EWHC 1377 (Admin) (2004) 7 CCLR 385 (care plan should be reconsidered); *R v Birmingham City Council, ex p Equal Opportunities Commission* [1989] 1 AC 1155, 1197A-B (explaining what the council's "proper course must surely be"); *R v Commission for Racial Equality, ex p Hillingdon London Borough Council* [1982] AC 779, 793F (hinting that it was "difficult to believe that the commission will persist in trying afresh to embark upon a formal investigation"); *R v Secretary of State for the Home Department, ex p Hickey (No.2)* [1995] 1 WLR 734, 741A-D (expected behaviour in areas not directly under review).

(C) POSSIBLE SOLUTIONS. *R v Secretary of State for the Home Department, ex p Read* [1989] AC 1014, 1055D (exercise of powers "may be a matter which the Secretary of State will wish to consider"); *R v Legal Aid Board, ex p Bruce* [1992] 1 WLR 694, 701G (claimant's inclusion "merits the serious consideration of the Lord Chancellor"); *R v Wandsworth County Court, ex p Munn* (1994) 26 HLR 697, 701-2 (guidance as to endorsement of penal notices); *R v Middlesex Guildhall Crown Court, ex p Salinger* [1993] QB 564, 575C-576D (procedural guidance, absent any rules); *R v Secretary of State for the Home Department, ex p Ram* [1995] COD 250 (inviting Home Secretary to reconsider exercising power); *R v Secretary of State for the Home Department, ex p Moon* (1996) 8 Admin LR 477, 485G-H (suggesting distinction for Secretary of State to have in mind when reconsidering).

(D) BETTER PRACTICES. *R (Refugee Legal Centre) v Secretary of State for the Home Department* [2004] EWCA Civ 1481 [2005] 1 WLR 2219 at [23] (Home Office required to formulate a "written flexibility policy"), [25] ("a material part of the RLC's concern needs to be addressed"); *R v Secretary of State for the Home Department, ex p Oladehinde* [1991] 1 AC 254, 301G-302B (identifying a "much more satisfactory" procedure); *R v Secretary of State for Health, ex p Luff* (1991) 3 Admin LR 797, 817B (making of observations "in the hope that it may be of help in the carrying out of future policy").

(E) EXPECTING GREATER COOPERATION. *R v Northavon District Council, ex p Smith* [1994] 2 AC 402, 413E (hoping that parties "will explore the possibility of obtaining council accommodation informally and in a spirit of mutual cooperation"); *R v Secretary of State for the Environment, ex p Kent County Council* (1995) 93 LGR 322, 334 ("a sad reflection that the two public bodies themselves have felt it necessary to come to this court to have [their] difference resolved"); *R v Lord Chancellor, ex p Law Society* (1994) 6 Admin LR 833 (DC), 868A ("It is ... to be hoped that a satisfactory dialogue can be resumed in the near future").

(F) OTHER OBSERVATIONS. *R (SK) v Secretary of State for the Home Department* [2008] EWHC 98 (Admin) (comment on shocking manner in which officials had dealt with case); *R (Abbasi) v Secretary of State for Foreign and Commonwealth Affairs* [2002] EWCA Civ 1598 [2003] UKHRR 76 at [64], [66] (without directly ruling on legality of detention by US authorities at Guantanamo Bay, Court of Appeal commenting that detention arbitrary and in breach of human rights, as involving a "legal black hole"); *Rushbridger v HM Attorney-General* [2003] UKHL 38 [2004] 1 AC 357 (prosecution for anti-Royal articles inconceivable); *R (Howard League for Penal Reform) v Secretary of State for the Home Department* [2002] EWHC 2497 (Admin) [2003] 1 FLR 484 at [175] (claimant having "performed a most useful service in bringing to public attention matters which, on the face of it, ought to shock the conscience of every citizen"); *R v Forest Heath District Council, ex p West* (1992) 4 Admin LR 349, 352F ("on reflection", council might "think it to be more appropriate to rehouse [the claimants] rather than to incur [further] costs"); *R v Chief Constable of Devon & Cornwall, ex p Central Electricity Generating Board* [1982] QB 458, 472E ("I hope [the chief constable] will decide to use his men to clear the obstructors off the site"); *R v Secretary of State for the Home Department, ex p Stafford* [1998] 1 WLR 503, 518F (urging reconsideration).

3.4.4 **Reassurance in defeat.** *R v Secretary of State for Transport, ex p National Insurance Guarantee Corporation Plc* [1996] COD 425 (judicial review failing but providing the comfort that legislative provision not having the feared meaning).

3.5 **Wider impact/knock-on effect.** The outcome of a judicial review may have a very significant effect on the conduct and practices of public bodies, whether in lookalike cases or more generally.

3.5.1 **Many like cases.** *R (Limbuela) v Secretary of State for the Home Department* [2004] EWCA Civ 540 [2004] QB 1440 at [2] (666 judicial review cases awaiting disposal in the light of the CA's judgment) (HL is at [2005] UKHL 66 [2006] 1 AC 396); *In re Wilson* [1985] AC 750, 755F (Lord Roskill, recognising that "magistrates courts ... must be faced with this situation in many thousands of cases each year"); *R v Criminal Injuries Compensation Board, ex p Webb* [1987] QB 74, 77F-G (acknowledging that some 250 similar cases waiting in the wings); *R v Stockport Justices, ex p Conlon* [1997] 2 All ER 204, 205D (aware that "some hundred or so" like cases in the Administrative Court List); *R v Preston Supplementary Benefits Appeal Tribunal, ex p Moore* [1975] 1 WLR 624, 632A-B (statutory provisions applied daily by thousands of officers and 120 appeal tribunals); *R v Solihull Metropolitan Borough Council Housing Benefits Review Board, ex p Simpson* (1994) 92 LGR 719, 727-728, 730 (common practice of Review Boards); *R v Secretary of State for Wales, ex p Gwent County Council* [1995] ELR 87, 94C-F (recognising implications for local authority payments to central government under a range of statutes).

3.5.2 **Precipitating a change of practice.** *R v Secretary of State for the Home Department, ex p Doody* [1994] 1 AC 531, 554A (describing how a change in the Home Secretary's practice for setting initial parole review dates had been "prompted by" the decision in *R v Secretary of State for the Home Department, ex p Handscomb* (1987) 86 Cr App R 59); *R v Life Assurance and Unit Trust Regulatory Organisation Ltd, ex p Tee* (1995) 7 Admin LR 289 (considering the change in the Lautro rules, extending rights to challenge intervention notices to non-Lautro members, following the start of the litigation which became *R v Life Assurance and Unit Trust Regulatory Organisation, ex p Ross* [1993] QB 17); *R v Newham London Borough Council, ex p Dada* (1994) 26 HLR 738, 745-746 (council no longer applying policy which had been held in *R v London Borough of Newham, ex p Laronde* (1995) 27 HLR 215 to have been applied inflexibly); *R v Secretary of State for Social Services, ex p Sherwin* 16th February 1996 unrep. (making clear that standard letter of Benefits Agency should be altered in future to show that discretion had been exercised).

3.5.3 **Impact/experience of judicial review.**
(A) ANALYSIS OF IMPACT OF JUDICIAL REVIEW.[22] Bridges, Meszaros and Sunkin, *Judicial Review in Perspective* (2nd ed. 1995); Lord Woolf, "The Additional Responsibilities of the Judiciary in the New Millennium", in Markesinis (ed), *The Clifford Chance Millennium Lectures: The Coming Together of the Common Law and the Civil Law* at p.139 (advantages of "structured research" into practical benefits of judicial review).
(B) PRACTICAL EXPERIENCE OF JUDICIAL REVIEW.[23]

---

[22] George Meszaros, Lee Bridges & Maurice Sunkin [1997] JR 51; Maurice Sunkin, Kerman Calvo & Varda Bondy [2006] JR 275.

[23] Jane Ridley [1996] JR 45; Diane Blood [2002] JR 146; Amit Kapadia [2008] JR 191.

> **P4 Materiality.** A claim may fail if lacking substance, as where non-material, non-prejudicial, futile, academic or premature.

4.1 Practical substance and judicial review
4.2 Materiality/material flaw
4.3 Lack of prejudice
4.4 Futility
4.5 Dangers of materiality, prejudice and futility
4.6 Hypothetical/academic issues
4.7 Prematurity

4.1 Practical substance and judicial review. The fact that judicial review is essentially concerned with legality and not merits gives rise to a mismatch, between the reason why a claimant is inviting judicial interference (merits-disagreement) and the basis on which they are inviting it (anything but merits-disagreement). Courts are alive to this inescapable reality. Indeed, a clear lack of practical substance in the claim can be a reason not to entertain it. There too, however, the Court must avoid the forbidden function of being driven by its own perception of the merits.

4.1.1 **A Steyn maxim: substance over form.***R v Hammersmith and Fulham London Borough Council, ex p Burkett* [2002] UKHL 23 [2002] 1 WLR 1593 at [31] (Lord Steyn: "In public law the emphasis should be on substance rather than form"); *R v Secretary of State for the Home Department, ex p Pierson* [1998] AC 539, 585D (Lord Steyn: "In public law the emphasis should be on substance rather than form"); *Secretary of State for the Home Department v Khalif Mohamed Abdi* [1994] Imm AR 402 (CA), 423 (Steyn LJ: "in administrative law it is not the form that matters but the substance"); <4.1.4> (emphasising substance rather than form).

4.1.2 **Recognising the reality of the grievance.** *R (Mount Cook Land Ltd) v Westminster City Council* [2003] EWCA Civ 1346 [2004] 1 PLR 29 at [46] (Auld LJ: "judicial review applications by would-be developers or objectors to development in planning cases are by their very nature driven primarily by commercial or private motive rather than a high-minded concern for the public weal"); *R v Ogwr Borough Council, ex p Carter Commercial Developments Ltd* [1989] 2 PLR 54 58H ("The fact that the real motive for seeking [judicial review] is to advance the [claimant]'s cause is really neither here nor there"); *R v Monopolies & Mergers Commission, ex p Argyll Group Plc* [1986] 1 WLR 763, 774B (claimant's "interest may not represent a pure and burning passion to see that public law is rightly administered, but that could be said of most [claimants] for judicial review"); *R v Lord Chancellor, ex p Child Poverty Action Group* [1999] 1 WLR 347, 353H ("many, indeed most judicial review challenges ..., even if they do raise issues of general importance ... are cases in which the [claimant] is seeking to protect some private interest of his or her own"); *Mass Energy Ltd v Birmingham City Council* [1994] Env LR 298, 306 ("really a commercial dispute between a successful and an unsuccessful tenderer"); *Ridge v Baldwin* [1964] AC 40, 68 (claimant's "real interest in this appeal is to try to save his pension rights"); *R (Quintavalle) v Secretary of State for Health* [2001] EWHC Admin 918 [2001] 4 All ER 1013 at [39]-[40] (even if claimant's motive were "to force these issues back on to the Parliamentary agenda", the court "should exercise jurisdiction" where claimant having standing and legitimate concern raised as to a question of statutory interpretation); *R v Birmingham City Council, ex p O* [1983] 1 AC 578, 592B-C (although dispute "basically one between social workers ... and the council", not detracting from "the importance of the issue").

4.1.3 **Inapt uses of judicial review.**[24] *R (Fudge) v South West Strategic Health Authority* [2007] EWCA Civ 803 at [68] ("these proceedings were wholly disproportionate to the limited utility of the result achieved"), [67] ("Public law falls into disrepute if it causes an unnecessary diversion of work and resources"); *R v Licensing Authority established under Medicines Act 1968, ex p Smith Kline & French Laboratories Ltd (No.1)* [1990] 1 AC 64, 107C-F (judicial review part of a "campaign" intended "to harass and obstruct the licensing authority"); *R v Secretary of State for the Environment, ex p Nottinghamshire County Council* [1986] AC 240, 267F-H ("Judicial review is not just a move in an interminable chess tournament"); *R v Hammersmith and Fulham London Borough Council, ex p Burkett* [2001] Env LR 684 (CA) at [17] (describing "the discovery by commercial lawyers in recent years that wherever central or local government happens to have become involved, judicial review can become a way of conducting a trade war by other means"); *R (Noble Organisation) v Thanet District Council* [2005] EWCA Civ 782 [2006] Env LR 185 at [68] (expressing "dissatisfaction at the way the availability of the remedy of judicial review can be exploited - some might say abused - as a commercial weapon by rival potential developers"); *R (B) v Lambeth London Borough Council* [2006] EWHC 639 (Admin) (2006) 9 CCLR 239 at [35] (inappropriate to use judicial review "as a means of monitoring and regulating the performance by a public authority of its public duties and responsibilities"); <13.6.3> (curbing inappropriate action).

4.1.4 **Whether the challenge has substance.** *R v Monopolies & Mergers Commission, ex p Argyll Group Plc* [1986] 1 WLR 763 (MMC's chairman held to have acted without power, but remedy nevertheless refused as a matter of discretion), 774E ("Good public administration is concerned with substance rather than form"); *R v Chief Constable of the Thames Valley Police, ex p Cotton* [1990] IRLR 344, 350-351 ("natural justice is not concerned with the observance of technicalities, but with matters of substance"), 351 ("the court is concerned with matters of substance and not mere form"); *R v Central Criminal Court, ex p Hutchinson* [1996] COD 14 (refusing judicial review of a search warrant, emphasising that claimant not submitting that the same material would have been outside a legitimate, more narrowly-drawn, warrant); *R v Tottenham Youth Court, ex p Fawzy* [1999] 1 WLR 1350, 1357E-H (claimant not "exposed to any substantial unfairness or disadvantage"; *Lubrizol Ltd v Tyndallwoods Solicitors* 8th April 1998 unrep. (emphasising "the importance of all parties looking beyond the purely legal issues to the practical and commercial realities of the case"); *R v Secretary of State for the Home Department, ex p Chugtai* [1995] Imm AR 559, 567 ("This court has ample power in the exercise of its discretion to avoid giving [a remedy] in cases which do not appear to have any merit"); *R v London Borough of Newham, ex p Watkins* (1994) 26 HLR 434, 451 (referring to cases of "trivial default"); *R (M) v Commissioner of Police of the Metropolis* [2001] EWHC Admin 553 (concluding that no interference in substance with an HRA:ECHR right: Court not required "to divorce itself from reality, nor to avert its gaze from the substance of a case"); *R (Edwards) v Environment Agency* [2008] UKHL 22 (substantial EIA compliance); *R (Wembley Field Ltd) v Brent London Borough Council* [2005] EWHC 2978 (Admin) [2006] Env LR 891 (consultation shorter than statutorily-required period but substantial compliance and no prejudice); *R v Department of Health, ex p Gandhi* [1991] 1 WLR 1053, 1068A-B (finding procedural unfairness, but granting declaration only); *R v Oxford Crown Court, ex p Smith* (1990) 2 Admin LR 389, 396F, 401H (declaration only, where crown court should have entertained argument, but it proving "worthless"); *R v Manchester Crown Court, ex p Taylor* [1988] 1 WLR 705, 718H (declaration needs a "practical point"); *R (Fingle Glen Junction Business & Community Action Group) v Highways Agency* [2007] EWHC 2446 (Admin) (in considering non-consultation complaint "it is important to look at the substance of the matter").

---

[24] Jonathan Lewis [2007] JR 107.

/**material flaw**.[25] There are several interrelated ways in which the Court can ... ...stance of the case and conclude that a public law wrong does not warrant interfere... ...ooking at the case in the round. One way is by asking whether a given flaw in the defendant's approach was a "material" one. Might it have made a difference? Would the decision inevitably have been the same anyway? Then only, the Court may say the flaw did not vitiate the decision, or that a remedy is not warranted.

4.2.1 **Materiality: need more than a mistake.** *R v Independent Television Commission, ex p TSW Broadcasting Ltd* [1994] 2 LRC 414, 425i ("[A claimant] for judicial review must show more than a mistake on the part of the decision maker or his advisers"), applied in *R v Independent Television Commission, ex p Virgin Television Limited* [1996] EMLR 318; *West Coast Wind Farms Ltd v Secretary of State for the Environment* [1996] Env LR 29, 48 (no "fundamental" error: no "reasonable prospect that the Inspector would have done other than reach the same conclusion"); *R (Nadesu) v Secretary of State for the Home Department* [2003] EWHC 2839 (Admin) at [34] (Court "satisfied that if the Secretary of State had taken the ... [matter] into consideration ... he would have come to the same conclusion"); *R v Epsom Justices, ex p Gibbons* [1984] QB 574 (magistrates reached the right answer, albeit for an "inappropriate" reason); *R v Secretary of State for Education, ex p London Borough of Southwark* [1995] ELR 308, 324H-325A (decision reasonable even if arrived at "more by good luck than judgment"); *Dobie v Burns International Security Services (UK) Ltd* [1985] 1 WLR 43, 49B-C (no remittal on appeal if decision plainly and unarguably right); *A v Kirklees Metropolitan Borough Council* [2001] EWCA Civ 582 [2001] ELR 657 at [17] ("objective question" whether relevant material "could have made any difference"), [25] (whether, if remitted, "[t]he outcome would inevitably be the same"); *R (E) v JFS Governing Body* [2008] EWHC 1535 (Admin) at [214] (declaration only where breach of race equality duty but even "the fullest and most conscientious compliance" would not have made "any difference").

4.2.2 **Materiality and mixed reasons/separable reasons.** *R (UNISON) v First Secretary of State* [2006] EWHC 2373 (Admin) [2007] LGR 188 at [17] (a reason given for pension changes wrong in law, but court satisfied that same conclusion would have been reached in any event as a matter of policy); *R v Broadcasting Complaints Commission, ex p Owen* [1985] QB 1153, 1177A-B ("Where the reasons given by a statutory body for taking or not taking a particular course of action are not mixed and can clearly be disentangled, but where the court is quite satisfied that even though one reason may be bad in law, nevertheless the statutory body would have reached precisely the same decision on the other valid reasons, then this court will not interfere by way of judicial review"); *Suisse Security Bank and Trust Ltd v Governor of the Central Bank of The Bahamas* [2006] UKPC 11 [2006] 1 WLR 1660 at [44] (applying *Owen*); *R (Eliot) v Crown Court at Reading* [2001] EWHC Admin 464 [2001] 4 All ER 625 at [7] (whether "two separate reasons were being given"); *R v Housing Benefit Review Board for Allerdale District Council, ex p Doughty* [2000] COD 462 (whether lawful strand of reasoning untainted by being interwoven with unlawful strand); <52.2.6> (approach to mixed purposes/mixed motives).

4.2.3 **Material misconstitution/participation.** *R v Monopolies & Mergers Commission, ex p Argyll Group Plc* [1986] 1 WLR 763 (properly constituted group of members of the MMC would reach the same conclusion); *R v Governors of Small Heath School, ex p Birmingham*

---

[25] This paragraph in a previous edition was cited in *Re E* [2006] NICA 37 at [108].

City Council (1990) 2 Admin LR 154, 166G-168D (although 4 governors ought to have disqualified themselves, DC entitled to refuse remedy where "the fact that they voted did not have any direct effect on the result of the ballot"); *R v Surrey Coroner, ex p Wright* [1997] QB 786, 797H (assessor ought not to have given evidence in coroner's inquest but court "not persuaded that [it] will have made any material difference to the outcome"); cf. *R (B) v Head Teacher of Alperton Community School* [2001] EWHC Admin 229 at [23] (where panel was "without jurisdiction" because not "duly constituted in accordance with the statute", "no question of discretion arises. The claimant is entitled to [a remedy] as of right").

4.2.4 Material procedural flaw. *R (Abbey Mine Ltd) v Coal Authority* [2008] EWCA Civ 353 at [44] (matters were not put but no material effect on outcome); *R (O'Connell) v Parole Board* [2007] EWHC 2591 (Admin) [2008] 1 WLR 979 at [24] (decision could not be affected by anything said at oral hearing); *R (National Association of Health Stores) v Secretary of State for Health* [2005] EWCA Civ 154 at [22] (defective consultation non-material since missing option could not rationally have been adopted); *R (Smith) v North East Derbyshire Primary Care Trust* [2006] EWCA Civ 1291 [2006] 1 WLR 3315 at [10] (defendant "would have to show that the decision would inevitably have been the same"); *R (Mlloja) v Secretary of State for the Home Department* [2005] EWHC 2833 (Admin) at [34] (ask whether "the outcome would necessarily or inevitably have been the same if the correct procedures had been adopted"); *London Borough of Merton v Williams* [2002] EWCA Civ 980 [2003] HLR 257 at [43] (whether "the decision would inevitably have been the same"); *R (Lichfield Securities Ltd) v Lichfield District Council* [2001] EWCA Civ 304 [2001] 3 PLR 33 at [23] (materiality goes to finding of unfairness, not to discretion as to remedy); *Sheridan v Stanley Cole (Wainfleet) Ltd* [2003] EWCA Civ 1046 [2003] 4 All ER 1181 at [50] ("the outcome would inevitably be the same"); *R (S) v London Borough of Brent* [2002] EWCA Civ 693 [2002] ELR 556 at [26] ("it is not ordinarily open ... to a decision-maker who has failed to give a fair hearing to assert that a fair hearing would have made no difference"); *R (Morley) v Nottinghamshire Healthcare NHS Trust* [2002] EWCA Civ 1728 [2003] 1 All ER 784 at [48] (whether a "reasonable possibility" that the outcome would have been different); *Nwabueze v General Medical Council* [2000] 1 WLR 1760, 1775-1776D (no unfairness because no "points of substance" to raise); *R (Madden) v Bury Metropolitan Borough Council* [2002] EWHC 1882 (Admin) (2002) 5 CCLR 622 at [74] (Court must be "certain", "mere likelihood" insufficient); *R (O'Callaghan) v Charity Commission* [2007] EWHC 2491 (Admin) (inadequate consultation and not shown that decision would inevitably be the same).

4.2.5 Material inflexible policy. *R v Brent London Borough Council, ex p Baruwa* (1997) 29 HLR 915, 927 (any illegality from excessively rigid policy not vitiating decision as to intentional homelessness in the present case).

4.2.6 Materiality and other grounds for judicial review. <48.1.6> (material misdirection in law/error of law); <56.1.6> (materiality and relevancy/irrelevancy); <49.2.4> (material error of fact); <61.3.6> (operative bias).

4.3 **Lack of prejudice.** A second interrelated way in which the Court can look to the "substance" of the case, in the light of an error of approach, is to ask whether the claimant can in truth be said to have suffered no "prejudice" as a result of the public law wrong. In other words, was the flaw in the decision-maker's approach one which did no conceivable harm. If so, the Court may decide not to interfere.

4.3.1 Whether prejudice/injustice from flawed approach. *R v Aston University Senate, ex p Roffey* [1969] 2 QB 538, 551B ("prerogative writs are a discretionary remedy designed to remedy real and substantial injustice"); *R (Ghadami) v Harlow District Council* [2004] EWHC 1883 (Admin) [2005] LGR 24 at [73] (defective advertisement but "neither the claimant nor the public at large suffered any prejudice"); *R v Joint Higher Committee on Surgical Training, ex p Milner* (1995) 7 Admin LR 454, 463D (no injustice from considering oral rather than written references); *R v Panel on Take-overs and Mergers, ex p Guinness Plc* [1990] 1 QB 146, 192B ("[the claimant] has failed in the end to satisfy me that there has been any real injustice, or even any real risk of injustice, in this case"); *R v Liverpool Magistrates' Court, ex p Ansen* [1998] 1 All ER 692, 699d ("no substantial injustice"); *R (Garg) v Criminal Injuries Compensation Authority* [2007] EWCA Civ 797 at [44] (error of law not having "produced any real injustice"); <50.3.6> (prejudice and improper delegation).

4.3.2 Reasons and prejudice. *South Bucks District Council v Porter (No.2)* [2004] UKHL 33 [2004] 1 WLR 1953 at [36] (Lord Brown, speaking in a statutory planning challenge: "A reasons challenge will only succeed if the party aggrieved can satisfy the court that he has genuinely been substantially prejudiced by the failure to provide an adequately reasoned decision"); *R v Immigration Appeal Tribunal, ex p Dhaliwal* [1994] Imm AR 387, 392 ("To provide a remedy based on the absence of proper reasoning, there should be some element of prejudice"); *R (C) v Leeds Youth Court* [2005] EWHC 1216 (Admin) (youth court should have given reasons but committal was the only available decision on the facts here); *R (Wall) v Brighton and Hove City Council* [2004] EWHC 2582 (Admin) [2004] 4 PLR 115 at [62] (Sullivan J: "While the extent to which a claimant has been prejudiced by a local planning authority's failure to include summary reasons in a decision notice will be a relevant factor in the exercise of the court's discretion, there is no requirement that an applicant for judicial review must show that he or she has been prejudiced, or substantially prejudiced, by the unlawful act complained of").

4.3.3 Prejudice and procedural flaws. *R v Chief Constable of the Thames Valley Police, ex p Cotton* [1990] IRLR 344 (absent any statutory or contractual procedure, court asking whether any breach of natural justice in substance; not here, where no substantial chance that would have made any difference); *R v East Dereham Justices, ex p Clarke* [1996] COD 196 (failure to allow opportunity for representations but no detriment); *R v South Northamptonshire District Council, ex p Crest Homes Plc* (1995) 93 LGR 205, 210 (remedy refused because "nothing to suggest that there has been any prejudice to any objecting party caused by the irregular ... consultation"); *R v Powys County Council, ex p Andrews* [1997] Env LR 170, 187 (where failure to consult other officers, ask whether loss of a "real, as opposed to fanciful, chance" of a contrary decision); *R (Clegg) v Secretary of State for Trade and Industry* [2002] EWCA Civ 519 at [30] ("if procedural unfairness is established, it would be enough to show that, but for that procedural unfairness, the outcome might have been different"); *R v Chelsea College of Art and Design, ex p Nash* [2000] ELR 686 at [50] (only "in the very plainest of cases ... one can say that the breach could have made no difference"); *R v Secretary of State for Foreign and Commonwealth Affairs, ex p Everett* [1989] 1 QB 811, 819B (although Secretary of State should have given reasons and an opportunity to persuade, claimant now knowing the reasons and no real prejudice); *Hobbs v London Borough of Sutton* (1994) 26 HLR 132, 146 ("no need" to put matters to the claimants, since "even if some explanation could have been given... it could not, in my judgment, have affected the decision itself"); *R v Secretary of State for the Home Department, ex p Georghiades* (1993) 5 Admin LR 457 (Parole Board's decision quashed for failure to put material to the claimant), 468H-469A ("The court does not ... enquire whether this material did work to the [claimant]'s prejudice. Sufficient that it might have done so"); *R v North & East Devon Health Authority, ex p Pow* (1998) 1 CCLR 280, 293E-F (remedy granted where failure to consult because, even though the grounds for opposition to the decision were well-known, proper consultation ought to produce positive suggestions of alternative proposals); *R v Tandridge District Council, ex p Al Fayed* [2000] 1 PLR 58, 62 C-D ("established beyond argument" that defendant would have come to same conclusion), 63B; *Berkeley v Secretary of State for the Environment* [2001] 2 AC 603 (where no environmental impact assessment as required by EC law, Court not entitled to refuse remedy on the basis that the result would have been the same); *R v Secretary of State for the Home Department, ex p Amin* [2001] ACD 66 (technical breach involving no prejudice); *Magill v Porter* [2001] UKHL 67 [2002] 2 AC 357 at [106] (assuming that not necessary to show prejudice, if breach of Article 6 because unreasonable delay); *R (Varma) v Duke of Kent* [2004] EWHC 1705 (Admin) [2004] ELR 616 at [27] ("entirely satisfied that [the claimant] could not have made any representation which could have affected the result"); *R (Siborurema) v Office of the Independent Adjudicator* [2007] EWCA Civ 1365 at [66] ("no real possibility" that disclosure of information for comment would have affected the decision); <60.4.4> (whether procedural ultra vires needs prejudice); <60.1.8> (material irregularity); <60.1.14> (procedural fairness: whether need for prejudice).

4.3.4 Flaw having been subsequently corrected. <36.4> (whether breach cured on appeal/ reconsideration); *R v Bath City Council, ex p Nankervis & Wilson* [1994] COD 271 (decision to commence possession proceedings flawed, but subsequent decision to continue them lawful and proper); *R v Newham London Borough Council, ex p Begum* (1996) 28 HLR 646 (errors cured when matter eventually properly reconsidered); *R v Wolverhampton Municipal Borough Council, ex p Dunne* (1997) 29 HLR 745, 751, 753-754 (inquiries not undertaken but refuse remedy only if inquiries would not, if made at the time, have affected the decision).

4.4 Futility.[26] A third way in which the Court may focus upon "substance" is to ask whether granting a remedy would be "futile". Judges sometimes say that judicial review remedies ought not to be granted, as a matter of discretion, where there is no realistic prospect that they would lead to a different eventual outcome. The question is whether the decision would inevitably be the same if required to be taken afresh. If so, a Court may decline to give a remedy.

4.4.1 Remedy would serve no useful purpose. *R (Edwards) v Environment Agency* [2008] UKHL 22 at [65] (pointless to quash where overtaken by events); *R (Middleton) v West Somerset Coroner* [2004] UKHL 10 [2004] 2 AC 182 at [48] ("No purpose is served by a declaration"); *R v Secretary of State for the Home Department, ex p Fire Brigades Union* [1995] 2 AC 513, 576H-577A, 566C-D (sending the matter back to the Secretary of State to consider afresh would be a pointless exercise); *R (Arbab) v Secretary of State for the Home Department* [2002] EWHC 1249 (Admin) [2002] Imm AR 536 at [64] (declaration would serve no useful purpose); *R v Head Teacher and Governors of Fairfield Primary School, ex p W* [1998] COD 106 (no practical significance in disciplinary matter where those concerned about to leave for separate secondary schools); *R v Southwark Coroner's Court, ex p Epsom Health Care NHS Trust* [1995] COD 92 (no useful purpose in ordering new inquest); *R v Gloucestershire County Council, ex p P* [1994] ELR 334, 340D (declaration sought having "little or no value for the future"); *R v Horseferry Road Magistrates, ex p Prophet* [1995] Env LR 104, 111-112 (judicial review proceedings having become pointless); *R v Comptroller-General of Patents Designs & Trade Marks, ex p Gist-Brocades* [1986] 1 WLR 51, 66G-H

---

[26] This paragraph in a previous edition was cited in *Lawrence v Attorney General* [2007] UKPC 18 [2007] 1 WLR 1474 at [65]; also *Lam Yuet Mei v Permanent Secretary for Education and Manpower* [2004] HKCU 922 at [61].

("the passage of time has by now made any prerogative remedy of no practical use"); *R v Mansfield Justices, ex p Sharkey* [1985] QB 613, 629H-630B (re-hearing "could not fail to impose the same or a similar condition"); *R v North West Thames Regional Health Authority, ex p Daniels (Rhys William)* [1994] COD 44 (order would not benefit the claimant nor do any good); *R v Cumbria County Council ex p P* [1995] ELR 337, 345E ("A declaration in the terms asked would clarify nothing"); *R v Secretary of State for Employment, ex p Seymour-Smith* [1997] 1 WLR 473 (declaration discharged since would serve no useful purpose as to any claim in an industrial tribunal or any need for the UK to take remedial action); *R (Machi) v Legal Services Commission* [2001] EWCA Civ 2010 [2002] 1 WLR 983 at [34] (no futility once "a reasoned decision of the Administrative Court had been delivered on the questions of illegality and fairness"); *R (C) v Secretary of State for Justice* [2008] EWCA Civ 882 at [49] (appropriate to quash regulations for absence of race equality impact assessment, where assessment done subsequently, but served to validate the decision and refusing relief would send the wrong message to public authorities).

4.4.2 **No material capable of producing different decision.** *R (Martin) v Secretary of State for the Home Department* [2003] EWHC 1512 (Admin) at [19] (defective parole dossier but omitted material not capable of leading to a different result); *R v Secretary of State for the Home Department & Others ex p Tania Luiza Stefan* [1995] Imm AR 410, 423 (misdirection in law, but no material such as would have persuaded the adjudicator to alter the determination); *R v Rochester-upon-Medway City Council, ex p Williams* (1994) 26 HLR 588, 595-596 (if required to reconsider, the facts "would drive it to the same conclusion"); *R v London Borough of Newham, ex p Campbell* (1994) 26 HLR 183, 190 (misdirection, but "on the evidence before this court, the only conclusion which a local authority could come to would be [the same]"); *R v Canterbury City Council, ex p Springimage Ltd* [1993] 3 PLR 58, 74H (material misdirection, but no "real possibility of the decision on this application being different, were the matter now to go back to the committee"); *R v Oxford City Justices, ex p Berry* [1988] QB 507 (magistrates should have addressed admissibility of confession, but ample other evidence on which could commit); *Warren v Uttlesford District Council* [1997] COD 483 (declining to order fresh public inquiry where claimants unable to point to any specific new material with a realistic possibility of causing the council to change its mind); *A v Kirklees Metropolitan Borough Council* [2001] EWCA Civ 582 [2001] ELR 657 at [24] (not realistic that would have made any difference), [25] (if remitted "[t]he outcome would inevitably be the same").

4.4.3 **Open-minded defendant willing to consider representations.** *R (S) v Education Action (Waltham Forest)* [2006] EWHC 3144 (Admin) [2007] ELR 185 at [38] (no order needed where defendant having offered to reconsider); *R v Secretary of State for the Home Department, ex p Pierson* [1998] AC 539, 593E-F (defendant "willing to consider any further representations", so order would not "serve any useful purpose"); *R v Radio Authority, ex p Bull* [1998] QB 294, 309B-F ("preferable that the whole issue should be reconsidered in the light of our judgments on the up to date information"); *R v Secretary of State for the Home Department, ex p Venables* [1998] AC 407, 437D (consideration of reports "after the decision has been reached is not the same as for them to be taken into account before the decision is reached"); *R (Q) v Secretary of State for the Home Department* [2003] EWCA Civ 364 [2004] QB 36 at [91] (willingness to reconsider an adverse decision as to welfare benefits for asylum-seekers "not a substitute for proper and fair primary decision making"); *R (SP) v Secretary of State for the Home Department* [2004] EWCA Civ 1750 at [58] ("once a decision is made, it is difficult to change it", especially where would mean seeking to persuade that wrong factual basis); <13.5.5> (restraint and defendant's open-mindedness).

4.4.4 Ask whether judicial review *might* make a difference. *R v Inner West London Coroner, ex p Dallaglio* [1994] 4 All ER 139, 155e (Simon Brown LJ: "Although there must inevitably be formidable difficulties in resuming these inquests now ... not prepared to say that a fresh coroner would be bound to refuse a resumption"); *Simplex GE (Holdings) Ltd v Secretary of State for the Environment* [1988] 3 PLR 25, 42 (Purchas LJ: "It is not necessary for [counsel for the claimant] to show that the minister would, or even probably would, have come to a different conclusion. He has to exclude only the contrary contention, namely that the minister necessarily would still have made the same decision"); *R (Tataw) v Immigration Appeal Tribunal* [2003] EWCA Civ 925 [2003] INLR 585 at [28] (not "so plain and obvious" that appeal to IAT would fail so that "this court should refuse relief"); *R v Director of Passenger Rail Franchising, ex p Save Our Railways* [1996] CLC 589, 607C ("It is not ... apparent that the grant of [a remedy] will serve no useful purpose because the Secretary of State may simply amend his instructions... [W]hether he does so is a matter for him").

4.5 Dangers of materiality, prejudice and futility.[27] Judges will not readily accede to the argument that a public law flaw was non-material or non-prejudicial, or that a remedy would be futile. Public law standards matter, and public bodies should not be encouraged to breach them in the belief that they will be "let off" by the Court. Moreover, it is wrong in principle for the Court to become drawn into appraising the strength of the merits, or speculating as to how they would have been or would now be decided. There is therefore a heavy onus on a public body to show that judicial review should be refused because the decision "inevitably" would have been, or would now be, the same.

4.5.1 Onus of proof and materiality/prejudice/futility. <42.2.5(C)>.

4.5.2 Refusing a remedy: a discretion to be exercised sparingly. <24.3.4>; *R v Inner London Crown Court, ex p Sitki* [1994] COD 342 (residual discretion to refuse to quash, where the result would inevitably have been the same; but ought to be sparingly exercised, so as not to encourage unlawfulness); *R v Tynedale District Council, ex p Shield* (1990) 22 HLR 144, 148 ("the court has jurisdiction not to quash the decision if satisfied that there would be no purpose in so doing" but where manifestly flawed decision letter "in general the court would be slow not to quash").

4.5.3 Beware: procedural flaws and clear-cut cases. *John v Rees* [1970] 1 Ch 345, 402C-E (Megarry J: "It may be that there are some who would decry the importance which the courts attach to the observance of the rules of natural justice. `When something is obvious', they may say, `why force everybody to go through the tiresome waste of time involved in framing charges and giving an opportunity to be heard? The result is obvious from the start'. Those who take this view do not, I think, do themselves justice. As everybody who has anything to do with the law well knows, the path of the law is strewn with examples of open and shut cases which, somehow, were not; of unanswerable charges which, in the event, were completely answered; of inexplicable conduct which was fully explained; of fixed and unalterable determinations that, by discussion, suffered a change. Nor are those with any knowledge of human nature who pause to think for a moment likely to underestimate the feelings of resentment of those who find that

---

[27] This paragraph in a previous edition was cited in *R (Smith) v North East Derbyshire Primary Care Trust* [2006] EWCA Civ 129 at [10]; also *R (O'Callaghan) v Charity Commission* [2007] EWHC 2491 (Admin) at [41].

a decision against them has been made without their being afforded any opportunity to influence the course of events"); *R v Ealing Magistrates' Court, ex p Fanneran* (1996) 8 Admin LR 351, 356E (Staughton LJ: "the notion that when the rules of natural justice have not been observed, one can still uphold the result because it would not have made any difference, is to be treated with great caution. Down that slippery slope lies the way to dictatorship. On the other hand, if it is a case where it is demonstrable beyond doubt that it would have made no difference, the court may, if it thinks fit, uphold a conviction even if natural justice had not been done"), 359E (Rougier J); *R v Chief Constable of the Thames Valley Police, ex p Cotton* [1990] IRLR 344, 352 (Bingham LJ: "While cases may no doubt arise in which it can properly be held that denying the subject of a decision an adequate opportunity to put his case is not in all the circumstances unfair, I would expect these cases to be of great rarity. There are a number of reasons for this: 1. Unless the subject of the decision has had an opportunity to put his case it may not be easy to know what case he could or would have put if he had had the chance. 2. As memorably pointed out by Megarry J in *John v Rees* [1970] Ch 345 at p.402, experience shows that that which is confidently expected is by no means always that which happens. 3. It is generally desirable that decision-makers should be reasonably receptive to argument, and it would therefore be unfortunate if the complainant's position became weaker as the decision-maker's mind became more closed. 4. In considering whether the complainant's representations would have made any difference to the outcome the court may unconsciously stray from its proper province of reviewing the propriety of the decision-making process into the forbidden territory of evaluating the substantial merits of a decision. 5. This is a field in which appearances are generally thought to matter. 6. Where a decision-maker is under a duty to act fairly the subject of the decision may properly be said to have a right to be heard, and rights are not to be lightly denied"); *R (Amin) v Secretary of State for the Home Department* [2003] UKHL 51 [2004] 1 AC 653 at [52] (Lord Steyn, referring to *John v Rees*, and warning against "the assumption that, although there has not been an adequate enquiry, it may be refused because nothing useful is likely to turn up. That judgment cannot fairly be made until there has been an enquiry"); *R v Broxtowe Borough Council, ex p Bradford* [2000] LGR 386, 387f-g (where claimant "denied a right to be heard which should have been granted to him, the courts should exercise considerable caution before concluding that the absence of the hearing has not resulted in any injustice"); *R v Secretary of State for the Home Department, ex p Kingdom of Belgium* 15th February 2000 unrep. (rejecting argument that disclosure "pointless": "The governing interest is the public interest in operating a procedure which would be perceived and accepted by the great majority to be fair"); *R v Life Assurance and Unit Trust Regulatory Organisation Ltd, ex p Tee* (1995) 7 Admin LR 289, 307F ("the Court has to be very careful before it concludes, that it would have made no difference if the representations had been made or the appeal had taken place"), 311A-B ("Where a person has unjustly been denied a fair hearing it is only in the most exceptional circumstances that it can be proper to deny him a further opportunity"), but 311C-D ("it is to my mind inconceivable that any future repetition or elaboration of [Mr Tee's] representations would lead Lautro to reverse or vary their decision").

4.5.4 **"Futility" and dangers of Court substituting its view on the merits.** *R v Governors of the Sheffield Hallam University, ex p R* [1995] ELR 267, 288B (refusing "to decline ... to grant the [claimant] the [remedy] which is otherwise her due on the basis of my own appraisal of her chances. To do so would be, precisely, to substitute the court for the university as the decision-making body"); *R v Legal Aid Area No.8 (Northern) Appeal Committee, ex p Angell* (1991) 3 Admin LR 189, 223H-224C (remittal for reconsideration albeit seeming "quite pointless" because "the final decision ... is more properly taken by the Appeal Committee than by the court"); *R (Bushell) v Newcastle Upon Tyne Licensing Justices* [2004] EWHC 446 (Admin) at [29] (conclusion that "the decision-maker should have taken a particular view of the facts when

the decision-maker has not addressed his mind to those facts ... should be confined to clear and obvious cases") (HL is [2006] UKHL 7 [2006] 1 WLR 496);*R v British Coal Corporation, ex p Union of Democratic Mineworkers* [1988] ICR 36, 43H-45F, 46D-E (declaration granted that union representing substantial proportion of persons; although still open to Board to refuse to accept sufficient representation, by no means certain that such a pessimistic prognosis justified); *R v North West Lancashire Health Authority, ex p A* [2000] 1 WLR 977, 1000A ("if this Court were to assert that the health authority, reviewing those factors, would necessarily come to the same decision as previously ... it would be making exactly the error of substituting its own judgement for that of the health authority"); *R v Tandridge District Council, ex p Al Fayed* [2000] 1 PLR 58, 63C-D ("Once it is apprised of a procedural impropriety the court will always be slow to say, in effect, `no harm has been done'. That usually would involve arrogating to itself a value judgment which Parliament has left to others. But the facts of the present case are exceptional and in my judgment the judge was right to refuse [a remedy]").

4.5.5 Dangers of speculating. *R v Director of Public Prosecutions, ex p C* (1995) 7 Admin LR 385, 393D-E (Kennedy LJ: "What conclusion [the decision-maker] would have reached if he had had regard to [certain matters] ... is not a matter which in my judgment should be speculated upon in this court. The decision is one for the Director of Public Prosecutions not for this court"); *Diedrichs-Shurland v Talanga-Stiftung* [2006] UKPC 58 at [37] (wrong to speculate as to whether judge saw representations lodged behind other party's back); *R v Ealing Magistrates' Court, ex p Fanneran* (1996) 8 Admin LR 351, 359E (wrong "for this court to employ its imagination to postulate facts which might or might not have occurred or arguments which might or might not have succeeded had the rules of natural justice been followed"); *R v West Dorset District Council, ex p Gerrard* (1995) 27 HLR 150, 166 ("Not all shut doors are, in truth, shut, not all minds are closed when it comes to representation of a case"); *R v Immigration Appeal Tribunal, ex p Bastiampillai* [1983] 2 All ER 844, 853g ("I cannot say what the Secretary of State's decision would have been").

4.5.6 Fairness as an end in itself/unfairness as injustice. *R (Khatun) v London Borough of Newham* [2004] EWCA Civ 55 [2005] QB 37 at [27] (Laws LJ: "a right to be heard truly so called ... is an end in itself: it is simply the doing of justice, which requires no utilitarian justification"); *R v Bank of England, ex p Mellstrom* [1995] CLC 232, 241B (where no opportunity to deal with relevant adverse information, may be "not sufficient for the repository of the power to endeavour to shut information of that kind out of his mind and to reach a decision without reference to it"); *Errington v Wilson* The Times 2nd June 1995 (prejudice amounting from the fact of the denial of the opportunity to test the evidence); *R v Inner West London Coroner, ex p Dallaglio* [1994] 4 All ER 139, 155j-156b (rejecting "futility argument" because decision "fairly taken", claimants in a different position as to whether they "would reluctantly accept it"); *R v Secretary of State for Education and Science, ex p Islam* (1993) 5 Admin LR 177, 188B-C (important that "any unfairness will be swept away"); *Lichfield* <4.2.4>; *R (Turpin) v Commissioner for Local Administration* [2001] EWHC Admin 503 [2003] LGR 133 (no need for prejudice, sufficient that risk of prejudice).

4.6 Hypothetical/academic issues.[28] Courts do not like holding moots. In general, judges need a lot of persuading that it is right to entertain a judicial review challenge where the sole issues are, or have become, academic or hypothetical.

4.6.1 House of Lords and "hypothetical"/"academic" matters. *Rushbridger v HM Attorney-*

---

[28] David Elvin QC, `Hypothetical, Academic and Premature Challenges' [2006] JR 307.

General [2003] UKHL 38 [2004] 1 AC 357 at [35] (Lord Hutton: "It is not the function of the courts to decide hypothetical questions which do not impact on the parties before them"), *R v Secretary of State for the Home Department, ex p Salem* [1999] 1 AC 450, 456G-457B ("appeals which are academic between the parties should not be heard unless there is a good reason in the public interest for doing so"); *R v Secretary of State for the Home Department, ex p Wynne* [1993] 1 WLR 115, 120A-B ("It is well established that this House does not decide hypothetical questions"); *R v Secretary of State for the Home Department, ex p Adan* [2001] 2 AC 477 (academic appeals entertained because of general importance of the issues); *Neill v North Antrim Magistrates' Court* [1992] 1 WLR 1220, 1232H & 1234E (guidance although question had "become entirely academic"); *Chief Adjudication Officer v Foster* [1993] AC 754, 761F ("academic" issue dealt with, since having "far-reaching procedural implications for the future, it has been very fully argued and it is important that your Lordships should resolve it"); *R v Secretary of State for the Home Department, ex p Abdi* [1996] 1 WLR 298, 302F (dealing with "a question of fundamental importance"); *R (Ullah) v Secretary of State for the Home Department* [2004] UKHL 26 [2004] 2 AC 323 at [5] (given the factual position, issue of principle "academic. But it is a question of legal and practical importance. It has been fully argued... The House should give such assistance as, on the present state of the Strasbourg authorities, it can"); *A v Secretary of State for the Home Department* [2005] UKHL 71 [2006] 2 AC 221 at [1] & [90] (deciding whether torture-obtained evidence legally inadmissible albeit Secretary of State's present policy not to rely on it); *R (Bushell) v Newcastle Upon Tyne Licensing Justices* [2006] UKHL 7 [2006] 1 WLR 496 at [7]-[8] (although could no longer secure a licence, favourable ruling could affect compensation and costs); *R (Limbuela) v Secretary of State for the Home Department* [2005] UKHL 66 [2006] 1 AC 396 at [81] (no longer live issue for claimants, but importance undiminished).

4.6.2 Declarations and real questions/proper contradictors. *Russian Commercial and Industrial Bank v British Bank for Foreign Trade Ltd* [1921] 2 AC 438, 448 (Lord Dunedin: "The question must be a real and not a theoretical question; the person raising it must have a real interest to raise it; he must be able to secure a proper contradictor, that is to say, someone presently existing who has a true interest to oppose the declaration sought"); *R v Bromley London Borough Council, ex p Lambeth London Borough Council* The Times 16th June 1984 (proper contradictor); *R v Manchester Crown Court, ex p Taylor* [1988] 1 WLR 705, 717A (point theoretical rather than real); *R v Director of Public Prosecutions, ex p London Borough of Merton* [1999] COD 358 (proceedings unlikely to be of interest to another party).

4.6.3 Reluctance to deal with hypothetical/academic matters. *R (Smeaton) v Secretary of State for Health* [2002] EWHC 886 (Admin) [2002] 2 FLR 146 at [420] (courts "exist to resolve real problems and not disputes of merely academic significance"); *R (Howard League for Penal Reform) v Secretary of State for the Home Department* [2002] EWHC 2497 (Admin) [2003] 1 FLR 484 at [140] (not "the task of a judge when sitting judicially - even in the Administrative Court - to set out to write a textbook or practice manual or to give advisory opinions"); *R (European Surgeries Ltd) v Cambridgeshire Primary Care Trust* [2007] EWHC 2758 (Admin) at [21] (inappropriate to entertain claim for declaration regarding rights of NHS reimbursement where patient was not seeking reimbursement); *R v Inland Revenue Commissioners, ex p Bishopp* (1999) 11 Admin LR 575 (Court declining to make declaration regarding Revenue's pre-transaction advice, inter alia because dispute based to a large extent on hypothetical facts); *R v Portsmouth Hospitals NHS Trust, ex p Glass* [1999] 2 FLR 905, 910G ("For the court to act in anticipation in this area to try and produce clarity where, alas, there is no clarity at the moment, would, in my judgment, be a task fraught with danger"); *R (Anti-Waste Ltd) v Environment Agency* [2007] EWCA Civ 1377 [2008] 1 WLR 923 at [49] (need for utility as to declaration).

4.6.4 Whether an appropriate "test case". *R v British Broadcasting Corporation, ex p Quintavelle* (1998) 10 Admin LR 425 (sometimes appropriate to approach a case in terms of the need for guidance on an issue of general principle, rather than the merits and prospects of success of the individual case), 426E-427C (two principal considerations: whether there is any remedy which the claimant could be granted, which would be of value to the decision-maker; and whether the present application an appropriate vehicle for such guidance); *R (Morris) v Westminster City Council* [2004] EWHC 1199 (Admin) (appropriate test case); *R (Tshikangu) v Newham London Borough Council* [2001] EWHC Admin 92 (where claimant no longer needs judicial review, wrong for claimant's lawyers to decide without reference to defendant or Court to proceed as test case); *R (Cronin) v Sheffield Magistrates' Court* [2002] EWHC 2568 (Admin) [2003] 1 WLR 752 at [30] ("It is very important ... that the limited resources which are available from public funds for testing points of principle are confined to cases where it is really necessary"); *R v Secretary of State for the Home Department, ex p Adan* [2001] 2 AC 477 (CA), 486F-H (deciding "a question of general importance ... which may be considered and decided irrespective of the facts of these particular cases"; "Given the number of cases in the pipeline in which, we understand, the issue is raised, it is in our judgment in the public interest that we should determine it in these proceedings"); *R (Zeqiri) v Secretary of State for the Home Department* [2002] UKHL 3 [2002] INLR 291 at [40] (referring to a `test case' where the parties "agreed to abide by whatever the ... case decided"); *R (C) v Secretary of State for Justice* [2008] EWCA Civ 882 at [43] (claimant no longer at secure training centre but test case).

4.6.5 Matter no longer disputed. *R (Jones) v Chief Constable of Cheshire* [2005] EWHC 2457 (Admin) (appropriate to give judgment and make a declaration, albeit no longer disputed, to make clear the absence of police power)

4.6.6 Resolving an issue in the public interest. *R v Oxfordshire County Council, ex p P* [1996] ELR 153, 157B-D (Laws J: "A decision to refuse [a remedy] as a matter of discretion on the footing that the claim is academic ought not in my view to be made without some appreciation of the force of the arguments. In a public law case ... [a claimant] may have an important point to bring to the court's attention, whose resolution might be required in the public interest, even if the [claimant] himself has suffered no perceptible prejudice as a result of the decision in question"); *R v Horseferry Road Magistrates Court, ex p K* [1997] QB 23, 41C-D (although ruling not necessary "not purely hypothetical and, in any event, ... there is a general public interest to be served by expressing our conclusions on the merits"); *R v Board of Visitors of Dartmoor Prison, ex p Smith* [1987] QB 106, 115F ("questions of general public interest"); *London Borough of Islington v Camp* (1999) [2004] LGR 58 (serving a useful purpose in the public interest); cf. *Bowman v Fels* [2005] EWCA Civ 226 [2005] 1 WLR 3083 at [7] & [15] (underlying litigation settled but CA deciding important issue in the public interest).

4.6.7 Hypothetical/academic matters entertained: illustrations. *R (W) v Commissioner of Police for the Metropolis* [2006] EWCA Civ 458 [2007] QB 399 at [17] (appropriate to decide meaning and effect of police power); *R v Horseferry Road Magistrates' Court, ex p Bennett (No.2)* [1994] 1 All ER 289, 297h (difficult to see how otherwise question would arise for direct decision); *R v Cleveland County Council, ex p Commission for Racial Equality* [1994] ELR 44, 45G ("an important point of principle"); *R v Sunderland Juvenile Court, ex p G* [1988] 1 WLR 398 (appropriate to give guidance on whether document, now available, should have been disclosed); *R v Governor of Her Majesty's Prison Swaleside, ex p Wynter* (1998) 10 Admin LR 597, 600E-G (similar cases would arise in future); *R v Secretary of State for the Home Department, ex p Norgren* [2000] QB 817, 826D (although claimant would stay out of the UK if extradition challenge failed, "obvious importance" for him to learn whether "free to return to the United Kingdom without risk of arrest"); *R (Farrakhan) v Secretary of State for the Home Department* [2002] EWCA Civ 606 [2002] QB 1391 at [10] (sole "practical significance" lying in "guidance" for future); *R (B) v Stafford Combined Court* [2006] EWHC 1645 (Admin) [2007] 1 WLR 1524 at [14] (historic violation but actual relevant facts and keen interest in deciding lawfulness).

4.6.8 **Matter becoming academic.**

(A) COURT NOT DECIDING THE ISSUES. *R (Zoolife International Ltd) v Secretary of State for Environment, Food and Rural Affairs* [2007] EWHC 2995 (Admin) (wrong to entertain claim overtaken by events, especially given court's case-load and fact-sensitive issue); *R (Yaseetharan) v Secretary of State for the Home Department* [2002] EWHC 1467 (Admin) [2003] Imm AR 62 at [28] (applying *Salem*, lawfulness of policy preventing legal representation at Stansted asylum interviews having become academic, the policy now having been changed); *R v Headteacher of Crug Glas School, ex p D* [2000] ELR 69 (case relating to school's policy regarding seriously ill child serving no useful purpose where child now receiving agreed home tuition); *Marco's Leisure v West Lothian District Licensing Board* The Times 14th January 1993 (date of public performance having passed and so issue academic); *R v Secretary of State for the Home Department, ex p Adams* [1995] 3 CMLR 476 (Article 234 reference lifted and proceedings dismissed, the exclusion order challenged having been lifted); *R v Legal Aid Board, ex p Clement Garage Ltd* The Times 3rd June 1996 (staying challenge to reinstatement of legal aid (now Community Legal Service funding) for opponent in litigation, having become moot when beneficiary asked of own motion for legal aid to be discharged); *R v Secretary of State for Social Security, ex p Armstrong* (1996) 8 Admin LR 626 (issue as to compatibility of UK Act with EC Directive having become academic from claimant's point of view, she having succeeded in an appeal to a higher rate of benefit); *R v Secretary of State for the Home Department, ex p Pinfold* [1997] COD 338 (given imminent removal of Secretary of State's power to (re-)consider the matter, challenge to his past decision academic, and not appropriate to give guidance in advance to new decision-maker); *R v Rotherham Metropolitan Borough Council, ex p Clark* The Times 4th December 1997 (by time of council's appeal against judicial review of decisions refusing school places, such places having been allocated to the claimants).

(B) COURT DECIDING THE ISSUES. *R (Gilboy) v Liverpool City Council* [2008] EWCA Civ 751 [2008] LGR 521 at [2] (claimant having obtained accommodation but important point which parties wanting resolved); *R (Ware) v Neath Port Talbot County Borough* [2007] EWCA Civ 1359 [2008] LGR 176 at [43] (appeal overtaken by events but issues of wider and ongoing importance); *R (M) v Gateshead Metropolitan Borough Council* [2006] EWCA Civ 221 [2006] QB 650 at [14] (important point which could not otherwise be decided); *R (Robinson) v Torridge District Council* [2006] EWHC 877 (Admin) [2007] 1 WLR 871 (deciding issue of interpretation for guidance of magistrates); *R (William Hill Organisation Ltd) v Batley and Dewsbury Betting Licensing Committee* [2004] EWHC 1201 (Admin) at [25] (question of widespread practice and continuing interest); *R (National Anti-Vivisection Society) v First Secretary of State* [2004] EWHC 2074 (Admin) at [7] (although developer not now intending to take advantage of impugned planning permission, matter not academic since position could change and permission running with the land, and too late to challenge later); *Francis v Royal Borough of Kensington and Chelsea* [2003] EWCA Civ 443 [2003] 2 All ER 1052 at [3] ("issue of principle" and "too good an opportunity to miss to provide ... clarification"); *R (Maxhuni) v Commissioner for Local Administration for England* [2002] EWCA Civ 973 [2003] LGR 113 at [5] (issue of "very considerable general importance"); *R (Sim) v Parole Board* [2003] EWCA Civ 1845 [2004] QB 1288 at [9] (questions of principle arising from declarations granted below); *R v Secretary of State for the Home Department, ex p Mersin* [2000] INLR 511, 513C-E (dealing with historic unreasonable asylum delay because of "the scale of difficulties facing [others] similarly placed"); *R (Director of Public Prosecutions) v*

Camberwell Green Youth Court [2003] EWHC 3217 (Admin) at [4] (question of principle regarding youth court's supposed inherent power) [15] (permission, limited to declaratory remedy).
(C) OTHER. *R (Tshikangu) v Newham London Borough Council* [2001] EWHC Admin 92 (claimant's lawyers criticised for not informing Court at permission stage that claimant now given accommodation); *R (Murray) v Parole Board* [2003] EWCA Civ 1561 at [9] (claimant now released from detention, but "issue" not "academic" as to whether resources an answer to parole review delays not "academic"), [25] (nevertheless "no value" in applying the law to these facts); *R (Napier) v Secretary of State for the Home Department* [2004] EWHC 936 (Admin) [2004] 1 WLR 3056 at [58] (violation of Art 6 but acknowledged by Secretary of State in removing extra prison disciplinary days), [61] (therefore claimant no longer a "victim" and judicial review refused); *R (Newsum) v Welsh Assembly (No.2)* [2005] EWHC 538 (Admin) [2006] Env LR 1 at [48] (although European Commission and ECJ now seized of the matter, domestic court expressing conclusions since would be relied on before those bodies).

4.7 **Prematurity.**[29] Judicial review may be characterised as "too soon". The Court may regard it inappropriate to rule on a grievance which is not yet "ripe" for review, and which may turn out not to have practical significance.

4.7.1 **Prematurity and the need for a "decision".**[30] *R v Immigration Appeal Tribunal, ex p Khatib-Shahidi* [2000] INLR 491 (adjudicator's recommendation or refusal to make one not a decision susceptible to judicial review, because a "pre-executive decision");*R v Hammersmith and Fulham London Borough Council, ex p Burkett* [2002] UKHL 23 [2002] 1 WLR 1593 at [43] (observing that judicial review of a provisional decision could be dismissed as premature); *R (MacNeil) v Parole Board* [2001] EWCA Civ 448 at [15] (leaving open whether Parole Board recommendation amenable to judicial review); *R v Portsmouth Hospitals NHS Trust, ex p Glass* [1999] 2 FLR 905, 910G (declining "to act in anticipation in this area to try and produce clarity" as "a task fraught with danger"); *R v Bromley London Borough Council, ex p Lambeth London Borough Council* The Times 16th June 1984 (declaration granted that subscriptions would be intra vires, there being jurisdiction notwithstanding that there was no `decision' yet); *R v Secretary of State for Health, ex p Imperial Tobacco Ltd* [1999] EuLR 582 (existence of Directive and Treaty obligation constitute the "substantive act" of which complaint made); *R v Secretary of State for the Environment, ex p Omega Air Ltd* [2000] EuLR 254 (judicial review to test validity of EC Regulation albeit not yet into force and no domestic legislation yet in existence); *R v British Advertising Clearance Centre, ex p Swiftcall Ltd* 16th November 1995 unrep. (in "an area in which decisions are made very quickly", where documents giving "a clear indication of how [the defendant] is minded to act", if "the course they are suggesting is fundamentally unlawful, the sooner that is decided the better"); *Ex p Amnesty International* The Times 11th December 1998 (Court assuming that jurisdiction in relation to imminent decision even though no yet made); *R v Commissioners of Inland Revenue, ex p Ulster Bank Ltd* [1997] STC 832, 842g-843c (premature to challenge rationality until decision reached); *R (Mahmood) v Secretary of State for the Home Department* [2001] 1 WLR 840 at [29] (court not generally required to review future implementation of past

---

[29] Jack Beatson QC, `The Need to Develop Principles of Prematurity and Ripeness for Review' [1998] JR 79.

[30] This subparagraph in a previous edition was cited in *NH International (Caribbean) Ltd v Urban Development Corporation of Trinidad and Tobago* [2005] TTHC 38.

decision; primary role on judicial review "historic"); *R (Medway Council) v Secretary of State for Transport* [2002] EWHC 2516 (Admin) (judicial review granted of unreasonable and unfair consultation document); *R (Garden and Leisure Group Ltd) v North Somerset Council* [2003] EWHC 1605 (Admin) at [35] (judicial review of planning resolution as a "decision in principle"); <5.1.3> (judicial restraint because no "decision").

4.7.2 **Judicial review of intended course of conduct.** *R v Avon Magistrates' Courts Committee, ex p Bath Law Society* [1988] QB 409 (future magistrates court scheme); *R v Secretary of State for Foreign & Commonwealth Affairs, ex p Rees-Mogg* [1994] QB 552 (decision to proceed to ratify Maastricht); *R v Secretary of State for Transport, ex p Richmond-upon-Thames London Borough Council* [1994] 1 WLR 74, 91G-H (review of announcement of proposed scheme); *R v Bromley London Borough Council, ex p Lambeth London Borough Council* The Times 16th June 1984 (declaration that subscriptions to the Association of London Authorities would be intra vires); *R v Amber Valley District Council, ex p Jackson* [1985] 1 WLR 298 (whether resolution meant forthcoming planning decision would be biased); *R v Islington London Borough Council, ex p the Building Employers Confederation* (1989) 1 Admin LR 97 (judicial review granted of council's proposed contract terms (intended to be included in draft agreements with contractors), these being ultra vires); *County Properties Ltd v Scottish Ministers* [2000] 4 PLR 83 (judicial review of decision as to procedure to adopt in planning matter, because procedure claimed to be incompatible with ECHR Art 6 (which claim eventually failed: [2001] 4 PLR 122); claimant not obliged to wait for decision-making process to run its course); *R (Alconbury Developments Ltd) v Secretary of State for the Environment Transport and the Regions* [2001] UKHL 23 [2003] 2 AC 295 at [171] (appropriate to clarify important issue at the outset; "the practical advantages of testing the issue at this early stage are obvious"); *R (Heath) v Doncaster Metropolitan Borough Council* [2001] ACD 273 (judicial review of proposed contract terms); *R (A) v Lord Saville of Newdigate* [2001] EWCA Civ 2048 [2002] 1 WLR 1249 (judicial review of Bloody Sunday Tribunal's preliminary ruling); *Wiseman v Borneman* [1971] AC 297 (application for a declaration that intended procedure (confirmed in correspondence) would be a breach of natural justice); *British Oxygen Co Ltd v Board of Trade* [1971] AC 610, 626-627C (review of intended stance and current rule).

4.7.3 **Judicial review of draft measures.** *R v HM Treasury, ex p Smedley* [1985] QB 657 (whether draft Order in Council ultra vires and unreasonable); *R (Plowman) v Secretary of State for Foreign and Commonwealth Affairs* [2001] EWHC Admin 617 (judicial review of draft Order in Council); *R v Electricity Commissioners, ex p London Electricity Joint Committee Co* [1924] 1 KB 171 (prohibiting order granted where scheme in draft Order ultra vires); *Bates v Lord Hailsham* [1972] 1 WLR 1373 (application for an injunction to prevent holding of a meeting where draft order likely to be approved, rejected because (a) no duty to consult and (b) delay); *R v Local Government Commission, ex p Cambridgeshire District Council & County Council* [1995] COD 149 (LGC's draft report); *R v Secretary of State for Health, ex p Imperial Tobacco Ltd* [1999] EuLR 582 (in challenge relating to validity of EC Directive, no need to wait until draft measures published); *R (A & B) v East Sussex County Council (No.2)* [2003] EWHC 167 (Admin) (2003) 6 CCLR 194 at [24] (Court considering lawfulness of draft protocols on manual lifting of disabled persons), [27] (deciding only to "address the matters of general principle").

4.7.4 **Whether to let proceedings take their course.**[31] <13.6.2> (timing of intervention: avoiding disruption).
(A) MAGISTRATES' PROCEEDINGS. *R (Singh) v Stratford Magistrates Court* [2007] EWHC 1582 (Admin) [2007] 1 WLR 3119 at [7] (generally better to await result of proceedings), [8] (deciding question of law here to avoid further delay and because resolution of issues sought by the parties); *R (Hoar-Stevens) v Richmond-upon-Thames Magistrates' Court* [2003] EWHC 2660 (Admin) at [2] ("Normally this court will not entertain an application for a quashing order in relation to a decision made in a magistrate's court where the proceedings in that court are not complete"); *R (Watson) v Dartford Magistrates Court* [2005] EWHC 905 (Admin) (judicial review of decision to grant prosecution adjournment), [6] (normal rule is court keeps out until magistrates have made their determination), [7] (but no restriction here where straightforward issue and clear principle); *R v Bow Street Metropolitan Stipendiary Magistrate, ex p Noncyp Ltd* [1990] 1 QB 123 (preliminary decision whether to admit evidence); *Government of the United States of America v Bowe* [1990] 1 AC 500, 526G-H ("generally speaking, the entire case ... should be presented to the magistrate before either side applies for a prerogative remedy"); *R (Durham County Council) v North Durham Justices* [2004] EWHC 1073 (Admin) at [32] (judicial review of adjournments to require personal service of summonses, appropriate because real challenge directed to unlawful policy guidance).
(B) OTHER PROCESSES. *R (Wani) v Secretary of State for the Home Department* [2005] EWHC 2815 (Admin) [2006] Imm AR 125 (normally an abuse of process to challenge AIT's decision to remit an appeal, being only a preliminary decision and all issues remaining open for argument); *R (Mahfouz) v General Medical Council* [2004] EWCA Civ 233 at [44] (generally preferable for disciplinary proceedings to take their course), [45] (but should have adjourned here to allow judicial review); *R v Chief Constable of the Merseyside Police, ex p Merrill* [1989] 1 WLR 1077, 1088D (rare to consider judicial review before final decision); *R v Personal Investment Authority Ombudsman, ex p Burns-Anderson Independent Network Plc* (1998) 10 Admin LR 57 (premature to challenge PIA ombudsman's provisional conclusion dealing with jurisdiction); *Huntley v Attorney-General for Jamaica* [1995] 2 AC 1, 17F-G (test case as to procedural rights entertained, although usually more appropriate to await prisoner classification decision); *R v Secretary of State for the Home Department, ex p Hickey (No.2)* [1995] 1 WLR 734 (judicial review of Secretary of State's decision as to referral of conviction to the CA), 757H-758A (court would not "readily intervene to regulate procedures in advance of a substantive decision", but exceptional here); *R (S) v Knowsley NHS Primary Care Trust* [2006] EWHC 26 (Admin) at [68] (court not powerless to prevent unfair procedure merely because of existence of later way of remedying consequences).

4.7.5 **Clarification better at the start.** *R v Lord Saville of Newdigate, ex p B* The Times 15th April 1999 (although only an interim decision, nevertheless a decision which would influence future conduct of the inquiry and which ought, if erroneous, to be corrected); *R v Lord Saville of Newdigate, ex p A* [2000] 1 WLR 1855 at [43] ("The fact that a court would not quash the final decision of a tribunal on a procedural ground does not mean that a preliminary decision would not be quashed. The unfair refusal of an interpreter or an adjournment are very much the type of decisions which, if the subject of an immediate application for judicial review, will be reversed by the courts although the final decision would not be. The concern of the court is whether what has happened has resulted in real injustice"); *R (Warren) v HM Assistant Coroner for Northamptonshire* [2008] EWHC 966 (Admin) (judicial review of ruling at inquest

---

[31] This paragraph in a previous edition was cited in *R v Hammersmith and Fulham London Borough Council, ex p Burkett* [2002] UKHL 23 [2002] 1 WLR 1593 at [38]; also *Financial Secretary v Felix Wong* [2003] HKCU 1304 at [14].

pre-trial review); *R (Kurdistan Workers Party) v Secretary of State for the Home Department* [2002] EWHC 644 (Admin) at [81] (suggesting that best to deal with procedural defect when it arose); *R v Secretary of State for the Environment, ex p Kensington and Chelsea Royal Borough Council* The Times 30th January 1987 (apt to challenge inspector's decision not to admit certain evidence because stultifying party's presentation of their case and rendering inquiry a barren exercise); *R v Horseferry Road Justices, ex p Independent Broadcasting Authority* [1987] QB 54, 73A-F (appropriate to establish whether or not offence existing, before further expense incurred in criminal proceedings); *R v Secretary of State for Transport, ex p London Borough of Richmond Upon Thames (No.3)* [1995] Env LR 409, 412-413 ("If it is arguable that the new consultation is proceeding on a false basis which is justiciable in law, there will be every reason to lean in favour of deciding the issue sooner rather than later"); *R v Broadcasting Complaints Commission, ex p British Broadcasting Corporation* (1994) 6 Admin LR 714, 718A-E (correct to challenge BCC's preliminary decision that it had jurisdiction to entertain a complaint; not obliged to wait for outcome of complaint); also *R v Broadcasting Complaints Commission, ex p Channel Four Television Corporation* [1995] COD 289; cf. *R v Personal Investment Authority Ombudsman, ex p Burns Anderson Independent Network Plc* [1997] COD 379 (explaining *BBC* as involving a final decision which related to press freedom).

4.7.6 Ouster meaning judicial review only available prospectively. *R v Wiltshire County Council, ex p Lazard Brothers & Co Ltd* The Times 13th January 1998 (judicial review granted of resolution to make order, despite statutory ouster clause as to order once made, because of error of law).

> **P5 Targets.** A wide range of measures, acts, decisions, policies and omissions can be the subject of a judicial review challenge.

5.1 Judicial review and "decisions"
5.2 Spectrum of possible targets
5.3 Multiple targets/target-selection

5.1 Judicial review and "decisions". The most common target for judicial review is a "decision" of a public authority, often communicated in a decision letter. It is sometimes said that, absent a "decision", judicial review will not lie. In truth there are a wide range of things which public bodies do, fail to do, or even may be about to do, which can be the focus of a judicial review claim in an appropriate case. The focal point can change, for example where the defendant reaches a fresh "decision" after the commencement of the claim for judicial review.

5.1.1 Communication of "decision".*R v Oldham Metropolitan Borough Council, ex p Garlick* [1993] AC 509, 519A ("the decision letter"); *R v Northavon District Council, ex p Smith* [1994] 2 AC 402, 408F-G ("the decisions contained in the letter"); *R (Yogathas) v Secretary of State for the Home Department* [2002] UKHL 36 [2003] 1 AC 920 (Secretary of State's certification decisions communicated in letters); *R v Secretary of State for Trade and Industry, ex p Lonrho Plc* [1989] 1 WLR 525, 530E & 533A (decisions announced in press releases); *Council of Civil Service Unions v Minister for the Civil Service* [1985] AC 374 (Minister's "instruction" was "issued orally" and later confirmed by an announcement in the House of Commons and a letter); *Chief Constable of the North Wales Police v Evans* [1982] 1 WLR 1155 (chief constable's statement to an officer that he could either resign or be dismissed disclosing a "decision" which could be challenged by judicial review, notwithstanding that he took the former option); *Padfield v Minister of Agriculture Fisheries & Food* [1968] AC 997 (decision letter refusing to refer complaint); *R v Eastleigh Borough Council, ex p Betts* [1983] 2 AC 613, 620E, 623C (housing decision communicated in letter); *In re Wilson* [1985] AC 750, 755A-B (justices' clerk's letter); *Cinzano (UK) Ltd v Customs & Excise Commissioners* [1985] 1 WLR 484, 485D, 487D-E (letter refusing to acknowledge effect of proposed scheme); *R v Secretary of State for Trade and Industry, ex p Lonrho Plc* [1989] 1 WLR 525, 532A (letter affirming minister's decision); *Champion v Chief Constable of the Gwent Constabulary* [1990] 1 WLR 1, 15H ("the decision embodied in the chief superintendent's letter"); *R v Richmond upon Thames London Borough Council, ex p McCarthy & Stone (Developments) Ltd* [1992] 2 AC 48, 49G, 66D, 75D ("decision" refusing to revoke a policy of charging for pre-application advice); cf. *R v Secretary of State for Employment, ex p Equal Opportunities Commission* [1995] 1 AC 1, 26E-F (letter not constituting a decision but a view as to statutory compatibility with EC law; proper focus of challenge the statute itself).

5.1.2 Judicial review of "decisions": illustrations. *R (Anufrijeva) v Secretary of State for the Home Department* [2003] UKHL 36 [2004] 1 AC 604 (judicial review of decision to remove welfare benefits on refusal of asylum); *R (Beresford) v Sunderland City Council* [2003] UKHL 60 [2004] 1 AC 889 (judicial review of decision refusing to register land as a town or village green); *R (ProLife Alliance) v British Broadcasting Corporation* [2003] UKHL 23 [2004] 1 AC 185 (judicial review of BBC's decision not to show a party election broadcast depicting abortion); *R (Anderson) v Secretary of State for the Home Department* [2002] UKHL 46 [2003] 1 AC 837 (judicial review of decision to set mandatory lifer tariff); *R v Hammersmith and Fulham London Borough Council, ex p Burkett* [2002] UKHL 23 [2002] 1 WLR 1593 (judicial review of decision granting planning permission); <32.2> (decisions regarding legal process).

5.1.3 Judicial restraint because no "decision". *R (P) v Essex County Council* [2004] EWHC

2027 (Admin) at [33] ("the Administrative Court exists to adjudicate upon specific challenges to discrete decisions. It does not exist to monitor and regulate the performance of public authorities"); *R (Onuegbu) v Hackney London Borough Council* [2005] EWHC 1277 (Admin) (no housing decision yet for consideration by judicial review); *R (Shrewsbury and Atcham Borough Council) v Secretary of State for Communities and Local Government* [2008] EWCA Civ 148 [2008] 3 All ER 548 at [32]-[36] (focus should generally be on ultimate actions having substantive legal consequences, not preparatory steps); *Bobb v Manning* [2006] UKPC 22 [2006] 4 LRC 735 at [16] (Prime Minister's speech not "a formulated policy statement or decision susceptible to challenge by judicial review");*R v Devon County Council, ex p L* (1992) 4 Admin LR 99, 118B-C (letter not amounting to a decision); *R v Secretary of State for the Home Department, ex p Wynne* [1993] 1 WLR 115, 119F (failure to make a request meaning "no relevant decision"); *R v Immigration Appeal Tribunal, ex p Khatib-Shahidi* [2000] INLR 491 (declined recommendation merely a "pre-executive decision"); <4.7.1> (prematurity and the need for a decision).

5.1.4 **Absence of a "decision" not fatal.** *R v Secretary of State for Transport, ex p London Borough of Richmond Upon Thames (No.3)* [1995] Env LR 409, 413 (Sedley J: "the want of an identifiable decision is not fatal to an application for judicial review"); *R v Secretary of State for Health, ex p Imperial Tobacco Ltd* [1999] EuLR 582 (in challenge regarding validity of EC Directive, statutory obligation to take implementing measures a sufficient `act' to constitute the subject-matter of the proceedings); *London Borough of Islington v Camp* (1999) [2004] LGR 58 (appropriate claim for declaration albeit no decision nor proposed action, because useful purpose in the public interest); *R (MacNeil) v Parole Board* [2001] EWCA Civ 448 at [15] (leaving open whether Parole Board recommendation apt for judicial review).

5.1.5 **Position where fresh/further "decision".** *E v Secretary of State for the Home Department* [2004] EWCA Civ 49 [2004] QB 1044 at [77] (at least where defendant has "a continuing public responsibility ... [i]t is often sensible ... for the matter to be looked at in the light of the ... most recent consideration of the matter, and the judicial review procedure is flexible enough to allow that"); *R v Secretary of State for the Home Department, ex p Turgut* [2001] 1 All ER 719, 735j-736b (generally convenient to substitute fresh immigration decision as the decision challenged in the proceedings), 736e-f (but not where case had already reached the CA); *R v Secretary of State for the Home Department, ex p Alabi* [1997] JR 254 (permissible to challenge awaited fresh decision in existing proceedings, with stay when reconsideration awaited); *R v Institute of Chartered Accountants, ex p Bruce* 22nd October 1986 unrep. (where post-permission decision challenged on different grounds, pragmatic solution of applying arguability threshold to the question of permission to amend); *R (Holub) v Secretary of State for the Home Department* [2001] 1 WLR 1359 at [10] (where fresh decision post-dating first instance hearing, focus of hearing in CA on new decision, thus "considering the matter as a reviewing court of first instance"); *R (Assisted Reproduction and Gynaecology Centre) v Human Fertilisation and Embryology Authority* [2002] EWCA Civ 20 [2003] 1 FCR 266 at [2] (amendment at permission stage in CA given fresh decision); *R v Commissioner for Local Administration, ex p Abernethy* [2000] COD 56 (stay of proceedings where defendant had agreed to reconsider); *R (Khan) v Secretary of State for the Health* [2003] EWCA Civ 1129 [2004] 1 WLR 971 (post-judgment adjournment to allow amending regulations to secure HRA-compatibility); *R v Lambeth London Borough Council, ex p A* (1998) 10 Admin LR 209, 225G-H (where fresh decision reached following hearing of the judicial review at first instance, CA declining to consider propriety of the fresh decision); *R v Secretary of State for the Home Department, ex p Canbolat* [1997] Imm AR 281 (DC), 296-297 and [1997] 1 WLR 1569 (CA), 1576D (focus on original certification albeit having regard to subsequent exchanges); *R (on the application of Wandsworth London Borough Council) v Schools Adjudicator* [2003] EWHC 2969 (Admin) at [9] (appropriate here to focus on position as it was before the judge below, not on subsequent developments); *R (P) v Essex County Council* [2004] EWHC 2027 (Admin) at [35] & [38] (where judicial review focusing on new decision, need promptly notified clear proposed amended grounds).

5.2 Spectrum of possible targets. Aside from "decisions", there is a wide range of types of act (and inaction) of public bodies whose legality the claimant may seek to impugn by means of judicial review.

5.2.1 Targets for judicial review: CPR 54. See CPR 54.1(2)(a) (referring to enactment, decision, action and failure to act) <64.2>.

5.2.2 Primary Legislation/EC Legislation. <35.1.3> (judicial review of primary legislation); *R v Secretary of State for Health, ex p Imperial Tobacco Ltd* [1999] EuLR 582 (Art 234 reference as to whether Directive invalid); *R v Secretary of State for the Environment, ex p Omega Air Ltd* [2000] EuLR 254 (Art 234 reference to test whether EC Regulation invalid); *R (Unitymark Ltd) v Department of the Environment, Food and Rural Affairs* [2003] EWHC 2748 (Admin) (challenge to domestic implementing measure, where Art 234 reference because of doubts as to legality of the EC Regulation).

5.2.3 Regulation/Rule/Order/Standing Order. *R (C) v Secretary of State for Justice* [2008] EWCA Civ 882 (regulations quashed); *R v Secretary of State for Health, ex p United States Tobacco International Inc* [1992] QB 353 (regulations quashed for procedural unfairness in making them); *R v Secretary of State for Trade and Industry, ex p Orange Personal Communications Ltd* The Times 15th November 2000 (regulations unlawful because disapplying primary legislation without saying so explicitly); *R v Secretary of State for the Home Department, ex p Saleem* [2001] 1 WLR 443 (immigration rule ultra vires and unreasonable); *R v Lautro, ex p Kendall* [1994] COD 169 (lawfulness of Lautro Rule); *Raymond v Honey* [1983] 1 AC 1 (Prison Rules ultra vires); *R (Bancoult) v Secretary of State for Foreign & Commonwealth Affairs* [2007] EWCA Civ 498 [2008] QB 365 (Order in Council unfair); *R (Asif Javed) v Secretary of State for the Home Department* [2001] EWCA Civ 789 [2002] QB 129 (asylum Order irrational); *R v Secretary of State for Trade and Industry, ex p Thomson Holidays Ltd* The Times 12th January 2000 CA (quashing ultra vires articles of Order); *R v Lord Chancellor, ex p Witham* [1998] QB 575 (court fees Order unlawful); *R (Edison First Power Ltd) v Secretary of State for the Environment, Transport and the Regions* [2003] UKHL 20 [2003] 4 All ER 209 (rating order); cf. *A v Secretary of State for the Home Department* [2004] UKHL 56 [2005] 2 AC 68 (derogation order quashed); *R v Secretary of State for the Home Department, ex p Anderson* [1984] QB 778 (prison standing orders ultra vires); *R v Flintshire County Council, ex p Armstrong-Braun* [2001] EWCA Civ 345 [2001] LGR 344 (quashing council's standing order); *R (Howard League for Penal Reform) v Secretary of State for the Home Department* [2002] EWHC 2497 (Admin) [2003] 1 FLR 484 at [160], [185(vi)] (judicial review granted of Secretary of State's policy, contained in Prison Service Order, for error of law); *R (Partridge Farms Ltd) v Secretary of State for Environment, Food & Rural Affairs* [2008] EWHC 1645 (Admin) (Order breaching EC principle of equality).

5.2.4 Policy/scheme. *R (S) v Secretary of State for the Home Department* [2006] EWCA Civ 1157 [2006] INLR 575 (ultra vires policy of maintaining temporary admission); *R (Faarah) v Southwark London Borough Council* [2008] EWCA Civ 807 (unlawful housing allocation scheme); *R v Secretary of State for the Home Department, ex p Daly* [2001] UKHL 26 [2001] 2 AC 532 (unlawful correspondence search policy); *R v Secretary of State for the Home Department, ex p Simms* [2000] 2 AC 115 (unlawful journalist interview policy); *R (Smith) v Secretary of State for the Home Department* [2005] UKHL 51 [2006] 1 AC 159 (unlawful policy of not undertaking periodic tariff reviews); *Lindsay v Commissioners of Customs and Excise* [2002] EWCA Civ 267 [2002] 1 WLR 1766 (unlawful policy of confiscating cars involved in tobacco smuggling); *R (A) v Secretary of State for the Home Department* [2002] EWHC 1618 (Admin) [2003] 1 WLR 330 at [49] (policy based on error of law); *R (Ann Summers Ltd) v Jobcentre Plus* [2003] EWHC 1416 (Admin) (irrational policy); *R (Wandsworth London Borough Council) v Secretary of State for Transport* [2005] EWHC 20 (Admin) at [58] (judicial review of decisions contained in White Paper).

5.2.5 **Ordinance/Byelaw/Practice/Scheme/Resolution.** *R (Bancoult) v Secretary of State for the Foreign and Commonwealth Office* [2001] QB 1067 (Ordinance ultra vires); *DPP v Hutchinson* [1990] 2 AC 783 (byelaw held ultra vires in criminal proceedings); *Boddington v British Transport Police* [1999] 2 AC 143 (public law challenge to byelaw raised as defence to prosecution); *R v Secretary of State for the Home Department, ex p Doody* [1994] 1 AC 531 (practice regarding tariff-setting for mandatory lifers); *R v Weston-super-Mare Justices, ex p Shaw* [1987] QB 640 (magistrates' "listing practice"); *R v Minister of Agriculture Fisheries and Food, ex p S.P. Anastasiou (Pissouri) Ltd* [1995] 1 CMLR 569 (practice of allowing importation of fruit without proper certification); *R (Association of Pharmaceutical Importers) v Secretary of State for Health* [2001] EWCA Civ 1986 [2002] EuLR 197 (judicial review of voluntary price regulation scheme, being a state measure albeit not binding); *R v Herrod, ex p Leeds City Council* [1978] AC 403 (judicial review of local authorities' resolutions refusing to entertain applications for the grant or renewal of gaming licences over certain classes of premises).

5.2.6 **Proposal/Draft.** *R v Chief Constable of Kent Constabulary, ex p Kent Police Federation Joint Branch Board* [2000] COD 169 (judicial review of proposal of reviews of detention by video link); <4.7.3> (judicial review of draft measures).

5.2.7 **Direction/Directive/Instruction.** *R v Secretary of State for the Environment, Transport and the Regions, ex p Channel Tunnel Group Ltd* [2001] EWCA Civ 1185 (directions quashed on judicial review); *R (Quark Fishing Ltd) v Secretary of State for Foreign and Commonwealth Affairs* [2002] EWCA Civ 1409 (judicial review granted of direction given by Secretary of State to licensing decision-maker); *R (Sullivan) v Maidstone Crown Court* [2002] EWHC 967 (Admin) [2002] 1 WLR 2747 (local practice direction declared unlawful, since approach taken therein exceeding crown court's jurisdiction); *R v Secretary of State for Transport, ex p Greater London Council* [1986] QB 556 (GLC establishing unlawfulness, irrationality and unfairness of direction given to it by the Secretary of State); *R v London Transport Executive, ex p Greater London Council* [1983] QB 484 (GLC establishing lawfulness of own direction issued to the LTE); *R v Secretary of State for the Environment, ex p Oswestry Borough Council* [1995] COD 357 (direction under Local Government Act challenged as ultra vires, and the conclusion which underpinned it as irrational); *R v Social Fund Inspector, ex p Healey* (1992) 4 Admin LR 713 (judicial review of Social Fund directions); *R (London and Continental Stations and Property Ltd) v Rail Regulator* [2003] EWHC 2607 (Admin) at [3] (judicial review sought of statutory direction requiring station access contract). *R v Secretary of State for the Home Department, ex p Brind* [1991] 1 AC 696, 752A-B (judicial review of "directives" banning the use by TV companies of recorded speech of members of specified organisations); *R v Chief Constable of Avon & Somerset, ex p Robinson* [1989] 1 WLR 793 (vires of instructions); *R v City of Sunderland, ex p Baumber* [1996] COD 211 (instructions to educational psychologists).

5.2.8 **Notice/Declaration/Circular.** *R (Morgan Grenfell & Co Ltd) v Inland Revenue Commissioners* [2002] UKHL 21 [2003] 1 AC 563 (judicial review of notice requiring bank to disclose to the Inland Revenue its instructions to and advice of Counsel); *R v Secretary of State for Health, ex p Macrae Seafoods Ltd* [1995] COD 369 (challenge to declaration by Secretary of State); *R v Secretary of State for Health, ex p Pfizer Ltd* (1999) 2 CCLR 270 (judicial review granted of Circular, being advice intended to be relied on, as being contrary to domestic and EC law); *Royal College of Nursing of the United Kingdom v Department of Health and Social Security* [1981] AC 800 (whether DHSS advice contained in a "circular" letter interpreting the Abortion Act 1967 s.1(1) erroneous in law); *R v Secretary of State for the Home Department, ex p Northumbria Police Authority* [1989] QB 26 (judicial review of scheme introduced by Circular); *R v Chief Constable of Leicestershire, ex p Henning* [1994] COD 256 (judicial review of decision to send circular restricting individual solicitor's clerk's access to persons in police custody); *R v Secretary of State for the Home Department, ex p Westminster Press Ltd* [1992] COD 303 (no misstatements in Circular, as to statute or common law); *R v Wandsworth London Borough Council, ex p Beckwith* [1996] 1 WLR 60 (on judicial review of council's decision, considering whether Department of Health circular incorrect in law); *R v Secretary of State for Health, ex p K* (1998) 1 CCLR 495 (judicial review of Circular for alleged error of law).

5.2.9 **Guidance.** *R (A) v Secretary of State for Health* [2008] EWHC 855 (Admin) (Secretary of State's guidance to NHS trusts wrong in law); *R (Association of British Travel Agents Ltd) v Civil Aviation Authority* [2006] EWCA Civ 1299 (CAA guidance wrong in law being misleading as to reach of the legislation); *R (Axon) v Secretary of State for Health* [2006] EWHC 37 (Admin) [2006] QB 539 (judicial review of Best Practice Guidance on contraceptive advice to young persons without parental consent); *R v Secretary of State for the Environment, ex p Nottinghamshire County Council* [1986] AC 240 (statutory "guidance"); *R v Secretary of State for the Environment, ex p Tower Hamlets London Borough Council* [1993] QB 632 (Code of Guidance); *R v Secretary of State for the Environment, ex p Lancashire County Council* [1994] 4 All ER 165 (policy guidance); *R v Securities and Investments Board, ex p Independent Financial Advisers Association* [1995] 2 BCLC 76 (non-statutory Guidance); *Laker Airways Ltd v Department of Trade* [1977] QB 643 (statutory "guidance" cutting across the main purpose of the Act); *R (National Association of Colliery Overman Deputies and Shot Firers) v Secretary of State for Work and Pensions* [2003] EWHC 607 (Admin) (failure to amend and clarify guidance notes on diagnosis of prescribed diseases for welfare benefits purposes); *R v Department of Health, ex p Source Informatics Ltd* [2001] QB 424 (guidance document incorrectly stating the law); *Gillick v West Norfolk and Wisbech Area Health Authority* [1986] AC 112 (lawfulness of non-statutory DHSS "Memorandum of Guidance"); *R (Jarrett) v Legal Services Commission* [2001] EWHC Admin 389 (Lord Chancellor's directions and guidance incompatible with HRA:ECHR Art 6); *R v Newham London Borough Council, ex p P* [1990] 1 WLR 482, 489G (Secretary of State's guidance erroneous); *R (United Kingdom Renderers Association Ltd) v Secretary of State for the Environment, Transport and the Regions* [2002] EWCA Civ 749 [2003] Env LR 178 (process guidance note); *R (Quintavalle) v Secretary of State for Health* [2001] EWHC Admin 918 [2001] 4 All ER 1013 at [38] ("definitive government response" allowing research on embryos); *R (Burke) v General Medical Council* [2005] EWCA Civ 1003 [2006] QB 273 (GMC's artificial nutrition guidance).

5.2.10 **Opinion/Comment/Publication.** *R v Worthing Borough Council, ex p Burch* (1985) 50 P & CR 53 (Secretary of State's "opinion" as to likely planning permission); *R (Tree and Wildlife Action Committee Ltd) v Forestry Commissioners* [2007] EWHC 1623 (Admin) [2008] Env LR 100 (EIA opinion for planning process); *R (Mowlem Plc) v HM Assistant Deputy Coroner for Avon* [2005] EWHC 1359 (Admin) at [30] (coroner's post-verdict comments unlawful); *R v Secretary of State for the Environment, ex p Greenwich London Borough Council* [1989] COD 530 (whether information leaflet misstating the law); *R v Liverpool City Council, ex p Baby Products Association* [2000] LGR 171 (press release circumventing statutory machinery); *R v Secretary of State for Transport, ex p Richmond-upon-Thames London Borough Council* [1994] 1 WLR 74 (press notice announcing proposed scheme); *R v*

Secretary of State for Trade and Industry, ex p Lonrho Plc [1989] 1 WLR 525 at 530E & 533A (decisions announced in press releases).

5.2.11 **Action/Failure/Refusal.** *R (Rottman) v Commissioner of Police for the Metropolis* [2002] UKHL 20 [2002] 2 AC 692 (judicial review of search of premises for evidence following arrest, in an extradition case); *R (L (A Minor)) v Governors of J School* [2003] UKHL 9 [2003] 2 AC 633 (judicial review of reintegration response by school following independent appeal panel direction of pupil's reinstatement); *R (Saadi) v Secretary of State for the Home Department* [2002] UKHL 41 [2002] 1 WLR 3131 (judicial review of detention of asylum-seekers for speedy decision-making); *R v Secretary of State for the Home Department, ex p Fire Brigades Union* [1995] 2 AC 513 (judicial review of failure to bring statutory scheme into force); *R v Ministry of Agriculture Fisheries & Food, ex p Bostock* [1994] I ECR 955 (failure to introduce compensation scheme for earlier period); <24.4.5> (mandatory order); <39.2.3> (duty not to delay); *R (Mayor of London) v Enfield London Borough Council* [2008] EWCA Civ 202 [2008] LGR 615 at [29] (refusal to withdraw direction); *R (Pretty) v Director of Public Prosecutions* [2001] UKHL 61 [2002] 1 AC 800 (refusal to agree not to prosecute); *R (Green) v Police Complaints Authority* [2004] UKHL 6 [2004] 1 WLR 725 (refusal to disclose material); *R (O'Byrne) v Secretary of State for the Environment, Transport and the Regions* [2002] UKHL 45 [2002] 1 WLR 3250 (refusal to consent to sale to council tenant); *R v Independent Television Commission, ex p TV Danmark 1 Ltd* [2001] UKHL 42 [2001] 1 WLR 1604 (refusing consent to exclusive TV transmission); *R v Richmond upon Thames London Borough Council, ex p McCarthy & Stone (Developments) Ltd* [1992] 2 AC 48, 49G (refusal to revoke charging policy); *R v General Medical Council, ex p Gee* [1987] 1 WLR 564 (refusal to amend disciplinary charges); *R v Northavon District Council, ex p Smith* [1994] 2 AC 402 (refusal to accede to request); *R v Chief Constable of the West Midlands Police, ex p Wiley* [1995] 1 AC 274 (refusal to give undertaking).

5.3 **Multiple targets/target-selection.** Judicial review claims frequently involve several interrelated potential targets. They may be connected "vertically" (eg. an enactment and a decision pursuant to it) or "horizontally" (eg. a decision and its implementation). The claimant's dilemma is whether to challenge early and risk criticism for prematurity, or later and risk being found to have fatally delayed.

5.3.1 **Vertical examples.**
(A) REGULATION/SCHEME OR DECISION. *R v Secretary of State for Social Security, ex p Britnell* [1991] 1 WLR 198 (challenge to "decision" to deduct overpayment, challenged on basis that regulation ultra vires); *Bromley London Borough Council v Greater London Council* [1983] 1 AC 768 (challenge to rating precept, though turning on legality of scheme being funded); *Singh (Pargan) v Secretary of State for the Home Department* [1992] 1 WLR 1052 (regulation and decision to serve notice under it); *Maynard v Osmond* [1977] QB 240 (disciplinary regulations and decision under them); *Cinnamond v British Airports Authority* [1980] 1 WLR 582 (byelaw and notice); *R v Secretary of State for the Environment, ex p Brent London Borough Council* [1982] QB 593 (Order and decision); *R v Criminal Injuries Compensation Board, ex p P* [1995] 1 WLR 845, 852E-G (following refusal of compensation, challenge to decision revising scheme).
(B) CIRCULAR/GUIDANCE/POLICY OR DECISION. *Daymond v Plymouth City Council* [1976] AC 609 (charges imposed under DoE circular); *R v Barnet London Borough Council, ex p Nilish Shah* [1983] 2 AC 309 (decisions quashed because guidance erroneous in law); *Newbury District Council v Secretary of State for the Environment* [1981] AC 578, 621F & 628H-629A (decision "uninfected" by erroneous government circular); *R v Secretary of State for the Home Department, ex p Simms* [2000] 2 AC 115 (policy and decisions); *R v General*

Medical Council ex p Colman [1990] 1 All ER 489 (judicial review of GMC's guidance banning advertising and decision refusing to allow permission in claimant's case); *R v Secretary of State for the Home Department, ex p Flynn* [1995] Imm AR 594 (border check policy and specific decision); *R v Chief Constable of the North Wales Police, ex p AB* [1999] QB 396 (policy and conduct pursuant to it); *R v Felixstowe Justices, ex p Leigh* [1987] QB 582 (journalist obtaining judicial review of magistrates' policy, but not decision); *R v East Lancashire Health Authority, ex p B* [1997] COD 267 (whether policy a fetter depending on attitude to individual cases); *R v Accrington Youth Court, ex p Flood* [1998] 1 WLR 156 (committal pursuant to unlawful policy).
(C) DECISION OR APPEAL. *R v Secretary of State for the Home Department, ex p Oladehinde* [1991] 1 AC 254, 257D-H (deportation notices and IAT appeal decisions); *R v Governors of the Bishop Challoner Roman Catholic Comprehensive Girls' School, ex p Choudhury* [1992] 2 AC 182, 187F (governors' decision and tribunal's dismissal of appeals); *R v Secretary of State for the Home Department, ex p Abdi* [1996] 1 WLR 298 (Home Secretary's asylum certificates and immigration judges' decisions upholding them); *R v Law Society, ex p Singh & Choudry* (1995) 7 Admin LR 249, 250B (decision and its confirmation on appeal); cf. *R v Secretary of State for the Home Department, ex p Mande Ssenyonjo* [1994] Imm AR 310 (having exhausted his rights of appeal, claimant could not now seek to challenge the underlying decision); <36.4.2> (whether appeal curing procedural unfairness); <36.3.10> (appeal as alternative remedy).

5.3.2 **Horizontal examples.** *R v Hammersmith and Fulham London Borough Council, ex p Burkett* [2002] UKHL 23 [2002] 1 WLR 1593 (discussing planning resolution and consequential planning permission); *R v Inland Revenue Commissioners, ex p T.C.Coombs & Co* [1991] 2 AC 283, 303G-304A (inspector's notice not commissioner's approval); *R v Secretary of State for Education, ex p Cumbria County Council* [1994] ELR 220, 227A-B (governors' proposal not Minister's approval); *R v Secretary of State for the Home Department, ex p Broom* [1986] QB 198 (Secretary of State's implementation of decision dismissing prison officer); *R v Secretary of State for the Home Department, ex p McCartney* [1994] COD 528 (certificate and decision not to "revise" it); *R v Secretary of State for the Home Department, ex p Adams* [1995] All ER (EC) 177, 180b (order and refusal to revoke it); *R (Edward) v Secretary of State for the Environment, Transport and the Regions* [2001] ACD 164 (decision to make a compulsory purchase order operative); *R (Interbrew SA) v Competition Commission* [2001] EWHC Admin 367 (judicial review granted of Competition Commission's recommendation and Secretary of State's acceptance of it).

5.3.3 **Whether target-selection solving problems of non-reviewability.** *R v Lord Chancellor, ex p Stockler* (1996) 8 Admin LR 590 (judicial review of Lord Chancellor's decisions as to High Court listing, in circumstances where High Court itself not reviewable); *R v Comptroller of Patents, Designs and Trade Marks, ex p Lenzing AG* [1997] EuLR 237 (impermissible to get round immunity from review of European Patent Office Board of Appeal by challenging consequential entry in UK register); *R v Wiltshire County Council, ex p Lazard Brothers & Co Ltd* The Times 13th January 1998 (judicial review available of resolution to make order, despite statutory ouster applying to orders once made); *R v Lewes Crown Court, ex p Sinclair* (1993) 5 Admin LR 1 (since Crown Court sentence not amenable to judicial review, court refusing circumvention by challenge to warrant of committal).

5.3.4 **Delay and multiple targets.** <26.2.8>.

51

P6 Power sources. Powers or duties can arise under or by reference to EC and domestic legislation, common law or prerogative, even policy guidance or international law.

6.1 Powers/duties: basic sources
6.2 Policy guidance
6.3 International law

6.1 Powers/duties: basic sources and hierarchy. There are many varied legal sources which help delineate the proper functions of public bodies. Action by a public authority cannot be lawful unless based on positive power and falling within relevant legal restrictions.

6.1.1 Need for positive authority (no free-standing powers).*R v Richmond London Borough Council, ex p Watson* [2001] QB 370 (CA), 385C (Buxton LJ: "A public body can only do that which it is authorised to do by positive law"); *R v Secretary of State for Health, ex p B* [1999] 1 FLR 656, 668G (public body does not have a free-standing function, but can only act according to the terms of the statute or delegated legislation giving it power, referring to *Fewings* [1995] 1 WLR 1037); *R v Somerset County Council, ex p Fewings* [1995] 1 All ER 513 (Laws J), 524f.

6.1.2 The basic legislative hierarchy.
(A) ULTRA VIRES. <P46>.
(B) READING DOWN. <46.3.3>.

6.1.3 Fundamental/constitutional sources.
(A) BILL OF RIGHTS. *R v Commissioners of Customs and Excise, ex p Kay and Co* [1996] STC 1500, 1520j-1521a (contrary to the Bill of Rights for Customs and Excise to impose a cut-off on claims for overpaid tax, where Act containing right to repayment); *R v Secretary of State for the Home Department, ex p Herbage (No 2)* [1987] QB 1077, 1095F & 1096C-D (CA using Bill of Rights); *Boodram v Baptiste* [1999] 1 WLR 1709 (Bill of Rights cut down by clear subsequent legislative provisions); *R (Pretty) v Director of Public Prosecutions* [2001] UKHL 61 [2002] 1 AC 800 at [39] (referring to the Bill of Rights); *Wilson v First County Trust Ltd* [2003] UKHL 40 [2004] 1 AC 816 at [60] (having regard to Hansard as background and on judicial review of ministerial decisions not "questioning" what said in Parliament, so compatible with Bill of Rights); *Buchanan v Jennings* [2004] UKPC 36 [2005] 1 AC 115 (Bill of Rights not violated where use of historical Hansard record to support defamation action based on statement confirmed but not repeated outside the House).
(B) MAGNA CARTA. *In Re S-C (Mental patient: Habeas corpus)* [1996] QB 599, 603C (no confinement without authority of law as a "fundamental constitutional principle, traceable back to ... Magna Carta"); *R v Secretary of State for the Home Department, ex p Muboyayi* [1992] QB 244, 254F-G (duty of the courts to uphold classic statement of the law in Magna Carta); *R (Bancoult) v Secretary of State for the Foreign and Commonwealth Office* [2001] QB 1067 at [30]-[34] (discussing guarantee in Magna Carta); *R v Secretary of State for the Home Department, ex p Wynne* [1993] 1 WLR 115, 121H-122E (Magna Carta considered in CA).
(C) CONSTITUTIONAL STATUTES. <7.5.7>.
(D) HUMAN RIGHTS ACT. <P9>; <64.7>.

6.1.4 Status/influence of miscellaneous other sources.*R v Royal Pharmaceutical Society of Great Britain, ex p Mahmood* [2001] EWCA Civ 1245 [2002] 1 WLR 879 (RPS Charter); *R (ProLife Alliance) v British Broadcasting Corporation* [2003] UKHL 23 [2004] 1 AC 185 at [1] (BBC contract and Charter); *R (Al-Jedda) v Secretary of State for Defence* [2007] UKHL 58 [2008] 1 AC 332 (UN Security Council Resolution qualifying HRA:ECHR Art 5); *R (M) v*

HM Treasury [2006] EWHC 2328 (Admin) (UN Security Council Resolution aid to interpretation of EU Regulation intended to implement it); *R (Tum) v Secretary of State for the Home Department* [2004] EWCA Civ 788 [2004] INLR 442 (EC-Turkey Association Agreement); *R (G) v Barnet London Borough Council* [2003] UKHL 57 [2004] 2 AC 208 at [68] (UK's First Report to UN Committee on the Rights of the Child); *T v Secretary of State for the Home Department* [1996] AC 742, 786B (UNHCR Handbook); *Meyrick Estate Management Ltd v Secretary of State for Environment, Food and Rural Affairs* [2007] EWCA Civ 53 [2007] Env LR 558 at [57] (relevance of new legislation, meaning quashing order may serve no useful purpose); *R (Cole) v Secretary of State for the Home Department* [2003] EWHC 1789 (Admin) at [90] (proper for Secretary of State to decline tariff re-setting function where imminent legislation would remove that function to secure HRA:ECHR Art 6-compatibility); *R (Shrewsbury and Atcham Borough Council) v Secretary of State for Communities and Local Government* [2008] EWCA Civ 148 [2008] 3 All ER 548 (new Act retrospectively approving procedure adopted); <6.2> (policy guidance).

6.1.5 **Implied/incidental powers: general.** *R (Leicester Gaming Club Ltd) v Gambling Commission* [2007] EWHC 531 (Admin) (implied power to extend time); *R (Government of Bermuda) v Office of Communications* [2008] EWHC 2009 (Admin) (incidental power of dispute resolution); *Ward v Metropolitan Police Commissioner* [2005] UKHL 32 [2006] 1 AC 23 (no implied power to impose conditions on mental health warrant requiring named professionals be present), [24]; *Director of Public Prosecutions v Haw* [2007] EWHC 1931 (Admin) [2008] 1 WLR 379 at [33] (implied power to delegate where responsibilities of statutory office mean delegation inevitable); *R v Bristol City Council, ex p Everett* [1999] 1 WLR 1170, 1180A (implied power to withdraw an abatement notice); *R (Barry) v Liverpool City Council* [2001] EWCA Civ 384 [2001] LGR 361 (incidental power to set up registration scheme, but not to impose charge for participation); *R v Director of Public Prosecutions, ex p Duckenfield* [2000] 1 WLR 55 (police authority power to fund legal proceedings); *R (Dixon) v Secretary of State for the Environment, Food and Rural Affairs* [2002] EWHC 831 (Admin) (implied power to burn foot-and-mouth carcasses); *R (Risk Management Partners Ltd) v Brent London Borough Council* [2008] EWHC 692 (Admin) [2008] LGR 331 (local government incidental powers); *R v Governor of Frankland Prison, ex p Russell* [2000] 1 WLR 2027 at [11] (implied power to interfere with fundamental rights needing self-evident and pressing need, applying *R v Secretary of State for the Home Department, ex p Leech* [1994] QB 198).

6.1.6 **Other residual powers.**[32] *R (Wilkinson) v Commissioners of Inland Revenue* [2005] UKHL 30 [2005] 1 WLR 1718 at [21] (limits on Revenue's taxes management powers); *R v West Yorkshire Coroner, ex p Smith (No.2)* [1985] QB 1096 (coroner's "ancient jurisdiction"); *R v Secretary of State for Health, ex p Kamal* (1992) 4 Admin LR 730 (Secretary of State's residual power); *R v Chief National Insurance Commissioner, ex p Connor* [1981] QB 758, 765A-B (NIC power under "the rules of public policy"); *R v Director General of Fair Trading, ex p F.H. Taylor & Co Ltd* [1981] ICR 292, 294C-D (DGFT needing no statutory power for free speech publishing work); *R v Industrial Tribunal, ex p Cotswold Collotype Co Ltd* [1979] ICR 190 (IT's inherent power); *Independent Publishing Co Ltd v Attorney General of Trinidad and Tobago* [2004] UKPC 26 [2005] 1 AC 190 (criminal court having no inherent power to order postponed reporting of proceedings); *R (Mathialagan) v Southwark London Borough Council* [2004] EWCA Civ 1689 at [37] (magistrates self-correction where judicial review quashing would arise); *R (Newham London Borough Council) v Stratford Magistrates Court* [2008] EWHC 125 (Admin) (magistrates' common law power to set aside previous civil decisions).

---

[32] John Howell QC, `Section 2 of the Local Government Act 2000' [2004] JR 72.

6.1.7 **Duty/power to reconsider a decision?** *R v Hertfordshire County Council, ex p Cheung* The Times 4th April 1986 (see transcript) (council having "power to reconsider their decision"); <49.2.15> (duty to reconsider where error of fact pointed out); *R v Criminal Injuries Compensation Board, ex p Moore* [1999] COD 241 (CICB having power to reconsider where criminal conviction prior to acceptance of award); *R v Brent London Borough Council, ex p Sadiq* (2001) 33 HLR 525 at [35] (council having no power to reconsider lawful decision to provide housing under Housing Act 1996 s.193); *R v Southwark London Borough Council, ex p Campisi* (1999) 31 HLR 560 (local authority having duty here to consider whether sufficient change of circumstances to warrant possible reversal of housing decision); *Crawley Borough Council v B* The Times 28th March 2000 (council entitled to revisit conclusion as to whether to refuse housing and if so on what grounds); *E v Secretary of State for the Home Department* [2004] EWCA Civ 49 [2004] QB 1044 (discussing IAT's new power to direct a rehearing: r.30 of the Immigration and Asylum Appeals (Procedure) Rules 2003); <49.2.15> (duty to reconsider where error of fact); <49.2.16> (power to reopen decision where error of fact).

6.1.8 **No residual power: illustrations.** *Credit Suisse v Allerdale Borough Council* [1997] QB 306 and *Credit Suisse v Waltham Forest London Borough Council* [1997] QB 362 (local government incidental powers (Local Government Act 1972 s.111) not capable of circumventing restrictions in comprehensive borrowing powers); *Macharia v Secretary of State for the Home Department* [2000] INLR 156 at [17] (IAT having no implied power to allow further evidence without notice as required by express rule); *R v P Borough Council, ex p S* [1999] Fam 188, 213F-215F (no implied power of suspension, because inconsistent with express, limited powers); *R v Liverpool City Council, ex p Baby Products Association* [2000] LGR 171 (no power to issue press release where would circumvent detailed statutory code as to enforcement action).

6.1.9 **Whether power to levy a charge.** *R v Richmond upon Thames London Borough Council, ex p McCarthy & Stone (Developments) Ltd* [1992] 2 AC 48 (considering the principle in *Wilts Dairies* against the levying of charges without express statutory authority); *R (Passenger Transport UK) v Humber Bridge Board* [2003] EWCA Civ 842 [2004] QB 310 (rectifying construction of regulations to correct drafting mistake, by reading in words, providing the clear statutory authority necessary to empower the imposing of a charge), at [27] (clear statutory authority needed).

6.1.10 **Residual prerogative powers.** <34.3.3> (prerogative powers); *R v Secretary of State for the Home Department, ex p Northumbria Police Authority* (1993) 5 Admin LR 489 (Home Secretary entitled to set up central store of riot equipment under prerogative powers for maintaining law and order); *R v Secretary of State for Health, ex p C* [2000] 1 FLR 627, 631G-632A (Crown's prerogative power including common law powers enjoyed by ordinary citizens); *R (Bancoult) v Secretary of State for the Foreign and Commonwealth Office* [2001] QB 1067 at [61] (prerogative power not extending to exiling subjects from territory where they belong). As to whether prerogative powers ousted by statutory powers sufficiently covering the same ground, see *R v Royal Pharmaceutical Society of Great Britain, ex p Mahmood* [2001] EWCA Civ 1245 [2002] 1 WLR 879 (discussing *Attorney-General v De Keyser's Royal Hotel Ltd* [1920] AC 508).

6.1.11 **Common law powers.** *R (Shrewsbury and Atcham Borough Council) v Secretary of State for Communities and Local Government* [2008] EWCA Civ 148 [2008] 3 All ER 548 at [44] (Secretary of State having general powers to do anything which can be done by natural person); *R (Charlton) v Secretary of State for Education and Skills* [2005] EWHC 1378 (Admin) [2005] 2 FCR 603 at [117] (Secretary of State exercising prerogative or common law powers); *R v Brent Health Authority, ex p Francis* [1985] QB 869, 878B-C (health authority's "common law power"); *Council of Civil Service Unions v Minister for the Civil Service* [1985] AC 374, 407C, 410C-D (prerogative power as having "common law" source).

6.2 Policy guidance. Many areas of action by public bodies involve policy guidance, directions or instructions. Policy guidance may be received (external), as when a local authority has regard to the Secretary of State's guidance; or it may be self-adopted (internal), as when a local authority has regard to its own policy. It may be statutory or non-statutory. Its legal relevance and implications will depend on its character and context, though there will often be a duty (1) to interpret it correctly (or at least reasonably) and (2) to depart from it only for good reason.

6.2.1 Guidance and direction. *R v North Derbyshire Health Authority, ex p Fisher* (1998) 10 Admin LR 27, 32A-E (as to "guidance", duty is to have regard to it, properly to construe it, and give reasons for departing from it; as to "direction", duty is an "absolute duty to comply"); *Laker Airways Ltd v Department of Trade* [1977] QB 643, 714 ("Guidance is assistance in reaching a decision proffered to him who has to make that decision, but guidance does not compel any particular decision. Direction on the other hand ... is compulsive in character"); *R v Social Fund Inspector, ex p Ali* (1994) 6 Admin LR 205, 208G-H, 212D (mandatory statutory duty to determine questions in accordance with Minister's guidance set out in Social Fund Directions); *R v Director of Passenger Rail Franchising, ex p Save Our Railways* [1996] CLC 589, 597H ("An instruction is a direction with which the recipient must comply. Guidance is advice which the recipient should heed and respect; it should ordinarily be followed but need not if there are special reasons for not doing so"); *R (Girling) v Parole Board* [2006] EWCA Civ 1779 [2007] QB 783 (Secretary of State's statutory directions not binding on parole board); *Royal Mail Group Plc v Postal Services Commission* [2007] EWHC 1205 (Admin) (context where duty to have regard to guidance being tantamount to duty to act in accordance with it).

6.2.2 Statutory guidance. *R v Islington London Borough Council, ex p Rixon* [1997] ELR 66 (explaining that duty to comply with statutory guidance unless good reason for departure; non-statutory guidance manifestly a relevancy to be conscientiously taken into account); *R v London Borough of Barnet, ex p B* [1994] ELR 357, 360B-C (statutory duty to "act" under statutory guidance); *R v London Borough of Croydon, ex p Jarvis* (1994) 26 HLR 194, 205, 209-210 (statutory duty to "have regard to" Code of Practice, not "follow" it); *R (Munjaz) v Mersey Care NHS Trust* [2005] UKHL 58 [2006] 2 AC 148 at [21] (statutory guidance "should be given great weight"; duty to "consider with great care, and ... depart only if it has cogent reasons for doing so"), [69] (need for "cogent reasons if in any respect they decide not to follow it. These reasons must be spelled out clearly, logically and convincingly"); *R (Khatun) v London Borough of Newham* [2004] EWCA Civ 55 [2005] QB 37 at [47] (recipient of statutory guidance (circular) "must (a) take it into account and (b) if they decide to depart from it, give clear reasons for doing so"); *R (Prospect) v Ministry of Defence* [2008] EWHC 2056 (Admin) (whether Early Release Scheme compatible with code issued under Order in Council); *R v Tameside Metropolitan Borough Council, ex p J* [2000] 1 FLR 942, 951G (statutory guidance "a helpful aid to the way the legislation is intended to be implemented, and it should not be departed from without good reason"); *R v Sutton London Borough Council, ex p Tucker* (1998) 1 CCLR 251 (decision unlawful and/or irrational for failure to follow s.7 guidance); *R v Bolsover District Council, ex p East Midlands Development* (1996) 28 HLR 329 (asking, where statutory duty to have regard to those matters specified by Secretary of State, whether misunderstood Circular specified by Secretary of State); *R v Cornwall County Council, ex p LH* [2000] 1 FLR 236 (council's policy contrary to statutory guidance, applying *Rixon*, and therefore unlawful); *R (Bodimeade) v Camden London Borough Council* [2001] EWHC Admin 271 (2001) 4 CCLR 246 at [22], [25] (failure to adopt a needs-led approach contrary to statutory guidance); *R (G) v Legal Services Commission* [2004] EWHC 276 (Admin) (misdirection as to test in statutory guidance); *R (M) v Islington London Borough Council* [2004] EWCA Civ 235 [2005] 1 WLR 884 at [59] (council entitled to decide "inappropriate" to follow the guidance here), [79] (guidance allowing the divergent response); cf. *R (Coghlan) v Chief Constable of Greater Manchester Police* [2004] EWHC 2801 (Admin) [2005] 2 All ER 890 at [54] (non-statutory guidance "so obviously material to the decision ... that anything short of direct consideration ... would not be in accordance with the intention of the statutory scheme").

6.2.3 **Non-statutory scheme.** *R v Secretary of State for the Home Department, ex p Chahal* [1995] 1 WLR 526, 544F (immigration rules "do not have statutory force, but they set out the practice which the Secretary of State is expected to follow"); *R v Criminal Injuries Compensation Board, ex p Ince* [1973] 1 WLR 1334 (asking whether Board had correctly applied provisions of the non-statutory Criminal Injuries Compensation Scheme); *R v Ministry of Defence, ex p Walker* [2000] 1 WLR 806 (non-statutory scheme for compensating service personnel); *R v Inspector of Taxes, Reading, ex p Fulford-Dobson* [1987] QB 978, 991A-H (Revenue concession, meaning duty to "act fairly and evenhandedly in the administration of the scheme"); *R (British Telecommunications Plc) v Revenue and Customs Commissioners* [2005] EWHC 1043 (Admin) at [20] (tax concessions lawfully made but available only to those falling clearly within their terms).

6.2.4 **General consequences of adopting policy guidance.** *R (Alconbury Developments Ltd) v Secretary of State for the Environment Transport and the Regions* [2001] UKHL 23 [2003] 2 AC 295 at [143] (Lord Clyde: "The formulation of policies is a perfectly proper course for the provision of guidance in the exercise of an administrative discretion. Indeed policies are an essential element in securing the coherent and consistent performance of administrative functions. There are advantages both to the public and the administrators in having such policies. Of course there are limits to be observed in the way policies are applied. Blanket decisions which leave no room for particular circumstances may be unreasonable. What is crucial is that the policy must not fetter the exercise of the discretion. The particular circumstances always require to be considered. Provided that the policy is not regarded as binding and the authority still retains a free exercise of discretion the policy may serve the useful purpose of giving a reasonable guidance both to applicants and decision-makers"); *R v Secretary of State for the Home Department, ex p Hastrup* [1996] Imm AR 616, 623-624 (policy will generally "promote consistency of practice", not fetter the discretion but may give rise to a legitimate expectation); Sir Stephen Sedley, `Policy and Law' in Andenas and Fairgrieve, *Judicial Review in International Perspective* (Kluwer, 2000) chapter 18 (describing four analytical bases for the "presumption that ministers will follow their policies").

6.2.5 **Policy guidance must not be a fetter.** *R v Police Complaints Board, ex p Madden* [1983] 1 WLR 447 (fetter by erroneously treating policy guidance as binding); *R v Brent London Borough Council, ex p Macwan* (1994) 26 HLR 528 (not unlawful for council to decline to comply with Secretary of State's `guidance'); *Laker Airways Ltd v Department of Trade* [1977] QB 643 (guidance ultra vires as cutting across the statute and requiring CAA to revoke licence); *R v Worthing Borough Council, ex p Burch* (1985) 50 P & CR 53 (circular unlawful as having the practical effect of constraining the local authority); *R (S) v London Borough of Brent* [2002] EWCA Civ 693 [2002] ELR 556 (no unlawful fetter in Secretary of State's statutory guidance having provided that pupil exclusion order made in accordance with a published discipline policy should "normally" be upheld), [15] (appeal panel must not neglect Secretary of State's guidance, but must not treat it as "something to be strictly adhered to").

6.2.6 **Policy guidance giving rise to legitimate expectation.** *R (Corby District Council) v*

Secretary of State for Communities and Local Government [2007] EWHC 1873 (Admin) [2008] LGR 109 (unjustified departure from substantive legitimate expectation engendered by scheme as published); *R (Jeeves) v Gravesham Borough Council* [2006] EWHC 1249 (Admin) at [35] (legitimate expectation that council would have regard to planning circular); *R (Asha Foundation) v Millennium Commission* [2002] EWHC 916 (Admin) (Administrative Court) at [9] (guidelines giving rise to legitimate expectation of being "the rules of the competition"); *R (Saadi) v Secretary of State for the Home Department* [2001] EWCA Civ 1512 [2002] 1 WLR 356 (CA) at [7] ("The lawful exercise of [statutory] powers can ... be restricted, according to established principles of public law, by government policy and the legitimate expectation to which such policy gives rise"); *R v Secretary of State for the Home Department, ex p Popatia* [2000] INLR 587 at [117] (legitimate expectation from `long residence' immigration policy); *R v Secretary of State for the Home Department, ex p Asif Mahmood Khan* [1984] 1 WLR 1337, 1352C-D (legitimate expectation from stated criteria); <54.2> (unjustified breach of a substantive legitimate expectation).

6.2.7 Policy guidance and COE:COM R(80)2. See Recommendation No.R(80)2 of the Committee of Ministers (adopted 11 March 1980) <45.1.4(B)> ("Basic principles", including that: "An administrative authority, when exercising a discretionary power: ... applies any general administrative guidelines in a consistent manner while at the same time taking account of the particular circumstances of each case; ... (7) Any general administrative guidelines which govern the exercise of a discretionary power are: (i) made public; or (ii) communicated in an appropriate manner and to the extent that is necessary to the person concerned, at his request, be it before or after the taking of the act concerning him; (8) Where an administrative authority, in exercising a discretionary power, departs from a general administrative guideline in such a manner as to affect adversely the rights, liberties or interests of a person concerned, the latter is informed of the reasons for this decision. This is done either by stating the reasons in the act or by communicating them, at his request, to the person concerned in writing within a reasonable time").

6.2.8 Basic duties arising from guidance/policy.[33]
(A) *GRANSDEN*. See *Gransden v Secretary of State for the Environment* (1987) 54 P & CR 86, 93-94 ("the body determining an application must have regard to the policy ... [which] does not mean that it needs necessarily to follow the policy. However, if it is going to depart from the policy, it must give clear reasons for ... doing so ... If the body making the decision fails to properly understand the policy, then the decision will be as defective as it would be if no regard had been paid to the policy"); *R (Swords) v Secretary of State for Communities and Local Government* [2007] EWCA Civ 795 [2007] LGR 757 at [50].
(B) DUTY TO UNDERSTAND/MISDIRECTION. *R (Heath & Hampstead Society) v Camden London Borough Council* [2008] EWCA Civ 193 [2008] 3 All ER 80 at [38] (error of law in misinterpreting planning policy guidance); *R (S) v Secretary of State for the Home Department* [2008] EWHC 2069 (Admin) (Secretary of State acting contrary to plain meaning of immigration policy); *R v Secretary of State for the Home Department, ex p Pierson* [1998] AC 539 (considering whether decision consistent with own policy), 568G-569G (Lord Goff), 576E-577A (Lord Browne-Wilkinson), 583H (Lord Lloyd); *R v Secretary of State for the Home Department, ex p Popatia* [2000] INLR 587 (Secretary of State erring as to meaning/ effect of own `long residence' policy); *Horsham District Council v Secretary of State for the Environment* [1992] 1 PLR 81, 92E (McCowan LJ: "It is not enough for the decision-maker merely to have regard to the plan if he misinterprets it"); cf. *R v Governing Body of Irlam & Cadishead Community High School, ex p Salford City Council* [1994] ELR 81, 87D

---

[33] Kate Markus & Martin Westgate, `The Duty to Follow Guidance' [1997] JR 154.

("misapprehension" as to Secretary of State's guidance not a "misdirection in law", since the guidance "does not have statutory effect"); *R v Secretary of State for the Home Department, ex p Pilditch* [1994] COD 352 (failure to consider relevant part of own policy); *R (G) v Legal Services Commission* [2004] EWHC 276 (Admin) (misdirection as to serious wrongdoing test in statutory guidance); *R v Secretary of State for the Environment, ex p West Oxfordshire District Council* (1994) 26 HLR 417, 425 (Minister's decision "flawed, having been arrived at by a departure from or misinterpretation of the published policy", referring (at 423) to legitimate expectation and duty to apply Circular and its underlying intent); *R v Leeds City Council, ex p Hendry* (1994) 6 Admin LR 439, 442C-E (decision ultra vires/unlawful, having wrongly applied stated policy); <29.5.10> (whether meaning of policy a hard-edged question for the Court).

(C) DUTY TO HAVE PROPER REGARD. *R (Jeeves) v Gravesham Borough Council* [2006] EWHC 1249 (Admin) at [35] (planning decision flawed for failure to have regard to circular); *R v North Derbyshire Health Authority, ex p Fisher* (1998) 10 Admin LR 27 (health authority's policy unlawful because failure to have proper regard to NHS Circular); *R v London Borough of Newham, ex p Ugbo* (1994) 26 HLR 263, 268 ("failure to refer to the specific paragraph in the Code of Guidance ... [constituting] the kind of procedural error which would lead this court to intervene"); *R (Lichfield Securities Ltd) v Lichfield District Council* [2001] EWCA Civ 304 [2001] 3 PLR 33 at [13] ("in general", public authority "obliged" to "have regard to its established policy"); *R (Coghlan) v Chief Constable of Greater Manchester Police* [2004] EWHC 2801 (Admin) [2005] 2 All ER 890 (unlawful termination of disciplinary suspension, for failure to have regard to non-statutory guidance).

(D) DUTY TO JUSTIFY DEPARTURE. *R (B) v Lewisham London Borough Council* [2008] EWHC 738 (Admin) at [54] (unjustified departure from guidance); *Philomena Gangadeen v Secretary of State for the Home Department* [1998] Imm AR 106, 111 ("the Home Secretary is in ordinary circumstances obliged to act in accordance with his declared policy, and that, if he departs from it, it is incumbent on him to explain why"); *R v Secretary of State for the Home Department, ex p Urmaza* [1996] COD 479 (decision-maker can be held in public law to his policy, with departure requiring the articulation of a good reason).

6.2.9 Whether duty to promote the purpose/objective of policy guidance. *R (Dabrowski) v Secretary of State for the Home Department* [2003] EWCA Civ 580 [2003] Imm AR 454 at [17] ("whatever the literal ambit", common ground that purpose of immigration enforcement policy equally applicable to port cases); *Shala v Secretary of State for the Home Department* [2003] EWCA Civ 233 [2003] INLR 349 at [21] (Schiemann LJ, emphasising "the need for adjudicators to bear in mind the *reasons* for the policies which they are enforcing and not just the *wording* of the policies"); *R v Secretary of State of Transport, ex p Berkshire, Buckinghamshire and Oxfordshire Naturalists' Trust Ltd* [1997] Env LR 80, 87 (Court unable to "enlarge" the ambit of the policy, by holding the Government to its "underlying purpose"); *R v Secretary of State for the Home Department, ex p Urmaza* [1996] COD 479 (Secretary of State having erred in law in excluding claimant from Home Office policy whose meaning and purposes applied to him); *R v Secretary of State for Trade and Industry, ex p McCormick* [1998] COD 160 (not irrational, unreasonable or inconsistent for Secretary of State not to apply similar policy to directors' disqualification proceedings as to criminal proceedings); *Afunyah v Secretary of State for the Home Department* [1998] Imm AR 201, 204 (entitled to decide not to extend the policy); *R v Brighton & Hove Council, ex p Marmont* [1998] 2 PLR 48 (in evicting travellers under RSC O.113, no duty to have regard to approach set out in Government Circular on gypsy eviction under Criminal Justice and Public Order Act 1994 ss.77-80); *R (Saadi) v Secretary of State for the Home Department* [2001] EWCA Civ 1512 [2002] 1 WLR 356 (CA) at [23] (Lord Phillips MR: "If the policy reason for detention is that this is necessary in order to effect speedy processing of applications for asylum and, in fact, it is not necessary for this purpose, then the decision to detain may be open to attack on the ground of irrationality"); *R (Gashi) v Secretary of State for the Home Department* [2003] EWHC 1198 (Admin) at [11] (interpretation of policy by reference to "the purpose of the policy").

6.2.10 **Policy guidance and other duties.**
(A) PROCEDURAL DUTY ARISING FROM POLICY GUIDANCE. *R (Gleaves) v Secretary of State for the Home Department* [2004] EWHC 2522 (Admin) (failure to follow prison discipline manual and record reasons not rendering the decision unlawful); *R v Governor of HM Prison Long Lartin, ex p Ross* The Times 9th June 1994 (duty to give reasons contained in Home Office circular, stating that "reasons given should be as full as is reasonably possible"); *R v Secretary of State for Education, ex p Cumbria County Council* [1994] ELR 220, 224G-225F (circular making clear that wide consultation should ordinarily take place); *R v Lambeth London Borough Council, ex p N* [1996] ELR 299 (ministerial guidance indicating that parents important consultees and what kinds of matters important to hear their representations upon); *R v Governors of the Sheffield Hallam University, ex p R* [1995] ELR 267, 282B-284F (failure to follow own procedural rules); *R v Monopolies and Mergers Commission, ex p Stagecoach Holdings Plc* The Times 23rd July 1996 (whether MMC followed "self-direction" as to procedural standards in own Fact Sheet, but legitimate expectation adding nothing to ordinary procedural fairness analysis); *R (Haringey Consortium of Disabled People and Carers Association) v Haringey London Borough Council* (2002) 5 CCLR 422 at [48] (consultation required under the General Conditions of Grant Aid for Voluntary Organisations Agreement); <60.1.20> (fairness following choice).
(B) OTHER DUTIES. *R (D) v Secretary of State for the Home Department* [2003] EWHC 155 (Admin) [2003] 1 FLR 979 (policy prescribing a relevant consideration), [16] (Prison Service policy as one source of obligation to have regard to the best interests of the child); *R v Wolverhampton Metropolitan Borough Council, ex p Dunne* (1997) 29 HLR 745 (duty to investigate humanitarian questions, in relation to eviction of travellers, as required by Government policy); cf. *R v Hillingdon London Borough Council, ex p McDonagh* [1999] 1 PLR 22 (circular indicating good practice, not imposing any legally binding obligation to conduct investigations); *R v Lincolnshire County Council and Wealden District Council, ex p Atkinson, Wales and Stratford* (1996) 8 Admin LR 529, 535G (concession that legally relevant matters being as identified in departmental circular); *R v Hillingdon London Borough Council, ex p McDonagh* [1999] 1 PLR 22 (circular not directly applicable in law but an indication of matters which may be material); *R v Secretary of State for Education, ex p S* [1994] ELR 252, 263E-F (Sedley J: although "the Secretary of State ought in fairness to practise what he preaches to local education authorities ... [this] is not a source of law. If the Secretary of State ought in fairness to disclose any advice which he himself obtains, the obligation has to be derived from the statutory context of the Secretary of State's own appellate obligations. It cannot be derived from non-statutory advice given by him to others").

6.2.11 **Whether duty to publish/publicise policy guidance.** *R (Walmsley) v Lane* [2005] EWCA Civ 1540 [2006] LGR 280 at [57] ("it is inimical to good public administration for a public authority to have and operate ... a policy without making it public"); *R (Salih) v Secretary of State for the Home Department* [2003] EWHC 2273 (Admin) at [52] (rule of law meaning Government should make "hard cases" asylum support policy known to those who may need it; "constitutional imperative" not to "withhold information about its policy relating to the exercise of a power conferred by statute"); *R (Refugee Legal Centre) v Secretary of State for the Home Department* [2004] EWCA Civ 1481 [2005] 1 WLR 2219 at [19] (making policy public "will enable applicants and their legal representatives to know what [the proper] ingredients are taken to be; and if anything is included in or omitted from them which renders the process legally unfair, the courts will be in a position to say so"); *B v Secretary of State for Work and Pensions* [2005] EWCA Civ 929 [2005] 1 WLR 3796 at [43] ("If ... a policy has been formulated and is regularly used by officials, it is the antithesis of good government to keep it

in a departmental drawer"); *R (Faarah) v Southwark London Borough Council* [2008] EWCA Civ 807 at [47(4)] (administrative practice should have been published); *R v Secretary of State for the Home Department, ex p Stafford* [1998] 1 WLR 503 (CA), 521G ("because what is involved is an executive ... restriction on liberty, the policy and the decisions taken under it need to be transparent ... the Secretary of State's policy needs to be clearly stated"), 530F ("sufficient general indication has been given of the terms of the policy"); *R v Secretary of State for the Home Department, ex p Ruddock* [1987] 1 WLR 1482, 1497B ("if the practice has been to publish the current policy, it would be encumbent upon [the Secretary of State] in dealing fairly to publish the new policy"); *R v Newham London Borough Council, ex p Miah* (1996) 28 HLR 279, 288 (important to publicise housing policy, but policy not ultra vires if failure to publish); *R v Ministry of Defence, ex p Walker* [2000] 1 WLR 806 (better if MoD had publicised change in policy but change not unfair in the circumstances); *R (Collaku) v Secretary of State for the Home Department* [2005] EWHC 2855 (Admin) (sufficient here that reasons given reflecting the policy); *R v Chief Constable of the North Wales Police, ex p AB* [1999] QB 396, 429H ("both so as to accord with the principles of good administrative practice and to comply with the requirement that a public authority should act `in accordance with the law' ... should have made the policy which it was applying available to the public. To do so provides a safeguard against arbitrary action"); <59.1.4> (requirement of measures "prescribed by law" etc); *R (L) v Secretary of State for the Home Department* [2003] EWCA Civ 25 [2003] 1 WLR 1230 at [17] ("legal certainty is an aspect of the rule of law"), [25] ("It is an aspect of the rule of law that individuals and those advising them, since they will be presumed to know the law, should have access to it in authentic form").

6.2.12 Guidance/policy in action: further examples. <32.2.4> (policy guidance and prosecutorial decisions); *Tesco Stores Ltd v Secretary of State for the Environment* [1995] 1 WLR 759 (analysing role of planning policies); *City of Edinburgh Council v Secretary of State for Scotland* [1997] 1 WLR 1447, 1450E-H, 1458C-H (as to effect of statutory presumption on a planning decision-maker to apply the development plan); *R v Governors of the Hasmonean High School, ex p N & E* [1994] ELR 343, 348B-C (school governors "required to decide in accordance with their own published criteria for admission"); <29.3.19> (whether policy guidance assists statutory interpretation).

6.3 International law.[34] Questions of compatibility with international law obligations can be highly relevant. An international instrument which has been "incorporated" by domestic statute becomes part of domestic law through the statute. A non-incorporated international instrument can be legally relevant in a number of ways (hence the pre-HRA effect of the ECHR[35]), as can general principles of customary international law.

6.3.1 International law: presumption of domestic law compatibility. *R v Lyons* [2002] UKHL 44 [2003] 1 AC 976 at [27] (Lord Hoffmann: "there is a strong presumption in favour of interpreting English law (whether common law or statute) in a way which does not place the United Kingdom in breach of an international obligation"); *A v Secretary of State for the Home Department* [2005] UKHL 71 [2006] 2 AC 221 at [27] (Lord Bingham, referring to "the well-established principle that the words of a United Kingdom statute, passed after the date of a treaty and dealing with the same subject matter, are to be construed, if they are reasonably

---

[34] See generally Shaheed Fatima, *Using International Law in Domestic Courts* (2005, Hart Publishing); and her overview articles at [2003] JR 81, 138 & 235

[35] Lord Lester QC [1996] JR 21; James Maurici [1996] JR 29.

capable of bearing such a meaning, as intended to carry out the treaty obligation and not to be inconsistent with it"); *Mabon v Mabon* [2005] EWCA Civ 634 [2005] Fam 366 at [26] (Family Proceedings Rules construed "to meet our obligations to comply with ... article 12 of the United Nations Convention on the Rights of the Child"); *R (Al-Skeini) v Secretary of State for Defence* [2007] UKHL 26 [2008] 1 AC 153 at [147]-[149] (presumption of compatibility albeit international instrument not itself requiring domestication); <6.3.5> (international law and legislative ambiguity).

6.3.2 **International law via ECHR/HRA.** *A v Secretary of State for the Home Department* [2005] UKHL 71 [2006] 2 AC 221 at [29] (Lord Bingham, describing the influence of international law instruments on the interpretation of the ECHR); *R (Al-Skeini) v Secretary of State for Defence* [2007] UKHL 26 [2008] 1 AC 153 (international law influencing ECHR jurisdiction and so HRA territorial reach); *Singh v Entry Clearance Officer, New Delhi* [2004] EWCA Civ 1075 [2005] QB 608 at [30] (CA considering UN Convention on Rights of the Child and Hague Convention 1993, as the relevant international law in the context of analysing Art 8 family life); *R (B) v Secretary of State for the Foreign and Commonwealth Office* [2004] EWCA Civ 1344 [2005] QB 643 at [84] (emphasising international law in extra-territorial application of ECHR Art 3/5, as to actions of consular staff); *R (R) v Durham Constabulary* [2005] UKHL 21 [2005] 1 WLR 1184 at [26] (UN Convention on the Rights of the Child "reflected in the interpretation and application" of the ECHR by the ECtHR), [44] (but ECHR rights "less extensive" than those under the CRC).

6.3.3 **International law/ECHR via EC Law.** *R (Omar) v Secretary of State for the Home Department* [2005] EWCA Civ 285 [2005] INLR 470 (Dublin Convention via EC Regulation 343/2003); EC Treaty Art 6(3) ("The Union shall respect fundamental rights, as guaranteed by the [ECHR] and as they result from the constitutional traditions common to the Member States, as general principles of Community law"); *A v Chief Constable of West Yorkshire* [2004] UKHL 21 [2004] ICR 806 (decision incompatible with EC law as influenced by ECHR, rather than by HRA standing alone since ECtHR decisions characterised as prospective only) at [13] (ECHR "shaping the current European understanding of what fundamental human rights mean and require"); *R v Hertfordshire County Council, ex p Green Environmental Industries Limited* [2000] 2 AC 412, 422B (statute giving effect to Directive so "it must be interpreted according to principles of Community law, including its doctrines of fundamental human rights"); *A v Chief Constable of West Yorkshire* [2002] EWCA Civ 1584 [2003] HRLR 137 at [42] ("the Convention jurisprudence is introduced into domestic law ... by the medium of the Equal Treatment Directive"); *Booker Aquaculture Ltd v Secretary of State for Scotland* The Times 24th September 1998 (freedom of property under Human Rights Convention as a general principle of EC law, rendering unlawful the exercise of statutory power without compensation); *R v Secretary of State for Health, ex p Eastside Cheese Company* [1999] EuLR 968 (whether breach of Art 1P to Human Rights Convention so as to prevent reliance on EC Treaty (Article 36) defence of justification); *B v Secretary of State for the Home Department* [2000] UKHRR 498 (ECHR Art 8 relevant to deportation decision relating to EC national).

6.3.4 **"Domesticated" international instruments.**
(A) DOMESTIC EMBODIMENT. See European Communities Act 1972 (EC Treaty) <8.1.1>; Human Rights Act 1998 <9.1.4> (ECHR through the HRA); *Re M (Abduction: Rights of Custody)* [2007] UKHL 55 [2007] 3 WLR 975 (Hague Convention on Civil Aspects of Child Abduction, scheduled to Child Abduction and Custody Act 1985); *Re Deep Vein Thrombosis and Air Travel Group Litigation* [2005] UKHL 72 [2006] 1 AC 495 (Warsaw Convention 1929, scheduled to the Carriage By Air Act 1961); *Kirin-Amgen Inc v Hoechst Marion Roussel Ltd* [2004] UKHL 46 [2005] 1 All ER 667 (Convention on the Grant of European Patents 1973, given effect by the Patents Act 1977); *R (G) v Barnet London Borough Council* [2003] UKHL

57 [2004] 2 AC 208 at [68] (Part III of the Children Act 1989 "intended to reflect the obligation in article 18(2) of the United Nations Convention on the Rights of the Child"); *In re Nielsen* [1984] AC 606, 616E (extradition treaty); *In re McFarland* [2004] UKHL 17 [2004] 1 WLR 1289 at [10] (ICCPR Art 14(6) treated as "incorporated" in Ministerial policy statement which referred to it); *In re D (A Child) (Abduction: Rights of Custody)* [2006] UKHL 51 [2007] 1 AC 619 at [65] (human rights provision of 1980 Child Abduction Convention not scheduled to 1985 domesticating Act, but now given effect via the Human Rights Act 1998); *Gomez v Goz-Monche Vives* [2008] EWHC 259 (Ch) [2008] 3 WLR 309 at [64] (1984 Hague Convention, via the Recognition of Trusts Act 1987).

(B) DOMESTICATING STATUTE: COMPATIBLE CONSTRUCTION. *R (Mullen) v Secretary of State for the Home Department* [2004] UKHL 18 [2005] 1 AC 1 at [5] (Lord Bingham, explaining that since Criminal Justice Act 1988 s.133 "enacted to give effect ... in domestic law" to Art 14(6) of the International Convention on Civil and Political Rights, "the key to interpretation of s.133 is a correct understanding of Art 14(6)"), [35] (Lord Steyn); *R v Asfaw* [2008] UKHL 31 [2008] 2 WLR 1178 at [28] (although statute intended to give effect to international instrument, disparity arising and "no legitimate process of interpretation" enabling symmetry); *R v Southwark Crown Court, ex p Customs & Excise Commissioners* [1990] 1 QB 650, 659D-660H (construing Drug Trafficking Offences Act 1986 to accord with the Convention on Narcotics); *Litster v Forth Dry Dock & Engineering Co Ltd* [1990] 1 AC 546, 559D-F ("[if] primary and subordinate legislation enacted to give effect to the United Kingdom's obligations under the EEC Treaty ... can reasonably be construed so as to conform with those obligations"); *Lesotho Highlands Development Authority v Impregilo SpA* [2005] UKHL 43 [2006] 1 AC 221 at [30] (interpreting Arbitration Act 1996 s.68 in the light of the New York Arbitration Convention 1958, being its "likely ... inspiration"); *Reid v Secretary of State for Scotland* [1999] 2 AC 512, 549G-H (Convention case-law treated as relevant in considering statutory provision passed to give effect to ruling of the European Court of Human Rights).

(C) EXTENDED RIGHTS UNDER DOMESTICATING ACT. *R (Ullah) v Secretary of State for the Home Department* [2004] UKHL 26 [2004] 2 AC 323 at [20] ("It is of course open to member states to provide for rights more generous than those guaranteed by the Convention"; *R (Mullen) v Secretary of State for the Home Department* [2004] UKHL 18 [2005] 1 AC 1 at [35] ("there is nothing to prevent Parliament when giving effect to the United Kingdom's international obligations from giving the citizen more rights than those obligations require that he be given"); *R (Williamson) v Secretary of State for Education and Employment* [2002] EWCA Civ 1926 [2003] QB 1300 (CA) at [181] ("Compatibility with the Convention does not necessarily prevent English law from enhancing or further entrenching a Convention right").

6.3.5 Using international law to resolve legislative ambiguity. *R v Secretary of State for the Home Department, ex p Brind* [1991] 1 AC 696, 747H-748A ("it is already well settled that, in construing any provision in domestic legislation which is ambiguous in the sense that it is capable of a meaning which either conforms to or conflicts with the Convention, the courts will presume that Parliament intended to legislate in conformity with the Convention, not in conflict with it"); *Garland v British Rail Engineering Ltd* [1983] 2 AC 751, 771 (Lord Diplock); *R v Broadcasting Complaints Commission, ex p Granada Television Ltd* [1995] 3 EMLR 163 (interpreting "privacy" in the Broadcasting Act 1990 in accordance with ECHR Art 8(1)); *R v Khan (Sultan)* [1997] AC 558, 580D; *R v Crown Court at Manchester, ex p H* [2000] 1 WLR 760, 771C (arguable ambiguity meaning need to construe Supreme Court Act 1981 s.29(3) compatibly with Article 6); *MacDonald v Ministry of Defence* [2001] HRLR 77 (apply ECHR pre-HRA because legislation ambiguous); *JA Pye (Oxford) Ltd v Graham* [2002] UKHL 30 [2003] 1 AC 419 at [65] (common law principle of compatible construction unavailable since statute not ambiguous); *R v Lyons* [2002] UKHL 44 [2003] 1 AC 976 (pre-HRA, ECHR overridden by domestic statute); *HM Attorney-General v Associated Newspapers Ltd* [1994]

2 AC 238 (Convention irrelevant since statute unambiguous); *R v Registrar General of Births, Deaths and Marriages, ex p P and G* [1996] 2 FLR 90, 98A-B ("no relevant ambiguity ... which Art 8 can help to resolve"); *Quazi v Quazi* [1980] AC 744, 808 (domesticating Act interpreted compatible with relevant treaty where "ambiguous or vague" or involving "ambiguity or obscurity"); cf. *Sultan Abid Mirza v Secretary of State for the Home Department* [1996] Imm AR 314 (suggesting ECHR capable of use in resolving ambiguity in Home Office policy).

6.3.6 **International law yielding to domestic statute.** *R v Lyons* [2002] UKHL 44 [2003] 1 AC 976 at [14] (ECHR obligation "cannot override an express and applicable provision of domestic statutory law"), [28] ("If Parliament has plainly laid down the law, it is the duty of the courts to apply it, whether that would involve the Crown in breach of an international treaty or not"), [40] ("In domestic law, the courts are obliged to give effect to the law as enacted by Parliament. This obligation is entirely unaffected by international law"), [67], [69], [77]; *Re M & H (Minors) (Local Authority: Parental Rights)* [1990] 1 AC 686, 721G-H (Lord Brandon: "while English courts will strive when they can to interpret statutes as conforming with the obligations of the United Kingdom under the Convention, they are nevertheless bound to give effect to statutes which are free from ambiguity in accordance with their terms, even if those statutes may be in conflict with the Convention"); *R (Norris) v Secretary of State for the Home Department* [2006] EWHC 280 (Admin) [2006] 3 All ER 1011 at [44] (extradition treaty not conferring municipal rights enforceable against own government, these being provided solely by domestic legislation); *R v Asfaw* [2008] UKHL 31 [2008] 2 WLR 1178 at [29] ("no ground in domestic law for failing to give effect to an enactment in terms unambiguously inconsistent with [an international law] obligation").

6.3.7 **Undomesticated international instruments: no direct effect.** *A v Secretary of State for the Home Department* [2005] UKHL 71 [2006] 2 AC 221 at [27] (Lord Bingham: "a treaty, even if ratified by the United Kingdom, has no binding force in the domestic law of this country unless it is given effect by statute or expresses principles of customary international law"); *R v Lyons* [2002] UKHL 44 [2003] 1 AC 976 at [39] (rejecting an "attempt to give direct domestic effect to an international treaty, contrary to the principle in the *International Tin Council* case [1990] 2 AC 418"); *Friend v Lord Advocate* [2007] UKHL 53 at [8]-[9] (hunting legislation not reviewable by reference to undomesticated international obligations); *Briggs v Baptiste* [2000] 2 AC 40, 54A ("international conventions do not alter domestic law except to the extent that they are incorporated into domestic law by legislation"); *R v Asfaw* [2008] UKHL 31 [2008] 2 WLR 1178 at [69] ("It is for Parliament to determine the extent to which [international obligations] are to be incorporated domestically. That determination having been made, it is the duty of the courts to give effect to it"); *R (Lika) v Secretary of State for the Home Department* [2002] EWCA Civ 1855 (Dublin Convention not part of domestic law); *Thomas v Baptiste* [2000] 2 AC 1, 23B ("the terms of a treaty cannot effect any alteration to domestic law or deprive the subject of existing legal rights unless and until enacted into domestic law by or under authority of the legislature"); *Higgs v Minister of National Security* [2000] 2 AC 228, 241C-G ("the domestic courts have no jurisdiction to construe or apply a treaty" and "unincorporated treaties cannot change the law of the land"); *R (Campaign for Nuclear Disarmament) v Prime Minister* [2002] EWHC 2759 (Admin) [2003] 3 LRC 335 at [47(i)] ("The court has no jurisdiction to declare the true interpretation of an international instrument which has not been incorporated into English domestic law and which it is unnecessary to interpret for the purposes of determining a person's rights or duties under domestic law"), [23], [36]-[37]; *R v Khan (Sultan)* [1997] AC 558, 581D-E (relevant decision of European Court of Human Rights "is no more a part of our law than the Convention itself"); *In re McKerr* [2004] UKHL 12 [2004] 1 WLR 807 at [49]-[50] (referring to the view of some commentators that "human rights treaties enjoy a special status" and that there may be room for "an estoppel against the Crown in favour of individuals in human rights cases").

6.3.8 Undomesticated international instrument: relevant nevertheless. *Republic of Ecuador v Occidental Exploration and Production Co* [2005] EWCA Civ 1116 [2006] QB 432 (unincorporated treaty relevant to determine rights and duties in English arbitration), at [31] ("English courts are not ... precluded from interpreting or having regard to the provisions of unincorporated treaties. Context is always important"); *R v G* [2003] UKHL 50 [2004] 1 AC 1034 at [53] (Lord Steyn, referring to Art 40(1) of the UN Convention on the Rights of the Child (need to have regard to special position of children in criminal justice system): "the House cannot ignore the norm created by the Convention"); *A v Secretary of State for the Home Department* [2005] UKHL 71 [2006] 2 AC 221 at [112] (reliance on Torture Convention); *R (E) v JFS Governing Body* [2008] EWHC 1535 (Admin) at [141]-[142] (Convention on the Elimination of Racial Discrimination relevant); *In re McFarland* [2004] UKHL 17 [2004] 1 WLR 1289 at [10] (ICCPR Art 14(6) treated as "incorporated" in Ministerial policy statement which referred to it); *R (Mullen) v Secretary of State for the Home Department* [2004] UKHL 18 [2005] 1 AC 1 at [40] (UK not having signed or ratified ECHR Protocol VII, but "It is, however, relevant to an understanding of the European jurisprudence"); *A v Secretary of State for the Home Department* [2004] UKHL 56 [2005] 2 AC 68 at [63] (non-binding international materials supporting conclusion under HRA); *R (Howard League for Penal Reform) v Secretary of State for the Home Department* [2002] EWHC 2497 (Admin) [2003] 1 FLR 484 at [45]-[46] (UN Convention on the Rights of the Child 1989 and the Charter of Fundamental Rights of the European Union as important sources), [51] ("both can ... properly be consulted insofar as they proclaim, reaffirm or elucidate the content of those human rights that are generally recognised throughout the European family of nations, in particular the nature and scope of those fundamental rights that are guaranteed by the [ECHR]").

6.3.9 International law and developing common law. *A v Secretary of State for the Home Department* [2005] UKHL 71 [2006] 2 AC 221 at [27] (Lord Bingham: "If, and to the extent that, development of the common law is called for, such development should ordinarily be in harmony with the United Kingdom's international obligations and not antithetical to them"); *Director of Public Prosecutions v Jones* [1999] 2 AC 240, 259B (appropriate to have regard to the ECHR where common law uncertain and developing, in resolving the uncertainty and deciding how the law should develop); *R v Secretary of State for the Home Department, ex p McQuillan* [1995] 4 All ER 400, 422f-j (since ECHR "standards ... both march with those of the common law and inform the jurisprudence of the European Union, it becomes unreal and potentially unjust to continue to develop English public law without reference to them"); *R v Secretary of State for the Home Department, ex p Simms* [2000] 2 AC 115, 131H-132A (Lord Hoffmann: "much of the Convention reflects the common law: see *Derbyshire County Council v Times Newspapers Ltd* [1993] AC 534, 551. That is why the United Kingdom government felt able in 1950 to accede to the Convention without domestic legislative change. So the adoption of the text as part of domestic law [by the Human Rights Act 1998] is unlikely to involve radical change in our notions of fundamental human rights"); *R (the Secretary of State for the Home Department) v Mental Health Review Tribunal* [2001] ACD 334 (HRA not a "sea change", since most aspects of domestic law already compliant); <59.5.14> (relationship between the common law and ECHR Art 6); <P58> (proportionality); <7.5> (common law protection of basic rights); <32.3> (anxious scrutiny: common law principles of justification); <7.3> and <46.2> (common law principle of legality).

6.3.10 International instrument and legitimate expectation. <41.1.7> (substantive legitimate expectation and international instruments).

6.3.11 International law as a relevancy. *R v Secretary of State for the Home Department, ex* *p Venables* [1998] AC 407, 499F-H (conclusion in relation to tariff-setting and child offender that Secretary of State required to remain free to take account of welfare of child), supported by reference to UN Convention on the Rights of the Child); cf. *R v Secretary of State for the Home Department, ex p Brind* [1991] 1 AC 696, 761H-762A (ECHR not a relevancy); *R v Director of Public Prosecutions, ex p Kebilene* [2000] 2 AC 326, 371D-E (DPP not bound to come to a view as to whether prosecution compatible with ECHR Art 6); *R v Ministry of Defence, ex p Smith* [1996] QB 517, 558E (failure to take account of ECHR obligations "is not of itself a ground for impugning that exercise of discretion"); *R v Secretary of State for the Home Department, ex p Engin Ozminnos* [1994] Imm AR 287, 291-293 (ECHR articles having "at least some role [here] as relevant factors in the taking of a decision"); *R v Secretary of State for the Home Department, ex p Rosa Maria Moreno Lopez* [1997] Imm AR 11, 15 (Dyson J: "when the Secretary of State exercises his discretion and his powers, he is required to have regard to the Convention"); *R (Hurst) v London Northern District Coroner* [2007] UKHL 13 [2007] 2 AC 189 at [56], [58] (not sound here to have regard to ECHR Art 2 rights as international law obligations); *R v Secretary of State for the Home Department, ex p Norney* (1995) 7 Admin LR 861, 871C-D ("where it is clear that the statutory provision which creates the discretion was passed in order to bring the domestic law into line with the Convention, it would ... be perverse to hold that, when considering the lawfulness of the exercise of the discretion, the court must ignore the relevant provisions of the Convention"); *R (C) v Secretary of State for Justice* [2008] EWCA Civ 882 at [61] (CA referring to UN Human Rights Committee General Comment); <56.1.5> (relevancy/irrelevancy and fundamental rights).

6.3.12 **Public body choosing to apply international law.** *R v Secretary of State for the Home Department, ex p Launder* [1997] 1 WLR 839, 867C-F (decision could be "flawed because the decision-maker has misdirected himself on the Convention which he himself says he took into account"); *R v Director of Public Prosecutions, ex p Kebilene* [2000] 2 AC 326, 982A (Lord Steyn, endorsing Lord Hope's general approach in *Launder*), 989B-E (claimants entitled to effective remedy if legal basis for decision unsound in this way); *R (Gentle) v Prime Minister* [2008] UKHL 20 [2008] 2 WLR 879 at [26] (discussing *Launder*); *R (Corner House Research) v Director of the Serious Fraud Office* [2008] UKHL 60 [2008] 3 WLR 568 at [47] (*Launder* principle inapplicable where defendant had made clear would have reached the same conclusion even if incorrect as to international law), [51], [56], [66]; *R (Barclay) v Secretary of State for Justice* [2008] EWHC 1354 (Admin) at [101] (agreeing with *Launder* approach); *R (Hurst) v London Northern District Coroner* [2005] EWCA Civ 890 [2005] 1 WLR 3892 at [33] (doubting the *Launder* principle, and treating it as now largely overtaken by HRA) (HL is [2007] UKHL 13 [2007] 2 AC 189); *R (Campaign for Nuclear Disarmament) v Prime Minister* [2002] EWHC 2759 (Admin) [2003] 3 LRC 335 at [33] (*Launder*-type challenge as to UN-compatibility of War on Iraq rejected).

6.3.13 **Court exercising a power.** *R v Secretary of State for the Environment, ex p National & Local Government Officers' Association* (1993) 5 Admin LR 785, 795B (considering relevance of the Convention when Court considering how its discretion may be exercised, citing *Attorney General v Guardian Newspapers* [1987] 1 WLR 1248, 1296-1297); *Re M (Petition to European Commission of Human Rights)* [1997] 1 FLR 755, 757D-E ("where an English court has to exercise a discretion, that is to say, it can act in one way or another, one or more of which violates the Convention and another of which does not, the court will seek to act in a way which does not violate the Convention"); *R v Khan (Sultan)* [1997] AC 558, 580E, 583C (Convention relevant to exercise of criminal court's statutory discretion to exclude evidence improperly obtained); *Camelot Group Plc v Centaur Communications Ltd* [1999] QB 124 (Convention relevant to court's decision (of fact) as to the public interest balance under s.10 of the Contempt of Court Act 1981).

6.3.14 Customary international law and the common law. *R (European Roma Rights Centre) v Immigration Officer at Prague Airport* [2004] UKHL 55 [2005] 2 AC 1 at [23] (Lord Bingham, identifying the principles by which customary international law identified, specifically "a general and consistent practice of states followed by them from a sense of legal obligation"); *In re McKerr* [2004] UKHL 12 [2004] 1 WLR 807 at [52] (no customary international law obligation at the relevant time, requiring state investigation into deaths, but: "The impact of evolving customary international law on our domestic legal system is a subject of increasing importance"); *R v Jones* [2006] UKHL 16 [2007] 1 AC 136 (assimilation of crime recognised in customary international law into domestic criminal law not automatic, it being a matter for Parliament to create a new crime); *R (Abbasi) v Secretary of State for Foreign and Commonwealth Affairs* [2002] EWCA Civ 1598 [2003] UKHRR 76 at [68]-[69] (relevant obligation "not yet recognised" in international law); *R v Lyons* [2002] UKHL 44 [2003] 1 AC 976 at [39] (recognising that an obligation may arise as an "established feature of customary international law", but here "ancillary to a treaty obligation" so reliance on customary international law an impermissible "attempt to give direct domestic effect to an international treaty"); *R (Campaign for Nuclear Disarmament) v Prime Minister* [2002] EWHC 2759 (Admin) [2003] 3 LRC 335 (rejecting reliance on customary international law where focus on UN Security Council Resolution and no domestic law rights or obligations); *Sepet v Secretary of State for the Home Department* [2003] UKHL 15 [2003] 1 WLR 856 at [20], [53] and *Krotov v Secretary of State for the Home Department* [2004] EWCA Civ 69 [2004] 1 WLR 1825 (considering in the context of the Refugee Convention, by reference to customary international law, whether any established core human right of conscientious objection); *A v Secretary of State for the Home Department* [2005] UKHL 71 [2006] 2 AC 221 at [33] (prohibition on torture jus cogens (peremptory norm) in international law); *R (Binyan Mohamed) v Secretary of State for Foreign and Commonwealth Affairs* [2008] EWHC 2048 (Admin) at [161]-[183] (no customary international law duty to disclose evidence of Guantanamo torture), [184] (leaving open how such a duty would enter the common law).

> **P7 Constitutional fundamentals.** Core common law principles can constitute fundamentals of the UK's unwritten constitution.

7.1 Legislative supremacy. The basic rule is straightforward: Parliament can do what it likes. Primary legislation is enforced and respected by the Courts, subject to: (1) EC-incompatibility (given the subordination to EC law through the European Communities Act 1972); (2) declared ECHR-incompatibility (given the special remedy in the Human Rights Act 1998). The Courts' basic duty is to respect what Parliament has said ("plain words" or "necessary implication"), has not said ("easy to say so") or not not yet said ("change is for Parliament").

7.1.1 Legislative supremacy as a paramount constitutional principle. *R (Anderson) v Secretary of State for the Home Department* [2002] UKHL 46 [2003] 1 AC 837 at [39] (Lord Steyn: "the supremacy of Parliament is the paramount principle of our constitution"); <9.1.8> (HRA and legislative supremacy); *R (Jackson) v Attorney General* [2005] UKHL 56 [2006] 1 AC 262 at [9] ("the supremacy of the Crown in Parliament").

7.1.2 Legislative supremacy: basic limits of the judicial role. *R (Quintavalle) v Secretary of State for Health* [2003] UKHL 13 [2003] 2 AC 687 at [15] (Lord Bingham, describing "the constitutional imperative that the courts stick to their interpretative role and do not assume the mantle of legislators"); *Duport Steels Ltd v Sirs* [1980] 1 WLR 142, 157B-158C (Lord Diplock: "the British constitution, though largely unwritten, is firmly based upon the separation of powers; Parliament makes the laws, the judiciary interpret them... [T]he role of the judiciary is confined to ascertaining from the words that Parliament has approved as expressing its intention what that intention was, and to giving effect to it").

7.1.3 Plain words. *R v J* [2004] UKHL 42 [2005] 1 AC 562 at [15] (Lord Bingham: "It is the duty of the court to give full and fair effect to the meaning of a statute. In a purely domestic context such as this, it cannot construe the statute by reference to any extraneous legal instrument. It must seek to give effect to all the provisions of a statute. It cannot pick and choose, giving effect to some and discounting others. It has no warrant, in a case such as this where no Convention right is engaged, to resort to the unique interpretative technique required by section 3 of the Human Rights Act 1998. If a statutory provision is clear and unambiguous, the court may not decline to give effect to it on the ground that its rationale is anachronistic, or discredited, or unconvincing"), [37] (Lord Steyn: "Parliament does not intend the plain meaning of its legislation to be evaded. And it is the duty of the courts not to facilitate the circumvention of the parliamentary intent"), [38] ("The courts must loyally give effect to the statutes as enacted by Parliament. The judiciary may not render a statutory provision, such as a time limit, nugatory on the ground that it disagrees with the reason underlying it"); *In re W (An Infant)* [1971] AC 682, 698C-D ("It is not for the courts to embellish, alter, subtract from or add to words which, for once at least, Parliament has employed without any ambiguity at all"); *R v Inland Revenue Commissioners, ex p Rossminster* [1980] AC 952, 1008D-E (Lord Diplock: "judges in performing their constitutional function of expounding what words used by Parliament in legislation mean, must not be over-zealous to search for ambiguities or obscurities in words which on the face of them are plain, simply because the members of the court are out of sympathy with the policy to which the Act appears to give effect"); *Inland Revenue Commissioners v Hinchy* [1960] AC 748, 767 (unless "these words are capable of a more limited construction ... then we must apply them as they stand, however unreasonable or unjust the consequences, and however strongly we may suspect that this was not the real intention of Parliament"); *R v Chief Constable of the Royal Ulster Constabulary, ex p Begley* [1997] 1 WLR 1475, 1480H (HL having "power to develop the law. But it is a limited power. And it can be exercised only in the gaps left by Parliament. It is impermissible for the House to develop the law in a direction which is contrary to the expressed will of Parliament"); *R v Governor of Pentonville Prison, ex p Azam* [1974] AC 18, 59D ("Parliament can, if it uses sufficiently clear words, give legislation retroactive effect"); *R v Inland Revenue Commissioners, ex p Woolwich Equitable Building Society* [1990] 1 WLR 1400, 1412H ("well-established presumptions ... are clearly rebuttable if sufficiently clear express words are used"); <6.3.5> plain words and international law; <29.1.5> (plain mistakes: rectifying construction); <28.1.3> (ouster by plain words); <29.3.15> (gateways to external aids: ambiguity, obscurity or absurdity).

7.1.4 **"Necessary implication"**. *R v Lord Chancellor, ex p Lightfoot* [2000] QB 597[36] (necessary implication sufficient to override protection of common law fundamental rights); *A v HM Treasury* [2008] EWHC 869 (Admin) [2008] 3 All ER 361 at [25] (need "clear indication that, even in the absence of express words, fundamental rights are overridden"); *R v Hertfordshire County Council, ex p Green Environmental Industries Limited* [2000] 2 AC 412 (statute impliedly excluding freedom from self-incrimination); *B (A Minor) v Director of Public Prosecutions* [2000] 2 AC 428 (no express words or necessary implication to override common law presumption); *A v Secretary of State for the Home Department* [2005] UKHL 71 [2006] 2 AC 221 at [51] (common law abhorrence of torture incapable of being "overridden by a statute and a procedural rule which make no mention of torture"), [96] (provision for use of torture "would have to be expressly provided in primary legislation"), [114] ("This is not a matter that can be left to implication. Nothing short of an express provision will do, to which Parliament has unequivocally committed itself"); *R (Bright) v Central Criminal Court* [2001] 1 WLR 662, 697A-B (statute authorising interference with privilege against self-incrimination, by "necessary implication"); *R (Edison First Power Ltd) v Secretary of State for the Environment, Transport and the Regions* [2003] UKHL 20 [2003] 4 All ER 209 at [5] (asking whether "inevitable inference" that Parliament intended to displace the presumption against double taxation), [17] (whether "clear Parliamentary intent"); *R (W) v Metropolitan Police Commissioner* [2005] EWHC 1586 (Admin) [2005] 1 WLR 3706 at [21]-[22] (difficult to establish necessary implication); <46.2.4> (principle of legality and necessary implication); <7.4.6> (access to justice and necessary implication); *R (Morgan Grenfell & Co Ltd) v Inland Revenue Commissioners* [2002] UKHL 21 [2003] 1 AC 563 at [45] ("reasonable implication" insufficient); *R v Children and Family Court Advisory and Support Service* [2003] EWHC 235 (Admin) [2003] 1 FLR 953 at [76] ("necessary implication connotes an implication that is compellingly clear").

7.1.5 **"Easy to say so"**.
(A) GENERAL. *Ward v Metropolitan Police Commissioner* [2005] UKHL 32 [2006] 1 AC 23 at [22] ("if ... Parliament had wished to include the power ..., it would have been simple to say so"); *R v Barnet London Borough Council, ex p Nilish Shah* [1983] 2 AC 309, 345E-

---

[36] Mark Elliott [1998] JR 217.

F (concept of "domicile" and its difficulties "must have been known to Parliament when enacting the Act"); *R v Oldham Metropolitan Borough Council, ex p Garlick* [1993] AC 509, 518B ("If this had been the intention of Parliament it would surely have said so"); *Re S (Minors)* [1995] ELR 98, 104G-H (if Parliament had meant "school" rather than attendance arrangements, it would have said so); *R v Radio Authority, ex p Guardian Media Group Plc* [1995] 1 WLR 334 (Parliament could have prohibited this kind of arrangement); *R v Secretary of State for Foreign & Commonwealth Affairs, ex p World Development Movement Ltd* [1995] 1 WLR 386, 402A (defendant relying on absence of the word "sound" preceding "development"; Court preferring to rely on absence of the word "unsound", which Parliament could easily have inserted); *R (Crown Prosecution Service) v Registrar General of Births, Deaths and Marriages* [2002] EWCA Civ 1661 [2003] QB 1222 at [19] (Parliament could easily have included public policy exception to prevent accused from marrying prosecution witness rendering them non-compellable); *R v Monopolies & Mergers Commission, ex p South Yorkshire Transport Ltd* [1993] 1 WLR 23, 29D ("The courts have repeatedly warned against the dangers of taking an inherently imprecise word, and by redefining it thrusting on it a spurious degree of precision"); *R v Sheffield City Council Housing Benefits Review Board, ex p Smith* (1995) 93 LGR 139, 151 (term left undefined showing that Parliament intended the decision-maker to decide its meaning).
(B) JUDICIAL REVIEW. *R v Solicitor-General, ex p Taylor* (1996) 8 Admin LR 206, 219A ("if [Parliament] had intended the Attorney-General's discretion to be reviewable ... it would have said so"); *Anisminic Ltd v Foreign Compensation Commission* [1969] 2 AC 147, 170D-F (if Parliament intended complete ouster "I would have expected to find something much more specific"; "it would be easy to say so"); *R v Gloucestershire County Council, ex p Barry* [1996] 4 All ER 421 (CA), 442a ("Parliament knows very well how to confer a power"; "if it uses language apt to impose a duty it presumably means what it says"); *R v Commissioners of Customs and Excise, ex p Kay and Co* [1996] STC 1500, 1521d, 1522e (if Parliament had intended to confer a cut-off power it would have said to); *R v Tower Hamlets London Borough Council, ex p Chetnik Developments Ltd* [1988] AC 858, 880B-E (Parliament could have made the need to budget a relevancy through "express provision"); *Pearlberg v Varty* [1972] 1 WLR 534, 548F (if right to a hearing intended, "it would have been easy and natural to insert an express provision"); *R v Army Board of the Defence Council, ex p Anderson* [1992] QB 169, 187D ("Had Parliament wished to impose those detailed procedures on the Army Board, it could have done so").

7.1.6 Wrong to "read in words". *Thompson v Goold & Co* [1910] AC 409, 420 (Lord Mersey: "It is a strong thing to read into an Act of Parliament words which are not there, and in the absence of clear necessity it is a wrong thing to do"), cited in *Grunwick Processing Laboratories Ltd v Advisory Conciliation & Arbitration Service* [1978] AC 655, 699G, 692E; *R v Director of the Serious Fraud Office, ex p Smith* [1993] AC 1, 44A ("neither history nor logic demands that any qualification of what Parliament has so clearly enacted ought to be implied"); *Daymond v Plymouth City Council* [1976] AC 609, 645E ("If there is ... a defect, it is not for us sitting judicially to remedy it by legislating to put into section 30 words which Parliament could, if it had wished, have inserted"); *R v Secretary of State for the Home Department, ex p Oladehinde* [1991] 1 AC 254, 303E ("very slow to read into the statute a further implicit limitation"); *R v City of London Corporation, ex p Mystery of the Barbers of London* [1996] 3 PLR 69, 77E ("Where statutory words are clear, and their literal meaning does not lead to an absurdity, then they are to be given their natural and ordinary meaning. It is not permissible in such circumstances to read into the statute words that are not there"); *R (Gnezele) v Leeds City Council* [2007] EWHC 3275 (Admin) at [22]-[23] (reading in words justified by necessary implication of statute read as a whole); <29.1.5> (rectifying construction: altering language to give effect to Parliament's intention).

7.1.7 **"Change is for Parliament".** *R v Secretary of State for Home Department, ex p Virk* [1996] COD 134 (granting judicial review on the basis that the effect of the statute was plain, albeit unlikely, and if the result was `cloud cuckoo land' it was for Parliament to remedy the defect); *R v Trent River Authority, ex p National Coal Board* [1971] AC 145, 154E ("Rectification of the defect in the Act, if it be a defect, is a matter for the legislature and not for this House in the exercise of its judicial functions"); *Barnard v Gorman* [1941] AC 378, 384 ("Our duty in the matter is plain. We must not give the statutory words a wider meaning merely because, on a narrower construction the words might leave a loophole for frauds against the Revenue. If, on the proper construction, of the section, that is the result, it is not for judges to attempt to cure it. That is the business of Parliament"); *Webb v Chief Constable of Merseyside Police* [2000] 1 All ER 209, 224d-e ("If statutory provision[s] for civil confiscation are inadequate, it is for Parliament to strengthen them after proper consideration of all the implications"); *R v Hull University Visitor, ex p Page* [1993] AC 682, 694E (Lord Griffiths: "If it is thought that the exclusive jurisdiction of the visitor has outlived its usefulness, which I beg to doubt, then I think that it should be swept away by Parliament and not undermined by judicial review"); *Wandsworth London Borough Council v Winder* [1985] AC 461, 510C ("If the public interest requires that persons should not be entitled to defend actions brought against them by public authorities, where the defence rests on a challenge to a decision by the public authority, then it is for Parliament to change the law"); *Murphy v Brentwood District Council* [1991] 1 AC 398, 482C ("It is pre-eminently for the legislature to decide whether [the] policy reasons should be accepted as sufficient for imposing on the public the burden of providing compensation"); *In re F (Adult: Court's Jurisdiction)* [2001] Fam 38 (court entitled to use inherent jurisdiction to fill statutory lacuna), 56E (Sedley LJ: "the courts ... have from time to time had to speak where Parliament, although the more appropriate forum, was silent. Both can find themselves left behind by time and tide, and that is what has happened here"); *R v Secretary of State for the Home Department, ex p Pegg* [1995] COD 84, 85 (although up to Parliament to remedy unsatisfactory state of affairs, reviewing court to be extra vigilant on judicial review).

7.1.8 **Unconstitutional legislation: steps towards an enhanced constitutional role.** <7.2.3> (dual sovereignty); <7.5.1> (constitutional rights); <7.5.3> (constitutional rights and legislative supremacy); *R (Jackson) v Attorney General* [2005] UKHL 56 [2006] 1 AC 262 (ruling on validity of the Hunting Act) at [102] (Lord Steyn, querying whether Parliamentary supremacy would extend to "oppressive and wholly undemocratic legislation" such as "to abolish judicial review of flagrant abuse of power by a government or even the role of the ordinary courts in standing between the executive and citizens", given that "the supremacy of Parliament is ... a construct of the common law"), [104] (Lord Hope, referring to developing qualifications to the principle of Parliamentary sovereignty), [107] ("the rule of law enforced by the courts is the ultimate controlling factor on which our constitution is based ... the courts have a part to play in defining the limits of Parliament's legislative sovereignty"), [110] ("no absolute rule that the courts could not consider the validity of a statute"); *B (A Minor) v Director of Public Prosecutions* [2000] 2 AC 428, 470B-G (Lord Steyn, referring to presumptions which "operate at a higher level as expressions of fundamental principles governing both civil liberties and the relations between Parliament, the executive and the courts"); *Anisminic Ltd v Foreign Compensation Commission* [1969] 2 AC 147 (using presumption in the face of apparently clear statutory ouster); *R (Bancoult) v Secretary of State for the Foreign and Commonwealth Office* [2001] QB 1067 at [46] (Laws LJ: "a legislature created by a measure passed by a body which is legally prior to it must act within the confines of the power thereby conferred... [N]othing could be more elementary"); *R (Southall) v Secretary of State for Foreign and Commonwealth Affairs* [2003] EWCA Civ 1002 at [11] (referring to "what has been much discussed in the legal literature, namely, whether the courts could in some circumstances refuse to enforce an Act of Parliament which said that all babies under two years of age should be slaughtered"); Professor Geoffrey Wilson, *The Courts, Law and Convention* in *The Making and Remaking of the British Constitution* (1997) at p.116 ("Nobody should be surprised if in a real case of legislative enormity the courts did not discover a higher principle of law by which they felt free or even obliged to ignore the current version of the doctrine [of Parliamentary sovereignty] not only in the name of constitutional convention but also in the name of law").

7.2 **Rule of law/separation of powers.** The rule of law is a first principle of public law which, together with the separation of powers, explains the constitutional imperative of judicial supervision of public authorities, through the Courts' discharge of their sovereign constitutional function.

7.2.1 **The rule of law as a constitutional principle.** *R (Anufrijeva) v Secretary of State for the Home Department* [2003] UKHL 36 [2004] 1 AC 604 at [28] ("the constitutional principle requiring the rule of law to be observed"); *R v Horseferry Road Magistrates' Court, ex p Bennett* [1994] 1 AC 42, 67F ("There is ... no principle more basic to any proper system of law than the maintenance of the rule of law itself"); <12.1.14> (the rule of law and preventing abuse of power); *A v Secretary of State for the Home Department* [2004] UKHL 56 [2005] 2 AC 68 at [42] (Lord Bingham: "the judges in this country are not elected and are not answerable to Parliament ... But the function of independent judges charged to interpret and apply the law is universally recognised as a cardinal feature of the modern democratic state, a cornerstone of the rule of law itself"), [113] (Lord Hope: "review by the courts" as "a constitutive element of democratic government"); *State of Mauritius v Khoyratty* [2006] UKPC 13 [2007] 1 AC 80 at [12] ("The idea of a democracy involves a number of different concepts. The first is that the people must decide who should govern them. Secondly, there is the principle that fundamental rights should be protected by an impartial and independent judiciary. Thirdly, in order to achieve a reconciliation between the inevitable tensions between these ideas, a separation of powers between the legislature, the executive, and the judiciary is necessary").

7.2.2 **The separation of powers as a constitutional principle.**[37] *R (Anderson) v Secretary of State for the Home Department* [2002] UKHL 46 [2003] 1 AC 837 at [39] (Lord Steyn: "the separation of powers between the judiciary and the legislative and executive branches of government is a strong principle of our system of government"); *Director of Public Prosecutions v Mollison (No.2)* [2003] UKPC 6 [2003] 2 AC 411 at [13] (separation of powers requiring Jamaican statute involving detention at the Governor-General's pleasure to be read as being at the court's pleasure); <13.1.4> (so-called deference and allocational legal principle); *Independent Jamaica Council for Human Rights (1998) Ltd v Marshall-Burnett* [2005] UKPC 3 [2005] 2 AC 356 at [12] (Lord Bingham: "independence of the judges (or, put negatively, the protection of judges from executive pressure or interference) is all but universally recognised as a necessary feature of the rule of law").

7.2.3 **Dual sovereignty: Parliament and Judiciary.** *X Ltd v Morgan-Gampian Ltd* [1991] 1 AC 1, 48E (Lord Bridge: "The maintenance of the rule of law is in every way as important in a free society as the democratic franchise. In our society the rule of law rests upon twin foundations: the sovereignty of the Queen in Parliament in making the law and the sovereignty of the Queen's courts in interpreting and applying the law"); *In re F (Adult: Court's*

---

[37] Lord Hoffmann [2002] JR 137; Martin Chamberlain [2003] JR 12; Philip Sales [2006] JR 94; Cheryl Saunders [2006] JR 337.

Jurisdiction) [2001] Fam 38, 56D (Sedley J: "The relationship between [Parliament and the courts] is a working relationship between two constitutional sovereignties", referring to *R v Parliamentary Commissioner for Standards, ex p Al Fayed* [1998] 1 WLR 669, 670, per Lord Woolf MR); *R (Jackson) v Attorney General* [2005] UKHL 56 [2006] 1 AC 262 at [102] (Lord Steyn, using the concept of "divided sovereignty").

7.2.4 **Judicial review and the rule of law.** <12.1>.

7.3 **Principles of legality.** Using the rule of law, the Courts use "the principle of legality" to counterbalance legislative supremacy. Constitutional imperatives can thus be protected, by implying limitations into enabling statutory powers. In this way the common law has protected against statutory powers being exercised to breach human rights, at least absent plain words (or necessary implication). But principles of legality have an unmistakable wider potential, capable of reaching beyond fundamental rights and impervious even to plain words.

7.3.1 **The principle of legality and fundamental rights.** <46.2>

7.3.2 **Broader potential/reach of "principles of legality".**
(A) BASIC FAIRNESS. *R v Secretary of State for the Home Department, ex p Pierson* [1998] AC 539, 588G-589B (Lord Steyn, identifying the cases where natural justice `supplements' the legislative scheme <60.3> as part of a broader "principle of legality"); *R (McNally) v Secretary of State for Education* [2001] EWCA Civ 332 [2001] ELR 773 at [39] (using principle of legality to ensure wide statutory provisions, and involving duties rather than powers, read as consistent with natural justice).
(B) REASONABLENESS/OTHER BASIC TENETS OF COMMON LAW. *R (Morgan Grenfell & Co Ltd) v Inland Revenue Commissioners* [2002] UKHL 21 [2003] 1 AC 563 at [8] (Lord Hoffmann: "the courts will ordinarily construe general words in a statute, although literally capable of having some startling or unreasonable consequence, such as overriding fundamental human rights, as not having been intended to do so ... [T]he wider principle itself [ie. beyond human rights] is hardly new. It can be traced back at least to *Stradling v Morgan* (1560) 1 Pl 199"), [44] (Lord Hobhouse: "the principle of statutory construction [the principle of legality] is not new and has long been applied in relation to the question whether a statute is to be read as having overridden some basic tenet of the common law", referring to *Viscount Rhondda's Claim* [1922] 2 AC 339 and *B (A Minor) v Director of Public Prosecutions* [2000] 2 AC 428).
(C) LIMITING GENERAL STATUTORY WORDS. *R v Secretary of State for the Home Department, ex p Stafford* [1999] 2 AC 38, 48C-D (Lord Steyn, referring to Lord Browne-Wilkinson's formulation in the context of "the principle of construction which requires the court, in certain cases, to construe general words in a statute as impliedly limited").
(D) SUPPLEMENTING THE TEXT. *B (A Minor) v Director of Public Prosecutions* [2000] 2 WLR 452, 470B (Lord Steyn: "Parliament does not write on a blank sheet. The sovereignty of Parliament is the paramount principle of our constitution. But Parliament legislates against the background of the principle of legality"), 470G ("in the absence of express words or a truly necessary implication, Parliament must be presumed to legislate on the assumption that the principle of legality will supplement the text").
(E) OTHER. *R (Morgan Grenfell & Co Ltd) v Inland Revenue Commissioners* [2002] UKHL 21 [2003] 1 AC 563 at [44] (considering the principle of legality in the context of "basic tenet[s] of the common law"); *R (Anufrijeva) v Secretary of State for the Home Department* [2003] UKHL 36 [2004] 1 AC 604 at [27] (principle of legality used to support duty to notify

citizen of decision before it can adversely affect citizen's rights).

7.3.3 **Principle of legality and "necessary implication".** <46.2.4>.

7.4 **Access to justice.** The citizen's right of recourse to the Courts is a core right recognised by the common law. It is a paradigm example of a "constitutional right". In vindicating it, the Courts are simultaneously recognising both the citizen's interests and their own judicial responsibilities.

7.4.1 **Access to justice as a "constitutional right".** *R (Anufrijeva) v Secretary of State for the Home Department* [2003] UKHL 36 [2004] 1 AC 604 at [26] ("the right of access to justice ... is a fundamental and constitutional principle of our legal system"); *R v Secretary of State for the Home Department, ex p Leech* [1994] QB 198, 210A ("It is a principle of our law that every citizen has a right of unimpeded access to a court... Even in our unwritten constitution it must rank as a constitutional right"); *R v Lord Chancellor, ex p Witham* [1998] QB 575 (access to law a constitutional right); *R v Secretary of State for the Home Department, ex p Pierson* [1998] AC 539, 589B-E (Lord Steyn), 575B-C (Lord Browne-Wilkinson); *Colley v Council for Licensed Conveyancers* [2001] EWCA Civ 1137 [2002] 1 WLR 160 at [26] (Sir Andrew Morritt V-C: "the right of access to a court is of fundamental constitutional importance"); *Cullen v Chief Constable of the Royal Ulster Constabulary* [2003] UKHL 39 [2003] 1 WLR 1763 at [18] (referring to the constitutional right of access to justice); <7.5.1> (constitutional rights).

7.4.2 **Access to the Court.**[38] *A v HM Treasury* [2008] EWHC 869 (Admin) [2008] 3 All ER 361 at [17] (access to the court as a constitutional right); *R v Legal Aid Board, ex p Duncan* [2000] COD 159 (see transcript at [456]) ("there is a common law right of access to the courts which is of fundamental importance in our legal system"); *R (Kehoe) v Secretary of State for Work and Pensions* [2004] EWCA Civ 225 [2004] QB 1378 at [79] and [84] (recourse to the court to enforce maintenance payments as "a constitutional safeguard") (HL is [2005] UKHL 48 [2006] 1 AC 42); *A v Secretary of State for the Home Department* [2004] EWCA Civ 1123 at [143] (access to law applicable to the special immigration appeals tribunal) (HL is [2005] UKHL 71 [2006] 2 AC 221).

7.4.3 **Access to a lawyer.** *R v Secretary of State for the Home Department, ex p Anderson* [1984] QB 778 (judicial review of standing orders restricting access to legal advice, as being ultra vires enabling Act given that infringing fundamental human right of access to the courts); *R v Secretary of State for the Home Department, ex p Leech* [1994] QB 198, 210A-H, 216D-E, H (judicial review of prison rule enabling governor to read letters from solicitor, ultra vires as hindering right of access to the courts); *R v Chief Constable of the Royal Ulster Constabulary, ex p Begley* [1997] 1 WLR 1475 (considering extent of common law right of access to a solicitor); *R v Legal Aid Board, ex p Duncan* [2000] COD 159 (see transcript at [456]) (right of access to the court not extending to right to have publicly funded lawyer of choice); *R v Shayler* [2002] UKHL 11 [2003] 1 AC 247 at [73] (Lord Hope: "Access to legal advice is one of the fundamental rights enjoyed by every citizen under the common law"); *Ramsarran v Attorney-General of Trinidad and Tobago* [2005] UKPC 8 [2005] 2 AC 614 (PC recognising constitutional right of informed access to lawyer, whenever individual detained).

7.4.4 **Right to a fair trial/hearing.** *R v Secretary of State for the Home Department, ex p Q*

---

[38] Dan Squires [2001] JR 38; Lord Justice Brooke [2006] JR 1.

[2000] UKHRR 386, 391E (right to a fair trial as a constitutional right); *Locabail (UK) Ltd v Bayfield Properties Ltd* [2000] QB 451 at [2] (right to a fair hearing before an impartial tribunal "properly described as fundamental"); also Lord Steyn at [1999] PL 51, 55; referring in particular to *R v Brown* [1994] 1 WLR 1599, 1606E and [1998] AC 367, 374G; <7.6.5> (natural justice/due process and the rule of law).

7.4.5 Access to law/tribunal. *R (L) v Secretary of State for the Home Department* [2003] EWCA Civ 25 [2003] 1 WLR 1230 at [17] ("legal certainty is an aspect of the rule of law"), [25] ("It is an aspect of the rule of law that individuals and those advising them, since they will be presumed to know the law, should have access to it in authentic form"); *R v Secretary of State for the Home Department, ex p Khawaja* [1984] AC 74, 111H (Lord Scarman: "Every person within the jurisdiction enjoys the equal protection of our laws. There is no distinction between British nationals and others. He who is subject to English law is entitled to its protection"); *R v Secretary of State for the Home Department, ex p Saleem* [2001] 1 WLR 443, 458F-G ("if the state establishes [a right of appeal] it must ensure that people within its jurisdiction enjoy the fundamental guarantees in art 6"); *R v Secretary of State for the Home Department, ex p Saleem* [2001] 1 WLR 443 (access to court extending, by analogy, to right of access to specialist tribunals: here, immigration tribunals); *R (G) v Immigration Appeal Tribunal* [2004] EWHC 588 (Admin) [2004] 1 WLR 2953 at [8] (Collins J: "Access by a citizen or a person who is entitled while in this country to the protection of its laws to the Court is a right of the highest constitutional importance. Legislation which removes that right is inimical to the rule of law") (CA is [2004] EWCA Civ 1731 [2005] 1 WLR 1445).

7.4.6 Access to law excluded only by plain words/necessary implication. *Pyx Granite Co Ltd v Ministry of Housing and Local Government* [1960] AC 260, 286 ("the subject's recourse to Her Majesty's courts for the determination of his rights is not to be excluded except by clear words"), applied in *Boddington v British Transport Police* [1999] 2 AC 143, 161E and in *Seal v Chief Constable South Wales Police* [2007] UKHL 31 [2007] 1 WLR 1910 at [18]; *Raymond v Honey* [1983] 1 AC 1, 14G ("a citizen's right to unimpeded access to the courts can only be taken away by express enactment"); *Leech v Deputy Governor of Parkhurst Prison* [1988] AC 533, 577H ("a citizen should have unimpeded access to the courts unless such right has been expressly removed by statute"); *R v Secretary of State for the Home Department, ex p Ruddock* [1987] 1 WLR 1482, 1492F (need "the most clear and unequivocal words"); *Hoffmann-La Roche (F) & Co AG v Secretary of State for Trade and Industry* [1975] AC 295, 366C (Lord Diplock: "the courts lean heavily against a construction of the Act which would have this effect"); *R v Lord Chancellor, ex p Lightfoot* [2000] QB 597 (right capable of being overridden by irresistible inference as opposed to express provision); *R v Chief Constable of the Royal Ulster Constabulary, ex p Begley* [1997] 1 WLR 1475, 1480H, 1481D-G (beyond the power of the HL to extend the common law right of access to a solicitor to cover a situation contrary to the expressed will (deliberate legislative policy) of Parliament); <7.1.4> (necessary implication).

7.5 Constitutional/common law rights Beyond and behind the HRA:ECHR the common law recognises core "constitutional" rights, protected by: (1) anxious scrutiny (a common law parallel to HRA s.6); and (2) the principle of legality (a common law parallel to HRA s.3). Such rights are said to yield to plain statutory words or necessary implication, at the present state of constitutional evolution.

7.5.1 "Constitutional rights". *Thoburn v Sunderland City Council* [2002] EWHC 195 (Admin) [2003] QB 151 at [62] ("In the present state of its maturity the common law has come to recognise that there exist rights which should properly be classified as constitutional or fundamental"); *R v Lord Chancellor, ex p Lightfoot* [2000] QB 597 (Laws J), 609B (referring to the concept of a "constitutional right" as meaning "that special class of rights which, in truth, everyone living in a democracy under the rule of law ought to enjoy"); *R v Secretary of State for the Home Department, ex p Simms* [2000] 2 AC 115, 125G ("primary right"); *Watkins v Secretary of State for the Home Department* [2006] UKHL 17 [2006] 2 AC 395 at [61]-[62] (Lord Rodger, cautioning against "constitutional rights" label to define class of rights for tort actionability without proof of damage), [64] ("heroic efforts" to develop "constitutional rights" now superseded by HRA), [73(3)] ("constitutional rights" remaining relevant to statutory interpretation and judicial review of secondary legislation).

7.5.2 **A "constitutional shift"**. *Redmond-Bate v Director of Public Prosecutions* 23rd July 1999 unrep. (rights-recognition as part of "the constitutional shift which is now in progress"); *R (Beeson) v Dorset County Council* [2002] EWCA Civ 1812 [2003] UKHRR 353 at [18] (pre-HRA, "the common law was more and more inclined to give autonomous recognition to the notion of constitutional rights"); *R (Laporte) v Chief Constable of Gloucestershire* [2006] UKHL 55 [2007] 2 AC 105 at [34] (HRA as "a constitutional shift").

7.5.3 **Constitutional rights and legislative supremacy.** *R v Lord Chancellor, ex p Witham* [1998] QB 575, 581E (Laws J, emphasising that on the *present* state of the law, the common law continues to afford legislative supremacy to Parliament); *R (International Transport Roth GmbH) v Secretary of State for the Home Department* [2002] EWCA Civ 158 [2003] QB 728 at [71] (Laws LJ: "In its present state of evolution, the British system may be said to stand at an intermediate stage between parliamentary supremacy and constitutional supremacy"); *Director of Public Prosecutions v Mollison (No.2)* [2003] UKPC 6 [2003] 2 AC 411 at [19] ("Provisions derogating from [constitutional] rights should receive a strict and narrow rather than a broad construction"); *In re McKerr* [2004] UKHL 12 [2004] 1 WLR 807 at [30] (wrong to recognise a new common law right in an area where Parliament has legislated); *R (Hooper) v Secretary of State for Work and Pensions* [2005] UKHL 29 [2005] 1 WLR 1681 at [92] (Lord Scott: "There are not, under English domestic law, any fundamental constitutional rights that are immune from legislative change").

7.5.4 **Recognised rights beyond the ECHR.** *R (Anufrijeva) v Secretary of State for the Home Department* [2003] UKHL 36 [2004] 1 AC 604 at [27] (Lord Steyn, discussing the "principle of legality" recognised in *Simms*, as extending beyond the ECHR: "the Convention is not an exhaustive statement of fundamental rights under our system of law. Lord Hoffmann's dictum [in *Simms*] applies to fundamental rights beyond the four corners of the Convention. It is engaged in the present case"); *R (Q) v Secretary of State for the Home Department* [2003] EWCA Civ 364 [2004] QB 36 at [115] (anxious scrutiny, under the *Smith* test <32.3.5>, not "confined to rights set out in the European Convention on Human Rights", but "apt ... to apply to the right to seek asylum, which is not only the subject of a separate international convention but is expressly recognised by Article 14 of the Universal Declaration of Human Rights").

7.5.5 **Values and principles.** *Wainwright v Home Office* [2003] UKHL 53 [2004] 2 AC 406 at [31] (Lord Hoffmann, referring to freedom of speech and privacy as "underlying values", rather than "rules of law", being "a value which underlies the existence of a rule of law"); *State of Trinidad and Tobago v Boyce* [2006] UKPC 1 [2006] 2 AC 76 (PC, explaining that common law principle of no criminal appeal against acquittal, but not having status of an entrenched constitutional due process guarantee).

7.5.6 **Protection of fundamental rights at common law.**
(A) ANXIOUS SCRUTINY: NEED FOR JUSTIFICATION. <32.3>.
(B) PRINCIPLE OF LEGALITY. <7.3> and <46.2>.

7.5.7 **"Constitutional statutes".** *Thoburn v Sunderland City Council* [2002] EWHC 195 (Admin) [2003] QB 151 at [62] ("a constitutional statute is one which (a) conditions the legal relationship between citizen and state in some general, overarching manner, or (b) enlarges or diminishes the scope of what we would now regard as fundamental constitutional rights"; examples being Magna Carta 1297; the Bill of Rights 1689; the Union with Scotland Act 1706; the Representation of the People Acts 1832, 1867, 1884; the European Communities Act 1972; the Human Rights Act 1998; the Scotland Act 1998; the Government of Wales Act 1998), [63] ("Ordinary statutes may be impliedly repealed. Constitutional statutes may not... A constitutional statute can only be repealed, or amended in a way which significantly affects its provisions touching fundamental rights or otherwise the relation between citizen and state, by unambiguous words on the face of the later statute").

7.5.8 **Life.** *R (Amin) v Secretary of State for the Home Department* [2003] UKHL 51 [2004] 1 AC 653 at [30] (Lord Bingham: "A profound respect for the sanctity of human life underpins the common law").

7.5.9 **Common humanity/human dignity/freedom from destitution.**[39] *R v Secretary of State for Social Security, ex p Joint Council for the Welfare of Immigrants* [1997] 1 WLR 275, 292F-G (human rights at issue so basic that unnecessary to resort to the ECHR; applying "the law of humanity"); *R (Othman) v Secretary of State for Work and Pensions* [2001] EWHC Admin 1022 (2002) 5 CCLR 148 at [52] (referring to the "humanitarian safety net"), [56] ("the law of humanity applies as much to a European directive as it does to any other law which is applicable in this country"); *R v Lincolnshire County Council and Wealden District Council, ex p Atkinson, Wales and Stratford* (1996) 8 Admin LR 529, 535H (shelter); *R v Governor of Frankland Prison, ex p Russell* [2000] 1 WLR 2027 (prisoner's right to food); *R v Secretary of State for the Home Department, ex p Irfan Ahmed* [1995] Imm AR 210, 219 ("if the policy of the Home Office were one which ignored the obvious humanitarian principle of respect for family life, that would be a factor in favour of holding the policy to be unreasonable"); *R v Secretary of State for the Home Department, ex p Herbage (No 2)* [1987] QB 1077, 1095F-G (if "cruel and unusual punishment", "it would be an affront to common sense that the court should not be able to afford [a remedy]"); *Yildiz v Secretary of State for Social Security* [2001] EWCA Civ 309 at [18] (Buxton LJ: "If the Secretary of State really wished to implement the policy suggested on his behalf in this case, and subject [the claimant] and other asylum seekers in his position to ... a life so destitute that no civilised nation can tolerate it, then he would have to use very clear words to that effect"); *R v Wandsworth London Borough Council, ex p O* [2000] 1 WLR 2539 (freedom from destitution); *R (Limbuela) v Secretary of State for the Home Department* [2005] UKHL 66 [2006] 1 AC 396 (approaching destitution by applying statutory human rights).

7.5.10 **Non-torture.** *A v Secretary of State for the Home Department* [2005] UKHL 71 [2006] 2 AC 221 at [11]-[12] (Lord Bingham, describing the common law prohibition on torture "as a constitutional principle"), [52] ("The principles of the common law, standing alone, ... compel the exclusion of third party torture evidence as unreliable, unfair, offensive to ordinary standards of humanity and decency and incompatible with the principles which should animate a tribunal seeking to administer justice"), [64] (Lord Nicholls: "for centuries the common law has set its face against torture"), [83] (Lord Hoffmann: "the rejection of torture by the common law has a special iconic importance as the touchstone of a humane and civilised legal system ... a constitutional resonance for the English people which cannot be overestimated"), [129] (Lord Rodger), [152] (Lord Carswell); *Jones v Ministry of Interior of Saudi Arabia* [2006]

---

[39] Declan O'Callaghan and Rajesh Bhasvar [2001] JR 25; Justin Bates [2005] JR 165.

UKHL 26 [2007] 1 AC 270 (prohibition on torture in international law).

7.5.11 Liberty. <6.1.3(B)> (Magna Carta); *A v Secretary of State for the Home Department* [2004] UKHL 56 [2005] 2 AC 68 at [36] (Lord Bingham: "fundamental importance of the right to personal freedom", reflected in "the long libertarian tradition of English law ... upheld in a series of landmark decisions down the centuries and embodied in the substance and procedure of the law to our own day"), [86] (Lord Hoffmann); *R (Saadi) v Secretary of State for the Home Department* [2001] EWCA Civ 1512 [2002] 1 WLR 356 (CA) at [69] (Lord Phillips MR, referring to the "recognition, that is part of our heritage, of the fundamental importance of liberty"); *Naidike v Attorney-General of Trinidad and Tobago* [2004] UKPC 49 [2005] 1 AC 538 at [48] (need clear words to interfere with liberty); *R (W) v Metropolitan Police Commissioner* [2005] EWHC 1586 (Admin) [2005] 1 WLR 3706 at [21] (the "right to walk the streets without interference from police ... unless they possess common law or statutory powers to stop us"); *D v Home Office* [2005] EWCA Civ 38 [2006] 1 WLR 1003 at [69] (importance attached by English law to the right to liberty); *R (Abbasi) v Secretary of State for Foreign and Commonwealth Affairs* [2002] EWCA Civ 1598 [2003] UKHRR 76 at [60] ("The underlying principle, fundamental in English law, is that every imprisonment is prima facie unlawful"); *Eshugbayi Eleko v Government of Nigeria* [1931] AC 662, 670 (Lord Atkin: "no member of the executive can interfere with the liberty or property of a British subject except on the condition that he can support the legality of his action before a court of justice"); *In re Wilson* [1985] AC 750, 757H (Lord Roskill: "in principle, the subject must not be deprived of his liberty save after the performance of a judicial act effected with judicial propriety"); *R v Maidstone Crown Court, ex p Clark* [1995] 1 WLR 831 (important in cases involving liberty that courts can grant redress); *R v Secretary of State for the Home Department, ex p Khawaja* [1984] AC 74, 111F ("If Parliament intends to exclude effective judicial review of the exercise of a power in restraint of liberty, it must make its meaning crystal clear"), 122E-F (Lord Bridge: duty to "regard with extreme jealousy any claim by the executive to imprison a citizen without trial and allow it only if it is clearly justified by the statutory language relied on"; "a robust exercise of the judicial function in safeguarding the citizen's rights"); *Tan Te Lam v Superintendent of Tai A Chau Detention Centre* [1997] AC 97, 111E ("the courts should construe strictly any statutory provision purporting to allow the deprivation of individual liberty by administrative detention"); *R v London (North) Industrial Tribunal, ex p Associated Newspapers Ltd* [1998] ICR 1212, 1224 ("a provision which enables interference to take place with basic constitutional rights should be narrowly construed"); *R (Kelly) v Secretary of State for Justice* [2008] EWCA Civ 177 [2008] 3 All ER 844 (rectifying construction albeit penal statute affecting liberty, because no settled right to liberty being interfered with).

7.5.12 Due process & related rights. <7.4> (access to justice); <7.6.5> (natural justice/ due process and the rule of law); *R v Davis* [2008] UKHL 36 [2008] 3 WLR 125 at [5] (accused's right to confront their accusers); *R (Bright) v Central Criminal Court* [2001] 1 WLR 662 (discussing the privilege against self-incrimination at common law); *R v Hertfordshire County Council, ex p Green Environmental Industries Limited* [2000] 2 AC 412 (self-incrimination); *R v Director of the Serious Fraud Office, ex p Smith* [1993] AC 1, 40D ("strong presumption against interpreting a statute as taking away the right of silence"); *R (Morgan Grenfell & Co Ltd) v Inland Revenue Commissioners* [2002] UKHL 21 [2003] 1 AC 563 at [7], [43] (legal professional privilege as a fundamental human right); *B v Auckland District Law Society* [2003] UKPC 38 [2003] 2 AC 736 at [37] (legal professional privilege); *R (Kelly) v Warley Magistrates Court* [2007] EWHC 1836 (Admin) (general provisions incapable of empowering interference with litigation privilege); *R v Islington North Juvenile Court, ex p Daley* [1983] 1 AC 347, 364B ("The right of an accused to be tried by a jury of his fellow countrymen for any offence which ordinary people would regard as involving a grave reflection on his character ... is a right that is deeply rooted in tradition").

7.5.13 **Privacy.** *Douglas v Hello! Ltd (No.3)* [2005] EWCA Civ 595 [2006] QB 125 (privacy through the tort of breach of confidence); *Wainwright v Home Office* [2003] UKHL 53 [2004] 2 AC 406 at [31] (privacy as an underlying value rather than a rule of law); *HRH Prince of Wales v Associated Newspapers Ltd* [2006] EWCA Civ 1776 [2008] Ch 57.

7.5.14 **Religion.** *R v Secretary of State for the Home Department, ex p Moon* (1996) 8 Admin LR 477, 480F-G ("The common law, like the European Convention on Human Rights, recognises the freedom of individuals to adopt, practise and ... change their religion").

7.5.15 **Freedom of expression/speech.** *R v Shayler* [2002] UKHL 11 [2003] 1 AC 247 at [21] (Lord Bingham: "The fundamental right of free expression has been recognised at common law for very many years"); *McCartan Turkington Breen v Times Newspapers Ltd* [2001] 2 AC 277, 297F (Lord Steyn: "Even before the coming into operation of the Human Rights Act 1998 the principle of freedom of expression attained the status of a constitutional right with attendant high normative force"); *Rushbridger v HM Attorney-General* [2003] UKHL 38 [2004] 1 AC 357 at [7] ("freedom of political speech is a core value of our legal system. Without it the rule of law cannot be maintained"); *R v Secretary of State for the Home Department, ex p Brind* [1991] 1 AC 696, 757B-C (Lord Ackner: "In a field which concerns a fundamental human right - namely that of free speech - close scrutiny must be given to the reasons provided as justification for interference with that right"); *R v Secretary of State for the Home Department, ex p Simms* [2000] 2 AC 115, 125G (Lord Steyn, speaking of "the right of freedom of expression": "In a democracy it is the primary right: without it an effective rule of law is not possible"), 126B (ECHR Art 10 reflected in the common law); *Reynolds v Times Newspapers Ltd* [2001] 2 AC 127, 207G-H (Lord Steyn, dissenting in the result, referring to freedom of expression as a constitutional right); *Wainwright v Home Office* [2003] UKHL 53 [2004] 2 AC 406 at [31] (Lord Hoffmann, referring to freedom of speech as an "underlying value", rather than "a rule of law", being "a value which underlies the existence of a rule of law"); *R (Bright) v Central Criminal Court* [2001] 1 WLR 662, 681B (freedom of speech as a "fundamental freedom"); *Worme v Commissioner of Police of Grenada* [2004] UKPC 8 [2004] 2 AC 430 at [19] (PC, describing "the importance that is attached to the right of freedom of expression, particularly in relation to public and political matters").

7.5.16 **Assembly/association.** *McEldowney v Forde* [1971] AC 632, 657F (Lord Pearson: "In construing this regulation one has to bear in mind that it authorises very drastic interference with freedom of association ... Therefore it should be narrowly interpreted").

7.5.17 **Property.** *Chesterfield Properties Plc v Secretary of State for the Environment* [1998] JPL 568, 579-580 (ownership of land recognised as a constitutional right); *Attorney-General v Blake* [2001] 1 AC 268, 289G (endorsing "the established general principle, of high constitutional importance, that there is no common law power to take or confiscate property without compensation"); *R v Secretary of State for the Environment, Transport and the Regions, ex p Spath Holme* [2001] 2 AC 349, 383B-H (presumption that Parliament does not intend to take away property rights without clear language); *Attorney-General of Jamaica v Williams* [1998] AC 351, 354H ("The fundamental human right to protection against unlawful searches and seizures is part of the English common law"); *R (Bright) v Central Criminal Court* [2001] 1 WLR 662, 679G-681A (autonomy of premises and freedom from search as constitutional rights); *Secretary of State for Defence v Guardian Newspapers Ltd* [1985] AC 339, 363 ("the principle of construction ... that the courts must be slow to impute to Parliament an intention to override property rights in the absence of plain words to that effect"); *R v Independent Television Commission, ex p Flextech Plc* [1999] COD 108 (interference with existing contractual rights requiring clear and unambiguous express power or duty); *R v Herrod, ex p Leeds City Council* [1978] AC 403, 424B-E (anxious to avoid a construction which "would have the effect of causing grave hardship by depriving very many people of their livelihood"); *R v Coventry City Council, ex p Phoenix Aviation* [1995] 3 All ER 37, 62e-63b (decision yielding to disruption of a lawful trade reviewed "with particular rigour").

7.5.18 Other key rights and interests. *R (Bancoult) v Secretary of State for the Foreign and Commonwealth Office* [2001] QB 1067 at [39] (Laws LJ: "I would certainly accept that a British subject enjoys a constitutional right to reside in or return to that part of the Queen's dominions of which he is a citizen"); *Hipperson v Newbury District Electoral Officer* [1985] QB 1060 (considering the right to vote); *R v Flintshire County Council, ex p Armstrong-Braun* [2001] EWCA Civ 345 [2001] LGR 344 (standing order having "restrictive effect on the functioning of individual elected representatives") at [60] (as part of collective rights of citizens); *Sepet v Secretary of State for the Home Department* [2003] UKHL 15 [2003] 1 WLR 856 at [20], [53] (whether core human right of conscientious objection); *Raymond v Honey* [1983] 1 AC 1, 10G-H ("under English law, a convicted prisoner, in spite of his imprisonment, retains all civil rights which are not taken away expressly or by necessary implication").

7.6 **Basic fairness.** Natural justice is the traditional name for legal standards of basic fairness protected by the law. This common law doctrine, rooted in centuries of legal tradition, readily adds procedural protections into statutory frameworks. Though conventionally associated with standards which are (a) procedural and (b) applicable to public bodies, in truth basic fairness is broader in each respect.

7.6.1 Natural justice: a sense of history. *R v University of Cambridge* (1723) 1 Stra 557, 567 (Fortescue J: "The laws of God and man both give the party an opportunity to make his defence, if he has any"); *Cooper v Wandsworth Board of Works* (1863) 14 CB (NS) 180, 190 (Willes J: "a tribunal which is by law invested with power to affect the property of one of Her Majesty's subjects, is bound to give such subject an opportunity of being heard before it proceeds ... that rule is of universal application, and founded upon the plainest principles of justice"); *Board of Education v Rice* [1911] AC 179, 182 (Lord Loreburn LC: "they must act in good faith and fairly listen to both sides, for that is a duty lying upon every one who decides anything"); <2.1.5(A)> (historical context).

7.6.2 Natural justice/procedural fairness as a ground for judicial review. <P60>.

7.6.3 Natural justice as a fundamental principle. *Ridge v Baldwin* [1964] AC 40, 113-114 ("the essential requirements of natural justice at least include that before someone is condemned he is to have an opportunity of defending himself, and in order that he may do so that he is to be made aware of the charges or allegations or suggestions which he has to meet"; "here is something which is basic to our system"), 133 ("There is imposed a clog on the discretion in that it cannot be exercised arbitrarily without regard to natural justice"); *Chief Constable of the North Wales Police v Evans* [1982] 1 WLR 1155, 1161C-D (defendant "should have directed his mind to the criteria laid down in the regulation in accordance with the appropriate principles of natural justice"); *R v Inland Revenue Commissioners, ex p Unilever Plc* [1996] STC 681, 690f ("duty to act fairly and in accordance with the highest public standards"), 692c-d ("a general public law discretion must in the ordinary way be exercisable in favour of the citizen when its non-exercise would involve unfairness or injustice to him"); *R (Hampstead Heath Winter Swimming Club) v Corporation of London* [2005] EWHC 713 (Admin) [2005] 1 WLR 2930 at [33] ("the values of the common law are dictated by current concepts of justice and fairness and reasonableness").

7.6.4 Natural justice having a common law source. *Cooper v Wandsw*

(1863) 14 CBNS 180 per Byles J at 194 (referring to "the justice of the common law"), cited in *Pearlberg v Varty* [1972] 1 WLR 534 per Lord Hailsham at 537D; *Wiseman v Borneman* [1971] AC 297, 309B (Lord Morris: "Natural justice, it has been said, is only `fair play in action'. Nor do we wait for directions from Parliament. The common law has abundant riches: there may we find what Byles J called `the justice of the common law'"); *Reid v Secretary of State for Scotland* [1999] 2 AC 512, 541G (Lord Clyde, referring to whether "the tribunal whose decision is being challenged has ... departed from the procedures which either by statute or at common law as a matter of fairness it ought to have observed"); *Stefan v General Medical Council* [1999] 1 WLR 1293, 1297C-D ("an obligation to give reasons ... may arise through construction of the statutory provisions as a matter of implied intention. Alternatively it may be held to exist by operation of the common law as a matter of fairness").

7.6.5 Natural justice/due process and the rule of law. <P59> (right to a fair trial/hearing); *Chuan v Public Prosecutor* [1981] AC 648,670G (approaching the concept of "law" as meaning a system which includes common law natural justice); *Thomas v Baptiste* [2000] 2 AC 1 (considering common law due process rights, reflected in Constitution of Trinidad and Tobago), 22B-C; *Bushell v Secretary of State for the Environment* [1981] AC 75, 95B (Lord Diplock, speaking of a public authority with a discretionary function as owing "a constitutional duty to perform it fairly"); *Higgs v Minister of National Security* [2000] 2 AC 228, 245H (PC discussing constitutional and common law principle of due process).

7.6.6 Natural justice/procedural fairness supplementing the statutory scheme. <60.3>.

7.6.7 Basic fairness and the principle of legality. <7.3.2(A)>.

7.6.8 Broader senses of basic fairness/natural justice.
(A) SUBSTANTIVE FAIRNESS. *R v Secretary of State for the Home Department, ex p Pierson* [1998] AC 539, 591F (Lord Steyn: "the rule of law enforces minimum standards of fairness, both substantive and procedural"); *R (Anufrijeva) v Secretary of State for the Home Department* [2003] UKHL 36 [2004] 1 AC 604 at [30] (Lord Steyn: "fairness is the guiding principle of our public law"); *In Re Officer L* [2007] UKHL 36 [2007] 1 WLR 2135 at [22], [27]-[29] (overlap between common law duty of fairness to a witness and Art 2 safeguarding duty).
(B) NEED FOR A SUBSTANTIVE FACTUAL BASIS. *Mahon v Air New Zealand Ltd* [1984] AC 808, 820G-H (Lord Diplock, referring to a principle of "natural justice" that an investigative decision-maker "must base his decision upon evidence that has some probative value").
(C) RESTITUTION. *Moses v Macferlan* (1760) 2 Burr 1005 per Lord Mansfield CJ at 1012 ("the defendant, upon the circumstances of the case, is obliged by the ties of natural justice and equity to refund the money"), cited in *Woolwich Equitable Building Society v Inland Revenue Commissioners* [1993] AC 70, 178G, 201G.
(D) ABUSE OF PROCESS. *Atkinson v United States of America Government* [1971] AC 197, 231E-F (Lord Reid: asking whether proceedings "oppressive and contrary to natural justice").

7.6.9 Procedural fairness applicable to private bodies/functions. *Gray v Marlborough College* [2006] EWCA Civ 1262 [2006] ELR 516 (public law principles an indicative starting-point for independent school's contractual duty to act fairly); *Modahl v British Athletic Federation (No.2)* [2001] EWCA Civ 1447 [2002] 1 WLR 1192 at [117] (fairness in a domestic contractual context involving "a measure of consistency with parallel principles of fairness" in public law and human rights cases); *Wright v Jockey Club* The Times 16th June 1995 (fairness as an implied term of contractual relationship with Jockey Club); *Weinberger v Inglis* [1919] AC 606, 636 (suggesting Stock Exchange obliged to comply with principles of natural justice);

Lakeside Colony of Hutterian Brethren v Hofer [1992] 3 SCR 165 (Supreme Court of Canada holding that breach of natural justice by religious community in expelling a Church member); *Wandsworth London Borough Council v A* [2000] 1 WLR 1246 (local education authority having a duty to act reasonably and fairly even where acting, in relation to a parent, as landowner); *R (Oxford Study Centre Ltd) v British Council* [2001] EWHC Admin 207 [2001] ELR 803 (declaration granted that council having acted in breach of implied contractual term of fairness); *Pratt Contractors Ltd v Transit New Zealand* [2003] UKPC 83 at [46]-[47] (in claim for breach of contract by public authority conducting a competitive tendering process, implied contractual term of fair dealing not "impos[ing] under the guise of contract law, the obligation to avoid making its decision or otherwise conducting itself in ways which would render it amenable to judicial review of administrative action").

7.6.10 Statutory interpretation and basic fairness. <29.3.6>.

7.7 Basic reasonableness. Unreasonableness is a recognised ground for judicial review. But it runs deeper, rooted in a strong common law resistance to unreasonableness. That is why, for example, Courts strive to avoid statutory interpretations which are unreasonable and an affront to justice and good sense.

7.7.1 Unreasonableness as a ground for judicial review. <P57>.

7.7.2 Unreasonableness: a sense of history. *Rooke's Case* (1598) 5 Co Rep 99b (Lord Coke: "notwithstanding that the words of the commission give authority to the commissioners to do according to their discretions, yet their proceedings ought to be limited and bound with the rule of reason and law"); *Westminster Corporation v London & North Western Railway* [1905] AC 426, 430 (Lord Macnaghten: "It is well settled that a public body invested with statutory powers ... must take care not to exceed or abuse its powers... it must act reasonably"); *Roberts v Hopwood* [1925] AC 578, 613 (Lord Wrenbury, explaining that the decision-maker "must, by use of his reason, ascertain and follow the course which reason directs. He must act reasonably"); <2.1.5(A)> (historical context).

7.7.3 Avoiding startling/unreasonable statutory interpretation. *R (Morgan Grenfell & Co Ltd) v Inland Revenue Commissioners* [2002] UKHL 21 [2003] 1 AC 563 at [8] (Lord Hoffmann: "the courts will ordinarily construe general words in a statute, although literally capable of having some startling or unreasonable consequence ... as not having been intended to do so"; this "can be traced back at least to *Stradling v Morgan* (1560) 1 Pl 199"), [44] (Lord Hobhouse: "the principle of statutory construction is not new and has long been applied in relation to the question whether a statute is to be read as having overridden some basic tenet of the common law"); <7.3> (principles of legality); <29.3.5> (construction to avoid unreasonableness/absurdity); <29.3.15> (resort to external aids); <29.4> (use of Hansard).

7.7.4 Unreasonableness applicable to private bodies/functions. *Weinberger v Inglis* [1919] AC 606 (HL considering whether proprietors of stock exchange had acted arbitrarily or capriciously); *McAllister v Society of Lloyd's* 2nd December 1998 unrep. (even if not amenable to judicial review, arguable that Lloyd's owing a general duty not to act *Wednesbury* unreasonably, given that performing functions in the public interest within a statutory framework); *Wandsworth London Borough Council v A* [2000] 1 WLR 1246 (local education authority having a duty to act reasonably and fairly even where authority acting as a landowner); *James D'Avila v Tom Sawyer* 22nd March 1996 unrep. (considering whether decision of Labour Party's National Executive Committee irrational); *Edge v Pensions Ombudsman* [2000] Ch 602, 628D (considering analogy between duties of trustees and

Wednesbury principles); *Colgan v Kennel Club* 26th October 2001 unrep. (Kennel Club sanction manifestly excessive and disproportionate); *Paragon Finance Plc v Nash* [2001] EWCA Civ 1466 [2002] 1 WLR 685 at [38] (*Wednesbury* test relevant where contract conferring a discretion on one party); *Modahl v British Athletic Federation* [2001] EWCA Civ 1447 [2002] 1 WLR 1192 at [44]-[48] (declaratory remedy (not damages) available against domestic body, even absent an implied contract); cf. *Saeed v Royal Wolverhampton Hospitals NHS Trust* The Times 17th January 2001 (whether NHS Trust entitled to discipline employee depending on interpretation of the contract of employment; court's role to decide true meaning of the contract).

> **P8 EC law.** Domestic statutes, rules and decisions must be compatible
> with applicable EC legislation and legal principle.

8.1 EC law supremacy
8.2 EC Treaty rights
8.3 Judicial review for EC-incompatibility
8.4 Article 234 references to the ECJ
8.5 EC law damages/reparation

8.1 EC law supremacy.[40] EC legislation prescribes rights to be respected and obligations to be performed by member states, to which the European Communities Act 1972 subordinated the United Kingdom. EC supremacy works through concepts which include in particular: (1) direct effect; (2) effective protection; (3) compatible interpretation; and (4) relevant general principles.

8.1.1 **The European Communities Act 1972.** See s.2(1) (enforceable EC rights and remedies); s.2(2) (power to make implementing provisions); s.2(4) (effect on domestic legislation); s.3(1) (EC questions as questions of law); *Thoburn v Sunderland City Council* [2002] EWHC 195 (Admin) [2003] QB 151 at [62]-[64], [69] (ECA 1972 as a constitutional statute); <7.5.7> (constitutional statutes).

8.1.2 **Principal sources of EC law.** See the Treaty Establishing the European Community (Consolidated Version); EC Treaty Art 249 (referring to EC Regulations, Directives and Decisions); ECA 1972 s.3(1) (applicability of principles laid down by the ECJ).

8.1.3 **Supremacy of EC law.** *A v Chief Constable of West Yorkshire* [2004] UKHL 21 [2004] ICR 806 at [9] (Lord Bingham: "It is ... well-established that the law of the [European] Community prevails over any provision of domestic law inconsistent with it"); *Thoburn v Sunderland City Council* [2002] EWHC 195 (Admin) [2003] QB 151 at [1] ("The law of the EU is itself part of our domestic law, by force of the European Communities Act 1972"), [69] ("All the specific rights and obligations which EU law creates are by the 1972 Act incorporated into our domestic law and rank supreme: that is, anything in our substantive law inconsistent with any of these rights and obligations is abrogated or must be modified to avoid the inconsistency. This is true even where the inconsistent municipal provision is contained in primary legislation"), [59]-[60] (Parliament not binding its successors but Act not capable of being impliedly repealed); *R v Secretary of State for Transport, ex p Factortame Ltd (No.2)* [1991] 1 AC 603, 659A-C ("whatever limitation of its sovereignty Parliament accepted when it enacted the European Communities Act 1972 was entirely voluntary... there is nothing in any way novel in according supremacy to rules of Community law in those areas to which they apply and to insist that, in the protection of rights under Community law, national courts must not be inhibited by rules of national law ... is no more than a logical recognition of that supremacy"); *Stoke-on-Trent City Council v B&Q plc* [1991] Ch 48, 56D (Hoffmann J: "The EEC Treaty is the supreme law of this country, taking precedence over Acts of Parliament"); *R v Ministry of Agriculture Fisheries and Food, ex p Lower Burytown Farms Ltd* [1999] EuLR 129, 135D-E (important not to be mesmerised by fact that claimant's legal entitlement arising under an EC Directive, which should be approached as if provisions were contained in a British statute); *R v Ministry of Agriculture Fisheries and Food, ex p SP Anastasiou* [1995] COD 339 (ECJ decisions binding on High Court in the same way as are Court of Appeal and House of Lords decisions); *R (Watts) v Bedford Primary Care Trust* [2003] EWHC 2228 (Admin) (2003)

---

[40] David Anderson QC [2003] JR 127; Nicholas Blake QC [2003] JR 198.

6 CCLR 566 at [98] (Court's "obligation to apply ... statements of principle to be found in the relevant parts of the ECJ's judgment"); *R v Secretary of State for Employment, ex p Equal Opportunities Commission* [1995] 1 AC 1, 28A-C (domestic Court the appropriate forum to decide issue of compatibility of domestic statute with EC law).

8.1.4 **"Direct effect".** See ECA 1972 s.2(1) (enforceable rights and remedies); *R v Secretary of State for Transport, ex p Factortame Ltd* [1990] 2 AC 85, 151C (Lord Bridge: "Directly enforceable Community rights ... are automatically available and must be given unrestricted retroactive effect. The persons entitled to the enjoyment of such rights are entitled to direct and immediate protection against possible infringement of them. The duty to provide such protection rests with the national court. The remedy to be provided against infringement must be effective, not merely symbolic or illusory. The rules of national law which render the exercise of directly enforceable Community rights excessively difficult or virtually impossible must be overridden"); *Marshall v Southampton and South West Hampshire AHA* [1986] ECR 723 (direct effect principle discussed and applied); *R v Durham County Council, ex p Huddleston* [2000] 1 WLR 1484 at [12] ("Because no state may lawfully take advantage of its own failure to implement a directive, state bodies are to be treated in domestic law as if an unimplemented directive had been implemented"); *Van Duyn v Home Office* [1975] Ch 358 (directly effective Directive, where unconditional and sufficiently precise, and implementation date has expired); *Foster v British Gas Plc* [1991] 2 AC 306, 308 (meaning of "emanation of the state" for purposes of direct effect); *R v London Borough of Hammersmith, ex p CPRE London Branch* [2000] Env LR 565 at [32] ("once a Directive has been correctly transposed into domestic legislation, an individual is thereafter confined to his remedies under the domestic legislation"); *R (Omar) v Secretary of State for the Home Department* [2005] EWCA Civ 285 [2005] INLR 470 at [21] (certain Dublin Convention provisions having direct effect via EC Regulation 343/2003).

8.1.5 **"Effective protection".** See EC Treaty Art 10 (duty to take measures); *Autologic Holdings Plc v Inland Revenue Commissioners* [2004] EWCA Civ 680 [2004] 3 All ER 957 at [25] (Peter Gibson LJ: "The importance of the principle of effectiveness in Community law cannot be overstated. Any provision of national law which makes the exercise of a right conferred by Community law practically impossible or extremely difficult cannot prevail"); *R (Noble Organisation) v Thanet District Council* [2005] EWCA Civ 782 [2006] Env LR 185 at [60] ("proceedings for judicial review afford adequate protection for Community law rights in respect of the validity of public actions"); *R v Secretary of State for the Home Department, ex p Gallagher* [1996] 2 CMLR 951 at [10] (Lord Bingham CJ: "It is a cardinal principle of Community law that the laws of Member States should provide effective and adequate redress for violations of Community law by Member States where these result in infringement of specific individual rights conferred by the law of the Community"); *Preston v Wolverhampton Healthcare NHS Trust (No.2)* [2001] UKHL 5 [2001] 2 AC 455 at [4] (Lord Slynn, explaining that: "where reliance is placed on the performance of domestic procedural conditions those conditions must not be such as to make the enforcement of Community law rights impossible in practice and they must not be less favourable than those applying to a similar claim of a domestic nature"); *R v Secretary of State for Transport, ex p Factortame Ltd (No.2)* [1991] 1 AC 603, 644F (duty to set aside rule of international law preventing interim remedy); *R v London Borough of Hammersmith & Fulham, ex p CPRE* [2000] Env LR 532, 540 (domestic judicial review delay rules compatible with effective protection) (upheld by CA at [2000] Env LR 549); *Autologic Holdings Plc v Inland Revenue Commissioners* [2004] EWCA Civ 680 [2004] 3 All ER 957 (contrary to EC law for High Court to decline to entertain EC-based restitution claims on basis that alternative remedy of statutory appeal not followed).

8.1.6 **"Compatible interpretation".** See the principle in *Marleasing* [1990] ECR I-4135 at

4159, considered in *Ghaidan v Godin-Mendoza* [2004] UKHL 30 [2004] 2 AC 557 at [45] and [48] (discussing the principle and key authorities); *Murphy v Media Protection Services Ltd* [2007] EWHC 3091 (Admin) [2008] 1 WLR 1869 at [25] ("the *Marleasing* principle requires us to construe the provisions so nearly as possible as to achieve the result required by the Directive, once the time for the implementation of the latter has passed"); *Campbell v MGN Ltd* [2002] EWCA Civ 1373 [2003] QB 633 at [96] (domestic statute to be interpreted consistently with an EC Directive which it is intended to implement) (HL is [2004] UKHL 22 [2004] 2 AC 457); *R (Equal Opportunities Commission) v Secretary of State for Communities and Local Government* [2007] EWHC 483 (Admin) (considering what interpretation "possible"); *Webb v Emo Air Cargo Ltd* [1993] 1 WLR 49, 59F (duty "to construe domestic legislation in any field covered by a Community Directive so as to accord with the interpretation of the Directive as laid down by the European Court of Justice, if that can be done without distorting the meaning of the domestic legislation... This is so whether the domestic legislation came after or, as in this case, preceded the Directive"), 60F (but "the domestic law must be open to an interpretation consistent with the Directive"); *General Building & Maintenance Plc v Greenwich Borough Council* (1994) 6 Admin LR 266 (construing Regulations according to purposes of Directive); *Ken Lane Transport Ltd v County Trading Standards Officer of North Yorkshire County Council* [1995] 3 CMLR 140 (construing Order compatibly with Directive it was passed to implement); *R v Ministry of Agriculture Fisheries and Food ex p National Farmers Union* [1995] 3 CMLR 116 (regulations unlawful in that seeking to introduce additional restriction upon Directive purported to be implemented by them); *White v White* [2001] UKHL 9 [2001] 2 All ER 43 at [21] (Lord Nicholls), [31] (Lord Cooke); *Clarke v Kato* [1998] 1 WLR 1647, 1656A-D (compatible interpretation may be "a construction which departs boldly from the ordinary meaning of the language of the statute ... to strain to give effect to the design and purpose behind the legislation, and to give weight to the spirit rather than the letter... But even in this context the exercise must still be one of construction and it should not exceed the limits of what is reasonable"); *R v Durham County Council, ex p Huddleston* [2000] 1 WLR 1484 at [10] (primary legislation incompatible with EC Directive, and "convergent construction" solution not possible, so direct effect solution adopted); *Ghaidan v Godin-Mendoza* [2004] UKHL 30 [2004] 2 AC 557 at [45] (recognising the parallel between the *Marleasing* principle and s.3 HRA); *Litster v Forth Dry Dock & Engineering Co Ltd* [1990] 1 AC 546, 577A-B (Court able "where necessary, to supply by implication words appropriate to comply"); *CR Smith Glaziers (Dunfermline) Ltd v Customs and Excise Commissioners* [2003] UKHL 7 [2003] 1 WLR 656 at [29] (Lord Hoffmann) and [48] (Lord Hope); *Imperial Chemical Industries Plc v Colmer (Inspector of Taxes)* [2000] 1 All ER 129, 134c (effect of ECA 1972 s.2 is "the same as if a subsection were incorporated" in the statutory provision so as to be "without prejudice to the directly enforceable Community rights of companies established in the Community"); *Relaxion Group Plc v Rhys-Harper* [2003] UKHL 33 [2003] 4 All ER 1113 at [104] (albeit no horizontal direct effect, "a directive works its way into our domestic system by means of the legislation which is designed to give effect to it. It is then for the courts to interpret that legislation, as far as possible, in a way that gives effect to this country's obligations under the treaty").

8.1.7 **"General principles" of EC law.**[41] *A v HM Treasury* [2008] EWHC 869 (Admin) [2008] 3 All ER 361 at [30] (effective judicial review); <P37> (proportionality template); <41.1.4> (legitimate expectation); *R (Partridge Farms Ltd) v Secretary of State for Environment, Food & Rural Affairs* [2008] EWHC 1645 (Admin) (EC principle of equality); *Dow Benelux v Commission* [1989] ECR 3137 (right to be heard); <6.3.3> (ECHR via EC law); <62.2.5> (reasons and EC law); *R v Ministry of Agriculture Fisheries and Food, ex p First City Trading*

---

[41] David Anderson QC, 'Abuse of Rights' [2006] JR 348.

[1997] EuLR 195 (EC fundamental principle of equal treatment inapplicable since challenged scheme not implementing any powers or duties conferred or imposed by EC law).

8.2 EC Treaty rights. The EC Treaty contains codified rights with which a member state is not entitled unjustifiedly to interfere. Whether an interference with a Treaty right can be justified depends on applying the structured principle of proportionality, having regard to the particular right in question and the types of codified justification formulated in the Treaty article. An unjustified interference is a ground for judicial review, as the many working examples demonstrate.

8.2.1 Article 28: Freedom of import. EC Treaty Art 28 (prohibition) and Art 30 (justification); *R (Countryside Alliance) v Attorney General* [2007] UKHL 52 [2008] 1 AC 719 (Hunting Act not breaching Art 28); *R (International Transport Roth GmbH) v Secretary of State for the Home Department* [2002] EWCA Civ 158 [2003] QB 728 (immigration carrier penalty scheme not interfering with Art 28); *R (British American Tobacco) v Secretary of State for Health* [2004] EWHC 2493 (Admin) (exception to statutory tobacco advertising ban compatible with Art 28).

8.2.2 Articles 29: Freedom of export. EC Treaty Art 29 (prohibition) and Art 30 (justification); *R v Ministry of Agriculture Fisheries and Food, ex p Hedley Lomas (Ireland) Ltd* [1997] QB 139 (refusal of licence for live exports (based on belief that Spain would not comply with EC Directive) unjustified restriction on exports); *R v Chief Constable of Sussex, ex p International Trader's Ferry Ltd* [1999] 2 AC 418 (decision restricting police protection for live calf exporters justified and so not a breach of Article 29).

8.2.3 Article 39: Free movement of workers. EC Treaty Art 39 (duty and justifiable exceptions); *R v Secretary of State for Social Services, ex p Urbanek* (1995) 7 Admin LR 781 (income support regulations not contrary to Article 39); *R v Secretary of State for the Home Department, ex p Vitale* [1996] All ER (EC) 461 (decisions discontinuing income support consistent with Article 39); *B v Secretary of State for the Home Department* [2000] UKHRR 498 (deportation of an EC national disproportionate); *R (Conde) v Lambeth London Borough Council* [2005] EWHC 62 (Admin) (2005) 8 CCLR 486 (refusal of housing assistance for an EEA national seeking work Art 39-compatible).

8.2.4 Article 18: Free movement of citizens. EC Treaty Art 18 (right and justifiable exceptions); *R v Secretary of State for the Home Department, ex p Adams* [1995] All ER (EC) 177 (proportionality of exclusion order); *Phull v Secretary of State for the Home Department* [1996] Imm AR 72 (Article 18 not applicable to internal situation, nor directly effective); *R v Secretary of State for the Home Department, ex p Vitale* [1996] All ER (EC) 461 (income support restrictions not contrary to Article 18); *R (Kaur) v Secretary of State for the Home Department* [2001] All ER (EC) 250 (UK entitled to lay down conditions as to when individuals becoming "nationals" for purposes of Article 18 rights).

8.2.5 Article 43: Freedom of establishment. EC Treaty Art 43 (prohibition) and Art 46 (justification); *R v HM Treasury, ex p Daily Mail & General Trust Plc* [1989] QB 446 (scheme preventing transfer of company's central management abroad without Revenue's consent not a contravention of Article 43); *Centros Ltd v Erhvervs-og Selskabsstyrelsen* [2000] Ch 446 (whether unlawful to refuse to register a company formed in another member state); *R v Westminster City Council, ex p Dinev* 24th October 2000 unrep. (licensing scheme not an infringement of Article 43).

8.2.6 **Article 49: Freedom of services.** EC Treaty Art 49 (prohibition) and Art 46 (justification); *R (Countryside Alliance) v Attorney General* [2007] UKHL 52 [2008] 1 AC 719 (Hunting Act not breaching Art 49); *Gough v Chief Constable of Derbyshire* [2002] EWCA Civ 351 [2002] QB 1213 (football banning orders proportionate and so not a breach of Art 49); *R (International Transport Roth GmbH) v Secretary of State for the Home Department* [2002] EWCA Civ 158 [2003] QB 728 (immigration carrier penalty scheme not interfering with Article 49 rights); *R (Theophilus) v London Borough of Lewisham* [2002] EWHC 1371 (Admin) [2002] 3 All ER 851 (restriction on student support not a breach of Art 49).

8.2.7 **Equal treatment/freedom from discrimination.** See eg. EC Treaty Art 141 (equal pay obligation) and Art 12 (prohibition on nationality-based discrimination); *R v Secretary of State for Employment, ex p Equal Opportunities Commission* [1995] 1 AC 1 (statutory requirement for 5 years' minimum period for redundancy/unfair dismissal protections incompatible with Article 141, not being objectively justified); *R v Secretary of State for Employment, ex p Seymour-Smith* [1999] 2 AC 554 and [2000] 1 WLR 435 (applicability of Article 141 to an Order imposing a 2-year minimum work period for any unfair dismissal claim); *R v Ministry of Agriculture Fisheries and Food, ex p First City Trading* [1997] EuLR 195 (claimant not entitled to rely on EC fundamental principles of equal treatment, since scheme challenged not devised in order to implement any powers or duties conferred or imposed by EC law); *R v Secretary of State for Social Security, ex p Taylor* [2000] All ER (EC) 80 (winter fuel payments not objectively justified and so in breach of social security/equal treatment Directive); *R v Ministry of Agriculture Fisheries and Food, ex p Astonquest* [2000] EuLR 371 (fishing catch restrictions justified and proportionate, for purposes of EC Treaty Art 34(2)); *Harmon CFEM Facades (UK) Ltd v Corporate Officer of the House of Commons* (1999) 67 Con LR 1 (breach of EC Treaty Art 12 in favouring domestic tendering company).

8.2.8 **State aid.**[42] EC Treaty Art 87 (prohibition) *R v Commissioners of Customs and Excise, ex p Lunn Poly Ltd* [1999] EuLR 653 (Finance Act 1997 s.21, introducing differential rates of insurance premium tax, incompatible with Article 87, as an unnotified unjustified state aid); *R v Ministry of Agriculture Fisheries and Food, ex p British Pig Industry Support Group* [2000] EuLR 724 (not unlawful or unreasonable for Minister to refuse to apply to Commission for permission for state aid); *R (Lidl (UK) GmbH) v Swale Borough Council* 23rd February 2001 unrep. (no question of state aid where land sold for best consideration reasonably obtainable); *R v Secretary of State for Trade and Industry, ex p BT3G Ltd* [2001] EWCA Civ 1448 [2001] EuLR 822 (decisions permitting two mobile phone companies to have and retain third generation licences pending their disassociation not an impermissible state aid); *R (Professional Contractors Ltd) v Commissioners of Inland Revenue* [2001] EWCA Civ 1945 [2002] EuLR 329 (tax legislation not a state aid); *R (British Aggregates Associates) v Her Majesty's Treasury* [2002] EWHC 926 (Admin) [2002] EuLR 394 (aggregate levy not an impermissible state aid).

8.3 **Judicial review for EC-incompatibility.**[43] It follows from the supremacy of EC law that enactments, rules or decision-making which are incompatible with EC law stand to be overturned on judicial review, as being unlawful. In an EC law context, all grounds for judicial review are capable of being informed by the rights, obligations and principles of EC law.

---

[42] Thomas de la Mare [2000] JR 100; Aidan Robertson [2002] JR 91.

[43] Clive Lewis [2002] JR 272; Richard Gordon QC [2007] JR 19.

8.3.1 Legislation incompatible with EC law.
(A) PRIMARY LEGISLATION. *R v Secretary of State for Employment, ex p Equal Opportunities Commission* [1995] 1 AC 1 (declaring primary legislation incompatible with Community law); *R v Commissioners of Customs and Excise, ex p Lunn Poly Ltd* [1999] EuLR 653 (declaration Finance Act 1987 s.21 incompatible with EC law).
(B) SECONDARY LEGISLATION/RULES. *R (Barker) v Bromley London Borough Council* [2006] UKHL 52 [2007] 1 AC 470 (regulations failing to implement EC Directive); *Hockenjos v Secretary of State for Social Security (No.2)* [2004] EWCA Civ 1749 [2005] 1 FLR 1009 (welfare regulations violating EC Directive); *R v Secretary of State for Employment, ex p Seymour-Smith (No.2)* [2000] 1 WLR 435 (1985 Order violating EC Equal Treatment Directive and EC Art 141 (ex Art 119)); *R (Equal Opportunities Commission) v Secretary of State for Communities and Local Government* [2007] EWHC 483 (Admin) (regulations not properly implementing EC Directive); *R (Partridge Farms Ltd) v Secretary of State for Environment, Food & Rural Affairs* [2008] EWHC 1645 (Admin) (2006 Order breaching EC principle of equality).

8.3.2 Acts of public authorities incompatible with EC law. <8.2> (EC Treaty rights); <8.1.4> (direct effect); <8.1.6> (compatible interpretation).

8.3.3 EC law and particular grounds for judicial review. As to misdirection as to EC law, see eg. *R v Secretary of State for the Environment, ex p Greenpeace Ltd* [1994] 4 All ER 352; *R v National Rivers Authority, ex p Moreton* [1996] Env LR 234 (whether misunderstood EC Directive); <37.1.7> (proportionality under EC law); <41.1.4> (legitimate expectation under EC law); <6.3.3> (ECHR via EC law). As to relevancies/irrelevancies under EC law, see eg. *R v Secretary of State for the Home Department, ex p Evans (Medical) Ltd* [1995] All ER (EC) 481 (EC Directive referring to "criteria" upon which decision could be based; ECJ ruling that matter in question falling within that category and so Secretary of State entitled to have regard to it); *R v Secretary of State for the Environment, ex p Royal Society for the Protection of Birds* [1997] QB 206 (Secretary of State not entitled to take account of economic considerations when designating a special protection area for wild birds under Wild Birds Directive). <62.2.5> (duty to give reasons under EC law).

8.4 Article 234 references to the ECJ. The Court of Justice in Luxembourg has a special advisory role, to give rulings on dispositive points of interpretation of EC law, upon questions referred to it by the national court.

8.4.1 Article 234 references: the rules. See EC Treaty Art 234; CPR 68.[44]

8.4.2 Whether to make a reference.[45] *R v International Stock Exchange, ex p Else* [1993] QB 534, 545D-F ("if the facts have been found and the Community law issue is critical to the court's final decision, the appropriate course is ordinarily to refer the issue to the Court of Justice unless the national court can with complete confidence resolve the issue itself ... fully mindful of the differences between national and Community legislation, of the pitfalls which face a national court venturing into what may be an unfamiliar field, of the need for uniform interpretation throughout the Community and of the great advantages enjoyed by the Court of

---

[44] Information Note on References from National Courts for a Preliminary Ruling [2005] JR 361.

[45] David Anderson [1996] JR 142; Mark Hoskins [2002] JR 162.

Justice in construing Community instruments. If the national court has any real doubt, it should ordinarily refer"); *R v Secretary of State for Defence, ex p Perkins* [1997] IRLR 297, 300 (only refuse "if the answer to the question of construction is so obvious as to leave no scope for reasonable doubt"); *R v Chief Constable of Sussex, ex p International Trader's Ferry Ltd* [1999] 2 AC 418, 436D & 440C (reference unnecessary as to whether Art 34 triggered, because Art 36 justification satisfied); *R v Ministry of Agriculture Fisheries and Food, ex p Astonquest* [2000] EuLR 371, 390G (no reference "because the principles to be applied are clear. The difficulty is in taking a correct view of the facts, which is a matter for the national court"); *R (Unitymark Ltd) v Department of the Environment, Food and Rural Affairs* [2003] EWHC 2748 (Admin) (Administrative Court applying *Else*, where issue of validity of EC measure); *R (Synthon BV) v Licensing Authority* [2006] EWHC 1759 (Admin) (whether point of general importance likely to promote uniform application of the law in the EU).

8.4.3 **Article 234 references: other matters.** *R (Mellor) v Secretary of State for Communities and Local Government* [2008] EWCA Civ 213 (Art 234 reference ordered at the permission stage); <22.2.8(B)> (third party participation in an Art 234 reference); *Royscot Leasing Ltd v Commissioners of Customs and Excise* (1999) 11 Admin LR 251 (power to withdraw reference); *R (International Air Transport Association) v Department of Transport* [2004] EWHC 1721 (Admin) (Court requesting ECJ President to consider directing priority/urgency under Arts 55 and 104A); *R (A) v Secretary of State for the Home Department* [2002] EWCA Civ 1008 [2002] EuLR 580 (appeal against order for reference); *R (SPCMA SA) v Secretary of State for Environment, Food and Rural Affairs* [2007] EWHC 2610 (Admin) (referring such questions as arguable).

8.5 EC law damages/reparation.[46] EC law confers some rights to monetary remedies against public bodies, including the State itself.

8.5.1 **Routes to damages.** *Three Rivers District Council v Bank of England* [2003] 2 AC 1, 198G-199B (Lord Hope: "Community law, as it has been developed by the European Court of Justice, is capable of conferring upon individuals the right to claim damages from a national authority by one or other or both of two distinct routes... The first route by which the right to claim damages against the state or an emanation of the state for the non-implementation or misimplementation of a Directive may be asserted is based upon the principle of direct effect... The second route is based upon the principle of state liability"), 199B-200B (situations where direct effect giving a damages right), 200B-G (state liability for failure to implement a Directive), 200H-201G (both routes involving "three conditions ... the rule of law infringed must have been intended to confer rights on individuals, the breach must have been sufficiently serious, and there must be a direct causal link between the breach of the obligation resting on the state and the damage sustained by the injured parties").

8.5.2 **State liability: *Francovich* reparation.** Key cases include: *Francovich v Republic (Italy)* [1995] ICR 722 at 772C-773A (3 conditions: "that the result prescribed by the directive should entail the grant of rights to individuals"; "that it should be possible to identify the content of those rights on the basis of the provisions of the directive"; and "the existence of a causal link between the breach of the State's obligation and the loss and damage suffered by the injured parties"); *Brasserie du Pêcheur v Federal Republic of Germany* [1996] QB 404; *R v HM Treasury, ex p British Telecommunications Plc* [1996] QB 615; *R v Ministry of Agriculture*

---

[46] Thomas de la Mare [1996] JR 225, [1997] JR 143; Daniel Denman [2008] JR 126; Dr Paolisa Nebbia [2008] JR 136.

Fisheries and Food, ex p Hedley Lomas (Ireland) Ltd 1997] QB 139; *R v Secretary of State for the Home Department, ex p Gallagher* [1996] 2 CMLR 951; *Dillenkofer v Federal Republic of Germany* [1997] QB 259; *Norbrook Laboratories v Ministry of Agriculture, Fisheries and Food* [1998] ECR I-1531, at [106]-[107] (ECJ); *R v Secretary of State for Transport, ex p Factortame Ltd* [2000] 1 AC 524. Other illustrations include: *Three Rivers District Council v Bank of England* [2003] 2 AC 1 (Directive not intended to confer such rights); *Boyd Line Management Services Ltd v Ministry of Agriculture Fisheries and Food* [1999] EuLR 44 (relevant EC provisions not shown to be intended to confer rights on individuals); *R v Ministry of Agriculture, Fisheries and Food, ex p Lay and Gage* [1998] COD 387 (breach not sufficiently serious; bona fide misinterpretation of unclear provision). As to liability of the domestic court[47], see *Kobler v Republik Osterreich* [2004] QB 848.

8.5.3 Other monetary remedies via EC law. As to whether there is a duty under EC law to enact a compensation scheme, see *R v Ministry of Agriculture Fisheries & Food, ex p Bostock* [1994] I ECR 955; also *R v Minister of Agriculture, Fisheries and Food, ex p Country Landowners' Association* [1996] 2 CMLR 193; *Booker Aquaculture Ltd v Secretary of State for Scotland* The Times 24th September 1998 (exercise of power to order destruction of property, without any compensation scheme, contrary to ECHR and therefore EC general principles). As to whether domestic compensation restrictions contravene EC law, see *Marshall v Southampton & South West Hampshire Health Authority (Teaching) (No.2)* [1994] QB 126 (domestic ceiling on compensation required by EC Directive unlawful); *Brasserie du Pêcheur v Federal Republic of Germany* [1996] QB 404, 504D (legislation excluding loss of profits "not compatible with Community law"); *R v Ministry of Agriculture Fisheries and Food, ex p Lower Burytown Farms Ltd* [1999] EuLR 129 (on judicial review, declaration granted that entitled to be paid interest on payments due under EC Directive; such payments constituting a statutory debt just as where entitlement arising under domestic legislation).

---

[47] Mark Hoskins [2004] JR 278.

> **P9 The HRA.** Domestic legislation must be read, and public authorities must act, compatibly with HRA:ECHR rights.

9.1 HRA: key features and themes
9.2 Codified Convention rights
9.3 HRA ss.3-4: legislative compatibility/DOI
9.4 HRA s.6: compatible public authority action
9.5 HRA just satisfaction

9.1 HRA: key features and themes.[48] By the Human Rights Act 1998 (HRA) Parliament enacted into domestic law protections reflecting those in the European Convention on Human Rights (ECHR). The HRA enhanced the Courts' role in protecting rights and changed the face of judicial review.

9.1.1 **A new and elegant constitutional text.** *McCartan Turkington Breen v Times Newspapers Ltd* [2001] 2 AC 277, 297G (HRA meaning that the ECHR "fulfills the function of a Bill of Rights in our legal system"; "the Human Rights Act 1998 is a constitutional measure"); *Thoburn v Sunderland City Council* [2002] EWHC 195 (Admin) [2003] QB 151 at [62]-[64] (HRA as a constitutional statute <7.5.7>); *R v Secretary of State for the Home Department, ex p Simms* [2000] 2 AC 115, 131G-132B (HRA meaning "the principles of fundamental human rights which exist at common law [are] supplemented by a specific text, namely the European Convention on Human Rights and Fundamental Freedoms"); *Wilson v First County Trust Ltd* [2003] UKHL 40 [2004] 1 AC 816 at [179] (Lord Rodger: "The 1998 Act is beautifully drafted. Its structure is tight and elegant"), [182] (referring to the HRA's "unusual" and "perhaps unique" range); *In re McKerr* [2004] UKHL 12 [2004] 1 WLR 807 at [77] (Lord Rodger: an "elegant and comprehensive solution"); *R (M) v Secretary of State for Health* [2003] EWHC 1094 (Admin) [2003] UKHRR 746 at [18] ("The architecture of the Act and its paradigmatic relationship with the doctrine of separation of powers were the product of great legal and constitutional ingenuity").

9.1.2 **The new rights-based culture.** *R (International Transport Roth GmbH) v Secretary of State for the Home Department* [2002] EWCA Civ 158 [2003] QB 728 at [27] (Simon Brown LJ: "the court's role under the [HRA] is as the guardian of human rights"); *R (P and Q) v Secretary of State for the Home Department* [2001] EWCA Civ 1151 [2001] 1 WLR 2002 at [56] ("the introduction of a rights-based culture into English public law"); *Redmond-Bate v Director of Public Prosecutions* 23rd July 1999 unrep. ("the constitutional shift which is now in progress"); *Douglas v Hello! Ltd* [2001] QB 967 at [64] (describing the change from the position in which English law was "historically based on freedoms, not rights"); *Venables v News Group Newspapers Ltd* [2001] Fam 430 at [100] (HRA as "a new era"); *R (Wooder) v Feggetter* [2002] EWCA Civ 554 [2003] QB 219 at [45] ("a new and different paradigm of superimposed law"); *R v Lambert* [2001] UKHL 37 [2002] 2 AC 545 at [6] ("It is clear that the 1998 Act must be given its full import and that long or well entrenched ideas may have to be put aside, sacred cows culled"); *Sheffield City Council v Smart* [2002] EWCA Civ 4 [2002] HLR 639 at [20] ("not an extension of the jurisdiction. That has not changed. What has changed is the substantive law which governs the actions and omissions of public authorities");

---

[48] Thomas de la Mare [1999] JR 32; Lord Lester QC [1999] JR 171, [2002] JR 179; David Pannick QC [1999] JR 177; Andrew Henderson [1999] JR 267; Michael Fordham [2000] JR 262, [2001] JR 205; Cherie Booth QC [2001] JR 1; Gerry Moynihan QC [2000] JR 274; Margaret Gray [2000] JR 114; Varda Bondy [2003] JR 149; Thomas de la Mare & David Pievsky [2003] JR 221.

R v Kansal (No.2) [2001] UKHL 62 [2002] 2 AC 69 at [51] ("The development of our jurisprudence on [the HRA 1998] has only just begun. New problems are being revealed every week, if not every day"); *R (Khan) v Secretary of State for the Health* [2003] EWCA Civ 1129 [2004] 1 WLR 971 at [99] ("human rights law casts long shadows in exceptional cases"); *Rowland v Environment Agency* [2003] EWCA Civ 1885 [2005] Ch 1 at [101] ("a fundamental watershed in the development of both substantive and procedural law").

9.1.3 **Practical and effective rights.** *R v Shayler* [2002] UKHL 11 [2003] 1 AC 247 at [61] (Lord Hope, emphasising the need for "the fundamental rights enshrined in the Convention ... to remain practical and effective"); *Jones v Ministry of Interior of Saudi Arabia* [2004] EWCA Civ 1394 [2005] QB 699 at [87] ("It is a fundamental principle that rights conferred by the [ECHR] should be interpreted so as to be practical and effective") (HL is [2006] UKHL 26 [2007] 1 AC 270).

9.1.4 **Mirroring the ECHR.** *In re McKerr* [2004] UKHL 12 [2004] 1 WLR 807 at [63] (Lord Hoffmann, describing "incorporation" as "a misleading metaphor. What the Act has done is to create domestic rights expressed in the same terms as those contained in the Convention. But they are domestic rights, not international rights. Their source is the statute, not the Convention. They are available against specific public authorities, not the United Kingdom as a state. And their meaning and application is a matter for domestic courts, not the court in Strasbourg"), [26] (Lord Nicholls); *R (Animal Defenders International) v Secretary of State for Culture Media and Sport* [2008] UKHL 15 [2008] 2 WLR 781 at [37], [53] (HRA matching ECHR); *R (Quark Fishing Ltd) v Secretary of State for Foreign and Commonwealth Affairs* [2005] UKHL 57 [2005] 3 WLR 837 (mirror as to territoriality).

9.1.5 **Autonomous human rights jurisprudence.** *Kay v Lambeth London Borough Council* [2006] UKHL 10 [2006] 2 AC 465 at [44] (Lord Bingham: "it is for national authorities, including national courts particularly, to decide in the first instance how the principles expounded in Strasbourg should be applied in the special context of national legislation, law, practice and social and other conditions"); *R (M) v Commissioner of Police of the Metropolis* [2001] EWHC Admin 553 (HRA meaning "we are to fashion a municipal jurisprudence of human rights"); *R (International Transport Roth GmbH) v Secretary of State for the Home Department* [2002] EWCA Civ 158 [2003] QB 728 at [81] (task "to develop an autonomous, and not merely an adjectival, human rights jurisprudence"); *Begum v Tower Hamlets London Borough Council* [2002] EWCA Civ 239 [2002] 1 WLR 2491 (CA) at [17] (task "to develop a municipal law of human rights by the incremental method of the common law, case by case, taking account of the Strasbourg jurisprudence").

9.1.6 **HRA canons of interpretation.** <9.3.1> (HRA s.3 rule of interpretation); *R v Secretary of State for the Home Department, ex p Simms* [2000] 2 AC 115, 131G-132B (Lord Hoffmann, referring to "the principle of legality ... expressly enacted as a rule of construction in section 3" and which gains "further support from the obligation of the minister in charge of a Bill to make a statement of compatibility under section 19"); <29.5.4> (interpretation of the ECHR).

9.1.7 **ECHR principles of legality.** <59.1.4> (prescribed by law/in accordance with law); <37.1.8> (proportionality under the HRA); <32.3.8> (pressing social need); <58.5.7> (fair balance); <58.5.2> (beware of the Strasbourg margin of appreciation); <58.5.3> (HRA latitude).

9.1.8 **The HRA and legislative supremacy.** *R v Director of Public Prosecutions, ex p Kebilene* [2000] 2 AC 326, 367A (Lord Steyn: "the carefully and subtly drafted Human Rights Act 1998 preserves the principle of parliamentary sovereignty. In a case of incompatibility ...

the courts may not disapply the legislation. The court may merely issue a declaration of incompatibility which then gives rise to a power to take remedial action: see section 10"); *R v Lyons* [2002] UKHL 44 [2003] 1 AC 976 at [58] (Lord Hutton: "Parliament is the supreme law-making body for the United Kingdom and a statute enacted by Parliament which cannot be read under section 3(1) of the Human Rights Act 1998 in a way which is compatible with the Convention prevails over any provision of the Convention or any judgment of the European Court [of Human Rights]"); *Doherty v Birmingham City Council* [2008] UKHL 57 [2008] 3 WLR 636 at [21] (HRA preserving Parliamentary sovereignty); *Wilson v First County Trust Ltd* [2003] UKHL 40 [2004] 1 AC 816 at [127] (Lord Hobhouse); <9.3.11> (declaration of incompatibility); <7.1.1> (legislative supremacy as a paramount constitutional principle).

9.1.9 The Strasbourg safety-net: resort to the ECtHR.[49] See eg. *Pretty v UK* [2002] 2 FCR 97; *Smith and Grady v United Kingdom* (1999) 29 EHRR 493.

9.1.10 Citing Strasbourg authority: the need for discipline. <11.1.10>.

9.1.11 Issues of retrospectivity: matters pre-2 October 2000.[50]
(A) HRA NOT RETROSPECTIVE. *JA Pye (Oxford) Ltd v Graham* [2002] UKHL 30 [2003] 1 AC 419 at [65], [73] (HRA not retrospective); *Wilson v First County Trust Ltd* [2003] UKHL 40 [2004] 1 AC 816 (no jurisdiction to grant declaration of incompatibility here, in respect of events pre-2.10.00); *Pearce v Mayfield School* [2003] UKHL 34 [2004] 1 All ER 339 at [23] (HRA not applying to pre-2.10.00 discriminatory ill-treatment of teacher); *R v Lambert* [2001] UKHL 37 [2002] 2 AC 545 (HRA not applying where post-2.10.00 criminal appeal arising out of pre-2.10.00 summing up and conviction); *R v Kansal (No.2)* [2001] UKHL 62 [2002] 2 AC 69 (HL applying *Lambert* in the interests of certainty, even though considering (3-2) that it was wrongly decided); *R v Lyons* [2002] UKHL 44 [2003] 1 AC 976 at [18], [25], [61] (HRA not retrospective, applying *Lambert* and *Kansal*); *R v Benjafield; R v Rezvi* [2002] UKHL 1 & 2 [2003] 1 AC 1099 (applying *Kansal*); *In re McKerr* [2004] UKHL 12 [2004] 1 WLR 807 (HRA not requiring Art 2 procedural duty of investigation in relation to pre-2.10.00 death); *R v Dimsey; R v Allen* [2001] UKHL 46 & 45 [2002] 1 AC 509 (HRA not retrospective so pre-October 2000 convictions not challengeable on basis of Article 6 self-incrimination point) at [29] (Lord Scott), [23] (Lord Hutton); *R v Director of Public Prosecutions, ex p Kebilene* [2000] 2 AC 326 (rejecting argument that, pending the coming into force of the HRA, DPP obliged to form a concluded view as to whether prosecution would be compatible with the ECHR).
(B) HRA SECTION 3 NOT RETROSPECTIVE. *R (Hurst) v London Northern District Coroner* [2007] UKHL 13 [2007] 2 AC 189 (s.3 inapplicable to pre-2.10.00 death, so as to trigger Art 2 investigative duty); *JA Pye (Oxford) Ltd v Graham* [2002] UKHL 30 [2003] 1 AC 419, [65], [73] (HRA, including s.3, not retrospective); *Wilson v First County Trust Ltd* [2003] UKHL 40 [2004] 1 AC 816 (s.3 not applying to pre-2.10.00 civil cause of action to alter vested rights).
(C) CASES WHERE CONSIDERED APPROPRIATE TO APPLY THE ACT/ECHR. *R v Director of Public Prosecutions, ex p J* [2000] 1 WLR 1215 (ECHR relevant because possible future effect on trial or any appeal); *R (Montana) v Secretary of State for the Home Department* [2001] 1 WLR 552 at [14] (ECHR applied even though decision predated the Act); *R (Mahmood) v Secretary of State for the Home Department* [2001] 1 WLR 840 (although strictly HRA not applicable, CA recognising artificiality of such an approach, especially where defendant had had regard to ECHR); *R (Isiko) v Secretary of State for the Home Department*

---

[49] The Hon Mr Justice Bratza & Alison Padfield [1998] JR 220; Alison Padfield [2000] JR 141.

[50] Carine Patry [2001] JR 145.

[2001] UKHRR 385 at [4] (treating HRA as if in force, even though policy and implementation in question predated 2.10.00); *R (Fleurose) v Securities and Futures Authority* [2001] EWCA Civ 2015 at [3] (Court content to assume that ECHR should apply); *R (Wright) v Secretary of State for the Home Department* [2001] EWHC Admin 520 [2001] UKHRR 1399 (continuing failure including post-2.10.00); *R (Mellor) v Secretary of State for the Home Department* [2001] EWCA Civ 472 [2002] QB 13 at [21] (treating HRA as applicable even though decision pre-2.10.00); *R (MacNeil) v Parole Board* [2001] EWCA Civ 448 at [14] (apply the Act anyway); *MacDonald v Ministry of Defence* [2001] HRLR 77 (apply ECHR to pre-October 2000 decision because legislation ambiguous); *Aston Cantlow and Wilmcote with Billesley Parochial Church Council v Wallbank* [2003] UKHL 37 [2004] 1 AC 546 at [4], [31], [80], [141] (in case concerning recovery of church repair levy, assuming as agreed by the parties that HRA applicable where ongoing proceedings for recovery of repair liability); *R (Bewry) v Norwich City Council* [2001] EWHC Admin 657 [2002] HRLR 21 (immaterial that decision pre-October 2000, because common law matching HRA:ECHR Art 6 as to independent and impartial tribunal); *R (Wilkinson) v Responsible Medical Officer Broadmoor Hospital* [2001] EWCA Civ 1545 [2002] 1 WLR 419 at [25] (focus on legality of future certified treatment, not just past decisions, so HRA treated as applicable); *R (Waite) v Hammersmith and Fulham London Borough Council* [2002] EWCA Civ 482 [2003] HLR 24 (although acts in question pre-dated October 2000, parties inviting the Court to decide the case on the basis of the HRA); *A v Chief Constable of West Yorkshire* [2002] EWCA Civ 1584 [2003] HRLR 137 at [42] ("because of the date at which the acts complained of took place, the Convention jurisprudence is introduced into domestic law not by the medium of the HRA, but by the medium of the Equal Treatment Directive").

(D) RETROSPECTIVITY UNDER HRA S.22(4). HRA s.7(1)(b) and s.22(4) <64.7>; *R v Lambert* [2001] UKHL 37 [2002] 2 AC 545 (distinguishing between proceedings brought by public authority and criminal appeal), applied in *R v Kansal (No.2)* [2001] UKHL 62 [2002] 2 AC 69; *Magill v Porter* [2001] UKHL 67 [2002] 2 AC 357 at [82] (assuming that HRA applicable to a *civil* appeal relating to a pre-October 2000 decision); *R (Ben-Abdelaziz) v Haringey London Borough Council* [2001] EWCA Civ 803 [2001] 1 WLR 1485 (although nominally in the name of the Crown, judicial review not "proceedings brought by or at the instigation of a public authority" for the purposes of HRA s.22(4)); *Mabey v Secretary of State for the Environment, Transport and the Regions* [2001] ACD 278 (s.22(4) not applying to an appeal against a planning enforcement notice, albeit that the enforcement notice was served by the planning authority); *Pearce v Mayfield School* [2003] UKHL 34 [2004] 1 All ER 339 at [23] (post-2.10.00 appeal from the EAT, concerning pre-2.10.00 discriminatory ill-treatment of a teacher, not constituting "proceedings brought by ... a public authority" under s.22(4), since "brought" meaning when proceedings first started).

(E) OTHER. *R (L) v Manchester City Council* [2001] EWHC Admin 707 (2002) 5 CCLR 268 at [99] (damages only available under the HRA in relation to acts or omissions taking place after 2.10.00); *R (Wright) v Secretary of State for the Home Department* [2006] EWCA Civ 67 [2006] HRLR 727 (judicial review of refusal of compensation not capable of creating pre-HRA entitlement to Art 5 damages); *A v Chief Constable of West Yorkshire* [2004] UKHL 21 [2004] ICR 806 at [13] (ECtHR decisions on transsexuals characterised as "prospective" only); *C v Home Office* [2004] EWCA Civ 234 [2004] UKHRR 813 at [29] (room for argument as to appropriateness of challenging failure post-2.10.00 to enact ECHR-complaint delegated legislation, given that not possible to challenge pre-2.10.00 enactment of non-compliant delegated legislation); *R (Hooper) v Secretary of State for Work and Pensions* [2005] UKHL 29 [2005] 1 WLR 1681 at [58] (sufficient that claimant reaffirmed wish to claim discriminatorily denied welfare benefit after 2.10.00); *R (Juncal) v Secretary of State for the Home Department* [2008] EWCA Civ 869 (applying common law principle of legality where impugned hospital order preceded HRA).

9.1.12 **Positive obligations/horizontal effect.**[51] *R (Ullah) v Secretary of State for the Home Department* [2004] UKHL 26 [2004] 2 AC 323 at [34] (Lord Bingham: "For the purpose of rendering fundamental rights under the ECHR more effective, the ECtHR has developed certain positive obligations viz obligations which require states to take action"); *Douglas v Hello! Ltd* [2001] QB 967, at [129] (development of privacy, by reference to Article 8, precisely an incremental common law change for which the HRA designed, given court's role as a "public authority"); *Douglas v Hello! Ltd (No.3)* [2005] EWCA Civ 595 [2006] QB 125 at [50]-[53] (court's Art 8 obligation in relation to tort law and privacy); *Copsey v WWB Devon Clays Ltd* [2005] EWCA Civ 932 [2005] HRLR 1136 (HRA:ECHR application in employment context); <59.2.3> (Article 2: positive obligation); <59.3.2> (Article 3: positive obligations); <59.6.2> (Article 8: positive obligations).

9.1.13 **Issues of territoriality.** See ECHR Art 1 ("The high contracting parties shall secure to everyone within their jurisdiction the rights and freedoms defined in section I of this Convention"); *R (Al-Skeini) v Secretary of State for Defence* [2007] UKHL 26 [2008] 1 AC 153 (HRA extra-territorial reach matching ECHR Art 1 jurisdiction; HRA applicable to British detention in occupied Iraq); *R (Quark Fishing Ltd) v Secretary of State for Foreign and Commonwealth Affairs* [2005] UKHL 57 [2006] 1 AC 529 (refusal of fishing licence not engaging Art 1P since Protocol I not extended to this British Overseas Territory); *Government of the United States of America v Montgomery (No.2)* [2004] UKHL 37 [2004] 1 WLR 2241 (UK's ECHR Art 6 responsibility treated as engaged where registering a foreign judgment secured by "flagrant denial" of justice); *R (Ullah) v Secretary of State for the Home Department* [2004] UKHL 26 [2004] 2 AC 323 (ECHR rights engaged in immigration removal or extradition to state where flagrant denial of rights); *Singh v Entry Clearance Officer, New Delhi* [2004] EWCA Civ 1075 [2005] QB 608 (entry clearance refusal engaging Art 8 rights of appellant child in India, seeking to establish family life with adoptive parents in the UK); *R (Smith) v Oxfordshire Assistant Deputy Coroner* [2008] EWHC 694 (Admin) (Art 2 applicable to MOD safeguarding of British soldier from hyperthermia in Iraq).

9.1.14 **Duty to take account of Strasbourg case-law: HRA s.2.**
(A) GENERAL. See HRA s.2 <64.7>; *In re McKerr* [2004] UKHL 12 [2004] 1 WLR 807 at [64] (court not "bound by a decision of the Strasbourg court"); *R (S) v Chief Constable of South Yorkshire* [2004] UKHL 39 [2004] 1 WLR 2196 at [66] (Strasbourg decisions "provide authoritative guidance"); *R v Lyons* [2002] UKHL 44 [2003] 1 AC 976 at [46] ("obviously highly desirable that there should be no divergence between domestic and ECtHR jurisprudence" but may decline to follow if apparent that "the ECtHR has misunderstood or been misinformed about some aspect of English law"); *Pelling v Bruce-Williams* [2004] EWCA Civ 845 [2004] Fam 155 at [35] (not "strictly bound" but it would "challenge the fundamental purpose of the Convention were we to prefer the conclusions of the minority to those of the majority without any fresh development or argument to justify departure"); *R (Beeson) v Dorset County Council* [2002] EWCA Civ 1812 [2003] UKHRR 353 at [19] ("not precedent" but "the integrity of our law as a whole presses in favour of shared principle between London and Strasbourg"); *Wilkinson v Kitzinger* [2006] EWHC 2022 (Fam) [2006] HRLR 1141 at [63] (purpose of s.2 to enforce same Convention rights as would be enforced as in Strasbourg, but not to develop the jurisprudence beyond a clear line of authority); <9.1.5> (fashioning an autonomous human rights jurisprudence).
(B) FOLLOWING A CLEAR AND CONSTANT LINE OF STRASBOURG AUTHORITY.

---

[51] Thomas de la Mare & Kate Gallafent [2001] JR 29; Claire McDougall [2003] JR 98; Rabinder Singh QC [2008] JR 94.

R (Alconbury Developments Ltd) v Secretary of State for the Environment Transport and the Regions [2001] UKHL 23 [2003] 2 AC 295 at [26] (Lord Slynn: "In the absence of some special circumstances ... the court should follow any clear and constant jurisprudence of the European Court of Human Rights"); *R (Ullah) v Secretary of State for the Home Department* [2004] UKHL 26 [2004] 2 AC 323 at [20] (Lord Bingham: "the Convention is an international instrument, the correct interpretation of which can be authoritatively expounded only by the Strasbourg Court. From this it follows that a national court subject to a duty such as that imposed by section 2 should not without strong reason dilute or weaken the effect of the Strasbourg case-law"), applied in *N v Secretary of State for the Home Department* [2005] UKHL 31 [2005] 2 AC 296 at [24]; *R (Al-Skeini) v Secretary of State for Defence* [2007] UKHL 26 [2008] 1 AC 153 at [90], [105]-[106] (duty to keep pace, but not leap ahead).

(C) DECISION OF THE GRAND CHAMBER. *R (Anderson) v Secretary of State for the Home Department* [2002] UKHL 46 [2003] 1 AC 837 at [18] (although "not strictly binding, the House will not without good reason depart from the principles laid down in a carefully considered judgment of the [Strasbourg] Court sitting as a Grand Chamber"); *R (Harrison) v Secretary of State for the Home Department* [2003] EWCA Civ 432 [2003] INLR 284 at [28] (Court even less likely to depart from jurisprudence reflected in a "recent judgment of the Grand Chamber").

(D) DECISION OF THE COMMISSION. *R (Williamson) v Secretary of State for Education and Employment* [2002] EWCA Civ 1926 [2003] QB 1300 at [37] (s.2 duty applying to "the jurisprudence of the Convention organs, including the Commission") (HL is at [2005] UKHL 15 [2005] 2 AC 246); *Copsey v WWB Devon Clays Ltd* [2005] EWCA Civ 932 [2005] HRLR 1136 (taking account of Commission decisions under s.2).

(E) DECISION ON INTERPRETATION. *M v Secretary of State for Work and Pensions* [2006] UKHL 11 [2006] 2 AC 91 at [29] (wrong to "depart from a decision of the ECtHR on the interpretation of an article in the Convention save for good reason").

(F) PRINCIPLES LAID DOWN. *Kay v Lambeth London Borough Council* [2006] UKHL 10 [2006] 2 AC 465 (Lord Bingham: "it is ordinarily the clear duty of our domestic courts ... to give practical recognition to the principles laid down by the Strasbourg Court as governing the Convention rights"); *Aston Cantlow and Wilmcote with Billesley Parochial Church Council v Wallbank* [2001] EWCA Civ 713 [2002] Ch 51 at [44] ("task is not to cast around in the European Human Rights Reports like blackletter lawyers seeking clues", but "to draw out the broad principles which animate the Convention") (HL is [2003] UKHL 37 [2004] 1 AC 546).

(G) SITUATION FALLING WITHIN THE MARGIN OF APPRECIATION. *In re G (Adoption: Unmarried Couple)* [2008] UKHL 38 [2008] 3 WLR 76 (HL finding HRA violation albeit ECtHR would uphold) at [31] (where ECtHR would uphold measure as within the UK's margin of appreciation, domestic court entitled to decide for itself whether justified), [36], [120].

(H) OTHER. *Doherty v Birmingham City Council* [2008] UKHL 57 [2008] 3 WLR 636 (following previous HL decision, with adjustment, notwithstanding that minority view since endorsed by ECtHR); *R (Animal Defenders International) v Secretary of State for Culture Media and Sport* [2008] UKHL 15 [2008] 2 WLR 781 (declining to follow unpersuasive Strasbourg decision); *R (Alconbury Developments Ltd) v Secretary of State for the Environment Transport and the Regions* [2001] UKHL 23 [2003] 2 AC 295 at [76] (doubting applicability of decisions if they "compelled a conclusion fundamentally at odds with the distribution of powers under the British constitution"); *Napier v Scottish Ministers* [2005] UKHRR 268 (domestic court not required to have regard to ECtHR decisions as to standard of proof).

9.1.15 **HRA and authority/precedent.** <11.1.9>.

9.1.16 **Relationship between the ECHR and the common law.** <6.3.9>.

9.1.17 **Textbook commentary.** See especially Lester and Pannick, *Human Rights Law and Practice*; Grosz, Beatson and Duffy, *Human Rights: The 1998 Act and the European Convention*; and Clayton and Tomlinson, *The Law of Human Rights*.

9.1.18 **HRA and proper defendant.** *R (Amin) v Secretary of State for the Home Department* [2002] EWCA Civ 390 [2003] QB 581 (CA) at [39] (central government as "the proper body to stand in the shoes of the state when it is called on to answer an alleged violation of article 2") (HL is at [2003] UKHL 51 [2004] 1 AC 653).

9.2 **Codified Convention rights.** The HRA gives domestic protection to rights by listing them as "the Convention rights" in HRA Schedule 1. It is to these codified rights that the statutory rule of compatible interpretation (s.3) and the statutory prohibition on incompatible public authority action (s.6) apply.

9.2.1 **Supplementary nature of the HRA.** See the long title to the 1998 Act ("An Act to give *further effect* to rights and freedoms guaranteed under the European Convention on Human Rights ..." (emphasis added)); and s.11.

9.2.2 **Meaning of "the Convention".** See HRA s.21(1) <64.7>.

9.2.3 **Meaning of "the Convention rights".** See HRA s.1 <64.7>; *In re McKerr* [2004] UKHL 12 [2004] 1 WLR 807 at [25] (Lord Nicholls, referring to rights "created by the 1998 Act by reference to the Convention"); *R (S) v Chief Constable of South Yorkshire* [2004] UKHL 39 [2004] 1 WLR 2196 at [66] (importance of "the equivalent rights in the Convention"); *Wilson v First County Trust Ltd* [2003] UKHL 40 [2004] 1 AC 816 at [181] ("Convention rights are to be seen as an expression of fundamental principles rather than as a set of mere rules").

9.2.4 **Questions as to Convention Rights: relevant sources.** See HRA s.2 <64.7>.

9.2.5 **Undomesticated ECHR provisions.**
(A) ARTICLE 1. <9.1.13> (territoriality).
(B) ARTICLE 13. <32.3.14> and <59.10.11>.
(C) PROTOCOL VI. *R (Aru) v Chief Constable of Merseyside* [2004] EWCA Civ 199 [2004] 1 WLR 1697 at [13] (ECHR Protocol VI not domesticated).
(D) PROTOCOL VII. *R (Mullen) v Secretary of State for the Home Department* [2004] UKHL 18 [2005] 1 AC 1 (UK not having signed or ratified Protocol VII but relevant to understanding the jurisprudence).

9.2.6 **The Convention rights and their violation.** <P59> (HRA-violation).

9.2.7 **Derogation.** See ECHR Art 15 and HRA s.14(6) <64.7>.

9.3 **HRA ss.3-4: legislative compatibility/DOI.** HRA s.3 imposes a strong obligation to interpret domestic legislation, wherever "possible", compatibly with the Convention rights. In rare cases where it is truly impossible for primary legislation to be read so that it (or secondary legislation made under it) is ECHR-compatible, there is the last resort "declaration of incompatibility", triggering a fast-track mechanism of amendment by Parliament.

9.3.1 **Rule of interpretation (s.3): reading legislation ECHR-compatibly.**[52] See HRA s.3 <64.7>; *Ghaidan v Godin-Mendoza* [2004] UKHL 30 [2004] 2 AC 557 at [26] (Lord Nicholls, describing s.3 as "a key section" in the HRA: "It is one of the primary means by which Convention rights are brought into the law of this country"), [39] (Lord Steyn, calling s.3 "the principal remedial measure"); cf. <8.1.6> (compatible interpretation in EC law). [53]

9.3.2 **Legislative compatibility: focus in time.** *Ghaidan v Godin-Mendoza* [2004] UKHL 30 [2004] 2 AC 557 at [23] (question is not whether the legislation was compatible when enacted, but whether it is compatible when the issue arises for determination); *Wilson v First County Trust Ltd* [2003] UKHL 40 [2004] 1 AC 816 at [144] (date when applied not enacted).

9.3.3 **Key guidance on s.3.** *R v Lambert* [2001] UKHL 37 [2002] 2 AC 545 at [79] (Lord Hope: "Resort to [s.3] will not be possible if the legislation contains provisions, either in the words or phrases which are under scrutiny or elsewhere, which expressly contradict the meaning which the enactment would have to be given to make it compatible [or] ... which have this effect by necessary implication... Section 3(1) preserves the sovereignty of Parliament. It does not give power to the judges to overrule decisions which the language of the statute shows have been taken on the very point at issue by the legislator"); *Poplar Housing and Regeneration Community Association Ltd v Donoghue* [2001] EWCA Civ 595 [2002] QB 48 at [75] ("section 3 does not entitle the court to *legislate*"); *R v A (No.2)* [2001] UKHL 25 [2002] 1 AC 45 at [13] and [43] ("possible" interpretation under s.3 may be one which ordinary literal and purposive approaches could not yield), [44] (Lord Steyn: "the interpretative obligation under section 3 of the 1998 Act is a strong one"; "it will sometimes be necessary to adopt an interpretation which linguistically may appear strained. The techniques to be used will not only involve the reading down of express language in a statute but also the implication of provisions. A declaration of incompatibility is a measure of last resort"); *In re S (Care Order: Implementation of Care Plan)* [2002] UKHL 10 [2002] 2 AC 291 at [40] ("a meaning which departs substantially from a fundamental feature of an Act of Parliament is likely to have crossed the boundary between interpretation and amendment. This is especially so where the departure has important practical repercussions which the court is not equipped to evaluate"); *Ghaidan v Godin-Mendoza* [2004] UKHL 30 [2004] 2 AC 557 at [30] ("the interpretative obligation decreed by section 3 is of an unusual and far-reaching character" which bids the Court to "depart from the unambiguous meaning the legislation would otherwise bear" and from "the intention reasonably to be attributed to Parliament in using the language in question"), [32] ("a court can modify the meaning, and hence the effect, of primary and secondary legislation"), [33] (but "cannot ... adopt a meaning inconsistent with a fundamental feature of legislation", the adopted meaning being one which "must be compatible with the underlying thrust of the legislation being construed"); *Sheldrake v Director of Public Prosecutions* [2004] UKHL 43 [2005] 1 AC 264 at [28] (Lord Bingham, discussing *Ghaidan* guidance).

9.3.4 **Interpreting, not legislating.** *R (Anderson) v Secretary of State for the Home Department* [2002] UKHL 46 [2003] 1 AC 837 at [30] (compatible interpretation "would not be judicial interpretation but judicial vandalism: it would give the section an effect quite different from that which Parliament intended and would go well beyond any interpretative process sanctioned by section 3 of the 1998 Act"), [59] ("It would ... be ...interpolation inconsistent with the plain legislative intent ... Section 3(1) is not available where the suggested interpretation is contrary to express statutory words or is by implication necessarily contradicted by the statute"); *R v*

---

[52] David Manknell [2000] JR 109; Andrew Henderson [2000] JR 258.

[53] Abigail Schaeffer [2005] JR 72.

Shayler [2002] UKHL 11 [2003] 1 AC 247 at [52] ("If compatibility cannot be achieved without overruling decisions which have already been taken on the very point at issue by the legislator, or if to do so would make the statute unintelligible or unworkable, it will be necessary to leave it to Parliament to amend the statute"); *R (Wilkinson) v Commissioners of Inland Revenue* [2005] UKHL 30 [2005] 1 WLR 1718 at [17] (Lord Hoffmann, s.3 not "requiring the courts to give the language of statutes acontextual meanings"; "the question is still one of *interpretation*, i.e. the ascertainment of what, taking into account the presumption created by section 3, Parliament would reasonably be understood to have meant by using the actual language of the statute"), [19] (reinterpretation one which "no way ... any reasonable reader" could have understood the words used); *Bellinger v Bellinger* [2003] UKHL 21 [2003] 2 AC 467 (refusing to give "male" and "female" a novel and extended meaning); *R (International Transport Roth GmbH) v Secretary of State for the Home Department* [2002] EWCA Civ 158 [2003] QB 728 at [66] (impossible to construe the statute compatibly without turning the scheme "inside out"; "we cannot create a wholly different scheme").

9.3.5 **Least intrusive reinterpretation.** *R (Middleton) v West Somerset Coroner* [2004] UKHL 10 [2004] 2 AC 182 at [34] (HL accepting that there should be "no greater revision of the existing regime than is necessary to secure compliance with the Convention"; "the scheme enacted by and under the authority of Parliament should be respected save to the extent that a change of interpretation (authorised by section 3 of the Human Rights Act 1998) is required to honour the international obligations of the United Kingdom expressed in the Convention").

9.3.6 **Section 3: further cases.** *R (Middleton) v West Somerset Coroner* [2004] UKHL 10 [2004] 2 AC 182 at [35] (reinterpreting coroner's statutory function to ensure Art 2-compatibility); *Secretary of State for the Home Department v MB* [2007] UKHL 46 [2008] 1 AC 440 at [72], [92] (implied proviso to secure fairness under Art 6); *R (Baiai) v Secretary of State for the Home Department* [2008] UKHL 53 [2008] 3 WLR 549 at [32] (implied limiting proviso to secure Art 12-compatibility); *R (Hammond) v Secretary of State for the Home Department* [2005] UKHL 69 [2006] 1 AC 603 (implied condition to ensure Art 6-compatibility); *R v Director of Public Prosecutions, ex p Kebilene* [2000] 2 AC 326, 373F (s.3 as "a strong adjuration"); *R v Z* [2005] UKHL 22 [2005] 2 WLR 709 at [62] ("a strong obligation"; "a strong rebuttable presumption"); *R (Wooder) v Feggetter* [2002] EWCA Civ 554 [2003] QB 219 at [48] (s.3 as "a strong canon of construction"); *R (Fuller) v Chief Constable of Dorset Constabulary* [2001] EWHC Admin 1057 [2003] QB 480 at [38] ("Only *in extremis* will a statutory provision be construed to be incompatible"); *R (Khan) v Oxfordshire County Council* [2004] EWCA Civ 309 [2004] LGR 257 at [54] (s.3 not requiring "a statutory provision to be interpreted in a particular way to provide for the possibility, however remote, that there would otherwise be a breach of the Convention"); *Goode v Martin* [2001] EWCA Civ 1899 [2002] 1 WLR 1828 (modified interpretation of CPR for Art 6-compatibility); *R (Wright) v Secretary of State for Health* [2007] EWCA Civ 999 [2008] QB 422 (CA able to read statute compatibly).

9.3.7 **Relationship between HRA s.3 and common law position.** *R (McLellan) v Bracknell Forest Borough Council* [2001] EWCA Civ 1510 [2002] QB 1129 at [76] (Waller LJ, referring to the *Simms* principle of legality as "subsumed by section 3 of the Human Rights Act"); *Sheffield City Council v Smart* [2002] EWCA Civ 4 [2002] HLR 639 at [42] ("we have reached the point, and did so before incorporation of ECHR, where if Parliament is to legislate so as to deny or frustrate what the law recognises as a fundamental or constitutional right, the courts will look for specific provision or necessary implication to that effect"); *R v Shayler* [2001] EWCA Crim 1977 [2001] 1 WLR 2206 (CA) at [77]-[78] (position "different" under the Human Rights Act compared to situation where common law rights yielding to "language of the statute" which is "clear"); <46.2> (principle of legality).

9.3.8 **HRA s.3: further matters.** *R (South Gloucestershire Local Education Authority) v South Gloucestershire Schools Appeal Panel* [2001] EWHC Admin 732 [2002] ELR 309 at [49] (in determining the meaning of a policy, duty to have regard to the ECHR and so far as possible adopt a compatible interpretation); <46.3.5> (s.3 as a form of reading down/reading in); cf. *Director of Public Prosecutions v Mollison (No.2)* [2003] UKPC 6 [2003] 2 AC 411 at [17] (Privy Council substituting "the Court's pleasure" for "Her Majesty's pleasure" in Jamaican statute so as to be lawful by reference to the Jamaican Constitution).

9.3.9 **Position where incompatibility mandated by primary legislation (s.3).** See HRA s.3(2) <64.7>; *C v Home Office* [2004] EWCA Civ 234 [2004] UKHRR 813 at [27] (HRA approach to compatibility and delegated legislation involves: (1) applying s.3 duty of compatible interpretation; (2) where no compatible finding possible, finding the act of making the delegated legislation (even if approved by Parliament) to be a s.6 violation; (3) unless the content were mandated by primary legislation (HRA s.4(3)).

9.3.10 **Statements of legislative compatibility.** See HRA s.19 <64.7>; *R v A (No.2)* [2001] UKHL 25 [2002] 1 AC 45 at [69] (statement of compatibility merely an expression of minister's opinion; not binding); *R (Animal Defenders International) v Secretary of State for Culture Media and Sport* [2008] UKHL 15 [2008] 2 WLR 781 (statute compatible albeit no statement of compatibility made given Strasbourg jurisprudence).

9.3.11 **Declaration of incompatibility (DOI): HRA s.4.**[54] See HRA s.4 <64.7>; *R (Kurdistan Workers Party) v Secretary of State for the Home Department* [2002] EWHC 644 (Admin) at [86] (inferior tribunal not able to make DOI); HRA s.5 (Crown's rights of notification, joinder and appeal); HRA s.10 and Sch 2 (remedial action following DOI); *R (Hooper) v Secretary of State for Work and Pensions* [2005] UKHL 29 [2005] 1 WLR 1681 at [52] (no point in DOI where relevant sections now repealed); *R (Morris) v Westminster City Council* [2005] EWCA Civ 1184 [2006] 1 WLR 505 at [57] (no good reason not to make DOI).

9.3.12 **DOI granted: examples.** *R (Black) v Secretary of State for Justice* [2008] EWCA Civ 359 (Secretary of State statutory release decision-making function); *R (Baiai) v Secretary of State for the Home Department* [2008] UKHL 53 [2008] 3 WLR 549 (upholding DOI in relation to discriminatory aspect of impugned legislation); *R (Clift) v Secretary of State for the Home Department* [2006] UKHL 54 [2007] 1 AC 484 (statutory bar on parole board review for long-term prisoners liable to deportation); *R (Nasseri) v Secretary of State for the Home Department* [2007] EWHC 1548 (Admin) [2008] 2 WLR 523 (statutory deeming of ECHR-compatible action by Dublin states); *A v Secretary of State for the Home Department* [2004] UKHL 56 [2005] 2 AC 68 (detention without trial of non-nationals); *Ghaidan v Godin-Mendoza* [2004] UKHL 30 [2004] 2 AC 557 (Lord Steyn's Appendix of DOIs granted); *R (Morris) v Westminster City Council* [2005] EWCA Civ 1184 [2006] 1 WLR 505 (statutory disentitlement to priority housing need based on child's immigration control status); *Bellinger v Bellinger* [2003] UKHL 21 [2003] 2 AC 467 (statutory invalidity of marriage unless between "male and female"); *R (M) v Secretary of State for Health* [2003] EWHC 1094 (Admin) [2003] UKHRR 746 (statutory automatic appointment of mental health detainee's nearest relative); *R (Anderson) v Secretary of State for the Home Department* [2002] UKHL 46 [2003] 1 AC 837 (Crime (Sentences) Act 1997 s.29 incompatible with Art 6); *R (International Transport Roth GmbH) v Secretary of State for the Home Department* [2002] EWCA Civ 158 [2003] QB 728 (immigration carrier

---

[54] Caroline Neenan [2000] JR 247; Owain Thomas & Robert Kellar [2001] JR 135; Rabinder Singh QC [2002] JR 237.

penalty regime); *R (D) v Secretary of State for the Home Department* [2002] EWHC 2805 (Admin) [2003] 1 WLR 1315 (non-referral to parole board of post-tariff discretionary lifers detained on mental health grounds); *R (H) v Mental Health Review Tribunal, North and East London Region* [2001] EWCA Civ 415 [2002] QB 1 (statutory burden of proof in mental health case); *R (Chief Constable of Lancashire) v Preston Crown Court* [2001] EWHC Admin 928 [2002] 1 WLR 1332 (crown court rules requiring licensing justices to sit on crown court appeal).

9.3.13 **DOI: guidance and illustrations.** <9.1.8> (HRA and legislative supremacy); *R v Secretary of State for the Home Department, ex p Simms* [2000] 2 AC 115, 132A-B (Lord Hoffmann: "in those unusual cases in which the legislative infringement of fundamental human rights is so clearly expressed as not to yield to the principle of legality, the courts [are] able to draw this to the attention of Parliament by making a declaration of incompatibility. It will then be for the sovereign Parliament to decide whether or not to remove the incompatibility"); *R v A (No.2)* [2001] UKHL 25 [2002] 1 AC 45 at [44] ("A declaration of incompatibility is a measure of last resort"); *R (F) v Enfield London Borough Council* [2002] EWHC 432 (Admin) [2002] 2 FLR 1 at [67] (DOI inappropriate where incompatibility arising from "the body of legislation taken together", rather than "any particular statutory provision"); but see *R (Rose) v Secretary of State for Health* [2002] EWHC 1593 (Admin) [2002] 2 FLR 962 at [58]-[61] (leaving open whether a DOI need identify a specific provision or could involve looking at the legislative scheme as a whole).

9.3.14 **DOI: notice to the Crown.** CPR 54PD <64.3> para 8.2; ACO:NFG <64.4> para 11.2; *Poplar Housing and Regeneration Community Association Ltd v Donoghue* [2001] EWCA Civ 595 [2002] QB 48 at [20] (guidance re notifying the Crown); *Wilson v First County Trust Ltd* [2001] 2 WLR 302 (CA adjourning appeal in consumer credit case, to allow Crown to be notified as to question whether statute compatible with Convention rights); *Matthews v Ministry of Defence* [2002] EWHC 13 (QB) at [51] (requirement of notice dispensed with, since Counsel for MoD able to argue the incompatibility point fully) (HL is at [2003] UKHL 4 [2003] 1 AC 1163); *R (Ward) v Hillingdon London Borough Council* [2001] EWHC Admin 91 [2001] LGR 457 at [40] (court not willing to deal with statutory incompatibility issue where Crown had not been notified); *R v A* [2001] 1 WLR 789 (HL giving permission for minister to be joined in appeal, to consider question of compatibility, even though neither of the other parties intending to ask for DOI); *R (F) v Enfield London Borough Council* [2002] EWHC 432 (Admin) [2002] 2 FLR 1 at [3] (adjournment for Secretary of State to be joined); *R v Kearns* [2002] EWCA Crim 748 [2002] 1 WLR 2815 at [16] (no need for joinder or service of the Crown, where Counsel acting for both the prosecution and the Secretary of State); *R (Morris) v Westminster City Council* [2003] EWHC 2266 (Admin) [2004] HLR 265 at [19] (although Treasury Solicitors had been served and previously indicated no wish to make representations, no notice by the court as required), [20] (adjourning questions of compatible construction (s.3) and DOI so as to ensure Crown on notice); *R (S) v Governing Body of YP School* [2003] EWCA Civ 1306 [2004] ELR 37 at [9] (claimant having succeeded, so that case "now moot", CA declining to permit proceedings to be used as a "platform to debate the consistency of [the statute] with the Convention, which would require service on the Secretary of State and a further adjourned hearing").

9.3.15 **DOI: other matters.** *R (Hooper) v Secretary of State for Work and Pensions* [2003] EWCA Civ 813 [2003] 1 WLR 2623 at [78] ("the state is entitled not merely to a wide margin of appreciation when considering whether and when a change is required to the law in order to ensure that it remains Convention compliant in changing circumstances, but ..., having so decided, it is entitled to such time as is reasonable to make the necessary change") (HL is at [2005] UKHL 29 [2005] 1 WLR 1681); *M v Secretary of State for Work and Pensions* [2006] UKHL 11 [2006] 2 AC 91 (former unequal treatment for homosexual and heterosexual relationships for child support calculation was justified where law and social values were in state of transition at that time); *Rushbridger v HM Attorney-General* [2003] UKHL 38 [2004] 1 AC 357 (declining to entertain a hypothetical and unnecessary claim for a DOI) at [58] (Lord Rodgers: "not the function of the courts to keep the statute book up to date"), [61] (Lord Walker), [36] (Lord Hutton); *In re K (A Child) (Secure Accommodation Order: Right to Liberty)* [2001] Fam 377 at [118]-[128] (wrong in principle, by reference to s.6(2), to treat DOI as triggering damages); *Bellinger v Bellinger* [2003] UKHL 21 [2003] 2 AC 467 at [55] (considering all the circumstances, in approaching the discretion as to DOI; rejecting objection that no useful purpose; here, right to "formally record that the present state of statute law is incompatible with the Convention"), [79]; *R (M) v Secretary of State for Health* [2003] EWHC 1094 (Admin) [2003] UKHRR 746 (DOI granted albeit that the incompatibility admitted and stated intention to legislate, and albeit that court making clear that it was for the Secretary of State to decide what should happen as a result), [18] ("it is not for the court to insulate the Minister from ... pressure [to adopt the HRA s.10 route]"); *R (Laing Homes Ltd) v Buckinghamshire County Council* [2003] EWHC 1578 (Admin) [2003] 3 PLR 60 at [161] (unnecessary to decide on DOI where decision flawed on domestic law grounds); *Lancashire County Council v Taylor* [2005] EWCA Civ 284 [2005] 1 WLR 266 at [37]-[44] (DOI inappropriate where grounds for making it would not apply to or assist the person seeking it); *R (Morris) v Westminster City Council* [2005] EWCA Civ 1184 [2006] 1 WLR 505 at [71] (abuse of power for a public authority to sue other powers to circumvent or replace non-compliant statutory provision).

9.4 **HRA s.6: compatible public authority action.**Section 6 of the Human Rights Act prohibits "public authority" action (or inaction) which is incompatible with the Convention rights. Under section 7 the "victim" of an ECHR-violation is enabled to bring proceedings, including by judicial review.

9.4.1 **Public authority duty to act ECHR-compatibly: s.6.** See HRA s.6 <64.7>; *Attorney General's Reference No.2 of 2001* [2003] UKHL 68 [2004] 2 AC 72 at [32] (Lord Nicholls: "The object of ... section 6(1) is plain: such conduct should not occur. Public authorities cannot lawfully, that is, properly, conduct themselves in a way which is incompatible with a Convention right"); *R (Rose) v Secretary of State for Health* [2002] EWHC 1593 (Admin) [2002] 2 FLR 962 at [50] (s.6(6)(a) "prevents the claimants from complaining of any failure to enact primary legislation or of any failure to make regulations [which] ... require the positive approval of both Houses of Parliament ... [but] the claimants are not debarred from claiming the Secretary of State has acted unlawfully in failing to make regulations [which] ... would fall within the negative resolution procedure"); *R (Morris) v Westminster City Council* [2005] EWCA Civ 1184 [2006] 1 WLR 505 at [66] (s.6 can turn a statutory power into a statutory duty, as where the failure to exercise the power would mean acting ECHR-incompatibly).

9.4.2 **The HRA s.6(2) defences: exceptions of legislative incompatibility.** See HRA s.6(2) <64.7>; *Doherty v Birmingham City Council* [2008] UKHL 57 [2008] 3 WLR 636 (considering s.6(2)(b) in the context of HRA defences to possession proceedings); *R (Wilkinson) v Commissioners of Inland Revenue* [2005] UKHL 30 [2005] 1 WLR 1718 at [22] (s.6(2)(a) defence meaning no power to act), [23] (s.6(2)(b) defence where giving effect to legislative provisions, even if power); *R (Hooper) v Secretary of State for Work and Pensions* [2005] UKHL 29 [2005] 1 WLR 1681 (discussing s.6(2)(a) and (b) in context of discriminatory widowed mother's allowance); *Togher v Revenue and Customs Prosecution Office* [2007] EWCA Civ 686 [2008] QB 476 at [68]-[70] (compatible interpretation of statutory discretion impossible by reference to s.6(2)(b)); *Aston Cantlow and Wilmcote with Billesley Parochial Church Council v Wallbank* [2003] UKHL 37 [2004] 1 AC 546 (s.6(2)(b) applicable where Act

providing for liability even if incompatible with ECHR); *Friends Provident Life and Pensions Ltd v Secretary of State for Transport, Local Government and Regions* [2001] EWHC Admin 820 [2002] 1 WLR 1450 at [99] (Court not prevented by s.6(2)(b) from giving a remedy albeit involving treating a statutory discretion as becoming a duty in some, but not all, circumstances); *R (Bono) v Harlow District Council* [2002] EWHC 423 (Admin) [2002] 1 WLR 2475 (s.6(2)(b) inapplicable unless action in question required by subordinate legislation as a necessary consequence of primary legislation).

9.4.3 **The s.6 duty: meaning of "public authority" (HRA s.6(3)).**[55] See HRA s.6(3) <64.7>; *Aston Cantlow and Wilmcote with Billesley Parochial Church Council v Wallbank* [2003] UKHL 37 [2004] 1 AC 546 (PCC pursuing statutory chancel repair costs not a public authority) at [7] (core public authorities including "government departments, local authorities, the police and the armed forces", indicated by "special powers, democratic accountability, public funding in whole or in part, an obligation to act only in the public interest, and a statutory constitution"), [11]-[12] (factors as to whether a hybrid public authority include extent to which "publicly funded, or is exercising statutory powers, or is taking the place of central government or local authorities, or is providing a public service"); *YL v Birmingham City Council* [2007] UKHL 27 [2008] 1 AC 95 (private care home not exercising a public function in relation to local authority-placed residents); *Attorney General's Reference No.2 of 2001* [2003] UKHL 68 [2004] 2 AC 72 at [30] (Court a public authority not able properly to act in a manner rendered unlawful by s.6 of the HRA); *A v Head Teacher and Governors of Lord Grey School* [2004] EWCA Civ 382 [2004] QB 1231 (headteacher and governors treated as HRA "public authorities") (HL is [2006] UKHL 14 [2006] 2 AC 363); *Marcic v Thames Water Utilities Ltd* [2002] QB 929 (High Court) (statutory sewerage undertaker treated as "public authority" for HRA) (HL is [2003] UKHL 66 [2004] 2 AC 42); *R (D) v Secretary of State for the Home Department* [2006] EWHC 980 (Admin) at [59] (independent contractor running immigration detention centre a functional public authority). *R (Weaver) v London & Quadrant Housing Trust* [2008] EWHC 1377 (Admin) (registered social landlord an HRA public authority); *RSPCA v Attorney-General* [2002] 1 WLR 448 at [37] (RSPCA not an HRA "public authority"); *R (A) v Lord Saville of Newdigate* [2001] EWCA Civ 2048 [2002] 1 WLR 1249 at [6] (Bloody Sunday Tribunal a "public authority" for HRA purposes); *R (A) v Partnerships in Care Ltd* [2002] EWHC 529 (Admin) [2002] 1 WLR 2610 (managers of private psychiatric hospital a "public authority" for HRA); *R (West) v Lloyds of London* [2004] EWCA Civ 506 [2004] 3 All ER 251 at [39] (Lloyds not an HRA public authority); *Cameron v Network Rail Infrastructure Ltd* [2006] EWHC 1133 (QB) [2007] 1 WLR 163 (NRI not an HRA public authority for running railway nor safety function).

9.4.4 **Proceedings alleging s.6 breach: HRA s.7.** See HRA s.7 <64.7>; also s.9 (judicial acts), s.11(b) (safeguard for existing proceedings); *R (Wilkinson) v Responsible Medical Officer Broadmoor Hospital* [2001] EWCA Civ 1545 [2002] 1 WLR 419 at [61] (proceedings under s.7(1) not confined to judicial review); *CF v Secretary of State for the Home Department* [2004] EWHC 111 (Fam) [2004] 1 FCR 577 at [212] (HRA case relating to separation of prison mother and baby could be brought under CPR 8 in Family Division or in Administrative Court under CPR 54).

9.4.5 **Standing and proceedings alleging s.6 breach: the victim test (s.7).** <38.4>.

9.4.6 **Delay and proceedings under the Human Rights Act: the one year rule (s.7(5)).** See

---

[55] Jennifer Johnston [2001] JR 250; Claire McDougall [2002] JR 23; Vikram Sachdeva [2002] JR 248 & [2004] JR 43; Richard Drabble QC [2006] JR 38.

HRA s.7(5) <64.7>; *R (Quark Fishing Ltd) v Secretary of State for Foreign and Commonwealth Affairs* [2003] EWHC 1743 (Admin) (permission to extend time to include damages claim) at [38] (considering reasons for delay and prejudice) (HL is [2005] UKHL 57 [2006] 1 AC 529); *Weir v Secretary of State for Transport* [2004] EWHC 2772 (Ch) [2005] UKHRR 154 (time extended having regard to nature of and reason for delay and lack of prejudice); *Cameron v Network Rail Infrastructure Ltd* [2006] EWHC 1133 (QB) [2007] 1 WLR 163 at [47] (not equitable to extend time); *Somerville v Scottish Ministers* [2007] UKHL 44 [2007] 1 WLR 2734 (s.7(5) inapplicable under Scotland Act).

9.4.7 **HRA remedies.** See HRA s.8 <64.7> (any just and appropriate available remedy); s.7(8) (no criminal offence created), s.12 (position where remedy affecting freedom of expression); *Greene v Associated Newspapers Ltd* [2004] EWCA Civ 1462 [2005] QB 972 (s.12(3) and restraining alleged defamation); *Ashdown v Telegraph Group Ltd* [2001] EWCA Civ 1142 [2002] Ch 149 (s.12 and breach of copyright); *Cream Holdings Ltd v Banerjee* [2004] UKHL 44 [2005] 1 AC 253 at [22] (explaining s.12(3) flexible test); *X (a woman formerly known as Mary Bell) v O'Brien* [2003] EWHC 1101 (QB) [2003] 2 FCR 686 (applying s.12 in context of exceptional order to restrain present identity).

9.5 **HRA just satisfaction.**[56] The victim of an HRA violation can claim the remedy of monetary "just satisfaction".

9.5.1 **Just satisfaction: HRA s.8.** See HRA s.8 <64.7> (just satisfaction), s.9 (judicial acts); *Anufrijeva v London Borough of Southwark* [2003] EWCA Civ 1406 [2004] QB 1124 at [53] (just satisfaction included in judicial review), [77]-[78] (guidance as to dealing with just satisfaction).

9.5.2 **Approach to HRA just satisfaction.** *Anufrijeva v London Borough of Southwark* [2003] EWCA Civ 1406 [2004] QB 1124 at [57] (damages "should be no less liberal than those applied at Strasbourg... The difficulty lies in identifying from the Strasbourg jurisprudence clear and coherent principles governing the award of damages"), [53] (in a human rights claim "the concern will usually be to bring the infringement to an end and any question of compensation will be of secondary, if any, importance"), [56] (need "to adopt a balanced approach", there being "a balance to be drawn between the interests of the victim and those of the public as a whole"), [63] ("The approach is an equitable one. The `equitable basis' has been cited by the ECtHR both as a reason for awarding damages and as a basis upon which to calculate them"); *Re V (A Child)* [2004] EWCA Civ 1575 [2005] UKHRR 144 at [36] (CA emphasising that just satisfaction discretionary); *R (Wilkinson) v Commissioners of Inland Revenue* [2005] UKHL 30 [2005] 1 WLR 1718 at [28] (no just satisfaction award because, if discrimination removed, claimant would have been no better off); *R (Greenfield) v Secretary of State for the Home Department* [2005] UKHL 14 [2005] 1 WLR 673 at [3] (primary aim of ECHR to protect against and prevent human rights violations), [8] (finding of violation generally sufficing in Art 6 cases), [13] (just satisfaction may be appropriate if sufficient causal connection between the violation and an otherwise favourable outcome); *R (H) v Secretary of State for the Home Department* [2003] UKHL 59 [2004] 2 AC 253 at [30] (just satisfaction not called for because "(a) the violation has been publicly acknowledged and the appellant's right thereby vindicated, (b) the law has been amended in a way which should prevent similar violations in future, and (c) the appellant has not been the victim of unlawful detention, which article 5 is intended to avoid"); *Watkins v Secretary of State for the Home Department* [2006] UKHL 17 [2006] 2 AC

---

[56] Richard Clayton QC [2005] JR 124, [2006] JR 230.

395 at [64] (exemplary damages no part of the ECtHR jurisprudence), [26] (but could arise as compensation for non-pecuniary loss, rather than to punish).

9.5.3 **HRA just satisfaction: further cases.** *R (Johnson) v Secretary of State for the Home Department* [2007] EWCA Civ 427 [2007] 1 WLR 1990 (HRA s.7 damages securing compensation guaranteed by Art 5(5)); *R (Bernard) v Enfield London Borough Council* [2002] EWHC 2282 (Admin) [2003] UKHRR 148 (£10,000 just satisfaction for 20 months of unsuitable accommodation); *R (KB) v Mental Health Review Tribunal* [2003] EWHC 193 (Admin) [2004] QB 936 at [47], [53] (compensatory approach using tort parallel); *Cullen v Chief Constable of the Royal Ulster Constabulary* [2003] UKHL 39 [2003] 1 WLR 1763 at [79] (Lord Millett, referring to the absence of principles in the Strasbourg jurisprudence), [81]-[84] (wrong to award HRA damages where no damage to compensate); *In re K (A Child) (Secure Accommodation Order: Right to Liberty)* [2001] Fam 377 at [118]-[128] (wrong in principle to treat DOI as triggering damages); *In re Medicaments and Related Classes of Goods (No.4)* [2001] EWCA Civ 1217 [2002] 1 WLR 269 (refusing costs reimbursement as HRA damages, where proceedings had violated Art 6); *R (A) v Secretary of State for the Home Department* [2002] EWHC 1618 (Admin) [2003] 1 WLR 330 at [74] (Art 5(4) liability for damages not that of the Secretary of State, but the hospital authority); *R (Wilkinson) v Commissioners of Inland Revenue* [2003] EWCA Civ 814 [2003] 1 WLR 2683 at [63] (HRA damages inappropriate where anomalous and discriminatory tax concession provided to comparators now abolished); *R (W) v Doncaster Metropolitan Borough Council* [2004] EWCA Civ 378 [2004] LGR 743 at [65] (erroneous perception "that damages under the Human Rights Act 1998 might be of a lower order than those for a tortious award"); *Re P* [2007] EWCA Civ 2 (just satisfaction not appropriate for procedural Art 8 violation regarding care plan).

P10 Cooperation & candour. The Court will expect from all parties cooperative behaviour and candid disclosure.

10.1 A cooperative enterprise
10.2 ADR/mediation
10.3 Claimant's duty of candour
10.4 Defendant/interested party's duty of candour

10.1 A cooperative enterprise. The supervisory jurisdiction works best as a relationship of mutual respect and cooperation between Court and defendant public authority. This is illustrated by judicial review remedies, which can involve the defendant being relied on to act in accordance with: (1) remittal (for reconsideration); (2) declarations (clarificatory orders); and (3) rulings embodied in a judgment (no formal order being necessary). Judges have high expectations of the behaviour of judicial review parties and their representatives, and will expect cooperation with the Court, with each other, and with the process.

10.1.1 **Judicial review: relationships of mutual respect and cooperation.** *R v Lancashire County Council, ex p Huddleston* [1986] 2 All ER 941, 945c (Sir John Donaldson MR, describing judicial review as a "relationship between the courts and those who derive their authority from the public law, one of partnership based on a common aim, namely the maintenance of the highest standards of public administration"); *M v Home Office* [1992] 1 QB 270 (CA), 314F-315A (Nolan LJ, referring to "the crucial need ... for mutual respect between the judges and the executive": "judgments and orders of the courts are meaningless without the willingness and ability of the executive to enforce them"; "the proper constitutional relationship of the executive with the courts is that the courts will respect all acts of the executive within its lawful province, and that the executive will respect all decisions of the court as to what its lawful province is"); *Fothergill v Monarch Airlines Ltd* [1981] AC 251, 279G (Lord Diplock: "when it is engaged in reviewing the legality of administrative action, [the court] is doing so as mediator between the state in the exercise of its legislative power and the private citizen for whom the law made by Parliament constitutes a rule binding upon him and enforceable by the executive power of the state"); *R (Cowl) v Plymouth City Council* [2001] EWCA Civ 1935 [2002] 1 WLR 803 at [3] ("the courts should deter the parties from adopting an unnecessarily confrontational approach to the litigation"); <13.1.3> (mutual respect between Parliament and the Courts)

10.1.2 **Remedies and cooperation.** <3.1.1> (quash and remit); <24.2> (declarations); *R v Secretary of State for Transport, ex p Factortame Ltd* [1990] 2 AC 85, 150D ("A declaration of right made in proceedings against the Crown is invariably respected and no injunction is required"); *M v Home Office* [1994] 1 AC 377, 423A ("the Crown can be relied upon to co-operate fully with such declarations"); *R v Licensing Authority established under Medicines Act 1968, ex p Smith Kline & French Laboratories Ltd (No.2)* [1990] 1 QB 574, 596B (no need to consider final injunction, rather than a declaration); *R v Hillingdon London Borough Council, ex p Royco Homes Ltd* [1974] QB 720, 732F (decision quashed and so falls to be reconsidered; mandamus adjourned "with liberty to apply in case it proves necessary hereafter to achieve the proper solution to this problem"); *R v Rochdale Metropolitan Borough Council, ex p Schemet* [1994] ELR 89, 109A-D (declaration, and terms of judgment, sufficient; no need for mandatory order); <24.4.10> (no need for formal order); <3.4.3(B)> (Court commenting as to what public body expected to do); <12.1.11> (the rule of law and coercive remedies).

10.1.3 **Case-management.** <2.6> (strict case-management); CPR 1.4(2) (active case-management including "encouraging the parties to cooperate with each other in the conduct of the proceedings").

10.1.4 **Cooperation between the parties.** *Secretary of State for Employment v ASLEF (No.2)* [1972] 2 QB 455, 487E-F & 500B (CA expressing "indebtedness ... for the co-operation which the court has received from all parties ... by means of which alone it has been possible to deal with a complex and difficult case as swiftly"); *R v Secretary of State for the Home Department, ex p Moon* (1996) 8 Admin LR 477, 479H (parties cooperating so that permission granted as a formality and Court proceeding immediately to hear as hearing of the judicial review); *West Glamorgan County Council v Rafferty* [1987] 1 WLR 457, 471B ("Much was agreed between the parties. The [authority] have contested the issues with complete candour and have wasted no time whatever on peripheral matters"); *R v Life Assurance and Unit Trust Regulatory Organisation, ex p Ross* [1993] QB 17, 42B (Court assisted by statement of agreed facts).

10.1.5 **Special responsibility of lawyers drafting reasons.** <62.3.2> (drafting reasons: proper limits of the lawyer's function).

10.1.6 **Early candour.** See Pre-Action Protocol; *Ford v GKR Construction Ltd* [2000] 1 WLR 1397, 1400H (Judge LJ: "Civil litigation is now developing into a system designed to enable the parties involved to know where they stand in reality at the earliest possible stage, and at the lowest practicable cost, so that they may make informed decisions about their prospects and the sensible conduct of their cases"), 1403B (Lord Woolf MR, referring to "the need when conducting litigation to make prompt disclosure of all relevant matters").

10.1.7 **Candour in supplying documents lodged at Court.** *R v Secretary of State for the Home Office, ex p Shahina Begum* [1995] COD 176 (criticising the claimant's advisers' failure to put the defendant's letter to the judge, and their refusal to provide it with a copy of the bundle lodged with the Administrative Court Office).

10.1.8 **Defendant facilitating judicial review.** *In re Wilson* [1985] AC 750, 755A-B (magistrates acting to "enable" judicial review to be sought); *R v Horseferry Road Magistrates' Court, ex p Bennett* [1994] 1 AC 42 (magistrates staying criminal proceedings for judicial review on extradition abuse); *Panday v Virgil* [2008] UKPC 24 [2008] 3 WLR 296 at [33]-[34] (abuse of process normally to be decided by criminal court, not by adjourning for judicial review); *R v Huddersfield Justices, ex p D* [1997] COD 27 (rather than adjourning to allow judicial review challenge, better to make a ruling so that an appeal could ensue); *R v Lee* [1993] 1 WLR 103, 111A-B (crown court discretion to stay pending judicial review); *R (McLellan) v Bracknell Forest Borough Council* [2001] EWCA Civ 1510 [2002] QB 1129 (county court judge should adjourn possession proceeding to enable HRA judicial review); *London Borough of Merton v Williams* [2002] EWCA Civ 980 [2003] HLR 257 at [44] (wrong to adjourn possession proceedings if judicial review would have no real prospect of success); *R (Mahfouz) v General Medical Council* [2004] EWCA Civ 233 at [40] ("it was important that the committee should not impede [the claimant's] undoubted right to test their decision before the High Court"), [41] (unfair of GMC's professional conduct committee not to adjourn for a short period for application to the High Court for judicial review and a stay based on apparent bias through knowledge of prejudicial material); *R (London Borough of Hounslow) v School Admission Appeals Panel for the London Borough of Hounslow* [2002] EWCA Civ 900 [2002] 1 WLR 3147 at [51] (wrong in principle for appeals panel to adjourn for judicial review); <20.1.11> (defendant staying its hand); <20.1.13(A)> (dangers of deciding to press ahead).

10.1.9 **Judicial expectations.** <2.6> (strict case-management); *Gouriet v Union of Post Office Workers* [1978] AC 435, 507D (citing *Deare v Attorney-General* (1835) 1 Y & C Ex 197, 208 per Abinger CB: "it has been the practice, which I hope never will be discontinued, for the officers of the Crown to throw no difficulty in the way of any proceeding for the purpose of bringing matters before a court of justice, where any real point of difficulty that requires judicial decision has occurred"); *R v Reading Justices, ex p South West Meat Ltd* (1992) 4 Admin LR 401 (dismissal of a late and `cynical' application that judicial review proceedings should continue as if begun by claim form); *R v Somerset County Council, ex p Fewings* [1995] 1 All ER 513, 523c-d (Laws J: "In taking their decisions on behalf of the local community, members of local authorities are entitled to, and should, receive accurate advice from the council's lawyers as to the extent of their powers"); *R v Secretary of State for Education, ex p Prior* [1994] ELR 231, 251A-B (Brooke J: "this case shows very vividly how important it is that the governors of a grant-maintained school should have access to good legal advice before they set in motion dismissal procedures"); *R v Minister for Roads and Traffic, ex p McCreery* 15th September 1994 unrep. (Minister should consent to quashing of order, in the light of a related decision of CA); <18.1.12> (costs against magistrates etc where unreasonable refusal to sign consent orders); *Levey* <21.1.6> (position where Court inviting defendant to attend oral permission hearing); *R (Adriano) v Surrey County Council* [2002] EWHC 2471 (Admin) [2003] Env LR 559 at [51] (criticising lack of "member involvement in the preparation of the defendant's response to this judicial review", "leading counsel was instructed by Officers to submit that the Local Waste Plan should be construed to precisely the opposite effect" to what "councillors had made ... perfectly clear" was their wish when adopting the plan).

10.2 **ADR/mediation.**[57] Alternative dispute resolution (ADR) and mediation are said to have an important role in public law. The Courts may encourage recourse to ADR in appropriate cases, but in truth the nature of public authority functions and responsibilities mean that, absent voluntary pragmatic action, there may be little alternative to the Court ruling on a contested issue of public law.

10.2.1 **ADR/mediation and active case-management.** CPR 1.4 (active case management including "encouraging the parties to use an alternative dispute resolution procedure if the court considers that appropriate and facilitating the use of such procedure" and "helping the parties to settle the whole or part of the case").

10.2.2 **Guidance on ADR/mediation.** *R (Cowl) v Plymouth City Council* [2001] EWCA Civ 1935 [2002] 1 WLR 803 (closure of a residential home) at [1] (Lord Woolf CJ: "even in disputes between public authorities and the members of the public for whom they are responsible, insufficient attention is paid to the paramount importance of avoiding litigation whenever this is possible" and "the contribution alternative dispute resolution can make to resolving disputes in a manner which both meets the needs of the parties and the public and saves time, expense and stress"), [2] ("The courts should ... make appropriate use of their ample powers under the CPR to ensure that the parties try to resolve the dispute with the minimum involvement of the courts"), [3] ("the court may have to hold, on its own initiative, an inter partes hearing at which the parties can explain what steps they have taken to resolve the dispute without the involvement of the courts. In particular the parties should be asked why a complaints procedure or some other form of ADR has not been used or adapted to resolve or reduce the issues which are in dispute"); *Halsey v Milton Keynes General NHS Trust* [2004] EWCA Civ 576 [2004] 4 All ER 920 at [11] ("All members of the legal profession who conduct litigation should now routinely consider with their clients whether their disputes are suitable for ADR. But ... the court's role is to encourage, not to compel"), [9] ("to oblige truly unwilling parties to refer their disputes to mediation would be to impose an unacceptable obstruction on their right of access to the court"), [32]-[33] (describing a form of order requiring the parties to consider ADR and file a witness statement

---

[57] On ADR/mediation, see Martin Smith [2002] JR 148; Presiley Baxendale QC [2002] JR 212; Varda Bondy [2004] JR 306; Vardy Bondy, Margaret Doyle & Val Reid [2005] JR 220.

explaining why it was considered inappropriate).

10.2.3 ADR/mediation in judicial review. See Lord Chancellor's Department Consultation Paper (4/2001) on the Judicial Review Proposed Pre-Action Protocol (March 2001) para 5 and Annex A (Law Commission's paper); *Clark v University of Lincolnshire and Humberside* [2000] 1 WLR 1988 at [10] (mediation successful in dispute between student and university); *R (Lloyd) v Barking and Dagenham London Borough Council* (2001) 4 CCLR 27 at [14] (CA granting permission to appeal but expecting the parties' "undertakings to engage in mediation availing themselves if they are requested of the Court's ADR service with a view to compromising all of the outstanding issues or at least of reducing the differences between them so as to limit the eventual appeal to the true and essential areas of dispute"); *R (Lloyd) v Dagenham London Borough Council* [2001] EWCA Civ 533 (2001) 4 CCLR 196 at [12]-[13] (ADR having failed because mediation had begun from "entrenched positions"); *R (Arca) v Cumbria County Council* [2003] EWHC 232 (Admin) at [21] (urging the parties to enter into discussions and seek to avoid further litigation); *Halsey v Milton Keynes General NHS Trust* [2004] EWCA Civ 576 [2004] 4 All ER 920 at [7] (describing Government pledge 23.3.01 that "Government Departments and agencies" made "commitments" that ADR "will be considered and used in all suitable cases wherever the other party accepts it") [34]-[35] (no special rule when considering ADR and public bodies).

10.2.4 Costs and non-pursuit of ADR/mediation.<18.1.6>.

10.3 Claimant's duty of candour. Judicial review claimants have always been under an important duty to make full and frank disclosure to the Court of material facts, and known impediments to judicial review (eg. alternative remedy, delay, adverse authority, statutory ouster). Before the CPR, this was policed by the right to set aside permission granted without notice. Under CPR 54, although a candour duty remains, defendants and third parties are directly protected by provision for sending a letter of response and lodging an acknowledgment of service.

10.3.1 Claimant's duty of candour.[58] *Cocks v Thanet District Council* [1983] 2 AC 286, 294G (need for "frank disclosure of all relevant facts"); *R v Leeds City Council, ex p Hendry* (1994) 6 Admin LR 439, 444D ("fundamental importance that applications for judicial review should be made with full disclosure of all material available"); *R (Gillan) v Commissioner of Police of the Metropolis* [2004] EWCA Civ 1067 [2005] QB 388 (CA) at [54] ("the general obligation on parties conducting judicial review proceedings to do so openly"); *R (Madan) v Secretary of State for the Home Department* [2007] EWCA Civ 770 [2007] 1 WLR 2891 at [17] (importance of candour where immigration removal challenged and injunction sought); *R v Wirral Metropolitan Borough Council, ex p Bell* (1995) 27 HLR 234, 238-239 (refusing to dismiss permission application for serious non-disclosure alone since notice to defendant meant no prejudice); *R v Durham County Council, ex p Huddleston* [2000] Env LR D20 (adequate disclosure where defendant's letter exhibited in claimant's bundle); *R (F) v Head Teacher of Addington High School* [2003] EWHC 228 (Admin) (wasted costs ordered against claimant's solicitors where grounds not provided to defendant and defendant's letter not drawn to attention of permission judge, and so misleading impression given as to defendant's inaction); *R (I) v Secretary of State for the Home Department* [2007] EWHC 3103 (Admin) at [9] (claimant should have included immigration history, especially original immigration judge decision, in claim bundle).

---

[58] Daniel Kolinsky [1998] JR 23.

10.3.2 **Duty to up-date the Court.** *R (Tshikangu) v Newham London Borough Council* [2001] EWHC Admin 92 at [23] (duty to inform court of "material change in circumstances" or if claimant "no longer needed judicial review").

10.3.3 **Aspects of candour (pre-CPR).** *R v Secretary of State for the Home Department, ex p Li Bin Shi* [1995] COD 135 (duty to cite adverse authority); *R v Cornwall County Council, ex p Huntington* [1992] 3 All ER 566, 576f-g (duty to point out existence of ouster clause in claim form); *R v Law Society, ex p Bratsky Lesopromyshlenny Complex* [1995] COD 216 (duty to identify alternative remedy); *R v Lloyd's of London, ex p Briggs* (1993) 5 Admin LR 698, 707D (duty to point out delay and give reason to extend time).

10.3.4 **Pre-CPR 54: setting aside permission for non-disclosure.** *R v Secretary of State for the Home Department, ex p Ketowoglo* The Times 6th April 1992 (affidavit misleading as to facts); *R v General Medical Council, ex p Chadha* 17th May 1996 unrep. (inaccurate and misleading affidavit); *R v Metropolitan Police Force Disciplinary Tribunal, ex p Lawrence* The Times 13th July 1999 (non-disclosure of date and nature of disciplinary hearing); *R v Bromley London Borough Council, ex p Barker* [2001] Env LR 1 (insufficiently candid as to delay); *R (Tshikangu) v Newham London Borough Council* [2001] EWHC Admin 92 (setting aside permission at the substantive hearing, because claimant had not informed court at permission stage that no longer needed judicial review); *R v Bromley London Borough Council, ex p Barker* [2001] Env LR 1 (permission set aside, at substantive hearing); *R v Secretary of State for the Home Department, ex p Beecham* [1996] Imm AR 87, 89 (discussing position where "innocent misrepresentation").

10.3.5 **Other (pre-CPR) responses to non-disclosure.** *R v Wealden District Council, ex p Pinnegar* [1996] COD 64 (setting aside interim prohibiting order, which could not conceive judge would have made had he known of the relevant facts not disclosed to him); *R v Leeds City Council, ex p Hendry* (1994) 6 Admin LR 439 (at substantive hearing, remedy refused for non-disclosure at permission stage); *R v Liverpool City Council, ex p Filla* [1996] COD 24 (claimant refused costs of judicial review proceedings which had become moot post-permission, because of serious breaches of duty of disclosure when applying for permission; emphasising the need of the Court to be able to rely on the claimant's solicitors); *R v Secretary of State for the Home Office, ex p Shahina Begum* [1995] COD 176 (wasted costs order made against solicitor and barrister, for failure to put Treasury Solicitors' letter (and enclosures) before the Court (despite a request to do so) and refusal to send them the bundle).

10.4 **Defendant/interested party's duty of candour.**[59] A defendant public authority and its lawyers owe a vital duty to make full and fair disclosure of relevant material. That should include: (1) due diligence in investigating what material is available; (2) disclosure which is relevant or assists the claimant, including on some as yet unpleaded ground; and (3) disclosure at the permission stage if permission is resisted. An interested party is also under a duty of candour. A main reason why disclosure is not ordered in judicial review is because Courts trust public authorities to discharge this self-policing duty, which is why such anxious concern is expressed where it transpires that they have not done so.

---

[59] This paragraph in a previous edition was cited in *Chan Mei Yiu Paddy v Secretary of State for Justice (No.2)* [2008] 3 HKC 182 at [46] (Saunders J); also *Capital Rich Development Ltd v Town Planning Board* [2007] HKCU 90 at [51].

10.4.1 **Defendant's duty of candour.**[60] *R (Quark Fishing Ltd) v Secretary of State for Foreign and Commonwealth Affairs* [2002] EWCA Civ 1409 at [50] (Laws LJ: "there is ... a very high duty on public authority respondents, not least central government, to assist the court with full and accurate explanations of all the facts relevant to the issue the court must decide"); *Belize Alliance of Conservation Non-Governmental Organisations v Department of the Environment* [2004] UKPC 6 [2004] Env LR 761 at [86] (Lord Walker: "A [defendant] authority owes a duty to the court to cooperate and to make candid disclosure, by way of [witness statement], of the relevant facts and (so far as they are not apparent from contemporaneous documents which have been disclosed) the reasoning behind the decision challenged in the judicial review proceedings"); *R v Lancashire County Council, ex p Huddleston* [1986] 2 All ER 941, 945g (judicial review "to be conducted with all the cards face upwards on the table"), 947e (defendant "should set out fully what they did and why, *so far as is necessary, fully and fairly to meet the challenge*"); *R v Secretary of State for Education, ex p S* [1995] ELR 71, 85D ("It was of course incumbent on the Secretary of State in giving his decision to explain adequately how he has come to his conclusion"); *R v Kensington and Chelsea Royal Borough Council, ex p Assiter* The Times 20th August 1996 (incumbent on authority to explain to the court the basis of decision); *Fayed* <17.4.5>.

10.4.2 **Opportunities for candour.** <19.1.5> (letter of response); <19.3> (summary grounds); <22.1.3> (detailed response/evidence); <2.5.7> (whether non-appearing/ non-adversarial defendant should respond).

10.4.3 **Defendant's candour: beyond the pleaded case.** *R v Barnsley Metropolitan Borough Council, ex p Hook* [1976] 1 WLR 1052, 1058C-D (claimant permitted to raise matters not in original grounds, because: "It must be remembered that, in applications for [quashing orders], the [claimant] knows very little of what has happened behind the scenes. He only knows that a decision has been taken which is adverse to him, and he complains of it. His statement of grounds ... should not be treated as rigidly as a pleading in an ordinary civil action. If the Divisional Court give [permission] (as it did here) the practice is for the [defendant] to put on affidavits the full facts as known to them. The matter is then considered at large upon the affidavits. If there then appear to be other grounds on which [a quashing order] may be granted, the court can inquire into them without being bound by the grounds stated in the original statement. The Divisional Court will always look into the substance of the matter. So here"); *R v Waltham Forest London Borough Council, ex p Baxter* [1988] QB 419, 422A-B (Sir John Donaldson MR commenting that: "the council rightly responded with additional information, as a result of which four principal issues emerged").

10.4.4 **Interested parties and candour.** *Belize Alliance of Conservation Non-Governmental Organisations v Department of the Environment* [2004] UKPC 6 [2004] Env LR 761 at [87] (Lord Walker, explaining that duty of candour also applicable to third party developer, since in effect partners with the defendant Department in the development project).

10.4.5 **Praising defendants for candour.** *R (Bancoult) v Secretary of State for the Foreign and Commonwealth Office* [2001] QB 1067 at [63] (commending "the wholly admirable conduct of the relevant government servants and counsel instructed for the [defendants] who have examined and then disclosed without cavil or argument all the material documents contained in the files of government departments, some of which ... are embarrassing and worse. This has exemplified a high tradition of cooperation between the executive and the judiciary in the doing of justice, and upholding the rule of law"); *Anisminic Ltd v Foreign Compensation Commission*

---

[60] Jonathan Auburn [1999] JR 156; Michael Fordham [2007] JR 195.

[1969] 2 AC 147, 171G-H (albeit no duty to give reasons, FCC "acted with complete propriety" in giving them), 199D-E ("it very properly disclosed its reasons"); *R v Army Board of the Defence Council, ex p Anderson* [1992] QB 169, 179D (paying tribute to the "total candour" of the defendant's affidavit); *R v Secretary of State for the Home Department, ex p Launder* [1997] 1 WLR 839, 856H (Secretary of State having "decided, in a commendable departure from the normal procedure in extradition cases, to give reasons for his decision"); *M v Home Office* [1994] 1 AC 377, 425H (privilege "commendably" waived).

10.4.6 Criticising defendants for lack of candour. *R (S) v Secretary of State for the Home Department* [2006] EWHC 1111 (Admin) at [117] (indemnity costs awarded where defendant providing no grounds, evidence or explanation); *R (Quark Fishing Ltd) v Secretary of State for Foreign and Commonwealth Affairs* [2002] EWCA Civ 1409 at [55] (defendant having "fallen short of those high standards of candour which are routinely adhered to by government departments faced with proceedings for judicial review"), [68] ("the approach taken to the public decisions that had to be made fell unhappily short of the high standards of fairness and openness which is now routinely attained by British government departments"); *R (Rashid) v Secretary of State for the Home Department* [2005] EWCA Civ 744 [2005] INLR 550 at [52] (criticising failure to cooperate and make candid disclosure of relevant facts and reasoning behind challenged decision); *Central Broadcasting Services Ltd v Attorney General of Trinidad and Tobago* [2006] UKPC 35 [2006] 1 WLR 2891 at [26]-[27] (non-disclosure of relevant facts), [36] ("highly regrettable" that lower courts allowed to proceed on false premise); *R v London Borough of Lambeth, ex p Campbell* (1994) 26 HLR 618, 622 ("lamentable" failure of duty "to disclose all the facts which it ought reasonably to appreciate are relevant to the issue or issues arising in a judicial review"); *Jordan Abiodun Iye v Secretary of State for the Home Department* [1994] Imm AR 63, 67 ("unsatisfactory" inability "to make clear" Secretary of State's position).

10.4.7 Duty not to be selective. *Lancashire County Council v Taylor* [2005] EWCA Civ 284 [2005] 1 WLR 266 (discussing evidence on HRA justification and legislative compatibility) at [60] ("Departments of state need ... to bear in mind that they have an advantage in this field. They have access to materials to which other parties have no access or which it would be difficult and expensive for them to search out. But axiomatically an exercise of this kind, if it is to be carried out at all, must disclose the unwelcome along with the helpful"; "the cautionary reminder that if research of this kind is to be placed before the court, it cannot be selective in what it tends to show"); *R (National Association of Health Stores) v Secretary of State for Health* [2005] EWCA Civ 154 at [47] (Government not entitled to withhold ministerial briefing and give secondary account instead); <17.1.4(B)> (need to exhibit primary evidence).

11.1 Use of case-law
11.2 Academic commentary/comparative case-law

11.1 Use of case-law. The same general rules of precedent and citation apply in judicial review as in other proceedings. The Court is bound by the result and decisive reasoning of a higher court's substantive decision and will follow a same-level decision unless satisfied that it is plainly wrong. Permission decisions will not generally assist. Judicial review authorities are frequently illustrative or helpful, rather than technically binding, as case-specific applications of flexible principles. The best way to use the cases is as working examples which guide, rather than a straitjacket which constrains.

11.1.1 Proper citation practice: advocates' duties.[61]
(A) GENERAL NEED FOR SELECTIVITY. *Practice Direction (Citation of Authorities)* [2001] 1 WLR 1001 at [2] (important that courts not "burdened with a weight of inappropriate and unnecessary authority"); *R (Countryside Alliance) v Attorney General* [2006] EWCA Civ 817 [2007] QB 305 (CA) at [3] (criticising excessive number of authorities and absence of consolidated index); *R (C) v Secretary of State for Justice* [2008] EWCA Civ 882 at [1] (number of authorities and lack of focus); <11.1.10> (warning against excessive citation of Strasbourg authorities); *R (Schmelz) v Immigration Appeal Tribunal* [2004] EWCA Civ 29 at [24] (criticising excessive and irrelevant authorities).
(B) DUTY TO CITE ADVERSE AUTHORITY. *Practice Direction (Citation of Authorities)* [2001] 1 WLR 1001 at [4] (emphasising "the duty of advocates to draw the attention of the court to any authority not cited by an opponent which is adverse to the case being advanced"); *Re V (A Child) (Care Proceedings: Human Rights Claims)* [2004] EWCA Civ 54 [2004] 1 All ER 997 at [103] ("Counsel has a plain duty to bring to the attention of the court any authority, which may be on the point, particularly if it is contrary to the argument which counsel is advancing").
(C) NEED TO IDENTIFY THE PROPOSITION OF LAW. *Practice Direction (Citation of Authorities)* [2001] 1 WLR 1001 at [8.1] ("Advocates ... required to state, in respect of each authority that they wish to cite, the proposition of law that the authority demonstrates, and the parts of the judgment that support that proposition"), [8.4] (statement to "demonstrate, in the context of the advocate's argument, the relevance of the authority or authorities to that argument and that the citation is necessary for a proper presentation of that argument").
(D) NEED REASON FOR MULTIPLE CITATION ON SINGLE PROPOSITION. *Practice Direction (Citation of Authorities)* [2001] 1 WLR 1001 at [8.1] ("If it is sought to cite more than one authority in support of a given proposition, advocates must state the reason for taking that course"), [8.4] (statement to "demonstrate, in the context of the advocate's argument, the relevance of the authority or authorities to that argument and that the citation is necessary for a proper presentation of that argument").
(E) PROPOSITIONS/REASONS TO BE IN SKELETON/NOTICE. *Practice Direction (Citation of Authorities)* [2001] 1 WLR 1001 at [8.2] ("The demonstration referred to in para 8.1 will be required to be contained in any skeleton argument and in any appellant's or respondent's notice in respect of each authority referred to in that skeleton or notice"), [8.4] ("The statements referred to in para 8.1 should not materially add to the length of submissions or of skeleton arguments, but should be sufficient to demonstrate, in the context of the advocate's argument, the relevance of the authority or authorities to that argument and that the citation is

---

[61] Jonathan Auburn [2001] JR 142.

necessary for a proper presentation of that argument").

(F) CERTIFICATION IN BUNDLES/LISTS OF AUTHORITIES.*Practice Direction (Citation of Authorities)* [2001] 1 WLR 1001 at [8.3] ("Any bundle or list of authorities prepared for the use of any court must in future bear a certification by the advocate responsible for arguing the case that the requirements of this paragraph have been complied with in respect of each authority included"); *R (Prokopp) v London Underground Ltd* [2003] EWCA Civ 961 [2004] Env LR 170 at [90] (Buxton LJ, emphasising the requirement of certification); CPR 52PD para 15.11(5) (need for certification of bundle of authorities in the CA) <23.2.2>.

(G) CITING "ESTABLISHED LAW" CASES: NEED JUSTIFICATION. *Practice Direction (Citation of Authorities)* [2001] 1 WLR 1001 at [7.1] ("Courts will in future pay particular attention ... to any indication given by the court delivering the judgment [cited] that it was seen by that court as only applying decided law to the facts of the particular case; or otherwise as not extending or adding to the existing law"), [7.2] ("Advocates who seek to cite a judgment that contains indications of the type referred to in para 7.1 will be required to justify their decision to cite the case").

(H) ARGUABILITY DECISIONS.*Practice Direction (Citation of Authorities)* [2001] 1 WLR 1001 at [6.1] (certain judgments "may not in future be cited before any court unless it clearly indicates that it purports to establish a new principle or to extend the present law", in future cases in "the form of an express statement to that effect"), [6.2] (para 6.1 applying to "decisions on applications that only decide that the application is arguable ..."); *R (England) v Tower Hamlets London Borough Council* [2006] EWCA Civ 1742 at [17] (direction given); *R (Ipsea Ltd) v Secretary of State for Education and Skills* [2003] EWCA Civ 7 [2003] ELR 393 at [1] (novel point, fully argued); *R (L) v Secretary of State for the Home Department* [2003] EWCA Civ 25 [2003] 1 WLR 1230 (direction given); *R (Pharis) v Secretary of State for the Home Department* [2004] EWCA Civ 654 [2004] 1 WLR 2590 at [22] (direction given); *R (Securiplan plc) v Security Industry Authority* [2008] EWHC 1762 (Admin) (direction given); *R (William Hill Organisation Ltd) v Batley and Dewsbury Betting Licensing Committee* [2004] EWHC 1201 (Admin) (direction where judgment at substantive hearing but only one party participating).

(I) CITING COMPARATIVE CASE-LAW. <11.2.7>.

(J) NEUTRAL CITATION OF JUDGMENTS. *Practice Direction (Judgments: Form and Citation)* [2001] 1 WLR 194; and *Practice Direction (Judgments: Neutral Citations)* [2002] 1 WLR 346. The form is [2008] EWHC 1 (Admin), [2008] EWCA Civ 1 and [2008] UKHL 1.

(K) OFFICIAL REPORTS/ ELECTRONIC REPORTS.*Practice Direction (Judgments: Form and Citation)* [2001] 1 WLR 194 at [3.1]-[3.2] (cite official Law Reports ahead of other series; electronic reproductions permissible if legible and non-garbled).

(L) PROPER TRANSCRIPTS, AND NOT SUMMARIES.*Practice Direction (Supreme Court: Judgments) (No.2)* [1999] 1 WLR 1, 2B and *Practice Note (Court of Appeal)* [1999] 1 WLR 1027 at [9.6.5] (reference to unreported judgment must be approved official transcript if available); *Hamblin v Field* The Times 26th April 2000 (deploring the use of summaries instead of the judgments); *R v Bolsover District Council, ex p Pepper* [2001] LGR 43 at [25] (Keene J, commenting on the sole reliance on summaries from COD: "I do say, for the guidance of counsel, that it is important that those seeking to rely upon such decisions should seek to obtain the full judgments in cases where only a summary is available in the reports").

(M) CITATION/BUNDLES OF AUTHORITIES IN THE COURT OF APPEAL. <23.2.2>.

11.1.2 **Caution as to precedent in public law.** *R (Greenpeace Ltd) v Secretary of State for Trade and Industry* [2007] EWHC 311 (Admin) [2007] Env LR 623 at [61] ("Judgments are not to be construed as though they were enactments of general application); *R v Inland Revenue Commissioners, ex p Unilever Plc* [1996] STC 681, 690f ("precedent should act as a guide not a cage"); *R v Secretary of State for Transport, ex p Richmond upon Thames London Borough Council (No.4)* [1996] 1 WLR 1460, 1472E ("It is always unwise to transfer principles established in one branch of administrative law too slavishly into another"); *R v Ministry for Agriculture Fisheries & Food, ex p Hamble Fisheries (Offshore) Ltd* [1995] 2 All ER 714, 728j (case-law approached with "caution, looking not for analogy but for principle"); *R (Wooder) v Feggetter* [2002] EWCA Civ 554 [2003] QB 219 at [42] (Sedley LJ, warning in the context of reasons against "treating the categories so far acknowledged in the reactive and exploratory growth of the common law as exhaustive. Rather than try to fit given shapes into pre-formed slots like toddlers in a playgroup ..., the courts have to continue the process of working out and refining, case by case, the relevant principles of fairness").

11.1.3 **Cases turning on their facts.** *R v Independent Television Commission, ex p TSW Broadcasting Ltd* [1994] 2 LRC 414, 430d (Lord Templeman: "Of course in judicial review proceedings, as in any other proceedings, everything depends on the facts"), applied in *R v Inland Revenue Commissioners, ex p Unilever Plc* [1996] STC 681, 686a; *R (PD) v West Midlands and North West Mental Health Review Tribunal* [2004] EWCA Civ 311 at [8] ("The natural reaction of the lawyer to any problem is to look for case precedent and this is true even where the issue is essentially one of fact. In such circumstances precedent can be helpful in focussing the mind on the relevant issues and producing consistency of approach. In a case such as the present, however, [where] the search is for the reaction of the fair-minded and informed observer ... citation of authorities may cloud rather than clarify perception. The court must be careful when looking at case precedent not to permit it to drive common sense out of the window"); *R v Secretary of State for the Home Department, ex p Ku* [1995] QB 364 (rejecting previous authority as resting on finding of fact with which the Court disagreed); *R v Chief Constable of the Merseyside Police, ex p Merrill* [1989] 1 WLR 1077, 1084H-1085A ("Judgments apply specifically to the facts of the case under consideration and only incidentally may have more general application"); *R v Central Criminal Court, ex p Hutchinson* [1996] COD 14 (reference to previous cases on highly variable context of legality of search warrants unhelpful); *Ridge v Baldwin* [1964] AC 40, 64-65 (Lord Reid, warning as to "opinions [that] have sometimes been expressed to the effect that natural justice is so vague as to be practically meaningless. But I would regard these as tainted by the perennial fallacy that because something cannot be cut and dried or nicely weighed or measured therefore it does not exist"); *R v Secretary of State for the Home Department, ex p Bobby Gangadia* [1994] Imm AR 341, 345 (alternative remedy cases "which depend entirely on their facts get reported in the Immigration Appeal Reports as if they laid down some new principles of law"); *Henry Boot Homes Ltd v Bassetlaw District Council* [2002] EWCA Civ 983 [2002] 4 PLR 108 at [56] (declining to adopt an "absolute .. proposition" regarding legitimate expectation); cf. *Robinson v Secretary of State for Northern Ireland* [2002] UKHL 32 at [33] (Lord Hoffmann: "A judicial decision must ... rest on `reasons that in their generality and their neutrality transcend any immediate result that is involved'").

11.1.4 **Older cases.** <2.1.5(A)> (historical context); *Palacegate Properties Ltd v Camden London Borough Council* [2000] 4 PLR 59, 79F ("clear that in the context we are presently called on to consider, the earlier decisions in the planning field upon which [Counsel] relied have to be regarded with a degree of care"); *R v Inland Revenue Commissioners, ex p National Federation of Self-Employed and Small Businesses Ltd* [1982] AC 617, 639H-640D (Lord Diplock: "Any judicial statements on matters of public law if made before 1950 are likely to be a misleading guide to what the law is today"), 656E-H (Lord Roskill: "today of little assistance"); *Council of Civil Service Unions v Minister for the Civil Service* [1985] AC 374, 400D-E (declining to follow a "case ... decided long before the modern development of judicial review").

11.1.5 **Pre-CPR authority: beware.** Cf. *Vinos v Marks & Spencer Plc* [2001] 3 All ER 784 at [17] (May LJ: "The CPR are a new procedural code, and the question for this court in this case

115

concerns the interpretation and application of the relevant provisions of the new procedural code as they stand untrammelled by the weight of authority that accumulated under the former rules"); *Biguzzi v Rank Leisure Plc* [1999] 1 WLR 1926 (where CPR applicable, old authorities on matters of civil procedure generally no longer relevant); *Thurrock Borough Council v Secretary of State for the Environment, Transport and the Regions* The Times 20th December 2000 at [23] ("decisions of courts under the former procedural regime are very often not of much assistance in relation to decisions that have to be made under the new regime ... [and] on occasion they may be positively misleading"); *R (Melton) v School Organisation Committee* [2001] EWHC Admin 245 (approach to delay no less rigorous than it had been under the former RSC Order 53).

11.1.6 **Permission decisions.**[62]

(A) GENERAL. <11.1.1(H)> (*Practice Direction* describing advocates' duty in respect of judgments on "applications attended by one party only" or "applications that only decide that the application is arguable"); *R v Hammersmith and Fulham London Borough Council, ex p Burkett* [2002] UKHL 23 [2002] 1 WLR 1593 at [41] ("judgments on applications for permission to apply for judicial review ... are *generally* not regarded as authoritative", referring to *Clark v University of Lincolnshire and Humberside* (see [2000] 1 WLR 1988 at [43]); *Bugg v DPP* [1993] QB 473, 506D-E (Woolf LJ: "caution should be exercised in seeking to rely on judgments given for applications for [permission]");.

(B) COURT OF APPEAL PERMISSION DECISIONS. *R v Secretary of State for the Home Department, ex p Syed Majid Kazmi (No.2)* [1995] Imm AR 73, 82-83 (Dyson J, treating CA decision on leave (permission) for judicial review as binding on him); *R v Secretary of State for the Home Department, ex p Manvinder Singh* [1996] Imm AR 41, 51-52 (discussing CA permission decision regarding arguability; upheld at [1996] COD 476); *R v City and County of Swansea, ex p Granada Hospitality Ltd* 13th November 1998 unrep. (Richards J: "I ... consider myself to be bound by what was said in *ex p Woods* since, although the [Court of Appeal] was concerned only with a renewed application for [permission], it heard argument *inter partes* and the observations that I have quoted formed part of the *ratio* for the decision"); *R v Immigration Appeal Tribunal, ex p Anderson* The Times 22nd March 2000 (CA permission decision treated as binding save in exceptional circumstances); *R v Newham London Borough Council, ex p Lumley* (2001) 33 HLR 124 at [43] (CA decision on permission application as not being binding but highly persuasive); cf. *Clark v University of Lincolnshire and Humberside* [2000] 1 WLR 1988 at [43] (CA decisions on permission to appeal not "binding authorities" but "are at best only of persuasive weight"); *R (S) v Secretary of State for the Home Department* [2003] EWHC 1941 (Admin) (2004) 7 CCLR 32 at [8] (CA decision on permission to appeal treated as persuasive).

11.1.7 **Bindingness of same-level decisions.** *R v Greater Manchester Coroner, ex p Tal* [1985] QB 67, 81A-B (High Court judge "will follow a decision of another judge of first instance, unless he is convinced that that judgment is wrong"); *Hertfordshire County Council v National Grid Gas Plc* [2007] EWHC 2535 (Admin) [2008] 1 All ER 1137 at [55] (test for departure not met); *R v Governor of Brockhill Prison, ex p Evans* [1997] QB 443 (departure); *R (W) v Lambeth London Borough Council* [2002] EWCA Civ 613 [2002] 2 All ER 901 (CA) at [29], [73] (CA departing from earlier incorrect Court of Appeal decisions); *R v R* [2003] EWCA Crim 2199 [2004] 1 WLR 490 at [32] (explaining the *per incuriam* principle: "a decision given in the absence of relevant information cannot be safely relied on", as here where "only the appellant was represented" and cases not cited were "important to the proper consideration of [the] issue"), [33] (2-judge CA overruling 3-judge CA decision as per incuriam); *Horton v Sadler*

---

[62] Kate Olley [1999] JR 235.

[2006] UKHL 27 [2006] 2 WLR 1346 (HL departing from previous decision where producing criticism and anomalies and restricting development of the law); *Cave v Robinson Jarvis & Rolf (a firm)* [2001] EWCA Civ 245 [2002] 1 WLR 581 (two-judge CA decision treated as binding on full CA).

11.1.8 Precedent and basic human rights. *Lewis v Attorney-General of Jamaica* [2001] 2 AC 50, 75C (where subject's life at stake "rigid adherence to a rule of stare decisis is not justified"); *Ifzal Ali v Secretary of State for the Home Department* [1994] Imm AR 69, 77 (Evans LJ, accepting that "the doctrine of precedent should not apply with its full rigour [where] the liberty of the subject is involved").

11.1.9 The HRA and authority/precedent.[63]
(A) PRE-HRA CASE-LAW NOT BINDING UNDER HRA.*Kay v Lambeth London Borough Council* [2006] UKHL 10 [2006] 2 AC 465 at [45] (not bound by pre-HRA authority); *C Plc v P* [2006] EWHC 1226 (Ch) [2006] Ch 549 at [80] (not bound by pre-HRA HL decisions); *R (H) v Secretary of State for the Home Department* [2003] UKHL 59 [2004] 2 AC 253 at [27] (endorsing departure from pre-HRA HL decision); *R v Lambert* [2001] UKHL 37 [2002] 2 AC 545 at [81] (given new HRA s.3 duty of interpretation, "clear that the courts are not bound by previous authority as to what the statute means"); *R (K) v Camden and Islington Health Authority* [2001] EWCA Civ 240 [2002] QB 198 at [19] (HRA ss.2-3 "override the respect that would otherwise have to be given to binding precedent"); *NHS Trust A v M* [2001] Fam 348 at [18] (post-HRA, "no longer bound by the decision in *Bland*'s case"); *R (Shields) v Crown Court at Liverpool* [2001] EWHC Admin 90 [2001] UKHRR 610 at [15] (DC asking whether Supreme Court Act 1981 s.29(3) having a different meaning under the HRA); *Greenfield v Irwin* [2001] EWCA Civ 113 [2001] 1 WLR 1279 (CA examining whether HL decision incompatible with the HRA).
(B) BINDING DOMESTIC AUTHORITY ON HRA:ECHR.*Mendoza v Ghaidan* [2002] EWCA Civ 1533 [2003] Ch 380 (CA) at [6] ("a court is bound by any decision within the normal hierarchy of domestic authority as to the meaning of an article of the Convention, in the same way as it is bound by such a decision as to the meaning of purely domestic law") (HL is [2004] UKHL 30 [2004] 2 AC 557); *R (Williamson) v Secretary of State for Education and Employment* [2002] EWCA Civ 1926 [2003] QB 1300 at [41] ("the court ... is bound by any decision within the normal hierarchy of domestic authority as to the meaning of an article of the [ECHR], in the same way as it is bound by such a decision as to the meaning of purely domestic law") (HL is at [2005] UKHL 15 [2005] 2 AC 246); *R (Bright) v Central Criminal Court* [2001] 1 WLR 662, 682E-H (inappropriate to re-examine and reinterpret decisions of the ECtHR which have authoritatively been examined by HL or CA); *Kay v Lambeth London Borough Council* [2006] UKHL 10 [2006] 2 AC 465 at [43] (domestic court bound, in the usual way, by post-HRA decision of the HL or CA as to the content of the ECHR, even if inconsistent with later ECtHR decision); *Doherty v Birmingham City Council* [2008] UKHL 57 [2008] 3 WLR 636 (HL declining to overrule itself, notwithstanding ECtHR decision applying minority approach from previous case); *R (RJM) v Secretary of State for Work and Pensions* [2007] EWCA Civ 614 [2007] 1 WLR 3067 at [21]-[22] (proper concession enabling reliance on ECtHR decision overriding binding domestic case).
(C) HRA s.2 DUTY TO HAVE REGARD TO STRASBOURG JURISPRUDENCE. <9.1.14>.

11.1.10 Citing Strasbourg authority: the need for discipline.[64] *Williams v Cowell* [2000] 1

---

[63] Neil Sheldon [2001] JR 208.

[64] Michael Fordham [2000] JR 139.

WLR 187, 198D-E (wrong "to turn a judicial hearing of a particular case into an international human rights seminar... There should only be put before the court that part of the researched material which is reasonably required for the resolution of the particular [case]"); *Daniels v Walker* [2000] 1 WLR 1382, 1386F-1387C ("it is essential that counsel, and those who instruct counsel, take a responsible attitude as to when it is right to raise a Human Rights Act point"); *Barclays Bank Plc v Ellis* 9th August 2000 unrep. at [37] (Counsel relying on HRA argument under a "duty to have available for the information of the court any material in terms of decisions of the European Court of Human Rights upon which they wish to rely or which will help the court in its adjudication"); *Re V (A Child)* [2004] EWCA Civ 1575 [2005] UKHRR 144 at [33] (family judges needing to avoid irrelevant human rights arguments); *R (Bright) v Central Criminal Court* [2001] 1 WLR 662, 679D-F (lamenting "vast and increasingly lengthy" ECtHR citations "simply repeating in different language long standing and well understood principles of the common law"); *R (London Borough of Hounslow) v School Admission Appeals Panel for the London Borough of Hounslow* [2002] EWCA Civ 900 [2002] 1 WLR 3147 at [62] (HRA adding nothing in the context of schools admissions); *R (W) v Metropolitan Police Commissioner* [2005] EWHC 1586 (Admin) [2005] 1 WLR 3706 at [21] ("the resolution of points of statutory interpretation ... can very often be achieved without any need to refer to Strasbourg law at all"); *R (Williamson) v Secretary of State for Education and Employment* [2002] EWCA Civ 1926 [2003] QB 1300 at [72] (Court directing further oral hearing because discovering line of Strasbourg authority which was considered potentially relevant and which had not been put before the Court), [183] (new point decisive) (HL is at [2005] UKHL 15 [2005] 2 AC 246).

11.1.11 Other. *R v James* [2006] EWCA Crim 14 [2006] QB 588 (since now open to PC to overrule HL, also now open to CA exceptionally to treat PC as having done so); *Kadhim v Housing Benefit Board, London Borough of Brent* [2001] QB 955 (discussing meaning of "ratio"; and explaining that court not bound by proposition of law assumed by an earlier court without argument); *R v Simpson* [2003] EWCA Crim 1499 [2004] QB 118 at [27] ("The rules as to precedent reflect the practice of the courts and have to be applied bearing in mind that their objective is to assist in the administration of justice. They are of considerable importance because of their role in achieving the appropriate degree of certainty as to the law. This is an important requirement of any system of justice. The principles should not, however, be regarded as so rigid that they cannot develop in order to meet contemporary needs").

11.2 Academic commentary/comparative case-law

As especially befits a dynamic and developing area of law, judicial review Courts draw where appropriate on relevant academic analysis and comparative jurisprudence.

11.2.1 Academic commentary: general. *R v Shayler* [2002] UKHL 11 [2003] 1 AC 247 at [76] (Lord Hope: "much useful guidance on the difference between the traditional grounds of judicial review and the proportionality approach can be found in the work of academic public lawyers on this subject"); *R v G* [2003] UKHL 50 [2004] 1 AC 1034 at [34] (Lord Bingham: "a decision which attracts reasoned and outspoken criticism by the leading scholars of the day, respected as authorities in the field, must command attention"); *Spiliada Maritime Corporation v Cansulex Ltd* [1987] AC 460, 488B-C (referring to academic commentators as "pilgrims with us on the endless road to unattainable perfection"); *R v Local Commissioner for Administration for the North & East Area of England, ex p Bradford Metropolitan City Council* [1979] QB 287, 311F-H (Lord Denning MR, describing the Courts' indebtedness to "the writings of the teachers of law"); *Kleinwort Benson Ltd v Lincoln City Council* [1999] 2 AC 349, 378A (Lord Goff: "Nowadays [the judge] derives much assistance from academic writings in interpreting statutes and, more especially, the effect of reported cases").

11.2.2 **Judicial review: journals.** The leading academic journal on administrative law is *Public Law* (Sweet & Maxwell); the leading practitioner journal is *Judicial Review* (Hart Publishing).[65]

11.2.3 **Textbook commentary.** The leading textbook commentaries on administrative law are *De Smith's Judicial Review of Administrative Action* ; and *Wade and Forsyth, Administrative Law*.[66] See too *Craig, Administrative Law*; *Lewis, Judicial Remedies in Public Law* and *Supperstone and Goudie*.

11.2.4 **Expert legal evidence.** *R v Secretary of State for the Home Department, ex p Simms* [2000] 2 AC 115 (HL accepting evidence from a well-known solicitor as to the role of prisoners' access to the media in uncovering miscarriages of justice); *Poplar Housing and Regeneration Community Association Ltd v Donoghue* [2001] EWCA Civ 595 [2002] QB 48 at [56] (CA considering witness statements from two academics on the question of whether a housing association was exercising a public function for the purposes of the Human Rights Act).

11.2.5 **Significance of comparative jurisprudence.**[67] *Kleinwort Benson Ltd v Lincoln City Council* [1999] 2 AC 349, 378B (Lord Goff, referring to judges as having "regard, where appropriate, to decisions of judges in other jurisdictions"); *Practice Direction (Citation of Authorities)* [2001] 1 WLR 1001 at [9.1] ("Cases decided in other jurisdictions can, if properly used, be a valuable source of law in this jurisdiction"); Markesinis, "Our Debt to Europe: Past, Present and Future" in Markesinis (ed), *The Clifford Chance Millennium Lectures: The Coming Together of the Common Law and the Civil Law* at p.66 (referring to Lord Goff's statement in his Child Lecture, that: "we are bound to see an enrichment of our legal culture on an unparalleled scale through the increasing study of comparative law").

11.2.6 **Comparative jurisprudence: examples.** *R (Ullah) v Secretary of State for the Home Department* [2004] UKHL 26 [2004] 2 AC 323 at [23] (Lord Bingham, considering the reach of the HRA by reference to analysis including decisions of the Human Rights Chamber of Bosnia and Herzegovina, the Human Rights Committee of the UN, and the Supreme Court of Canada); *DPP v Hutchinson* [1990] 2 AC 783, 805F (United States and Australian authority providing "the fullest exploration and exposition of the principles governing the severability of legislative instruments"); *Rees v Crane* [1994] 2 AC 173, 191G-H; *R v Secretary of State for the Home Department, ex p O'Brien* (1996) 8 Admin LR 121 (DC), 134B-C (United States case-law "persuasive"); *In re Medicaments and Related Classes of Goods (No.2)* [2001] 1 WLR 700 (analysing the law of apparent bias by reference to the Strasbourg jurisprudence, together with that of the Commonwealth and Scotland); *Cullen v Chief Constable of the Royal Ulster Constabulary* [2003] UKHL 39 [2003] 1 WLR 1763 at [18] (reliance by minority in HL on comparative material), cf. [47] (Lord Hutton); *Re Deep Vein Thrombosis and Air Travel Group Litigation* [2005] UKHL 72 [2006] 1 AC 495 at [11] (in interpreting Convention, "assistance

---

[65] See Nicholas Bamforth's invaluable surveys of key academic articles: from 1995 at [1996] JR 41; 1996 at [1997] JR 38; 1997 at [1998] JR 111; 1998 at [1999] JR 134; for 1999 at [2000] JR 127; 2000 at [2001] JR 180; 2001 at [2002] JR 277; 2002 at [2003] JR 208; 2003/4 [2005] JR 174; 2005/6 [2008] JR 20.

[66] Both texts were recommended, together with this Handbook, in *Office of Fair Trading v IBA Health Ltd* [2004] EWCA Civ 142 [2004] 4 All ER 1103 at [89] (Carnwath LJ).

[67] Lord Lester QC [2001] JR 13; Jean-Marie Woehrling [2005] JR 311.

can and should be sought from relevant decisions of the courts of other Convention countries, but the weight to be given to them will depend upon the standing of the court concerned and the quality of the analysis"); *D v East Berkshire Community Health NHS Trust* [2005] UKHL 23 [2005] 2 AC 373 at [49] (Lord Bingham, referring to state liability position in France and Germany; also CA at [2003] EWCA Civ 1151 [2004] QB 558, considering New Zealand cases in context of negligence liability and child abuse investigation cases); *Anufrijeva v Southwark London Borough Council* [2003] EWCA Civ 1406 [2004] QB 1124 at [54] (CA referring to Indian authority (*Nilabathbehara v State of Orpassa* [1993] 2 SCC 746) as to role of public law damages); *Chester v Afshar* [2004] UKHL 41 [2004] 3 WLR 927 (HL heavily influenced by decision of High Court of Australia, in context of negligence and causation).

11.2.7 **Citing comparative case-law.** *Practice Direction (Citation of Authorities)* [2001] 1 WLR 1001 at [9.1] ("Cases decided in other jurisdictions can, if properly used, be a valuable source of law in this jurisdiction. At the same time, however, such authority should not be cited without proper consideration of whether it does indeed add to the existing body of law"), [9.2] ("In future, therefore, any advocate who seeks to cite an authority from another jurisdiction must (i) comply, in respect of that authority, with the rules set out in para 8 above; (ii) indicate in respect of each authority what that authority adds that is not to be found in authority in this jurisdiction; or, if there is said to be justification for adding to domestic authority, what that justification is; (iii) certify that there is no authority in this jurisdiction that precludes the acceptance by the court of the proposition that the foreign authority is said to establish"), [9.3] ("For the avoidance of doubt, paras 9.1 and 9.2 do not apply to cases decided in either the Court of Justice of the European Communities or the organs of the European Convention [of Human Rights]. Because of the status in English law of such authority, as provided by, respectively, section 3 of the European Communities Act 1972 and section 2(1) of the Human Rights Act 1998, such cases are covered by the earlier paragraphs of this Direction").

11.2.8 **Comparative public law: commentaries.**[68] The multitude of textbook sources include: Delaney, *Judicial Review of Administrative Action: A Comparative Analysis* (Round Hall, Sweet and Maxwell 2001); Markesinis (ed), *The Clifford Chance Millennium Lectures: The Coming Together of the Common Law and the Civil Law*; *Brown and Bell, French Administrative Law*; Allison, *A Continental Distinction in the Common Law* (OUP); Zamir and Zysblat, *Public Law in Israel* (1996); Sorabjee [1994] PL 39 (India).

11.2.9 **Cautious approach to comparative rights jurisprudence.**[69] *Sheldrake v Director of Public Prosecutions* [2004] UKHL 43 [2005] 1 AC 264 at [33] ("valuable insights from the reasoning of Commonwealth judges deciding issues under different human rights instruments", but "[s]ome caution is ... called for in considering different enactments decided under different

---

[68] Scotland: Tom Mullen [1996] JR 107, [1997] JR 102, [2002] JR 29, Timothy Straker QC [1998] JR 234; Northern Ireland: Brigid Hadfield [1996] JR 170; Australia: Karyl Nairn [1997] JR 173, Paul D Evans & Jennan A Ambikapathy [2001] JR 188, Lisa Busch [2006] JR 363; New Zealand: Michael Taggart [1997] JR 236, James Maurici [1999] JR 196, John Guess [2005] JR 334; Canada: Tim Costigan [1998] JR 102; South Africa: Andrew Henderson [1998] JR 174, [1999] JR 118; India: Soli Sorabjee [1999] JR 126, Madhav Khosla [2007] JR 191; Pakistan: Neil Moloney [1999] JR 201, [2000] JR 61; Hong Kong: Kate Olley [2003] JR 109; USA: Louis H Pollak [2005] JR 188.

[69] Joanne Clement [2004] JR 159 & 207.

constitutional arrangements", especially since "the United Kingdom courts must take their lead from Strasbourg"); *Brown v Stott (Procurator Fiscal, Dunfermline)* [2003] 1 AC 681, 724C-F ("care needs to be taken" in citing Canadian authority in relation to the approach to the ECHR; not "a reliable guide"); *R (Pretty) v Director of Public Prosecutions* [2001] UKHL 61 [2002] 1 AC 800 at [23] (s.7 of the Canadian Charter having "no close analogy in the European Convention"); *A, X and Y v Secretary of State for the Home Department* [2002] EWCA Civ 1502 [2004] QB 335 (CA) at [94] ("it is always dangerous to refer to an interpretation of a different human rights charter, however distinguished the source of that interpretation, without taking into account any significant differences in the language of that charter") (HL is [2004] UKHL 56 [2005] 2 AC 68); *Myles v Director of Public Prosecutions* [2004] EWHC 594 (Admin) [2004] 2 All ER 902 at [16] ("very limited assistance is to be derived from the Canadian decisions given the unanimity of English authority on this issue"); *Wilkinson v Kitzinger* [2006] EWHC 2022 (Fam) [2006] HRLR 1141 at [124]-[127] (neither Canadian nor South African case-law assisting).

> **P12 Vigilance.** Courts promote their interventionist capacities, driven by the rule of law and the need to protect against abuse.

12.1 Judicial review and the rule of law
12.2 Abuse models

12.1 **Judicial review and the rule of law.**Judicial review is the Courts' way of enforcing the rule of law: ensuring that public authorities' functions are undertaken according to law and that they are accountable to law. In other words, ensuring that public bodies are not "above the law".

12.1.1 The rule of law as a constitutional principle. <7.2.1>.

12.1.2 Judicial review: the rule of law in action. *R (Alconbury Developments Ltd) v Secretary of State for the Environment Transport and the Regions* [2001] UKHL 23 [2003] 2 AC 295 at [73] ("The principles of judicial review give effect to the rule of law"); *Bobb v Manning* [2006] UKPC 22 [2006] 4 LRC 735 at [14] ("The rule of law requires that those exercising public power should do so lawfully");*Toussaint v Attorney General of Saint Vincent & the Grenadines* [2007] UKPC 48 [2007] 1 WLR 2825 at [29] (judicial review as part of the rule of law); *R (Corner House Research) v Director of the Serious Fraud Office* [2008] UKHL 60 [2008] 3 WLR 568 at [41] (referring to "the rule of law, to which the principles of judicial review give effect"); *R v HM the Queen in Council, ex p Vijayatunga* [1988] QB 322, 343E-F ("Judicial review is the exercise of the court's inherent power at common law to determine whether action is lawful or not; in a word to uphold the rule of law"); *R v Secretary of State for Trade and Industry, ex p Greenpeace Ltd* [1998] Env LR 415, 424 (Court "primarily concerned with the maintenance of the rule of law by the imposition of objective legal standards upon the conduct of public bodies");*R v Horseferry Road Magistrates' Court, ex p Bennett* [1994] 1 AC 42, 62B ("the judiciary accept a responsibility for the maintenance of the rule of law that embraces a willingness to oversee executive action and to refuse to countenance behaviour that threatens either basic human rights or the rule of law"); *Attorney General's Reference No.2 of 2001* [2003] UKHL 68 [2004] 2 AC 72 at [30] (Court's "purpose is to uphold, vindicate and apply the law"), [35] ("Courts exist to uphold the law"); *Begum v Tower Hamlets London Borough Council* [2003] UKHL 5 [2003] 2 AC 430 at [57] (Art 6 "founded on the rule of law ... that there should be the possibility of adequate judicial review"); *A v HM Treasury* [2008] EWHC 869 (Admin) [2008] 3 All ER 361 at [30] (effective judicial review as a general principle of EC law); *R (C) v Secretary of State for Justice* [2008] EWCA Civ 882 at [55] (role of law supporting quashing of regulations).

12.1.3 The rule of law outweighs inconvenience/chaos. *R v Secretary of State for the Home Department, ex p Fayed* [1998] 1 WLR 763, 777B ("Administrative convenience cannot justify unfairness"); *R (Abbey Mine Ltd) v Coal Authority* [2008] EWCA Civ 353 at [34] ("no question of sacrificing fairness to administrative convenience", but the "duty of fairness always takes its place in a practical setting"); *R (Refugee Legal Centre) v Secretary of State for the Home Department* [2004] EWCA Civ 1481 [2005] 1 WLR 2219 at [8] (Government "not entitled to sacrifice fairness on the altar of speed and convenience, much less of expediency; and whether it has done so is a question of law for the courts"); *Bradbury v Enfield London Borough Council* [1967] 1 WLR 1311, 1324H ("Even if chaos should result, still the law must be obeyed"); *R v Paddington Valuation Officer, ex p Peachey Property Corporation Ltd* [1966] 1 QB 380, 418D ("inconvenience" not "a justification for ignoring invalidity"), 419D (remedy albeit that "to do so would produce inconvenience and chaos for the rating authority"; "otherwise the law could be flouted and injustice perpetrated with impunity"); *Hourigan v Secretary of State for Work and Pensions* [2002] EWCA Civ 1890 [2003] 3 All ER 924 (administrative convenience not a reason to give income support regulations a manifestly unfair meaning); *R v Secretary of State for Trade, ex p Vardy* [1993] ICR 720, 762G ("enormous problems" but which "must be resolved within the law, not outside it"); <14.4.1> (the Spackman observation); *Francis v Secretary of State for Work and Pensions* [2005] EWCA Civ 1303 [2006] 1 WLR 3202 at [30] ("administrative convenience cannot in itself be a sufficient justification for discrimination").

12.1.4 **Judicial review as a protection.** *R v Secretary of State for Trade and Industry, ex p Lonrho Plc* [1989] 1 WLR 525, 535F (Lord Keith: "Judicial review is a protection and not a weapon"); *DPP v Hutchinson* [1990] 2 AC 783, 819F (Lord Lowry: "the sounder aspects of judicial review ... have promoted freedom and have afforded protection from power"); *Nagle v Feilden* [1966] 2 QB 633, 654F-G (Salmon LJ: "One of the principal functions of our courts is, whenever possible, to protect the individual from injustice and oppression. It is important ... that we should not abdicate that function"); *R v Secretary of State for the Home Department, ex p Moon* (1996) 8 Admin LR 477, 485C (Sedley J: "it is precisely the unpopular [claimant] for whom the safeguards of due process are most relevant in a society which acknowledges the rule of law"); *R v Norfolk County Council, ex p M* [1989] QB 619, 628D-E (Waite J: "it is not the law that local authorities are free to exercise arbitrary control over the entry of names of alleged abusers on a child abuse register with total immunity from supervision by the courts. Any such immunity would seriously erode the rights of the citizen"); *R v Lord Chancellor, ex p Child Poverty Action Group* [1999] 1 WLR 347, 355F-G (Dyson J: "the role of the court in all public law cases is to ensure that public bodies do not exceed or abuse their powers"); *Hazell v Hammersmith & Fulham London Borough Council* [1992] 2 AC 1, 36F-G (Lord Templeman: "The object of the doctrine of ultra vires is the protection of the public").

12.1.5 **Wrong to abdicate an important role.** *R (International Transport Roth GmbH) v Secretary of State for the Home Department* [2002] EWCA Civ 158 [2003] QB 728 at [27] (Simon Brown LJ: "the court's role under the 1998 [Human Rights] Act is as the guardian of human rights. It cannot abdicate this responsibility"), [54] ("Constitutional dangers exist no less in too little judicial activism as in too much"); *Laker Airways Ltd v Department of Trade* [1977] QB 643, 707H-708B (Lord Denning MR: "It is a serious matter for the courts to declare that a minister of the Crown has exceeded his powers. So serious that we think hard before doing it. But there comes a point when it has to be done. These courts have the authority - and I would add, the duty - in a proper case, when called upon to inquire into the exercise of a discretionary power by a minister or his department. If it found that the power has been exercised improperly or mistakenly so as to impinge unjustly on the legitimate rights or interests of the subject, then these courts must so declare"); *McEldowney v Forde* [1971] AC 632, 653-D (Lord Pearce: "the duty of surveillance entrusted to the courts for the protection of the citizen" means the Court "cannot take the easy course of `passing by on the other side' when it seems clear to it that the Minister is using a power in a way which Parliament, who gave him that power, did not intend... The fact that this is not an easy line to draw is no reason why the courts should give up the task and abandon their duty to protect the citizen"); *R v Inland Revenue Commissioners, ex p National Federation of Self-Employed and Small Businesses Ltd* [1982] AC 617, 652E-F (Lord Scarman: "The courts have a role, long established, in the public law. They are available to the citizen who has a genuine grievance if he can show that it is one in respect of which prerogative relief is appropriate. I would not be a party to the retreat of the courts from this field of public law merely because the duties imposed upon the revenue are complex and call for management decisions in which discretion must play a significant role").

12.1.6 **Guardians of the public interest.** *Estate of M Kingsley (dec'd) v Secretary of State for Transport* [1994] COD 358 (as guardians of the public interest, judges having to approve discontinuance of proceedings, and grant of remedy by consent); <38.2.7> (standing and the public interest); <18.4> (costs and the public interest).

12.1.7 **Righting wrongs/protecting rights.** *R (Bancoult) v Secretary of State for Foreign & Commonwealth Affairs* [2007] EWCA Civ 498 [2008] QB 365 at [61] (Sedley LJ: "What modern public law focuses upon are wrongs - that is to say, unlawful acts of public administration. These often, of course, infringe correlative rights, but they do not necessarily do so: hence the test of standing for public law claimants, which is interest-based rather than rights-based"); *R v Secretary of State for the Environment, ex p Kirkstall Valley Campaign Ltd* [1996] 3 All ER 304, 325a (Sedley J: "Public law is concerned not only with the vindication of positive rights, but with the redress of public wrongs wherever the court's attention is called to them by a person or body with a sufficient interest"); *R v Somerset County Council, ex p Dixon* [1998] Env LR 111, 121 (Sedley J: "Public law is not at base about rights, even though abuses of power may and often do invade private rights; it is about wrongs - that is to say misuses of public power"), applied in *R (Corner House Research) v Secretary of State for Trade and Industry* [2005] EWCA Civ 192 [2005] 1 WLR 2600 at [145]; <P9> (HRA); <7.5.1> (constitutional rights).

12.1.8 **The rule of law and reviewability.** *R v Hull University Visitor, ex p Page* [1993] AC 682, 704B (Lord Browne-Wilkinson, citing *Czarnikow v Roth, Schmidt & Co* [1922] 2 KB 478, 488 per Scrutton CJ: "There must be no Alsatia in England where the King's writ does not run"); *R v Commissioner of the Metropolis, ex p Blackburn* [1968] 2 QB 118, 148E-G (Edmund-Davies LJ, explaining that policy duty enforceable by mandatory order, since otherwise "however brazen the failure of the police to enforce the law, the public would be wholly without a remedy ... The very idea is as repugnant as it is startling ... How ill it accords with the seventeenth century assertion of Thomas Fuller that, `Be you never so high, the law is above you' ... its effect would be to place the police above the law");*R v Board of Visitors of Hull Prison, ex p St Germain* [1979] QB 425, 455B-E (Shaw LJ, referring to the courts as "ultimate custodians of the rights and liberties of the subject" so that declining jurisdiction would be "tantamount to abdicating a primary function of the judiciary"); *R v Panel on Take-overs and Mergers, ex p Datafin Plc* [1987] QB 815, 827A-B (Sir John Donaldson MR, characterising the "principal issue" as "whether this remarkable body is above the law"), 839A-B ("unthinkable that ... the panel should go on its way cocooned from the attention of the courts in defence of the citizenry") and 846C (Lloyd LJ: "The courts must remain ready, willing and able to hear a legitimate complaint in this as in any other field of our national life"); *R v Tower Hamlets London Borough Council, ex p Chetnik Developments Ltd* [1988] AC 858, 872B-F (Lord Bridge, citing with approval this passage from *Wade* (5th ed. at 357): "Unreviewable administrative action is just as much a contradiction in terms as is unfettered discretion, at any rate in the case of statutory powers"); *R v Ministry of Defence, ex p Smith* [1996] QB 517 (DC) at 539E (Simon Brown LJ: "I have no hesitation in holding this challenge justiciable. To my mind only the rarest cases will today be ruled strictly beyond the court's purview"); *R v J* [2004] UKHL 42 [2005] 1 AC 562 at [38] (Lord Steyn: "The CPS as an independent law enforcement agency carry out duties of a public character. It must act fairly and within the law. It must observe statute law as Parliament framed it. In our Parliamentary democracy nobody is above the law").

12.1.9 **The rule of law and no unfettered powers.** <39.1> (no unfettered powers); *R v Tower Hamlets London Borough Council, ex p Chetnik Developments Ltd* [1988] AC 858, 872B-F (Lord Bridge, citing with approval the comment by Professor Wade that: "in a system based on the rule of law, unfettered governmental discretion is a contradiction in terms"); *R v Somerset County Council, ex p Fewings* [1995] 1 All ER 513, 524d-e (Laws J: "a truly unfettered discretion will at once put the decision-maker outside or, as I would prefer to say, above the law"); *Laker Airways Ltd v Department of Trade* [1977] QB 643, 707H-708B (prerogative powers not unfettered).

12.1.10 The rule of law and standing. *R v Inland Revenue Commissioners, ex p National Federation of Self-Employed and Small Businesses Ltd* [1982] AC 617, 644E-G (Lord Diplock, describing the "grave lacuna in our system of public law if a pressure group, like the federation, or even a single public-spirited taxpayer, were prevented by outdated technical rules of locus standi from bringing the matter to the attention of the court to vindicate the rule of law and get the unlawful conduct stopped"; central government officers and departments are "responsible to a court of justice for the lawfulness of what they do, and of that the court is the only judge"); *R v Secretary of State for Foreign and Commonwealth Affairs, ex p World Development Movement Ltd* [1995] 1 WLR 386, 395G-H.

12.1.11 The rule of law and coercive remedies. *M v Home Office* [1994] 1 AC 377 (injunction/contempt available against the Crown), 395G (Lord Templeman: "the argument that there is no power to enforce the law by injunction or contempt proceedings ... would, if upheld, establish the proposition that the executive obey the law as a matter of grace and not as a matter of necessity, a proposition which would reverse the result of the Civil War"); *R v Commissioners of Inland Revenue, ex p Kingston Smith* [1996] STC 1210, 1211a, 1212e (Court initiating consideration of contempt powers against Inland Revenue of its own motion, so as to uphold the rule of law, where the Revenue had disregarded a pre-permission injunction).

12.1.12 The rule of law and transparency/certainty. *R (Anufrijeva) v Secretary of State for the Home Department* [2003] UKHL 36 [2004] 1 AC 604 at [26] ("Notice of a decision is required before it can have the character of a determination with legal effect"), [28] ("the constitutional principle requiring the rule of law to be observed ... requires that a constitutional state must accord to individuals the right to know of a decision before their rights can be adversely affected"); *R (Salih) v Secretary of State for the Home Department* [2003] EWHC 2273 (Admin) at [45] (Stanley Burnton J: "It is a fundamental requisite of the rule of law that the law should be made known"), [52] ("constitutional imperative" applied to extra-statutory policy, that Government should not "withhold information about its policy relating to the exercise of a power conferred by statute"); *R (L) v Secretary of State for the Home Department* [2003] EWCA Civ 25 [2003] 1 WLR 1230 at [17] ("legal certainty is an aspect of the rule of law"), [25] ("It is an aspect of the rule of law that individuals and those advising them, since they will be presumed to know the law, should have access to it in authentic form"); <55.1.19> (uncertainty).

12.1.13 The rule of law and basic fairness/due process. *R v Secretary of State for the Home Department, ex p Pierson* [1998] AC 539, 591F (Lord Steyn: "the rule of law enforces minimum standards of fairness, both substantive and procedural"), 590G-591A (true analysis not legitimate expectation but the rule of law); *R v Secretary of State for the Home Department, ex p Fayed* [1998] 1 WLR 763, 778A (Lord Woolf MR: "[The claimants] have not had the fairness to which they were entitled and the rule of law must be upheld"); *R (Anderson) v Secretary of State for the Home Department* [2002] UKHL 46 [2003] 1 AC 837 at [39] (Lord Steyn, emphasising the importance of the rule of law in the context of incompatibility of Ministerial tariff-setting with ECHR Art 6 under the Human Rights Act); *Thomas v Baptiste* [2000] 2 AC 1 (considering common law due process rights, reflected in Constitution of Trinidad and Tobago), 22B-C ("'due process of law' is a compendious expression in which the word `law' ... invokes the concept of the rule of law itself and the universally accepted standards of justice observed by civilised nations which observe the rule of law", referring to *Lassalle v Attorney-General* (1971) 18 WIR 379); *Higgs v Minister of National Security* [2000] 2 AC 228, 245H (considering common law principle of due process); *R v Secretary of State for the Home Department, ex p Hindley* [2000] 1 QB 152 (CA), 163B-164H (Lord Woolf MR, considering the related principles of due process and abuse of process); *R v Horseferry Road Magistrates' Court, ex p Bennett* [1994] 1 AC 42, applying *Connelly v Director of Public Prosecutions*

[1964] AC 1254, 1354 (Lord Devlin, describing the courts' "inescapable duty to secure fair treatment for those who come or are brought before them"; "The courts cannot contemplate for a moment the transference to the Executive of the responsibility for seeing that the process of law is not abused"); *In re Schmidt* [1995] 1 AC 339, 377H-378A ("in relation to a pending trial in England ... the High Court in its supervisory jurisdiction is the only bulwark against any abuse of process").

12.1.14 **The rule of law and preventing abuse of power.** *A v Secretary of State for the Home Department* [2004] EWCA Civ 1123 at [248] (Laws LJ, identifying "a general constitutional principle ... It is the most elementary principle in our books. It is that the law forbids the exercise of State power in an arbitrary, oppressive or abusive manner. This is, simply, a cardinal principle of the rule of law. The rule of law requires, not only that State power be exercised within the express limits of any relevant statutory jurisdiction, but also fairly and reasonably and in good faith"), [251] ("a basic truth which applies in any jurisdiction where public power is subject to the rigour of democracy and the rule of law ... is that State power is not only constrained by objective law - that is, the imperative that it be exercised fairly, reasonably and in good faith and within the limits of any relevant statute. More than this: the imperative is one which cannot be set aside on utilitarian grounds, as a means to a further end. It is not in any way to be compromised"), [252] ("the constitutional principle which forbids abuse of State power") (HL is [2005] UKHL 71 [2006] 2 AC 221).

12.2 "Abuse models". The availability of judicial review and delineation of grounds for review have frequently been informed by asking this hypothetical question: `what if things were to go (or to have gone) badly wrong?'. The Courts' instinctive and principled answer is that they must retain the capacity to deal with abuses of power, were they to happen.

12.2.1 **Abuse models and reviewability.** *Leech v Deputy Governor of Parkhurst Prison* [1988] AC 533, 582E (Lord Oliver: "One has to postulate, for the question to be a live one at all, that there has been an error of law or an abuse or excess of power"); *R v Panel on Take-overs and Mergers, ex p Datafin Plc* [1987] QB 815, 827C ("what is to happen if the panel goes off the rails? Suppose, perish the thought, that it were to use its powers in a way which was manifestly unfair. What then?"), 845H (posing an "obvious example": "if it reached a decision in flagrant breach of the rules of natural justice"); *R v Ethical Committee of St Mary's Hospital (Manchester), ex p H* [1988] 1 FLR 512, 518H-519A ("If the committee had advised, for instance, that the IVF unit should in principle refuse all such treatment to anyone who was a jew or coloured, then I think the courts might well grant a declaration that such a policy was illegal"); *R v Secretary of State for the Home Department, ex p Herbage (No 2)* [1987] QB 1077, 1095F-G (were there "cruel and unusual punishment", "it would be an affront to common sense that the court should not be able to afford [a remedy]"); *R v Inland Revenue Commissioners, ex p Mead* [1993] 1 All ER 772, 782e ("Absurd examples, such as a policy only to prosecute black men or the political opponents of an outgoing government, which are virtually unthinkable, do however point to the theoretical existence of the jurisdiction to review"); *R v Criminal Injuries Compensation Board, ex p P* [1995] 1 WLR 845, 863D-E (using "the fanciful but archetypal example of perversity, [namely] if the scheme had been revised in 1979 to exclude only redheaded victims of crimes committed by persons under the same roof"); *R v Secretary of State for the Home Department, ex p Ruddock* [1987] 1 WLR 1482, 1491G-H (rejecting the contention "that the court should never inquire into a complaint against a minister" relying on national security: "To take an extreme and one hopes unlikely example, suppose an application were put before the court alleging a warrant was improperly issued by a Secretary of State against a political opponent ... to see if anything discreditable could be learnt ...").

12.2.2 Abuse models and statutory ousters. <P28> (ouster); *Anisminic Ltd v Foreign Compensation Commission* [1969] 2 AC 147, 170B-E (Lord Reid: "Let me illustrate the matter by supposing a simple case. A statute provides that a certain order may be made by a person who holds a specified qualification or appointment... A person aggrieved by an order alleges that it is a forgery or that the person who made the order did not hold that qualification or appointment... If the draftsman or Parliament had intended to introduce a new kind of ouster clause so as to prevent any inquiry even as to whether the document relied on was a forgery, I would have expected to find something much more specific"), 199F-H (Lord Pearce); *Ex p Waldron* [1986] QB 824, 846G-H (comfort in narrow construction of ouster, since would have left "a serious inadequacy in the powers of the courts to protect the citizen from an actual or potential loss of liberty arising out of a serious error of law").

12.2.3 Abuse models and standing. *R v Inland Revenue Commissioners, ex p National Federation of Self-Employed and Small Businesses Ltd* [1982] AC 617, 641C (Lord Diplock's objective of avoiding a "grave lacuna" was based on the prospect of "flagrant and serious breaches of the law by persons and authorities exercising governmental functions which are continuing unchecked").

12.2.4 Rejecting the "reductio ad absurdum". *R v Director of the Serious Fraud Office, ex p Smith* [1993] AC 1, 43D-G (Lord Mustill, dismissing as "unreal" this "reductio ad absurdum": "Counsel conjured up for us the picture of the accused person, after a gruelling day in court, returning to the cells to be met with the sight of an official of the Serious Fraud Office, armed with a further batch of questions, which he would be forced to answer on pain of being prosecuted for another offence"); *R v Secretary of State for Health, ex p United States Tobacco International Inc* [1992] QB 353, 365D-F; cf. *R v Secretary of State for the Home Department, ex p Al-Mehdawi* [1990] 1 AC 876, 900F-901E.

> **P13 Restraint.** Courts adopt a primary self-restraint, preserving for public bodies a latitude for judgment and discretion.

13.1 "Soft" review: reasonableness
13.2 Restraint and factual questions
13.3 Restraint and discretion/judgment
13.4 Restraint and expertise
13.5 Judicial restraint in action
13.6 Protecting public authorities
13.7 Review from the decision-maker's point of view

13.1 "Soft" review: reasonableness. Public authorities have an important role and function. There must necessarily be questions which it is for them, rather than judges, to decide. In considering whether a public body has abused its powers, Courts must not abuse theirs. In constitutional terms, just as judicial vigilance is underpinned by the rule of law, so judicial restraint is underpinned by the separation of powers. There are three categories: (1) those rare questions which are non-reviewable or non-justiciable; (2) "soft" questions, reviewable on a conventional basis (a reasonableness standard); and (3) "hard-edged" questions, correctable by review (a correctness standard). Under conventional ("soft") review, the decision-maker has a "latitude", "area of judgment" or "margin of discretion". This is better language than "margin of appreciation", which is a Strasbourg Court concept having added international-deference. So, conventional review is "review with built-in latitude".[70]

13.1.1 **"Latitude".** *Tweed v Parades Commission for Northern Ireland* [2006] UKHL 53 [2007] 1 AC 650 at [36] ("latitude", to describe the margin of discretion applicable under the HRA); *R (G) v Barnet London Borough Council* [2003] UKHL 57 [2004] 2 AC 208 at [15] (statutes affording local authorities "latitude"); *R (Mullen) v Secretary of State for the Home Department* [2004] UKHL 18 [2005] 1 AC 1 at [12] (Secretary of State enjoying some "latitude" in administering an gratia scheme); *Schindler* [1994] ECR I-1039 at [61] (ECJ describing national authorities as having a "degree of latitude"); *R (Pelling) v Bow County Court* [2001] UKHRR 165 at [33] ("a latitude for judgment"); *Knight v Nicholls* [2004] EWCA Civ 68 [2004] 1 WLR 1653 at [39] ("latitude" under HRA:ECHR Art 3P); cf. *R v Secretary of State for the Environment, ex p Greater London Council* 3rd April 1985 unrep. ("target area"); *R v Manchester Crown Court, ex p McDonald* [1999] 1 WLR 841, 851A ("field of judgment"); *R v Criminal Cases Review Commission, ex p Pearson* [1999] 3 All ER 498, 523 ("area of judgment"); <58.5.8> ("margin of discretion"); <58.5.2> (beware of the Strasbourg margin of appreciation); *Grape Bay Ltd v Attorney-General of Bermuda* [2000] 1 WLR 574, 585F ("wide margin of appreciation"); *R v Chief Constable of Sussex, ex p International Trader's Ferry Ltd* [1999] 2 AC 418, 430C-D ("the margin of appreciation or discretion").

13.1.2 **Constitutional role of judicial restraint.** <7.2.2> (separation of powers as a constitutional principle); *R v Secretary of State for the Environment, ex p Nottinghamshire County Council* [1986] AC 240, 250H-251A (Lord Scarman: "Judicial review is a great weapon in the hands of the judges: but the judges must observe the constitutional limits set by our parliamentary system upon their exercise of this beneficent power"); Lord Hoffmann, *Separation of Powers*, COMBAR Lecture 23 October 2001 at [30] (referring to "questions of policy which are more appropriately decided by the democratically elected organs of the state", requiring "a

---

[70] The phrase "review with built-in latitude" (from a previous edition of this Handbook) was endorsed in

R (Levy) v Environment Agency [2002] EWHC 1663 (Admin) [2003] Env LR 245 at [23] (Silber J).

degree of restraint on the part of judges" since "there is a legitimacy about the decisions of elected institutions to which judges, however enlightened, can never lay claim"); *R v Inland Revenue Commissioners, ex p Rossminster* [1980] AC 952, 1027D-E (Lord Scarman, referring to "the fundamental limits of the judicial function"); *Mercury Energy Ltd v Electricity Corporation of New Zealand Ltd* [1994] 1 WLR 521, 529G ("The exploitation and extension of remedies such as judicial review beyond their proper sphere should not be encouraged"); *R v Independent Television Commission, ex p TSW Broadcasting Ltd* [1994] 2 LRC 414, 430d (Lord Templeman: "judicial review should not be allowed to run riot"), applied in *R v Independent Television Commission, ex p Virgin Television Limited* [1996] EMLR 318; *R v Crown Court at Manchester, ex p McDonald* [1999] 1 WLR 841, 850H-851A (Lord Bingham CJ: "This court['s] ... only role, as in any other application for judicial review, is to see whether the decision in question is open to successful challenge on any of the familiar grounds which support an application for judicial review"; not to "trespass into a field of judgment which is reserved to the court of trial").

13.1.3 **Parliament and the Courts: mutual respect.** *In re McFarland* [2004] UKHL 17 [2004] 1 WLR 1289 at [7] (Lord Bingham: "Just as the courts must apply Acts of Parliament whether they approve of them or not, and give effect to lawful official decisions whether they agree with them or not, so Parliament and the executive must respect judicial decisions whether they approve of them or not, unless and until they are set aside"); *R v HM Treasury, ex p Smedley* [1985] QB 657, 666C-D (Sir John Donaldson MR: "it is a constitutional convention of the highest importance that the legislature and the judicature are separate and independent of one another, subject to certain ultimate rights of Parliament over the judicature which are immaterial for present purposes. It therefore behoves the courts to be ever sensitive to the paramount need to refrain from trespassing upon the province of Parliament or, so far as this can be avoided, even appearing to do so... I would hope and expect that Parliament would be similarly sensitive to the need to refrain from trespassing upon the province of the courts").

13.1.4 **So-called "deference" and allocational legal principle.** *R (ProLife Alliance) v British Broadcasting Corporation* [2003] UKHL 23 [2004] 1 AC 185 at [76] (Lord Hoffmann: "the courts themselves often have to decide the limits of their own decision-making power. That is inevitable. But it does not mean that their allocation of decision-making power to the other branches of government is a matter of courtesy or deference. The principles upon which decision-making powers are allocated are principles of law. The courts are the independent branch of government and the legislature and executive are, directly and indirectly respectively, the elected branches of government. Independence makes the courts more suited to deciding some kinds of questions and being elected makes the legislature or executive more suited to deciding others. The allocation of these decision-making responsibilities is based upon recognised principles. The principle that the independence of the courts is necessary for a proper decision of disputed legal rights or claims of violation of human rights is a legal principle. It is reflected in article 6 of the Convention. On the other hand, the principle that majority approval is necessary for a proper decision on policy or allocation of resources is also a legal principle. Likewise, when a court decides that a decision is within the proper competence of the legislature or executive, it is not showing deference. It is deciding the law"), [144] (Lord Walker: "deference ... may not be the best word to use").

13.1.5 **Matter entrusted to the primary decision-maker.** *R v Secretary of State for the Home Department, ex p Launder* [1997] 1 WLR 839, 857D (question "entrusted to the Secretary of State by Parliament"); *Ashbridge Investments Ltd v Minister of Housing & Local Government* [1965] 1 WLR 1320, 1326E-F (a question "entrusted ... to the Minister for decision"); *In re A Company* [1981] AC 374, 383G (question which public body has "jurisdiction to decide for itself"); *R v Governor of Pentonville Prison, ex p Azam* [1974] AC 18, 64C ("the decision whether to remove or not is made by the Secretary of State"); *R v Secretary of State for the Home Department, ex p Brind* [1991] 1 AC 696, 766H ("The decision-makers, very often elected, are those to whom Parliament has entrusted the discretion"); *Re W (A Minor) (Wardship: Jurisdiction)* [1985] AC 791, 797C ("If Parliament in an area of concern defined by statute ... prefers power to be exercised administratively instead of judicially, so be it").

13.1.6 **Avoiding abuse by the courts: the forbidden substitutionary approach.** <15.1> (forbidden substitutionary approach); *R v Secretary of State for the Home Department, ex p Brind* [1991] 1 AC 696, 766H (Lord Lowry: "to interfere with [the Secretary of State's] discretion beyond the limits as hitherto defined would itself be an abuse of the judges' supervisory jurisdiction"); *Chief Constable of the North Wales Police v Evans* [1982] 1 WLR 1155, 1160E-H (judicial review "is not intended to take away from those authorities the powers and discretions properly vested in them by law and to substitute the courts as the bodies making the decisions"); cf. *Council of Civil Service Unions v Minister for the Civil Service* [1985] AC 374, 405G (to review the rationality of national security matters would be to "substitute its opinion for the opinion of those responsible for national security") and 418C (to review the legality of treaty-making would be to "determine whether a treaty should be concluded"); *R v Chief Rabbi, ex p Wachmann* [1992] 1 WLR 1036, 1043A (to review the procedural fairness of religious decisions would involve "adjudicating upon matters intimate to a religious community").

13.2 **Restraint and factual questions.** A classic context calling for restraint is where the public body's relevant conclusion concerned a question of fact, or `fact and degree'. The Courts do not, and could not possibly, interfere by judicial review every time the judge might have reached an appraisal of the facts different from that reached by the primary decision-maker. However, unjustified conclusions of fact can be overturned on judicial review, in a clear and appropriate case.

13.2.1 **Questions of fact for the primary decision-maker (public body).** *R v Hillingdon London Borough Council, ex p Puhlhofer* [1986] AC 484, 518D-E (Lord Brightman: "Where the existence or non-existence of a fact is left to the judgment and discretion of a public body and that fact involves a broad spectrum ranging from the obvious to the debatable to the just conceivable, it is the duty of the court to leave the decision of that fact to the public body to whom Parliament has entrusted the decision-making power save in a case where it is obvious that the public body, consciously or unconsciously, are acting perversely"); *R (Ireneschild) v Lambeth London Borough Council* [2007] EWCA Civ 234 [2007] LGR 619 at [44] (*Puhlhofer* approach still pertinent); *R v Brighton and Hove Borough Council, ex p Nacion* (1999) 11 Admin LR 472 (CA expressing "reservations as to how far those comments of Lord Brightman are of general application"); *Edwards v Bairstow* [1956] AC 14, 38-39 (Lord Radcliffe: courts' "duty is no more than to examine those facts with a decent respect for the tribunal ... and if they think that the only reasonable conclusion on the facts found is inconsistent with the determination come to, to say so without more ado"); *Lee Ting Sang v Chung Chi-Keung* [1990] ICR 409, 415C-H (Court "must not abdicate its responsibility"); *R v Director General of Telecommunications, ex p Cellcom Ltd* [1999] COD 105 (see transcript) ("The resolution of disputed questions of fact is for the decision-maker, and the Court can only interfere if his decision is perverse eg. if his reasoning is logically unsound").

13.2.2 **The distinction between fact and law.** *R v Barnet London Borough Council, ex p Nilish Shah* [1983] 2 AC 309, 341B-C (Lord Scarman: "If a local education authority gets the law right, or, as lawyers would put it, directs itself correctly in law, the question of fact ... is for the authority, not the court, to decide"); <48.1.4> (fact/law and ordinary words); *R v Local*

Government Commission for England, ex p North Yorkshire County Council 11th March 1994 unrep. (Laws J, referring to the "distinction between law and fact" as "particularly important", it being "in the public interest that the LGC, which has a pivotal role in the practical and constitutional arrangements to be made for public administration at the local level, should be allowed to get on with its task untrammelled by technicality and uninhibited by any excessive legalisms"); *R v Poplar Coroner, ex p Thomas* [1993] QB 610, 630C-D (although statute using "an ordinary word of the English language", application not "a pure question of fact", but "some guidance at least can and should be given as a matter of law by the courts to coroners so that they may focus their attention upon the real considerations material to the decision and, one hopes, thereby achieve an essential measure of consistency in their approach to the section"); *R v Radio Authority, ex p Bull* [1998] QB 294, 304E ("The courts exercising their supervisory jurisdiction have the responsibility for providing guidance where it is practical to do so"); *R v National Insurance Commissioner, ex p Secretary of State for Social Services* [1981] 1 WLR 1017, 1022E ("These provisions have to be applied, day in and day out, by delegated medical practitioners all over the country. They should be applied uniformly"); *In re A Company* [1981] AC 374, 383G-H ("interrelated questions of law, fact and degree"; "a typical question of mixed law, fact and degree which only a scholiast would think it appropriate to dissect"); *R v Medicines Control Agency, ex p Pharma Nord Ltd* (1998) 10 Admin LR 646, 659C (questions of fact become questions of law "where the application of the statutory language to the facts as a matter of law requires only one answer"); *R (Cherwell District Council) v First Secretary of State* [2004] EWCA Civ 1420 [2005] 1 WLR 1128 at [50] (whether development of Crown land by private contractor could constitute Crown development a matter of law; if so, whether this development properly did so a question of fact); <16.3> (error of law as hard-edged review).

13.2.3 **Questions of "fact and degree".** *R v Monopolies & Mergers Commission, ex p Argyll Group Plc* [1986] 1 WLR 763, 771B ("a question of fact and degree" as "supremely a matter for the commission"), 777H ("a question of fact and degree for the judgment of the commission"); *R (Cherwell District Council) v First Secretary of State* [2004] EWCA Civ 1420 [2005] 1 WLR 1128 at [50] and [57] (questions of "fact and degree", where conclusion would need to be "outside the bounds of reasonable judgment"); *R v Broadcasting Complaints Commission, ex p Granada Television Ltd* [1995] 3 EMLR 163 (Parliament "considered it more appropriate that the difficult questions of fact and degree, and the value of judgment ... are best left to a specialist body, such as the BCC, whose members have experience of broadcasting"); *R v Yorkshire Regional Health Authority, ex p Suri* (1995) 30 BMLR 78, 81-82 ("Provided the proper approach is adopted, the answer ... will inevitably become a question of fact and degree eminently suitable to resolution by a committee of laymen, and not susceptible to sophisticated legal analyses").

13.2.4 **Questions of credibility.** *R v Secretary of State for the Home Department, ex p Panther* (1996) 8 Admin LR 154 (impossible to go behind adjudicator's adverse findings on credibility); *R v Secretary of State for the Home Department, ex p Agbonmenio* [1996] Imm AR 69 (adverse conclusions as to credibility a matter of fact for the adjudicator); *R v Criminal Injuries Compensation Board, ex p Milton* [1996] COD 264 (open to the CICB to make an adverse credibility finding if it simply disbelieved the claimant; cf. specific contradictory evidence); *R v Special Adjudicator, ex p Paulino* [1996] Imm AR 122 (adverse conclusion as to credibility on peripheral matters not sufficient to support conclusion that asylum claim frivolous).

13.2.5 **Questions of educated prediction.** *R v Director General of Telecommunications, ex p Cellcom Ltd* [1999] COD 105 (see transcript) (Lightman J: "If (as I have stated) the Court should be very slow to impugn decisions of fact made by an expert and experienced decision-maker, it must surely be even slower to impugn his educated prophesies and predictions for the future"); *Secretary of State for the Home Department v Rehman* [2001] UKHL 47 [2003] 1 AC

153 at [22] (Lord Slynn, referring to deportation decisions on grounds that "conducive to the public good" as "an executive judgment" having regard to "precautionary and preventative principles" rather than "merely finding facts"); *R (London and Continental Stations and Property Ltd) v Rail Regulator* [2003] EWHC 2607 (Admin) at [30] (exercise incapable of "exact precision"), [34] ("predictions for the future incapable of any exact measurement").

13.2.6 **Error of fact as a ground for judicial review.** <P49>.

13.3 **Restraint and discretion/judgment.**Another classic context for restraint on the part of the Court is where a public body has a "discretion" (ie. the function of making a choice). Since discretion is never "unfettered", and there are always limits on the proper exercise of power to prevent arbitrariness and abuse, it will often be better to speak of the public authority as exercising a "judgment". The Courts' general starting-point is and must be that the primary decision, on matters of discretion and judgment, is for the public body.

13.3.1 **Discretion and judgment.** *R v Secretary of State for the Home Department, ex p Yousaf* [2000] 3 All ER 649 at [48] (Sedley LJ: "Although it is described in other authorities as a discretion, the word `discretion' is most apt to describe a circumscribed area of decision-making which depends on an often incommunicable sense of what is fair rather than on the kind of reasoning which characterises judgment. Statutes constitutive of public authority rarely create a true discretion in this sense. They generally give ministers authority to do things at their own election in order to promote ... the policy and objects of the statute"); <39.1.4> (better to speak of "judgment" rather than discretion); *Rushbridger v HM Attorney-General* [2003] UKHL 38 [2004] 1 AC 357 at [20] (Lord Steyn, referring to the difference between discretion and judgment in the context of whether to entertain a claim for a declaration of the criminal legality of proposed conduct <24.2.6>); *R (Tofik) v Immigration Appeal Tribunal* [2003] EWCA Civ 1138 at [17] (IAT's decision as to extension of time for appeal not a discretion but a judgment); *R v Bradford Metropolitan Borough Council, ex p Sikander Ali* [1994] ELR 299, 308G (Jowitt J: "[the] application of a criterion involves the making of judgments and there will be questions of degree"), applied in *R v South Gloucestershire Education Appeals Committee, ex p Bryant* [2001] ELR 53 (school admissions criteria), at [28].

13.3.2 **Discretion: power to choose.** *Secretary of State for Education and Science v Tameside Metropolitan Borough Council* [1977] AC 1014, 1064 (Lord Diplock: "The very concept of administrative discretion involves a right to choose between more than one possible course of action upon which there is room for reasonable people to hold differing opinions as to which is to be preferred"), cited in *R v Secretary of State for the Environment, ex p Nottinghamshire County Council* [1986] AC 240, 248E-F (Lord Scarman); *Hill v Chief Constable of West Yorkshire* [1989] AC 53, 59D-F (Lord Keith).

13.3.3 **Discretion/judgment: the need for judicial restraint.** *Chertsey Urban District Council v Mixnam's Properties Ltd* [1965] AC 735, 753G-754A (where "Parliament ... hands over the power of control to local authorities in general terms which imply full confidence in their use of their discretion, a court of law has no right to approach the question of the validity of some exercise of it with an a priori belief or intuition as to what Parliament is likely to have intended to allow"); *Mercury Energy Ltd v Electricity Corporation of New Zealand Ltd* [1994] 1 WLR 521, 528C (matter "for the defendant and nobody else to decide in its discretion"); *Julius v Bishop of Oxford* (1880) 5 App Cas 214, 247 (Lord Blackburn, explaining that any decision-maker is human "and being human may misuse any discretion entrusted to them; but so are Judges").

13.3.4 **Statutory discretion: "soft" nature of review.** *Associated Provincial Picture Houses Ltd v Wednesbury Corporation* [1948] 1 KB 223, 228 ("an exercise of ... discretion can only be challenged in the courts in a strictly limited class of case"); *Cocks v Thanet District Council* [1983] 2 AC 286, 292F ("strictly limited grounds"); *Chertsey Urban District Council v Mixnam's Properties Ltd* [1965] AC 735, 761A (describing "functions entrusted to them by Parliament. Courts should not be astute to find they have acted outside the scope of their powers. They should be supported if possible").

13.3.5 **Limits of discretion/judgment.** <P39> (discretion/duty); <39.1> (no unfettered discretion).

13.4 **Restraint and expertise.**Another classic context warranting judicial restraint is where the issue was within the particular expertise of the public body. Here, general restraint is reinforced by the insight that the primary decision-maker is better placed than the Court to evaluate matters falling within its area of expertise.

13.4.1 **Special knowledge/experience.** *R (Great North Eastern Railway Ltd) v Office of Rail Regulation* [2006] EWHC 1942 (Admin) at [39] (referring to "the ORR's expertise in this highly technical field" which "the Court would be very slow indeed to impugn"); *Presho v Insurance Officer* [1984] 1 AC 310, 318F (referring to "a question of fact of a kind which insurance officers, local tribunals and the commissioner are, by reason of their wide knowledge and experience of matters pertaining to industrial relations, exceptionally well qualified to answer"); *R v Social Fund Inspector, ex p Ali* (1994) 6 Admin LR 205, 210E ("when Parliament entrusts an expert body of people ... with the task of fulfilling the intentions of Parliament in a specialist sphere, the courts should be very slow to interfere"); *Associated Provincial Picture Houses Ltd v Wednesbury Corporation* [1948] 1 KB 223, 230 (matters "which the knowledge and experience of that authority can best be trusted to deal with"); *R v Inland Revenue Commissioners, ex p Preston* [1985] AC 835, 864E-F ("unique knowledge of fiscal practices and policy"); *W v Education Appeal Committee of Lancashire County Council* [1994] ELR 530, 536H-537A ("especially knowledgeable men and women with experience of education").

13.4.2 **Specialised statutory body/tribunal.** *Napp Pharmaceutical Holdings Ltd v Director General of Fair Trading* [2002] EWCA Civ 796 [2002] 4 All ER 376 at [34] (Buxton LJ, speaking of "findings, as the conclusion of an expert and specialist tribunal, specifically constituted by Parliament to make judgements in an area in which judges have no expertise, they fall exactly into ... an area which this court would be very slow indeed to enter"); *R (Kwik-fit Ltd) v Central Arbitration Committee* [2002] EWCA Civ 512 at [2] (Central Arbitration Committee treated as an expert tribunal in a specialist area); *R v Parole Board, ex p Watson* [1996] 1 WLR 906, 917C ("It is not for the court to second-guess the judgment of a specialist tribunal"); *United Kingdom Association of Professional Engineers v Advisory Conciliation & Arbitration Service* [1981] AC 424, 439G ("Acas is the chosen instrument for promoting good industrial relations"); *R v Broadcasting Standards Commission, ex p British Broadcasting Corporation* [2001] QB 885 at [14] (BSC having expertise enabling it to exercise judgment and discretion, in relation to such matters as what constitutes an interference with "privacy"); *R v London Metal Exchange Ltd, ex p Albatros Warehousing BV* 31st March 2000 unrep. at [57] (LME appeal committee "an expert body which was well placed to assess the needs of the market, the impact of a breach of the rules and what was required in order to deter future breaches and secure confidence in the market"); *R (Levy) v Environment Agency* [2002] EWHC 1663 (Admin) [2003] Env LR 245 at [77]-[79] (Environment Agency's expertise as to pollution control); *R (London and Continental Stations and Property Ltd) v Rail Regulator* [2003] EWHC 2607 (Admin) at [29] (Moses J: "[The Rail Regulator] is better placed than a court to make an overall assessment of what is in the interest of the rail network ... [which] explains why the court has limited scope for intervention"), [34] ("expert and experienced").

13.4.3 **Specialised judgment.** *R (Campaign to End All Animal Experiments) v Secretary of State for the Home Department* [2008] EWCA Civ 417 at [1] ("scientific judgment is not immune from lawyers' analysis. But the court must be careful not to substitute its own inexpert view of the science for a tenable expert opinion... the court should be very slow to conclude that this expert and experienced Chief Inspector reached a perverse scientific conclusion"); *R v Hampshire County Council, ex p W* [1994] ELR 460, 472A ("a question of professional judgment upon which a court of law would embark at the peril of everybody concerned"); *R (Assisted Reproduction and Gynaecology Centre) v Human Fertilisation and Embryology Authority* [2002] EWCA Civ 20 [2003] 1 FCR 266 at [15] ("It is not the function of the court to enter the scientific debate, nor is it the function of the court to adjudicate on the merits of the [defendant]'s decisions or any advice it gives"), [65]; *Begum v Tower Hamlets London Borough Council* [2003] UKHL 5 [2003] 2 AC 430 at [56] (referring to "areas of the law such as regulatory and welfare schemes in which decision-making is customarily entrusted to administrators"), [104].

13.5 **Judicial restraint in action.** Measured restraint by the Court is a strong theme of judicial review; an important "default setting" ensuring that, absent a demonstrable public law wrong, the Court should not interfere. Certain contexts are most clearly associated with restraint, but the general starting-point is that public bodies should be "left to get on with it".

13.5.1 Judicial restraint: examples of particular contexts.

(A) EXPENDITURE/DISTRIBUTION/RESOURCES. *R v Secretary of State for the Environment, ex p Hammersmith & Fulham London Borough Council* [1991] 1 AC 521, 593F (Lord Bridge: "What is the appropriate level of public expenditure and public taxation is, and always has been, a matter of political opinion"); <32.4.8> (modified review and Westminster-approved measures); *R (Waite) v Hammersmith and Fulham London Borough Council* [2002] EWCA Civ 482 [2003] HLR 24 at [37] ("the distribution of state benefit lies particularly within the constitutional responsibility of elected Government"); *R (T) v Secretary of State for the Home Department* [2003] EWCA Civ 1285 [2003] UKHRR 1321 at [11] (Art 3 positive obligation "inevitably means that funds have to be expended, and because the allocation of resources is normally a matter exclusively for the executive courts must be careful not to set too low the threshold at which the duty to act does arise"); *R (Otley) v Barking and Dagenham NHS Primary Care Trust* [2007] EWHC 1927 (Admin) (unreasonable to refuse cancer drug); *R (Walker) v Secretary of State for Justice* [2008] EWCA Civ 30 [2008] 3 All ER 104 at [40] (unlawful not to fund adequate offending behaviour courses in prisons).

(B) POLICY-LADEN DECISIONS. *R v Secretary of State for the Home Department, ex p Launder* [1997] 1 WLR 839, 854E-G (Lord Hope: "we are dealing here with decisions in which there is obviously a substantial policy content, where ... the court must exercise great caution in holding a decision to be irrational"); *R (Gurung) v Ministry of Defence* [2008] EWHC 1496 (Admin) at [55] ("the greater the policy content of a decision ... the more hesitant the court must be in holding a decision to be irrational"); *R v Ministry of Defence, ex p Smith* [1996] QB 517, 556B-C ("Where decisions of a policy-laden, esoteric or security-based nature are in issue even greater caution than normal must be shown"); *R v Lord Chancellor, ex p Maxwell* [1997] 1 WLR 104 (endorsing that the greater the element of policy in a decision, the greater should be the judicial reticence in reviewing it); <58.5> (HRA latitude and policy content).

(C) COMPLEX ASSESSMENTS/MATTERS OF DETAIL. *R v London Borough of Southwark, ex p Cordwell* (1995) 27 HLR 594, 601 (rejecting application attempting to give "spurious precision to what is inevitably an extremely difficult exercise in value judgment"); *R v Camden*

London Borough Council, ex p Cran (1996) 94 LGR 8, 27-28 (ie. McCullough J's discussion of court's "approach to matters of detail"); *Upjohn Ltd v Licensing Authority established by the Medicines Act 1968* [1999] 1 WLR 927 at [34] ("where a Community authority is called on, in the performance of its duties, to make complex assessments, it enjoys a wide measure of discretion").

(D) SPECIALISED MATTERS/EXPERT ADVICE. *R (London and Continental Stations and Property Ltd) v Rail Regulator* [2003] EWHC 2607 (Admin) at [32] (Moses J, commenting that the "nature of the subject matter ... reinforces the reluctance a court must feel in intervening ... the Regulator was concerned with issues of economic policy and of economic theory and practice"), [105] (inappropriate for court to resolve "rival arguments as to the appropriate method of calculating elasticities in relation to increased walking time"); *R (Corner House Research) v Director of the Serious Fraud Office* [2008] UKHL 60 [2008] 3 WLR 568 at [40] (DSFO "obliged and entitled to rely on the expert assessments of others"); *R v Council of Legal Education, ex p Eddis* (1995) 7 Admin LR 357, 380E-H ("central" that defendant "consulted experts at every stage"); *R v Ministry of Defence, ex p Smith* [1996] QB 517, 558A-B (policy "supported ... by those to whom the ministry properly looked for professional advice"); *R v Secretary of State for Health, ex p Eastside Cheese Company* [1999] EuLR 968, 987G ("on public health issues which require the evaluation of complex scientific evidence, the national court may and should be slow to interfere with a decision which a responsible decision-maker has reached after consultation with its expert advisers"); *R v London Borough of Bromley, ex p Crystal Palace Campaign* 21st December 1998 unrep. (impossible to impugn decision as to architectural style, in the light of expert advice obtained by defendant).

(E) OTHER. *R (Da Silva) v Director of Public Prosecutions* [2006] EWHC 3204 (Admin) at [54] ("lengthy, careful and thorough" consideration); *R v Independent Television Commission, ex p Virgin Television Limited* [1996] EMLR 318 (restraint "a logical consequence of the perceived care and meticulous approach which the Commission brought to bear on its task of assessment and evaluation"); *R v London Borough of Lambeth, ex p G* [1994] ELR 207, 213F-G ("It is not for this court to take decisions of educational policy in substitution for the local education authority"); *Clark v University of Lincolnshire and Humberside* [2000] 1 WLR 1988 at [12] ("issues of academic or pastoral judgment ... may be unsuitable for adjudication in the courts"); *R v Hillingdon London Borough Council, ex p Puhlhofer* [1986] AC 484, 518D-E (calling for "great restraint" in the housing context), 517D (local authority having "to balance the priority needs of the homeless on the one hand, and the legitimate aspirations of those on their housing waiting list on the other hand"); *Philomena Gangadeen v Secretary of State for the Home Department* [1998] Imm AR 106, 115 ("the court should be very slow to interfere with the Home Secretary's decision not to grant what is essentially a concession on extra-statutory grounds"); *Tesco Stores Ltd v Secretary of State for the Environment* [1995] 1 WLR 759, 780H ("matters of planning judgment are within the exclusive province of the local planning authority or the Secretary of State"); *R v Lord Chancellor, ex p Law Society* (1994) 6 Admin LR 833 (DC), 857D-E (Neill LJ: "hard and difficult choices have to be made by those whose responsibilities include the apportionment of finite resources between competing public services"); <31.2.3> (circumstances where limited resources); *R (Burke) v General Medical Council* [2005] EWCA Civ 1003 [2006] QB 273 at [21] (dangers of enunciating propositions "where the issues raised involve ethical questions that any court should be reluctant to address").

13.5.2 Judicial restraint: examples of particular decision-makers.

(A) MINISTERS. *Hoffmann-La Roche (F) & Co AG v Secretary of State for Trade and Industry* [1975] AC 295, 352G ("it was for the Minister to form certain opinions and for the Minister to decide what, if any, action to take. Questions of policy were for him subject to the control of Parliament"); *R v Secretary of State for the Home Department, ex p Launder* [1997] 1 WLR 839, 857C-D (whether to extradite a matter entrusted to the Home Secretary).

(B) LOCAL AUTHORITIES. *R (Johnson) v Reading Borough Council* [2004] EWHC 765

(Admin) at [61] ("Real deference should be paid to the decision of decision takers who are democratically elected and who take their decision following ... adequate consultation"); *R v Devon County Council, ex p L* (1992) 4 Admin LR 99, 114F-115B (local authority "should be allowed to perform their task without looking over their shoulder all the time for the possible intervention of the court").

(C) COMMERCIAL REGULATORS. *R v Securities & Futures Authority, ex p Panton* 20th June 1994 unrep. (speaking of "the self-regulatory organisations": "it is not the function of the court in anything other than a clear case to second guess their decisions or, as it were, to look over their shoulder"; "these bodies are amenable to judicial review, but are, in anything other than very clear circumstances, to be left to get on with it"); *A v B Bank (Governor and Company of the Bank of England Intervening)* [1993] QB 311, 329B-C ("the importance which should be attached to the Bank of England having, within the limits laid down by the Act and the general law, unfettered and unimpeded scope for the exercise of their most important public duties of regulation under the Act in the interests of the public"), cited in *R v Chance, ex p Coopers & Lybrand* (1995) 7 Admin LR 821, 833D-F.

(D) OTHER. *Bolton v Law Society* [1994] 1 WLR 512, 516H (endorsing the view that "in cases of professional misconduct ... it would require a very strong case to interfere with sentence ... because the disciplinary committee are the best possible people for weighing the seriousness of the professional misconduct"); *R v Licensing Authority Established under Medicines Act 1968, ex p Smith Kline & French Laboratories (No.1)* [1990] 1 AC 64 at 108B ("The courts should be reluctant to criticise the practices of the licensing authority or to grant injunctions or orders or declarations against the licensing authority which is endeavouring reasonably and conscientiously to discharge the onerous duties imposed by Parliament and is acting in good faith").

13.5.3 **Presumptions of validity.** <42.1.3>.

13.5.4 **Benevolent treatment of certain materials/targets.**
(A) DELEGATED LEGISLATION/BYELAWS. *McEldowney v Forde* [1971] AC 632, 645D (Lord Hodson: "the courts will be slow to interfere with the exercise of wide powers to make regulations"); *Kruse v Johnson* [1898] 2 QB 91 (courts should take a "benevolent" approach to byelaws made by public representative bodies, asking whether manifestly unjust, partial, made in bad faith or so gratuitous and oppressive that no reasonable person could think them justified), applied in *R v Dyfed County Council, ex p Manson* [1995] Env LR 83, 96.
(B) DECISIONS AS TO LEAVE/PERMISSION TO APPEAL. <32.2.10>.
(C) PLANNING MEASURES. *Newbury District Council v Secretary of State for the Environment* [1981] AC 578, 609F-G (giving a planning "condition the benevolent treatment to which, like a byelaw, it is entitled"); *Chertsey Urban District Council v Mixnam's Properties Ltd* [1965] AC 735, 760G-761B ("a benevolent interpretation given to the discretion"); *R v South Northamptonshire District Council, ex p Crest Homes Plc* (1995) 93 LGR 205, 211, 219 (benevolent interpretation to section 106 agreements).
(D) DECISIONS/REASONS/DECISION LETTERS. *R (Roberts) v Secretary of State for Communities and Local Government* [2008] EWHC 677 (Admin) (letter "not to be construed as though it was a statutory instrument"); *R (Assura Pharmacy Ltd) v NHS Litigation Authority* [2008] EWHC 289 (Admin) at [73] (straightforward down-to-earth reading of decision letter); *R (Campbell) v General Medical Council* [2004] EWHC 1288 (Admin) at [27] (wrong to approach GMC's reasons "in a pedantic and nit-picking spirit", nor "seize on occasional omission and infelicities") (CA is [2005] EWCA Civ 250 [2005] 1 WLR 3488); *Save Britain's Heritage v Number 1 Poultry Ltd* [1991] 1 WLR 153, 164E-G (decision letter approached by "reading it with a measure of benevolence"); *R (Puspalatha v Immigration Appeal Tribunal* [2001] EWHC Admin 333 at [43] (inappropriate to subject an adjudicator's determination "to the kind of legalistic scrutiny that might perhaps be appropriate in the case of a statutory

instrument, charter party or trust deed"); *United Kingdom Association of Professional Engineers v Advisory Conciliation & Arbitration Service* [1981] AC 424, 435C-E (as to Acas reports: necessary to "read between the lines"); *R v Local Commissioner for Administration for the South (etc), ex p Eastleigh Borough Council* [1988] QB 855, 866D-E (ombudsman's report having to be "written in everyday language", not intended to undergo "microscopic and somewhat legalistic analysis"); *R v Wandsworth London Borough, ex p Oteng* (1994) 26 HLR 413, 416 ("housing authorities are not to be criticised if they do not always use, in decision letters, the same language as a lawyer would have used, so long as their reasons are clear and complete"). (E) DEBATES/COLLECTIVE DECISIONS. *R v London County Council, ex p London and Provincial Electric Theatres Ltd* [1915] 2 KB 466, 490-491 ("probably hardly any decision of a body like the London County Council dealing with these matters could stand if every statement which a member made in debate were to be taken as a ground of the decision"); *R v Somerset County Council, ex p Fewings* [1995] 1 WLR 1037, 1051D.

13.5.5 Judicial restraint and defendant's reconsideration/willingness? <4.4.3> (open-minded defendant willing to consider representations); <36.4.4> (whether defect curable by reconsideration); *R v Radio Authority, ex p Guardian Media Group Plc* [1995] 1 WLR 334, 347B-D ("the authority left open the position should new material emerge ... The position of the authority was not an unreasonable one"); *R v Legal Aid Board, ex p Duncan* [2000] COD 159 (see transcript at [561]) (asking "whether, given the externally imposed time-frame, the scheme the Board devised is robust enough to accommodate the possibility of changes of tack once weaknesses in the scheme of the kind that are evident in this judgment are brought to its attention"); *R v Secretary of State for the Home Department, ex p Pierson* [1998] AC 539, 593E-F (upholding CA's approach in rejecting an unfairness challenge, referring to the Secretary of State's expressed willingness to hear any further representations); *R (Carlton-Conway) v London Borough of Harrow* [2002] EWCA Civ 927 [2002] 3 PLR 77 (where planning officer should not have dealt with matter under delegated powers, judicial review granted even though planning committee had since ratified the decision) at [27] (risk of "a potential motivation, as would be perceived by a fair-minded member of the public, that a wish to support their chief planning officer and to avoid the possibility of judicial review were factors that led to the relevant decisions"); *R (Goodman) v London Borough of Lewisham* [2003] EWCA Civ 140 [2003] Env LR 644 at [14] (as to "the decision undertaken ... after these proceedings were launched. A strong note of caution in respect of such reconsiderations was sounded by this court in [*Carlton-Conway*]); *R v Secretary of State for the Home Department, ex p Turgut* [2001] 1 All ER 719, 729g (need to "recognise at least the possibility that [the Secretary of State] has (even if unconsciously) tended to depreciate the evidence of risk and ... tended also to rationalise the further material adduced so as to maintain his pre-existing stance rather than reassess the position with an open mind"); *R (Kaur) v Ealing London Borough Council* [2008] EWHC 2062 (Admin) at [43] (unlawful to decide policy without prior impact assessment, on basis of monitoring impact after the event).

13.6 Protecting public authorities. One aspect of judicial restraint is control over the adverse impact which judicial review litigation could have on the exercise of public functions. Public authorities need protecting from unwarranted interference.

13.6.1 Principal protections. <P26> delay; <P21> (permission); <P38> (standing); <P4> (materiality); <27.3> (procedural exclusivity: abuse); <24.3> (discretion as to remedy); <2.6> (strict case-management).

13.6.2 Timing of intervention: avoiding disruption. <4.7.4> (whether to let proceedings take their course); *R v Chance, ex p Coopers & Lybrand* (1995) 7 Admin LR 821, 837C-E (judicial review not generally available "before ... disciplinary procedures were complete", since this would "frustrate [or] at least reduce the intended efficacy of disciplinary proceedings"); *R v Association of Futures Brokers and Dealers Ltd, ex p Mordens Ltd* (1991) 3 Admin LR 254, 263E ("it is only in the most exceptional circumstances that the court will grant judicial review of a decision taken during the course of a hearing ... before that hearing has been concluded"); *R v Panel on Take-overs and Mergers, ex p Datafin Plc* [1987] QB 815, 840H (take over panel should "ignore any application for [permission] to apply of which they become aware, since to do otherwise would enable such applications to be used as a mere ploy in take-over battles which would be a serious abuse of the process of the court"), 842C-E ("expect the relationship between the panel and the court to be historic rather than contemporaneous", to "allow contemporary decisions to take their course").

13.6.3 Curbing inappropriate action. <P10> (cooperation and candour); *R v Independent Television Commission, ex p TSW Broadcasting Ltd* [1994] 2 LRC 414, 425h-i ("it is not permissible to probe the advice received by the decision maker or to require particulars or administer interrogatories or ... cross-examine, in order to discover the existence of a mistake by the decision maker or the advisers of the decision makers"); *R v Secretary of State for Trade and Industry, ex p Lonrho Plc* [1989] 1 WLR 525, 535F ("Lonrho sought ... improperly to bully the DTI by threats of judicial review, to intimidate the DTI by insinuations of a political `cover up' and to obtain and exploit observations which, distorted and taken out of context, might lend some support to an application for judicial review. Judicial review is a protection and not a weapon"); *R v Secretary of State for Health, ex p London Borough of Hackney* 25th April 1994 unrep. ("deprecating" delayed claim then pursued urgently without notice); *R (Assisted Reproduction and Gynaecology Centre) v Human Fertilisation and Embryology Authority* [2002] EWCA Civ 20 [2003] 1 FCR 266 at [54] (concern "at the tone of some of the correspondence, which appeared designed to put pressure on the [defendant] to capitulate rather than to reconsider").

13.7 Review from the decision-maker's point of view One protection from over-intrusion is a default position of review from the point of view of the decision-maker, on material then available.

13.7.1 Looking through the decision-maker's eyes. *R v Kingston-Upon-Thames Justices, ex p Peter Martin* [1994] Imm AR 172, 179 (considering reasonableness "through the eyes of the magistrates at the relevant time, having regard to the existing circumstances"); *Re HK (An Infant)* [1967] 2 QB 617, 635G (whether "decision ... can be attacked in the light of the information then available to the immigration officer, and in the light of the consideration which he then gave to that information"); *R v Secretary of State for Social Services, ex p Association of Metropolitan Authorities* [1986] 1 WLR 1, 7D ("treating as material the facts as they appeared to the Secretary of State, and not necessarily as they were"); *R v Commissioners of Customs and Excise, ex p British Sky Broadcasting Group* [2001] EWHC Admin 127 [2001] STC 437 (review by reference to "the factors which were known or ought to have been known by the administrator when the decision was taken").

13.7.2 Failure to request/complain. <31.4>.

13.7.3 Fresh evidence in judicial review. <17.2>.

13.7.4 Material which was not before the decision-maker: illustrations. *R v Secretary of State for Education & Science, ex p Parveen Malik* [1994] ELR 121, 129C-D & H ("the fundamental flaw in [counsel]'s argument is that his submissions ... are founded on material which was not before the Secretary of State"); *R v Secretary of State for the Home Department, ex p Syed Majid Kazmi* [1994] Imm AR 94, 101 ("this application has to be considered on the material before the Secretary of State"); *R v Secretary of State for Transport, ex p Richmond-upon-Thames London Borough Council* [1994] 1 WLR 74, 96D-E (since defendant "was not bound by law to obtain specific expert material", argument not advanced by exhibiting expert articles which "were not before the Secretary of State"); *R v West Sussex Quarter Sessions, ex p Albert & Maud Johnson Trust Ltd* [1974] QB 24 (emergence of fresh evidence, even if it might have made a difference had it been available before the defendant, not of itself a ground for judicial review); *R v Westminster City Council, ex p Ali* (1997) 29 HLR 580, 582 (HHJ Rich: "it may be improper to go beyond the scope of the material that was actually before the City Council"); *R v MacDonald (Inspector of Taxes), ex p Hutchinson and Co Ltd* [1998] STC 680, 695a (evidence "strictly irrelevant to the legality of the decision taken in 1996, since the evidence was not available to those making the decision").

13.7.5 **Hindsight/unavailable material.** *R v Registrar General of Births, Deaths and Marriages, ex p P and G* [1996] 2 FLR 90, 96A ("none of the post-1993 material upon which [counsel] now relies could reasonably be expected to be available to the Registrar General ... when he was making the decisions challenged in this case"); *R v Secretary of State for Transport, ex p Richmond upon Thames London Borough Council (No.4)* [1996] 1 WLR 1460, 1482B (Brooke LJ: "the minister could not reasonably be criticised for not relying on evidence that did not at present exist... the present state of the research evidence on sleep disturbance was a factor he could reasonably take into account"); *R v Council of Legal Education, ex p Eddis* (1995) 7 Admin LR 357, 372B ("With the wisdom of hindsight, that decision might be wrong, but in our judgment it was not irrational in the circumstances in which it was taken").

13.7.6 **Special cases.** <17.2> (whether fresh evidence permissible); *R (Ivanauskiene) v Special Adjudicator* [2001] EWCA Civ 1271 [2002] INLR 1 (although special adjudicator was bound to follow a relevant Court of Appeal decision, nevertheless amounting to misapplication of law given that HL had since overturned CA); *R v Governor of Brockhill Prison, ex p Evans (No.2)* [2001] 2 AC 19 (no defence of justification to false imprisonment where following line of authorities subsequently overturned); *R v Inner London North Coroner, ex p Touche* [2001] EWCA Civ 383 [2001] QB 1206 at [36] (although decision was originally correct, coroner should have changed his mind on information subsequently brought to his attention); *R (Haqq) v HM Coroner for Inner West London* [2003] EWHC 3366 (Admin) (although insufficient evidence before the coroner for him to release body to claimant, court on judicial review granting declaration that body should be released to her, domicile and entitlement to letters of administration having been established on the evidence before the court).

13.7.7 **Judicial review for ignorance of established and material fact.** <49.2.2>.

> **P14 Balancing.** Judicial review principles are a careful evolving equilibrium serving the dual imperatives of vigilance and restraint.

14.1 Judicial review and striking a balance. The principles governing judicial review are the product of the tension between vigilance and restraint. It is tempting to regard vigilance as dominant in relation to reviewability (when the Courts preserve the capacity to intervene) and restraint as dominant in relation to grounds for review (when the Courts will actually do so). But the truth is that a "critical balance" is being struck throughout the law and practice.

14.1.1 Striking a balance in judicial review. *R v Inland Revenue Commissioners, ex p National Federation of Self-Employed and Small Businesses Ltd* [1982] AC 617, 662A-C ("judicial review should be freely available in whatever form may be appropriate in a particular case" but "it is equally important that the courts do not by use or misuse of the weapon of judicial review cross that clear boundary between what is administration, whether it be good or bad administration, and what is an unlawful performance of the statutory duty by a body charged with the performance of that duty"); *R (International Transport Roth GmbH) v Secretary of State for the Home Department* [2002] EWCA Civ 158 [2003] QB 728 at [54] (Simon Brown LJ: "Constitutional dangers exist no less in too little judicial activism as in too much"); *R v Lord Saville of Newdigate, ex p A* [2000] 1 WLR 1855 at [31] ("the courts have to bear in mind at all times that the members of the tribunal have a much greater understanding of their task than the courts. However, subject to the courts confining themselves to their well-recognised role on applications for judicial review, it is essential that they should be prepared to exercise that role regardless of the distinction of the body concerned and the sensitivity of the issues involved"); *R v Ministry of Defence, ex p Smith* [1996] QB 517 (DC) at 538E (describing the "tension ... between the suggested defence interests of the state and the fundamental human rights of the individuals affected").

14.1.2 The critical balance: "two-tiered review". <16.6.4> (two-tiered review); <13.1> & <15.1> (soft review); <P16> (hard-edged review).

14.1.3 The critical balance: discretions and duties. <13.3> (restraint and discretion/judgment); <39.1> (no unfettered discretion/power); <39.2> (discretion/power: the essential duties); <P39> (discretion/duty).

14.1.4 Striking a balance: reviewability. <32.4.10> (modified review and national security); <35.1.5(C)> (prerogative of mercy); <34.3.5> (judicial review of delegated legislation); <13.5.4(A)> (benevolent treatment of delegated legislation); <P28> (statutory ousters); <P32> (modified review).

14.1.5 Striking a balance: onus. <P42>.

14.1.6 Striking a balance: special responses. <P43> (severance): see eg. *DPP v Hutchinson* [1990] 2 AC 783, 819C-F (textual severability as "a concession to the erring law-maker") <46.3.3> (reading down).

14.1.7 Damages for maladministration: searching for the right balance. <25.2.2>.

14.2 Striking a balance: grounds for judicial review Behind the articulation of every ground for judicial review, Courts are grappling with the question of where precisely to draw the line, in deciding when a public body goes so 'badly wrong' as to warrant interference by the Court.

14.2.1 Striking a balance: "unlawfulness" examples.
(A) THE FACT/LAW DISTINCTION. This distinction is designed to express a balance between vigilance (questions of law) and restraint (questions of fact); <13.2> (restraint and factual questions); <P48> (error of law); <P49> (error of fact).
(B) ERROR OF FACT: "DECENT RESPECT". *Edwards v Bairstow* [1956] AC 14, 38-39 (Lord Radcliffe: "The court is not a second opinion"; "Their duty is no more than to examine those facts with a decent respect for the tribunal"); <P49> (error of fact).
(C) BALANCING RIGHTS AND LEGISLATIVE SUPREMACY. *R v Lord Chancellor, ex p Witham* [1998] QB 575, 581E (Laws J: "at a time when the common law continues to accord a legislative supremacy to Parliament, the notion of a constitutional right can in my judgment inhere only in this proposition, that the right in question cannot be abrogated by the state save by specific provision in an Act of Parliament, or by regulations whose vires in main legislation specifically confers the power to abrogate. General words will not suffice"), applied in *Cullen v Chief Constable of the Royal Ulster Constabulary* [2003] UKHL 39 [2003] 1 WLR 1763 at [45] (Lord Hutton); <7.5.1> (constitutional rights).
(D) BALANCING STATE AND INDIVIDUAL: LATITUDE. <58.5>.
(E) BALANCING INDIVIDUAL AND PUBLIC RIGHTS *Attorney-General's Reference (No.2 of 2001)* [2001] EWCA Crim 1568 [2001] 1 WLR 1869 (CA) at [19] (Lord Woolf CJ: "As is the case with many of the rights which are contained in the Convention, the courts are called upon to hold the balance between the rights of the individual and the rights of the public") (HL is at [2003] UKHL 68 [2004] 2 AC 72).
(F) CONSTITUTIONAL STATUTES: STRIKING A BALANCE. <7.5.7>.
(G) ART 6 INDEPENDENCE AND IMPARTIALITY: STRIKING A BALANCE. *Begum v Tower Hamlets London Borough Council* [2003] UKHL 5 [2003] 2 AC 430 at [35] (Lord Hoffmann, encapsulating the critical balance by which the ECHR Art 6 requirement of independence is applied broadly to include "administrative" functions, but accompanied by an appropriate restraint in the scrutiny of judicial review which ensures compatibility, thus: "An English lawyer can view with equanimity the extension of the scope of article 6 because the English conception of the rule of law requires the legality of virtually all governmental decisions affecting the individual to be subject to the scrutiny of the ordinary courts... But this breadth of scope is accompanied by an approach to the grounds of review which requires that regard be had to democratic accountability, efficient administration and the sovereignty of Parliament").

14.2.2 Striking a balance: unreasonableness/abuse of power. *R (Bancoult) v Secretary of State for Foreign & Commonwealth Affairs* [2007] EWCA Civ 498 [2008] QB 365 at [78] ("Notwithstanding the great latitude which the prerogative power of Colonial governance enjoys", Court characterising Order in Council as an abuse of power); *Wheeler v Leicester City Council* [1985] AC 1054, 1077II-1078A (Lord Roskill, referring to the important "line which divides a proper exercise of a statutory discretion based on a political judgment, in relation to which the courts must not and will not interfere, from an improper exercise of such a discretion in relation to which the courts will interfere"); *R v Director of Public Prosecutions, ex p Manning* [2001] QB 330, at [23] (Court slow to interfere with DPP's judgment as to whether to prosecute, but: "At the same time, the standard of review should not be set too high, since judicial review is the only means by which the citizen can seek redress against a decision not to prosecute and if the test were too exacting an effective remedy would be denied"); *R v Secretary of State for the Home Department, ex p Brind* [1991] 1 AC 696, 749A-B (Lord

Bridge: "The primary judgment as to whether the particular competing public interest justifies the particular restriction imposed falls to be made by the Secretary of State to whom Parliament has entrusted the discretion. But we are entitled to exercise a secondary judgment by asking whether a reasonable Secretary of State, on the material before him, could reasonably make that primary judgment"); *R v Ministry for Agriculture Fisheries & Food, ex p Hamble Fisheries (Offshore) Ltd* [1995] 2 All ER 714, 722a-c (Sedley J, describing the "two conflicting imperatives" of consistency and non-rigidity); <56.2> (discretionary/obligatory relevancies); <56.3> (relevance and weight).

14.2.3 Striking a balance: "unfairness" examples. <30.3> (judicial/ administrative distinction); <60.7.10> (practical limits of the duty to tell); <60.1.19> (fairness not best practice); <40.2> (legitimate expectation/ estoppel and inalienability).

14.3 Striking a balance: nothing personal.One way of managing the tension between vigilance and restraint has been to emphasise that the Courts' intervention, where it is appropriate, does not mean criticism or disrespect for the public decision-makers themselves.

14.3.1 Nothing personal and objective standards. *R v London Borough of Camden, ex p Paddock* [1995] COD 130 (see transcript) (Sedley J: "it is never pleasant for officers or members of a public body to be told that they have departed from standards of public administration required by law. But to be told this is not to be `condemned'. The critical question is not the subjective intention of the decision-maker but the objective effect of what was done"); <45.2.6> (need for objective standards).

14.3.2 Nothing personal: unreasonableness. *Champion v Chief Constable of the Gwent Constabulary* [1990] 1 WLR 1, 16F-17A (Lord Lowry: "The conclusion therefore is that he was guilty of *Wednesbury* unreasonableness and, to adopt the words used in that case, came to a conclusion so unreasonable that no reasonable Chief Constable could ever have come to it. The use of this stark language may be a salutary reminder of the heavy burden assumed by those who would attack administrative decisions, but I regret the identification which it implies of unreasonableness with the decision-maker as well as with the decision... When the decision is made by a statutory authority or a public officer, I feel that it would be more becoming and more accurate to condemn (where that step must be taken) a decision `so unreasonable that no statutory authority/public officer' (to be specified) `acting reasonably could ever have come to it', because it by no means follows that the authority or officer concerned has not in the past behaved or will not in future behave in the most reasonable way imaginable"); *R v London Borough of Brent, ex p Omar* (1992) 4 Admin LR 509, 524E (conclusion "unintentionally perverse"); *In re W (An Infant)* [1971] AC 682, 695F (Lord Hailsham: "Unreasonableness is one thing. Culpability is another. It may be that all or most culpable conduct is unreasonable. But the converse is not necessarily true").

14.3.3 Nothing personal: unfairness. *Fairmount Investments Ltd v Secretary of State for the Environment* [1976] 1 WLR 1255, 1266E (no "moral blame" from unfairness conclusion); *R v Inner West London Coroner, ex p Dallaglio* [1994] 4 All ER 139, 156c-d (no "condemnation" for coroner's "single intemperate comment"); *R v Secretary of State for Education and Science, ex p Islam* (1993) 5 Admin LR 177, 187C-D ("manifest unfairness" in the Secretary of State's decision, simply "a gap in the thinking about the procedure which should have been adopted"); *R v National Lottery Commission, ex p Camelot Group Plc* [2001] EMLR 3 at [83] (Commission intended to act fairly; nevertheless "conspicuous unfairness").

14.3.4 Nothing personal: unlawfulness. *R (Ivanauskiene) v Special Adjudicator* [2001] EWCA

Civ 1271 [2002] INLR 1 at [23] (adjudicator having committed an error of law, albeit that entirely blameless; followed a decision of the Court of Appeal which had subsequently been overturned as incorrect); *R (JE) v Criminal Injuries Compensation Appeals Panel* [2003] EWCA Civ 234 at [37] (judicial review granted because of case-law which post-dated the decision, and on the basis of fuller argument than the defendant had heard); *R (Sussex Police Authority) v Cooling* [2004] EWHC 1920 (Admin) at [42] (no stigma attaching to getting the law wrong).

14.4 Convenience and floodgates.Judicial review is popular and the Administrative Court faces a heavy workload. Nevertheless, the Courts take a principled stance in refusing to draw defensive lines which would restrict the law or its development, on the basis of workload, convenience, or "floodgates".

14.4.1 Justice trumps convenience: the *Spackman* observation.

General Medical Council v Spackman [1943] AC 627, 638 (Lord Atkin: "Convenience and justice are often not on speaking terms"), cited in *Leech v Deputy Governor of Parkhurst Prison* [1988] AC 533, 578B (Lord Oliver); *R v Secretary of State for the Environment, ex p Brent London Borough Council* [1982] QB 593, 646F-G; *R (Murray) v Parole Board* [2003] EWCA Civ 1561 at [24] ("logistical difficulties" no answer to question whether parole review delays excessive in breach of HRA:ECHR Art 5(4)).

14.4.2 Refusing to adopt "defensive lines".

(A) GENERAL. *R v Bolton Justices, ex p Scally* [1991] 1 QB 537, 555C-D (Watkins LJ: "the overriding principle ... must surely be that justice should be done and if it be demonstrated that another principle rigidly applied is or would seem to be getting in the way of doing justice, the bounds of that principle require to be very critically examined in a modern light and without the so often deployed floodgates argument being given undue prominence"); *R v Lambert* [2001] UKHL 37 [2002] 2 AC 545 at [30] (Lord Steyn: "A healthy scepticism ought to be observed about practised predictions of an avalanche of dire consequences likely to flow from any new development").

(B) REVIEWABILITY. *Leech v Deputy Governor of Parkhurst Prison* [1988] AC 533, 566B-F (Lord Bridge: "[Counsel] held out the prospect, as one which should make our judicial blood run cold, that opening the door to judicial review of governors' awards would make it impossible to resist an invasion by what he called `the tentacles of the law' of many other departments of prison administration"; "In a matter of jurisdiction it cannot be right to draw lines on a purely defensive basis and determine that the court has no jurisdiction over one matter which it ought properly to entertain for fear that acceptance of jurisdiction may set a precedent which will make it difficult to decline jurisdiction over other matters which it ought not to entertain. Historically the development of the law in accordance with coherent and consistent principles has all too often been impeded, in diverse areas of the law besides that of judicial review, by the court's fear that unless an arbitrary boundary is drawn it will be inundated by a flood of unmeritorious claims").

(C) FAIRNESS. *R v Secretary of State for the Home Department, ex p Duggan* [1994] 3 All ER 277, 287h (principles of fairness applying to security reviews, since "in a matter of jurisdiction, lines are not to be drawn on a purely defensive basis").

(D) SUFFICIENT EVIDENTIAL BASIS. *R v Bedwellty Justices, ex p Williams* [1997] AC 225, 237G (no flood of judicial review of committals following *Neill v North Antrim Magistrates' Court* [1992] 1 WLR 1220); see *Neill* at 1233D-G (posing the question "whether as a matter of policy the court should entirely abstain from intervening, for fear of being submerged by a flood of worthless applications").

(E) HRA DAMAGES. *R (N) v Secretary of State for the Home Department* [2003] EWHC 207

(Admin) [2003] HRLR 583 at [198] (Silber J: "Even if the floodgate argument had any application to the fact-sensitive decision whether or not to award damages in a particular case, I do not consider that it has any value or relevance to this case") (CA is *Anufrijeva v Southwark London Borough Council* [2003] EWCA Civ 1406 [2004] QB 1124); cf. *D v Home Office* [2005] EWCA Civ 38 [2006] 1 WLR 1003 at [109] (rejecting floodgates in context of tort of false imprisonment).

14.4.3 The litigation flood: a threat more illusory than real. *Leech v Deputy Governor of Parkhurst Prison* [1988] AC 533, 582F-583B (Lord Oliver: "the spectre of the courts being flooded with frivolous applications for [permission] to apply for judicial review is more likely to be illusory than real"); *R v Secretary of State for the Home Department, ex p Tarrant* [1985] QB 251, 297D-G; *Gouriet v Union of Post Office Workers* [1978] AC 435, 510A-B ("it was urged that any change in the present law would open what were called the `floodgates' to a multiplicity of claims by busybodies. But it is difficult to see why such people should be more numerous or active than private prosecutors are at the present day"); *Williams* <14.4.2(D)>.

14.4.4 Principled responses to the floodgates fear.
(A) A FLOOD OF JUDICIAL REVIEW CASES MAY BE NECESSARY.*Edwards v Bairstow* [1956] AC 14, 32 (Viscount Simonds: "We were warned by learned counsel for the [defendants] that to allow this appeal would open the floodgates to appeals against the decisions of the General Commissioners up and down the country. That would cause me no alarm, if decisions such as that we have spent some time in reviewing were common up and down the country").
(B) NO FLOOD IF NO ABUSE OF POWER.*R v Horseferry Road Magistrates' Court, ex p Bennett* [1994] 1 AC 42, 77A (Lord Lowry: "No `floodgates' argument applies because the executive can stop the flood at source by refraining from impropriety").
(C) PARLIAMENT COULD ACT. *Leech v Deputy Governor of Parkhurst Prison* [1988] AC 533, 582H-583B (Lord Oliver: "the remedy, in the end, lies in the hands of the courts or, in the ultimate analysis, with Parliament"); *Woolwich Equitable Building Society v Inland Revenue Commissioners* [1993] AC 70, 177B and 200E; *R v Kansal (No.2)* [2001] EWCA Crim 1260 [2002] 2 AC 69 (CA) at [24] (HL is [2001] UKHL 62 [2002] 2 AC 69).
(D) THE FORBIDDEN SUBSTITUTIONARY APPROACH. <15.1>(forbidden substitutionary approach); *R v Secretary of State for the Home Department, ex p Doody* [1994] 1 AC 531, 566D-E (Lord Mustill: "this will not be a signal for a flood of successful applications for judicial review... Only if it can be shown that the decision may have been arrived at through a faulty process, in one of the ways so familiar to practitioners of judicial review, will [prisoners] have any serious prospect of persuading the court to grant [a remedy]"); *Puhlhofer* (Lord Brightman) <13.2.1>; *R v Preston Supplementary Benefits Appeal Tribunal, ex p Moore* [1975] 1 WLR 624, 631G-H (to avoid the courts becoming "engulfed with streams of cases", they should "leave the tribunals to interpret the Act in a broad reasonable way, according to the spirit and not to the letter").
(E) MODIFIED REVIEW. <P32>.
(F) LIBERAL APPROACH TO EXCLUSIVITY. <27.3.8>;*Chief Adjudication Officer v Foster* [1993] AC 754, 766H-767A (Lord Bridge, "pleased" to conclude that exclusivity did not apply, since "it avoids a cumbrous duplicity of proceedings which could only add to the already over-burdened list of applications for judicial review awaiting determination by the Divisional Court"), applied in *Boddington v British Transport Police* [1999] 2 AC 143, 175B.
(G) REFUSAL TO SPECULATE.*R (Asif Javed) v Secretary of State for the Home Department* [2001] EWCA Civ 789 [2002] QB 129 at [79] (referring to submission that remedy should be refused because of potential large number of like claims: "This submission is speculative and we do not consider it to afford a good reason for refusing the [claimants] the [remedy] to which they would otherwise be entitled").

14.4.5 Fear of the flood: stunting development of the law?

(A) COMMON LAW PROPORTIONALITY. <P58>; *R v Secretary of State for the Home Department, ex p Brind* [1991] 1 AC 696, 767B-C (Lord Lowry: "Stability and relative certainty would be jeopardised if the new doctrine [of proportionality] held sway, because there is nearly always something to be said against any administrative decision and parties who felt aggrieved would be even more likely than at present to try their luck with a judicial review application both at first instance and on appeal... The increase in applications for judicial review of administrative action (inevitable if the threshold of unreasonableness is lowered) will lead to the expenditure of time and money by litigants, not to speak of the prolongation of uncertainty for all concerned with the decisions in question, and the taking up of court time which could otherwise be devoted to other matters. The losers in this respect will be members of the public, for whom the courts provide a service").

(B) BLAMELESS UNFAIRNESS. <60.1.16> (blameless unfairness); *R v Secretary of State for the Home Department, ex p Al-Mehdawi* [1990] 1 AC 876, 901D-E (blameless unfairness rejected for fear of "opening such a wide door which would indeed seriously undermine the principle of finality in decision making").

(C) REVIEWABILITY. *R v Chief Constable of the Kent County Constabulary, ex p L* [1993] 1 All ER 756, 771a (Watkins LJ:"The danger of opening too wide the door of review of the discretion to continue a prosecution is manifest and such review, if it exists, must, therefore, be confined to very narrow limits"); *R v Football Association Ltd, ex p Football League Ltd* [1993] 2 All ER 833, 849c-d (judicial review of the FA would be "a misapplication of increasingly scarce judicial resources"; "not, of course, a jurisprudential reason for refusing judicial review, but it will be cold comfort to the seven or eight other substantive applicants and the many more [claimants for permission] who have had to be displaced from the court's lists in order to accommodate the present litigation to learn that, though they may have a remedy for their complaints about the arbitrary abuse of executive power, it cannot be granted to them yet").

> **P15 The forbidden method.** Judges will not intervene as if matters for the public body's judgment were for the Court's judgment.

15.1 "Soft" review: the forbidden substitutionary approach
15.2 "Not an appeal"
15.3 "Legality not correctness"
15.4 "Not the merits"
15.5 "Court does not substitute its own judgment"

15.1 "Soft" review: the forbidden substitutionary approach Every public body has its own proper role and has matters which it is to be trusted to decide for itself. The Courts are careful to avoid usurping that role and interfering whenever they might disagree as to those matters. There are various ways of formulating the warning against impermissible interference. But however it is expressed, the idea of a forbidden approach is essential in understanding and applying principles of judicial review. This idea is at the heart of "soft" review (with built-in "latitude").

15.1.1 **The "forbidden" method.** The "forbidden appellate approach" was Lord Lowry's phrase in *R v Secretary of State for the Home Department, ex p Brind* [1991] 1 AC 696 at 767G. *R v Chief Registrar of Friendly Societies, ex p New Cross Building Society* [1984] QB 227, 241H-242A ("it is not for the court to consider whether the chief registrar's decisions were `right' or `wrong', or to entertain an appeal from them or to substitute the court's discretion for his"); *Laker Airways Ltd v Department of Trade* [1977] QB 643, 724D-E (Lawton LJ: "In a case such as this I regard myself as a referee. I can blow my judicial whistle when the ball goes out of play; but when the game restarts I must neither take part in it nor tell the players how to play").

15.1.2 **Beware of the forbidden method: some basic warnings.** *R (Abbey Mine Ltd) v Coal Authority* [2008] EWCA Civ 353 at [25] ("These grounds ... are fact dressed up as law. Time and again, despite repeated protests in this court and in the Administrative Court, points are taken in judicial review cases which are not points of law at all. This is a waste of scarce resources and an impediment to the clear and transparent development of public law principles"); *R v Secretary of State for Trade and Industry, ex p Lonrho Plc* [1989] 1 WLR 525, 535B-C (Lord Keith, warning of "the danger of judges wrongly though unconsciously substituting their own views for the views of the decision-maker who alone is charged and authorised by Parliament to exercise a discretion. The question is not whether the Secretary of State came to a correct solution or to a conclusion which meets with the approval of the ... Court but whether the discretion was properly exercised"); *R v Nat Bell Liquors Ltd* [1922] 2 AC 128, 142-143 (warning against "rehearing the whole case by way of appeal on the evidence"); *R v Secretary of State for Transport, ex p Richmond-upon-Thames London Borough Council* [1994] 1 WLR 74, 95G (rejecting "a disguised, though elegant, plea upon the merits").

15.1.3 **Understanding "soft" review/reasonableness.** <13.1> (soft review: reasonableness); *R v Secretary of State for the Home Department, ex p Hindley* [1998] QB 751 (DC), 777A (Lord Bingham CJ: "The threshold of irrationality for purposes of judicial review is a high one. This is because responsibility for making the relevant decision rests with another party and not with the court. It is not enough that we might, if the responsibility for making the relevant decision rested with us, make a decision different from that of the appointed decision-maker. To justify intervention by the court, the decision under challenge must fall outside the bounds of any decision open to a reasonable decision-maker"); *R v Secretary of State for the Home Department, ex p Brind* [1991] 1 AC 696, 757G-H (Lord Ackner, explaining that the unreasonableness principle "has to be expressed in terms that confine the jurisdiction exercised by the judiciary to a supervisory, as opposed to an appellate, jurisdiction... It would be a wrongful usurpation of power by the judiciary to substitute its, the judicial view, on the merits and on that basis to quash the decision"); *R v Secretary of State for the Home Department, ex p Khawaja* [1984] AC 74, 110A (unreasonableness principle "excludes the court from substituting its own view of the facts for that of the authority"); <13.1.1> (latitude); <13.7> (review from the decision-maker's point of view).

15.1.4 **Process rather than decision?** *Chief Constable of the North Wales Police v Evans* [1982] 1 WLR 1155, 1173F (Lord Brightman: "Judicial review is concerned, not with the decision, but with the decision-making process"), 1174G ("Judicial review, as the words imply, is not an appeal from a decision, but a review of the manner in which the decision was made"), but see 1173D-E and 1174F-1175B ("Other considerations arise when an administrative decision is attacked on the ground that it is vitiated by self-misdirection, by taking account of irrelevant or neglecting to take account of relevant factors, or is so manifestly unreasonable that no reasonable authority, entrusted with the power in question, could reasonably have made such a decision").

15.2 **"Not an appeal".**[71] This is a first common formula for warning against the forbidden substitutionary approach. But it is not the best one. Whether judicial review is like "an appeal" depends on what sort of "appeal", and what sort of issue, is in mind. There is no universal model of an "appeal", and some appeals (eg. on a "point of law") are like judicial review. On some issues (eg. questions of law or precedent fact), judicial review is like a "substitutionary" appeal.

15.2.1 **Judicial review is "not an appeal".** *R (Malik) v Manchester Crown Court* [2008] EWHC 1362 (Admin) at [31] ("these are judicial review proceedings. This is not an appeal. The decision of the judge cannot be quashed unless he erred in law in one or more of the respects in which a decision can be impugned on public law grounds"); *R v Secretary of State for the Home Department, ex p Launder* [1997] 1 WLR 839, 857C (Lord Hope: "The function of the court in the exercise of its supervisory jurisdiction is that of review. This is not an appeal against the Secretary of State's decision on the facts"); *Kemper Reinsurance Company v Minister of Finance* [2000] 1 AC 1, 14H-15A ("judicial review is quite different from an appeal. It is concerned with the legality rather than the merits of the decision"); *R v Crown Court at Manchester, ex p McDonald* [1999] 1 WLR 841, 855A-B ("It is important to remember always that this is judicial review of, and not an appeal against, the judge's decision"); *R v Northumberland Compensation Appeal Tribunal, ex p Shaw* [1952] 1 KB 338, 357 ("not ... the cloak of an appeal in disguise"); *General Medical Council v Spackman* [1943] AC 627, 640 ("not an appellate power"); *R v Greater Manchester Coroner, ex p Tal* [1985] QB 67, 80G-H ("not sitting in an appellate capacity"); *R v Inland Revenue Commissioners, ex p Rossminster* [1980] AC 952, 1013E-H ("not a court of appeal"); *Associated Provincial Picture Houses Ltd v Wednesbury Corporation* [1948] 1 KB 223, 234 (not "an appellate authority"); *R v Secretary of State for Education and Science, ex p Islam* (1993) 5 Admin LR 177, 179G-180A ("This court does not act as a Court of Appeal from the Secretary of State's decision; that cannot be emphasized too much").

15.2.2 **Parliament provided no appeal: Court must not invent one.** *R v Independent Television Commission, ex p TSW Broadcasting Ltd* [1994] 2 LRC 414, 424c-e (Lord Templeman: "Parliament may by statute confer powers and discretions and impose duties on a

---

[71] This paragraph in a previous edition was cited in *R v Director of Immigration, ex p Yunus* [2005] FJHC 512.

decision maker who may be an individual, a body of persons or a corporation... Where Parliament has not provided for an appeal from a decision maker the courts must not invent an appeal machinery... The courts have invented the remedies of judicial review not to provide an appeal machinery but to ensure that the decision maker does not exceed or abuse his powers"); *R v Broadcasting Complaints Commission, ex p Granada Television Ltd* [1995] 3 EMLR 163 ("Parliament has not provided any right of appeal against the decisions of the BCC. This indicates a clear intention to leave to the BCC alone the determination of [these] difficult questions"); cf. <36.1.2> (absence of other safeguards and judicial vigilance).

15.2.3 **Different "appeal" models.** CPR 52.11 (CA generally conducting a "review of the decision of the lower court" rather than a "re-hearing"); <27.2.3> (public law principles in statutory appeals); *In re J (A Child) (Custody Rights: Jurisdiction)* [2005] UKHL 40 [2006] 1 AC 80 at [12] (appeal against exercise of discretion only if plainly wrong, referring to *G v G (Minors: Custody Appeal)* [1985] 1 WLR 647); *Assicurazioni Generali SpA v Arab Insurance Group (Practice Note)* [2003] 1 WLR 577 at [6]-[23] (role of CA in relation to questions of fact, depending on whether trial judge having advantage in relation to witnesses); *Lloyd v McMahon* [1987] AC 625, 697D-F (statutory appeal as "a rehearing of the broadest possible scope"); *Cook v Southend Borough Council* [1990] 2 QB 1, 18F (appeal as "a statutory right to judicial review"); *Kawarindrasingh v White* [1997] 1 WLR 785 ("review", where court should exercise discretion afresh); *General Medical Council v Hiew* [2007] EWCA Civ 369 [2007] 1 WLR 2007 at [26] (in dealing with suspension orders, "the exercise in decision-making is to be performed by the court as the primary decision-maker").

15.2.4 **Judicial review is not that different from an "appeal".** *Begum v Tower Hamlets London Borough Council* [2003] UKHL 5 [2003] 2 AC 430 at [47] (Lord Hoffmann: "the gap between judicial review and a full right of appeal is seldom in practice very wide. Even with a full right of appeal it is not easy for an appellate tribunal which has not itself seen the witnesses to differ from the decision-maker on questions of primary fact and ... on questions of credibility"), [99] (Lord Millett, describing the limitations on an appeal "on a point of law" as "not very different from the limitations which practical considerations impose on an appellate court with full jurisdiction to entertain appeals on fact or law but which deals with them on the papers only and without hearing oral evidence").

15.3 **"Legality not correctness".** This formulation draws an important distinction, but introduces two pitfalls. First, because "legality" needs to be understood in its broader sense of all grounds for judicial review (eg. reasonableness and fairness). Secondly, because "legality" can itself involve a "correctness"-review (eg. on questions of law or precedent fact).

15.3.1 **Legality not correctness.** *R (Corner House Research) v Director of the Serious Fraud Office* [2008] UKHL 60 [2008] 3 WLR 568 at [41] (Lord Bingham: "The issue ... is not whether his decision was right or wrong, nor whether the [Court] agrees with it, but whether it was a decision which the Director was lawfully entitled to make"); *Sutton London Borough Council v Davis* [1994] Fam 241, 249F ("A decision can be lawful without being correct"); *R (Persey) v Secretary of State for the Environment, Food and Rural Affairs* [2002] EWHC 371 (Admin) [2003] QB 794 at [66] (not whether the court thinks the decision was the "right" one); *Chief Constable of the North Wales Police v Evans* [1982] 1 WLR 1155, 1161A (question is not whether reaches "a conclusion which is correct in the eyes of the court"); *R v Inland Revenue Commissioners, ex p National Federation of Self-Employed and Small Businesses Ltd* [1982] AC 617, 663C (no interference with "administration whether good or bad which is lawful"); *R v Criminal Cases Review Commission, ex p Pearson* [1999] 3 All ER 498, 523e-f ("If this court were to hold that a decision one way or the other was objectively right or objectively wrong, it would be exceeding its function"); *R v Secretary of State for Trade, ex p Anderson Strathclyde Plc* [1983] 2 All ER 233, 243f ("Whether he was right or wrong ... is a matter of political judgment, and not a matter of law"); *Secretary of State for Education and Science v Tameside Metropolitan Borough Council* [1977] AC 1014, 1074H-1075C ("it is quite unacceptable ... to proceed from `wrong' to `unreasonable'... History is replete with genuine accusations of unreasonableness when all that is involved is disagreement, perhaps passionate, between reasonable people"); *R v Secretary of State for the Home Department, ex p Fire Brigades Union* [1995] 2 AC 513, 560H-561A ("A claim that a decision under challenge was wrong leads nowhere, except in the rare case where it can be characterised as so obviously and grossly wrong as to be irrational")

15.3.2 Lawfulness not wisdom. *R v Secretary of State for Trade and Industry, ex p Lonrho Plc* [1989] 1 WLR 525, 536D-E (Lord Keith at 536D-E: "the courts must be careful not to invade the political field and substitute their own judgment for that of the Minister. The courts judge the lawfulness not the wisdom of the decision"); *R v Cumbria County Council, ex p NB* [1996] ELR 65, 72H ("The wisdom of its decision is not a matter upon which this court is empowered to express a view"); *R v Local Government Boundary Commission, ex p Somerset, Avon & Cleveland County Councils* [1994] COD 517 (see transcript) ("ours not to reason why; we have to see whether there was a judicially reviewable error").

15.3.3 Not whether the Court agrees. *R v Home Secretary, ex p Bateman & Howse* (1995) 7 Admin LR 175, 183G-H (Sir Thomas Bingham MR: "it was open to him so to conclude. It is not a question whether I, as a member of this court, agree with him or not"); *R v General Medical Council ex p Colman* [1990] 1 All ER 489, 511d ("it is quite beside the point to consider whether I would have reached the same conclusion"); *R v Secretary of State for Health, ex p Luff* (1991) 3 Admin LR 797, 816D-817A (enough that defendant's view "tenable").

15.4 "Not the merits". This is another favourite formulation of the warning against the forbidden substitutionary approach. It works, provided that what is ruled out is (1) substitutionary (correctness) review, in relation to (2) "soft" questions (eg. judgment, discretion, policy). Beyond those restrictions, there may well be "merits review" (a term which is perhaps apt to mislead), at least in "correcting" certain hard-edged questions and closely scrutinising others (eg. justification for rights-interference).

15.4.1 Judicial review is not "merits" review. *R v Secretary of State for Education and Employment and the North East London Education Authority, ex p M* [1996] ELR 162, 205C-E (Simon Brown LJ: "It has been said time without number that in exercising its supervisory jurisdiction this court is not concerned with the substantive merits of an administrative decision and will not entertain an appeal on the facts"); *Council of Civil Service Unions v Minister for the Civil Service* [1985] AC 374, 401G (Lord Fraser: "The issue here is not whether the minister's instruction was proper or fair or justifiable on its merits. These matters are not for the courts to determine"); *R v Somerset County Council, ex p Fewings* [1995] 1 All ER 513 (Laws J), 515c-g ("one of [judicial review's] most important characteristics is ... that in most cases, the judicial review court is not concerned with the merits of the decision under review. The court does not ask itself the question, 'Is this decision right or wrong?'. Far less does the judge ask himself whether he would himself have arrived at the decision in question... The only question for the judge is whether the decision taken by the body under review was one which it was legally permitted to take in the way that it did"); *Champion v Chief Constable of the Gwent Constabulary* [1990] 1 WLR 1, 12C-D (judicial review is "not concerned with the merits); *R (P) v Essex County Council* [2004] EWHC 2027 (Admin) at [32] (Munby J, contrasting the merits function of the "best interests" jurisdiction, with "review by reference to public law criteria");

R (St Helens Borough Council) v Manchester Primary Care Trust [2008] EWCA Civ 931 at [13] ("the court will not normally examine the merits of the factual determination").

15.4.2 **HRA and whether a "merits review".** *R (Rayner) v Secretary of State for Justice* [2008] EWCA Civ 176 at [43] (under HRA, courts "prepared to investigate more closely the merits of a decision challenged by way of judicial review");*R v Secretary of State for the Home Department, ex p Daly* [2001] UKHL 26 [2001] 2 AC 532 at [27] ("the doctrine of proportionality may require the reviewing court to assess the balance which the decision maker has struck, not merely whether it is within the range of rational or reasonable decisions" and "may require attention to be directed to the relative weight accorded to interests and considerations"), [28] ("This does not mean that there has been a shift to merits review"); *R (Alconbury Developments Ltd) v Secretary of State for the Environment Transport and the Regions* [2001] UKHL 23 [2003] 2 AC 295 at [52] (HRA proportionality "does not go as far as to provide for a complete rehearing on the merits of the decision"); *Wilson v First County Trust Ltd* [2003] UKHL 40 [2004] 1 AC 816 at [62]-[63] (proportionality of legislation a question involving a "value judgment"), [141]-[142] (ECHR-compatibility of legislation "an objective question to be answered having regard to all relevant evidence"; and involving "a sociological assessment"); *R (JB) v Haddock* [2006] EWCA Civ 961 [2006] HRLR 1237 at [13], [64] (in relation to forced medical treatment, "full merits review" with patient entitled to require oral evidence and cross-examination), applying *R (Wilkinson) v Responsible Medical Officer Broadmoor Hospital* [2001] EWCA Civ 1545 [2002] 1 WLR 419 at [36] ("a full merits review"); *CF v Secretary of State for the Home Department* [2004] EWHC 111 (Fam) [2004] 1 FCR 577 at [31] (HRA challenge "not a review of the merits"); *R (G) v London Borough of Ealing* [2002] EWHC 250 (Admin) at [15] ("in some contexts nothing short of a full merits review will suffice even in a judicial review case"); *Huang v Secretary of State for the Home Department* [2007] UKHL 11 [2007] 2 AC 167 (on human rights appeal, immigration judge required to decided compatibility of removal as primary not reviewing function); *Langley v Liverpool City Council* [2005] EWCA Civ 1173 [2006] 1 WLR 375 at [58] (Art 8 not merits review); *R (Suryananda) v Welsh Ministers* [2007] EWCA Civ 893 at [103] (not a merits review); <58.5.3> (HRA latitude).

15.5 **"Court does not substitute its own judgment".** This is perhaps the best of the formulations warning against an impermissible approach on judicial review. It has three advantages. First, it recognises that the warning applies only to certain types of question: labelled here as matters of "judgment". Secondly, it explains what judges should not do regarding those questions: substitute their own view. Thirdly, it reflects the position as to remedy: in general the Court will remit for reconsideration rather than impose a preferred outcome.

15.5.1 **Court does not substitute its own judgment.** *R (Western Riverside Waste Authority) v Wandsworth London Borough Council* [2005] EWHC 536 (Admin) [2005] LGR 846 at [56] ("The court must not attempt to substitute its own judgment"); *WM (DRC) v Secretary of State for the Home Department* [2006] EWCA Civ 1495 at [16] (wrong for court to take the short cut of deciding the issue for itself, even if well-placed to do so); *Luby v Newcastle-under-Lyme Corporation* [1964] 2 QB 64, 72 ("It is not for the court to substitute its own view of what is a desirable policy"), approved in *Wandsworth London Borough Council v Winder* [1985] AC 461, 506D; *R v Birmingham City Council, ex p O* [1983] 1 AC 578, 594H-595A ("The court has no jurisdiction to substitute its own opinion"); *O'Reilly v Mackman* [1983] 2 AC 237, 282G (warning against the "temptation, not always easily resisted, to substitute its own view of the facts"); *In re Westminster City Council* [1986] AC 668, 715G ("Whether a court ... would have made the same decision is irrelevant"); *Chief Constable of the North Wales Police v Evans*

[1982] 1 WLR 1155, 1160G ("it is no part of [the] purpose [of judicial review] to substitute the opinion of the judiciary or of individual judges for that of the authority constituted by law to decide the matters in question"); *R (Director of Public Prosecutions) v Camberwell Youth Court* [2004] EWHC 1805 (Admin) [2005] 1 WLR 810 at [7] (not sufficient that Court would have decided differently).

15.5.2 **No substitution and nature of remedy.** *R v Entry Clearance Officer Bombay, ex p Amin* [1983] 2 AC 818, 829B-C (Lord Fraser: "Judicial review ... is made effective by the court quashing an administrative decision without substituting its own decision"); <3.1> (remittal for reconsideration).

> **P16 Hard-edged questions.** There are certain matters which the Court considers afresh for itself, imposing its own judgment.

16.1 Hard-edged[72] review: correctness. "Hard-edged" questions represent an important exception to the rule against the forbidden substitutionary approach. They can be thought of as questions which the public body has to decide, but is not permitted to get wrong. In reviewing such questions, the Court does precisely what is forbidden on "soft" review: it does "substitute its own view". That is because the role of the reviewing Court here is to ensure objective "correctness".

16.1.1 A "hard-edged" question. *R v Monopolies & Mergers Commission, ex p South Yorkshire Transport Ltd* [1993] 1 WLR 23, 32D-F (Lord Mustill, distinguishing between "a broad judgment whose outcome could be overturned only on the ground of irrationality" and "a hard-edged question [where t]here is no room for legitimate disagreement"); *R v Medicines Control Agency, ex p Pharma Nord Ltd* (1998) 10 Admin LR 646, 664A-B; *Mahmut Cakabay v Secretary of State for the Home Department (No.2)* [1999] Imm AR 176, 188.

16.1.2 Matters of objective judgment for the Court. *R v Secretary of State for the Home Department, ex p Khawaja* [1984] AC 74 ("illegal entrant" as a question for the Court); *R v Swansea City Council, ex p Elitestone Ltd* [1993] 2 PLR 65, 73C-D (whether property constituting "buildings" treated "as a matter of objective judgment"); *R v Secretary of State for the Home Department, ex p Zeenat Bibi* [1994] Imm AR 326, 329 (legal status of marriage one a question on which "the court must make up its own mind"); *White & Collins v Minister of Health* [1939] 2 KB 838 (whether land part of a park a question for the Court to decide for itself); *R v Secretary of State for the Environment, Transport and the Regions, ex p Spath Holme* [2001] 2 AC 349, 396G ("the `intention of Parliament' as an objective concept, not subjective"); *R (L) v Secretary of State for the Home Department* [2003] EWCA Civ 25 [2003] 1 WLR 1230 (certification of human rights claims as clearly unfounded) at [56] ("The test is an objective one: it depends not on the Home Secretary's view but upon a criterion which a court can readily re-apply once it has the materials which the Home Secretary had. A claim is either clearly unfounded or it is not").

16.2 Precedent fact. A "precedent fact" (or "antecedent fact") is a question of fact, regarded as a fundamental condition precedent to the proper exercise of the public body's function, such that the body is not permitted to answer it incorrectly. Having identified a precedent fact question, the Court simply asks the question for itself, and can consider evidence which was not before the decision-maker. The idea is that a necessary "trigger" to the decision-making function must, objectively, have been met for the body's action to have been lawful.

16.2.1 Judicial review for error as to precedent fact. <49.1>.

---

[72] For an adoption of the label "hard-edged" as used in an earlier edition of this Handbook, see *R v East Sussex County Council, ex p T* [1997] ELR 311 at 319E (Keene J).

16.2.2 **Precedent fact: Court investigating the issue for itself.** *R (Maiden Outdoor Advertising Ltd) v Lambeth London Borough Council* [2003] EWHC 1224 (Admin) at [35] (precedent fact meaning "a matter of fact which must be established before any [enforcement] action can be taken"), [36] (so that "the court is entitled, if there is a material dispute, to resolve it for itself"); *Eshugbayi Eleko v Government of Nigeria* [1931] AC 662, 670 (Lord Atkin: "the duty of the Courts to investigate the issue"); *Cendiz Doldur v Secretary of State for the Home Department* [1998] Imm AR 352 (court investigating whether "illegal entrant", applying *R v Secretary of State for the Home Department, ex p Khawaja* [1984] AC 74); *R v Oldham Metropolitan Borough Council, ex p Garlick* [1993] AC 509, 520E (Lord Griffiths, referring to "a question of precedent fact going to the jurisdiction and so to be decided by the court"); *Silver Mountain Investments Ltd v Attorney-General of Hong Kong* [1994] 1 WLR 925, 934A (referring to the situation where there is a "precondition of objective fact"); *Tan Te Lam v Superintendent of Tai A Chau Detention Centre* [1997] AC 97, 112C-114E; *R v Secretary of State for the Home Department, ex p Rahman* [1998] QB 136 (in deciding precedent fact the court is still reviewing the Secretary of State's decision, and entitled therefore to look at hearsay evidence which was before the Secretary of State); *R (Ullah) v Secretary of State for the Home Department* [2003] EWCA Civ 1366 at [28] (Potter LJ: under "*Khawaja*, exceptionally in the realm of judicial review ... the court must itself decide whether the evidence relied on by the Secretary of State is sufficient to resolve the question of precedent fact against the [claimant]").

16.2.3 **Fresh evidence and precedent fact.** <17.2.5(B)>.

16.2.4 **EC challenge drawing Court into legitimate fact-finding role.** <49.2.14>).

16.3 **Error of law as hard-edged review.**[73] Errors of law are correctable by judicial review. Questions of law are therefore "hard-edged" questions, which the reviewing Court is entitled to answer for itself, substituting its own conclusion for that of the public authority. A material error of law is a ground for intervention.

16.3.1 **Judicial review for error of law.** <P48> (error of law); <P4> (materiality.

16.3.2 **Error of law as hard-edged review.** *R v Central Arbitration Committee, ex p BTP Tioxide Ltd* [1981] ICR 843, 856B-D ("A tribunal either misdirects itself in law or not according to whether it has got the law right or wrong, and that depends on what the law is and not on what a lay tribunal might reasonably think it was. In this field there are no marks for trying hard but getting the answer wrong"); *R v Elmbridge Borough Council, ex p Health Care Corporation Ltd* [1991] 3 PLR 63, 68G ("In order to decide whether they have misapplied the law the court itself has to come to the conclusion as to what the law is. It cannot duck the issue by saying the law is very difficult and there are conflicting views and therefore the local authority are not unreasonable in taking one view"); *Davies v Presbyterian Church of Wales* [1986] 1 WLR 323, 328F-G ("The question to be determined is a question of law... If the industrial tribunal erred in deciding that question, the decision must be reversed and it matters not that other industrial tribunals might have reached a similar erroneous conclusion in the absence of an authoritative decision by a higher court"); *R (Campaign for Nuclear Disarmament) v Prime Minister* [2002] EWHC 2759 (Admin) [2003] 3 LRC 335 at [10] (question of international law as "a sharp-edged question of law").

---

[73] This paragraph in a previous edition was cited in *R v East Sussex County Council, ex p Tandy* [1997] 3 FCR 525.

16.3.3 **Treating questions of law as "soft" questions.** <48.2> (error of law: restricted categories); *R v Inland Revenue Commissioners, ex p S.G. Warburg & Co Ltd* [1994] STC 518, 540d (relevant revenue law treated as a question of fact, assessed on the material before the tax inspector); *R (Atilla) v Secretary of State for the Home Department* [2006] EWHC 1203 (Admin) at [19] (question of foreign law an issue of fact for reasonableness review); *Kershaw Mechanical Services Ltd v Kendrick Construction Ltd* [2006] EWHC 727 (TCC) [2006] 3 All ER 79 at [57] (some deference to arbitrator determining question of law).

16.3.4 **Error of law: an appellate approach except for Court's discretion.** *Mallinson v Secretary of State for Social Security* [1994] 1 WLR 630, 638H-639B (Lord Woolf, explaining the court's hard-edged approach to a "statutory appeal on a point of law", but contrasting "the residual discretion which it has on an application for judicial review to limit the circumstances in which it grants [permission] or [remedy]").

16.4 Interpretation as a hard-edged question

In general, a question of "interpretation" (or "construction") will be an objective legal question for the Court to decide, whereas a question of "application" will be a "soft" review. Interpretation of legislation is a question of law, but interpretation of other materials is similarly often treated as hard-edged review, in which the Court asks whether the public body's interpretation was "correct".

16.4.1 **Statutory interpretation as a hard-edged question.** *R (Gillan) v Commissioner of Police of the Metropolis* [2004] EWCA Civ 1067 [2005] QB 388 at [30] ("The interpretation of the 2000 Act is a matter of law for the courts. There is no question of this court showing deference or respect to the views of the [defendants] because of the subject matter of the legislation") (HL is [2006] UKHL 12 [2006] 2 AC 307); *E's Applications* [1983] RPC 231, 253 (Lord Diplock, referring to "the important constitutional principle that questions of construction of all legislation primary or secondary are questions of law to be determined authoritatively by courts of law; that errors in construing primary or secondary legislation made by inferior tribunals that are not courts of law, however specialised and prestigious they may be, are subject to correction by judicial review"); *R v Barnet London Borough Council, ex p Nilish Shah* [1983] 2 AC 309, 341A (Lord Scarman: "the meaning to be attributed to enacted words is a question of law, being a matter of statutory interpretation"); *R v Director of Public Prosecutions, ex p Kebilene* [2000] 2 AC 326 (DC), 344B (Lord Bingham CJ: "In their interpretation of statutes British judges have no discretion: they must give the statutory language what they take to be its ordinary and natural meaning"); *R v Director General of Water Services, ex p Oldham Metropolitan Borough Council* (1998) 96 LGR 396, 409e-f (whether water supply cut off a question of interpretation and therefore "a question of law for this Court to decide"); *R v Secretary of State for the Environment, Transport and the Regions, ex p Spath Holme* [2001] 2 AC 349, 396G ("the `intention of Parliament' is an objective concept"); *R (Goodman) v London Borough of Lewisham* [2003] EWCA Civ 140 [2003] Env LR 644 at [8] (as to "the authority's understanding of the meaning in law of the expression used in the Regulation": "If the authority reaches an understanding of those expressions that is wrong as a matter of law, then the court must correct that error: and in determining the meaning of the statutory expressions the concept of reasonable judgment as embodied in *Wednesbury* simply has no part to play").

16.4.2 **Interpretation of non-statutory sources.** *R v East Sussex County Council, ex p Reprotech (Pebsham) Ltd* [2001] Env LR 14 (CA) (objective construction of council resolution) (HL is at [2002] UKHL 8 [2003] 1 WLR 348); *R v Secretary of State for the Home Department, ex p Adan* [2001] 2 AC 477 (CA), 497B-D (questions of interpretation of the Refugee Convention as questions of law for the court); *R v Secretary of State for the Environment,*

Transport and the Regions, ex p Channel Tunnel Group Ltd [2001] EWCA Civ 1185 at [57] (interpretation of an international instrument as a question for the Court); *Dunlop v Secretary of State for the Environment* (1996) 94 LGR 427, 430 (Sedley J, referring to construction of an 1820 award: "Construction being a matter for the court, it is accepted that I am not limited to supervisory review on *Wednesbury* grounds"); *R v Secretary of State for the Environment, ex p Enfield London Borough Council* (1994) 92 LGR 525 (proper construction of a 1990 Determination); *R v Director of Passenger Rail Franchising, ex p Save Our Railways* [1996] CLC 589, 601D (as to Secretary of State's directions: "the Court ... cannot ... in case of dispute, abdicate its responsibility to give the document its proper meaning. It means what it means, not what anyone ... would like it to mean"); *Mercury Communications Ltd v Director General of Telecommunications* [1996] 1 WLR 48 (HL treating interpretation of licence as question for the Court); cf. *R v Director General of Electricity Supply, ex p First Hydro Company* 2nd March 2000 unrep. (meaning of "connection charges" a matter of judgment for the DGES, distinguishing *Mercury*); *R v Paul* The Times 17th September 1998 (construction of a firearms certificate, being a public document concerned with public safety, a question of law for the Court); *Stancliffe Stone Co Ltd v Peak District National Park Authority* [2005] EWCA Civ 747 [2006] Env LR 158 (CA expressing different views on whether any deference appropriate as to construction of planning permission).

16.4.3 **Whether meaning of policy/guidance a hard-edged question.** <29.5.10>.

16.4.4 **Distinction between interpretation and application.** *R v Secretary of State for the Home Department, ex p Adan* [2001] 2 AC 477 (CA), 497B-D (questions of interpretation of the Refugee Convention as questions of law for the court; questions of application as questions of fact for review on basis of `anxious scrutiny' reasonableness <32.3>); *R (Yogathas) v Secretary of State for the Home Department* [2001] EWCA Civ 1611 (CA) at [51]-[54] (maintaining the distinction between interpretation and application) (HL is [2002] UKHL 36 [2003] 1 AC 920); *R v South Hams District Council, ex p Gibb* [1995] QB 158, 170G ("if as a matter of law the local authorities applied the right test" then whether persons are "gypsies" was for them); *R v Broadcasting Complaints Commission, ex p British Broadcasting Corporation* (1995) 7 Admin LR 575, 593B (once necessary issues of law established, questions of fact and degree left to the BCC's expertise and experience); *R v Sefton Metropolitan Borough Council, ex p Help The Aged* [1997] 4 All ER 532, 543j-544a ("any appropriate application of the language of the statutory provisions to the facts of this case does not allow any other result"); <16.6.5> (the *South Yorks Transport* principle).

16.5 **Procedural fairness as hard-edged review.** The basic objective standards of procedural fairness are determined directly by the Courts. What fairness demands is for the primary judgment of the Court. Public bodies do enjoy some procedural latitude in that, beyond the core minimum standards required by the Courts, procedural choices remain for the body's judgment or discretion.

16.5.1 **Requirements of fairness as a question for the Court.** *Gillies v Secretary of State for Work and Pensions* [2006] UKHL 2 [2006] 1 WLR 781 at [6] ("whether a tribunal ... was acting in breach of the principles of natural justice is essentially a question of law"); *R (Mahfouz) v General Medical Council* [2004] EWCA Civ 233 at [19] (Carnwath LJ: "Where it is alleged that a lower tribunal has acted in breach of the rules of fairness or natural justice, the court is not confined to reviewing the reasoning of the tribunal on *Wednesbury* principles. It must make its own independent judgment ... Furthermore, the question whether there has been a breach of those principles is one of law, not fact"); *R (Refugee Legal Centre) v Secretary of State for the Home Department* [2004] EWCA Civ 1481 [2005] 1 WLR 2219 at [8] (court decides whether system intrinsically unfair); *R v Panel on Take-overs and Mergers, ex p Guinness Plc* [1990] 1 QB 146, 184C-E (rejecting the argument "that the correct test is *Wednesbury* unreasonableness... It confuses substance and procedure"; "Of course the court will give great weight to the tribunal's own view of what is fair, and will not lightly decide that a tribunal has adopted a procedure which is unfair ... But in the last resort the court is the arbiter of what is fair"); *R (Brooks) v Parole Board* [2003] EWHC 1458 (Admin) [34] (fairness a matter for the court but giving great weight to the tribunal's own view); *R v Lord Saville of Newdigate, ex p A* [2000] 1 WLR 1855 at [41] (endorsing *Guinness*); *R (A) v Lord Saville of Newdigate* [2001] EWCA Civ 2048 [2002] 1 WLR 1249 at [7] (tribunal `master of its own procedure', but reviewing Court deciding question of what fairness required); *R v Secretary of State for the Home Department, ex p Kingdom of Belgium* 15th February 2000 unrep. (applying *De Smith, Woolf and Jowell*: "Whether fairness is required and what is involved in order to achieve fairness is for the decision of the courts as a matter of law. The issue is not one for the discretion of the decision-maker. The test is not whether no reasonable body would have thought it proper to dispense with a fair hearing. The *Wednesbury* reserve has no place in relation to procedural propriety").

16.5.2 **Further illustrations.** *R (Medway Council) v Secretary of State for Transport* [2002] EWHC 2516 (Admin) at [32] ("It is for the Court to decide what is or is not fair. If a consultation procedure is unfair, it does not lie in the mouth of the public authority to contend that it had a discretion to adopt such a procedure"); *R v P Borough Council, ex p S* [1999] Fam 188, 220B ("It is for the court to determine what is or is not required to satisfy the requirements of fairness"); *R v National Lottery Commission, ex p Camelot Group Plc* [2001] EMLR 3 at [59] ("it is for the court to decide whether the procedure in this case was unfair, but ... in reaching that decision the court should take into account the views of the Commission as to the appropriateness of the procedure"); *R v Monopolies and Mergers Commission, ex p Stagecoach Holdings Plc* The Times 23rd July 1996 ("in the vast majority of cases the court will be unlikely to regard what the MMC has reasonably believed to be fair as unfair", but: "it is not what the MMC believed, however reasonably, to have been fair that should prevail but what was in fact fair... [T]he court must be the arbiter of whether in any given circumstances there has been unfairness resulting in injustice and a need to intervene"); *R v Cheshire County Council, ex p C* [1998] ELR 66, 73G-74B ("the court itself will decide on the relevant material whether fairness required an adjournment"); *R v Secretary of State for the Home Department, ex p Q* [2000] UKHRR 386, 393G (whether decision an infringement of constitutional right to a fair trial being a question for the primary judgment of the Court); *R (Tromans) v Cannock Chase District Council* [2004] EWCA Civ 1036 [2004] LGR 735 at [16] ("no real difference" between unfairness and unreasonableness here: if council did not act fairly here "it could not properly be said to have acted reasonably").

16.5.3 **Other aspects of fairness as questions for the Court.** *R v Secretary of State for the Home Department, ex p Q* [2000] UKHRR 386, 393F (HRA:ECHR Art 6: "it must be for the court to form its own primary judgment as to whether the right to a fair trial is infringed"); *R v Secretary of State for Social Services, ex p Association of Metropolitan Authorities* [1986] 1 WLR 1, 6F-G (procedural ultra vires as a question "for the court to determine yea or nay"); *Wang v Commissioner of Inland Revenue* [1994] 1 WLR 1286, 1293A-G (whether breach of express duty to reach determination within "a reasonable time" a "question of fact" for the reviewing Court "in the light of all the circumstances"); *R v Secretary of State for Employment, ex p National Association of Colliery Overmen, Deputies & Shotfirers* [1994] COD 218 (questions of fact as to whether adequate consultation took place); <17.3.8> (procedural sequence: resolving disputed facts); *In re Medicaments and Related Classes of Goods (No.2)* [2001] 1 WLR 700 (apparent bias) at [33] ("in a case such as this, it is for the Court to consider the facts and to decide for itself whether having regard to those facts the tribunal or any member of it is disqualified from continuing to sit").

16.5.4 **Procedural latitude/procedural discretion.** <60.1.19> (fairness not best practice); *R (Greenpeace Ltd) v Secretary of State for Trade and Industry* [2007] EWHC 311 (Admin) [2007] Env LR 623 at [62]-[63] (broad discretion as to how to carry out consultation); *R v Secretary of State for the Home Department, ex p Doody* [1994] 1 AC 531, 560H-561A (question is not whether "some procedure other than the one adopted by the decision-maker would be better or more fair" but that chosen "procedure is actually unfair. The court must constantly bear in mind that it is to the decision maker, not the court, that Parliament has entrusted not only the making of the decision but also the choice as to how the decision is made"), applied in *R (Bennion) v Chief Constable of Merseyside Police* [2001] EWCA Civ 638 at [39]; *Bushell v Secretary of State for the Environment* [1981] AC 75, 94H-95B ("the procedure to be followed at the inquiry" as a matter "left to the discretion of the minister or the inspector"); *Local Government Board v Arlidge* [1915] AC 120, 132 (body entitled "to follow the procedure which is its own"); *General Medical Council v Spackman* [1943] AC 627, 634 (GMC as "master of its own procedure"); *R (Liverpool City Council) v Secretary of State for Health* [2003] EWHC 1975 (Admin) [2004] LGR 635 at [40] (statutory language giving Secretary of State "considerable scope as to who is consulted"); *R v Panel on Take-overs and Mergers, ex p Guinness Plc* [1990] 1 QB 146, 184D ("the court will give great weight to the tribunal's own view of what is fair, and will not lightly decide that a tribunal has adopted a procedure which is unfair"); *R (WB) v Leeds School Organisation Committee* [2002] EWHC 1927 (Admin) [2003] ELR 67 at [30] (approaching on rationality grounds the question whether committee choosing to exercise "power" to hear representations).

16.6 **Hard-edged questions: further matters.** The contrast between those questions which are and are not matters for (hard-edged) "correctness" review produces a two-tier system. In truth, all administrative law standards are objective and determined by the Courts, but some are substitutionary in nature while others are designed with built-in latitude for the public body.

16.6.1 **Judicial review imposes objective standards.** <45.2.6> (need for objective standards); <14.3.1> (nothing personal and objective standards).

16.6.2 **Nature of other grounds for review.** *R v Secretary of State for Foreign and Commonwealth Affairs, ex p World Development Movement Ltd* [1995] 1 WLR 386, 401H (treating statutory purpose a question for the reviewing court on the evidence before it); *Padfield v Minister of Agriculture Fisheries & Food* [1968] AC 997 (purpose of the statute treated as a question of law for the Court, involving construction of the statute); *R v Secretary of State for the Environment, Transport and the Regions, ex p Spath Holme* [2001] 2 AC 349, 396G ("the `intention of Parliament' is an objective concept"); <58.5.10> (proportionality as a question for the court); <56.2> (obligatory and discretionary relevance); <56.3> (relevance and weight); <54.2.4> (substantive legitimate expectation: rationality test); <54.2.5> (fairness/justification test); <49.2.2> (unfair disregard of an established and relevant fact); <P63> (external wrongs); <39.3.6> (statutory formulae: role of the court).

16.6.3 **Hard-edged questions and fresh evidence.** <17.2> (fresh evidence); <17.2.5(B)> (fresh evidence and precedent fact); <17.2.5(D)> (fresh evidence and procedural fairness).

16.6.4 **Soft and hard-edged questions: "two-tiered review".** *R (Goodman) v London Borough of Lewisham* [2003] EWCA Civ 140 [2003] Env LR 644 at [8] (meaning of "Schedule 2 development" as a matter of law where "the court must correct [an] error"), [9] (whether "likely to have significant effects on the environment" as "an enquiry of a nature to which the *Wednesbury* principle does apply"); *R (B) v Calderdale Metropolitan Borough Council* [2004] EWCA Civ 134 [2004] 1 WLR 2017 at [6] (statutory grant eligibility "a matter of law depending on the ascertained facts"; but whether works "necessary and appropriate is a matter for the council's judgment, subject to the ordinary constraints of public law"); *R v Governor of Brixton Prison, ex p Schtraks* [1964] AC 556, 579 (sufficiency of evidence reviewed on basis of reasonableness), 586 (whether offences "of a political nature" to be addressed by the court "as a substantive matter"); *Holgate-Mohammed v Duke* [1984] AC 437, 443B-C ("an executive discretion" as to whether to arrest, reviewable on *Wednesbury* grounds), 442F ("reasonable cause" as a precedent fact for the court); *R v Secretary of State for the Home Department, ex p Rahim Miah (Note)* [1990] 1 WLR 806, 812G-H (on "illegal entrant" question, court "forms its own judgment on the facts"; otherwise performs "its normal role, which is to review the decision which has been reached by the administrators"); <13.2.2> (fact/law distinction); <16.3> (error of law as hard-edged review); *R v Monopolies & Mergers Commission, ex p South Yorkshire Transport Ltd* [1993] 1 WLR 23, 32D-F (whether hard-edged question raises a matter going to "the proper function of the courts"); *R v Oldham Metropolitan Borough Council, ex p Garlick* [1993] AC 509, 520e (distinguishing a question "entrusted to the authority and so can only be reviewed on *Wednesbury* grounds" from "a question of precedent fact going to the jurisdiction and so to be decided by the court"); *R (Bloggs 61) v Secretary of State for the Home Department* [2003] EWCA Civ 686 [2003] 1 WLR 2724 at [81] (leaving open whether "it is for the court to make its own judgment as to whether there would be an interference with the right to life"); <47.2.3> (jurisdiction as two-tiered review).

16.6.5 **The *South Yorkshire Transport* approach.** *R v Monopolies & Mergers Commission, ex p South Yorkshire Transport Ltd* [1993] 1 WLR 23 (although statutory criterion absent which "no jurisdiction to proceed", nevertheless "the criterion ... may itself be so imprecise that different decision-makers, each acting rationally, might reach differing conclusions when applying it to the facts of a given case"; "a meaning broad enough to call for the exercise of judgment" needing to be "within the permissible field of judgment"); applied eg. in *R (BBC) v Information Tribunal* [2007] EWHC 905 (Admin) [2007] 1 WLR 2583 at [57]; and in *R (Goodman) v London Borough of Lewisham* [2003] EWCA Civ 140 [2003] Env LR 644 at [8].

16.6.6 **Equal and opposite decisions.** *R (St Helens Borough Council) v Manchester Primary Care Trust* [2008] EWCA Civ 931 (whether comparable conflicting decisions from which the Court would have to decide on the substantive merits) at [33] & [37] (here, PCT the primary decision-maker reviewable on orthodox *Wednesbury* grounds).

P17 Evidence and fact. Judicial review is generally conducted on written evidence and regarded as an unsuitable forum for resolving factual disputes, though this can be appropriate and necessary.

17.1 Judicial review evidence. Evidence in judicial review cases is almost invariably in written form (witness statements) with relevant documents.

17.1.1 General rules about evidence. See CPR 32 (evidence).

17.1.2 Rules about judicial review evidence. See CPR 54.14, 54.16(2), 54.17 <64.2>; also CPR 8.5; CPR 54PD <64.3> paras 5.6-5.7, 10.1; <17.4.1> (rules about disclosure/ cross-examination/ further information).

17.1.3 Argumentative evidence and overburdensome documents *Alex Lawrie Factors Ltd v Morgan* The Times 18th August 1999 (purpose of witness statement is for witness to give relevant evidence in own words; not a vehicle for lawyer to put forward complex legal argument); *R v Ministry of Agriculture Fisheries and Food ex p National Farmers Union* [1995] 3 CMLR 116, 118 ("widespread tendency ... to overburden the court with documents and with argumentative affidavits"); *R (Crouch) v South Birmingham Primary Care Trust* [2008] EWHC 605 (Admin) (court inundated with large amount of unnecessary material); *R (Parents for Legal Action Ltd) v Northumberland County Council* [2006] EWHC 1081 (Admin) [2006] ELR 397 at [87] (need for careful thought in preparation of hearing bundles; "a properly constructed Core Bundle would have been of inestimable advantage"); *R v Secretary of State for the Environment, ex p Merton London Borough Council* The Times 22nd March 1990 (large quantities of entirely superfluous papers); *Bruce v Worthing Borough Council* (1994) 26 HLR 223, 224 ("unnecessary compilation of files"); *R (Prokopp) v London Underground Ltd* [2003] EWCA Civ 961 [2004] Env LR 170 at [52] ("grotesque waste" of trees, public money and "judicial time and energy in laying one's hand on the few documents and authorities which are relevant. It is the duty of Counsel and solicitors to go through material in order to decide what is relevant"), [90].

17.1.4 Appropriate extent of defendant's evidence.
(A) NEED TO PROVIDE AN EXPLANATION. *R v Gloucester Crown Court, ex p Chester* [1998] COD 365 (deprecating position where nothing from defendant court to indicate basis of impugned decision or stance in relation to the judicial review proceedings, whether by letter or otherwise); *R v Feltham Justices, ex p Haid* [1998] COD 440 (see transcript) (response should "make it clear" that claimant's witness statement has been read and what is not accepted).
(B) NEED TO EXHIBIT PRIMARY EVIDENCE. *Tweed v Parades Commission for Northern Ireland* [2006] UKHL 53 [2007] 1 AC 650 at [4] (Lord Bingham: "Where a public authority relies on a document as significant to its decision, it is ordinarily good practice to exhibit it as the primary evidence ... the document itself is the best evidence of what it says"), [33] (Lord Carswell: "A party whose [witness statements] contain a reference to documents should ... exhibit them in the absence of a sufficient reason (which may include the length or volume of the documents, confidentiality or public interest immunity)"), [57] (Lord Brown, endorsing the practice of exhibiting the main documents).
(C) AVOID INAPPROPRIATE COMMENT. *R (C) v Secretary of State for Justice* [2008] EWCA Civ 882 at [24] (criticising "aggressively justificatory tone"); *R (C) v Brent, Kensington and Chelsea and Westminster Mental Health NHS Trust* [2002] EWHC 181 (Admin) (2003) 6

CCLR 335 at [13] (claimant's evidence containing "impermissible comment and argument"); *Richard Read (Transport) Ltd v Secretary of State for the Environment* [1995] 3 PLR 59, 65D-E (ill-judged comments); *R v Poole Borough Council, ex p Ross* (1996) 28 HLR 351, 360 ("entirely inappropriate" to put in evidence asserting confidence that the decision was fair and untainted); *A v Kirklees Metropolitan Borough Council* [2001] EWCA Civ 582 [2001] ELR 657 at [17] ("not appropriate" to express a view on whether omitted evidence would have made a difference, the issue turning "not on what the decision-maker may with hindsight say he would have made of the evidence but on the objective question whether the evidence was capable of having made a difference"), [20] ("not a topic for ex post facto evidence"); *R v Tunbridge Wells Health Authority, ex p Goodridge* The Times 21st May 1988 (individual's view irrelevant); *R v Leeds City Council, ex p Hendry* (1994) 6 Admin LR 439, 442E-H (unsupported affidavit assertion).

(D) REASONS AND RATIONALISATION. <62.4> (timing of reasons); <62.3.2> (drafting reasons: proper limits of the lawyer's function).

(E) OTHER. *R v Humberside County Council, ex p Bogdal* [1991] COD 66 (application to strike out some of defendant's exhibits refused; claimant not entitled to pick and choose issues; once seeking to quash decision, Court not excluded from having all relevant background documents); *R v Southwark London Borough Council, ex p Campisi* (1999) 31 HLR 560, 565 ("Their files were in such a state that one can have absolutely no confidence that somebody actually sat back and seriously thought about it, as opposed to a lawyer afterwards reconstructing from various bits of mosaic to be found in various files, something which could have been a perfectly reasonable decision"); *R v Secretary of State for the Home Department, ex p Gashi* [1999] INLR 276, 305C-H ("rationalisation" provided by defendant's Counsel not corresponding to anything in the written evidence to show that the Secretary of State or his officials had followed this line of reasoning); *R v Secretary of State for the Home Department, ex p Elshani* [1999] INLR 265, 274G-H (defendant's evidence not required expressly to deal with every point made by claimant; failure to do so may lead to conclusion that the matter was not properly taken into account, but depends on the circumstances whether it will do so).

17.1.5 **Materials/evidence and HRA justification.** *Lancashire County Council v Taylor* [2005] EWCA Civ 284 [2005] 1 WLR 266 at [53]-[59] (caution as to use of Parliamentary materials where HRA justification and declaration of incompatibility arising); *Evans v Amicus Healthcare Ltd* [2004] EWCA Civ 727 [2005] Fam 1 at [44]-[56], [114]-[115] (discussing and querying appropriateness of witness statement and Government policy evidence dealing with legislative intent, in the context of HRA questions and statutory interpretation); *R (Wilson) v Wychavon District Council* [2007] EWCA Civ 52 [2007] QB 801 at [36], [107] (Hansard inadmissible to evaluate proportionality of statutory measure); *Wilson v First County Trust Ltd* [2003] UKHL 40 [2004] 1 AC 816 (discussing the admissibility of Hansard material in addressing ECHR-compatibility of primary legislation) at [63]-[67], [116]-[117], [142]; *R (Morris) v Westminster City Council* [2005] EWCA Civ 1184 [2006] 1 WLR 505 at [39] ("extrinsic evidence of legislative policy can only be admissible, if admissible at all, in relation to a claim for a declaration of incompatibility"); *R (British American Tobacco) v Secretary of State for Health* [2004] EWHC 2493 (Admin) at [65] (detailed evidence lodged in response to judicial review proceedings not an "'ex post facto' rationalisation", the Minister being "entitled to justify the application of the regulations made in the particular context of the criticism raised").

17.1.6 **Expert evidence.**[74] See CPR 35 and CPR 35PD; *R (Lynch) v General Dental Council* [2003] EWHC 2987 (Admin) [2004] 1 All ER 1159 at [22] (Collins J, explaining that "fresh evidence involving expert evidence should in general not be admitted unless it falls within the

---

[74] Andrew Lidbetter [2004] JR 194.

P17 EVIDENCE AND FACT

Powis guidelines"), [24] ("But ... the Court must be enabled to carry out its function. To do this it must understand the material which is put before it"; "in a truly technical field, where the significance of a particular process is in issue expert evidence can be admitted to explain the process and its significance"), [25] ("its purpose is in reality to explain to the court matters which it needs to understand in order to reach a just conclusion"); *R v Haringey London Borough Council, ex p Norton* (1998) 1 CCLR 168, 180E-G (Roger Henderson QC: "It is not permissible to adduce, either by way of expert evidence or at all, evidence which purports to answer the question which it is for the Court to answer"; "the Court may in certain rare circumstances be assisted by knowing ex post facto how an expert in the field would have assessed the needs of a particular [claimant] (eg a case where deficient enquiry led to ignorance of material facts or opinion and the evidence being proffered goes to the issue of what would have been discovered had due enquiry been made)"); *Field v Leeds City Council* (2000) 32 HLR 618 (permissible to use in-house expert evidence if court satisfied that appropriate expert witness); *R (Seahawk Marine Foods Ltd) v Southampton Port Health Authority* [2002] EWCA Civ 54 at [19] (expert evidence relevant to question of proportionality), [34] (Buxton LJ: "While in some cases it will be possible for a court to reach a conclusion on an issue of proportionality on the basis of commonsense and its own understanding of the process of government and administration, I doubt whether it will often be wise for a court to undertake that task in a case involving technical or professional decision-making without the benefit of evidence as to normal practices and the practicability of the suggested alternatives"); *CF v Secretary of State for the Home Department* [2004] EWHC 111 (Fam) [2004] 1 FCR 577 at [217] (expert evidence admissible in HRA proportionality cases (eg. mental health) but misgivings as to routine use of expert evidence in public law community care, child welfare etc cases), [218] (need for restraint and case-management, including clear identification of "what precise point the evidence being adduced really goes to"); *R (Middlebrook Mushrooms Ltd) v Agricultural Wages Board of England and Wales* [2004] EWHC 1447 (Admin) at [84] (expert evidence could be relied on in relation to question of justification under HRA:ECHR Art 14); *R (Watkins-Singh) v Aberdare Girls High School Governors* [2008] EWHC 1865 (Admin) at [28]-[29], [64] (accepting evidence of claimant's evidence as to significance of Sikh kara bangle; rejecting defendant's so-called expert evidence for non-compliance with CPR).

17.1.7 Hearsay.[75] See CPR 33 and CPR 33PD; *R v Camden London Borough Council, ex p Adair* (1997) 29 HLR 236, 248 (fact that affidavit containing hearsay evidence not a good enough reason to exclude it); *R v Secretary of State for the Home Department, ex p Lillycrop* 27th November 1996 unrep. (civil servant entitled to give evidence explaining basis of decision-maker's approach, provided that sources of knowledge and belief stated, and given "the limited extent to which such evidence is likely to be acted upon by a Court"); *R v Secretary of State for the Environment, Transport and the Regions, ex p Alliance Against the Birmingham Northern Relief Road* 23rd March 1999 unrep. (hearsay evidence not inappropriate); *R v Secretary of State for the Home Department, ex p Rahman* [1998] QB 136 (entitled to look at hearsay evidence which was before the decision-maker, even when deciding precedent fact).

17.1.8 Departmental realities and evidence. *R v Secretary of State for Health, ex p London Borough of Hackney* [1994] COD 432 (see transcript) (rejecting the criticism that the evidence put forward on behalf of the defendant was "hearsay and inadmissible", since "although it is true that the Secretary of State personally made the decision, and there is no affidavit from her, nonetheless, litigation of this kind has always proceeded in our Courts by reference to the principle that a department of State is indivisible"); *R v Secretary of State for Health, ex p London Borough of Hackney* 22nd April 1994 unrep. ("Although it is the Secretary of State who

---

[75] Ben Rayment [1998] JR 19.

is answerable to Parliament for her department, officials of it may, with her authority, explain its workings, including those in which her own role has been determinative"); <30.4.2> (departmental realities); *R v Secretary of State for the Department of Environment, ex p London Borough of Islington* (1991) [1997] JR 121, 125 (Secretary of State giving evidence "through his mouthpiece"); *R v Ministry for Agriculture Fisheries & Food, ex p Hamble Fisheries (Offshore) Ltd* [1995] 2 All ER 714, 732h-j ("ministerial policy is not something [which] can ordinarily be deposed to by a senior executive officer, however experienced and knowledgeable"); *R v Secretary of State for the Home Department, ex p Rose* 9th March 1995 unrep. (although decision was that of the Secretary of State, unreasonable and unrealistic to expect him rather than senior civil servant to swear affidavit explaining its basis); *R v Secretary of State for the Home Department, ex p Fayed* [2001] Imm AR 134 at [59] (no need for witness statement from Home Secretary personally); *R v Secretary of State for the Home Department, ex p Pierson* [1998] AC 539, 544G (Secretary of State named as defendant only because responsible for department within which decisions made); *R v Gloucestershire County Council, ex p H* [2000] ELR 357 (on appeal to special educational needs tribunal, authority entitled to give evidence by its representative before the tribunal).

17.1.9 **Litigation privilege.** *R v Secretary of State for the Home Department, ex p Gashi* [1999] INLR 276, 308D-E, G (suggesting that since judicial review not purely adversarial and the court having an overriding interest to promote a welfare consideration, litigation privilege may not allow the defendant to refuse production of an expert report).

17.2 **Fresh evidence in judicial review.**The starting-point is to focus on evidence which was before, or available to, the public body at the time of its impugned action. But other evidence can be relevant and admissible in judicial review, including where it relates to: (1) the impugned action; (2) background information; (3) a ground for judicial review; (4) a further issue arising; and sometimes even (5) material which is now, or would now be, before the decision-maker.

17.2.1 **Fresh evidence in judicial review: general points.** See Schiemann LJ in *R v Secretary of State for the Home Department, ex p Turgut* [2001] 1 All ER 729 (accepting and summarising amicus submissions[76]), 735g ("The Court will not shut out evidence which is relevant to the issues"; "The evidence is not strictly limited to evidence which was or should have been before the Secretary of State at the time of the decision. This was the unanimous view of the House of Lords in *R v Secretary of State for the Home Department, ex p Launder* [1997] 1 WLR 839, 860H-861B"), 735j-736b ("What quite often happens is that ... the Secretary of State asks permission to put before the court evidence seeking to explain and justify his original decision. Such permission is frequently given"; "Sometimes the Secretary of State will seek permission to adduce evidence to the effect that he has considered the evidence filed by the [claimant] and that he has made a new, second, decision in the light of that evidence. Where that new decision is in favour of the [claimant] the case is usually disposed of by consent. Where however the second decision is to the same effect as the first decision and the [claimant] challenges the legality of the second decision ... [the claimant] may apply for permission to amend his application for permission so as to substitute the new decision and generally the court will grant such an application"), 736e ("the principles governing the admission by the Court of Appeal of new evidence are different. At that stage it will not usually be appropriate for an attempt to be made before this court to substitute a new decision for the old and to litigate the legality of that new decision before this court"); <5.1.6> (position where fresh/ further

[76] Reproduced at [2000] JR 18.

"decision"); <62.4> (timing of reasons); *R (Limbuela) v Secretary of State for the Home Department* [2004] EWCA Civ 540 [2004] QB 1440 at [113] (in HRA:ECHR Art 3 challenge as to destitution and asylum-seekers, relevant to focus on the up-to-date position) (HL is at [2005] UKHL 66 [2006] 1 AC 396).

17.2.2 The *Powis* default position. *R v Secretary of State for the Environment, ex p Powis* [1981] 1 WLR 584, 595G (Dunn LJ, describing "the principles on which fresh evidence should be admitted on judicial review": "(1) that the court can receive evidence to show what material was before the minister or inferior tribunal; (2) where the jurisdiction of the minister or inferior tribunal depends on a question of fact or where the question is whether essential procedural requirements were observed, the court may receive and consider additional evidence to determine the jurisdictional fact or procedural error ...; and (3) where the proceedings are tainted by misconduct on the part of the minister or member of the inferior tribunal or the parties before it ... [where] fresh evidence is admissible to prove the particular misconduct alleged"; *Dwr Cymru Cyfyngedig v Environment Agency of Wales* [2003] EWHC 336 (Admin) at [58] ("judicial review is a developing area of the law where it can be said that the grounds of judicial review are not closed but ... the principles in *Powis* provide an approved and sensible basis on which to proceed which should only be departed from in exceptional circumstances where it can be justified in order to achieve justice and fairness. One of the dangers of admitting fresh evidence in judicial review proceedings is that the court may thereby find itself put in the position of being asked to decide the merits of the case rather than acting as a court of review").

17.2.3 Material not before the decision-maker.
(A) REVIEW FROM THE DECISION-MAKER'S POINT OF VIEW. <13.7>.
(B) WHETHER MATERIAL WAS BEFORE THE DECISION-MAKER.*R v Secretary of State for the Environment, ex p Powis* [1981] 1 WLR 584, 595G ("the court can receive evidence to show what material was before the minister or inferior tribunal"); *Hollis v Secretary of State for the Environment* (1983) 47 P & CR 351 (material taken to have been before the decision-maker, because within the knowledge of the relevant Department).
(C) MATERIAL WOULD BE BEFORE DECISION-MAKER IF CASE RECONSIDERED.*R v Secretary of State for the Home Department, ex p Launder* [1997] 1 WLR 839, 860H-861B (Lord Hope: "The situation has changed since 1995 when the decisions were taken... Although we are concerned primarily with the reasonableness of the decisions at the time when they were taken we cannot ignore these developments. We are dealing in this case with concerns which have been expressed about human rights and the risks to the [claimant]'s life and liberty. If the expectations which the Secretary of State had when he took his decisions have not been borne out by events or are at risk of not being satisfied by the date of the [claimant]'s proposed return to Hong Kong, it would be your Lordships' duty to set aside the decisions so that the matter may be reconsidered in the light of the changed circumstances"); cf. *R (Gorlov) v Institute of Chartered Accountants in England and Wales* [2002] EWHC 2202 (Admin) at [69] (wrong to use judicial review "to quash a decision in order to introduce fresh evidence").
(D) DECISION-MAKER SHOULD HAVE RECONSIDERED. *R v Inner London North Coroner, ex p Touche* [2001] EWCA Civ 383 [2001] QB 1206 at [36] (although decision was originally correct, coroner should have changed his mind on information subsequently brought to his attention).

17.2.4 Background information. *R (Pelling) v Bow County Court* [2001] UKHRR 165 at [14] (evidence serving as "useful background information"); *R v Humberside County Council, ex p Bogdal* [1991] COD 66 (claimant not entitled to pick and choose issues; once seeking to quash decision, Court not excluded from having all relevant background documents); *R (Wagstaff) v Secretary of State for Health* [2001] 1 WLR 292 (Sir Louis Blom-Cooper QC giving a witness statement setting out his experience of inquiries being held in public).

17.2.5 **Material going to a ground for judicial review.**
(A) GENERAL. *R v Secretary of State for the Environment, ex p Powis* [1981] 1 WLR 584, 595H-596A ("where the jurisdiction of the minister or inferior tribunal depends on a question of fact or where the question is whether essential procedural requirements were observed, the court may receive and consider additional evidence to determine the jurisdictional fact or procedural error"; "where the proceedings are tainted by misconduct on the part of the minister or member of the inferior tribunal or the parties before it. Examples of such misconduct are bias by the decision-making body, or fraud or perjury by a party. In each case fresh evidence is admissible to prove the particular misconduct alleged"); *R v Criminal Injuries Compensation Board, ex p A* [1998] QB 659 (CA), 682B-C (Simon Brown LJ: "it is only in certain narrowly defined circumstances that the rule against judicially reviewing decisions by reference to fresh evidence is tempered"); *R v West Sussex Quarter Sessions, ex p Albert and Maud Johnson Trust Ltd* [1974] 1 QB 24 (judicial review does not lie on the basis that fresh evidence has come to light which undermines a factual conclusion of the defendant) *Ashbridge Investments Ltd v Minister of Housing & Local Government* [1965] 1 WLR 1320, 1327C (court "cannot receive evidence ... so as to decide the whole matter afresh"); *R v London Residuary Body, ex p Inner London Education Authority* (1987) [1998] JR 238, 247-248 (declining to permit reliance on a report so as to seek to show that the decision-maker should have decided differently); *R v Director General of Telecommunications, ex p Cellcom Ltd* [1999] COD 105 (see transcript) ("A party can in judicial review proceedings adduce evidence to show what material was before the decision-maker, but not fresh material not available to the decision-maker designed to persuade the Court that the decision-maker's decision was wrong").
(B) PRECEDENT FACT. *R v Secretary of State for the Environment, ex p Powis* [1981] 1 WLR 584, 595H ("where the jurisdiction of the minister or inferior tribunal depends on a question of fact ... the court may receive and consider additional evidence to determine the jurisdictional fact"); *Eshugbayi Eleko v Government of Nigeria* [1931] AC 662, 675 (on addressing precedent facts, Court to "give such directions as it thinks fit as to the production of other evidence, whether written or oral, and by cross-examination of deponents or otherwise"); *White & Collins v Minister of Health* [1939] 2 KB 838, 847-848 (issue decided "upon the evidence before us"); *R v Secretary of State for the Home Department, ex p Momin Ali* [1984] 1 WLR 663, 670H (Court required to consider "the evidence which is now available"); *R v Commissioners of Customs and Excise, ex p Lunn Poly Ltd* [1999] Eu LR 653, 662B-D (questions of fact which EC law requires the domestic Court to decide for itself); <17.3.7> (disputed facts and precedent fact).
(C) FUNDAMENTAL FACTUAL ERROR. <49.2.2> (unfair disregard of an established and relevant fact); *E v Secretary of State for the Home Department* [2004] EWCA Civ 49 [2004] QB 1044 at [68] ("assuming the relevance of showing a mistake of fact in the Tribunal's decision, there may need to be evidence to prove it"); *R v Criminal Injuries Compensation Board, ex p A* [1999] AC 330, 344G-345C (Lord Slynn).
(D) PROCEDURAL FAIRNESS. *R v Secretary of State for the Environment, ex p Powis* [1981] 1 WLR 584, 595H ("where the question is whether essential procedural requirements were observed, the court may receive and consider additional evidence to determine the ... procedural error"); *R v Nat Bell Liquors Ltd* [1922] 2 AC 128, 160 ("How is it ever to appear within the four corners of the record that the members of the inferior Court were unqualified, or were biased, or were interested in the subject matter?"); *R v Chief Constable of West Midlands Police, ex p Carroll* (1995) 7 Admin LR 45, 49H-51B (evidence going to factual question whether a document had been made available to the claimant); <17.3.8> (disputed facts and procedural sequence).
(E) MISCONDUCT BY DECISION-MAKER/THIRD PARTY. *R v Mid-Glamorgan County Council, ex p B* [1995] ELR 168, 179C (evidence going to whether bias and hostility at hearing); *R v Knightsbridge Crown Court, ex p Goonatilleke* [1986] QB 1 (whether perjury by witness); *R v Horseferry Magistrates Court, ex p Bennett* The Times 1st April 1994 (whether

extradition abuse by prosecuting authorities).

(F) DEFECTIVE INQUIRY.[77] *R v Rochford District Council, ex p Ferdinando* 8 September 1992 unrep. (evidence admissible "to show what could, upon proper inquiry, have been elicited..."); *R v Haringey London Borough Council, ex p Norton* (1998) 1 CCLR 168, 180F-G ("the Court may in certain rare circumstances be assisted by knowing ex post facto how an expert in the field would have assessed the needs of a particular [claimant] (eg. a case where deficient enquiry led to ignorance of material facts or opinion and the evidence being proffered goes to the issue of what would have been discovered had due enquiry been made)"); *R v Criminal Injuries Compensation Board, ex p A* [1999] AC 330 (judicial review was granted on the basis of a report which was not, but should have been, before the decision-maker; ultimately analysed the matter as involving procedural unfairness: see 345C and 347C).

(G) IMPACT/FORESEEABLE IMPACT. *R v Secretary of State for the Home Department, ex p Simms* [2000] 2 AC 115, 127D-128H (evidence of impact and implications of restriction); *R v Warwickshire County Council, ex p Collymore* [1995] ELR 217, 223D-E (practical effect of over-rigidly applied policy); *JL Engineering v Secretary of State* (1994 & 1995) 68 P & CR 504 ("Evidence as to facts which arose later can only be relevant and admissible in so far as it throws light on what the [decision-maker] might reasonably have expected to happen").

(H) PROPORTIONALITY/JUSTIFICATION. *R (Middlebrook Mushrooms Ltd) v Agricultural Wages Board of England and Wales* [2004] EWHC 1447 (Admin) at [84] (Stanley Burnton J: "In deciding whether there is an objective justification for the different treatment of the class complaining of the infringement of its rights under [HRA:ECHR] Article 14, the Court is not restricted to the matters before the decision maker. Under this head, therefore, the Court is free to consider the expert evidence adduced by the parties for the purposes of these proceedings"); *Wilson v First County Trust Ltd* [2003] UKHL 40 [2004] 1 AC 816 at [141] (Lord Hobhouse: "Whether a particular statutory provision offends against any of the `Convention rights' is an objective question to be answered having regard to all relevant evidence"), [142] ("The questions of justification and proportionality involve a sociological assessment - an assessment of what are the needs of society. This in part involves a legal examination of the content and legal effect of the relevant provision. But it also involves consideration of what is the mischief, social evil, danger etc which it is designed to deal with. Often these matters may already be within the knowledge of the court. But equally there will almost always be other evidentially valuable material which can be placed before the court which is relevant, such as reports that have been made, statistics that have been collected, and so on. Oral witnesses may have important evidence to give").

17.2.6 Fresh evidence going to a further issue arising. Fresh evidence could go to questions such as (1) reviewability, (2) prejudicial delay, (3) standing, (4) alternative remedy and (5) discretionary refusal of relief (eg. utility); *R (Malik) v Manchester Crown Court* [2008] EWHC 1362 (Admin) at [32] (new developments not relevant to whether decision was lawful, but relevant to utility of remedy if retaken decision would be bound to be the same); *R (C) v Secretary of State for Justice* [2008] EWCA Civ 882 (question of discretionary refusal of remedy in light of new impact assessment).

17.2.7 Fresh evidence and appeal.
(A) COURT OF APPEAL: GENERAL. See CPR 52.11(2); *Ladd v Marshall* [1954] 1 WLR 1489, 1491 (three conditions: "first, it must be shown that the evidence could not have been obtained with reasonable diligence for use at the trial; secondly, the evidence must be such that,

---

[77] This subparagraph in a previous edition was cited in *Smart Gain Investment Ltd v Town Planning Board* [2007] HKCU 1817 at [95].

if given, it would probably have an important influence on the result of the case, though it need not be decisive; thirdly, the evidence must be such as is presumably to be believed, or in other words, it must be apparently credible, though it need not be incontrovertible").

(B) COURT OF APPEAL: PUBLIC LAW. *E v Secretary of State for the Home Department* [2004] EWCA Civ 49 [2004] QB 1044 at [81] ("wrong to say that the *Ladd v Marshall* principles have not been treated as applicable at all in judicial review ... It is clear, however, that some flexibility has been allowed where the `interests of justice' so require"), [82] ("*Ladd v Marshall* principles ... remain the starting point [in public law], but there is a discretion to depart from them in exceptional circumstances"), [91(iii)] (" *Ladd v Marshall* principles, which may be departed from in exceptional circumstances where the interests of justice require"); *R (B) v S* [2006] EWCA Civ 28 [2006] 1 WLR 810 at [38]-[39] (applying *Ladd v Marshall*); *Haile v Immigration Appeal Tribunal* [2001] EWCA Civ 663 [2002] Imm AR 170 at [25] (Simon Brown LJ: "the old *Ladd v Marshall* principles ... never did apply strictly in public law and judicial review").

(C) COURT OF APPEAL DEALING WITH PERMISSION/SUBSTANTIVE HEARING. *R v Secretary of State for the Home Department, ex p Turgut* [2001] 1 All ER 719, 736d (where Court of Appeal considering permission or the hearing of the judicial review, having reserved the matter to itself, same principles applicable to fresh evidence as in the High Court); cf. *R (Young) v Oxford City Council* [2002] EWCA Civ 990 [2002] 3 PLR 86 at [23] (CA, appearing to assume that *Ladd v Marshall* would apply on an appeal against a refusal of permission for judicial review; but fresh evidence allowed because of claimant's difficulties in having adduced the evidence before the judge); <23.1.12> (CA reserving substantive hearing to itself).

(D) COURT OF APPEAL DEALING WITH SUBSTANTIVE APPEAL. *R v Secretary of State for the Home Department, ex p Turgut* [2001] 1 All ER 719, 736e-f (Schiemann LJ: "If the trial takes place before the High Court and either party seeks to appeal, ... [t]he normal rules governing the reception of evidence on appeals will normally apply"); *R v Secretary of State for the Home Department, ex p Gardian* [1996] COD 306 (CA) (further evidence not admitted); *R v Chief Constable of Sussex, ex p International Traders' Ferry Ltd* [1998] QB 477 (CA), 490F-491G (further evidence reluctantly considered, at the request of the parties); *R v Secretary of State for the Home Department, ex p Simms* [1999] QB 349 (CA), 357C (further evidence relating to reasons for impugned ban); *R v Human Fertilisation and Embryology Authority, ex p Blood* [1999] Fam 151, 174E (CA considering legality of fresh post-judgment decision); cf. *R v Lambeth London Borough Council, ex p A* (1998) 10 Admin LR 209, 225G-226C (CA declining to consider whether recent events showing defendant now discharging its statutory duty); *R v Criminal Injuries Compensation Board, ex p B* 7th December 1998 unrep. (CA declining to admit evidence that reasons were the opposite of those presented to the High Court); *Vernon v Bosley (No.2)* [1998] 1 FLR 304 (asking whether exclusion an affront to common sense and justice); *R v Royal Pharmaceutical Society of Great Britain, ex p Mahmood* [2001] EWCA Civ 1245 [2002] 1 WLR 879 at [32] (fresh evidence appropriate to "fresh issue" in CA); *A v Secretary of State for the Home Department* [2003] EWCA Civ 175 [2003] INLR 249 at [20] (in asylum/ human rights case "the proper approach [is] to consider the wider interests of justice"); *R (Bagdanavicius) v Secretary of State for the Home Department* [2003] EWCA Civ 1605 [2004] 1 WLR 1207 at [71] (CA considering fresh evidence, given obligation of "anxious scrutiny" <32.3>).

(E) FRESH EVIDENCE ON AN APPEAL TO HL. *R v Secretary of State for the Home Department, ex p Simms* [2000] 2 AC 115, 127D-128G (material made available to House of Lords, describing "in compelling detail" as to importance of communications between prisoners and journalists), considered in *E v Secretary of State for the Home Department* [2004] EWCA Civ 49 [2004] QB 1044 at [75]; *R (S) v Chief Constable of South Yorkshire* [2004] UKHL 39 [2004] 1 WLR 2196 at [18] (strongly deprecating last minute attempt to introduce letter).

17.3 **Judicial review and factual disputes.**[78] Judicial review has often been said to be unsuitable for deciding disputed facts. Undeniably, in general: (1) questions of fact are for the defendant body; (2) a fact-adjudication alternative remedy will be preferable; and (3) judicial review claims with factual disputes can be transferred out of CPR 54. Nevertheless, the judicial review Court may need to make findings of fact (with or without oral evidence), especially if crucial to whether a ground for intervention is made out.[79]

17.3.1 **Not generally necessary or appropriate to resolve disputed facts.** *Tweed v Parades Commission for Northern Ireland* [2006] UKHL 53 [2007] 1 AC 650 at [2] (Lord Bingham: "applications for judicial review ... characteristically, raise an issue of law, the facts being common ground or relevant only to show how the issue arises"), [32] (Lord Carswell: "applications for judicial review ... generally raise legal issues"); *Anufrijeva v London Borough of Southwark* [2003] EWCA Civ 1406 [2004] QB 1124 at [53] ("the Administrative Court ... does not normally concern itself with issues of disputed fact"); *R v Derbyshire County Council, ex p Noble* [1990] ICR 808, 813C-D ("Cross-examination and [disclosure] can take place on applications for judicial review, but in the ordinary way judicial review is designed to deal with matters which can be resolved without resorting to those procedures"); *R v Inland Revenue Commissioners, ex p T.C.Coombs & Co* [1991] 2 AC 283, 302A ("Proceedings in which [witness statement] evidence is the general rule are not well suited to resolving factual questions"); *R v Horsham District Council, ex p Wenman* [1995] 1 WLR 680, 709G ("judicial review proceedings are wholly inappropriate as the forum for the resolution of issues of disputed fact"); *R v Chief Constable of the Warwickshire Constabulary, ex p Fitzpatrick* [1999] 1 WLR 564, 579D ("Judicial review is not a fact-finding exercise"); *R (St Helens Borough Council) v Manchester Primary Care Trust* [2008] EWCA Civ 931 at [13] ("a court hearing a judicial review application normally receives evidence in writing only, and does not set about determining questions of disputed fact"; "The court does not often itself make a factual decision which the primary decision maker has not made").

17.3.2 **Fact-finding generally best left to public bodies.** <13.2> (restraint and factual questions); *R v West Sussex County Council, ex p Wenman* (1993) 5 Admin LR 145, 154A-B (judicial review "is not appropriate for the kind of fact finding exercise on disputed facts that a court at first instance, or a statutory body with statutory responsibilities to investigate facts, is equipped to perform"); *R v City of Westminster, ex p Moozary-Oraky* (1994) 26 HLR 213, 221 ("Since the issue [here] would always in the first instance be determined by the local authority under its [statutory] duty to inquire... there is good reason for not substituting the courtroom for the town hall in deciding an unresolved factual dispute"); *R v East Sussex County Council, ex p Tandy* [1998] AC 714 (CA), 724F ("cross-examination is rare in judicial review proceedings, ... rightly since a decision can if necessary be remitted to the deciding authority for reconsideration").

17.3.3 **Alternative remedy more suitable for resolving disputed facts.** *R v Secretary of State for the Home Department, ex p Swati* [1986] 1 WLR 477, 487H ("statutory appeal procedure ... clearly the appropriate method of challenging the immigration officer's decision. It is a procedure which enables the full facts to be ascertained. The process of judicial review is not appropriate for a purely factual challenge"); *R v London Borough of Brent, ex p Sawyers* [1993]

---

[78] David Abrahams [1999] JR 221.

[79] This paragraph in a previous edition was cited in *Chan Mei Yiu Paddy v Secretary of Justice* [2007] HKCU 1241 at [6]; also *Lai Tak Shing v Director of Home Affairs* [2006] HKCU 1692 at [50].

COD 416 (statutory appeal to the Secretary of State much more suitable than judicial review, for determination what was reasonably practicable for local authority to do in relation to suitability of housing); *R v Folkestone Magistrates' Court, ex p Bradley* [1994] COD 138 (appropriate remedy appeal to the Crown Court, which could resolve questions of fact); *R v London Borough of Hackney, ex p GC* [1995] ELR 144 (Auld J), 154F-G (Secretary of State, on statutory appeal, "far better equipped" for fact-finding exercise); *R v Oldbury Justices, ex p Smith* (1995) 7 Admin LR 315, 327C-D ("In a case such as the present, which bristles with factual difficulties, the only convenient and proper way to get it before the Divisional Court is by case stated and not by way of application for judicial review"); *R v Croydon Justices, ex p Dean* [1993] QB 769, 776E ("If it is necessary for the disputed issues of fact in this case to be resolved by oral evidence", better to "leave it to the Crown Court to decide whether there is abuse of process"); *R v Birmingham City Council, ex p A* [1997] 2 FLR 841 (issues needing oral evidence, better suited to a statutory complaints investigation); *R v Westminster City Council, ex p P* (1998) 1 CCLR 486, 492D, G (disputed issue of fact more appropriate for Secretary of State's default powers than judicial review); *R (Davies) v Revenue & Customs Commissioners* [2008] EWCA Civ 933 at [7] ("if a tribunal of fact exists which can find the relevant facts it is normally good practice to postpone judicial review until after the facts have been found").

17.3.4 Fact-resolution and transfer out. <21.2.15> (transfer out of CPR 54); *R v Chief Constable of Lancashire, ex p Parker* [1993] QB 577, 581C-D ("common ground that the issues of principle should be determined by this court and that the factual issues, including the question whether the damages should include aggravated and exemplary damages, should be determined by a single judge as if the proceedings had been begun by [claim form action]"); *R v London Commodity Exchange (1986) Ltd, ex p Brealey* [1994] COD 145 (order for transfer out, because essentially private law claim and disputed facts); cf. *Attorney General of Trinidad and Tobago v Ramanoop* [2005] UKPC 15 [2006] 1 AC 328 at [30] (constitutional motion may be appropriate for continuance by writ where factual dispute emerging).

17.3.5 May be appropriate to resolve factual dispute on judicial review. *R (Corner House Research) v Director of the Serious Fraud Office* [2008] EWHC 714 (Admin) at [8] (not necessary to resolve factual questions "unless omission inhibits a correct legal conclusion") (HL is [2008] UKHL 60 [2008] 3 WLR 568); *R v Secretary of State for the Department of Environment, ex p London Borough of Islington* (1991) [1997] JR 121, 128 (Nolan LJ: "Disputed questions of fact do not normally arise in judicial review cases, but they can of course arise and they may be crucial"); <17.4> (disclosure, further information and cross-examination); *Leech v Deputy Governor of Parkhurst Prison* [1988] AC 533, 582E (judicial review of prison governors for error of law or abuse of power "may and almost certainly will in some cases involve questions of fact which are inevitably more appropriately dealt with by the court"), 567F-H (need to "ascertain the facts on which the validity of the governor's adjudication essentially depends"); *Doherty v Birmingham City Council* [2008] UKHL 57 [2008] 3 WLR 636 at [68], [138] (if necessary, judicial review can be "adjusted so as to enable issues of fact to be judicially resolved").

17.3.6 Whether to make findings of fact on written evidence.
(A) GENERAL. *S v Airedale NHS Trust* [2002] EWHC 1780 (Admin) at [18] (Stanley Burnton J: "It is a convention of our litigation that at trial in general the evidence of a witness is accepted unless he is cross-examined and is thus given the opportunity to rebut the allegations made against him. There may be an exception where there is undisputed objective evidence inconsistent with that of the witness that cannot sensibly be explained away (in other words, the witness's testimony is manifestly wrong) ... The general rule applies as much in judicial review proceedings as in other litigation, although in judicial review proceedings it is relatively unusual for there to be a conflict of testimony and even more unusual for there to be cross-examination

of witnesses") (HL is *R (Munjaz) v Mersey Care NHS Trust* [2005] UKHL 58 [2006] 2 AC 148). (B) MAKING FINDINGS ON WRITTEN EVIDENCE. *R (European Roma Rights Centre) v Immigration Officer at Prague Airport* [2004] UKHL 55 [2005] 2 AC 1 at [97] (concluding that the evidence, albeit no oral evidence, supporting the inference that system had been operated in a directly discriminatory fashion); *R (C) v Secretary of State for Justice* [2008] EWCA Civ 882 at [24] (rejecting assertion in witness statement); *Attorney General v News Group Newspapers Plc* [1989] QB 110, 127-128 (observations as to rejecting contents of affidavits); *Chief Constable of the North Wales Police v Evans* [1982] 1 WLR 1155, 1165F ("conflict of evidence relating to the interview", as to which preferring one version "on the probabilities"); *R v London Borough of Newham, ex p Gentle* (1994) 26 HLR 466, 470 (rejecting defendant's affidavit evidence); *R v Highbury Corner Metropolitan Stipendiary Magistrate, ex p Di Matteo* [1991] 1 WLR 1374, 1378F (accepting affidavit evidence of claimant's solicitors "in preference to the recollection of the magistrate, as recorded in his affidavit"); *R v Central Criminal Court, ex p Randle* [1991] 1 WLR 1087, 1110A-B ("There are inevitably situations in which facts have necessarily to be found, albeit the evidence is on affidavit"); *Attorney-General of Trinidad and Tobago v Phillip* [1995] 1 AC 396, 405D-H (PC unravelling picture from affidavit evidence); *R v North Derbyshire Health Authority, ex p Fisher* (1998) 10 Admin LR 27, 44C-45B, 47A-C (expressing serious doubts about what Court told in the evidence as to the authority's true position); *London Borough of Islington v Camp* (1999) [2004] LGR 58, 66g ("In each case the court has to make a judgment on the basis of the factual material before it. There are often gaps in the evidence. That is something with which the court has to cope as best it can"); *R v Northavon District Council, ex p Smith* [1994] 2 AC 402, 411E-G ("question of fact, to be answered in the light of the evidence which was placed before the trial judge"); *R (Professional Contractors Ltd) v Commissioners of Inland Revenue* [2001] EWHC Admin 236 [2001] EuLR 514 at [20] (court making findings) (CA is [2001] EWCA Civ 1945 [2002] EuLR 329); *R (Maqsood) v Special Adjudicator* [2002] Imm AR 268 at [21]-[27] (making findings on the written evidence, as to whether notice of a hearing had been received by solicitors); *R (Salih) v Secretary of State for the Home Department* [2003] EWHC 2273 (Admin) at [55] (Court finding that "no evidence" to justify the view that publication of asylum welfare policy would encourage undeserved applications"); *R (Ullah) v Secretary of State for the Home Department* [2003] EWCA Civ 1366 at [28] (discussing the precedent fact issue of "illegal entrant", and the court's scrutiny of written evidence with cross-examination where appropriate), [34] (here, written evidence not of sufficient weight to decide the issue of fact against the claimant, to the necessary level of proof).

(C) DECLINING TO GO BEHIND THE WRITTEN EVIDENCE. *R v Board of Visitors of Hull Prison, ex p St Germain (No.2)* [1979] 1 WLR 1401, 1410H ("Since we have had to decide this matter on affidavit evidence without the benefit of cross-examination, we are obliged to take the facts where they are in issue as they are deposed to on behalf of the board"); *R v Camden London Borough Council, ex p Cran* (1996) 94 LGR 8, 11-12, 72, 73 (impossible for the Court to form a view as to credibility, as would be possible in a witness action); *R v Neale, ex p S* [1995] ELR 198, 206E ("I cannot attempt to resolve this conflict of evidence, nor is it necessary that I should do so"); *R (Fernback) v Harrow London Borough Council* [2001] EWHC Admin 278 [2002] Env LR 231 at [63]; *R (MWH & H Ward Estates Ltd) v Monmouthshire County Council* [2002] EWCA Civ 1915 at [29] (wrong to "go behind the evidence" as to whether options were considered); *R (Watkins-Singh) v Aberdare Girls High School Governors* [2008] EWHC 1865 (Admin) at [101] & [135] (proceeding on basis of defendant's written evidence).

(D) STATEMENTS OF DECISION-MAKERS RELATING TO BIAS. *Locabail (UK) Ltd v Bayfield Properties Ltd* [2000] QB 451 at [19] (as to real danger of bias, and whether decision-maker aware of an alleged disqualifying matter: "While a reviewing court may receive a written statement from any judge, lay justice or juror specifying what he or she knew at any relevant time, the court is not necessarily bound to accept such statement at its face value. Much will depend on the nature of the fact of which ignorance is asserted, the source of the statement, the effect of any corroborative or contradictory statement, the inherent probabilities and all the circumstances of the case in question"; "Nor will the reviewing court pay attention to any statement by the judge concerning the impact of any knowledge on his mind or his decision: the insidious nature of bias makes such a statement of little value, and it is for the reviewing court and not the judge whose impartiality is challenged to assess the risk that some illegitimate extraneous consideration may have influenced the decision"); *R (A1 Veg Ltd) v Hounslow London Borough Council* [2003] EWHC 3112 (Admin) [2004] LGR 536 at [79] (disregarding witness statement evidence on the issue of apparent bias).

17.3.7 Resolving disputed facts: precedent fact. *R (Beckett) v Secretary of State for the Home Department* [2008] EWHC 2002 (Admin) at [3] (Court hearing oral evidence on judicial review because "issues of precedent fact can require that course to be followed"); *R v Arts Council of England, ex p Women's Playhouse Trust* [1998] COD 175 (see transcript) ("cases in which it is the court's duty to resolve questions of primary fact" including "where some jurisdictional fact has to be established"); *R (Lim) v Secretary of State for the Home Department* [2006] EWHC 3004 (Admin) at [47] (cross-examination appropriate for precedent fact); *R v City of Westminster, ex p Moozary-Oraky* (1994) 26 HLR 213 (although precedent fact which the Court could resolve itself, with cross-examination, prefer to quash the decision and remit it for consideration by the council); *R (Maiden Outdoor Advertising Ltd) v Lambeth London Borough Council* [2003] EWHC 1224 (Admin) at [36]-[37] (Court entitled to decide question of precedent fact for itself; including by directing for continuation of the proceedings as if begun by ordinary claim form action).

17.3.8 Resolving disputed facts: procedural sequence. *R v Bank of England, ex p Mellstrom* [1995] CLC 232, 238E-240B (finding as a fact that detrimental material not disclosed to claimant was not relied on by decision-maker); *R v Harrow Crown Court, ex p Dave* [1994] 1 WLR 98, 101H-102D (resolving whether prosecution disclosed its witness's prior convictions to the defence); *R v Mid-Glamorgan County Council, ex p B* [1995] ELR 168, 179C ("necessary for me to come to a conclusion on [the] conflict of evidence before determining the issue of bias and unfair conduct"); *Chief Constable of the North Wales Police v Evans* [1982] 1 WLR 1155, 1165F ("conflict of evidence relating to the interview", as to which Lord Bridge preferring Evans's version "on the probabilities"); *R v Reigate Justices, ex p Curl* [1991] COD 66 (factual dispute as to what had occurred in magistrates' proceedings; position presumed to be as asserted by defendant); *R v Her Majesty's Prison Featherstone, ex p Bowen* 26th October 1998 unrep. (disputed facts as to whether claimant given opportunity to make representations prior to decisions, but court's function not permitting it to make findings of disputed fact unless defendant's affidavits disclose some inherent improbability); *R v London Borough of Camden, ex p Paddock* [1995] COD 130 (see transcript) (Sedley J, having permitted cross-examination on affidavits, which "made it possible to discern what had in all probability happened in relation to a critical aspect of the procedure"); *R v Mid-Glamorgan County Council, ex p B* [1995] ELR 168, 173G (cross-examination allowed, by consent, limited to the question of the conduct of the appeal committee); *R v Chief Constable of the West Midlands Police, ex p Carroll* (1995) 7 Admin LR 45, 53G-H (CA accepting Divisional Court's analysis of the facts, as to the disputed question of whether or not the claimant had been shown a report (see 50A), Lloyd LJ (see 50C) having approached that issue in this way: "As with disputed issues of fact in other fields, we have to go by three things: our impression of the witnesses, the documentary evidence, such as it is, and the inherent probabilities").

17.3.9 Resolving disputed facts and justification. <17.4.17> (disclosure etc and HRA/proportionality); *R (G) v Nottinghamshire Healthcare NHS Trust* [2008] EWHC 1096 (Admin) at [96]-[97] (caveat that court proceeded without live evidence or cross-examination); *CH v Sutton & Merton Primary Care Trust* [2004] EWHC 2984 (Admin) (2005) 8 CCLR 5 at [20] (need to resolve factual issues to decide whether overriding public interest for justified breach of legitimate expectation).

17.3.10 EC challenge drawing Court into legitimate fact-finding role. <49.2.14>.

17.3.11 Resolving disputed facts: bad faith. <52.1> (bad faith); *R v Derbyshire County Council, ex p Times Supplements Ltd* (1991) 3 Admin LR 241, 247G-248C (although "open to us ... to reject the contents of those affidavits in whole or in part (see *Attorney General v News Group Newspapers Plc* [1989] QB 110 at pages 127 and 128)", counsel "sought and obtained [permission] to cross-examine ... the councillors who appeared before us"), 252E ("I did not believe them. The longer they were cross-examined the more manifest it became that they were implausibly endeavouring to buttress the insupportable... their evidence ... displayed an unworthy lack of candour"); cf. *R v Bassetlaw District Council, ex p Oxby* The Times 18th December 1997 (allegation of fraud against individual councillors appropriate for writ action rather than judicial review); *R v Tower Hamlets London Borough Council, ex p Luck* [1999] COD 294 (whether bad faith allegation, to be pursued in private law action, could be sustained likely to be illuminated by disclosure).

17.3.12 Resolving disputed facts: extradition abuse. <63.1.3>; *R v Horseferry Road Magistrates' Court, ex p Bennett* [1994] 1 AC 42, 52B-53A (court having "jurisdiction to inquire into such matters"); *R v Horseferry Road Magistrates' Court, ex p Bennett (No.2)* [1994] 1 All ER 289, 291b (disclosure ordered of documents which "go to the very heart of a factual dispute between the parties, a dispute which if resolved in the [claimant]'s favour could well bring an end to the criminal proceedings against him"), 292c-d (court needing to resolve the "direct conflict" in the evidence filed); *R v Horseferry Road Magistrates' Court, ex p Bennett* [1994] COD 321 (see transcript) (Henry LJ, ordering cross-examination by video link: "This is very different from the run of the mill of Ord 53 cases where cross-examination and [disclosure] are both unusual because normally unnecessary. Here they are necessary for the Court properly to discharge the task that the House of Lords has remitted to them"); *R v Horseferry Road Magistrates' Court, ex p Bennett (No.2)* The Times 1st April 1994 (DC resolving the dispute, on the basis that: "Against the well-intentioned oral evidence there is one decisive contemporary document"). Note that the Scottish courts subsequently even made a contrary finding as to the disputed facts: see *Bennett v H.M. Advocate* The Times 2nd December 1994.

17.3.13 Fresh evidence in judicial review. <17.2>.

17.4 Disclosure, further information and cross-examination[80]. It being generally unnecessary to resolve factual disputes, and given the defendant's duty of candour, Courts will not normally order disclosure, further information or cross-examination. However, such orders can and should be made, where justice requires it, as where it is necessary for the fair disposal of the case.[81]

---

[80] Robin Allen QC & Mark Shaw [1998] JR 12; Martin Smith [2001] JR 138; Oliver Sanders [2006] JR 194.

[81] This paragraph in a previous edition was cited in *Cullen v Chief Constable of the Royal Ulster Constabulary* [2003] UKHL 39 [2003] 1 WLR 1763 at [5]; also *Julita F Raza v Chief Executive in Council* [2006] HKCU 1199 at [22].

17.4.1 **Rules about disclosure/further information/cross-examination.**CPR 54PD <64.3> para 12.1; CPR 31.12 (specific disclosure); CPR 8.6(2)-(3) (oral evidence); CPR 18.1 (further information). The original CPR 54 did not incorporate the relevant provisions of CPR 8.6, and an interim judicial solution was necessary until CPR 54.16(1) was amended: see *R (G) v London Borough of Ealing* [2002] EWHC 250 (Admin) at [27].

17.4.2 **Codified/common law rights to information.**[82] Freedom of Information Act 2000; Data Protection Act 1998; Data Protection Act 1998; *R (Lord v Secretary of State for the Home Department* [2003] EWHC 2073 (Admin) (Secretary of State having shown no proper basis for declining disclosure of reports underlying a parole `gist', under Data Protection Act 1998 s.7); *London Regional Transport v Mayor of London* 24th August 2001 unrep. (discussing freedom of information in the context of HRA:ECHR Art 10; there, public interest in publication of report); *R (Roberts) v Nottinghamshire Healthcare NHS Trust* [2008] EWHC 1934 (QB) (psychiatric patient not entitled to NHS trust's medical report under Data Protection Act 1998); *R (Binyan Mohamed) v Secretary of State for Foreign and Commonwealth Affairs* [2008] EWHC 2048 (Admin) (claimant entitled to disclosure under *Norwich Pharmacal* [1974] AC 133 principle, based on facilitation of wrongdoing).

17.4.3 **Duties of candour.** <10.3> (claimant's duty of candour); <10.4> (defendant/interested party's duty of candour); <19.1.1> (provision of information: pre-action protocol).

17.4.4 **Best evidence rule.** *Tweed v Parades Commission for Northern Ireland* [2006] UKHL 53 [2007] 1 AC 650 at [4] (defendant authority should ordinarily exhibit the primary documents, rather than referring to them and summarising them); *R (National Association of Health Stores) v Secretary of State for Health* [2005] EWCA Civ 154 at [47] (CA explaining that where Government declining to produce ministerial briefing, wrong to seek to give a secondary account instead), [49] (best evidence rule applying).

17.4.5 **Disclosure generally unnecessary given duty of candour.** *R (Quark Fishing Ltd) v Secretary of State for Foreign and Commonwealth Affairs* [2002] EWCA Civ 1409 at [50] (Laws LJ: "there is no duty of general disclosure in judicial review proceedings. However there is - of course - a very high duty on public authority respondents, not least central government, to assist the court with full and accurate explanations of all the facts relevant to the issue the court must decide. The real question here is whether in the evidence put forward on his behalf the Secretary of State has given a true and comprehensive account of the way the relevant decisions in the case were arrived at"); *R v Secretary of State for the Home Department, ex p Fayed* [1998] 1 WLR 763, 775C (Lord Woolf MR: "On an application for judicial review there is usually no [disclosure] because [disclosure] should be unnecessary because it is the obligation of the [defendant] public body in its evidence to make frank disclosure to the court of the decision-making process"); *R v Arts Council of England, ex p Women's Playhouse Trust* [1998] COD 175 (see transcript) (Laws J, explaining that disclosure and cross-examination not automatic, but that "it is generally the duty of a public body made [defendant] in judicial review proceedings to make full and fair disclosure as necessary to assist the court").

17.4.6 **Documents referred to in grounds/statements.** CPR 31.14; *Tweed v Parades Commission for Northern Ireland* [2006] UKHL 53 [2007] 1 AC 650 (not automatic that disclosure of documents referred to appropriate), [33] (documents referred to in witness

---

[82] Tim Treuherz [1998] JR 184; Claire McDougall [2002] JR 199 & 253; Philip Coppel [2004] JR 266 & [2005] JR 289; Gemma White [2006] JR 224; Anna Condliffe [2007] JR 246.

statements should be exhibited absent a good reason); *R v Inland Revenue Commissioners, ex p Taylor* [1989] 1 All ER 906 (not sufficient that reports referred to in defendant's affidavit; not necessary for fair disposal).

17.4.7 Subpoenas.[83] *R v London Borough of Islington, ex p Erkul* 26th March 1996 unrep. (subpoena to attend for cross-examination); *R v Secretary of State for Transport, ex p Port of Felixstowe Ltd* [1997] COD 356 (subpoenas at permission stage, where evidence likely to be vital, not available without subpoenas, nor from any other source).

17.4.8 Disclosure/further information/cross-examination are important. *R (G) v London Borough of Ealing* [2002] EWHC 250 (Admin) at [14] ("there will be some cases ... where justice simply cannot be done unless there is cross-examination"), [20] ("There will be judicial review cases ... in which the court will simply not be able to meet its obligations under Article 6 of the Convention unless it is able to order cross-examination"); *R (Quark Fishing Ltd) v Secretary of State for Foreign and Commonwealth Affairs* [2002] EWCA Civ 1409 (unlawful approach becoming clear from documents disclosed following court order), [27] (important letter disclosed following order); *R (JB) v Haddock* [2006] EWCA Civ 961 [2006] HRLR 1237 at [64] (patient entitled to cross-examination where HRA-compatibility of forced medical treatment); <17.3> (resolving disputed facts); *R v Inland Revenue Commissioners, ex p Rossminster* [1980] AC 952, 1025E-G (importance of 1977 procedural reforms as to disclosure, further information and cross-examination); *O'Reilly v Mackman* [1983] 2 AC 237, 280B (previous "procedural disadvantages" removed); Recommendation No.R(80)2 of the Committee of Ministers (adopted 11 March 1980) <45.1.4(B)> ("Basic principles", including that: "A court or other independent body which controls the exercise of a discretionary power has such powers of obtaining information as are necessary for the exercise of its function").

17.4.9 Disclosure etc: not usually necessary. *Tweed v Parades Commission for Northern Ireland* [2006] UKHL 53 [2007] 1 AC 650 at [4] (judicial review characteristically raising issues of law, with facts common ground or of background relevance only, so disclosure of documents usually unnecessary), [56] ("likely to remain exceptional"); *R v Inland Revenue Commissioners, ex p Rossminster* [1980] AC 952, 1027A-B (powers "to be sparingly used"); *R v Secretary of State for the Home Department, ex p Zamir* [1980] AC 930, 949C-D ("cross-examination, though allowable, does not take place in practice"); *R v Arts Council of England, ex p Women's Playhouse Trust* [1998] COD 175 (see transcript) (Laws J: "neither [disclosure] nor cross-examination is automatic"); *R (G) v London Borough of Ealing* [2002] EWHC 250 (Admin) at [14] (referring to "cases - no doubt not very many - where justice simply cannot be done unless there is cross-examination"); *Cullen v Chief Constable of the Royal Ulster Constabulary* [2003] UKHL 39 [2003] 1 WLR 1763 at [5] (explaining, by reference to passages in this *Handbook*, that historically cross-examination has been "in practice rarely permitted" in judicial review proceedings); *R v Bow County Court, ex p Pelling* [1999] 1 WLR 1807, 1826E-F (further information not appropriate to seek to obtain judge's reasons for impugned decision, court able to give remedy if breach of any duty to give reasons).

17.4.10 Disclosure ordered. *R (Ministry of Defence) v Wiltshire & Swindon Coroner* [2005] EWHC 889 (Admin) [2006] 1 WLR 134 at [16] (disclosure ordered in relation to tapes of inquest under challenge); *R v Inland Revenue Commissioners, ex p J. Rothschild Holdings Plc* [1986] STC 410 (disclosure ordered of internal Revenue documents relating to tax exemption practice); *R v Secretary of State for the Home Department, ex p Herbage (No 2)* [1987] QB 1077 (disclosure ordered of medical reports relevant to conditions of imprisonment); *R*

---

[83] Parishil Patel [1998] JR 17.

(Deutsch) v Hackney London Borough Council [2003] EWHC 2692 at [3] (grant of permission for judicial review of controlled parking designation order accompanied by order for standard disclosure within 14 days): *Tweed v Parades Commission for Northern Ireland* [2006] UKHL 53 [2007] 1 AC 650 (disclosure to judge for evaluation of relevance and confidentiality).

17.4.11 **Cross-examination ordered.** *R v Waltham Forest London Borough Council, ex p Baxter* [1988] QB 419, 422D (councillors cross-examined on their affidavits), 426E, 427C; *R v Derbyshire County Council, ex p Times Supplements Ltd* (1991) 3 Admin LR 241, 247G-248C (bad faith shown by cross-examination); *R (H) v Commissioners of Inland Revenue* [2002] EWHC 2164 (Admin) [2002] STC 1354 at [44] (cross-examination permitted in relation to legality of Revenue seizure of computer hard disk); *R (Wilkinson) v Responsible Medical Officer Broadmoor Hospital* [2001] EWCA Civ 1545 [2002] 1 WLR 419 (cross-examination in judicial review claim raising question whether mental health treatment compatible with HRA); *S v Airedale NHS Trust* [2002] EWHC 1780 (Admin) The Times 5th September 2002 at [13] (cross-examination granted, in human rights mental health context, but limited to expert witnesses) (HL is *R (Munjaz) v Mersey Care NHS Trust* [2005] UKHL 58 [2006] 2 AC 148); cf. *Locabail (UK) Ltd v Bayfield Properties Ltd* [2000] QB 451 at [19] (not appropriate to cross-examine or seek disclosure from a judge, in order to decide whether bias); *R (Beckett) v Secretary of State for the Home Department* [2008] EWHC 2002 (Admin) (oral evidence and cross-examination in precedent fact case); *R (Binyan Mohamed) v Secretary of State for Foreign and Commonwealth Affairs* [2008] EWHC 2048 (Admin) at [76] (cross-examination in claim for documents).

17.4.12 **A flexible, case-specific approach.** *Tweed v Parades Commission for Northern Ireland* [2006] UKHL 53 [2007] 1 AC 650 at [32] (Lord Carswell, recognising "a more flexible and less prescriptive principle, which judges the need for disclosure in accordance with the requirements of the particular case, taking into account the facts and circumstances"), [56] (Lord Brown); *R v Inland Revenue Commissioners, ex p National Federation of Self-Employed and Small Businesses Ltd* [1982] AC 617, 638F ("a wide discretion as to what ... orders [are] appropriate to the particular case"); *Cocks v Thanet District Council* [1983] 2 AC 286, 294H ("the court's discretionary control of both [disclosure] and cross-examination"); *R v Radio Authority, ex p Wildman* [1999] COD 255 (cross-examination essentially a matter on which the judge hearing the substantive application to have the final word); *R (Ghadami) v Harlow District Council* [2004] EWHC 1883 (Admin) [2005] LGR 24 at [26] (cross-examination deferred to the judge hearing the substantive hearing); <31.5.9> (discretionary control and disclosure/further information/cross-examination).

17.4.13 **Necessary for fair disposal.** *Tweed v Parades Commission for Northern Ireland* [2006] UKHL 53 [2007] 1 AC 650 at [3] (Lord Bingham: "The test will always be whether, in the given case, disclosure appears to be necessary in order to resolve the matter fairly and justly"), [52] (Lord Brown); *R (Charlton) v Secretary of State for Education and Skills* [2005] EWHC 1378 (Admin) [2005] 2 FCR 603 at [80] (further disclosure necessary for fair disposal of the issues); *R (Ghadami) v Harlow District Council* [2004] EWHC 1883 (Admin) [2005] LGR 24 at [26] (cross-examination not "necessary for the just and proper disposal of the case"); *R (Da Silva) v Director of Public Prosecutions* [2006] EWHC 3204 (Admin) at [62] (disclosure not necessary for determination of lawfulness of decision); *R v Secretary of State for Foreign and Commonwealth Affairs, ex p World Development Movement Ltd* [1995] 1 WLR 386, 396C-397H (whether disclosure necessary either for disposing fairly of the matter or for saving costs); *R v Secretary of State for Health, ex p London Borough of Hackney* 29th July 1994 unrep. (whether "factual issue of sufficient substance to lead the court to conclude that it may, or will, be unable to resolve the issue fairly, fairly that is to all parties, without [disclosure] of documents bearing on the issue one way or the other"); *R (Husain) v Asylum Support Adjudicator* [2001] EWHC

Admin 852 at [16] (disclosure not "necessary for the determination of the issues").

17.4.14 **When justice requires.** *R v Arts Council of England, ex p Women's Playhouse Trust* [1998] COD 175 (see transcript) ("ordered only to the extent that the justice of the individual case requires"); *O'Reilly v Mackman* [1983] 2 AC 237, 282C (Lord Diplock: disclosure "whenever, and to the extent that, the justice of the case requires"), 283A ("whenever the justice of the particular case so requires"); *Jones v Secretary of State for Wales* [1995] 2 PLR 26, 30B (cross-examination "when the justice of the case requires").

17.4.15 **Relevance.** *Tweed v Parades Commission for Northern Ireland* [2006] UKHL 53 [2007] 1 AC 650 at [58] (whether disclosure could realistically affect the outcome); *R v Inland Revenue Commissioners, ex p National Federation of Self-Employed and Small Businesses Ltd* [1982] AC 617, 654E-F (Lord Scarman: "Upon general principles, [disclosure] should not be ordered unless and until the court is satisfied that the evidence reveals reasonable grounds for believing that there has been a breach of public duty; and it should be limited strictly to documents relevant to the issue which emerges from the affidavits"); *R v Secretary of State for the Home Department, ex p Benson* The Independent 16th November 1988 (claimant having to show medical report not just relevant but central to application for judicial review of parole decision); *R v Inland Revenue Commissioners, ex p Rothschild Holdings* [1986] STC 410 (court needing to make factual finding as to departmental practice); *Re Quark Fishing Ltd* [2001] EWHC Admin 920 at [19] (document "not relevant to any real issue in the proceedings"), [27] (disclosure ordered of letter referred to in decision document and potentially relevant); *R (Corner House Research) v Director of the Serious Fraud Office* [2008] EWHC 71 (Admin) (disclosure of relevant letters ordered).

17.4.16 **No fishing expeditions.** *Tweed v Parades Commission for Northern Ireland* [2006] UKHL 53 [2007] 1 AC 650 at [56] (Lord Brown: "the courts should continue to guard against what appear to be merely 'fishing expeditions' for adventitious further grounds of challenge"); *R v Inland Revenue Commissioners, ex p National Federation of Self-Employed and Small Businesses Ltd* [1982] AC 617, 635H (no disclosure "in the hope of eliciting some impropriety"), 664C-D ("no reason to allow ... a fishing expedition in the hope of obtaining on [disclosure] something which might counter that which appears clearly from the affidavits filed on behalf of the appellants"); *R v Secretary of State for Health, ex p London Borough of Hackney* [1994] COD 432 & 29th July 1994 unrep. (impermissible to order disclosure "to see whether something might turn up"); *R (Ministry of Defence) v Wiltshire & Swindon Coroner* [2005] EWHC 889 (Admin) [2006] 1 WLR 134 at [13]-[14] (although point not yet pleaded, appropriate to order disclosure of inquest tapes for Counsel to consider whether to pursue the point having heard them).

17.4.17 **Doubt and incompleteness.** *Tweed v Parades Commission for Northern Ireland* [2006] UKHL 53 [2007] 1 AC 650 at [4] (where documents referred to and not exhibited, not necessary "to suggest some inaccuracy or incompleteness"), [56] (agreeing "that the time has come to do away with the rule that there must be a demonstrable contradiction or inconsistency or incompleteness in the [defendant's witness statements] before disclosure will be ordered"); *R v Secretary of State for Health, ex p London Borough of Hackney* [1994] COD 432 (see transcript) ("[disclosure] of documents may be ordered where there is a prima facie case for suggesting that an affidavit is in some respect incorrect, or if an affidavit has dealt inadequately with any particular issue").

17.4.18 **Factual dispute going to the ground for judicial review.** <17.3.7> (resolving disputed facts: precedent fact); <17.3.8> (resolving disputed facts: procedural sequence); <17.3.11> (resolving disputed facts: bad faith); <63.1.3> (resolving disputed facts: extradition abuse).

17.4.19 **Disclosure etc and HRA/proportionality.** *Tweed v Parades Commission for Northern Ireland* [2006] UKHL 53 [2007] 1 AC 650 at [38] (proportionality forming part of context for deciding whether disclosure necessary for fair disposal of the issues), [54] (proportionality meaning "a closer factual analysis of the justification ... is required than used to be undertaken on judicial review challenges"); *R (JB) v Haddock* [2006] EWCA Civ 961 [2006] HRLR 1237 at [64]-[65] (right to cross-examination, if requested, where HRA-compatibility of forced medical treatment); *R (G) v London Borough of Ealing* [2002] EWHC 250 (Admin) at [18] (referring to "cases in which, such is the intensity of the review demanded by some challenge based on alleged breach of Convention rights, that compliance [by] the court itself with the Convention will demand that there be cross-examination"); *C v Bury Metropolitan Borough Council* [2002] EWHC 1438 (Fam) [2002] 2 FLR 868 at [57] (court hearing oral evidence in human rights challenge to revised care plan); *R (Wilkinson) v Responsible Medical Officer Broadmoor Hospital* [2001] EWCA Civ 1545 [2002] 1 WLR 419 (cross-examination in judicial review claim raising question whether mental health treatment); *R (N) v Dr M* [2002] EWCA Civ 1789 [2003] 1 WLR 562 (oral evidence and cross-examination allowed, in a case concerning the legality of forced medical treatment), [36] (more generally: "cross-examination should only be ordered if this is necessary to enable the court to determine the factual disputes for itself"), [39] ("it should not often be necessary to adduce oral evidence with cross-examination where there are disputed issues of fact and opinion in cases where the need for forcible medical treatment of a patient is being challenged on human rights grounds"); *CF v Secretary of State for the Home Department* [2004] EWHC 111 (Fam) [2004] 1 FCR 577 at [217]-[218] (need for caution as to expert evidence and cross-examination in HRA challenges); *R (B) v S* [2006] EWCA Civ 28 [2006] 1 WLR 810 at [64] (no conflict between *Wilkinson* and *N (M)*); *R (H) v Secretary of State for Health* [2005] UKHL 60 [2006] 1 AC 441 at [31] (judicial review court may be "obliged to conduct a sufficient review of the merits to satisfy itself that the requirements of article 5(1)(e) were indeed made out. But it is not well equipped to do so... [I]t is not used to hearing oral evidence and cross examination. It will therefore take some persuading that this is necessary"); *R (E) v Ashworth Hospital Authority* [2001] EWHC Admin 1089 (conflict of expert opinion, and Court deciding that defendant's approach justified by reference to HRA:ECHR Art 8); *R (Mullen) v Secretary of State for the Home Department* [2002] EWHC 230 (Admin) [2002] 1 WLR 1857 (DC referring to *Wilkinson* in context of judicial review extending to questions of fact where necessary to ensure Art 6 compliance, in the face of a decision-maker not being independent and impartial); *R (Carson) v Secretary of State for Work and Pensions* [2005] UKHL 37 [2006] 1 AC 173 at [69] (Lord Walker, explaining that although the state has the burden of justifying discrimination, "the court ... rarely has to make a detailed assessment of the credibility and cogency of factual evidence").

17.4.20 **Disclosure/further information/cross-examination: other aspects.** *Jones v Secretary of State for Wales* [1995] 2 PLR 26, 32F ("usually undesirable that a person holding a quasi-judicial office should be exposed to cross-examination"); *Richard Read (Transport) Ltd v Secretary of State for the Environment* [1995] 3 PLR 59, 65C (cross-examination of planning inspector inappropriate; need compellingly pressing reasons); *Tweed v Parades Commission for Northern Ireland* [2006] UKHL 53 [2007] 1 AC 650 at [30] (doubting previously stated principle that judicial review only concerned with "terminus", not route by which decision reached); *R v Secretary of State for Home Affairs, ex p Harrison* (1987) [1997] JR 113, 119-120 (terminus argument); *R v Secretary of State for Transport, ex p APH Road Safety Limited* [1993] COD 150 (rejecting submission that in an irrationality case Court concerned only with whether the claimant could show with the material at his disposal that the decision was irrational); *R v Secretary of State for Education & Science, ex p G* The Times 7th July 1989 (defendant having conceded that decision should be quashed and remitted, Court having no jurisdiction to order disclosure of documents for use as to redetermination); *R v Legal Aid Board, ex p London Docklands Development Corporation* [1994] COD 247 (further information refused because of legal professional privilege); *Roylance v General Medical Council (No.2)* [2000] 1 AC 311 (refusal to admit witness statement relating to GMC's deliberations in camera, because of need for deliberations as to corporate judicial decision to remain confidential); <17.1.9> (litigation privilege); *R v Lewes Justices, ex p the Gaming Board of Great Britain* [1973] AC 388, 413E-F (referring to "the old fallacy that any official in the government service would be inhibited from writing frankly and possibly at all unless he could be sure that nothing which he wrote could ever be exposed to the light of day"); *R v Secretary of State for Education, ex p S* [1994] ELR 252 (Sedley J), 262E-G (having not seen critical document: "More than once in the course of the argument I have felt like Lord Bowen's blind man looking for a black hat in a dark room"; but cf. CA at [1995] ELR 71); *R (JB) v Haddock* [2006] EWCA Civ 961 [2006] HRLR 1237 at [65] (cross-examination not necessary in HRA forced medical treatment case if not requested by claimant); *R v Secretary of State for the Home Department, ex p Oladehinde* [1991] 1 AC 254, 302B-C (no application to cross-examine); *R v Secretary of State for the Home Department, ex p Gardian* [1996] COD 306 (approach as to disclosure in the Court of Appeal).

18.1 **Costs: general matters.**[84] Costs are of vitally practical importance, yet principles have too often unquestioningly been imported from private law and their application can be a rushed epilogue to a case. Costs orders are always in the Court's discretion, structured by general principles or conventions.

18.1.1 **Some key costs rules.** See generally section 51 of the Supreme Court Act 1981 and CPR 44.3; CPR 54.9(1)-(2) <64.2> (failure to file AOS); CPR 54PD <64.3> paras 8.5-8.6 (permission hearing); JR:PAP <64.5> para 7 (non-compliance with JR:PAP); ACO:NFG <64.4> para 17.1 (responsibility for costs); CPR 44.4 (basis of assessment); CPR 44.8 (time for complying with costs orders); CPR 43-48PD (Practice Direction about Costs) section 8, at para 8.5 and the accompanying table (common costs orders at preliminary stages).

18.1.2 **The costs discretion.** See SCA s.51(1); CPR 44.3(1). *Bolton Metropolitan District Council v Secretary of State for the Environment (Practice Note)* [1995] 1 WLR 1176, 1178F (Lord Lloyd: "in all questions to do with costs, the fundamental rule is that there are no rules. Costs are always in the discretion of the court, and a practice, however widespread and longstanding, must never be allowed to harden into a rule"); *Lownds v Home Office* [2002] EWCA Civ 365 [2002] 1 WLR 2450 at [10] (focus on "proportionality"), [31] ("global approach": whether "the costs as a whole are ... disproportionate"; if so, as whether each item necessary; if not, whether each item reasonable); *Rushbridger v HM Attorney-General* [2003] UKHL 38 [2004] 1 AC 357 (claimant ordered to pay costs of unnecessary and hypothetical proceedings), [47] (Lord Scott: "if unnecessary litigation is commenced in order to obtain obvious results, the claimant must expect to have to pay the costs of the exercise"); *R (Corner House Research) v Secretary of State for Trade and Industry* [2005] EWCA Civ 192 [2005] 1 WLR 2600 at [24]-[27] (discussing features of costs in public law); *R (Davey) v Aylesbury Vale District Council* [2007] EWCA Civ 1166 [2008] 1 WLR 878 AT [18] (public law not necessarily following the practice in civil litigation generally).

18.1.3 **Starting-point: costs follow the event.** See CPR 44.3(2)(a); *R (Davey) v Aylesbury Vale District Council* [2007] EWCA Civ 1166 [2008] 1 WLR 878 at [29] ("costs should ordinarily follow the event and ... it is for the claimant who has lost to show that some different approach should be adopted on the facts of a particular case"); *R (Smeaton) v Secretary of State for Health* [2002] EWHC 886 (Admin) [2002] 2 FLR 146 at [406] ("the starting point is the same in judicial review proceedings as in other types of cases"); *R v Lord Chancellor, ex p Child Poverty Action Group* [1999] 1 WLR 347, 355F ("The starting point must be the basic rule ... that costs follow the event"); *R v Intervention Board for Agricultural Produce, ex p Fish Producers' Organisation Ltd* [1993] 1 CMLR 707, 710 ("the court's discretion is not applied differently or in any special way in circumstances where the costs arise in judicial review proceedings"); *R (Boxall) v Mayor and Burgesses of Waltham Forest London Borough Council* (2001) 4 CCLR 258 at [9] (CPR 44.3 allowing "a wide discretion to depart" from costs following the event

---

[84] Zoe Leventhal [2005] JR 139; Stephen Cragg [2008] JR 51.

"depending on the circumstances of the particular case").

18.1.4 **Issue-based orders.**[85] See CPR 44.3(6); *R (Bateman) v Legal Services Commission* [2001] EWHC Admin 797 (CPR 44.3 a break with the past; successful claimant deprived of costs attributable to issues on which had failed); *R v Secretary of State for Transport, ex p Factortame Ltd (No.5)* [1998] EuLR 456 (CA), 478-481 (suggesting that different approach justified in complex litigation where failed issues have increased costs); *R v Bacon's City Technology College, ex p W* [1998] ELR 488, 501E (claimant awarded 75% of costs); *R v Hambledon District Council, ex p Somerfield Stores Ltd* [1999] 1 PLR 66, 91C-D (successful claimant securing 50% of costs because successful only on one point, which did not occupy much of court time or costs of parties' preparation); *R v Hampshire County Council, ex p H* [1999] 2 FLR 359, 373C (defendant to pay 50% of claimant's costs); *R v North West Lancashire Health Authority, ex p A* [2000] 1 WLR 977, 1003H (successful parties in CA only awarded 66% of their costs); *R v Kirklees Metropolitan Borough Council, ex p Beaumont* [2001] ELR 204 (see transcript at [105]) (claimant recovering full costs, even though failed on an issue, because hearing not materially lengthened and evidence relevant background); *R (Jarrett) v Legal Services Commission* [2001] EWHC Admin 389 (claimant awarded 50% of costs because in substance succeeded albeit that 4 or 5 arguments not pursued); *Boxall* <18.5.4(A)>; *R (Turpin) v Commissioner for Local Administration* [2001] EWHC Admin 503 [2003] LGR 133 (defendant to pay 80% of claimant's costs where one of 3 grounds had failed); *R (Adriano) v Surrey County Council* [2002] EWHC 2471 (Admin) [2003] Env LR 559 at [88] (claimants recovering full costs even though unnecessary for some grounds to be advanced because "plain that the three principal points were going to succeed"); *R (Munjaz) v Mersey Care NHS Trust* [2003] EWCA Civ 1036 [2003] 3 WLR 1505 at [89] (declining to deprive claimant of costs on unsuccessful issues: "fundamental human rights and the liberty of the subject are involved ... There is a public interest in these issues beyond those of the individual parties. It would be wrong to discourage any party from raising any proper and reasonable argument even if it ultimately failed") (HL is [2005] UKHL 58 [2006] 2 AC 148); *R (Coghlan) v Chief Constable of Greater Manchester Police* [2004] EWHC 2801 (Admin) [2005] 2 All ER 890 (partially successful claimant receiving two-thirds costs order); *R (Longfield Care Homes Ltd) v HM Coroner for Blackburn* [2004] EWHC 2467 (Admin) (no order for costs where "a curate's egg of a judgment for both sides" and "impossible to disentangle the costs of arguing each issue"); *R (Chorion Plc) v Westminster City Council* [2002] EWCA Civ 1126 at [16]-[17] <18.5.2(B)>.

18.1.5 **Costs consequences of procedural non-compliance.**
(A) FAILURE TO COMPLY WITH PRE-ACTION PROTOCOL. CPR 44.3(5)(a); JR:PAP <64.5> para 7; *R (Aegis Group Plc) v Inland Revenue Commissioners* [2005] EWHC 1468 (Ch) (defendant deprived of 15% of costs to reflect unexplained and unacceptably late response to letter before claim).
(B) FAILURE TO LODGE ACKNOWLEDGMENT OF SERVICE. CPR 54.9(1)-(2) <64.2>; *R (Kelly) v Hammersmith and Fulham London Borough Council* [2004] EWHC 435 (Admin) (2004) 7 CCLR 542 at [58] (defendant awarded costs even though acknowledgment of service did not take alternative remedy point, since fact remaining that claimant brought "a misconceived claim").
(C) GENERAL. *R (Montpeliers & Trevors Association) v City of Westminster* [2005] EWHC 16 (Admin) [2006] LGR 304 at [59] (court would have deprived defendant of some of its costs, had it succeeded, given its inactivity in defiance of the rules).

18.1.6 **Costs and failure to explore alternative dispute resolution (ADR).** <10.2>

---

[85] Shaheen Rahman [2001] JR 149.

(ADR/mediation); *R (Nurse Prescribers Ltd) v Secretary of State for Health* [2004] EWHC 403 (Admin) at [116] (no order for costs, despite failed challenge, because claimant had established a disappointed legitimate expectation and the Secretary of State had declined an ADR offer); *Halsey v Milton Keynes General NHS Trust* [2004] EWCA Civ 576 [2004] 4 All ER 920 at [13] ("In deciding whether to deprive a successful party of some or all of his costs on the grounds that he has refused to agree to ADR ... [t]he fundamental principle is that such departure is not justified unless it is shown (the burden being on the unsuccessful party) that the successful party acted unreasonably in refusing to agree to ADR"); *Dunnett v Railtrack plc* [2002] EWCA Civ 303 [2002] 1 WLR 2434 (Railtrack winning but no order for costs because Railtrack having refused to explore ADR, being confident of succeeding); *R (Johnson) v Reading Borough Council* [2004] EWHC 765 (Admin) (council awarded its costs of failed judicial review, notwithstanding that claimants requested ADR in letter before claim); *R (A) v East Sussex County Council* [2005] EWHC 585 (Admin) (2005) 8 CCLR 228 at [43] (fanciful to suggest mediation would have been successful), [44] (position might be different, had defendant been proposing mediation without preconditions).

18.1.7 Costs in favour of third parties: opposing unsuccessful challenge.[86]

(A) THE *BOLTON* GUIDANCE. *Bolton Metropolitan District Council v Secretary of State for the Environment (Practice Note)* [1995] 1 WLR 1176, 1178F-1179A (Lord Lloyd, stating the general position in planning appeals, where the Secretary of State's decision granting planning permission to a developer has been upheld: "(1) The Secretary of State, when successful in defending his decision, will normally be entitled to the whole of his costs. He should not be required to share his award of costs by apportionment... (2) The developer will not normally be entitled to his costs unless he can show that there was likely to be a separate issue on which he was entitled to be heard... or unless he has an interest which requires separate representation... (3) A second set of costs is more likely to be awarded at first instance, than in the Court of Appeal or House of Lords... (4) An award of a third set of costs will rarely be justified, even if there are in theory three or more separate interests"). Although a planning appeal, *Bolton* is treated as being of assistance in judicial review cases.

(B) THE NORMAL RULE. *R (Smeaton) v Secretary of State for Health* [2002] EWHC 886 (Admin) [2002] 2 FLR 146 at [431] (Munby J: "the normal rule ... is that two sets of respondents' costs are not awarded against an unsuccessful claimant for judicial review"), [437] (here, alleged criminality arising, which was that of the interested party); *Wychavon District Council v Secretary of State for the Environment* [1994] 3 PLR 42 (normally appropriate to make only one order on statutory review, where issues identical); *R v Secretary of State for the Environment, ex p Kirkstall Valley Campaign Ltd* [1996] 3 All ER 304, 342f-343b ("it is not the normal practice in this court to give two sets of costs"); *R v Registrar of Companies, ex p Central Bank of India* [1986] QB 1114, 1162F-H ("undoubtedly the general rule ... that, if several parties appear in the same interest on an application for judicial review, they will only be allowed one set of costs between them"); *R v Industrial Disputes Tribunal, ex p American Express Co Inc* [1954] 1 WLR 1118 ("The court does not like having to give two sets of costs in these cases... The opinion of the court is that, in future, in matters of this sort, we shall not grant more than one set of costs"; "the court will consider very carefully whether or not they will give two sets of costs"); *R v Intervention Board for Agricultural Produce, ex p Fish Producers' Organisation Ltd* [1993] 1 CMLR 707, 710 (speaking of protecting claimant "from having to pay costs to all of a number of [defendants] who have intervened and chosen not to leave it to one [defendant] to carry the argument").

(C) SOME FURTHER ILLUSTRATIONS. *Berkeley v Secretary of State for the Environment (No.2)* The Times 7th April 1998 (not sufficient reason for second set, in terms of a separate

---

[86] Mark Shaw [1997] JR 4.

issue requiring representation) (HL is at [2001] 2 AC 603); *R (Trustees of the Friends of the Lake District) v Secretary of State for the Environment, Transport and the Regions* [2001] EWHC Admin 281 (third party's costs refused because, although differences in emphasis, essentially covered the same ground as the defendant); *R (Friends of the Earth and Greenpeace) v Secretary of State for Environment Food and Rural Affairs* [2001] EWCA Civ 1950 (intervener not recovering costs in High Court or Court of Appeal; second set of costs in the Court of Appeal "very unusual" and "no question of two sets of costs here", where unsuccessful claimants were "public interest groups"); *R (Alliance Spring Co Ltd) v First Secretary of State* [2005] EWHC 18 (Admin) [2005] 3 PLR 76 (second set of costs, but limited to preparation of evidence to answer a particular factual allegation); *R (Great North Eastern Railway Ltd) v Office of Rail Regulation* [2006] EWHC 1942 (Admin) (claimant ordered to pay costs of defendant and two interested parties).

(D) NATURE OF "SEPARATE INTEREST". *R (Bedford) v London Borough of Islington* [2002] EWHC 2044 (Admin) [2003] Env LR 463 at [296] (developer not awarded its costs, commenting that "[it] does have a separate interest, but it was not at the time a conflicting interest. [T]he entitlement to separate representation, and an interest separately to protect, does not of itself warrant the grant of a second set of costs. It is ... almost inevitable that the interested party ... will be able to make a significant contribution to the argument and that the interested party will be able to make a significant contribution to the evidence").

(E) SECOND SET OF COSTS GRANTED: EXAMPLES. *R (Smeaton) v Secretary of State for Health* [2002] EWHC 886 (Admin) [2002] 2 FLR 146 at [438] (second set of costs ordered because the "simple reality is that this case without the active participation of [the interested party] would have been a `Hamlet without the Prince'"); *R (the Secretary of State for the Home Department) v Mental Health Review Tribunal* [2002] EWCA Civ 1868 (2003) 6 CCLR 319 at [32]-[33] (wrong in principle to deny the third party his costs where he had the "very special interest" that his liberty was at stake); *R v Ogwr Borough Council, ex p Carter Commercial Developments Ltd* [1989] 2 PLR 54, 63G-H (exceptional case justifying two costs orders, although "there has not, as it turned out, been much difference of argument from the point of view of the two [defendants], ... in view of the way in which the matter was launched and the risk that the local authority might well have been involved primarily in defeating an allegation of bad faith"); *R v North Staffordshire Health Authority, ex p Worthington* [1997] COD 272 (see transcript) (appropriate to order second set of costs on the particular facts and because of stance taken by defendant); *R v Secretary of State for the Environment, Transport and the Regions, ex p Alliance Against the Birmingham Northern Relief Road* 23rd March 1999 unrep. (costs awarded to third party, but limited to "costs of being represented at the hearing by experienced counsel properly instructed", ie. so that "in a position to deal with any additional points" where could not be assured of "unity of view" with the defendant); *R v Secretary of State for National Heritage, ex p J Paul Getty Trust* [1997] EuLR 407, 419B ("this was a case where there was a separate interest for the Fund to represent and it was appropriate for them to be separately represented); *R v Cotswold District Council, ex p Barrington* (1998) 75 P & CR 515 (two sets of costs granted at the permission stage); *R v Ministry of Agriculture Fisheries and Food, ex p Monsanto Plc* [1999] QB 1161, 1174B (having failed in application for interim remedy, claimant ordered to pay defendant's costs and 75% of third party's costs); *R v Secretary of State for the Home Department, ex p Arthur H Cox Ltd* [1999] EuLR 677 (see transcript) (third party awarded half its costs because, although additional arguments unsuccessful, claimant had made a serious allegation which, notwithstanding a clear warning, had only be withdrawn at the last moment); *R v Secretary of State for Agriculture Fisheries and Food, ex p ISK Biosciences Ltd* 8th October 1997 unrep. (second set of costs granted because discrete issue argued by third party, even though not necessary to decide that issue); *R v Medicines Control Agency, ex p Rhone-Poulenc Rorer Ltd* [1999] EuLR 181 (see transcript) (one intervener awarded half its costs, another one-third); *R v Director General of Electricity Supply, ex p First Hydro Company* 2nd March 2000 unrep. (second set of costs, where important case and claimant must have appreciated what taking on in launching these proceedings); *R v Tandridge District Council, ex p Al Fayed* [2000] 1 PLR 58 (see transcript) (3rd party obtaining half of its costs in Court of Appeal); *R (Association of Pharmaceutical Importers) v Secretary of State for Health* [2001] EWCA Civ 1986 [2002] EuLR 197 (second set of costs awarded).

18.1.8 Costs and third parties: supporting successful challenge. *R v Secretary of State for Health, ex p Eastside Cheese Company* (1999) 11 Admin LR 254 (Moses J) (defendant ordered to pay costs of third party (of instructing counsel, but not solicitors), where could have brought own proceedings, which could have been consolidated or heard together, and would have succeeded) (order not disturbed by CA [1999] EuLR 968); *R v Legal Aid Board, ex p Duncan* [2000] COD 159 (Law Society, although not having formally intervened, supporting the application for judicial review and having provided witness statements).

18.1.9 Costs against third parties: resisting successful challenge. *R (Mills) v Birmingham Magistrates Court* [2005] EWHC 2732 (Admin) (costs against CPS, who sought and defended the impugned magistrates' order); *R v Hastings Licensing Justices, ex p John Lovibond & Sons Ltd* [1968] 1 WLR 735 (costs against third party supporting defendant justices' decision); *R (Holmes) v General Medical Council* [2001] EWHC Admin 321 (third party having to pay costs or claimant and defendant, where they each agreed that judicial review should be granted and the third party alone had (unsuccessfully) sought to uphold the decision); *R v Manchester Stipendiary Magistrate, ex p Granada Television Ltd* [1999] QB 1202 (DC), 1213A-B (costs against interested party unsuccessful in defending magistrate's decision); *R (Munjaz) v Mersey Care NHS Trust* [2003] EWCA Civ 1036 [2003] 3 WLR 1505 at [90] (Secretary of State to pay claimant's costs regarding issues which Secretary of State introduced) (HL is [2005] UKHL 58 [2006] 2 AC 148); *R (Holme) v Liverpool Magistrates Court* [2004] EWHC 3131 (Admin) (court declining costs against CPS who had attended to assist the court, the defendant magistrates not appearing); *R v Family Health Services Appeal Authority, ex p E Moss Ltd* 29th April 1998 unrep. (claimant's costs paid, as to 75% by defendant and as to 25% by third party); *R (Towry Law Financial Services plc) v Financial Services Ombudsman Service Ltd* [2002] EWHC 1603 (Admin) at [23] (declining costs against interested party who did not concede claim against ombudsman immediately, given the absence of a warning from the claimant at the outset as to costs and because settlement should not be discouraged); *R (Pilot Foods Ltd) v Horseferry Road Magistrates' Court* [2003] EWHC 1447 (Admin) at [29] (costs against local authority whose regulatory breach led to impugned liability orders and who could have agreed a consent order allowing the claim); *R (Sussex Police Authority) v Cooling* [2004] EWHC 1920 (Admin) (post-permission costs against third party who unsuccessfully defended impugned decision of certifying medical officer); *R (O'Callaghan) v Charity Commission* [2007] EWHC 2491 (Admin) (50% of claimant's costs from third party who had made much of the running in unsuccessfully defending).

18.1.10 Costs and friend of the court (amicus curiae). See eg. Justice/PLP Report, *A Matter of Public Interest: Reforming the Law and Practice on Interventions in Public Interest Cases* (1996) at 34 ("Orders for costs are made neither against nor in favour of an amicus"); *B v Croydon Health Authority (No.2)* [1996] 1 FLR 253 (as to official solicitor).

18.1.11 Costs and separately-represented claimants. *R (A) v East Sussex County Council* [2005] EWHC 585 (Admin) (2005) 8 CCLR 228 at [47] ("it would in the circumstances be appropriate - fair, just and appropriate - to depart from ... the typical starting point and to award the claimants two sets of costs").

18.1.12 **Costs and (non-appearing/neutrally appearing) courts/tribunals.**[87]
(A) GENERAL GUIDANCE. *R (Davies) v Birmingham Deputy Coroner* [2004] EWCA Civ 207 [2004] 1 WLR 2739 at [47] (Brooke LJ: "(i) The established practice of the courts was to make no order for costs against an inferior court or tribunal which did not appear before it except when there was a flagrant instance of improper behaviour or when the inferior court or tribunal unreasonably declined or neglected to sign a consent order disposing of the proceedings; (ii) The established practice of the courts was to treat an inferior court or tribunal which resisted an application actively by way of argument in such a way that it made itself an active party to the litigation, as if it was such a party, so that in the normal course of things costs would follow the event; (iii) If, however, an inferior court or tribunal appeared in the proceedings in order to assist the court neutrally on questions of jurisdiction, procedure, specialist case-law and such like, the established practice of the courts was to treat it as a neutral party, so that it would not make an order for costs in its favour or an order for costs against it whatever the outcome of the application; (iv) There are, however, a number of important considerations which might tend to make the courts exercise their discretion in a different way today in cases in category (iii) above, so that a successful [claimant] ..., who has to finance his own litigation without external funding, may be fairly compensated out of a source of public funds and not be put to irrecoverable expense in asserting his rights after a coroner (or other inferior tribunal) has gone wrong in law, and there is no other very obvious candidate available to pay his costs"); *R v Bristol Magistrates Court, ex p Hodge* [1997] QB 974, 982C-D (whether "they had done something which calls for strong disapproval"); *R v Newcastle under Lyme Justices, ex p Massey* [1994] 1 WLR 1684, 1691H-1693H (need for exceptional circumstances, such as unreasonable refusal to sign a consent order); <2.5.7> (non-appearing/non-adversarial defendants).
(B) COSTS ORDERED AGAINST MAGISTRATES: ILLUSTRATIONS. *R v Huntingdon Magistrates' Court, ex p Percy* [1994] COD 323 (magistrates' unreasonable continued refusal to state a case, even after permission to move for judicial review of that decision granted by the Court); *R v Aldershot Justices, ex p Rushmoor Borough Council* [1996] COD 21 (costs against justices for refusing to state a case notwithstanding the grant of permission for judicial review) and the sequel *R v Aldershot Justices, ex p Rushmoor Borough Council (No.2)* [1996] COD 280 (Court declining to set aside the costs order); *R v Lincoln Justices, ex p Count* (1996) 8 Admin LR 233 (perverse decision in flagrant disregard of elementary principles); *R v Stafford Justices, ex p Johnson* [1995] COD 352 (serious failure to conduct proper inquiry); *R v Reading Family Justices Panel, ex p DSS* 28th November 1995 unrep. and *R v Stoke-on-Trent Justices, ex p Booth* The Independent 9th February 1996 (unreasonable failure to sign consent orders); *R v Metropolitan Stipendiary Magistrate, ex p Ali* The Independent 12th May 1997 (continued refusal to state a case, as here, notwithstanding judge's comments in granting permission); *R v Newcastle Upon Tyne Justices, ex p Devine* [1998] COD 420 (awarding costs against magistrates who had made elementary error and not taken the opportunity to accept it); *R v Doncaster Justices, ex p Jack* The Times 26th May 1999 (rare case where costs order against non-appearing magistrates appropriate); *R v Feltham Justices, ex p Haid* [1998] COD 440 (costs against magistrates refused). Note that until 1997 magistrates had no indemnity (see eg. *R v Coventry Justices, ex p Director of Public Prosecutions* [1991] 1 WLR 1153, 1157H), after which the Justices of the Peace Act 1997 s.54 provided for indemnification from local funds.
(C) THE CHANCE TO APPLY TO SET ASIDE THE ORDER. The practice, with any non-appearing person or body (including the Legal Services Commission) is to make an order `nisi' (ie. not to take effect for a specified period so as to allow an application to set aside the costs order): see eg. *R v Doncaster Justices, ex p Christison* [2000] COD 5 (magistrates successfully applying to set aside costs order as unjustified, by further explaining the evidence which had

---

[87] Mark Shaw [1996] JR 133.

been put before the court).

(D) COSTS AGAINST CORONERS. *Davies* (above); *R v West Yorkshire Coroner, ex p Kenyon* The Times 11th April 1984 (general principle no costs order if coroner not appearing and error of law not calling for strong disapproval); *R v Inner London North Coroner, ex p Touche* [2001] EWCA Civ 383 [2001] QB 1206 (costs appropriate where coroner appeared and lost, even though no disapproval), [56] (different (and anomalous) if judicial officer chooses not to appear; in which case costs only if disapproval); *In the matter of an inquest into the death of Catherine Lucy Clegg* [1997] COD 166 (costs against non-appearing coroner).

(E) COSTS AGAINST AN OMBUDSMAN. *Moore's (Wallisdown) Ltd v Pensions Ombudsman* [2002] 1 WLR 1649 (costs ordered in full against pensions ombudsman, having appeared to defend decision on statutory appeal), concluding that approach incorrect in both *Elliott v Pensions Ombudsman* The Times 20th November 1997 (costs appropriate only to the extent that the Ombudsman had participated and that participation had increased the costs incurred) and *University of Nottingham v Eyett* [1999] 1 WLR 594 (Pensions Ombudsman only liable for costs to the extent that they had been increased by his attendance); *Seifert v Pensions Ombudsman* [1997] 4 All ER 947, 956d (on appeal against decision of Pensions Ombudsman, fact that determinations set aside not enough to justify order for costs against the Ombudsman); *R (Towry Law Financial Services plc) v Financial Services Ombudsman Service Ltd* [2002] EWHC 1603 (Admin) at [20] (need for "flagrant disregard of principle" to award costs against non-participating inferior tribunal such as the Financial Services Ombudsman).

(F) INFERIOR COURT AND TWO OPPOSING PARTIES. *R (Davies) v Birmingham Deputy Coroner* [2004] EWCA Civ 207 [2004] 1 WLR 2739 at [5] (Brooke LJ, explaining that where judicial review of county court: "in those cases a lis is generally joined between the competing parties and no question tends to arise in relation to the possibility of an order for costs against the judge himself").

18.1.13 Costs and discretionary refusal of a remedy.

(A) COSTS AGAINST DEFENDANT. *R v Lambeth London Borough Council, ex p Touhey* (2000) 32 HLR 707, 728 (suggesting appropriate to order costs against defendant where continuing breach of housing duty but no remedy because council now making proper efforts); *R v North West Thames Regional Health Authority, ex p Daniels (Rhys William)* [1994] COD 44 (see transcript) (costs awarded to claimant where breach of statutory duty to consult CHC, but no remedy granted because would serve no useful purpose); *In the matter of an inquest into the death of Catherine Lucy Clegg* [1997] COD 166 (costs where grounds made out but not in the interests of justice to order a new inquest); *R (Guiney) v Greenwich London Borough Council* [2008] EWHC 2012 (Admin) (claimant awarded 75% of costs where obtaining declaration only, and not partial quashing).

(B) COSTS AGAINST CLAIMANT. *R v Trafford Borough Council, ex p Colonel Foods Ltd* [1990] COD 351 (costs against claimant where grounds for judicial review satisfied, but remedy refused as a matter of discretion given existence of alternative remedy by way of appeal).

(C) NO ORDER FOR COSTS/OTHER ORDERS. *R (Bloggs) v Secretary of State for the Home Department* [2002] EWHC 1921 (Admin) (where unsuccessful claimant had a "strong and justified sense of grievance", "the Prison Service in this case must be content with the victory rather than with any imposition of costs") (CA is at [2003] EWCA Civ 686 [2003] 1 WLR 2724); *R v Swale Borough Council & Medway Ports Authority, ex p Royal Society for the Protection of Birds* (1990) 2 Admin LR 790, 808H-816E (breach of legitimate expectation but remedy refused for delay, given third party reliance; no order for costs as between claimant and defendant, but claimant having to pay interested party's costs); *Berkeley v Secretary of State for the Environment (No.2)* The Times 7th April 1998 (see transcript) (where Secretary of State was in breach of his legal obligations, albeit "in the end it has not affected the outcome of the proceedings": "It is appropriate for the court, which has its own interest in preserving the high standards of civil administration which we expect in this country, to mark its disapproval of that breach by depriving the Secretary of State of a proportion of his costs, although only in the court below") (NB. the HL granted the remedy: see [2001] 2 AC 603); *R v Sheffield City Council, ex p H* [1999] ELR 242 (Owen J), 248E (where quashing order (certiorari) refused because would serve no useful purpose, but declarations granted, claimants awarded one-third of costs); *R (L) v Independent Appeal Panel of St Edward's College* [2001] EWHC Admin 108 [2001] ELR 542 (no order for costs where remedy refused as a matter of discretion because not sensible to reconvene schools admissions panel during present school year).

18.1.14 **Costs and CLS funding (legal aid).** <19.1.8> (CLS funding); Access to Justice Act 1999 s.22(4) (CLS funding "shall not affect (a) the rights or liabilities of other parties to the proceedings, or (b) the principles on which the discretion of any court or tribunal is normally exercised"); *R v Wandsworth London Borough Council, ex p Heshmati* [1998] COD 67 (costs should follow the event, even where successful claimant legally-aided and defendant a public body); *R (Boxall) v Mayor and Burgesses of Waltham Forest London Borough Council* (2001) 4 CCLR 258 at [10] ("The court should not normally take into account that a party is publicly funded when deciding whether and if so what costs order to make between the parties"); *R (Gunn) v Secretary of State for the Home Department* [2001] EWCA Civ 891 [2001] 1 WLR 1634 (explaining that costs judge can order costs against Legal Services Commission in favour of a public body); *R v Gloucestershire County Council, ex p P* [1994] ELR 334, 341B-342C (judge refusing to order costs against one public body (the defendant authority) in favour of another (legal aid board, now LSC)); <18.1.15> (costs set off).

18.1.15 **Costs set off.** *R (Burkett) v Hammersmith and Fulham London Borough Council* [2004] EWCA Civ 1342 (where CLS-funded claimant obtaining costs order in JR, appropriate to direct a set-off in respect of earlier costs order made against the same claimant); *R (Supportways Community Services Ltd) v Hampshire County Council (No.2)* [2006] EWCA Civ 1170 (2006) 9 CCLR 498 (inquiry for damages, conditional on first paying costs ordered).

18.1.16 **Costs out of central funds.** *Practice Direction (Criminal Proceedings: Costs)* [2004] 1 WLR 2657 at [II 3.1] (Administrative Court "may make a defendant's costs order [from central funds] on determining proceedings in a criminal cause or matter"). For examples, see *R (Hale) v Southport Justices* [2002] EWHC 257 (Admin) The Times 29th January 2002; *R v Manchester Stipendiary Magistrate, ex p Hill* [1983] 1 AC 328, 346E-G; *R v Middlesex Crown Court, ex p Khan* [1997] COD 186; *R v Preston Crown Court, ex p Lancashire County Council* [1999] 1 WLR 142; *R v Southwark Crown Court, ex p Gross* [1998] COD 445. There is no power in a civil case: *Holden & Co v Crown Prosecution Service (No.2)* [1994] 1 AC 22; also *R v Moore* [2003] EWCA Crim 1574 [2003] 1 WLR 2170 (considering, in a contempt context, the limited jurisdiction to order costs out of central funds); *R (Davies) v Birmingham Deputy Coroner* [2004] EWCA Civ 207 [2004] 1 WLR 2739 at [44] (Brooke LJ, lamenting "the government's continuing unwillingness to permit the courts to make an order that an applicant's costs be borne by central funds in an appropriate case"), [45] (no heed paid to the pleas of the courts or the Law Commission), [48].

18.1.17 **Incorporating for costs-protection.** *R v Leicestershire County Council, ex p Blackfordby & Boothorpe Action Group Ltd* [2001] Env LR 2 at [37] (advantages of incorporation including "the avoidance of substantial personal liability of members for the costs of unsuccessful legal proceedings", but the "costs position can be dealt with adequately by requiring the provision of security for costs in a realistically large sum... [That is] the right approach in principle"); *R (Residents Against Waste Sites Ltd) v Lancs County Council* [2007] EWHC 2558 (Admin) at [19] (position dealt with by security for costs); *R v Ministry of Agriculture Fisheries and Food, ex p British Pig Industry Support Group* [2000] EuLR 724 at [108] (security for costs appropriate solution where incorporated claimant; requiring co-claimant as a condition of permission an appropriate solution where unincorporated claimant); *R (PPG11 Ltd) v Dorset County Council* [2003] EWHC 1311 (Admin) [2004] Env LR 84 at [3] (where claimant "a limited company formed as an action group from those opposed to the scheme"); *R (Hereford Waste Watchers Ltd) v Hereford Council* [2005] EWHC 191 (Admin) [2005] Env LR 586 at [2] (claimant company "formed specifically to challenge the development in this case"); <21.2.11(A)> (security for costs); *Village Residents Association Ltd v An Bord Pleanala* 23rd March 2000 (Irish High Court ordering security for costs against company incorporated to bring a planning judicial review claim).

18.2 **Summary assessment/detailed assessment of costs.**Where the Court makes a costs order it can either direct a subsequent "detailed assessment" or can conduct an immediate "summary assessment" of the appropriate amount to be paid.

18.2.1 **Detailed assessment or summary assessment.** See CPR 43.3 and 43.4, 44.7; CPR 43-48PD section 12.

18.2.2 **Interim payment pending detailed assessment.** See CPR 44.3(8); *Mars Ltd v Teknowledge Ltd* [2000] FSR 138 (applicable principles discussed); *Dyson Ltd v Hoover Ltd* [2003] EWHC 624 (Ch) [2004] 1 WLR 1264 (presumption in favour of interim payment applicable only where judge had had benefit of hearing whole trial); *R (Montpeliers & Trevors Association) v City of Westminster* [2005] EWHC 16 (Admin) [2006] LGR 304 (defendant ordered to pay £27,500 within 7 days as interim payment, where claimant could expect to recover say 75% (£36,000) of total costs of £48,000).

18.2.3 **Whether to conduct summary assessment.**See CPR 43-48PD (Practice Direction about Costs) section 13. As to the CA, see CPR 52PD paras 14.1-14.2.

18.2.4 **Summary assessment: basis of assessment.**See CPR 44.4-44.5; CPR 43-48PD (Practice Direction about Costs) section 11.

18.2.5 **Summary assessment and CLS funding (legal aid).**CPR 43-48PD (Practice Direction about Costs) paras 13.9-13.10.

18.3 **Costs and the permission stage.**Generally speaking: (1) where permission is granted, costs are reserved or costs in the case; (2) where permission is refused, a defendant can recover (a) reasonable costs of an acknowledgment of service, but not (b) costs of attending an oral permission hearing; (3) where permission becomes unnecessary, no order for costs is made.

18.3.1 **Power to order costs at the permission stage.**[88] Supreme Court Act 1981 s.51(1)-(2); *R (Mount Cook Land Ltd) v Westminster City Council* [2003] EWCA Civ 1346 [2004] 1 PLR 29; *R v Camden London Borough Council, ex p Martin* [1997] 1 WLR 359, 365A (permission stage costs covered by SCA 1981 s.51).

---

[88] Mark Shaw [1996] JR 8.

18.3.2 **Costs of failed applications for permission.**[89]
(A) COSTS OF THE AOS. *R (Mount Cook Land Ltd) v Westminster City Council* [2003] EWCA Civ 1346 [2004] 1 PLR 29 at [76(1)] ("certainly in a case to which the Pre-Action Protocol applies and where a defendant or other interested party has complied with it ... a successful defendant or other party at the permission stage who has filed an acknowledgment of service pursuant to CPR 54.8 should generally recover the costs of doing so from the claimant, whether or not he attends any permission hearing"); *R (Ewing) v Office of the Deputy Prime Minister* [2005] EWCA Civ 1583 [2006] 1 WLR 1260 (endorsing *Mount Cook*); *R (Davey) v Aylesbury Vale District Council* [2007] EWCA Civ 1166 [2008] 1 WLR 878 at [16] (rule of practice that "an unsuccessful applicant for permission must expect to pay the defendant's costs of putting in an acknowledgment of service"), [21] (included if ultimate defendant's costs order silent), [33] (but limited to the costs of discharging the proper, narrow function of the AOS).
(B) COSTS OF ORAL HEARING. CPR 54PD <64.3> paras 8.5-8.6; *R (Mount Cook Land Ltd) v Westminster City Council* [2003] EWCA Civ 1346 [2004] 1 PLR 29 at [76(2)-(7)] ("a defendant who attends and successfully resists the grant of permission at a renewal hearing should not generally recover from the claimant his costs of and occasioned by doing so"; need for "exceptional circumstances" which "may consist ... of ...: (a) the hopelessness of the claim; (b) the persistence in it by the claimant after having been alerted to facts and/or of the law demonstrating its hopelessness; (c) the extent to which the court considers that the claimant, in the pursuit of his application, has sought to abuse the process of judicial review for collateral ends - a relevant consideration as to costs at the permission stage, as well as when considering discretionary refusal of relief at the stage of substantive hearing, if there is one; and (d) whether, as a result of the deployment of full argument and documentary evidence by both sides at the hearing of a contested application, the unsuccessful claimant has had, in effect, the advantage of an early substantive hearing of the claim"; relevant to consider "the extent to which the unsuccessful claimant has substantial resources which it has used to pursue the unfounded claim and which are available to meet an order for costs"); *R (Payne) v Caerphilly County Borough Council* [2004] EWCA Civ 433 (overturning costs order of permission hearing, there being no exceptional circumstances under the *Mount Cook* principle); *R (Davey) v Aylesbury Vale District Council* [2007] EWCA Civ 1166 [2008] 1 WLR 878 at [16] (rule of practice whereby "a defendant which chooses to attend and oppose an oral application for permission cannot ordinarily expect to recover its costs of doing so even if permission is refused, but may exceptionally be allowed them - for example where it has been able to alert the court to an abuse of its process"), [21] (oral hearing costs excluded from eventual defendant's costs order if silent); *R (Islamic Human Rights Commission) v Civil Aviation Authority* [2006] EWHC 2465 (Admin) (£10,000 awarded to each defendant in respect of permission hearing).

18.3.3 **Approach to permission costs.**
(A) NEED FOR PROPORTIONALITY. *R (Ewing) v Office of the Deputy Prime Minister* [2005] EWCA Civ 1583 [2006] 1 WLR 1260 at [41] (need to avoid costs principles "applied in a way which seriously impedes the right of citizens to access to justice, particularly when seeking to protect their environment"), [42] ("the court must be particularly careful to ensure that the costs falling on the judicial review claimant are not disproportionately inflated by the involvement of the other parties at the permission stage"), [43] (summary grounds should not be detailed, especially if pre-action protocol followed first);*R (Davey) v Aylesbury Vale District Council* [2007] EWCA Civ 1166 [2008] 1 WLR 878 at [33] (limited to proper, narrow function

---

[89] Robert McCracken & Gregory Jones [2002] JR 4; James Cornwell [2004] JR 49; Robert Palmer & Stephen Whale [2004] JR 55.

of AOS); *R (Roudham & Larling Parish Council) v Breckland Council* [2008] EWCA Civ 714 at [29] (need to give fair weight to the work necessary for even short-form summary grounds). (B) PROCEDURE. *R (Ewing) v Office of the Deputy Prime Minister* [2005] EWCA Civ 1583 [2006] 1 WLR 1260 at [47] (pending a CPR change, suggesting: (i) AOS should include any *Mount Cook* costs application; (ii) paper refusal of permission should include indication of whether/what proposed to order; (iii) 14 days for claimant to respond; (iv) 7 further days for defendant/third party to reply; (v) decision then made on paper). (C) ORDER IN FAVOUR OF THIRD PARTY. *R (Ewing) v Office of the Deputy Prime Minister* [2005] EWCA Civ 1583 [2006] 1 WLR 1260 (third parties awarded costs of lodging AOS); *R v Secretary of State for National Heritage, ex p J Paul Getty Trust* [1997] EuLR 407, 419B (costs of failed permission awarded to defendant and third party); *R v Cotswold District Council, ex p Barrington* (1998) 75 P & CR 515 (two sets of costs granted at the permission stage).

18.3.4 **Pre-permission costs.**
(A) CLAIMANT'S COSTS. *R v Royal Borough of Kensington & Chelsea, ex p Ghebregiogis* (1995) 27 HLR 602 (appropriate in exceptional cases to order costs against defendant where failing to concede well-founded case until after judicial review lodged; here, admirably clear letter before claim); *R (Kemp) v Denbighshire Local Health Board* [2006] EWHC 181 (Admin) [2007] 1 WLR 639 at [75] (not a sufficiently clear case). (B) DEFENDANT'S COSTS. *R (Davey) v Aylesbury Vale District Council* [2007] EWCA Civ 1166 [2008] 1 WLR 878 at [21] (where claim fails, judge should deal with whether costs order includes defendant's pre-permission costs, which defendant must justify), [21] (reasonable costs included if defendant's costs order silent), [30] (must be proportionate).

18.3.5 **Permission costs: whether included in final costs order.**[90] *R (Davey) v Aylesbury Vale District Council* [2007] EWCA Civ 1166 [2008] 1 WLR 878 at [5] (court at substantive hearing awarding defendant's costs can exclude costs of unsuccessfully having opposed permission), [21] & [31] (judge should deal expressly with whether permission and pre-permission costs included; if order silent, includes reasonable pre-permission costs, costs of the AOS but not any oral hearing); *Practice Statement (Judicial Review: Costs)* [2004] 2 All ER 994 (unless otherwise stated, "grant of permission ... deemed to contain an order that costs be costs in the case"); *R v Director General of Electricity Supply, ex p Scottish Power Plc* 3rd February 1997 unrep. (CA expressly awarding successful claimant the costs of the permission application); *R v Metropolitan Stipendiary Magistrate, ex p Ali* The Independent 12th May 1997 (costs against magistrate limited to post-permission costs); *R v Wandsworth London Borough Council, ex p M* [1998] ELR 424, 429B (claimant awarded costs of proceedings, but no order as to costs of permission hearing).

18.3.6 **Wasted costs and permission hearings.** *R v Immigration Appeal Tribunal, ex p Gulbamer Gulsen* [1997] COD 430 (common law jurisdiction to order wasted costs regarding permission stage); *R v Secretary of State for the Home Department, ex p Mahmood* [1999] COD 119 (wasted costs granted in relation to additional permission hearing caused by non-attendance); *R (F) v Head Teacher of Addington High School* [2003] EWHC 228 (Admin) (wasted costs ordered against claimant's solicitors where grounds not provided to defendant and defendant's letter not drawn to attention of permission judge, and so misleading impression given as to defendant's inaction); cf. *R v Camden London Borough Council, ex p Martin* [1997] 1 WLR 359 (doubting whether statutory jurisdiction pre-CPR, absent any permission stage service).

---

[90] James Maurici [1998] JR 140.

18.4 Costs and the public interest. The public interest is increasingly recognised as influencing costs in judicial review. Courts can decide in appropriate cases that claimants: (1) should have early certainty that they will be responsible for no or capped costs; or (2) should not face costs orders where their claims have failed. In truth, public law costs principles need a bold and far-reaching re-examination.

18.4.1 **General observations.** *R (Corner House Research) v Secretary of State for Trade and Industry* [2005] EWCA Civ 192 [2005] 1 WLR 2600 at [70] ("there is a public interest in the elucidation of public law by the higher courts in addition to the interests of the individual parties. One should not therefore necessarily expect identical principles to govern the incidence of costs in public law cases, much less the `arterial hardening' of guidance into rule"); *R (Ministry of Defence) v Wiltshire & Swindon Coroner* [2005] EWHC 889 (Admin) [2006] 1 WLR 134 at [34] (Collins J: "The principle must be that in the court's general discretion in relation to costs, and, more importantly, in ensuring that there is proper access to justice and if the needs of justice require, appropriate orders can be made").

18.4.2 **No order as to costs: public interest cases.** *R (Davey) v Aylesbury Vale District Council* [2007] EWCA Civ 1166 [2008] 1 WLR 878 at [21] ("In contrast to a judicial review claim brought wholly or mainly for commercial or proprietary reasons, a claim brought partly or wholly in the public interest, albeit unsuccessful, may properly result in a restricted or no order for costs"); *R (Smeaton) v Secretary of State for Health* [2002] EWHC 886 (Admin) [2002] 2 FLR 146 at [410] ("cases where public interest or analogous considerations will make it inappropriate in all the circumstances to [order] costs"), [421] (here, "not a matter of genuine public concern at all"); *New Zealand Maori Council v Attorney-General of New Zealand* [1994] 1 AC 466, 485G-H (no order as to costs on the appeal since important to examine point raised by the claimant "not ... out of any motive of personal gain [but] ... in the interest of ... an important part of the heritage of New Zealand"); *R (Friends of the Earth and Greenpeace) v Secretary of State for Environment Food and Rural Affairs* [2001] EWCA Civ 1950 at [5] (no order for costs in CA, in part because "the public interest in this particular area, the area of public health and well-being, is obviously very great and very exceptional"); *R v Secretary of State for the Environment, ex p Challenger* [2001] Env LR 209 (no costs order where human rights case of potential importance and claimants of limited means); *R v Secretary of State for the Environment, ex p Shelter* [1997] COD 49 (no order against claimant charity where pending cases raising the same issue, being of genuine public concern, claimant's involvement assisted the Court and likely alternative would have been legally-aided claimant from whom defendant unlikely to recover costs); *R (Greenpeace Ltd) v Secretary of State for the Environment, Food and Rural Affairs* [2005] EWCA Civ 1656 [2006] Env LR 627 at [38]-[40] (judge entitled to decide no order for costs, where important issues and public interest); Woolf Report, *Access to Justice* (1996) at p.255 (no order where "the proceedings have been brought in the public interest"); *Oshlack v Richmond River Council* [1998] HCA 11 (High Court of Australia upholding no costs order in "public interest litigation"); *British Columbia Minister of Forests v Okanagan Indian Band* [2003] 3 SCR 371 (Supreme Court of Canada) at [38] (issues "of broad social significance" where "the public interest is served by a proper resolution").

18.4.3 **Protective costs/cost-capping orders.**[91]
(A) GENERAL. See *R (Corner House Research) v Secretary of State for Trade and Industry*

---

[91] Kate Markus & Martin Westgate [1998] JR 76; Richard Stein & Jamie Beagent [2005] JR 206; Ben Jaffey [2006] JR 171.

[2005] EWCA Civ 192 [2005] 1 WLR 2600 and *R (Compton) v Wiltshire Primary Care Trust* [2008] EWCA Civ 749.

(B) GUIDANCE. *R (Corner House Research) v Secretary of State for Trade and Industry* [2005] EWCA Civ 192 [2005] 1 WLR 2600 at [74] (court should be "satisfied that: (i) The issues raised are of general public importance. (ii) The public interest requires that those issues should be resolved. (iii) The applicant has no private interest in the outcome of the case. (iv) Having regard to the financial resources of the applicant and the respondent(s) and to the amount of costs that are likely to be involved it is fair and just to make the order. (v) If the order is not made the applicant will probably discontinue the proceedings and will be acting reasonably in so doing"), [76] ("When making any PCO where the applicant is seeking an order for costs in its favour if it wins, the court should prescribe by way of a capping order a total amount of the recoverable costs which will be inclusive, so far as a CFA-funded party is concerned, of any additional liability"); *R (Compton) v Wiltshire Primary Care Trust* [2008] EWCA Civ 749 (CA explaining that (1) general public importance and public interest not meaning national interest; (2) no added criterion of exceptionality; (3) PCO made on paper should only be set aside where compelling reasons shown).

(C) CASES. *King v Telegraph Group Ltd* [2004] EWCA Civ 613 [2005] 1 WLR 2282 (general guidance on CCOs); *Campbell v MGN Ltd (No.2)* [2005] UKHL 61 [2005] 1 WLR 3394 at [33]-[34] (considering *King*); *Henry v British Broadcasting Corporation* [2005] EWHC 2503 (QB) [2006] 1 All ER 154 (need to apply promptly for CCO); *Wilkinson v Kitzinger* [2006] EWHC 835 (Fam) [2006] 2 FCR 537 (£25,000 costs cap ordered); *R (Campaign for Nuclear Disarmament) v Prime Minister* [2002] EWHC 2712 (Admin) (£25,000 CCO); *R (BUAV) v Secretary of State for the Home Department* [2006] EWHC 250 (Admin) (£40,000 CCO); *R (Corner House Research) v Director of the Serious Fraud Office* [2008] EWHC 71 (Admin) (£70,000 CCO); *R (Compton) v Wiltshire Primary Care Trust* [2008] EWCA Civ 749 (2 claims with CCOs involving caps of £25,000 (from defendant) and £20,000 CCO (from claimant) upheld by CA).

(D) PROCEDURAL GUIDANCE. *R (Corner House Research) v Secretary of State for Trade and Industry* [2005] EWCA Civ 192 [2005] 1 WLR 2600 at [78] (PCO should normally be sought on face of claim form; defendant may resist but should not expect to recover costs more than £1,000), [79] (judge should decide on the papers, if refused and unsuccessfully sought at oral hearing, defendant should not expect to recover more than £2,500), [80]-[81] (similar position, and additional potential costs exposure, where participating interested party).

(E) APPLYING *CORNER HOUSE*. *R (Goodson) v Bedfordshire and Luton Coroner* [2004] EWHC 2931 (Admin) [2006] 1 WLR 432 at [28] (no PCO where private interest in securing fresh inquiry into father's death), [31] (*Corner House* guidelines "are not to be regarded as inflexible"); *Wilkinson v Kitzinger* [2006] EWHC 835 (Fam) [2006] 2 FCR 537 (issue not one whose general public importance requiring resolution); *Weir v Secretary of State for Transport* [2005] EWHC 2192 (Ch) (discussing *Corner House* in private law context); *R (England) v Tower Hamlets London Borough Council* [2006] EWCA Civ 1742 at [14] (doubting appropriateness and workability of no private interest criterion), [15] (different considerations where environmental access to justice).

(F) PRIOR CASE-LAW. *R v Lord Chancellor, ex p Child Poverty Action Group* [1999] 1 WLR 347 (pre-CPR guidance); *R (Refugee Legal Centre) v Secretary of State for the Home Department* [2004] EWCA Civ 1239 (indicating a more liberal approach); *Village Residents Association Ltd v An Bord Pleanala* 23rd March 2000 (Irish High Court refusing PCO in an ordinary planning case); <18.4.4(B)> (defendant agreeing to bear own costs).

(G) INTERVENERS AND PRE-EMPTIVE ORDERS. CPR 54PD <64.3> paras 13.3-13.4; CPR 54.17 <64.2>.

(H) DEFENDANTS AND PROTECTIVE COSTS ORDERS. *R (Ministry of Defence) v Wiltshire & Swindon Coroner* [2005] EWHC 889 (Admin) [2006] 1 WLR 134 at [34] ("no reason in principle why a protective costs order should not in an appropriate case extend to protect the position of a defendant", albeit "unusual and no doubt exceedingly rare"), [35] (inapt here where coroner having backing of local authority).

18.4.4 No costs: other protective arrangements.
(A) DEFENDANT'S AGREEMENT TO BEAR COSTS IN ANY EVENT. See *Barnard v Gorman* [1941] AC 378, 388.
(B) DEFENDANT AGREEING TO BEAR ITS OWN COSTS. *Gillick v West Norfolk and Wisbech Area Health Authority* [1986] AC 112, 179B ("Fortunately in this case there is no issue between the parties as to costs. If the department succeeds, it does not ask for costs against Mrs Gillick here or below"); *R (Refugee Legal Centre) v Secretary of State for the Home Department* [2004] EWHC 684 (Admin) [2004] Imm AR 142 at [8] ("The claimant ... requested and in due course received an assurance that the [Secretary of State] would not seek costs if he succeeded in resisting the claim for judicial review") (CA is at [2004] EWCA Civ 1481 [2005] 1 WLR 2219).
(C) COSTS RECOVERY AS A CONDITION OF PERMISSION TO APPEAL. *Chief Constable of the North Wales Police v Evans* [1982] 1 WLR 1155, 1164C ("the Appeal Committee, as a condition of giving [permission] to appeal, directed that the appellant bear the [defendant]'s costs of the appeal in any event"); *R (Corner House Research) v Director of the Serious Fraud Office* [2008] EWHC 714 (Admin) (permission to appeal to HL on basis that claimant would recover costs in any event) (HL is [2008] UKHL 60 [2008] 3 WLR 568).
(D) NO COSTS AS CONDITION OF PERMISSION TO PARTICIPATE. *R v Secretary of State for the Environment, ex p O'Byrne* The Times 12th November 1999 (local authority joined as second defendant, on terms that even if unsuccessful claimant would not have to bear its costs).

18.5 Costs and discontinuance/early disposal.[92] A claimant who chooses to discontinue judicial review can expect to pay the costs, as can a defendant which reverses its decision recognising likely defeat. Where the case has been overtaken by events, the default position is no order as to costs.

18.5.1 Discontinuance: costs against a conceding claimant. See ACO:NFG <64.4> para 16.2; *R v Liverpool City Council, ex p Newman* (1992) [1998] JR 178, 179 (Simon Brown LJ: "I have no doubt that if judicial review proceedings are discontinued there is ... a general rule that that will be at the [claimant]'s cost, in other words the [defendants] will recover their costs, provided ... that such discontinuance can be shown to be consequent upon the [claimant]'s recognition of the likely failure of his challenge").

18.5.2 Costs against a conceding defendant. *R v Secretary of State for the Home Department, ex p Tim Fat Wong* [1995] COD 331 (costs against Secretary of State, having conceded in illegal entrant case); *R v London Borough of Islington, ex p Hooper* [1995] COD 76 (claimant entitled to costs where late concession by defendant necessarily involved clarification and time for consideration); *R v Herefordshire Magistrates, ex p Hereford and Worcestershire County Council* (1996) 72 P & CR 226 (where, following grant of permission for judicial review of refusal to state case, magistrates agree to state a case, inappropriate to order costs against them); *R (Chorion Plc) v Westminster City Council* [2002] EWCA Civ 1126 at [16] (Pill LJ: "There may be cases in which a party discontinues its claim, having achieved by concession a considerable measure of success, and yet that party is not entitled to all its costs. Issues besides the one the concession on which led to discontinuance may have been raised"), [17] ("Not

---

[92] James Hope & David Wilson [1997] JR 64.

191

having heard the case, [the judge] may find it difficult to decide which are the good points of the successful party and which are the points to which the principle should apply ... [Here, the judge] should have but did not consider the merit or absence of merit of the points claimed to be unnecessary to the relief sought"); <18.1.4> (issue-based approach to costs).

18.5.3 **Costs and favourable reconsideration.**[93] *R (DB) v Worcestershire County Council* [2006] EWHC 2613 (Admin) (costs not ordered against defendant where properly changed its mind as a sensible means of dispute resolution); *R v Independent Television Commission, ex p Church of Scientology* [1996] COD 443 (see transcript) (Dyson J: "the mere fact that there has been a favourable reconsideration of a decision on the merits in the course of judicial review proceedings will rarely without more entitle the [claimant] to his costs. If the Court is able, on the material before it, to conclude that the application for judicial review would probably have been successful and that it was for this reason that the [defendant] conceded the [remedy] sought by agreeing to reconsider or even reverse the decision, then on the face of it the [claimant] may well be entitled to his costs. It may be possible to determine that an application for judicial review would or would probably not have been successful, by a cursory glance at the material. Sometimes this will not be possible. The Court will, of course, always be alive to the crucial distinction between an attack on the lawfulness of a decision and a challenge to the merits of the decision. The Court will also, no doubt, bear in mind the public interest in ensuring as far as possible that decision-makers are not discouraged from reconsidering decisions during the course of judicial review proceedings if circumstances arise which justify their reconsideration"); *R v Secretary of State for the Home Department, ex p Richard* 24th October 1995 unrep. (claimant securing 50% of his costs because plain that the proceedings secured the reconsideration, whether or not the earlier decision was unlawful, and that the bulk of the costs had been incurred by him).

18.5.4 **Costs where proceedings have become academic: general principles.**
(A) THE *BOXALL* GUIDANCE.[94] *R (Boxall) v Mayor and Burgesses of Waltham Forest London Borough Council* (2001) 4 CCLR 258 (claimant succeeding in costs even though may well not have succeeded on all contested issues, there being "little doubt" that defendant would have been "found to have acted unlawfully in some respect"), at [22] (Scott Baker J: "Having considered the authorities, the principles I deduced to be applicable are as follows: (i) The court has power to make a costs order when the substantive proceedings have been resolved without a trial but the parties have not agreed about costs. (ii) It will ordinarily be irrelevant that the claimant is legally aided. (iii) The overriding objective is to do justice between the parties without incurring unnecessary court time and consequently additional cost. (iv) At each end of the spectrum there will be cases where it is obvious which side would have won had the substantive issues been fought to a conclusion. In between, the position will, in differing degrees, be less clear. How far the court will be prepared to look into the previously unresolved substantive issues will depend on the circumstances of the particular case, not least the amount of costs at stake and the conduct of the parties. (v) In the absence of a good reason to make any other order the fall back is to make no order as to costs. (vi) The court should take care to ensure that it does not discourage parties from settling judicial review proceedings for example by a local authority making a concession at an early stage").
(B) THE *NEWMAN* GUIDANCE. *R v Liverpool City Council, ex p Newman* (1992) [1998] JR 178, 179 ("If, for instance, [discontinuance] has been brought about because the [defendant], recognising the high likelihood of a challenge against him succeeding, has pre-empted his

---

[93] Jane Mulcahy [1996] JR 208.

[94] Robert Kellar [2002] JR 208.

failure in the proceedings by doing that which the challenge is designed to achieve - even if perhaps no more than agreeing to take a fresh decision - it may well be just that he should not merely fail to recover his own costs but indeed pay the [claimant]'s. On the other hand, it may be that the challenge has become academic merely through the [defendant] sensibly deciding to short-circuit the proceedings, to avoid their expense or inconvenience or uncertainty without in any way accepting the likelihood of their succeeding against him. He should not be deterred from such a cause by the thought that he would then be liable for the [claimant]'s costs. Rather in those circumstances, it would seem to me appropriate that the costs should lie where they fall and there should accordingly be no order. That might equally be the case if some action wholly independent of the parties has rendered the outcome of the challenge academic. It would seldom be the case that on discontinuance this court would think it necessary or appropriate to investigate in depth the substantive merits of what had by then become an academic challenge. That ordinarily would be a gross misuse of this court's time and further burden its already full list"); *R v Secretary of State for the Home Department, ex p Asif Ali Zardari* 11th March 1998 unrep. (similar observations by Lord Bingham CJ).

(C) ILLUSTRATIONS. *R (Salman) v Barking and Dagenham London Borough Council* [2005] EWHC 731 (Admin) [2005] ELR 514 (costs awarded because court regarding impugned decision as unlawful); *R (Bowhay) v North and East Devon Health Authority* [2001] ACD 159 (costs appropriate because case appearing to be in category where defendant had recognised that claimant appeared to have a strong case); *R (Bernard) v Dudley Metropolitan Borough Council* [2003] EWHC 147 (Admin) at [6] (describing *Boxall* as a "guideline judgment"), [14] (obvious that claim would have succeeded, so defendant ordered to pay costs); *Sengoz v Secretary of State for the Home Department* The Times 13th August 2001 (absent a good reason, fallback position is no order as to costs, referring to *Boxall*).

18.5.5 Holding a costs "moot": deciding the legal merits to dispose of costs.
(A) POSSIBLE TO CONTINUE TO A HEARING. *R v Greenwich London Borough Council, ex p Lovelace* [1991] 1 WLR 506, 517G, 524G ("litigation may sometimes be properly continued for the sole purpose of resolving an issue as to costs when all other matters in dispute have been resolved"); *R v Holderness Borough Council, ex p James Robert Developments Ltd* [1993] 1 PLR 108 (academic challenge considered, because question of costs remaining live); *R v Central Criminal Court, ex p Propend Finance Property Ltd* [1996] 2 Cr App R 26 (judicial review arguments resolved, although consent to quashing of impugned decisions, in order to decide costs issues); *R v British Coal Corporation, ex p Ibstock Building Products Ltd* [1995] Env LR 277 (claimant entitled in law to information subsequently provided, so entitled to costs); *R (Bushell) v Newcastle Upon Tyne Licensing Justices* [2006] UKHL 7 [2006] 1 WLR 496 (costs one factor in HL deciding academic appeal), [26]-[27] (doubtful whether could suffice on its own).

(B) STRONG RELUCTANCE TO HOLD A FULL HEARING. *R v Secretary of State for the Home Department, ex p Asif Ali Zardari* 11th March 1998 unrep. ("It would, however, be a deplorable waste of time and money if the court were routinely to conduct a full hearing in order to decide the question of costs"); *R v Liverpool City Council, ex p Newman* (1992) [1998] JR 178, 179 ("It would seldom be the case that on discontinuance this court would think it necessary or appropriate to investigate in depth the substantive merits of what had by then become an academic challenge. That ordinarily would be a gross misuse of this court's time and further burden its already full list"); *R (Tshikangu) v Newham London Borough Council* [2001] EWHC Admin 92 at [29] (recovery of costs not a good reason for pursuing claim rendered academic, the further costs being "disproportionate" to those already incurred); *R v Independent Television Commission, ex p Church of Scientology* [1996] COD 443 (see transcript) (court very slow to embark on exercise, particularly in a case of considerable complexity); *R (A) v East Sussex County Council* [2005] EWHC 585 (Admin) (2005) 8 CCLR 228 at [39] (inappropriate to "delve into the detail", as would be necessary for "any even provisional or tentative view of

where the overall merits lie").
(C) COURT READILY ABLE TO FORM A VIEW. *Freud Lemos Properties Ltd v Secretary of State for the Environment* 23rd March 1994 unrep. (claimant granted costs on discontinuance of statutory review: "in this case the question of costs can without too much difficulty be decided by reference to the merits of the substantive case"); *R v Calderdale Metropolitan Borough Council, ex p Houghton* (2000) 3 CCLR 228 (on looking at the papers briefly, Court able to say that application for judicial review was likely to have succeeded); *R v Cambridge County Council, ex p Leach* [1998] COD 101 (claimants granted their costs where defendant having taken the necessary action, because court satisfied that defendant's discharge of its statutory duty had been culpably slow and susceptible to challenge); *R (H) v Kingston upon Thames Royal London Borough Council* [2002] EWHC 3158 (Admin) (2003) 6 CCLR 240 (awarding claimant's costs, without going into case in detail, Court able to decide that defendant's legal argument unsustainable); *R (DG) v Worcestershire County Council* [2005] EWHC 2332 (Admin) (2006) 9 CCLR 21 (court not able to be satisfied that defendant had clearly acted unlawfully and clearly unlikely that claimant would have won).

18.5.6 **Costs and early disposal: other.**
(A) COSTS AND (INDEPENDENT) ACT RENDERING PROCEEDINGS ACADEMIC. *Newman* <18.5.4(B)>; *R v Legal Aid Board, ex p Clement Garage Ltd* The Times 3rd June 1996 (proceedings stayed with each side bearing their own costs); *R v Secretary of State for the Home Department, ex p Harrison* [2001] ACD 8 (reclassification of claimant prisoner an act rendering case academic).
(B) COSTS AND CLAIMANT'S LATE WITHDRAWAL. *R v Warley Justices, ex p Callis* [1994] COD 240 (third party entitled to costs of preparing to defend judicial review, where claim undermined by post-permission authority but only withdrawn 2 days before hearing of the judicial review date).
(C) THIRD PARTY COSTS AND DISCONTINUANCE. *Estate of M Kingsley (dec'd) v Secretary of State for Transport* [1994] COD 358 (third party to statutory review awarded its costs, following discontinuance by agreement between claimant and defendant); *R v Warley Justices, ex p Callis* [1994] COD 240 (local authority (third party) entitled to costs where judicial review application withdrawn at the last minute).
(D) DISCONTINUANCE AND TRANSFER. *R (Aegis Group Plc) v Inland Revenue Commissioners* [2005] EWHC 1468 (Ch) (claimant ordered to pay costs under CPR 38.6 where judicial review discontinued on transfer of issue to parallel Chancery Division proceedings).

18.6 **Special costs responses.** Particular steps are available to the Court, including in situations warranting disapproval or deterrence.

18.6.1 **Depriving successful party of costs order.** *R v Liverpool City Council, ex p Filla* [1996] COD 24 (claimant non-disclosure at the permission stage); *R v Borough of Milton Keynes, ex p Macklen* 30th April 1996 unrep. (failure to write letter before claim); *R (Arslan) v Secretary of State for the Home Department* [2006] EWHC 1877 (Admin) (Secretary of State successful but having to pay costs of issuing and interim relief, through unreasonable insistence on speedy removal); <18.1.5(A)> (deprivation of costs for non-compliance with Pre-Action Protocol).

18.6.2 **Costs against non-appearing tribunals.** <18.1.12>.

18.6.3 **Costs orders against non-parties.** See Supreme Court Act 1981 s.51(1); CPR 48.2; *Goodwood Recoveries Ltd v Breen* [2005] EWCA Civ 414 [2006] 1 WLR 2723 (considering exercise of this power); *R (Davies) v Secretary of State for the Environment, Food and Rural Affairs* [2002] EWHC 2762 (Admin) (directing that individual be joined as a party so that costs of failed judicial review could be sought against him); *R (Ewing) v Office of the Deputy Prime Minister* [2005] EWCA Civ 1583 [2006] 1 WLR 1260 (costs against pre-permission vexatious litigant, whether or not technically a "party"); *R v Darlington Borough Council, ex p Association of Darlington Taxi Owners (No.2)* [1995] COD 128 (costs ordered against individual members of unincorporated association, although non-parties, they having maintained and financed the failed proceedings); *R v Secretary of State for Foreign and Commonwealth Affairs, ex p British Council of Turkish Cypriot Associations* [1998] COD 336 (inappropriate to consider costs orders against individual members of claimant unincorporated association until clear that society as a whole not going to meet costs order); *R v Lambeth London Borough Council, ex p Wilson* (1998) 30 HLR 64 (no jurisdiction to make wasted costs orders under s.51(6) against individual council officer; jurisdiction under s.51(3) but generally needing fraud); *R v Secretary of State for the Home Department, ex p Eniah Mudzengi* [1993] Imm AR 320 (costs order against claimant's unqualified representative, for failure to notify defendant and Court that application being abandoned).

18.6.4 **Costs on an indemnity basis.**[95] See CPR 44.4; *R (S) v Secretary of State for the Home Department* [2006] EWHC 1111 (Admin) at [116] (inexcusable, deliberate wall of silence); *R v Governing Body of Irlam & Cadishead Community High School, ex p Salford City Council* [1994] ELR 81, 88C-D (indemnity costs against claimant); *R v Ministry of Agriculture Fisheries and Food, ex p SP Anastasiou* [1995] COD 339 (indemnity costs where unnecessary third party application for Art 234 reference); *R (Adriano) v Surrey County Council* [2002] EWHC 2471 (Admin) [2003] Env LR 559 at [89] (indemnity costs from date when "wholly unreasonable" for officers not to have taken the matter back to the committee). *R (Bernard) v Dudley Metropolitan Borough Council* [2003] EWHC 147 (Admin) at [15] (indemnity costs where prosecuting acted unreasonably to a high degree, "uncooperative and heedless of clear authority"); *R (British Telecommunications Plc) v Revenue and Customs Commissioners* [2005] EWHC 1043 (Admin) at [30] (indemnity costs where abortive claim through failure to put case forward on proper basis); *R (Montpeliers & Trevors Association) v City of Westminster* [2005] EWHC 16 (Admin) [2006] LGR 304 (indemnity costs of second day of hearing, caused by need to deal with defendant's default of the rules).

18.6.5 **Wasted costs orders against legal representatives.** See Supreme Court Act 1981 s.51(6) & (7); CPR 48.7; CPR 43-48PD (Practice Direction about Costs) section 53; *Ridehalgh v Horsefield* [1994] Ch 205 (general principles); *Medcalf v Medcalf* [2002] UKHL 27 [2003] 1 AC 120 at [13] (endorsing *Ridehalgh*, subject to *Arthur J Hall v Simons* [2002] 1 AC 615 and further observations (*Medcalf* at [23]) as to legal professional privilege in the context of wasted costs); *R v Horsham District Council, ex p Wenman* [1995] 1 WLR 680 (wasted costs order narrowly escaped; judge warning of possible wasted costs orders against those who are not adequately informed as to judicial review principles); *R v Secretary of State for the Home Department, ex p Abbassi* The Times 6th April 1992 (frivolous application, in the face of an alternative remedy); *R v Secretary of State for the Home Office, ex p Shahina Begum* [1995] COD 176 (wasted costs order made for unreasonable and negligent failure to make full and frank disclosure); *R v London Borough of Westminster, ex p Geehan & Butler* [1995] COD 204 (although no arguable ground for judicial review, not negligent to bring proceedings, given urgency of case and destitution faced by homeless claimant); *R v London Borough of Hackney, ex p Rowe* [1996] COD 155 (over-zealous; but not improper, unreasonable or negligent); *Lubrizol Ltd v Tyndallwoods Solicitors* 8th April 1998 unrep. (application misconceived but not negligent or unreasonable); *R v Secretary of State for the Home Department, ex p Tim Fat Wong* [1995] COD 331 (claimant's solicitor acted unreasonably in neither getting on with the

---

[95] Anna Riley [2004] JR 202.

case or going off the record, but no wasted costs order because the latter would have caused an injustice); *R v Lambeth London Borough Council, ex p Wilson* (1998) 30 HLR 64 (no jurisdiction to make wasted costs orders under Supreme Court Act 1981 s.51(6) against individual officer); *R (F) v Head Teacher of Addington High School* [2003] EWHC 228 (Admin) (wasted costs ordered against claimant's solicitors where grounds not provided to defendant and defendant's letter not drawn to attention of permission judge, and so misleading impression given as to defendant's inaction); *R (Yildrim) v Immigration Appeal Tribunal* [2002] EWHC 1939 (Admin) (wasted costs inappropriate because Court not satisfied as to causation, ie. that CLS funding would have been refused if claimant's solicitors had acted properly); *R (Hide) v Staffordshire County Council* [2007] EWHC 2441 (Admin) (declining wasted costs where impact would be solicitor's bankruptcy); <18.3.6> (wasted costs and the permission stage); JR:UCP <64.6> para 2.

18.6.6 **Reporting to LSC/taxing authorities.** *R v Secretary of State for the Home Department, ex p Stephen Kyasanku* [1994] Imm AR 547, 549 (Macpherson J, warning that "far too many of these applications are brought on the advice of counsel which never should have come before this court at all and the time will come very soon when steps will be taken to deprive those involved of any fees in respect of these applications"); *R v Secretary of State for the Home Office, ex p Shahina Begum* [1995] COD 176 (Court having no power to withdraw legal aid taxation, but direction made that judgment should be drawn to the attention of the taxing authority to consider whether appropriate to disallow costs); *R v Secretary of State for the Home Department, ex p Panther* (1996) 8 Admin LR 154 (following dismissal of hopeless renewed application for permission, papers to be forwarded to Legal Aid Board (now the LSC) and taxing master); *R v Liverpool City Justices, ex p Price* [1998] COD 453 (directing that judgment sent to taxing authorities to decide whether to disallow wasted costs).

18.6.7 **Powers in relation to misconduct.** See CPR 44.14; CPR 43-48PD (Practice Direction about Costs) section 18; *Practice Direction (Criminal Proceedings: Costs)* [2004] 1 WLR 2657 at [VIII.2.1].

> **P19 Making the claim.** Where pre-claim correspondence fails, claims are to be made and acknowledged in the prescribed way.

19.1 Pre-claim steps.[96] Before judicial review is claimed, the parties are generally expected to have engaged in prompt and cooperative correspondence, to avert unnecessary litigation, by explaining themselves and reconsidering their positions. An eye must be kept on the ticking clock, since the requirement of promptness is not suspended, though what is said and done can help explain the consequential delay or justify an extension of time.

19.1.1 **The Pre-Action Protocol (JR:PAP).**[97] See ACO Notes for Guidance (ACO:NFG) <64.4> para 3.2; and JR:PAP <64.5>.

19.1.2 **Letter Before Claim (LBC).** JR:PAP <64.5> paras 8-12 (LBC) and Annex A Section 1 (model LBC), Section 2 (address for sending LBC), Section 3 (required reference details).

19.1.3 **Importance of pre-action correspondence.**[98] *R v Horsham District Council, ex p Wenman* [1995] 1 WLR 680, 709E-F (need to give intended defendant an opportunity to put the matter right); *R (Tshikangu) v Newham London Borough Council* [2001] EWHC Admin 92 at [24] (Stanley Burnton J, referring to *Wenman*: "If anything, this statement should be given even greater weight today, after the introduction of the CPR, than in 1995"); *McGlinn v Waltham Contractors Ltd* [2005] EWHC 1419 (TCC) [2005] 3 All ER 1126 ("purpose of a pre-action protocol procedure is to narrow issues and to allow a prospective defendant, wherever possible, to demonstrate to a prospective claimant that a particular claim is doomed to failure"); <18.1 5(A)> (costs implications); *R (Ewing) v Office of the Deputy Prime Minister* [2005] EWCA Civ 1583 [2006] 1 WLR 1260 at [43], [54] (if JR:PAP followed properly, defendant's summary grounds can be briefer and *Mount Cook* costs lower); *R v Royal Borough of Kensington & Chelsea, ex p Ghebregiogis* (1995) 27 HLR 602 (claimant's pre-permission costs awarded against proposed defendant for unreasonable persistence despite admirably clear letter before claim).

19.1.4 **Pre-action correspondence: relationship with promptness.** ACO:NFG <64.4> para 3.4; JR:PAP <64.5> introduction (JR:PAP steps do not suspend time), para 14 (dealing with timing); CPR 54.5(2) <64.2> (no extension of time by agreement). *R v Borough of Milton Keynes, ex p Macklen* 30th April 1996 unrep. (Brooke J, pre-CPR, stressing importance of writing a LBC: "If adopting such a course turns out to be unsuccessful then there would surely be little danger of the application for judicial review being turned down on the grounds of delay, because the [claimant] had followed the very desirable procedure of seeking to have the dispute resolved by other means"); <26.3.7> (delay and pursuit of alternative remedy).

19.1.5 **Letter Of Response (LOR).** JR:PAP <64.5> paras 13-17 & Annex B (model LOR).

---

[96] Michael Fordham [1996] JR 16 & 76.

[97] Charles Banner [2008] JR 59.

[98] Stephen Cragg [1996] JR 71; Parishil Patel [1999] JR 96.

19.1.6 **Pre-claim notification of third parties.** The JR:PAP <64.5> requires both the LBC and LOR to be copied to interested parties. *R (Candlish) v Hastings Borough Council* [2005] EWHC 1539 (Admin) [2006] Env LR 278 at [25], [27] (claimant's solicitors should copy third party in on pre-claim correspondence); *R v London Docklands Development Corporation, ex p Frost* (1997) 73 P & CR 199, 211 (considering situation "where there has been delay and where third party rights may be at risk"); *R v Cotswold District Council, ex p Barrington* (1998) 75 P & CR 515 (need to inform planning authority and landowner of possibility of judicial review proceedings as soon as first seriously contemplated, certainly as soon as possible after challenge made); *R v Essex County Council, ex p Tarmac Roadstone Holdings Ltd* [1998] 1 PLR 79, 88D-H (remedy not refused even though delay and failure of notification that proceedings being brought; claimant deciding in good faith that writing letter before claim would have prejudiced on-going negotiations); *R v Leeds City Council, ex p N* [1999] ELR 324, 334C (need in education cases to "give early warning as to what is going on").

19.1.7 **ADR/mediation.** <10.2>.

19.1.8 **CLS funding.**[99] ACO:NFG <64.4> paras 4.2-4.4 (legal aid for judicial review); JR:PAP <64.5> Annex C (notes on public funding for judicial review); <2.5.5> (public interest litigation).

19.2 **Making the claim.** Starting a judicial review claim involves filling in the claim form (N461) and drafting the grounds for judicial review. They need to be put in a rule-compliant[100], paginated and indexed bundle which will also include (1) a list of essential reading, (2) any written evidence in support, (3) relevant documents and (4) key legislative material. The claim form and bundle are filed with the ACO, with the appropriate fee. There must then be (certified) service on the defendant(s) and any identified interested (directly-affected) third parties. There is a special procedure for urgent cases.

19.2.1 **Commencing the claim.** ACO:NFG <64.4> para 4.1; *R (Kemp) v Denbighshire Local Health Board* [2006] EWHC 181 (Admin) [2007] 1 WLR 639 at [91] (claim for judicial review "instituted", for purposes of Supreme Court Act 1981 s.35A, when lodged); ACO:NFG <64.4> para 6.1 (court fee payable when lodging claim); *R (Corner House Research) v Director of the Serious Fraud Office* [2008] EWHC 246 (Admin) (public entitled to judicial review grounds from court file under CPR 2.3(1), absent a special embargo request and direction).

19.2.2 **Time for commencing the claim.** Supreme Court Act 1981 s.31(6)-(7) <64.1>; CPR 54.5 <64.2>; ACO:NFG <64.4> paras 5.1-5.2.

19.2.3 **Claim form/bundle: prescribed contents.** See CPR 8.2; CPR 54.6 <64.2>; CPR 54PD <64.3> paras 5.1-5.10; CPR 16PD para 15; CPR 8.5(1), (2) & (7); ACO:NFG <64.4> paras 7.1-7.9; *R (Campaign for Nuclear Disarmament) v Prime Minister* [2002] EWHC 2712 (Admin) at [7] (desirable for claim form to contain notice of any application for a pre-emptive costs order).

19.2.4 **Clear identification of the issues of law.** *R v Vale of Glamorgan Borough Council, ex*

---

[99] Stephen Cragg [1996] JR 5; Charles George QC & Gregory Jones [1999] JR 14; Zoe Taylor [2000] JR 157; David Wolfe, Phil Shiner & Murray Hunt [2001] JR 227; Louise Christian [2002] JR 82.

[100] Cf. Sir Stephen Sedley, `Sedley's Laws of Documents' [1996] JR 37.

p James [1996] Env LR 102, 109 (grounds for judicial review "serves to direct the parties' minds to the issues which are alleged to arise and thereby concentrate their mind on the evidence to deal with those particular issues"); cf. *Somerville v Scottish Ministers* [2007] UKHL 44 [2007] 1 WLR 2734 (regarding Scottish procedure) at [65] ("The factual history should be set out succinctly and the issues of law should be clearly identified"); *R (Hargrave) v Stroud District Council* [2002] EWCA Civ 1281 [2002] 3 PLR 115 at [40] (irrationality ground "needs to be taken early and in detail, and not left to be expanded in this court"); <21.2.1> (amendment of the claim form).

19.2.5 Importance of focus: sifting the good from the bad. *R (Naing) v Immigration Appeal Tribunal* [2003] EWHC 771 (Admin) at [59] (Davis J: "the overloading of a case with hopeless points simply operates potentially to devalue points which otherwise might be made to appear arguable"); cf. *Ashmore v Corporation of Lloyds* [1992] 1 WLR 446, 453H (Lord Templeman: "It is the duty of counsel to assist the judge by simplification and concentration and not to advance a multitude of ingenious arguments in the hope that out of 10 bad points the judge will be capable of fashioning a winner ... [T]here has been a tendency in some cases for legal advisers, pressed by their clients, to make every point conceivable and inconceivable without judgment or discrimination"); *R (P) v Essex County Council* [2004] EWHC 2027 (Admin) at [31] (Munby J, lamenting those welfare cases where: "Too often in my experience inadequate thought is given to what precisely the court is being asked or can properly be asked to do"), [34] ("It is elementary that it is for the claimant to set out what his case is and then to adduce the necessary evidence in support"); <22.4.13> (oral argument).

19.2.6 Service of the claim form. CPR 54.7 <64.2>; CPR 54PD <64.3> para 6.1; ACO:NFG <64.4> paras 7.10-7.12.

19.2.7 Urgent cases procedure (JR:UCP <64.6>).[101] ACO:NFG <64.4> paras 8.1-8.5; JR:UCP <64.6> (published as Annex B to *Practice Statement (Administrative Court: Annual Statement) 2001/2* [2002] 1 All ER 633); *R (Director of Public Prosecutions) v Camberwell Youth Court* [2004] EWHC 1805 (Admin) [2005] 1 WLR 810 (DC explaining that judicial review more appropriate than voluntary bill of indictment in you court jurisdiction cases, provided that claim pursued expeditiously using the Form N463 urgent cases procedure); *R (Shergill) v Harrow Crown Court* [2005] EWHC 648 (Admin) at [2] (any judicial review of crown court refusal of bail should be subject of an oral hearing normally within 48 hours, on notice to the crown court and prosecuting authority); *R (BG) v Medway Council* [2005] EWHC 1932 (Admin) [2006] 1 FLR 663 at [40] (in urgent case, better to abridge time for AOS rather than deny defendant the opportunity to make representations regarding permission).

19.2.8 Claimant's duty of candour. <10.3>.

19.3 Acknowledging the claim Defendants and interested parties served with the claim form have 21 days to file an Acknowledgment of Service (AOS) on the relevant form (Form N462). The AOS is intended (1) to confirm whether permission is resisted (frequently, it ought not to be) and (2) to assist the permission judge (a) with summary grounds which explain why permission should be refused and (b) as to appropriate case-management directions. Key documents can be supplied, and a claim for costs of preparing the AOS included. There is nothing to stop the claimant submitting a prompt and brief reply.

---

[101] Richard Clayton [2001] JR 225; Kate Markus [2004] JR 256.

19.3.1 **Duty/status of acknowledgment.** CPR 54.8 <64.2>; CPR 54.9 (failure to file AOS) <64.2>; ACO:NFG <64.4> paras 9.1-9.3; CPR 54PD <64.3> para 7.1; CPR 8.3 and CPR 10.5; *R (Corner House Research) v Director of the Serious Fraud Office* [2008] EWHC 246 (Admin) (summary grounds a "defence" to which public entitled under CPR 2.3(1) from court file, absent a special embargo request and direction).

19.3.2 **Purpose of the AOS.** *R (Ewing) v Office of the Deputy Prime Minister* [2005] EWCA Civ 1583 [2006] 1 WLR 1260 at [43] ("The purpose of the `summary of grounds' is not to provide the basis for full argument of the substantive merits, but rather ... to assist the judge in deciding whether to grant permission, and if so on what terms"; "it may be appropriate simply to refer to [pre-action] letter"; "helpful to draw attention to any `knock-out points' or procedural bars, or the practical or financial consequences for other parties (which may, for example, be relevant to directions for expedition)"); *R (Davey) v Aylesbury Vale District Council* [2007] EWCA Civ 1166 [2008] 1 WLR 878 at [13] (where permission contested, proper course is generally "to explain its decision and any further grounds of opposition in short form" and wait and see whether permission granted), [32] (assisting judge as to grant of permission and terms), [33] (court should decline to look at anything going further), [33] (costs of AOS should be limited to proper function of the AOS); *R (Mount Cook Land Ltd) v Westminster City Council* [2003] EWCA Civ 1346 [2004] 1 PLR 29 at [71] ("The objects of the obligation on a defendant to file an acknowledgment of service setting out where appropriate his case are: (1) to assist claimants with a speedy and relatively inexpensive determination by the court of the arguability of their claims; and (2) to prompt defendants - public authorities - to give early consideration to and, where appropriate, to fulfil their public duties"); *R (Ministry of Defence) v Wiltshire & Swindon Coroner* [2005] EWHC 889 (Admin) [2006] 1 WLR 134 at [44] ("The purpose of an Acknowledgment of Service, whatever the CPR may say, is to assist the court in deciding whether permission should be granted or not").

19.3.3 **Including permission-stage points.**<26.1.7> (promptness/ good reason as a permission-stage issue); <36.3.7> (alternative remedy as a permission-stage issue).

19.3.4 **Include permission-costs application.** *R (Ewing) v Office of the Deputy Prime Minister* [2005] EWCA Civ 1583 [2006] 1 WLR 1260 at [47] (need to include any *Mount Cook* costs application and schedule with AOS).

19.3.5 **Defendant/interested party's duty of candour.** <10.4>.

19.3.6 **Failure to file AOS.** *R (Matthias Rath BV) v Advertising Standards Authority Ltd* [2001] HRLR 436 (court allowing evidence lodged by defendant to count as acknowledgment); *R (A) v National Asylum Support Service* [2003] EWHC 1402 (Admin) at [13] (Secretary of State permitted to participate despite absence of detailed grounds, or earlier summary grounds, because no prejudice and in the interests of justice to receive informed submissions) (CA is [2003] EWCA Civ 1473 [2004] 1 WLR 752).

19.3.7 **Waiting for the AOS.** *R (Webb) v Bristol City Council* [2001] EWHC Admin 696 (permission should not have been granted while defendant's acknowledgment was awaited and time-limit unexpired; if interim remedy was urgent, it should have been granted pre-permission).

19.3.8 **Urgent cases: abridging time for AOS.** *R (BG) v Medway Council* [2005] EWHC 1932 (Admin) [2006] 1 FLR 663 at [40] (in urgent case, better to abridge time for AOS rather than deny defendant the opportunity to make representations regarding permission).

19.3.9 **Extended-time cases.** *Practice Statement (Late claim for asylum: interim relief)* [2004] 1 All ER 923 (general extension of time to 2 months for Secretary of State's acknowledgment in cases under Nationality Immigration and Asylum Act 2002 s.55, where court has granted interim relief, the purpose of the longer period being to avoid unnecessary costs and facilitate compromise).

19.3.10 **Claimant's reply.**[102] A claimant wishing to lodge a brief and prompt reply, before the papers go to the judge, can do so and should liaise with the ACO.

---

[102] Gregory Jones & Jack Rabinowicz [2005] JR 121.

> **P20 Interim remedies.** The Court can make orders securing a particular state of affairs pending final resolution of the claim.

20.1 **Interim remedies.**[103] Judges have wide and flexible powers to make orders securing a particular position, where justice so requires, pending the final disposal of the judicial review claim.

20.1.1 **Interim remedies: rules and guidance.** See CPR 54.6(1)(c) <64.2>; CPR 25 and CPR 25PD; CPR 54.10(2) (stay of the proceedings under review); JR:PAP <64.5> paras 6-7 and 16(e); ACO:NFG <64.4> para 8.2; JR:UCP <64.6> paras 4-5 and 7.

20.1.2 **Established availability of interim remedies.** *M v Home Office* [1994] 1 AC 377, 421F-G (interim injunctions available in principle); *M v Home Office* [1994] 1 AC 377 (interim injunction against the Crown), 422E-G.

20.1.3 **Issues concerning the claim/action.** *R v Licensing Authority Established By The Medicines Act 1968, ex p Rhone Poulenc Rorer Ltd* [1998] EuLR 127, 142C-F (no need for a "cause of action", being "a private law concept"); *In re S (Hospital Patient: Court's Jurisdiction)* [1996] Fam 1, 10G-H (interim injunction in claim for a declaration); <22.2.8(C)> (interim remedy sought against third party).

20.1.4 **Pre-permission interim remedies.** CPR 25.2; *M v Home Office* [1994] 1 AC 377, 422A-B (interim remedy available in urgent cases pending consideration of permission); *R v Commissioners of Inland Revenue, ex p Kingston Smith* [1996] STC 1210, 1214d (interim remedy granted "in support of what was an intended application for judicial review"); *Ex p Amnesty International* The Times 11th December 1998 (assuming that Court having jurisdiction to grant a stay pending the application for permission to move for judicial review); *R (Webb) v Bristol City Council* [2001] EWHC Admin 696 (permission should not have been granted while defendant's acknowledgment was awaited and time-limit unexpired; if interim remedy was urgent, it should have been granted pre-permission).

20.1.5 **Stay of challenged proceedings.** CPR 54.10(2) <64.2> ("Directions under paragraph (1) may include a stay of proceedings to which the claim relates"); *R (H) v Ashworth Hospital Authority* [2002] EWCA Civ 923 [2003] 1 WLR 127 at [42] ("stay of proceedings" given "a wide interpretation so as to apply to administrative decisions" and "enhance the effectiveness of the judicial review jurisdiction"; "The purpose of a stay in a judicial review is clear. It is to suspend the `proceedings' that are under challenge pending the determination of the challenge. It preserves the status quo. This will aid the judicial review process and make it more effective. It will ensure, so far as possible, that, if a party is ultimately successful in his challenge, he will not be denied the full benefit of his success"), [46] (jurisdiction to grant a stay even where decision fully implemented); *R v Licensing Authority Established By The Medicines Act 1968, ex p Rhone Poulenc Rorer Ltd* [1998] EuLR 127; *R v Falmouth and Truro Port Health Authority, ex p South West Water Ltd* [2001] QB 445, 472B-473E (suggesting that stay should be rare in a case involving public safety where there is a statutory remedy); *R v HM Treasury, ex p British Telecommunications Plc* [1994] 1 CMLR 621 ("we have difficulty in understanding

---

[103] This paragraph in a previous edition was cited in *R v Public Service Commission, ex p Tokaibai* [2005] FJHC 107.

how a stay, if granted, could take effect in relation to enacted law which has come into force and calls for no further action by the party against whom the stay is granted"); *M v Home Office* [1994] 1 AC 377, 422G ("a stay could be granted against the Crown"); *R v Secretary of State for Education and Science, ex p Avon County Council* [1991] 1 QB 558, 561G-562C (preferring stay to injunction: "An order that a decision of a person or body whose decisions are open to challenge by judicial review shall not take effect until the challenge has finally been determined is, in my view, correctly described as a stay"); <20.2.3> (cross-undertaking).

20.1.6 **Interim declarations.**[104] CPR 25.1 (power to grant interim declaration); *Access to Justice* (1996) at p.253; *Amalgamated Metal Trading Ltd v City of London Police Financial Investigation Unit* [2003] EWHC 703 (Comm) [2003] 1 WLR 2711 at [10] (Tomlinson J: "It remains to be worked out what are the circumstances in which it might be appropriate to resort to this new jurisdiction"); *R v R (Interim Declaration)* [2000] 1 FLR 451, 453B ("Until recently there was no power even to consider an interim declaration"; "However, the lacuna in the law has been remedied by Part 25"); *Governor and Company of the Bank of Scotland v A Ltd* [2001] EWCA Civ 52 [2001] 1 WLR 751 at [45] ("It was at one time thought, that an interim declaration could have no practical purpose. The developments in other jurisdictions showed this was not the situation. Now the Civil Procedure Rules acknowledge that just as interim injunctions can be granted so can interim declarations"); *R v Secretary of State for Trade and Industry, ex p Trades Union Congress* [2000] EuLR 698 (DC) and The Times 17th October 2000 (CA) (both Courts considering, on its merits, application for interim declaration pending Article 234 reference to ECJ); *R v Environment Agency, ex p Mayer Parry Recycling Ltd* [2001] Env LR 630 (interim declaration addressed by reference to balance of convenience, especially because would amount in substance to interim injunction); *R (Ashworth Hospital Authority) v Mental Health Review Tribunal for West Midlands and North West Region* [2001] EWHC Admin 901 (2002) 5 CCLR 36 (Administrative Court) at [98] (interim declaration inappropriate to curtail liberty or force medical treatment); cf. *NHS Trust v T (Adult Patient: Refusal of Medical Treatment)* [2004] EWHC 1279 (Fam) [2005] 1 All ER 387 (in a best interests case, interim declaration appropriate to enable future emergency blood transfusions if refused by self-harming adult with mental incapacity).

20.1.7 **Bail.**[105] *R v Secretary of State for the Home Department, ex p Turkoglu* [1988] 1 QB 398, 399H, 401G (inherent jurisdiction to grant bail in judicial review); *R v Secretary of State for the Home Department, ex p Sezek* [2001] EWCA Civ 795 [2002] 1 WLR 348 at [16] (power of Admin Court and CA to grant bail in judicial review); *Re Vilvarajah* The Times 31st October 1987 (as to bail in an immigration context); *R v Secretary of State for the Home Department, ex p Swati* [1986] 1 WLR 477, 485H-486A; *R v Thanet Justices, ex p Dass* [1996] COD 77 (understandable pursuit of judicial review rather than case stated, to secure bail); <24.4.12> (bail granted alongside final remedy).

20.1.8 **Judicial review interim remedies should be on notice.** See the JR:UCP <64.6>; *R v Metropolitan Police Force Disciplinary Tribunal, ex p Lawrence* The Times 13th July 1999 (see transcript) (where stay being sought, "essential" that defendants "notified of the proposed application so that they are given the opportunity if they wish to be heard") *R v Kensington & Chelsea Royal London Borough Council, ex p Hammell* [1989] QB 518, 539B-C ("the applicant would be well advised to give notice to the other party"); *R v London Boroughs Transport Committee, ex p Freight Transport Association* [1989] COD 572, 573 (highly desirable that

[104] Stephen Houseman [1996] JR 34; Adam Solomon [2001] JR 10.

[105] Ben Rayment [1998] JR 129.

interim remedies dealt with at oral permission hearing, with notice to defendant);.

20.1.9 Interim remedies in action.
(A) HOUSING/WELFARE CASES. *R (Casey) v Restormel Borough Council* [2007] EWHC 2554 (Admin) (mandatory injunction to require temporary accommodation); *R (W) v Sheffield City Council* [2005] EWHC 720 (Admin) (interim order requiring housing, pending county court resolution, appropriate where claimant genuinely vulnerable and conclusions appearing unreasonable); *R v Cardiff City Council, ex p Barry* (1989) 22 HLR 261, 263 (interim injunction to secure temporary accommodation usually following grant of permission, where necessary); *R v Kensington & Chelsea Royal London Borough Council, ex p Hammell* [1989] QB 518; *R v Camden London Borough Council, ex p Mohammed* (1997) 9 Admin LR 639, 643E-H; *R (AA) v Lambeth London Borough Council* [2001] EWHC Admin 741 (2002) 5 CCLR 36 (interim injunction to require reinstatement of welfare support for asylum-seeker); *Practice Statement (Late claim for asylum: interim relief)* [2004] 1 All ER 923 (describing practice in interim relief cases involving Nationality Immigration and Asylum Act 2002 s.55, where Secretary of State's decision rejecting asylum support on basis that asylum not claimed promptly).
(B) IMMIGRATION REMOVAL CASES. *R (Madan) v Secretary of State for the Home Department* [2007] EWCA Civ 770 [2007] 1 WLR 2891 at [17] (setting out principles for interim injunctions in immigration removal cases); *R v Secretary of State for the Home Department, ex p Muboyayi* [1992] QB 244, 257H-258A (Lord Donaldson MR: "The court should not permit a would-be immigrant to be compulsorily removed from its jurisdiction if he has sought the protection and assistance of the court and the result would be to render any subsequent order quashing a decision to refuse leave to enter less effective"); *R (Pharis) v Secretary of State for the Home Department* [2004] EWCA Civ 654 [2004] 1 WLR 2590 at [15] (describing prior practice of treating permission for judicial review as triggering suspension of removal); *R (Anton) v Secretary of State for the Home Department* [2004] EWHC 2730/2731 (Admin/Fam) [2005] 2 FLR 818 (interim injunction to prevent immigration removal); *YD (Turkey) v Secretary of State for the Home Department* [2006] EWCA Civ 52 [2006] 1 WLR 1646 (CA's inherent power to grant stay of removal directions); <23.1.8> (stay of immigration removal pending appeal to the CA).
(C) SUSPENDING ENACTED LAW. *R v Secretary of State for Transport, ex p Factortame Ltd (No.2)* [1991] 1 AC 603, 678G; applying *Hoffmann-La Roche (F) & Co AG v Secretary of State for Trade and Industry* [1975] AC 295 per Lord Reid at 341F-G (where resisting the upholding of enacted law, whether as defendant or claimant, need "to show special reason why justice requires" this); cf. *William Sinclair Holdings Ltd v English Nature* [2001] EWHC Admin 408 [2002] Env LR 132 (interim injunction granted to prevent designation of protected site, on basis that firmly-based claim for declaration of incompatibility of primary legislation).
(D) RESTRAINING PUBLICATION. *R (Debt Free Direct Ltd) v Advertising Standards Authority Ltd* [2007] EWHC 1337 (Admin) (need compelling case to restrain publication of adjudication); *R v Advertising Standards Authority Ltd, ex p Vernons Organisation Ltd* [1992] 1 WLR 1289 (need especially pressing grounds to restraining publication of decision); *R v Advertising Standards Authority Ltd, ex p Direct Line Financial Services Ltd* [1998] COD 20 (doubting *Vernons* and applying a balance of convenience approach); *R (Matthias Rath BV) v Advertising Standards Authority Ltd* [2001] HRLR 436 at [30] (preferring *Vernons* to *Direct Line*); *Douglas v Hello! Ltd* [2001] QB 967 at [151] (referring to *Vernons*); *R v National Health Service Executive, ex p Ingoldby* [1999] COD 167 (granting interim remedy to prevent publication of a report); *R (Ealing London Borough Council) v Audit Commission* [2002] EWHC 2852 (Admin) (refusing interim injunction to restrain announcement of local government league table, since essentially sought to protect reputation of local authority and restraint would unduly interfere with free speech); <9.4.7> (HRA remedies).
(E) RESTRAINING COMMERCIAL ACTIVITY. *R v Ministry of Agriculture Fisheries and*

Food, ex p Monsanto Plc [1999] QB 1161, 1172F ("judicial review proceedings give rise. Such proceedings are ... neither intended for nor well suited to inhibiting commercial activity, particularly over an indefinite, substantial period of time").

(F) OTHER. *R (Martin) v Harrow Crown Court* [2007] EWHC 3193 (Admin) at [9] (suspension of driving disqualification pending judicial review); *R (OSS Group Ltd) v Environment Agency* [2006] EWHC 2390 (Admin) (order to prevent prosecution based on impugned waste-classification, pending judicial review); *R (H) v Ashworth Hospital Authority* [2002] EWCA Civ 923 [2003] 1 WLR 127 at [44] and [47] (need for "strong" case to grant interim remedy in challenge to MHRT discharge, resulting in claimant's detention); *R (G) v Barnet London Borough Council* [2005] EWHC 1946 (Admin) [2006] ELR 4 (interim remedy available, albeit sparingly, in special educational needs case where arguable error of law, pending tribunal appeal); *R v Newham London Borough Council, ex p X* [1995] ELR 303, 306E-307B (exceptional case where appropriate to grant interim remedy to ensure child back at the same school, given that strong prima facie case of unfairness or disproportionate penalty); *R v Servite Houses and Wandsworth London Borough Council, ex p Goldsmith* (2000) 3 CCLR 354 (mandatory interim order granted by CA, requiring that residential home be kept open pending appeal); *R v Humberside Family Health Services Authority, ex p Dr Moore* [1995] COD 343 (restraining action without prior consultation); *Pett v Greyhound Racing Association Ltd (No.1)* [1969] 1 QB 125 (restraining disciplinary proceedings without legal representation); *Highland Regional Council v British Railways Board* 1996 SLT 274 (restraining withdrawal of train service without following statutory procedure); *R v Westminster City Council, ex p Augustin* [1993] 1 WLR 730, 734A-C, F-H (interim remedy pending appeal to CA refused; need strong prima facie case); *Atlanta Fruchthandelsgesellschaft v Bundesamt für Ernährung und Forstwirtschaft* [1996] All ER (EC) 31 (as to interim remedy pending ECJ ruling on validity of EC regulation); *Napier v Scottish Ministers* [2002] UKHRR 308 (mandatory order to compel transfer of prisoner to facilities with integral toilet rather than `slopping out'); *R (S) v Norfolk County Council* [2004] EWHC 404 (Admin) [2004] ELR 259 (interim injunction granted requiring continued funding for college placement in special educational needs case).

20.1.10 Dealing with Interim remedy problems by expedition. A good example is *R (British Aggregates Associates) v Her Majesty's Treasury* [2002] EWHC 926 (Admin) [2002] EuLR 394 at [14] (difficulties regarding interim injunction met by urgent substantive hearing).

20.1.11 Interim remedy by consent/undertaking in lieu. *AB (Jamaica) v Secretary of State for the Home Department* [2007] EWCA Civ 1302 [2008] 1 WLR 1893 at [37] ("ministers of the Crown can and do give undertakings to the court in appropriate cases ... it is consonant with the dignity of the Crown that, where an interim measure of this kind is appropriate, its ministers should undertake rather than be ordered"); *Practice Direction (Administrative Court: Uncontested Proceedings)* [2008] 1 WLR 1377 at [2] (where interim order agreed, proposed order and statement of matters relied on to be lodged with supporting authorities, to be dealt with by Master/Deputy Master of Crown Office); *R v Liverpool City Council, ex p May* [1994] COD 144 (undertaking to pay housing benefit until further order); *R v Ministry of Agriculture Fisheries & Food, ex p Cox* (1994) 6 Admin LR 421, 425A (undertaking in lieu of a stay); *Beggs v Scottish Ministers* [2007] UKHL 3 [2007] 1 WLR 455 at [18] (contempt for breach of undertaking given to judicial review court in lieu of interim remedy); *R v Monopolies & Mergers Commission, ex p Elders IXL Ltd* [1987] 1 WLR 1221, 1231D (MCC agreeing not to disclose the information until after determination of the proceedings).

20.1.12 Interim remedies in EC law challenges. *R v HM Treasury, ex p British Telecommunications Plc* [1994] 1 CMLR 621 ("Where an interim injunction is sought which will have the effect of disapplying national legislation pending a reference to the Court of Justice", relevant to have regard to "the general undesirability of disturbing enacted law"); *R v*

Secretary of State for Health, ex p Imperial Tobacco Ltd [2002] QB 161 (CA) (whether interim remedy to prevent implementing legislation pending challenge to legality of EC Directive); and see [2001] 1 WLR 127 (HL, commenting on CA approach); *R v Licensing Authority Established By The Medicines Act 1968, ex p Rhone Poulenc Rorer Ltd* [1998] EuLR 127, 134F-G (generally wrong for Court considering interim remedy to go behind conclusion underpinning Art 234 reference, that serious question to be tried); *R v Ministry of Agriculture Fisheries and Food, ex p Monsanto Plc* [1999] QB 1161, 1173H (refusing interim remedy pending Art 234 reference, taking into account the length of time involved and absence of Court control over it).

20.1.13 Position where no interim remedy.
(A) DANGERS OF DECIDING TO PRESS AHEAD. *R v Secretary of State for Education and Science, ex p Hardy* (1989) 153 LG Rev 592 (McNeill J: "So far as good administration is concerned, the LEA has only itself to blame if it went ahead with its proposals in the teeth of an application for judicial review... [W]e can hardly regard it as conducive to anything but the prospect of administrative chaos to press on with substantial educational changes in the teeth of a challenge to the validity of the authority under which it is acting"); *R (the Transport and General Workers Union) v Walsall Metropolitan Borough Council* [2001] EWHC Admin 452 [2002] ELR 329 at [45] (remedy granted, declaring contract unlawful, in situation where local authority and contractor "went into it with their eyes open").
(B) SIGNIFICANCE OF FAILURE TO SEEK INTERIM REMEDY. *Mass Energy Ltd v Birmingham City Council* [1994] Env LR 298, 318 (relying on fact that claimants had "conspicuously failed to apply for [an] interim [remedy]"); *R v Legal Aid Board, ex p Donn & Co (a Firm)* [1996] 3 All ER 1, 15j-17b (granting judicial review notwithstanding argument that contract in operation for 6 months and claimants having chosen not to seek a stay when obtaining permission); also *Hardy* and *TGWU* <20.1.13>; *R (Gavin) v Haringey London Borough Council* [2003] EWHC 2591 (Admin) [2004] 1 PLR 61 at [60] (referring to the absence of an interim injunction, in deciding that post-proceedings expense relevant to hardship/prejudice and refusal of remedy for delay); *R v Birmingham City Council, ex p Dredger* (1994) 6 Admin LR 553, 577E ("That [the claimants] did not apply for a stay is hardly a ground for refusing [a remedy] now").

20.1.14 Action in the light of interim remedy.
(A) APPLICATION TO DISCHARGE INTERIM REMEDY. *R v Secretary of State for Health, ex p Scotia Pharmaceuticals International Ltd (No.2)* [1997] EuLR 650 (application to remove stay); *R v Wealden District Council, ex p Pinnegar* [1996] COD 64 (application to remove interim prohibiting order).
(B) APPEAL AGAINST GRANT OR REFUSAL OF INTERIM REMEDY. *R v Secretary of State for Health, ex p Imperial Tobacco Ltd* [2002] QB 161 (CA) (appeal against grant of interim remedies); *R v Secretary of State for the National Heritage, ex p Continental Television BVio* [1994] COD 121 (appeal against refusal of interim remedies).
(C) INTERIM ORDER NOT PRECLUDING RECONSIDERATION. *Jones v Welsh Rugby Union* The Times 6th January 1997 (effect of an interim order in a case of procedural unfairness; interim injunction not preventing fresh decision by adoption of fair procedure).

20.2 The balance of convenience.[106] The basic approach to interim remedies, borrowed from private law, is (1) to require a prima facie (arguable) case for granting judicial review and then (2) to identify and avoid the greater risk of an injustice (from an interim loser becoming

---

[106] This paragraph in a previous edition was cited in *Garvin v National Housing Authority* [2003] TTHC 36.

an ultimate winner). The Court looks at the case in the round, taking into account matters such as: the strength of the challenge; whether some monetary order is available providing an adequate ultimate remedy for one side or the other (which will be rare in public law); the status quo; and the wider public interest.

20.2.1 **The balance of convenience.** *American Cyanamid Co v Ethicon Ltd* [1975] AC 396; *R v Ministry of Agriculture Fisheries and Food, ex p Monsanto Plc* [1999] QB 1161, 1166D & 1172F (*American Cyanamid* principles applicable in public law proceedings); *R v Secretary of State for Transport, ex p Factortame Ltd (No.2)* [1991] 1 AC 603, 672D (Lord Goff, describing "the balance of convenience" approach); *R v Secretary of State for Transport, ex p Factortame Ltd* [1990] 2 AC 85, 139G (the "exercise of holding the ring"); *R v HM Treasury, ex p British Telecommunications Plc* [1994] 1 CMLR 621 (not applied "in a mechanistic way"); *R v Secretary of State for Health, ex p Scotia Pharmaceuticals International Ltd (No.1)* [1997] EuLR 625 (strong prima facie case; no practical remedy in damages; policy considerations; interests of the wider public; and claimant's reasonable and prompt action); *Ex p Scott* [1998] 1 WLR 226, 228B (Tucker J: "not ... so strong a prima facie case as to justify the granting of [an] interim [remedy]"); *Francis v Royal Borough of Kensington and Chelsea* [2003] EWCA Civ 443 [2003] 2 All ER 1052 at [16] (need "strong" prima facie case for interim mandatory injunction to enforce a statutory duty), [18] (even stronger test appropriate where interim mandatory injunction to enforce an exercise of a statutory power); *Films Rover International Ltd v Canon Film Studios Ltd* [1987] 1 WLR 670, 680 ("A fundamental principle is ... that the court should take whichever course appears to carry the lower risk of injustice if it should turn out to have been `wrong' in the sense I have described"), referred to in *R v Licensing Authority Established By The Medicines Act 1968, ex p Rhone Poulenc Rorer Ltd* [1998] EuLR 127, 145A (Laws J calling the *Films Rover* test as "the test of lesser injustice"); *R v Secretary of State for Transport, ex p Factortame Ltd (No.2)* [1991] 1 AC 603, 659F ("the course which, in all the circumstances, appears to offer the best prospect that eventual injustice will be avoided or minimised"); *R v Secretary of State for Transport, ex p Factortame Ltd* [1990] 2 AC 85, 139G ("a pragmatic decision as to who is likely to suffer the greater injustice").

20.2.2 **Special considerations.**
(A) RELEVANCE OF THE PUBLIC INTEREST. *Smith v Inner London Education Authority* [1978] 1 All ER 411, 422h (Browne LJ: where a public authority is involved, "one must look at the balance of convenience more widely, and take into account the interests of the public in general to whom these duties are owed"), cited in *R v Secretary of State for Transport, ex p Factortame Ltd (No.2)* [1991] 1 AC 603, 673C; *R v Ministry of Agriculture Fisheries and Food, ex p Monsanto Plc* [1999] QB 1161, 1173E (referring to public interest that decision of public body should be respected until set aside, although a matter having rather less weight in the present circumstances); *R v Durham County Council, ex p Huddleston* [2000] Env LR D21 (interim injunction granted to prevent irreversible damage to the environment, because of wider environmental interests going beyond claimant's interests in preventing noise etc); *Sierbein v Westminster City Council* (1987) 86 LGR 431 (importance of public interest where seeking to restrain enforcement of the criminal law).
(B) SITUATION WHERE PRACTICAL EFFECT IS FINAL. *NWL Ltd v Woods* [1979] 1 WLR 1294, 1307 (more stringent threshold required where effect of interim remedy application will be final); *Douglas v Hello! Ltd* [2001] QB 967 at [51].
(C) RESOLVING QUESTIONS OF LAW. *R v Secretary of State for Transport, ex p Factortame Ltd (No.2)* [1991] 1 AC 603, 677G ("If the only question at issue between the parties is one of law it may be possible in many cases to decide this at the stage of a contested application for an interim injunction"); *R v Secretary of State for Transport, ex p Factortame Ltd* [1990] 2 AC 85, 140E-F (situations where the Court "confronted with the issue at any level would decide it and no question of interim [remedy] could possibly arise").

(D) SPECIAL DIFFICULTIES AS TO ADEQUACY OF DAMAGES. *R v Secretary of State for Transport, ex p Factortame Ltd (No.2)* [1991] 1 AC 603, 672G-673B (Lord Goff, referring to problems in seeking to resolve public law cases at the "adequacy of damages" stage, because claimant has "no general right to indemnity by reason of damage suffered through invalid administrative action" and defendant defendant "cannot normally be protected by a remedy in damages because it will itself have suffered none"); *R v Secretary of State for Health, ex p Scotia Pharmaceuticals International Ltd (No.2)* [1997] EuLR 650, 652F (a *Francovich* claim <8.5.2> "would not be easy"); *Primecrown Ltd v Medicines Control Agency* [1997] EuLR 657, 661D (Latham J: "the principles set out in [*Francovich*] have not yet been sufficiently worked out to be able to say other than that there is an arguable claim").

20.2.3 **Claimant's cross-undertaking in damages.**[107] CPR 25PD; *R v Secretary of State for Health, ex p Scotia Pharmaceuticals International Ltd (No.1)* [1997] EuLR 625, 642D (no problem as to adequacy of damages from defendant's point of view, since claimant required to give cross-undertaking in damages and having ability to pay); *R v Secretary of State for the Environment, ex p Royal Society for the Protection of Birds* (1995) 7 Admin LR 434, 443B-C (RSPB "not prepared to give any cross undertaking in damages"); *R v Darlington Borough Council, ex p Association of Darlington Taxi Owners* [1994] COD 424 (legal capacity of claimant important because of requirement of cross-undertaking in damages); *St George's Healthcare NHS Trust v S* [1999] Fam 26, 61A (referring to the cross-undertaking "which is required as a matter of course"); *R v Durham County Council, ex p Huddleston* [2000] Env LR D21 (interim injunction granted, where wider questions of public interest, despite claimant's inability to give a cross-undertaking); *R v Servite Houses and Wandsworth London Borough Council, ex p Goldsmith* (2000) 3 CCLR 354, at [37]-[38] (no cross-undertaking required from elderly women challenging decision to close residential home; court granting interim mandatory injunction); *R v London Borough of Lambeth, ex p Sibyll Walter* 2nd February 1989 unrep. (whether interim remedy absent cross-undertaking); *R v Inspectorate of Pollution, ex p Greenpeace Ltd* [1994] 1 WLR 570, 574H (cross-undertaking "essentially a matter for the discretion of the judge"); *The Bellize Alliance of Conservation Non-Governmental Organisations v Department of the Environment* [2003] UKPC 63 [2003] 1 WLR 2839 (claim not appearing sufficiently strong to hold up major dam project with no cross-undertaking in damages) at [39] (wide discretion as to whether to grant interim relief despite cross-undertaking), [40] (important to form some view on strength of claim); *R v Secretary of State for the Environment, ex p Rose Theatre Trust Company* [1990] COD 47 (jurisdiction to grant interlocutory injunction without a cross-undertaking, but court extremely slow to do so); cf. *Coventry City Council v Finnie* (1997) 29 HLR 658, 661 ("circumstances in which the court would grant an injunction without a cross-undertaking as to damages" not "closed. It is, after all, a rule of practice rather than [a] rule of law"); *R v Inspectorate of Pollution, ex p Greenpeace Ltd* [1994] 1 WLR 570, 577C (cross-undertaking an "entirely permissible condition" of the grant of interim relief where stay affecting third party); *R v Medicines Control Agency, ex p Smith and Nephew Pharmaceuticals Ltd* 26th March 1999 unrep. (scope of the cross-undertaking representing reasonable royalty for lost sales rather than full trading losses); *SmithKline Beecham Plc v Apotex Europe Ltd* [2005] EWHC 1655 (Ch) [2006] 1 WLR 872 (whether cross-undertaking extending to cover third parties).

---

[107] Michael Fordham [1997] JR 136.

> **P21 Permission.** The claimant must obtain permission for judicial review, by prompt and candid papers disclosing an arguable case.

21.1 Granting or refusing permission
21.2 Case-management at the permission stage

21.1 Granting or refusing permission.[108] The permission stage filters out unsustainable claims and allows early case-management. Permission is considered on paper or at an oral hearing and is appropriate if there is a properly arguable case and no discretionary bar.

21.1.1 Permission.[109] ACO:NFG <64.4> paras 9.4-9.7; Supreme Court Act 1981 s.31(3) <64.1>; CPR 54.4 <64.2>; cf. *Seal v Chief Constable South Wales Police* [2007] UKHL 31 [2007] 1 WLR 1910 (absent statutory requirement of permission of the High Court under Mental Health Act 1983 s.139(2), proceedings a nullity).

21.1.2 Nature and purpose of permission.
(A) AN IMPORTANT FILTER.[110] *R v Secretary of State for Trade and Industry, ex p Eastaway* [2000] 1 WLR 2222, 2227H (Lord Bingham: "The requirement of permission to apply for judicial review is imposed primarily to protect public bodies against weak and vexatious claims"); *S v Knowsley Borough Council* [2004] EWHC 491 (Fam) [2004] 2 FLR 716 at [72] ("a safeguard" which "protects [public authorities] against having to spend time in dealing with points that are not arguable. It is well known that the resources of local authorities are stretched, and ... the judicial review procedure provides an appropriate sieve in the public interest"); *R (Davey) v Aylesbury Vale District Council* [2007] EWCA Civ 1166 [2008] 1 WLR 878 at [11]-[12] (permission as expeditious perusal, not a full exploration of evidence or argument); *R v Secretary of State for the Home Department, ex p Cheblak* [1991] 1 WLR 890, 901C-D ("a filter to exclude cases which are unarguable").
(B) JUDGE MUST BE SATISFIED THAT THERE IS AN ISSUE. *R v Social Security Commissioner, ex p Pattni* (1993) 5 Admin LR 219, 223G (claimant must satisfy judge at permission stage that there is a basis for seeking judicial review; judge not entitled to grant permission without such an issue being identified).
(C) COMPLEXITY/VOLUME OF MATERIAL. *R v Local Government Commission for England, ex p North Yorkshire County Council* 11th March 1994 unrep. (Laws J: judge's task is "essentially the same whether the papers are few or voluminous, whether the putative issues are simple or complex: there should be no greater tendency to grant [permission] in the latter class of case than the former"); *R v London Docklands Development Corporation, ex p Frost* (1997) 73 P & CR 199, 204 ("it is not to be assumed that there is an arguable point simply because a number, even a large number, of different points are raised and expanded upon at length in skeleton arguments and in oral argument. The approach of `never mind the quality, feel the width' has no application in these proceedings").
(D) PERMISSION AS "PROCEEDINGS". *R v Commissioners of Inland Revenue, ex p Mead and Cook* [1993] COD 324 (application for permission "proceedings" under Supreme Court Act 1981 s.51); *R v Westminster City Council, ex p Castelli* (1995) 7 Admin LR 840 (application for permission constituting "proceedings" under Contempt of Court Act 1981); *R v Secretary*

---

[108] This paragraph in a previous edition was cited in *Sharma v Antoine* [2006] UKPC 57 at [14(4)]; also *Omagh District Council v Minister for Health* [2004] NICA 10 at [5].

[109] Michael Fordham, `Permission Principles' [2006] JR 176.

[110] Jane Mulcahy, `Grounds for Refusing Leave' [1998] JR 126.

of State for the Home Department, ex p Chetta [1996] COD 463 (judicial review proceedings instituted, for the purposes of the Extradition Act 1989 s.16(1), when notice of an application for permission lodged with Administrative Court Office); *Ex p Ewing (No.2)* [1994] 1 WLR 1553 (considering nature of renewed permission application, in context of vexatious litigant); *R v Camden London Borough Council, ex p Martin* [1997] 1 WLR 359 (discussing nature of permission jurisdiction).

(E) ACO LAWYER'S NOTES.[111] When papers are lodged, the practice is for a lawyer in the Administrative Court Office to prepare a note for the judge. These notes were described in *R v Lord Chancellor's Department, ex p O'Toole* [1998] COD 269, where it was held that there was no right of disclosure, and any new practice of greater transparency would need a Practice Direction (as with notes in the Court of Appeal Criminal Division: [1992] 1 WLR 938). In *O'Toole* it was emphasised that the judge would disclose any adverse matter which might affect his decision and which was unknown to the claimant. The position was reinforced in *Parker v Law Society* [1999] COD 183 (where the Court of Appeal held that its bench memoranda in civil cases did not require disclosure, but that any unknown adverse point would be raised).

(F) WHETHER PERMISSION PUTTING ONUS ON DEFENDANT. <42.2.3>.

21.1.3 Letters to be placed before the judge. *Aaron v Law Society* [2003] EWHC 2271 (Admin) at [75] (as to "communications relevant to their consideration by the Judge, an applicant must, and is entitled to, depend upon their transmission by court staff to the Judge", since the "documents, by their very nature, should have alerted any reasonably experienced and diligent court officer responsible for the file of the need for their inclusion in the papers placed before the Judge").

21.1.4 Court service of permission order. See CPR 54.11 <64.2>; CPR 54PD <64.3> para 9.1.

21.1.5 Consideration on the papers. See CPR 54.12 <64.2>; CPR 54PD <64.3> para 8.4; *Practice Statement (Administrative Court: Annual Statement) 2001/2* [2002] 1 All ER 633, 633g (welcoming better informed and "more structured allocation of paper applications").

21.1.6 Oral hearing. CPR 54.12 <64.2>; ACO:NFG <64.4> paras 10.1-10.5; CPR 54PD <64.3> paras 8.5-8.6; *Practice Statement (Administrative Court: Annual Statement) 2001/2* [2002] 1 All ER 633, 636d ("when completing the form used for renewing applications for permission to apply for judicial review, claimants must set out the grounds for renewal in the light of the reasons given by the single judge when refusing permission on the papers"); *R (Mount Cook Land Ltd) v Westminster City Council* [2003] EWCA Civ 1346 [2004] 1 PLR 29 at [71] (Auld LJ: "if a defendant or other interested party chooses to attend and contest the grant of permission at a renewal hearing, the hearing should be short and not a rehearsal for, or effectively a hearing of, the substantive claim"; wrong to "clog up [the permission] stage with full-scale rehearsals of what would be the substantive hearing of a claim if permission is granted"); *R v Secretary of State for the Home Department, ex p Kingdom of Belgium* 15th February 2000 unrep. (DC granting permission in criminal case, following refusal by single judge at oral hearing); *R v Secretary of State for the Home Department, ex p Bulger* [2001] EWHC Admin 119 [2001] 3 All ER 449 at [72] (DC refusing permission to appeal, having refused permission for judicial review); <23.2.1(B)> (CA having no jurisdiction); *R (Yildrim) v Immigration Appeal Tribunal* [2002] EWHC 1939 (Admin) at [13] (criticising the "large number of hopeless applications for permission to apply for judicial review [which] are renewed orally after a clear indication from the judge on paper that they have little prospect of success"); *R v Oxford, ex p Levey* (1987) 151 LG Rev 371, 373 ("it has long been the practice in

---

[111] David Abrahams [1999] JR 22.

appropriate cases for judges to invite a proposed [defendant] to assist the court upon the application for [permission] and to adjourn the application for this purpose"; "it is particularly desirable that such invitations should be accepted"); *R v Secretary of State for the Home Department, ex p Gunn* 14th July 2000 unrep. (in many asylum cases "the Secretary of State will appear and in many cases will be expected by the court to appear", the Court wishing "always to be certain that it has the benefit of full information"); *R v Secretary of State for the Home Department, ex p Fadia Nader* [1998] Imm AR 33 (importance of accurate time estimate); *R v North West Leicestershire District Council, ex p Moses* [2000] Env LR 443, 459 ("Judges must be astute to ensure that disproportionate time is not taken up at the permission stage").

21.1.7 Permission and arguability.[112] *Sharma v Antoine* [2006] UKPC 57 [2007] 1 WLR 780 at [14(4)] ("the court will refuse [permission] to claim judicial review unless satisfied that there is an arguable ground for judicial review having a realistic prospect of success and not subject to a discretionary bar such as delay or an alternative remedy"); *R v Number 8 Area Committee of the Legal Aid Board, ex p Megarry* [1994] PIQR 476 ("no sensible prospect of success"); *R v Secretary of State for Social Security, ex p Lloyd* [1995] 1 FLR 856, 857D ("fanciful, unrealistic and not supported by the Act"); *R v Secretary of State for the Home Department, ex p Fielding* 23rd November 1998 unrep. (point worthy of consideration); *R v Inland Revenue Commissioners, ex p National Federation of Self-Employed and Small Businesses Ltd* [1982] AC 617, 644A (Lord Diplock, referring to what "on a quick perusal of the material then available, the court thinks that it discloses what might on further consideration turn out to be an arguable case"); *R v Legal Aid Board, ex p Hughes* (1993) 5 Admin LR 623, 628D-G (Lord Donaldson MR, commenting that "things have moved on since" Lord Diplock's comments, and that need for an arguable case); *R v Secretary of State for Trade and Industry, ex p Greenpeace Ltd* [1998] Env LR 415, 418 (Laws J, describing the Diplock test as "most certainly the general rule"); *R v Royal Life Saving Society, ex p Heather Rose Mary Howe* [1990] COD 440 (no public law element); *R v Chief Rabbi, ex p Wachmann* [1992] 1 WLR 1036, 1037H (unarguable as to reviewability); *R (Rhodes) v Kingston upon Hull City Council* [2001] ELR 230 (permission refused because court would not give a remedy in the exercise of its discretion); *R (Gentle) v Prime Minister* [2006] EWCA Civ 1078 at [23] (CA granting permission for judicial review, not on grounds of real prospect of success, but because of importance of the issues); *R v HM Customs and Excise, ex p Davies Products (Liverpool) Ltd* 25th June 1991 unrep. (sufficient that "very real grievance" and conceivable need for Art 234 reference to the ECJ).

21.1.8 Substantive/summary resolution of issues.
(A) RESOLVING A QUESTION OF JURISDICTION. *Ex p Scott* [1998] 1 WLR 226, 229F (resolving issue as to whether challenge constituting "charity proceedings" for which Court having no jurisdiction absent authorisation from the Charity Commissioners or the Chancery Division); *R v Parliamentary Commissioner for Standards, ex p Al Fayed* [1998] 1 WLR 669 (deciding no jurisdiction to review Parliamentary Commissioner for Standards).
(B) RESOLVING A POINT OF LAW/PRINCIPLE. *R v Secretary of State for Trade and Industry, ex p Greenpeace Ltd* [1998] Env LR 415, 418 (Laws J: "cases occasionally arise where the question whether [permission] should be granted involves substantial issues of principle"); *Rashed Masoud Al-Zagha v Secretary of State for the Home Department* [1994] Imm AR 20, 26 (Leggatt LJ: "in the same way that the court, on an application ... for summary judgment, will consider any point of law or construction, if it can readily deal with and dispose of the matter by reference to that question, so it seems to me should the court approach an application for [permission]"); *R (Persimmon Homes (Thames Valley) Ltd) v North Hertfordshire District*

---

[112] Michael Fordham [2007] JR 219.

Council [2001] EWHC Admin 565 [2001] 1 WLR 2393 at [2] (dealing with point of construction by treating permission as substantive hearing); *R v Attorney-General, ex p Rockall* [2000] 1 WLR 882 (dealing with issue as to applicability of statutorily reversed burden of proof) cf. *Re Polly Peck International Plc (in administration) (No.2)* [1998] 3 All ER 812, 820e, 827h-j (as to appropriateness of resolving points of law at stage of permission to commence writ proceedings); *R (SPCMA SA) v Secretary of State for Environment, Food and Rural Affairs* [2007] EWHC 2610 (Admin) (Court granting final declaration at permission stage on one statutory interpretation issue on which parties were now agreed).
(C) PROMPTNESS/GOOD REASON AS A PERMISSION-STAGE ISSUE. <26.1.7>.
(D) ALTERNATIVE REMEDY AS A PERMISSION-STAGE ISSUE. <36.3.7>.
(E) TREATING AS SUBSTANTIVE HEARING. <21.2.3> (rolled-up hearing).
(F) SUMMARY JUDGMENT/DISPOSAL. <22.1.6> (summary judgment).

21.1.9 **Enhanced arguability.** *R (Federation of Technological Industries) v Commissioners of Customs and Excise* [2004] EWHC 254 (Admin) at [8] (Lightman J: "The orthodox approach is to give permission to apply for judicial review if the claimant shows an arguable case. But the court in the exercise of its discretion whether to give permission may impose a higher hurdle if the circumstances require this. Factors of substantial importance in this context may include the nature of the issue, the urgency of resolution of the dispute and how detailed and complete is the argument before the court on the application for permission") (CA is at [2004] EWCA Civ 1020); *Mass Energy Ltd v Birmingham City Council* [1994] Env LR 298, 307-308, 310-311, 318 (CA adopting a deliberately heightened threshold of whether the claim was "strong", ie. "likely to succeed"; rather than whether it was "arguable", because it had seen extensive material and heard detailed argument, and speed reasons applied); *R v London Docklands Development Corporation, ex p Frost* (1997) 73 P & CR 199, 203 (suggesting that *Mass Energy* approach appropriate where "the court was satisfied that it had heard as much argument and dealt with the matter in as much depth as was normally likely at a substantive hearing"); *R v Cotswold District Council, ex p Barrington* (1998) 75 P & CR 515 (Keene J: "where the court seems to have all the relevant material and have heard full argument at the [permission] stage ... [i]t may then require [a claimant] to show a reasonably good chance of success"); *R v Derbyshire County Council, ex p Woods* [1998] Env LR 277, 280-281 (as "a discretionary matter", CA adopting "an approach that is somewhere between" showing "a reasonable prospect of success" and the *Mass Energy* test); *R v Northampton Borough Council, ex p Northampton Rapid Transit System* 10th July 2000 unrep. (applying *Woods*); *R (Johnson) v Professional Conduct Committee of Nursing & Midwifery Council* [2008] EWHC 885 (Admin) at [124] (3 day permission hearing "as full a hearing as there would have been had permission been granted", so would have been a "classic case for the application of the modified test for permission").

21.1.10 **Permission and non-disclosure/service.** *R (I) v Secretary of State for the Home Department* [2007] EWHC 3103 (Admin) at [10] (Court entitled to refuse permission, in an appropriate case, for breach of claimant's candour duty); *R (Koyama) v University of Manchester* [2007] EWHC 1868 (Admin) (commenting that permission would have been refused in any event for deliberate failure to serve defendant under CPR 54.7).

21.1.11 **Permission and alternative remedy.** <36.3.6> and <36.3.7>.

21.1.12 **Permission and standing.**
(A) SCA S.31(3). <P64.1>.
(B) REFUSING PERMISSION FOR LACK OF STANDING. <38.3.2>.
(C) LEGAL INCAPACITY. <38.1.7>.

21.1.13 Permission and delay.
(A) TIME FOR COMMENCING THE CLAIM. <P26>.
(B) REFUSING PERMISSION FOR DELAY. <26.1.7>.
(C) EXTENSION OF TIME. <26.3>.

21.1.14 Court striking out completely hopeless/abusive case. *R (Kumar) v Secretary of State for Constitutional Affairs* [2006] EWCA Civ 990 [2007] 1 WLR 536 at [65] (strike out power extends to judicial review); *R (Nine Nepalese Asylum Seekers) v Immigration Appeal Tribunal* [2003] EWCA Civ 1892 at [15] (appropriate to strike out judicial review permission appeals where totally devoid of merits, of own motion under CPR 3.3(4) giving 10 days for hearing speedily to be sought); *R (Davies) v Secretary of State for the Environment, Food and Rural Affairs* [2002] EWHC 2762 (Admin) (judicial review struck out as manifestly an abuse of process, where claim relating to moribund company whose interests claimant had no authority to advance).

21.1.15 Partial/limited/conditional permission.[113] See CPR 54.12(1)(b) <64.2>; CPR 54PD <64.3> para 9.1; also CPR 1.1-1.4; CPR 54.15 <64.2> (application to extend partial/ limited permission); *R v Secretary of State for Transport, ex p Richmond-upon-Thames London Borough Council* [1994] 1 WLR 74, 98B ("pressing" need for rules allowing permission to be refused "on some grounds, while granting it on others"); *R v Staffordshire County Council, ex p Ashworth* (1997) 9 Admin LR 373, 378B-F (court's "inherent power to control its own processes" so as "not to permit [the claimant] to reopen the ground of application for which [permission] had been refused"); *R v Advertising Standards Authority, ex p City Trading Ltd* [1997] COD 202 (see transcript) (applying *Ashworth* and permitting argument "only on the basis upon which [permission] was granted"); *R v Falmouth and Truro Port Health Authority, ex p South West Water Ltd* [2001] QB 445, 472F-473C (where alternative remedy by means of statutory right of appeal, permission should have been for a "limited judicial review" restricted to two issues); *R v London Borough of Hammersmith, ex p CPRE London Branch* [2000] Env LR 532 (permission given in respect of one challenged decision but refused as to another (see too the CA at [2000] Env LR 549)); *R v East Sussex County Council, ex p Ward* (2000) 3 CCLR 132 at [37] (permission granted on condition that remedy be limited to a particular period in time, given considerations of delay); *R (Evans) v University of Cambridge* [2002] EWHC 1382 (Admin) [2003] ELR 8 at [3] (permission limited to whether decisions amenable to judicial review, with permission on remaining issues to await the outcome of that hearing); <22.4.9> (effect of partial permission at substantive hearing); <23.1.9> (appeal and partial/ conditional permission).

21.1.16 Fresh permission application. *R (Opoku) v Principal of Southwark College* [2002] EWHC 2092 (Admin) [2003] 1 All ER 272 at [9] (permission decision interlocutory so no res judicata, but may be abuse of process to make repeat application absent new material), [16] ("The court should only exercise its discretion to grant permission where the claimant establishes that there has been a significant change of circumstances or that he has become aware of significant new facts which he could not reasonably have known or found out on the previous unsuccessful application or that a proposition of law is now maintainable which was not previously open to him").

21.1.17 Security for costs/cost conditions. <21.2.11>.

21.1.18 Defendant inviting quashing order, on grant of permission. This happens on

---

[113] Helen Mountfield [1996] JR 65, [1997] JR 61, [2004] JR 26; Richard Leiper [1999] JR 20.

occasion, as a pragmatic course which allows reconsideration rather than a substantive hearing: see eg. *Pitchaiappah Gnanavarathan v A Special Adjudicator* [1995] Imm AR 64, 72; *R v Immigration Appeal Tribunal, ex p Probakaran* [1996] Imm AR 603, 606.

21.1.19 Setting aside permission.
(A) UNDER CPR 54. See CPR 54.13 (person served may not apply to set aside); *R v Association of British Travel Agents, ex p Sunspell Ltd* [2001] ACD 88 at [2] (Keene J, expressing doubts as to whether court still possessing power to set aside permission under CPR 54); *R (Webb) v Bristol City Council* [2001] EWHC Admin 696 (using inherent jurisdiction to set aside permission granted where defendant had not yet lodged AOS and time for doing so had not expired); *R v Commissioner for Local Administration, ex p Field* [2000] COD 58 (where late application to set aside permission, court emphasising that having inherent jurisdiction to set aside permission); *R (Candlish) v Hastings Borough Council* [2005] EWHC 1539 (Admin) [2006] Env LR 278 at [15] (permission revoked where interested party's AOS not brought to paper judge's attention); *R (Tataw) v Immigration Appeal Tribunal* [2003] EWCA Civ 925 [2003] INLR 585 at [13] (permission for judicial review set aside where granted by mistake, in erroneous reliance on consent from Secretary of State given in a different case); *R v Chief Constable of West Yorkshire, ex p Wilkinson* [2002] EWHC 2353 (Admin) at [43] ("The court has always had power to recall and reopen orders and decisions in cases of fraud and mistake").
(B) PREVIOUS POSITION. Under RSC Ord 53 an application to set aside was required to explain its precise basis (*R v Lloyd's of London, ex p Briggs* [1992] COD 456); it had to be made speedily (*R v Derbyshire County Council, ex p Noble* [1989] COD 285); and the power was to be used sparingly (*R v Secretary of State for the Home Department, ex p Sholola* [1992] Imm AR 135). Grounds included[114]: material non-disclosure <10.3.4>; want of arguability (*R v Luton Borough Council, ex p Riaz Ahmed Mirza* [1995] COD 231); non-reviewability (*R v London Borough of Hackney, ex p Kadir* 13th December 1991 unrep.); alternative remedy (*R v Secretary of State for the Home Department, ex p Watts* [1997] COD 152); delay (*R v Commissioner for Local Administration, ex p Field* [2000] COD 58); legal incapacity (*R v Darlington Borough Council, ex p Association of Darlington Taxi Owners* [1994] COD 424); cf. *Sharma v Antoine* [2006] UKPC 57 [2007] 1 WLR 780 at [14(6)] (leave set aside "very sparingly" but appropriate "if satisfied on inter partes argument that the leave is one that plainly should not have been granted"); *R v Customs & Excise Commissioners, ex p Eurotunnel Plc* [1995] CLC 392, 399D-E (third parties had locus to raise issues of delay on an application to set aside permission).
(C) NO APPEAL FROM THE GIVING OF PERMISSION. <23.1.2>.

21.1.20 Costs and permission.
(A) PERMISSION GRANTED: COSTS IN THE CASE. <18.3.5>.
(B) PERMISSION REFUSED: DEFENDANT/THIRD PARTY COSTS. <18.3.3(C)>.
(C) SUMMARY ASSESSMENT OF COSTS. <18.2>.

21.1.21 Effect of permission on CLS funding.
The grant of permission provides a strong basis for a (renewed) application for CLS funding, where the problem was prior doubts as to prospects of success); *R v Legal Aid Board, ex p Hughes* (1993) 5 Admin LR 623, 628B (Lord Donaldson MR: tests for permission and legal aid not "essentially different"), 629G ("In form they are different questions, but in substance they are not"), 629G-H (legal aid committee may, in a "borderline case", take a different view from the single Judge, eg, if they have "more information than the Judge"); cf. *R v Legal Aid Board, ex p Owners Abroad Group plc* [1998] COD 224 (although Lord Donaldson's guidance helpful, in fact the threshold for permission for

---

[114] Parishil Patel [1997] JR 204.

judicial review lower than that for granting legal aid).

21.1.22 Precedent: status of permission decisions. <11.1.6>.

21.1.23 Permission: rights of appeal. <23.1>.

21.2 Case-management at the permission stage

The permission stage provides the perfect opportunity for early case-management. The Court can make any necessary or desirable orders or directions as to how the case should be dealt with.

21.2.1 Amendment of the claim form. Cf. CPR 54.15 (post-permission amendment). The claimant can invite the Court to grant permission for judicial review, by reference to grounds which have been amended since they were lodged. The Court will consider the usual questions of arguability, but may also wish to take into account any additional consideration of lack of promptness. The pre-CPR rules contained express provision (Order 53 r.3(6)) for amendment at the permission stage ("The court hearing an application for permission may allow the [claimant]'s statement to be amended, whether by specifying different or additional grounds or [remedy] or otherwise, on such terms, if any, as it thinks fit").

21.2.2 Partial/limited/conditional permission. <21.1.15>.

21.2.3 Rolled-up hearing. *R v Criminal Injuries Compensation Board, ex p A* [1999] 2 AC 330, 341B-F (permission can be "adjourned to the substantive hearing" so that "the question under both Ord 53, r.4(1) (good reason for an extension of time) and section 31(6) (hardship, prejudice, detriment, justifying a refusal of [permission]) may fall for determination"), 347F-348A; *R (Candlish) v Hastings Borough Council* [2005] EWHC 1539 (Admin) [2006] Env LR 278 at [15] (rolled-up hearing to keep promptness point open); *R (Paul) v Coroner of the Queen's Household* [2007] EWHC 408 (Admin) [2008] QB 172 (Diana inquest); *R (Da Silva) v Director of Public Prosecutions* [2006] EWHC 3204 (Admin) (police shooting); *R (Westminster City Council) v Mayor of London* [2002] EWHC 2440 (Admin) [2003] LGR 611 (Congestion Charging Scheme); *R (BMW AG) v Revenue & Customs Commissioners* [2008] EWHC 712 (Admin) (VAT accounting changes).

21.2.4 Permission treated as substantive hearing.
(A) GENERAL. *R (Persimmon Homes (Thames Valley) Ltd) v North Hertfordshire District Council* [2001] EWHC Admin 565 [2001] 1 WLR 2393 at [2] (dealing with point of construction by treating permission as substantive hearing); *R (Green) v Police Complaints Authority* [2001] EWHC Admin 1160 at [3] (judge at contested permission hearing deciding sensible to treat as substantive hearing); *R (Noble Organisation) v Thanet District Council* [2004] EWHC 2576 (Admin) [2005] Env LR 513 at [33] (treating the hearing as the substantive hearing in the interests of justice, despite the claimant's refusal to consent to that course).
(B) TO PRESERVE APPEAL RIGHTS. *R v Director of Public Prosecutions, ex p Camelot Group Plc* (1998) 10 Admin LR 93, 105E-F (permission treated as hearing of the judicial review by CA so that dismissal not necessarily the end for claimant's arguments); *R v Parliamentary Commissioner for Standards, ex p Al Fayed* [1998] 1 WLR 669 (permission given by CA so case able to be pursued to HL); *R v Her Majesty's Treasury, ex p Shepherd Neame Ltd* (1999) 11 Admin LR 517, 518b (permission given by CA to preserve position as to petition to HL).

21.2.5 Expedition/abridgment.
(A) EXPEDITION. An order for expedition is important because it means that the case will be fast-tracked, by means of the expedited list. Expedition is only appropriate where there is a good

reason why the case needs to be dealt with more urgently than the big queue of cases awaiting resolution. See *R v Secretary of State for the Home Department, ex p Harrison* [2001] ACD 8 (importance of all parties ensuring Court informed, at the permission stage and thereafter, if circumstances warranting expedition).

(B) ABRIDGMENT. See CPR 3.1(2)(a). An order for expedition may be accompanied by orders for abridgment of time: a truncated timetable for evidence, detailed statement of grounds of opposition and perhaps skeleton arguments. So, the Court may abridge time for defendants/third parties to serve their detailed response and written evidence more speedily than the prescribed 35 days (CPR 54.14), or a tighter timetable for service of skeleton arguments <22.1.15> and <22.1.16>.

21.2.6 Hearing of a preliminary issue. <22.4.8>.

21.2.7 Cross-examination/further information/disclosure. <17.4>.

21.2.8 Interim remedy.
(A) INTERIM REMEDIES. <P20>.
(B) BAIL. <20.1.7>.
(C) STAY OF THE PROCEEDINGS UNDER REVIEW. <20.1.5>.

21.2.9 Anonymity/hearing in private. See CPR 39.2.
(A) ANONYMITY. *R v Westminster City Council, ex p P* (1998) 1 CCLR 486, 493C-494H (need for the Court to be satisfied (especially where the parties are agreed) that anonymity of claimant necessary on basis that the parties would be deterred from seeking justice if their names were revealed to the public); *In the matter of D* (1998) 1 CCLR 190, 196K ("the test is ... whether the proposed derogation from open justice is necessary in order to prevent a real risk that the administration of justice will be rendered impracticable"); *R v Legal Aid Board, ex p Kaim Todner* [1999] QB 966, 975H-977G; *R v Westminster City Council, ex p Castelli* (1995) 7 Admin LR 840[115]; *R v Cambridge District Health Authority, ex p B (No.2)* [1996] 1 FLR 375 (application to lift anonymity); *R v Huddersfield Justices, ex p D* [1997] COD 27 (anonymity order extended indefinitely); *In re R (Minor) (Court of Appeal: Order against identification)* The Times 9th December 1998 (CA practice of child anonymity); *Practice Note (Anonymisation in asylum and immigration cases in the Court of Appeal)* [2006] 4 All ER 928 (asylum cases automatically anonymised in CA).
(B) HEARINGS IN PRIVATE. *R (Amvac Chemical UK Ltd) v Secretary of State for Environment, Food and Rural Affairs* [2001] EWHC Admin 1011 at [5]-[12] (considering approach to CPR 39.2 and concluding that insufficient grounds for private hearing in the circumstances); also *Clibbery v Allan* [2002] EWCA Civ 45 [2002] Fam 261; HRA:ECHR Art 6 <59.5.9> (public hearing/judgment in public).

21.2.10 Vexatious litigant. *R (Ewing) v Office of the Deputy Prime Minister* [2005] EWCA Civ 1583 [2006] 1 WLR 1260 at [34]-[36] (vexatious litigant needing separate statutory permission under Supreme Court Act 1981 s.42); *R (Ewing) v Department of Constitutional Affairs* [2006] EWHC 504 (Admin) [2006] 2 All ER 993 (paper-only permission under CPR 3PD para 7); *R (Kumar) v Secretary of State for Constitutional Affairs* [2006] EWCA Civ 990 [2007] 1 WLR 536 (Administrative Court power to impose civil restraint order against litigant persistently making totally unmeritorious applications, following adjournment for notice and defence).

21.2.11 Costs protection.

---

[115] Emma Dixon [1996] JR 73.

(A) SECURITY FOR COSTS.[116] See CPR 25.12, CPR 25.13; *R v Westminster City Council, ex p Residents Association of Mayfair* [1991] COD 182 (security for costs ordered where corporate claimant unlikely to be able to pay costs, and highly likely that resources could be found by those who were behind the application); *R v Leicestershire County Council, ex p Blackfordby & Boothorpe Action Group Ltd* [2001] Env LR 2 at [37] (where action group incorporated at the time of the challenge (or for the purpose of bringing it), appropriate to address costs position by means of security for costs; here £15,000); *R (Residents Against Waste Sites Ltd) v Lancs County Council* [2007] EWHC 2558 (Admin) at [20] (£25,000 agreed as security for costs); *R v Hammersmith and Fulham London Borough Council, ex p People Before Profit Ltd* (1981) 45 P & CR 364 (had permission been granted, court would have awarded security for costs); *R v Common Professional Examination Board, ex p Mealing-McCleod* The Times 2nd May 2000 (CA had granted permission to appeal on condition of security for costs); <18.1.17> (security for costs and specially-incorporated claimant).

(B) COST CONDITIONS. *R v Ministry of Agriculture Fisheries and Food, ex p British Pig Industry Support Group* [2000] EuLR 724 at [108] (where claimant unincorporated, appropriate for court to make permission conditional on adequate costs provision, such as joinder of a co-claimant).

(C) PROTECTIVE COSTS ORDER/COST CAPPING ORDER. <18.4.3>.

21.2.12 Article 234 reference. <8.4>.

21.2.13 Application by person wishing to be heard: CPR 54.17. <22.2.3>.

21.2.14 Other directions. See CPR 54.10(1) <64.2>; CPR 54PD <64.3> paras 8.1-8.3; ACO:NFG <64.4> para 11.1; CPR 3.1(2)(a) (extension/ abridgment of time); <9.3.14> (HRA notice to the Crown); CPR 54PD <64.3> para 8.3 (direction for hearing outside London/ Cardiff): *R (Deepdock Ltd) v Welsh Ministers* [2007] EWHC 3346 (Admin) (judicial review of Welsh Minister should be heard in Wales); CPR 54.10(2) (stay of proceedings under review); *R v Dover Magistrates Court, ex p Kidner* [1983] 1 All ER 475 and *R (P and Q) v Secretary of State for the Home Department* [2001] EWCA Civ 1151 [2001] 1 WLR 2002 at [118] (suitability of certain cases for Family Division judges); ACO:NFG <64.4> para 2.2 (suitability for Divisional Court); CPR 54.18 <64.2> (determination without a hearing); *R (Santur) v Secretary of State for the Home Department* [2007] EWHC 741 (Admin) (open to paper judge in a hopeless asylum case to direct that removal able to take place notwithstanding any renewal of permission; claimant would need to apply for a stay); cf. <23.1.8>.

21.2.15 Transfer out.
(A) UNDER THE CPR. See CPR 54.20; *R (Mullins) v Appeal Board of the Jockey Club* [2005] EWHC 2197 (Admin) at [48]-[49] (transfer out available in principle where defendant not amenable to judicial review); *R (West) v Lloyds of London* [2004] EWCA Civ 506 [2004] 3 All ER 251 at [41] (not appropriate to transfer out, since claimant would need to "entirely reshape his case so as to identify the private law causes of action"; "he will have to begin again"); *R (Oxford Study Centre Ltd) v British Council* [2001] EWHC Admin 207 [2001] ELR 803 (where defendant not amenable to judicial review but implied contractual duty of fairness and no need for cross-examination, court treating case as transferred to ordinary action and granting a declaration); *R (Arthurworry) v Haringey London Borough Council* [2001] EWHC Admin 698 (no reference to transfer, but court simply proceeding to consider issues by reference to private law (relationship of trust and confidence) where matter not amenable to judicial review).
(B) TRANSFER OUT: PRE-CPR CASE-LAW. *R v Secretary of State for the Home*

---

[116] Caroline Neenan [1999] JR 231.

Department, ex p Dew [1987] 1 WLR 881, 892B (RSC Ord 53 r.9(5) "limited ... to cases where the claim is for declaration, injunction or damages"), 901E ("a rule 9(5) order can only be made where a breach of some public law obligation is propounded"); *R v Crown Prosecution Service, ex p Hogg* (1994) 6 Admin LR 778, 782D ("great wisdom ... in preventing the aborting of proceedings at a late stage if it becomes apparent that the wrong procedure has been chosen"); *R v Reading Justices, ex p South West Meat Ltd* (1992) 4 Admin LR 401 (refusal of defendant's late application for conversion to writ claim, designed to prevent the hearing of the judicial review from taking place); *R v Secretary of State for the Home Department, ex p Soylemez* [1992] COD 137 (conversion to writ, where damages the only live issue); *R v Blandford Justices, ex p Pamment* [1990] 1 WLR 1490, 1496D-E (where "judicial review is academic in the sense that its sole or main purpose is merely to prime the pump for the damages claim, the best course for the court would be to decline as a matter of discretion to deal with the application for judicial review and allow the damages claim to proceed as if begun by writ"); *R v Commissioners of Customs and Excise, ex p F & I Services Ltd* [2000] STC 364 (conversion where arguable that breach of duty of care in giving pre-transaction VAT advice); *O'Reilly v Mackman* [1983] 2 AC 237, 283H-284A (availability of ordering proceedings to continue as if they had begun by writ); *Trustees of the Dennis Rye Pension Fund v Sheffield City Council* [1998] 1 WLR 840, 848G ("If judicial review is used when it should not, the court can protect its resources either by directing that the application should continue as if begun by [ordinary action] or by directing it should be heard by a judge who is not nominated to hear cases in the [Administrative Court]"); *R v Jockey Club, ex p RAM Racecourses* [1993] 2 All ER 225, 244e-g (conversion inappropriate where no substance in the challenge, and anyway "only the costs of the writ and a little time would be saved"); *R v Provincial Court of the Church in Wales, ex p Williams* [1999] COD 163 (even though defendant not amenable to judicial review, need to consider whether arguable case of breach of implied contractual duties of reasonableness and fairness, in order to decide whether to order proceedings to continue as if begun by writ); *R v Medicines Control Agency, ex p Pharma Nord Ltd* (1998) 10 Admin LR 646, 658H-659A (transfer could be appropriate to allow fact-resolution); *R v Insurance Ombudsman, ex p Aegon Life Insurance Ltd* [1994] CLC 88, 94H-95A (declining to convert to writ because pleaded grounds for judicial review "not directed towards identifying the implied terms on the breach of which the [claimant] would wish to rely. The [defendant] is entitled to have the matter properly pleaded"); *R v London Borough of Hackney, ex p Kadir* 13th December 1991 unrep. (employment matter, where proceedings "not really in a suitable state" for conversion to writ).

21.2.16 **Transfer in.**

(A) UNDER THE CPR. See CPR 30.5 (transfer); CPR 54.4 <64.2> (need for permission); CPR 54PD <64.3> para 14.2; *R (Governor of HMP Wandsworth) v Kinderis* [2007] EWHC 998 (Admin) [2008] QB 347 at [1] (prisoner governor's claim to establish which of two inconsistent orders applicable, transferred to the Admin Court); *Independent Committee for the Supervision of Standards of Telephone Information Services v Andronikou* [2007] EWHC 2307 (Admin) (claim in debt under statutory scheme); *R (Lord v Secretary of State for the Home Department* [2003] EWHC 2073 (Admin) at [17] (claim for parole data protection disclosure order transferred to the Admin Court); *R (Johnson) v Reading Borough Council* [2004] EWHC 765 (Admin) at [5] (wrong to transfer HRA damages claim to the Admin Court).
(B) PRE-CPR.[117] *O'Reilly v Mackman* [1983] 2 AC 237, 284A-B (Lord Diplock: "There is no such converse power under the RSC to permit an action begun by writ to continue as if it were an application for judicial review"); *Davy v Spelthorne Borough Council* [1984] AC 262, 274G (Lord Fraser: "The court has no power to order the proceedings for damages to continue as if they had been made under Order 53. The converse power under Order 53 r.9 operates in one

---

[117] Matthew Holt [2000] JR 91 & 171.

direction only"); *R v Tower Hamlets London Borough Council, ex p Luck* [1999] COD 294 (QB Master having no power to transfer private law action to the Divisional Court to be considered as potential judicial review); *Trustees of the Dennis Rye Pension Fund v Sheffield City Council* [1998] 1 WLR 840, 849A.

> **P22 Substantive hearing.** At the hearing the Court decides whether there are grounds for intervening and whether to grant a remedy.

22.1 Post-permission/pre-hearing steps
22.2 Third party participation
22.3 Disposal without a hearing
22.4 The substantive hearing

22.1 Post-permission/pre-hearing steps. Following the grant of permission, the defendants and third parties lodge their detailed grounds and written evidence, to which the claimant may reply. In the run up to the hearing, the parties lodge bundles and skeleton arguments.

22.1.1 Post-permission service. See CPR 54.11 <64.2>; CPR 54PD <64.3> para 9.1 (court service of permission order).

22.1.2 Post-permission fee. ACO:NFG <64.4> para 9.7.

22.1.3 Defendant/third party's detailed response/evidence (35 days post-permission). See CPR 54.14(1) <64.2>; CPR 54PD <64.3> para 10.1; ACO:NFG <64.4> paras 11.4-11.7; <10.4> (defendant/ third party's duty of candour); *R (Ministry of Defence) v Wiltshire & Swindon Coroner* [2005] EWHC 889 (Admin) [2006] 1 WLR 134 at [44] (Collins J: "there is an obligation on the defendants to put in a detailed statement of the grounds of defence. That will supersede an Acknowledgment of Service, although nowadays it often seems to be the case, and it is understandable why it should be, that the Acknowledgment of Service effectively will stand as grounds of defence"); *R (Corner House Research) v Director of the Serious Fraud Office* [2008] EWHC 246 (Admin) (detailed grounds a "defence" to which public entitled under CPR 2.3(1) from court file, absent a special embargo request and direction).

22.1.4 Claimant reconsideration. *R (Bateman) v Legal Services Commission* [2001] EWHC Admin 797 at [21] (endorsing this statement in the ACO standard form notifying the grant of permission: "Where permission to apply has been granted, claimants and their legal advisers are reminded of their obligation to reconsider the merits of their application in the light of the defendant's evidence"); *R v Secretary of State for the Home Department, ex p Brown* The Times 6th February 1984 ("It is highly desirable for counsel and solicitors instructed by [a claimant] for judicial review to give further careful consideration on the merits of the application once they had received notice of the [defendant]'s evidence, even though [permission] to move for judicial review had already been obtained. If that were done, much time, expense and disappointment in the hearing of hopeless applications would be saved"), applied in *R v Horsham District Council, ex p Wenman* [1995] 1 WLR 680, 701D-E ("any solicitor or counsel holding themselves out as competent to handle judicial review proceedings ... should be taken as being familiar with it. One of the reasons for the warning ... is to avoid the wasting of time and incurring of expense in connection with hopeless applications"); *R v Liverpool City Justices, ex p Price* [1998] COD 453 (clear that legally aided challenge hopeless once defendant's evidence filed; direction that judgment be sent to taxing authorities to decide whether to disallow wasted costs); *R v Horseferry Road Magistrates, ex p Prophet* [1995] Env LR 104, 112 (Schiemann J: "[Claimants] should bear in mind that judicial review is a discretionary remedy. This Court will not grant it when it will no longer achieve anything useful... It is, therefore, advisable for [claimants] when they are given a hearing date to consider carefully whether or not it is sensible, in the light of intervening events and the passage of time, to continue to pursue the request for [a remedy]. If it is not, then whatever may have been the merits at the time of the application for [permission], an attempt should be made to come to terms with the [defendant] and to discontinue the proceedings"); *R v Secretary of State for the*

Home Department, ex p Kekana [1998] Imm AR 136, 140 ("severe criticism" of pursuit on legal aid of immigration judicial review to a hearing of the judicial review, notwithstanding that the claimant's stay had been completed and she had left the UK); <5.1.5> (position where the defendant has agreed to reconsider); *R (Bateman) v Legal Services Commission* [2001] EWHC Admin 797 at [21] (Munby J: "An applicant who has been granted permission to apply for judicial review nonetheless remains under an obligation to consider with care just which arguments ought and which arguments ought not to be pursued at the substantive hearing. Matters contained in the defendant's acknowledgment of service or the defendant's evidence may demonstrate that points which were initially thought by the claimant to have merit in fact do not ... The need for conscientious performance of this obligation has been pointed out on previous occasions ... People must appreciate that failure in this regard may be visited with adverse costs orders").

22.1.5 **Claimant's reply evidence.** CPR 54.16(2) (need for court's permission).

22.1.6 **Summary judgment/strike out?** See CPR 24 (summarily disposing of claim or issue); *R v Ministry of Agriculture, Fisheries and Food, ex p Lay and Gage* [1998] COD 387 (following an ECJ ruling in judicial review proceedings that there was a breach of EC law, defendant successfully inviting Court to rule by means of the old RSC Ord 14A (summary disposal on a point of law) that breach gave rise to no *Francovich* damages <8.5.2>); cf. *Evans v First Secretary of State* [2003] EWCA Civ 1523 [2004] Env LR 319 (summary judgment appropriate to dismiss an unarguable statutory review of a planning decision); *R (Quark Fishing Ltd) v Secretary of State for Foreign and Commonwealth Affairs* [2005] UKHL 57 [2006] 1 AC 529 (in judicial review proceedings, strike out application by defendant succeeding, there being no viable HRA damages claim).

22.1.7 **Pre-hearing applications.** See ACO:NFG <64.4> para 13.1.

22.1.8 **Disclosure, further information, cross-examination.** <17.4>.

22.1.9 **HRA notice to the Crown.** <9.3.14>.

22.1.10 **Notice of amendment of grounds.** See CPR 54.15 <64.2>; CPR 54PD <64.3> para 11.1; *R (B) v Lambeth London Borough Council* [2006] EWHC 639 (Admin) (2006) 9 CCLR 239 at [37] (need for clarity and prompt amendment, so defendant and court can see exactly what decisions challenged, on what grounds and evidence, and what remedy sought); *Gover v Propertycare Ltd* [2006] EWCA Civ 286 [2006] 4 All ER 69 at [12] (makes a mockery of court's pre-reading if parties come to court believing can advance wholly new case); *R (P) v Essex County Council* [2004] EWHC 2027 (Admin) at [35] ("the court will normally permit such amendments as may be required to ensure that the real dispute between the parties can be adjudicated upon", but "incumbent on [claimant] (a) to seek permission to amend his N461, (b) to give notice of his wish to amend at the earliest possible moment and in any event no later than 7 clear days before the hearing and (c) to formulate the new or additional case he wishes to make in a properly drafted document setting out, in the manner and with the detail required by CPR Part 54.6 and by Form N461, the precise amendments for which he is seeking permission"); <5.1.5> (fresh/further decision and need for promptly notified amendment).

22.1.11 **Adjournment/stay of the judicial review claim.**
(A) ADJOURNMENT. *R v Birmingham City Coroner ex p Najada* The Times 5th December 1995 (applications for judicial review should be heard as quickly as reasonably practicable; incumbent upon defendant seeking an adjournment to justify it); *R v London Borough of Newham, ex p Omo-Etiobio* 3rd March 1993 unrep. (refusal to adjourn even though parties had

agreed that course); *R v Immigration Officer, ex p Quaquah* [2000] INLR 196, 204A (Turner J describing how he had adjourned the substantive application pending a strike out application in related private law proceedings); *R v Legal Aid Board, ex p Duncan* [2000] COD 159 (see transcript at [2]) (DC explaining that had granted the defendants an adjournment of the hearing of the judicial review); *Poplar Housing and Regeneration Community Association Ltd v Donoghue* [2001] EWCA Civ 595 [2002] QB 48 at [28]-[30] (first instance court may appropriately deal with HRA issues summarily and without adjourning for full materials, especially where an appeal is likely); *R (Lloyd) v Dagenham London Borough Council* [2001] EWCA Civ 533 (2001) 4 CCLR 196 at [3]-[5] (judicial review adjourned on basis of undertakings given to the Court, and then restored when dispute arising as to whether those undertakings had been breached); *R (Davies) v Revenue & Customs Commissioners* [2008] EWCA Civ 933 at [7] ("if a tribunal of fact exists which can find the relevant facts it is normally good practice to postpone judicial review until after the facts have been found").
(B) STAY. *R v University of Cambridge, ex p Evans* [1998] ELR 515 (stay granted where no prospect of Court granting remedy to interfere with past decisions (to promote other individuals) and prospect of defendant taking steps, during the next round of promotions, to cure the legal problems identified in the grant of permission); *R v Hammersmith and Fulham London Borough Council, ex p Burkett* [2001] Env LR 684 (CA) at [14] ("an arguably premature application can often be stayed or adjourned to await events"); cf. *Sparks v Harland* The Times 9th August 1996 (staying proceedings pending outcome of European Court of Human Rights case: no reason why plaintiff should be required to `roll the ball back up the hill' by starting proceedings all over again).
(C) PENDING FRESH DECISION. <5.1.5>.
(D) PENDING RELATED CASE. *R (Rama) v Immigration Appeal Tribunal* [2003] EWHC 27 (Admin) at [6] (court "often requested to stand-out cases which may be affected by pending appeals in higher courts"), [7] (court needing to be satisfied that "two criteria" met: "(1) that there is uncertainty as to the relevant law, which is likely to be resolved by a forthcoming decision of the higher court; and (2) that the facts of the case which it is sought to adjourn are such that the decision which is awaited is likely to be determinative or substantially affect the outcome of the present case"), [8] (no uncertainty as to the law where unequivocal and unanimous CA decision, notwithstanding pending petition to the HL); *R v Secretary of State for the Home Department, ex p McQuillan* [1995] 4 All ER 400, 426a-e (claim stayed pending outcome of Article 234 references in *Adams* and *Gallagher*).

22.1.12 Effect of fresh decision/offered reconsideration. <5.1.5>.

22.1.13 Partial/limited permission notification. <21.1.15>.

22.1.14 Listing/listing policy. See ACO:NFG <64.4> paras 12.1-12.5. *Practice Statement (Administrative Court: Annual Statement) 2001/2* [2002] 1 All ER 633 (Annex C), 639-640 (fixing substantive hearings); *R (Ghadami) v Harlow District Council* [2004] EWCA Civ 891 (CA overturning judge's listing directions in special circumstances where made without sufficient regard to previous judge's directions).

22.1.15 Claimant's bundle/skeleton (21 working days pre-hearing). See CPR 54PD <64.3> para 15.1 (skeleton), paras 16.1-16.2 (bundle); ACO:NFG <64.4> para 12.9 (claimant's skeleton), para 12.12 (bundle).

22.1.16 Defendant/third party's skeleton (14 working days pre-hearing). See CPR 54PD <64.3> para 15.2; ACO:NFG <64.4> para 12.10 (defendant/ third party's skeleton).

22.1.17 Adhering to the timetable for skeletons. *Haggis v Director of Public Prosecutions*

[2003] EWHC 2481 (Admin) [2004] 2 ALL ER 382 at [30] (Brooke LJ: "the judges of [the Administrative Court] and the Court of Appeal are likely in future to be very much less forbearing in relation to the late service of skeleton arguments. Their lack of forbearance may well lead to disagreeable orders in relation to costs if this is the only way in which discipline can be achieved"), [34] (lamenting "the court ... being bombarded at a very late stage, sometimes after it has already done its pre-reading, with the late arrival of skeleton arguments and important authorities").

22.1.18 **Content of skeletons.** See CPR 54PD <64.3> para 15.3; <11.1.1> (citation of authority); <11.1.10> (need for careful use of Strasbourg authority); *R (Prokopp) v London Underground Ltd* [2003] EWCA Civ 961 [2004] Env LR 170 at [90] (Buxton LJ: "The skeleton should ... clearly identify what authorities, and what parts of what authorities, are relied on, and carry the certification of counsel as required by the Lord Chief Justice's *Practice Direction* [2001] 1 WLR 1001"); CPR 52PD para 5.10 (requirements as to citation of authorities in skeleton for the CA) and para 15.11(5) (certification duty as to CA bundle of authorities); ACO:NFG <64.4> para 12.11.

22.1.19 **Importance of the time estimate.** In assisting with listing, it is important that Counsel give an accurate time estimate for the hearing, and notify any subsequent change in the estimate. Pre-CPR these points were emphasised in *Practice Direction (Crown Office List)* [1987] 1 WLR 232 and *Practice Note (Crown Office List)* [1987] 1 All ER 1184. See too *Planning High Court Practice* [2008] JR 161 (parties in planning cases asked to provide dual time estimate, based on judge with and without planning experience).

22.1.20 **Bundles of authorities.** <11.1.1(F)> (citation rules).

22.1.21 **Hansard warning (5 working days).** *Practice Direction* [1995] 1 WLR 192 ("Any party intending to refer to any extract from Hansard in support of any such argument as is permitted by the decisions in *Pepper v Hart* [1993] AC 593 and *Pickstone v Freemans Plc* [1989] AC 66 or otherwise must, unless the judge otherwise directs, serve upon all other parties and the court copies of any such extract together with a brief summary of the argument intended to be based upon such extract... Unless the judge otherwise directs, service upon other parties to the proceedings and the court of the extract and summary of argument ... shall be effected not less than five clear working days before the first day of the hearing. This applies whether or not there is a fixed date").

22.1.22 **Summary costs schedule/statement.** <18.2>.

22.2 **Third party participation.**[118] The rules and practice allow for involvement by persons directly affected by the claim, or other persons wishing to be heard.

22.2.1 **Interested party (person directly affected): procedural rules.** <19.1.2> (letter before claim); <19.1.5> (letter of response); CPR 54.1(2)(f) <64.2> (person directly affected); CPR 54PD <64.3> para 8.5 (involvement at permission hearing); CPR 54.6(1)(a) <64.2> (identification in claim form); CPR 54PD <64.3> paras 5.1-5.2 (claim form); CPR 54.7(b) (service of claim form); CPR 54.8 (AOS); CPR 54.14(1) (detailed grounds).

---

[118] Deana Smith [2002] JR 10.

22.2.2 **Meaning of person "directly affected".**[119] *R v Rent Officer Service, ex p Muldoon* [1996] 1 WLR 1103, 1105E (Lord Keith: "That a person is directly affected by something connotes that he is affected without the intervention of any intermediate agency"); *R v Legal Aid Board, ex p Megarry* [1994] COD 468 (tobacco companies' application, to be served with judicial review proceedings against Legal Aid Board's decision refusing legal aid for personal injuries actions against them, refused); *R v Seeboard Plc, ex p Guildford* The Times 6th March 1998 (Seeboard Plc heard as a person directly affected); *R v Monopolies and Mergers Commission, ex p Milk Marque Ltd* [2000] COD 329 (Dairy Industry Federation not directly affected, unless and until reorganisation following one possible outcome in ECJ); *R v Secretary of State for the Environment, Transport and the Regions, ex p Garland* 10th November 2000 unrep. at [8] (district auditor not a person directly affected); *R (Fuller) v Chief Constable of Dorset Constabulary* [2001] EWHC Admin 1057 [2003] QB 480 at [34] (wrong not to have named local authority as interested party in a case about police power to remove travellers from the local authority's land); *R (Telefonica O2 Europe plc) v Secretary of State for Business & Regulatory Reform* [2007] EWHC 3018 (Admin) at [2] (H3G as a person directly affected).

22.2.3 **Other person.** See CPR 54.17 <64.2> (power/application); CPR 54PD <64.3> paras 13.1-13.5. The old RSC O.53 r.9(1) provided for hearing a "proper" person to be heard "in opposition to" the claim.[120] *R v Coventry City Council, ex p Phoenix Aviation* [1995] 3 All ER 37, 51c ('Compassion in World Farming' appearing under Ord. 53 r.9(1)); *R v Secretary of State for Foreign & Commonwealth Affairs, ex p Indian Association of Alberta* [1982] QB 892, 904C-D (Government of Canada); *R v Broadcasting Complaints Commission, ex p Barclay* (1997) 9 Admin LR 265 (whether or not BBC ought to have been served as a person directly affected, undoubtedly a proper person to be heard); *R v Bow Street Metropolitan Stipendiary Magistrate, ex p South Coast Shipping Co Ltd* [1993] QB 645, 651A-B (Lloyd LJ: "In the course of the hearing, it occurred to us that the Director [of Public Prosecutions] might himself be affected by the result of this application and ought therefore to have been given the opportunity to be heard. [Counsel] has appeared this morning on behalf of the Director ... We gave him [permission] to be joined under the provisions of RSC Ord. 53 r.9"); *R v Seeboard Plc, ex p Guildford* The Times 6th March 1998 (Electricity Association heard as a proper person); *R v Monopolies and Mergers Commission, ex p Milk Marque Ltd* [2000] COD 329 & 330 (Dairy Industry Federation a proper person to be heard, and so entitled to copies of the papers lodged by the claimant with the Administrative Court, so as to be able to make informed representation); *R v Secretary of State for the Environment, Transport and the Regions, ex p Garland* 10th November 2000 unrep. at [9] (district auditor a proper person to be heard).

22.2.4 **Third party supporting the claim.** *R (Bushell) v Newcastle Upon Tyne Licensing Justices* [2004] EWHC 446 (Admin) at [1] (judicial review supported by 5 interested parties) (HL is [2006] UKHL 7 [2006] 1 WLR 496). The old RSC O.53 r.9 was limited to opposing the claim, but there were several cases in which ways were found to permit such intervention. Now, CPR 54 has removed the difficulty: *R v Independent Television Commission, ex p Virgin Television Limited* [1996] EMLR 318 (other unsuccessful licence bidders permitted to intervene in support of the application, being "directly affected"); *R v Secretary of State for the Environment, ex p Standley* [1997] Env LR 589, 597 (NFU permitted to make short written and oral submissions, with permission, in support of the application, "as an interested party"), and then [1999] QB 1279, 1285B (given permission, by national court, to make submissions on the reference to the ECJ, in support of the claimant); *R v Legal Aid Board, ex p Kaim Todner*

---

[119] James Maurici [1997] JR 7.

[120] Daniel Denman [1999] JR 98.

[1999] QB 966, 971D (Law Society permitted to make representations in support of claimant's claim to anonymity, although not a "party"); *R v Secretary of State for Health, ex p Eastside Cheese Company* (1999) 11 Admin LR 254 (Moses J) (interested party appearing in support of grant of judicial review) (CA is [1999] EuLR 968).

22.2.5 Third party participation: general.
(A) IMPORTANCE WHERE NON-APPEARING TRIBUNAL. *R (Morris) v Woolwich Magistrates Court* [2005] EWHC 781 (Admin) at [29] (emphasising that CPS should be more pro-active in appearing in judicial review cases where defendant court not appearing, especially where an allegation of unfairness against the court).
(B) THIRD PARTY PARTICIPATION: TYPICAL EXAMPLES. *R (Amicus - MSF Section) v Secretary of State for Trade and Industry* [2004] EWHC 860 (Admin) [2004] ELR 311 at [7] (three evangelical Christian organisations intervening in EC challenge to employment sex-orientation regulations); *R v Secretary of State for Trade and Industry, ex p Lonrho Plc* [1989] 1 WLR 525, 528D (subject-company of report and possible monopolies reference); *R v Independent Television Commission, ex p TSW Broadcasting Ltd* [1994] 2 LRC 414, 416c (successful bidder); *R v Panel on Take-overs and Mergers, ex p Datafin Plc* [1987] QB 815, 817B-C (take-over bidder and their merchant bankers as interveners); *Bromley London Borough Council v Greater London Council* [1983] 1 AC 768, 813E-F (recipient of grant); *R v Licensing Authority established under Medicines Act 1968, ex p Smith Kline & French Laboratories Ltd (No.1)* [1990] 1 AC 64, 101H-102C and 107F (other licence applicants); *R v Bournewood Community and Mental Health NHS Trust, ex p L* [1999] 1 AC 458, 481D (HL expressing gratitude for assistance from Mental Health Act Commission, Registered Nursing Home Association and Secretary of State); *Horvath v Secretary of State for the Home Department* [2001] 1 AC 489, 493B (Refugee Legal Centre intervening in HL by way of written submissions); *R v Wandsworth London Borough Council, ex p O* [2000] 1 WLR 2539, 2548C (CA inviting Secretary of State to intervene); *R v Secretary of State for the Environment, ex p Kent County Council* (1995) 93 LGR 322, 334 (footpath modification order case where, "as almost invariably happens in this class of case, the Ramblers' Association was permitted to appear as having a general interest in the subject matter of this litigation"); *R v Secretary of State for the Home Department, ex p Sivakumaran* [1988] AC 958, 992D (UN High Commissioner for Refugees); *R v Central Criminal Court, ex p Francis & Francis* [1989] AC 346 (Law Society intervening on question regarding legal professional privilege, but failing to impress (see 385C, cf. 389F) and ordered to pay the extra costs caused by their intervention (see 397G)); *Estate of M Kingsley (dec'd) v Secretary of State for Transport* [1994] COD 358 (in statutory review, third party seeking to be joined, for purpose of costs of compromised proceedings); *R v General Commissioners of Income Tax, ex p Hood-Barrs* (1947) 27 TC 506 (in challenging tax decisions, claimant should seek directions as to whom to serve); *R (Sivasubramaniam) v Wandsworth County Court* [2002] EWCA Civ 1738 [2003] 1 WLR 475 at [1] (Lord Chancellor's Department intervening because of points of principle arising as to the availability of judicial review of decisions of the county court);*Begum v Tower Hamlets London Borough Council* [2003] UKHL 5 [2003] 2 AC 430 at [25] (Article 6 case regarding local authority decision-making where "the First Secretary of State was, on account of the general importance of the case for the public administration, given leave to intervene"); *R (A & B) v East Sussex County Council (No.2)* [2003] EWHC 167 (Admin) (2003) 6 CCLR 194 at [182] (intervention by Disability Rights Commission having "greatly assisted" in case regarding HRA:ECHR Art 8 and manual lifting of disabled persons); *R (Blewett) v Derbyshire County Council* [2004] EWCA Civ 1508 [2004] Env LR 293 at [2] (Friends of the Earth submitting written intervention in the CA, on an environmental and planning case); *R (Compton) v Wiltshire Primary Care Trust* [2008] EWCA Civ 749 (PLP intervening in protective costs order case).
(C) SHARED REPRESENTATION. *R (Girling) v Parole Board* [2005] EWHC 5469 [2006]

1 WLR 1917 at [61] (Parole Board and Secretary of State entitled to share legal representation if both satisfied that agreeing on the issues raised) (CA is at [2006] EWCA Civ 1779 [2007] QB 783); *R (Murungaru) v Secretary of State for the Home Department* [2008] EWCA Civ 1015 at [14] (Counsel not able to speak for both Secretary of State and Attorney General in his public interest role regarding appointment of special advocates).
(D) SOCIAL SECURITY COMMISSIONER CASES. *R (Latif) v Social Security Commissioners* [2002] EWHC 2355 (Admin) at [15] ("in a normal case ... the Administrative Court would not expect the Secretary of State to participate in the proceedings, so as to provide the only element of resistance to a claim. It is really a matter for the Secretary of State to seek to participate only when his interests and those of his Department are seen by him to require his participation").
(E) OTHER. *R (Corner House Research) v Director of the Serious Fraud Office* [2008] EWHC 246 (Admin) (non-party media obtaining declaration in judicial review proceedings, as to right of access to pleadings from court file).

22.2.6 General powers of joinder.
(A) CPR PART 19. See especially CPR 19.1(2) & (3).
(B) INHERENT JURISDICTION TO JOIN PARTIES/ALLOW INTERVENTIONS. *R v Minister of Agriculture Fisheries and Food, ex p SP Anastasiou (Pissouri)* [1994] COD 329 (Court having inherent jurisdiction to ensure that all those who might be affected by the decision have the opportunity to present their case); *R v National Lottery Commission, ex p Camelot Group Plc* [2001] EMLR 3 at [3] (court having jurisdiction to hear person although not falling within old RSC Ord 53 rules); *Warren, Felsted Parish Council v Uttlesford District Council* [1996] COD 262 (inherent jurisdiction to allow third party intervention in planning statutory review); *Roe v Sheffield City Council* [2003] EWCA Civ 1 [2004] QB 653 at [85] (just as public interest interveners allowed by CPR 54, "no reason why the High Court in the exercise of its inherent jurisdiction should not be able to act likewise").
(C) JOINDER AS A DEFENDANT. *R v Secretary of State for the Environment, ex p O'Byrne* The Times 12th November 1999 (local authority joined as second defendant, on terms that even if unsuccessful claimant would not have to bear its costs); *R v Secretary of State for Education, ex p Cumbria County Council* [1994] ELR 220, 222C (although Governing Body joined as second defendant, remedy sought only against Secretary of State; late application to amend to seek remedy against the Governors rejected) and 227A-B (any thwarting of a legitimate expectation of consultation was by the Governors not the Secretary of State).
(D) JOINDER AS A CLAIMANT. *Gulf Insurance Ltd v Central Bank of Trinidad and Tobago* [2005] UKPC 10 (Bank joined so that could recover damages for conversion).

22.2.7 Judicial review opposed/resisted only by third party. *R (Reading Borough Council) v Admissions Appeal Panel for Reading Borough Council* [2005] EWHC 2378 (Admin) [2006] ELR 186 (school admissions decisions defended only by interested third parties); *R (Friends of the Earth Ltd) v Environment Agency* [2003] EWHC 3193 (Admin) [2004] Env LR 615 (judicial review conceded by Environment Agency but contested unsuccessfully by beneficiary of impugned decision); *R (Secretary of State for the Home Department) v Mental Health Review Tribunal* [2004] EWHC 1029 (Admin) at [1] (third party alone opposing judicial review); *R (Holmes) v General Medical Council* [2001] EWHC Admin 321 at [14] (judicial review of GMC's decision (declining to entertain a complaint against a doctor) not opposed by GMC, but only by the doctor); *R v Tunbridge Wells Justices, ex p Tunbridge Wells Borough Council* [1996] Env LR 88, 91 (judicial review conceded by defendant justices but resisted by third party accused); *R v Secretary of State for the Environment, ex p Sutton London Borough Council* (1997) 95 LGR 509 (preliminary issue fought out between claimant and third party); *R v Durham County Council, ex p Huddleston* [2000] 1 WLR 1484 (judicial review supported by defendant but resisted by intervening Secretary of State and beneficiary third party); *R v*

General Medical Council, ex p Toth [2000] 1 WLR 2209 (GMC accepting that decisions should be quashed, but remedy unsuccessfully resisted by directly affected third party);*R v Independent Appeals Tribunal of Hillingdon London Borough Council, ex p Governing Body of Mellow Lane School* [2001] ELR 200 (court refusing to set aside consent order even though third party pupil not having consented to it and so having been denied the opportunity to defend it in court, given that his rights fully protected on reconsideration of the decision); *R v Knowsley Metropolitan Borough Council, ex p Williams* [2001] Env LR 28 (magistrates' decision not quashed even though they accepting that it should be; court persuaded that magistrates entitled to reach conclusion in question); *R (Douglas) v North Tyneside Metropolitan Borough Council* [2003] EWCA Civ 1847 [2004] 1 WLR 2363 at [3] (local authority leaving it to Secretary of State to defend claim, since had merely been implementing his regulations).

22.2.8 Third party participation: other matters.

(A) INTERVENTION ON CONDITIONS. *R (Countryside Alliance) v Attorney General* [2005] EWHC 1677 (Admin) [2006] UKHRR 73 at [28] (RSPCA permission to intervene on terms that no costs order for or against them); *R v Department of Health, ex p Source Informatics Ltd* [2001] QB 424 at [11] (permission to intervene "on stringent terms as to the length of oral argument and costs"); *R v Minister of Agriculture, Fisheries & Food, ex p S.P. Anastasiou (Pissouri)* [1994] COD 329 (late application to intervene granted subject to undertaking not to raise certain political issues); *R v Secretary of State for the Environment, ex p O'Byrne* The Times 12th November 1999 (local authority joined as second defendant, on terms that even if unsuccessful claimant would not have to bear its costs); *R v Broadcasting Standards Commission, ex p British Broadcasting Corporation* [2001] QB 885 at [5] (Liberty permitted to intervene, but "confined by the Court to making written submissions").

(B) THIRD PARTY PARTICIPATION ON AN ART 234 REFERENCE.[121] *R v Secretary of State for the Environment, ex p Standley* [1999] QB 1279, 1285B (NFU given permission, by national court, to make submissions on the reference to the ECJ, in support of the claimant); *R v Minister of Agriculture Fisheries and Food, ex p SP Anastasiou (Pissouri)* [1994] COD 329 (order that third party participate in an existing Article 234 reference), *Anastasiou* [1995] COD 339 (third party making application for a reference itself); *R v Monopolies and Mergers Commission, ex p Milk Marque Ltd* [2000] COD 329 and 330 (although not a person directly affected, and so not formally a "party", court ruling that Dairy Industry Federation a proper person to be heard and indicating that appropriate to be heard on reference to ECJ, though ultimately that was a matter for the ECJ); *R (First Corporate Shipping Ltd) v Secretary of State for the Environment, Transport and the Regions* [2001] All ER (EC) 177 (domestic court had ordered that WWF be joined for the purpose of the reference it had made at the permission stage); *R (International Air Transport Association) v Department of Transport* [2004] EWHC 1721 (Admin) (Court directing that witness statements by European and German airline associations stand as evidence in the Art 234 reference proceedings, at their own costs).

(C) INTERIM REMEDY SOUGHT AGAINST THIRD PARTY.[122] *R v Secretary of State for Health, ex p Scotia Pharmaceuticals International Ltd (No.1)* [1997] EuLR 625, 646B (concluding, if necessary, that applicant could at domestic law obtain interim remedy against third party by reason of the latter's status in the proceedings; notwithstanding the *Siskina* [1979] AC 210 (no interim remedy where no cause of action)); *R v Secretary of State for the Environment, ex p Rose Theatre Trust Company* [1990] COD 47 (third party successfully applying to discharge interim remedy); *R v Licensing Authority Established By The Medicines*

---

[121] Daniel Denman [2001] JR 211.

[122] This subparagraph in a previous edition was cited in *R (Brent London Borough Council) v Fed 2000* [2006] EWHC 2282 (Admin) at [52].

Act 1968, ex p Rhone Poulenc Rorer Ltd [1998] EuLR 127, 142F (Laws J: "there is [no] ... rule that an injunction in judicial review may be granted only against the public body whose decision is impugned; a third party, such as the importers in this case, who are `directly affected' within Order 53 r.5(3), may be enjoined if it is just and convenient to do so"), 134G-135B (refusing to allow third parties, at hearing of application for stay pending reference, to go behind judge's findings when making the reference (especially where they had notice of that hearing and did not appear)); *R v Medicines Control Agency, ex p Smith and Nephew Pharmaceuticals Ltd* 26th March 1999 unrep. (comments as to when might be appropriate for third parties to seek protection of cross-undertaking in damages); *R v Durham County Council, ex p Huddleston* [2000] Env LR D21 (interim injunction against third party, granted in the wider public interest, notwithstanding absence of a cross-undertaking in damages); *R (Prokopp) v London Underground Ltd* [2003] EWHC 960 (Admin) at [15] (Collins J: "If a developer is about to take what may be irrevocable steps which are said to be unlawful ... an individual can seek and, if appropriate, obtain interim relief... His claim will initially be against the developer, but he must notify the [local planning authority] and add it ... as defendant") (CA is at [2003] EWCA Civ 961 [2004] Env LR 170).

(D) APPEAL BY THIRD PARTY. <23.2.5>.

(E) COSTS IN FAVOUR OF THIRD PARTY. <18.1.7> and <18.1.8> (costs in favour third party); <18.3.3(C)> (permission costs in favour of third party); <18.5.6(C)> (third party costs and discontinuance).

(F) COSTS AGAINST THIRD PARTY. <18.1.9>.

(G) THIRD PARTY INTERVENTION IN THE HOUSE OF LORDS. *R v Secretary of State for the Home Department, ex p Sivakumaran* [1988] AC 958, 992D (UN High Commissioner for Refugees); *R v Immigration Appeal Tribunal, ex p Shah* [1999] 2 AC 629 (UNHCR); *R v Bournewood Community and Mental Health NHS Trust, ex p L* [1999] 1 AC 458, 481D (Mental Health Act Commission, Registered Nursing Home Association and Secretary of State); *R v Bow Street Metropolitan Stipendiary Magistrate, ex p Pinochet Ugarte* [2000] 1 AC 61 and *R v Bow Street Metropolitan Stipendiary Magistrate, ex p Pinochet Ugarte (No.3)* [2000] 1 AC 147 (oral submissions by Amnesty International and others; written submissions from Human Rights Watch); *R v Khan (Sultan)* [1997] AC 558, 565H, 579C-D (written submissions); *R (Alconbury Developments Ltd) v Secretary of State for the Environment Transport and the Regions* [2001] UKHL 23 [2003] 2 AC 295 at [3] (intervention by the Lord Advocate, since related case had arisen in Scotland); *R v Independent Television Commission, ex p TV Danmark 1 Ltd* [2001] UKHL 42 [2001] 1 WLR 1604 at [32] (oral participation by the Secretary of State; written submissions by BBC and ITV); *R v Shayler* [2002] UKHL 11 [2003] 1 AC 247 (intervention by newspapers); *Wilson v First County Trust Ltd* [2003] UKHL 40 [2004] 1 AC 816 at [2] (Secretary of State intervening as to declaration of incompatibility, and Speaker of House of Commons and Clerk to the Parliaments intervening as to the use of Hansard); *R (Middleton) v West Somerset Coroner* [2004] UKHL 10 [2004] 2 AC 182 at [7] (written submissions by the Coroners' Society, the Northern Ireland Human Rights Commission, and Inquest); *R (Ullah) v Secretary of State for the Home Department* [2004] UKHL 26 [2004] 2 AC 323 at [5] ("valuable interventions on behalf of JUSTICE, Liberty and the Joint Council for the Welfare of Immigrants"); *R (Jackson) v Attorney General* [2005] UKHL 56 [2006] 1 AC 262 (League Against Cruel Sports).

22.2.9 Third party intervention by the State/Government.[123] *Doherty v Birmingham City Council* [2008] UKHL 57 [2008] 3 WLR 636 (Secretary of State intervening as to whether HRA defence available to local authority possession proceedings); *Wilson v First County Trust Ltd* [2003] UKHL 40 [2004] 1 AC 816 at [2] (Secretary of State intervening in consumer credit case

---

[123] Philip Havers QC & Christopher Mellor [2004] JR 130.

where declaration of incompatibility in issue); *R v Bournewood Community and Mental Health NHS Trust, ex p L* [1999] 1 AC 458, 481D (intervention by Secretary of State); *R v Wandsworth London Borough Council, ex p O* [2000] 1 WLR 2539, 2548C (Court of Appeal inviting Secretary of State to intervene); *R v Rent Officer Service, ex p Muldoon* [1996] 1 WLR 1103 (HL rejecting Secretary of State's application to be served as a person directly affected); *Begum v Tower Hamlets London Borough Council* [2003] UKHL 5 [2003] 2 AC 430 at [25] (Article 6 case regarding local authority decision-making where "the First Secretary of State was, on account of the general importance of the case for the public administration, given leave to intervene"); *R (Alconbury Developments Ltd) v Secretary of State for the Environment Transport and the Regions* [2001] UKHL 23 [2003] 2 AC 295 at [3] (intervention by the Lord Advocate, since related case had arisen in Scotland); *R v Independent Television Commission, ex p TV Danmark 1 Ltd* [2001] UKHL 42 [2001] 1 WLR 1604 at [32] (oral participation by the Secretary of State); *Roe v Sheffield City Council* [2003] EWCA Civ 1 [2004] QB 653 at [87] (Sedley LJ, considering actionability for breach of statutory duty not to be a proper issue for third party intervention by the Secretary of State, just because of its knock-on effect), [104] (Hale LJ, disagreeing, given the "strong policy element"); *R (Sivasubramaniam) v Wandsworth County Court* [2002] EWCA Civ 1738 [2003] 1 WLR 475 at [1] (Lord Chancellor's Department intervening because of points of principle arising as to the availability of judicial review of decisions of the county court); *Lawal v Northern Spirit Ltd* [2003] UKHL 35 [2004] 1 All ER 187 (Lord Chancellor's Department intervening on question of apparent bias where counsel had acted as part-time chairman of EAT); *Evans v Amicus Healthcare Ltd* [2004] EWCA Civ 727 [2005] Fam 1 at [42] (Secretary of State intervening because of HRA-compatibility and questions of "construction of legislation affecting a material aspect of the public interest").

22.2.10 Public interest intervention. See generally the Justice/PLP Report, *A Matter of Public Interest: Reforming the Law and Practice on Interventions in Public Interest Cases* (1996), endorsed in *R v Chief Constable of the North Wales Police, ex p AB* [1999] QB 396, 426B-C; *Public Law Project, Third Party Interventions in Judicial Review: An Action Research Study* (PLP, May 2001); *Jones v Ministry of Interior of Saudi Arabia* [2006] UKHL 26 [2007] 1 AC 270 (Redress, Amnesty, Interights and JUSTICE); *R (Munjaz) v Mersey Care NHS Trust* [2005] UKHL 58 [2006] 2 AC 148 (Mind and Mental Health Act Commission); *R (Ullah) v Secretary of State for the Home Department* [2004] UKHL 26 [2004] 2 AC 323 (various NGOs); *R (McCann) v Crown Court at Manchester* [2002] UKHL 39 [2003] 1 AC 787 at [38] (Liberty); *R (Saadi) v Secretary of State for the Home Department* [2002] UKHL 41 [2002] 1 WLR 3131 (Liberty, Justice and Aire Centre); *R (Limbuela) v Secretary of State for the Home Department* [2005] UKHL 66 [2006] 1 AC 396 at [35] (Shelter); *R (Corner House Research) v Secretary of State for Trade and Industry* [2005] EWCA Civ 192 [2005] 1 WLR 2600 at [4] (Public Law Project); *Roe v Sheffield City Council* [2003] EWCA Civ 1 [2004] QB 653 at [84] (Sedley LJ: "The most apparent value of interventions is in public law cases, where aspects of the public interest in a legal issue of general importance may be represented by neither of the two parties before the court. Both NGOs and ministers may play a valuable role here").

22.2.11 Friend of the Court (amicus curiae). *R (Secretary of State for Defence) v Pensions Appeal Tribunal* [2005] EWHC 1775 (Admin) at [12] (adjournment for AG to consider providing amicus to avoid one-sided argument on important point); *R v Cambridge District Health Authority, ex p B (No.2)* [1996] 1 FLR 375 (Official Solicitor acting as an amicus curiae); *R (Ministry of Defence) v Wiltshire & Swindon Coroner* [2005] EWHC 889 (Admin) [2006] 1 WLR 134 at [42] (court can request, but up to Attorney-General to decide whether to appoint); *London Borough of Islington v Camp* (1999) [2004] LGR 58, 66c ("Recourse to an amicus should be sparing, given the cost to central funds, but in an appropriate case it is capable of remedying a deficiency arising out of the unwillingness or inability of one of the parties to present full submissions"); <18.1.10> (costs and amicus curiae).

22.3 **Disposal without a hearing.**[124] Judicial review can be disposed of without a hearing, where: (1) the claim is withdrawn; (2) the defendant (and interested parties) concede; or (3) the parties agree to determination on the papers.

22.3.1 **Substantive decision without a hearing.** See CPR 54.18 <64.2>; ACO:NFG <64.4> para 14.1; Woolf Report, *Access to Justice* (1996) at p.255 (proposal for disposal of some contested applications without a hearing of the judicial review, where the case is suitable and the parties agree); *R (Sinclair Gardens Investments (Kensington) Ltd v Lands Tribunal* [2004] EWHC 1910 (Admin) at [21] (by agreement, key issue dealt with on the basis of written submissions) (CA is [2005] EWCA Civ 1305 [2006] 3 All ER 650); *R (Reading Borough Council) v Admissions Appeal Panel for Reading Borough Council* [2005] EWHC 2378 (Admin) [2006] ELR 186 at [10] (where defendant agreeing decisions unlawful, order for determination on documents under CPR 54.18 unless third parties objecting within 7 days), [11] (CPR 54.18 inapt if third party not agreeing); *R (Baiai) v Secretary of State for the Home Department (No.2)* [2006] EWHC 1454 (Admin) [2007] 1 WLR 735 at [6] (further issues resolved on written submissions only), [76] (unsatisfactory that urgency denying judge benefit of oral argument) (HL is [2008] UKHL 53 [2008] 3 WLR 549).

22.3.2 **Discontinuance by the claimant.** *Practice Direction (Administrative Court: Uncontested Proceedings)* [2008] 1 WLR 1377 at [3c] (discontinuance on notice under CPR 38).

22.3.3 **Agreed final orders.** *Practice Direction (Administrative Court: Uncontested Proceedings)* [2008] 1 WLR 1377 at [1] (agreed determination, requiring a court order, dealt with by parties lodging proposed order and supporting statement with authorities, to be dealt with by Crown Office Master/ Deputy Master), [3a] (agreed withdrawal, where no court order or costs order sought, dealt with by ACO staff on basis of letter from parties); *R v St Helen's Justices, ex p Jones* [1999] 2 All ER 73 (Court declining to sign consent order agreed by the parties, not being persuaded of its power to grant the remedy in question); *R (Meredith) v Merthyr Tydfil County Borough Council* [2002] EWHC 634 (Admin) (application not opposed, indeed supported, by defendant council) at [7] (Elias J: "it is incumbent upon the court to be satisfied that any orders it makes can properly be given as a matter of law ... [so] that the integrity of the legal process itself should be respected"); *R v Legal Aid Board, ex p Kaim Todner* [1999] QB 966 (CA proceeding to deal with anonymity issue despite claimant's threat to withdraw if no interim anonymity granted); *Estate of M Kingsley (dec'd) v Secretary of State for Transport* [1994] COD 358 (since reviewing court is guardian of the public interest, any order agreeing to discontinuance of the proceedings or agreeing to the granting of consent requiring the court's approval); *R v Secretary of State for the Home Department, ex p Gashi* 15th June 2000 unrep. (although claims being withdrawn, appropriate to rule on certain issues because raised or likely to be raised in several pending cases); *R v Independent Appeals Tribunal of Hillingdon London Borough Council, ex p Governing Body of Mellow Lane School* [2001] ELR 200 (court refusing to set aside consent order even though third party not consenting, because his rights protected on reconsideration).

22.3.4 **Refusal to consent and costs against non-appearing tribunal.** <18.1.12>.

22.3.5 **Costs and discontinuance/early disposal.** <18.5>.

---

[124] Gavin Eynon [1999] JR 153.

22.4 **The substantive hearing.** At the substantive hearing the Court will hear oral submissions, look at key documents and authorities, and raise questions. Judgment will then be delivered, having first been circulated in draft, and consequential matters will be dealt with in open court or on the papers.

22.4.1 **Rolled-up hearing.** <21.2.3>.

22.4.2 **Live evidence/cross-examination.** <17.4>.

22.4.3 **Amendment of grounds for judicial review.**<22.1.10>; *R v Hammersmith and Fulham London Borough Council, ex p Burkett* [2002] UKHL 23 [2002] 1 WLR 1593 at [31] (amendment to challenge later decision and overcome delay objection); *R (Middlebrook Mushrooms Ltd) v Agricultural Wages Board of England and Wales* [2004] EWHC 1447 (Admin) at [12] (amendment allowed, arising out of defendant's evidence and documents disclosed by it, and where issue important and arguable and would be unfair not to decide it); *R v Tower Hamlets London Borough Council, ex p Khalique* (1994) 26 HLR 517, 521, 523, 527 ("fundamental" grounds arising "in the course of the proceedings" and court granting declarations sought by way of amendment); *R v Chief Constable of the North Wales Police, ex p AB* [1999] QB 396, 426G-H (in CA claimant focusing on entirely new procedural fairness point); *R v Secretary of State for the Home Department, ex p Benwell* [1985] QB 554, 567C-D (no injustice from allowing amendment to include what had emerged as the most serious matter); *R v Immigration Appeal Tribunal, ex p Syeda Khatoon Shah* [1997] Imm AR 145 (Sedley J), 148 ("in the area of asylum law, potentially involving as it always does the right to life, the court ought not in my view to be difficult or rigid provided a sensible endeavour is being made to crystallise in serviceable form the legal issue thrown up by the evidence and findings"); *R v Secretary of State for the Home Department, ex p Bugdaycay* [1987] AC 514 (Musisi's successful unreasonableness challenge taken up for the first time in the HL); *R v Kent County Council, ex p C* [1998] ELR 108, 119G-H (not permitting new point to be advanced; defendant not having had notice of it and the opportunity of answering it by evidence); *R v Institute of Chartered Accountants, ex p Bruce* 22nd October 1986 unrep. (where substantial amendment, appropriate to apply same test as for permission to seek judicial review); *Steinberg v McLeod Russel Holdings plc* [1996] COD 25 (refusing permission to amend, in statutory appeal, on grounds of delay); *R v Airport Coordination Ltd, ex p States of Guernsey Transport Board* 16th October 1998 unrep. (desirability of determining the real question, whether causing prejudice or lengthening the proceedings); *R v Portsmouth City Council, ex p Faludy* [1999] ELR 115 (CA declining to consider new argument; emphasising importance of taking points at the outset); *R v London Borough of Bromley, ex p Crystal Palace Campaign* 21st December 1998 unrep. (permission to argue new point "a pragmatic decision by the court. To hear the arguments for and against granting [permission] would, in the present case, have taken the same amount of time as to hear the arguments on the substantive point"); *R v Secretary of State for the Home Department, ex p Dinc* [1999] INLR 256, 262A (unsatisfactory that Secretary of State "never invited to address his mind (and so his evidence) to objections formulated on the wing"); *R (O'Byrne) v Secretary of State for the Environment, Transport and the Regions* [2001] EWCA Civ 499 [2002] HLR 567 (CA) at [15] (claimant given permission to amend the notice of appeal to take the only seriously arguable point in the case) (HL is at [2002] UKHL 45 [2002] 1 WLR 3250); *Cachia v Faluyi* [2001] EWCA Civ 998 [2001] 1 WLR 1966 at [16] (permission to amend granted to take HRA point, "since the court would in any event have been obliged to consider it pursuant to our duty under section 6(1) of the Act"); *R (Association of Pharmaceutical Importers) v Secretary of State for Health* [2001] EWCA Civ 1986 [2002] EuLR 197 at [39] (reply point, as to breach of EC Transparency Directive, not open to claimant because not pleaded); *R (M-P) v London Borough of Barking* [2002] EWHC 2483 (Admin) [2003] ELR 144 at [29] (amendment refused because too late); *R (Smith) v Parole Board* [2003]

EWCA Civ 1014 [2003] 1 WLR 2548 at [16] ("It is the obligation of parties to applications for judicial review, as in the case of oral litigation, to give as much notice as possible of their full case and to bring forward their full case at the start. However ... there are going to be ... situations where good sense makes it clear that the argument should be wider than it would otherwise be if it was confined to the grounds where permission has been granted"); *R (Hargrave) v Stroud District Council* [2002] EWCA Civ 1281 [2002] 3 PLR 115 at [40] (Buxton LJ: "if an irrationality challenge is to be taken it needs to be taken early and in detail, and not left to be explained in this court"); *B v Secretary of State for Work and Pensions* [2005] EWCA Civ 929 [2005] 1 WLR 3796 at [17] (CA allowing reliance for first time on HRA argument, although "regrettable" that arising "so late in the day"; "wrong to shut the argument out" since "akin to submissions going to jurisdiction"); *R (Greenpeace Ltd) v Secretary of State for the Environment, Food and Rural Affairs* [2005] EWCA Civ 1656 [2006] Env LR 627 at [15] ("the responsible approach now is surely to have the substantial issues ... properly settled by the court's adjudication"); <10.4.3> (defendant's candour leading to emergence of additional grounds); <22.4.13> (late plum-picking undesirable).

22.4.4 Substitution of claimant.[125] *R v Secretary of State for the Environment, ex p Friends of the Earth* (1995) 7 Admin LR 793, 794E-F (following death of individual claimant since hearing at first instance, CA granting permission for judicial review, refusing judicial review and granting permission to appeal to a replacement individual); *R v Gloucestershire County Council, ex p Barry* [1996] 4 All ER 421 (CA), 424c (substitution of daughter and RADAR, for deceased claimant); *R v North West Leicestershire District Council, ex p Moses* [2000] Env LR 443, 458 ("had the challenge from every other standpoint been soundly based, it would be unfortunate to have to reject it - rather, say, than substitute for Ms Moses another [claimant] who, as a resident of Kegworth, was equally concerned about the airport's extension - merely because of Ms Moses' move"); *R v Richmond London Borough Council, ex p Watson* [2002] UKHL 34 [2002] 2 AC 1127 at 585D (substitution after death of named claimant); *R (Beeson) v Dorset County Council* [2002] EWCA Civ 1812 [2003] UKHRR 353 at [2] (personal representatives substituted for deceased claimant since issues affected his estate and were "of some general importance").

22.4.5 Judge/venue. See ACO:NFG <64.4> para 2.2; *R (Mohamad) v Special Adjudicator* [2002] EWHC 2496 (Admin) (Munby J, commenting that "normal practice" for a substantive application not to come before the same judge who originally refused permission on the papers, but that no objection here); cf. *Sengupta v Holmes* [2002] EWCA Civ 1104 (not unfair for judge who had refused permission to appeal on the papers to sit on substantive appeal); <21.2.14> (Chancery/Family judge); *R v Council of the Society of Lloyds, ex p Johnson* 16th August 1996 unrep. (single Lord Justice sitting in the Admin Court); *R (Spiro) v Immigration Appeal Tribunal* [2001] EWCA Civ 2094 [2002] Imm AR 356 at [7] (not inappropriate for Collins J, albeit President of the Immigration Appeal Tribunal, to consider judicial review of the IAT "in his role as a judge of the High Court"); *R (Deepdock Ltd) v Welsh Ministers* [2007] EWHC 3346 (Admin) (judicial review of Welsh Minister should be heard in Wales).

22.4.6 Divisional Court. Civil examples include *R (Alconbury Developments Ltd) v Secretary of State for the Environment Transport and the Regions* [2001] UKHRR 270; *R (Campaign for Nuclear Disarmament) v Prime Minister* [2002] EWHC 2759 (Admin) [2003] 3 LRC 335; <21.2.14>; <23.2.1> (criminal cause or matter); *Douglas v Hello! Ltd (No.3)* [2003] EWHC 786 (Ch) [2003] 3 All ER 996 at [94] (split 2-judge CA aborting appeal for listing before a 3-judge court because unable to agree).

---

[125] Martha Grekos [2003] JR 174.

22.4.7 Court of Appeal reserving the substantive hearing to itself. <23.1.12>.

22.4.8 Hearing of a preliminary issue. See CPR 1.4(1), (2)(d) & (i); *R v Disciplinary Committee of the Jockey Club, ex p Aga Khan* [1993] 1 WLR 909 (whether Jockey Club amenable to judicial review); *R (Evans) v University of Cambridge* [2002] EWHC 1382 (Admin) [2003] ELR 8 at [3] (permission limited to whether decisions amenable to judicial review, with permission on remaining issues to await the outcome of that hearing); *R v Association of British Travel Agents, ex p Sunspell Ltd* [2001] ACD 88 (whether ABTA disciplinary decisions amenable to judicial review); *R (A) v Partnerships in Care Ltd* [2002] EWHC 529 (Admin) [2002] 1 WLR 2610 (reviewability of managers of private psychiatric hospital); *R (Mullins) v Appeal Board of the Jockey Club* [2005] EWHC 2197 (Admin) (reviewability of Jockey Club appeal board); *R (Lim) v Secretary of State for the Home Department* [2006] EWHC 3004 (Admin) (preliminary issues of precedent fact and alternative remedy); *R (Balbo B & C Auto Transporti Internationali) v Secretary of State for the Home Department* [2001] EWHC Admin 195 [2001] 1 WLR 1556 (alternative remedy); *R (Carvill) v Commissioners of Inland Revenue* [2002] EWHC 1488 (Ch) [2002] STC 1167 (fairness and legality); *R (Rose) v Secretary of State for Health* [2002] EWHC 1593 (Admin) [2002] 2 FLR 962 (whether Art 8 engaged); *R (Khatun) v London Borough of Newham* [2004] EWCA Civ 55 [2005] QB 37 at [4] (applicability of statute); *R (Friends of the Earth Ltd) v Environment Agency* [2003] EWHC 3193 (Admin) [2004] Env LR 615 (claim succeeding on preliminary issue); *R (Cardiff County Council) v Customs and Excise Commissioners* [2003] EWCA Civ 1456 at [1] (recoverability of `overpaid' VAT); *R (M) v Lambeth London Borough Council* [2008] EWHC 1364 (Admin) (age-determination function); *A v B* [2008] EWHC 1512 (Admin) (whether judicial review ousted by statute).

22.4.9 Partial/limited permission: whether to extend. See CPR 54.15 <64.2>; *R (Smith) v Parole Board* [2003] EWCA Civ 1014 [2003] 1 WLR 2548 (discussing approach to be taken to whether Court hearing substantive judicial review should give claimant permission to argue ground for which permission originally refused) at [16] (need for "good reason for altering the view of the single judge taken at the permission stage, no further sensible guidance can be provided"), [17] (need for advance notification); *R (Hunt) v Criminal Cases Review Commission* [2001] QB 1108 at [14] (sensible and convenient approach is for claimant to intimate to the defendant the wish to develop argument on a point for which permission was refused); *R (Smith) v Parole Board* [2003] EWCA Civ 1014 [2003] 1 WLR 2548 (claimant not needing to appeal where restricted permission, not following *R (Opoku) v Principal of Southwark College* [2002] EWHC 2092 (Admin) [2003] 1 All ER 272); *R v Bow Street Stipendiary Magistrate, ex p Roberts* [1990] 1 WLR 1317 (claimant should serve notice of intention to rely on grounds for which permission refused); *R v Salisbury Magistrates Court, ex p G* 28th June 1999 unrep. (DC permitting claimant to take point at hearing of the judicial review on which permission had been refused); *R (A) v Hertfordshire County Council* [2001] LGR 435 at [11] (CA allowing another ground to be advanced, beyond that for which permission had been granted); *Nahar v Social Security Commissioners* [2001] EWHC Admin 1049 [2002] 2 FCR 442 (Administrative Court) at [17]-[19] (claimant given permission to argue human rights point on which permission had been refused).

22.4.10 Non-appearing/non-adversarial defendants. <2.5.7>.

22.4.11 Article 234 reference. <8.4>.

22.4.12 Defaulting defendant's participation. CPR 54.9(1)-(2) <64.2> (failure to lodge acknowledgment of service); *R (Montpeliers & Trevors Association) v City of Westminster* [2005] EWHC 16 (Admin) [2006] LGR 304 at [17] (granting permission to defendant to participate notwithstanding disobedience/ defiance of the rules).

22.4.13 **The oral argument.** *R (Lambert) v London Borough of Southwark* [2003] EWHC 2121 (Admin) at [39] (Jackson J, referring to Counsel as having "modified, and in one or two cases abandoned, contentions set out in his skeleton argument. I make no complaint whatsoever about the changes in position of the claimant's legal advisors. It is inevitable that issues become more focussed in the run up to a court hearing. It is also sensible for any advocate to concentrate on his stronger points and to pass over or to drop his weaker ones"); *R (Bateman) v Legal Services Commission* [2001] EWHC Admin 797 at [17] (Munby J, discussing by reference to an exchange between Pliny and Regalus the "tension between the desirable pursuit of forensic brevity and the advocate's understandable fear of inadvertently betraying his client's interests by not taking every possible point"), [18] ("one of the merits of great advocates ... has been the ability ruthlessly to sacrifice nine points and win on the tenth and best ... [T]he `leave no stone unturned' approach is no longer to be encouraged. Indeed, in the ordinary run of litigation - I leave on one side cases in which fundamental human rights are engaged, where somewhat different considerations may apply - it is simply no longer acceptable. On the contrary, CPR 44.3 can properly and where appropriate should be applied in such a way as positively to encourage litigants to be selective as to the points they take and positively to discourage litigants taking a multiplicity of `bad' points"); *R v Independent Television Commission, ex p Virgin Television Limited* [1996] EMLR 318 (criticising the "`pick out a plum' school of advocacy [which] is particularly dangerous (as well as being futile) in judicial review", involving "plum-picking" where "an unpleaded case is raised, effectively too late for any evidential reply").

22.4.14 **Post-hearing communication.** *Uphill v BRB (Residuary) Ltd* [2005] EWCA Civ 60 [2005] 1 WLR 2070 at [31] (important new authority should have been drawn to the judge's attention after the hearing, with a request to make further submissions).

22.4.15 **Draft judgment.**[126] *Egan v Motor Services (Bath) Ltd (Note)* [2007] EWCA Civ 1002 [2008] 1 WLR 1589 at [49]-[51] (inappropriate to write to judge on receipt of draft judgment requesting reconsideration of conclusions; exceptionally could seek further reasons or opportunity to make submissions on a decisive unargued point); *R (Edwards) v Environment Agency* [2008] UKHL 22 [2008] 1 WLR 1587 at [66] & [73] (draft HL judgment not an opportunity to reargue the case or introduce new arguments).

22.4.16 **Duty to take a note of the judgment.**[127] *Hertsmere Borough Council v Harty* [2001] EWCA Civ 1238 (Counsel's duty to take a note of judgment, in case of need for urgent appeal).

22.4.17 **Consequential matters.**
(A) COSTS. <P18>.
(B) SUMMARY ASSESSMENT OF COSTS. <18.2>.
(C) PERMISSION TO APPEAL. <23.2.3>.
(D) OTHER. *R (Khan) v Secretary of State for the Health* [2003] EWCA Civ 1129 [2004] 1 WLR 971 (post-judgment adjournment to allow amending regulations to secure HRA-compatibility); *R (Cash) v Northamptonshire Coroner* [2007] EWHC 1354 (Admin) [2007] 4 All ER 903 at [55] (dealing with consequential matters on written submissions).

22.4.18 **Closed hearings.** *R (Roberts) v Parole Board* [2005] UKHL 45 [2005] 2 AC 738

---

[126] James Maurici [2008] JR 193.

[127] Alexander Booth [2002] JR 176.

(judicial review involving closed hearing in High Court with special advocates); *R (Binyan Mohamed) v Secretary of State for Foreign and Commonwealth Affairs* [2008] EWHC 2048 (Admin) at [4] (closed sessions with special advocate); *R (Murungaru) v Secretary of State for the Home Department* [2008] EWCA Civ 1015 (closed hearing, with no need for special advocate).

> **P23 Appeal.** An Administrative Court refusal of permission, or substantive grant or refusal of judicial review, can be appealed.

23.1 Permission appeal
23.2 Substantive appeal

23.1 Permission appeal. Where, in a "civil" case, the Administrative Court refuses permission for judicial review on paper and on oral reconsideration, an appeal lies to the Court of Appeal (CA). The claimant needs double-permission: (1) permission to appeal; and then (2) permission for judicial review. Where the CA grants both (1) and (2), it may reserve the substantive decision to itself. Where (1) is granted but (2) refused, the claimant can appeal to the House of Lords. In a "criminal" case the CA has no jurisdiction, and permission will be for the Divisional Court (or, with permission, the House of Lords).

23.1.1 Permission appeal rules. See CPR 52.15 (judicial review appeals); ACO:NFG <64.4> para 18.1.

23.1.2 No appeal from the grant of permission. *R v Chief Constable of West Yorkshire, ex p Wilkinson* [2002] EWHC 2353 (Admin) at [40] (common ground "that the rules do not permit an appeal from the decision ... in granting permission"); *R (Kurdistan Workers Party) v Secretary of State for the Home Department* [2002] EWHC 644 (Admin) at [99] (referring to "the absence of any right of appeal against the grant of permission").

23.1.3 Civil and criminal cases. <23.2.1>; ACO:NFG <64.4> para 18.1 (civil), para 18.4 (criminal: no further remedy).

23.1.4 Permission appeal and claimant duty of candour. *R (Bown) v Secretary of State for Transport* [2003] EWCA Civ 1170 [2003] 3 PLR 100 (where permission to appeal being sought in a "without notice procedure" in the CA, and where issues as to delay or expedition, appellant obliged to make "full disclosure" of "countervailing considerations", or to notify the respondent) at [50] (CA referring to a "possible gap in the procedures for permission to appeal" as a "without notice procedure", where factors relating to delay or need for expedition: "Such factors should be known to the court, since they may be very relevant to its exercise of any discretion, particularly as to the significance of delay or the need for expedition. In our view, in such cases, the claimant should, as part of his duty of full disclosure, provide the court with information about countervailing considerations, so far as not apparent from the documents, or alternatively give notice to the proposed respondents to enable them to put any relevant information before the court").

23.1.5 Importance of permission recourse to the CA. *Kemper Reinsurance Company v Minister of Finance* [2000] 1 AC 1, 15B (Lord Hoffmann: "The law reports reveal a number of important points of administrative law which have been decided by the Court of Appeal or House of Lords in cases in which [permission] was refused at first instance"); *R v Oxfordshire County Council, ex p Sunningwell Parish Council* [2000] 1 AC 335, 349B-C (CA granting permission, dismissing substantive application and giving permission to bring (ultimately successful) appeal in HL); *R v Commissioner for the Special Purposes of the Income Tax Acts, ex p Stipplechoice* The Times 23rd January 1985 and *R v Beverley County Court, ex p Brown* The Times 25th January 1985 (expressing the constitutional importance of the right of renewal to the Court of Appeal, at a time of a legislative proposal to remove it); *Leech v Deputy Governor of Parkhurst Prison* [1988] AC 533 (permission originally refused).

23.1.6 The approach of the CA. *R (Werner) v Inland Revenue Commissioners* [2002] EWCA

Civ 979 [2002] STC 1213[128] at [31] (Brooke LJ: "Under [CPR 52.15] the Court of Appeal will apply the now familiar test of determining whether an appeal against a judge's refusal of permission would have a real prospect of success, in the sense that the prospect of success is not merely 'fanciful' (*Swain v Hillman* [2001] 1 All ER 91). In applying this test it will inevitably examine the merits of the original application, and if it considers that the application is fit for consideration at a substantive judicial review hearing it will of course decide that the prospects of a successful appeal are not fanciful. It will probably go on to grant permission to apply for judicial review itself under CPR 52.15(3)"), [32] ("If it considers that there is a real prospect of the appellant being able to show at a contested appeal hearing that the application is fit for consideration at a substantive judicial review hearing but it wishes to hear the respondent on the matter, it will probably adjourn the application to be heard on notice, with the appeal to follow if permission is granted. This will represent a speedier and more convenient way of dealing with the matter than merely granting permission to appeal there and then, and then holding things up until a substantive appeal hearing can be heard on the question whether the appeal should be allowed and permission to apply for judicial review granted"), [33] ("The House of Lords has now made it clear that if this court refuses permission to appeal against a refusal of permission to apply for judicial review there is no further right of appeal (*R v Secretary of State for Trade and Industry, ex p Eastaway* [2000] 1 WLR 2222). If, on the other hand, this court grants permission to appeal but then refuses permission to apply for judicial review at the substantive appeal hearing, there is potentially a right of appeal to the House of Lords (see *R v Hammersmith and Fulham London Borough Council, ex p Burkett* [2002] UKHL 23 [2002] 1 WLR 1593)").

23.1.7 **Double-permission.**

(A) GENERAL. *R (M) v Homerton University Hospital* [2008] EWCA Civ 197 at [1] (permission to appeal granted at beginning of hearing, then hearing argument on appeal against refusal of permission for judicial review); *R v Hammersmith and Fulham London Borough Council, ex p Burkett* [2001] Env LR 684 (CA) at [7] (permission to appeal granted after hearing appellant only, then hearing all parties on permission for judicial review); *R (Plowman) v Secretary of State for Foreign and Commonwealth Affairs* [2001] EWHC Admin 617 (in post-judgment argument, parties accepting that Administrative Court judge having power to give permission to appeal against refusal of permission to claim judicial review).
(B) IMPLICATIONS FOR HL JURISDICTION.[129] *R v Secretary of State for Trade and Industry, ex p Eastaway* [2000] 1 WLR 2222 (where CA has refused permission to appeal, HL having no jurisdiction); *R v Hammersmith and Fulham London Borough Council, ex p Burkett* [2002] UKHL 23 [2002] 1 WLR 1593 (HL having jurisdiction to consider whether to grant permission for judicial review where CA had (a) granted permission to appeal from Administrative Court refusal of permission for judicial review but (b) had dismissed the appeal).
(C) CA ACTING TO PRESERVE APPEAL RIGHTS. *R v Oxfordshire County Council, ex p Sunningwell Parish Council* [2000] 1 AC 335, 349B-C (CA granting permission, but in light of CA authority which may have been wrongly decided, refusing substantive application and granting permission to appeal to HL); *R v Director of Public Prosecutions, ex p Camelot Group Plc* (1998) 10 Admin LR 93, 105E-F (permission treated as hearing of the judicial review by CA so that dismissal not necessarily the end for claimant's arguments); *R v Her Majesty's Treasury, ex p Shepherd Neame Ltd* (1999) 11 Admin LR 517, 518b (permission given by CA to preserve position as to petition to HL); *R v Parliamentary Commissioner for Standards, ex p Al Fayed* [1998] 1 WLR 669 (on a permission appeal, CA recognising the importance of the

---

[128] Michael Fordham & James Maurici [2003] JR 97.

[129] Michael Beloff QC & Helen Mountfield [1998] JR 119; Richard Fisher [2001] JR 69.

issue, dismissing the proceedings by granting permission and treating the hearing as the substantive application, to leave permission open to the HL).

23.1.8 **Stay of immigration removal.** *R (Pharis) v Secretary of State for the Home Department* [2004] EWCA Civ 654 [2004] 1 WLR 2590 at [19] (CA explaining that: "in future the lodging of a notice of appeal in the Court of Appeal in an immigration or asylum case when the refusal of a High Court judge to grant permission to apply for judicial review is under challenge should not be interpreted as giving rise to an automatic stay of deportation process. If the appellant wishes to seek a stay, he/she must make an express application for this purpose which the staff of the Civil Appeals Office must place before a judge of this court for a ruling on paper, as already happens when a stay is sought in connection with possession proceedings when the execution of a warrant of possession is imminent"): cf. *Santur* <21.2.14>.

23.1.9 **Appeal and partial/conditional permission.**
(A) ADMINISTRATIVE COURT PARTIAL PERMISSION. <22.4.9> (effect of partial permission at substantive hearing); *R (Smith) v Parole Board* [2003] EWCA Civ 1014 [2003] 1 WLR 2548 (CA allowing appeal from decision by judge at substantive hearing, refusing to allow permission to rely on ground for which permission originally refused; judge entitled to allow such a ground to be advanced where good reason).
(B) POSITION WHERE CA PARTIAL PERMISSION. *R v Radio Authority, ex p Wildman* [1999] COD 255 (open to first instance judge to allow reliance on a ground on which permission had been refused by CA, if some development had occurred, but natural to pay greatest of attention to views expressed by CA in refusing permission on that ground); *R (Pelling) v Bow County Court* [2001] UKHRR 165 at [13] (DC suggesting that where CA granting partial permission, "the substance of the decision stands on the same level with regard to this court as would the decision of any permission granting judge"), at [14] (permission to re-open grounds following partial permission refused in the circumstances).

23.1.10 **Appeal and directions/orders.** <20.1.14> (appeal and interim remedy); <31.5.8> (interim remedy and discretionary control); <8.4.3> (appeal and Art 234 reference); *R (Ghadami) v Harlow District Council* [2004] EWCA Civ 891 (successful appeal against listing directions since, although CA slow to interfere with case-management decisions, here made without sufficient regard to directions originally made).

23.1.11 **Hopeless permission appeals.** *R v Secretary of State for the Home Department, ex p Panther* (1996) 8 Admin LR 154, 162F-G (not surprising that application for permission launched, but "a wholly different matter to renew the application, after refusal by the Judge, to this court"); *In re Southgate's Application* The Times 8th November 1994; *R (Nine Nepalese Asylum Seekers) v Immigration Appeal Tribunal* [2003] EWCA Civ 1892 (Brooke LJ: "applications of this kind represent an abuse of the processes of this court, which exists to resolve genuine points of law in judicial review cases, and is not a fourth tier appellate court of fact when the original tribunal of fact has disbelieved an applicant").

23.1.12 **CA reserving substantive hearing to itself.** See CPR 52.15(4); *R (B) v Secretary of State for the Foreign and Commonwealth Office* [2004] EWCA Civ 1344 [2005] QB 643 at [2] (CA reserving an issue of extra-territorial application of the HRA to itself, the issue being "both novel and important"); *R (M) v Gateshead Metropolitan Borough Council* [2006] EWCA Civ 221 [2006] QB 650 at [14]; *R (Young) v Oxford City Council* [2002] EWCA Civ 990 [2002] 3 PLR 86 at [2], [41] (on appeal from refusal of permission for judicial review, Court of Appeal proceeding to determine the case itself); ditto *R (Ozcan) v Immigration Appeal Tribunal* [2002] EWCA Civ 1133 at [1] and *R (Zhou) v Secretary of State for the Home Department* [2003] EWCA Civ 51 [2003] INLR 211 at [4] (each treating appeal from refusal of permission as substantive judicial review); *R (Sacker) v HM Coroner for West Yorkshire* [2003] EWCA Civ 217 [2003] 2 All ER 278 (CA hearing substantive judicial review claim); *R (Greenpeace Ltd) v Secretary of State for the Environment, Food and Rural Affairs* [2002] EWCA Civ 1036 [2002] 1 WLR 3304 at [1] ("given that there had been a full hearing below with all parties represented"); *R v Secretary of State for the Home Department, ex p Adan* [2001] 2 AC 477, 483C-485D (CA having jurisdiction to entertain substantive application); *R v Secretary of State for the Home Department, ex p Turgut* [2001] 1 All ER 719, 736d (CA "will not usually reserve the trial of the matter to itself"); *R v Secretary of State for the Home Department, ex p Gallagher* [1996] 2 CMLR 951 (appeal likely in any event); *R v Commissioners of Inland Revenue, ex p Ulster Bank Ltd* [1997] STC 832, 844d-e (correctness of earlier decision being questioned); *R v Secretary of State for the Home Department, ex p Sanusi* [1999] IRLR 198, 199E (point of law of general importance on which early definitive ruling desirable); *R v Oxfordshire County Council, ex p Sunningwell Parish Council* [2000] 1 AC 335, 349B-C (CA granting permission but refusing substantive application and granting permission to appeal to HL); *R v Secretary of State for the Home Department, ex p Daly* [1999] COD 388 (challenge to previous authority); *R v Secretary of State for the Environment, Transport and the Regions, ex p Spath Holme* [2001] 2 AC 349, 354C (CA) at [2] ("We are therefore exercising an original jurisdiction, but as the Court of Appeal and not as a Divisional Court"); *R (W) v Lambeth London Borough Council* [2002] EWCA Civ 613 [2002] 2 All ER 901 (CA) at [1] (questioning earlier CA authority); *R (Smith) v Parole Board* [2003] EWCA Civ 1014 [2003] 1 WLR 2548 at [20] ("final disposal ... most unlikely to be achieved by a decision below the Court of Appeal"); *R (West) v Lloyds of London* [2004] EWCA Civ 506 [2004] 3 All ER 251 at [1] (CA directing reviewability issue to be decided first, and reserving that issue to itself), [2] (such a course being appropriate given a line of first instance authority).

23.1.13 **Summary assessment of costs.** See CPR 52PD para 14.1-14.2.

23.2 Substantive appeal.

An appeal lies, in a civil case, from an Administrative Court decision on a substantive hearing, with the permission of that Court or of the CA itself. Adherence to the rules on timing and documents is important. From the CA there is a further appeal, with permission, to the House of Lords. In a criminal matter, appeal is direct from the Administrative Court (a Divisional Court) to the HL, with permission and a certification of public importance.

23.2.1 Appeals: civil and criminal matters.[130]
(A) GENERAL. ACO:NFG <64.4> para 18.2 (civil), para 18.5 (criminal); Administration of Justice Act 1960 s.1(1); Supreme Court Act 1981 s.18(1)(a); *R v Secretary of State for the Home Department, ex p Ogilvy* [1996] COD 497 (CA having no jurisdiction over criminal cause or matter).
(B) "CRIMINAL CAUSE OR MATTER".[131] *Government of the United States of America v Montgomery* [2001] UKHL 3 [2001] 1 WLR 196 (restraint order, to enforce external confiscation order, essentially civil in character even though granted in consequence of criminal proceedings); *R (McCann) v Crown Court at Manchester* [2001] EWCA Civ 281 [2001] 1 WLR 1084 (anti-social behaviour orders civil matters); *R (South West Yorkshire Mental Health NHS Trust) v Bradford Crown Court* [2003] EWCA Civ 1857 [2004] 1 WLR 1664 (crown court orders for secure detention following jury trial of defendant unfit to stand trial criminal); *R*

---

[130] Jonathan Lewis [2007] JR 204.

[131] Ben Rayment [1999] JR 26.

(Aru) v Chief Constable of Merseyside [2004] EWCA Civ 199 [2004] 1 WLR 1697 (police caution a criminal cause or matter).

23.2.2 Civil appeals: rules/compliance. See CPR 52 and CPR 52PD; *Scribes West Ltd v Relsa Anstalt (No.1)* [2004] EWCA Civ 835 at [31] ("the judges of the Court of Appeal attach great importance to the need for all the papers for an appeal to be filed at least seven days before the hearing"); *Haggis v Director of Public Prosecutions* [2003] EWHC 2481 (Admin) [2004] 2 All ER 382 at [32] ("what is really important is that [the] agreed bundle [of authorities] should be filed not less than seven days before the hearing"), [33] ("I draw particular attention to the need to mark in the authorities the passages on which the advocates wish to rely"); *R (Jeyeapragash) v Immigration Appeal Tribunal* [2004] EWCA Civ 1260 [2005] 1 All ER 412 (re-emphasising the requirements as to skeletons and bundles 7 days before the hearing).

23.2.3 Permission to appeal. CPR 52.3(6); CPR 52PD para 3.2; *Tanfern Ltd v Cameron-MacDonald* [2000] 1 WLR 1311 at [21] ("the word `real' means that the prospect of success must be realistic rather than fanciful"); *R (Ben-Abdelaziz) v Haringey London Borough Council* [2001] EWCA Civ 803 [2001] 1 WLR 1485 at [1] (permission to appeal granted because of the importance of the issue rather than the prospects of success); *R (Richardson) v North Yorks County Council* [2003] EWCA Civ 1860 [2004] 1 WLR 1920 at [4] (issues sufficiently important to justify appeal hearing).

23.2.4 Appeal from substantive hearing on partial permission. *R (Smith) v Parole Board* [2003] EWCA Civ 1014 [2003] 1 WLR 2548 at [17] ("if permission [for judicial review] is refused in respect of a particular ground, the Court of Appeal on an appeal from the hearing at first instance will not be able to consider that matter").

23.2.5 Appeal by third party. *R (Bushell) v Newcastle Upon Tyne Licensing Justices* [2006] UKHL 7 [2006] 1 WLR 496 (judicial review granted to objectors, successful appeal by licensee); *R (Walmsley) v Lane* [2005] EWCA Civ 1540 [2006] LGR 280 at [27] (successful appeal by TfL, joined as a party post-judgment); *Wilson v First County Trust Ltd* [2003] UKHL 40 [2004] 1 AC 816 at [9] (appeal by Secretary of State against declaration of incompatibility); *R (Middleton) v West Somerset Coroner* [2004] UKHL 10 [2004] 2 AC 182 (Secretary of State appealing coroner Art 2 case); *R v Manchester Stipendiary Magistrate, ex p Granada Television Ltd* [2001] 1 AC 300 (appeal by Lord Advocate); *R v Secretary of State for the Environment, Transport and the Regions, ex p Garland* 10th November 2000 unrep. at [9] (district auditor a proper person to be heard, but not a person directly affected, so would have no right of appeal); *R (Officers A & B) v HM Coroner for Inner South London* [2004] EWCA Civ 1439 [2005] UKHRR 44 (appeal by deceased's family, from judicial review of coroner granted to police officers seeking anonymity); *R (Hurst) v London Northern District Coroner* [2005] EWCA Civ 890 [2005] 1 WLR 3892 at [7] (appeal by Metropolitan Police Commissioner in judicial review of coroner) (HL is [2007] UKHL 13 [2007] 2 AC 189); cf. *George Wimpey UK Ltd v Tewkesbury Borough Council* [2008] EWCA Civ 12 [2008] 1 WLR 1649 (third party permitted to appeal albeit not a party to the proceedings in the High Court).

23.2.6 Appeal judge's previous involvement. *Khreino v Khreino* [2000] 1 FLR 578 (CA properly constituted where including single Lord Justice who had previously refused permission to appeal on the papers); *Sengupta v Holmes* [2002] EWCA Civ 1104 (not unfair for judge who had refused permission to appeal on the papers to sit on substantive appeal).

23.2.7 **Favourable decision: appeal against adverse reasoning.**[132] *R v London Borough of Lambeth, ex p Ekpo-Wedderman* 23rd October 1998 unrep. (appeal only available from "judgment or order" of the Court); *R v Lord Saville of Newdigate, ex p B* The Times 15th April 1999 (exceptional case where appeal appropriate against unfavourable decision, but only on the basis of one aspect of the reasoning); *Curtis v London Rent Assessment Committee* [1999] QB 92 (in statutory appeal from rent assessment committee, appellant entitled to appeal to CA where High Court having quashed the impugned decision (on procedural grounds) but rejected other (substantive) grounds); *R v A (No.2)* [2001] UKHL 25 [2002] 1 AC 45 at [170]-[171] (in the circumstances, HL having jurisdiction over appeal which concerned obiter statements by CA rather than the actual decision, given the importance of the matters); *R (Green) v Police Complaints Authority* [2002] EWCA Civ 389 [2002] UKHRR 985 at [72] (CA entertaining "an appeal essentially against the reasons", despite "the general principle ... that appeals are against orders, not against the reasons given for them") (HL is [2004] UKHL 6 [2004] 1 WLR 725); *R (Beeson) v Dorset County Council* [2002] EWCA Civ 1812 [2003] UKHRR 353 at [13] (common ground that judicial review should be granted for error of law, but Secretary of State nevertheless appealing on questions of HRA compatibility); *R (Watts) v Bedford Primary Care Trust* [2004] EWCA Civ 166 at [3] (judicial review refused below, but judge nevertheless "reached certain conclusions of law, embodied as declarations in his order, which the Secretary of State challenges on this appeal"); *R (M) v Islington London Borough Council* [2004] EWCA Civ 235 [2005] 1 WLR 884 at [13] (appeal entertained where judge quashed the decision but claimant contending that he should have gone further); *MH v Special Educational Needs and Disability Tribunal* [2004] EWCA Civ 770 [2004] LGR 844 at [9] (explaining that judge below had allowed special educational needs appeal and remitted the case, but had gone on to give guidance as to the statutory scheme, against which guidance the appellant appealing to the CA).

23.2.8 **Fresh evidence and appeal.** <17.2.7>.

23.2.9 **Appeals: matters of High Court discretionary control.** <31.5.4>.

23.2.10 **Further appeal to House of Lords.**[133] See HL Standing Orders; Administration of Justice Act 1960 s.1(2) (criminal matter: need for "certified by the court below that a point of law of general public importance is involved in the decision"); ACO:NFG <64.4> para 18.6.

---

[132] Gregory Jones & Carine Patry [2000] JR 15.

[133] Victoria Wakefield [2005] JR 135; Charles Banner & Richard Moules [2007] JR 24.

P24 Remedies. The Court has discretionary power to quash, mandate, prevent and clarify.

24.1 Unified remedies
24.2 The declaration
24.3 Remedy as a discretionary matter
24.4 The remedies in action

24.1 Unified remedies. Judicial review has ancient roots in the trilogy of separate prerogative remedies: certiorari, mandamus and prohibition. These were renamed (as quashing, mandatory and prohibiting orders) and brought within a single judicial review procedure, in which were also included the remedies of declarations, injunctions and damages.

24.1.1 Remedies under CPR 54.
(A) REMEDIES FOR WHICH CPR 54 MUST BE USED. See Supreme Court Act 1981 s.31(1) <64.1>; CPR 54.2 <64.2>.
(B) REMEDIES FOR WHICH CPR 54 MAY BE USED. See Supreme Court Act 1981 s.31(2) and (4) <64.1>; CPR 54.3 <64.2>.
(C) MONETARY REMEDY MUST NOT BE THE SOLE REMEDY. See CPR 54.3(2) <64.2>.
(D) NAMING THE REMEDIES. <2.3> (terminology).

24.1.2 The 1977 unification of remedies. *O'Reilly v Mackman* [1983] 2 AC 237, 283D (Lord Diplock, explaining that the new 1977 RSC Ord 53 r.1 "enables an application for a declaration or an injunction to be included in an application for judicial review"), 283H ("a procedure by which every type of remedy for infringement of the rights of individuals that are entitled to protection in public law can be obtained in one and the same proceeding by way of an application for judicial review"); <2.1.5(B)> (the 1977/1981 reforms).

24.2 The declaration. The flexible and adaptable nature of the declaratory remedy gives it a special function and importance in public law.

24.2.1 Discretion to make a declaration: basic conditions.[134] See Supreme Court Act 1981 s.31(2) <64.1> (whether just and convenient); CPR 54.3 <64.2>; *R v Gloucestershire County Council, ex p P* [1994] ELR 334, 340F (declaration would not have been "just and convenient in all the circumstances of the case so to do"); <24.2.1> (whether just and convenient); *Greenwich Healthcare NHS Trust v London and Quadrant Housing Trust* [1998] 1 WLR 1749, 1756A-B (applying the 3 conditions from *In re F* [1990] 1 AC 1, 82: "that the question under consideration is a real question; that the person seeking the declaration has a real interest and that there has been proper argument"); <4.6.2> (Lord Dunedin's test); *Financial Services Authority v Rourke* The Times 12th November 2001 (court taking into account justice to the claimant and defendant, whether it would serve a useful purpose, and whether any other special reasons not to make such an order). See generally Zamir and Woolf, *The Declaratory Judgment*.

24.2.2 Declaration can be sole remedy sought. See CPR 40.20; *R v Secretary of State for Employment, ex p Equal Opportunities Commission* [1995] 1 AC 1, 36G-H (declaration available "whether or not the court could also make a prerogative order"); *R v Gloucestershire County Council, ex p P* [1994] ELR 334, 338B-C ("somewhat unusual for a bare declaration to be sought in a case where other relief is not granted").

---

[134] Barbara Hewson [1996] JR 204

24.2.3 In praise of the declaration. *Governor and Company of the Bank of Scotland v A Ltd* [2001] EWCA Civ 52 [2001] 1 WLR 751 at [45] (declarations having "performed a crucial function" in the emerging "modern law of judicial review"); *R v Ministry of Agriculture, Fisheries and Food, ex p Dairy Trade Federation Limited* [1998] EuLR 253, 257E-F (Dyson J: "Declarations are a useful discretionary remedy, and the courts are increasingly adopting a flexible and pragmatic approach to their use"); *In re S (Hospital Patient: Court's Jurisdiction)* [1996] Fam 1, 19G (importance of the law being able to give "practical help in cases such as this"); *Gouriet v Union of Post Office Workers* [1978] AC 435, 501C-D (declaration "a useful power" which "over the course of the last hundred years it has become more and more extensively used"), 513G ("it was recognised no later than 1899 that it was an `innovation of a very important kind'").

24.2.4 Declaration in action. *R (Faarah) v Southwark London Borough Council* [2008] EWCA Civ 807 at [49] (declaration appropriate to ensure practice corrected generally); *R (Infant & Dietetics Foods Association Ltd) v Secretary of State for Health* [2008] EWHC 575 (Admin) (declaration that regulations not accurately transposing EC Directive); *R (Teeside Power Ltd) v Gas and Electricity Market Authority* [2008] EWHC 1415 (Admin) (declaration as to scheme amendment power); *R (Page) v Secretary of State for Justice* [2007] EWHC 2026 (Admin) (declaration so that release reconsidered); *R (Vovk) v Secretary of State for the Home Department* [2006] EWHC 3386 (Admin) (declaration that detention unlawful); *R v Hillingdon London Borough Council, ex p Islam (Tafazzul)* [1983] 1 AC 688 (declaration that finding of intentional homelessness unsustainable); *Chief Constable of the North Wales Police v Evans* [1982] 1 WLR 1155 (declaration that unfair treatment of probationary police officer); *R v Secretary of State for the Home Department, ex p Doody* [1994] 1 AC 531 (declarations as to procedural duties owed to mandatory lifers); *R v Rochdale Metropolitan Borough Council, ex p Schemet* [1994] ELR 89, 108G (declaration as to lawfulness of change of policy); *R v Secretary of State for Social Services, ex p Association of Metropolitan Authorities* [1986] 1 WLR 1, 15H-16A (declaration that regulations made unfairly); *R v Dorset County Council and Further Education Funding Council, ex p Goddard* [1995] ELR 109, 135F (declaration of continuing duty to maintain special educational needs statement); *R v Secretary of State for Social Services, ex p Association of Metropolitan Authorities* (1993) 5 Admin LR 6, 16F (declaration of failure to comply with procedural duty); *R v Parole Board, ex p Wilson* [1992] QB 740, 757A (declaration of entitlement to information); *R v Investors Compensation Scheme Ltd, ex p Weyell* [1994] QB 749, 767H (narrow declaration rather than quashing whole decision); cf. *R (Burke) v General Medical Council* [2005] EWCA Civ 1003 [2006] QB 273 at [23] (declaration refused where unnecessary for the claimant's protection and inappropriate as far as impugning defendant's guidance concerned); *R (Beck) v Chief Constable of Hertfordshire* [2008] EWHC 1909 (Admin) declaration that firearms licence application should be determined); *R (Looe Fuels Ltd) v Looe Harbour Commissioners* [2007] EWHC 1141 (Admin) (declaration that no power to buy and sell fuel for harbour-using vessels); *R (Guiney) v Greenwich London Borough Council* [2008] EWHC 2012 (Admin) (declaration that planning permission decision breached duty of consultation, but not affecting its validity).

24.2.5 Advisory declarations/advisory opinions.[135]
(A) DEVELOPMENT OF ADVISORY DECLARATIONS. *In re S (Hospital Patient: Court's Jurisdiction)* [1996] Fam 1, 18A ("the development of a new advisory declaratory jurisdiction"); *R v Secretary of State for the Home Department, ex p Mehari* [1994] QB 474, 491G-H ("there are circumstances in which the public law court ought to exercise the jurisdiction, which it certainly possesses, to give advisory opinions"); Woolf Report, *Access to Justice* (1996) at 252

---

[135] Daniel Kolinsky [1999] JR 225.

(advocating "advisory declarations when it is in the public interest" but "limited to cases where the issue was of public importance and was defined in sufficiently precise terms, and where the appropriate parties were before the court"); Law Com No.226, *Administrative Law: Judicial Review and Statutory Appeals* at 120.

(B) USE SPARINGLY. *R (Campaign for Nuclear Disarmament) v Prime Minister* [2002] EWHC 2759 (Admin) [2003] 3 LRC 335 at [46] ("advisory declarations" as "valuable tools" which "should be sparingly used. Their essential purposes are, first, to reduce the danger of administrative activities being declared illegal retrospectively, and, secondly, to assist public authorities by giving advice on legal questions which is then binding on all"), [47(iii)] (need "demonstrably good reason"), [52] (jurisdiction "to be exercised only in exceptional circumstances"); *R v Ministry of Agriculture, Fisheries and Food, ex p Live Sheep Traders Ltd* [1995] COD 297 (advisory opinion "will be looking prospectively to the future, not retrospectively at the past"); *R (Mahmood) v Secretary of State for the Home Department* [2001] 1 WLR 840 at [29] (court "not generally concerned to give advisory opinions as to how public authorities ought to act" but "there may be circumstances when it is its duty to do so"); *R (Burke) v General Medical Council* [2005] EWCA Civ 1003 [2006] QB 273 at [21] ("The court should not be used as a general advice centre. The danger is that the court will enunciate propositions of principle without full appreciation of the implications that these will have in practice").

(C) APPLICATION ENTERTAINED IN THE PUBLIC INTEREST. *R (Customs and Excise Commissioners) v Canterbury Crown Court* [2002] EWHC 2584 (Admin) at [27] (Laws LJ: "there is a plain public interest in this court entertaining what has become an application for an advisory declaration"); *London Borough of Islington v Camp* (1999) [2004] LGR 58 (claim entertained albeit no dispute or proposed action, because serving a useful purpose in the public interest); *P v P (Ancillary Relief: Proceeds of Crime)* [2003] EWHC 2260 (Fam) [2004] Fam 1 (declarations clarifying legal advisers' duties in relation to assets being proceeds of crime).

(D) APPLICATION DECLINED. *R (Campaign for Nuclear Disarmament) v Prime Minister* [2002] EWHC 2759 (Admin) [2003] 3 LRC 335 (declining to rule on interpretation of UN Resolution, relevant to imminent decision as to war on Iraq); *R v Portsmouth Hospitals NHS Trust, ex p Glass* [1999] 2 FLR 905 (Court declining declaration as to circumstances where doctors could override wishes of next-of-kin; inapt to seek prospective clarity given need for focus on particular circumstances); *R v Secretary of State for the Home Department, ex p Pinfold* [1997] COD 338 (wrong to embark on giving guidance as to how the new Criminal Cases Review Commission should discharge its functions); *R v Director of Public Prosecutions, ex p London Borough of Merton* [1999] COD 358 (declining to entertain hypothetical matter where likely to be of limited assistance for the future); *R (Henlow Grange Health Farm Ltd) v Bedfordshire County Council* [2001] EWHC Admin 179 (judicial review inappropriate where in effect would be an advisory declaration while Secretary of State's planning decision awaited); *Amalgamated Metal Trading Ltd v City of London Police Financial Investigation Unit* [2003] EWHC 703 (Comm) [2003] 1 WLR 2711 (whether monies were proceeds of crime should be left for resolution between parties between whom it arose); <4.6> (hypothetical/ academic matters).

(E) OTHER CASES. *Oxfordshire County Council v Oxford City Council* [2006] UKHL 25 [2006] 2 AC 674 (CPR8 claim by registration authority for guidance on issues arising from town green registration inquiry); *R (Governor of HMP Wandsworth) v Kinderis* [2007] EWHC 998 (Admin) [2008] QB 347 (prisoner governor's judicial review to establish which of two inconsistent orders applicable); *R (Howard League for Penal Reform) v Secretary of State for the Home Department* [2002] EWHC 2497 (Admin) [2003] 1 FLR 484 at [140] (not the court's task "to set out to write a textbook or practice manual or to give advisory opinions"); *R v Inland Revenue Commissioners, ex p Bishopp* (1999) 11 Admin LR 575, 588f-589a ("the greater the extent to which the dispute between the parties is based on hypothetical facts, the more likely it is that, as a matter of discretion, the court will refuse"); *R v Birmingham City Council, ex p*

Equal Opportunities Commission [1994] ELR 282, 292E-293B (permission set aside "because what was being sought was a declaration of an advisory nature which was not connected with any relevant decision"); *R (Ellis) v Chief Constable of Essex Police* [2003] EWHC 1321 (Admin) [2003] 2 FLR 566 (legality of police "Offender Naming Scheme") at [37] ("If the situation was one where the scheme was obviously lawful or obviously unlawful, then the court could grant a declaration to this effect. This would be desirable because it would remove any doubt as to the legality of the scheme"); *R (Lord Chancellor) v Chief Land Registrar* [2005] EWHC 1706 (Admin) [2006] QB 795 (Lord Chancellor seeking declarations as to lawfulness or otherwise of his scheme, doubts having been expressed by the Chief Land Registrar).

24.2.6 Declaration as to criminality of conduct.[136] *Rushbridger v HM Attorney-General* [2003] UKHL 38 [2004] 1 AC 357 (discussing the principle from *Imperial Tobacco Ltd v Attorney-General* [1981] AC 718, that only in an exceptional case would it be appropriate to entertain civil proceedings for a declaration as to the legality in criminal law of a proposed course of conduct); *R (I-CD Publishing Ltd) v Secretary of State* [2003] EWHC 1761 (Admin) at [27] (wrong in principle to entertain claim for declaration as to whether proposed future modified conduct would bring claimant within statutory provision and so be non-criminal); *R (Haynes) v Stafford Borough Council* [2006] EWHC 1366 (Admin) [2007] 1 WLR 1365 at [32], [52] (appropriate to decide issue in the public interest, where construing statutory scheme and not declaring commission of any offence by any individual); *R v Director of Public Prosecutions, ex p Camelot Group Plc* (1998) 10 Admin LR 93, 104C (adopting a flexible approach, the only rigid rule being that Court should not entertain the matter where criminal proceedings already on foot); *R v Medicines Control Agency, ex p Pharma Nord Ltd* (1998) 10 Admin LR 646, 660F-H (court would not be interfering with imminent criminal proceedings); *R v Environment Agency, ex p Dockgrange Ltd* [1997] Env LR 575 (Court dealing with the matter); *R (Smeaton) v Secretary of State for Health* [2002] EWHC 886 (Admin) [2002] 2 FLR 146 (whether use of morning-after pill would constitute criminal offence); *R (NTL Group Ltd) v Ipswich Crown Court* [2002] EWHC 1585 (Admin) [2003] QB 131 (whether claimant would commit criminal offence by diverting e-mails to obey special protection order); *Blackland Park Exploration Ltd v Environment Agency* [2003] EWCA Civ 1795 [2004] Env LR 652 (CA granting a declaration that claimant operating a "landfill"), [16] (parties having genuine and anxious interest in resolution of issue); *R (Hampstead Heath Winter Swimming Club) v Corporation of London* [2005] EWHC 713 (Admin) [2005] 1 WLR 2930 at [21]-[25] (appropriate to deal with whether defendant would be exposed to criminal liability, where issue genuinely arising as alleged error of law in its decision, and the prosecuting authority having been served as an interested party); *Bowman v Fels* [2005] EWCA Civ 226 [2005] 1 WLR 3083 at [18] (CA proceeding despite being "wary of usurping the function of the criminal courts by interpreting a criminal statute unless it is very desirable").

24.2.7 Declaration that primary legislation incompatible with EC law. <8.3.1(A)>.

24.2.8 Declaration in favour of the defendant. *Rowland v Environment Agency* [2003] EWCA Civ 1885 [2005] Ch 1 (claim rejected and declarations granted in favour of defendant); *R v Secretary of State for the Home Department, ex p Gashi* 15th June 2000 unrep. at [6] and [15] (no declaration needed, in favour of defendant, because judgment speaking for itself).

24.3 Remedy as a discretionary matter. It is a first principle of judicial review that remedies are discretionary. One specific basis on which a remedy can be refused in the Court's discretion is where the claimant unduly delayed and granting a remedy would cause

---

[136] Alice Robinson [2006] JR 30.

relevant prejudice or detriment.

24.3.1 **The discretion as to remedy.**[137] *R (Edwards) v Environment Agency* [2008] UKHL 22 at [63] (court's discretion to be exercised having regard to "the nature of the flaw in the decision and the ground for exercise of the discretion"); *R (Bibi) v Newham London Borough Council* [2001] EWCA Civ 607 [2002] 1 WLR 237 at [40] ("The court has two functions - assessing the legality of actions by administrators and, if it finds unlawfulness on the administrators' part, deciding what [remedy] it should give"); *Credit Suisse v Allerdale Borough Council* [1997] QB 306, 355D ("The discretion of the court in deciding whether to grant any remedy is a wide one. It can take into account many considerations, including the needs of good administration, delay, the effect on third parties, the utility of granting the relevant remedy. The discretion can be exercised so as partially to uphold and partially quash the relevant administrative decision or act"); *R v Panel on Take-overs and Mergers, ex p Datafin Plc* [1987] QB 815, 840B ("the court has an ultimate discretion ... and may refuse to [set aside] in the public interest, notwithstanding that it holds and declares the decision to have been made ultra vires"); *Nichol v Gateshead Metropolitan Borough Council* (1988) 87 LGR 435, 460 ("The court has an overall discretion as to whether to grant [a remedy] or not. In considering how that discretion should be exercised, the court is entitled to have regard to such matters as the following: (1) The nature and importance of the flaw in the challenged decision. (2) The conduct of the [claimant]. (3) The effect on administration of granting [the remedy]"); *R v Secretary of State for the Environment, ex p Walters* (1998) 30 HLR 328, 381 (need for "close attention both to the nature of the illegality of the decision, and its consequences"), applied in *R (Fudge) v South West Strategic Health Authority* [2007] EWCA Civ 803 at [67]; *R v Inner London South District Coroner, ex p Douglas-Williams* [1999] 1 All ER 344, 347d-f (whether remedy "necessary or desirable ... in the interests of justice"), applied in *R (Onwumere) v Secretary of State for the Home Department* [2004] EWHC 1281 (Admin) at [22]; *R v Monopolies & Mergers Commission, ex p Argyll Group Plc* [1986] 1 WLR 763, 774C-775B (remedy refused for reasons relating to "the needs of public administration"); *R v Islington London Borough Council, ex p Degnan* (1998) 30 HLR 723, 730 (balancing exercise, as to "the individual right and the public interest in decisions being taken lawfully" and "the practical effect - or lack of it - of the illegality found"); *R (Sacupima) v Newham London Borough Council* [2001] 1 WLR 563, 572E (effects of impugned decision only for short duration); *R v Avon County Council, ex p Terry Adams Ltd* [1994] Env LR 442, 477-478 (public interest consequences of granting remedy); *R (Mount Cook Land Ltd) v Westminster City Council* [2003] EWCA Civ 1346 [2004] 1 PLR 29 at [45]-[46] (commercial motives of claimant not a reason to refuse relief).

24.3.2 **Refusal of remedy: particular reasons.** <26.1.8> (delay); <38.3.6> (standing); <36.3.8> (alternative remedy); <10.3.5> (non-disclosure); <31.3.4> (unclean hands).

24.3.3 **Whether to refuse remedy: examples.**
(A) REMEDY REFUSED. *R (Dimmock) v Secretary of State for Education and Skills* [2007] EWHC 2288 (Admin) [2008] 1 All ER 367 at [44] (remedy not needed where deficiency solved by new clarificatory guidance); *R (Tu) v Secretary of State for the Home Department* [2002] EWHC 2678 (Admin) [2003] Imm AR 288 (no remedy where nationality unclear) at [24] ("pragmatic and sensible" solution); *R v Criminal Injuries Compensation Board, ex p Aston* [1994] PIQR 460 (technical flaw could have made no difference); *R v Walton Street Justices, ex p Crothers* [1995] COD 159 (no injustice caused and not in the interests of justice); *R v Chief*

---

[137] This paragraph in a previous edition was cited in *R (Jones) v Mansfield District Council* [2003] EWCA Civ 1408 [2004] Env LR 391 at [59].

Constable of Devon and Cornwall, ex p Hay [1996] 2 All ER 711, 726e (not proper to "wind the film back" and put an officer back in service); *King v East Ayrshire Council* The Times 3rd November 1997 (successful ground of challenge had not been advanced originally); *R v Secretary of State for the Home Department, ex p Harry* [1998] 1 WLR 1737, 1748F-G (relief not needed given indication of change of process and assurances as to future cases); *R v Legal Aid Board, ex p W (Minors)* [2000] 1 WLR 2502, 2510H (remittal would cause delay "incompatible with the welfare of the children"); *R v Secretary of State for the Environment, Transport and the Regions, ex p Garland* 10th November 2000 unrep. at [44] (inequitable where claimant had previously agreed not to challenge).

(B) REMEDY GRANTED. *R (C) v Secretary of State for Justice* [2008] EWCA Civ 882 (regulations quashed), [49] ("wrong message to public authorities" if race equality impact assessment breach "cured" by conducting assessment to validate impugned decision); *R (Carlton-Conway) v London Borough of Harrow* [2002] EWCA Civ 927 [2002] 3 PLR 77 (where planning officer should not have dealt with matter under delegated powers, judicial review granted even though planning committee had since ratified the decision); *R v Immigration Appeal Tribunal, ex p Iqbal Ali* [1994] Imm AR 295, 298-299 (fact that claimant now 21 not "in principle, a reason why I should refuse, in my discretion, to quash a decision made when he was younger and which may have been the wrong decision and the reasoning for which is, in any event, not clear"); *R v Criminal Injuries Compensation Board, ex p A* [1999] 2 AC 330, 347B-C (quashing the decision, "a breach of the rules of natural justice having been established", albeit that "the difficulties of reopening the matter now are obvious"); *R v Manchester City Council, ex p S* [1999] ELR 414 (remedy granted to require school to admit the claimant, having been unlawfully not admitted, even though school now full); *R v Hillingdon Health Authority, ex p Goodwin* [1984] ICR 800, 811D-E (remedy meaning delay but not so serious as to justify refusal); *R (Mount Cook Land Ltd) v Westminster City Council* [2003] EWCA Civ 1346 [2004] 1 PLR 29 at [45]-[46] (commercial motives of claimant, in seeking to put pressure on lessee, not a reason to refuse relief); <20.1.13(A)> (dangers of deciding to press ahead); <24.3.4> (whether wrong in principle to deny remedy).

(C) CHOICE OF REMEDY. *R (E) v JFS Governing Body* [2008] EWHC 1535 (Admin) at [214] (declaration only where breach of race equality duty but policy and application would have been the same); *R (Guiney) v Greenwich London Borough Council* [2008] EWHC 2012 (Admin) (declaration only where aspect of planning permission complained of not capable of partial quashing); *R (Rashid) v Secretary of State for the Home Department* [2005] EWCA Civ 744 [2005] INLR 550 at [37] (wrong to declare entitlement to refugee status where claimant could no longer meet the criteria), [39] (declaring entitlement to indefinite leave to remain as "the appropriate response in the circumstances"); *R v Secretary of State for Social Services, ex p Association of Metropolitan Authorities* [1986] 1 WLR 1 (declining to quash regulations, but declaring that they had been made unfairly), 14G-15B; *R v Bristol Corporation, ex p Hendy* [1974] 1 WLR 498 (mandatory order refused where breach of statutory duty caused by circumstances beyond defendant's control); *R (Murray) v Parole Board* [2003] EWCA Civ 1561 at [24] ("logistical difficulties" no answer to question whether parole review delays excessive in breach of HRA:ECHR Art 5(4), but "answer would be, generally speaking, that no mandatory relief should be granted despite the breach"); *C.O. Williams Construction v Donald George Blackman* [1995] 1 WLR 102, 109E-H (impossible to "put the clock back and reverse the effect of the cabinet's decision", albeit leaving questions as to possible damages); *R v Southwark Coroner's Court, ex p Epsom Health Care NHS Trust* [1995] COD 92 (quash part of coroner's verdict, but decline to order a new inquest, since no practical purpose, no need to remove any stigma and public interest in leaving central finding in place).

(D) OTHER. *R v Inner London South District Coroner, ex p Douglas-Williams* [1999] 1 All ER 344, 347d-f (where judicial review of coroner on grounds of misdirection of jury, test for remedy whether it is necessary or desirable to grant remedy in the interests of justice). Note *R v Secretary of State for the Environment Transport and the Regions, ex p Watson* [1999] Env LR

310, 325 ("even within proceedings indubitably limited to public law interests [a claimant] will be restricted to the [remedy] that adequately recognises the public law interest that he asserts"); *R (Hammerton) v London Underground Ltd* [2002] EWHC 2307 (Admin) at [214] (fact that only one claimant relevant to the discretion as to remedy).

24.3.4 Whether wrong in principle to deny remedy where unlawfulness shown.

R (Edwards) v Environment Agency [2008] UKHL 22 at [63] (Lord Hoffmann: "the discretion must be exercised judicially and in most cases in which a decision has been found to be flawed, it would not be a proper exercise of the discretion to refuse to quash it"); *Berkeley v Secretary of State for the Environment* [2001] 2 AC 603[138], 616F ("exceptional" not to quash ultra vires decision), 608C-D (discretion "very narrow"), 615G (directly enforceable EC right); *R (Gavin) v Haringey London Borough Council* [2003] EWHC 2591 (Admin) [2004] 1 PLR 61 at [40]-[41] (delay objection remains); *R (Jones) v Mansfield District Council* [2003] EWCA Civ 1408 [2004] Env LR 391 at [59] (need for "care" in applying *Berkeley*); *R (Richardson) v North Yorks County Council* [2003] EWCA Civ 1860 [2004] 1 WLR 1920 at [42] (leaving open whether *Berkeley*'s true reach narrow); *R (Mount Cook Land Ltd) v Westminster City Council* [2003] EWCA Civ 1346 [2004] 1 PLR 29 at [46] (referring to *Berkeley*); *R (Blewett) v Derbyshire County Council* [2004] EWCA Civ 1508 [2004] Env LR 293 at [119] (applying *Berkeley*); *R v Attorney General, ex p Imperial Chemical Industries* [1987] 1 CMLR 72, 109 ("wrong in principle" to deny remedy "unless, at any rate, there are extremely strong reasons in public policy for doing so"); *R v General Medical Council, ex p Toth* [2000] 1 WLR 2209 at [6] (need "strong reasons in public policy"); *R v Restormel Borough Council, ex p Corbett* [2001] EWCA Civ 330 [2001] 1 PLR 108 at [17] ("the judge should incline to quash what is shown to be an unlawful decision"); *R v Director General of Water Services, ex p Oldham Metropolitan Borough Council* (1998) 96 LGR 396, 416b (wrong to refuse a remedy where unlawful failure of statutory enforcement); *Chief Constable of the North Wales Police v Evans* [1982] 1 WLR 1155, 1172F ("regrettable" if wronged litigant "sent away from a court of justice empty-handed"); *R (South Wales Sea Fisheries Committee) v National Assembly for Wales* [2001] EWHC Admin 1162 at [54]-[55] (Court should be slow to leave in place invalid Order); *R (Barwise) v Chief Constable of West Midlands Police* [2004] EWHC 1876 (Admin) at [37] ("only in exceptional cases that relief will be refused if unlawful conduct is established"); *R (Brent London Borough Council) v Fed 2000* [2005] EWHC 2679 (Admin) [2006] ELR 169 at [67] (inappropriate to deny remedy where effect would be to qualify a clear statutory duty or usurp approving body's function); *R (Pridmore) v Salisbury District Council* [2004] EWHC 2511 (Admin) [2005] 1 PLR 39 at [39]-[41] (where cavalier disregard of planning requirements, denial of remedy "would come close to undermining the mandatory scheme of the legislation"); *R (B) v Head Teacher of Alperton Community School* [2001] EWHC Admin 229 at [23] (panel lacking jurisdiction and so "no question of discretion arises. The claimant is entitled to [a remedy] as of right"); *R v Lincolnshire County Council and Wealden District Council, ex p Atkinson, Wales and Stratford* (1996) 8 Admin LR 529, 539G (lacking jurisdiction), 549H (means entitled to a remedy "*ex debito justiciae*"); *Grunwick Processing Laboratories Ltd v Advisory, Conciliation and Arbitration Service* [1978] AC 655, 695A (ultra vires meaning normally entitled to quashing order "ex debito justiciae"); *Credit Suisse v Allerdale Borough Council* [1997] QB 306, 342B-H ("general discretion" remains); *Boddington v British Transport Police* [1999] 2 AC 143, 176A-C ("grave objections to giving courts discretion to decide whether governmental action is lawful or unlawful"); *Attorney General's Reference No.2 of 2001* [2003] UKHL 68 [2004] 2 AC 72 at [176] (whether relief could be automatic under HRA:ECHR Art 6), [122] ("paradox" of the "illegal act which the court nevertheless does not restrain"); *R (C) v Secretary of State for Justice* [2008] EWCA Civ 882 at [41] (discretion to withhold relief "if there are

---

[138] Andrew Lidbetter & Reimar Buchner [2003] JR 36.

pressing reasons for not disturbing the status quo"), [85] (finding of ultra vires "should normally lead to the delegated legislation being quashed").

24.4 The remedies in action. The judicial review case-law provides a wealth of ready working examples of ways in which the remedies operate, in various contexts, in practice.

24.4.1 **Quashing order (formerly "certiorari").** *R (C) v Secretary of State for Justice* [2008] EWCA Civ 882 (quashing unlawfully-made regulations); *R (Redknapp) v Commissioner of the City of London Police* [2008] EWHC 1177 (Admin) (quashing unlawfully issued warrant); *R (Kaur) v Ealing London Borough Council* [2008] EWHC 2062 (Admin) (quashing unlawful funding decision); *R (S) v Secretary of State for the Home Department* [2008] EWHC 2069 (Admin) (quashing decision to refuse exceptional leave to remain); *R (MH) v Bedfordshire County Council* [2007] EWHC 2435 (Admin) [2008] ELR 191 (quashing decision to discontinue funding for special educational needs); *R (W) v Chief Constable of Hampshire* [2006] EWHC 1904 (Admin) (quashing a police caution); *R (Pridmore) v Salisbury District Council* [2004] EWHC 2511 (Admin) [2005] 1 PLR 39 (quashing planning permission for default of prior notice duty); *R v Barnet London Borough Council, ex p Nilish Shah* [1983] 2 AC 309 (quashing refusal of student grants for error of law); *Wheeler v Leicester City Council* [1985] AC 1054 (quashing ban on rugby club training on council land); *R v Secretary of State for Education and Employment, ex p National Union of Teachers* 14th July 2000 unrep. (quashing a statutory instrument); <3.1.1> (quash and remit).

24.4.2 **Substitutionary remedy: Court's power of retaking the decision.** See CPR 54.19(3)[139] <64.2>; *R (Mowlem Plc) v HM Assistant Deputy Coroner for Avon* [2005] EWHC 1359 (Admin) at [26] (substituting words for inapt coroner's verdict); *R (Thames Water Utilities Ltd) v Bromley Magistrates Court* [2005] EWHC 1231 (Admin) at [5] (where district judge wrongly declining to determine point of law, Court able "to resolve the question of law" since "no useful purpose would seem to be served by remitting the matter"); *R (Secretary of State for the Home Department) v Chief Asylum Support Adjudicator* [2003] EWHC 269 (Admin) (Court directing dismissal of asylum support appeal by reference to CPR 54.19(3)) (CA is [2003] EWCA Civ 1673); *R (Cunningham) v Exeter Crown Court* [2003] EWHC 184 (Admin) at [22] (where irrational costs refusal appropriate to "direct the Crown Court to award the claimant his costs"); *R v Inner London Crown Court, ex p Provis* [2000] COD 481 (court substituting order whereby licensing appeal allowed, because unfair to remit and allow police a second opportunity to resist); *R (Longfield Care Homes Ltd) v HM Coroner for Blackburn* [2004] EWHC 2467 (Admin) at [32] (coroner's verdict "quashed and amended"); *R (Governing Body of London Oratory School) v Schools Adjudicator* [2005] EWHC 1842 (Admin) [2005] ELR 484 at [17] (remedy of quashing but not remitting to schools adjudicator not constituting a substitutionary decision under CPR 54.19(3)); Law Com No.226, *Administrative Law: Judicial Review and Statutory Appeals* at 120.

24.4.3 **Power to vary sentences/orders on conviction.** See Supreme Court Act 1981 s 43; *R (Corner) v Southend Crown Court* [2005] EWHC 2334 (Admin) (substituting 2 year driving ban for 4 year ban); *R v Exeter Crown Court, ex p Chennery* [1996] COD 207 (substituting 12 for 18 months sentence); *R v Pateley Bridge Justices, ex p Percy* [1994] COD 453 (substituting 1 day for 1 month imprisonment); *R v Truro Crown Court, ex p Adair* [1997] COD 296 (substituting lower fine); *R v St Helen's Justices, ex p Jones* [1999] 2 All ER 73 (s.43(3) not apt to apply to an order subsequent to conviction, made for a new intervening cause; here, neglect or default in paying fine).

---

[139] Anya Proops [2001] JR 216; John Campbell [2002] JR 72; Alexander Horne [2007] JR 135.

24.4.4 **Partial quashing.** <43.1.6>.

24.4.5 **Mandatory order (formerly "mandamus").**
(A) GENERAL. *R v Inland Revenue Commissioners, ex p National Federation of Self-Employed and Small Businesses Ltd* [1982] AC 617, 650B (Lord Scarman, describing mandamus as "the most elusive of the prerogative writs and orders").
(B) REQUIRING PERFORMANCE/PREVENTING BREACH OF DUTY.*R (P) v Newham London Borough Council* [2004] EWHC 2210 (Admin) (2004) 7 CCLR 553 (ordering a pathway plan); *R v Camden London Borough Rent Officer, ex p Ebiri* [1981] 1 WLR 881 (requiring setting of fair rent); *Wang v Commissioner of Inland Revenue* [1994] 1 WLR 1286, 1296F-G (failure to act within reasonable time could be compelled by mandatory order); *R (Khan) v London Borough of Newham* [2001] EWHC Admin 589 (mandatory order to require discharge of housing duty, notwithstanding council's lack of resources); *Fleming v Lees* [1991] COD 50 (preventing breach of duty).
(C) SOLE LEGALLY PERMISSIBLE RESULT.*R v Ealing London Borough Council, ex p Parkinson* (1996) 8 Admin LR 281, 287F (situation "where the public law court is able to conclude that only one result was legally open to the body in question"); *R v Inner London North District Coroner, ex p Linnane* [1989] 1 WLR 395, 403B (mandatory order to achieve what was "the right conclusion"); *R (S) v Secretary of State for the Home Department* [2007] EWCA Civ 546 at [46] (situation of "unfairness ... so obvious ... that there was only one way in which the Secretary of State could reasonably exercise his discretion"); *R (Luminar Leisure Ltd) v Norwich Crown Court* [2004] EWCA Civ 281 [2004] 1 WLR 2512 at [20] (whether the only manner in which a case could properly have been resolved).
(D) WRONGLY DECLINING JURISDICTION. *Lewisham London Borough Council v Lewisham Juvenile Court Justices* [1980] AC 273 (mandatory order against justices for erroneously declining jurisdiction to hear the Council's complaint); *R v Statutory Committee of the Pharmaceutical Society of Great Britain, ex p Pharmaceutical Society of Great Britain* [1981] 1 WLR 886 (mandatory order where committee erroneously concluded that no jurisdiction because of conditional discharge in criminal proceedings); *R v Oxford Justices, ex p D* [1987] QB 199 (mandatory order for magistrates' clerk's refusal to issue a summons for access, on the erroneous basis that magistrates lacking jurisdiction); *R v Reading Crown Court, ex p Hutchinson* [1988] QB 384 (mandatory order where wrongly declining to examine lawfulness of byelaws); cf.*R v Comptroller-General of Patents Designs & Trade Marks, ex p Gist-Brocades* [1986] 1 WLR 51, 66F (preferring "a declaration or certiorari to quash as being erroneous in law his decision denying his own jurisdiction"); <47.1.4(B)> (wrongly declining jurisdiction).
(E) REQUIRING PROCEDURAL STEPS.*R v St Albans Magistrates' Court, ex p Read* (1994) 6 Admin LR 201 (following magistrates' ex parte order, court making mandatory order that inter partes hearing take place, as required by fairness); *R v Wandsworth County Court, ex p Munn* (1994) 26 HLR 697 (mandatory order to require chief clerk and district judges of the County Court to indorse a penal notice on an injunction); *R v Hereford Corporation, ex p Harrower* [1970] 1 WLR 1424 (mandatory order to require performance of duty of inviting tenders); *R v HM Coroner for Greater London, ex p Ridley* [1985] 1 WLR 1347 (mandatory order where refusal to order second inquest `unsustainable'); *R v British Coal Corporation, ex p Union of Democratic Mineworkers* [1988] ICR 36 (mandatory order following failure to consult); *R v Newham East Magistrates, ex p London Borough of Newham* [1995] Env LR 113 (requiring magistrates to state a case).
(F) ENSURING SUFFICIENCY OF INQUIRY.*R v Newcastle Justices, ex p Skinner* [1987] 1 WLR 312 (failure to conduct a means inquiry); *R v Inner London North District Coroner, ex p Linnane* [1989] 1 WLR 395 (coroner's decision not to empanel a jury); *R (AB and SB) v Nottingham City Council* [2001] EWHC Admin 235 (2001) 4 CCLR 295 at [53] (mandatory order to require full assessment of needs, within the maximum period laid down in relevant

guidance document); <P51> (insufficient inquiry).
(G) OTHER. <24.4.13(A)> (mandatory order and nullity acquittals); *R (Association of British Travel Agents Ltd) v Civil Aviation Authority* [2006] EWCA Civ 1299 at [65] (mandatory order directing misleading guidance note to be withdrawn); *R v Brent London Borough Council, ex p Miyanger* (1997) 29 HLR 628 (mandatory order to require housing decision within 28 days); *R (Stewart) v Wandsworth London Borough Council* [2001] EWHC Admin 709 (2001) 4 CCLR 466 at [33] (order made requiring needs assessment); *R (A) v Lord Saville of Newdigate* [2001] EWCA Civ 2048 [2002] 1 WLR 1249 at [57] (matter remitted to Tribunal "with a direction that ... evidence should not be taken in Londonderry"); <24.4.14(D)> (no fetter by mandatory order).

24.4.6 Prohibiting order (formerly "prohibition"). *R (Watson) v Dartford Magistrates Court* [2005] EWHC 905 (Admin) (prohibiting order to prevent prosecution from adducing certain witness evidence, where adjournment had been unlawfully granted); *R v Liverpool Corporation, ex p Liverpool Taxi Fleet Operators' Association* [1972] 2 QB 299 (prohibiting order granted where unlawful decision to increase taxi licence numbers, in breach of undertaking to consult); *R v Electricity Commissioners, ex p London Electricity Joint Committee Co* [1924] 1 KB 171 (prohibiting order in respect of proposed scheme, being ultra vires); *R v Horseferry Road Magistrates' Court, ex p Bennett* [1994] 1 AC 42, 79H-80B (Lord Lowry, approving the use of prohibiting order against magistrates in *R v Bow Street Magistrates, ex p Mackeson* (1981) 75 Cr App R 24 and *R v Telford Justices, ex p Badhan* [1991] 2 QB 78); *R v Dudley Justices, ex p Gillard* [1986] AC 442, 448G (Lord Bridge, referring to prohibiting order as "the effective and sufficient remedy"); *R v Horseferry Road Justices, ex p Independent Broadcasting Authority* [1987] QB 54 (prohibiting order granted in context of criminal proceedings commenced in a magistrates court, since Broadcasting Act 1981 s.4(3) not creating a criminal offence); *R v Faversham and Sittingbourne Justices, ex p Stickings* [1996] COD 439 (prohibiting order to prevent fresh trial, where unlawful decision setting aside ruling as to admissibility of evidence).

24.4.7 Declaration. <24.2>.

24.4.8 Injunction. <P20> (interim remedy); *R v North Yorkshire County Council, ex p M* [1989] QB 411 (parents obtaining injunction of local authority's decision to foster their daughter without consulting a court-appointed guardian ad litem); *Bradbury v Enfield London Borough Council* [1967] 1 WLR 1311 (injunction to prevent local authority from ceasing to maintain school, without going through statutory procedure); *R v Environment Agency, ex p Dockgrange Ltd* [1997] Env LR 575 (see transcript) (order to restrain any enforcement action inconsistent with the declaration of the Court); *R v Secretary of State for the Home Department, ex p Sarbjit Kaur* [1996] Imm AR 359 (court declining injunction to restrain deportation, pending petition to the ECtHR, absent any domestic/EC law right); Supreme Court Act 1981 s.37 (whether just and convenient).

24.4.9 Prospective-only remedy/overruling: limiting retrospective effect.[140] *R v Governor of Brockhill Prison, ex p Evans (No.2)* [1999] QB 1043 (CA), 1058F-G (declaration may be prospective only); the HL is at [2001] 2 AC 19: see 26H ("there may be situations in which it would be desirable, and in no way unjust, that the effect of judicial rulings should be prospective or limited to certain claimants"); *In Re Spectrum Plus Ltd* [2005] UKHL 41 [2005] 2 AC 680 (discussion as to whether and when it might be appropriate for the HL, wholly exceptionally, to overrule a previous case with prospective effect only); *R v Warwickshire County Council, ex p Collymore* [1995] ELR 217 (court ruling that council's policy had been applied over-rigidly,

---

[140] Richard McManus QC [2007] JR 228.

but not retrospective); *R v East Sussex County Council, ex p Ward* (2000) 3 CCLR 132 at [37] (permission granted on condition that no remedy would be granted in respect of an earlier period); cf. *R (Carson) v Secretary of State for Work and Pensions* [2005] UKHL 37 [2006] 1 AC 173 at [104] (Lord Carswell, dissenting, indicating that he would have been inclined to declare the invalidity of the pension uprating restriction, but "making the invalidity prospective only"); <13.6.2> (timing of intervention); cf. *R (Bidar) v Ealing London Borough Council* [2005] QB 812 at [66]-[70] (ECJ, describing the exceptional power to limit the temporal effect of its ruling).

24.4.10 No order/declaratory judgment. *R (O) v Parkview Academy* [2007] EWCA 592 [2007] ELR 454 at [46] (acceptance of undertakings a sensible exercise of discretion); *R (Purja) v Ministry of Defence* [2003] EWCA Civ 1345 [2004] 1 WLR 289 at [73] ("Very often the court allows its judgment to speak for itself rather than grant express declaratory relief"); *R (Zeqiri) v Secretary of State for the Home Department* [2002] UKHL 3 [2002] INLR 291 at [12] ("In cases affecting the Secretary of State, the court frequently adopts the view that the Secretary of State will be guided by its opinion without the necessity of a formal order of mandamus or declaration"); *R (Barry) v Liverpool City Council* [2001] EWCA Civ 384 [2001] LGR 361 at [27] ("When the [defendant] is a responsible public body it is often considered unnecessary to make a formal declaration"); *R (Wandsworth London Borough Council) v Secretary of State for Transport* [2005] EWHC 20 (Admin) at [313] ("a declaration in the terms of this judgment should suffice"); <23.2.7> (appeal against reasoning).

24.4.11 Liberty to apply/consequential applications.
(A) ORDER FOR LIBERTY TO APPLY. *Wheeler v Leicester City Council* [1985] AC 1054, 1079F (liberty to apply in case injunction becoming necessary); *R v West Yorkshire Coroner, ex p Smith* [1983] QB 335, 359G (liberty to apply for mandatory order); *R v Rochdale Metropolitan Borough Council, ex p Schemet* [1994] ELR 89, 109G-110D (liberty to re-apply for mandatory order, "in the unlikely event of the local education authority ... seeking to continue to apply a policy which the court has said is unlawful"); *R v Human Fertilisation and Embryology Authority, ex p Blood* [1999] Fam 151 (no formal order except liberty to apply (to CA)); *R v Director General of Electricity Supply, ex p Scottish Power Plc* 3rd February 1997 unrep. (liberty to apply to CA for further directions); *R v Wandsworth London Borough Council, ex p M* [1998] ELR 424, 429A-B (declaration and liberty to apply); *R v Investors Compensation Scheme Ltd, ex p Weyell* [1994] QB 749, 767H (declaration "if necessary with liberty to apply"); *R (Dube) v Secretary of State for the Home Department* [2002] EWHC 2032 (Admin) (Administrative Court) at [26] (matter to be referred back to the same judge to make an order, if the outcome of a pending IAT appeal made this necessary); *R (Arca) v Cumbria County Council* [2003] EWHC 232 (Admin) (discharging earlier order for "liberty to apply", and dismissing attempt to rely on it to show continuing unlawfulness); *R (Kind) v Secretary of State for the Environment, Food and Rural Affairs* [2005] EWHC 1324 (Admin) [2006] QB 113 (liberty to apply granted).
(B) ADJOURNMENT AS TO (FURTHER) REMEDY. *R v St Albans Magistrates' Court, ex p Read* (1994) 6 Admin LR 201, 204B-E (mandatory order; adjourning quashing order to be pursued if no urgent hearing); *R v Social Fund Inspector, ex p Ali* (1994) 6 Admin LR 205, 224A (application adjourned, so that "if the promised review does not take place ... the court can hear argument if necessary on the natural justice point"); *R v London Borough of Newham, ex p Watkins* (1994) 26 HLR 434, 441 (judicial review adjourned, on council's undertaking to recommend re-hearing by appeals panel, and revived on panel's refusal to conduct such a re-hearing); *R (Lloyd) v Dagenham London Borough Council* [2001] EWCA Civ 533 (2001) 4 CCLR 196 at [3]-[5] (judicial review adjourned on basis of undertakings given to the Court, and then restored when dispute arising as to whether those undertakings had been breached).
(C) APPLICATION ARISING OUT OF ORDER MADE. *R v Ministry of Agriculture Fisheries*

and Food, ex p Anastasiou (Pissouri) Ltd [1999] EuLR 168 (application for an injunction to restrain modified conduct adopted in the light of declaratory remedy granted at hearing of the judicial review of existing judicial review proceedings; application regarded as "arising from" the declaratory remedy); *R v Secretary of State for Trade, ex p Vardy* [1993] ICR 720, 762E-F (referring to a matter "which any court which had to consider the matter in future might well conclude was within the declaration [granted]"); *R v British Coal Corporation, ex p Price (No.2)* [1993] COD 323 (Court unable to add to declaration made, being now functus; and in any event premature until clear what defendant had decided to do; but granting liberty to apply); *R v British Coal Corporation, ex p Price* [1993] COD 482 (application for declaration of non-compliance with the earlier order, rejected on the facts).
(D) NEW/FURTHER ISSUE: NEW APPLICATION. *Silver Mountain Investments Ltd v Attorney-General of Hong Kong* [1994] 1 WLR 925, 937C (refusing to allow claimant to amend pleadings and adduce fresh evidence to support new ground: "these matters, if they have merit, could more appropriately be dealt with by a fresh application for [permission] to apply for judicial review"); *R v Oldham Metropolitan Borough Council, ex p Garlick* [1993] AC 509, 521A-B ("As the local housing authority is in any event going to review its decision there is no purpose in entering upon a *Wednesbury* review at this stage"); <2.5.12> (issue estoppel/ res judicata etc).

24.4.12 **Other special orders.** *R (A) v Secretary of State for the Home Department* [2008] EWHC 142 (Admin) at [39] (mandatory order for release, by grant of bail); *R (Rockware Glass Ltd) v Chester City Council* [2007] Env LR 32 (suspending quashing of permit for industrial plant, pending fresh and lawful decision, to avoid disproportionate effect of closing down or unlawful operation); *R v Secretary of State for the Home Department, ex p Sanusi* [1999] INLR 198 (directing judgment brought to personal attention of Minister); <18.6.6> (directions that judgment to be brought to attention of CLS funding authorities); *R v Feltham Justices, ex p Haid* [1998] COD 440 (directing judgment be sent to Criminal Policy Division of Lord Chancellor's Department, and to Judicial Studies Board, to ensure magistrates properly advised and trained); *R v Secretary of State for the Home Department, ex p Bulger* [2001] EWHC Admin 119 at [60] (directing transcript to go to DPP to consider forgery of documents); *R (A) v Lord Saville of Newdigate* [2001] EWCA Civ 2048 [2002] 1 WLR 1249 at [57] (matter remitted to Tribunal "with a direction that ... evidence should not be taken in Londonderry"); *R v Stoke-on-Trent Crown Court, ex p Marsden* [1999] COD 114 (ordering release of claimant and directing attendance at crown court the following day for bail conditions to be set); *R v Bow Street Magistrates Court, ex p Mitchell* [2000] COD 282 (magistrates' costs order quashed and remitted on condition of claimant giving an undertaking that full disclosure of his financial position would be given to the magistrates).

24.4.13 **Remedy: other special situations.**
(A) ACQUITTALS. *R v Hendon Justices, ex p Director of Public Prosecutions* [1994] QB 167, 174G-175A, 178F ("certiorari can go to quash a decision which is a nullity and which by hypothesis is accordingly not an acquittal... However, it will usually be more appropriate to issue mandamus [requiring the information to be heard] where the prosecution wishes to proceed upon the information"); *R v Dorking Justices, ex p Harrington* [1984] AC 743; <35.1.7> (judicial review of acquittals).
(B) REMEDY WHERE FAILURE TO GIVE REASONS. <62.5>.
(C) REMEDY WHERE DEFENDANT IS FUNCTUS. <47.1.4(F)> (functus).
(D) REMEDY AND REINSTATING EMPLOYEES. *Chief Constable of the North Wales Police v Evans* [1982] 1 WLR 1155 (HL declining to grant mandatory order, although "very tempted"); *Malloch v Aberdeen Corporation* [1971] 1 WLR 1578, 1584D-E (Lord Reid, wrong to grant remedy if "would involve the reinstatement of the appellant"); *Vine v National Dock Labour Board* [1957] AC 488 (declaration granted).

(E) REMEDY AND SETTING ASIDE A CONTRACT. *R (Structadene Ltd) v Hackney London Borough Council* [2001] 2 All ER 225 (where decision to dispose of land unlawful, court quashing the decision and declaring that the contract invalid); *R (the Transport and General Workers Union) v Walsall Metropolitan Borough Council* [2001] EWHC Admin 452 [2002] ELR 329 (on judicial review, Court quashing a decision to enter into a contract, the decision being procedurally flawed since parent governors should not have been excluded; declaration granted that contract void and of no effect).
(F) SEVERANCE. <P43>.

24.4.14 Remedy and avoiding fetter/forbidden substitutionary approach.
(A) FORBIDDEN SUBSTITUTIONARY APPROACH. <15.1>.
(B) AVOIDING FETTERING THE DEFENDANT: GENERAL. *R (Hammerton) v London Underground Ltd* [2002] EWHC 2307 (Admin) at [187] (avoiding, in relation to the consequences of finding a breach of planning control, any remedy which would "substitute the court for the planning authorities"); *Rajkumar v Lalla* 29th November 2001 unrep. (PC) at [23] ("While there may be cases in which the result of a successful judicial review is that the legal considerations provide a unique admissible decision which the statutory authority could lawfully give in the circumstances, that is not the position in the present case"); *R (Hughes) v Commissioner of Local Administration* [2001] EWHC Admin 349 (inappropriate to make order that on reconsideration ombudsman bound to find injustice, being inappropriate as it would fetter her discretion, although Court making clear that it expected such a finding and that there would inevitably be a further reference to the Courts if a contrary conclusion was reached); *R (the Howard League for Penal Reform) v Secretary of State for the Home Department* [2002] EWHC 2497 (Admin) [2003] 1 FLR 484 at [176], [178]-[179] (declining to rule on questions of possible reorganisation of the prison service and responsibility for welfare of child detainees, including policy questions and whether legislation should be amended); *R (D) v Secretary of State for the Home Department* [2003] EWHC 155 (Admin) [2003] 1 FLR 979 at [30] ("I am not in a position to conclude that such reconsideration could have only one possible outcome. It is for the Prison Service to reach a lawful decision following a procedurally and substantively correct reconsideration").
(C) NO FETTER BY QUASHING ORDER. *R (Hirst) v Secretary of State for the Home Department* [2002] EWHC 602 (Admin) [2002] 1 WLR 2929 at [86] (declaration granted that policy unlawful, but quashing order inappropriate because court "would in effect be dictating the policy").
(D) NO FETTER BY MANDATORY ORDER. *R (Hughes) v Commissioner of Local Administration* [2001] EWHC Admin 349 (order that on reconsideration ombudsman bound to find injustice would be inappropriate as would fetter her discretion, but Court making clear that it expected such a finding and that there would inevitably be a further reference to the Courts if a contrary conclusion was reached); *R v Secretary of State for the Home Department, ex p Chugtai* [1995] Imm AR 559, 569 (although appearing inevitable that IAT would need to grant permission to appeal, not "appropriate in these cases to make an order of mandamus ... the proper course is to quash the decision and for them to reconsider in the light of this judgment").
(E) NO FETTER BY INJUNCTION. *R v Secretary of State for the Home Department, ex p Mersin* [2000] INLR 511, 513H-514B (court "can identify breaches of the law by the Secretary of State" but it would be "trespassing on the [defendant]'s own discretion if I were to formulate an injunction or [mandatory order] directing him how to deal with these cases in the future"), applied in *R (Arbab) v Secretary of State for the Home Department* [2002] EWHC 1249 (Admin) [2002] Imm AR 536 (not appropriate for Court to rule on proper management of Government department).
(F) NO FETTER BY DECLARATION. *R v Barnet London Borough Council, ex p Nilish Shah* [1983] 2 AC 309, 350F-351A (certiorari and mandamus granted, but declaration refused, to avoid "any semblance of the courts assuming the function assigned by Parliament to the local

education authority"); *R (T) v Secretary of State for Health* [2002] EWHC 1887 (Admin) (2003) 6 CCLR 277 at [62] (declaration would have involved "trespassing in matters over which Parliament enjoys exclusive jurisdiction, namely making legislation").

> **P25 Monetary remedies.** Recognised debt, restitution and damages
> (not maladministration) claims are available on judicial review.

25.1 Availability of debt, restitution and damages
25.2 No damages for maladministration
25.3 Recognised species of reparation claim

25.1 Availability of debt, restitution and damages.

Reforms in 1977/1981 made it permissible to include a claim for damages in judicial review proceedings, including now just satisfaction under the Human Rights Act 1998. CPR 54 also allows the inclusion of claim in debt or restitution. All such monetary claims need a viable cause of action. They will often be adjourned (or transferred) for separate hearing, and the Court may be cautious about entertaining a judicial review solely designed as a vehicle for a monetary remedy.

25.1.1 Debt, restitution and damages in judicial review: procedural rules. Supreme Court Act 1981 s.31(4) <64.1>; CPR 54.3(2); CPR 16PD para 15; <9.5> (HRA just satisfaction).

25.1.2 The 1977/1981 introduction of damages. *O'Reilly v Mackman* [1983] 2 AC 237, 283A-C (Lord Diplock, describing as the prior "handicap ... that a claim for damages for breach of a right in private law of the applicant resulting from an invalid decision of a public authority could not be made in an application under Order 53. Damages could only be claimed in a separate action begun by writ ... Rule 7 of the new Order 53 permits the applicant for judicial review to include ... a claim for damages and empowers the court to award damages on the hearing of the application if satisfied that such damages could have been awarded to him in an action begun by him by writ at the time of making the application"); cf. *Gulf Insurance Ltd v Central Bank of Trinidad and Tobago* [2005] UKPC 10 (damages for tort of conversion awarded in judicial review proceedings).

25.1.3 Debt/interest. CPR 54.3(2); *R (Elite Mobile Plc) v Customs and Excise Commissioners* [2004] EWHC 2923 (Admin) (debt claim for statutory VAT repayment in judicial review claim, giving rise to interest under s.35A of the Supreme Court Act 1981); *R (Kemp) v Denbighshire Local Health Board* [2006] EWHC 181 (Admin) [2007] 1 WLR 639 (judicial review claim seeking healthcare funding as restitution constituting recovery of a "debt"); *R (Kemp) v Denbighshire Local Health Board* [2006] EWHC 1339 (Admin) (claimant awarded interest under Supreme Court Act 1981 s.35A at special account rate); *R v Ministry of Agriculture Fisheries and Food, ex p Lower Burytown Farms Ltd* [1999] EuLR 128 (declaration granted on judicial review, of claimant's entitlement to interest under Supreme Court Act 1981 s.35A on statutory debt payable pursuant to an EC Directive); *Steed v Secretary of State for the Home Department* [2000] 1 WLR 1169 (statutory right to compensation); cf. *Trustees of the Dennis Rye Pension Fund v Sheffield City Council* [1998] 1 WLR 840, 850H ("An order for payment of money could not be granted on judicial review").

25.1.4 Restitution.[141] CPR 54.3(2) <64.2>; *Kemp* <25.1.3>; *Waikato Regional Airport Ltd v Attorney General* [2003] UKPC 50 (restitution granted in New Zealand judicial review proceedings, where airport levy unfairly imposed); cf. *Woolwich Equitable Building Society v Inland Revenue Commissioners* [1993] AC 70, 170H-171D; *R v Barnet Magistrates Court, ex p Cantor* [1999] 1 WLR 334, 344-346 (declining mandamus to order repayment of money as indirect restitution remedy); *R v East Sussex County Council, ex p Ward* (2000) 3 CCLR 132 at [39]-[40] (judicial review inapt for restitution issues arising out of unlawful agreement); *R*

---

[141] Felicity Toube [1996] JR 92; Graham Virgo [2006] JR 370; Patrick Halliday [2007] JR 178.

(Carvill) v Commissioners of Inland Revenue [2002] EWHC 1488 (Ch) [2002] STC 1167 (claim form action for restitution of taxes, listed together with judicial review as to lawfulness of their retention).

25.1.5 Judicial review as an indirect route to compensation.

(A) COMPENSATION SCHEMES. *R (Mullen) v Secretary of State for the Home Department* [2004] UKHL 18 [2005] 1 AC 1 (judicial review of refusal to pay statutory and ex gratia compensation following quashing of criminal conviction); *R v Investors Compensation Scheme Ltd, ex p Bowden* [1996] 1 AC 261 (Investors Compensation Scheme); *R v Criminal Injuries Compensation Board, ex p Lain* [1967] 2 QB 864 (Criminal Injuries Compensation Scheme); *R v Secretary of State for the Home Department, ex p Fire Brigades Union* [1995] 2 AC 513 (failure to implement statutory scheme); *R v Criminal Injuries Compensation Board, ex p P* [1995] 1 WLR 845 (decision how to modify an existing common law scheme); *R v Eurotunnel Developments Ltd, ex p Stephens* (1997) 73 P & CR 1 (no public law element, in relation to undertakings given by Eurotunnel to introduce scheme); <25.3.14> (statutory compensation). (B) NON-PAYMENT/FAILURE TO PAY.[142] *R v Liverpool City Corporation, ex p Ferguson & Ferguson* [1985] IRLR 501 (judicial review for a declaration of entitlement to be paid); *R v Commissioners of Customs and Excise, ex p Kay and Co* [1996] STC 1500 (declaration of entitlement to be paid forthwith); *R v Tower Hamlets London Borough Council, ex p Chetnik Developments Ltd* [1988] AC 858 (judicial review of the failure to make restitution); *R v Barnet Magistrates Court, ex p Cantor* [1999] 1 WLR 334, 344D (mandatory order to enforce a civil claim in restitution would be an unwarranted extension of the jurisdiction of the court); *R (Wright) v Secretary of State for the Home Department* [2006] EWCA Civ 67 [2006] HRLR 727 (refusal of compensation not capable of creating pre-HRA entitlement to Art 5 damages); *R v Inland Revenue Commissioners, ex p Matrix-Securities Ltd* [1994] 1 WLR 334, 346H-347A (had claimant spent money promoting scheme in reliance on Revenue clearance, "fairness demands that [it] should be reimbursed for this out of pocket expense and it could be regarded as an abuse of power for the revenue to refuse to do so"); *R v Coventry City Council, ex p Coventry Heads of Independent Care Establishments* (1998) 1 CCLR 379, 386E-387H (whether council obliged to increase payments for residential home places in line with DSS rates essentially a contractual dispute and so unsuitable for judicial review).

25.1.6 Adjourning damages for separate hearing. *R (Kurdistan Workers Party) v Secretary of State for the Home Department* [2002] EWHC 644 (Admin) at [87] (Richards J: "In practice, where there is a claim for damages as part of an otherwise appropriate claim for judicial review, the claim for damages would normally be left over to be dealt with as a discrete issue, if still relevant, after the main issues of public law had been determined. Even if still dealt with under CPR Part 54, rather than transferred out of the Administrative Court, it would still generally be subject to directions bringing it broadly into line with a damages claim commenced in the normal way"); *R v Secretary of State for the Home Department, ex p Naheed Ejaz* [1994] QB 496, 508E (claim for damages for false imprisonment remitted for separate hearing); *R v London Borough of Lambeth, ex p Campbell* (1994) 26 HLR 618, 623 (damages adjourned, claimant to issue a summons before the Administrative Court Master for directions); *R v Tower Hamlets London Borough Council, ex p Khalique* (1994) 26 HLR 517, 527 (damages to be assessed); *R v Sandwell Metropolitan Borough Council, ex p Thomas* 22nd December 1992 unrep. (transfer to the county court); *Slough Estates Plc v Welwyn Hatfield District Council* [1996] 2 PLR 50 (damages for deceit continuing as if begun by writ).

---

[142] This subparagraph in a previous edition was cited in *Touchwood Services Ltd v Revenue and Customs Commissioners* [2007] EWHC 105 (Ch) at [12].

25.1.7 **Caution where judicial review solely to underpin damages.** CPR 54.3(2); *R (Bamber) v Revenue & Customs Commissioners* [2007] EWHC 798 (Admin) at [6]-[7] (damages not as sole remedy); *D v Home Office* [2005] EWCA Civ 38 [2006] 1 WLR 1003 at [58] ("no jurisdiction to entertain a claim for damages alone"); *R (Kurdistan Workers Party) v Secretary of State for the Home Department* [2002] EWHC 644 (Admin) at [87] (damages claim "not in itself a good reason for permitting judicial review"); *R v Ministry of Agriculture, Fisheries and Food, ex p Live Sheep Traders Ltd* [1995] COD 297 (see transcript) (refusing declaration as to unlawfulness of scheme/decision, where simply to underpin damages claim, it being wrong "needlessly to invoke this court's jurisdiction to establish that which not only can, but can more conveniently, be established elsewhere"); *R v Dorset Police Authority, ex p Vaughan* [1995] COD 153 (declaration would have been appropriate to form the basis for a civil claim to enforce pension rights); *R v Chief Constable of the West Midlands Police, ex p Carroll* (1995) 7 Admin LR 45, 47C (appeal entertained and allowed, being "not academic" since "if it succeeds the appellant would be entitled to damages for lost salary); *R (Machi) v Legal Services Commission* [2001] EWHC Admin 580 at [24] (Court deciding to hear the case because ruling on unlawfulness "would create an issue estoppel ... and might be of assistance" to a damages claim) (CA is [2001] EWCA Civ 2010 [2002] 1 WLR 983); *R (N) v Secretary of State for the Home Department* [2003] EWHC 207 (Admin) [2003] HRLR 583 (declaration and HRA damages entertained: CA is *Anufrijeva v Southwark London Borough Council* [2003] EWCA Civ 1406 [2004] QB 1124); *R (Mohamed) v Secretary of State for the Home Department* [2003] EWHC 1530 (Admin) (declaration that previous detention unlawful; with directions as to disposal of consequential damages claim); *R v Deputy Governor of Parkhurst Prison, ex p Hague* [1992] 1 AC 58, 156H-157B (CA declaration that segregation unlawful the backcloth to HL dealing with damages); *Chief Constable of the North Wales Police v Evans* [1982] 1 WLR 1155, 1175H ("declaration would clarify the status of the [claimant] ... and would leave him free to pursue such remedies, short of reinstatement, as may be open to him"); *R v Lambeth London Borough Council, ex p Sarbrook Ltd* (1995) 27 HLR 380 (declaration granted of failure to comply with statutory duty, but damages refused because Act not intended to confer right to damages); *C.O. Williams Construction v Donald George Blackman* [1995] 1 WLR 102, 109E-H (Privy Council refusing to strike out judicial review proceedings seeking a declaration, which "alone would be academic", because of possibility of damages under the Barbados Act); *Sita Kamara Vafi v Secretary of State for the Home Department* [1996] Imm AR 169 (not appropriate to grant permission for judicial review for purpose of founding private law remedy); *R v Gloucestershire County Council, ex p P* [1994] ELR 334, 340D (declaration would have "little or no value for the future because if there is to be a claim for damages ... it would have to be heard on the basis of oral evidence"); *R v Secretary of State for Social Security, ex p Armstrong* (1996) 8 Admin LR 626 (refusing permission where issues academic as regards claimant, save for alleged *Francovich* reparation claim); *R v Secretary of State for Employment, ex p Equal Opportunities Commission* [1995] 1 AC 1, 32B-D (although incompatibility with EC law, wrong to grant declaration of *Francovich* breach, the issues being appropriate for separate damages actions), applied in *R v Secretary of State for Employment, ex p Seymour-Smith* [1997] 1 WLR 473, 480E; *Davy v Spelthorne Borough Council* [1984] AC 262, 278E (doubting declaration or damages available if no prerogative order could be sought), doubted in *R v Chelmsford Crown Court, ex p Chief Constable of the Essex Police* [1994] 1 WLR 359, 368G-369F; *R v London Commodity Exchange (1986) Ltd, ex p Brealey* [1994] COD 145 (essentially a private claim for damages and therefore a matter for private law); *R v Tower Hamlets London Borough Council, ex p Luck* [1999] COD 294 (challenge to tendering decision should be by private law action for damages).

25.1.8 **Other general matters.** *Matthews v Ministry of Defence* [2003] UKHL 4 [2003] 1 AC 1163 (whether immunity from liability under the Crown Proceedings Act 1947 compatible with the HRA); *Jones v Department of Employment* [1989] QB 1 (negligence precluded by statutory ouster); *R v Ministry of Agriculture Fisheries and Food, ex p Lower Burytown Farms Ltd* [1999] EuLR 129 (declaration that interest payable under Supreme Court Act 1981 in respect of statutory debt).

25.2 No damages for maladministration.The mere existence of a recognised species of unlawfulness or `public law wrong' does not give rise to any right to damages. Sadly, nor is there yet even a residual power on the part of the Court to award a monetary sum where necessary in the interests of justice. Parliament and the Courts have yet to fashion a public law solution to the well-recognised problem of the injustice where maladministration calls for a monetary response.

25.2.1 No general right to damages. *R (Quark Fishing Ltd) v Secretary of State for Foreign and Commonwealth Affairs* [2005] UKHL 57 [2006] 1 AC 529 at [96] (Baroness Hale: "Our law does not recognise a right to claim damages for losses caused by unlawful administrative action ... There has to be a distinct cause of action in tort or under the Human Rights Act 1998"); *R (Nurse Prescribers Ltd) v Secretary of State for Health* [2004] EWHC 403 (Admin) at [82] (compensation "not available directly in judicial review proceedings arising out of a claim for disappointment of a legitimate expectation"); *R v Secretary of State for Transport, ex p Factortame Ltd (No.2)* [1991] 1 AC 603, 672H (Lord Goff: "in this country there is no general right to indemnity by reason of damage suffered through invalid administrative action"); *R v Ealing London Borough Council, ex p Parkinson* (1996) 8 Admin LR 281, 285C-F (Laws J, referring to the "general principle of administrative law, namely that the law recognises no right of compensation for administrative tort"), 291H; *K v Secretary of State for the Home Department* [2002] EWCA Civ 775 at [30] (CA insistence on proximity requirement for a common law duty of care lest "the court would have in effect created a category of administrative tort sounding in damages"); *Mercury Energy Ltd v Electricity Corporation of New Zealand Ltd* [1994] 1 WLR 521, 526A (difference between basis for judicial review and "actionable wrong"); *R (Banks) v Secretary of State for the Environment, Food and Rural Affairs* [2004] EWHC 416 (Admin) at [117] (where unfair herd movement restriction order, Court "not ... able to award damages in these proceedings to the claimants even though they have suffered substantial financial loss"); <3.3.1> (tort claim following successful judicial review); <25.3.7(E)> (public law unlawfulness not negligent per se).

25.2.2 The need for a solution.[143] *Somerville v Scottish Ministers* [2007] UKHL 44 [2007] 1 WLR 2734 at [77] (Lord Scott: "A chapter of public law still, however, largely unwritten relates to the ability of courts, in actions where public law challenges to administrative action have succeeded, to award compensation to those who have sustained loss as a consequence of the administrative action in question"); *Stovin v Wise* [1996] AC 923, 931F-G ("a coherent, principled control mechanism has to be found"), 933F-G (Lord Nicholls, referring to the "knotty problem" and "unease over the inability of public law, in some instances, to afford a remedy matching the wrong"), 940E ("public law is unable to give an effective remedy ... A concurrent common law duty is needed to fill the gap"); *Hoffmann-La Roche (F) & Co AG v Secretary of State for Trade and Industry* [1975] AC 295, 359B-C (Lord Wilberforce, speaking of English law's "unwillingness to accept that a subject should be indemnified for loss sustained by invalid administrative action... In more developed legal systems this particular difficulty does not arise"); Justice/All Souls Report, *Administrative Justice: Some Necessary Reforms* (1988), p.364 ("A remedy should be available where a person suffers loss as a result of wrongful administrative action not involving negligence"; and "where loss is caused by excessive or

---

[143] Michael Fordham [2003] JR 104; John Corkindale [2004] JR 61.

unreasonable delay in reaching a decision"); *R v Commissioners of Customs and Excise, ex p F & I Services Ltd* [2001] EWCA Civ 762 at [73] (Sedley LJ: "That the cases do not include damages for abuses of power falling short of [misfeasance] in public office does not necessarily mean that door is closed to them in principle. But the policy implications of such a step are immense, and it may well be that - despite the presence for some years in the rules of a power to award damages on an application for judicial review - a legal entitlement to them cannot now come into being without legislation"); *R (Quark Fishing Ltd) v Secretary of State for Foreign and Commonwealth Affairs* [2003] EWHC 1743 (Admin) at [44] (Collins J: "this case is yet another which shows that consideration should be given by Parliament to providing some possibility of a claim for damages for unlawful executive action which causes loss. It is clearly not something which can be done by the courts"); *Cullen v Chief Constable of the Royal Ulster Constabulary* [2003] UKHL 39 [2003] 1 WLR 1763 at [71] (solution in addressing any lacuna in the law, is for public law not private law); *Gorringe v Calderdale Metropolitan Borough Council* [2004] UKHL 15 [2004] 1 WLR 1057 at [2] (Lord Steyn: "This is a subject of great complexity and very much an evolving area of the law"; "On the one hand the courts must not contribute to the creation of a society bent on litigation, which is premised on the illusion that for every misfortune there is a remedy. On the other hand, there are cases where the courts must recognise on principled grounds the compelling demands of corrective justice"); *Watkins v Secretary of State for the Home Department* [2006] UKHL 17 [2006] 2 AC 395 at [10] (ongoing work of the Law Commission in relation to monetary remedies in public law), [26] (describing the "undesirability of introducing by judicial decision, without consultation, a solution which the consultation and research conducted by the Law Commission may show to be an unsatisfactory solution to what is in truth a small part of a wider problem"); *Sandhar v Department of Transport, Environment and the Regions* [2004] EWCA Civ 1440 [2005] 1 WLR 1632 at [57] (Brooke LJ: "I do not see how this court can remedy what appears to be a significant injustice", but "I for one would welcome it if some administrative means could be found of assisting [the claimant] out of public funds").

25.2.3 **Damages for maladministration: other aspects.** *R v Knowsley Borough Council, ex p Maguire* [1992] COD 499 (rejecting, in the context of refusal of taxi licences, ingenious arguments as to contract, breach of statutory duty and negligence, attempting to remedy the absence of damages for breach of administrative law); *Cullen v Chief Constable of the Royal Ulster Constabulary* [2003] UKHL 39 [2003] 1 WLR 1763 at [49] (rejecting the idea of a new innominate tort); *R (Quark Fishing Ltd) v Secretary of State for Foreign and Commonwealth Affairs* [2003] EWHC 1743 (Admin) at [42] (Collins J, rejecting the suggestion of a "novel" claim for "breach of common law rights", being a hopeless "attempt to elevate a claimed legitimate expectation to become a right at common law"); *Chagos Islanders v Attorney General* [2004] EWCA Civ 997 at [20]-[26] (Sedley LJ, explaining the problem that common law tort claims are not available in English law against "the State" or "the Crown" as such, but only against limbs of the state having "corporate legal personality" or for personal responsibility of individuals or Crown vicarious liability for individuals' conduct; but, beyond the HRA, "the state is not a potential tortfeasor"); Bell and Bradley, *Governmental Liability: A Comparative Study* (1991) (comparative survey); *Ramesh Lawrence Maharaj v Attorney-General of Trinidad and Tobago (No.2)* [1979] AC 385, 399F-G (constitutional "redress", not in tort but in public law); *C.O. Williams Construction v Donald George Blackman* [1995] 1 WLR 102, 109H (statutory damages under s.5(2)(f) of the Administrative Justice Act of Barbados) Recommendation No.R(84)15 of the Committee of Ministers (18th September 1984) (reparation from public authorities); *R v Ealing London Borough Council, ex p Parkinson* (1996) 8 Admin LR 281, 287C-288A (commenting that damages could make the court "a fact-finding tribunal").

25.3 **Recognised species of reparation claim.**[144] Absent a much-needed statutory or public law solution, claims for reparation have to fit within established causes or rights of action. They include claims in negligence and breach of statutory duty, misfeasance in public office, *Francovich* reparation, and just satisfaction under HRA s.7.

25.3.1 *Francovich* **reparation.** <8.5.2>.

25.3.2 **Just satisfaction under the HRA.** <9.5>.

25.3.3 **Damages for breach of contract.** *Harmon CFEM Facades (UK) Ltd v Corporate Officer of the House of Commons* (1999) 67 Con LR 1 (liability to tenderer for breach of implied contract); *R (Supportways Community Services Ltd) v Hampshire County Council (No.2)* [2006] EWCA Civ 1170 (2006) 9 CCLR 498 (damages to be assessed as to breach of contractual duty to conduct services review).

25.3.4 **Tort claims: general considerations.**
(A) TORT AVAILABLE IN PRINCIPLE. *Stovin v Wise* [1996] AC 923, 946G (well-established that a public body is, in principle, liable in tort; but such liability can be restricted by statutory authority or wide discretionary powers); <25.3.7(A)> (negligence available in principle); <25.3.6(A)> (breach of statutory duty available in principle).
(B) VICARIOUS LIABILITY. *Phelps v Hillingdon London Borough Council* [2001] 2 AC 619 (council vicariously liable for negligence by educational psychologists and teachers); *Racz v Home Office* [1994] 2 AC 45 (possible Home Office vicarious liability for misfeasance by prison officers); *Majrowski v Guy's and St Thomas's NHS Trust* [2006] UKHL 34 [2007] 1 AC 224 (NHS Trust capable of being vicariously liable for breach of harassment obligation).
(C) AGGRAVATED AND EXEMPLARY DAMAGES. *Watkins v Secretary of State for the Home Department* [2006] UKHL 17 [2006] 2 AC 395 at [26] ("the policy of the law is not in general to encourage the award of exemplary damages"); *Rowlands v Chief Constable of Merseyside Police* [2006] EWCA Civ 1773 [2007] 1 WLR 1065 (exemplary damages); *Thompson v Commissioner of Police of the Metropolis* [1998] QB 498 (approach to quantum in relation to exemplary damages); *Attorney General of Trinidad and Tobago v Ramanoop* [2005] UKPC 15 [2006] 1 AC 328 (exemplary-type damages appropriate as constitutional "redress"); <25.3.5> (aggravated/exemplary damages and misfeasance).

25.3.5 **Misfeasance in public office.**[145] *Three Rivers District Council v Bank of England* [2003] 2 AC 1, 191B-196E (need for: (1) a public officer; (2) exercising power as a public officer; (3) targeted malice (conduct specifically intended to injure a person or persons) or action with knowledge or reckless indifference (ie. subjective recklessness - not caring) to the illegality of the act and the probability of causing injury to the claimant (or his class); (4) no separate requirement of proximity; (5) causation necessary; (6) losses only recoverable if actually foreseen as probable); *R Cruickshank Ltd v Chief Constable of Kent County Constabulary* [2002] EWCA Civ 1840 at [28]-[29] (summarising the effect of *Three Rivers*); *Southwark London Borough Council v Dennett* [2007] EWCA Civ 1091 [2008] LGR 94 (need for subjective recklessness); *Akenzua v Secretary of State for the Home Department* [2002] EWCA Civ 1470 [2003] 1 WLR 741 (applicable to personal death or personal injury; no need to be "the predictable victim"); *Watkins v Secretary of State for the Home Department* [2006] UKHL 17 [2006] 2 AC 395 (need for proof of special damage; exemplary damages only if special

---

[144] Michael Fordham & Gemma White [2001] JR 44 & 109.

[145] David Elvin [1998] JR 26, Sarah Hannett [2005] JR 227; Duncan Fairgrieve [2007] JR 169.

damage); *Karagozlu v Metropolitan Police Commissioner* [2006] EWCA Civ 1691 [2007] 1 WLR 1881 (transfer to closed conditions sufficiently special damage); *Harmon CFEM Facades (UK) Ltd v Corporate Officer of the House of Commons* (1999) 67 Con LR 1 (misfeasance where operated a "buy British" policy in a tendering context, knowing or reckless as to its unlawfulness, and had falsified the reasons for the decision); *Kuddus v Chief Constable of Leicestershire Constabulary* [2001] UKHL 29 [2002] 2 AC 122 at [3], [30] (police officer's forgery of a statement constituting misfeasance), [3] (aggravated damages available); *Racz v Home Office* [1994] 2 AC 45 (possibility of Home Office vicarious liability for any misfeasance by prison officers); *Darker v Chief Constable of the West Midlands Police* [2001] 1 AC 435 (considering extent of any immunity from liability for misfeasance, in the context of criminal investigations); *O'Brien v Chief Constable of South Wales Police* [2005] UKHL 26 [2005] 2 WLR 1038 (admissibility of similar fact evidence in claim for misfeasance).

25.3.6 **Breach of statutory duty.**
(A) AVAILABLE IN PRINCIPLE. *M v Home Office* [1994] 1 AC 377, 412H-413A ("no reason in principle why, if a statute places a duty on a specified minister or other official which creates a cause of action, an action cannot be brought for breach of statutory duty claiming damages or for an injunction"); *Kirvek Management and Consulting Services Ltd v Attorney General of Trinidad and Tobago* [2002] UKPC 43 [2002] 1 WLR 2792 at [16]-[19] (actionable breach of statutory duty under Trinidad and Tobago legislation, for failure by court registry to place money into an interest-bearing account); *Mitchell v Department of Transport* [2006] EWCA Civ 1089 [2006] 1 WLR 3356 (actionable statutory duty to maintain the highway).
(B) STATUTORY DUTIES NOT GENERALLY ACTIONABLE. *O'Rourke v Camden London Borough Council* [1998] AC 188 (homelessness duties under the Housing Act 1985 not intended to create private law cause of action since part of social welfare scheme (in the public interest); largely dependent on exercise of judgment and discretion; and enforceable in public law); *T v Surrey County Council* [1994] 4 All ER 577, 597g (describing the "considerable reluctance on the part of the courts to impose upon local authorities any liability for breach of statutory duty other than that expressly imposed in the statute"); *Clunis v Camden and Islington Health Authority* [1998] QB 978 (no liability for breach of statutory duty under Mental Health Act 1983 s.117(2)); *Cullen v Chief Constable of the Royal Ulster Constabulary* [2003] UKHL 39 [2003] 1 WLR 1763 (statutory duty to give reasons for deferring access to lawyer not actionable in damages, at least absent loss or injury); *Bowden v South West Water Services Ltd* [1998] Env LR 445 (no liability under Water Resources Act 1991 or Water Industry Act 1991); *Neil Martin Ltd v Revenue & Customs Commissioners* [2007] EWCA Civ 1041 (statutory duty to issue tax certificate not an actionable duty).
(C) TEST OF LEGISLATIVE INTENTION. *R v Deputy Governor of Parkhurst Prison, ex p Hague* [1992] 1 AC 58, 170H-171A (asking "whether the legislature intended that private law rights of action should be conferred upon individuals in respect of breaches of the relevant statutory provision"); *Phelps v Hillingdon London Borough Council* [2001] 2 AC 619, 652F ("The general nature of the duties imposed on local authorities in the context of a national system of education and the remedies available by way of appeal and judicial review indicate that Parliament did not intend to create a statutory remedy by way of damages").
(D) OTHER FACTORS. *Wentworth v Wiltshire County Council* [1993] QB 654 (right to damages for breach of statutory duty not extending to this loss on the part of this claimant); *Customs & Excise Commissioners v Barclays Bank Plc* [2006] UKHL 28 [2006] 3 WLR 1 (discussing bases for liability for economic loss); *Cullen v Chief Constable of the Royal Ulster Constabulary* [2003] UKHL 39 [2003] 1 WLR 1763 at [44] (actionability of statutory duty to give reasons for deferring access to lawyer would need harm); *Attorney-General of the British Virgin Islands v Hartwell* [2004] UKPC 12 [2004] 1 WLR 1273 at [27] (no hard and fast rule in deciding which types of damage reasonably foreseeable); *Butchart v Home Office* [2006] EWCA Civ 239 [2006] 1 WLR 1155 (prison service duty of care extending to psychiatric

injury); *Phelps v Hillingdon London Borough Council* [2001] 2 AC 619, 652F (referring to "the remedies available by way of appeal and judicial review" as among the indicators "that Parliament did not intend to create a statutory remedy by way of damages"); *X (Minors) v Bedfordshire County Council* [1995] 2 AC 633, 747E-F, 751B, 769H (absence or existence of another remedy an indicator for or against liability for breach of statutory duty); *Clunis v Camden and Islington Health Authority* [1998] QB 978, 991F (Secretary of State's default powers "the primary method of enforcement of the obligations").

(E) BREACH OF RULES/REGULATIONS. *Calveley v Chief Constable of Merseyside* [1989] AC 1228, 1237C-H (whether breach of Regulations sounded in damages); *P v Liverpool Daily Post & Echo Newspapers Plc* [1991] 2 AC 370, 419G-420D (whether Rules conferring cause of action in damages); *R v Deputy Governor of Parkhurst Prison, ex p Hague* [1992] 1 AC 58 (whether breach of Prison Rules sounded in damages); *Dugmore v Swansea NHS Trust* [2002] EWCA Civ 1689 [2003] 1 All ER 333 (hospital's actionable duty as employer, owed to nurse employee, for breach of Control of Substances Hazardous to Health Regulations); *Smith v Northamptonshire County Council* [2008] EWCA Civ 181 [2008] 3 All ER 1054 (scope of liability as employer for breach of regulations).

25.3.7 Negligence: general points.

(A) NEGLIGENCE AVAILABLE IN PRINCIPLE. *Davy v Spelthorne Borough Council* [1984] AC 262, 276C (Lord Wilberforce: "There is no doubt that, side by side with their statutory duties, local authorities may in certain limited circumstances become liable for negligence at common law in the performance of their duties"); *Phelps v Hillingdon London Borough Council* [2001] 2 AC 619 (local authorities capable of being vicariously liable for negligence by educational psychologists and teachers).

(B) DUTY OF CARE: ILLUSTRATIONS. *Butchart v Home Office* [2006] EWCA Civ 239 [2006] 1 WLR 1155 (duty of care capable of arising where prison authorities knowingly putting vulnerable prisoner with suicidal cellmate); *Lennon v Metropolitan Police Commissioner* [2004] EWCA Civ 130 [2004] 1 WLR 2594 (police personnel officer's actionable duty of care where negligent advice as to housing allowance implications of inter-force transfer); *R (A) v Secretary of State for the Home Department* [2004] EWHC 1585 (Admin) (actionable duty of care where maladministration resulting in denial of asylum welfare benefits); *Attorney-General of the British Virgin Islands v Hartwell* [2004] UKPC 12 [2004] 1 WLR 1273 (actionable duty of care breached in entrusting an unsuitable officer with firearms); *A v Essex County Council* [2003] EWCA Civ 1848 [2004] 1 WLR 1881 (having decided what information to provide to adoptive parents, council having breached actionable duty of care in failing to take reasonable care in passing on that information); *Barber v Somerset County Council* [2004] UKHL 13 [2004] 1 WLR 1089 (local education authority liable in damages for breach of employer's duty of care arising out of inaction during onset of teacher's breakdown through work-related stress).

(C) NO DUTY OF CARE: ILLUSTRATIONS. *Van Colle v Hertfordshire Chief Constable* [2008] UKHL 50 [2008] 3 WLR 593 (no duty of care in protecting from death threats); *Jain v Trent Strategic Health Authority* [2007] EWCA Civ 1186 [2008] QB 246 (no duty of care by registration authority applying for court order against nursing home); *Rowley v Secretary of State for Work and Pensions* [2007] EWCA Civ 598 [2007] 1 WLR 2861 (no duty of care for defaults of Child Support Agency); *Lawrence v Pembrokeshire County Council* [2007] EWCA Civ 446 [2007] 1 WLR 2991 (no duty of care owed to parent regarding child protection registration of children); *D v Bury Metropolitan Borough Council* [2006] EWCA Civ 1 [2006] 1 WLR 917 (no actionable duty of care in context of interim care order based on child abuse allegations).

(D) THE DEVELOPING LAW. <25.3.11> (Lord Bingham's new dawn); *Gorringe v Calderdale Metropolitan Borough Council* [2004] UKHL 15 [2004] 1 WLR 1057 at [2] (Lord Steyn, observing in relation to "negligence and statutory duties and powers": "This is a subject of great complexity and very much an evolving area of the law"); *R v Commissioners of Customs and*

Excise, ex p F & I Services Ltd [2000] STC 364, 380c-d (Carnwath J, referring to negligence and public authorities as "a developing area of the law" in a "fluid state") (CA is [2001] EWCA Civ 762); *W v Essex County Council* [2001] 2 AC 592 (arguable negligence claim in respect of placement of foster child with claimants); *Barrett v Enfield London Borough Council* [2001] 2 AC 550 (duty of care capable of arising, depending on proven facts, in relation to children in care); *Phelps v Hillingdon London Borough Council* [2001] 2 AC 619 (duty of care capable of arising in educational contexts), applied in *Carty v Croydon London Borough Council* [2004] EWHC 228 (QB) [2004] ELR 226 (local education authority not liable in negligence in special educational needs case); *R (A) v Secretary of State for the Home Department* [2004] EWHC 1585 (Admin) (recognising actionable duty of care in asylum welfare benefits context, as an incremental step in the development of the law).

(E) PUBLIC LAW UNLAWFULNESS NOT NEGLIGENT PER SE. *Rowling v Takaro Properties Ltd* [1988] AC 473, 502B ("misconstruing a statute ... can be severely criticised without attracting the epithet `negligent'"); *Dunlop v Woollahra Municipal Council* [1982] AC 158, 172D ("failure by a public authority to give a person an adequate hearing before deciding to exercise a statutory power in a manner which will affect him or his property, cannot by itself amount to a breach of a duty of care sounding in damages"); *R v Deputy Chief Constable of Thames Valley Police, ex p Cotton* [1989] COD 318, 320 ("The mere fact of succeeding in judicial review proceedings does not supply [a cause of action]").

(F) WHETHER BREACH. *Faulkner v Enfield London Borough Council* [2003] ELR 426 (school and local education authority owing duty of care to pupils in respect of bullying, but duty discharged here); *Jenney (A Minor) v North Lincolnshire County Council* [2000] LGR 269 (council in breach of common law duty of care because claimant had been able to wander out onto the road and school was unable to show that it had taken all reasonable precautions); *Phelps v Hillingdon London Borough Council* [2001] 2 AC 619, 655B, 672F (in asking whether negligence in educational services, appropriate to apply the medical negligence test: whether acted in accordance with a practice accepted as proper by a responsible body of opinion).

(G) TYPE OF LOSS. *R (A) v Secretary of State for the Home Department* [2004] EWHC 1585 (Admin) (negligence action permissible albeit that pure economic loss); *Harris v Evans* [1998] 1 WLR 1285 (emphasising that economic loss); *Perrett v Collins* The Times 23rd June 1998 (duty of care of air certifying authority as to physical injury); *Adams v Bracknell Forest Borough Council* [2004] UKHL 29 [2004] 3 All ER 897 (impaired literacy as a consequence of unidentified dyslexia capable of constituting personal injury for limitation period purposes); *Stovin v Wise* [1996] AC 923, 948G-949A; *Marc Rich & Co AG v Bishop Rock Marine Co Ltd* [1996] 1 AC 211, 237D-G; *Murphy v Brentwood District Council* [1991] 1 AC 398.

(H) CAUSATION. *Chester v Afshar* [2004] UKHL 41 [2004] 3 WLR 927 (causation considered and modified, to provide a remedy in the interests of policy and corrective justice, in a medical negligence context).

25.3.8 Negligence: 3 preconditions. See *Caparo Industries Plc v Dickman* [1990] 2 AC 605, applied in *Phelps v Hillingdon London Borough Council* [2001] 2 AC 619, 653C:

(A) FORESEEABILITY. *X & Y v Hounslow London Borough Council* [2008] EWHC 1168 (QB) (reasonably foreseeable that failure to transfer vulnerable couple would result in injuries by local youths); *Attorney-General of the British Virgin Islands v Hartwell* [2004] UKPC 12 [2004] 1 WLR 1273 at [21] (reasonable foreseeability requirement); *Kent v Griffiths* [2001] QB 36 (reasonably foreseeable injuries from ambulance delay)*Jebson v Ministry of Defence* [2000] 1 WLR 2055 (reasonably foreseeable that drunken officer would fall from unsupervised vehicle).

(B) PROXIMITY/ASSUMPTION OF RESPONSIBILITY. *Neil Martin Ltd v Revenue & Customs Commissioners* [2007] EWCA Civ 1041 (voluntary assumption of responsibility in relation to tax certificate application); *Phelps v Hillingdon London Borough Council* [2001] 2 AC 619 (sufficient nexus or assumption of responsibility where educational psychologist assessing child or teacher providing for educational needs); *Rowley v Secretary of State for*

Work and Pensions [2007] EWCA Civ 598 [2007] 1 WLR 2861 at [54] (no assumption of responsibility); *K v Secretary of State for the Home Department* [2002] EWCA Civ 775 (insufficient proximity nexus); *Sandhar v Department of Transport, Environment and the Regions* [2004] EWCA Civ 1440 [2005] 1 WLR 1632 (no voluntary assumption of responsibility).
(C) FAIR, JUST AND REASONABLE. *Rowley v Secretary of State for Work and Pensions* [2007] EWCA Civ 598 [2007] 1 WLR 2861 at [84] (not fair just and reasonable to impose actionable duty of care); *D v East Berkshire Community Health NHS Trust* [2005] UKHL 23 [2005] 2 AC 373 (applying fair, just and reasonable test); *R (A) v Secretary of State for the Home Department* [2004] EWHC 1585 (Admin) at [43] (fair just and reasonable; indeed, unjust if not a remedy).

25.3.9 **Negligence: impact of the HRA.** *Z v United Kingdom* (2001) 34 EHRR 97 (no Art 6 violation if "immunity" simply expression of principles of substantive law); *Matthews v Ministry of Defence* [2003] UKHL 4 [2003] 1 AC 1163 (statutory immunity against tort action by armed forces a rule of substantive law and not a procedural bar, so not incompatible with Art 6); *S v Gloucestershire County Council* [2001] Fam 313 (can be appropriate and compatible with ECHR Art 6 to strike out a negligence claim on basis that no duty of care capable of arising); *Mowan v Wandsworth London Borough Council* (2001) 33 HLR 616 (strike out compatible with Art 6); *Jones v Ministry of Interior of Saudi Arabia* [2006] UKHL 26 [2007] 1 AC 270 (Art 6 implications of immunity for state officials re torture); *D v Home Office* [2005] EWCA Civ 38 [2006] 1 WLR 1003 (considering suggested immunity for immigration officials from tort of false imprisonment, in HRA context).

25.3.10 **Negligence and statutory powers/duties.** *Stovin v Wise* [1996] AC 923, 946G-947A (Lord Hoffmann: "in the absence of express statutory authority, a public body is in principle liable for torts in the same way as a private person. But its statutory powers or duties may restrict its liability"); *Phelps v Hillingdon London Borough Council* [2001] 2 AC 619 (duty of care arising in the context of statutory powers); *R (A) v Secretary of State for the Home Department* [2004] EWHC 1585 (Admin) (actionable duty of care albeit relating to omissions in failing to exercise statutory powers); *Barrett v Enfield London Borough Council* [2001] 2 AC 550 (whether irrationality an appropriate precondition for showing negligence); *Carty v Croydon London Borough Council* [2005] EWCA Civ 19 [2005] 1 WLR 2312 (whether liability for actionable duty of care by education officer performing statutory duties); *Dorset Yacht Co Ltd v Home Office* [1970] AC 1004 (whether performance of statutory duty actionable in negligence); *Stovin v Wise* [1996] AC 923, 952F-953A ("Whether a statutory duty gives rise to a private cause of action is a question of construction").

25.3.11 **Lord Bingham's new dawn.** *D v East Berkshire Community Health NHS Trust* [2005] UKHL 23 [2005] 2 AC 373 at [49] (Lord Bingham, dissenting: "the concept of duty has proved itself a somewhat blunt instrument for dividing claims which ought reasonably to lead to recovery from claims which ought not"), [50] ("the law of tort should evolve, analogically and incrementally, so as to fashion appropriate remedies to contemporary problems"), [92] (Lord Nicholls, explaining the attractiveness of the idea that "the common law should jettison the concept of duty of care as a universal prerequisite to liability in negligence"), [93] ("identifying the parameters of an expanding law of negligence is proving difficult, especially in fields involving the discharge of statutory functions by public authorities"; in human rights law "In deciding whether overall the end result was acceptable the court makes a value judgment based on more flexible notions than the common law standard of reasonableness and does so freed from the legal rigidity of a duty of care"), [94] (removal of the duty of care-based approach "would be likely to lead to a lengthy and unnecessary period of uncertainty in an important area of the law", at least "unless replaced by a control mechanism").

25.3.12 **Other species of tort liability: illustrations.**[146] *Gulf Insurance Ltd v Central Bank of Trinidad and Tobago* [2005] UKPC 10 (damages for tort of conversion awarded in judicial review proceedings); *Ashley v Chief Constable of Sussex Police* [2008] UKHL 25 [2008] 3 All ER 573 (assault and battery); *D v Home Office* [2005] EWCA Civ 38 [2006] 1 WLR 1003 (false imprisonment); *Slough Estates Plc v Welwyn Hatfield District Council* [1996] 2 PLR 50 (deceit); *Gregory v Portsmouth City Council* [2000] 1 AC 419 (malicious prosecution); *Tomlinson v Congleton Borough Council* [2003] UKHL 47 [2004] 1 AC 46 (occupiers liability); *In re Organ Retention Group Litigation* [2004] EWHC 644 (QB) [2005] QB 506 (wrongful interference); *S v Newham London Borough Council* [1998] 1 FLR 1061 (defamation); *Feakins v DEFRA* [2005] EWCA Civ 1535 [2006] Env LR 1099 (trespass); *Keegan v Chief Constable of Merseyside* [2003] EWCA Civ 936 (malicious procurement of warrant); *Darker v Chief Constable of the West Midlands Police* [2001] 1 AC 435 (conspiracy to injure); *R Cruickshank Ltd v Chief Constable of Kent County Constabulary* [2002] EWCA Civ 1840 (interference with contractual relations capable of lying against public officials); *Wainwright v Home Office* [2003] UKHL 53 [2004] 2 AC 406 (intentional infliction of harm); *Dennis v Ministry of Defence* [2003] EWHC 793 (QB) [2003] Env LR 741 (nuisance); *Transco Plc v Stockport Metropolitan Borough Council* [2003] UKHL 61 [2004] 2 AC 1 (rule in *Rylands v Fletcher*).

25.3.13 **Employment remedies.** *Dunnachie v Kingston upon Hull City Council* [2004] UKHL 36 [2005] 1 AC 226 (unfair dismissal).

25.3.14 **Statutory compensation.** *Steed* <25.1.3>; *Westminster City Council v Ocean Leisure Ltd* [2004] EWCA Civ 970 (statutory compensation under compulsory purchase legislation); *R (O'Brien) v Independent Assessor* [2007] UKHL 10 [2007] 2 AC 312 (level of statutory compensation for miscarriage of justice detention); *British Telecommunications Plc v Gwynedd Council* [2004] EWCA Civ 942 [2004] 4 All ER 975 (allowable costs under street works legislation).

---

[146] Heather Williams QC [2007] JR 145; Christopher Knight [2007] JR 165.

B. PARAMETERS OF JUDICIAL REVIEW

further dominant themes shaping the law and practice

P26 Delay
P27 Public/private
P28 Ouster
P29 Interpretation
P30 Function
P31 Context
P32 Modified review
P33 Flux
P34 Reviewability
P35 Non-reviewability
P36 Alternative remedy
P37 Proportionality template
P38 Standing
P39 Discretion/duty
P40 Inalienability
P41 Legitimate expectation
P42 Onus
P43 Severance
P44 Nullity

<1.1> means "see para 1.1"

> **P26 Delay.** Judicial review must be commenced promptly; undue delay may lead to refusal of permission or (if prejudicial) a remedy.

26.1 The approach to delay
26.2 Promptness and the running of time
26.3 Good reason to extend time
26.4 Hardship, prejudice and detriment

26.1 **The approach to delay.** Judicial review claims are required to be commenced promptly. At the permission stage the Court can refuse permission for lack of promptness if either: (1) there is no good reason for extending time; or (2) the combined effect of the delay and the likely hardship, prejudice or detriment from the remedy sought justifies dismissal of the case. At the substantive hearing, a remedy may be refused for delay, but on ground (2) alone.

26.1.1 **The delay rules.** See Supreme Court Act 1981 s.31(6) <64.1>; CPR 54.5 <64.2>; CPR 54PD <64.3> para 4.1; ACO:NFG <64.4> para 5.1-5.2. *R (Melton) v School Organisation Committee* [2001] EWHC Admin 245 (Administrative Court's approach to delay no less rigorous than it had been under RSC Ord 53); <9.4.6> (HRA: the one year rule).

26.1.2 **The interests of speedy certainty.** *O'Reilly v Mackman* [1983] 2 AC 237, 280H-281A (Lord Diplock: "The public interest in good administration requires that public authorities and third parties should not be kept in suspense as to the legal validity of a decision the authority has reached in purported exercise of decision-making powers for any longer period than is absolutely necessary in fairness to the person affected by the decision"), applied in *R v Dairy Produce Quota Tribunal, ex p Caswell* [1990] 2 AC 738, 749E; *R v Hammersmith and Fulham London Borough Council, ex p Burkett* [2002] UKHL 23 [2002] 1 WLR 1593 at [44] ("there is a need for public bodies to have certainty as to the legal validity of their actions. That is the rationale of" the delay rule); *R v Monopolies & Mergers Commission, ex p Argyll Group Plc* [1986] 1 WLR 763, 774H-775B ("good public administration requires decisiveness and finality, unless there are compelling reasons to the contrary"); *R v Aston University Senate, ex p Roffey* [1969] 2 QB 538, 555C ("The prerogative remedies are exceptional in their nature and should not be made available to those who sleep upon their rights"); *Wandsworth London Borough Council v A* [2000] 1 WLR 1246, 1259E ("it is of the essence of judicial review applications that they must be brought promptly"); *Regalbourne Ltd v East Lindsey District Council* (1994) 6 Admin LR 102, 111H-112A ("public law context", where "the reasonable requirements of public administration have a significance which is absent in ordinary *inter partes* litigation"); *R v Institute of Chartered Accountants in England and Wales, ex p Anreas Chry Andreou* (1996) 8 Admin LR 557, 562H-563B ("Public law litigation cannot be conducted at the leisurely pace too often accepted in private law disputes").

26.1.3 **The need for speedy certainty: illustrations.**
(A) EDUCATION. *R v Rochdale Metropolitan Borough Council, ex p Schemet* [1994] ELR 89, 100G (referring to the "plain detriment to good administration in quashing decisions made almost 2 years ago where, on the basis of those decisions, the local authority has organised its expenditure in a particular way"); *R v Rochdale Metropolitan Borough Council, ex p B* [2000] Ed CR 117, 120 ("absolutely essential that, if parents are to bring judicial review proceedings in relation to the allocation of places at secondary school for their children, the matter is heard and determined by a court, absent very exceptional circumstances, before the term starts"), approved in *R v Hammersmith and Fulham London Borough Council, ex p Burkett* [2002] UKHL 23 [2002] 1 WLR 1593 at [18] (Lord Steyn); *R v London Borough of Redbridge, ex p G* [1991] COD 398 (as to selection for school places, important for parents and pupils to know

precisely where they stand); *R v Northamptonshire County Council, ex p K* [1994] ELR 397, 404D (need for speedy certainty as to school closure); *R v Education Committee of Blackpool Borough Council, ex p Taylor* [1999] ELR 237, 241A (importance of promptness in education cases); *R (Melton) v School Organisation Committee* [2001] EWHC Admin 245 (importance of promptness in context of school reorganisation); *R (M-P) v London Borough of Barking* [2002] EWHC 2483 (Admin) (undue delay in challenging decision to remove pupil from register).

(B) RULES IN PLACE. *R v Secretary of State for Social Services, ex p Association of Metropolitan Authorities* [1986] 1 WLR 1, 15E-F (Webster J: "The regulations have been in force for about six months ... If [they] were to be [quashed] all applicants who had been refused benefit because of the new regulations would be entitled to make fresh claims, and all authorities would be required to consider each such claim"); *R v Ministry of Agriculture, Fisheries and Food, ex p Live Sheep Traders Ltd* [1995] COD 297.

(C) PLANNING CASES. *Bushell v Secretary of State for the Environment* [1981] AC 75, 104A ("schemes authorising the construction of motorways and decisions to act on such authorisations cannot be held up indefinitely because the current methods of estimating and predicting future traffic needs are imperfect and are likely to be improved as further experience is gained"); *R v Secretary of State for the Environment, ex p Rose Theatre Trust Co* [1990] 1 QB 504, 519B-C ("Suppose a decision to build a motorway turns out, once it has been built, to have been unlawful because the Secretary of State took into account something which he ought not have done? If everyone could challenge an unlawfully granted planning permission for a house, what would be the position of the innocent first or subsequent purchaser?").

26.1.4 "Promptness" requirement sufficiently "certain". *R (Hardy) v Pembrokeshire County Council* [2006] EWCA Civ 240 [2006] Env LR 659 at [11]-[18] (promptness requirement sufficiently certain to be HRA:ECHR-compatible); *R v Hammersmith and Fulham London Borough Council, ex p Burkett* [2002] UKHL 23 [2002] 1 WLR 1593[1] at [53] (question raised by Lord Steyn); *Lam v United Kingdom* Application No.41671/98 (ECtHR regarding promptness requirement as sufficiently certain, being "a proportionate measure taken in pursuit of a legitimate aim"; "a strict procedural requirement which serve[s] a public interest purpose, namely the need to avoid prejudice being caused to third parties who may have altered their situation on the strength of administrative decisions"); *R (A1 Veg Ltd) v Hounslow London Borough Council* [2003] EWHC 3112 (Admin) [2004] LGR 536 at [40] (promptness requirement remains).

26.1.5 Delay not fatal: some striking examples. <26.3> (good reason to extend time); *Chief Constable of the North Wales Police v Evans* [1982] 1 WLR 1155, 1157H, 1171B-C (14 months: where pursuit of industrial tribunal claim and legal aid); *R v Eastleigh Borough Council, ex p Betts* [1983] 2 AC 613, 622H-623C (14 months); *Gowa v Attorney-General* [1985] 1 WLR 1003, 1007F-1008E (26 months); *R v Secretary of State for Foreign & Commonwealth Affairs, ex p Ross-Clunis* [1991] 2 AC 439, 440G and 443G (8 years); *In re Sampson* [1987] 1 WLR 194, 195B-196A (permission to appeal granted 41 months after the decision of the Divisional Court); *R (Bancoult) v Secretary of State for the Foreign and Commonwealth Office* [2001] QB 1067 (successful judicial review quashing 1971 Immigration Ordinance, challenged in 1999).

26.1.6 The significance of s.31(6). See Supreme Court Act 1981 s.31(6) <64.1>; *R v Dairy Produce Quota Tribunal, ex p Caswell* [1990] 2 AC 738, 747B-C ("when an application for [permission] to apply is not made promptly and in any event within three months, the court may

---

[1] Reuben Taylor [2005] JR 249.

refuse [permission] on the ground of delay unless it considers that there is good reason for extending the period; but, even if it considers that there is such good reason, it may still refuse [permission] (or, where [permission] has been granted, [a] substantive [remedy]) if in its opinion the granting of the [remedy] sought would be likely to cause hardship or prejudice (as specified in section 31(6)) or would be detrimental to good administration"); *R v Hammersmith and Fulham London Borough Council, ex p Burkett* [2002] UKHL 23 [2002] 1 WLR 1593 at [18] (s.31(6) as "a useful reserve power in some cases, such as where an application made well within the three month period would cause immense practical difficulties").

26.1.7 **Delay: permission and post-permission issues.**[2]

(A) GENERAL GUIDANCE. *R v Criminal Injuries Compensation Board, ex p A* [1999] 2 AC 330, 341B-F (Lord Slynn, explaining that permission "may be given if the court considers that good reason for extending the period has been shown... If [permission] is given, then ... it does not fall to be reopened at the substantive hearing on the basis that there is no ground for extending time ... What the court can do under section 31(6) is to refuse to grant [a remedy]").

(B) DELAY AT THE PERMISSION STAGE. *R v Dairy Produce Quota Tribunal, ex p Caswell* [1990] 2 AC 738, 747B-G (Lord Goff: "when an application for [permission] to apply is not made promptly and in any event within three months, the court may refuse [permission] on the ground of delay unless it considers that there is good reason for extending the period; but, even if it considers that there is such good reason, it may still refuse [permission] ... if in its opinion the granting of the [remedy] sought would be likely to cause hardship or prejudice"); <26.1.7(B)> (delay at the substantive hearing); <10.3.3> (candour and duty to disclose delay); <26.3> (good reason to extend time); <26.4> (hardship, prejudice and detriment); <21.2.3> (deferring/adjourning the question of permission: rolled-up hearing); <21.1.6> (oral permission hearing).

(C) DELAY AT THE SUBSTANTIVE HEARING. *R v Dairy Produce Quota Tribunal, ex p Caswell* [1990] 2 AC 738, 747G (Lord Goff: "the fact that the single judge had granted [permission] ... did not preclude the court from subsequently refusing substantive [remedy] on the ground of undue delay in the exercise of its discretion under section 31(6)"); *R v Chief Constable of West Yorkshire, ex p Wilkinson* [2002] EWHC 2353 (Admin) at [41] ("If the judge in granting permission rules that delay does not preclude the grant of permission, and that, if necessary, an extension of time should be granted, that is intended to be dispositive of the point and, in the ordinary way at least, it cannot then be argued before the judge hearing the substantive application that permission should not have been granted and that an extension of time should have been refused. Of course at that stage the trial judge can still have regard to the question of delay in deciding what remedy, if any, to grant, but that is another point altogether"); *R (Lichfield Securities Ltd) v Lichfield District Council* [2001] EWCA Civ 304 [2001] 3 PLR 33 at [34] ("undue delay is placed by s.31(6)(b) on the agenda at the substantive hearing... But it does not follow ... that the judge at the substantive hearing should proceed as if the issue had never previously arisen in the case, at least where it has been properly argued out between the parties at the [permission] stage... While ultimately it is a matter for the judge hearing the substantive application, we consider that the appropriate course ... is that the [defendant] should be permitted to recanvass, by way of undue delay, an issue of promptness which has been decided at the [permission] stage in the [claimant]'s favour only (i) if the judge hearing the initial application has expressly so indicated; (ii) if new and relevant material is introduced on the substantive hearing; (iii) if, exceptionally, the issues as they have developed at the full hearing put a different aspect on the question of promptness; or (iv) if the first judge has plainly overlooked some relevant matter or otherwise reached a decision per incuriam. This is, today, no more than practical case management"); cf. *R (Holmes) v General Medical Council*

---

[2] Michael Fordham [1997] JR 208; Alec Samuels [2002] JR 216.

[2001] EWHC Admin 321 at [94] (*Lichfield* approach "essentially concerned with the problems that arise once a fully reasoned judgment after oral argument has been delivered on the issue [of delay and prejudice]").

26.1.8 Remedy refused for delay: examples. *R v Department of Transport, ex p Presvac Engineering Ltd* (1992) 4 Admin LR 121 (remedy inappropriate because (a) no good reason for extension of time and (b) would be wrong to exercise discretion to grant remedy on the merits); *R v Royal Borough of Kingston-upon-Thames, ex p Emsden* (1992) 4 Admin LR 550, 563A-E (not necessary to make a finding of fact because of delay); *R v Swale Borough Council & Medway Ports Authority, ex p Royal Society for the Protection of Birds* (1990) 2 Admin LR 790, 808H-816E (breach of legitimate expectation but remedy refused for delay, given third party reliance); *R v Director of Passenger Rail Franchising, ex p Save Our Railways* [1996] CLC 589, 606G-H (remedy as to certain orders refused because of undue delay); *R v Dorset Police Authority, ex p Vaughan* [1995] COD 153 (permission having been granted, up to defendant to show hardship etc; not for claimant to show good reason for extending time); *R v Secretary of State for Health, ex p London Borough of Hackney* 25th April 1994 unrep. (waiting until the last day of the 3 month period "should materially detract from the readiness of the court to grant [a remedy]"); *R v Governing Body of Gateway Primary School, ex p X* [2001] ELR 321 at [44] (remedy refused because of undue delay and detriment to good administration in allowing claimant to jump the queue and increase class size); *R (Gavin) v Haringey London Borough Council* [2003] EWHC 2591 (Admin) [2004] 1 PLR 61 at [39] (remedy refused for undue delay, under s.31(6)(b)).

26.1.9 Delay not fatal: examples. <26.3> (good reason to extend time); *R v Greenwich London Borough Council, ex p Patterson* (1994) 26 HLR 159 (Court of Appeal overturning decision to refuse remedy for delay, there being a good reason and no hardship/prejudice); *R v Secretary of State for the Home Department, ex p Bina Rajendra Patel* [1995] Imm AR 223, 227 (Brooke J: "if [permission] is granted, and the court, at the substantive stage, finds that there was something seriously defective, as a matter of law, with the decision, then, in the present context of an immigration case, as opposed to the context of a case where an overturning of an administrative decision might have an effect on a wider number of people ... it would be unlikely that the court would refuse to grant [a remedy] simply because the application, which has been granted [permission], was made too late"); *R v South Northamptonshire District Council, ex p Crest Homes Plc* (1995) 93 LGR 205, 209-210 (appropriate to "decide the substantive points before considering whether to refuse [a remedy] because of the delay. Clearly, the nature and importance of the flaw in the challenged decision must be a major factor in the exercise of discretion involved in the grant of [a remedy]").

26.1.10 Delay affecting type of remedy. *R (Crown Prosecution Service) v City of London Magistrates' Court* [2007] EWHC 1924 (Admin) at [24] (declaration granted, but mandatory orders refused because of delay by CPS); *R v Rochdale Metropolitan Borough Council, ex p Schemet* [1994] ELR 89 (refusing quashing order (certiorari), because of delay, but granting declarations that decision to introduce new policy unlawful, and that legitimate expectation existing that old policy (free travel passes) should continue until rational grounds given and opportunity to comment), 100G ("the delay ought not to lead to the rejection of the application, although it should affect the [remedy] granted"); *R v Dorset Police Authority, ex p Vaughan* [1995] COD 153 (even if delay a reason for refusing remedy, still appropriate to grant a declaration of unlawfulness); *R v Neath and Port Talbot Justices, ex p Director of Public Prosecutions* [2000] 1 WLR 1376, 1381G-H (setting out the factors which should affect whether or not to grant a remedy as a matter of discretion, so as to order a retrial, notwithstanding the lapse of time).

26.1.11 **Refusing remedy: reasons of speedy certainty albeit no delay.** <24.3> (discretion to refuse remedy); *R v Secretary of State for the Environment, ex p Walters* (1998) 30 HLR 328, 380-382 (court entitled to have regard to hardship, prejudice and detriment to good administration even where no undue delay by claimant in bringing proceedings); *R v Secretary of State for Social Services, ex p Association of Metropolitan Authorities* (1993) 5 Admin LR 6, 16C-D (referring to "a public interest in not upsetting regulations which have been made unless good reason can be shown for doing so"); cf. *R v Secretary of State for Education and Employment, ex p National Union of Teachers* 14th July 2000 unrep. (Order quashed, distinguishing *AMA*); *R v Birmingham City Council, ex p Dredger* (1994) 6 Admin LR 553, 577A-G (remedy granted notwithstanding disruption, expenditure and re-allocation of funds); *R v Chief Constable of Devon and Cornwall, ex p Hay* [1996] 2 All ER 711, 726d-g (Court unwilling to undo decision); *R v Hillingdon Health Authority, ex p Goodwin* [1984] ICR 800, 811D-E (Woolf J: "it does not seem to me that the additional short delay which will result from my decision could have such serious consequences as would justify my taking a course which would prevent the matter being reconsidered in accordance with the law").

26.1.12 **Speed during the proceedings.** <21.2.5> (expedition); <2.6> (strict case-management); <22.1.11> (approach to adjournment/stay); <22.4.3> (permission to amend); *R v Birmingham City Council, ex p Dredger* (1994) 6 Admin LR 553, 577E (Hutchison J: "small weight should be given to delay occasioned since the commencement of proceedings")[3].

26.1.13 **Judicial review as a speedy process: speedy courts.** *O'Reilly v Mackman* [1983] 2 AC 237, 281B (judicial review "a very speedy means, available in urgent cases within a matter of days rather than months, for determining whether a disputed decision was valid in law or not"); *Somerville v Scottish Ministers* [2007] UKHL 44 [2007] 1 WLR 2734 at [159] (judicial review should be disposed of promptly); *R (Shergill) v Harrow Crown Court* [2005] EWHC 648 (Admin) at [2] (bail challenge heard within 48 hours); *R (Paul) v Inner West London Assistant Deputy Coroner* [2007] EWCA Civ 1259 [2008] 1 WLR 1335 at [2]-[3] (to CA judgment within 21 days of decision); *Bromley London Borough Council v Greater London Council* [1983] 1 AC 768, 836C (remarkable speed of proceedings "an indication of the value of the procedure of judicial review"); *Secretary of State for Education and Science v Tameside Metropolitan Borough Council* [1977] AC 1014, 1045G (from start to HL in 7 weeks); *Gouriet v Union of Post Office Workers* [1978] AC 435, 473F-474E (CA sitting on a Saturday); *R (SR) v Huntercombe Maidenhead Hospital* [2005] EWHC 2361 (Admin) at [35] (claim to judgment within 3 weeks); *R v Monopolies & Mergers Commission, ex p Argyll Group Plc* [1986] 1 WLR 763 (less than one month from start to CA decision); *Mayor etc of London Borough of Wandsworth v National Association of Schoolmasters/Union of Women Teachers* [1994] ELR 170, 183B (8 days from claim to conclusion of hearing); *R v Council of the Society of Lloyds, ex p Johnson* 16th August 1996 unrep. (judgment within 9 working days of permission); *R (Crown Prosecution Service) v Registrar General of Births, Deaths and Marriages* [2002] EWCA Civ 1661 [2003] QB 1222 at [1] (decided by CA within 3 days of decision of Administrative Court); <21.2.3> (rolled-up hearing); <21.2.5> (expedition); *R (Heather) v Leonard Cheshire Foundation* [2002] EWCA Civ 366 [2002] 2 All ER 936 at [9] (decision with reasons to follow); *R (Bodimeade) v Camden London Borough Council* [2001] EWHC Admin 271 (2001) 4 CCLR 246 at [2]-[3] (brief reasons, with detailed reasons to follow); *R (Stanley) v Coroner for Inner North London* [2003] EWHC 1180 (Admin) at [8] (order, with reasons to follow).

---

[3] Tom Weisselberg [1996] JR 139.

26.2 **Promptness and the running of time.**A claimant has a duty to act promptly, not a right to wait for up to three months. Some contexts call for the utmost promptness. The clock starts when the grounds first arise and does not stop until the claim is lodged. Care is always needed in letting time elapse.

26.2.1 **Promptness and 3 months.**
(A) 3 MONTHS AS A STARTING-POINT. *R v Chief Constable of Devon and Cornwall, ex p Hay* [1996] 2 All ER 711, 732a (Sedley J: "the practice ... is to work on the basis of the three-month limit and to scale it down wherever the features of the particular case make that limit unfair to the [defendant] or to third parties"); *R (Crown Prosecution Service) v City of London Magistrates' Court* [2007] EWHC 1924 (Admin) at [21] (*Hay* merely a "rule of thumb"); *R (A1 Veg Ltd) v Hounslow London Borough Council* [2003] EWHC 3112 (Admin) [2004] LGR 536 at [40] ("a useful starting point is that when judicial review claims are brought within the prescribed three month period, there is a rebuttable presumption that they have been brought promptly").
(B) LACK OF PROMPTNESS EVEN WITHIN 3 MONTHS. *R v Hammersmith and Fulham London Borough Council, ex p Burkett* [2002] UKHL 23 [2002] 1 WLR 1593 at [18] (Lord Steyn, referring to s.31(6) as "a useful reserve power in some cases, such as where an application made well within the three month period would cause immense practical difficulties"); *R v Independent Television Commission, ex p TV NI Ltd* (1991) [1996] JR 60 (delay within 3 months); *R v Director of Passenger Rail Franchising, ex p Save Our Railways* [1996] CLC 589, 606G (3 months constituting "undue" delay in all the circumstances); *R v British Broadcasting Corporation, ex p Referendum Party* (1997) 9 Admin LR 553, 572B (tenable reasons for waiting 18 days to challenge BBC's allocation of party election broadcast time, given that waiting for ITC's decision and no prejudice); *R v Somerset County Council, ex p Dixon* [1998] Env LR 111, 115 (whether "the demands of promptness are such as to make it unfair or unreasonable to proceed with the claim even though it has been issued within three months"); *R v Secretary of State for Trade and Industry, ex p Greenpeace Ltd* [1998] Env LR 415; *R v Cotswold District Council, ex p Barrington* (1998) 75 P & CR 515 (permission refused for delay within 3 months); *R v Chief Constable of Ministry of Defence Police, ex p Sweeney* [1999] COD 122 (although commenced within 3 months, judicial review should have been commenced in time to secure a stay of the disciplinary hearing); *R (Crown Prosecution Service) v City of London Magistrates' Court* [2007] EWHC 1924 (Admin) (undue delay where lodged on last day of 3 months).

26.2.2 **Promptness especially important where other interests affected.**[4] *R v Secretary of State for Health, ex p Furneaux* [1994] 2 All ER 652, 658e ("The obligation ... to proceed promptly ... is of particular importance where third parties are concerned"); *R v Independent Television Commission, ex p TV NI Ltd* (1991) [1996] JR 60; *R v Avon County Council, ex p Terry Adams Ltd* [1994] Env LR 442, 478 ("There is much importance in the principle that, if objection is to be made by an objector to the conduct by a public authority of a continuing administrative process, in which costs will be incurred by the authority and by other interested parties, application should be made promptly"); *R v Director of Passenger Rail Franchising, ex p Save Our Railways* [1996] CLC 589, 606G ("imperative need for the [claimants] to take action with the utmost promptness"); *R v Secretary of State for Trade and Industry, ex p Greenpeace Ltd* [1998] Env LR 415, 438 ("The courts have very firmly stated that a judicial review [claimant] must proceed with particular urgency where third party interests are

---

[4] Christopher Forsyth [1998] JR 8; Nigel Pleming QC & Kate Markus [2000] JR 6; Andrew Lidbetter [1996] JR 51.

involved... [T]he principle is plainly established").

26.2.3 **When grounds first arose.** See CPR 54.5(1) <64.2>; CPR 54PD <64.3> para 4.1 (date when seeking to quash a judgment etc); *R v Hammersmith and Fulham London Borough Council, ex p Burkett* [2002] UKHL 23 [2002] 1 WLR 1593 at [38] (possible in principle to challenge preliminary decision such as planning resolution, or to wait and challenge grant of planning permission)[5]; HL disapproving the approach in *R v Secretary of State for Trade and Industry, ex p Greenpeace Ltd* [1998] Env LR 415, 424 ("a judicial review [claimant] must move against the substantive act or decision which is the real basis of his complaint"); *R (Catt) v Brighton and Hove County Council* [2007] EWCA Civ 298 [2007] Env LR 691 at [47] (applying *Burkett* to allow claimant to wait and challenge planning decision not screening opinion); *R (Garden and Leisure Group Ltd) v North Somerset Council* [2003] EWHC 1605 (Admin) at [35] (applying *Burkett* to allow claimant to challenge planning resolution and not wait for final decision); *R (British Aggregates Associates) v Her Majesty's Treasury* [2002] EWHC 926 (Admin) [2002] EuLR 394 at [154] (time starting to run from the date of Royal Assent of the legislation complained of, not its subsequent implementation by statutory instrument); *R v Customs & Excise Commissioners, ex p Eurotunnel Plc* [1995] CLC 392, 400E-F ("Prima facie the dates when the orders were made are the dates when the grounds for the application first arose. See *R v HM Treasury, ex p Smedley* [1985] QB 657 per Donaldson MR at p.667... However, there is an argument for saying that time did not begin to run until the dates when the orders came into force and for present purposes we would be prepared to assume in Eurotunnel's favour, without deciding the point, that these were the relevant dates"); *R (Eisai Ltd) v National Institute for Health and Clinical Excellence* [2008] EWCA Civ 438 at [70] (claimant entitled to challenge outcome of consultation process for unfairness, not required to have challenged the unfair act itself); *R v Cardiff City Council, ex p Gooding Investments Ltd* [1996] Env LR 288, 301 (relevant decision tender invitation, not award of contract); *R (A1 Veg Ltd) v Hounslow London Borough Council* [2003] EWHC 3112 (Admin) [2004] LGR 536 at [52] (*Gooding* not a "principle of general application"); *R v Port Talbot Borough Council, ex p Jones* [1988] 2 All ER 207, 215j (challenge properly to 1986 decision; challenge to 1984 resolution would have been premature); *R v Inland Revenue Commissioners, ex p Allen* [1997] STC 1141, 1151b-c (in truth, challenge to commencement not continuation of criminal proceedings); *R v Horse Race Betting Levy Board, ex p National Association of Bookmakers* 7th September 1998 unrep. (claimant should have challenged decision to appoint subcommittee, not wait for implementation of outcome).

26.2.4 **Relevance of date of claimant's knowledge.** <26.3.5> (claimant's lack of knowledge); *R v Department of Transport, ex p Presvac Engineering Ltd* (1992) 4 Admin LR 121 at 133D-H (relevant date is when grounds arose not claimant's knowledge); cf. *R (Anufrijeva) v Secretary of State for the Home Department* [2003] UKHL 36 [2004] 1 AC 604 at [26] ("Notice of a decision is required before it can have the character of a determination with legal effect"), [28] ("the constitutional principle requiring the rule of law to be observed ... requires that a constitutional state must accord to individuals the right to know of a decision before their rights can be adversely affected").

26.2.5 **Stopping the clock.** *R v Secretary of State for the Home Department, ex p Chetta* [1996] COD 463 (judicial review proceedings instituted when notice of application for permission to proceed with claim for judicial review made: ie. documents lodged with (and stamped by) Administrative Court Office); *Crichton v Wellingborough Borough Council* [2002] EWHC 2988 (Admin) [2004] Env LR 215 at [56] (Gibbs J, expressing the view that judicial review lodged

---

[5] James Maurici [2002] JR 152.

on 10.9.02 was one day outside the "three months" in challenging a decision of 10.6.02).

26.2.6 **Delay and the pre-action protocol: not stopping the clock.** See JR:PAP <64.5> preamble ("This protocol ... does not affect the time limit specified by Rule 54.5(1)"), para 14; <26.3.7> (pursuit of an alternative as a good reason to extend time).

26.2.7 **Delay and "continuing" activities.**
(A) GENERAL. *Somerville v Scottish Ministers* [2007] UKHL 44 [2007] 1 WLR 2734 at [51], [81], [145], [197] ("continuing" activity approach considered in discussing HRA s.7(5)); *R (Hammerton) v London Underground Ltd* [2002] EWHC 2307 (Admin) at [197] (operations in breach of planning control "a continuing state of affairs"); *Phonographic Performance Ltd v Department of Trade and Industry* [2004] EWHC 1795 (Ch) (non-implementation of Directive treated as a continuing breach for the purpose of *Francovich* reparation); *R (H) v London Borough of Brent* [2002] EWHC 1105 (Admin) [2002] ELR 509 at [15] ("continuing" nature of council's position as to payment of school transport costs treated as a good reason for entertaining the claim despite delay); *R v Eastleigh Borough Council, ex p Betts* [1983] 2 AC 613 (continuing duty to house); *R v Secretary of State for Foreign & Commonwealth Affairs, ex p Ross-Clunis* [1991] 2 AC 439 (continuing failure to recognise citizenship); *R v Birmingham City Council, ex p Equal Opportunities Commission* [1989] 1 AC 1155 (continuing education arrangements); *R v Richmond upon Thames London Borough Council, ex p McCarthy & Stone (Developments) Ltd* [1992] 2 AC 48 (continuing practice); *London & Clydeside Estates Ltd v Aberdeen District Council* [1980] 1 WLR 182, 197B-C (continuing duty to issue a valid certificate); *R v Ministry of Agriculture Fisheries & Food, ex p Bostock* [1994] I ECR 955 (failure to enact primary legislation); cf. *London Borough of Islington v Camp* (1999) [2004] LGR 58, 72d (time running from latest date when relevant action).
(B) CONTINUING POLICY/ARRANGEMENT. *R v Warwickshire County Council, ex p Collymore* [1995] ELR 217, 228G-229D (treating unlawfulness of (continuing) policy as a reason to extend time, especially insofar as remedy sought is prospective), applied in *R v East Sussex County Council, ex p Ward* (2000) 3 CCLR 132 at [37] (where permission had been granted on condition that no remedy would be granted in respect of an earlier period, in the light of delay considerations); *R v Westminster City Council, ex p Hilditch* 14th June 1990 unrep. (Nicholls LJ:"[i]f the policy is unlawful, prima facie it should be discontinued"), applied in *R v Rochdale Metropolitan Borough Council, ex p Schemet* [1994] ELR 89, 100H.
(C) CONTINUING QUESTION OF COMPATIBILITY WITH EC LAW. *R (Federation of Technological Industries) v Commissioners of Customs and Excise* [2004] EWHC 254 (Admin) at [2] (rejecting delay complaint, where "on-going legislative provisions" and question of consistency with EC law) (CA is at [2004] EWCA Civ 1020); *R v Secretary of State for Employment, ex p Seymour-Smith (No.2)* [2000] 1 WLR 435, 451G-452A (need to keep impact of measure under review); *R v Secretary of State for Employment, ex p Equal Opportunities Commission* [1995] 1 AC 1 (challenge to 1978 Act); *R v Ministry of Agriculture Fisheries & Food, ex p Bostock* [1994] I ECR 955 (delay in challenging failure to enact primary legislation); *R v Customs & Excise Commissioners, ex p Eurotunnel Plc* [1995] CLC 392, 401A-B (relevance of delay).

26.2.8 **Delay and multiple targets.** <5.3> (multiple targets).
(A) DELAY AND MULTIPLE TARGETS: ILLUSTRATIONS. *R v Hammersmith and Fulham London Borough Council, ex p Burkett* [2002] UKHL 23 [2002] 1 WLR 1593 at [42] (claimant entitled to challenge planning resolution or actual grant of planning permission); *Younger Homes (Northern) Ltd v First Secretary of State* [2003] EWHC 3058 (Admin) at [85] (Ouseley J: "*Burkett* makes it clear that the challenge can be made to the substantive decision at the end of the process on the grounds of an earlier reviewable error which itself had some legal consequences for the continuation of the process"); *R v Richmond upon Thames London*

Borough Council, ex p McCarthy & Stone (Developments) Ltd [1992] 2 AC 48 (judicial review of council's decision not to revoke its practice of charging (including the claimant) for pre-application advice); *R v Birmingham City Council, ex p Equal Opportunities Commission* [1989] 1 AC 1155 (challenge to current arrangements, directed at later meetings but which the EOC had considered illegal for some 18 months); *R v Secretary of State for Foreign & Commonwealth Affairs, ex p Ross-Clunis* [1991] 2 AC 439 (challenging "decisions" in both 1980 and 1988); *Newbury District Council v Secretary of State for the Environment* [1981] AC 578, 594B (condition imposed in 1962, could have been appealed against then; instead statutory challenge to enforcement notices served 10 years later); *R (Jackson) v Attorney General* [2005] UKHL 56 [2006] 1 AC 262 (judicial review challenge to validity of the Hunting Act 2004, albeit basis of challenge involving impugning Parliament Act 1949); *R v Lincoln City Council, ex p Wickes Building Supplies Ltd* (1994) 92 LGR 215, 222 (judicial review of magistrates' decision not to stay prosecutions as an abuse of process as "no doubt an acceptable alternative to a more [timeous] attack on the lawfulness of the local authority's decisions to prosecute"); *R v Secretary of State for Transport, ex p National Insurance Guarantee Corporation Plc* [1996] COD 425 (refusal to amend Regulations); *R v Islington London Borough Council, ex p East* [1996] ELR 74, 86B-C (subsequent decision by full council as "a substantive decision in its own right"); *R v Secretary of State for Trade and Industry, ex p Greenpeace* [2000] Env LR 221, 258-261 (further round of licensing decisions constituting relevant distinct events susceptible to judicial review); *R v London Borough of Hammersmith, ex p CPRE London Branch* [2000] Env LR 532 (able to challenge decision refusing to revoke planning permission); *R (Asif Javed) v Secretary of State for the Home Department* [2001] EWCA Civ 789 [2002] QB 129 (judicial review of 1999 asylum refusals on basis of unlawfulness of 1996 Order).

(B) DELAY: RESISTANCE TO USE OF LATER TARGETS. *R (Leitao) v Secretary of State for the Home Department* [2008] EWHC 1553 (Admin) at [27] (not open to claimant to avoid immigration appeal time limits by requesting discretionary leave and seeking judicial review); *R v Secretary of State for the Home Department, ex p Mohammed Akram* [1994] Imm AR 8, 9-10 (delay not side-stepped by challenging removal directions); *R v Newbury District Council, ex p Chieveley Parish Council* (1998) 10 Admin LR 676 (court looks to the decision which in substance is being challenged, not a later claimed acknowledgement of its validity); *Payne v Secretary of State for the Home Department* [1999] Imm AR 489 (operative decision the original refusal of asylum not a later `confirmation'); *R v Commissioner for Local Administration, ex p Field* [2000] COD 58 (delay problem not overcome merely by writing fresh letter and obtaining a reply which was then sought to be characterised as fresh decision).

26.2.9 Planning cases: no "6 week principle". *R v Hammersmith and Fulham London Borough Council, ex p Burkett* [2002] UKHL 23 [2002] 1 WLR 1593 at [53] (Lord Steyn, disapproving the previous case-law in which it had been suggested that judicial review in a planning context required to be commenced within 6 weeks: "The inference has sometimes been drawn that the three months limit has by judicial decision been replaced by a `six weeks rule'. This is a misconception. The legislative three months limit cannot be contracted by a judicial policy decision"); *R v North West Leicestershire District Council, ex p Moses* [2000] Env LR 443, 450 ("The rule that any application for judicial review must be made promptly applies with particular force when seeking to challenge the grant of planning permission by a local authority"); *R (Finn-Kelcey) v Milton Keynes Borough Council* [2008] EWHC 1650 (Admin) (wrong to wait 3 months after grant of planning permission). The 6-week cases [6] included: *R v Exeter City Council, ex p JL Thomas & Co Ltd* [1991] 1 QB 471, 484F-G; *R v Ceredigion County Council, ex p McKeown* [1998] 2 PLR 1, 2G; *R v Newbury District Council, ex p Chieveley Parish Council* (1998) 10 Admin LR 676; *R v Cotswold District Council, ex p*

---

[6] John Howell QC [1999] JR 9.

Barrington (1998) 75 P & CR 515; *R v Restormel Borough Council, ex p Corbett* [2001] EWCA Civ 330 [2001] 1 PLR 108 at [23]; cf. *R v Essex County Council, ex p Tarmac Roadstone Holdings Ltd* [1998] 1 PLR 79 (time extended); *R v Durham County Council, ex p Huddleston* [2000] Env LR D20 (acted reasonably); *R v Camden London Borough Council, ex p Williams* [2000] 2 PLR 93, 99A-C (look at all the circumstances).

26.3 **Good reason to extend time.** A claimant lacking promptness requires an extension of time, for which many good reasons exist.

26.3.1 **Extension of time.** See CPR 3.1(2)(a); CPR 3.9; *Sayers v Clarke Walker (a firm)* [2002] EWCA Civ 645 [2002] 1 WLR 3095 (CA endorsing the CPR 3.9 "checklist" in the context of an extension of time for appeal, as preferable to judges using their own checklists); ACO:NFG <64.4> para 5.2; CPR 54.5(2) (no extension of time by agreement).

26.3.2 **Good reason to extend time: general points.**[7] *R v Secretary of State for Trade and Industry, ex p Greenpeace* [2000] Env LR 221, 261-264 (Maurice Kay J, asking: "(i) Is there a reasonable objective excuse for applying late?; (ii) What, if any, is the damage, in terms of hardship or prejudice to third party rights and detriment to good administration, which would be occasioned if permission were now granted?; (iii) In any event, does the public interest require that the application should be permitted to proceed?"); *R v Warwickshire County Council, ex p Collymore* [1995] ELR 217, 228F-G ("it is ... for the [claimant] to establish that there is good reason for time to be extended"); *R (Rayner) v Secretary of State for the Home Department* [2007] EWHC 1028 (Admin) [2007] 1 WLR 2239 (Admin Ct) at [90] ("once there has been appreciable delay, for instance in obtaining public funding, then a litigant and/or his lawyers must act with particular promptitude thereafter")

26.3.3 **Whether adequate explanation for delay/default.** *R v London Docklands Development Corporation, ex p Frost* (1997) 73 P & CR 199, 210 ("No explanation, certainly no adequate explanation, has been advanced"); *R v Criminal Injuries Compensation Board, ex p A* [1998] QB 659 (CA), 682G ("Every [claimant] knows or must be taken to know that he or she must give an explanation for [the undue] delay if the application is not to be dismissed") (HL is at [1999] 2 AC 330); *R v Secretary of State for Trade and Industry, ex p Greenpeace* [2000] Env LR 221, 261 (no reasonable objective excuse for applying late); *R v Waveney District Council, ex p Bell* [2001] Env LR 465 (no obligation in the circumstances to provide an explanation why grounds for judicial review not prepared earlier; readily understandable why took 5 weeks); cf. *Hashtroodi v Hancock* [2004] EWCA Civ 652 [2004] 1 WLR 3206 (although highly material to ask whether good reason for failure to serve claim form within prescribed time, wrong in principle to approach extension of time under CPR 7.6(2) as a necessary threshold condition).

26.3.4 **Position adopted by other parties.** CPR 54.5(2) (no extension of time by agreement); *R (International Masters Publishers Ltd) v Revenue & Customs Commissioners* [2006] EWHC 127 (Admin) at [13] (claimant should have written asking commissioners whether they would agree not to take a delay point if a proposed judicial review awaited the outcome of the claimant's related appeal).

26.3.5 **Claimant's lack of knowledge.** *R v Licensing Authority, ex p Novartis Pharmaceuticals Ltd* [2000] COD 232 (good reason to extend time where claimant lacked essential information needed for purpose of knowing whether anything capable of being subject of judicial review; not a case where delaying in order to obtain more or better evidence to support case; not obliged to

---

[7] Richard Leiper [1996] JR 212.

make improbable assumption as to facts, or to adopt a confrontational stance with government branch); *R v Department of Transport, ex p Presvac Engineering Ltd* (1992) 4 Admin LR 121 at 133H-134A ("the [claimant's] subjective experience and state of knowledge ... may ... be relevant when the court comes to consider the proviso contained in the second part of Order 53 r.4, namely: `... unless the court considers that there is good reason for extending the period within which the application shall be made'"); *R v Secretary of State for the Home Department, ex p Ruddock* [1987] 1 WLR 1482, 1485F ("before the television programme, the [claimant] had and could have had no suspicion that a warrant to tap his phone might have been signed in 1983. I therefore think it is plain that on the question of delay, there was good reason for no application being made before March 1985"); *R v Warwickshire County Council, ex p Collymore* [1995] ELR 217, 228D ("Until the letter of 16 September 1993, the [claimant] cannot have been aware of the basis on which the refusal to grant her a discretionary award could have been attacked in judicial review proceedings"); *R v London Borough of Redbridge, ex p G* [1991] COD 398 (Court would readily have extended time in relation to period of ignorance of the policy); *R v Secretary of State for Foreign and Commonwealth Affairs, ex p World Development Movement Ltd* [1995] 1 WLR 386, 402H (delay no bar (to remedy) because "[i]t was not until earlier this year that material matters could be known to the [claimants]"); *R v Milling (Medical Referee), ex p West Yorkshire Police Authority* [1997] 8 Med LR 392, 395 (good reason for extending time where delay in the challenged certificate reaching the claimant was the fault of the Home Office, and where acted reasonably promptly thereafter); *R v Cotswold District Council, ex p Barrington* (1998) 75 P & CR 515 (ignorance of the decision not a good reason here, where aware of the scheme and should have enquired as to the decision); *R v North West Leicestershire District Council, ex p Moses* [2000] Env LR 443, 451-452 (ignorance not an excuse in the particular circumstances; absurd to allow a late challenge to a development by identifying an ignorant individual); *R v Commissioners of Customs and Excise, ex p British Sky Broadcasting Plc* 14th July 2000 unrep. (Langley J: "knowledge or the lack of it are relevant to the discretion to extend time"); *R (Young) v Oxford City Council* [2002] EWCA Civ 990 [2002] 3 PLR 86 at [34] (claimant "was entitled first to seek information from the [defendant] as to the procedures which had been followed. He could not know whether he had an arguable case. Had an explanation demonstrating a correct procedure been provided, the application would probably not have been made, at any rate in its present form").

26.3.6 **Sensible and reasonable behaviour (causing no prejudice).** *R v Commissioner for Local Administration, ex p Croydon London Borough Council* [1989] 1 All ER 1033, 1046g (Woolf LJ: "While in the public law field, it is essential that the courts should scrutinise with care any delay in making an application and a litigant who does delay in making an application is always at risk, the [rules] are not intended to be applied in a technical manner. As long as no prejudice is caused ... the courts will not rely on those provisions to deprive a litigant who has behaved sensibly and reasonably of [a remedy] to which he is otherwise entitled"); *R v Council of the Society of Lloyds, ex p Johnson* 16th August 1996 unrep. (tolerance described by Woolf LJ only where no prejudice has been caused by the delay); *R v Durham County Council, ex p Huddleston* [2000] Env LR D20 (unfair to hold delay against claimant, where had acted reasonably in the light of defendant's stance); *R (Young) v Oxford City Council* [2002] EWCA Civ 990 [2002] 3 PLR 86 at [33] (claimant "acted reasonably in the circumstances in seeking by his letters ... further information before commencing proceedings"), [43] ("it is undesirable for a litigant to proceed blindly towards challenge of a decision in relation to which he suspects a fault or omission susceptible of review in a case where, for the purposes of clarification, he reasonably requires further information from the decision-making body so that he can consider in an informed manner whether proceedings are justified or worthwhile"); *R v Commissioners of Customs and Excise, ex p British Sky Broadcasting Plc* 14th July 2000 unrep. (applying *Croydon*); *R (Quintavalle) v Secretary of State for Health* [2001] EWHC Admin 918 [2001] 4 All ER 1013 at [33] (reasonable behaviour).

26.3.7 **Alternative solutions/pursuit of other avenues.**

(A) GENERAL. *R v Hammersmith and Fulham London Borough Council, ex p Burkett* [2001] Env LR 684 (CA) at [14] ("Judicial review is in principle a remedy of last resort. It follows, as it always does when a potential [claimant] for judicial review expeditiously seeks a reasonable way of resolving the issue without litigation, that the court will lean against penalising him for the passage of time and will where appropriate enlarge time if the alternative expedient fails"); *R v University College London, ex p Ursula Riniker* [1995] ELR 213, 215 ("the discretion to enlarge time ... will be sympathetically approached by the court where the [claimant] in the meantime has not been sleeping on her rights but has been attempting to canvass them by other legitimate means"); *R (Cowl) v Plymouth City Council* [2001] EWCA Civ 1935 [2002] 1 WLR 803 (judicial review should not have been pursued where complaints procedure available); *R v Stratford-on-Avon District Council, ex p Jackson* [1985] 1 WLR 1319, 1323E-F (claimant was making an approach to the Secretary of State); *R v Customs & Excise Commissioners, ex p Eurotunnel Plc* [1995] CLC 392, 402D ("an attempt to resolve one's problems by extra-judicial activity may amount to sensible and reasonable behaviour and give grounds for extending the period"); *Catchpole v Buckinghamshire County Council* [1998] ELR 463, 471E ("a complainant must first avail himself of any appropriate remedy made available by statute"); *R v Education Committee of Blackpool Borough Council, ex p Taylor* [1999] ELR 237, 240H (need for promptness even where exploring other avenues).

(B) DELAY DURING COMMUNICATIONS WITH DEFENDANT. <26.2.6> (delay and Pre-Action Protocol); *R v Borough of Milton Keynes, ex p Macklen* 30th April 1996 unrep. (if pre-action correspondence "turns out to be unsuccessful then there would surely be little danger of the application for judicial review being turned down on the grounds of delay, because the [claimant] had followed the very desirable procedure of seeking to have the dispute resolved by other means"); *R (British Aggregates Associates) v Her Majesty's Treasury* [2002] EWHC 926 (Admin) [2002] EuLR 394 at [155] ("The claimants have been far from idle. The long lead-in time has been used for substantial consultation and negotiation ... It is trite to observe that claimants cannot delay making claims merely because they are seeking to persuade the decision-maker to change its mind. But such negotiations are a relevant factor"); *R v London Borough of Harrow, ex p Carter* (1994) 26 HLR 32 (good reason for extending time where during the delay the claimant had been in communication with the defendant (and another authority), during which there appeared to be some prospect that the matter would be resolved); *R v Greenwich London Borough Council, ex p Patterson* (1994) 26 HLR 159, 167-168 (delay when district judge requested authority to reconsider the matter was "good reason"); *R v Law Society, ex p First National Commercial Bank Plc* [1996] COD 22 (attempt to negotiate a settlement arguably a good reason to extend time); *R v Ministry of Agriculture Fisheries and Food, ex p Bostock* [1991] 1 CMLR 687, 695 ("those advising the [claimant] here behaved in a perfectly proper and reasonable way allowing a reasonable time for the Minister to consider his position and, if he formed the view that he should take legislative action to implement the European regulations, to do so"); *R v Department of Transport, ex p Presvac Engineering Ltd* (1992) 4 Admin LR 121 (as to delay while adopting a conciliatory approach).

(C) DELAY WHILE EXHAUSTING ALTERNATIVE REMEDIES. *R v Commissioners of Customs and Excise, ex p Greenwich Property Ltd* [2001] EWHC Admin 230 [2001] STC 618 at [1] (good reason to extend time where pursuing an appeal, albeit misconceived); *R (Asif Javed) v Secretary of State for the Home Department* [2001] EWCA Civ 789 [2002] QB 129 at [78] (delay "technical because the [claimants] sensibly first pursued appeals to special adjudicators"); *R (International Masters Publishers Ltd) v Revenue & Customs Commissioners* [2006] EWHC 127 (Admin) at [13] (where related appeal being pursued, claimant should have written asking defendant to agree not to take a delay point, absent which judicial review should have been lodged), [16]-[17] (inexcusable delay, through commercial decision to pursue appeal only); *R (T) v A School* [2002] EWCA Civ 1349 [2003] ELR 160 at [22] (sensible "to try the appellate process first" but wise "to give a clear indication straightaway that he also has a potential judicial review challenge", so defendant "can decide what is the most sensible way forward"); *Chief Constable of the North Wales Police v Evans* [1982] 1 WLR 1155, 1171B-C (appeal to an industrial tribunal); *R v Secretary of State for the Home Department, ex p Oladehinde* [1991] 1 AC 254 (pursuit of statutory appeal); *R v Rochdale Metropolitan Borough Council, ex p Cromer Ring Mill Ltd* [1982] 3 All ER 761, 764j ("wholly understandable" that claimants "sought to exhaust all possible remedies").

(D) DELIBERATE CHOICE TO PURSUE ALTERNATIVE MEANS. *R v Essex County Council, ex p Jackson Projects Ltd* [1995] COD 155 (permission refused for delay where claimant had initially decided to pursue compensation claim rather than challenge compulsory purchase order); *R v London Borough of Redbridge, ex p G* [1991] COD 398 (claimant not permitted to rely on fact that elected to seek to persuade by political means, rather than seeking legal remedy); *R v London Borough of Bexley, ex p Barnehurst Golf Club Limited* [1992] COD 382 (fact that claimant trying to use political means of redress first not a good reason for extending time); *Din (Taj) v Wandsworth London Borough Council* [1983] 1 AC 657, 685E-F (suggesting that if appeal dismissed on ground that "the wrong procedure", claimants would then succeed on judicial review).

(E) DELAY AND AWAITING A TEST CASE. *R v Hertfordshire County Council, ex p Cheung* The Times 4th April 1986 (see transcript) (Sir John Donaldson MR: "if a test case is in progress in the public law court, others who are in a similar position to the parties should not be expected themselves to begin proceedings in order to protect their positions"; "it could be assumed that the result of the test case would be applied to them by the authorities concerned without the need for proceedings and that, if this did not in the event occur, the court would regard this as a complete justification for a late application for judicial review"), considered in *R (Zeqiri) v Secretary of State for the Home Department* [2002] UKHL 3 [2002] INLR 291 at [40] (referring to a `test case' where the parties "agreed to abide by whatever the ... case decided"); *R (Wilkinson) v Commissioners of Inland Revenue* [2003] EWCA Civ 814 [2003] 1 WLR 2683 at [59] (referring to *Cheung*: Strasbourg case not a test case, so no duty to treat other look-alike cases in the same way when friendly settlement reached).

26.3.8 Delay in securing CLS funding (legal aid). *R v Stratford-on-Avon District Council, ex p Jackson* [1985] 1 WLR 1319, 1324A (Ackner LJ: "it is a perfectly legitimate excuse for delay to be able to say that the delay is entirely due to the fact that it takes a certain time for a certificate to be obtained from the legal aid authorities"); *R (Sacker) v HM Coroner for West Yorkshire* [2003] EWCA Civ 217 [2003] 2 All ER 278 at [29] (applying *Jackson*) (HL is [2004] UKHL 11 [2004] 1 WLR 796); *R v University of Portsmouth, ex p Lakareber* [1999] ELR 135, 139G-140C (not applying *Jackson*, where lack of evidence as to efforts being made, and where need for promptness obvious); *Chief Constable of the North Wales Police v Evans* [1982] 1 WLR 1155, 1157H, 1171B-C (referring to legal aid); *R v Metropolitan Borough of Sandwell, ex p Cashmore* (1993) 25 HLR 544 (delay in obtaining legal aid not normally a good reason); *R v Governors of La Sainte Union Convent School, ex p T* [1996] ELR 98, 99E ("legal aid history" going "a very great distance" in providing a good reason to extend time); *In re Wilson* [1985] AC 750, 755B (delays "no doubt ... occasioned by the necessity for obtaining legal aid"); *R v Surrey Coroner, ex p Wright* [1997] QB 786, 789H ("the delay is attributable to problems in obtaining legal aid for which no blame should be attributed to the [claimant]"); *Re F* [1999] ELR 251 (delay in obtaining legal aid treated as acceptable reason in context of special educational needs appeal); *R v Leeds City Council, ex p N* [1999] ELR 324, 334C-D (legal aid delays not treated as sufficient reason to extend time in a case where speed and need for early warning so important); *R v Headteacher of Crug Glas School, ex p D* [2000] ELR 69, 73B (need for utmost promptness where delay, once legal aid received); *R (H) v London Borough of Brent* [2002] EWHC 1105 (Admin) [2002] ELR 509 at [15] (delay in securing legal aid as a good reason).

26.3.9 **Importance of the issues.** *Re S (Application for Judicial Review)* [1998] 1 FLR 790, 795H (Butler-Sloss LJ: "The general importance of the matter raised in the application to move may, therefore, as a matter of public policy, constitute a good reason to extend time even though in most cases the delay would be a complete bar to granting [permission]. The issues raised must be genuinely of public importance and must be such that they can best be ventilated in the public law context. Such cases are likely to be exceptional"); *R v North West Leicestershire District Council, ex p Moses* [2000] Env LR 443, 452 (referring to "cases which recognise that the importance of the substantive issue raised is material to the exercise of the court's discretion with regard to delay"); *R v Secretary of State for the Home Department, ex p Ruddock* [1987] 1 WLR 1482, 1485G (although "unimpressed by the reasons for [the delay]": "since the matters raised are of general importance, it would be a wrong exercise of my discretion to reject the application on grounds of delay"); *R v Department of Transport, ex p Presvac Engineering Ltd* (1992) 4 Admin LR 121, 137A-B (asking "whether in the circumstances ... there are good reasons for extending the time based on public policy"); *R v Secretary of State for Foreign and Commonwealth Affairs, ex p World Development Movement Ltd* [1995] 1 WLR 386, 402H ("the general importance of the matter may itself be a reason for resolving the substantive issues, even where there has been delay"); *R v Ministry of Agriculture, Fisheries and Food, ex p Dairy Trade Federation Limited* [1998] EuLR 253, 262F ("there are circumstances in which the court will extend time for reasons of public policy"; but for the alternative remedy "I would have been disposed to extend time simply because the points are so important"); *R v Customs & Excise Commissioners, ex p Eurotunnel Plc* [1995] CLC 392, 402C (Balcombe LJ: "the importance of the issues raised by an application can constitute a reason for extending the period"); *R (Robertson) v City of Wakefield Metropolitan Council* [2001] EWHC Admin 915 [2002] QB 1052 at [12] ("strong public interest in the matter receiving substantive judicial consideration"); *In re Friends of the Earth and James Savage* 1st December 1994 (application years out of time but in the public interest to extend time); *R v Secretary of State for Trade and Industry, ex p Greenpeace* [2000] Env LR 221, 263 (extension of time granted, despite some prejudice to third parties and detriment to good administration, on public interest grounds); *R (Quintavalle) v Secretary of State for Health* [2001] EWHC Admin 918 [2001] 4 All ER 1013 at [33] (points of general importance).

26.3.10 **Strength of the claim.** *PJG v Child Support Agency* [2006] EWHC 423 (Fam) [2006] 2 FLR 857 at [14] (extending time where miscarriage of justice conceded); *R v Warwickshire County Council, ex p Collymore* [1995] ELR 217, 228B-229E (unlawfulness of matter under challenge a good reason to extend time); *R v Secretary of State for the Home Department, ex p Bina Rajendra Patel* [1995] Imm AR 223, 227 (where good grounds for judicial review, reluctant at the hearing of the judicial review to refuse a remedy on grounds of delay, at least where no widespread effect on third parties); *Selliah Arulanandam v Secretary of State for the Home Department* [1996] Imm AR 587, 592 (in considering delay "it is appropriate also to have an eye to the general merits of the case"); *Crest Homes* <26.1.9>; *Soinco SACI v Novokuznetsk Aluminium Plant* The Times 29th December 1997 (on any application to extend time relevant to examine the merits); *R v Council for Licensed Conveyancers, ex p Bradford and Bingley Building Society* [1999] COD 5 (where unjustifiable delay, good reason having to be supplied by analysis of merits of challenge; the better the prospects of success, the readier the court should be to extend time; even a substantial degree of merit would be appropriate basis of finding good reason); *R (Ford) v Press Complaints Commission* 31st July 2001 unrep. at [45] (arguability not a good reason to extend time, or delay rule would be otiose); cf. *Sayers v Clarke Walker (a firm)* [2002] EWCA Civ 645 [2002] 1 WLR 3095 (regarding extension of time for appeal) at [34] ("In cases where the arguments for granting or refusing an extension of time were otherwise evenly balanced, a court will have to evaluate the merits of the proposed appeal"); *R (Customs and Excise Commissioners) v Maidstone Crown Court* [2004] EWHC 1459 (Admin) at [37] (merits of appeal from magistrates a key consideration in crown court's decision whether to give leave to appeal out of time).

26.3.11 **Possibility of collateral challenge.** <27.3.11> (collateral challenge); *R (British Waterways Board) v First Secretary of State* [2006] EWHC 1019 (Admin) at [16]-[17] (time extended for delayed judicial review where could have raised illegality as a defence to rates demand); *R v Department of Trade and Industry, ex p Alba Radio Ltd* 30th November 2000 unrep. (extend time where challenge to Regulations could have been mounted in criminal proceedings and in appeal by case stated); *R v Commissioners of Customs and Excise, ex p British Sky Broadcasting Plc* 14th July 2000 unrep. (good reason where important issues, no prejudice and risk of their being litigation in any event); cf. *R v Customs & Excise Commissioners, ex p Eurotunnel Plc* [1995] CLC 392, 401C (fact that legality could be challenged collaterally not a reason for disapplying delay principles in judicial review).

26.3.12 **Other factors.** *R v Hammersmith and Fulham London Borough Council, ex p Burkett* [2001] Env LR 684 (CA) at [25]-[26] ("prejudice" and "detriment to good administration" relevant to question of a "good reason" to extend time); *R (Ford) v Press Complaints Commission* 31st July 2001 unrep. at [46] (mere absence of prejudice not a sufficient legal basis for extension of time); *R (British Beer and Pub Association) v Canterbury City Council* [2005] EWHC 1318 (Admin) [2006] LGR 596 at [100] (conducting review to identify appropriate test cases); *R v Warwickshire County Council, ex p Collymore* [1995] ELR 217, 228G-229D (continuing policy and remedy prospective-only); *R v Secretary of State for the Home Department, ex p Florence Jumoke Oyeleye* [1994] Imm AR 268, 274 (claimant badly let down by legal advisers, not to be criticised for not having legal expertise); *R v London Borough of Newham, ex p Laronde* (1995) 27 HLR 215, 226 (delay "in no way is down to the fault of the [claimant]"); *R v London Borough of Newham, ex p Gentle* (1994) 26 HLR 466 (delay fault of former solicitors and had caused no detriment); *R v Tavistock General Commissioners, ex p Worth* [1985] STC 564 (delay caused by non-legal adviser not a good reason); *Boddington v British Transport Police* [1999] 2 AC 143, 161H, 173D (observing in the context of collateral challenge in criminal proceedings that where a measure is promulgated generally the first time that the individual may have been affected by it will be when it is sought to be enforced against him); *Mariam Ahmad v Secretary of State for the Home Department* [1999] Imm AR 356, 357 ("Normally, in the case of asylum seekers, this court will be circumspect about being too rigorous in applying the normal principles of judicial review in relation to delay because" dismissal based on delay "may have very grave consequences for the asylum seeker"); *Birmingham City Council v Birmingham College of Food* [1996] ELR 1, 36F-G (although incorporated, claimant having no assets under own control until 'operative date'); *R v Warrington Justices, ex p Shone* (1996) 72 P & CR 7 (delay outweighed by hardship and prejudice to claimant in having to pay (or be committed for non-payment of) rates for which he was not liable); *Sage v South Gloucestershire County Council* [1998] ELR 525, 531A-B (claimant encouraged by defendant to pursue an application for a review, which "sent him off on the wrong horse"); *R v Customs & Excise Commissioners, ex p Eurotunnel Plc* [1995] CLC 392, 401E-404C (hardship etc caused by the claimant's delay treated as relevant to whether good reason; *R v Essex County Council, ex p C* [1994] ELR 54 (Jowitt J), 56G-H ("The [defendants] have suffered no hardship from the delay, and it is right that the matter of principle should be decided"); *R (Tofik) v Immigration Appeal Tribunal* [2003] EWCA Civ 1138 at [25] (CA explaining the lawyer default a difficult issue in immigration context); *Flaxmann-Binns v Lincolnshire County Council* [2004] EWCA Civ 424 [2004] 1 WLR 2232 at [41] (explaining, in the context of lifting an automatic stay imposes for delay under CPR 51PD para 19, that: "The fact that the delay was attributable to fault on the part of his solicitor rather than fault on the part of the claimant is a factor which weighs in the claimant's favour").

26.3.13 **Absence of good reason not necessarily fatal.** *R v London Borough of Newham, ex* *p Ajayi* (1996) 28 HLR 25 (suggesting that, in an exceptional case, Court may entertain judicial review even though claimant has failed to show a good reason for extending time).

26.4 Hardship, prejudice and detriment. In any case of lack of promptness or of undue delay, a key justification for refusing (1) permission or (2) a remedy at the substantive hearing is the likelihood that granting judicial review would cause substantial hardship or prejudice to a person, or detriment to good administration.

26.4.1 Focus on hardship etc caused by the remedy, not by the delay. Supreme Court Act 1981 s.31(6) <64.1>; *R v Secretary of State for Health, ex p Furneaux* [1994] 2 All ER 652 (no need for nexus between delay and hardship, prejudice or detriment); *R v Ipswich Borough Council, ex p Bartlett* [1997] COD 470 (Court entitled to take account of prejudice resulting from the delay).

26.4.2 Hardship/prejudice and third party reliance. *R v Monopolies & Mergers Commission, ex p Argyll Group Plc* [1986] 1 WLR 763, 779A ("possible serious detriment to shareholders"), 782H-783A ("third parties have acted in reliance on the announcement"); *R v Secretary of State for Trade and Industry, ex p Greenpeace Ltd* [1998] Env LR 415 (licensees had accepted the risks of the venture in question on the strength of what must have seemed a firm decision to grant licences); *R v Secretary of State for Trade and Industry, ex p Greenpeace* [2000] Env LR 221, 263 (extension of time granted on public interest grounds, although some prejudice to third parties); *R v Bassetlaw District Council, ex p Oxby* The Times 18th December 1997 (rejecting third party prejudice arguments where unjust for third party to keep benefit of improperly granted planning consents); *R v North West Leicestershire District Council, ex p Moses* [2000] Env LR 443, 450 (third parties having incurred substantial expenditure in reliance on planning permission for runway); *R v Licensing Authority, ex p Novartis Pharmaceuticals Ltd* [2000] COD 232 (special need for utmost promptness where interfering with future acts of third parties; but extending time here where acts all in the past); *R (Comninos) v Bedford Borough Council* [2003] EWHC 121 (Admin) [2003] LGR 271 at [29] (delayed challenge to council's decision to underwrite costs of officers' libel proceedings, and substantial hardship to the officers); *R v Hammersmith and Fulham London Borough Council, ex p Burkett* [2001] Env LR 684 (CA) at [28] ("the fact of expenditure may matter, though it is unlikely to be decisive, if the issue of time reaches the question of prejudice. But it does not ... follow that the quantum of expenditure can by itself enhance this aspect of a [defendant]'s case"); *R (Gavin) v Haringey London Borough Council* [2003] EWHC 2591 (Admin) [2004] 1 PLR 61 at [60] ("not unreasonable of [the developer] to carry on with the works even after the commencement of proceedings"), [61] (rejecting the submission "that the costs incurred since ... the date when the claim for judicial review was lodged should be left out of account").

26.4.3 Detriment to good administration.[8]
(A) NEED FOR CAUTION. *R v Hammersmith and Fulham London Borough Council, ex p Burkett* [2001] Env LR 684 (CA) at [29] ("Administration beyond law is bad administration. The courts exist to protect the former as jealously as to stop the latter; but they cannot know which they are dealing with unless they can hear out and decide viable challenges to the legality

---

[8] This subparagraph in a previous edition was cited in *R (Lichfield Securities Ltd) v Lichfield District Council* [2001] EWCA Civ 304 [2001] 3 PLR 33 at [39]; also *R (Raines) v Orange Grove Foster Care Agency Ltd* [2006] EWHC 1887 (Admin) at [68]; *R (Gavin) v Haringey London Borough Council* [2003] EWHC 2591 (Admin) at [81].

of administrative acts. This cannot be regarded as a universal rule ... but it heavily qualifies the availability of a `good administration' answer to a plea of promptness or an application to enlarge time, and it is doubtless the reason why public authorities rarely consider it appropriate to use it"); *R v Restormel Borough Council, ex p Corbett* [2001] EWCA Civ 330 [2001] 1 PLR 108 at [32] ("If there are reasons for not interfering with an unlawful decision ... they operate not in the interests of good administration but in defiance of it"); *R (Lichfield Securities Ltd) v Lichfield District Council* [2001] EWCA Civ 304 [2001] 3 PLR 33 at [39] (detriment to good administration as "a relatively unexplored ground", partly because "it can come into play only ... in practice, where the consequent hardship or prejudice to others is insufficient by itself to cause [a remedy] to be refused. In such a situation it can rarely, if ever, be in the interests of good administration to leave an abuse of public power uncorrected"); *R (Gavin) v Haringey London Borough Council* [2003] EWHC 2591 (Admin) [2004] 1 PLR 61 at [82] (*Lichfield* to "be read not as precluding the refusal of relief on the ground of detriment to good administration, but as serving to emphasise the need for caution in deciding whether the grant of relief really would be detrimental to good administration and, if so, how much weight to attach to that detriment"), [84] (here, "a net detriment to good administration if the planning permission were quashed so long after it was granted").

(B) WHETHER NEED FOR EVIDENCE. *R v Elmbridge Borough Council, ex p Health Care Corporation Ltd* [1991] 3 PLR 63, 83F ("no evidence ... of actual detriment to good administration other than the bare facts", but court "entitled to take a broad view of this matter..."); *R v Middlesbrough Borough Council, ex p I.J.H. Cameron (Holdings) Limited* [1992] COD 247 (remedy would not have been refused on this ground, absent evidence of hardship, prejudice or detriment); *R v Newbury District Council, ex p Chieveley Parish Council* (1998) 10 Admin LR 676 (detriment to good administration inherent in late challenge to planning permission); *R v Law Society, ex p Vokes* 18th February 1998 unrep. (inherent detriment to good administration); *R (Gavin) v Haringey London Borough Council* [2003] EWHC 2591 (Admin) [2004] 1 PLR 61 at [83] (detriment to good administration including developer and other third parties, where not capable of being identified or proving specific hardship or prejudice).

(C) GOOD ADMINISTRATION AND A TAILORED REMEDY. *R v Warwickshire County Council, ex p Collymore* [1995] ELR 217, 228G-229D (detriment to good administration met by flexibility as to remedy: treating unlawfulness of (continuing) policy as a reason to extend time, especially insofar as remedy sought is prospective); *R (Gavin) v Haringey London Borough Council* [2003] EWHC 2591 (Admin) [2004] 1 PLR 61 at [91] (where undue delay in planning case, declaration granted but quashing order refused), [92] (choice of remedy described as "the outcome ... that produces the lesser injustice").

(D) OTHER. *R v Secretary of State for the Home Department, ex p Oyeleye* [1994] Imm AR 268 (need more than inconvenience); *R v Secretary of State for Education and Science, ex p Hardy* (1989) 153 LG Rev 592 (local authority only having itself to blame where went ahead with scheme knowing that it was the subject of a judicial review challenge); *R v Dairy Produce Quota Tribunal, ex p Caswell* [1990] 2 AC 738, 749F (not "wise to attempt to formulate any precise definition or description of what constitutes detriment to good administration"), 749G-750A (suggesting relevant factors); *R v Mid-Warwickshire Licensing Justices, ex p Patel* [1994] COD 251 (advantageous to good administration for Court to remove the confusion); *R v Secretary of State for Trade and Industry, ex p Greenpeace Ltd* [1998] Env LR 415 (detriment to good administration, in that pursuit of challenge now generating severe and undesirable uncertainty within relevant licensing scheme, and possibly other regimes); *R v Law Society, ex p Vokes* 18th February 1998 unrep. (inherent detriment to good administration where delayed challenges to decision making payments from compensation fund); *R v Governing Body of Gateway Primary School, ex p X* [2001] ELR 321 at [44] (highly detrimental to allow claimant to jump the queue and increase a class size).

26.4.4 Leaving hardship, prejudice and detriment to the substantive hearing. *R v Stratford-on-Avon District Council, ex p Jackson* [1985] 1 WLR 1319, 1325H (consideration of delay issues "may well necessitate (inter alia) some assessment of the substantial merits or otherwise of the [claimant]'s complaints and that this assessment can be made far more appropriately and satisfactorily on the hearing of the substantive application"), endorsed in *R v Dairy Produce Quota Tribunal, ex p Caswell* [1990] 2 AC 738, 747D-E ("Questions of hardship or prejudice, or detriment" capable of arising "on a contested application for [permission] ... but even then ... it may be thought better to grant [permission] where there is considered to be good reason to extend the period under rule 4(1), leaving questions arising under section 31(6) to be explored in depth on the hearing of the substantive application"); *R v Ministry of Agriculture Fisheries and Food, ex p Bostock* [1991] 1 CMLR 687, 694 ("questions of good administration and prejudice to third parties are essentially matters for examination in depth at an inter partes hearing"); *R v Ministry of Agriculture, Fisheries and Food, ex p Dairy Trade Federation Limited* [1998] EuLR 253, 263F (would have left "questions arising under section 31(6) to be explored in depth on the hearing of the substantive application"); cf. *R v Secretary of State for Trade and Industry, ex p Greenpeace Ltd* [1998] Env LR 415 (permission refused where prejudice and detriment to good administration); *R v Customs & Excise Commissioners, ex p Eurotunnel Plc* [1995] CLC 392, 399G-400B ("exceptional" case, justifying resolution of these issues at permission stage).

> **P27 Public/private.** Judicial review applies "public law" principles, but is not the exclusive procedure for their application.

27.1 The public/private distinction
27.2 Public law principles outside CPR 54
27.3 Procedural exclusivity: abuse of process

27.1 The public/private distinction[9]. The difficult distinction between public law and private law is inescapably necessary in identifying: (1) grounds on which it is appropriate to interfere with action by public authorities ("public law grounds"); and (2) bodies exercising functions which are amenable to such review ("public functions"). It is necessary to ask whether a body "can" be judicially reviewed under CPR 54 (reviewability). Symmetry with public law can often be found in other litigation, including where relating to private bodies

27.1.1 **The development of "public law".** *O'Reilly v Mackman* [1983] 2 AC 237, 277B (Lord Diplock: "the appreciation of the distinction in substantive law between what is private law and what is public law has itself been a latecomer to the English legal system. It is a consequence of the development that has taken place in the last 30 years of the procedures available for judicial control of administrative action"); *Davy v Spelthorne Borough Council* [1984] AC 262, 276F (referring to the development of "a system of public law"); *In re State of Norway's Application* [1987] QB 433, 475G-H (no "clear distinction between public and private law", but "the division is beginning to be recognised"); *Attorney-General v Blake* [2001] 1 AC 268 (distinguishing public law and private law claims for injunction against a former employee).

27.1.2 **The public/private distinction in context.** *R v Institute of Chartered Accountants of England and Wales, ex p Taher Nawaz* [1997] COD 111 (see transcript) (Sedley J: "the division between private and public law has no rationale beyond the procedural" and "there is a series of cases where [the] two have been found to coexist"); <P34> (reviewability); *R v Panel on Take-overs and Mergers, ex p Datafin Plc* [1987] QB 815, 845A (referring to "the new-found distinction between public and private law"), 848G-H ("if the duty is a public duty, then the body in question is subject to public law"); *R v Fernhill Manor School, ex p A* [1994] ELR 67, 79F ("the law as it stands now makes a clear distinction between public law cases and private law cases"); <9.4.3> ("public authority" for HRA purposes); *Credit Suisse v Allerdale Borough Council* [1997] QB 306 (no discretion to refuse remedy where contract found to be ultra vires in private law and so unenforceable).

27.1.3 **A difficult distinction.** *R (Alconbury Developments Ltd) v Secretary of State for the Environment Transport and the Regions* [2001] UKHL 23 [2003] 2 AC 295 at [78] (Lord Hoffmann, referring to English law's "lack of a clear distinction between public and private law"); *McClaren v Home Office* [1990] ICR 824, 829F-G (referring to the "cases where it is not immediately clear whether the rights which the plaintiff claims and which he claims have been infringed by a public authority, are truly to be classified as rights under public law or rights under private law"); *Lonrho Plc v Tebbit* [1992] 4 All ER 280, 288h (Kerr LJ: "our law ... has already suffered too much from the undesirable complexities of this overlegalistic procedural dichotomy"); *Trustees of the Dennis Rye Pension Fund v Sheffield City Council* [1998] 1 WLR 840, 842G ("despite the hopes to the contrary, a very substantial volume of the resources of the parties and the courts are still being consumed to little or no purpose over largely tactical issues as to whether the correct procedure has been adopted"), 848A ("this constant unprofitable litigation over the divide between public and private law proceedings"), 849B-C ("increasingly

---

[9] Andrew Denny [2005] JR 65.

complex and technical"); *Andreou v Institute of Chartered Accountants of England and Wales* [1998] 1 All ER 14, 19g ("a subject which regrettably has become highly arbitrary"); *An Bord Bainne Co-operative Ltd v Milk Marketing Board* [1984] 2 CMLR 584, 589 (public and private law issues "homogenised"); *Roy v Kensington & Chelsea & Westminster Family Practitioner Committee* [1992] 1 AC 624 (bundle of private and public law rights); <35.2.2> (reviewability and contract); <35.2.4> (reviewability and employment).

27.2 Judicial review principles outside CPR 54

Many of the "public law" principles which govern the Court's supervisory jurisdiction on judicial review of public bodies under CPR 54(I) are also present in other forms of proceeding. Sometimes administrative law principles are parallel to, and even derived from, legal standards which apply in private law litigation against private entities. Moreover, not all issues in judicial review cases are "public law" issues.

27.2.1 **Express statutory incorporation of judicial review principles.** See eg. Housing Act 1996 s.204A(4) (county court "shall apply the principles applied by the High Court on an application for judicial review"); Enterprise Act 2002 s.120(4) (CAT required to "apply the same principles as would be applied by a court on an application for judicial review").

27.2.2 **Public law principles in "statutory review" cases.** *Chesterfield Properties Plc v Secretary of State for the Environment* [1998] JPL 568, 569 (Laws J: describing a statutory application to quash as "a statutory judicial review"); *Bushell v Secretary of State for the Environment* [1981] AC 75 (natural justice); *Save Britain's Heritage v Number 1 Poultry Ltd* [1991] 1 WLR 153 (procedural ultra vires); *Hazell v Hammersmith & Fulham London Borough Council* [1992] 2 AC 1 (ultra vires); *British Railways Board v Secretary of State for the Environment* [1993] 3 PLR 125 (irrationality); *Bolton Metropolitan Borough Council v Secretary of State for the Environment* [1995] 3 PLR 37 (adequacy of reasons).

27.2.3 **Public law principles in statutory appeals.**[10] *E v Secretary of State for the Home Department* [2004] EWCA Civ 49 [2004] QB 1044 (immigration appeal on basis of "error of law" reflecting all judicial review grounds), [42] (referring to judicial review and appeal on a point of law: "it has become a generally safe working rule that the substantive grounds for intervention are identical"); *Begum (Nipa) v Tower Hamlets London Borough Council* [2000] 1 WLR 306, 312G-313F, 327B (appeal to county court "on any point of law arising from [the decision]" (Housing Act 1996 s.204) including all judicial review grounds), applied in *Begum v Tower Hamlets London Borough Council* [2003] UKHL 5 [2003] 2 AC 430 at [7] (Lord Bingham), [17] (Lord Hoffmann), [98] (Lord Millett); *Enfield London Borough Council v Kruja* [2004] EWCA Civ 1769 at [21] (Laws LJ, describing s.204 appeal as "a statutory judicial review").

27.2.4 **Public law principles: other proceedings against public bodies.**
(A) HABEAS CORPUS. *R v Governor of Brixton Prison, ex p Armah* [1968] AC 192 (error of law); *R v Governor of Pentonville Prison, ex p Alves* [1993] AC 284 (misdirection in law/unreasonableness); *Tan Te Lam v Superintendent of Tai A Chau Detention Centre* [1997] AC 97 (precedent fact).
(B) ORDINARY CLAIM FORM ACTIONS. *Vine v National Dock Labour Board* [1957] AC 488 (delegation of power); *Ceylon University v Fernando* [1960] 1 WLR 223 (natural justice); *Pyx Granite Co Ltd v Ministry of Housing and Local Government* [1960] AC 260 (vires of

---

[10] Brian Kennelly [2006] JR 160; Clare Radcliffe [2007] JR 197.

planning refusal/conditions); *Kanda v Government of Malaya* [1962] AC 322 (ultra vires/natural justice); *Ridge v Baldwin* [1964] AC 40 (natural justice); *Pfizer Corporation v Ministry of Health* [1965] AC 512 (ultra vires); *Chertsey Urban District Council v Mixnam's Properties Ltd* [1965] AC 735 (ultra vires/unreasonableness); *Wiseman v Borneman* [1971] AC 297 (natural justice); *Pearlberg v Varty* [1972] 1 WLR 534 (natural justice); *Daymond v Plymouth City Council* [1976] AC 609 (delegated legislation); *Grunwick Processing Laboratories Ltd v Advisory Conciliation & Arbitration Service* [1978] AC 655 (ultra vires); *Engineers & Managers Association v Advisory Conciliation & Arbitration Service* [1980] 1 WLR 302 (ultra vires); *Calvin v Carr* [1980] AC 574 (natural justice); *United Kingdom Association of Professional Engineers v Advisory Conciliation & Arbitration Service* [1981] AC 424 (irrationality); *Din (Taj) v Wandsworth London Borough Council* [1983] 1 AC 657 (error of law); *Cheall v Association of Professional Executive Clerical & Computer Staff* [1983] 2 AC 180 (natural justice); *Air Canada v Secretary of State for Trade (No.2)* [1983] 2 AC 394 (vires of airport charges); *London Borough of Islington v Camp* (1999) [2004] LGR 58 (action by claim form for a declaration, in circumstances where a decision either way likely to give rise to judicial review); *CF v Secretary of State for the Home Department* [2004] EWHC 111 (Fam) [2004] 1 FCR 577 at [25] ("choice of forum or of remedy cannot affect substantive law").
(C) TORT CLAIMS. *In re McC (A Minor)* [1985] AC 528 (jurisdictional error relevant to action for damages against magistrates); *Holgate-Mohammed v Duke* [1984] AC 437, 443C ("The *Wednesbury* principles, as they are usually referred to, are applicable to determining the lawfulness of the exercise of the statutory discretion of a constable ... for the purpose of founding a cause of action at common law for damages"), applied in *Henderson v Chief Constable of Cleveland Police* [2001] EWCA Civ 335 [2001] 1 WLR 1103 at [20]; *Taylor v Chief Constable of Thames Valley* [2004] EWCA Civ 858 [2004] 3 All ER 503 at [3] (application of *Wednesbury* test to discretion and powers of arrest).

27.2.5 Public law principles in claims against private bodies.[11] <7.6.9> (procedural fairness applicable to private bodies); <7.7.4> (unreasonableness applicable to private bodies); *Law v National Greyhound Racing Club Ltd* [1983] 1 WLR 1302 (ultra vires challenge by private law action); <9.1.12> (horizontal effect of the HRA); *Bradley v Jockey Club* [2005] EWCA Civ 1056 at [17]-[18] (supervisory jurisdiction by claim form action); *R v Association of British Travel Agents, ex p Sunspell Ltd* [2001] ACD 88 at [22] (requirement of proportionality of sanction capable of being implied contract term); *Stevenage Borough Football Club Ltd v Football League Ltd* (1998) 10 Admin LR 609 (judicial review-type challenge to rules, via modified restraint of trade doctrine); *R v Servite Houses and Wandsworth London Borough Council, ex p Goldsmith* (2000) 3 CCLR 325 (declining to apply public law principles to a housing association); *R (Arthurworry) v Haringey London Borough Council* [2001] EWHC Admin 698 (judicial review-type remedy granted by reference to the implied duty of trust and confidence between employer and employee);*Amec Civil Engineering Ltd v Secretary of State for Transport* [2005] EWCA Civ 291 [2005] 1 WLR 2339 at [47]-[48] (pre-arbitration engineer duty to act independently, honestly and fairly).

27.2.6 Public law principles in criminal proceedings. *Rogers v Essex County Council* [1987] AC 66 (illegality); *R v Gough* [1993] AC 646 (bias); *Boddington v British Transport Police* [1999] 2 AC 143 (questions of vires entitled to be raised by criminal defendant); *R v Latif* [1996] 1 WLR 104, 111B-113D (relying on the principle in *R v Horseferry Road Magistrates' Court, ex p Bennett* [1994] 1 AC 42 in a criminal appeal); *D'Souza v DPP* [1992] 1 WLR 1073 (lawfulness of entry by force decisive on prosecution for assault).

---

[11] Andrew Lidbetter & Jasveer Randhawa [2005] JR 326; Jennifer Bruce [2008] JR 12.

27.2.7 **Public law principles in other proceedings.** *Re Golden Chemicals Ltd* [1976] Ch 300 (delegability in insolvency proceedings); *Scott v National Trust for Places of Historic Interest or Natural Beauty* [1998] 2 All ER 705, 715-716a (abuse of power in charity proceedings); *Sieff v Fox* [2005] EWHC 1312 (Ch) [2005] 1 WLR 3811 (relevancy/irrelevancy principle in the context of trustees' discretionary power); *Credit Suisse v Allerdale Borough Council* [1997] QB 306 (ultra vires in contract claim); *Paragon Finance Plc v Nash* [2001] EWCA Civ 1466 [2002] 1 WLR 685 at [38] (*Wednesbury* test relevant where contract conferring a discretion); *Thomas v University of Bradford (No.2)* [1992] 1 All ER 964, 976d-f (judicial review grounds applied in Visitorial proceedings); *Rees v Crane* [1994] 2 AC 173 (public law principles in constitutional motion case).

27.2.8 **Private law issues in judicial review proceedings.** *R (Balding) v Secretary of State for Work and Pensions* [2007] EWCA Civ 1327 [2008] 1 WLR 564 (meaning of "bankruptcy debt"); *R v Investors Compensation Scheme Ltd, ex p Weyell* [1994] QB 749 (approach to compensation for default of financial adviser); *R (Rowe) v Vale of White Horse District Council* [2003] EWHC 388 (Admin) at [1] (private law restitution issue).

27.3 Procedural exclusivity: abuse of process.[12]

Although it is necessary to ask whether a body "can" be judicially reviewed under CPR 54 (reviewability), it is wrong to conclude that such a body "can only" (and so must) be challenged by that means. Certain remedies against public bodies (quashing, mandatory and prohibiting orders) are "exclusive" to CPR 54. And a claim which is not, but by its nature should have been, by judicial review can in a clear case be dismissed as an abuse of process, especially if it was not brought promptly. Beyond that situation, choice of forum is not an abuse, though transfer into or out of CPR 54 may prove necessary to ensure just and effective resolution of the issues.

27.3.1 **Remedies for which CPR 54(I) must be used.** <24.1.1(A)>.

27.3.2 **Abuse of process.** *O'Reilly v Mackman* [1983] 2 AC 237, 285E (Lord Diplock, suggesting that it would "as a general rule be contrary to public policy, and as such an abuse of the process of the court, to permit a person seeking to establish that a decision of a public authority infringed rights to which he was entitled to protection under public law to proceed by way of an ordinary action and by this means to evade the provisions of Order 53 for the protection of such authorities"); *Link Organisation Plc v North Derbyshire Tertiary College* [1999] ELR 20, 26B-D (Buxton LJ, treating the principle as one of "judgment" rather than "law"); *Cocks v Thanet District Council* [1983] 2 AC 286, 295C (abuse where "no valid reason" for proceeding otherwise than by judicial review).

27.3.3 **Delay as abuse.** *Clark v University of Lincolnshire and Humberside* [2000] 1 WLR 1988 at [39] ("What is likely to be important ... will not be whether the right procedure has been adopted but whether the protection provided by Order 53 has been flouted in circumstances which are inconsistent with the proceedings being able to be conducted justly"), [17] (Sedley LJ); *Mann Singh Shingara v Secretary of State for the Home Department* [1999] Imm AR 257, 266 ("it would be an abuse of process to bring private law proceedings", being "so long out of time for challenging the ... decision"); *O'Reilly v Mackman* [1983] 2 AC 237, 285H (claims "blatant attempts to avoid the protections for the defendants for which Order 53 provides"); *Stancliffe Stone Co Ltd v Peak District National Park Authority* [2005] EWCA Civ 747 [2006] Env LR 158 at [44] (judicial review would face "formidable difficulties" of delay) [54] (inapt

---

[12] Thomas de la Mare [1998] JR 133; Tom Hickman [2000] JR 178; Rachel Bateson [2004] JR 140.

"attempt to challenge in a private law action for declaratory relief matters solely of public law which ought more properly to have been raised (if at all) by action for judicial review"); *Bahamas Telecommunications Company Ltd v Public Utilities Commission* [2008] UKPC 10 at [25] (claim for declaration of licensing entitlements struck out because should have been a prompt judicial review or statutory appeal and delay was prejudicial).

27.3.4 Other clear-cut case as abuse. *Link Organisation Plc v North Derbyshire Tertiary College* [1999] ELR 20, 26C-D (Buxton LJ: "I am quite clear that the present case falls well outside even the most generous limits within which it is permissible to assert public law issues in a writ action... The public law complaint is at present hypothetical"); *Andreou v Institute of Chartered Accountants of England and Wales* [1998] 1 All ER 14 (abuse because seeking to rely simply on public law claims previously advanced in judicial review proceedings which had been dismissed for delay).

27.3.5 Lord Woolf's practical guidance. See *Trustees of the Dennis Rye Pension Fund v Sheffield City Council* [1998] 1 WLR 840 and in *Clark v University of Lincolnshire and Humberside* [2000] 1 WLR 1988:
(A) JUDICIAL REVIEW NORMALLY PREFERABLE WHERE PUBLIC BODY *Clark* at [29] ("[The defendant] is a public body... Court proceedings would, therefore, normally be expected to be commenced under [CPR Part 54]"), [32] ("the preferable procedure would usually be by way of judicial review").
(B) WHERE DOUBT, START JUDICIAL REVIEW, AND TRANSFER IF NECESSARY *Rye* at 848F-G ("If it is not clear whether judicial review or an ordinary action is the correct procedure it will be safer to make an application for judicial review than commence an ordinary action"; "the court can protect its resources either by directing that the application should continue as if begun by [ordinary action] or by directing it should be heard by a judge who is not nominated to hear cases in the [Administrative Court]").
(C) DOUBTFUL ORDINARY ACTION: USE PERMISSION/TRANSFER *Rye* at 848H-849B ("in cases where it is unclear whether proceedings have been correctly brought by an ordinary action it should be remembered that after consulting the [Administrative Court Office] a case can always be transferred to the [Administrative Court] as an alternative to being struck out").
(D) LOOK AT THE PRACTICAL CONSEQUENCES. *Rye* at 849D-E (need to consider "the practical consequences of the choice of procedure which has been made" and whether the choice has any "significant disadvantages for the parties, the public or the court").

27.3.6 Powers of transfer. <21.2.16> (transfer into the Administrative Court); <21.2.15> (transfer out of CPR 54).

27.3.7 Golden rule 1: avoid arid and costly procedural debate. *Clark v University of Lincolnshire and Humberside* [2000] 1 WLR 1988 at [37] (Lord Woolf MR: "The intention of the CPR is to harmonise procedures as far as possible and to avoid barren procedural disputes which generate satellite litigation") *R (Heather) v Leonard Cheshire Foundation* [2002] EWCA Civ 366 [2002] 2 All ER 936 at [38] (referring to "the old demarcation disputes as to when judicial review was or was not appropriate under Order 53. Part 54 CPR is intended to avoid any such disputes which are wholly unproductive"); *R v Ministry of Agriculture Fisheries and Food, ex p Lower Burytown Farms Ltd* [1999] EuLR 129, 137F-138A (tensions in the law, now resolved by *Rye*).

27.3.8 Golden rule 2: need to be flexible and permissive. *Mercury Communications Ltd v Director General of Telecommunications* [1996] 1 WLR 48, 57D-E (Lord Slynn: "some flexibility as to the use of different procedures is necessary. It has to be borne in mind that the overriding question is whether the proceedings constitute an abuse of the process of the court");

British Steel Plc v Commissioners for Customs & Excise [1997] 2 All ER 366 (Saville LJ: "In this day and age it is surely possible to devise procedures which avoid this form of satellite litigation, while safeguarding both the private rights of individuals and companies and the position and responsibilities of public authorities"); *Roy v Kensington & Chelsea & Westminster Family Practitioner Committee* [1992] 1 AC 624, 655A (Lord Lowry: "unless the procedure adopted by the moving party is ill suited to dispose of the question at issue, there is much to be said in favour of the proposition that a court having jurisdiction ought to let a case be heard rather than entertain a debate concerning the form of the proceedings"); *R (Heather) v Leonard Cheshire Foundation* [2002] EWCA Civ 366 [2002] 2 All ER 936 at [38] (since a "bona fide contention is being advanced (although incorrect) that LCF was performing a public function, that is an appropriate issue to be brought to the court by way of judicial review"), [39] ("We wish to make clear that the CPR provides a framework which is sufficiently flexible to enable all the issues between the parties to be determined... In view of a possibility of a misunderstanding as to the scope of judicial review we draw attention to this and the powers of transfer under Part 54"); *Phonographic Performance Ltd v Department of Trade and Industry* [2004] EWHC 1795 (Ch) (not an abuse of process to bring *Francovich* reparation claim for non-implementation of EC Directive by ordinary claim form action), [49] ("essentially private law proceedings which can and prima facie should be brought by an ordinary claim"); *D v Home Office* [2005] EWCA Civ 38 [2006] 1 WLR 1003 at [105] (false imprisonment damages could be claimed in the county court and did not need to be by judicial review only).

27.3.9 Golden rule 3: onus on the objector. *Davy v Spelthorne Borough Council* [1984] AC 262, 278F (Lord Wilberforce: "prima facie the rule applies that the plaintiff may choose the court and the procedure which suits him best. The onus lies upon the defendant to show that in doing so he is abusing the court's procedure"); *R v East Berkshire Health Authority, ex p Walsh* [1985] QB 152, 173G ("A party inviting the court to take this draconian step assumes a heavy burden").

27.3.10 The rise and fall of the condition precedent principle. *Cocks v Thanet District Council* [1983] 2 AC 286, 294E (Lord Bridge, describing the exclusivity principle as applicable in cases where claimant's failure to overturn a "decision of the public authority ... prevents him establishing a necessary condition precedent to the statutory private law right which he seeks to enforce"), 293B (where overturning a "public law decision ... is a condition precedent to the establishment of the private law duty"); *The Great House at Sonning Ltd v Berkshire County Council* (1997) 95 LGR 350 (claim in nuisance from road closure necessarily involving challenge to reasonableness or fairness of closure order or its implementation, these being matters for judicial review); *Roy v Kensington & Chelsea & Westminster Family Practitioner Committee* [1992] 1 AC 624, 653B-D (not applying *Cocks*); *Stovin v Wise* [1996] AC 923 (damages action for non-exercise of statutory powers, but no suggestion that unlawfulness needing to be established via judicial review); *Trustees of the Dennis Rye Pension Fund v Sheffield City Council* [1998] 1 WLR 840, 847H-848A (commenting that the law "has moved on from *Cocks*"); *Andreou v Institute of Chartered Accountants of England and Wales* [1998] 1 All ER 14, 21e ("appropriate to proceed in a private law action even though there is a public law issue to be determined as long as there is a private law right which is clearly identified which has also to be determined"); *Boddington v British Transport Police* [1999] 2 AC 143, 172G-H (exclusivity rule "does not apply in a civil case when an individual seeks to establish private law rights which cannot be determined without an examination of the validity of a public law decision"); *Clark v University of Lincolnshire and Humberside* [2000] 1 WLR 1988 at [16] (recognising the difficulties created by *Cocks*).

27.3.11 The defendant exception/collateral challenge. *Wandsworth London Borough Council v Winder* [1985] AC 461, 509E-510A (not an abuse to defend proceedings brought against him by challenging local authority decision); *Kay v Lambeth London Borough Council* [2006] UKHL 10 [2006] 2 AC 465 at [60] (affirming *Winder* principle); *Doherty v Birmingham City Council* [2008] UKHL 57 [2008] 3 WLR 636 (applying *Kay*; as to HRA points as defence to possession proceedings); *Panday v Virgil* [2008] UKPC 24 [2008] 3 WLR 296 at [33]-[34] (abuse of process normally to be decided by criminal court, not by adjourning for judicial review); *Bunney v Burns Anderson Plc* [2007] EWHC 1240 (Ch) [2007] 4 All ER 246 at [47] (entitled to raise defence of illegality of Financial Ombudsman Service direction in proceedings to enforce it); *Derbyshire County Council v Akrill* [2005] EWCA Civ 308 (2005) 8 CCLR 173 (public law defence to local authority claim for residential accommodation fees); *R v Inland Revenue Commissioners, ex p T.C.Coombs & Co* [1991] 2 AC 283, 304C ("challenging ... the validity of the notice by way of defence to penalty proceedings");*R v Secretary of State for Transport, ex p Factortame Ltd* [1990] 2 AC 85, 142B-C (raising EC incompatibility as criminal defence); *Credit Suisse v Allerdale Borough Council* [1997] QB 306 (raising ultra vires of contract as defence to action to enforce it); *Boddington v British Transport Police* [1999] 2 AC 143 raising by way of defence the legal validity of an instrument under which prosecuted); *R v Wicks* [1998] AC 92 (criminal planning enforcement context where not possible to raise as defence procedural impropriety in decision to issue the notice); *Dilieto v Ealing London Borough Council* [2000] QB 381 (distinguishing *Wicks*, where enforcement notice out of time); *R v Medicines Control Agency, ex p Pharma Nord Ltd* (1998) 10 Admin LR 646, 660D (criminal court's jurisdiction not excluded).

> **P28 Ouster.** Statutory prohibition of judicial review is theoretically possible, unlikely in practice, and constitutionally questionable.

28.1 The approach to legislative preclusive clauses
28.2 Time-limit ousters

28.1 The approach to legislative preclusive clauses Legislative provisions which suggest a curtailment of the Courts' powers of judicial review strike at the heart of the Courts' constitutional self-image, in upholding the rule of law and access to the courts, and test the limits of the principle of legislative supremacy. Although recognising the theoretical possibility of ouster, the starting-point is that only the clearest wording would do, and even that is questionable. There are many cases of apparent ousters not having prevented judicial review.

28.1.1 Aversion to ouster. *R (G) v Immigration Appeal Tribunal* [2004] EWCA Civ 1731 [2005] 1 WLR 1445 at [13] ("The common law power of the judges to review the legality of administrative action is a cornerstone of the rule of law in this country and one that the judges guard jealously. If Parliament attempts by legislation to remove that power, the rule of law is threatened. The courts will not readily accept that legislation achieves that end"); *Farley v Secretary of State for Work and Pensions (No.2)* [2006] UKHL 31 [2006] 1 WLR 1817 at [18] (not an ouster where jurisdictional limitation part of a statutory scheme locating jurisdiction to another court); cf. *State of Mauritius v Khoyratty* [2006] UKPC 13 [2007] 1 AC 80 (statutory exclusion of bail unconstitutional given democratic guarantee).

28.1.2 Construction to preserve jurisdiction. *Anisminic Ltd v Foreign Compensation Commission* [1969] 2 AC 147, 170C-D (Lord Reid: "a provision ousting the ordinary jurisdiction of the court must be construed strictly"; "that meaning shall be taken which preserves the ordinary jurisdiction of the court"); *R (Sivasubramaniam) v Wandsworth County Court* [2002] EWCA Civ 1738 [2003] 1 WLR 475 at [44] (statute not impliedly ousting judicial review of a county court permission to appeal decision); *R (Bancoult) v Secretary of State for Foreign & Commonwealth Affairs* [2007] EWCA Civ 498 [2008] QB 365 (Colonial Laws Validity Act 1865 not restricting challenge to colonial legislation to repugnancy).

28.1.3 Ouster by plain words. *R v Hull University Visitor, ex p Page* [1993] AC 682, 693H-694A ("Parliament can by the use of appropriate language provide that a decision .... shall ... not be subject to challenge either by way of appeal or judicial review"); *R v Acting Returning Officer for Devon (etc), ex p Sanders* [1994] COD 497 (ouster by the Parliamentary Election Rules); <7.4.6> (access to law excluded only by plain words or necessary implication); *Adams v Lord Advocate* [2002] UKHRR 1189, [62]-[64] (effect of Scotland Act 1998 being that "the jurisdiction of this court to review Acts of the Scottish Parliament on traditional common law grounds is excluded"); *R (Sivasubramaniam) v Wandsworth County Court* [2002] EWCA Civ 1738 [2003] 1 WLR 475 at [44] (need for clear and explicit words), [42] (no presumption that an ouster provision does not mean what it says, when applied to courts of law); *R (Hilali) v Governor of Whitemoor Prison* [2008] UKHL 3 [2008] 1 AC 805 at [21] (habeas corpus excluded here by clear statutory words); *A v B* [2008] EWHC 1512 (Admin) at [14] (no clear words ousting judicial review); cf. *Anisminic Ltd v Foreign Compensation Commission* [1969] 2 AC 147 (judicial review even though statute apparently clear and emphatic).

28.1.4 Replacement of judicial review. *R (G) v Immigration Appeal Tribunal* [2004] EWCA Civ 1731 [2005] 1 WLR 1445 (paper statutory review meaning judicial review on equivalent grounds an abuse of process).

28.1.5 **Exclusive alternative remedy.** <36.2>.

28.1.6 **Ouster of judicial review: constitutionally dubious.**[13] <7.1.8> (towards an enhanced constitutional role).

28.1.7 **"No certiorari" clauses not excluding certiorari.** *Anisminic Ltd v Foreign Compensation Commission* [1969] 2 AC 147, 200F (citing *Ex p Bradlaugh* (1878) 3 QBD 509, 513 per Mellor J: "It is well established that the provision taking away the certiorari does not apply where there was an absence of jurisdiction"). Note too the Tribunals and Inquiries Act 1992 s.12, formerly s.14 of the 1971 Act, repealing most pre-1958 'no certiorari' clauses.

28.1.8 **Approach to other statutory formulations.**
(A) `FINALITY' CLAUSES. *R v Medical Appeal Tribunal, ex p Gilmore* [1957] 1 QB 574 (provision that decision "final" simply meaning no appeal); *R (Revenue and Customs Commissioners) v Machell* [2005] EWHC 2593 (Admin) [2006] 1 WLR 609 at [24] ("final and conclusive" simply meaning no appeal and binding); *HMB Holdings Ltd v Antigua and Barbuda* [2007] UKPC 37 at [30] ("a clause which confers finality ... can only relate to decisions which have been given within the field of operation that has been entrusted to the decision-maker").
(B) `NOT TO BE CALLED INTO QUESTION' CLAUSES. *Anisminic Ltd v Foreign Compensation Commission* [1969] 2 AC 147 (judicial review available despite provision stating that determinations of FCC "not to be called into question in any legal proceedings whatsoever").
(C) `NO PROCEEDINGS' CLAUSES. *R v Bradford Metropolitan Borough Council, ex p Sikander Ali* [1994] ELR 299, 315C-316B (suggesting that judicial review for racial discrimination available despite statutory preclusion of "proceedings, whether civil or criminal", since judicial review not within "civil proceedings" for that purpose).
(D) `NO REVIEW' CLAUSES. *R v Secretary of State for the Home Department, ex p Fayed* [1998] 1 WLR 763, 771B-773C (statute providing that decision "shall not be subject to appeal to, or review in, any court", but this "does not prevent the court exercising its jurisdiction to review a decision on the traditional grounds available on an application for judicial review", specifically for breach of natural justice, this rendering the decision a "nullity"); *Attorney-General v Ryan* [1980] AC 718, 730C-E ("It is by now well-established law that to come within the prohibition of appeal or review by an ouster clause of this type, the decision must be one which the decision-making authority ... had jurisdiction to make. If in purporting to make it he has gone outside his jurisdiction, it is ultra vires and is not a `decision' under the Act"); *R v Secretary of State for the Home Department, ex p Mehta* [1992] COD 484 (legislative provision stating that Secretary of State's decision "shall not be subject to appeal to, or review in, any court" not preventing court from pointing out error in construction of the Act which rendered the decision a nullity).
(E) `CONCLUSIVE EVIDENCE' CLAUSES. *R v Registrar of Companies, ex p Central Bank of India* [1986] QB 1114 (effect of statutory provision that certificate of incorporation conclusive evidence of compliance with statutory requirements); *R v Registrar of Companies, ex p Attorney General* [1991] BCLC 476 (provision not binding on Crown, so Attorney General entitled to seek judicial review).

28.1.9 **Ouster not applying to nullity/jurisdictional error.** *Anisminic Ltd v Foreign*

---

[13] Michael Fordham [2004] JR 86; Lord Lester QC [2004] JR 95; Clause 14 [2004] JR 97; Constitutional Affairs Committee [2004] JR 100; Lord Steyn [2004] JR 107; Lord Falconer's Statement [2004] JR 109; Martin Chamberlain [2004] JR 112; Thomas de la Mare [2004] JR 119.

Compensation Commission [1969] 2 AC 147, 170E-F (ouster "protects every determination which is not a nullity"), 211H ("the preclusive clause can have no application except to a determination made within the limits, whatever they turn out to be, fixed by Parliament"), 196C (importance of "jurisdiction" and "nullity" as to effect of ouster), 170F ("there are no degrees of nullity"), 208B-C (in ensuring "that the limits of that area which have been laid down are observed", court is "carrying out the intention of the legislature"); *Fayed* <28.1.8(D)>; *South East Asia Fire Bricks v Non-Metallic Mineral Products Manufacturing Employers Union* [1981] AC 363 (jurisdictional error not excluded); *R v Miall* [1992] QB 836, 841H-842A; *Mehta* <28.1.8(D)>; *R v Paddington Valuation Officer, ex p Peachey Property Corporation Ltd* [1966] 1 QB 380, 404E ("error which goes to the root"; "[valuation list] vitiated by fundamental error"); <32.1.5(A)> (s.29(3) and jurisdictional error/ nullity).

28.1.10 Ouster does not prevent challenge to antecedent/subsequent steps. *R v Wiltshire County Council, ex p Lazard Brothers & Co Ltd* The Times 13th January 1998 (statutory ouster in relation to order not preventing judicial review of resolution to make an order); *R v Wiltshire County Council, ex p Nettlecombe Ltd* (1998) 96 LGR 386 (ouster in relation to orders made not preventing judicial review challenge to antecedent step of decision to make an order); *R (Richards) v Pembrokeshire County Council* [2004] EWCA Civ 1000 [2005] LGR 105 at [47] (even if Order not open to challenge given statutory time-limit ouster, could be possible to challenge validity of subsequent instruments made under the Order and replicating the lack of vires).

28.2 Time-limit ousters. A special type of statutory ouster provides for both (1) a right of challenge (eg. appeal or statutory review) within a limited time (eg. 6 weeks) and (2) the matter not otherwise to be questionable in legal proceedings. Courts have tended to treat judicial review as thereby ousted, where a challenge is sought to be made beyond the specified time-limit.

28.2.1 Strict enforcement of time-limit ouster. *R v Cornwall County Council, ex p Huntington* [1994] 1 All ER 694 (statutory time-limit ouster effectively ousting judicial review); *R (Deutsch) v Hackney London Borough Council* [2003] EWHC 2692 at [17] (statutory time-limit ouster effectively ousting challenge to parking designation order), [25] (emphasising that order "bears no brand of invalidity on its forehead"), [27] (leaving open situation where any question of HRA-compatibility); *Smith v East Elloe Rural District Council* [1956] AC 736 (strict enforcement of time-limit ouster even in the face of an allegation of fraud/bad faith); *R v Secretary of State for the Environment, ex p Ostler* [1977] 1 QB 122 (Court of Appeal concluding that *Smith* survived *Anisminic*); *R v Secretary of State for the Environment, ex p Kent* [1990] COD 78 (CA refusing permission in the face of 6 week time-limit ouster); *Khan v Newport Borough Council* [1991] COD 157 (CA declining permission in the face of 6 week time-limit ouster to challenge tree preservation order); *R v Secretary of State for the Environment, ex p Upton Brickworks Ltd* [1992] COD 301 (permission set aside because of time-limit ouster); *R v London Borough of Camden, ex p Woolf and Others* [1992] COD 456 (permission set aside in light of time-limit ouster); *R v Devon County Council, ex p Isaac and Another* [1992] COD 371 (refusal of judicial review of (unconfirmed) modification order in light of time-limit ouster); *R v Dacorum District Council, ex p Cannon* [1996] 2 PLR 45 (judicial review of listed building enforcement notice refused, because available appeal (with time limit) an exclusive remedy); *Enterprise Inns Plc v Secretary of State for the Environment, Transport and the Regions* [2000] 4 PLR 52 (strict approach to whether application within the 6 week period; no jurisdiction where application lodged prior to start-date).

28.2.2 Judicial review despite time-limit ouster. *R v Wiltshire County Council, ex p Nettlecombe Ltd* (1998) 96 LGR 386 (distinguishing *Huntington* where challenge to an `antecedent step' and plain error of law); <28.1.10> (antecedent/subsequent steps).

28.2.3 **Delay and planning cases (6 week parallel).** <26.2.9>.

28.2.4 **Time to overrule** *Ostler?* *R (Richards) v Pembrokeshire County Council* [2004] EWCA Civ 1000 [2005] LGR 105 at [37] (CA suggesting that "the advent of the Human Rights Act 1998, and in particular the consequent introduction into English Law of Article 6 of the European Convention on Human Rights, may have an impact on the continuing effectiveness of the reasoning in *Ostler*. Even if it does not, it may be that the reasoning in *Smith v East Elloe District Council* [1956] AC 735 (which drove the decision in *Ostler*) had been rendered obsolete by the reasoning in *Anisminic Limited v Foreign Compensation Commission* [1969] 2 AC 147. But that point is very probably not open in this court: see *R v Cornwall County Council, ex p Huntington* [1994] 1 All ER 694").

29.1 The purposive approach to interpretation
29.2 Legislative purpose and judicial review
29.3 Statutory interpretation
29.4 Using Hansard
29.5 Interpreting other sources

29.1 The purposive approach to interpretation. An enactment is to be interpreted by focusing on its purpose and intent, approached by reference to the language, context and background. The meaning derived must be one which the words used can bear, but strong interpretative techniques promote compatibility with EC, HRA:ECHR or common law rights and principles. And the Court may correct an obvious drafting error by means of a rectifying construction.

29.1.1 **Purposive approach to statutory interpretation.** *R (Quintavalle) v Secretary of State for Health* [2003] UKHL 13 [2003] 2 AC 687[14] at [8] (Lord Bingham: "The court's task, within the permissible bounds of interpretation, is to give effect to Parliament's purpose"), [21] (Lord Steyn, describing "the shift towards purposive interpretation", agreeing that: "statutes always have some purpose or object to accomplish, whose sympathetic and imaginative discovery is the surest guide to their meaning"), [38] (Lord Millett: "the task of the court is to ascertain the intention of Parliament as expressed in the words it has chosen"); *Pepper v Hart* [1993] AC 593, 617E-F ("The courts now adopt a purposive approach which seeks to give effect to the true purpose of legislation"), 635D ("the purposive approach to construction now adopted by the courts in order to give effect to the true intentions of the legislature"); *Macniven (HM Inspector of Taxes) v Westmoreland Investments Ltd* [2001] UKHL 6 [2003] 1 AC 311 at [6] ("When searching for the meaning with which Parliament has used the statutory language in question, courts have regard to the underlying purpose that the statutory language is seeking to achieve"), [29] ("There is ultimately only one principle of construction, namely to ascertain what Parliament meant by using the language of the statute"); *In re C (A Minor)* [1997] AC 489, 501F ("The Act should be construed purposively so as to give effect to the underlying intentions of Parliament"); *R (Kelly) v Secretary of State for Justice* [2008] EWCA Civ 177 [2008] 3 All ER 844 at [27] (purposive interpretation of criminal statute); *Re M (a Minor) (Care Order: Threshold Conditions)* [1994] 3 All ER 298, 309 (referring to "the tyranny of language and the importance of ascertaining and giving effect to the intentions of Parliament by construing a statute in accordance with the spirit rather than the letter of the Act"); *R v Rotherham Metropolitan Borough Council, ex p Clark* (1998) 10 Admin LR 153, 159C (purposive construction of Regulations), 170G (Lord Bingham CJ: "On a wholly literal approach to the statutory language [the LEA's] argument is sustainable. But it does not in my view give effect to the spirit or purpose of the section").

29.1.2 **The purpose from the text.** *Seal v Chief Constable South Wales Police* [2007] UKHL 31 [2007] 1 WLR 1910 at [5] (Lord Bingham: "In construing any statutory provision the starting point must always be the language of the provision itself"); *R (Westminster City Council) v National Asylum Support Service* [2002] UKHL 38 [2002] 1 WLR 2956 at [6] (Lord Steyn: "The object is to see what is the intention expressed by the words enacted"); *Wilson v First County Trust Ltd* [2003] UKHL 40 [2004] 1 AC 816 at [56] (Lord Nicholls: "When a court is carrying out its constitutional task of interpreting legislation it is seeking to identify the

---

[14] Angela Gruenberg [2002] JR 264, [2003] JR 178.

intention of Parliament expressed in the language used. This is an objective concept. In this context the intention of Parliament is the intention the court reasonably imputes to Parliament in respect of the language used"); *R v Z (Attorney General for Northern Ireland's Reference)* [2005] UKHL 35 [2005] 2 AC 645 at [16]-[17] (Lord Bingham: "the task of the court is to interpret the provision which Parliament has enacted and not to give effect to an inferred intention of Parliament not fairly to be derived from the language of the statute"), [33] (Lord Woolf); *Black-Clawson International Ltd v Papierwerke Waldhof-Aschaffenburg AG* [1975] AC 591, 613G ("We are seeking the meaning of the words which Parliament used. We are seeking not what Parliament meant but the true meaning of what they said"), applied in *Roodal v The State* [2003] UKPC 78 [2005] 1 AC 328 at [15]; *R v Inland Revenue Commissioners, ex p Woolwich Equitable Building Society* [1990] 1 WLR 1400, 1411G ("the question is ultimately not one of what, subjectively, Parliament may (or must) have intended to do but whether, by the words which it has used, it has effectively done it"); *R (O'Byrne) v Secretary of State for the Environment, Transport and the Regions* [2002] UKHL 45 [2002] 1 WLR 3250 at [3] ("the intention of Parliament must be inferred by considering the terms and purposes of both Acts in their respective contexts"); *R (Wilkinson) v Commissioners of Inland Revenue* [2005] UKHL 30 [2005] 1 WLR 1718 at [18] ("the intention of Parliament" normally means "the interpretation which the reasonable reader would give to the statute read against its background, including, now, an assumption [under HRA s.3] that it was not intended to be incompatible with Convention rights").

29.1.3 **The purpose from the context.** *R (Haw) v Secretary of State for the Home Department* [2006] EWCA Civ 532 [2006] QB 780[15] at [17] (questions of construction "must be answered by considering the statutory language in its context, which of course includes the purpose of the Act. The search is for the meaning intended by Parliament. The language used by Parliament is of central importance but that does not mean that it must always be construed literally. The meaning of language always depends upon its particular context"); *Inland Revenue Commissioners v McGuckian* [1997] 1 WLR 991, 999D (Lord Steyn: "Where there is no obvious meaning of a statutory provision the modern emphasis is on a contextual approach designed to identify the purpose of a statute and to give effect to it"); *R (Westminster City Council) v National Asylum Support Service* [2002] UKHL 38 [2002] 1 WLR 2956 at [5] (Lord Steyn: "The starting point is that language in all legal texts conveys meaning according to the circumstances in which it was used. It follows that the context must always be identified and considered before the process of construction or during it... [T]here is no need to establish an ambiguity before taking into account the objective circumstances to which the language relates").

29.1.4 **Purpose and plain words.** *Inland Revenue Commissioners v Hinchy* [1960] AC 748, 767 (Lord Reid: "we can only take the intention of Parliament from the words which they have used in the Act, and therefore the question is whether these words are capable of a more limited construction. If not, then we must apply them as they stand, however unreasonable or unjust the consequences, and however strongly we may suspect that this was not the real intention of Parliament"); *Beswick v Beswick* [1968] AC 58, 73 (Lord Reid: "If the words of the Act are only capable of one meaning we must give them that meaning no matter how they got there"); *In re Arrows Ltd (No.4)* [1995] 2 AC 75, 109F-G (albeit "hard to believe that Parliament ... meant [this]", it being "anomalous in the extreme"; "Yet that is the result which is produced by the language of [the] section"); *R v Clwyd County Council, ex p A* [1993] COD 35 (Parliament having achieved by plain words something which was no doubt not intended); *R v Moore* [1995] QB 353, 362A-C ("this is a situation in which loyalty to the literal wording of the statute will

---

[15] Thomas A Cross [2007] JR 122.

frustrate the plain legislative intent"); *Director of Public Prosecutions v Bull* [1995] QB 88, 95B (conflict between legislator's expressed intention and actual intention); *R v Registrar General, ex p Smith* [1991] 2 QB 393, 401F-G, 402G, 403H-404C, 405C (presumption, despite plain words, that Parliament did not intend to reward serious crime).

29.1.5 **Rectifying construction: altering the language to effect Parliament's intention.** *Inco Europe Ltd v First Choice Distribution* [2000] 1 WLR 586, 592C-593A (Lord Nicholls: "The court must be able to correct obvious drafting errors. In suitable cases, in discharging its interpretative function the court will add words, or omit words or substitute words... This power is confined to plain cases of drafting mistakes... Before interpreting a statute in this way the court must be abundantly sure of three matters: (1) the intended purpose of the statute or provision in question; (2) that by inadvertence the draftsman and Parliament failed to give effect to that purpose in the provision in question; and (3) the substance of the provision Parliament would have made, although not necessarily the precise words Parliament would have used, had the error in the Bill been noticed"); *R (Passenger Transport UK) v Humber Bridge Board* [2003] EWCA Civ 842 [2004] QB 310 (rectifying a statutory instrument); *R (Kelly) v Secretary of State for Justice* [2008] EWCA Civ 177 [2008] 3 All ER 844 (rectifying construction, reading in words into Order); *R (Zenovics) v Secretary of State for the Home Department* [2002] EWCA Civ 273 [2002] INLR 219 at [26] (rectifying construction); *R (Buddington) v Secretary of State for the Home Department* [2006] EWCA Civ 280 at [26] (supplying the missing comma); *R (Crown Prosecution Service) v Bow Street Magistrates Court* [2006] EWHC 1763 (Admin) [2007] 1 WLR 291 (reading in words to correct obvious drafting error); *Haw v City of Westminster Magistrates Court* [2007] EWHC 2960 (Admin) [2008] 3 WLR 465 at [28] (applying *Inco*).

29.1.6 **Ensuring a compatible interpretation.** <9.3> (HRA s.3); <8.1.6> (EC law compatible interpretation); <46.3> (interpretation to allow validity: reading down/ reading in).

29.2 **Legislative purpose and judicial review.**The concept of legislative purpose has a central role in judicial review, relevant statutory objectives being crucial to the operation of grounds for judicial review.

29.2.1 **Legislative purpose at the heart of judicial review.** *R v Hull University Visitor, ex p Page* [1993] AC 682, 693A (Lord Griffiths: "the purpose of judicial review clearly ... is to ensure that those bodies that are susceptible to judicial review have carried out their public duties in the way it was intended they should"); *In re Findlay* [1985] AC 318, 335B-C ("legislative purpose" as the critical factor in relation to illegality grounds); *R v Secretary of State for the Home Department, ex p Fire Brigades Union* [1995] 2 AC 513, 572E-G (describing "the court's duty to determine whether the minister has ... acted within the powers conferred on him by Parliament": "the court is not acting in opposition to the legislature, or treading on Parliamentary toes. On the contrary: it is ensuring that the powers conferred by Parliament are exercised within the limits, and for the purposes, which Parliament intended"); *R v Secretary of State for the Home Department, ex p Yousaf* [2000] 3 All ER 649 at [48] (Sedley LJ: "Statutes constitutive of public authority rarely create a true discretion ... They ... generally give ministers authority to do things at their own election in order to promote ... the policy and objects of the statute"); *R v Secretary of State for Foreign and Commonwealth Affairs, ex p World Development Movement Ltd* [1995] 1 WLR 386, 398B-402G; <45.4.3> (whether ultra vires the sole underpinning for judicial review grounds).

29.2.2 **Power is held on trust: to be used for the purpose for which conferred.** <39.1.2>.

29.2.3 **Legislative purpose in action in judicial review.** <P34> (reviewability); <P46> (ultra vires); <P53> (frustrating the legislative purpose); <P39> (discretion/duty); <50.3> (improper delegation); <P56> (relevancy/irrelevancy); <60.4> (procedural ultra vires); also *R (Asif Javed) v Secretary of State for the Home Department* [2001] EWCA Civ 789 [2002] QB 129 at [49] (Lord Phillips MR: "The extent to which the exercise of a statutory power is in practice open to judicial review on the ground of irrationality will depend critically on the nature and purpose of the enabling legislation").

29.2.4 **Beware of hypothetical legislative purpose.** *Chertsey Urban District Council v Mixnam's Properties Ltd* [1965] AC 735, 754C (unhelpful to ask what "Parliament would have been likely to intend", where "a purely speculative question"); *R v Inland Revenue Commissioners, ex p Woolwich Equitable Building Society* [1990] 1 WLR 1400, 1415F-1416A ("The draftsman's hypothetical intention is by no means obvious... What form the regulation might have taken if the invalidity of paragraph (4) had been appreciated is a matter of pure speculation"); <P43> (severability: not hypothetical legislative purpose); <34.2.9> (reviewability and the "but for" test).

29.3 **Statutory interpretation.** There are a wide range of tools and techniques by which Courts unlock the meaning of a statutory provision. Every administrative lawyer needs to be familiar with the tool-kit and its use.

29.3.1 **The Interpretation Act 1978.**[16] See eg. *In re Wilson* [1985] AC 750 (s.12(1)); *R v West London Stipendiary Magistrate, ex p Simeon* [1983] 1 AC 234 (s.16(1)); *R v General Medical Council, ex p Gee* [1987] 1 WLR 564 (s.17(2)(b)); *R v Brentwood Justices, ex p Nicholls* [1992] 1 AC 1 (s.6(c)); *R (Oy) v Bristol Magistrates' Court* [2003] UKHL 55 [2004] 2 All ER 555 (s.18); *R (Wilkinson) v Commissioners of Inland Revenue* [2005] UKHL 30 [2005] 1 WLR 1718 (s.6 of the 1978 Act not available in conjunction with HRA s.3, to read widow as including widower, where clear contrary intent).

29.3.2 **Ordinary and natural meaning.** *R (G) v Westminster City Council* [2004] EWCA Civ 45 [2004] 1 WLR 1113 at [42] (Lord Phillips MR: "In the absence of any case precedent, or any extrinsic aid to construction, we shall seek to give [the relevant section] a meaning that accords with the natural meaning of the language used and makes sense, having regard to the overall scheme of the legislation"); *R (W) v Commissioner of Police for the Metropolis* [2006] EWCA Civ 458 [2007] QB 399 at [28] (natural meaning of "remove"); *R v Barnet London Borough Council, ex p Nilish Shah* [1983] 2 AC 309, 345H-346A ("giving the words their natural and ordinary meaning ... helps to prevent the growth and multiplication of refined and subtle distinctions in the law's use of common English words").

29.3.3 **Established legal meaning.** *B v Secretary of State for Work and Pensions* [2005] EWCA Civ 929 [2005] 1 WLR 3796 at [35] and [50] (approach to use of words having a previous legal history).

29.3.4 **Mischief.** *R v Z (Attorney General for Northern Ireland's Reference)* [2005] UKHL 35 [2005] 2 AC 645 at [17] (Lord Bingham: "the interpretation of a statute ... is directed to a particular statute, enacted at a particular time, to address (almost invariably) a particular problem or mischief"), [37] (Lord Woolf: "the controversial provision ... has to be read not only in the context of the statute as a whole but in the context of the situation which led to its enactment"), [49] (Lord Carswell, referring to "the principle of statutory construction that in seeking to ascertain the mischief towards which a statute is directed it can be of prime

---

[16] James Maurici [1996] JR 47.

importance to have regard to the historical context"); *Malloch v Aberdeen Corporation* [1971] 1 WLR 1578, 1583H-1584A ("legislation should be interpreted in light of the mischief which it appears to have been intended to remedy"); *R (Westminster City Council) v National Asylum Support Service* [2002] UKHL 38 [2002] 1 WLR 2956 at [5] ("Insofar as the Explanatory Notes cast light on the objective setting or contextual scene of the statute, and the mischief at which it is aimed, such materials are ... always admissible aids to construction"); *R v Kensington and Chelsea London Borough Council, ex p Lawrie Plantation Services Ltd* [1999] 1 WLR 1415 (HL adopting purposive interpretation, identifying mischief which Parliament was intending to counter); <29.3.16> (Official Reports etc); <29.4.8> (Hansard and mischief).

29.3.5 **Construction to avoid unreasonableness/absurdity.***R (Jackson) v Attorney General* [2005] UKHL 56 [2006] 1 AC 262 at [28] (Lord Bingham: "in accordance with long-established principles of statutory interpretation, the courts will often imply qualifications into the literal meaning of wide and general words in order to prevent them having some unreasonable consequence which Parliament could not have intended"); *Burton v Mellham Ltd* [2006] UKHL 6 [2006] 1 WLR 2820 at [19] (whether tax statute involving "so disproportionate a penalty as to raise real doubt whether Parliament can have intended the system to work like that"); *R (Quintavalle) v Secretary of State for Health* [2003] UKHL 13 [2003] 2 AC 687 at [49] (avoiding an interpretation which "would produce an incoherent and irrational regulatory code"), [15]; *R (Stellato) v Secretary of State for the Home Department* [2007] UKHL 5 [2007] 2 AC 70 at [45] (surprising result unlikely to have been intended and so needing clearest of language); *R (Edison First Power Ltd) v Secretary of State for the Environment, Transport and the Regions* [2003] UKHL 20 [2003] 4 All ER 209 at [25] ("courts will often imply qualifications into the literal meaning of wide and general words in order to prevent them from having some unreasonable consequence which it is considered that Parliament could not have intended"), [116] ("the presumption that Parliament intends to act reasonably... The Courts will presume that Parliament did not intend a statute to have consequences which are objectionable or undesirable; or absurd; or unworkable or impracticable; or merely inconvenient; or anomalous or illogical; or futile or pointless"), [139] ("interpretative presumption that Parliament does not intend that legislation should bring about results that are unreasonable or unfair or arbitrary"); *R (Haw) v Secretary of State for the Home Department* [2006] EWCA Civ 532 [2006] QB 780 at [23] (avoiding conclusion which would be "wholly irrational and could fairly be described as manifestly absurd"); *Hourigan v Secretary of State for Work and Pensions* [2002] EWCA Civ 1890 [2003] 3 All ER 924 (declining to give regulations a manifestly unfair meaning); *R v Secretary of State for Health, ex p K* (1998) 1 CCLR 495, 500B-F ("The more absurd or inconvenient the result ... the clearer the language must be if it is to prevail"); *R v Hammersmith and Fulham London Borough Council, ex p Burkett* [2002] UKHL 23 [2002] 1 WLR 1593 at [46] (presumption "that the legislature intended to legislate for a certain and predictable regime"); *R (Hampstead Heath Winter Swimming Club) v Corporation of London* [2005] EWHC 713 (Admin) [2005] 1 WLR 2930 at [33] ("The courts presume that Parliament intended to legislate justly, fairly and reasonably ... the values of the common law are dictated by current concepts of justice and fairness and reasonableness").

29.3.6 **Preserving basic fairness.**
(A) GENERAL. *R (Hampstead Heath Winter Swimming Club) v Corporation of London* [2005] EWHC 713 (Admin) [2005] 1 WLR 2930 at [33] (Stanley Burnton J: "It has always been a principle of the interpretation of statutes that the courts should seek to construe them so as to produce a just and fair law. The courts presume that Parliament intended to legislate justly, fairly and reasonably ... the values of the common law are dictated by current concepts of justice and fairness and reasonableness"); Lord Steyn, *The Weakest and Least Dangerous Department of Government* [1997] PL 84, 85 ("Judges are ... entitled to assume, unless a statute make crystal clear provision to the contrary, that Parliament would not wish to make unjust laws. Indeed, as

the House of Lords made clear in the *Boucraa* [*L'Office Cherifien Des Phosphates v Yamashita-Shinnihon Steamship Co Ltd* [1994] 1 AC 486 at 525A-B], in the context of statutory interpretation legal reasoning may proceed on the initial premise that `simple fairness ought to be the basis of every legal rule'"); *R (South Tyneside Metropolitan Borough Council) v Lord Chancellor* [2007] EWHC 2984 (Admin) at [41] (preferring interpretation avoiding injustice); <60.3> (natural justice supplementing the legislative scheme); <7.6> (basic fairness as a common law fundamental).

(B) PRESUMPTION AGAINST RETROSPECTIVITY. *L'Office Cherifien Des Phosphates v Yamashita-Shinnihon Steamship Co Ltd* [1994] 1 AC 486; *Wilson v First County Trust Ltd* [2003] UKHL 40 [2004] 1 AC 816 (presumption against retrospectivity considered in the context of the HRA s.3); *Plewa v Chief Adjudication Officer* [1995] 1 AC 249, 256E-258D ("presumption against retrospectivity should apply", to avoid "unfairness"); *R (Khadir) v Secretary of State for the Home Department* [2003] EWCA Civ 475 [2003] INLR 426 (retrospective statute determinative of issue in appeal to CA, as to lawfulness of grant of temporary admission, albeit High Court correct as to the law at the time of its decision).

(C) PENAL PROVISION CONSTRUED NARROWLY. *R v Z (Attorney General for Northern Ireland's Reference)* [2005] UKHL 35 [2005] 2 AC 645 at [16]-[17], [33] (penal statute interpreted strictly); *R (Oy) v Bristol Magistrates' Court* [2002] EWHC 566 (Admin) [2002] 4 All ER 965 at [54] ("in relation to a penal provision" it is "right to adopt the interpretation which is more favourable to the subject") (HL is at [2003] UKHL 55 [2004] 2 All ER 555); *Cartwright v Superintendent of Her Majesty's Prison* [2004] UKPC 10 [2004] 1 WLR 902 at [15] ("Even in regard to criminal statutes the presumption in favour of strict construction is nowadays rarely applied. There has been a shift to purposive construction of penal statutes"); *R (Hampstead Heath Winter Swimming Club) v Corporation of London* [2005] EWHC 713 (Admin) [2005] 1 WLR 2930 at [32] (penal statute narrowly interpreted but also needing purposive interpretation).

(D) PRESUMPTION AGAINST DOUBLE TAXATION. *R (Edison First Power Ltd) v Secretary of State for the Environment, Transport and the Regions* [2003] UKHL 20 [2003] 4 All ER 209 (electricity rating Order held (3-2) not ultra vires as constituting "double taxation").

29.3.7 Antecedent legislation/legislative history.

(A) GENERAL. *R v Carrick District Council, ex p Prankerd* [1999] QB 1119, 1130D (Lightman J: "A construction should not be adopted which disturbs long standing and well established features of earlier legislation where there is no apparent reason for such change and no apparent intention on the part of the legislature to make the change and where the language of the statute does not manifest a clear intention to do so"); *R v Lord Chancellor, ex p Lightfoot* [2000] QB 597 (legislative history irresistibly showing that Parliament intended to authorise Order of the kind under attack); *Goodes v East Sussex County Council* [2000] 1 WLR 1356, 1360H ("quite impossible, in construing the Act of 1959, to shut one's eyes to the fact that it was not a code which sprang fully formed from the legislative head but was built upon centuries of highway law. The provisions of the Act itself invited reference to the earlier law and in some cases were unintelligible without them"); *R v West Yorkshire Coroner, ex p Smith* [1983] QB 335, 355A, 356B-C (no ambiguity or obscurity, so impermissible to have regard to earlier statutory enactment replaced by current Act).

(B) CONSOLIDATING LEGISLATION. *Farrell v Alexander* [1977] AC 59, 73 (Lord Wilberforce: "self-contained statutes, whether consolidating previous law, or so doing with amendments, should be interpreted, if reasonably possible, without recourse to antecedents, and that the recourse should only be had when there is a real and substantial difficulty or ambiguity which classical methods of construction cannot resolve"); *R v Secretary of State for the Environment, Transport and the Regions, ex p Spath Holme* [2001] 2 AC 349 (consolidating statute and restricted use of legislative history), applied in *British Waterways Board v Severn Trent Water Ltd* [2001] EWCA Civ 276 [2002] Ch 25 at [6]; *R (Persimmon Homes (Thames*

Valley) Ltd) v North Hertfordshire District Council [2001] EWHC Admin 565 [2001] 1 WLR 2393 at [13]-[19] (regard had to predecessor provisions because ambiguity).

29.3.8 **Related Acts of Parliament.**
(A) GENERAL. *Chief Adjudication Officer v Foster* [1993] AC 754, 769E (Lord Bridge: "the social security legislation as a whole"); *Anyanwu v South Bank Student Union* [2001] UKHL 14 [2001] 1 WLR 638 at [2] (legitimate and necessary to consider all three discrimination Acts); *R v Secretary of State for the Home Department, ex p Malhi* [1991] 1 QB 194, 203E, 208E-F, 211E (related immigration legislation); *R v Coventry City Council, ex p Phoenix Aviation* [1995] 3 All ER 37, 53h-j (statutory provision subservient to another provision in another Act); *R v Secretary of State for Social Security, ex p Taylor* [1996] COD 332 (effect of Insolvency Act 1986 on 1992 Social Security legislation); *R v Thames Magistrates' Court, ex p Horgan* [1998] QB 719 (reading one statutory provision together with an earlier one to which express reference made).
(B) RELATED SUBSEQUENT ACTS. *R v Richmond upon Thames London Borough Council, ex p McCarthy & Stone (Developments) Ltd* [1992] 2 AC 48, 72G (Lord Lowry: "The circumstances in which resort can be had to later legislation for the purpose of statutory interpretation are not entirely clear"); *R v Barnet London Borough Council, ex p Nilish Shah* [1983] 2 AC 309, 348H (such an exercise "cannot be permissible"); *Cape Brandy Syndicate v Inland Revenue Commissioners* [1921] 2 KB 403, 414 ("subsequent legislation on the same subject may be looked to in order to see what is the proper construction to be put upon an earlier Act where that earlier Act is ambiguous"), applied in *Commissioner of Inland Revenue v Hand Seng Bank Ltd* [1991] 1 AC 306, 324A-C; *R (H) v Commissioners of Inland Revenue* [2002] EWHC 2164 (Admin) [2002] STC 1354 at [27] (statements in Parliament in debating new legislation "cannot be relevant or admissible for the purpose of interpreting previous legislation"); *Fullwood v Chesterfield Borough Council* (1994) 26 HLR 126, 131 ("The 1987 Regulations had a certain meaning when they were made and this meaning cannot be retrospectively affected by Regulations made in 1990"); *Hyde Park Residence Ltd v Secretary of State for the Environment, Transport and the Regions* [2000] 1 PLR 85 (whether section impliedly repealed by later enactment); *R (O'Byrne) v Secretary of State for the Environment, Transport and the Regions* [2002] UKHL 45 [2002] 1 WLR 3250 (later Act disapplying the earlier provision).

29.3.9 **Common law backcloth.** *R v Secretary of State for the Home Department, ex p Pierson* [1998] AC 539, 587C (Lord Steyn: "Parliament does not legislate in a vacuum. Parliament legislates for a European liberal democracy founded on the principles and traditions of the common law"), 573G (Lord Browne-Wilkinson); *R (Rottman) v Commissioner of Police for the Metropolis* [2002] UKHL 20 [2002] 2 AC 692 at [75] (Lord Hutton: "It is a well-established principle that a rule of the common law is not extinguished by a statute unless the statute makes this clear by express provision or by clear implication"); *National Assistance Board v Wilkinson* [1952] 2 QB 648, 661 ("a statute is not to be taken as effecting a fundamental alteration in the general law unless it uses words that point unmistakably to that conclusion"), cited in *Black-Clawson International Ltd v Papierwerke Walhof-Aschaffenburg AG* [1975] AC 591, 650F; *R v Chief Constable of Devon and Cornwall, ex p Hay* [1996] 2 All ER 711, 724d ("while statute can modify the common law it cannot, by revealing Parliament's or the draftsman's view of the common law, determine what the common law is").

29.3.10 **Relevance of parts of the same statute.**
(A) SAME WORD, SAME MEANING; DIFFERENT WORD, DIFFERENT MEANING? *R v Hertfordshire County Council, ex p Green Environmental Industries Limited* (1998) 96 LGR 417 (CA), 431c (unlikely that "reasonable excuse" meaning something different in ss.69 and 71 of the Environmental Protection Act 1990) (HL is at [2000] 2 AC 412); *Hounslow London*

Borough Council v Thames Water Utilities [2003] EWHC 1197 (Admin) [2004] QB 212 ("premises" capable of meaning different things in different subsections of same section of the statute); *R (Secretary of State for the Home Department) v Immigration Appeal Tribunal* [2001] EWHC Admin 261 [2001] QB 1224 at [35] (if necessary, court willing to give same word different meaning in same sentence of the statute); *R v Barnet London Borough Council, ex p Nilish Shah* [1983] 2 AC 309, 340C-D; *R v Director of the Serious Fraud Office, ex p Smith* [1993] AC 1, 39H; *R v Crown Court at Maidstone, ex p Harris* [1994] COD 514; *R v Secretary of State for the Environment, ex p Nottinghamshire County Council* [1986] AC 240, 261C-E (rejecting the argument that slightly different phrases had "crucially different" meanings); *Associated Dairies Ltd v Baines* [1997] AC 524, 532F-G ("It is wrong to rely upon linguistic dissimilarities as indicative of an intended meaning with far reaching consequences when those consequences, seen in the wider context of the Act as a whole, lack all rhyme and reason"); *R (Saadat) v Rent Service* [2001] EWCA Civ 1559 [2002] HLR 613 at [11] (observing, in relation to legislative use of the word "locality": "wholly different meanings of this very word within a few lines are not unknown").

(B) EFFECT OF OTHER PROVISIONS. *Bromley London Borough Council v Greater London Council* [1983] 1 AC 768, 814H (Lord Wilberforce: the empowering provision "cannot ... be read in isolation, and it is necessary to examine the rest of the Act in order to ascertain the framework in which this power is exercisable"); *Cinzano (UK) Ltd v Customs & Excise Commissioners* [1985] 1 WLR 484, 488E ("the pattern of the Act"); *R (Morgan Grenfell & Co Ltd) v Inland Revenue Commissioners* [2002] UKHL 21 [2003] 1 AC 563 (other safeguards in the Act not sufficient to conclude that interference with legal professional privilege a necessary implication of the Act as a whole); *R v Secretary of State for the Environment, ex p Kingston upon Hull City Council* [1996] Env LR 248 (EC Directive expressly providing for relevance of cost in relation to collecting systems; supporting the conclusion that cost irrelevant in relation to estuarial limits); *R v Waltham Forest London Borough Council, ex p Holder* (1997) 29 HLR 71 (housing benefit Regulations making clear when requirement of financial `availability' of alternative accommodation relevant).

(C) EFFECT ON OTHER PROVISIONS. *R v Dudley Justices, ex p Gillard* [1986] AC 442, 453G (avoiding unsatisfactory overlap); *R v Radio Authority, ex p Guardian Media Group Plc* [1995] 1 WLR 334, 349D-E (other provisions would be "surplusage"); *R v Canons Park Mental Health Review Tribunal, ex p A* [1995] QB 60, 86C-D (other provisions would be redundant); *R (Law Society) v Master of the Rolls* [2005] EWHC 146 (Admin) [2005] 1 WLR 2033 at [14] (weight of argument on surplusage depends on context).

29.3.11 **"Easy to say so".** <7.1.5>.

29.3.12 **The general yields to the specific.** *R v Director of the Serious Fraud Office, ex p Smith* [1993] AC 1, 43H-44A ("the principle of common sense, expressed in the maxim generalia specialibus non derogant"); *R v Secretary of State for the Home Department, ex p H* [1995] QB 43, 56D-E (general enactment yields to earlier specific provision); *R (Oy) v Bristol Magistrates' Court* [2003] UKHL 55 [2004] 2 All ER 555 (HL ruling, 3-2, that prosecution under general domestic Health and Safety legislation permissible albeit outside specific EC legislation).

29.3.13 **Updating interpretation/always speaking.** *R v G* [2003] UKHL 50 [2004] 1 AC 1034 at [29] (Lord Bingham: "Since a statute is always speaking, the context or application of a statutory expression may change over time, but the meaning of the expression itself cannot change"); *In re McFarland* [2004] UKHL 17 [2004] 1 WLR 1289 at [25] (Lord Steyn: "legislation, primary or secondary, must be accorded an always-speaking construction unless the language and structure of statute reveals an intention to impress on the statute a historic meaning. Exceptions to the general principle are a rarity"); *R v Ireland* [1998] AC 147, 158-159 ("a statute of the `always speaking type': the statute must be interpreted in the light of the best current scientific appreciation of the link between the body and psychiatric injury"); *Fitzpatrick v Sterling Housing Association Ltd* [2001] 1 AC 27, 35B (Lord Slynn), 45F-G (Lord Nicholls), 50A (Lord Clyde); *Victor Chandler International Ltd v Customs and Excise Commissioners* [1999] 1 WLR 2160, 2167H (treat Act as always speaking, but wording must be wide enough fairly to embrace the changes in question); *Birmingham City Council v Oakley* [2001] 1 AC 617, 631F-G (content of statutory concept may change over time, but the concept remains the same); *R (Quintavalle) v Secretary of State for Health* [2003] UKHL 13 [2003] 2 AC 687 (applying the *RCN* approach), at [9], [22]-[23]; *R (Smeaton) v Secretary of State for Health* [2002] EWHC 886 (Admin) [2002] 2 FLR 146 at [350] (statutory offence "always speaking", so "miscarriage" interpreted "as it would be *currently* understood ... in the light of the best current scientific and medical knowledge that is available to the court"); *Glen v Korean Airlines Co Ltd* [2003] EWHC 643 (QB) [2003] QB 1386 at [22]-[30] ("always speaking" approach applied), [28] (doubting whether Hansard admissible to show statute a "bargain or contract" with a single historical meaning).

29.3.14 Realities of the legislative process. *R v Herrod, ex p Leeds City Council* [1978] AC 403, 424D-E ("It cannot be supposed that members of Parliament have the time meticulously to examine the large number of schedules which seem to have become a normal feature of modern statutes, let alone to scrutinise what are described as minor and consequential amendments tucked away in an eleventh schedule"); *Chertsey Urban District Council v Mixnam's Properties Ltd* [1965] AC 735, 751B ("In construing a provision of doubtful meaning I think we are entitled to have some regard to the legislative habits of Parliament").

29.3.15 General gateways to external aids: ambiguity, obscurity or absurdity. *R v Secretary of State for the Environment, Transport and the Regions, ex p Spath Holme* [2001] 2 AC 349, 398C-D (Lord Nicholls: "the constitutional implications point to a need for courts to be slow to permit external aids to displace meanings which are otherwise clear and unambiguous and not productive of absurdity"); *R v Northumbrian Water Ltd, ex p Able UK Ltd* [1996] 2 PLR 28 (impermissible to look outside the Act where words clear).

29.3.16 Official Reports etc. <29.3.4> (mischief); *Wilson v First County Trust Ltd* [2003] UKHL 40 [2004] 1 AC 816 at [56] (Lord Nicholls, discussing the use of White Papers on the question of mischief); *R (G) v Barnet London Borough Council* [2003] UKHL 57 [2004] 2 AC 208 at [84] (White Paper relied on); *R (Bradley) v Secretary of State for Work and Pensions* [2008] EWCA Civ 36 at [38] (relying on White Paper to understand statutory purpose); *Cooke v United Bristol Healthcare NHS Trust* [2003] EWCA Civ 1370 [2004] 1 WLR 251 at [54] ("Where a Bill is based wholly or partly on a Law Commission recommendation, it is appropriate to take account of the Report to find the mischief to which the provision was directed"); *Black-Clawson International Ltd v Papierwerke Walhof-Aschaffenburg AG* [1975] AC 591; *Davis v Johnson* [1979] AC 264, 329H-330B, 345C-D, 350C-E (mischief); *Duke v Reliance Systems Ltd* [1988] AC 618, 632G, 637D, 638G-H; *Owens Bank Ltd v Bracco* [1992] 2 AC 443, 488E (recommendations); *Pepper v Hart* [1993] AC 593, 635B-F (suggesting broadening of mischief rule); *Bushell v Secretary of State for the Environment* [1981] AC 75, 105A-107E (Franks Report as to function of inquiries); *Stevenson v Rogers* 8th December 1998 (use of Law Commission Report); *R (Heather) v Leonard Cheshire Foundation* [2001] EWHC Admin 429 (2001) 4 CCLR 211 (Administrative Court) at [84] (as to position regarding White Papers).

29.3.17 Using international instruments. <6.3>.

29.3.18 **Effect of subordinate legislation on primary legislation.**
(A) USING SUBORDINATE LEGISLATION TO CONSTRUE PRIMARY LEGISLATION.[17]
Hanlon v Law Society [1981] AC 124, 193F ("Subordinate legislation may be used in order to construe the parent Act, but only where power is given to amend the Act by regulations or where the meaning of the Act is ambiguous"); *Deposit Protection Board v Dalia* [1994] 2 All ER 577, 585 (Regulations must be at same time as the Act); *R v Lord Chancellor, ex p Lightfoot* [2000] QB 597, 625G-627C (appropriate to look at subordinate legislation because ambiguity as to whether general words empowering restriction with fundamental rights and because an entire and continuing code); *R v Oxford Regional Mental Health Review Tribunal, ex p Secretary of State for the Home Department* [1988] AC 120, 129B (use of regulation to construe Act doubtful); *R v Berkshire County Council, ex p Parker* [1997] COD 64 (see transcript) (proper to "look at subordinate legislation to assist in the construction of main legislation where the subordinate measure forms part of a code with the statute"); *R (Machi) v Legal Services Commission* [2001] EWCA Civ 2010 [2002] 1 WLR 983 at [21] (although regulations "not in the present circumstances an aid to the construction of the Act ... the statute is nevertheless given shape and definition by regulations which spell out in interlocking form the specific ways in which the wide statutory powers may be exercised").
(B) WHETHER SUBORDINATE CUTTING DOWN PRIMARY LEGISLATION. *R v Secretary of State for Social Security, ex p Joint Council for the Welfare of Immigrants* [1997] 1 WLR 275, 290A (Simon Brown LJ: "Specific statutory rights are not to be cut down by subordinate legislation passed under the vires of a different Act"), 293E (Waite LJ); considered in *R v Secretary of State for Trade and Industry, ex p Mercury Personal Communications Ltd* The Times 20th October 1999; *Hyde Park Residence Ltd v Secretary of State for the Environment, Transport and the Regions* [2000] 1 PLR 85 (power to make subordinate legislation modifying primary legislation to be narrowly and strictly construed); *R v Secretary of State for Trade and Industry, ex p Orange Personal Communications Ltd* The Times 15th November 2000 (where subordinate legislation disapplying primary legislation, including when made under European Communities Act 1972 s.2(2), regulations must say so explicitly).

29.3.19 **Using policy guidance to interpret legislation?** *R (Gillan) v Commissioner of Police of the Metropolis* [2006] UKHL 12 [2006] 2 AC 307 at [15] (Circular cannot affect construction of the statute); *R v Wandsworth London Borough Council, ex p Beckwith* [1996] 1 WLR 60 (circular entitled to respect but wrong); *R v Brent London Borough Council, ex p Awua* [1996] 1 AC 55, 70B-D (Code of Guidance incorrectly stating position under the Act); *R v Richmond upon Thames London Borough Council, ex p McCarthy & Stone (Developments) Ltd* [1992] 2 AC 48 (reliance on Circular neither "justifiable or necessary"); *R v Gloucestershire County Council, ex p Barry* [1997] AC 584, 612D (not "proper material for the construction of the critical provision"); *Chief Constable of Cumbria v Wright* [2006] EWHC 3574 (Admin) [2007] 1 WLR 1407 at [16]-[20] (Government guidance persuasive but no special legal status); *R v Wandsworth London Borough Council, ex p Mansoor* [1997] QB 953, 967D-E (Codes of Guidance "can amount at best to persuasive authority on the construction of the Acts"); *R (Jeeves) v Gravesham Borough Council* [2006] EWHC 1249 (Admin) at [35] (circular not overriding the Act but ensuring consistency in exercise of statutory discretion); *R v Tameside Metropolitan Borough Council, ex p J* [2000] 1 FLR 942, 951G (statutory guidance "a helpful aid to the way the legislation is intended to be implemented, and it should not be departed from without good reason"); *R v Royal Borough of Kensington and Chelsea, ex p Amarfio* (1995) 27 HLR 543, 545-547 (CA relying on Code of Guidance).

---

[17] John Tillman [2000] JR 255.

29.3.20 **Explanatory notes/notes on clauses.**[18] *R (S) v Chief Constable of South Yorkshire* [2004] UKHL 39 [2004] 1 WLR 2196 at [4] (Lord Steyn: "Explanatory notes are not endorsed by Parliament. On the other hand, in so far as they cast light on the setting of a statute, and the mischief at which it is aimed, they are admissible in aid of construction of the statute. After all, they may potentially contain much more immediate and valuable material than other aids regularly used by the courts, such as Law Commission Reports, Government Committee reports, Green Papers, and so forth"); *R (Westminster City Council) v National Asylum Support Service* [2002] UKHL 38 [2002] 1 WLR 2956 at [5] ("Insofar as the Explanatory Notes cast light on the objective setting or contextual scene of the statute, and the mischief at which it is aimed, such materials are ... always admissible aids to construction"), [6] ("If exceptionally there is found in Explanatory Notes a clear assurance by the executive to Parliament about the meaning of a clause, or the circumstances in which a power will or will not be used, that assurance may in principle be admitted against the executive in proceedings in which the executive places a contrary contention before a court"); *R v St Helen's Justices, ex p Jones* [1999] 2 All ER 73 (reliance by the Court on Notes on Clauses), 79c-d, 81f; *R v A (No.2)* [2001] UKHL 25 [2002] 1 AC 45 at [82] (Lord Hope, making use of Government's explanatory notes on the Act: "I think that it is legitimate to refer for the purposes of clarification to the notes to this section in the explanatory notes to the Act prepared by the Home Office. I would use it in the same way as I would use the explanatory note attached to a statutory instrument: see *Coventry and Solihull Waste Disposal Co Ltd v Russell* [1999] 1 WLR 2093, 2103D-G"); *Chief Adjudication Officer v Clarke* [1995] ELR 259, 264B-C (use of Explanatory and Financial Memorandum to the Bill); *Callery v Gray (No.2)* [2001] EWCA Civ 1246 [2001] 1 WLR 2142 at [51]-[53] (explanatory notes to Bill admissible under *Pepper v Hart* principles); *R (Theophilus) v London Borough of Lewisham* [2002] EWHC 1371 (Admin) [2002] 3 All ER 851 at [19] (reference to Explanatory Notes for the purpose of clarification).

29.3.21 **Use of Hansard.** <29.4>.

29.3.22 **Other aids to construction: illustrations.**
(A) DICTIONARY DEFINITIONS. *Wolman v Islington London Borough Council* [2007] EWCA Civ 823 [2008] 1 All ER 1259 at [9] (dictionary definitions not capable of providing meaning of expression read in context); *R v Barnet London Borough Council, ex p Nilish Shah* [1983] 2 AC 309, 342C; *R v Devon County Council, ex p G* [1989] 1 AC 573, 604A.
(B) LONG TITLE/RECITAL/PREAMBLE. *R (Quintavalle) v Secretary of State for Health* [2003] UKHL 13 [2003] 2 AC 687 at [26], [41] (long title); *Vibixa Ltd v Komori UK Ltd* [2006] EWCA Civ 536 [2006] 1 WLR 2472 (preamble relevant in considering purpose of statutory instrument); *R (Hampstead Heath Winter Swimming Club) v Corporation of London* [2005] EWHC 713 (Admin) [2005] 1 WLR 2930 at [52] (preamble "no more than a guide to Parliament's intention"); *R (L) v Metropolitan Police Commissioner* [2007] EWCA Civ 168 [2008] 1 WLR 681 at [33] (long title not displacing clear meaning).
(C) SIDENOTES/SECTION HEADINGS. *R v Montila* [2004] UKHL 50 [2004] 1 WLR 3141 at [36] (headings and sidenotes admissible aids to construction); *R (Quintavalle) v Human Fertilisation and Embryology Authority* [2002] EWHC 2785 (Admin) [2003] 2 All ER 105 (Admin Court) at [12] (Court referring to section heading in construing the statute) (HL is at [2005] UKHL 28 [2005] 2 AC 561).
(D) OTHER. *R (Passenger Transport UK) v Humber Bridge Board* [2003] EWCA Civ 842 [2004] QB 310 at [51] (decision letter and inspector's report "admissible extraneous materials", providing "the immediate context" and making clear a statutory purpose); *R v Special Adjudicator, ex p Paulino* [1996] Imm AR 122 (Rules of the Supreme Court not a guide to

---

[18] Tim Buley [2003] JR 7.

interpretation of asylum appeals legislation); *Callery v Gray (No.2)* [2001] EWCA Civ 1246 [2001] 1 WLR 2142 at [48]-[50] (consultation paper and response treated not aids to construction).

29.3.23 **Interpretation of other measures/sources.** <29.5>.

29.4 **Using Hansard.** In carefully restricted circumstances Courts will allow a question of statutory interpretation to be illuminated by a clear statement as to the meaning of the relevant provision, made in Parliament by a promoter of the Bill. Hansard may also be put to other uses, whether creative or mundane.

29.4.1 **Use of Hansard: the required practice.** <22.1.21> (Hansard notice).

29.4.2 **Hansard: the three *Pepper v Hart* conditions.** *Pepper v Hart* [1993] AC 593, 640B-C (Lord Browne-Wilkinson, describing permissible "reference to Parliamentary materials where (a) legislation is ambiguous or obscure, or leads to an absurdity; (b) the material relied upon consists of one or more statements by a minister or other promoter of the Bill together if necessary with such other Parliamentary material as is necessary to understand such statements and their effect; (c) the statements relied upon are clear"); *R v Secretary of State for the Environment, Transport and the Regions, ex p Spath Holme* [2001] 2 AC 349, 391E (Lord Bingham: "each of these conditions is critical"), 392D-E ("important that the conditions laid down by the House in *Pepper v Hart* should be strictly insisted upon"); *Mirvahedy v Henley* [2003] UKHL 16 [2003] 2 AC 491 at [159] ("reluctance to extend the clear guidelines" set out); *Wilson v First County Trust Ltd* [2003] UKHL 40 [2004] 1 AC 816 at [58] (Lord Nicholls, referring to the conditions as "practical safeguards ... intended to keep references to Hansard within reasonable bounds"), [140] (Lord Hobhouse, explaining the importance that there be no "relaxing [of] the strict observation of the safeguards"); *R (South Wales Sea Fisheries Committee) v National Assembly for Wales* [2001] EWIIC Admin 1162 at [31] (conditions applied to admissibility of statements in the Welsh Assembly in promoting the impugned Order).

29.4.3 **Use of Hansard: a strict approach.** *Pepper v Hart* [1993] AC 593, 617A-B (Lord Bridge: "It should ... only be in the rare cases where the very issue of interpretation which the courts are called on to resolve has been addressed in Parliamentary debate and where the promoter of the legislation has made a clear statement directed to that very issue, that reference to Hansard should be permitted"); *Robinson v Secretary of State for Northern Ireland* [2002] UKHL 32 at [39] (Lord Hoffmann, describing observations in HL "insisting that the conditions for admissibility must be strictly complied with"); *R v Richmond London Borough Council, ex p Watson* [2001] QB 370 (CA), 387F ("the *Pepper v Hart* jurisprudence should only be used in those cases where the House of Lords clearly intended it to be used"); *Director of Public Prosecutions v Bull* [1995] QB 88, 95A-C (no resort to Hansard, even though parliamentary debates making answer plain); *Thoburn v Sunderland City Council* [2002] EWIIC 195 (Admin) [2003] QB 151 at [76] ("If a minister gives the House a false impression of the potential effect of a Bill's provisions ... the cost and the sanction are political"); *R (Quintavalle) v Human Fertilisation and Embryology Authority* [2005] UKHL 28 [2005] 2 AC 561 at [34] ("almost invariably the case" that Hansard statements do not assist: cf. CA at [2003] EWCA Civ 667 [2004] QB 168 at [41]).

29.4.4 **Hansard in action.**[19] *Chief Adjudication Officer v Foster* [1993] AC 754, 772E-G

---

[19] Richard Clayton [1996] JR 77; David Manknell [2004] JR 30; Elisabeth Laing [2006] JR 44.

(describing that case, *R v Warwickshire County Council, ex p Johnson* [1993] AC 583 and *Stubbings v Webb* [1993] AC 498 as cases in which Hansard was "found to provide the answer"); *Harding v Wealands* [2006] UKHL 32 [2007] 2 AC 1 at [37]-[38] (clear statement by ministerial promoter), [83]; *AE Beckett & Sons (Lyndons) Ltd v Midland Electricity Plc* [2001] 1 WLR 281 at [39] ("a rare case where material admitted under *Pepper v Hart* has resolved an ambiguity in the statute"); *Nikonovs v Governor of Brixton Prison* [2005] EWHC 2405 (Admin) [2006] 1 WLR 1518 at [16], [18] (sufficient ambiguity and passages making answer clear beyond peradventure); *Culnane v Morris* [2005] EWHC 2438 (QB) [2006] 1 WLR 2880 (relying on Hansard); *Chief Constable of Merseyside Police v Harrison* [2006] EWHC 1106 (Admin) [2007] QB 79 at [16] (unequivocal ministerial statement); *Haw v City of Westminster Magistrates Court* [2007] EWHC 2960 (Admin) [2008] 3 WLR 465 at [26] (use where ambiguity).

29.4.5 The three conditions not met: illustrations. *R (National Grid Gas Plc) v Environment Agency* [2007] UKHL 30 [2007] 1 WLR 1780 at [23] (no ambiguity); *R (L) v Metropolitan Police Commissioner* [2007] EWCA Civ 168 [2008] 1 WLR 681 at [32] (no ambiguity); *Commissioner of Police of the Metropolis v Hooper* [2005] EWHC 199 (Admin) [2005] 1 WLR 1995 at [28] (no ambiguity etc); *Thoburn v Sunderland City Council* [2002] EWHC 195 (Admin) [2003] QB 151 at [75]-[76] (no ambiguity); *In re OT Computers Ltd* [2004] EWCA Civ 653 [2004] Ch 317 at [39] (meaning of ambiguity); *R v Dorset County Council and Further Education Funding Council, ex p Goddard* [1995] ELR 109, 127A (not statement by promoter of Bill); *Melluish (Inspector of Taxes) v BMI (No.3) Ltd* [1996] 1 AC 454, 481F-482A ("The parliamentary materials sought to be introduced by the Revenue in the present case were not directed to the specific statutory provision under consideration or to the problem raised by the litigation but to another provision and another problem"); *R v Wandsworth London Borough Council, ex p Mansoor* [1997] QB 953, 967F ("To be of value as an aid to construction such statements must be directed to the intended meaning of the provisions which the court is being asked to construe"); *R v Southwark Borough Council, ex p Udu* (1996) 8 Admin LR 25, 28C-E (no assistance from passage relating to an amendment which was rejected); *Robinson v Secretary of State for Northern Ireland* [2002] UKHL 32 at [35] (Lord Hoffmann: "nothing that was said in the debate addressed the question presently before your Lordships and ... did not therefore satisfy the requirements of admissibility laid down in *Pepper v Hart*"), [17] (Lord Bingham); *Chief Adjudication Officer v Wolke* [1997] 1 WLR 1640, 1658C (statement not sufficiently clear); *R v Newham London Borough Council, ex p Barking and Dagenham London Borough Council* [1993] COD 427 (speech obscure); *R (Transport for London) v London Underground Ltd* [2001] EWHC Admin 637 (statements not "clear", because Minister evaded the question); *R (G) v Westminster City Council* [2004] EWCA Civ 45 [2004] 1 WLR 1113 at [36] (no "clear Ministerial statement as to the meaning of [the] word" in question, where various inconsistent comments on a range of amendments, including a differently-worded version of the relevant provision).

29.4.6 An "executive estoppel" explanation of *Pepper v Hart*. *Wilson v First County Trust Ltd* [2003] UKHL 40 [2004] 1 AC 816 at [113] (Lord Hope, referring to the purpose of *Pepper v Hart* as being "to prevent the executive seeking to place a meaning on words used in legislation which is different from that which ministers attributed to those words when promoting the legislation in Parliament"), [59] (Lord Nicholls); *R v A (No.2)* [2001] UKHL 25 [2002] 1 AC 45 at [81] ("strictly speaking, this exercise [of resort to Hansard] is available for the purpose only of preventing the executive from placing a different meaning on words used in legislation from that which they attributed to those words when promoting the legislation in Parliament"); *McDonnell v Congregation of Christian Brothers Trustees* [2003] UKHL 63 [2004] 1 AC 1101 at [29] (Lord Steyn: "A difficulty has ... arisen about the true ratio of *Pepper v Hart*. It is certainly at least authority for the proposition that a categorical assurance given by the government in debates as to the meaning of the legislation may preclude the government vis-a-vis an individual from contending to the contrary. This may be seen as an estoppel or simply a principle of fairness. This view of *Pepper v Hart* restricts its ratio to the material facts of that case. There is, however, a possible broader interpretation of *Pepper v Hart*, viz that it may be permissible to treat the intentions of the government revealed in debates as reflecting the will of Parliament. This interpretation gives rise to serious conceptual and constitutional difficulties which I summarised elsewhere: `Pepper v Hart: A re-examination' (2001) 21 OJLS 59. In *Wilson v First County Trust Ltd* [2003] UKHL 40 [2004] 1 AC 816 at [59], Lord Nicholls of Birkenhead discussed this distinction. In my view the narrower interpretation of *Pepper v Hart* ought to be preferred").

29.4.7 Misgivings about *Pepper v Hart*. *Robinson v Secretary of State for Northern Ireland* [2002] UKHL 32 at [40] (Lord Hoffmann, referring to "the conceptual and constitutional difficulties which are discussed by my noble and learned friend Lord Steyn in his Hart Lecture ((2001) 21 Oxford Journal of Legal Studies 59) and were not in my view fully answered in *Pepper v Hart*"); Lord Steyn, "Interpretation: Legal Texts and their Landscape", in Markesinis (ed), *The Clifford Chance Millennium Lectures: The Coming Together of the Common Law and the Civil Law* eg. at p.87 (questioning whether in the light of experience *Pepper v Hart* had been shown to be desirable, and referring to Lord Renton QC's criticisms and prediction in his Statute Law Society Lecture, that *Pepper v Hart* "will one day be superseded"); *Wilson v First County Trust Ltd* [2003] UKHL 40 [2004] 1 AC 816 at [140] (Lord Hobhouse: "the attempt by advocates to use Parliamentary material from Hansard as an aid to statutory construction has not proved helpful and the fears of those pessimists who saw it as simply a cause of additional expense in the conduct of litigation have been proved correct"); cf. *R (Jackson) v Attorney General* [2005] UKHL 56 [2006] 1 AC 262 at [65] (Lord Nicholls: "it would be unfortunate if *Pepper v Hart* were now to be sidelined. The *Pepper v Hart* ruling is sound in principle, removing as it did a self-created judicial anomaly. There are occasions when ministerial statements are useful in practice as an interpretive aid, perhaps especially as a confirmatory aid").

29.4.8 Hansard and mischief. *McDonnell v Congregation of Christian Brothers Trustees* [2003] UKHL 63 [2004] 1 AC 1101 at [29] (Lord Steyn: "It is permissible to use Hansard to identify the mischief at which a statute is aimed. It is, therefore, unobjectionable to use ministerial and other promoters' statements to identify the objective background to the legislation [and] to the extent that *Pepper v Hart* [1993] AC 593 permits such use of Hansard the point is uncontroversial"); *R (Jackson) v Attorney General* [2005] UKHL 56 [2006] 1 AC 262 at [97] (Lord Steyn, considering Hansard and mischief); *Building Societies Commission v Halifax Building Society* [1997] Ch 255, 274C-F (discerning mischief in relation to obscure words); *State of Mauritius v Khoyratty* [2006] UKPC 13 [2007] 1 AC 80 at [17] (mischief to which constitutional section directed "made crystal clear in ... parliamentary debates as reported in Hansard"); <29.3.4> (mischief).

29.4.9 Using Hansard to discern purpose/width of discretionary power. *R v Secretary of State for the Environment, Transport and the Regions, ex p Spath Holme* [2001] 2 AC 349 (Hansard only available to interpret purpose of discretionary power where "ambiguous"; House of Lords expressing differing views as to what could constitute ambiguity and whether ambiguity in that case); *R (Bradley) v Secretary of State for Work and Pensions* [2008] EWCA Civ 36 [2008] 3 All ER 1116 at [43] (Hansard relevant to statutory purpose); *R v Secretary of State for Education and Employment, ex p Liverpool Hope University College* [2001] EWCA Civ 362 [2001] ELR 552 at [46] (Hansard used to decide whether defendant had frustrated the legislative purpose by defeating a clear and unambiguous statement of that purpose); *R v Northumbrian Water Ltd, ex p Newcastle and North Tyneside Health Authority* [1999] Env LR

715, 726-727 (Hansard crucial in determining width of discretion and legislative purpose); *Pepper v Hart* [1993] AC 593, 639A-B ("Hansard has frequently been referred to with a view to ascertaining whether a statutory power has been improperly exercised for an alien purpose or in a wholly unreasonable manner"); *R v London (North) Industrial Tribunal, ex p Associated Newspapers Ltd* [1998] ICR 1212, 1221A, 1223F-G (use of Hansard to discern the purpose of the provision).

29.4.10 **Using Hansard to identify decision/policy/basis of review.** *Wilson v First County Trust Ltd* [2003] UKHL 40 [2004] 1 AC 816 at [60] (Lord Nicholls: "courts, when adjudicating upon an application for judicial review of a ministerial decision, may have regard to a ministerial statement made in Parliament"), [142] (Lord Hobhouse: "ministerial statements made in the House may be referred to when they are relevant to a question to be determined by a court. An example which immediately comes to mind is the ministerial statements concerning immigration policy which used to be made at the time when immigration law was largely extra-statutory"); *Toussaint v Attorney General of Saint Vincent & the Grenadines* [2007] UKPC 48 [2007] 1 WLR 2825 at [34] (statement in Parliament admissible "to explain executive action and to enable its judicial review"); *R (Anderson) v Secretary of State for the Home Department* [2002] UKHL 46 [2003] 1 AC 837 at [38] (Hansard relevant to see "how the system [of Ministerial tariff-setting] worked and still works"); *Prebble v Television New Zealand Ltd* [1995] 1 AC 321, 337B-F (use of Hansard to establish, "as a matter of history", things said in Parliament).

29.4.11 **Hansard and HRA justification/proportionality.** <17.1.5> (evidence and HRA justification).

29.4.12 **Hansard and questions of EC-compatibility.** *Three Rivers District Council v Bank of England (No.2)* [1996] 2 All ER 363 (restrictions in *Pepper v Hart* applicable only where ordinary domestic legislation and the issue is the construction of certain sections; not where the issue is the wider purpose and object of the statute, such as questions whether the Act was consistent with EC legislation or sought to introduce into English law an EC Directive or international convention).

29.4.13 **Other uses of Hansard.**
(A) HANSARD AND VIRES OF REGULATIONS. Hansard is acknowledged to have a special role in judicial review, at least in relation to this: see *Pepper v Hart* [1993] AC 593, 630H-631D and 635F-G, referring to *Pickstone v Freemans Plc* [1989] AC 66, 112B; and see *Chief Adjudication Officer v Foster* [1993] AC 754, 772B-E.
(B) HANSARD AND EC LAW IMPLEMENTATION. *R (Amicus - MSF Section) v Secretary of State for Trade and Industry* [2004] EWHC 860 (Admin) [2004] ELR 311 at [62] (Richards J, discussing the "wider principle" applicable "when considering legislation implementing a Community obligation"), applying *Pickstone* at 112B-C (Lord Keith: "entirely legitimate for the purpose of ascertaining the intention of Parliament to take into account the terms in which the draft was presented by the responsible Minister and which formed the basis of its acceptance").
(C) HANSARD AND ECHR. *R v Broadcasting Complaints Commission, ex p Barclay* (1997) 9 Admin LR 265, 272C-D (discussing complex situation where conflict between Hansard intended meaning and ECHR-compatible interpretation).
(D) HANSARD AND CRIMINAL LIABILITY. *Thet v Director of Public Prosecutions* [2006] EWHC 2701 (Admin) [2007] 1 WLR 2022 at [15] (doubting use of Hansard to extend criminal liability).
(E) LEGITIMATE EXPECTATION AND PROMISES IN PARLIAMENT. <41.1.13(A)>.

29.4.14 **Reliance on Select Committees.** *Office of Government Commerce v Information*

Commissioner [2008] EWHC 774 (Admin) at [63] (views of Select Committee an illegitimate and irrelevant matter); *R (Federation of Tour Operators) v HM Treasury* [2007] EWHC 2062 (Admin) (Select Committee reports and evidence inadmissible in relation to increase in air passenger duty; discussing Parliamentary privilege) (CA is [2008] EWCA Civ 752); *R (Wheeler) v Office of the Prime Minister* [2008] EWHC 1409 (Admin) at [54] (opinion of Select Committee not admissible on a question of fact for the Court, nor where opinion contested and impugned).

29.5 Interpreting other sources. The bread and butter exercise of interpretation involves construing statutory enactments, but there are many other instruments and sources whose proper (or permissible) interpretation may be relevant to the disposal of a judicial review claim.

29.5.1 Towards purposive and contextual interpretation in the general law. *Investors Compensation Scheme Ltd v West Bromwich Building Society* [1998] 1 WLR 896, 912F-913G (describing the "fundamental change" in construction of contracts); *Wheatley v Drillsafe Ltd* The Times 25th July 2000 (purposive approach to interpreting patent claims).

29.5.2 Interpreting delegated legislation.
(A) GENERAL. *Liversidge v Sir John Anderson* [1942] AC 206, 223 (Viscount Maugham, emphasising the need to remember that "Orders in Council making regulations pursuant to an Act of Parliament do not in general receive the same attention and scrutiny as statutes").
(B) EXPLANATORY NOTE. *Coventry and Solihull Waste Disposal Co Ltd v Russell (Valuation Officer)* [2000] 1 All ER 97, 107g-j (explanatory note attached to statutory instrument used as aid to construction of statutory instrument where ambiguous, referring to *Pickstone v Freemans Plc* [1989] AC 66, 127); *R (Passenger Transport UK) v Humber Bridge Board* [2003] EWCA Civ 842 [2004] QB 310 at [49] (explanatory note in statutory instrument could be used "to help to resolve the question whether any words were omitted from the statutory instrument by mistake").
(C) DELEGATED LEGISLATION WHICH MODIFIES PRIMARY LEGISLATION. *R v Secretary of State for Social Security, ex p Britnell* [1991] 1 WLR 198, 204 (restrictive approach to power and exercise of power to modify primary legislation by means of subordinate legislation), applied in *R v Secretary of State for the Environment, Transport and the Regions, ex p Spath Holme* [2001] 2 AC 349, 382H (Lord Bingham).
(D) OTHER. <30.1.1> (importance of function in interpreting statutory sources including regulations); <46.3> (interpretation to allow validity: reading down/reading in).

29.5.3 Interpreting EC instruments. *R v HM Treasury, ex p Smedley* [1985] QB 657, 669C (EC instruments are "not expressed against the background of English canons of construction and should not be so construed", referring to *H.P. Bulmer Ltd v J. Bollinger SA* [1974] Ch 401, 410), *R v International Stock Exchange of the UK & Eire, ex p Else Ltd* [1993] QB 534 (identifying primary purpose of EC Directive); *R v Medicines Control Agency, ex p Rhone-Poulenc Rorer Ltd* [1999] EuLR 181, 190F (Directive to be construed purposively even though may involve doing some violence to the language); *R v Commissioners of Customs and Excise, ex p Shepherd Neame Ltd* (1999) 11 Admin LR 517 (whether primary legislation incompatible with Treaty objectives of approximation of excise rates); *R (Amicus - MSF Section) v Secretary of State for Trade and Industry* [2004] EWHC 860 (Admin) [2004] ELR 311 at [158] (recitals "can assist in the interpretation of the substantive provisions of a directive" but not where reliance "on a recital alone as establishing an important limitation on the scope of a directive"), [159] (avoiding an interpretation which would frustrate the intention as expressed in recital).

29.5.4 Interpreting the ECHR.

(A) LIVING INSTRUMENT. *R (Pretty) v Director of Public Prosecutions* [2001] UKHL 61 [2002] 1 AC 800 at [56] (Lord Steyn, emphasising that the ECHR is a living instrument whose general language is adaptable); *Brown v Stott (Procurator Fiscal, Dunfermline)* [2003] 1 AC 681, 703 (limits of living instrument principle); *N v Secretary of State for the Home Department* [2005] UKHL 31 [2005] 2 AC 296 at [21] (Lord Hope: "humanitarian principles ... may also be used to enlarge the scope of the Convention beyond its express terms ... The question must always be whether the enlargement is one which the contracting parties would have accepted and agreed to be bound by"); *R (Saadi) v Secretary of State for the Home Department* [2001] EWCA Civ 1512 [2002] 1 WLR 356 (CA) at [36] ("its effect may change in step with changes in the standards applied by the member States. As a starting point, however, it seems to us sensible to consider the position in 1951, when the Convention was agreed").

(B) OTHER. *Coppard v Customs and Excise Commissioners* [2003] EWCA Civ 511 [2003] QB 1428 at [39] ("the Convention is not a United Kingdom statute, and that we should be concerned less with close analysis of its language than with the principles which animate it"); *R v Director of Public Prosecutions, ex p Kebilene* [2000] 2 AC 326, 375A-C (Lord Hope, describing the ECHR as one of those "instruments [which] call for a generous interpretation suitable to give to individuals the full measure of the fundamental rights and freedoms referred to"); *R v Lambert* [2002] QB 1112 (CA) at [13] ("giving a broad and purposive approach not a rigid approach to the language of the Convention, an approach which will make the Convention a valuable protection of the fundamental rights of individual members of the public as well as society as a whole").

29.5.5 Interpreting international instruments.

(A) GENERAL. *Januzi v Secretary of State for the Home Department* [2006] UKHL 5 [2006] 2 AC 426 at [4] (approach to interpretation of the Refugee Convention); *R v Secretary of State for the Home Department, ex p Adan* [2001] 2 AC 477, 515G-517B (principles applicable to the search for an "autonomous" meaning of a treaty); *R (Mullen) v Secretary of State for the Home Department* [2004] UKHL 18 [2005] 1 AC 1 at [36] ("true autonomous and international meaning", "untrammelled by notions of its national legal culture" or "the ordinary use of English"), [50] ("a court may in appropriate cases have regard to travaux preparatoires in construing a treaty" but "such an aid is only helpful if the materials clearly and indisputably point to a definite treaty intention"); *Re P (a Child) (abduction: acquiescence)* [2004] EWCA Civ 971 [2005] Fam 293 at [40] (autonomous meaning approach adopted in the context of the Hague Convention on the Civil Aspects of International Child Abduction); *Re Deep Vein Thrombosis and Air Travel Group Litigation* [2005] UKHL 72 [2006] 1 AC 495 at [11] (Lord Scott, describing these as important principles: "(1) the starting point is to consider the natural meaning of the language [of the Convention]"; (2) the Convention should be considered as a whole and given a purposive interpretation; (3) the language of the Convention should not be interpreted by reference to domestic law principles or domestic rules of interpretation; and (4) assistance can and should be sought from relevant decisions of the courts of other Convention countries"); *Sepet v Secretary of State for the Home Department* [2003] UKHL 15 [2003] 1 WLR 856 at [6] (Refugee Convention as "a living instrument"); *R v Immigration Appeal Tribunal, ex p Shah* [1999] 2 AC 629, 646F-G, 649G (approving Sedley J: interpreting the Refugee Convention "not a conventional lawyer's exercise of applying a legal litmus test to ascertained facts; it is a global appraisal of an individual's past and prospective situation in a particular cultural, social, political and legal milieu, judged by a test which, though it has legal and linguistic limits, has a broad humanitarian purpose"); *R (Bleta) v Secretary of State for the Home Department* [2004] EWHC 2034 (Admin) [2005] 1 WLR 3194 at [10] (extradition treaty to be given a liberal and purposive interpretation, as a working contractual arrangement).

(B) HUMAN RIGHTS INSTRUMENTS. *R (European Roma Rights Centre) v Immigration Officer at Prague Airport* [2004] UKHL 55 [2005] 2 AC 1 at [18] (Lord Bingham, referring to

a "generous and purposive interpretation, bearing in mind its humanitarian objects and purpose"; but "the court's task remains one of interpreting the written document to which the contracting states have committed themselves").
(C) USING THE VIENNA CONVENTION. *R v Secretary of State for the Home Department, ex p Read* [1989] AC 1014, 1053E-F (Explanatory Report on a Convention, "available as an aid to construction as part of the `travaux préparatoires' and under article 31 of the Vienna Convention on the Law of Treaties 1969"); *R (European Roma Rights Centre) v Immigration Officer at Prague Airport* [2004] UKHL 55 [2005] 2 AC 1 at [17] (travaux as legitimate guide to interpretation, under the Vienna Convention Art 32), [19] (good faith requirement, under Vienna Art 26); *R (Hoxha) v Special Adjudicator* [2005] UKHL 19 [2005] 1 WLR 1063 (HL considering the meaning of the Refugee Convention, by reference to the Vienna Convention on the interpretation of treaties).

29.5.6 Interpreting written constitutions. *Matthew v The State* [2004] UKPC 33 [2005] 1 AC 433 at [42] (minority in the PC discussing the cases on special approach to interpreting written constitutions); *Minister of Home Affairs v Fisher* [1980] AC 319, 329D (constitutional instrument "sui generis, calling for principles of interpretation of its own"); *Matadeen v Pointu* [1999] AC 98, 108C-F; *Elloy De Freitas v Permanent Secretary of Ministry of Agriculture Fisheries Lands and Housing* [1999] AC 69, 75F ("in construing constitutional provisions a liberal approach is required"); *Thomas v Baptiste* [2000] 2 AC 1, 24B-C ("A Constitution embodies fundamental rights and freedoms, not their particular expression at the time of its enactment. The due process clause must therefore be broadly interpreted. It does not guarantee the particular forms of legal procedure existing when the Constitution came into force; the content of the clause is not immutably fixed at that date"); *Vasquez v R* [1994] 3 All ER 674, 682e-f (Lord Jauncey, commenting that Privy Council having "stated ... on many occasions that a Constitution should be construed generously in relation to fundamental rights and freedoms of individuals").

29.5.7 Interpreting the immigration rules/non-statutory rules. *R v Immigration Appeal Tribunal, ex p Singh (Bakhtaur)* [1986] 1 WLR 910, 917H-918B (Lord Bridge, explaining that: "Immigration rules ... are discursive in style, in part merely explanatory and, on their face, frequently offer no more than broad guidance as to how discretion is to be exercised in different typical situations. In so far as they lay down principles to be applied, they generally do so in loose and imprecise terms"); *R v Secretary of State for the Home Department, ex p Paul Okello* [1995] Imm AR 269, 272 (immigration rules "essentially rules of practice laid down to ensure like treatment in like cases" which "should not be construed as though they were statutes"); *R v Investors Compensation Board, ex p Bowden* [1994] 1 WLR 17 (DC), 24G (compensation scheme rules "not drawn with the tightness to be found in primary or secondary legislation and we approach the arguments with a caution against adopting the approach which is appropriate to enactments") (also HL at [1996] 1 AC 261, 276H and 279E-F: commenting on looseness of drafting).

29.5.8 Interpreting directions/instructions. *R v Secretary of State for Social Services, ex p Stitt* 21st February 1990 unrep. (Woolf LJ: "Although the [Social Fund] directions have the force of law and have to be complied with, in approaching their construction and approaching the construction of the guidance, it is important to remember that they are not the ordinary form of delegated legislation. As in the case of the Immigration Rules, they should be interpreted in a common sense manner so as to give effect to their obvious intent"), applied in *R v Social Fund Inspector, ex p Ali* (1994) 6 Admin LR 205, 212B; *R v Director of Passenger Rail Franchising, ex p Save Our Railways* [1996] CLC 589, 601B (Secretary of State's instructions had to be read in a practical, down to earth way, as a communication with a responsible public official); *R (KR) v Secretary of State for Work and Pensions* [2008] EWHC 1881 (Admin) at [13] (Social Fund

Directions to be interpreted in a common sense manner).

29.5.9 Interpreting policy guidance: general. *R v Secretary of State for the Home Department, ex p Engin Ozminnos* [1994] Imm AR 287, 292 (Auld J: "the internal policy document against which the exercise of this discretion is to be measured, is not a statutory document. It is not to be subjected to fine analysis so as to interpret it in the way one would a statute"); *R v Secretary of State for the Home Department, ex p Benjamin Yaw Amankwah* [1994] Imm AR 240, 245 (policy is "not an Act of Parliament and is not fixed in tablets of stone"); *R v Secretary of State for the Home Department, ex p Urmaza* [1996] COD 479 (purposive construction of policy); *R v Secretary of State for the Home Department, ex p Pierson* [1998] AC 539, 568G-569G (Lord Goff, adopting a strict interpretation of Home Secretary's policy), cf. 576H and 583H (Lord Browne-Wilkinson and Lord Lloyd, dissenting, preferring a less "technical" approach); *R v Secretary of State for the Home Department, ex p Stafford* [1998] 1 WLR 503, 524B; *R (Gashi) v Secretary of State for the Home Department* [2003] EWHC 1198 (Admin) at [11] (interpretation of policy by reference to "the Rules within which it operates" and "the purpose of the policy"); *R (Prospect) v Ministry of Defence* [2008] EWHC 2056 (Admin) at [30] (Code "should be interpreted flexibly").

29.5.10 Meaning of policy guidance[20]: whether a hard-edged question.[21]
(A) GENERAL. *R (Raissi) v Secretary of State for the Home Department* [2008] EWCA Civ 72 [2008] 3 WLR 375 at [123] (meaning of ex gratia compensation scheme a question for the Court to decide), [122] (reservations about the "reasonable meaning" approach); *R (Humphries) v Secretary of State for Work and Pensions* [2008] EWHC 1585 (Admin) at [73] (interpretation of Government guidance a question for the Court); *In re McFarland* [2004] UKHL 17 [2004] 1 WLR 1289 at [24] (where ministerial statements "an important source of individual rights and corresponding duties", must be "interpreted objectively" as a question "of interpretation" and "of law"); *R v Ministry of Defence, ex p Walker* [2000] 1 WLR 806, 810D (court could consider whether scheme "correctly interpreted"), 813A (indicating "imprecise" phrase involving question whether Minister's interpretation "rational"); *R v Secretary of State for the Home Department, ex p Urmaza* [1996] COD 479 (meaning of policy primarily a question for the Court); *R v Director of Passenger Rail Franchising, ex p Save Our Railways* [1996] CLC 589, 601D (as to Secretary of State's directions, "the Court ... cannot ... in case of dispute, abdicate its responsibility to give the document its proper meaning. It means what it means, not what anyone ... would like it to mean"); *R v Secretary of State for the Home Department, ex p Pierson* [1998] AC 539, 568G-569G; *R v Secretary of State for the Home Department, ex p Stafford* [1998] 1 WLR 503 (deciding true meaning of policy); *R v Secretary of State for the Environment, ex p Oldham Metropolitan Borough Council* [1998] ICR 367, 376F-G, 377D (court deciding meaning of statutory guidance); *R v Director of Public Prosecutions, ex p Duckenfield* [2000] 1 WLR 55, 73B (although policy not subjectively believed to cover this situation, "the policy has to be read objectively"); *R (Norwich and Peterborough Building Society) v Financial Ombudsman Service Ltd* [2002] EWHC 2379 (Admin) at [69]-[71] (treating interpretation of Banking Code as a question for the Court).
(B) PLANNING. *R (Heath & Hampstead Society) v Camden London Borough Council* [2008] EWCA Civ 193 [2008] 3 All ER 80 at [38] (Court interpreting national planning policy), [16]

---

[20] This paragraph in a previous edition was cited in *R (Raissi) v Secretary of State for the Home Department* [2008] EWCA Civ 72 [2008] 3 WLR 375 at [118]; also *Cranage Parish Council v First Secretary of State* [2004] EWHC 2949 (Admin) at [44].

[21] James Maurici [1998] JR 85; Nicholas Blake QC [2006] JR 298.

(importance of consistency where national policy applied); cf. *R (Springhall) v Richmond upon Thames London Borough Council* [2006] EWCA Civ 19 [2006] LGR 419 at [7] (planning decision-maker's approach to policy only interfered with "if it goes beyond the range of reasonable meanings that can be given to the language used"), [29] (whether giving "a meaning to the words of a planning policy that they cannot reasonably bear"); *Gransden* <6.2.8>; *R v Derbyshire County Council, ex p Woods* [1998] Env LR 277, 290 (whether decision-maker giving "a meaning to the words they are not properly capable of bearing"); *R (Adriano) v Surrey County Council* [2002] EWHC 2471 (Admin) [2003] Env LR 559 (meaning of policy a matter for the planning authority, but not entitled to adopt an interpretation which had been expressly rejected during the formal process by which the policy had been adopted).

(C) IMMIGRATION. *R v Secretary of State for the Home Department, ex p Engin Ozminnos* [1994] Imm AR 287 (matter for the Home Secretary to construe his own policy, subject to Court's power to intervene on *Wednesbury* grounds), applied in *Philomena Gangadeen v Secretary of State for the Home Department* [1998] Imm AR 106, 115); *R (Gashi) v Secretary of State for the Home Department* [2003] EWHC 1198 (Admin) at [15] (applying *Ozminnos*; "the interpretation relied upon by the Secretary of State was not reasonably open to him"); *R (Nadesu) v Secretary of State for the Home Department* [2003] EWHC 2839 (Admin) at [25] (Maurice Kay J: "the Secretary of State's construction is not correct in law, nor is it one which he is reasonably entitled to adopt"); *R (S) v Secretary of State for the Home Department* [2008] EWHC 2069 (Admin) at [22] (leaving open whether *Raissi* applicable to immigration policies).

29.5.11 Interpretation as a hard-edged question. <16.4>.

> **P30 Function.** It is essential to understand the role and responsibilities of the decision-maker under review.

    30.1 Understanding the defendant's function
    30.2 Traditional functional labels
    30.3 The judicial/administrative distinction
    30.4 Other aspects of function

30.1 Understanding the defendant's function Judicial review principles demand a proper understanding of the defendant body's function, to decide whether its conduct: (1) is reviewable at all; (2) engages "soft" or "hard-edged" review; and (3) involves a public law wrong warranting the Court's interference. Functional insight is essential to the Court's approach, complementing the contextualism which is the hallmark of judicial review.

30.1.1 The importance of understanding function. <34.2.3> (reviewability and emphasis on function not office/status); <34.2.7> (public function); <9.4.3> (public function for HRA); <P27> (public/private); *In Re Duffy* [2008] UKHL 4 at [25] (mediation and reconciliation role of Parades Commission key to reasonableness of appointments); *R (Lewis) v Redcar & Cleveland Borough Council* [2008] EWCA Civ 746 at [69] (function of planning committee in deciding approach to apparent bias); *Bromley London Borough Council v Greater London Council* [1983] 1 AC 768, 822H-823A ("[the] structural characteristics of the GLC need to be borne in mind in applying ... a purposive construction to the [statute]"); *R v HM Attorney-General for Northern Ireland, ex p Devine* [1992] 1 WLR 262, 267E-F (Lord Goff, rejecting a statutory interpretation which "would impose an extraordinary fetter upon a tribunal whose function is to ascertain the truth by an inquisitorial process"); *R v Monopolies & Mergers Commission, ex p South Yorkshire Transport Ltd* [1993] 1 WLR 23 <16.6.5>; *R v Secretary of State for the Home Department, ex p Edwards* [1994] COD 443 (distinguishing between advisory and determinative functions of Parole Board); *R v Chief Registrar of Friendly Societies, ex p New Cross Building Society* [1984] QB 227, 264H (registrar "engaged in an inquisitorial, not an adversarial, process"); *R v Director of Public Prosecutions, ex p Thom* [1995] COD 194 (DPP's statutory powers of discontinuance not applying in the context of extradition proceedings, since DPP's function not that of prosecutor but as lawyer for the foreign government concerned).

30.1.2 Function and grounds for judicial review: examples. *R v General Council of the Bar, ex p Percival* [1991] 1 QB 212, 234D-E ("the limits of review" depend on "the powers, functions and procedures of the body concerned"); *McInnes v Onslow-Fane* [1978] 1 WLR 1520 (dividing licensing cases into application, forfeiture and expectation cases, with heightened fairness obligations arising in relation to forfeiture, and expectation cases as an intermediate category); *R (Abbey Mine Ltd) v Coal Authority* [2008] EWCA Civ 353 at [31] (*McInnes* distinction merely a pointer); *Local Government Board v Arlidge* [1915] AC 120, 132 (Viscount Haldane LC: "what [a fair] procedure is to be in detail must depend on the nature of the tribunal"); *Bushell v Secretary of State for the Environment* [1981] AC 75 (fairness assessed with an accurate understanding of purpose of public inquiry); <61.3.7> (bias and function); *W (a Minor) v Education Appeal Committee of Lancashire County Council* [1994] ELR 530, 538E (adequacy of reasons "must be considered in the light of the type of committee which is under consideration"); *Fairmount Investments Ltd v Secretary of State for the Environment* [1976] 1 WLR 1255, 1265G (inspector's own impressions were not an irrelevancy: "Part of his function lies in his own knowledge of the subject"); *R v Secretary of State for the Home Department, ex p Causabon-Vincent* [1997] COD 245 (function of Home Secretary in setting mandatory lifer's tariff dictating considerations which entitled to take into account); *Vine v National Dock Labour Board* [1957] AC 488, 512 (Lord Somervell: "In deciding whether a `person' has power to delegate one has to consider the nature of the duty and the character of the person"); *United Kingdom Association of Professional Engineers v Advisory Conciliation & Arbitration Service* [1981] AC 424, 442C-F (unreasonableness involving asking "no reasonable person charged with the body's responsibilities under the statute could have exercised its power in the way that it did").

30.2 Traditional functional labels. At one time judicial review Courts would use simple labels to identify functions to which a certain principle, standard or approach did or did not apply. However, all attempted bright-line distinctions are problematic in administrative law and such labels should be seen as shorthand indicative factors, drawn from a spectrum.

30.2.1 **"Judicial"/"administrative".** <30.3>.

30.2.2 **"Quasi-judicial".** *Vine v National Dock Labour Board* [1957] AC 488, 510-511 (Lord Somervell: "the functions of a local board under these provisions have been said to be judicial or quasi-judicial and this has been regarded as conclusive on the question whether the functions could be delegated... The phrase `quasi-judicial' suggests that there is a well-marked category of activities to which certain judicial requirements attach. An examination of the cases shows, I think, that this is not so... [In fact] the administrative and quasi-judicial functions are closely intermingled"); *Race Relations Board v Charter* [1973] AC 868, 901F-G (Lord Simon (in a different context): "The word `quasi' is apt to confuse rather than clarify; though it may legitimately be used to denote a twilight area and to signify to which of the neighbouring areas the situation in question is more akin"); *R v Commission for Racial Equality, ex p Hillingdon London Borough Council* [1982] AC 779, 787F-G (Lord Diplock: "I do not think that in administrative law as it has developed over the last 20 years attaching the label `quasi-judicial' to it is of any significance").

30.2.3 **"Inferior" tribunal/court.** *Anisminic Ltd v Foreign Compensation Commission* [1969] 2 AC 147, 182C ("inferior tribunal" as "a categorising but not a derogatory description"); *Council of Civil Service Unions v Minister for the Civil Service* [1985] AC 374, 414D-F (Lord Roskill: "Historically the use of the old prerogative writs of certiorari, prohibition and mandamus was designed to establish control by the Court of King's Bench over inferior courts or tribunals. But the use of those writs, and of their successors the corresponding prerogative orders, has become far more extensive. They have come to be used for the purpose of controlling what would otherwise be unfettered executive action whether of central or local government"); *In re McC (A Minor)* [1985] AC 528 (statutory liability of magistrates in damages), 541H-542A (Lord Bridge: "Whatever the juridical basis for the distinction between superior and inferior courts in this regard, and however anomalous it may seem to some, the distinction unquestionably remains part of the law affecting justices and will continue to do so as long as the language of ... [the relevant section] remains in legislative force"); *Peach Grey & Co (a firm) v Sommers* [1995] 2 All ER 513, 519f-520j (industrial tribunal an inferior court for purpose of contempt).

30.3 The judicial/administrative distinction. Distinguishing between "judicial" and "administrative" (alongside "legislative") functions was once regarded as fundamental. Three things have happened: (1) judicial review principles were applied to "administrative" as well as "judicial" (and quasi-judicial) functions; (2) the Courts acknowledged a continuum of functions, in which one function was at most*comparatively* more "administrative" or "judicial" than another; and (3) the distinction made a come-back in the context of the Human Rights Act.

30.3.1 **Judicial/administrative and reviewability.** <34.3.2> (judicial review extending to administrative functions).

30.3.2 **Judicial/administrative and procedural fairness.** *Amec Civil Engineering Ltd v Secretary of State for Transport* [2005] EWCA Civ 291 [2005] 1 WLR 2339 at [47]-[48] (CA referring to the natural justice rules applicable to those acting judicially); *Wiseman v Borneman* [1971] AC 297, 308B ("Natural justice requires that the procedure before any tribunal which is acting judicially shall be fair in all the circumstances"); *Engineers & Managers Association v Advisory Conciliation & Arbitration Service* [1980] 1 WLR 302, 317D ("a judicial element substantial enough to impose ... the obligations of natural justice"); *R (Wooder) v Feggetter* [2002] EWCA Civ 554 [2003] QB 219 at [41] (Sedley LJ, referring to an argument seeking to distinguish cases as involving "adjudication": "To collapse substance into form in this way would be to invert the logic of modern public law and to turn it back towards the arid categories of judicial, quasi-judicial, administrative and discretionary acts which dogged it in its postwar resurgence"); *Board of Education v Rice* [1911] AC 179, 182 (Lord Loreburn, recognising that even for a "determination ... of an administrative kind ... they must ... fairly listen to both sides"); *Re HK (An Infant)* [1967] 2 QB 617, 630B-C ("even if an immigration officer is not in a judicial or quasi-judicial capacity, he must ... act fairly"); *In re Pergamon Press Ltd* [1971] Ch 388, 399H ("the inspectors must act fairly. This is a duty which rests on them, as on many other bodies, even though they are not judicial, nor quasi-judicial, but only administrative"); *R v Commission for Racial Equality, ex p Hillingdon London Borough Council* [1982] AC 779, 787F-G (presumption of need for fairness applicable to functions of an administrative body); *Chief Constable of the North Wales Police v Evans* [1982] 1 WLR 1155, 1160E (Lord Hailsham, referring to fairness in the context of "a wide range of authorities, judicial, quasi-judicial, and ... administrative"); *Council of Civil Service Unions v Minister for the Civil Service* [1985] AC 374, 407E-F ("ancient restrictions in the law relating to the prerogative writs and orders have not prevented the courts from extending the requirement of natural justice, namely the duty to act fairly, so that it is required of a purely administrative act"); *Pearlberg v Varty* [1972] 1 WLR 534, 542H ("Whether the commissioner's function in deciding to give leave is to be described as judicial or administrative, he must obviously act fairly"); *R v Norfolk County Council, ex p M* [1989] QB 619, 628F-H (administrative function with serious consequences, so duty to act fairly); *R v Secretary of State for the Environment, ex p Kirkstall Valley Campaign Ltd* [1996] 3 All ER 304, 323g-324g (Sedley J, explaining that apparent bias not limited to "judicial or quasi-judicial proceedings"); *R v Higher Education Funding Council, ex p Institute of Dental Surgery* [1994] 1 WLR 242, 258E-F (duty to give reasons not limited to judicial and quasi-judicial functions; "In the modern state the decisions of administrative bodies can have a more immediate and profound impact on people's lives than the decisions of a court, and public law has since *Ridge v Baldwin* [1964] AC 40 been alive to that fact"); *Stefan v General Medical Council* [1999] 1 WLR 1293, 1301H-1302B ("the fact that an administrative function is being performed does not exclude the possibility that reasons may require to be given for a decision... But the carrying out of a judicial function remains ... `a consideration in favour of a requirement to give reasons'").

30.3.3 **Judicial/administrative and HRA:ECHR Art 6.** *Begum v Tower Hamlets London Borough Council* [2003] UKHL 5 [2003] 2 AC 430 (approaching the Art 6 requirements of independence as being contextual, with judicial review readily ensuring compatibility in the context of an "administrative" decision-making context); *R (Anderson) v Secretary of State for the Home Department* [2002] UKHL 46 [2003] 1 AC 837 at [50] (analysing the extent to which tariff-setting for mandatory lifers was a "judicial" function, in order to decide the proper impact of HRA:ECHR Art 6); *R (Beeson) v Dorset County Council* [2002] EWCA Civ 1812 [2003] UKHRR 353 (treating the "administrative" nature of the decision-making process as a strong indicator that judicial review would suffice to ensure that the statutorily-intended scheme satisfied Art 6).

30.3.4 **Judicial/administrative and other grounds for review.** *R v Legal Aid Board, ex p Bateman* [1992] 1 WLR 711, 719B (Nolan LJ: *Wednesbury* "equally appropriate no matter whether the role of the board is regarded as administrative or as quasi judicial"); *Champion v Chief Constable of the Gwent Constabulary* [1990] 1 WLR 1, 15H (Lord Lowry: "an administrative discretion... accordingly reviewable on *Wednesbury* principles"); <50.3> (improper delegation); *Vine v National Dock Labour Board* [1957] AC 488 (activity judicial and so incapable of delegation); *Metropolitan Borough & Town Clerk of Lewisham v Roberts* [1949] 2 KB 608; *Barnard v National Dock Labour Board* [1953] 2 QB 18; *R v Gateshead Justices, ex p Tesco Stores Ltd* [1981] QB 470 (no power to delegate a judicial function).

30.3.5 **The modern view: a continuum of functions.** *R v Secretary of State for Education, ex p S* [1994] ELR 252 (Sedley J) at 268E-F ("While public law has moved well beyond any formal classification of obligations according to whether a proceeding is administrative or judicial or something in between, it is recognised that there is a continuum of public functions along which duties of openness in decision-making vary. All, however, are subject to the duty memorably described by Lord Loreburn LC in *Board of Education v Rice* <7.6.1>"); *Chief Constable of the North Wales Police v Evans* [1982] 1 WLR 1155, 1160E (Lord Hailsham, referring to fairness in the context of the "wide range of authorities, judicial, quasi-judicial, and ... administrative").

30.4 **Other aspects of function.** There are a host of illustrative ways in which the Courts address judicial review principles by grappling with the particular nature of the function under consideration. Function is an important part of the "context" which, of course, "is everything".

30.4.1 **Politics and political process.** *R v Southwark London Borough Council, ex p Udu* (1996) 8 Admin LR 25 (council a political body entitled to adopt policies for political reasons); *R v Avon County Council, ex p Crabtree* [1996] 1 FLR 502, 511B-E (nature of local authorities); *Magill v Porter* [2001] UKHL 67 [2002] 2 AC 357 at [21] (Lord Bingham, recognising the realities of the party political process); *R v Secretary of State for the Environment, ex p Haringey London Borough Council* (1994) 92 LGR 538, 546-547 (Court's awareness of realities of party political 'point-scoring'); *R v Waltham Forest London Borough Council, ex p Baxter* [1988] QB 419, 422G-424H, 427B-428H (whip system); *R v Local Commissioner for Administration in North and North East England, ex p Liverpool City Council* [2001] 1 All ER 462 at [36] (system of agreed voting preventing proper debate and amounting to maladministration, because where party political influence decisive an immaterial consideration had been taken into account); *R (Island Farm Development Ltd) v Bridgend County Borough Council* [2006] EWHC 2189 (Admin) [2007] LGR 60 at [23] (councillors entitled to have regard to party policy and manifesto promises, provided that not having a closed mind); *Bromley London Borough Council v Greater London Council* [1983] 1 AC 768, 829C-G (not "irrevocably bound to carry out pre-announced policies contained in election manifestos"), 814B, 853B-C; *Secretary of State for Education and Science v Tameside Metropolitan Borough Council* [1977] AC 1014, 1067F ("rightly considered that they had a mandate from the electors"), 1055B.

30.4.2 **Departmental realities.**
(A) GENERAL. *Local Government Board v Arlidge* [1915] AC 120, 136 (courts not "blind to the well-known facts applicable not only to the constitution but to the working of such branches of the Executive"); *Bushell v Secretary of State for the Environment* [1981] AC 75, 95E-96A (fairness "to be judged ... in the light of the practical realities as to the way in which administrative decisions involving forming judgments based on technical considerations are

reached"); *M v Home Office* [1994] 1 AC 377, 425G-H, 426B (Lord Woolf: "Normally it will be more appropriate to make the [contempt] order against the office which a minister holds... [since] default [will have been] by the department for which the minister is responsible"); *R v Secretary of State for Education, ex p S* [1995] ELR 71, 78F, 84H-85D (wide consultation by civil servants inter se a necessary part of public decision-making); *Secretary of State for the Home Department v Khalif Mohamed Abdi* [1994] Imm AR 402 (CA), 429 (Peter Gibson LJ: "The Crown being one and indivisible, the Home Secretary may well have a mass of material from his own and other Government departments available to him"); *R v Secretary of State for the Home Department, ex p Pierson* [1998] AC 539, 544G-H (Secretary of State "named as [defendant] only because responsible for department within which decisions taken"); *R (Alconbury Developments Ltd) v Secretary of State for the Environment Transport and the Regions* [2001] UKHL 23 [2003] 2 AC 295 at [47] (Lord Slynn: "On the decision making process I do not suggest that one can make artificial distinctions between different branches of a government department"), [127] ("the process of consultation within the department is simply the Secretary of State advising himself"); <17.1.8> (departmental realities and evidence).

(B) PRACTICALITIES AND DELEGATION. *Local Government Board v Arlidge* [1915] AC 120, 133-134 ("The Minister ... is not only at liberty but is compelled to rely on the assistance of his staff"); *R v Secretary of State for the Home Department, ex p Oladehinde* [1991] 1 AC 254, 300A-B ("It is obvious that the Secretary of State cannot personally take every decision to deport an immigrant"; the "devolution of responsibility [is] recognised as a practical necessity in the administration of government"); *R v Commission for Racial Equality, ex p Cottrell & Rothon* [1980] 1 WLR 1580, 1589B; *R v Southwark London Borough Council, ex p Bannerman* (1990) 2 Admin LR 381, 385B-E; <50.3.1> (the *Carltona* principle); <50.4.2> (practicalities and the need to adopt a policy).

30.4.3 **The Crown and modern convention.** *Council of Civil Service Unions v Minister for the Civil Service* [1985] AC 374, 417B-C (Lord Roskill: "To speak today of the acts of the sovereign as `irresistible and absolute' when modern constitutional convention requires that all such acts are done by the sovereign on the advice of and will be carried out by the sovereign's ministers currently in power is surely to hamper the continual development of our administrative law"); *Town Investments v Department of the Environment* [1978] AC 359, 380F-381C, 397G-398G ("the fiction" of action by the Crown); *British Medical Association v Greater Glasgow Health Board* [1989] AC 1211; *Spook Erection Ltd v Secretary of State for the Environment* [1989] QB 300 (although market franchise granted by royal prerogative, holder not acting on Crown's behalf and so not entitled to Crown exemption from planning control); *Lord Advocate v Dumbarton District Council* [1990] 2 AC 580; *R (Cherwell District Council) v First Secretary of State* [2004] EWCA Civ 1420 [2005] 1 WLR 1128 (considering the extent of crown immunity from statutory planning control for development of Crown land on behalf of the Crown).

30.4.4 **Special position of privatised body.** *R v Northumbrian Water Ltd, ex p Newcastle and North Tyneside Health Authority* [1999] Env LR 715, 724 (water company "carries out functions which can be described as public", but "as a commercial organisation [it] cannot be said to possess powers solely in order that it may use them for the public good"), 729 ("it does not have the same duty that a public body, which is not a commercial undertaking, has. It is entitled to look to the interests of its shareholders").

30.4.5 **Choosing from competing claims/sharing the pie.** *R v Entry Clearance Officer Bombay, ex p Amin* [1983] 2 AC 818, 828F-G (function involving "weighing the needs of one applicant against those of others who are in competition with him"); *Din (Taj) v Wandsworth London Borough Council* [1983] 1 AC 657, 663H ("every allocation of priority housing to homeless persons must have the effect of deferring the hopes of persons in other categories, some of whom may have been waiting for a long time"), 674F-G ("the real contest here is not between the homeless citizen and the state: the duty of the housing authority is to hold the balance fairly among all homeless persons and to exercise a fair discretion according to law"); *R (Quark Fishing Ltd) v Secretary of State for Foreign and Commonwealth Affairs* [2002] EWCA Civ 1409 (impugned licensing decision involving allocation of fishing licences to others, yet judicial review still successful).

30.4.6 Analysing interrelated functions: illustrations. *R (G) v Barnet London Borough Council* [2003] UKHL 57 [2004] 2 AC 208 (social services and housing authorities); *R (Bradley) v Secretary of State for Work and Pensions* [2008] EWCA Civ 36 [2008] 3 All ER 1116 (Secretary of State and Parliamentary ombudsman); *R (K) v West London Mental Health NHS Trust* [2006] EWCA Civ 118 [2006] 1 WLR 1865 (responsible medical officer and NHS Trust); *R (Director of Revenue & Customs Prosecutions) v Criminal Cases Review Commission* [2006] EWHC 3064 (Admin) [2008] 1 All ER 383 (CCRC and Court of Appeal Criminal Division); *R (L (A Minor)) v Governors of J School* [2003] UKHL 9 [2003] 2 AC 633 (school and appeal panel); *R (Von Brandenburg) v East London and The City Mental Health NHS Trust* [2003] UKHL 58 [2004] 2 AC 280 (mental health review tribunal and social worker); *R v Northavon District Council, ex p Smith* [1994] 2 AC 402, 408D (district and county councils); *Gateshead Metropolitan Borough Council v Secretary of State for the Environment* [1994] 1 PLR 85 (planning and pollution control); *M v Secretary of State for the Home Department* [2003] EWCA Civ 146 [2003] 1 WLR 1980 at [25] (Home Secretary and criminal court as to deportation); *R (Bantamagbari) v City of Westminster* [2003] EWHC 1350 (Admin) (notifying and notified housing authorities); *R (A) v National Asylum Support Service* [2003] EWCA Civ 1473 [2004] 1 WLR 752 (NASS and local authority); *R (Girling) v Parole Board* [2006] EWCA Civ 1779 [2007] QB 783 (Secretary of State and Parole Board); *R (St Helens Borough Council) v Manchester Primary Care Trust* [2008] EWCA Civ 931 (social services and primary care trust); *R (TB (Jamaica)) v Secretary of State for the Home Department* [2008] EWCA Civ 977 (Home Secretary and AIT).

> **P31 Context.** Context is everything: the Court will always respond to the nature and circumstances of the individual case.

31.1 Contextualism
31.2 Circumstances
31.3 Characteristics and conduct of the claimant
31.4 Claimant's failure to complain/raise the concern at the time
31.5 The Court's controlling discretion/judgment
31.6 "Flexi-principles"

31.1 **Contextualism.** The delineation and application of administrative law principles depends on the context. The outcome of a case depends on its particular facts and circumstances.

31.1.1 A Steyn maxim: context is everything. *R v Secretary of State for the Home Department, ex p Daly* [2001] UKHL 26 [2001] 2 AC 532 at [28] (Lord Steyn: "In law context is everything"); *R (G) v London Borough of Ealing* [2002] EWHC 250 (Admin) at [16] (applying the Steyn maxim in relation to intensity of review and the need for oral evidence and cross-examination); *R (Howard League for Penal Reform) v Secretary of State for the Home Department* [2002] EWHC 2497 (Admin) [2003] 1 FLR 484 at [139(ii)] (applying the Steyn maxim to the application of the Children Act 1989 to detainees); *R (British American Tobacco) v Secretary of State for Health* [2004] EWHC 2493 (Admin) at [27] (applying the Steyn maxim); *Gorringe v Calderdale Metropolitan Borough Council* [2004] UKHL 15 [2004] 1 WLR 1057 at [2] (Lord Steyn, himself describing public authority negligence as "a subject on which an intense focus on the particular facts and on the particular statutory background, seen in the context of the contours of our social welfare state, is necessary").

31.1.2 Everything depends on the circumstances. *Neill v North Antrim Magistrates' Court* [1992] 1 WLR 1220, 1230G (Lord Mustill, speaking of availability of judicial review of committal for receipt of inadmissible evidence: "As with many problems of judicial review, this question does not admit of an outright answer. Everything depends on the circumstances"); *R v Secretary of State for Health, ex p London Borough of Hackney* 25th April 1994 unrep. (Buxton J: "The actual application of the orthodox principles of judicial review will of course vary according to the subject-matter of the case and, in particular, according to the specific administrative function under review"); *Secretary of State for Education and Science v Tameside Metropolitan Borough Council* [1977] AC 1014, 1047G (Lord Wilberforce: "there is no universal rule as to the principles on which the exercise of a discretion may be reviewed: each statute or type of statute must be individually looked at"); *Locabail (UK) Ltd v Bayfield Properties Ltd* [2000] QB 451 at [25] (whether real danger of bias depending on all the circumstances); *R (Q) v Secretary of State for the Home Department* [2003] EWCA Civ 364 [2004] QB 36 at [112] ("the courts ... have developed an issue-sensitive scale of intervention"); *R (Watkins-Singh) v Aberdare Girls High School Governors* [2008] EWHC 1865 (Admin) at [162] (decision unjustified in the special circumstances).

31.1.3 Cases turning on their facts. <11.1.3>.

31.1.4 Context and procedural fairness. <60.2> (procedural fairness as a flexi-principle); <60.3.7> (supplementing the legislative scheme with ad hoc/generalised duties); *Calvin v Carr* [1980] AC 574 (curing procedural unfairness), 592G (need for "examination of the whole hearing structure, in the context of the particular activity to which it relates"); *R v Higher Education Funding Council, ex p Institute of Dental Surgery* [1994] 1 WLR 242, 261A (adopting a "case-specific" approach to the incidence of a duty to give reasons); *Save Britain's*

Heritage v Number 1 Poultry Ltd [1991] 1 WLR 153, 167C ("the degree of particularity required [of reasons] will depend entirely on the nature of the issues falling for decision"); <60.4> (procedural ultra vires).

31.1.5 Context: other principles. <33.1.6> (incremental approach to legal development); *R v Secretary of State for the Department of Environment, ex p London Borough of Islington* (1991) [1997] JR 121, 123 (approach to disclosure "depends to a large extent on the actual circumstances of the case"); *R v Director of Public Prosecutions, ex p Camelot Group Plc* (1998) 10 Admin LR 93, 104C (importance of flexibility in relation to declarations regarding criminal conduct); *R v Secretary of State for the Home Department, ex p Pierson* [1998] AC 539, 592B (as to severability: "Always the context will be determinative"); *R v Secretary of State for Health, ex p Eastside Cheese Company* [1999] EuLR 968, 985F (proportionality principle "must be related to the particular situation in which it is invoked"); <29.1.3> (contextual approach to statutory interpretation); <35.1.5(A)> (justiciability depending on subject matter and suitability); *Watson v British Boxing Board of Control Ltd* [2001] QB 1134 at [7]-[8] (whether actionable duty of care depending on all the circumstances).

31.2 Circumstances. Alongside appreciating the public body's function and latitude, the reviewing Court will strive to understand the nature of the situation in which that body was seeking to act. The circumstances, viewed from the decision-maker's point of view and at the relevant time, are crucial in asking whether there is a public law wrong warranting intervention.

31.2.1 Circumstances in which defendant was acting: general. *R (Legal Remedy UK Ltd) v Secretary of State for Health* [2007] EWHC 1252 (Admin) at [128] (very difficult issues with far-reaching implications and irreconcilable interests); *R v Chief Constable of the North Wales Police, ex p AB* [1999] QB 396, 430D (acting "in a very difficult situation"); *R v Personal Investment Authority Ltd, ex p Lucas Fettes and Partners (Financial Services) Ltd* [1995] OPLR 187[22], 191G-H ("a serious crisis"); *R v Commission for Racial Equality, ex p Hillingdon London Borough Council* [1982] AC 779, 784B (combatting covert racism); *Engineers & Managers Association v Advisory Conciliation & Arbitration Service* [1980] 1 WLR 302, 320D ("the confused situation").

31.2.2 Urgency. *Langley v Liverpool City Council* [2005] EWCA Civ 1173 [2006] 1 WLR 375 at [76] (urgent state intervention in family life); *Wiseman v Borneman* [1971] AC 297, 308F-G (need for "a balance between the need for expedition and the need to give full opportunity to the defendant to see the material against him"); *Durayappah v Fernando* [1967] 2 AC 337, 346A ("while great urgency may rightly limit such opportunity timeously, perhaps severely, there can never be a denial of that opportunity if the principles of natural justice are applicable"); *Pickwell v Camden London Borough Council* [1983] QB 962, 989E ("a decision taken in an emergency must not be scrutinised as closely as one taken not under such pressure"), 990H; *R v Eastleigh Borough Council, ex p Betts* [1983] 2 AC 613, 621E-G (housing legislation having "purposes [which] demand speedy solutions to questions of doubt"); *R v Rochdale Metropolitan Borough Council, ex p Brown* [1997] Env LR 100 (need for urgency not justifying failure to make copy documents available to the claimant or to put summary representations before committee members); *R v Secretary of State for the Home Department, ex p Moon* (1996) 8 Admin LR 477 (urgency not justifying unfairness: provisional conclusion could have been faxed); *R v Life Assurance and Unit Trust Regulatory Organisation, ex p Ross* [1993] QB 17 (having decided

---

[22] Clare McGlynn [1996] JR 54.

to serve notice urgently, Lautro not obliged to allow/consider representations prior to so doing); *R v Brent Health Authority, ex p Francis* [1985] QB 869, 879C-D (in urgent circumstances, chairman having authority to act, subsequently ratified by committee); *A v B Bank (Governor and Company of the Bank of England Intervening)* [1993] QB 311, 324C-D, 325D (Bank of England's need to act with urgency); *In re Evans* [1994] 1 WLR 1006, 1008D ("Extradition treaties and legislation are designed to combine speed and justice"); *R v Secretary of State for Education and Employment, ex p Morris* The Times 15th December 1995 (urgency meaning absence of consultation duty explicable); *Bolton Metropolitan District Council v Secretary of State for the Environment* [1995] 3 PLR 37, 40A-C (adequacy of reasons where "circumstances are changing all the time" and "a tension between the proper examination of all relevant material, and the need to come to *some* decision, sooner rather than later"); *R v Secretary of State for Education and Employment and the North East London Education Authority, ex p M* [1996] ELR 162, 206A-210D (consultation and urgency); *R (Amvac Chemical UK Ltd) v Secretary of State for Environment, Food and Rural Affairs* [2001] EWHC Admin 1011 at [54]-[64] (urgency, but nevertheless failure to give fair and prompt warning and opportunity for comment).

31.2.3 **Limited resources.** *R v Chief Constable of Sussex, ex p International Trader's Ferry Ltd* [1999] 2 AC 418 (reduced policing for live exports), 1268F-H (referring to "the undesirability of the court stepping in too quickly" in cases "where the use of limited resources has to be decided"); *R v Brent and Harrow Health Authority, ex p London Borough of Harrow* [1997] ELR 187 (statute entitling health authority to ration its scarce resources); *R v Harrow London Borough Council, ex p M* [1997] ELR 62 (health authority's refusal to make funding available no answer to council's failure to perform its statutory duty to provide for special educational needs); *R v London Borough of Barnet, ex p B* [1994] ELR 357, 377E-F (balancing circumstances of children's needs against financial and budgetary constraints); <56.1.9> (whether limited resources are relevant); cf. *R (H) v Ashworth Hospital Authority* [2002] EWCA Civ 923 [2003] 1 WLR 127 at [76] ("If tribunals do not have the time and back-up resources that they need to discharge their statutory obligation to provide adequate reasons, then the time and resources must be found").

31.2.4 **"Polycentric" questions.** *R v Criminal Injuries Compensation Board, ex p P* [1995] 1 WLR 845, 857E-G (describing "decisions [which] involve a balance of competing claims on the public purse and the allocation of economic resources" as involving "a polycentric task ... perhaps most easily explained by thinking of a spider's web: `A pull on one strand will distribute tensions after a complicated pattern throughout the web as a whole ...'"); *R (Corner House Research) v Director of the Serious Fraud Office* [2008] UKHL 60 [2008] 3 WLR 568 at [31] (referring to polycentric questions).

31.2.5 **Whether something has gone wrong of a nature warranting intervention.** *R v Panel on Take-overs and Mergers, ex p Guinness Plc* [1990] 1 QB 146, 178H (asking "whether something has gone wrong of a nature and degree which require the intervention of the court").

31.3 **Characteristics and conduct of the claimant** Circumstances relating to the claimant are relevant to the question of standing to bring the claim, but also to the questions whether there are grounds for intervention and whether the Court should grant a remedy.

31.3.1 **Standing.** <P38>.

31.3.2 **Procedural fairness and particular claimants.** *David Eves v Hambros Bank (Jersey) Ltd* [1996] 1 WLR 251 (claimant lacking a legal interest in order to be able to complain about bias); *Lewis v Attorney-General of Jamaica* [2001] 2 AC 50 (condemned person having procedural rights in relation to exercise of prerogative of mercy); *R v Secretary of State for the Home Department, ex p Goswell* [1995] COD 438 (complainant in disciplinary proceedings not having additional fairness rights); *R v Secretary of State for the Home Department, ex p Moon* (1996) 8 Admin LR 477, 485C (Sedley J: "it is precisely the unpopular [claimant] for whom the safeguards of due process are most relevant in a society which acknowledges the rule of law"); *R (Anufrijeva) v Secretary of State for the Home Department* [2003] UKHL 36 [2004] 1 AC 604 at [36] (Lord Steyn: "even in unprepossessing cases fundamental principles must be upheld. The rule of law requires it"); *R v Higher Education Funding Council, ex p Institute of Dental Surgery* [1994] 1 WLR 242, 260D (in the context of fairness and reasons, rejecting the "suggestion that an institutional [claimant] is fundamentally different from an individual" in terms of "its expectations of the protection of the law").

31.3.3 Fact that claimant CLS funded (legally-aided) irrelevant. Access to Justice Act 1999 s.22(4) (legally-aided position "shall not affect (a) the rights or liabilities of other parties to the proceedings, or (b) the principles on which the discretion of any court or tribunal is normally exercised"); <18.1.14> (costs and CLS funding).

31.3.4 Unclean hands etc. *Nichol v Gateshead Metropolitan Borough Council* (1988) 87 LGR 435, 460 (conduct of the claimant relevant to discretion as to remedy); *R v Greenwich London Borough Council, ex p Glen International* 20th October 1998 unrep. (court not satisfied, to requisite high standard of proof, that dishonest conduct by claimant); *R v Cambridgeshire County Council, ex p Darnell* [1995] COD 434 (remedy would have been refused given claimant's cooperation in a dishonest scheme); *R v Secretary of State for the Environment, Transport and the Regions, ex p Garland* 10th November 2000 unrep. at [44] (inequitable and unjust to allow remedy where claimant had escaped action by district auditor because of settlement agreement on which Auditor had relied); *Cinnamond v British Airports Authority* [1980] 1 WLR 582, 590H and 592A (claimant taxi drivers' past bad records counting against them); *R v Brent London Borough Council, ex p Dorot Properties* The Times 7th March 1990 (remedy refused because, despite claimant ratepayer having overpaid, past conduct as to arrears); *R v Kirklees Metropolitan Borough Council, ex p Tesco Stores Ltd* (1994) 92 LGR 279, 292 ("plain unwillingness to comply with the law"); *R v Secretary of State for the Home Department, ex p Awais Karni Butt* [1994] Imm AR 11, 13 (claimant "should not be permitted to rely upon the fact that he absconded and thereby prevented any further examination"); <10.3> (claimant's duty of candour: whether lack of full and frank disclosure); *R v Ministry of Agriculture Fisheries and Food, ex p SP Anastasiou* [1995] COD 339 (refusing third party application for a further Art 234 reference, and ordering indemnity costs, where application brought for an extraneous purpose); *R v Greater London Council, ex p Royal Borough of Kensington and Chelsea* The Times 7th April 1982 (improper to come to court to seek to make political capital); *R v Hereford & Worcester County Council, ex p Smith (Tommy)* [1994] COD 129 (remedy inappropriate where sought to further unlawful purpose); *R v London Borough of Southwark, ex p Davies* (1994) 26 HLR 677, 680-1 (remedy not to be refused merely because of alleged dishonesty by claimant); *R v Chief Constable of the British Transport Police, ex p Farmer* [1998] COD 484 (caution as to plea that claimant should be refused a remedy because guilty of unmeritorious conduct); *R v Pembrokeshire County Council, ex p Coker* [1999] 4 All ER 1007, 1014e-g (behaviour raising serious questions as to the good faith of the application); *Brabazon-Drenning v United Kingdom Central Council for Nursing Midwifery and Health Visiting* [2001] HRLR 91 (unfair not to adjourn disciplinary proceedings, even though claimant's inability to attend was due to own failure to take medication); *R (Quintavalle) v Secretary of State for Health* [2001] EWHC Admin 918 [2001] 4 All ER 1013 at [39]-[40] (even if claimant's motive "to force these issues back on to the Parliamentary agenda", court "should exercise jurisdiction" where claimant having standing and legitimate concern raised as to a question of statutory interpretation); *R (Barwise) v Chief Constable of West Midlands*

Police [2004] EWHC 1876 (Admin) at [37] ("wrong ... to refuse relief based upon conduct grounds in circumstances where the precise rights and wrongs of the parties' actions have not been established").

31.4 Claimant's failure to complain/raise the concern at the time A common problem in judicial review is where claimants are raising with the reviewing Court points which were not raised with the public body at the time of its impugned action. The Court will grapple with the appropriateness of that course, effectively balancing fairness (a) to the claimant (having now raised a viable point) and (b) to the defendant (with whom it could have been raised at the time).

31.4.1 **Points not raised/taken at the time.** *R (Chelfat) v Tower Hamlets London Borough Council* [2006] EWHC 303 (Admin) at [26] (judicial review refused as a matter of discretion where inconsistent with course of action previously agreed); *R (A) v General Medical Council* [2004] EWHC 880 (Admin) at [106] (judicial review confined to the "issues as put before the PCC"); *R v Leeds Crown Court, ex p Redfearn* [1998] COD 437 (not open to claimant to rely on arguments not raised before Crown Court); *R (Shields) v Criminal Injuries Compensation Appeals Panel* [2001] ELR 164 at [26] (claimant not able to rely on point not argued before the decision-maker); *R (Crown Prosecution Service) v Bolton Magistrates' Court* [2003] EWHC 2697 (Admin) [2004] 1 WLR 835 at [8] (absence of objection meaning no remediable magistrates' ruling but Court could give guidance by declaratory relief); <13.7> (judicial review from the decision-maker's point of view); <60.8.8> (whether a right of proactivity or assistance by the decision-making body).

31.4.2 **Failed appeals: unpleaded grounds of appeal.**[23] *R v Secretary of State for the Home Department, ex p Robinson* [1998] QB 929, 946A-D (IAT, in deciding leave to appeal, should focus primarily on grounds advanced, but also any obvious point of law); *A (Iraq) v Secretary of State for the Home Department* [2005] EWCA Civ 1438 [2006] INLR 97 (discussing *Robinson* test); *R v Secretary of State for the Home Department, ex p Kolcak* [2001] Imm AR 666 (*Robinson* approach applicable to errors of fact as well as errors of law); *B v London Borough of Harrow* [1998] ELR 351 (CA), 355E-356C (permitting point to be relied on although not raised before the Special Educational Needs Tribunal, this being in the public interest).

31.4.3 **Bias: whether waiver.** <61.3.9> (apparent bias and waiver); *R v Secretary of State for the Home Department, ex p Fayed* [2001] Imm AR 134 at [84]-[89] and [120] (claimant having waived any objection based on apparent bias, because full knowledge of relevant circumstances but did not object to Secretary of State taking decision) at [86]-[89] and [111] (clear cases of actual bias not able to be waived, in public interest); *Modahl v British Athletic Federation Ltd* 28th July 1997 unrep. (CA) (waiver/ estoppel in relation to one bias objection, not raised at the time; but entitled to rely on broader bias matters of which no knowledge at the time); *R v Secretary of State for the Environment, ex p Kirkstall Valley Campaign Ltd* [1996] 3 All ER 304, 327e (where issue a lis inter partes, appropriate for person to declare their interest to see whether either party objects); citing *R v Altrincham Justices, ex p Pennington* [1975] QB 549, 554 (magistrate should bring the matter to the attention of the parties to see whether any objection); *R v Board of Visitors of Frankland Prison, ex p Lewis* [1986] 1 WLR 130, 133D-E, 135H; *R v HM Coroner for South Yorkshire, ex p Stringer* [1994] COD 176; *R v Mid-Glamorgan County Council, ex p B* [1995] ELR 168, 177G-179H.

---

[23] Ben Collins [1998] JR 147.

31.4.4 Procedural fairness: failure to request/complain.
(A) FAILURE TREATED AS FATAL/RELEVANT. *R (Thompson) v Law Society* [2004] EWCA Civ 167 [2004] 1 WLR 2522 at [47] ("the claimant's failure to ask for an oral hearing ... is fatal to his argument at common law"); *R v London Borough of Barnet, ex p B* [1994] ELR 357, 375E (not open to criticise consultation as a charade when participated in it); *R (J) v Head teacher and Governing Body of A School and College* [2003] EWHC 1747 (Admin) [2003] ELR 743 at [24] (lack of request at the time for an adjournment or attendance of teacher witnesses, being circumstances supporting the conclusion that no unfairness); *Ceylon University v Fernando* [1960] 1 WLR 223, 235 (absence of cross-examination "might have been a more formidable objection" but "he never made any such request"); *R v Secretary of State for the Environment, Transport and the Regions, ex p Alliance Against the Birmingham Northern Relief Road* 23rd March 1999 unrep. (referring to absence of request for the relevant document at the time: "The absence of such a request will usually signify a lack of prejudice"); *R v HM Coroner for South Yorkshire, ex p Stringer* [1994] COD 176 (treated as relevant that claimants had not objected to the procedure now criticised); *R v Solicitor-General, ex p Taylor* (1996) 8 Admin LR 206, 222C (in rejecting challenge based on non-consultation, commenting that the claimants "had shown no interest" at the relevant time); *R v Governing Body of Irlam & Cadishead Community High School, ex p Salford City Council* [1994] ELR 81, 86D (not suggested at the time that a different timetable should be adopted); *R v Secretary of State for Transport, ex p Richmond-upon-Thames London Borough Council* [1994] 1 WLR 74, 97H (failure to ask for clarification of consultation document); *R v Milk Marketing Board, ex p Brook* (1994) 6 Admin LR 369 (Hutchison J), 379B (failure to secure attendance of relevant witnesses or ask for an adjournment); *South Oxfordshire District Council v Secretary of State for the Environment* [1994] 1 PLR 72, 84E-G (no request for a subpoena); *R v Secretary of State for the Home Department ex p Osei Yaw Yeboah* [1995] Imm AR 393, 395 (legal adviser's failure to attend and seek adjournment); *R v Northamptonshire County Council, ex p W* [1998] ELR 291, 303E (parents had been offered postponement of hearing before panel, to permit them to attend and appear, but had declined); *R v University of the West of England, ex p M* [2001] ELR 77 (Richards J), at [19] ("Since the [claimant] did not request particulars of those contacts, either at the meeting or in subsequent correspondence relating to the decision or in connection with the rehearing, she cannot now complain of a lack of opportunity to make comments on them"); *R v Secretary of State for Education, ex p Bandtock* [2001] ELR 333 at [37] (claimant could have checked with defendant if something was unclear in the information provided during consultation).
(B) FAILURE NOT FATAL. *R v Governors of Dunraven School, ex p B* [2000] ELR 156, 193 ("The governors' duty to ensure fairness is not conditional upon applications or demands more appropriate to adversarial litigation"); *R v Northern & Yorks Regional Health Authority, ex p Trivedi* [1995] 1 WLR 961, 975C (unfairness, despite claimants' failure to ask for adjournment); *R (West) v Parole Board* [2002] EWCA Civ 1641 [2003] 1 WLR 705 at [44] ("A prisoner who does not ask for an oral hearing cannot ordinarily expect one; but even here it may become apparent to the Parole Board that a hearing is needed if it is to reach a safe conclusion on a disputed issue") (HL is [2005] UKHL 1 [2005] 1 WLR 350); *R (Chaston) v Devon County Council* [2007] EWHC 1209 (Admin) at [61], [66] (unfair not to refer new material back to inspector who had conducted inquiry, even though claimants provided with the material and made no such request).
(C) FAIRNESS AND WAIVER/ACQUIESCENCE. <60.1.18> (fairness and waiver/ failure to complain); *Thomas v University of Bradford (No.2)* [1992] 1 All ER 964, 979H (considering whether acquiescence to procedural irregularity); <61.3.9> (apparent bias and waiver); <61.1.6> (automatic disqualification and waiver).
(D) FAILURE TO TAKE OPPORTUNITY OF CURE. <36.4.6> (future opportunity to cure unfairness); *R v Norfolk County Council, ex p M* [1989] QB 619 (Waite J, referring to the offer of a hearing "before a body which had already condemned him in his absence. He refused it, and

in my view had every justification for doing so").

(E) ONUS. *R (Lichfield Securities Ltd) v Lichfield District Council* [2001] EWCA Civ 304 [2001] 3 PLR 33 at [26] (Sedley LJ: "it is for [the] public authority to make out any case that the remedy for its own unfairness lay in the [claimant's] hands").

(F) OTHER. *R v Director General of Telecommunications, ex p Cellcom Ltd* [1999] COD 105 (see transcript) (claimant not entitled to adduce "fresh material not available to the decision-maker ... *a fortiori* ... where (as here) there was a statutory consultation period before the decision was made and the fresh evidence could and should have been put before the decision-maker during that period"); *R (Edwards) v Environment Agency* [2004] EWHC 736 (Admin) [2004] 3 All ER 21 (standing to challenge decision even though no participation in the consultation exercise now alleged to have been flawed) at [16] (Keith J: "You should not be debarred from subsequently challenging the decision on the ground of inadequate consultation simply because you chose not to participate in the consultation exercise, provided that you are affected by its outcome").

31.4.5 **Procedural ultra vires: failure to complain.** *Thomas v University of Bradford (No.2)* [1992] 1 All ER 964 (acquiescence in fundamental procedural errors); *R v Bradford Metropolitan Borough Council, ex p Sikander Ali* [1994] ELR 299, 318C ("It was open to the [claimant] to ask questions about the admissions and catchment areas"); *R v Governors of the Sheffield Hallam University, ex p R* [1995] ELR 267, 286B-F; *Wang v Commissioner of Inland Revenue* [1994] 1 WLR 1286, 1296F-G (could have applied for mandatory order).

31.4.6 **Lack of jurisdiction: failure to object.** *R v Inner London Quarter Sessions, ex p D'Souza* [1970] 1 WLR 376 (Lord Parker CJ: "If a party to litigation applies to this court for certiorari, certiorari will not be granted if no objection to the jurisdiction was taken before the court below, unless the party was unaware of the absence of jurisdiction"); *R v Broadcasting Complaints Commission, ex p British Broadcasting Corporation* (1995) 7 Admin LR 575, 595A-B (no waiver of absence of jurisdiction by participating in process).

31.4.7 **Relevancy/irrelevancy: whether pointed out at the time.** *R v Secretary of State for the Home Department, ex p Harry Olugwagbohunmi Payne* [1995] Imm AR 48, 50 ("If in the context of the immigration rules the Secretary of State does not have a submission directed to him which raises the issue, he cannot be criticised for not applying his mind to it"); *R v Bow Street Magistrates' Court, ex p Paloka* The Times 16th November 1995 (claimant's failure to take foreign limitation point in extradition committal); *R v Sedgemoor District Council, ex p McCarthy* (1996) 28 HLR 607, 613 (no duty to investigate matter where no reasonable grounds for believing it to be a live issue); *R v Merton, Sutton and Wandsworth Health Authority, ex p Perry* (2000) 3 CCLR 378 at [81]-[84] (council should have considered promise of home for life even though not pointed out in response to consultation); *R v Sheffield City Council, ex p H* [1999] ELR 511, 516G (Laws LJ: "I would find it very difficult to see that the committee's decisions can properly be condemned as unlawful on the ground that they failed to take account of something never drawn to their attention"; cf. Pill and Peter Gibson LJJ, explaining that matter would have been relevant if decision quashed and remitted).

31.4.8 **Error as own fault.** *R (Assura Pharmacy Ltd) v NHS Litigation Authority* [2008] EWHC 289 (Admin) at [125] (material error of fact but claimant's own fault).

31.4.9 **Reasons: failure to complain/request reasons.** <62.2.12>.

31.4.10 **Relevant person did not complain.** *Durayappah v Fernando* [1967] 2 AC 337, 352G (Lord Upjohn: "Though the council should have been given the opportunity of being heard in its defence, if it deliberately chooses not to complain and takes no step to protest against its dissolution, there seems no reason why any other person should have the right to interfere"); *Century National Merchant Bank and Trust Co Ltd v Davies* [1998] AC 628, 638A-B (where bank failing to exercise its statutory remedy of appeal, directors and others may lack standing or may be guilty of an abuse of process in bringing a later action of their own).

31.4.11 **Failure to request/complain: other.** *R v Cambridge University, ex p Beg* (1999) 11 Admin LR 505, 512d (appellate body's "decision as to penalty cannot be criticised in this court, since they were not asked to address the issue"); *South Oxfordshire District Council v Secretary of State for the Environment, Transport and the Regions* [2000] 2 All ER 667 (in general, failure to take a point on a planning appeal not preventing that ground being raised in challenging the planning appeal decision; unlike enforcement notice appeal); *R (S) v Inner West London Coroner* [2001] EWHC Admin 105 at [13] (judicial review of coroner for failure to ask the jury to consider a verdict involving neglect, even though claimants had not sought such a direction); *R (B) v Head Teacher of Alperton Community School* [2001] EWHC Admin 229 at [23] (although no objection to appointment of statutorily-disqualified panel member, acquiescence not capable of conferring legal status).

31.5 **The Court's controlling discretion/judgment.**Many judicial review questions are matters for the Administrative Court judge's discretion and judgment, and may therefore not be readily appealable to the Court of Appeal.

31.5.1 **Appeal.** <P23>.

31.5.2 **Strict case-management.** <2.6>.

31.5.3 **Fact and judgment for the High Court judge.** *R (T) v Secretary of State for the Home Department* [2003] EWCA Civ 1285 [2003] UKHRR 1321 at [19] ("The question whether the effect of the State's treatment of an asylum-seeker is inhuman or degrading is a mixed question of fact and law ... [t]his court [the CA] is as well placed as the judge at first instance to answer the question"); <15.2.3> (appeal and CPR); *Rowland v Environment Agency* [2003] EWCA Civ 1885 [2005] Ch 1 at [48] (CA analysing factual position for itself); *R (Blewett) v Derbyshire County Council* [2004] EWCA Civ 1508 [2004] Env LR 293 at [114] (approaching factual question on judicial review claim as matter for the Administrative Court, to be overturned on appeal only if the "findings of secondary fact" were "so ill-founded as to be perverse", applying *G v G (Minors: Custody Appeal)* [1985] 1 WLR 647, 652).

31.5.4 **Discretionary control in general.** *R v Panel on Take-overs and Mergers, ex p Guinness Plc* [1990] 1 QB 146, 177E ("the judicial review jurisdiction of the High Court, and of this court on appeal, is a supervisory or `long stop' jurisdiction. It also has a large discretionary content, which contributes to its value"); *R v London Borough of Newham, ex p R* [1995] ELR 156, 163B-164H (guidance on discretion in judicial review, including as to alternative remedy and delay); *An Bord Bainne Co-operative Ltd v Milk Marketing Board* [1984] 2 CMLR 584, 589 (as to whether public or private law claim appropriate, "no grounds for interfering with such a discretionary decision"); *R (Abbey Mine Ltd) v Coal Authority* [2008] EWCA Civ 353 at [27] (conclusion on unfairness one of "principle" being "open in this court to be fully re-considered").

31.5.5 **Discretionary control: delay.** *R v Restormel Borough Council, ex p Corbett* [2001] EWCA Civ 330 [2001] 1 PLR 108 at [29] (decision as to refusal of remedy an exercise of "judgment", so "closer re-examination on appeal than a pure exercise of discretion"); *R v Secretary of State for Health, ex p Furneaux* [1994] 2 All ER 652, 657f-658h; *R v Vale of Glamorgan Borough Council, ex p James* [1997] Env LR 195, 202 ("delay was entirely a matter for his discretion and there was no error of principle which would justify this court in interfering with his decision upon it"); *R v Greenwich London Borough Council, ex p Patterson* (1994) 26 HLR 159 (CA overturning dismissal for delay); *R (T) v A School* [2002] EWCA Civ 1349 [2003] ELR 160 at [23] (on appeal from refusal of permission for judicial review, CA treating delay as a matter of discretion for the Administrative Court judge); *R v Dairy Produce Quota Tribunal, ex p Caswell* [1990] 2 AC 738, 750D (treating refusal of a remedy for delay as a matter for discretion not to be disturbed provided the Administrative Court takes into account the relevant factors), 749C (suggesting that question of what constitutes "detriment to good administration" resting on findings of fact with which appellate courts reluctant to interfere).

31.5.6 Discretionary control and standing. <38.1.4> (whether standing is a matter of discretion).

31.5.7 Discretionary control and alternative remedy. *R (M) v London Borough of Bromley* [2002] EWCA Civ 1113 [2002] 3 FCR 193 at [36] (CA declining to interfere with Administrative Court on question of alternative remedy unless "plainly wrong").

31.5.8 Discretionary control and interim remedy. *R v Secretary of State for Transport, ex p Factortame Ltd (No.2)* [1991] 1 AC 603, 664E-665B; *R v Inspectorate of Pollution, ex p Greenpeace Ltd* [1994] 1 WLR 570, 574H-575A, 576B-C, 578C; *R v Secretary of State for the National Heritage, ex p Continental Television BVio* [1994] COD 121 (Court of Appeal declining to interfere with judge's discretion); *Francis v Royal Borough of Kensington and Chelsea* [2003] EWCA Civ 443 [2003] 2 All ER 1052 at [30] (interim relief as a matter of discretion for the first instance judge); <20.1.14> (appeal and interim remedy).

31.5.9 Discretionary control and disclosure/further information/cross-examination. *R v Secretary of State for Health, ex p London Borough of Hackney* [1995] COD 80; cf. *Jones v Secretary of State for Wales* [1995] 2 PLR 26 (CA allowing an appeal from a decision refusing cross-examination); *R v Secretary of State for the Department of Environment, ex p London Borough of Islington* (1991) [1997] JR 121 (allowing an appeal from an order for disclosure).

31.5.10 Discretionary control and remedy.[24] *R (Edwards) v Environment Agency* [2006] EWCA Civ 877 [2007] Env LR 126 (CA) at [127] (discretionary refusal of remedy a matter for the High Court judge) (HL is [2008] UKHL 22); *R (C) v Secretary of State for Justice* [2008] EWCA Civ 882 (CA overturning DC's decision to refuse a remedy); *R v Restormel Borough Council, ex p Corbett* [2001] EWCA Civ 330 [2001] 1 PLR 108 at [29] (decision as to remedy an exercise of "judgment", so "closer to re-examination on appeal than a pure exercise of discretion" albeit that judge's conclusion "carries great weight"); *R v Tandridge District Council, ex p Al Fayed* [2000] 1 PLR 58, 62E (leaving open whether CA "free to exercise its discretion afresh"); *R v Civil Service Appeal Board, ex p Bruce* [1989] 2 All ER 907 (CA refusing to intervene); *R (Smith) v North East Derbyshire Primary Care Trust* [2006] EWCA Civ 1291 [2006] 1 WLR 3315 (CA interfering with judge's refusal of remedy as to whether material procedural flaw); *R v Secretary of State for the Environment, ex p Walters* (1998) 30 HLR 328 (CA refusing to interfere); *R v Islington London Borough Council, ex p Degnan* (1998) 30 HLR 723, 732 (whether "the discretion was clearly exercised on wrong principles"); *R v Sheffield City Council, ex p H* [1999] ELR 511, 520H (whether "satisfied that the first instance court erred in principle or arrived at a conclusion that was clearly wrong"); *R (Wainwright) v Richmond upon Thames London Borough Council* [2001] EWHC Admin 1090

---

[24] Timothy Straker QC [2000] JR 153.

at [53] (CA interfering as to discretionary refusal of remedy).

31.6 "Flexi-principles". Judicial review courts have an aversion to hard and fast rules. They prefer to formulate principles which have an in-built capacity to accommodate the context and circumstances of any given case. The most celebrated of judicial review's flexi-principles is procedural fairness, though in truth all review principles display a similar adaptability.

31.6.1 **Importance of (principled) flexibility.** *Office of Fair Trading v IBA Health Ltd* [2004] EWCA Civ 142 [2004] 4 All ER 1103 at [100] (Carnwath LJ: "the ordinary principles of judicial review ... are flexible enough to be adapted to the particular statutory context"); *R v Department for Education and Employment, ex p Begbie* [2000] 1 WLR 1115, 1130B (Laws LJ: "Fairness and reasonableness (and their contraries) are objective concepts; otherwise there would be no public law, or if there were it would be palm tree justice. But each is a spectrum, not a single point, and they shade into one another"); *R v Oldham Justices, ex p Cawley* [1997] QB 1, 16G (Simon Brown LJ: "judicial review has developed into an ever more flexible and responsive jurisdiction"); *R (A) v Lord Saville of Newdigate* [2001] EWCA Civ 2048 [2002] 1 WLR 1249 at [28] (using "common sense and humanity" approach to risk to life under HRA:ECHR Art 2); *Chief Constable of the North Wales Police v Evans* [1982] 1 WLR 1155, 1160E-G (Lord Hailsham: "Since the range of authorities, and the circumstances ... are almost infinitely various, it is of course unwise to lay down rules for the application of the remedy which appear to be of universal validity in every type of case"); *R v Bolton Justices, ex p Scally* [1991] 1 QB 537, 555D (Watkins LJ: "the overriding principle ... must surely be that justice should be done and if it be demonstrated that another principle rigidly applied is or would seem to be getting in the way of doing justice, the bounds of that principle require to be very critically examined in a modern light"); *R v Governor of Brockhill Prison, ex p Evans (No.2)* [2001] 2 AC 19, 28F (Lord Steyn, contrasting the "all or nothing" quality of "rules" and the "general norms", often competing, which are "principles"); *R (Wooder) v Feggetter* [2002] EWCA Civ 554 [2003] QB 219 at [42] (Sedley LJ. commenting that "lawyers seem to have manifested their classic learnt response" to the reasons case-law "by treating the categories so far acknowledged in the reactive and exploratory growth of the common law as exhaustive. Rather than try to fit given shapes into pre-formed slots like toddlers in a playgroup ..., the courts have to continue the process of working out and refining, case by case, the relevant principles of fairness"); *R (Bhatt Murphy) v Independent Assessor* [2008] EWCA Civ 755 at [28] (approach to fairness in "all the circumstances" showing that "the law's heart is in the right place, but it provides little guidance for the resolution of specific instances").

31.6.2 **Procedural fairness as a flexi-principle.** <60.2>.

31.6.3 **Unreasonableness as a flexi-principle.** *Office of Fair Trading v IBA Health Ltd* [2004] EWCA Civ 142 [2004] 4 All ER 1103 at [90] (Carnwath LJ, referring to "the flexibility of the legal concept of `reasonableness' dependent on the statutory context"); *R (Farrakhan) v Secretary of State for the Home Department* [2002] EWCA Civ 606 [2002] QB 1391 at [66] ("it [is] not merely in cases involving fundamental rights that the *Wednesbury* test should be replaced with a more flexible approach"); *R (Asif Javed) v Secretary of State for the Home Department* [2001] EWCA Civ 789 [2002] QB 129 at [49] (Lord Phillips MR: "The extent to which the exercise of a statutory power is in practice open to judicial review on the ground of irrationality will depend critically on the nature and purpose of the enabling legislation"); *R v Inland Revenue Commissioners, ex p Unilever Plc* [1996] STC 681, 694j-695a (Simon Brown LJ, saying of the *Wednesbury* principle that: "The flexibility necessarily inherent in that guiding principle should not be sacrificed on the altar of legal certainty"); *United Kingdom Association of Professional Engineers v Advisory Conciliation & Arbitration Service* [1981] AC 424, 444D (asking whether "no reasonable advisory, conciliation and arbitration body charged with the statutory duties of Acas could have reached in the circumstances of this case").

31.6.4 Substantive fairness as a flexi-principle. <54.1.8> (substantive unfairness in all the circumstances); *R v Inland Revenue Commissioners, ex p Unilever Plc* [1996] STC 681.

31.6.5 HRA/ECHR principles as flexi-principles. <58.5.9> (proportionality as a flexi-principle); *R (ProLife Alliance) v British Broadcasting Corporation* [2003] UKHL 23 [2004] 1 AC 185 at [144] (Lord Walker, explaining the need for a "complex and contextually sensitive approach" to justification and the discretionary area of judgment; "it is clear that any simple 'one size fits all' formulation of the test would be impossible"); *Huang v Secretary of State for the Home Department* [2005] EWCA Civ 105 [2006] QB 1 at [50] (HRA review "not so far susceptible to principles with sharp edges") (HL is [2007] UKHL 11 [2007] 2 AC 167); *R (M) v Commissioner of Police of the Metropolis* [2001] EWHC Admin 553 (Laws LJ, describing the "great mistake" to treat the Convention rights as "set in stone: that is, as if their efficacy and applicability were somehow at a distance from the actual facts of the case in which they were invoked"; similarly in "municipal jurisprudence of human rights": "like quicksilver, their shape moves to fit the place where they lie - that is, the facts of the particular case. This condition of robust flexibility is a virtue of the common law. So also it must be a virtue of our domestic law of human rights"); *R (Bloggs) v Secretary of State for the Home Department* [2002] EWHC 1921 (Admin) at [100] ("difficult, indeed pointless, ... to deploy a single phrase apt for all circumstances to express the degrees of risk to life and the nature of the state's duty in respect of that risk which Article 2 ECHR imposes") (CA is at [2003] EWCA Civ 686 [2003] 1 WLR 2724); *R (Rose) v Secretary of State for Health* [2002] EWHC 1593 (Admin) [2002] 2 FLR 962 at [45] (Scott Baker J, describing Article 8: "Private and family life is a flexible and elastic concept incapable of precise definition"); <59.5.15> (HRA:ECHR Art 6 as a flexi-principle).

31.6.6 Mandatory/directory/nullity as flexi-principles. <60.4.3> (whether intended vitiating consequence); <P44> (nullity); *London & Clydeside Estates Ltd v Aberdeen District Council* [1980] 1 WLR 182, 190A-C ("misleading" to use language suggesting the Courts are "necessarily bound to fit the facts of a particular case and a developing chain of events into rigid legal categories or to stretch or cramp them on a bed of Procrustes invented by lawyers for the purposes of convenient exposition"; "The jurisdiction is inherently discretionary and the court is frequently in the presence of differences of degree which merge almost imperceptibly into differences of kind"); *R v Immigration Appeal Tribunal, ex p Jeyeanthan* [2000] 1 WLR 354 <39.3.6(B)> & <60.4.3>; *R v London Borough of Newham, ex p Watkins* (1994) 26 HLR 434, 451 ("a spectrum of possibilities in which to place the particular non-compliance, along a continuum from the trivial default, which can properly be overlooked, to the flagrant defiance of a statutory obligation, which cannot be condoned or even countenanced").

31.6.7 Other examples of flexi-principles. *Rowland v Environment Agency* [2003] EWCA Civ 1885 [2005] Ch 1 at [135] (Mance LJ: "The common law principle of legitimate expectation is ... flexible and fact-responsive. Regard must be had to all the circumstances"); *R (Marsh) v Lincoln District Magistrates Court* [2003] EWHC 956 (Admin) at [44] (Munby J, emphasising by reference to the *Scally* case that principle of external unfairness <63.1.5> a flexible principle); *R v Dairy Produce Quota Tribunal, ex p Caswell* [1990] 2 AC 738 (discussing delay), 749F (Lord Goff: "I do not consider that it would be wise to attempt to formulate any precise definition or description of what constitutes detriment to good administration"); *Matthews v Ministry of Defence* [2003] UKHL 4 [2003] 1 AC 1163 at [33] ("The distinction between substance and procedure is a slippery one"); *R v Inland Revenue Commissioners, ex p National Federation of Self-Employed and Small Businesses Ltd* [1982] AC 617, 658F (test of "sufficient interest" for standing "one which could sufficiently embrace all classes of those who might apply, and yet permit sufficient flexibility in any particular").

> **P32 Modified review.** Matters may involve part-availability
> of judicial review; or restricted or enhanced grounds.

32.1 Part-reviewability of Crown Courts
32.2 Judicial review of decisions regarding legal process
32.3 Anxious scrutiny
32.4 Other modified review situations

32.1 Part-reviewability of Crown Courts. Reviewability of a public body in respect of some only of its functions is familiar: eg. a public body's employment decisions are generally a matter for employment law. One special case is the Crown Court, which by statute is judicially reviewable except in relation to "matters relating to trial on indictment". That is an unsatisfactory and complex exclusion, which may not be absolute.

32.1.1 **Restricted reviewability of Crown Courts.**[25] Supreme Court Act 1981 s.29(3) (judicial review of crown court except matters relating to trial on indictment); *In re Smalley* [1985] AC 622, 640H-641B (Lord Bridge, explaining the historical reason: "The Crown Court is a single court which has inherited the combined functions of both the former courts of quarter sessions and assize courts. Courts of quarter sessions were subject to the supervisory jurisdiction of the High Court exercised by the prerogative writs and orders; assize courts, as superior courts of record, were not").

32.1.2 **Tackling s.29(3).** *R v Crown Court at Manchester, ex p H* [2000] 1 WLR 760, 766C (s.29(3) "has, in recent years, attracted perhaps more judicial consideration, in not always apparently reconcilable decisions, than any other statutory provision"), 765H-766B ("now time for Parliament to introduce, as a matter of urgency, clarifying legislation which addresses the problems arising not only from s.29(3) itself, but also from its relationship with other legislation"); *In re Ashton* [1994] 1 AC 9 (endorsing guidance indicating non-reviewability of: (a) "any decision affecting the conduct of a trial on indictment, whether given in the course of the trial or by way of pre-trial directions" (*In re Smalley* [1985] AC 622 at 642G); and (b) "certain orders made at the conclusion of a trial on indictment ... [which] are themselves an integral part of the trial process" (*In re Sampson* [1987] 1 WLR 194, 196F)); *R v Manchester Crown Court, ex p Director of Public Prosecutions* [1993] 1 WLR 1524, 1528C (recognising the "extremely imprecise" wording of s.29(3)), 1530E-G (suggesting a "third helpful pointer" (c): "`Is the decision sought to be reviewed one arising in the issue between the Crown and the defendant formulated by the indictment (including the costs of such issue)?"); *R v Horseferry Road Magistrates' Court, ex p K* [1997] QB 23 (asking whether procedural step having a direct and immediate bearing on conduct and content of process of determining guilt or innocence).

32.1.3 **Issues of HRA:ECHR-compatibility.** *R (Regentford Ltd) v Canterbury Crown Court* [2001] HRLR 362 (declining to hold that s.29(3) incompatible with the HRA:ECHR Art 6); *R (Shields) v Crown Court at Liverpool* [2001] EWHC Admin 90 [2001] UKHRR 610 (Art 6 satisfied despite s.29(3) because defendant could appeal to CA Criminal Division if unfair trial); *R (O) v Central Criminal Court* [2006] EWHC 256 (Admin) at [44]-[46], [50] (no incompatibility because common law, statutory and bail remedies allowing challenge to legality of detention, and because Art 5(4) not requiring a right of appeal); *R v Crown Court at Manchester, ex p H* [2000] 1 WLR 760, 770D-771D (arguments for revisiting the meaning of s.29(3) in the light of Art 6); *R v Lichniak* [2001] EWHC Admin 294 [2002] QB 296 (CA) at

---

[25] Kris Gledhill [1996] JR 230; Kris Gledhill & Andrew Bodnar [2000] JR 193; Iain Steele [2008] JR 180.

[12]-[13] (HRA issues regarding mandatory statutory sentences, where judicial review difficult because of s.29(3); using HRA s.3 to modify effect of statutory restriction on appeal to CA Criminal Division) (HL is at [2002] UKHL 47 [2003] 1 AC 903); *R (Faithfull) v Crown Court at Ipswich* [2007] EWHC 2763 (Admin) [2008] 1 WLR 1636 (no violation of HRA:ECHR Art 1P here).

32.1.4 **The scope of s.29(3): examples.**
(A) NON-REVIEWABLE. *R (CPS) v Guildford Crown Court* [2007] EWHC 1798 (Admin) [2007] 1 WLR 2886 (sentence); *R (Faithfull) v Crown Court at Ipswich* [2007] EWHC 2763 (Admin) [2008] 1 WLR 1636 (failure to make compensation order alongside forfeiture order); *R (H) v Wood Green Crown Court* [2006] EWHC 2683 (Admin) [2007] 1 WLR 1670 (remanding hostile witness in custody during trial); *R (O) v Central Criminal Court* [2006] EWHC 256 (Admin) (non-dismissal of charge); *R v Sheffield Crown Court, ex p Brownlow* [1980] QB 530 (order allowing jury vetting); *R v Central Criminal Court, ex p Raymond* [1986] 1 WLR 710 (order that counts lie on file); *R v Leeds Crown Court, ex p Hussain* [1995] 1 WLR 1329 (arraignment); *R v Chelmsford Crown Court, ex p Chief Constable of the Essex Police* [1994] 1 WLR 359 (decision during trial as to disclosure of material); *R v Southwark Crown Court, ex p Michael Ward* (1995) 7 Admin LR 395 (decision as to commencement date of trial); *R v Maidstone Crown Court, ex p Shanks & McEwan (Southern) Ltd* [1993] Env LR 340 (refusal to stay indictment as abuse of process); *R v Southwark Crown Court, ex p Tawfick* (1995) 7 Admin LR 410, 418A-419B (decision that no power to allow a private prosecution to be conducted in person); *R v Greenwich Justices, ex p DeLeon* [1999] COD 116 (drawing up of confiscation order); *R (Shields) v Crown Court at Liverpool* [2001] EWHC Admin 90 [2001] UKHRR 610 (refusal of legal aid); *R (Regentford Ltd) v Canterbury Crown Court* [2001] HRLR 362 (refusal to make defendant's costs order); *R (Salubi) v Bow Street Magistrates Court* [2002] EWHC 919 (Admin) [2002] 1 WLR 3073 (crown court ruling as to whether to quash the indictment).
(B) REVIEWABLE. *R (O) v Harrow Crown Court* [2003] EWHC 868 (Admin) [2003] 1 WLR 2756 at [14] (bail decision) (HL is [2006] UKHL 42 [2006] 3 WLR 195); *In re McC (A Minor)* [1985] AC 528, 550C (appeal from magistrates); *R v Maidstone Crown Court, ex p Gill* [1986] 1 WLR 1405 (forfeiture order in relation to accused's parent); *R v Central Criminal Court, ex p Hutchinson* [1996] COD 14 (decision to issue a search warrant); *R v Maidstone Crown Court, ex p Clark* [1995] 1 WLR 831 (sham arraignment); *R v Central Criminal Court, ex p Randle* [1991] 1 WLR 1087, 1103D-G (decision whether to stay proceedings as abuse of process); *R v Wood Green Crown Court, ex p Director of Public Prosecutions* [1993] 1 WLR 723 (orders for costs after prosecution offered no evidence); *R (Eliot) v Crown Court at Reading* [2001] EWHC Admin 464 [2001] 4 All ER 625 (extension of custody time limit); *R v Crown Court at Manchester, ex p H* [2000] 1 WLR 760 (decision lifting a reporting restriction); *R (Commissioners of Inland Revenue) v Kingston Crown Court* [2001] EWHC Admin 581 [2001] 4 All ER 721 (dismissal of charges under Criminal Justice Act 1987 s.6); *R (Sullivan) v Maidstone Crown Court* [2002] EWHC 967 (Admin) [2002] 1 WLR 2747 (local practice direction requiring defendants to sign defence statements); *R (Customs and Excise Commissioners) v Canterbury Crown Court* [2002] EWHC 2584 (Admin) at [23] (directions as to mutual assistance proceedings in magistrates court); *R (Hallinan Blackburn Gittings & Nott (a firm)) v Middlesex Guildhall Crown Court* [2004] EWHC 2726 (Admin) [2005] 1 WLR 766 (production order).

32.1.5 **Avoiding the limitations on Crown Court reviewability.**
(A) NULLITY/JURISDICTIONAL ERROR. <P44> (nullity); <P47> (jurisdictional error); *R v Maidstone Crown Court, ex p Harrow London Borough Council* [2000] QB 719 (although supervision and treatment order unarguably a matter relating to trial on indictment, so jurisdictionally flawed that Court would not decline jurisdiction); *R v Leicester Crown Court,*

ex p Commissioners for Customs and Excise [2001] EWHC Admin 33 at [22] (parties agreeing that reviewable if jurisdictional error); *R (Kenneally) v Snaresbrook Crown Court* [2001] EWHC Admin 968 [2002] QB 1169 at [38]-[40] (jurisdictional error so reviewable); *R v Maidstone Crown Court, ex p Hollstein* [1995] 3 All ER 503 (arraignment a sham and therefore reviewable); cf. *R (CPS) v Guildford Crown Court* [2007] EWHC 1798 (Admin) [2007] 1 WLR 2886 at [16] (sentence passed without jurisdiction but s.29(3) applying); *R (Faithfull) v Crown Court at Ipswich* [2007] EWHC 2763 (Admin) [2008] 1 WLR 1636 (error of law but s.29(3) applying).
(B) DECLARATION ONLY. *R (B) v Stafford Combined Court* [2006] EWHC 1645 (Admin) [2007] 1 WLR 1524 at [14] (jurisdiction to grant declaration, where no mandatory, prohibiting or quashing order sought, no appeal right, and remedy not having effect of delaying trial); cf. *R (Faithfull) v Crown Court at Ipswich* [2007] EWHC 2763 (Admin) [2008] 1 WLR 1636 at [36], [41] (declining declaration where s.29(3) applying).
(C) HABEAS CORPUS. *R v Maidstone Crown Court, ex p Clark* [1995] 1 WLR 831, 842D, 843B-C, 844B-C (habeas corpus available in arraignment/bail context); *R (O) v Harrow Crown Court* [2003] EWHC 868 (Admin) [2003] 1 WLR 2756 at [14] (s.29(3) would not preclude habeas corpus as also sought here) (HL is [2006] UKHL 42 [2006] 3 WLR 195).
(D) INHERENT JURISDICTION AND JUDICIAL REVIEW OF CROWN COURT. *R v Maidstone Crown Court, ex p Harrow London Borough Council* [2000] QB 719, 736E (suggesting a "residual jurisdiction in this court to supervise the Crown Court in respect of a matter relating to trial on indictment if the challenge is to jurisdiction"); *R (Kenneally) v Snaresbrook Crown Court* [2001] EWHC Admin 968 [2002] QB 1169 (restriction order made without conviction being a matter relating to trial on indictment, but reviewable under residual jurisdiction); cf. *R v Chelmsford Crown Court, ex p Chief Constable of the Essex Police* [1994] 1 WLR 359 (no inherent jurisdiction to grant declaration in relation to matter "relating to trial on indictment").
(E) MULTIPLE TARGETS. <5.3> (multiple targets); *R (Sullivan) v Maidstone Crown Court* [2002] EWHC 967 (Admin) [2002] 1 WLR 2747 (decision to apply local practice direction requiring defendant to sign his defence statement not reviewable, but judicial review granted of practice direction itself).
(F) RELATED DECISION-MAKER. *R v Director of Public Prosecutions, ex p Kebilene* [2000] 2 AC 326, 369C (s.29(3) only restricting review of Crown Court, not other bodies such as DPP, but similar restraint appropriate); cf. *R (D) v Central Criminal Court* [2003] EWHC 1212 (Admin) at [6] and [33] (exceptional case where appropriate to allow judicial review of prosecution decision to continue with criminal proceedings, albeit crown court decision not to stay the prosecution non-reviewable under s.29(3)).
(G) CIRCUMVENTION IMPERMISSIBLE. *R v Lewes Crown Court, ex p Sinclair* (1993) 5 Admin LR 1 (claimant not permitted to circumvent inability to challenge sentence by challenging warrant of committal to prison); *R v Chester Crown Court, ex p Cheshire County Council* [1996] 1 FLR 651 (rejecting *Anisminic* arguments as to lack of jurisdiction); *R v Chelmsford Crown Court, ex p Chief Constable of the Essex Police* [1994] 1 WLR 359 (no inherent jurisdiction to grant declaration in relation to matter "relating to trial on indictment"); *R v B (Extradition: Abuse of Process)* The Times 18th October 2000 (no circumvention by using special category of extradition abuse).

32.2 Judicial review of decisions regarding legal process.

One situation treated with special restraint, where grounds for judicial review are applicable in a restricted way, is where the public body function concerns decisions about commencing or permitting legal proceedings.

32.2.1 Modified review and prosecutorial decisions.

Sharma v Antoine [2006] UKPC 57 [2007] 1 WLR 780 at [14(5)] ("judicial review of a prosecutorial decision, although available in principle, is a highly exceptional remedy"); *R (Bermingham) v Director of the Serious Fraud Office* [2006] EWHC 200 (Admin) [2007] QB 727 at [63] (judicial review of public authority's decision whether to launch a prosecution is to be exercised sparingly); *R v Director of Public Prosecutions, ex p Kebilene* [2000] 2 AC 326[26], 369H-371G ("absent dishonesty or mala fides or an exceptional circumstance, the decision of the Director to consent to the prosecution of the [claimants] is not amenable to judicial review"); *R v Hertfordshire County Council, ex p Green Environmental Industries Limited* [2000] 2 AC 412, 426B-427E (*Kebilene* approach not directly relevant to statutory notice precursor to criminal prosecution); *Mohit v Director of Public Prosecutions of Mauritius* [2006] UKPC 20 [2006] 1 WLR 3343 at [18] (English DPP's prosecutorial decisions amenable to judicial review in principle); *R (Pepushi) v Crown Prosecution Service* [2004] EWHC 798 (Admin) [2004] INLR 638 at [49] ("save in wholly exceptional circumstances, applications in respect of pending prosecutions that seek to challenge the decision to prosecute should not be made to this court. The proper course to follow ... is to take the point in accordance with the procedures of the Criminal Courts"); *R v Director of Public Prosecutions, ex p C* (1995) 7 Admin LR 385, 388B-C, 389E-G (decision not to prosecute reviewable but to be interfered with "sparingly", namely for unlawful policy, failure to act in accordance with an established policy or perversity); *R (D) v Central Criminal Court* [2003] EWHC 1212 (Admin) at [33] (in exceptional case regarding protection of accused and family).

32.2.2 Prosecutorial decisions: further cases.[27] *R (C) v Chief Constable of A* [2006] EWHC 2352 (Admin) at [32] (judicial review of ongoing police investigations only in "the most exceptional cases"); *R (Da Silva) v Director of Public Prosecutions* [2006] EWHC 3204 (Admin) at [23] (decision not to prosecute reviewable); *R v HM Commissioners of Inland Revenue, ex p Dhesi* The Independent 13th November 1995 (decision to apply for voluntary bill of indictment reviewable on limited grounds); *R v Attorney-General, ex p Rockall* [2000] 1 WLR 882 (refusal to revoke consent to prosecution); *R v Attorney-General, ex p Ferrante* The Independent 3rd April 1995 (refusal to authorise proceedings); *R v Panel on Take-overs and Mergers, ex p Fayed* [1992] BCC 524, 536C-D ("in the absence of evidence of fraud, corruption or mala fides, judicial review will not be allowed to probe a decision to charge individuals in criminal proceedings"); *R v Director of Public Prosecutions, ex p Manning* [2001] QB 330 (judicial review granted of DPP's decision not to prosecute following unlawful killing inquest verdict); *R (Pullen) v Health and Safety Executive* [2003] EWHC 2934 (Admin) (whether error of law or unreasonableness in HSE's decision not to prosecute); *R v Director of Public Prosecutions, ex p Jones* 23rd March 2000 unrep. (decision not to prosecute vitiated for error of law); *R v Inland Revenue Commissioners, ex p Mead* [1993] 1 All ER 772 (Revenue decision to prosecute); *R v Chief Constable of Kent, ex p L* [1993] 1 All ER 756 (whether decision to prosecute, rather than caution, contrary to settled policy); *R v Director of Public Prosecutions, ex p Camelot Group Plc* (1998) 10 Admin LR 93 (refusing judicial review of decision not to prosecute, private prosecution being effective and convenient alternative remedy); *R (Compassion in World Farming) v Secretary of State for the Environment Food and Rural Affairs* [2004] EWCA Civ 1009 at [47] (rare if ever for Court to make mandatory order requiring public authority to prosecute); *R (Charlson) v Guildford Magistrates Court* [2006] EWHC 2318 (Admin) [2006] 1 WLR 3494 (judicial review granted of refusal to issue summons for private prosecution); *R (Dennis) v Director of Public Prosecutions* [2006] EWHC 3211 (Admin) (inadequately reasoned decision not to prosecute for criminal negligence after coroner's verdict of unlawful killing).

---

[26] Ben Rayment [2000] JR 52.

[27] Derek Obadina [1997] JR 98.

32.2.3 **Decision to administer a caution.** *R (Mondelly) v Metropolitan Police Commissioner* [2006] EWHC 2370 (Admin) at [43] (whether police caution unreasonable or breach of clear and settled policy); *R (Omar) v Chief Constable of Bedfordshire Constabulary* [2002] EWHC 3060 (Admin) at [47] (caution quashed for "failure to consult the victim without sufficient good cause, the lack of a sufficiently comprehensive investigation, the mistakes as to fact and the consideration of irrelevant matters"); *R v Commissioner of Police of the Metropolis, ex p P* (1996) 8 Admin LR 6 (formal caution of 12-year-old quashed for clear breach of Home Office guidelines); *R v Commissioner of the Metropolitan Police, ex p Thompson* [1997] 1 WLR 1519 (judicial review granted of a police caution secured by inducement, contrary to relevant codes of guidance).

32.2.4 **Policy guidance and prosecutorial decisions.** *R v Chief Constable of the Kent County Constabulary, ex p L* [1993] 1 All ER 756, 770d (Watkins LJ: "the discretion of the CPS to continue or to discontinue criminal proceedings is reviewable by this court but only where it can be demonstrated that the decision was made regardless of or clearly contrary to a settled policy"); *R (F) v Crown Prosecution Service* [2003] EWHC 3266 (Admin) at [79] (applying *L*); *R v Director of Public Prosecutions, ex p C* (1995) 7 Admin LR 385 (judicial review granted of decision not to prosecute claimant's husband, for failure to act in accordance with established policy), 393C-D; *R v Commissioner of Police of the Metropolis, ex p P* (1996) 8 Admin LR 6 (police caution quashed for breach of guidelines in Home Office circular); *R v Inland Revenue Commissioners, ex p Allen* [1997] STC 1141 (asking whether decision to take criminal proceedings an unjustified departure from established practice); *R v Commissioner of the Metropolitan Police, ex p Thompson* [1997] 1 WLR 1519 (judicial review granted of a police caution secured by inducement, contrary to relevant codes of guidance).

32.2.5 **Decision as to enforcement action.** *R v Commissioners of Customs and Excise, ex p International Federation for Animal Welfare* [1998] Env LR D3 (prosecuting or enforcement authority's failure to act examinable by judicial review but court will interfere only in truly exceptional situations); *R v Director General of Water Services, ex p Oldham Metropolitan Borough Council* (1998) 96 LGR 396 (granting judicial review, Director General having a statutory duty to take enforcement action); *R v Hackney London Borough Council, ex p Adebiri* The Times 5th November 1997 (neither ultra vires nor unreasonable to take council tax enforcement action against asylum seekers); *R v Elmbridge Borough Council, ex p Active Office Ltd* (1998) 10 Admin LR 561 (decision to take and pursue planning enforcement proceedings not irrational).

32.2.6 **Decision to seek possession.** *West Glamorgan County Council v Rafferty* [1987] 1 WLR 457; *R v South Hams District Council, ex p Gibb* [1995] QB 158 (judicial review of decisions to institute proceedings to evict `gypsies'); *R v Bath City Council, ex p Nankervis & Wilson* [1994] COD 271 (decision to seek possession); *R v London Borough of Southwark, ex p Solomon* (1994) 26 HLR 693 (successful judicial review of decisions (a) that accommodation offered suitable and (b) to commence possession proceedings); *R v London Borough of Lambeth, ex p Campbell* (1994) 26 HLR 618 (decision to serve a notice to quit); *Manchester City Council v Cochrane* [1999] 1 WLR 809 (in certain possession proceedings, county court's only power in the face of a public law point being to adjourn the proceedings to allow an application for judicial review to proceed); *R v Hammersmith and Fulham London Borough Council, ex p Quigley* (2000) 32 HLR 379 (judicial review of decision to issue notice to quit, for failure to take account of cohabitee's right to apply for assignment of tenancy); *R (McLellan) v Bracknell Forest Borough Council* [2001] EWCA Civ 1510 [2002] QB 1129 (where arguable Human Rights Act:ECHR Art 8 challenge raised in possession proceedings, county court judge should adjourn to allow claim for judicial review to be pursued); *R (McCann) v Birmingham City Council* [2004] EWHC 2156 (Admin) (judicial review of decision to obtain notice to quit; as to decision to seek possession, not impugnable by reference to HRA:ECHR Art 8, referring to *Harrow London Borough Council v Qazi* [2003] UKHL 43 [2004] 1 AC 983 and *Bradney* [2003] EWCA Civ 1783).

32.2.7 Refusal to pursue/continue with proceedings. *R (Corner House Research) v Director of the Serious Fraud Office* [2008] UKHL 60 [2008] 3 WLR 568 (decision to discontinue bribery investigation), [30] (Lord Bingham: "only in highly exceptional cases will the court disturb the decisions of an independent prosecutor and investigator"); *R v Director of Public Prosecutions, ex p C* (1995) 7 Admin LR 385 (refusal to prosecute claimant's husband); *R v Flax Bourton Magistrates Court, ex p Commissioners of Customs and Excise* The Times 6th February 1996 (refusal to commit for trial on indictment); *R v Secretary of State for the Environment, ex p Friends of the Earth Ltd* (1995) 7 Admin LR 793 (decision to accept water companies' undertakings and not take enforcement action); *R v Commissioners of Customs and Excise, ex p International Federation for Animal Welfare* [1998] Env LR D3 (prosecuting or enforcement authority's failure to act only interfered with in truly exceptional situations); *R v North Thames Regional Health Authority and Chelsea & Westminster NHS Trust, ex p L* [1996] Med LR 385 (decision not to continue with disciplinary action); *Secretary of State for Trade and Industry v Davies* 19th November 1997 unrep. (decision to continue with directors disqualification proceedings).

32.2.8 Refusal to adjourn proceedings. *R (Fana) v Special Adjudicator* [2002] EWHC 777 (Admin) (unreasonable not to adjourn immigration appeal to allow psychiatric report to be adduced); *R v Birmingham City Council, ex p Dredger* (1994) 6 Admin LR 553, 554E-G (judicial review of refusal to adjourn meetings in relation to proposals for which there had been inadequate consultation); *R v Redbridge Justices, ex p Gurmit Ram* [1992] QB 384 (split bench of two magistrates under duty to adjourn to bench of 3); *L v Royal Borough of Kensington and Chelsea* [1997] ELR 155 (unfair refusal to adjourn); *R v Cheshire County Council, ex p C* [1998] ELR 66 (unfair refusal to adjourn); *R v Neath and Port Talbot Justices, ex p Director of Public Prosecutions* [2000] 1 WLR 1376 (refusal to adjourn); *R v South Tyneside Justices, ex p Mill Garages Ltd* The Times 17th April 1995 (refusal of a stay of prosecution); *Brabazon-Drenning v United Kingdom Central Council for Nursing Midwifery and Health Visiting* [2001] HRLR 91 (statutory appeal allowed, it being breach of natural justice not to adjourn disciplinary proceedings where livelihood at stake and unchallenged medical evidence of unfitness to attend); <60.8.1> (time to prepare).

32.2.9 Refusal to state a case. <2.5.10(D)> (mode of reviewing refusals to state a case).

32.2.10 Court/tribunal's decision as to permission to appeal.[28]
(A) COUNTY COURT: NARROW JURISDICTIONAL ERROR. *R (Sivasubramaniam) v Wandsworth County Court* [2002] EWCA Civ 1738 [2003] 1 WLR 475 at [54] (absent exceptional circumstances, Courts should dismiss "summarily in the exercise of their discretion" a judicial review of a county court decision as to permission to appeal, since "Parliament has put in place an adequate system for reviewing the merits of decisions made by District Judges and it is not appropriate that there should be further review of these by the High Court"); *R (Strickson) v Preston County Court* [2007] EWCA Civ 1132 at [27] (need for a pre-*Anisminic* jurisdictional error <47.1.3>, or "grave procedural irregularity"), [32] (whether "the judicial process itself has been frustrated or corrupted"), [34] (leaving open whether would include error of law on the face of the record" <48.2.4>).
(B) SOCIAL SECURITY. *R v Social Security Commissioner, ex p Pattni* (1993) 5 Admin LR

---

[28] Robert Kellar [2005] JR 244.

219, 220G ("Where the right to grant or refuse leave to appeal is that of courts or tribunals which are not courts of record, there is, however, a safety net or long stop which can be invoked if the refusal of leave to appeal is plainly wrong. This is the judicial review procedure. It is to be invoked only in the plainest possible case"); *R (Latif) v Social Security Commissioners* [2002] EWHC 2355 (Admin) at [6] (need to "show that the reasons ... were improper or insufficient, or that there were no good grounds on which leave would have been refused in the proper exercise of the commissioner's discretion").

(C) AIT. *R v Immigration Appeal Tribunal, ex p Shah* [1999] 2 AC 629 (judicial review of refusal of permission to appeal); *R (G) v Immigration Appeal Tribunal* [2004] EWCA Civ 1731 [2005] 1 WLR 1445 (abuse of process to pursue judicial review, where failed statutory review).

(D) OTHER. *R (Sinclair Gardens Investments (Kensington) Ltd) v Lands Tribunal* [2005] EWCA Civ 1305 [2006] 3 All ER 650 (applying *Sivasubramaniam* to Lands Tribunal refusal of leave to appeal from leasehold valuation tribunal); *R (Customs and Excise Commissioners) v Maidstone Crown Court* [2004] EWHC 1459 (Admin) (granting judicial review of crown court's decision to grant leave to appeal from the magistrates, because erroneous approach to extension of time).

32.2.11 Special cases. *R v HM Commissioners of Inland Revenue, ex p Dhesi* The Independent 13th November 1995 (decision to apply to High Court for voluntary bill of indictment might be amenable to judicial review); *R v Solicitor-General, ex p Taylor* (1996) 8 Admin LR 206, 218C-D (given Attorney-General's unique constitutional position, refusal to commence contempt proceedings not amenable to judicial review); *R v Thames Stipendiary Magistrate, ex p Bates* [1995] COD 6 (judicial review of a conviction available on grounds of unjustifiable commencement of proceedings by the prosecution); <24.2.6> (declaration as to criminal legality of conduct).

32.3 Anxious scrutiny.[29] Prior to and independently of the HRA, the common law applies especially rigorous standards of review in cases engaging fundamental rights. Under the doctrine of "anxious scrutiny" a defendant public body is required to demonstrate proper justification and high standards of fairness. Anxious scrutiny is the common law equivalent to HRA s.6's external prohibition from HRA s.6; just as the principle of legality is to HRA s.3's internal inhibition.

32.3.1 Common law/constitutional rights. <7.5.1>.

32.3.2 The principle of legality. <7.3> and <46.2>.

32.3.3 The anxious scrutiny principle. *R (Yogathas) v Secretary of State for the Home Department* [2002] UKHL 36 [2003] 1 AC 920 at [9] (anxious scrutiny as a "fundamental principle"); *R (D) v Secretary of State for Health* [2006] EWCA Civ 989 at [26]-[31] (common law anxious scrutiny involving a "pressing need" test); *R v Secretary of State for the Home Department, ex p Bugdaycay* [1987] AC 514, 531E-G (court applying "the more rigorous examination ... according to the gravity of the issue"; "the most anxious scrutiny"), 537H ("a special responsibility lies on the court in the examination of the decision-making process"); *R v Secretary of State for the Home Department, ex p Brind* [1991] 1 AC 696, 757B-C (where fundamental right, "close scrutiny must be given to the reasons provided as justification for interference with that right"); *R v Secretary of State for the Home Department, ex p Launder* [1997] 1 WLR 839, 855H, 867D-E (anxious scrutiny in extradition context); *R (Razgar) v*

---

[29] Michael Fordham [1996] JR 81; Michael Fordham & Thomas de la Mare [2000] JR 40.

Secretary of State for the Home Department [2004] UKHL 27 [2004] 2 AC 368 at [16] ("such careful scrutiny as is called for where an irrevocable step, potentially involving a breach of fundamental human rights, is in contemplation"), [69] (Lord Carswell); *R (Gibson) v Winchester Crown Court* [2004] EWHC 361 (Admin) [2004] 1 WLR 1623 at [35] (need to "scrutinise" the decision "rigorously"); *R (Da Silva) v Director of Public Prosecutions* [2006] EWHC 3204 (Admin) at [49] (anxious scrutiny means asking whether decision reasonably open); *Doherty v Birmingham City Council* [2008] UKHL 57 [2008] 3 WLR 636 at [135] (comparing anxious scrutiny and HRA proportionality).

32.3.4 **Limits of anxious scrutiny.** *E v Secretary of State for the Home Department* [2004] EWCA Civ 49 [2004] QB 1044 (anxious scrutiny not meaning automatic admissibility of fresh evidence on an asylum appeal) at [85] ("the `anxious scrutiny' principle, though very relevant to consideration of the facts of any case, cannot alter the statutory limits of the [asylum appeal] procedure. The Court of Appeal does not have an all-purpose role to prevent or correct any breaches of the Refugee or Human Rights Conventions"); *Begum v Tower Hamlets London Borough Council* [2003] UKHL 5 [2003] 2 AC 430 at [7] (unnecessary to apply "anxious scrutiny" in order for the court's role to constitute a "full jurisdiction" to render an administrative decision-making process compatible with HRA:ECHR Art 6, albeit that the decision-maker is not independent and impartial); *R (Mahmood) v Secretary of State for the Home Department* [2001] 1 WLR 840 (distinguishing between the common law justification test and the direct question whether there has been a breach of a Convention right).

32.3.5 **Substantial objective justification: the *Smith* test.** David Pannick QC's formulation, endorsed by the CA in *R v Ministry of Defence, ex p Smith* [1996] QB 517, 554D-G, 563A and 564H-565B ("The court may not interfere with the exercise of an administrative discretion on substantive grounds save where the court is satisfied that the decision is unreasonable in the sense that it is beyond the range of responses open to a reasonable decision-maker. But in judging whether the decision-maker has exceeded this margin of appreciation the human rights context is important. The more substantial the interference with human rights, the more the court will require by way of justification before it is satisfied that the decision is reasonable in the sense outlined above"). Cases applying the Pannick formulation include: *R v Secretary of State for the Home Department, ex p Stafford* [1999] 2 AC 38, 47G; *R v Secretary of State for the Home Department, ex p Simms* [2000] 2 AC 115, 130B; *R v Lord Saville of Newdigate, ex p A* [2000] 1 WLR 1855 at [34]; *R v A Local Authority, ex p LM* [2000] 1 FLR 612 (disclosure of information would be irrational under the *Smith* test); *R (Q) v Secretary of State for the Home Department* [2003] EWCA Civ 364 [2004] QB 36 at [115] (*Smith* test not "confined to rights set out in the European Convention on Human Rights", but "apt ... to apply to the right to seek asylum, which is not only the subject of a separate international convention but is expressly recognised by Article 14 of the Universal Declaration of Human Rights"); *R (Rogers) v Swindon NHS Primary Care Trust* [2006] EWCA Civ 392 [2006] 1 WLR 2649 at [56] (*Smith* test applied, whether or not HRA:ECHR Art 2 engaged, because could be life or death decision).

32.3.6 **Substantial objective justification.** *R v Lord Saville of Newdigate, ex p A* [2000] 1 WLR 1855 at [37] ("when a fundamental right such as the right to life is engaged, the options available to the reasonable decision-maker are curtailed ... because it is unreasonable to reach a decision which contravenes or could contravene human rights unless there are sufficiently significant countervailing considerations. In other words it is not open to the decision-maker to risk interfering with fundamental rights in the absence of compelling justification"), applied in *R (A) v Lord Saville of Newdigate* [2001] EWCA Civ 2048 [2002] 1 WLR 1249 at [24]; *R v Immigration Officer, ex p Quaquah* [2000] INLR 196, 206C (interference with rights requiring "explanation that will withstand `careful scrutiny'"), 206G ("a necessity for there to be identified countervailing circumstances which would have compellingly outweighed the [claimant]'s rights, which are presently under discussion"); *R (Mahmood) v Secretary of State for the Home Department* [2001] 1 WLR 840 at [18] (Laws LJ, referring to the common law test as a requirement of "substantial objective justification").

32.3.7 Justification: other illustrations. *R v Secretary of State for the Home Department, ex p Turgut* [2001] 1 All ER 719, 729e-j ("rigorous examination ... considering the underlying factual material for itself to see whether or not it compels a different conclusion to that arrived at by the Secretary of State"), 728j-729a (decision "rigorously examined and subjected to the most anxious scrutiny"); *R v Secretary of State for the Home Department, ex p Moon* (1996) 8 Admin LR 477, 483F-G ("the Court will demand clear justification for an executive decision which interferes with an important right; not, however, so as to persuade the Court to agree with the executive view, but simply to demonstrate that there was a sufficient basis on which the view could sensibly be reached"); *Chesterfield Properties Plc v Secretary of State for the Environment* [1998] JPL 568, 579-580 ("where ... a fundamental or constitutional right is threatened by an administrative decision of the state, the court on judicial review will require the public decision-maker to demonstrate that there existed substantial public interest grounds for his interference with the right"; "a substantial justification in the public interest"); *R v Secretary of State for the Home Department, ex p Iyadurai* [1998] Imm AR 470, 481-482 ("the court has jurisdiction to review to a higher standard than is adopted in at least the conventional statements of *Wednesbury*").

32.3.8 Pressing social need/self-evident and pressing need test. <6.1.5> (self-evident and pressing need test as to existence of implied power affecting fundamental rights); *R (D) v Secretary of State for Health* [2006] EWCA Civ 989 at [26]-[31] ("pressing need" test, demonstrating "the distance the law has travelled" from "the *Wednesbury* bludgeon"); *R v Secretary of State for the Home Department, ex p Simms* [2000] 2 AC 115, 129D (evidence not establishing "a case of pressing need which might prevail over the prisoners' attempt to gain access to justice"); *R v A Local Authority, ex p LM* [2000] 1 FLR 612 ("pressing social need" test for disclosing information about child abuse allegations to another authority); *R v Governor of Frankland Prison, ex p Russell* [2000] 1 WLR 2027 at [11] ("Where the question arises as to the extent to which a power is impliedly conferred by statute to interfere with fundamental rights, there must be established a self-evident and pressing need for that power and the interference must be the minimum necessary to fulfil that need"); *R (MWH & H Ward Estates Ltd) v Monmouthshire County Council* [2002] EWCA Civ 1915 at [31] ("pressing social need" not the appropriate test for property rights under Art 1P).

32.3.9 A fair balance. *R v Secretary of State for the Home Department, ex p Chahal* [1995] 1 WLR 526, 533A-534F (CA accepting, by reference to the principle of proportionality, that Secretary of State owing in a deportation context an important duty to balance the competing interests of national security and the rights and interests of the deportee); *R v Chief Constable of Sussex, ex p International Trader's Ferry Ltd* [1999] 2 AC 418 (Lord Slynn, emphasising, as a matter of domestic *Wednesbury* Review, that the Chief Constable had carried out a carefully considered balancing exercise); *R v O'Kane and Clarke, ex p Northern Bank Ltd* [1996] STC 1249, 1269e-f (unlawful because "no regard to the burden thereby imposed on the recipients or to the proportionality of that burden and the benefit which is sought to be achieved"); *R v Lord Saville of Newdigate, ex p A* [2000] 1 WLR 1855 at [68] (failure to attach adequate significance to particular matters).

32.3.10 Anxious scrutiny and the proportionality template.
(A) LEGITIMATE AIM. *Chesterfield Properties Plc v Secretary of State for the Environment* [1998] JPL 568, 579-580 (need for "substantial public interest grounds for his interference with the right"; "Only another interest, a public interest, of greater force may override it").

(B) SUITABILITY. <58.2.6>.
(C) NECESSITY. *R v O'Kane and Clarke, ex p Northern Bank Ltd* [1996] STC 1249, 1269f-g (response unnecessary: "if there were thought to be a need for protection I see no reason why this could not be achieved by the method suggested by the [claimant]").
(D) PROPORTIONALITY. <P58>.

32.3.11 **Fundamental rights and relevancy/irrelevancy.** <56.1.4> (anxious scrutiny and relevancy/ irrelevancy); <56.3.7> (weight and fundamental rights); <56.1.5> (fundamental rights as a relevant consideration).

32.3.12 **Anxious scrutiny and procedural fairness.** *R v Secretary of State for the Home Department, ex p Sittampalam Thirukumar* [1989] Imm AR 402, 414 ("asylum decisions are of such moment that only the highest standards of fairness will suffice"); *R (Refugee Legal Centre) v Secretary of State for the Home Department* [2004] EWCA Civ 1481 [2005] 1 WLR 2219 at [8] (applying *Thirukumar*); *R (Dirshe) v Secretary of State for the Home Department* [2005] EWCA Civ 421 at [13] (applying *Thirukumar*); *Mohammed Kerrouche v Secretary of State for the Home Department* [1997] Imm AR 610, 616 (anxious scrutiny a special approach "in relation to procedural failures than would be the case if a less important issue were at stake"); *R v Secretary of State for the Home Department, ex p Duggan* [1994] 3 All ER 277, 288d (approach where decision having "a direct impact on the liberty of the subject"); *R v Army Board of the Defence Council, ex p Anderson* [1992] QB 169, 187E (Board "dealing with an individual's fundamental statutory rights, must by its procedures achieve a high standard of fairness"); *R v Southwark Crown Court, ex p Gross* [1998] COD 445, 452 (Court must be "vigilant" to guard against erosion of "stringent safeguards" appropriate for executive powers to encroach on privacy and liberty of the subject); <62.2.7> (fundamental rights and duty to give reasons).

32.3.13 **Anxious scrutiny and decision-maker's reasoning.** *WM (DRC) v Secretary of State for the Home Department* [2006] EWCA Civ 1495 at [10] (decision "irrational if it is not taken on the basis of anxious scrutiny"), [26] ("the necessary level of scrutiny was not applied").

32.3.14 **Whether judicial review satisfies ECHR Art 13.**[30] Article 13 ("Everyone whose rights and freedoms as set forth in this Convention are violated shall have an effective remedy before a national authority"); *R (European Roma Rights Centre) v Immigration Officer at Prague Airport* [2004] UKHL 55 [2005] 2 AC 1 at [42] (HRA means ECHR is "incorporated into our law without article 13"); *R (Regentford Ltd) v Canterbury Crown Court* [2001] HRLR 362 ("Article 13 has not been incorporated into English law, but not to provide a remedy would seem to run the risk of rendering the United Kingdom in breach of its Treaty obligations, something which the English courts should strive to avoid"); *R (K) v Camden and Islington Health Authority* [2001] EWCA Civ 240 [2002] QB 198 at [53] ("important that the courts, as part of the State, should satisfy themselves so far as possible that the common law affords adequate control, in conformity with [ECHR] article 13"); *R v Secretary of State for the Home Department, ex p Turgut* [2001] 1 All ER 719 (adopting a rigorous reasonableness test having regard to Art 13); *Attorney General's Reference No.2 of 2001* [2003] UKHL 68 [2004] 2 AC 72 at [164] (Lord Rodger (dissenting in the result): "Parliament did not incorporate article 13 into our domestic law: it assumed that under the Human Rights Act 1998 courts would have at their disposal all the necessary remedies for dealing with violations of the Convention. Experience suggests this is indeed so"); *Secretary of State for the Home Department v MB* [2006] EWCA Civ 1140 [2007] QB 415 at [34] (Art 13 given "partial effect" by HRA ss.6-9,

---

[30] Michael Beloff QC & Rupert Beloff [2001] JR 154.

albeit remedy may be limited to declaration of incompatibility) (HL is [2007] UKHL 46 [2008] 1 AC 440).

32.4 Other modified review situations.[31] There are many situations where the context and subject-matter means judicial review is available only on some grounds, or only in an adapted way. But there are no neat pigeon-holes or rigid adjustments. All grounds for judicial review are contextual and adaptable to meet the interests of justice in the particular context and circumstances.

32.4.1 **Acts of Parliament.** <35.1.3> (judicial review of primary legislation).

32.4.2 **Courts of law: whether error of law available.** <48.2.2>.

32.4.3 **Modified review and visitors etc applying special law.**[32] <48.2.1> (Visitors: error of law unavailable); cf. *R v Hull University Visitor, ex p Page* [1993] AC 682, 709C-E (Lord Slynn, dissenting: "in my opinion if certiorari can go to a particular tribunal it is available on all the grounds which have been judicially recognised"); *R v Visitors to the Inns of Court, ex p Calder & Persaud* [1994] QB 1, 42B-D, 58D-E (Visitor's decisions as to whether natural justice satisfied not reviewable); *R v HM the Queen in Council, ex p Vijayatunga* [1990] 2 QB 444; *R (Varma) v Duke of Kent* [2004] EWHC 1705 (Admin) [2004] ELR 616 at [21] (judicial review of Visitor available for alleged improper delegation and unfairness).

32.4.4 **Non-statutory functions: whether modified review.** *R v Criminal Injuries Compensation Board, ex p P* [1995] 1 WLR 845, 864B-C ("It will ... be a very rare case where the court will be able to interfere with such a decision on the ground of irrationality"), 858C-D; *Gillick v West Norfolk and Wisbech Area Health Authority* [1986] AC 112, 192F-193B (doubting whether non-statutory guidance "is open to review on `Wednesbury' principles ... Such a review must always begin by examining the nature of the statutory power which the administrative authority whose action is called in question has purported to exercise, and asking, in the light of that examination, what were, and what were not, relevant considerations for the authority to take into account in deciding to exercise that power. It is only against such a specific statutory background that the question whether the authority has acted unreasonably, in the *Wednesbury* sense, can properly be asked and answered. Here there is no specific statutory background by reference to which the appropriate *Wednesbury* questions could be formulated"); *R v Ealing London Borough Council, ex p Parkinson* (1996) 8 Admin LR 281, 282G (because decision not an administrative function under statutory powers, defendant not entitled to rely on *Wednesbury* restraint but obliged to make out its case substantively); *R v Panel on Take-overs and Mergers, ex p Guinness Plc* [1990] 1 QB 146 (take-over panel exercising non-statutory functions), 159D-160A (discussing conventional grounds), 178H (asking "whether something has gone wrong of a nature and degree which require the intervention of the court").

32.4.5 **Prerogative powers: whether modified review.** *R v Criminal Injuries Compensation Board, ex p P* [1995] 1 WLR 845; *In re McFarland* [2004] UKHL 17 [2004] 1 WLR 1289 at [41] (Lord Scott: "the scope of the courts' powers of intervention are ... limited by the nature of the prerogative power in question"); *R (Elias) v Secretary of State for Defence* [2006] EWCA Civ 1293 [2006] 1 WLR 3213 at [191] (fetter principle inapplicable to prerogative power)

---

[31] This paragraph in a previous edition was cited in *Re Shuker* [2004] NIQB 20 at [16].

[32] Michael Beloff QC & Nicholas Bamforth [2002] JR 221.

Council of Civil Service Unions v Minister for the Civil Service [1985] AC 374, 411D-F (as to "irrationality", "difficult to envisage in any of the various fields in which the prerogative remains the only source of the relevant decision-making power a decision of a kind that would be open to attack through the judicial process upon this ground").

32.4.6 Preliminary matters: whether modified review. *Pearlberg v Varty* [1972] 1 WLR 534, 546B-C (natural justice rules not applying "to a judicial determination of the question whether there is a prima facie case ... with the same force or as much force as they do to decisions which determine the rights of persons"); *Wiseman v Borneman* [1971] AC 297, 311C-D (principles of natural justice not applicable "in their full vigour"); *Rees v Crane* [1994] 2 AC 173, 191G-192A (approach where decision "purely preliminary"); *R v Secretary of State for the Home Department, ex p Seton* 25th April 1996 unrep. (*Duggan* duties of fair disclosure not applying to initial category A classification, being a provisional decision not impacting on release dates); <32.2> (decisions regarding legal process).

32.4.7 Special commercial contexts: whether modified review. *R v Bridgend County Borough Council, ex p Jones* 1st October 1999 unrep. (in tendering context, where ultimately a commercial decision, focus of judicial review is on performance of duties arising expressly or by necessary implication from the statutory scheme); *Mass Energy Ltd v Birmingham City Council* [1994] Env LR 298, 319 (Evans LJ: "the council was entitled to deal with the tenderers on a commercial basis, subject only to the statutory restrictions as outlined. In commerce, life is not always fair"), 315 (Scott LJ, refusing to imply, on fairness grounds, obligations lacking "commercial realism"); *Mercury Energy Ltd v Electricity Corporation of New Zealand Ltd* [1994] 1 WLR 521, 529B (not "likely that a decision by a state enterprise to enter into or determine a commercial contract to supply goods or services will ever be the subject of judicial review in the absence of fraud, corruption or bad faith"); *R v Northumbrian Water Ltd, ex p Newcastle and North Tyneside Health Authority* [1999] Env LR 715, 724-729 (duty to act in the public interest inapplicable to commercial organisation/ privatised body).

32.4.8 Westminster-approved measures: whether modified review. *M v Home Office* [1994] 1 AC 377, 413D-G (Lord Woolf, explaining when of schemes "laid ... before Parliament for approval ... it could be difficult to persuade a court to intervene"); *R v Secretary of State for Trade and Industry, ex p Lonrho Plc* [1989] 1 WLR 525 at 536C-E (where report laid before Parliament "the courts must be careful not to invade the political field and substitute their own judgment for that of the Minister"); *O'Connor v Chief Adjudication Officer* [1999] 1 FLR 1200, 1210F-1211B (Auld LJ: "Irrationality is a separate ground for challenging subsidiary legislation ... It is wrong to deduce from [the] dicta a notion of `extreme' irrationality", albeit that "in cases where the minister has acted after reference to Parliament, usually by way of the affirmative or negative resolution procedure, there is a heavy evidential onus on a claimant for judicial review to establish the irrationality of a decision which may owe much to political, social and economic considerations in the underlying enabling legislation"); *R (Asif Javed) v Secretary of State for the Home Department* [2001] EWCA Civ 789 [2002] QB 129 (delegated legislation unlawful because underlying factual conclusions irrational) at [33] (Court retaining "the role of determining the legality of the subordinate legislation"), [37] (review not precluded by fact that statements were made in Parliament), [51] (no "principle of law which circumscribes the extent to which the court can review an order that has been approved by both Houses of Parliament under the affirmative resolution procedure"); *R v Secretary of State for the Environment, ex p Greater London Council* 3rd April 1985 unrep. (delegated legislation approved by House of Commons reviewable, including for unfairness and unreasonableness, albeit in practice grant of remedy on the latter ground likely to be rare); *R v Secretary of State for Social Security, ex p Joint Council for the Welfare of Immigrants* [1997] 1 WLR 275, 292C (conventional approach where regulations contravening express or implied requirements of a statute); *R v Criminal*

Injuries Compensation Board, ex p P [1995] 1 WLR 845, 861G-862B (Parliamentary approval not a "constitutional bar ... to the exercise of the court's powers of judicial review"); *Laker Airways Ltd v Department of Trade* [1977] QB 643 (statutory "guidance" approved by Parliament not the equivalent of an Act of Parliament); *R v HM Treasury, ex p Smedley* [1985] QB 657, 672C (discretion of Her Majesty in Council as to whether or not to make approved draft Order in Council, reviewable on *Wednesbury* principles); *R v Parliamentary Commissioner for Administration, ex p Dyer* [1994] 1 WLR 621, 623H, 625G-626E (refusing to apply "limited basis" of review to judicial review of the Parliamentary Ombudsman); *R v Secretary of State for the Environment, ex p British Telecommunications Plc* The Independent 5th September 1991 (since equipment rating Order approved by Parliament, amenable to judicial review only on grounds of illegality); *Ex p Williamson* The Times 9th March 1994 (Church of England Measure, being duly enacted and having received the Royal Assent, treated as enjoying the same invulnerability as an Act of Parliament); cf. *Adams v Lord Advocate* [2002] UKHRR 1189 at [62]-[64] (irrationality not available as a ground of challenge to an enactment of the Scottish Parliament).

32.4.9 National economic policy: whether modified review. *Hammersmith & Fulham London Borough Council* [1991] 1 AC 521, 596F-597H ("The formulation and the implementation of national economic policy are matters depending essentially on political judgment"; since needing "the approval of the House of Commons, it is not open to challenge on the grounds of irrationality short of the extremes of bad faith, improper motive or manifest absurdity"); *R v Secretary of State for the Environment, ex p Nottinghamshire County Council* [1986] AC 240, 250E-251A, 247H; *R v Commissioners of Customs and Excise, ex p Service Authority for the National Crime Squad* [2000] STC 638 (specification of police authorities for purposes of VAT a matter of national economic policy with which court should not interfere); *R v Secretary of State for Trade and Industry, ex p Isle of Wight Council* [2000] COD 245 (unreasonableness challenge to assisted areas scheme, being national economic policy, so would have to show that manifestly inappropriate); *R (South Cambridgeshire District Council) v First Secretary of State* [2005] EWHC 1746 (Admin) [2006] LGR 529 at [22] ("the lowest level of scrutiny available on grounds of rationality"); *R (Asif Javed) v Secretary of State for the Home Department* [2001] EWCA Civ 789 [2002] QB 129 at [49] (explaining *Nottinghamshire* and *Hammersmith* as "at an extreme end of the spectrum. In each case the decisions on how to exercise the statutory power turned on political and economic considerations to be evaluated by the minister and Parliament, whose rationality could not be measured by any yardstick available to the court"); *Howker v Secretary of State for Work and Pensions* [2002] EWCA Civ 1623 (Regulations laid before Parliament but nevertheless ultra vires because advisory committee misled and statutory procedure therefore breached), at [38] ("every member of the public adversely affected by a new regulation is entitled to challenge the lawfulness of that regulation on proper grounds. The courts have never shrunk from declaring the invalidity of a defective measure affecting the allocation of public monies"); *R (Gurung) v Ministry of Defence* [2002] EWHC 2463 (Admin) at [40]-[41] (judicial review granted of exclusionary criterion in compensation scheme, albeit involving public expenditure and announced in Parliament, as unequal and so irrational); *R (Gurung) v Ministry of Defence* [2008] EWHC 1496 (Admin) at [59]-[61] (restraint in context of revised pensions scheme).

32.4.10 National security: whether modified review. *R (Bancoult) v Secretary of State for Foreign & Commonwealth Affairs* [2007] EWCA Civ 498 [2008] QB 365 at [102], [118] (national security context may render an issue non-justiciable); *Secretary of State for the Home Department v Rehman* [2001] UKHL 47 [2003] 1 AC 153 at [31] (Lord Steyn: "It is well established in the case law that issues of national security do not fall beyond the competence of the courts ... It is, however, self-evidently right that national courts must give great weight to the views of the executive on matters of national security"), [53]-[54] (Lord Hoffmann); *R v*

Shayler [2002] UKHL 11 [2003] 1 AC 247 (discussing the role of ECHR Art 10 and judicial review in the context of the Official Secrets Act); *R v Secretary of State for the Home Department, ex p Cheblak* [1991] 1 WLR 890, 902G ("National security is the exclusive responsibility of the executive"); *Council of Civil Service Unions v Minister for the Civil Service* [1985] AC 374 (Government's obligation to produce evidence that the decision was in fact based on grounds of national security), 412F-G (Lord Diplock: "par excellence a non-justiciable question. The judicial process is totally inept to deal with the sort of problems which it involves"), 404H (but "the court does not abdicate its judicial function"); *R v Secretary of State for the Home Department, ex p Ruddock* [1987] 1 WLR 1482, 1490E-1492B (national security not a "plea in bar"); *R v Secretary of State for the Home Department, ex p Chahal* [1995] 1 WLR 526 (although national security a matter for the Secretary of State, duty to balance it against the interests of the individual); *A v Secretary of State for the Home Department* [2004] UKHL 56 [2005] 2 AC 68 (proportionality and justification of derogation order and statutory provision for detention of non-nationals without charge, in a national security context); *R (Tucker) v Director General of the National Crime Squad* [2003] EWCA Civ 2 at [43] (lower standards of fairness required where decision involving "sensitive intelligence information"), [47] ("In this type of case the duty of fairness requires no more than that the decision-maker acts honestly and without bias or caprice"); *R v Secretary of State for the Home Department, ex p Gallagher* [1994] 3 CMLR 295 (limited process rights where exclusion order based on national security).

32.4.11 Whether modified review: other cases. *R (Begum) v Tower Hamlets London Borough Council* [2006] EWCA Civ 733 [2006] LGR 674 at [20]-[21] (judicial review very rare to interfere with pending local election); *R v Barnet & Camden Rent Tribunal, ex p Frey Investments Ltd* [1972] 2 QB 342, 358B-C, 364G-365C, 368D-H (referral to Rent Tribunal not reviewable on relevancy/irrelevancy grounds); *R v Secretary of State for the Home Department, ex p Hepworth* [1998] COD 146 (Laws J: judicial review of "executive decisions arising wholly within the context of internal prison management" needing "crude irrationality").

P33 Flux. Judicial review is dynamic: new faiths emerge, old ones decay, the general trend being towards empowering the Court.

33.1 The developing law
33.2 Lessons from the past
33.3 "Two-stage" approaches to legal development
33.4 Forecasting

33.1 The developing law. The law of judicial review shifts, as it develops and matures. The common law tradition favours case-by-case development of the law, focusing the analysis on the particular context under consideration.

33.1.1 **Keeping up with the developing law.**[33] *Copeland v Smith* [2000] 1 WLR 1371, 1375H (Brooke LJ, describing it as "quite essential for advocates who hold themselves out as competent to practise in a particular field to bring and keep themselves up to date with recent authority in their field").

33.1.2 **The tide of change.** *R v Inland Revenue Commissioners, ex p National Federation of Self-Employed and Small Businesses Ltd* [1982] AC 617, 653C-D (Lord Scarman: "the tide of the developing law"), 631F (Lord Wilberforce: "recognition of the value of guiding authorities does not mean that the process of judicial review must stand still"); *Council of Civil Service Unions v Minister for the Civil Service* [1985] AC 374, 407H (Lord Diplock: "the English law relating to judicial control of administrative action has been developed upon a case to case basis which has virtually transformed it over the last three decades"), 414D-F (Lord Roskill: "as a result of a series of judicial decisions since about 1950 ... there has been a dramatic and indeed a radical change in the scope of judicial review. That change has been described - by no means critically - as an upsurge of judicial activism... [The] branch of judicial review which is concerned with the control of executive action ... has evolved, as with much of our law, on a case by case basis and no doubt hereafter that process will continue"); *R v Hull University Visitor, ex p Page* [1993] AC 682, 709B (Lord Slynn: "there has been a considerable development in the scope of judicial review in the second half of this century"); *R v Liverpool Corporation, ex p Liverpool Taxi Fleet Operators' Association* [1972] 2 QB 299, 310G (Roskill LJ: "The long legal history of the former prerogative writs and of their modern counterparts, the orders of prohibition, mandamus and certiorari, shows that their application has always been flexible as the need for their use in differing social conditions down the centuries has changed").

33.1.3 **A Steyn maxim: never say never.** *R v Panel on Take-overs and Mergers, ex p Fayed* [1992] BCC 524, 536C (Steyn LJ: "In the developing field of judicial review it is usually unwise to say `never'"); *R (Ullah) v Secretary of State for the Home Department* [2004] UKHL 26 [2004] 2 AC 323 at [48] (Lord Steyn: "Saying never in law often requires courts to swallow their words in circumstances not previously contemplated").

33.1.4 **Steps towards a developed system.** *Ridge v Baldwin* [1964] AC 40, 72-73 (Lord Reid:

---

[33] Surveys of important cases include Richard Gordon QC [1996] JR 38 & 105, [2008] JR 144; Gemma White [1997] JR 42; Richard Stein [1998] JR 57; Ian McLeod [1999] JR 130. Michael Fordham's Top 20 Cases for 1999 at [2000] JR 134; 2000 at [2001] JR 121; 2001 at [2002] JR 62; 2002 at [2003] JR 59; 2003 at [2004] JR 167; 2004 at [2006] JR 266; 2005 at [2006] JR 270; 2006 at [2008] JR 196; 2007 at [2008] JR 200.

"We do not have a developed system of administrative law - perhaps because until fairly recently we did not need it. So it is not surprising that in dealing with new types of cases the courts have had to grope for solutions, and have found that old powers, rules and procedure are largely inapplicable to cases which they were never designed or intended to deal with"); *O'Reilly v Mackman* [1983] 2 AC 237, 279H-280A (Lord Diplock: "We did have by [1977] a developed system of administrative law"); *Mahon v Air New Zealand Ltd* [1984] AC 808, 816G ("The extension of judicial control of the administrative process has provided over the last 30 years the most striking feature of the development of the common law in those countries of whose legal systems it provides the source: and although it is a development that has already gone a long way towards providing a system of administrative law as comprehensive in its content as the droit administratif of countries of the Civil Law, albeit differing in procedural approach, it is a development that is still continuing. It has not yet become static"); *R (Q) v Secretary of State for the Home Department* [2003] EWCA Civ 364 [2004] QB 36 at [112] ("The common law of judicial review in England and Wales has not stood still in recent years. Starting from the received checklist of justiciable errors set out by Lord Diplock in the *CCSU* case [1985] AC 374, the courts (as Lord Diplock himself anticipated they would) have developed an issue-sensitive scale of intervention to enable them to perform their constitutional function in an increasingly complex polity. They continue to abstain from merits review - in effect, retaking the decision on the facts - but in appropriate classes of case they will today look very closely at the process by which facts have been ascertained and at the logic of the inferences drawn from them"); *R v Inland Revenue Commissioners, ex p National Federation of Self-Employed and Small Businesses Ltd* [1982] AC 617, 639H-640B (rules of standing changed "over the years to meet the need to preserve the integrity of the rule of law despite changes in the social structure, methods of government and the extent to which the activities of private citizens are controlled by governmental authorities, that have been taking place continuously").

33.1.5 **Legal development and the common law tradition.** *Kuddus v Chief Constable of Leicestershire Constabulary* [2001] UKHL 29 [2002] 2 AC 122 at [33] (Lord Mackay: "The genius of the common law is its capacity to develop"); *Kleinwort Benson Ltd v Lincoln City Council* [1999] 2 AC 349, 377D-378G (Lord Goff, describing the nature of judicial development of the common law); *Wainwright v Home Office* [2003] UKHL 53 [2004] 2 AC 406 at [31] (Lord Hoffmann, pointing out that "the common law works" by identifying "underlying values", being "a value which underlies the existence of a rule of law"); *Douglas v Hello! Ltd* [2001] QB 967 at [109] ("The common law, and equity with it, grows by slow and uneven degrees. It develops reactively, both in the immediate sense that it is only ever expounded in response to events and in the longer-term sense that it may be consciously shaped by the perceived needs of legal policy. The modern law of negligence exemplifies both senses"); *Gillick v West Norfolk and Wisbech Area Health Authority* [1986] AC 112, 183B-E (Lord Scarman, describing the "task ... to search the overfull and cluttered shelves of the law reports for a principle, or set of principles recognised by the judges over the years but stripped of the detail which, however appropriate in their day, would, if applied today, lay the judges open to a justified criticism for failing to keep the law abreast of the society in which they live and work. It is, of course, a judicial commonplace to proclaim the adaptability and flexibility of the judge-made common law. But this is more frequently proclaimed than acted upon. The mark of the great judge from Coke through Mansfield to our day has been the capacity and the will to search out principle, to discard the detail appropriate (perhaps) to earlier times, and to apply the principle in such a way as to satisfy the needs of their own time. If judge-made law is to survive as a living and relevant body of law, we must make the effort, however inadequately, to follow the lead of the great masters of the judicial art"); *In re S (Hospital Patient: Court's Jurisdiction)* [1996] Fam 1, 19G ("the common law should respond to social needs as they are manifested, case by case"); *R v Governor of Brockhill Prison, ex p Evans (No.2)* [2001] 2 AC 19, 48A (Lord Hobhouse).

33.1.6 The incremental approach: developing on a case-by-case basis. <11.1.3> (cases turning on their facts); <31.6> (flexi-principles); *In re Smalley* [1985] AC 622 (crown court reviewability), 643H-644A (Lord Bridge: "it may well be impossible to prescribe in the abstract a precise test to determine on which side of the line any case should fall and, therefore, necessary to proceed ... on a case by case basis"); *R v Manchester Crown Court, ex p Director of Public Prosecutions* [1993] 1 WLR 1524, 1528C ("the law has developed on a case by case basis, not always with happy results"); *O'Reilly v Mackman* [1983] 2 AC 237 (procedural exclusivity), 285B-G (Lord Diplock: "I do not think that your Lordships would be wise to use this as an occasion to lay down categories of cases ... Whether there should be other exceptions should, in my view, at this stage in the development of procedural public law, be left to be decided on a case to case basis"); *R v Kensington & Chelsea Royal London Borough Council, ex p Hammell* [1989] QB 518 (interim remedies), 538B (declining to "try to state any formula for the exercise of the discretion to grant a mandatory injunction" in judicial review); *R v Kensington and Chelsea Royal London Borough Council, ex p Grillo* (1996) 28 HLR 94 (reasons), 105 (Neill LJ: "for the time being the law will have to develop on a case by case basis and I think it is too early to attempt to formulate any general principle"); *R (Bibi) v Newham London Borough Council* [2001] EWCA Civ 607 [2002] 1 WLR 237 (legitimate expectation) at [25] (Schiemann LJ: "Several attempts have been made to find a formulation which will provide a test for all cases. However, history shows that wide-ranging formulations, while capable of producing a just result in the individual case, are seen later to have needlessly constricted the development of the law"); *R v Latif* [1996] 1 WLR 104 (extradition abuse <63.1.3>), 113A-B (declining to give general guidance as to the exercise of the discretion in *R v Horseferry Road Magistrates' Court, ex p Bennett* [1994] 1 AC 42); *K v Secretary of State for the Home Department* [2002] EWCA Civ 775 (negligence) at [11] (Laws LJ: "The conditions upon which the common law will impose a duty of care so as to give rise to a cause of action in negligence are by no means precisely fixed. This typifies the common law's virtue, that claims are decided case by case so as to do justice in a myriad of different circumstances. This however has to be tempered by the influence of another virtue, which is the common law's capacity to develop firm principle. That is virtuous because it affords a strong measure of legal certainty. The tension between these two virtues is a major characteristic of the common law's method. It is important that we should not make too great a sacrifice of the principle of legal certainty on the altar of the common law's flexibility, or *vice versa*").

33.1.7 Limitations of the incremental approach: the need for guidance. *Wiseman v Borneman* [1971] AC 297, 310F (Lord Guest: "Where a question arises as to whether the principles of natural justice should be followed in any particular case it is important ... that the principles upon which this question is to be decided should be reasonably clear and definite. Inferior tribunals should be in a position to know whether, in any particular case, they were called on to apply the principles of natural justice and to what extent those principles should be followed. It would be unsatisfactory if cases where statutory tribunals had been set up were to be decided ex post facto upon some uncertain basis"); *R v Tower Hamlets London Borough Council, ex p Chetnik Developments Ltd* [1988] AC 858, 878H-879A (Lord Bridge, explaining that the House of Lords "must accept the obligation to give whatever guidance is possible as to the matters which may and those which may not be taken into consideration in exercising the discretion"); *R v Higher Education Funding Council, ex p Institute of Dental Surgery* [1994] 1 WLR 242, 257C-D (Sedley J: "No doubt the common law will develop, as the common law does, case by case. It is not entirely satisfactory that this should be so, not least because experience suggests that in the absence of a prior principle irreconcilable or inconsistent decisions will emerge"); *R v Secretary of State for Education, ex p London Borough of Southwark* [1995] ELR 308, 320D-F (Laws J: "I am quite sure that the courts... have not imposed on public bodies substantial duties to consult others merely as a knee-jerk response to the facts of the particular case, without regard to principle. If they did, we should have palm tree justice; or, to employ another overworked aphorism, the duty to consult would be as long as the Chancellor's foot. It is important to have in mind that while this area of the law is pre-eminently concerned with fairness - notoriously a concept giving rise to different views as to its application in practice - we are obliged, sitting here, to pay due respect to another principle: the principle of legal certainty. It would be intolerable if our jurisprudence did not make it reasonably clear to public administrators, whose task extends not to a single case but to the management of a continuing regime, when the law obliges them to consult persons or bodies affected by their decisions, and when it does not").

33.2 Lessons from the past. It is instructive to look back at the path which the developing law has taken and the analytical tools discarded along the way. Doing so should engender doubt as to the immutability of principle and convention. The legal highlights indicate a general promotion of supervisory control by reviewing Courts. Not necessarily "interventionism"; rather, preserving the capacity to intervene in an appropriate case.

33.2.1 Pushing back the frontiers of reviewability. <34.3> (conquests of reviewability).

33.2.2 Empowering highlights: grounds for judicial review.
(A) ERROR OF LAW ON THE FACE OF THE RECORD REDISCOVERED. *R v Northumberland Compensation Appeal Tribunal, ex p Shaw* [1952] 1 KB 338, re-discovering error of law on the face of the record <48.2.4>, as explained by Lord Diplock in *R v Inland Revenue Commissioners, ex p National Federation of Self-Employed and Small Businesses Ltd* [1982] AC 617, 640B (*Shaw* said to have "resurrected error of law upon the face of the record") and *O'Reilly v Mackman* [1983] 2 AC 237, 277C (an "expansion of the grounds upon which orders of certiorari could be obtained").
(B) UNSUSTAINABLE CONCLUSION OF FACT. *Edwards v Bairstow* [1956] AC 14, treating irrational conclusion of fact as an error of law <49.2.6>.
(C) FRUSTRATING THE LEGISLATIVE PURPOSE. *Padfield v Minister of Agriculture Fisheries & Food* [1968] AC 997, introducing the duty not to frustrate the legislative intention <P53>: see *O'Reilly v Mackman* [1983] 2 AC 237, 280A (Lord Diplock, referring to *Padfield* as a "landmark [case] ... in which a too-timid judgment of my own in the Court of Appeal was (fortunately) overruled").
(D) ERROR OF LAW. *Anisminic Ltd v Foreign Compensation Commission* [1969] 2 AC 147, introducing error of law, not on the face of the record, at least as to administrative bodies <P48>: as explained in *In re A Company* [1981] AC 374, 382G-H (Lord Diplock: "it has made possible the rapid development in England of a rational and comprehensive system of administrative law on the foundation of the concept of ultra vires").
(E) PRECEDENT FACT REGALVANISED. *R v Secretary of State for the Home Department, ex p Khawaja* [1984] AC 74, recognising illegal entrant as a precedent fact <49.1>, emphatically overturning *R v Secretary of State for the Home Department, ex p Zamir* [1980] AC 930.
(F) EXTRADITION ABUSE. *R v Horseferry Road Magistrates' Court, ex p Bennett* [1994] 1 AC 42, recognising judicial review of committal on basis of prior extradition abuse <63.1.3>.
(G) SUBSTANTIVE FAIRNESS. *R v Inland Revenue Commissioners, ex p Preston* [1985] AC 835 and *R v Inland Revenue Commissioners, ex p Unilever Plc* [1996] STC 681, cementing the notion of substantive unfairness <P54>.
(H) ANXIOUS SCRUTINY. See especially *R v Ministry of Defence, ex p Smith* [1996] QB 517, 554D-G, explaining the common law principle of anxious scrutiny <32.3.5> (the *Smith* test).
(I) PRINCIPLE OF LEGALITY. See especially *R v Lord Chancellor, ex p Witham* [1998] QB 575 and *R v Secretary of State for the Home Department, ex p Simms* [2000] 2 AC 115, explaining the common law principle of legality <7.3> and <46.2>.
(J) SUBSTANTIVE LEGITIMATE EXPECTATION. *R v North and East Devon Health*

Authority, ex p Coughlan [2001] QB 213, recognising the unfair and unjustified breach of a substantive legitimate expectation <54.2>.

(K) HUMAN RIGHTS. *A v Secretary of State for the Home Department* [2004] UKHL 56 [2005] 2 AC 68 (discriminatory anti-terrorism detention) and *A v Secretary of State for the Home Department* [2005] UKHL 71 [2006] 2 AC 221 (torture-obtained evidence), demonstrating a new and robust protection of human rights in the new HRA era.

(L) UNFAIR ERROR OF FACT. *E v Secretary of State for the Home Department* [2004] EWCA Civ 49 [2004] QB 1044, recognising unfairness resulting from misunderstanding or ignorance of an established and relevant fact (after *R v Criminal Injuries Compensation Board, ex p A* [1999] 2 AC 330, 344G-345C and *R (Alconbury Developments Ltd) v Secretary of State for the Environment Transport and the Regions* [2001] UKHL 23 [2003] 2 AC 295 at [53] <49.2.2>.

(M) JUDICIAL REVIEW AND PRIMARY LEGISLATION.*R (Jackson) v Attorney General* [2005] UKHL 56 [2006] 1 AC 262, considering the constitutional legality of primary legislation.

33.2.3 **Empowering highlights: other matters.**
(A) STANDING. *R v Inland Revenue Commissioners, ex p National Federation of Self-Employed and Small Businesses Ltd* [1982] AC 617 (confirming the relaxation of standing rules and establishing aversion to the standing lacuna <38.2.8>).

(B) HANSARD.*Pepper v Hart*, introducing the use of Hansard to interpret unclear legislation <29.4>.

(C) INJUNCTION/CONTEMPT AND THE CROWN. *M v Home Office* [1994] 1 AC 377, recognising the availability of injunctions against the Crown at domestic law (notwithstanding *R v Secretary of State for Transport, ex p Factortame Ltd* [1990] 2 AC 85 and *British Medical Association v Greater Glasgow Health Board* [1989] AC 1211).

(D) PROTECTIVE COSTS ORDERS. *R (Corner House Research) v Secretary of State for Trade and Industry* [2005] EWCA Civ 192 [2005] 1 WLR 2600, recognising the importance of PCOs in judicial review.

33.3 **"Two-stage" approaches to legal development.**The law often develops using "two-stage" methods, rather than single dramatic steps. One method ("temporary-masking") involves: (1) addressing a problem by stretching an established principle (masking); then later (2) reinterpreting that development as in truth a new principle (unmasking). Another method ("temporary-divergence") involves: (1) addressing a problem by taking a narrow new step which distinguishes the existing orthodoxy (divergence); and then later (2) addressing the divergence by preferring the new and overruling the old orthodoxy (overruling).

33.3.1 **The "temporary masking" dynamic: some examples.**
(A) USING JURISDICTIONAL ERROR TO INTRODUCE ERROR OF LAW. Step one: *Anisminic Ltd v Foreign Compensation Commission* [1969] 2 AC 147 (error of law described in the language of jurisdictional error). Step two: *In re A Company* [1981] AC 374 and *R v Hull University Visitor, ex p Page* [1993] AC 682 (recognising that *Anisminic* introduced error of law independently of whether the error went to jurisdiction).

(B) USING UNREASONABLENESS TO INTRODUCE SUBSTANTIVE FAIRNESS. Step one: *R v Inland Revenue Commissioners, ex p Unilever Plc* [1996] STC 681 (describing unfairness as an abuse of power, inter alia by reference to unreasonableness). Step two: *R v North and East Devon Health Authority, ex p Coughlan* [2001] QB 213 (recognising that substantive unfairness not wedded to a test of unreasonableness).

(C) USING ERROR OF LAW TO INTRODUCE FUNDAMENTAL ERROR OF FACT. Step one: *Edwards v Bairstow* [1956] AC 14 (gross factual error described in the language of error of law). Step two: *R v Criminal Injuries Compensation Board, ex p A* [1999] 2 AC 330, 344G-345C (treating misunderstanding or ignorance of an established and relevant fact as a self-standing ground <49.2>).

(D) USING UNREASONABLENESS TO INTRODUCE PROPORTIONALITY. Step one:*R v Secretary of State for the Home Department, ex p Brind* [1991] 1 AC 696 (proportionality treated as an aspect of unreasonableness). Step two: still under development <P58>.

(E) USING UNREASONABLENESS TO INTRODUCE INCONSISTENCY. Step one:*HTV Ltd v Price Commission* [1976] ICR 170 (treating inconsistency as a facet of unreasonableness). Step two: still under development <P55>.

33.3.2 The "temporary divergence" dynamic.

(A) INJUNCTIONS AGAINST THE CROWN. Step one:*R v Secretary of State for Transport, ex p Factortame Ltd* [1990] 2 AC 85 and *R v Secretary of State for Transport, ex p Factortame Ltd (No.2)* [1991] 1 AC 603 (injunction against the Crown available but only in EC law and not in a·domestic law context). Step two: *M v Home Office* [1994] 1 AC 377 (injunction available against the Crown even in a domestic law context).

(B) SUBSTANTIVE LEGITIMATE EXPECTATION. <54.2>. Step one: *R v North and East Devon Health Authority, ex p Coughlan* [2001] QB 213 (substantive legitimate expectation protected by means of a justification test, but only in certain circumstances, distinguishing *R v Secretary of State for the Home Department, ex p Hargreaves* [1997] 1 WLR 906). Step two: awaited (a future case which would overrule *Hargreaves* and *In re Findlay* [1985] AC 318).

(C) COMMON LAW PROPORTIONALITY. <P58>. Step one: *R v Secretary of State for the Home Department, ex p Simms* [2000] 2 AC 115 (recognising that domestic common law, in effect already applying proportionality though only in a common law rights context). Step two: awaited (a future case which will take the step contemplated in *R (British Civilian Internees - Far Eastern Region) v Secretary of State for Defence* [2003] EWCA Civ 473 [2003] QB 1397 at [32]-[37]).

(D) JUDICIAL REVIEW AND PRIMARY LEGISLATION. Step one:*R (Jackson) v Attorney General* [2005] UKHL 56 [2006] 1 AC 262 (considering whether primary legislation valid for the purposes of the Parliament Acts). Step two: awaited (a future case which will recognise the constitutional limits on valid primary legislation).

33.4 Forecasting.[34] It is dangerous to think (and impossible to believe) that administrative law is at a point of self-satisfied maturity. Identifying the state of flux in the law, and the trend towards empowerment (in the landmark cases), can inspire those who would favour further bold and principled developments. Various areas can be identified as receiving (or needing) incremental groundwork, as candidates for development in the coming years and decades.

33.4.1 A general duty to give reasons. We await a case which would vindicate the approach taken in *R v Lambeth London Borough Council, ex p Walters* (1994) 26 HLR 170 (Sir Louis Blom-Cooper QC: suggesting a general duty to give reasons). For one of countless missed opportunities, see *Stefan v General Medical Council* [1999] 1 WLR 1293.

33.4.2 Proportionality as a self-standing domestic principle. We await cases which will endorse and cement the conclusion of Lord Slynn in *R (Alconbury Developments Ltd) v Secretary of State for the Environment Transport and the Regions* [2001] UKHL 23 [2003] 2

---

[34] Michael Fordham [2003] JR 67, [2004] JR 122 & [2008] JR 66; Richard Clayton QC [2006] JR 9; Rabinder Singh QC [2007] JR 1; Helen Mountfield [2008] JR 1.

AC 295 at [51] (time to recognise proportionality as a conventional ground for review). For the step described but not taken, see *R (British Civilian Internees - Far Eastern Region) v Secretary of State for Defence* [2003] EWCA Civ 473 [2003] QB 1397.

33.4.3 General justification test for substantive legitimate expectation. We await a case which will explain that, on analysis, *R v Secretary of State for the Home Department, ex p Hargreaves* [1997] 1 WLR 906 and *In re Findlay* [1985] AC 318 do not survive in the light of *R v North and East Devon Health Authority, ex p Coughlan* [2001] QB 213. So: if a legitimate expectation of a substantive benefit has arisen, the public authority cannot dishonour it without being able to identify a cogent justification for denying it.

33.4.4 Unjustified inconsistency. We await a case which will analyse the various cases of intervention for inconsistent treatment <P55>, by recognising that inequality/inconsistency requires an objective justification (and not an unreasonableness test). Cf. *Matadeen v Pointu* [1999] 1 AC 98.

33.4.5 International law. We await cases which will provide a principled platform for public law accountability based on international law rights and obligations found in (1) undomesticated instruments and (2) customary international law.

33.4.6 Public interest costs rules. We await the general recognition that private law costs principles and assumptions can operate unjustly and against te public interest in administrative law, and a new and radical approach is called for.

33.4.7 Enhanced disclosure. We await the judicial articulation of clear and robust principles as to how the self-policing duty of candid disclosure by public authorities of documents in judicial review should properly be approached.

33.4.8 Reparation for maladministration. We await a new approach to monetary remedies in administrative law, free from the on-off restrictions of tort law.

33.4.9 Judicial review of unconstitutional primary legislation. We await a constitutional rebalancing, as the Supreme Court recognises the proper function of holding primary legislation to fundamental constitutional principles reflected in the common law.

33.4.10 Proposals for reform.[35] <2.1.5(D)> (key reports).

---

[35] `Silk Survey' [1996] JR 144; Christopher Knight, `Silk Survey - Ten Years On' [2008] JR 184; `Solicitor Survey' [1997] JR 241 & [1998] JR 53.

> **P34 Reviewability.** Judicial review is available only against authorities exercising public law functions.

34.1 Surveying the field
34.2 Principles of reviewability
34.3 Conquests of reviewability

34.1 Surveying the field. In deciding whether a body is or is not amenable to judicial review the focus is on the particular function rather than the status and nature of the body. Nevertheless, a good starting-point for appreciating the scope of reviewability and non-reviewability is to survey some of the bodies whose activities have been treated as falling either side of the line.

34.1.1 Reviewable bodies/functions: some examples. Registered social landlord (*R (Weaver) v London & Quadrant Housing Trust* [2008] EWHC 1377 (Admin)); Professional Conduct Committee of the Bar Council (*R v General Council of the Bar, ex p Percival* [1991] 1 QB 212); a consultant psychiatrist (*R v Dr Caldbeck-Meenan, ex p Clerk to Cleveland Police Authority* [1995] COD 152); managers of private psychiatric hospital (*R (A) v Partnerships in Care Ltd* [2002] EWHC 529 (Admin) [2002] 1 WLR 2610); an approved social worker (*St George's Healthcare NHS Trust v S* [1999] Fam 26); a hospital's Infertility Services Ethical Committee (*R v Ethical Committee of St Mary's Hospital (Manchester), ex p H (or Harriott)* [1988] 1 FLR 512); Code of Practice Committee of the British Pharmaceutical Industry (*R v Code of Practice Committee of the British Pharmaceutical Industry, ex p Professional Counselling Aids Ltd* [1991] 3 Admin LR 697); Broadcasting Complaints Commission (*R v Broadcasting Complaints Commission, ex p Owen* [1985] QB 1153); Independent Broadcasting Authority (*R v IBA, ex p Whitehouse* The Times 4th April 1985); Advertising Standards Authority (*R v Advertising Standards Authority Ltd, ex p Insurance Service Plc* (1990) 2 Admin LR 77); BBC (*R (ProLife Alliance) v British Broadcasting Corporation* [2003] UKHL 23 [2004] 1 AC 185); Monopolies and Mergers Commission (*R v Monopolies & Mergers Commission, ex p Argyll Group Plc* [1986] 1 WLR 763); Panel of Take-overs and Mergers (*R v Panel on Take-overs and Mergers, ex p Datafin Plc* [1987] QB 815); Lautro (*R v Life Assurance and Unit Trust Regulatory Organisation, ex p Ross* [1993] QB 17); Bank of England (*R v Bank of England, ex p Mellstrom* [1995] CLC 232); Director General for Electricity (*R v Director General of Electricity Supply, ex p Redrow Homes (Northern) Ltd* The Times 21st February 1995); Post Office (*R v Post Office, ex p Association of Scientific, Technical & Managerial Staffs* [1981] ICR 76); Central Arbitration Committee (*R v Central Arbitration Committee, ex p Banking Insurance & Finance Union* [1983] ICR 27); Civil Service Appeal Board (*R v Civil Service Appeal Board, ex p Bruce* [1989] 2 All ER 907); Army Board (*R v Army Board of the Defence Council, ex p Anderson* [1992] QB 169); District Valuer (*R v Kidderminster District Valuer, ex p Powell* (1992) 4 Admin LR 193); regional Electricity Board (*R v Midlands Electricity Board, ex p Busby; R v Midlands Electricity Board, ex p Williamson* The Times 28th October 1987); university with no Visitor (*R (Galligan) v University of Oxford* [2001] EWHC Admin 965 [2002] ELR 494); visitors to the Inns of Court (*R v Visitors to the Inns of Court, ex p Calder & Persaud* [1994] QB 1); trustees of a Catholic Diocese (*R v Trustees of the Roman Catholic Diocese of Westminster, ex p Andrews* (1990) 2 Admin LR 142); local ombudsman (*R v Local Commissioner for Administration for the South etc, ex p Eastleigh Borough Council* [1988] QB 855); Parliamentary ombudsman (*R v Parliamentary Commissioner for Administration, ex p Dyer* [1994] 1 WLR 621); Director of GCHQ (*R v Director, Government Communications Headquarters, ex p Hodges* [1988] COD 123); Magistrates' Court Committee (*R v Avon Magistrates' Courts Committee, ex p Bath Law Society* [1988] QB 409); state school governors (*R v Board of Governors of Stoke Newington School, ex p M* [1994] ELR 131); city technology college (*R v Governors of Haberdashers' Aske's Hatcham College Trust, ex p T*

[1995] ELR 350); Supreme Court taxing office (*R v Supreme Court Taxing Office, ex p Singh & Co* (1995) 7 Admin LR 849); British Coal (*R v British Coal Corporation, ex p Ibstock Building Products Ltd* [1995] Env LR 277); Lord Chancellor (*R v Lord Chancellor, ex p Stockler* (1996) 8 Admin LR 590); Registrar of Births, Deaths and Marriages (*R v Registrar General of Births, Deaths & Marriages, ex p Minhas* [1977] QB 1); Industrial Tribunal (*R v Industrial Tribunal, ex p Cotswold Collotype Co Ltd* [1979] ICR 190); Lands Tribunal (*R v Lands Tribunal, ex p City of London Corporation* [1982] 1 WLR 258); VAT Tribunal (*R v Value Added Tax Tribunal, ex p Happer* [1982] 1 WLR 1261); Independent Committee supervising premium rate telephone services (*R v Independent Committee for the Supervision of Telephone Information Services, ex p Firstcode Limited* [1993] COD 325); PIA ombudsman (*R (Mooyer) v Personal Investment Authority Ombudsman Bureau Ltd* [2001] EWHC Admin 247 at [8]); independent school regarding assisted place (*R v Cobham Hall School, ex p S* [1998] ELR 389); National Trust (*Scott v National Trust for Places of Historic Interest or Natural Beauty* [1998] 2 All ER 705, 716f-h, 712d-e); privatised water company exercising statutory powers (*R v Northumbrian Water Ltd, ex p Newcastle and North Tyneside Health Authority* [1999] Env LR 715); airport operator (*R v Fairoaks Airport Ltd, ex p Roads* [1999] COD 168); airport coordinator (*R v Airport Coordination Ltd, ex p Aravco Ltd* [1999] EuLR 939); Secretary of the Central Office of Employment Tribunals (*R v Secretary of the Central Office of the Employment Tribunals, ex p Public Concern at Work* [2000] COD 302); London Metal Exchange (*R v London Metal Exchange Ltd, ex p Albatros Warehousing BV* 31st March 2000 unrep.); voluntary adoption agency (*R (Gunn-Russo) v Nugent Care Society* [2001] EWHC Admin 566 [2001] UKHRR 1320); London Underground (*R (Hammerton) v London Underground Ltd* [2002] EWHC 2307 (Admin) at [184]); farmers' markets operator (*R (Beer) v Hampshire Farmers Market Ltd* [2003] EWCA Civ 1056 [2004] 1 WLR 233); welsh assembly (*R (South Wales Sea Fisheries Committee) v National Assembly for Wales* [2001] EWHC Admin 1162); Independent Adjudicator (*R (Siborurema) v Office of the Independent Adjudicator* [2007] EWCA Civ 1365).

34.1.2 **Non-reviewable bodies/functions: some examples.** BBC's disciplinary tribunal (*R v BBC, ex p Lavelle* [1983] 1 WLR 23); the National Joint Council for the Craft of Dental Technicians (*R v National Joint Council for the Craft of Dental Technicians (Disputes Committee), ex p Neate* [1953] 1 QB 704); an official of the Post Office (*R v Post Office, ex p Byrne* [1975] ICR 221); the Royal Life Saving Society (*R v Royal Life Saving Society, ex p Heather Rose Mary Howe* [1990] COD 440); the IBA, acting under Articles of Association (*R v Independent Broadcasting Authority, ex p Rank Organisation Plc* The Times 14th March 1986); the Jockey Club (*R v Disciplinary Committee of the Jockey Club, ex p Aga Khan* [1993] 1 WLR 909); the Football Association (*R v Football Association Ltd, ex p Football League Ltd* [1993] 2 All ER 833); the Chief Rabbi (*R v Chief Rabbi, ex p Wachmann* [1992] 1 WLR 1036); the Insurance Ombudsman (*R v Insurance Ombudsman, ex p Aegon Life Insurance Ltd* [1994] CLC 88); the PIA ombudsman's voluntary jurisdiction (*R (Mooyer) v Personal Investment Authority Ombudsman Bureau Ltd* [2001] EWHC Admin 247); independent school governors (*R v Fernhill Manor School, ex p A* [1994] ELR 67); Registrar of Criminal Appeals (*R v Registrar of Criminal Appeals, ex p Pegg* [1993] COD 192); Lloyds when regulating members (*R (West) v Lloyds of London* [2004] EWCA Civ 506 [2004] 3 All ER 251); Channel Tunnel Group Ltd (*R v Eurotunnel Developments Ltd, ex p Stephens* (1997) 73 P & CR 1); Parliamentary Commissioner for Standards (*R v Parliamentary Commissioner for Standards, ex p Al Fayed* [1998] 1 WLR 669); the Showman's Guild's Appeal Tribunal (*R v Showman's Guild of Great Britain, ex p Print* 31st July 1997 unrep.); Court of the Chief Rabbi (*R v London Beth Din (Court of the Chief Rabbi), ex p Michael Bloom* [1998] COD 131); Federation of Communication Services (*R v Panel of the Federation of Communication Services Ltd, ex p Kubis* (1999) 11 Admin LR 43); Great Western Trains granting an exclusive taxi franchise (*R v Great Western Trains Co Ltd, ex p Frederick* [1998] COD 239); Head of the Administrative

Court Office's decision to refuse to release notes (*R v Lord Chancellor's Department, ex p O'Toole* [1998] COD 269); non-maintained school with no formal governmental arrangement (*R v Muntham House School, ex p R* [2000] LGR 255); local authority's refusal to sell land (*R v Bolsover District Council, ex p Pepper* [2001] LGR 43); ABTA's disciplinary decisions (*R v Association of British Travel Agents, ex p Sunspell Ltd* [2001] ACD 88); charitable housing association providing residential home, acting under arrangement with local authority (*R (Heather) v Leonard Cheshire Foundation* [2002] EWCA Civ 366 [2002] 2 All ER 936); British Council accrediting language schools (*R (Oxford Study Centre Ltd) v British Council* [2001] EWHC Admin 207 [2001] ELR 803); decision not to agree to structured settlement in meeting damages judgment (*R (Hopley) v Liverpool Health Authority* [2002] EWHC 1723 (Admin)); decision to terminate secondment to National Crime Squad (*R (Tucker) v Director General of the National Crime Squad* [2003] EWCA Civ 2); Medical Defence Union (*R (Moreton) v Medical Defence Union Ltd* [2006] EWHC 1948 (Admin)).

34.1.3 Reviewability arguable/left open. *R v Press Complaints Commission, ex p Stewart-Brady* (1997) 9 Admin LR 274, 277F and *R (Ford) v Press Complaints Commission* 31st July 2001 unrep. at [11] (arguable that PCC reviewable); *R v National Health Service Executive, ex p Ingoldby* [1999] COD 167 (arguable that panel set up by NHS Trust amenable to judicial review despite lack of statutory source); *Modahl v British Athletic Federation Ltd* 28th July 1997 unrep. (CA) (Lord Woolf MR, commenting that it "could well be the case" that judicial review would have been available of the British Athletics Federation); *Ex p Scott* [1998] 1 WLR 226 (arguable that National Trust a statutory body exercising public functions, but no jurisdiction where challenge to its management of trust property, absent authorisation from the Charity Commissioners or the Chancery Division), cf. *Scott v National Trust for Places of Historic Interest or Natural Beauty* [1998] 2 All ER 705, 716f-h, 712d-e; *R v Bishop of Stafford, ex p Owen* [2001] ACD 83 (Bishop's decision not to extend rector's term of office probably amenable to judicial review); *R v British Standards Institute, ex p Dorgard* [2001] ACD 86 (British Standards Institute arguably reviewable, but not in relation to complaint arising out of an agreement); *R (W) v Governors of B School* [2001] LGR 561 (CA) at [34] (posing the question whether "a trade union may fall to be treated as a public body amenable to the judicial review jurisdiction") (HL is at *R (L (A Minor)) v Governors of J School* [2003] UKHL 9 [2003] 2 AC 633).

34.1.4 "Public authority" for other purposes. <9.4.3> (HRA public authority); Freedom of Information Act 2000 s.3 and Sch 1 (defining "public authority" by reference to a list of bodies); *R v Natji* [2002] EWCA Crim 271 [2002] 1 WLR 2337 ("public authority" for the purposes of the Prevention of Corruption Act 1916 and "public body" under the Public Bodies Corrupt Practices Act 1889).

34.2 Principles of reviewability.[36] The voluminous case-law provides a host of working examples applying a series of interrelated principles regarding reviewability, with perhaps these main lessons: (1) treat no single factor as determinative; (2) look especially for statutory or governmental underpinning; and (3) focus on the substance and effects of the function being discharged.

34.2.1 Reviewability in a nutshell. *R v London Beth Din (Court of the Chief Rabbi), ex p Michael Bloom* [1998] COD 131 (see transcript) (Lightman J: "The stage presently reached is

---

[36] This paragraph in a previous edition, and the principles set out below, were cited in *Re Sheridan Millennium Ltd* [2007] NIQB 27 at [19]

that for a decision to be judicially reviewable (so far as relevant) it must be a decision reached by a body exercising a statutory or (*de facto* or *de jure*) governmental function; and [judicial review] is not available in case of a decision by a body whose legal authority arises from some consensual submission to its jurisdiction and has no such function"); *R (Hopley) v Liverpool Health Authority* [2002] EWHC 1723 (Admin) at [39] (Pitchford J: "there is a need to identify: first, whether the defendant is a public body exercising statutory powers ...; second, whether the function being performed in exercise of those powers was a private or public one; and third, whether the defendant was performing a public duty owed to the claimant in the particular circumstances under consideration"); *R (Tucker) v Director General of the National Crime Squad* [2003] EWCA Civ 2 at [24]-[25] (applying the "criteria" from *Hopley*).

34.2.2 **Principle 1: no litmus test of reviewability.** *R (Tucker) v Director General of the National Crime Squad* [2003] EWCA Civ 2 at [13] (Scott Baker LJ: "The boundary between public law and private law is not capable of precise definition, and whether a decision has a sufficient public law element to justify the intervention of the Administrative Court by judicial review is often as much a matter of feel, as deciding whether any particular criteria are met"), [14] ("The starting point ... is that there is no single test or criterion by which the question can be determined"); *R (Beer) v Hampshire Farmers Market Ltd* [2003] EWCA Civ 1056 [2004] 1 WLR 233 at [12] (Dyson LJ: "It is clear from the authorities that there is no simple litmus test of amenability to judicial review"); *R v Panel on Take-overs and Mergers, ex p Datafin Plc* [1987] QB 815, 838E ("In all the reports it is possible to find enumerations of factors giving rise to the jurisdiction, but it is a fatal error to regard the presence of all those factors as essential or as being exclusive of other factors"); *R v Derbyshire County Council, ex p Noble* [1990] ICR 808, 814F ("there is no universal test which will be applicable to all circumstances which will indicate clearly and beyond peradventure as to when judicial review is or is not available"); *Poplar Housing and Regeneration Community Association Ltd v Donoghue* [2001] EWCA Civ 595 [2002] QB 48 at [66] ("there is no clear demarcation line which can be drawn between public and private bodies and functions. In a borderline case, such as this, the decision is very much one of fact and degree"); *R v Legal Aid Board, ex p Donn & Co (a Firm)* [1996] 3 All ER 1, 11h (matter of overall impression); *R v National Health Service Executive, ex p Ingoldby* [1999] COD 167 (categories of public law reviewability not closed).

34.2.3 **Principle 2: emphasis is on function not office/status.** *R v Supreme Court Taxing Office, ex p Singh & Co* (1995) 7 Admin LR 849, 853E (Latham J: "the question of jurisdiction [on judicial review] has to be resolved by looking at the function being performed by the person or body whose decision is being challenged, and not the office held by that person, or the general description of that body"); *Leech v Deputy Governor of Parkhurst Prison* [1988] AC 533, 583B-C (Lord Oliver: "the susceptibility of a decision to the supervision of the courts must depend, in the ultimate analysis, upon the nature and consequences of the decision and not upon the personality or individual circumstances of the person called upon to make the decision"); *R v Jockey Club, ex p RAM Racecourses* [1993] 2 All ER 225, 246j (Simon Brown J: "merely because some public body is amenable to judicial review it by no means follows that it is reviewable in all its functions"); *R v British Broadcasting Corporation, ex p McAliskey* [1994] COD 498 (Buckley J: suggestion that a private body used to implement government policy would be reviewable as to the application of that policy); *R (Hopley) v Liverpool Health Authority* [2002] EWHC 1723 (Admin) at [48] (court "concerned primarily with the quality and purpose of the function which the [defendant] was performing at the material time"); *R v Northumbrian Water Ltd, ex p Able UK Ltd* [1996] 2 PLR 28 (privatised water utility exercising statutory powers); <34.2.7> (public function); <9.4.3> ("public authority" for purposes of HRA).

34.2.4 **Principle 3: whether reviewability statutorily-recognised/precluded.** Supreme Court Act 1981 s.8(1) (High Court judges are reviewable "when exercising the jurisdiction of the

Crown Court": see *R v Central Criminal Court, ex p Director of Serious Fraud Office* [1993] 1 WLR 949, 954H) and s.27(3) (Crown Courts reviewable other than in matters "relating to trial on indictment"); County Courts Act 1984 ss.83-84 (which "give explicit recognition to the function of the Divisional Court enabling it to review a determination in a county court and to deal with it by the issue of one of the prerogative writs": see *R v Leeds County Court, ex p Morris* [1990] 1 QB 523 per Watkins LJ at 530E); *R v Acting Returning Officer for Devon (etc), ex p Sanders* [1994] COD 497 (Parliament's clear intention that pre-voting judicial review precluded, the intended recourse to law being a post-voting election petition); cf. <P28> (ouster); <36.2> (exclusive alternative remedy).

34.2.5 **Principle 4: jurisdiction is not conferred by parties' agreement/consent.** *R v Durham City Council, ex p Robinson* The Times 31st January 1992 (parties cannot create jurisdiction by agreement); *R v Knightsbridge Crown Court, ex p Dunne* [1994] 1 WLR 296, 301B; *R v Walsall Metropolitan Borough Council, ex p Yapp* [1994] ICR 528, 530F-G; cf. *R v Secretary of State for Foreign & Commonwealth Affairs, ex p Indian Association of Alberta* [1982] QB 892, 920E-G (matter "only justiciable as a matter of concession by the court, faced with the wish of the [claimants] to have it decided and of the [defendants'] non-objection to its decision").

34.2.6 **Principle 5: statutory power/underpinning indicates reviewability.** *Mohit v Director of Public Prosecutions of Mauritius* [2006] UKPC 20 [2006] 1 WLR 3343 at [20] (presumption that statutory function reviewable absent compelling reason); *R v Panel on Take-overs and Mergers, ex p Datafin Plc* [1987] QB 815, 847A-B (judicial review available where "the source of power is a statute, or subordinate legislation under a statute"); *Leech v Deputy Governor of Parkhurst Prison* [1988] AC 533, 561G-H ("where any person or body exercises a power conferred by statute which affects the rights or legitimate expectations of citizens and is of a kind which the law requires to be exercised in accordance with the rules of natural justice, the court has jurisdiction to review the exercise of that power"); *R v Secretary of State for the Home Department, ex p Doody* [1994] 1 AC 531, 560D ("where an Act of Parliament confers an administrative power there is a presumption that it will be exercised in a manner which is fair in all the circumstances"); *R (A) v Partnerships in Care Ltd* [2002] EWHC 529 (Admin) [2002] 1 WLR 2610 (managers of private psychiatric hospital reviewable because sufficient statutory underpinning); *R (Siborurema) v Office of the Independent Adjudicator* [2007] EWCA Civ 1365 at [49] (process "set up by statute"); *R v Leeds City Council, ex p Cobleigh* [1997] COD 69 (local authority's decision refusing to sell land not reviewable due to absence of statutory underpinning), cf. <35.2.4> (decisions relating to land); *R v Cripps, ex p Muldoon* [1984] QB 68, 87B-F (statutory tribunals reviewable unless it "should properly be regarded in all the circumstances as having a status so closely equivalent to the High Court that the exercise of power of judicial review by the High Court is for that reason inappropriate").

34.2.7 **Principle 6: public function indicates reviewability, consensual powers not.** *R (Beer) v Hampshire Farmers Market Ltd* [2003] EWCA Civ 1056 [2004] 1 WLR 233 at [16] (Dyson LJ: "unless the source of power clearly provides the answer, the question whether the decision of a body is amenable to judicial review requires a careful consideration of the nature of the power and function that has been exercised to see whether the decision has a sufficient public element, flavour or character to bring it within the purview of public law"); *R v Panel on Take-overs and Mergers, ex p Datafin Plc* [1987] QB 815, 838E-F (Sir John Donaldson MR: "Possibly the only essential elements are what can be described as a public element, which can take many different forms, and the exclusion from the jurisdiction of bodies whose sole source of power is a consensual submission to its jurisdiction"); <35.2.1> (consensual bodies/powers); *R v Disciplinary Committee of the Jockey Club, ex p Massingberd-Mundy* [1993] 2 All ER 207, 219a-b (*Datafin* "likely to provide the surest answer"); *R v Association of British Travel Agents, ex p Sunspell Ltd* [2001] ACD 88 (no public or governmental element, rather powers deriving from contractual relationship); *R v Criminal Injuries Compensation Board, ex p Lain* [1967] 2 QB 864, 882 ("[in early cases] the only constant limits throughout were that [the body] was performing a public duty"); *R v London Metal Exchange Ltd, ex p Albatros Warehousing BV* 31st March 2000 unrep. at [23] (can be public law function even though contractual relationship); *R v Lloyd's of London, ex p Briggs* (1993) 5 Admin LR 698, 714G-715B (no sufficient public law element in relationship between Lloyd's and Names); *R v Wear Valley District Council, ex p Binks* [1985] 2 All ER 699, 703j (sufficient "public law element" in licensing market traders, whether for a public market or an informal market); *Mercury Energy Ltd v Electricity Corporation of New Zealand Ltd* [1994] 1 WLR 521, 526C-D (reviewable "state enterprise" with "shares ... held by ministers" and which "carries on its business in the interests of the public"); *R (A1 Veg Ltd) v Hounslow London Borough Council* [2003] EWHC 3112 (Admin) [2004] LGR 536 at [30] (sufficiently public function in regulating market under statutory powers); *R (Weaver) v London & Quadrant Housing Trust* [2008] EWHC 1377 (Admin) (registered social landlord managing housing stock permeated by state control).

34.2.8 **Principle 7: governmental function indicates reviewability.** *R (West) v Lloyds of London* [2004] EWCA Civ 506 [2004] 3 All ER 251[37] (Lloyds not governmental); *R v Disciplinary Committee of the Jockey Club, ex p Aga Khan* [1993] 1 WLR 909, 923H ("not ... woven into any system of governmental control of horse racing"; "in no sense governmental"), 931D ("the power needs to be identified as governmental in nature"); *R (Moreton) v Medical Defence Union Ltd* [2006] EWHC 1948 (Admin) (MDU not having governmental function nor woven into fabric of public regulation); *R v Governors of Haberdashers' Aske's Hatcham College Trust, ex p T* [1995] ELR 350, 357E-361H (college's existence and essential characteristics deriving from exercise by government of statutory power); *R v Panel on Take-overs and Mergers, ex p Datafin Plc* [1987] QB 815, 835F (panel set up as "an act of government"); *R v Criminal Injuries Compensation Board, ex p Lain* [1967] 2 QB 864, 881B (CICB "set up by executive government"), 884E-F ("established by acts of government"); *R v Showman's Guild of Great Britain, ex p Print* 31st July 1997 unrep. (Showman's Guild having no governmental underpinning and not exercising governmental powers); *R v London Beth Din (Court of the Chief Rabbi), ex p Michael Bloom* [1998] COD 131 (need for a "governmental function"); *R v Muntham House School, ex p R* [2000] LGR 255 (school not reviewable where no direct funding from government or formal government arrangement regarding admission or exclusion); *R (Beer) v Hampshire Farmers Market Ltd* [2003] EWCA Civ 1056 [2004] 1 WLR 233 (company responsible for farmers markets amenable to judicial review even though its functions not woven into a system of governmental control, because public function and having stepped into the shoes of the local authority).

34.2.9 **Principle 8: a legislative "but for" test suggests reviewability.** *R v Advertising Standards Authority Ltd, ex p Insurance Service Plc* (1990) 2 Admin LR 77, 86C-D (ASA "clearly exercising a public function which, if the Authority did not exist, would no doubt be exercised by the Director General of Fair Trading"); *R v Chief Rabbi, ex p Wachmann* [1992] 1 WLR 1036, 1041F-1042A (asking whether: "were there no self-regulatory body in existence, Parliament would almost inevitably intervene to control the activity in question"); *R v Panel on Take-overs and Mergers, ex p Datafin Plc* [1987] QB 815, 835G ("No one could have been in the least surprised if the panel had been instituted and operated under the direct authority of statute law"); *R v Football Association Ltd, ex p Football League Ltd* [1993] 2 All ER 833, 848j ("[no] evidence to suggest that, if the FA did not exist the state would intervene to create a public body to perform its functions"); *R v Disciplinary Committee of the Jockey Club, ex p Aga Khan* [1993] 1 WLR 909, 932B (Hoffmann LJ: "there is nothing to suggest that if the Jockey

---

[37] Nicholas Jordan [2004] JR 286.

Club had not voluntarily assumed the regulation of racing, the government would feel obliged or inclined to set up a statutory body for the purpose"), cf. 923F-G (Sir Thomas Bingham MR: "if the Jockey Club did not regulate this activity the government would probably be driven to create a public body to do so").

34.2.10 **Principle 9: reviewability focuses on substance, not form.**
(A) REALITY AND NOT JUST SOURCE. *Council of Civil Service Unions v Minister for the Civil Service* [1985] AC 374, 407F (Lord Scarman: "the controlling factor ... is not its source but its subject-matter"); *R v Criminal Injuries Compensation Board, ex p Lain* [1967] 2 QB 864, 884B (reviewability never "dependent upon the source of the tribunal's authority to decide ... except where such authority is derived solely from agreement of parties to the determination"); *R v Panel on Take-overs and Mergers, ex p Datafin Plc* [1987] QB 815, 838H-839A (disappointing "if the courts could not recognise the realities of executive power and allowed their vision to be clouded by the subtlety and sometimes complexity of the way in which it can be exerted"); <34.2.3> (function and not office/status).
(B) CONSEQUENCES/RIGHTS/EXPECTATIONS.*Council of Civil Service Unions v Minister for the Civil Service* [1985] AC 374, 408F-409C (Lord Diplock, suggesting that a decision "susceptible to judicial review" would involve a decision-maker "empowered by public law ... to make decisions" leading to "consequences which affect some person (or body of persons) ... either (a) by altering rights or obligations of that person which are enforceable by or against him in private law; or (b) by depriving him of some benefit or advantage"); *Leech v Deputy Governor of Parkhurst Prison* [1988] AC 533, 561G-562B (Lord Bridge: "where any person or body exercises a power conferred by statute which affects the rights or legitimate expectations of citizens and is of a kind which the law requires to be exercised in accordance with the rules of natural justice, the court has jurisdiction to review the exercise of that power"); *R (Hopley) v Liverpool Health Authority* [2002] EWHC 1723 (Admin) at [56]-[57] (matter treated as non-reviewable because no decision affecting rights or obligations); *R v Panel on Take-overs and Mergers, ex p Datafin Plc* [1987] QB 815, 847C (asking whether "the exercise of its functions [has] public law consequences"); *R (Molinaro) v Kensington and Chelsea Royal London Borough Council* [2001] EWHC Admin 896 [2002] LGR 336 at [69] ("Public law bodies should not be free to abuse their power by invoking the principle that private individuals can act unfairly or abusively without legal redress"); *R (Nurse Prescribers Ltd) v Secretary of State for Health* [2004] EWHC 403 (Admin) at [68] (preferring the "public function" test to the *Molinaro* approach); *R (Tucker) v Director General of the National Crime Squad* [2003] EWCA Civ 2 at [18] (decision not reviewable even though no private law remedy either).

34.3 **Conquests of reviewability.**As well as trying to extract principles and themes from the case-law, another way to understand reviewability is to consider the way judicial review has claimed new territories, de-mystifying public power and breaking down old barriers.

34.3.1 **The expanding jurisdiction: general.** *R v Criminal Injuries Compensation Board, ex p Lain* [1967] 2 QB 864, 882A (Parker CJ: "the exact limits of the ancient remedy by way of certiorari have never been and ought not to be specifically defined. They have varied from time to time being extended to meet changing conditions"); *R v Jockey Club, ex p RAM Racecourses* [1993] 2 All ER 225, 248c-d (judicial review as "a dynamic area of law, well able to embrace new situations as justice requires"); *R v Visitors to the Inns of Court, ex p Calder & Persaud* [1994] QB 1, 41H ("Novelty is not ground the courts should fear to tread, in this or any other appropriate case"); *R v National Health Service Executive, ex p Ingoldby* [1999] COD 167 (categories of public law not closed);*R v Panel on Take-overs and Mergers, ex p Datafin Plc* [1987] QB 815 at 838C-D (Sir John Donaldson MR: "The Criminal Injuries Compensation Board, in the form which it then took, was an administrative novelty. Accordingly it would have been impossible to find a precedent for the exercise of the supervisory jurisdiction of the court which fitted the facts. Nevertheless the court not only asserted its jurisdiction, but further asserted that it was a jurisdiction which was adaptable thereafter. This process has since been taken further in *O'Reilly v Mackman* [1983] 2 AC 237, 279 (per Lord Diplock) by deleting any requirement that the body should have a duty to act judicially; in *Council of Civil Service Unions v Minister for the Civil Service* [1985] AC 374 by extending it to a person exercising purely prerogative power; and in *Gillick v West Norfolk and Wisbech Area Health Authority* [1986] AC 112, where Lord Fraser of Tullybelton, at p.163F and Lord Scarman, at p.178F-H expressed the view obiter that judicial review would extend to guidance circulars issued by a department of state without any specific authority").

34.3.2 "Administrative" (not just "judicial") functions. *Nakkuda Ali v Jayaratne* [1951] AC 66, 77 (Lord Radcliffe: unless defendant "is acting judicially or quasi-judicially ... then it would not be according to law that his decision should be amenable to review"), 78 ("a general principle that is beyond dispute"); *R v Criminal Injuries Compensation Board, ex p Lain* [1967] 2 QB 864, 882D-E (judicial review available "provided always that it has a duty to act judicially"); *Leech v Deputy Governor of Parkhurst Prison* [1988] AC 533, 575F-G (Lord Oliver: "It is clear, in particular, since the decision of your Lordships' House in *Ridge v Baldwin* [1964] AC 40, that the susceptibility of a decision to the supervisory jurisdiction of the court does not rest upon some fancied distinction between decisions which are `administrative' and decisions which are `judicial' of `quasi-judicial'"); *R v Hillingdon London Borough Council, ex p Royco Homes Ltd* [1974] QB 720, 728 (Lord Widgery, referring to the judicial "obstacle ... cleared away" by Lord Reid); *O'Reilly v Mackman* [1983] 2 AC 237, 279C-G (Lord Diplock: "subtle distinctions ... destroyed" by Reid); *R v Secretary of State for the Home Department, ex p Bugdaycay* [1987] AC 514, 535F-H (judicial review of decisions although they "are administrative and discretionary rather than judicial and imperative").

34.3.3 The Crown/prerogative powers. *Council of Civil Service Unions v Minister for the Civil Service* [1985] AC 374 (judicial review of prerogative power); *M v Home Office* [1994] 1 AC 377, 416C (describing the "numerous cases where prerogative orders, including orders of prohibition and mandamus, have been made against ministers"); *R (Bancoult) v Secretary of State for Foreign & Commonwealth Affairs* [2007] EWCA Civ 498 [2008] QB 365 at [35] and [107] (Order in Council reviewable although prerogative power of colonial governance), [111] (potential reviewability of all exercises of royal prerogative); *Mohit v Director of Public Prosecutions of Mauritius* [2006] UKPC 20 [2006] 1 WLR 3343 at [21] (explaining position of Attorney-General by reference to prerogative powers); *R (Charlton) v Secretary of State for Education and Skills* [2005] EWHC 1378 (Admin) [2005] 2 FCR 603 at [114]-[115] (discussing judicial review of prerogative powers); *R v Secretary of State for the Home Department, ex p Fire Brigades Union* [1995] 2 AC 513, 553D ("judicial review is as applicable to decisions taken under prerogative powers as to decisions taken under statutory powers save to the extent that the legality of the exercise of certain prerogative powers (eg. treaty-making) may not be justiciable"); *Lewis v Attorney-General of Jamaica* [2001] 2 AC 50 (prerogative of mercy reviewable for procedural unfairness); *R v Secretary of State for Foreign and Commonwealth Affairs, ex p Everett* [1989] 1 QB 811 (direct prerogative power); <35.1.5> (special prerogative powers and non-justiciable issues).

34.3.4 Other non-statutory functions. *R v National Joint Council for the Craft of Dental Technicians (Disputes Committee), ex p Neate* [1953] 1 QB 704, 706 (Lord Goddard CJ: "unless there is a body set up by statute and which has duties conferred on it by statute so that the parties are bound to resort to it ... it would be a very novel proceeding indeed if we issued these prerogative writs to it"), 709 (Croom-Johnson LJ: a body is "in no sense a public body ... [whose] authority does not depend upon any statutory jurisdiction"); *R v Panel on Take-overs and Mergers, ex p Datafin Plc* [1987] QB 815 (judicial review of non-statutory body); *R v Entry*

Clearance Officer Bombay, ex p Amin [1983] 2 AC 818, 837G (judicial review albeit "no express statutory basis"); *Gillick v West Norfolk and Wisbech Area Health Authority* [1986] AC 112, 192E-F (judicial review of circular with "no statutory force whatever") and 193G-H ("non-statutory in form"); *R v Norfolk County Council, ex p M* [1989] QB 619, 622B (operation of child abuse registers, having "no statutory authority, but the basis of their operation has been prescribed by a series of departmental circulars").

34.3.5 **Delegated legislation.** *R (Norris) v Secretary of State for the Home Department* [2006] EWHC 280 (Admin) [2006] 3 All ER 1011 at [42] (jurisdiction to review subordinate legislation laid before Parliament); *R (C) v Secretary of State for Justice* [2008] EWCA Civ 882 (delegated legislation not in a "specially protected position"); *R (Asif Javed) v Secretary of State for the Home Department* [2001] EWCA Civ 789 [2002] QB 129 at [37] (referring to "the right and the duty of the court to review the legality of subordinate legislation"); *Toussaint v Attorney General of Saint Vincent & the Grenadines* [2007] UKPC 48 [2007] 1 WLR 2825 at [18] (judicial review of subordinate legislation approved by Parliament); *Howker v Secretary of State for Work and Pensions* [2002] EWCA Civ 1623 (regulations invalid for breach of statutorily-required procedure), [38] ("every member of the public adversely affected by a new regulation is entitled to challenge the lawfulness of that regulation on proper grounds"); <13.5.4(A)> (benevolent approach to delegated legislation).

34.3.6 **Other matters: whether reviewable.** See generally <P35>.

34.3.7 **Primary legislation: extent of judicial review of Acts of Parliament.** <35.1.3>.

> **P35 Non-reviewability.** Certain matters are beyond the reach of judicial review because "private", or even though "public".

    35.1 Special functions and immunity from review
    35.2 Private law matters

35.1 Special functions and immunity from review

Certain bodies or functions, although properly regarded as "public", have nevertheless traditionally been recognised as not amenable to judicial review (and therefore beyond the Courts' supervisory reach). It is unlikely that there are many true immunities: an appropriate issue of public law should in principle be justiciable.

35.1.1 **Judicial review of the High Court.** *R v Secretary of State for the Home Department, ex p Bulger* [2001] EWHC Admin 119 at [13] ("review has never been possible in relation to the decisions of High Court Judges sitting as such ... even when the High Court Judge is not actually sitting in court, if his decision is made as a High Court Judge"), [14]-[17] (leaving open whether judge reviewable where setting life tariff); *In re A Company* [1981] AC 374, 392G-H ("the High Court is ... a superior court of record. It was not, in the past, subject to control by prerogative writ or order, nor today is it subject to the judicial review which has taken their place"); *R v Manchester Crown Court, ex p Williams & Simpson* (1990) 2 Admin LR 817 (decision of High Court judge on application for leave to prefer voluntary bill of indictment a function conferred upon the Judge in his capacity as a High Court Judge, not amenable to judicial review); Supreme Court Act 1981 s.8(1) (High Court judges are reviewable "when exercising the jurisdiction of the Crown Court": see *R v Central Criminal Court, ex p Director of Serious Fraud Office* [1993] 1 WLR 949, 954H); *R (Law Society) v Master of the Rolls* [2005] EWHC 146 (Admin) [2005] 1 WLR 2033 (Master of the Rolls reviewable when acting in appellate capacity); *R (Okandeji) v Bow Street Magistrates Court* [2005] EWHC 2925 (Admin) [2006] 1 WLR 674 (Extradition Act 2003 s.104(7) meaning district judge extradition decision deemed to be decision of the High Court, so not amenable to judicial review); *R v Lord Chancellor, ex p Stockler* (1996) 8 Admin LR 590 (judicial review of Lord Chancellor instructing or permitting acting judge to hear part-heard case); *G v Secretary of State for the Home Department* [2004] EWCA Civ 265 [2004] 1 WLR 1349 at [21] (leaving open whether judicial review of Special Immigration Appeals Commission available despite its Court status).

35.1.2 **Judicial review of the Attorney-General.** *R v Solicitor-General, ex p Taylor* (1996) 8 Admin LR 206, 218F-G (Attorney-General's "unique constitutional position" meaning even his statutory powers not amenable to judicial review); *Gouriet v Union of Post Office Workers* [1978] AC 435, 487G-488G (Attorney-General's powers "not subject to ... control and supervision by the courts"); *Mohit v Director of Public Prosecutions of Mauritius* [2006] UKPC 20 [2006] 1 WLR 3343 at [14] (*Gouriet* the current state of English law); *R v Attorney-General, ex p Ferrante* The Independent 3rd April 1995 (no grounds for impugning decision refusing to authorise application to High Court to re-open coroner's inquest); *R v Attorney-General, ex p Rockall* [2000] 1 WLR 882 (permission for judicial review of Attorney-General's decision not to withdraw consent to a prosecution refused because no arguable ground).

35.1.3 **Judicial review of primary legislation.** *R (Countryside Alliance) v Attorney General* [2007] UKHL 52 [2008] 1 AC 719 at [134] (subject to HRA and EC law and "provided always that it follows a proper parliamentary process", Parliament "can do whatever it likes"); *R (Professional Contractors Ltd) v Commissioners of Inland Revenue* [2001] EWHC Admin 236 [2001] EuLR 514 at [54] ("Whereas a statutory provision contained in an Act of Parliament cannot be normally challenged before the courts, nevertheless not only can its compatibility with human rights now be considered as a result of the Human Rights Act 1998, but its very legality can, and indeed must, be considered by the national courts if it conflicts with a requirement of the [EC] Treaty"); *R (Southall) v Secretary of State for Foreign and Commonwealth Affairs* [2003] EWCA Civ 1002 at [10] ("so far no court in the last century and more has set aside any provision of an Act of Parliament as being unlawful save in the circumstances set out in the European Communities Act"); *Hoffmann-La Roche (F) & Co AG v Secretary of State for Trade and Industry* [1975] AC 295, 349B-C ("the courts of law could not declare that an Act of Parliament was ultra vires"); *Pickin v British Railways Board* [1974] AC 765, 798F ("the courts in this country have no power to declare enacted law to be invalid"); <8.3.1(A)> (primary legislation declared incompatible with EC law); <9.3.11> (HRA declaration of incompatibility); *R v Secretary of State for the Home Department, ex p Fire Brigades Union* [1995] 2 AC 513 (judicial review of failure to bring Act into force); *R v Secretary of State for Education and Employment, ex p Liverpool Hope University College* [2001] EWCA Civ 362 [2001] ELR 552 (judicial review of statutory instrument bringing Act of Parliament into force); *R (British Aggregates Associates) v Her Majesty's Treasury* [2002] EWHC 926 (Admin) [2002] EuLR 394 at [138]-[140] (measures to implement primary legislation treated as justiciable); *R (Jackson) v Attorney General* [2005] UKHL 56 [2006] 1 AC 262 at [27] (proper to investigate whether Hunting Act constituting enacted law), [51] (appropriate challenge to validity of statute, not investigating conduct of proceedings in Parliament and issue one of statutory interpretation of the Parliament Acts), [110] (justiciable because "no absolute rule that the courts could not consider the validity of a statute and ... the issue ... was one of statutory interpretation"); <7.1.8> (towards an enhanced constitutional role).

35.1.4 **Judicial review and proceedings in Parliament.** Article 9 of the Bill of Rights 1689 ("the freedome of speech and debates or proceedings in Parliament ought not to be impeached or questioned in any court or place out of Parliament"); *Prebble v Television New Zealand Ltd* [1995] 1 AC 321, 332D ("the courts ... will not allow any challenge to be made to what is said or done within the walls of Parliament in performance of its legislative functions and protection of its established privileges"); *R (Wheeler) v Office of the Prime Minister* [2008] EWHC 1409 (Admin) (no enforceable legitimate expectation from promise to hold a Referendum, being a political matter for Parliament), at [47]-[49] (immunity from review in relation to proceedings in Parliament); *Pickin v British Railways Board* [1974] AC 765, 787G (Lord Reid: "The court has no concern with the manner in which Parliament or its officers carrying out its Standing Orders perform these functions"); *Bradlaugh v Gossett* (1884) 12 QBD 271 (impermissible to challenge the internal proceedings of Parliament); *R v Parliamentary Commissioner for Standards, ex p Al Fayed* [1998] 1 WLR 669 (Parliamentary Commissioner for Standards not amenable to judicial review because concerned with activities of Parliament), 670G (Lord Woolf MR: "It is clearly established that the Courts exercise a self-denying ordinance in relation to interfering with the proceedings of Parliament"); *R (Asif Javed) v Secretary of State for the Home Department* [2001] EWCA Civ 789 [2002] QB 129 (judicial review available in relation to delegated legislation, including as to rationality of underlying factual conclusions, notwithstanding that measure laid before Parliament and debated in both Houses); *R (L) v Secretary of State for the Home Department* [2003] EWCA Civ 25 [2003] 1 WLR 1230 at [22] (Art 9 "puts it beyond our jurisdiction to seek information about or to comment in any way upon the period of time between the giving of the Royal Assent ... and the transmission of the perfected text to the Queen's Printer"); *Wilson v First County Trust Ltd* [2003] UKHL 40 [2004] 1 AC 816 at [60] (having regard to Hansard as background and on judicial review of ministerial decisions not "questioning" what said in Parliament); *Buchanan v Jennings* [2004] UKPC 36 [2005] 1 AC 115 (not questioning proceedings in Parliament where use of Hansard record to support defamation action based on statement confirmed but not repeated outside the House).

35.1.5 **Special "non-justiciable" (prerogative) functions?**
(A) RELEVANCE OF SUBJECT MATTER. *R (Abbasi) v Secretary of State for Foreign and*

Commonwealth Affairs [2002] EWCA Civ 1598 [2003] UKHRR 76 at [85] ("the issue of justiciability depends, not on general principle, but on subject matter and suitability in the particular case"), [106(iv)]; *R (Bancoult) v Secretary of State for Foreign & Commonwealth Affairs* [2007] EWCA Civ 498 [2008] QB 365 at [47] (prerogative power of colonial governance not excluded from judicial review by reference to subject-matter).

(B) SPECIAL PREROGATIVE FUNCTIONS: LORD ROSKILL'S LIST.[38] *Council of Civil Service Unions v Minister for the Civil Service* [1985] AC 374, 418B-C (Lord Roskill: "Prerogative powers such as those relating to the making of treaties, the defence of the realm, the prerogative of mercy, the grant of honours, the dissolution of Parliament and the appointment of ministers as well as others are not, I think susceptible to judicial review because their nature and subject matter are such as not to be amenable to the judicial process"), 398F (Lord Fraser); *R (Bancoult) v Secretary of State for Foreign & Commonwealth Affairs* [2007] EWCA Civ 498 [2008] QB 365 at [46] (Lord Roskill's examples may today be regarded as questionable); *Lewis v Attorney-General of Jamaica* [2001] 2 AC 50, 77B ("treaty-making and declaring war" may be beyond review); *R v Secretary of State for the Home Department, ex p Fire Brigades Union* [1995] 2 AC 513, 553D ("treaty-making ... may not be justiciable"); *R (Abbasi) v Secretary of State for Foreign and Commonwealth Affairs* [2002] EWCA Civ 1598 [2003] UKHRR 76 at [106(iii)] ("the court cannot enter the forbidden areas").

(C) PREROGATIVE OF MERCY. *R (Page) v Secretary of State for Justice* [2007] EWHC 2026 (Admin) (court ordering reconsideration, where claimant had been misled about his release date); *R v Secretary of State for the Home Department, ex p Bentley* [1994] QB 349 (prerogative of mercy treated as reviewable); *Reckley v Minister of Public Safety and Immigration (No. 2)* [1996] 1 AC 527, 537H-541F (prerogative of mercy non-reviewable under Constitution of the Bahamas); *Lewis v Attorney-General of Jamaica* [2001] 2 AC 50 (prerogative of mercy reviewable as to procedural fairness of decision-making).

(D) MILITARY OPERATIONS/DEFENCE OF THE REALM. *R v Jones* [2006] UKHL 16 [2007] 1 AC 136 at [30] (Lord Bingham: "the courts will be very slow to review the exercise of prerogative powers ... and the deployment of the armed services ... I do not suggest that these rules admit of no exceptions"), [66] (Lord Hoffmann: "It is of course open to the court to say that the act in question falls wholly outside the ambit of the discretionary power"); *R (Gentle) v Prime Minister* [2008] UKHL 20 [2008] 2 WLR 879 (justiciable issue under the HRA); *R (Campaign for Nuclear Disarmament) v Prime Minister* [2002] EWHC 2759 (Admin) [2003] 3 LRC 335 at [47(ii)] ("The court will ... decline to embark upon the determination of an issue if to do so would be damaging to the public interest in the field of international relations, national security or defence"); *R (Marchiori) v Environment Agency* [2002] EWCA Civ 3 [2002] EuLR 225 at [38] (no merits review of defence matters), [40]-[41] (different if bad faith or statutory duty of review, for example under HRA); *R (International Transport Roth GmbH) v Secretary of State for the Home Department* [2002] EWCA Civ 158 [2003] QB 728 at [85] ("executive decisions dealing directly with matters of defence, while not immune from judicial review (that would be repugnant to the rule of law), cannot sensibly be scrutinised by the courts on grounds relating to their factual merits"); *R v Ministry of Defence, ex p Smith* [1996] QB 517 (DC), 539F-G (judicial review of whether to allow homosexuals to serve in the military); *R (Bancoult) v Secretary of State for the Foreign and Commonwealth Office* [2001] QB 1067 (judicial review of Ordinance removing island peoples to make way for US military base).

(E) TREATY-MAKING/BREAKING. *R (Wheeler) v Office of the Prime Minister* [2008] EWHC 1409 (Admin) at [55] (whether decision to ratify a Treaty amenable to judicial review to be approached on a case by case basis); *Ex p Molyneaux* [1986] 1 WLR 331, 336A-B (Taylor J: "it is not the function of this court to inquire into the exercise of the prerogative in entering into such an agreement"); *R v Secretary of State for Foreign & Commonwealth Affairs, ex p*

---

[38] Caroline Neenan [1998] JR 36.

Rees-Mogg [1994] QB 552 (judicial review of decision to proceed to ratify Maastricht Treaty); *R v HM Treasury, ex p Smedley* [1985] QB 657 (judicial review of draft Order in Council declaring EC budget undertaking an "ancillary" treaty); *R v Secretary of State for Foreign & Commonwealth Affairs, ex p Indian Association of Alberta* [1982] QB 892, 920E-G, 937G-H (considering whether Crown still bound by treaties); *New Zealand Maori Council v Attorney-General of New Zealand* [1994] 1 AC 466; *R v Secretary of State for Foreign and Commonwealth Affairs, ex p British Council of Turkish Cypriot Associations* [1998] COD 336 (see transcript) (issue justiciable if engaging a question of domestic UK law).

(F) FOREIGN AFFAIRS. *R (Al Rawi) v Secretary of State for Foreign and Commonwealth Affairs* [2006] EWCA Civ 1279 [2008] QB 289 at [148] (foreign relations involving "an especially broad margin of discretion"); *R v Secretary of State for Foreign and Commonwealth Affairs, ex p British Council of Turkish Cypriot Associations* [1998] COD 336 (whether UK support for Cyprus EU accession "justiciable only if it engages a question of domestic United Kingdom law"; "the powers of the Crown, even in its diplomatic function, may be constrained by statute"); *R (Bancoult) v Secretary of State for the Foreign and Commonwealth Office* [2001] QB 1067 (judicial review of Ordinance removing island peoples to make way for US military base); *R (Abbasi) v Secretary of State for Foreign and Commonwealth Affairs* [2002] EWCA Civ 1598 [2003] UKHRR 76 at [80] (judicial review available of refusal to render diplomatic assistance to British subject suffering violation of fundamental human rights), [106(iii)] (reviewable if shown to be "irrational or contrary to legitimate expectation"), [99] (foreign policy non-justiciable but "that does not mean the whole process is immune from judicial scrutiny"), [104] (whether action contrary to stated practice); *R (Quark Fishing Ltd) v Secretary of State for Foreign and Commonwealth Affairs* [2002] EWCA Civ 1409 at [57] (no fairness duty to invite representations as to "foreign policy issues"); *R (Carson) v Secretary of State for Work and Pensions* [2003] EWCA Civ 797 [2003] 3 All ER 577 at [66] (situation where the "judicial taboo of foreign relations is a red herring"; HL is at [2005] UKHL 37 [2006] 1 AC 173).

(G) DISSOLUTION OF PARLIAMENT. Cf. *Bobb v Manning* [2006] UKPC 22 [2006] 4 LRC 735 (constitutionality of prime minister's delayed dissolution of Parliament treated as reviewable to see whether any unlawful act).

35.1.6 **Issues of territoriality.**[39] *Tehrani v Secretary of State for the Home Department* [2006] UKHL 47 [2007] 1 AC 521 (London IAT's decision on Scottish-resident asylum-seeker's claim amenable to judicial review in Scotland); *R v Commissioner of Police of the Metropolis, ex p Bennett* [1995] QB 313 (English court having no jurisdiction to entertain judicial review challenge to execution in England of warrant for arrest issued in Scotland); *R (Bancoult) v Secretary of State for the Foreign and Commonwealth Office* [2001] QB 1067 at [26]-[29] (judicial review jurisdiction available in respect of overseas territories which are subject to the Queen's dominion, especially where decision in question was procured by the UK Government); *R (Quark Fishing Ltd) v Secretary of State for Foreign and Commonwealth Affairs* [2002] EWCA Civ 1409 (judicial review of Secretary of State's direction regarding licences in the territorial waters of UK overseas territory).

35.1.7 **Judicial review of acquittals.** *R v Dorking Justices, ex p Harrington* [1984] AC 743 & *R v Bournemouth Crown Court, ex p Weight* [1984] 1 WLR 980 (whether, as a corollary of the principle of 'double jeopardy', judicial review would lie to quash a criminal acquittal); *R v Horseferry Road Magistrates Court, ex p Director of Public Prosecutions* [1997] COD 172 (magistrate's dismissal of an information a nullity); *R v Dorking Justices, ex p Harrington* [1984] AC 743, 753B; *R (Wirral Health Authority) v Mental Health Review Tribunal* The Times

---

[39] Michael Beloff QC & Helen Mountfield [1997] JR 131.

26th November 2001 (appropriate to quash decision of MHRT discharging a convicted patient, since in law it was as though the decision had never been made); *R (Director of Public Prosecutions) v Birmingham City Justices* [2003] EWHC 2352 (Admin) (magistrates' decision not to vacate a trial was unlawful, which justifies the quashing of the consequential acquittal); *R (Omar) v Chief Constable of Bedfordshire Constabulary* [2002] EWHC 3060 (Admin) (judicial review granted of police decision to caution, rather than prosecute), [45] (concluding that it was in the public interest for judicial review to be available, with the possibility of a prosecution ensuing); *R v Portsmouth Crown Court, ex p Director of Public Prosecutions* [1994] COD 13 (decision allowing appeal against magistrates' conviction not an acquittal); *R v Clerkenwell Metropolitan Stipendiary Magistrate, ex p Director of Public Prosecutions* [1984] QB 821, 832E-H (refusal to hear the matter at all not an acquittal); *R v Sutton Justices, ex p Director of Public Prosecutions* [1992] 2 All ER 129, 133f-g (declaration available, not quashing order); *R v Haringey Justices, ex p Director of Public Prosecutions* [1996] QB 351, 360E-F (quashing order (certiorari) to quash decision to dismiss prosecution as an abuse of process; but case not remitted to justices with a direction to continue the trial); *R v Neath and Port Talbot Justices, ex p Director of Public Prosecutions* [2000] 1 WLR 1376 (case remitted for retrial where justices had wrongly refused to adjourn, but had dismissed the prosecution; DC explaining the factors affecting the discretion whether to grant a remedy); *R (Campbell) v General Medical Council* [2005] EWCA Civ 250 [2005] 1 WLR 3488 (quashing order refused in all the circumstances, albeit unlawfulness in disciplinary acquittal, where would expose doctor to double jeopardy); *R (Director of Public Prosecutions) v North & East Hertfordshire Justices* [2008] EWHC 103 (Admin) (quashing for unreasonable refusal to adjourn for blameless non-attendance of prosecution witness); <24.4.13(A)> (remedy and acquittals).

35.1.8 Religious authorities/matters? *R v Chief Rabbi, ex p Wachmann* [1992] 1 WLR 1036, 1042H-1043A (Simon Brown J: "the court is hardly in a position to regulate what is essentially a religious function... [and] must inevitably be wary of entering so self-evidently sensitive an area ... [as] adjudicating upon matters intimate to a religious community"); *Clark v University of Lincolnshire and Humberside* [2000] 1 WLR 1988 at [12] (Sedley LJ, explaining that "religious or aesthetic questions" may fall into the class where the dispute "may be unsuitable for adjudication in the courts"); *R v Imam of Bury Park Jame Masjid Luton, ex p Sulaiman Ali* [1994] COD 142; *R v London Beth Din (Court of the Chief Rabbi), ex p Michael Bloom* [1998] COD 131; *Ex p Williamson* The Times 9th March 1994; *R v Ecclesiastical Committee of Both Houses of Parliament, ex p Church Society* (1994) 6 Admin LR 670, 672A-C; *Williamson v Archbishop of Canterbury* The Times 25th November 1994; *R v Bishop of Stafford, ex p Owen* [2001] ACD 83 (Bishop probably reviewable in relation to decision not to extend rector's term of office); *R (Amicus - MSF Section) v Secretary of State for Trade and Industry* [2004] EWHC 860 (Admin) [2004] ELR 311 at [36] (religious views illustrating the background for striking the relevant balance, in considering the legality of employment sex-orientation regulations, but "resolution of the theological dispute raised ... would take the court beyond its legitimate role").

35.1.9 Immunity: other matters/contexts.
(A) CERTAIN CROWN COURT FUNCTIONS. <32.1>.
(B) STATUTORY OUSTERS. <P28>.
(C) EXCLUSIVE ALTERNATIVE REMEDY. <36.2>.
(D) PROCEEDINGS AGAINST CHARITABLE BODIES. *Ex p Scott* [1998] 1 WLR 226 (no jurisdiction to entertain judicial review challenge to National Trust's decision as to management of its property, because challenge constituting "charity proceedings" requiring prior authorisation of the Charity Commissioners or the Chancery Division); *R (Heather) v Leonard Cheshire Foundation* [2001] EWHC Admin 429 (2001) 4 CCLR 211 (if charity defendant had been public body, judicial review would have been "charity proceedings" needing consent) (consent obtained by time of appeal: [2002] EWCA Civ 366 [2002] 2 All ER 936 at [2]); *R*

(Brent London Borough Council) v Fed 2000 [2005] EWHC 2679 (Admin) [2006] ELR 169 at [43] (consent not required here).
(E) OTHER. *R v Birmingham Crown Court, ex p Ali* The Times 16th October 1998 (no common law power of review in relation to surety forfeiture decisions properly made by immigration appellate authority under the Immigration Act 1971 Sch 2 para 31; instead, challenge should be to enforcing magistrates).

35.2 **Private law matters.**"Private law" functions (or questions) are generally thought inapt for judicial review. There may be a "private" body never challengeable by judicial review, or a "public" body exercising a "private" function (eg. employment). In either case, there is unlikely to be immunity from judicial scrutiny: rather, the scrutiny will be for some "private law" claim.

35.2.1 **Contractual/consensual relationship.**
(A) NON-REVIEWABLE. *R v Disciplinary Committee of the Jockey Club, ex p Aga Khan* [1993] 1 WLR 909[40], 924C (describing powers which "derive from the agreement of the parties and give rise to private rights"); *R v Fernhill Manor School, ex p A* [1994] ELR 67, 79D (although "private schools operate within a statutory framework of control ... the relationships between the private schools and those who attend them are founded on the contract which is made between the school and those who are paying for the teaching and education of the pupils"); *R v Provincial Court of the Church in Wales, ex p Williams* [1999] COD 163 (Provincial Court of the Church in Wales not amenable to judicial review because legal authority arising from consensual submission to its jurisdiction); *R (Mooyer) v Personal Investment Authority Ombudsman Bureau Ltd* [2001] EWHC Admin 247 at [12] (PIA ombudsman not reviewable because consensual, non-statutory jurisdiction); *R (Arthurworry) v Haringey London Borough Council* [2001] EWHC Admin 698 (disciplinary proceedings not reviewable, but court granting a remedy by reference to the implied duty of trust and confidence between employer and employee); *R v BBC, ex p Lavelle* [1983] 1 WLR 23, 31C (BBC disciplinary procedure based on contract); *R v Criminal Injuries Compensation Board, ex p Lain* [1967] 2 QB 864, 882B-C ("private or domestic tribunals have always been outside the scope of certiorari since their authority is derived solely from contract, that is, from the agreement of the parties concerned"); *R v Panel on Take-overs and Mergers, ex p Datafin Plc* [1987] QB 815, 838F (referring to "the exclusion from the jurisdiction of bodies whose sole source of power is a consensual submission to its jurisdiction").
(B) REVIEWABLE. *R (Crouch) v South Birmingham Primary Care Trust* [2008] EWHC 605 (Admin) (proposed services agreement clause inconsistent with statutory scheme); *R (Kilby) v Basildon District Council* [2007] EWCA Civ 479 [2007] HLR 586 (whether power to vary secure tenancy terms); *R (Molinaro) v Kensington and Chelsea Royal London Borough Council* [2001] EWHC Admin 896 [2002] LGR 336 (refusal under lease to consent to change of user); *R (ProLife Alliance) v British Broadcasting Corporation* [2003] UKHL 23 [2004] 1 AC 185 at [1] (BBC's duty not to broadcast offensive material contained in its agreement with the Secretary of State); *R (Nurse Prescribers Ltd) v Secretary of State for Health* [2004] EWHC 403 (Admin) (changes for prescription services); *R (A) v B Council* [2007] EWHC 1529 (Admin) [2007] LGR 813 at [29] (decision as to suitability of subcontractor providing school transport for local authority); *R (Mullins) v Appeal Board of the Jockey Club* [2005] EWHC 2197 (Admin) at [29] (existence of contractual relationship is not inconsistent with judicial review", for example eviction of council tenants); *R v Panel on Take-overs and Mergers, ex p Datafin*

---

[40] Michael Beloff QC & Tim Kerr [1996] JR 30; David Pannick QC [1997] JR 150; Alec Samuels [2003] JR 54.

Plc [1987] QB 815, 850G (Take-over Panel reviewable "whether or not there is a legally binding contract").

(C) PRIVATE AND MONOPOLISTIC POWERS. *R v Panel on Take-overs and Mergers, ex p Datafin Plc* [1987] QB 815, 846A-B ("the panel regulates not only itself, but all others who have no alternative but to come to the market in a case to which the code applies"); *R v Chief Rabbi, ex p Wachmann* [1992] 1 WLR 1036, 1040H (Simon Brown J: "an Orthodox Rabbi is pursuing a vocation and has no choice but to accept the Chief Rabbi's disciplinary decisions"), 1041A ("the exclusion from judicial review of those who consensually submit to some subordinate jurisdiction properly applies only to arbitrators or `private or domestic tribunals'"); *R v London Beth Din (Court of the Chief Rabbi), ex p Michael Bloom* [1998] COD 131 (real consensual submission to jurisdiction); *R v Insurance Ombudsman, ex p Aegon Life Insurance Ltd* [1994] CLC 88, 93D, 94E (voluntary membership of Insurance Ombudsman scheme by insurers, and voluntary submission to his jurisdiction by their aggrieved customers).

35.2.2 Contractual subject-matter. Also <35.2.5> (commercial matters).
(A) NON-REVIEWABLE: EXAMPLES. *R (Supportways) v Hampshire County Council* [2006] EWCA Civ 1035 [2006] LGR 836 (service review obligation purely contractual); *R (West) v Lloyds of London* [2004] EWCA Civ 506 [2004] 3 All ER 251 at [31] (decisions "concerned solely with the commercial relationship ... governed by the contracts into which he had chosen to enter"); *R v Coventry City Council, ex p Coventry Heads of Independent Care Establishments* (1998) 1 CCLR 379, 386E-387H (matter essentially a contractual dispute, unsuitable for judicial review); *R v Association of British Travel Agents, ex p Sunspell Ltd* [2001] ACD 88 (contractual relationship between travel agent and ABTA); *R v British Standards Institute, ex p Dorgard* [2001] ACD 86 (British Standards Institute not reviewable in relation to complaint arising out of an agreement).
(B) REVIEWABLE: EXAMPLES. *R (Law Society) v Legal Services Commission* [2007] EWCA Civ 1264 [2008] 2 WLR 803 (ultra vires provision in civil legal aid contracts); *R v Enfield London Borough Council, ex p TF Unwin (Roydon) Ltd* (1989) 1 Admin LR 50 (suspension of contractor from local authority's list); *R v Legal Aid Board, ex p Donn & Co (a Firm)* [1996] 3 All ER 1 (decision to award contract); *R v Hillingdon Health Authority, ex p Goodwin* [1984] ICR 800 (hospital closure unlawful for failure to have regard to terms of contract with doctors); *R (O'Sullivan) v Secretary of State for Health* [2001] EWHC Admin 297 (judicial review turning on whether NHS terms and conditions incorporated into employment contract and binding Secretary of State).

35.2.3 Decisions relating to land.
(A) NON-REVIEWABLE. *R v Bolsover District Council, ex p Pepper* [2001] LGR 43 (local authority's statutory function of selling land not reviewable unless public law element introduced); *R v Leeds City Council, ex p Cobleigh* [1997] COD 69 (local authority's refusal to sell land not reviewable absent a statutory underpinning); *R (Hopley) v Liverpool Health Authority* [2002] EWHC 1723 (Admin) at [53] (applying *Pepper*).
(B) REVIEWABLE. *HMB Holdings Ltd v Antigua and Barbuda* [2007] UKPC 37 at [31] (decision compulsorily to acquire land); *R (Island Farm Development Ltd) v Bridgend County Borough Council* [2006] EWHC 2189 (Admin) [2007] LGR 60 (decision not to proceed with sale of land); *R (Ise Lodge Amenity Committee (A Class Action)) v Kettering Borough Council* [2002] EWHC 1132 (Admin) at [65] (resolution to sell land); *R v Barnet London Borough Council, ex p Pardes House School Ltd* [1989] COD 512 (decision to sell land vitiated by failure to consider own policy); *R v Pembrokeshire County Council, ex p Coker* [1999] 4 All ER 1007 (decision to lease land); *R v Secretary of State for the Environment, Transport and the Regions, ex p Wheeler* [2000] 3 PLR 98 (decision to offer land to local authority); *R v London Borough of Camden, ex p Hughes* [1994] COD 253 (decision not to enter contract to sell land); *R (Lemon Land Ltd) v London Borough of Hackney* [2001] EWHC Admin 336 [2001] LGR 555 (decision

to sell land unlawful, for failure to obtain best consideration reasonably obtainable); *R (Structadene Ltd) v Hackney London Borough Council* [2001] 2 All ER 225 (decision to dispose of land breaching statutory duty to obtain best price, also breach of fiduciary duty and unreasonable; contract declared invalid); *R (Molinaro) v Kensington and Chelsea Royal London Borough Council* [2001] EWHC Admin 896 [2002] LGR 336 (local authority decision under a lease, not to consent to a change of user).

(C) RELATED CONTEXTS. *R v Somerset County Council, ex p Fewings* [1995] 1 WLR 1037 (ban on hunting); <32.2.6> (decision to seek possession); *Wheeler v Leicester City Council* [1985] AC 1054 (ban on rugby club using council land); *R (Kelly) v Hammersmith and Fulham London Borough Council* [2004] EWHC 435 (Admin) (2004) 7 CCLR 542 (decision not to apply to vacate land registry caution).

35.2.4 Employment.[41]

(A) NON-REVIEWABLE. *R v BBC, ex p Lavelle* [1983] 1 WLR 23, 30C (Woolf J: "An application for judicial review has not and should not be extended to a pure employment situation"); *McClaren v Home Office* [1990] ICR 824, 836B-838B; *Wandsworth London Borough Council v A* [2000] 1 WLR 1246, 1252G-H ("in the case of employment by a public body, that legal status of the employer does not per se inject any element of public law"); *R (Evans) v University of Cambridge* [2002] EWHC 1382 (Admin) [2003] ELR 8 (despite University's public functions and statutory underpinning, claimant lecturer's remedies for employment matters statutory or contractual), [23] ("essentially an employment or contractual dispute"); *R v East Berkshire Health Authority, ex p Walsh* [1985] QB 152 (decision to dismiss nursing officer not reviewable); *R v Secretary of State for Employment, ex p Equal Opportunities Commission* [1995] 1 AC 1, 25C-E (individual employee's claim a matter for the employment tribunal); *R v Secretary of State for the Home Department, ex p Moore* [1994] COD 67 (confirmation of the decision to dismiss a prison officer); *R v Trent Regional Health Authority, ex p Jones* The Times 19th June 1986 (decision refusing to appoint a consultant surgeon); *R v Derbyshire County Council, ex p Noble* [1990] ICR 808 (council dismissal of deputy police surgeon); *R v Lord Chancellor's Department, ex p Nangle* [1992] 1 All ER 897 (disciplinary decisions affecting civil servant working for Lord Chancellor's Department); *R v Crown Prosecution Service, ex p Hogg* (1994) 6 Admin LR 778 (dismissal of barrister employed by the CPS); *R (Arthurworry) v Haringey London Borough Council* [2001] EWHC Admin 698 (disciplinary proceedings not reviewable, but court granting a remedy by reference to the implied duty of trust and confidence between employer and employee); *R (Tucker) v Director General of the National Crime Squad* [2003] EWCA Civ 2 at [35] ("clear line between disciplinary issues where an officer has the right to public law safeguards such as fairness, and operational or management decisions where the police are entitled to run their own affairs without the intervention of the courts").

(C) REVIEWABLE. *R (Prospect) v Ministry of Defence* [2008] EWHC 2056 (Admin) (lawfulness of Early Release Scheme offering early retirement); *R (Hodgson) v South Wales Police Authority* [2008] EWHC 1183 (Admin) (decision requiring police officer to retire); *McLaughlin v Governor of the Cayman Islands* [2007] UKPC 50 [2007] 1 WLR 2839 (dismissal of public office-holder); *R (Dunbar) v Hampshire Fire and Rescue Service* [2004] EWHC 431 (Admin) (refusal, contrary to the statutory scheme, to reinstate fire fighters following successful disciplinary appeal); *Chief Constable of the North Wales Police v Evans* [1982] 1 WLR 1155 (dismissal of policeman); *R v Salford Health Authority, ex p Janaway* [1989] AC 537 (dismissal of receptionist); *Champion v Chief Constable of the Gwent Constabulary* [1990] 1 WLR 1 (refusal of permission to would-be policeman governor); *R v Hillingdon Health Authority, ex p Goodwin* [1984] ICR 800 (hospital closure, with failure to have regard to terms of contracts

---

[41] Andrew Lidbetter & Peter Frost [1996] JR 98.

with doctors); *R v Secretary of State for the Home Department, ex p Benwell* [1985] QB 554 (dismissal of prison officer); *R v Secretary of State for the Home Department, ex p Broom* [1986] QB 198 (judicial review of decision to dismiss prison governor); *R v Secretary of State for Employment, ex p Equal Opportunities Commission* [1995] 1 AC 1 (EOC successfully seeking judicial review on EU-incompatible legislative qualifying conditions for unfair dismissal and redundancy entitlements); *R v Walsall Metropolitan Borough Council, ex p Yapp* [1994] ICR 528 (council employees seeking judicial review of decision, having accepted a tender from its own works department, to invite new tenders for part of the work); *R v Secretary of State for Education, ex p Prior* [1994] ELR 231 (teacher obtaining judicial review of Secretary of State's refusal to intervene as to a grant-maintained school governors' decision to dismiss him); *Jhagroo v Teaching Service Commission* [2002] UKPC 63 (PC granting declaration as to employment status; refusing in the circumstances to order that still employed as a public office holder)); *R (Verner) v Derby City Council* [2003] EWHC 2708 (Admin) [2004] LGR 786 (judicial review concerning whether teachers' acceptance of ill-health retirement benefit constituting resignation).

35.2.5 Whether managerial/commercial/operational function reviewable.
(A) REVIEWABLE. *R v Inland Revenue Commissioners, ex p National Federation of Self-Employed and Small Businesses Ltd* [1982] AC 617, 635F-H (Lord Wilberforce, referring to judicial review of Revenue's "management powers"), 636G-H (Lord Diplock: "wide managerial discretion"); *Mercury Energy Ltd v Electricity Corporation of New Zealand Ltd* [1994] 1 WLR 521 (judicial review of a decision to (enter into or) terminate a commercial contract); *R v Cleveland County Council, ex p Cleveland Care Homes Association* (1993) 17 BMLR 122 (decision to negotiate with reference to standard contract terms); *R v Legal Aid Board, ex p Donn & Co (a Firm)* [1996] 3 All ER 1, 8j-11j (decision to award multi-party legal aid contract); *R v Birmingham City Council, ex p Dredger* (1994) 6 Admin LR 553 (calculation of market stall charges); *R v Norfolk County Council, ex p M* [1989] QB 619, 627G-628D (child abuse register amenable to judicial review); *R v Bridgend County Borough Council, ex p Jones* 1st October 1999 unrep. (judicial review in tendering context); *R v Cumbria County Council, ex p Cumbria Professional Care Ltd* (2000) 3 CCLR 79 (judicial review of decision not to enter block contracts).
(B) NON-REVIEWABLE. *R v Comptroller of Patents, Designs and Trade Marks, ex p Lenzing AG* [1997] EuLR 237 (non-reviewability of Comptroller's administrative function of recording in register (non-reviewable) decision of European Patent Office Board of Appeal); *Lawson v Housing New Zealand* [1997] 4 LRC 369 (New Zealand High Court concluding that state housing body's decision to increase rents a commercial decision and not amenable to judicial review); *R (Hopley) v Liverpool Health Authority* [2002] EWHC 1723 (Admin) (decision declining to agree to meet damages judgment by means of structured settlement not reviewable), [54] ("commercial"-type decisions only reviewable "if there is an additional public element introduced to the process"); *R (Arbab) v Secretary of State for the Home Department* [2002] EWHC 1249 (Admin) [2002] Imm AR 536 at [45] ("the court will not generally involve itself in questions concerning the management of a government department or similar body"); *R (Tucker) v Director General of the National Crime Squad* [2003] EWCA Civ 2 at [32] ("entirely operational decision" not reviewable); <35.2.3> (decisions relating to land).

> **P36 Alternative remedy.**[42] Judicial review is regarded as inappropriate where suitable alternative safeguards exist.

36.1 General effect of other safeguards
36.2 Exclusive alternative remedy
36.3 Alternative remedy and discretion/case-management
36.4 Other remedy curing public law wrong

36.1 General effect of other safeguards. Judicial review is not the sole or immediate protection against legal wrongs by public authorities. The existence and pursuit of other avenues of protection stand to affect how the Court will approach a judicial review claim.

36.1.1 **Existence of other safeguards and judicial restraint.** *R v Inland Revenue Commissioners, ex p T.C.Coombs & Co* [1991] 2 AC 283, 300D, 302D-F (independent commissioner as "the real and intended safeguard", "the monitor of the decision"); *R v Dyfed County Council, ex p Manson* [1995] Env LR 83, 98 (where defect could be cured by Secretary of State when confirming byelaws, court should not intervene); *R v Local Government Commission for England, ex p Hampshire County Council* 11th March 1995 unrep. (appropriate avenue of public law representations to the Secretary of State, who would make ultimate decision); *Reckley v Minister of Public Safety and Immigration (No.2)* [1996] 1 AC 527, 537H-540B (advisory committee, under Constitution of Bahamas, the constitutional safeguard with respect to the prerogative of mercy); *Jahromi v Secretary of State for the Home Department* [1996] Imm AR 20 (protection afforded by Independent Advisory Panel); *R v Director of the Serious Fraud Office, ex p Smith* [1993] AC 1, 43F-G ("ample remedies" to control hypothetical abuses).

36.1.2 **Absence of other safeguards and judicial vigilance.** *R v Local Commissioner for Administration for the South (etc), ex p Eastleigh Borough Council* [1988] QB 855, 866F-H ("the fact that Parliament has not created a right of appeal against the findings in a Local Commissioner's report ... coupled with the public law character of the ombudsman's office and powers, ... is the foundation of the right to [a remedy] by way of judicial review"); *General Medical Council v Spackman* [1943] AC 627, 640 ("Parliament has not provided for any appeal from the decisions of the council", so that judicial review the "only control of the court to which the council is subject"); *R v Governors of Haberdashers' Aske's Hatcham College Trust, ex p T* [1995] ELR 350, 361E-H (absence of any other remedy supporting finding that college amenable to judicial review); *R v Plymouth City Council, ex p Plymouth & South Devon Cooperative Society Ltd* [1993] 2 PLR 75, 90G-H ("If planning permission was granted for a superstore development without due regard to the limits of material considerations, then appeal procedures would be irrelevant, and the sections of the public most directly affected would be the local community ... and the local traders"); cf. <15.2.2> (Parliament provided no appeal: Court must not invent one).

36.1.3 **Accountability to Parliament.** *R v Secretary of State for Trade and Industry, ex p Lonrho Plc* [1989] 1 WLR 525, 536C-E (Lord Keith: "the Secretary of State must act by a draft order laid before Parliament... These provisions ensure that a decision which is essentially political in character will be brought to the attention of Parliament and subject to scrutiny and challenge therein, and the courts must be careful not to invade the political field and substitute their own judgment for that of the Minister. The courts judge the lawfulness not the wisdom of the decision"); *R v Secretary of State for Social Security, ex p Nessa* (1995) 7 Admin LR 402,

---

[42] This section in a previous edition was cited in *Case No.9168/01* [2002] 2 BCLR 171 at [62].

406H ("The appropriate medium of challenge is in Parliament not in the courts"); *R v Inland Revenue Commissioners, ex p National Federation of Self-Employed and Small Businesses Ltd* [1982] AC 617, 644f-G (Lord Diplock: "It is not, in my view, a sufficient answer to say that judicial review of the actions of officers or departments of central government is unnecessary because they are accountable to Parliament for the way in which they carry out their functions. They are accountable to Parliament for what they do so far as regards efficiency and policy, and of that Parliament is the only judge; they are responsible to a court of justice for the lawfulness of what they do, and of that the court is the only judge"); *R v Parliamentary Commissioner for Administration, ex p Dyer* [1994] 1 WLR 621, 625C-E (Parliamentary ombudsman amenable to judicial review notwithstanding accountability to Parliament; Simon Brown LJ: "Many in government are answerable to Parliament and yet answerable also to the supervisory jurisdiction of this court"); *R v Secretary of State for the Home Department, ex p Fire Brigades Union* [1995] 2 AC 513 (HL split as to whether purely a political matter where any duty and accountability was owed to Parliament only, answering (3-2) that it was not); *R (C) v Secretary of State for Justice* [2008] EWCA Civ 882 (statutory instrument had been laid before Parliament, but not lawfully made by executive so quashed by court).

36.1.4 **"Election": whether pursuing other safeguards rules out judicial review.** <26.3.7> (pursuit of other remedies as good reason to extend time); *Ridge v Baldwin* [1964] AC 40, 126 (claimant "made it abundantly clear that by his appeal to the Secretary of State he was not in any way abandoning his right to contend that the decision of the watch committee was invalid"); *Calvin v Carr* [1980] AC 574, 597E (rejecting the argument that "having elected to take his case to the committee on appeal, [the claimant] had lost his right of resort to the court"); *R v Civil Service Appeal Board, ex p Bruce* [1989] 2 All ER 907 (judicial review refused as a matter of discretion, given pursuit of alternative remedy); *R v Secretary of State for the Home Department, ex p Mande Ssenyonjo* [1994] Imm AR 310 (pursuit of appeal machinery precluding claimant from challenging the original underlying decision); *R v Secretary of State for the Home Department, ex p Gurnam Singh* [1995] Imm AR 616, 624 (judicial review not available "where the full statutory appeals procedure has been used except in very special circumstances"); cf. *R v Secretary of State for the Home Department ex p Resul Erdogan* [1995] Imm AR 430, 433; <36.3.10> (deliberate decision not to appeal).

36.1.5 **Statutory remedy and HRA damages.** *Marcic v Thames Water Utilities Ltd* [2003] UKHL 66 [2004] 2 AC 42 at [71] (recourse to statutory regulator constituting the claimant's human rights remedy, subject to the regulator making an ECHR-compatible decision), [83].

36.1.6 **Other safeguards as cure.** <36.4>.

36.1.7 **Judicial review and ADR.** <10.2> (ADR/mediation).

36.2 **Exclusive alternative remedy.** In certain contexts, usually under particular legislative provisions, special alternative mechanisms have been regarded as the exclusive means of challenge, so that judicial review is effectively ousted.

36.2.1 **Existence of alternative remedy not precluding Court's jurisdiction.** <36.3.5>.

36.2.2 **Whether statutory remedy exclusive.** *Pyx Granite Co Ltd v Ministry of Housing and Local Government* [1960] AC 260, 302 (Lord Jenkins: "Where a statute creates a new right which has no existence apart from the statute creating it, and the statute creating the right at the same time prescribes a particular method of enforcing it, then, in the words of Lord Watson in *Barraclough v Brown* ([1897] AC 615, 623), `the right and the remedy are given uno flatu, and the one cannot be dissociated from the other'"), 304 (need for "clear words" for statutory remedy to be "exclusive method of determining questions of the kind to which it relates, and deprives the courts of the jurisdiction which they ordinarily possess"); *Century National Merchant Bank and Trust Co Ltd v Davies* [1998] AC 628, 637E-H (although not expressly stated in the Act, legislature intending statutory right of appeal to be exclusive remedy); *R (R) v Leeds City Council* [2005] EWHC 2495 (Admin) [2006] ELR 25 at [48] (county court having exclusive jurisdiction to deal with discrimination claim under Race Relations Act 1976 ss.17-18); *R (Okandeji) v Bow Street Magistrates Court* [2005] EWHC 2925 (Admin) [2006] 1 WLR 674 (statute meaning district judge extradition decision non-reviewable; appeal to HL the sole remedy); *R v Acting Returning Officer for Devon (etc), ex p Sanders* [1994] COD 497 (Act making clear that appropriate recourse election petition); *R v Dacorum District Council, ex p Cannon* [1996] 2 PLR 45 (statutory provision preventing challenge save by appeal); *R v Inner London Education Authority, ex p Ali* (1990) 2 Admin LR 822, 831B-836C (Secretary of State's default powers not exclusive); *R (Cheltenham Builders Ltd) v South Gloucestershire District Council* [2003] EWHC 2803 (Admin) [2004] 4 PLR 95 at [53] (Sullivan J: "Where Parliament wishes to oust judicial review because of the availability of a statutory appeal, it has to do so in the clearest possible terms").

36.2.3 **Whether common law (Visitorial) remedy exclusive.** *Thomas v University of Bradford* [1987] AC 795 & *Joseph v Board of Examiners of the Council of Legal Education* [1994] ELR 407 (visitorial jurisdictions exclusive); *R v Hull University Visitor, ex p Page* [1993] AC 682, 703G-H ("no relevant distinction between a case where a statute has conferred such final and conclusive jurisdiction and the case where the common law has for 300 years recognised that the visitor's decision on questions of fact and law are final and conclusive and are not to be reviewed by the courts"); *R v University of Nottingham, ex p K* [1998] ELR 184, 192F, 193H (university visitor's exclusive jurisdiction)); *R v Dean and Chapter of St Paul's Cathedral* [1998] COD 130 (Visitor of St Pauls having exclusive jurisdiction); *R (Galligan) v University of Oxford* [2001] EWHC Admin 965 [2002] ELR 494 (decision of Vice-Chancellor reviewable, there being no Visitorial jurisdiction).

36.3 **Alternative remedy and discretion/case-management.**[43] An existing alternative remedy raises a question for the Court's discretion and judgment. Judicial review is regarded as a last resort and can be declined on the basis that the claimant should first pursue a suitable alternative remedy. This question is best addressed at the permission stage, having regard to all the circumstances.

36.3.1 **Alternative remedy in a nutshell.** *Kay v Lambeth London Borough Council* [2006] UKHL 10 [2006] 2 AC 465 at [30] (Lord Bingham, referring to "the principle that if other means of redress are conveniently and effectively available to a party they ought ordinarily to be used before resort to judicial review"); *R (Pepushi) v Crown Prosecution Service* [2004] EWHC 798 (Admin) [2004] INLR 638 at [50] ("the Legal Services Commission and those advising prospective applicants for judicial review should always realise that judicial review is very rarely appropriate where an alternative remedy is available"); *R v Ministry of Agriculture, Fisheries and Food, ex p Live Sheep Traders Ltd* [1995] COD 297 (see transcript) ("It is a cardinal principle that, save in the most exceptional circumstances, the jurisdiction to grant judicial review will not be exercised where other remedies are available and have not been used").

36.3.2 **Judicial review as a long-stop/last resort.** *R (G) v Immigration Appeal Tribunal* [2004]

---

[43] Michael Beloff QC & Helen Mountfield [1999] JR 143; Richard Moules [2005] JR 350.

EWCA Civ 1731 [2005] 1 WLR 1445 at [27] ("judicial review is a remedy of last resort"); *R (Cowl) v Plymouth City Council* [2001] EWCA Civ 1935 [2002] 1 WLR 803 at [1] (Lord Woolf CJ: "even in disputes between public authorities and the members of the public for whom they are responsible, insufficient attention is paid to the paramount importance of avoiding litigation whenever this is possible"); *R (Bancoult) v Secretary of State for the Foreign and Commonwealth Office* [2001] QB 1067 at [27] ("judicial review is a legal recourse of last resort and [a claimant] must exhaust any proper alternative remedy open to him before the judicial review court will consider his case"); *R v Hammersmith and Fulham London Borough Council, ex p Burkett* [2002] UKHL 23 [2002] 1 WLR 1593 at [42] ("the established principle that judicial review is a remedy of last resort"); *R v Panel on Take-overs and Mergers, ex p Guinness Plc* [1990] 1 QB 146, 177E, G-178A ("the judicial review jurisdiction of the High Court ... is a supervisory or 'long stop' jurisdiction.. [C]onsistently with this 'long stop' character, it is not the practice of the court to entertain an application for judicial review unless and until all avenues of appeal have been exhausted, at least in so far as the alleged cause for complaint could thereby be remedied"); *R v Metropolitan Stipendiary Magistrate, ex p London Waste Regulation Authority* [1993] 3 All ER 113, 120b-c ("judicial review is a remedy of last resort"); *R v Sandwell Metropolitan Borough Council, ex p Wilkinson* (1999) 31 HLR 22, 28 ("Principle and pragmatism combine to emphasise the legal fact that judicial review is a remedy of last resort. Where there is set in place an elaborate statutory structure for challenge to, and review of, an administrative decision, the structure must in the ordinary way be fully invoked before seeking to engage the judicial review jurisdiction"); *R v Portsmouth Hospitals NHS Trust, ex p Glass* [1999] 2 FLR 905, 909G ("Judicial review is always regarded as a procedure of last resort"); *R (Lloyd) v Dagenham London Borough Council* [2001] EWCA Civ 533 (2001) 4 CCLR 196 at [27] ("The Court is here as a last resort where there is illegality"); *R v Serumaga* [2005] EWCA Crim 370 [2005] 1 WLR 3366 at [9] ("the last resort remedy of judicial review").

36.3.3 Alternative resolution: rules. JR:PAP <64.5> paras 2-3; CPR 1.4(1) and (2)(e).

36.3.4 ADR/mediation. <10.2>.

36.3.5 Existence of alternative remedy not precluding Court's jurisdiction. *Leech v Deputy Governor of Parkhurst Prison* [1988] AC 533, 580C-D (Lord Oliver: "An alternative remedy for abuse or excess, whether effective or not, may be a factor, and a very weighty factor, in the assessment of whether the discretion which the court undoubtedly has to grant or refuse judicial review should be exercised. But it cannot ... bear on the question of the existence of the jurisdiction"), 581D-E (never "suggested that the mere existence of an alternative remedy, of itself and by itself, ousts the jurisdiction of the court, though it may be a powerful factor when it comes to the question of whether the discretion to review should be exercised"); *R (Cheltenham Builders Ltd) v South Gloucestershire District Council* [2003] EWHC 2803 (Admin) [2004] 4 PLR 95 at [53] ("The fact that the claimant could have raised all of its complaints under [a statutory High Court application] does not oust the court's power to grant judicial review"); *R v Secretary of State for the Environment, Transport and the Regions, ex p Channel Tunnel Group Ltd* [2001] EWCA Civ 1185 at [40] (arbitration clause under relevant Treaty not precluding court from deciding meaning of Treaty and whether Directions ultra vires the corresponding domestic statute); *R v Legal Aid Board, ex p Donn & Co (a Firm)* [1996] 3 All ER 1, 11j (decision to award contract to another firm amenable to judicial review whether or not any private law remedy available).

36.3.6 Alternative remedy as a basis for refusing permission. *R (Sivasubramaniam) v Wandsworth County Court* [2002] EWCA Civ 1738 [2003] 1 WLR 475 at [46]-[47] (referring to the "abundance of authority" for "the proposition that permission to claim judicial review should not be granted when a suitable alternative remedy is available"); *Roy v Kensington &*

Chelsea & Westminster Family Practitioner Committee [1992] 1 AC 624, 637F-H (claimant "may (but not must) be refused [permission] to apply for judicial review on the ground that he has not exhausted his statutory remedy"); *Scott v National Trust for Places of Historic Interest or Natural Beauty* [1998] 2 All ER 705, 716j-717d (permission refused because charity proceedings on foot in the Chancery Division a convenient alternative remedy).

36.3.7 **Alternative remedy as a permission-stage issue.**[44] *R v Chief Constable of West Yorkshire, ex p Wilkinson* [2002] EWHC 2353 (Admin) at [42] (Davis J, treating the permission stage as "critical" in relation to an alternative remedy objection); *R v Essex County Council, ex p EB* [1997] ELR 327, 329C (McCullough J: "questions about the availability of an alternative procedure will normally arise on the application for [permission] and not at the hearing on the merits"); *R v Falmouth and Truro Port Health Authority, ex p South West Water Ltd* [2001] QB 445, 472A (referring to the permission stage as "perhaps the most important decision"), 473D ("The critical decision in an alternative remedy case, certainly one which requires a stay, is that taken at the grant of permission stage"); *R v Lambeth London Borough Council, ex p Crookes* (1997) 29 HLR 28, 35 (emphasising "the opportunity, at the moment of considering the application for [permission] to apply for judicial review, to determine the right course of action for the [claimant] to pursue"); *R v Peterborough Justices, ex p Dowler* [1997] QB 911, 923H-924A (treating the question whether exceptional case appropriate for judicial review in the face of appellate avenue as a question for the permission stage, as to which the potential defendant should be heard); *R v Westminster City Council, ex p P* (1998) 1 CCLR 486 (permission refused because Secretary of State's default powers the more convenient, expeditious and effective course); *R v Secretary of State for Health, ex p British Association of European Pharmaceutical Distributors* [2001] EuLR 464 at [160]-[161] (alternative remedy question "should have been raised [by the defendant] at a much earlier stage"); *R v University of Cambridge, ex p Evans* [1998] ELR 515, 517H (holding that "arguable, that this is not a true alternative form of recourse at all"); *R v Secretary of State for Social Security, ex p West* [1999] 1 FLR 1233, 1235B (treated as sufficient that arguable that entitled to pursue judicial review); <10.3.3> (duty to disclose alternative remedy); *R v Falmouth and Truro Port Health Authority, ex p South West Water Ltd* [2001] QB 445, 472F-473D (where statutory right of appeal, permission should not have been granted on so wide-ranging a basis, but should have been for a "limited judicial review", "restricted to two issues"); <21.1.15> (partial permission); <22.4.8> (preliminary issue).

36.3.8 **Alternative remedy and discretion to grant/refuse remedy.** *R (M) v London Borough of Bromley* [2002] EWCA Civ 1113 [2002] 3 FCR 193 at [23] (Buxton LJ: "the jurisprudence relating to alternative remedies [is] only one aspect of a more general discretionary power of the court to refuse relief in an appropriate case"); *R (JD Wetherspoon Plc) v Guildford Borough Council* [2006] EWHC 815 (Admin) [2007] 1 All ER 400 at [90] (alternative remedy can be basis for refusing substantive application); *R v Mansfield District Council, ex p Ashfield Nominees Ltd* (1999) 31 HLR 805 (alternative remedy as ground for refusing substantive application); *R v Civil Service Appeal Board, ex p Bruce* [1989] 2 All ER 907 (remedy refused where alternative remedy being pursued), 912f-j (alternative remedy relevant to exercise of discretion); *R v Chief Constable of West Yorkshire, ex p Wilkinson* [2002] EWHC 2353 (Admin) at [43] ("even where permission has been granted in an alternative remedy case, the alternative remedy argument may possibly ... be available to be deployed at a substantive hearing on any discussion as to the appropriateness of relief, if any, to be granted"); *R v Secretary of State for the Environment, Transport and the Regions, ex p Channel Tunnel Group Ltd* [2001] EWCA Civ 1185 (deciding at substantive hearing whether judicial review

---

[44] Kate Olley [2000] JR 240.

appropriate in the light of an arbitration clause).

36.3.9 Alternative remedy and adjournment/costs. *R (Davies) v Revenue & Customs Commissioners* [2008] EWCA Civ 933 at [7] ("if a tribunal of fact exists which can find the relevant facts it is normally good practice to postpone judicial review until after the facts have been found"), [17] (inapt to adjourn here); *R v Sefton Metropolitan Borough Council, ex p Harrison* [1995] COD 178 (refusal of costs because of failure to use alternative remedy); *R v Inland Revenue Commissioners, ex p Opman International UK* [1986] 1 WLR 568 (costs refused because alternative remedy); *R v Trafford Borough Council, ex p Colonel Foods Ltd* (grounds for judicial review satisfied, but remedy refused as a matter of discretion given existence of alternative remedy by way of appeal; costs awarded against claimant).

36.3.10 Unused appeal: need for exceptional circumstances. *Harley Development Inc v Commissioner of Inland Revenue* [1996] 1 WLR 727, 736C (Lord Jauncey: "where a statute lays down a comprehensive system of appeals procedure against administrative decisions, it will only be in exceptional circumstances, typically an abuse of power, that the courts will entertain an application for judicial review of a decision which has not been appealed"); *R v Inland Revenue Commissioners, ex p Preston* [1985] AC 835, 852D-F ("Where Parliament has provided by statute appeal procedures ... it will only be very rarely that the courts will allow the collateral process of judicial review to be used to attack an appealable decision"); *R (Sivasubramaniam) v Wandsworth County Court* [2002] EWCA Civ 1738 [2003] 1 WLR 475 at [48] (would need "exceptional circumstances" to allow claimant who had failed to seek permission to appeal from a county court decision to proceed by judicial review, since that would defeat the sensible statutory scheme); *R v Secretary of State for the Home Department, ex p Swati* [1986] 1 WLR 477 (exceptional circumstances); *R (Arslan) v Secretary of State for the Home Department* [2006] EWHC 1877 (Admin) at [34] (out of country appeal would disrupt claimant's shopkeeping business); *R (Lim) v Secretary of State for the Home Department* [2006] EWHC 3004 (Admin) at [43] (out of country appeal "a wholly inadequate means of determining the issue of precedent fact"); *R (JD Wetherspoon Plc) v Guildford Borough Council* [2006] EWHC 815 (Admin) [2007] 1 All ER 400 at [91] (sufficient that question of principle affecting licensing law generally); *R (DR) v Head Teacher of St George's Catholic School* [2002] EWCA Civ 1822 [2003] ELR 104 at [45] (asking whether impropriety, a point of principle or need for interim remedy), [54] (or where otherwise-unachievable speedy determination needed); *R v London Borough of Newham, ex p R* [1995] ELR 156, 163B-D (appeal to Secretary of State more "appropriate" and "effective" than judicial review); *R (M) v London Borough of Bromley* [2002] EWCA Civ 1113 [2002] 3 FCR 193 (challenge to process by which claimant placed on child abuse register should have been by statutory appeal to a tribunal); *R (Kurdistan Workers Party) v Secretary of State for the Home Department* [2002] EWHC 644 (Admin) (in challenging the proscription of organisations, more appropriate at least in the first instance for the statutory remedy of appeal to the Proscribed Organisations Appeal Commission to be pursued), [91] ("any [judicial review] challenge should at the very least await the outcome of the appeals"); *R v Hereford Magistrates' Court, ex p Rowlands* [1998] QB 110 (where procedural unfairness leading to magistrates conviction, defendant entitled to judicial review notwithstanding availability of appeal to Crown Court); *R (DR) v Head Teacher of St George's Catholic School* [2002] EWCA Civ 1822 [2003] ELR 104 at [33], [35] (*Rowlands* not establishing that magistrates' conviction would be quashed even following a "fair but unsuccessful crown court appeal"); *R v Merton London Borough Council, ex p Sembi* (2000) 32 HLR 439 (importance of seeking review and appeal to county court under Housing Act 1996, rather than judicial review); *R v Falmouth and Truro Port Health Authority, ex p South West Water Ltd* [2001] QB 445, 473D (permission for judicial review very rare where unused appeal "in a case concerning public safety"); *R (Dolatabadi) v Transport for London* [2005] EWHC 1942 (Admin) at [19], [26] (judicial review granted to ensure only proper outcome despite unused appeal remedy).

36.3.11 **Relative suitability of alternative remedy/judicial review.**

(A) SUITABILITY/EFFECTIVENESS. *R v Birmingham City Council, ex p Ferrero Ltd* [1993] 1 All ER 530, 537c (necessary "to look carefully at the suitability of the statutory appeal in the context of the particular case"); *R v Leeds City Council, ex p Hendry* (1994) 6 Admin LR 439, 443D-F ("the question ... is not simply whether or not there is an alternative statutory appeal procedure but whether in the context of that procedure the real issue to be determined can sensibly be determined by that means"); *Leech v Deputy Governor of Parkhurst Prison* [1988] AC 533, 566H-567A (whether available remedy "falls short of adequacy"); *R v Hillingdon London Borough Council, ex p Royco Homes Ltd* [1974] QB 720, 728 (asking whether an "equally effective and convenient remedy"); *R v Huntingdon District Council, ex p Cowan* [1984] 1 WLR 501, 507 ("the court should always ask itself whether the remedy that is sought in court, or the alternative remedy ... is the most effective and convenient, in other words, which of them will prove to be the most effective and convenient in all the circumstances, not merely for the [claimant], but in the public interest"); *Ex p Waldron* [1986] QB 824, 852F-853A ("Whether the alternative statutory remedy will resolve the question at issue fully and directly; whether the statutory procedure would be quicker, or slower, than procedure by way of judicial review; whether the matter depends on some particular or technical knowledge which is more readily available to the alternative appellate body", and whether the alternative remedy "apt to decide the question"); *R v Devon County Council, ex p Baker* [1995] 1 All ER 73, 92f ("Which of two available ... avenues of redress, is to be preferred will depend ultimately upon which is the more convenient, expeditious and effective"); *R v Essex County Council, ex p EB* [1997] ELR 327, 329C ("whether the alternative procedure would be equally convenient and effective"); *R (Cheltenham Builders Ltd) v South Gloucestershire District Council* [2003] EWHC 2803 (Admin) [2004] 4 PLR 95 at [59] (claimant "not seeking to obtain any unfair procedural advantage or to evade any procedural obstacle").

(B) ABSENCE OF PARTICIPATORY RIGHTS. *Primecrown Ltd v Medicines Control Agency* [1997] EuLR 657, 659F (cross-application for judicial review because "no right to be heard" on competitor's statutory review); *R v London Borough of Southwark, ex p Dagou* (1996) 28 HLR 72, 81 ("the statutory arbitral procedure is not a remedy available to the [claimant]. It is an alternative resolution disposal between the notified and notifying authorities... The [claimant] has no say"); *R v Snaresbrook Crown Court, ex p Director of Serious Fraud Office* The Times 26th October 1998 (judicial review appropriate where Crown Court has dismissed counts on indictment, because defendant having no right to be heard on, nor any right of appeal or review following, application for leave to prefer a voluntary bill); *R (Director of Public Prosecutions) v Camberwell Youth Court* [2004] EWHC 1805 (Admin) [2005] 1 WLR 810 (affirming participatory advantages of judicial review).

(C) SCOPE: RANGE OF REMEDIES/FULLER REMIT. *R (G) v Barnet London Borough Council* [2005] EWHC 1946 (Admin) [2006] ELR 4 (judicial review appropriate to secure interim relief, pending special educational needs appeal); *R (Smith) v North East Derbyshire Primary Care Trust* [2006] EWCA Civ 1291 [2006] 1 WLR 3315 at [9] (Patient's Forum not an alternative remedy where "no power or status to require the [defendant] to reverse its decision"); *R (Manson) v Ministry of Defence* [2005] EWCA Civ 1678 (whether employment tribunal jurisdiction extended to the issue); *Raffile v Government of the United Stated of America* [2004] EWHC 2913 (Admin) [2005] 1 All ER 889 at [35] (whether circumstances covered by terms of statutory extradition appeal); *R v Inland Revenue Commissioners, ex p Mead* [1993] 1 All ER 772, 783a-b ("the fact that there is an alternative remedy in respect of some matters" should not "prevent direct access to this court if those remedies do not cover the whole ambit of the jurisdiction in judicial review. If there is a gap the litigant should be able to avail himself of it"); *R v Manchester Metropolitan University, ex p Nolan* [1994] ELR 380, 396D (internal review not "as certain or as full as the recourse to law"); *R (Kurdistan Workers*

Party) v Secretary of State for the Home Department [2002] EWHC 644 (Admin) at [85]-[87] (pursue appeal first, albeit not full range of remedies (including declaration of incompatibility and HRA damages), being available later on judicial review if appropriate); *R (Cowl) v Plymouth City Council* [2001] EWCA Civ 1935 [2002] 1 WLR 803 at [14] (alternative remedy need not "cover exactly the same ground as judicial review", sufficient that "a significant part of the issues between the parties could be resolved outside the litigation process" and legal issue could subsequently be examined by court); *GH v Secretary of State for the Home Department* [2005] EWCA Civ 1182 at [47] (judicial review appropriate against removal directions, where no appealable decision).

(D) LEGISLATIVE INTENT/PROPORTIONALITY. *R (G) v Immigration Appeal Tribunal* [2004] EWCA Civ 1731 [2005] 1 WLR 1445 at [20] ("Where Parliament enacts a remedy with the clear intention that this should be pursued in place of judicial review, it is appropriate to have regard to the considerations giving rise to that intention"; "the judges should, so far as consistent with the rule of law, have regard to legislative policy"; court should "consider whether an alternative remedy is proportionate when deciding whether to exercise its power of judicial review"), [23] (statutory review "a satisfactory judicial process for the question that it was designed to address"); *R (Sinclair Gardens Investments (Kensington) Ltd) v Lands Tribunal* [2005] EWCA Civ 1305 [2006] 3 All ER 650 at [40]-[41] (whether statutory scheme giving adequate and proportionate protection, having regard to the nature of the issues, the effect of the procedures, the nature of the tribunals and the legislative intention).

36.3.12 Suitable issue for judicial review. *R v Devon County Council, ex p Baker* [1995] 1 All ER 73, 87b-c (Dillon LJ: "[T]he issue is entirely one in law in a developing field which is peculiarly appropriate for decision by the courts rather than by the Secretary of State"), 92f-h (Simon Brown LJ: "Where..., as here, what is required is the authoritative resolution of a legal issue... then ... judicial review [is] the more convenient alternative remedy"); *R v Newham London Borough Council, ex p X* [1995] ELR 303 ("the issues raised are ... essentially matters of law"); *R v Governing Body of The Rectory School and The London Borough of Richmond, ex p WK (A Minor)* [1997] ELR 484 (questions of procedural propriety regarded as important questions of law for judicial review and not statutory appeal); *R v Leeds City Council, ex p Hendry* (1994) 6 Admin LR 439, 443G-444A (magistrates not generally the appropriate forum for deciding questions of vires); *R v Wiltshire County Council, ex p Lazard Brothers & Co Ltd* The Times 13th January 1998 (judicial review appropriate despite available public inquiry and appeal, where council threatening to make plain error of law); *R v London Borough of Ealing, ex p Times Newspapers Ltd* [1987] IRLR 129 (clear abuse of power, for which the remedy was for the Court, not requested Secretary of State intervention); *R v Lambeth London Borough Council, ex p A* (1998) 10 Admin LR 209, 228A ("the statutory complaints procedure ... may provide a more suitable means of redress in a case where no question of law arises"); *R v Sutton London Borough Council, ex p Tucker* (1998) 1 CCLR 251, 275B-G (neither statutory complaints procedure nor default powers as convenient, expeditious or effective as judicial review, where discrete point of law); *R v Wiltshire County Council, ex p Nettlecombe Ltd* (1998) 96 LGR 386 (plain error of law); *R v Gloucestershire County Council, ex p RADAR* (1998) 1 CCLR 476 (statutory complaints mechanism not a suitable alternative remedy in relation to general issue of principle arising); *R v London Leasehold Valuation Tribunal, ex p Daejan Properties Ltd* The Times 20th October 2000 (Administrative Court) at [15] (judicial review appropriate for "short point of statutory construction"); *Macharia v Secretary of State for the Home Department* [2000] INLR 156 at [32] (Sedley LJ: judicial review more appropriate than appeal to CA, where question of natural justice as to what IAT did); *R v Nottingham City Council, ex p Howitt* [1999] COD 530 (issue of inflexibility of policy evidently treated as appropriate question for judicial review; unlike matters going to individual facts which were more apt for resolution by statutory appeal).

36.3.13 **Suitability and alternative remedy: other factors.** <17.3.3> (alternative remedy more suitable for resolving disputed facts); *R v Ministry of Defence Police, ex p Byrne* [1994] COD 429 (inappropriate to require claimant to invoke internal appeals machinery where impugned decision made by head of police force); *R v Ministry of Agriculture, Fisheries and Food, ex p Dairy Trade Federation Limited* [1998] EuLR 253, 263G-265B (more appropriate to challenge alleged abuse of dominant position directly, rather than indirect judicial review challenge to MAFF for not preventing it); *R v Secretary of State for the Environment, ex p Davidson* (1990) 2 Admin LR 94 (wrong to allow restrictions in statutory remedy to be circumvented; ie. time limit and restricted scope of remedy); *R v Inspector of Taxes, ex p Kissane* [1986] 2 All ER 37, 39j-40d (judicial review appropriate given availability of costs); *R v Environment Agency, ex p Petrus Oils Ltd* [1999] Env LR 732 (appeal an adequate alternative remedy despite non-availability of costs); *R v London Borough of Tower Hamlets, ex p Bradford* [1997] COD 195 and 282 (remedy might have been refused because alternative remedy, but for fact that would have caused unacceptable delay); *R v Special Educational Needs Tribunal, ex p KL* [1997] ELR 504 (judicial review appropriate despite availability of statutory review by decision-maker, because no prospect of different decision being reached on such a review); *R v Bassetlaw District Council, ex p Oxby* The Times 18th December 1997 (legitimate for council to seek judicial review of its own decisions, acting by its leader, rather than to revoke them and pay statutory compensation); *R v Bristol City Council, ex p Everett* [1999] 1 WLR 92 (Richards J), 106H-107B (where local authority, as "primary enforcement authority" acted unlawfully in not pursuing statutory nuisance functions, judicial review appropriate despite availability to the claimant of complaint to magistrates); *R v Snaresbrook Crown Court, ex p Director of Serious Fraud Office* The Times 26th October 1998 (judicial review more appropriate than application for leave to prefer voluntary bill, inter alia because High Court's decision as to the latter not giving the accused a right of appeal, nor appealable or reviewable); *R v Royal Borough of Kingston-Upon-Thames, ex p T* [1994] 1 FLR 798, 813H (no point of general public importance); *R v Secretary of State for the Home Department, ex p Q* [2000] UKHRR 386, 402A (judicial review appropriate to decide whether decision threatening right to a fair trial, rather than seeking stay of criminal trial itself for abuse of process); *R v Portsmouth Hospitals NHS Trust, ex p Glass* [1999] 2 FLR 905 (child's best interests paramount, and court not therefore concerned about is whether the right procedure has been used); *R (P and Q) v Secretary of State for the Home Department* [2001] EWCA Civ 1151 [2001] 1 WLR 2002 at [119]-[120] (Family Division proceedings more appropriate than Administrative Court where issue whether separation of incarcerated mother and her child unlawful as seriously compromising welfare of the child); *R v Kensington and Chelsea Royal London Borough Council, ex p Byfield* (1999) 31 HLR 913 (judicial review appropriate, albeit that arising out of decisions amenable to statutory appeal, where the point of law in the case concerned legality of policy).

36.3.14 **Particular types of alternative remedy.**
(A) STATUTORY APPEAL. <36.3.10>.
(B) LOCAL GOVERNMENT MONITORING OFFICER. *R v Hammersmith and Fulham London Borough Council, ex p Burkett* [2001] Env LR 684 (CA) at [14] (claimants "should not overlook the possibility of going first to the local authority's monitoring officer under s.5 of the Local Government and Housing Act 1989").
(C) OMBUDSMAN. *R (Scholarstica Umo) v Commissioner for Local Administration in England* [2003] EWHC 3202 (Admin) [2004] ELR 265 at [17] (once judicial review proceedings instituted local ombudsman having no jurisdiction); *R v Lambeth London Borough Council, ex p Crookes* (1997) 29 HLR 28 (normally preferable to challenge procedural irregularity first by complaint of maladministration to the local ombudsman); *R v Local Commissioner for Administration in North and North East England, ex p Liverpool City Council* [2001] 1 All ER 462 at [28], [45] (ombudsman entitled to consider complaint even

though judicial review remedy available); *R v Inland Revenue Commissioners, ex p National Federation of Self-Employed and Small Businesses Ltd* [1982] AC 617, 663C-E (Parliamentary ombudsman not relevant where "allegations of illegality in the performance of statutory duties").
(D) DEFAULT POWERS ETC. *R v Inner London Education Authority, ex p Ali* (1990) 2 Admin LR 822 (Secretary of State's default powers not precluding judicial review); *R v South Tyneside Metropolitan Borough Council, ex p Cram* (1998) 10 Admin LR 477, 482G-H (Secretary of State's refusal to exercise default powers relevant to Court's exercise of its discretion as to whether to grant remedy); *R v London Borough of Brent, ex p F* [1999] ELR 32 (discretion as to remedy necessarily raising educational matters best left to Secretary of State's default powers); *R v Westminster City Council, ex p P* (1998) 1 CCLR 486, 492C-H (issues as to housing of asylum seekers more appropriate for Secretary of State's default powers); *R v Cumbria County Council, ex p Cumbria Professional Care Ltd* (2000) 3 CCLR 79, 85G-H ("the existence of such powers is highly relevant to the exercise of the court's discretion to grant or refuse [a remedy]"); *R (Henlow Grange Health Farm Ltd) v Bedfordshire County Council* [2001] EWHC Admin 179 (judicial review of council's planning resolution inappropriate while Secretary of State's call-in decision awaited).
(E) APPEAL BY CASE STATED. *R (P) v Liverpool City Magistrates* [2006] EWHC 887 (Admin) [2006] ELR 386 at [8] (judicial review granted although should have been case stated); *R (Sissen) v Newcastle Upon Tyne Crown Court* [2004] EWHC 1905 (Admin) [2005] Env LR 349 at [1] (judicial review allowed to proceed although should have been case stated); *R (Stace) v Milton Keynes Magistrates Court* [2006] EWHC 1049 (Admin) at [14]-[15] (judicial review not inapt where magistrates had given reasons); *R v Harrow Crown Court, ex p Dave* [1994] 1 WLR 98, 107E-F (discouraging judicial review where case stated available); *R v Thanet Justices, ex p Dass* [1996] COD 77 (judicial review rather than case stated understandable, to secure bail); *R v Derwentside Magistrates' Court, ex p Swift* [1997] RTR 96 (case stated better, to allow stay of conviction pending appeal); *R v Clerkenwell Metropolitan Stipendiary Magistrate, ex p Director of Public Prosecutions* [1984] QB 821, 833A-836D (matter should have been by case stated, but judicial review treated as successful case stated with permission to lodge it out of time); *R (Durham County Council) v North Durham Justices* [2004] EWHC 1073 (Admin) at [30] (no power to state a case where no final determination); *R (Brighton and Hove City Council) v Brighton and Hove Justices* [2004] EWHC 1800 (Admin) at [23] (case stated appropriate), [24] ("but the bar is discretionary"), [25] (court reluctant to defeat claim "unless prejudice is caused to a party, or there is some other good reason").
(F) HABEAS CORPUS.[45] *R (A) v Secretary of State for the Home Department* [2008] EWHC 142 (Admin) (considering judicial review and habeas in context of unlawful immigration detention); *R v Barking Havering and Brentwood Community Healthcare NHS Trust* [1999] 1 FLR 106, 114F-117C (favouring judicial review in context of mental health detention, especially because of wider range of available remedies); *R v Oldham Justices, ex p Cawley* [1997] QB 1, 16F-19D; *In Re S-C (Mental patient: Habeas corpus)* [1996] QB 599 (challenge to jurisdiction to detain, not to any underlying administrative decision, appropriate for habeas corpus); *R v Secretary of State for the Home Department, ex p Rahman* [1996] 4 All ER 945 (Collins J) (distinction between habeas corpus and judicial review not one of substance), *In Re John (Julie)* [1998] COD 306 (considering habeas corpus and judicial review in context of Mental Health Act detention); *Abdul Sheikh v Secretary of State for the Home Department* [2001] INLR 98 (abuse of process to challenge decision by habeas corpus when previous judicial review on same ground had been dismissed for delay), at [9] (challenge to legality of detention can be either habeas corpus or judicial review).
(G) COMPLAINTS MECHANISMS. *R (Cowl) v Plymouth City Council* [2001] EWCA Civ 1935 [2002] 1 WLR 803 (in case concerning duty to conduct needs assessments, complaints

---

[45] Owen Davies [1997] JR 11.

mechanism was a suitable alternative remedy which should have been used); *R v Royal Borough of Kingston-upon-Thames, ex p T* [1994] 1 FLR 798; *R v East Sussex County Council, ex p W* [1998] 2 FLR 1082, 1092F-1093E, 1094A (statutory complaints procedure normally an appropriate alternative remedy); *R v Royal Borough of Kingston-Upon-Thames, ex p T* [1994] 1 FLR 798, 815C; *R v Lambeth London Borough Council, ex p A* (1998) 10 Admin LR 209, 228A ("the statutory complaints procedure ... may provide a more suitable means of redress in a case where no question of law arises"); *R v Sutton London Borough Council, ex p Tucker* (1998) 1 CCLR 251, 275B-G (neither statutory complaints procedure nor default powers as convenient, expeditious or effective as judicial review, where discrete point of law); *R (Shi) v King's College London* [2008] EWHC 857 (Admin) at [45] (complaint to Independent Adjudicator for Higher Education a suitable alternative remedy to judicial review of university disciplinary decision).

(H) BAIL. *R (Konan) v Secretary of State for the Home Department* [2004] EWHC 22 (Admin) at [30] (Collins J, explaining that bail not an alternative remedy to judicial review where lawfulness of detention in issue).

(I) PRIVATE LAW ALTERNATIVE REMEDIES. *R v Ministry of Agriculture, Fisheries and Food, ex p Dairy Trade Federation Limited* [1998] EuLR 253, 263G-265A (complaint to EC Commission an adequate alternative remedy where contending new scheme abuse of dominant position, in breach of Treaty of Rome); *R v East Berkshire Health Authority, ex p Walsh* [1985] QB 152, 169H-170B ("in at least the great majority of cases involving disputes about the dismissal of an employee by his employer, the most appropriate forum for their resolution is an industrial tribunal"); *R v Ministry of Agriculture, Fisheries and Food, ex p Live Sheep Traders Ltd* [1995] COD 297 (see transcript) (where judicial review sought to underpin damages claim for malicious prosecution, that action treated as a suitable alternative remedy); *Re S (Application for Judicial Review)* [1998] 1 FLR 790, 796C ("there will occasionally be matters of public importance which might be capable of being litigated in the civil courts, but are predominantly issues of public law and would be better argued and adjudicated upon in the public arena"); *R (Mooyer) v Personal Investment Authority Ombudsman Bureau Ltd* [2001] EWHC Admin 247 (instead of judicial review of PIA ombudsman's decision as to whether insurance company had acted properly in stopping payments, alternative remedy of suing the company in the courts); *R (Corporation of London) v Secretary of State for Environment, Food and Rural Affairs* [2004] EWCA Civ 1765 [2005] 1 WLR 1286 at [27] (tort of disturbance not an alternative remedy in relation to prior question of vires of market activities consent) (HL is [2006] UKHL 30 [2006] 1 WLR 1721); *R (Cookson & Clegg Ltd) v Ministry of Defence* [2005] EWCA Civ 811[46] (judicial review of tendering decision inappropriate, since all grounds of challenge available in parallel CPR Part 7 proceedings).

(J) COLLATERAL CHALLENGE. <27.3.11>; *R (Balbo B & C Auto Transporti Internationali) v Secretary of State for the Home Department* [2001] EWHC Admin 195 [2001] 1 WLR 1556 (challenge to notice of liability under Immigration and Asylum Act 1999 s.32 should be by defence when sued for the applicable penalty, not judicial review); <26.3.11> (possibility of collateral challenge as good reason to extend time for judicial review); <35.2.4> (employment remedies).

(K) CHARITY PROCEEDINGS. *R (Heather) v Leonard Cheshire Foundation* [2001] EWHC Admin 429 (2001) 4 CCLR 211 at [103] (where charity amenable to judicial review, those proceedings constituting "charity proceedings", needing consent of Charity Commissioners (or Chancery Division), but no need to commence the legal challenge itself in the Chancery Division) (CA is [2002] EWCA Civ 366 [2002] 2 All ER 936).

(L) EC COMMISSION. *R (Association of Pharmaceutical Importers) v Secretary of State for Health* [2001] EWCA Civ 1986 [2002] EuLR 197 (most convenient method for scrutiny of EC

---

[46] Nusrat Zar [2006] JR 26.

compatibility of price regulation scheme would be investigation by the EC Commission).
(M) JUDICIAL REVIEW OR FAMILY PROCEEDINGS. *Re S (Habeas Corpus)* [2003] EWHC
2734 (Admin) [2004] 1 FLR 590 at [17] (court where care proceedings being tried representing
the proper forum for litigating issues); *A v A Health Authority* [2002] EWHC 18 (Fam/Admin)
[2002] Fam 213 at [97] (asking whether "the task facing the judge is to come to a decision for
and on behalf of a child or incompetent adult" or "to review the decision of a public authority
taken in the exercise of some statutory power then the governing principles are those of public
law"); *R v Portsmouth Hospitals NHS Trust, ex p Glass* [1999] 2 FLR 905 (Family Division
proceedings preferable to judicial review); *R (P and Q) v Secretary of State for the Home
Department* [2001] EWCA Civ 1151 [2001] 1 WLR 2002 at [119]-[120] (Family Division
proceedings more appropriate than Administrative Court where issue whether separation of
incarcerated mother and her child unlawful as seriously compromising welfare of the child); *C
v Bury Metropolitan Borough Council* [2002] EWHC 1438 (Fam) [2002] 2 FLR 868 at [55]
(human rights challenges to care plans and child-placements should be heard in the Family
Division, preferably by judges with Administrative Court experience); *Re M (Care Proceedings:
Judicial Review)* [2003] EWHC 850 (Admin) [2003] 2 FLR 171 at [35] (judicial review inapt
"where the object of the proceedings is, as here, to prevent a local authority commencing
emergency protection or care proceedings"); *S v Knowsley Borough Council* [2004] EWHC 491
(Fam) [2004] 2 FLR 716 at [67] (judicial review appropriate in context of local authority
functions and ongoing secure accommodation order); <2.5.11(D)> (dual listing: judicial review
and Family proceedings).
(N) VOLUNTARY BILL OF INDICTMENT. *R (Director of Public Prosecutions) v
Camberwell Youth Court* [2004] EWHC 1805 (Admin) [2005] 1 WLR 810 (judicial review
more appropriate than voluntary bill of indictment where issue as to youth court's decision
whether to take jurisdiction in criminal prosecution; provided that claim pursued expeditiously).
(O) STATUTORY REVIEW. *R (G) v Immigration Appeal Tribunal* [2004] EWCA Civ 1731
[2005] 1 WLR 1445 (statutory review being "final", treated as meaning that judicial review an
abuse of process).
(P) OTHER. *R (Smith) v North East Derbyshire Primary Care Trust* [2006] EWHC 1338
(Admin) (claimant should have approached patients forum before seeking judicial review
complaining of failure to consult the public); *R (Humphries) v Secretary of State for Work and
Pensions* [2008] EWHC 1585 (Admin) at [107]-[109] (claimant should have complained to
independent case examiner).

36.4 **Other remedy curing public law wrong.** Pursuit of a suitable alternative means of
recourse may be able to remedy a public law wrong, whether by virtue of the substantive
decision or curative approach.

36.4.1 **Fairness and rights of immediate recourse.** *R (Holloway) v Oxfordshire County
Council* [2007] EWHC 776 (Admin) [2007] LGR 891 at [44] (interim order not breaching
natural justice given safeguards allowing later challenge); *R (M) v Secretary of State for
Constitutional Affairs* [2004] EWCA Civ 312 [2004] 1 WLR 2298 at [39(1)] (interim ASBO
without notice but with safeguards of review/discharge); *Wiseman v Borneman* [1971] AC 297,
318F-G (decisions without a hearing but speedy annulment or amendment available); *R (SP)
v Secretary of State for the Home Department* [2004] EWCA Civ 1750 at [58] (duty to allow
representations prior to segregation order, rights of immediate challenge not sufficing); *R
(Wright) v Secretary of State for Health* [2007] EWCA Civ 999 [2008] QB 422 (provisional
listing of unsuitable care worker needing to be preceded by right to make representations).

36.4.2 **Whether appeal curing procedural unfairness.**
(A) APPEAL CAPABLE OF CURING UNFAIRNESS. *R (DR) v Head Teacher of St George's
Catholic School* [2002] EWCA Civ 1822 [2003] ELR 104 (in general, unfairness in the context

of school exclusion decisions capable of being cured by means of statutory appeal); *R v Secretary of State for the Home Department, ex p Sesay* [1995] Imm AR 521, 522-523 (full immigration appeal can mean justice overall); *R v Visitors to the Inns of Court, ex p Calder & Persaud* [1994] QB 1, 59C ("an appeal to the visitors is or should be a full rehearing on the merits and as such it should cure any procedural defect or breach of natural justice on the part of the tribunal"); *Modahl v British Athletic Federation* [2001] EWCA Civ 1447 [2002] 1 WLR 1192 (procedure as a whole fair, including appeal); *Century National Merchant Bank and Trust Co Ltd v Davies* [1998] AC 628, 639C ("the statutory right of appeal to the Court of Appeal, exercising wide original jurisdiction, should be sufficient to achieve justice to the bank").

(B) APPEAL NOT CURING UNFAIRNESS. *Calvin v Carr* [1980] AC 574, 592C-593C ("no clear and absolute rule can be laid down on the question whether defects in natural justice appearing at an original hearing, whether administrative or quasi-judicial, can be `cured' through appeal proceedings"); *Ridge v Baldwin* [1964] AC 40, 79, 113, 125, 129 (unfairness not cured); *Malloch v Aberdeen Corporation* [1971] 1 WLR 1578, 1598E-F ("A limited right of appeal on the merits affords no argument against the existence of a right to a precedent hearing"); *R v Hereford Magistrates' Court, ex p Rowlands* [1998] QB 110 (where procedural unfairness leading to magistrates conviction, accused entitled to judicial review notwithstanding availability of appeal to Crown Court); *R v Bedwellty Justices, ex p Williams* [1997] AC 225, 235E-G, 236C (trial on indictment not an adequate alternative to judicial review for committal on inadmissible evidence); *R (Haringey Consortium of Disabled People and Carers Association) v Haringey London Borough Council* (2002) 5 CCLR 422 at [49] (inadequate consultation not cured by appeal, because budgetary decision easier to overturn before firmly made); *R (S) v Knowsley NHS Primary Care Trust* [2006] EWHC 26 (Admin) at [71] (enforceable duty of fairness at first stage); *R (Refugee Legal Centre) v Secretary of State for the Home Department* [2004] EWCA Civ 1481 [2005] 1 WLR 2219 at [15] (availability of individual appeal to adjudicator not of itself an answer if Secretary of State's asylum decision-making system inherently unfair).

36.4.3 Whether other safeguards preventing/curing unfairness.

R v Secretary of State for Transport, ex p Gwent County Council [1988] QB 429, 435E-G (Secretary of State unable to cure defective local inquiry); *R v Secretary of State for Education, ex p Cumbria County Council* [1994] ELR 220, 228A-D (breach by school governors of legitimate expectation of consultation cured by Minister's lawful approval of their decision); *R v Swansea City Council, ex p Elitestone Ltd* [1993] 2 PLR 65, 70H-71E (full committee's confirmation "was a consideration afresh", curing sub-committee's procedural irregularity); *R v Gwent County Council, ex p Bryant* [1988] COD 19 (where legitimate expectation of consultation, later decision-maker could rectify earlier unfairness); *R (Ramda) v Secretary of State for the Home Department* [2002] EWHC 1278 (Admin) at [27] (availability of right of petition to the ECtHR not a right of appeal capable of curing national authorities' failure to provide a fair trial); *Re C (care proceedings: disclosure of local authority's decision-making process)* [2002] EWHC 1379 (Fam) [2002] FCR 673 at [240] (although unfairness and incompatibility with HRA:ECHR Art 6 in earlier stages of care proceedings, nevertheless fair trial overall); *Independent Publishing Co Ltd v Attorney General of Trinidad and Tobago* [2004] UKPC 26 [2005] 1 AC 190 at [92] (availability of bail making good shortcomings of contempt hearing, for purposes of constitutional due process guarantee).

36.4.4 Whether defect cured by reconsideration/further act.

Grant v Teacher's Appeal Tribunal [2006] UKPC 59 (decision invalid for expiry of board's terms of appointment but genuine consideration afresh fair and valid); *R (Sardar) v Watford Borough Council* [2006] EWHC 1590 (Admin) (reconsultation not sufficing because not at formative stage and leaving residual feeling of unfairness); *R (Martin) v Secretary of State for the Home Department* [2003] EWHC 1512 (Admin) (defective parole dossier remedied by later reconsideration); *R (Banks) v Secretary of State for the Environment, Food and Rural Affairs* [2004] EWHC 416 (Admin) at [107] (no evidence of a "fair, open-minded and comprehensive" reconsideration), [108] (not "a genuinely open-minded review" rather "striving to defend an earlier decision in the context of adversarial litigation"); *R v London Borough of Barnet, ex p B* [1994] ELR 357, 371G-H (where reconsultation, ask "whether the ultimate decision is a fair one reached by fair methods"); *R v Legal Aid Board, ex p Donn & Co (a Firm)* [1996] 3 All ER 1, 13b-14d (unfairness in not having all material not cured where committee not reconvened to meet together again as a committee); *R v P Borough Council, ex p S* [1999] Fam 188, 221G-222A (reconsideration insufficient because "the need for an open-minded approach by the local authority as the decision-maker is at an end and it was defending a final decision"); *R v Lincolnshire County Council and Wealden District Council, ex p Atkinson, Wales and Stratford* (1996) 8 Admin LR 529 (whether considering relevancies at a later stage in a multi-stage process and/or giving undertakings to those affected could cure initial failure to consider relevant matters/make relevant inquiries).

36.4.5 Failure to take opportunity of cure. <31.4> (failure to complain/request).

36.4.6 Future opportunity of cure. *R (Neptune Wharf Ltd) v Secretary of State for Trade and Industry* [2007] EWHC 1036 (Admin) [2007] 3 All ER 676 at [36] (no unfairness in lack of prewarning of CPO postponement, where open-minded receptiveness to subsequent representations); *R (British Beer and Pub Association) v Canterbury City Council* [2005] EWHC 1318 (Admin) [2006] LGR 596 at [106] (policy overrigid but proposed addendum making remedy unnecessary); *R (Broadbent) v Parole Board* [2005] EWHC 1207 (Admin) (Parole Board error of approach but next parole hearing imminent); *R v Commissioners of Customs and Excise, ex p Mortimer* [1999] 1 WLR 17, 23G-H (lack of reasons but full appeal to magistrates); *R v Secretary of State for the Home Department, ex p Pierson* [1998] AC 539, 593E-F (refusal to intervene on basis of unfairness because Secretary of State willing to consider any further representations); *R (Q) v Secretary of State for the Home Department* [2003] EWCA Civ 364 [2004] QB 36 at [91] (fact that Secretary of State's willingness to reconsider "not a substitute for proper and fair primary decision making"); *R v Oxford Regional Mental Health Review Tribunal, ex p Secretary of State for the Home Department* [1988] AC 120, 128A-F (further hearing no cure since issues would not all remain open); *R v Hereford Magistrates' Court, ex p Rowlands* [1998] QB 110 (where procedural unfairness leading to magistrates' conviction defendant entitled to judicial review notwithstanding availability of appeal to Crown Court); *R v Bedwellty Justices, ex p Williams* [1997] AC 225, 235C-236D (committal on inadmissible evidence not cured by challengeability of admissibility at trial); *R (S) v Knowsley NHS Primary Care Trust* [2006] EWHC 26 (Admin) (appropriate for court to intervene to prevent unfairness, where live evidence and legal representation wrongly refused by NHS Trust, rather than leaving consequences for possible cure on appeal).

36.4.7 Judicial review curing procedural deficiencies.
(A) ARTICLE 6: JUDICIAL REVIEW AS "FULL JURISDICTION". <59.5.7>
(B) OTHER. *R (L) v Secretary of State for the Home Department* [2003] EWCA Civ 25 [2003] 1 WLR 1230 at [29] ("a s.115 [Nationality and Immigration Act] decision [to certify a human rights claim as clearly unfounded] is one which the Court is as well placed as the Home Secretary to take, and we go on to review the evidence in that light. We consider that this cures, in the cases before us, the unfairness which we accept would otherwise have resulted from the use of s.115 before it was promulgated").

36.4.8 Nullity and cure. <44.3.3>.

387

> **P37 Proportionality template.** Proportionality means state proof of action as appropriate and necessary to achieve a legitimate aim.

37.1 Proportionality principles

37.1 Proportionality principles. Proportionality is well-developed in Luxembourg (ECJ), Strasbourg (ECtHR), Privy Council constitutional appeals and comparative[47] jurisprudence. Domestic Courts apply proportionality principles in EC and HRA cases and increasingly in other public law cases. The structured proportionality template involves the State having to prove that a measure is appropriate and necessary to achieve a legitimate aim.

37.1.1 Proportionality in a nutshell. *B v Secretary of State for the Home Department* [2000] UKHRR 498, 502C (Sedley LJ: "In essence [proportionality] amounts to this: a measure which interferes with a Community or human right must not only be authorised by law but must correspond to a pressing social need and go no further than strictly necessary in a pluralistic society to achieve its permitted purpose; or, more shortly, must be appropriate and necessary to its legitimate aim"); <P57> (proportionality); *R (G) v Nottinghamshire Healthcare NHS Trust* [2008] EWHC 1096 (Admin) at [97] (proportionality as a "value judgment").

37.1.2 Proportionality: the *De Freitas* formulation. *Elloy De Freitas v Permanent Secretary of Ministry of Agriculture Fisheries Lands and Housing* [1999] AC 69, 80F-G (Lord Clyde, asking "whether (i) the legislative objective is sufficiently important to justify limiting a fundamental right; (ii) the measures designed to meet the legislative objective are rationally connected to it; and (iii) the means used to impair the right or freedom are no more than is necessary to accomplish the objective");*Huang v Secretary of State for the Home Department* [2007] UKHL 11 [2007] 2 AC 167 at [19] (adding an overriding requirement balancing the interests of society and the individual/group). *De Freitas* was applied in the HL in *R v Secretary of State for the Home Department, ex p Daly* [2001] UKHL 26 [2001] 2 AC 532 at [27] (the familiar "contours of the principle of proportionality"); *R v A (No.2)* [2001] UKHL 25 [2002] 1 AC 45 at [38]; *R (Pretty) v Director of Public Prosecutions* [2001] UKHL 61 [2002] 1 AC 800 at [93]; *Attorney General v Scotcher* [2005] UKHL 36 [2005] 1 WLR 1867 at [29].

37.1.3 The basic proportionality template. *R v Secretary of State for Health, ex p Eastside Cheese Company* [1999] EuLR 968 at [41] (asking whether measures are "appropriate and necessary in order to achieve the objectives legitimately pursued by the legislation in question; when there is a choice between several appropriate measures recourse must be had to the least onerous, and the disadvantages caused must not be disproportionate to the aims pursued"); *Centros Ltd v Erhvervs-og Selskabsstyrelsen* [2000] Ch 446 at [34] ("national measures liable to hinder or make less attractive the exercise of fundamental freedoms guaranteed by the Treaty must fulfil four conditions: they must be applied in a non-discriminatory manner; they must be justified by imperative requirements in the general interest; they must be suitable for securing the attainment of the objective which they pursue, and they must not go beyond what is necessary in order to attain it"); *R (International Transport Roth GmbH) v Secretary of State for the Home Department* [2002] EWCA Civ 158 [2003] QB 728 at [52] ("not merely must the impairment of the individual's rights be no more than necessary for the attainment of the public policy objective sought, but also that it must not impose an excessive burden on the individual concerned"); <58.3.1> (proportionality and common law rights).

37.1.4 Proportionality as a structured approach/methodical concept. *R v Shayler* [2002]

---

[47] Tom Hickman [2007] JR 31; Maik Martin & Alexander Horne [2008] JR 169.

UKHL 11 [2003] 1 AC 247 at [76]-[77] (Lord Hope, discussing "the structure of analysis" and "carefully constructed set of criteria" or proportionality); *London Regional Transport v Mayor of London* 24th August 2001 unrep. at [57] (Sedley LJ, referring to "the methodical concept of proportionality. Proportionality ... replaces an elastic concept with which political scientists are more at home than lawyers with a structured inquiry: Does the measure meet a recognised and pressing social need? Does it negate the primary right or restrict it more than is necessary? Are the reasons given for it logical?").

37.1.5 **Proportionality and degree of intensity.** *R v Shayler* [2002] UKHL 11 [2003] 1 AC 247 at [33] (Lord Bingham: "in any application for judicial review alleging [a] violation of a Convention right the court will now conduct a much more rigorous and intrusive review than was once thought to be permissible", referring to *Daly*), [61] (Lord Hope: "A close and penetrating examination of the factual justification for the restriction is needed if the fundamental rights enshrined in the Convention are to remain practical and effective for everyone who wishes to exercise them"), [111] (Lord Hutton); <58.5.9> (proportionality and width of latitude).

37.1.6 **Need to start with the written instrument: `codified justification'.** *R (Mahmood) v Secretary of State for the Home Department* [2001] 1 WLR 840 at [40] (Lord Phillips MR: "Interference with human rights can only be justified to the extent permitted by the Convention itself"); *R (Saadi) v Secretary of State for the Home Department* [2002] UKHL 41 [2002] 1 WLR 3131 (particular approach to proportionality in the context of immigration detention under Article 5(1)(f)); *R (P and Q) v Secretary of State for the Home Department* [2001] EWCA Civ 1151 [2001] 1 WLR 2002 at [64] ("we have to determine ... whether the interference ... is really proportionate to the legitimate aim (sanctioned by [the relevant ECHR Article]) which it seeks to pursue"); <59.1.3>.

37.1.7 **Proportionality and EC law rights.** *R v Secretary of State for the Environment, ex p National & Local Government Officers' Association* (1993) 5 Admin LR 785, 799A-B (Neill LJ: "The principle of proportionality [requires] that the means used to attain a given end should be no more than what is appropriate and necessary to attain that end. In the context of an administrative decision this means that there must be a reasonable relationship between the objective which is sought to be achieved and the means used to that end"); *R v Secretary of State for the Environment, ex p Oldham Metropolitan Borough Council* [1998] ICR 367, 384H-385A (Laws J, explaining that proportionality "is one of the fundamental principles of Community law ... having been developed by the Court of Justice as an integral part of the legal discipline applied by that court to the Community institutions in relation to their implementation of the Community legal order. When member states also act to implement Community law, or take measures necessarily relying on exemptions from Treaty obligations provided by Community law, they too will be subject to this internal law"); *CR Smith Glaziers (Dunfermline) Ltd v Customs and Excise Commissioners* [2003] UKHL 7 [2003] 1 WLR 656 at [28] (formality as to provision of information serving no legitimate objective and so disproportionate).

37.1.8 **Proportionality and HRA/ECHR rights.**[48] *Attorney General's Reference No.2 of 2001* [2003] UKHL 68 [2004] 2 AC 72 at [120] (Lord Hobhouse: "a basic principle of human rights law is the principle of proportionality"); *R (Alconbury Developments Ltd) v Secretary of State for the Environment Transport and the Regions* [2001] UKHL 23 [2003] 2 AC 295 at [51] (Lord Slynn: "Reference to the Human Rights Act 1998 ... makes it necessary that the court should

---

[48] Richard Clayton QC [2002] JR 124.

ask whether what is done is compatible with Convention rights. That will often require that the question should be asked whether the principle of proportionality has been satisfied"); *R v Secretary of State for the Home Department, ex p Daly* [2001] UKHL 26 [2001] 2 AC 532 at [27] (Lord Steyn: "the doctrine of proportionality may require the reviewing court to assess the balance which the decision maker has struck, not merely whether it is within the range of rational or reasonable decisions" and "the proportionality test may go further than the traditional grounds of review inasmuch as it may require attention to be directed to the relative weight accorded to interests and considerations"); *Brown v Stott (Procurator Fiscal, Dunfermline)* [2003] 1 AC 681, 720D-E (Lord Hope, asking "(1) is the right which is in question an absolute right, or is it a right which is open to modification or restriction because it is not absolute? (2) if it is not absolute, does the modification or restriction which is contended for have a legitimate aim in the public interest? (3) if so, is there a reasonable relationship of proportionality between the means employed and the aim sought to be realised? The answer to the question whether the right is or is not absolute is to be found by examining the terms of the article in the light of the judgments of the court. The question whether a legitimate aim is being pursued enables account to be taken of the public interest in the rule of law. The principle of proportionality directs attention to the question whether a fair balance has been struck between the general interest of the community in the realisation of that aim and the protection of the fundamental rights of the individual"); *Ghaidan v Godin-Mendoza* [2004] UKHL 30 [2004] 2 AC 557 at [18] (measure "fall[ing]" at the first hurdle: the absence of a legitimate aim"); *A v Secretary of State for the Home Department* [2004] UKHL 56 [2005] 2 AC 68 (detention of non-nationals without trial not rationally connected with security objective, since nationals also posing similar threat), [43] (Lord Bingham), [83] (Lord Nicholls), [133] (Lord Hope); *R (Baiai) v Secretary of State for the Home Department* [2008] UKHL 53 [2008] 3 WLR 549 at [31] (HRA proportionality and marriage-approval requirement).

37.1.9 **Least intrusive means?** *R (Pascoe) v First Secretary of State* [2006] EWHC 2356 (Admin) [2007] 1 WLR 885 at [75] (no universal test of "least intrusive means"); *Smith v Secretary of State for Trade and Industry* [2007] EWHC 1013 (Admin) [2008] 1 WLR 394 (not always necessary to show that least intrusive measure chosen).

37.1.10 **Proportionality: onus on the state/defendant body.***R (Professional Contractors Ltd) v Commissioners of Inland Revenue* [2001] EWHC Admin 236 [2001] EuLR 514 at [71] (Burton J: "The onus is upon the claimant to show a contravention of the [Treaty] Article. The onus then shifts to the defendant to justify the restriction") (CA is at [2001] EWCA Civ 1945 [2002] EuLR 329); *R v Secretary of State for Employment, ex p Seymour-Smith* [1999] 2 AC 554 (ECJ) at [77] ("it is for the member state, as the author of the allegedly discriminatory rule, to show that the said rule reflects a legitimate aim of its social policy, that that aim is unrelated to any discrimination based on sex, and that it could reasonably consider that the means chosen were suitable for attaining that aim"), applied in *R v Secretary of State for Employment, ex p Seymour-Smith (No.2)* [2000] 1 WLR 435, 450C-452E; *R (Samaroo) v Secretary of State for the Home Department* [2001] EWCA Civ 1139 [2001] UKHRR 1150 at [39] ("What is required is that the Secretary of State justify a derogation from a Convention right, and that the justification be `convincingly established'"); *Mendoza v Ghaidan* [2002] EWCA Civ 1533 [2003] Ch 380 at [18] (special burden on the State in Article 14 cases, where discrimination said to be justified) (HL is [2004] UKHL 30 [2004] 2 AC 557).

37.1.11 **Proportionality and scrutiny of evidence/reasoning.** <58.4>.

38.1 The requirement of sufficient interest
38.2 The approach to sufficient interest
38.3 Standing at the permission/substantive stages
38.4 Standing under the HRA: the victim test

38.1 The requirement of sufficient interest.A claimant for judicial review must have a "sufficient interest" in the subject-matter.

38.1.1 The standing rules. See Supreme Court Act 1981 s.31(3) <64.1>; HRA s.7 <64.7> (the victim test) <38.4>.

38.1.2 Sufficient interest: a special broad test. *R v Inland Revenue Commissioners, ex p National Federation of Self-Employed and Small Businesses Ltd* [1982] AC 617, 642B-E (Lord Diplock: "the draftsman ... avoided using the expression `a person aggrieved', although it lay ready to his hand. He chose instead ... ordinary English words which, on the face of them, leave the court an unfettered discretion to decide what in its own good judgment it considers to be `a sufficient interest' on the part of [a claimant] in the particular circumstances of the case before it. For my part I would not strain to give them any narrower meaning"); *Cook v Southend Borough Council* [1990] 2 QB 1, 8B-C (Woolf LJ, referring to the test as "deliberately substituted" for the narrower test of "person aggrieved, which was the test which applied to applications for the prerogative orders prior to the introduction of judicial review in 1977").

38.1.3 A necessary condition: standing is not conferred by consent. *R v Inland Revenue Commissioners, ex p National Federation of Self Employed and Small Businesses Ltd* [1982] AC 617, 660B (Lord Roskill, referring to claimants having to satisfy standing as a "condition precedent to their obtaining the [remedy] which they seek"); *R v Secretary of State for Social Services, ex p Child Poverty Action Group* [1990] 2 QB 540, 556E-F (Woolf LJ: "we make it clear that in our view the question of locus standi goes to jurisdiction of the court... The parties are not entitled to confer jurisdiction, which the court does not have, on the court by consent"), applied in *R v Brent London Borough Council, ex p Connery* [1990] 2 All ER 353, 354e and in *R v Secretary of State for the Environment, ex p Friends of the Earth Ltd* [1994] 2 CMLR 760 (Schiemann J), 762-763.

38.1.4 Judgment, not discretion. *R v Inland Revenue Commissioners, ex p National Federation of Self-Employed and Small Businesses Ltd* [1982] AC 617, 659A (Lord Roskill, treating "sufficient interest" as "a mixed question of fact and law; a question of fact and degree ... having regard to all the circumstances of the case"), 631C (not a "pure discretion. The matter is one for decision, a mixed decision of fact and law, which the court must decide on legal principles"); *R v Secretary of State for the Environment, ex p Rose Theatre Trust Co* [1990] 1 QB 504, 520C ("not purely a matter of discretion"); *R v North West Leicestershire District Council, ex p Moses* 14th September 1999 unrep. (Scott Baker J) (standing not a discretion but a matter of judgment).

38.1.5 A unified test for the different judicial review remedies. *R v Somerset County Council, ex p Dixon* [1998] Env LR 111, 120 ("The time is past when doctrinal niceties as opposed to substantive merits could distinguish locus for prohibition from locus for mandamus or certiorari"); *R v Inland Revenue Commissioners, ex p National Federation of Self-Employed and Small Businesses Ltd* [1982] AC 617, 638C-F (describing the 1977 reforms as serving "to sweep away these procedural differences including, in particular, differences as to locus standi").

38.1.6 Sufficient interest in the remedy, not the particular ground. *R (Kides) v South Cambridgeshire District Council* [2002] EWCA Civ 1370 [2002] 4 PLR 66 at [132]-[134] (Jonathan Parker LJ: "there is an important distinction to be drawn between, on the one hand, a person who brings proceedings having no real or genuine interest in obtaining the relief sought, and on the other hand a person who, whilst legitimately and perhaps passionately interested in obtaining the relief sought, relies as grounds for seeking that relief on matters in which he has no personal interest. I cannot see how it can be just to debar a litigant who has a real and genuine interest in obtaining the relief which he seeks from relying, in support of his claim for that relief, on grounds (which may be good grounds) in which he has no personal interest. It seems to me that a litigant who has a real and genuine interest in challenging an administrative decision must be entitled to present his challenge on all available grounds"), applied in *R (Hammerton) v London Underground Ltd* [2002] EWHC 2307 (Admin) at [209] (in the case of a "public interest litigant").

38.1.7 Legal incapacity/unincorporated associations.[49] *R (Davies) v Secretary of State for the Environment, Food and Rural Affairs* [2002] EWHC 2762 (Admin) (judicial review struck out as an abuse of process, where claimant having no authority to advance the interests of a moribund company said in the proceedings to have been unlawfully deprived of its river navigation functions); *R v Ministry of Agriculture Fisheries and Food, ex p British Pig Industry Support Group* [2000] EuLR 724 at [108] (no "overriding requirement for [a claimant] for judicial review to have legal personality, but it is important in such a case that adequate provision should be made for the protection of the [defendant] in costs"); *R v London Borough of Tower Hamlets, ex p Tower Hamlets Combined Traders Association* [1994] COD 325; *R v Traffic Commissioner for the North Western Traffic Area, ex p BRAKE* [1996] COD 248; *R v Darlington Borough Council, ex p Association of Darlington Taxi Owners* [1994] COD 424 (treating unincorporated association as lacking legal capacity to bring any action, including an application for judicial review, quite apart from questions of standing); *R v Leeds City Council, ex p Alwoodly Golf Club* 15th September 1995 unrep. (following *Darlington Taxi* and holding that no legal capacity); *R v Sheffield City Council, ex p Power* The Times 7th July 1994; *R v Crown Court at Maidstone, ex p Harris* [1994] COD 514 (unincorporated association a "person" for the purposes of statutory application for revocation of a liquor licence); *R v Gloucestershire County Council, ex p Barry* [1996] 4 All ER 421 (CA), 424c (Royal Association for Disability and Rehabilitation substituted as claimant, following death of individual); *R v Secretary of State for Foreign and Commonwealth Affairs, ex p British Council of Turkish Cypriot Associations* [1998] COD 336 (challenge by unincorporated association rejected on substantive grounds); *R v Liverpool City Council, ex p Baby Products Association* [2000] LGR 171 (first claimant an unincorporated association; challenge succeeding); *R (West End Street Traders' Association) v City of Westminster* [2004] EWHC 1167 (Admin) [2005] LGR 143; *R (Hampstead Heath Winter Swimming Club) v Corporation of London* [2005] EWHC 713 (Admin) [2005] 1 WLR 2930 at [12] (judicial review sought by club and secretary); <18.1.17> (incorporating for protection against costs risks); <38.2.9(C)> (group not having enhanced interest merely by amalgamating).

38.2 The approach to sufficient interest. The approach to standing is liberal. Financial interest is sufficient but not necessary. Public interest considerations favour the testing of the legality of executive action, it being contrary to the public interest for public law wrongs to go unchecked because no person has standing. It is relevant to consider whether the claimant

---

[49] Kris Gledhill [1996] JR 67.

is a "busybody" and whether there is an obviously better-placed challenger choosing not to complain.

38.2.1 Liberal approach to standing: technical restrictions relaxed. *R v Inland Revenue Commissioners, ex p National Federation of Self-Employed and Small Businesses Ltd* [1982] AC 617, 641C-D (Lord Diplock, describing removal of "technical restrictions on locus standi" representing "progress towards a comprehensive system of administrative law that I regard as having been the greatest achievement of the English courts in my judicial lifetime"); *R (Feakins) v Secretary of State for the Environment, Food and Rural Affairs* [2003] EWCA Civ 1546 [2004] 1 WLR 1761 at [21] (Dyson LJ: "In recent years, there has unquestionably been a considerable liberalisation of what is required to found a sufficiency of interest for the purposes of standing"); *R v Secretary of State for Foreign and Commonwealth Affairs, ex p World Development Movement Ltd* [1995] 1 WLR 386, 395F (Rose LJ, describing the "increasingly liberal approach to standing on the part of the courts during the last 12 years").

38.2.2 Not rights, but public law wrongs. *R v Somerset County Council, ex p Dixon* [1998] Env LR 111, 121 (Sedley J: "Public law is not at base about rights, even though abuses of power may and often do invade private rights; it is about wrongs - that is to say misuses of public power; and the courts have always been alive to the fact that a person or organisation with no particular stake in the issue or the outcome may, without in any sense being a mere meddler, wish and be well placed to call the attention of the court to an apparent misuse of public power. If an arguable case of such misuse can be made out on an application for [permission], the court's only concern is to ensure that it is not being done for an ill motive. It is if, on a substantive hearing, the abuse of power is made out that everything relevant to the [claimant]'s standing will be weighed up, whether with regard to the grant or simply to the form of [remedy]").

38.2.3 Liberal access for individuals. *R v Legal Aid Board, ex p Bateman* [1992] 1 WLR 711, 718B (describing "the desirability of the courts recognising in appropriate cases the right of responsible citizens to enter the lists for the benefit of the public, or of a section of the public, of which they themselves are members"); *R v Secretary of State for Foreign & Commonwealth Affairs, ex p Rees-Mogg* [1994] QB 552 (individual challenging ratification of Maastricht Treaty); *R v HM Treasury, ex p Smedley* [1985] QB 657 (individual challenging draft Order in Council relating to EC budget); *Gillick v West Norfolk and Wisbech Area Health Authority* [1986] AC 112, 176C ("a notable public service in directing judicial attention to [these] problems"); *R v Somerset County Council, ex p Dixon* [1998] Env LR 111, 117 ("there will be, in public life, a certain number of cases of apparent abuse of power in which any individual, simply as a citizen, has a sufficient interest to bring the matter before the court"); *R (Hammerton) v London Underground Ltd* [2002] EWHC 2307 (Admin) at [200] ("deep and knowledgeable interest in historic railway buildings"; not a troublemaker or busybody); *R (Ewing) v Office of the Deputy Prime Minister* [2005] EWCA Civ 1583 [2006] 1 WLR 1260 at [37]-[39] (situation where vexatious litigants setting themselves up "as a public champion" where only "a tenuous connection with the subject matter").

38.2.4 Liberal access for groups. *R v Her Majesty's Inspectorate of Pollution, ex p Greenpeace Ltd* [1994] 4 All ER 329, 350c-j (standing for "an entirely responsible and respected body with a genuine concern for the environment ... who, with its particular experience in environmental matters, its access to experts in the relevant realms of science and technology (not to mention the law), is able to mount a carefully selected, focused, relevant and well-argued challenge"); *R v Secretary of State for Foreign and Commonwealth Affairs, ex p World Development Movement Ltd* [1995] 1 WLR 386 (WDM successfully challenging aid to Pergau Dam), 395C-396B; *R v Minister of Agriculture Fisheries and Food, ex p Protesters*

Animal Information Network Ltd 20th December 1996 unrep. (serious application raising issues of real concern, made by responsible body with serious interest in the subject matter); *R (Quintavalle) v Human Fertilisation and Embryology Authority* [2002] EWHC 2785 (Admin) [2003] 2 All ER 105 at [5] (judicial review proceedings brought on behalf of group concerned with ethical issues in assisted reproduction; HL is [2005] UKHL 28 [2005] 2 AC 561); *R v Hammersmith & Fulham London Borough Council, ex p People Before Profit Ltd* (1982) 80 LGR 322; *R v Poole Borough Council, ex p Beebee* [1991] COD 264 (representatives of British Herpetological Society);*R v Secretary of State for the Home Department, ex p Immigration Law Practitioners' Association* [1997] Imm AR 189 (practitioners' body concerned with implementation and effects of immigration laws treated as entitled to challenge vires of immigration rule change); *R v Sefton Metropolitan Borough Council, ex p Help The Aged* [1997] 4 All ER 532 (test case brought by charity); *R v Secretary of State for Employment, ex p Equal Opportunities Commission* [1995] 1 AC 1 (EOC having standing and capacity to bring judicial review, in context of sex discrimination); *R (Refugee Legal Centre) v Secretary of State for the Home Department* [2004] EWCA Civ 1481 [2005] 1 WLR 2219 at [5] (since individual challenge would "decide nothing about the system itself": "This application is thus a good example of how a body such as the RLC may not only have standing but be best placed to bring an important question such as the present one before the court").

38.2.5 **A relaxed attitude to claimant identity/substitution.** *Wheeler v Leicester City Council* [1985] AC 1054, 1073F ("In reality it is an appeal by the club and I shall so treat it"); *R v Life Assurance and Unit Trust Regulatory Organisation, ex p Ross* [1993] QB 17, 45B (overlooking as a "technicality" that "the proper [claimant] was probably Winchester rather than the [claimant] personally"); *R v Secretary of State for Education & Science, ex p Parveen Malik* [1994] ELR 121, 122F (ordering that Mrs Malik "be substituted for the original [claimant], Mr Amin, because his application was beset by difficulties in connection with legal aid"); *R v North West Leicestershire District Council, ex p Moses* 14th September 1999 unrep. (where claimant had moved house away from airport development complained of, CA commenting that: "had the challenge from every other standpoint been soundly based, it would be unfortunate to have to reject it - rather, say, than substitute for Ms Moses another [claimant] who, as a resident of Kegworth, was equally concerned about the airport's extension - merely because of Ms Moses' move"); <22.4.4> (substitution of claimant).

38.2.6 **Standing and financial interest.**
(A) FINANCIAL/COMMERCIAL CONCERN NOT NECESSARY. *R v Inland Revenue Commissioners, ex p National Federation of Self-Employed and Small Businesses Ltd* [1982] AC 617, 646B-C ("a direct financial or legal interest is not now required"); *R v Secretary of State for the Environment, ex p Rose Theatre Trust Co* [1990] 1 QB 504, 520D ("a direct financial or legal interest is not required").
(B) FINANCIAL/COMMERCIAL CONCERN SUFFICIENT. *R (Mount Cook Land Ltd) v Westminster City Council* [2003] EWCA Civ 1346 [2004] 1 PLR 29 at [45] at [46] ("judicial review applications by would-be developers or objectors to development in planning cases are by their very nature driven primarily by commercial or private motive rather than a high-minded concern for the public weal"); *R v Canterbury City Council, ex p Springimage Ltd* [1993] 3 PLR 58, 61H (sufficient that person's commercial interest realistically affected by decision); *Standard Commercial Property Securities Ltd v Glasgow City Council* [2006] UKHL 50 (judicial review by rival developer); *R v Ogwr Borough Council, ex p Carter Commercial Developments Ltd* [1989] 2 PLR 54, 58H ("competing developers are entitled to attack each other's grants [of planning permission] provided the legal basis for such attack exists"); *R v Monopolies & Mergers Commission, ex p Argyll Group Plc* [1986] 1 WLR 763, 774B (no need for "a pure and burning passion to see that public law is rightly administered"); *R v Lord Chancellor, ex p Child Poverty Action Group* [1999] 1 WLR 347, 353H (many judicial review

cases involving claimant "seeking to protect some private interest of his or her own").

38.2.7 **Standing and the public interest.**[50] <38.2.8> (avoiding the standing lacuna); <2.5.5> (public interest litigation); *R v Lord Chancellor, ex p Child Poverty Action Group* [1999] 1 WLR 347, 353G (public interest challenge one having the "essential characteristics ... that it raises public law issues which are of general importance, where the [claimant] has no private interest in the outcome of the case"); *R v Secretary of State for Trade and Industry, ex p Greenpeace Ltd* [1998] Env LR 415, 425 (Laws J: "a public interest plaintiff ... has to act as a friend of the court; precisely because he has no rights of his own, his only *locus* is to assert the public interest. Litigation of this kind is now an accepted and greatly valued dimension of the judicial review jurisdiction, but it has to be controlled with particular strictness. It is a field especially open to potential abuse... Strict judicial controls, particularly as regards time, will foster not hinder the development of such litigation in the future"); *R v Secretary of State for Trade and Industry, ex p Greenpeace* [2000] Env LR 221, 259 ("I cannot envisage many cases where, on the same facts, a public interest [claimant] would be refused permission to apply because of delay but a private [claimant] would be permitted to proceed"); *R (Hammerton) v London Underground Ltd* [2002] EWHC 2307 (Admin) at [203] (claimant a public interest litigant); *Hoffmann-La Roche (F) & Co AG v Secretary of State for Trade and Industry* [1975] AC 295, 365E-H (Lord Diplock, explaining that where a statutory instrument is held to be unlawful: "Although such a decision is directly binding only as between the parties to the proceedings in which it was made, the application of the doctrine of precedent has the consequence of enabling the benefit of it to accrue to all other persons whose legal rights have been interfered with in reliance on the law which the statutory instrument purported to declare").

38.2.8 **Avoiding the standing lacuna.** *R v Secretary of State for the Home Department, ex p Bulger* [2001] EWHC Admin 119 at [20] ("the threshold for standing in judicial review has generally been set by the courts at a low level. This ... is because of the importance in public law that someone should be able to call decision makers to account, lest the rule of law break down and private rights be denied by public bodies"); *R v Inland Revenue Commissioners, ex p National Federation of Self-Employed and Small Businesses Ltd* [1982] AC 617, 644E-G (Lord Diplock, anxious to avoid the "grave lacuna in our system of public law if a pressure group, like the federation, or even a single public-spirited taxpayer, were prevented by outdated technical rules of locus standi from bringing the matter to the attention of the court to vindicate the rule of law and get the unlawful conduct stopped"); *R v General Council of the Bar, ex p Percival* [1991] 1 QB 212, 231C ("Unless the disappointed complainant is regarded as having sufficient locus standi to challenge the decision it is difficult to see who else could be expected to do it"); *R v North Thames Regional Health Authority and Chelsea & Westminster NHS Trust, ex p L* [1996] Med LR 385 (Sedley J: "It is legitimate to ask who, if not B, would have a sufficient interest to seek the correction of a misunderstanding of its own powers by the employing body in such a situation, and whether such a vacuum could be in the public interest"); *R v Secretary of State for Foreign and Commonwealth Affairs, ex p World Development Movement Ltd* [1995] 1 WLR 386, 393H, 395G-H, 402G; cf. *Rape Crisis Centre Company v Secretary of State for the Home Department* The Times 18th July 2000 (fallacy to suppose that public interest in ministers acting lawfully confers a right on every member of the public to bring a challenge).

38.2.9 **Striking a balance.**
(A) STANDING TEST MUST MEAN SOMETHING. *R v Inland Revenue Commissioners, ex p National Federation of Self-Employed and Small Businesses Ltd* [1982] AC 617, 645H (Lord

---

[50] Edite Legere [2005] JR 128.

Fraser at 645H: "while the standard of sufficiency has been relaxed in recent years, the need to have an interest has remained and the fact that RSC Ord 53 r.3 requires a sufficient interest undoubtedly shows that not every [claimant] is entitled to judicial review as of right"); *R v Secretary of State for the Home Department, ex p Ruddock* [1987] 1 WLR 1482, 1485A-C.

(B) BUSYBODIES. *R v Inland Revenue Commissioners, ex p National Federation of Self-Employed and Small Businesses Ltd* [1982] AC 617, 646B-C (Lord Fraser: "a mere busybody does not have a sufficient interest. The difficulty is ... to distinguish between the desire of the busybody to interfere in other people's affairs and the interest of the person affected by or having a reasonable concern with the matter to which the application relates"); *R (Feakins) v Secretary of State for the Environment, Food and Rural Affairs* [2003] EWCA Civ 1546 [2004] 1 WLR 1761 at [23] (Dyson LJ: "if a claimant seeks to challenge a decision in which he has no private law interest, it is difficult to conceive of circumstances in which the court will accord him standing, even where there is a public interest in testing the lawfulness of the decision, if the claimant is acting out of ill-will or for some other improper purpose"); *R v Dean and Chapter of St Paul's Cathedral* [1998] COD 130 (permission refused because, in seeking to challenge ordination of women priests in Wales, Church of England priest a busybody); *R v Legal Aid Board, ex p Bateman* [1992] 1 WLR 711, 718C (Nolan LJ: "It would be inaccurate as well as discourteous to describe [the claimant] as a busybody, but her attempt to intervene is at best quixotic and cannot be upheld").

(C) NO ENHANCED INTEREST MERELY BY AMALGAMATING. *R v Inland Revenue Commissioners, ex p National Federation of Self-Employed and Small Businesses Ltd* [1982] AC 617, 633D (Lord Wilberforce: "an aggregate of individuals each of whom has no interest cannot of itself have an interest"), 646G; *R v Secretary of State for the Environment, ex p Rose Theatre Trust Co* [1990] 1 QB 504, 521F (conceded that an "agglomeration of individuals [could not] ... have a standing which any one individual lacked"), 520E ("The fact that some thousands of people join together and assert that they have an interest does not create an interest if the individuals did not have an interest").

(D) FINDING THE APPROPRIATE BALANCE. *R v Legal Aid Board, ex p Bateman* [1992] 1 WLR 711, 721D ("though the problem of definition is elusive common sense should enable one to identify a sufficient interest when it presents itself, like the horse which is difficult to define but not difficult to recognise when one sees it"); *R v Inland Revenue Commissioners, ex p National Federation of Self-Employed and Small Businesses Ltd* [1982] AC 617, 654D (asking whether claimant having "a genuine grievance reasonably asserted"); *R v Manchester City Council, ex p Baragrove Properties Ltd* (1992) 4 Admin LR 171, 184D (asking whether claimant having "a reasonable concern in the matter to which this application relates"); *R v Secretary of State for the Home Department, ex p Bulger* [2001] EWHC Admin 119 at [20] (victim's family not having standing to challenge tariff set by Lord Chief Justice, given that Crown and defendant able to challenge judicial decisions in criminal cases); cf. *In re S (Hospital Patient: Court's Jurisdiction)* [1996] Fam 1, 18G ("it can be suggested that where a serious justiciable issue is brought before the court by a party with a genuine and legitimate interest in obtaining a decision against an adverse party the court will not impose nice tests to determine the precise legal standing of that claimant").

38.2.10 Relevance of a better-placed challenger.

(A) OBVIOUS CHALLENGER COULD COMPLAIN BUT HAS NOT. *Durayappah v Fernando* [1967] 2 AC 337, 352G-353B (Lord Upjohn, explaining that where "the council should have been given the opportunity of being heard in its defence, if it deliberately chooses not to complain and takes no step to protest against its dissolution, there seems no reason why any other person should have the right to interfere"), 355D (different if circumstances meant "impracticable" for the directly affected council to challenge); *Hoffmann-La Roche (F) & Co AG v Secretary of State for Trade and Industry* [1975] AC 295, 366D-E (Lord Diplock: "locus standi to challenge the validity of subordinate legislation may be restricted, under the court's inherent power to control its own procedure, to a particular category of persons affected by the subordinate legislation, and if none of these persons chooses to challenge it the presumption of validity prevails"); *R v Bow County Court, ex p Pelling* [1999] 1 WLR 1807 (where court refusing to exercise discretion to allow litigant in person to be accompanied by McKenzie friend, challenge brought by potential McKenzie friend not litigant in person (who had suffered no prejudice)); *R v Commissioners of Inland Revenue, ex p Continental Shipping Ltd* [1996] STC 813 (refusing remedy because the taxpayers, to whom reasons statutorily required to be given, not a party to the proceedings).

(B) CLAIMANT NEED NOT BE THE MOST OBVIOUS CHALLENGER. *R (Hammerton) v London Underground Ltd* [2002] EWHC 2307 (Admin) at [201] (Ouseley J, describing it as not "essential, in order for the claimant to have ... standing, that there be no one else who could bring such proceedings"; this being "a relevant factor ... but ... not an essential prerequisite"); *R v Secretary of State for the Home Department, ex p Brind* [1991] 1 AC 696, 752E-F (challenge to the Home Secretary's "directives" restricting the broadcasting of certain matters was mounted not by the IBA or the BBC, to whom they were directed, but by "broadcast journalists"); *R v London Borough of Haringey, ex p Secretary of State for the Environment* [1991] COD 135 (Secretary of State having standing to challenge setting of community charge, even though no challenge by ratepayer or district auditor); *R v Manchester City Council, ex p Baragrove Properties Ltd* (1992) 4 Admin LR 171, 182C-H (circumstances in which landlord, and not just tenants, entitled to challenge council's approach to housing benefit); *R v Felixstowe Justices, ex p Leigh* [1987] QB 582, 596G-H (fact that others more directly affected not precluding standing).

(C) NO OBVIOUS BETTER-PLACED CHALLENGER. *R v Secretary of State for Foreign and Commonwealth Affairs, ex p World Development Movement Ltd* [1995] 1 WLR 386, 395H ("the likely absence of any other responsible challenger"); *R v General Council of the Bar, ex p Percival* [1991] 1 QB 212, 231C ("Unless the disappointed complainant is regarded as having sufficient locus standi to challenge the decision it is difficult to see who else could be expected to do it"); *R v North Thames Regional Health Authority and Chelsea & Westminster NHS Trust, ex p L* [1996] Med LR 385 (Sedley J: "It is legitimate to ask who, if not B, would have a sufficient interest").

(D) JUDICIAL DECISIONS IN CRIMINAL CASES: PROSECUTION AND DEFENCE. *R v Secretary of State for the Home Department, ex p Bulger* [2001] EWHC Admin 119 at [20] (victim's family not having standing to challenge tariff set by Lord Chief Justice, given that Crown and defendant able to challenge judicial decisions in criminal cases), [21] ("in criminal cases there is no need for a third party to seek to intervene to uphold the rule of law. Nor, in my judgment, would such intervention generally be desirable").

(E) REALISM AND THE BETTER-PLACED CHALLENGER. *R v Inland Revenue Commissioners, ex p National Federation of Self-Employed and Small Businesses Ltd* [1982] AC 617, 644E-F ("The Attorney-General, although he occasionally applies for prerogative orders against public authorities that do not form part of central government, in practice never does so against government departments"); *R v Birmingham City Council, ex p Equal Opportunities Commission* [1989] 1 AC 1155, 1196B C ("It must not be forgotten that, in the field of education, there must be some reluctance on the part of parents to become entangled in disputes with their children's schools, or with the authorities responsible for them, on this subject. Quite apart from fear of prejudicing their children's prospects, the simple fact is that children pass rapidly on to other things, and a complaint of this kind may soon become irrelevant in relation to them"); *R v Lambeth London Borough Council, ex p Crookes* (1999) 31 HLR 59, 67 (landlord having standing to challenge failure to pay housing benefit in respect of claimants, where money would be received by him; defaulting residents having "little or no interest in the implementation of these regulations").

38.2.11 Put-up challengers and CLS (legal aid) funding abuse. *R (Edwards) v Environment*

Agency [2004] EWHC 736 (Admin) [2004] 3 All ER 21 (not an abuse of process to bring environmental challenge to process in which had not participate, even as an individual put up as legally-aidable), [20] (recognising role of the Legal Services Commission in addressing legitimacy and appropriateness of claimant under the Funding Code; "The Commission must ... be taken to have addressed the question of whether granting a funding certificate ... would be an abuse of the system"), [21] (here "not ... an abuse of the court's process .. even if [the claimant] has been put up to front the claim in order to secure public funding for it"); *R v Richmond upon Thames London Borough Council, ex p JC* [2001] ELR 21 at [31] (whether abuse for challenge to be in name of legally-aidable child rather than parent); *R v Legal Aid Board, ex p Bateman* [1992] 1 WLR 711, 717D & H ("unedifying" for claim to be in name of legally-aided client, but benefiting solicitors firm).

38.3 **Standing at the permission/substantive stages.**By statute, standing is framed as a precondition for the grant of permission for judicial review. There is certainly a threshold test at the permission stage, to filter out cases brought by busybodies. But standing is not an isolated preliminary issue, is capable of being influenced by the substantive analysis, and so can be best viewed in the round at the substantive hearing in the context of whether to grant a remedy.

38.3.1 **The standing rule: emphasising permission.**SCA s.31(3) <64.1>. The same emphasis was found in the old RSC Ord 53 r.3(5).

38.3.2 **Threshold test at the permission stage: busybodies.** *R v Inland Revenue Commissioners, ex p National Federation of Self-Employed and Small Businesses Ltd* [1982] AC 617, 630C-E (Lord Wilberforce: "There may be simple cases in which it can be seen at the earliest stage that the person applying for judicial review has no interest at all, or no sufficient interest to support the application: then it would be quite correct at the threshold to refuse him [permission] to apply. The right to do so is an important safeguard against the courts being flooded and public bodies harassed by irresponsible applications"), 653G-H (describing permission as a stage which "enables the court to prevent abuse by busybodies, cranks, and other mischief-makers"); *R v Monopolies & Mergers Commission, ex p Argyll Group Plc* [1986] 1 WLR 763, 773H (Sir John Donaldson MR: "The first stage test, which is applied upon the application for [permission], will lead to a refusal if the [claimant] has no interest whatsoever and is, in truth, no more than a meddlesome busybody. If, however, the application appears to be otherwise arguable and there is no other discretionary bar, such as dilatoriness on the part of the [claimant], the [claimant] may expect to get [permission] to apply, leaving the test of interest or standing to be re-applied as a matter of discretion on the hearing of the substantive application"); *R v Somerset County Council, ex p Dixon* [1998] Env LR 111[51], 116-117 (Sedley J, distilling these propositions: "(a) The threshold at the point of the application for [permission] is set only at the height necessary to prevent abuse. (b) To have `no interest whatsoever' is not the same as having no pecuniary or special personal interest. It is to interfere in something with which one has no legitimate concern at all; to be, in other words, a busybody. (c) Beyond this point, the question of standing has no materiality at the [permission] stage"), 121 ("entirely misconceived" to seek "to elevate the question of standing at the [permission] stage above the elementary level of excluding busybodies and troublemakers and to demand something akin to a special private interest in the subject matter"); *R v Dean and Chapter of St Paul's Cathedral* [1998] COD 130 (permission refused because, in seeking to challenge ordination of women priests in Wales, Church of England priest a busybody).

---

[51] Daniel Kolinsky [1997] JR 213.

38.3.3 Standing may be affected by all the circumstances. *R v Inland Revenue Commissioners, ex p National Federation of Self-Employed and Small Businesses Ltd* [1982] AC 617 (HL criticising approach of treating standing as divorced from the substantive issues in the case), 656D-E (standing depending "upon the due appraisal of many different factors revealed by the evidence produced by the parties"); *R (Edwards) v Environment Agency* [2004] EWHC 736 (Admin) [2004] 3 All ER 21 (ruling on standing as a preliminary issue) at [8] (treating standing as "a discrete issue which could be decided irrespective of the merits of the claim"); *R v Somerset County Council, ex p Dixon* [1998] Env LR 111, 117 ("At the substantive hearing 'the strength of the [claimant]'s interest is *one* of the factors to be weighed in the balance': that is to say that there may well be other factors which properly affect the evaluation of whether the [claimant] in the end has a 'sufficient interest' to maintain the challenge and - what may be a distinct question - to secure [a remedy] in one form rather than another"); *R v Legal Aid Board, ex p Bateman* [1992] 1 WLR 711, 714F ("In some cases ... it will be necessary to decide whether the application for judicial review is well founded in substance before determining the question of the [claimant]'s sufficiency of interest"); *R v Secretary of State for Foreign and Commonwealth Affairs, ex p World Development Movement Ltd* [1995] 1 WLR 386, 395F-G; *R v Her Majesty's Inspectorate of Pollution, ex p Greenpeace Ltd* [1994] 4 All ER 329, 349d-j.

38.3.4 The importance of the precise context. *R v Traffic Commissioner for the North Western Traffic Area, ex p BRAKE* [1996] COD 248 (sufficiency of interest something which the Court should not decide until factual and legal context analysed); *R v Sheffield City Council, ex p Power* The Times 7th July 1994 ("sufficient interest" dependent on 'the nature of the [remedy] sought and ... the legal and factual context of the subject matter of the application'); *R v Inland Revenue Commissioners, ex p National Federation of Self-Employed and Small Businesses Ltd* [1982] AC 617, 631F-G (whether claimant within scope of defendant's duty), 636C-F (emphasising nature of the duty and alleged breaches), 646C-D (whether alleged duty giving rise to right on the part of the claimant to complain), 649H-650A (character of the duty and the nature of the claimant's interest), 656D-E & 662E-G (nature of the duty and the complaint made).

38.3.5 Standing affected by whether unlawfulness shown. <38.2.8> (avoiding the standing lacuna); *R v Inland Revenue Commissioners, ex p National Federation of Self-Employed and Small Businesses Ltd* [1982] AC 617, 635F-636A (suggesting that because Revenue acting perfectly lawfully, "the federation had shown no sufficient interest in that matter to justify its application for [a remedy]"), 637D-F (focusing on whether grounds made out), 645C-E (suggesting that in the light of a finding of legality that in the final analysis claimant not having a sufficient interest), 654H-655B ("The federation, having failed to show any grounds for believing that the revenue has failed to do its statutory duty, have not, in my view, shown an interest sufficient in law to justify any further proceedings by the court on its application"); *R v Secretary of State for Foreign and Commonwealth Affairs, ex p World Development Movement Ltd* [1995] 1 WLR 386, 395G, 402G.

38.3.6 Standing addressed at the stage of discretion as to remedy. *R v Inland Revenue Commissioners, ex p National Federation of Self-Employed and Small Businesses Ltd* [1982] AC 617, 656D-E (Lord Roskill: "the grant or refusal of the remedy sought by way of judicial review is, in the ultimate analysis, discretionary, and the exercise of that discretion and the determination of the sufficiency or otherwise of the [claimants'] interest will depend ... upon the due appraisal of many different factors revealed by the evidence produced by the parties, few if any of which will be able to be wholly isolated from the others"); *R v Department of Transport, ex p Presvac Engineering Ltd* (1992) 4 Admin LR 121, 145G-146B (Purchas LJ: "The court must ... review at [the substantive] stage the question of sufficiency of interest and exercise its discretion accordingly. Whether this is properly called an investigation of *locus standi* or the exercise of discretion whether to grant [a remedy] is probably a semantic distinction without a difference"); *R v Criminal Injuries Compensation Board, ex p P* [1995] 1 WLR 845, 863F-H ("The nature and extent of the interest of [a claimant] who has crossed the relatively low statutory threshold of having a sufficient interest for the purpose of obtaining [permission] to bring judicial review proceedings may be relevant at the substantive hearing in relation to the exercise of discretion"); *R v Head Teacher and Governors of Fairfield Primary School, ex p W* [1998] COD 106 (standing treated as having `lapsed' where matter having ceased to be of practical significance); *R v Pembrokeshire County Council, ex p Coker* [1999] 4 All ER 1007, 1014c-d (claimants lacking standing to challenge decision to lease council land on other than best consideration, since not ratepayers).

38.4 Standing under the HRA: the victim test.[52] The Human Rights Act uses a "victim" test, reflecting the ECHR and Strasbourg approach. That introduces a tension, in the light of the general liberal approach including in pre-HRA human rights cases.

38.4.1 **The HRA victim test.** See HRA s.7(1) <64.7>; *Lancashire County Council v Taylor* [2005] EWCA Civ 284 [2005] 1 WLR 266 (defendant to possession proceedings not an HRA victim because not adversely affected by any alleged discrimination and would not benefit from declaration of incompatibility); *R (Countryside Alliance) v Attorney General* [2006] EWCA Civ 817 [2007] QB 305 (CA) at [65] (sufficient that claimants run the risk of being directly affected by state interference violating their Convention rights); *R (Holub) v Secretary of State for the Home Department* [2001] 1 WLR 1359 at [14] (suggesting parent a sufficient victim where complaining of breach of child's rights); *R (H) v Ashworth Hospital Authority* [2001] EWHC Admin 872 [2002] 1 FCR 206 (mental patient a sufficient "potential and indirect" victim to challenge `no condoms' policy); *R v Shayler* [2001] EWCA Crim 1977 [2001] 1 WLR 2206 (CA) at [92] (press not "victims"); *In re Medicaments and Related Classes of Goods (No.4)* [2001] EWCA Civ 1217 [2002] 1 WLR 269 at [8], [18]-[19] (association not a "victim" where claim not a representative action); *R (Medway Council) v Secretary of State for Transport* [2002] EWHC 2516 (Admin) at [20] (local authority not capable of being HRA "victim"); *R (Napier) v Secretary of State for the Home Department* [2004] EWHC 936 (Admin) [2004] 1 WLR 3056 at [61] (claimant no longer a victim); *R (Amicus - MSF Section) v Secretary of State for Trade and Industry* [2004] EWHC 860 (Admin) [2004] ELR 311 at [201] (Secretary of State not objecting to reliance by group on the HRA in challenging employment regulations, notwithstanding "victim" test); *R (Hooper) v Secretary of State for Work and Pensions* [2005] UKHL 29 [2005] 1 WLR 1681 at [57] (sufficient, for claim that benefit discriminatorily unavailable, that claimant had done something to indicate to an appropriate official that he would have made a claim had it been possible). Cf. *R v Secretary of State for Social Security, ex p Joint Council for the Welfare of Immigrants* [1997] 1 WLR 275 (human rights claim brought by non-governmental organisation).

---

[52] Neil Garnham [1999] JR 39; Robert McCracken & Saira Kabir Sheikh [2002] JR 172.

P39 Discretion/duty. It is vital to analyse the extent to which a body is entrusted with a discretion or required to perform a duty.

39.1 No unfettered powers
39.2 Discretion/power: the essential duties
39.3 Discretion and duty in action

39.1 No unfettered powers.[53] No discretionary power, amenable to judicial review, is "unfettered". Power always has limits, which the Courts delineate and enforce, identifying public law duties and ensuring that they have not been breached.

39.1.1 **The rule of law and no unfettered powers.** <12.1.9>.

39.1.2 **Power is held on trust: to be used for the purpose for which conferred.** *R v Tower Hamlets London Borough Council, ex p Chetnik Developments Ltd* [1988] AC 858, 872B-F (Lord Bridge, approving this passage from *Wade, Administrative Law* 5th ed. at 355-356: "Statutory power conferred for public purposes is conferred as it were upon trust, not absolutely - that is to say, it can validly be used only in the right and proper way which Parliament when conferring it is presumed to have intended. Although the Crown's lawyers have argued in numerous cases that unrestricted permissive language confers unfettered discretion, the truth is that, in a system based on the rule of law, unfettered governmental discretion is a contradiction in terms. The real question is whether the discretion is wide or narrow, and where the legal line is to be drawn. For this purpose everything depends upon the true intent and meaning of the empowering Act"); *Credit Suisse v Allerdale Borough Council* [1997] QB 306, 333G-H ("The statutory powers conferred on local authorities to be exercised for public purposes can only be validly used if they are used in the way which Parliament, when conferring the powers, is presumed to have intended"), 334F ("Statutory powers are conferred on local authorities upon trust. These powers can only be used in the way which Parliament is presumed to have intended"); *Magill v Porter* [2001] UKHL 67 [2002] 2 AC 357 at [19(2)] (Lord Bingham: "It follows from the proposition that public powers are conferred as if upon trust that those who exercise powers in a manner inconsistent with the public purpose for which the powers were conferred betray that trust and so misconduct themselves"); *R v Secretary of State for Foreign and Commonwealth Affairs, ex p World Development Movement Ltd* [1995] 1 WLR 386, 398C-D (accepting that "statutory powers, however permissive, must be used with scrupulous attention to their true purposes and for reasons which are relevant and proper"); *R v Secretary of State for the Home Department, ex p Brind* [1991] 1 AC 696, 756F (power "not an absolute or unfettered discretion. It is a discretion which is to be exercised according to law and therefore must be used only to advance the purposes for which it was conferred. It has accordingly to be used to promote the policy and objects of the Act: see *Padfield*"); *R v Secretary of State for the Environment, Transport and the Regions, ex p Spath Holme* [2001] 2 AC 349, 381B-C, 404D, 412H (House of Lords referring to and discussing the *Padfield* principle); *Stewart v Perth and Kinross Council* [2004] UKHL 16 at [28] (Lord Hope: "the discretion which is vested in the licensing authority is not unlimited. The authority is not at liberty to use it for an ulterior object, however desirable that object may seem to it to be in the public interest").

39.1.3 **No unfettered discretion: power always has limits.** *R v Secretary of State for the Environment, Transport and the Regions, ex p Spath Holme* [2001] 2 AC 349, 381B (Lord

---

[53] This paragraph in a previous edition was cited in *T v H (Spousal Maintenance)* [2006] NZFLR 560 at [28].

Bingham: "no statute confers an unfettered discretion on any minister"), 396D-E (Lord Nicholls: "No statutory power is of unlimited scope"), 400B (Lord Cooke: "no statutory discretion is unlimited"), 404E (Lord Hope: "No minister who seeks to exercise a discretion which legislation has conferred on him can claim that the discretion, however widely expressed, is unfettered or unlimited"), 412H (Lord Hutton, citing *Chetnik*, to like effect); *R v Somerset County Council, ex p Fewings* [1995] 1 WLR 1037, 1042H; *R v Mid Glamorgan Family Health Services, ex p Martin* [1995] 1 WLR 110, 117E ("I do not accept that a health authority ... has an absolute right to deal with medical records in any way that it chooses"); *Anns v Merton London Borough Council* [1978] AC 728, 762B (discretion not "absolute" but having to "be responsibly exercised"); *Padfield v Minister of Agriculture Fisheries & Food* [1968] AC 997, 1060F-G ("unfettered" as an "unauthorised gloss ... [T]he use of that adjective, even in an Act of Parliament, can do nothing to unfetter the control which the judiciary have over the executive, namely that in exercising their powers the latter must act lawfully and that is a matter to be determined by looking at the Act and its scope and object in conferring a discretion upon the Minister rather than by the use of adjectives"); *R (Bancoult) v Secretary of State for the Foreign and Commonwealth Office* [2001] QB 1067 at [55] (power "not wholly unrestrained"; "a very large tapestry, but every tapestry has a border"); *R (Corner House Research) v Director of the Serious Fraud Office* [2008] UKHL 60 [2008] 3 WLR 568 at [32] (discretion not unfettered).

39.1.4 Better to speak of "judgment" than discretion. *R v Devon County Council, ex p G* [1989] 1 AC 573, 604E-F (Lord Keith: "It is for the authority, and no one else, to decide whether free transport is really needed for the purpose of promoting the attendance at school of a particular pupil. That must depend on the authority's view of the circumstances of the particular case ... The authority's function in this respect is capable of being described as a 'discretion', though it is not, of course, an unfettered discretion but rather in the nature of an exercise of judgment"); <13.3.1> (discretion and judgment); *Begum v Tower Hamlets London Borough Council* [2002] EWCA Civ 239 [2002] 1 WLR 2491 (CA) at [24] (distinguishing between discretionary benefits and exercise of judgment required under the homelessness legislation) (HL is [2003] UKHL 5 [2003] 2 AC 430).

39.1.5 Explanation for references to "unfettered" discretion.
(A) MEANING NOT AMENABLE TO JUDICIAL REVIEW. *Gouriet v Union of Post Office Workers* [1978] AC 435, 512C-F (referring to the Attorney-General's power to halt a criminal prosecution as "his unfettered discretion": "absolute and non-reviewable").
(B) MEANING "WIDE" DISCRETION. *In re Findlay* [1985] AC 318, 332F-G (Lord Scarman: "the Secretary of State has two unfettered discretions. It is entirely a matter for him whether or not to refer the case of a prisoner to the [parole] board for advice: and he has a complete discretion whether or not to accept the board's recommendation"); *R v Inner London Education Authority, ex p Brunyate* [1989] 1 WLR 542, 549G-H ("The authority has a wholly unfettered discretion as to whom it will appoint or reappoint"); *Brooks v Director of Public Prosecutions* [1994] 1 AC 568, 579B (Lord Woolf: "On the [statutory] language ... the DPP is entitled, if he chooses to do so in his unfettered discretion, to seek the directions or consent of a judge as to whether an indictment should be preferred"); *R v Secretary of State for the Environment, ex p Lancashire County Council* [1994] 4 All ER 165, 177j-178a ("an unfettered discretion on the Secretary of State to decide not to exercise his powers"); *R (Mohammad) v Secretary of State for the Home Department* 24th January 2002 unrep. at [55] (using "unfettered discretion" to mean that Secretary of State was "not required to form any opinion on [the suggested] matter").

39.2 Discretion/power: the essential duties. A public body entrusted with discretionary powers owes various basic duties, the breach of any of which can justify the Court's intervention.

39.2.1 Duty to understand the nature of the power, and ask the right question. *Chief Constable of the North Wales Police v Evans* [1982] 1 WLR 1155, 1164H (Lord Bridge: "erroneous assumption that he had an absolute discretion"), 1161H; *R v Secretary of State for the Home Department, ex p Launder* [1997] 1 WLR 839, 858E ("If [the Secretary of State] asked himself the wrong question his decision would be flawed on the ground of illegality"); *Secretary of State for Education and Science v Tameside Metropolitan Borough Council* [1977] AC 1014, 1065B (Lord Diplock: "the question for the court is, did the Secretary of State ask himself the right question ..."); *R v Carrick District Council, ex p Shelley* [1996] Env LR 273 (question was whether statutory nuisance existing, not whether appropriate to take action); *North Yorkshire County Council v Secretary of State for the Environment* [1995] 3 PLR 54, 57G-58C (although test not correctly stated, on reading planning decision as a whole clear that inspector had the right test in mind); *R v Social Fund Inspector, ex p Taylor* [1998] COD 152 (duty to ask questions in the correct sequence: assessing need and priority first, then considering resources); *R v Secretary of State for Education and Employment, ex p Portsmouth Football Club Ltd* [1998] COD 142 (although Secretary of State had not treated his policy as though a rigid criteria, those bodies whom he had consulted had adopted such an approach and therefore not asked the right question); *R v Secretary of State for the Environment, ex p Nottinghamshire County Council* [1986] AC 240, 249C-D ("Power can be abused in a number of ways: by a mistake of law in misconstruing the limits imposed by statute (or by common law in the case of a common law power) upon the scope of the power");*Anisminic Ltd v Foreign Compensation Commission* [1969] 2 AC 147, 174C-D (whether "a wrong conclusion as to the width of their powers");*R v Clerkenwell Metropolitan Stipendiary Magistrate, ex p Telegraph Plc* [1993] QB 462, 471G (magistrate wrong to conclude that no power to hear claimants); *R v Visitors to the Inns of Court, ex p Calder & Persaud* [1994] QB 1 (misunderstood role, by acting as reviewing rather than appellate body).

39.2.2 Duty to consider exercising the power. *Stovin v Wise* [1996] AC 923, 950B (Lord Hoffmann: "A public body almost always has a duty in public law to consider whether it should exercise its powers");*R v Barnet London Borough Council, ex p Nilish Shah* [1983] 2 AC 309, 349H ("duty to consider whether or not to make a discretionary award in the event of a failure to establish eligibility for a mandatory award"); *R (Uluyol) v Immigration Officer* [2001] INLR 194 at [43] (duty to consider discretion as to whether to treat claimants as illegal entrants); *R v Secretary of State for the Home Department, ex p Tarrant* [1985] QB 251, 283G-284C (failure to consider whether to exercise discretion to allow legal representation); *R v Governor of Brixton Prison, ex p Walsh* [1985] AC 154, 165E-F (where "discretionary power ... to have the prisoner brought to the court", duty "to consider any request"); *Anns v Merton London Borough Council* [1978] AC 728, 755C ("They are under a duty to give proper consideration to the question whether they should inspect or not"); *R v Hertfordshire County Council, ex p Cheung* The Times 4th April 1986 (see transcript) (identifying a "power to reconsider their decision" and "a duty to consider exercising this power"); *R v North Thames Regional Health Authority and Chelsea & Westminster NHS Trust, ex p L* [1996] Med LR 385 (Trust empowered and obliged to consider whether to pursue disciplinary action); <50.4> (duty not to fetter discretion); <60.8.9> (duty to consider exercising procedural powers); <6.1.7> (power to reconsider).

39.2.3 Duty not to delay.[54] <50.1.3> (delay as abdication of function); <46.1.5> (delay as ultra vires/ breach of statutory duty); <57.3.5> (delay as unreasonableness/ unreasonable delay); <58.1.8> (delay as lack of proportionality); <60.8.2> (delay as procedural unfairness); <63.1.4> (abuse of process); *R (Saadi) v Secretary of State for the Home Department* [2002] UKHL 41

---

[54] Suzanne Lambert & Andrew Lindsay Strugo [2005] JR 253.

[2002] 1 WLR 3131 at [26] (immigration detention must be for a reasonable time, applying *R v Governor of Durham Prison, ex p Hardial Singh* [1984] 1 WLR 704, 706 and *Tan Te Lam v Superintendent of Tai A Chau Detention Centre* [1997] AC 97, 111); *R (M) v Secretary of State for the Home Department* [2008] EWCA Civ 307 (whether immigration detention of unreasonable duration); <59.5.11> (HRA:ECHR Art 6: hearing within a reasonable time); <59.4> (violation of HRA:ECHR Art 5); *Anufrijeva v Southwark London Borough Council* [2003] EWCA Civ 1406 [2004] QB 1124 at [45] (positive obligations "in relation to the provision of welfare support"), [46] (need "substantial prejudice" in a "culpable delay" case); *R (Salih) v Secretary of State for the Home Department* [2003] EWHC 2273 (Admin) at [66] ("The court cannot ... specify what resources must be devoted to administering the scheme, or what delay in general is lawful and what delay is not"; declining to "make declarations divorced from the facts of individual cases of the time within which public authorities must fulfil their duties"); *R v Dental Practice Board, ex p Z* The Times 6th March 2001 at [37]-[44] (unlawful for Board to defer question of payments; deferment constituting de facto suspension and/or failure to keep the question under review); *R v Patent Office, ex p Chocoladefabriken Lindt* 5th December 1996 unrep. (basic obligation to take timeous steps to register trade mark, enforceable by mandatory order); *R v Secretary of State for the Home Department, ex p Harshad Jashbhai Patel* (1995) 7 Admin LR 56, 71H ("wherever law is practised, justice is reproached by delay"); *Wang v Commissioner of Inland Revenue* [1994] 1 WLR 1286, 1293G, 1296F-G; *R v Sefton Metropolitan Borough Council, ex p Help The Aged* [1997] 4 All ER 532, 543c (where statutory duty to make provision triggered, council not entitled to defer performance by reason of lack of resources); *R v Brent London Borough Council, ex p Miyanger* (1997) 29 HLR 628 (mandatory order (mandamus) to require council to make promised housing decision within 28 days); *R v Commissioners of Customs and Excise, ex p Kay and Co* [1996] STC 1500 (unlawful to defer payment in discharge of statutory duty, there being no room for general power to delay or defer payment); *R v Secretary of State for Social Security, ex p Sutherland* [1997] COD 222 (no power to withhold benefit pending appeal in a related case); *Sambasivam v Secretary of State for the Home Department* [2000] INLR 105 (4 months delay between adjudicator's hearing and determination, in a case involving credibility issues, should have led to matter being remitted for reconsideration); *R v Inland Revenue Commissioners, ex p Preston* [1985] AC 835, 870D ("would have been inspired by an improper motive and would have constituted an abuse of power" to have "deliberately waited from 1979 until 1982 in order that the claims of the appellant might be time barred"); <53.1.7> (delay as frustrating the legislative purpose); Recommendation No.R(80)2 of the Committee of Ministers (adopted 11 March 1980) <45.1.4(B)> (describing the "Basic principles" as including that "An administrative authority, when exercising a discretionary power: ... takes its decision within a time which is reasonable having regard to the matter at stake; ... Where no time-limit for the taking of the decision in the exercise of a discretionary power has been set by law and the administrative authority does not take its decision within a reasonable time, its failure to do so may be submitted to control by an authority competent for the purpose").

39.2.4 Duty of inquiry: to take reasonable steps to inform itself. <P51>.

39.2.5 Duty to act in the public interest. *R (TC Projects Ltd) v Newcastle Licensing Justices* [2008] EWCA Civ 428 at [12] (statutory powers to be exercise for the purpose they were conferred and on relevant grounds of public interest); *R v Tower Hamlets London Borough Council, ex p Chetnik Developments Ltd* [1988] AC 858, 872C-F (public authority must act "upon lawful and relevant grounds of public interest"); *R v Northumbrian Water Ltd, ex p Newcastle and North Tyneside Health Authority* [1999] Env LR 715, 724-729 (public interest duty inapplicable to commercial organisation/ privatised body); *R (Shrewsbury and Atcham Borough Council) v Secretary of State for Communities and Local Government* [2008] EWCA Civ 148 [2008] 3 All ER 548 at [48], [74], [81] (leaving open whether Secretary of State obliged to exercise general powers in the public interest).

39.2.6 Other basic duties: further examples.
(A) DUTY TO ACT IN GOOD FAITH. <P52>.
(B) DUTY TO ACT REASONABLY. <P57>.
(C) DUTY TO PROMOTE THE LEGISLATIVE PURPOSE. <P53>.
(D) DUTY TO ACT FAIRLY. <P60> (procedural fairness); <7.6.3> (natural justice as a fundamental principle).
(E) DUTY TO MEET AS A BODY. *R v Army Board of the Defence Council, ex p Anderson* [1992] QB 169, 187F (Taylor LJ: "There must be a proper hearing of the complaint in the sense that the board must consider, as a single adjudicating body, all the relevant evidence and contentions before reaching its conclusions. This means, in my view, that the members of the board must meet. It is unsatisfactory that the members should consider the papers and reach their individual conclusions in isolation and, perhaps as here, having received the concluded views of another member"), applied in *R v Legal Aid Board, ex p Donn & Co (a Firm)* [1996] 3 All ER 1, 13f-14c.

39.2.7 Basic local government duties.
(A) FIDUCIARY DUTY TO RATE/CHARGE-PAYERS. *Bromley London Borough Council v Greater London Council* [1983] 1 AC 768, 829G-H (Lord Diplock: "a local authority owes a fiduciary duty to the ratepayers from whom it obtains moneys needed to carry out its statutory functions, and ... this includes a duty not to expend those moneys thriftlessly but to deploy the full financial resources available to it to the best advantage"), 838H, 815B; *Hazell v Hammersmith & Fulham London Borough Council* [1992] 2 AC 1, 37H; *R (Structadene Ltd) v Hackney London Borough Council* [2001] 2 All ER 225 (decision to dispose of land breached fiduciary duty to ratepayers).
(B) DUTY TO ACT IN ACCORDANCE WITH BUSINESS PRINCIPLES. *Bromley London Borough Council v Greater London Council* [1983] 1 AC 768, 831C-H (Lord Keith), 839A-C and 842A-B (Lord Scarman); 851D-E (Lord Brandon); *Prescott v Birmingham Corporation* [1955] Ch 210.
(C) DUTY TO BALANCE INTERESTS. *Bromley London Borough Council v Greater London Council* [1983] 1 AC 768, 820D (Lord Wilberforce: "[duty] to hold the balance between the transport users and the ratepayers"); 825D-E, 827C and E, 828F-830D (Lord Diplock); 841F-842A (Lord Scarman); 853E (Lord Brandon); *Roberts v Hopwood* [1925] AC 578; *Luby v Newcastle-under-Lyme Corporation* [1964] 2 QB 64; *R v London Transport Executive, ex p Greater London Council* [1983] QB 484, 491C-E; *R v Newcastle-upon-Tyne City Council, ex p Dixon* (1995) 92 LGR 168, 178-179.
(D) DUTY TO CONDUCT FINANCES ON ANNUAL BASIS. *In re Westminster City Council* [1986] AC 668, 704E (Lord Templeman), 713F (Lord Oliver) and 689B-C (Lord Bridge); *R v Brent and Harrow Health Authority, ex p London Borough of Harrow* [1997] ELR 187 (health authority entitled to ration its scarce resources when setting annual budget, not obliged to recalculate and reallocate according to specific demands arising).
(E) DUTY TO ACT IN THE PUBLIC INTEREST. <39.2.5>.
(F) DUTY TO MANAGE LAND FOR THE BENEFIT OF THE AREA. Local Government Act 1972 s.120(1)(b), considered in *R v Somerset County Council, ex p Fewings* [1995] 1 WLR 1037 and in *R v Sefton Metropolitan Borough Council, ex p British Association of Shooting and Conservation Ltd* [2000] LGR 628.
(G) DUTY TO SPEAK THROUGH STATED REASONS/RESOLUTIONS. <62.4.3>.

39.2.8 Transparency duties.
(A) DUTY TO COMMUNICATE POLICY. <6.2.11> (whether duty to publicise policy guidance).

(B) DUTY TO COMMUNICATE DECISION. *R (Anufrijeva) v Secretary of State for the Home Department* [2003] UKHL 36 [2004] 1 AC 604 at [26] ("Notice of a decision is required before it can have the character of a determination with legal effect"), [28] ("the constitutional principle requiring the rule of law to be observed ... requires that a constitutional state must accord to individuals the right to know of a decision before their rights can be adversely affected").

(C) DUTY TO GIVE REASONS. <P62>.

39.3 Discretion and duty in action. Powers and duties co-exist and the Court will decide: (1) what are the parameters of discretion, and the applicable duties; (2) the width of a discretion; and (3) whether the role of the Court in relation to such matters is hard-edged (correctness) or soft (reasonableness).

39.3.1 **Duties and powers coupled together.**

(A) GENERAL. *Larner v Solihull Metropolitan Borough Council* [2001] LGR 255 at [9] (although "there is a distinction between the position where a statutory body has merely a power and where it is under a statutory duty", "that simple distinction cannot always be decisive. On the one hand, a statutory body must give proper consideration to the exercise of its powers, and a failure to exercise a power may in a particular factual situation be so unreasonable as to amount to a breach of duty. On the other hand, a statutory duty may involve [a] large ... degree of discretion (and in particular, discretion as to matters of policy)"); *Julius v Bishop of Oxford* (1880) 5 App Cas 214, 222-223 (Earl Cairns LC: "there may be something in the nature of the thing empowered to be done, something in the object for which it is to be done, something in the conditions under which it is to be done, something in the title of the person or persons for whose benefit the power is to be exercised, which may couple the power with a duty, and make it the duty of the person in whom the power is reposed, to exercise that power when called upon to do so"); *R v Secretary of State for the Home Department, ex p Fire Brigades Union* [1995] 2 AC 513 (discretion as to whether to implement statutory scheme accompanied by duty to consider exercising the power).

(B) POWER BECOMES DUTY WHEN PERSON HAS A RIGHT TO ITS EXERCISE. *Padfield v Minister of Agriculture Fisheries & Food* [1968] AC 997, 1039E-F (Lord Morris (dissenting in the result): "Where some legal right or entitlement is conferred or enjoyed, and for the purpose of effectuating such right or entitlement a power is conferred upon someone, then words which are permissive in character will sometimes be construed as involving a duty to exercise the power. The purpose and the language of any particular enactment must be considered"); *Julius v Bishop of Oxford* (1880) 5 App Cas 214, 243 (Lord Blackburn: "if the object of giving the power is to enable the donee to effectuate a right, then it is the duty of the donee of the powers to exercise the power when those who have the right call upon him so to do. And this is equally the case where the power is given by the word `may' if the object is clear"); <3.1.7> and <24.4.5(C)> (position where sole legally permissible result).

(C) DUTY AND ADDED POWER. *R (G) v Barnet London Borough Council* [2003] UKHL 57 [2004] 2 AC 208 at [15] (Lord Nicholls, describing duties where "the terms themselves give ... an area of discretion"); *Engineers & Managers Association v Advisory Conciliation & Arbitration Service* [1980] 1 WLR 302 (HL characterising Acas's function in connection with recognition references as involving (a) a duty to conduct an investigation (b) a "very wide discretion" as to how it will do so (c) a power to adjourn an investigation but (d) a duty not to "abdicate" or "abandon" one), 305B-D (Lord Diplock), 310F (Lord Edmund-Davies), 317A-318G (Lord Scarman).

39.3.2 **The discretion/duty distinction illustrated.** *R (G) v Barnet London Borough Council* [2003] UKHL 57 [2004] 2 AC 208 at [12] (Lord Nicholls: "A power need not be exercised, but a duty must be discharged"), [74] (Lord Hope); *Singh (Pargan) v Secretary of State for the*

Home Department [1992] 1 WLR 1052, 1056F-G (statutory power framed under the permissive "may" nevertheless interpreted as a duty); *R v East Sussex County Council, ex p Tandy* [1998] AC 714, 749A-F (statutory duty not to be downgraded, by allowing lack of resources as an excuse for non-performance, into a discretionary power); *R v Kensington and Chelsea London Borough Council, ex p Kujtim* [1999] 4 All ER 161 (duty to house claimant, but entitled to regard duty as discharged where serious failure to cooperate); *Laker Airways Ltd v Department of Trade* [1977] QB 643, 669-670 (duty as to ends, discretion as to means); *R v Bexley London Borough Council, ex p B* (2000) 3 CCLR 15, 22G-J (statutory duty of reassessment arising pro-actively notwithstanding absence of any formal request); <60.4.3> (whether intended vitiating consequence); *Hoffmann-La Roche (F) & Co AG v Secretary of State for Trade and Industry* [1975] AC 295, 364E-F (law enforcement duties); *R (K) v West London Mental Health NHS Trust* [2006] EWCA Civ 118 [2006] 1 WLR 1865 (discretion not duty as to funding placement favoured by responsible medical officer); *R v Secretary of State for the Home Department, ex p National Association of Probation Officers* [1996] COD 399 (discretion, not duty, to make regulations governing probation officers' qualifications).

39.3.3 **"Target duty".**[55] *R v Bath Mental Healthcare NHS Trust, ex p Beck* (2000) 3 CCLR 5 (referring to "a target duty, failure to achieve which without more will not constitute a justiciable breach"); *R (G) v Barnet London Borough Council* [2003] UKHL 57 [2004] 2 AC 208 at [14] & [87] (referring to *R v Inner London Education Authority, ex p Ali* (1990) 2 Admin LR 822); *R v Bexley London Borough Council, ex p B* (2000) 3 CCLR 15, 22E-23C (council's duty a specific duty not a mere "target duty"); *R v Kensington and Chelsea London Borough Council, ex p Kujtim* [1999] 4 All ER 161, 174d-175a (duty not merely a "target duty"); *R (Conville) v Richmond upon Thames London Borough Council* [2006] EWCA Civ 718 [2006] 1 WLR 2808 at [36] (duty conferring a coterminous right); *R (W) v Doncaster Metropolitan Borough Council* [2004] EWCA Civ 378 [2004] LGR 743 at [50] (statutory duty as a "best endeavours, or reasonable endeavours" duty).

39.3.4 **"General duty".** *R (G) v Barnet London Borough Council* [2003] UKHL 57 [2004] 2 AC 208 (HL, 3-2, treating Children Act 1989 s.17(1) as a "general duty", not owed to and enforceable by each child individually), at [83], [85] and [91] (Lord Hope), [106] (Lord Millett), [114] (Lord Scott).

39.3.5 **Wide or narrow discretion?** <39.1.5(B)> (references to "unfettered" meaning "wide"); *R (Johnson) v Reading Borough Council* [2004] EWHC 765 (Admin) at [62] ("the widest possible discretion is given to the Council"); *R v Comptroller-General of Patents Designs & Trade Marks, ex p Gist-Brocades* [1986] 1 WLR 51 (HL divided as to whether comptroller having a "wide" discretion (see 62A-B, 63A-B) or not (68F-70C)); *R v Tower Hamlets London Borough Council, ex p Chetnik Developments Ltd* [1988] AC 858, 877D-E (narrow discretion); *R v Wilson, ex p Williamson* [1996] COD 42 (narrow discretion); *R v Warwickshire County Council, ex p Powergen* [1997] 3 PLR 62 (in the circumstances, only one option reasonably open); <13.3> (restraint and discretion/judgment); *R v Inland Revenue Commissioners, ex p National Federation of Self-Employed and Small Businesses Ltd* [1982] AC 617, 632A (Lord Wilberforce: "very wide powers"), 636G (Lord Diplock: "a wide managerial discretion"); 651A (Lord Scarman: "very considerable discretion in the exercise of their powers"); *Hill v Chief Constable of West Yorkshire* [1989] AC 53, 59E-F (Lord Keith: "a wide discretion").

39.3.6 **Statutory formulae: discretion/duty and the role of the Court.**
(A) "MAY". *R (Hargrave) v Stroud District Council* [2002] EWCA Civ 1281 [2002] 3 PLR 115

---

[55] Catherine Callaghan [2000] JR 184.

at [14] ("`may' gives the authority a discretion, even in a case where the condition precedent is fulfilled, not to embark on the statutory process"); *Holgate-Mohammed v Duke* [1984] AC 437, 443B (prima facie, "may" denotes "an executive discretion ... the lawfulness of [which] ... cannot be questioned in any court of law except upon those principles [in *Wednesbury*]"); *R v Secretary of State for the Environment, ex p Rose Theatre Trust Co* [1990] 1 QB 504, 513F (referring to "cases where the draftsman has used `may' when he meant `shall'"); *R v Commissioners of Inland Revenue, ex p Newfields Developments Ltd* [2001] UKHL 27 [2001] 1 WLR 1111 (Inland Revenue having a duty and not a discretion, even though statute saying "may", especially given that person who would exercise the discretion was not identified) at [22] ("may" expressing "conditionality": ie. that tax relief only applicable if conditions met), [43] ("may" being used to reflect fact that different possible outcomes);*R v Secretary of State for the Home Department, ex p Fire Brigades Union* [1995] 2 AC 513, 563C; *Singh (Pargan) v Secretary of State for the Home Department* [1992] 1 WLR 1052, 1056F-G (statutory power framed under the permissive "may" nevertheless interpreted as a duty); *Paul Okello v Secretary of State for the Home Department* [1995] Imm AR 269, 272 (contrasting the discretionary "may" with the mandatory "should"); *R v Secretary of State for the Home Department, ex p National Association of Probation Officers* [1996] COD 399 (permissive language not necessarily precluding duty; but here drafter using appropriate language to distinguish between discretions and obligations).

(B) "SHALL". *Grunwick Processing Laboratories Ltd v Advisory Conciliation & Arbitration Service* [1978] AC 655, 698H (Lord Salmon: "Prima facie the word `shall' suggests that it is mandatory but that word has often been rightly construed as being directory. Everything turns upon the context in which it is used - the subject matter, the purpose and effect of the section in which it appears"); *London & Clydeside Estates Ltd v Aberdeen District Council* [1980] 1 WLR 182, 201H ("the word `shall' ... is normally to be interpreted as connoting a mandatory provision, meaning that what is thereby enjoined is not merely desired to be done but must be done"); *R v Immigration Appeal Tribunal, ex p Jeyeanthan* [2000] 1 WLR 354, 358H (Lord Woolf MR: "The requirement is never intended to be optional if a word such as `shall' or `must' is used"), 360C-E ("the word `shall' is normally inserted to show that something is required to be done" but "more important is to focus on the consequences of non-compliance"), also <60.4.3>; *Attorney-General's Reference (No.3 of 1999)* [2001] 2 AC 91, 117B, 120C (applying *Jeyeanthan*); *R v Carrick District Council, ex p Shelley* [1996] Env LR 273 (duty to serve abatement notice); *R v Commissioners of Customs and Excise, ex p Kay and Co* [1996] STC 1500, 1521e-g ("shall pay" meaning duty to pay forthwith; no room for general power to defer payment); *R v City of Westminster Housing Benefit Review Board, ex p Mehanne* [2001] UKHL 11 [2001] 1 WLR 539 at [13] ("shall" reduce the eligible rent (in the regulations) leaving a discretion as to the amount of any reduction); *Paul Okello v Secretary of State for the Home Department* [1995] Imm AR 269, 272 (treating "should" as mandatory).

(C) "APPEARS". *R (Asif Javed) v Secretary of State for the Home Department* [2001] EWCA Civ 789 [2002] QB 129 at [55] (matter not purely subjective even though statute stating "it appears to him that"); *Attorney-General of Hong Kong v Ng Yuen Shiu* [1983] 2 AC 629, 634D-E, 631C-D and 635G-H (considering approach in relation to the power to make a removal order "if it appears to him" that the person had entered and remained unlawfully); *R v Secretary of State for Health, ex p United States Tobacco International Inc* [1992] QB 353, 372D (duty to "consult such organisations as appear to him to be representative of interests substantially affected by the proposal", treated as a duty to consult an organisation which "clearly ... would be substantially affected"); *R v Secretary of State for the Home Department, ex p McQuillan* [1995] 4 All ER 400, 422C ("in the ordinary way... the courts would enforce rigorously the requirement that the Secretary of State is to take into account `everything which appears to him to be relevant' so as to ensure that nothing of real relevance is discounted by the Secretary of State solely because it appears to him not to be relevant"); *R v Lambeth London Borough Council, ex p N* [1996] ELR 299 (statutory phrase "shall consult such persons as appear to them to be appropriate"; here, parents particularly important consultees).

(D) "SATISFIED". *Office of Fair Trading v IBA Health Ltd* [2004] EWCA Civ 142 [2004] 4 All ER 1103 at [45] (statutory phrase "is satisfied" means court must inquire as to whether belief was "reasonable and objectively justified by relevant facts");*R (Banks) v Secretary of State for the Environment, Food and Rural Affairs* [2004] EWHC 416 (Admin) at [10] ("satisfied" connoting a subjective element whereby question for the Court is not whether Secretary of State had reasonable grounds, but review of reasonableness of his conclusion that he was "satisfied" that he had such grounds); *R v Diggines, ex p Rahmani* [1986] AC 475, 482B ("satisfied", but nevertheless: "The question for the House is therefore: do the facts of this case meet the conditions required by the rule to be met for the exercise by the adjudicator of the power"); *R v Secretary of State for the Home Department, ex p Fatima* [1986] 1 AC 527 ("satisfied", but HL applying no *Wednesbury* restraint); *Secretary of State for Education and Science v Tameside Metropolitan Borough Council* [1977] AC 1014, 1047C-E (speaking of "is satisfied": "If a judgment requires, before it can be made, the existence of some facts, then, although the evaluation of those facts is for the Secretary of State alone, the court must inquire whether those facts exist, and have been taken into account, whether the judgment has been made upon a proper self-direction as to those facts, whether the judgment has not been made upon other facts which ought not to have been taken into account. If these requirements are not met, then the exercise of judgment, however bona fide it may be, becomes capable of challenge"); *Din (Taj) v Wandsworth London Borough Council* [1983] 1 AC 657, 664H (Lord Wilberforce: "The words `are satisfied' must be noted: they leave the decision, on these issues of fact, to the local authority. On well-known principle, there is no appeal to a court against such a decision, but it may be subject to `judicial review' for error in law including no doubt absence of any material on which the decision could reasonably be reached"); *R v Royal Borough of Kensington and Chelsea, ex p Kassam* (1994) 26 HLR 455 (duty to "make such inquiries as are necessary to satisfy themselves as to whether [the claimant] is homeless or threatened with homelessness" (see 459), question whether no reasonable authority could have been satisfied that sufficient inquiries had been made).

(E) "THINKS APPROPRIATE"/"CONSIDERS APPROPRIATE".*R v City of Westminster Housing Benefit Review Board, ex p Mehanne* [2001] UKHL 11 [2001] 1 WLR 539 at [13] (referring to the phrase "as it considers appropriate" as being "the language of discretion"); *R (G) v Barnet London Borough Council* [2003] UKHL 57 [2004] 2 AC 208 at [15] (Lord Nicholls, discussing the phrase "consider appropriate"); *R (Liverpool City Council) v Secretary of State for Health* [2003] EWHC 1975 (Admin) [2004] LGR 635 at [40] (statutory language, requiring Secretary of State to consult those representatives considered by him to be appropriate, giving him "considerable scope as to who is consulted").

(F) "THINKS FIT". *R v Secretary of State for Trade and Industry, ex p Lonrho Plc* [1989] 1 WLR 525, 533D (Lord Keith: "the discretion of the Secretary of State whether, and when, to publish the report, must be exercised by him (and not at the dictation of another Minister or body) by reference to relevant and not irrelevant considerations and in a manner which is not unreasonable, in the *Wednesbury* sense"); *Roberts v Hopwood* [1925] AC 578; *Newbury District Council v Secretary of State for the Environment* [1981] AC 578; *R v Hillingdon London Borough Council, ex p Royco Homes Ltd* [1974] QB 720.

(G) "BELIEF"/"BELIEVES". *Office of Fair Trading v IBA Health Ltd* [2004] EWCA Civ 142 [2004] 4 All ER 1103 at [45] (CA treating "believes" as involving that: "the belief must be reasonable and objectively justified by relevant facts");*R v Commission for Racial Equality, ex p Hillingdon London Borough Council* [1982] AC 779, 791C (Lord Diplock, asking whether "material ... sufficient to raise in the minds of reasonable men, possessed of the experience ... that has been acquired by the commission, [the relevant] suspicion").

(H) "OPINION". *R v Eastleigh Borough Council, ex p Betts* [1983] 2 AC 613, 626D-H and 628G; *R v Surrey County Council, ex p G and H* [1995] COD 50; *R v Hampshire County Council, ex p W* [1994] ELR 460, 469H-470B; *R v Humberside Family Health Services*

Authority, ex p Dr Moore [1995] COD 343.

(I) "REASONABLE CAUSE/GROUNDS". *Nakkuda Ali v Jayaratne* [1951] AC 66, 76-77 (treating the formula `where the body with reasonable cause/grounds...' as connoting a precedent fact); *R v Inland Revenue Commissioners, ex p Rossminster* [1980] AC 952, 1011B-C (Lord Diplock: "These words appearing in a statute do not make conclusive the officer's own honest opinion, that he has reasonable cause for the prescribed belief. The grounds on which the officer acted must be sufficient to induce in a reasonable person the required belief"); and see 1000D (Lord Wilberforce); *Holgate-Mohammed v Duke* [1984] AC 437, 442F (Lord Diplock: "reasonable cause" as "a condition precedent to a constable's having any power lawfully to arrest a person ... Whether he had reasonable cause is a question of fact for the court to determine"); *Raymond v Honey* [1983] 1 AC 1, 9H-10A & 13D-E ("reason to suppose" treated as precedent fact); *R v Leeds Crown Court, ex p Quirk & Khan* [1994] COD 287 (conclusion as to whether "good and sufficient cause" unreasonable); *A v B Bank (Governor and Company of the Bank of England Intervening)* [1993] QB 311, 326B-327G (such documents as the BoE "may reasonably require" treated as a matter for the Bank of England); *R v Director General of Telecommunications, ex p Cellcom Ltd* [1999] COD 105 (see transcript) (question whether a demand "reasonable" under the statutory phrase "such telecommunication services as satisfy all reasonable demands for them" as an objective question for the Court).

(J) OTHER STATUTORY LANGUAGE. *R (G) v Barnet London Borough Council* [2003] UKHL 57 [2004] 2 AC 208 at [15] ("reasonable steps"); *R v Secretary of State for Employment, ex p National Association of Colliery Overmen, Deputies & Shotfirers* [1994] COD 218 (even where Parliament did not expressly use subjective language questions of fact not usually a "precedent fact"); *R v East Sussex County Council, ex p T* [1997] ELR 311 (Keene J), 321A ("suitable" not a hard-edged question for the Court, but a question for the authority, subject to normal supervisory review; the point was not pursued in the CA).

40.1 Preservation of powers and duties
40.2 Inalienability and estoppel/legitimate expectation

40.1 Preservation of powers and duties. The preservation of the proper lawful function of a public authority is a public law imperative. Courts resist the prospect of allowing or requiring a public body to act in a way which is incompatible with its continuing duties or powers. So, for example, power must not be surrendered, which means that the public body should: (1) keep an open mind; (2) make up its own mind; and (3) have the capacity to change its mind. A decision-maker should not compromise its own function, nor the function of another body.

40.1.1 Inalienability of powers and duties: the *Birkdale* principle. *Birkdale District Electricity Supply Co Ltd v Southport Corporation* [1926] AC 355, 364 (Lord Birkenhead, referring to the "well established principle of law, that if a person or public body is entrusted by the Legislature with certain powers and duties expressly or impliedly for public purposes, those persons or bodies cannot divest themselves of these powers and duties. They cannot enter into any contract or take any action incompatible with the due exercise of their powers or the discharge of their duties"), cited eg. in *R v Liverpool Corporation, ex p Liverpool Taxi Fleet Operators' Association* [1972] 2 QB 299, 308; *R v Greater London Council, ex p Burgess* [1978] ICR 991, 992G; *Kalra v Secretary of State for the Environment* [1994] 2 PLR 99 (David Widdicombe QC), 108B-109G.

40.1.2 Keeping an open mind. *Stoke-on-Trent City Council v B & Q (Retail) Ltd* [1984] AC 754, 768F (Lord Roskill: "A local authority charged with the duty of enforcing the Shops Act 1950 cannot of course properly say that it will never carry out its statutory duty because of the expense involved in so doing. Were it to adopt that attitude, I do not doubt that its decision would be subject to judicial review on*Wednesbury* principles"); *Bovis Homes Ltd v New Forest District Council* [2002] EWHC 483 (Admin) at [114] (planning authority having predetermined the decision to make a local plan, so that having a closed mind); <P50> (fetter).

40.1.3 Making up its own mind. *R v Secretary of State for the Environment, ex p Kirkstall Valley Campaign Ltd* [1996] 3 All ER 304, 321h (Sedley J, referring to the "important principle: that the decision of a body, albeit composed of disinterested individuals, will be struck down if its outcome has been predetermined whether by the adoption of an inflexible policy or by the effective surrender of the body's independent judgment"); *R v Police Complaints Board, ex p Madden* [1983] 1 WLR 447 (wrongly treating Secretary of State's guidance as binding); <50.2.1> (puppets), <50.2.2> (rubber-stamping); <50.3> (improper delegation).

40.1.4 Changing its mind/retaining the capacity for a change of mind. *Secretary of State for Education and Science v Tameside Metropolitan Borough Council* [1977] AC 1014, 1073G-H (Lord Russell: "There was no obligation whatever in law on the local authority to implement its 1975 proposals, albeit they had been approved by the Secretary of State. Prima facie the local authority was within its rights and duties to change its mind"); *R (Hargrave) v Stroud District Council* [2002] EWCA Civ 1281 [2002] 3 PLR 115 (council having power to withdraw footpath diversion order) at [19] ("no reason why, other things being equal, they should not change their mind"); *Akin Ali v Secretary of State for the Home Department* [1994] Imm AR 489, 492-493; *R v Secretary of State for Education, ex p C* [1996] ELR 93; *Rootkin v Kent County Council* [1981] 1 WLR 1186 (entitled to review decision if relevant mistake had been made); *Attorney-General of Trinidad and Tobago v Phillip* [1995] 1 AC 396 (no power to give prospective pardon); <30.4.1> (not bound by manifesto promises); *R v Bradford City Metropolitan Council, ex p Corris* [1990] 2 QB 363, 373D-374C; cf. *R v London Borough of Lambeth, ex p Miah* (1995) 27 HLR 21 (where local authority has made determination of homelessness and accepted duty to provide permanent accommodation, that decision cannot be revised); <40.2> (inalienability and estoppel/ legitimate expectation).

40.1.5 Defendant changing its policy. *R (Bhatt Murphy) v Independent Assessor* [2008] EWCA Civ 755 at [41] (referring to "the entitlement of central government to formulate and re-formulate policy"); *In re Findlay* [1985] AC 318, 338E-F (prisoner entitled to consideration "in the light of whatever policy the Secretary of State sees fit to adopt provided always that the adopted policy is a lawful exercise of the discretion conferred upon him by the statute"); *R (Abbasi) v Secretary of State for Foreign and Commonwealth Affairs* [2002] EWCA Civ 1598 [2003] UKHRR 76 at [82] (legitimate expectation "is not that the policy or practice will necessarily remain unchanged"); *Hughes v Department of Health and Social Security* [1985] AC 776, 788A-C ("Administrative policies may change with changing circumstances ... The liberty to make such changes is something that is inherent in our constitutional form of government. When a change in administrative policy takes place and is communicated in a departmental circular ... any reasonable expectations that may have been aroused ... by any previous circular are destroyed and are replaced"), considered in *R v Secretary of State for the Home Department, ex p Pierson* [1998] AC 539, 598B; *R v North and East Devon Health Authority, ex p Coughlan* [2001] QB 213, at [64] (public authority "cannot abdicate its general remit" and so must "remain free to change policy" so that "its undertakings are correspondingly open to modification or abandonment"); *R v Secretary of State for Health, ex p United States Tobacco International Inc* [1992] QB 353, 368E, 369B ("a Minister cannot fetter a discretion given him under statute. Providing he acts within his statutory powers, rationally and fairly, he is entitled to change his policy"), 372G; <54.2> (substantive legitimate expectation).

40.1.6 Defendant departing from its policy. *R (Mullen) v Secretary of State for the Home Department* [2004] UKHL 18 [2005] 1 AC 1 at [60] (not irrational to depart from policy); <6.2.7(D)> (departure from policy).

40.1.7 Allowing another body to make up its own mind: puppeteers. <50.2.3>.

40.1.8 Nature of remedy: not fettering the public body. <24.4.14>.

40.1.9 Inalienability and private law. *Islwyn Borough Council & Gwent County Council v Newport Borough Council* (1994) 6 Admin LR 386, 417C-D (Roch LJ: "it is open to the authority to decide not to continue with its bargain. That may lead to a remedy in damages or an injunction or both. A council's decision as to its future action will only be fettered in those cases where a court considers that the discretionary remedy of an injunction should be granted"); *Silver Mountain Investments Ltd v Attorney-General of Hong Kong* [1994] 1 WLR 925, 934C-935D (rejecting the argument that the LDC had "tied its hands by entering into a contract with a single developer thereby wrongly fettering its discretion"); *Tidman v Reading Borough Council* [1994] 3 PLR 72 (duty of care incompatible with council's overriding public duties to apply planning law and exercise its discretionary powers in the public interest); *X (Minors) v Bedfordshire County Council* [1995] 2 AC 633, 765F-H (authority's vicarious common law liability for teachers' negligence in respect of special educational needs not a 'fetter' on statutory duties merely because statutory scheme addressing the same problem).

40.2 Inalienability and estoppel/legitimate expectation. The principle that a public body's continuing functions (powers and duties) should not be compromised may clash with its duties to act fairly and reasonably and not abuse its powers. A classic illustration is where the claimant relies on a legitimate expectation or estoppel, and in response the defendant public body invokes the inalienability of its powers and duties as releasing it from any such constraint.

40.2.1 **Legitimate expectation and inalienability problems.**[56] <P41> (legitimate expectation). (A) EXPECTATIONS WHICH CONFLICT WITH DUTIES.*Attorney-General of Hong Kong v Ng Yuen Shiu* [1983] 2 AC 629, 638F ("when a public authority has promised to follow a certain procedure, it is in the interest of good administration that it should act fairly and should implement its promise, so long as implementation does not interfere with its statutory duty"); *R v Inland Revenue Commissioners, ex p MFK Underwriting Agents Ltd* [1990] 1 WLR 1545, 1566H, 1567E-F, 1568D-E, 1569B, 1574F-G; *R v Gaming Board of Great Britain, ex p Kingsley* [1996] COD 241 (rejecting notion of a legitimate expectation that decision-maker would decline to take known material matters into account, since this would breach its statutory duty); <41.1.12(A)> (legitimate expectation yielding to primary legislation).
(B) ACTION WOULD BE UNLAWFUL/LACK AUTHORITY?[57] *Rowland v Environment Agency* [2003] EWCA Civ 1885 [2005] Ch 1 at [102] (unjust that "orthodox English domestic law does not allow the individual to retain the benefit which is the subject of the legitimate expectation, however strong, if creating or maintaining that benefit is beyond the power of the public body"), [115]-[120] (discussing Professor Craig's critique of the position), [136] (Mance LJ, referring to *Stretch v West Dorset District Council* (1997) 96 LGR 637 as reflecting the orthodox position); *R (Bibi) v Newham London Borough Council* [2001] EWCA Civ 607 [2002] 1 WLR 237 at [46]; *R v Leicester City Council, ex p Powergen* [1999] 4 PLR 91, 102E (planning officers having no delegated authority to vary or waive a planning condition, so no legitimate expectation arising as to the meaning which the council would give to the condition); <40.2.4(C)> (estoppel and ostensible authority); *R (AP) v Leeds Youth Court* [2001] EWHC Admin 215 (no legitimate expectation from magistrates' order to act in excess of power); *R (Theophilus) v London Borough of Lewisham* [2002] EWHC 1371 (Admin) [2002] 3 All ER 851 at [17] (no legitimate expectation if no power to provide student support); *R (White) v Barking Magistrates' Court* [2004] EWHC 417 (Admin) at [32] (magistrates' sentencing indication giving rise to a legitimate expectation but judicial review refused because no reasonable bench of magistrates could have acted as indicated).
(C) DEFENDANT CAN CHANGE ITS POLICY. <40.1.5> (defendant changing its policy).
(D) DEFENDANT CAN CORRECT ITS MISTAKE. *R v Department for Education and Employment, ex p Begbie* [2000] 1 WLR 1115, 1127B-D ("Where the court is satisfied that a mistake was made by the minister or other person making the statement, the court should be slow to fix the public authority permanently with the consequences of that mistake"; depends whether in all the circumstances unfairness amounting to an abuse of power), 1131E-F, 1133H; *Rowland v Environment Agency* [2003] EWCA Civ 1885 [2005] Ch 1 at [96] ("Courts should be slow to fix a public authority permanently with the consequences of a mistake ..., particularly when it would deprive the public of their rights"); *R v Inland Revenue Commissioners, ex p Matrix-Securities Ltd* [1994] 1 WLR 334, 346G-H ("It is one thing to hold the revenue to a clearance that has been acted upon in good faith, but quite another to permit the correction of an error before it has been acted upon"); *R v Beatrix Potter School, ex p K* [1997] ELR 468 (not unlawful for school to correct its mistake); *Francisco Javier Jaramillo-Silva v Secretary of State for the Home Department* [1994] Imm AR 352, 356 ("the Secretary of State was simply making a mistake in suggesting there would be a right of appeal"), 358 ("neither unfair nor inconsistent with good administration to have corrected his mistake"); *R (Thompson) v Secretary of State*

---

[56] Chris Hilson [2006] JR 289.

[57] David Blundell [2005] JR 147.

for the Home Department [2003] EWHC 538 (Admin) at [49] (here "not possible to found a legitimate expectation on the mistaken statement of an official, in circumstances where the reality is that a statutory provision operates"); <40.2.4(B)> (estoppel and correcting a mistake). (E) DEFENDANT CAN CHANGE ITS MIND. *R v Aylesbury Vale District Council, ex p Chaplin* (Keene J) The Times 23rd July 1996 (change of mind not indicating irrationality; citing *R v East Devon District Council, ex p Church Commissioners* 5th December 1995 unrep.). (F) HONOURING PROMISES WHERE COMPATIBLE WITH FUNCTIONS.*R v Liverpool Corporation, ex p Liverpool Taxi Fleet Operators' Association* [1972] 2 QB 299, 308E-F (body not entitled to "give an undertaking and break it as they please. So long as the performance of the undertaking is compatible with their public duty, they must honour it", cited in *Attorney-General of Hong Kong v Ng Yuen Shiu* [1983] 2 AC 629, 637H), 311A-D (Roskill LJ); *R v Westminster City Council, ex p Union of Managerial and Professional Officers* [2000] LGR 611, 626c-g (legitimate expectation "must be subject to the council being satisfied that it had the legal power" to honour the expectation). (G) THE PUBLIC INTEREST. *R v East Sussex County Council, ex p Reprotech (Pebsham) Ltd* [2002] UKHL 8 [2003] 1 WLR 348 (legitimate expectation as analogous to estoppel, but with a built-in consideration of the public interest).

40.2.2 Substantive unfairness and inalienability problems. *R v Inland Revenue Commissioners, ex p Preston* [1985] AC 835 (HL asking whether Revenue's conduct an abuse of power in public law terms), 862B-C ("no remedy against the commissioners for breach of contract or breach of representations", "because the commissioners could not in 1978 bind themselves not to perform in 1982 the statutory duty of counteracting a tax advantage"); *R v Inland Revenue Commissioners, ex p Unilever Plc* [1996] STC 681 (Revenue having a duty to enforce tax legislation, but nevertheless substantively unfair so as to be an abuse of power); <P54> (substantive fairness).

40.2.3 Estoppel in public law: the need for caution.[58] *R v Immigration Appeal Tribunal, ex p Patel (Anilkumar Rabindrabhai)* [1988] 1 AC 910, 918H-919A (no estoppel from leave to re-enter); *R v Wirral Metropolitan Borough Council, ex p B* [2001] LGR 1 at [36]-[42] (no estoppel from educational needs statement sent to parents in error and not reflecting tribunal's order); *R v East Sussex County Council, ex p Reprotech (Pebsham) Ltd* [2002] UKHL 8 [2003] 1 WLR 348 at [32] (planning officer's opinion "could not reasonably have been taken as a binding representation that no planning permission was required"), [33] ("unhelpful to introduce private law concepts of estoppel into planning law"), applied in *South Bucks District Council v Flanagan* [2002] EWCA Civ 690 [2002] 1 WLR 2601 at [16] (Keene LJ: "Now that [the] concepts [of legitimate expectation and abuse of power] are recognised, there is no longer a place for the private law doctrine of estoppel in public law or for the attendant problems which it brings with it"); *Henry Boot Homes Ltd v Bassetlaw District Council* [2002] EWCA Civ 983 [2002] 4 PLR 108 (legitimate expectation and estoppel only capable in exceptional circumstances to override planning requirements of the statutory code); <54.1.14> (estoppel and pubic authorities); *Gowa v Attorney-General* [1985] 1 WLR 1003, 1005G (Lord Roskill, leaving open whether "where a statute confers a discretionary power on the Crown and the exercise of that discretionary power is essential before the desired consequences can follow, the need for the exercise of that discretionary power as a condition precedent to those consequences following cannot be by-passed by the invocation of the doctrine of estoppel");*R v Governor of Pentonville Prison, ex p Azam* [1974] AC 18, 64H-65A (leaving open whether could be waiver of unlawful residence).

---

[58] Mark Elliott [2003] JR 71.

40.2.4 Estoppel: inalienability problems.

(A) WHETHER ESTOPPEL CONSISTENT WITH POWERS AND DUTIES. *London Borough of Tower Hamlets v Sherwood* [2002] EWCA Civ 229 (estoppel not inconsistent with the council's statutory powers and duties), at [68]-[69] ("estoppel will not lie to oblige a public authority to do something which is beyond its powers or to fetter or prevent it from carrying out its statutory duties or powers"); *R v East Sussex County Council, ex p Reprotech (Pebsham) Ltd* [2002] UKHL 8 [2003] 1 WLR 348 at [35] (describing the reconciliation of "invocations of estoppel with the general principle that a public authority cannot be estopped from exercising a statutory discretion or performing a public duty"); *R v Secretary of State for the Home Department, ex p Naheed Ejaz* [1994] QB 496, 504C-E ("The Secretary of State cannot, by mistaking his own powers, enlarge them beyond what Parliament has granted and he cannot be estopped from asserting that he lacked the necessary power, if that be the case"), 507F ("estoppel cannot be invoked to give a minister or authority powers which he or it does not in law possess"); *Rhyl Urban District Council v Rhyl Amusements Ltd* [1959] 1 WLR 465, 474 ("a plea of estoppel cannot prevail as an answer to a claim that something done by a statutory body is ultra vires"); *Buckinghamshire County Council v Secretary of State for the Environment* [1998] 4 PLR 19, 28B ("since it is wrong to prevent the exercise of a statutory function by raising an estoppel, it must also be wrong to seek to extend the scope of a statutory function or the way in which it is to be exercised on the basis of proprietary estoppel"); *Calder Gravel Ltd v Kirklees Metropolitan Borough Council* (1990) 2 Admin LR 327, 350C-F (difficulties in reconciling the authorities as to when estoppel could be "raised against a body which has a statutory duty to perform, such as a planning authority, and the effect of the estoppel would be to prevent it carrying out its statutory duty").

(B) ESTOPPEL AND CHANGING POLICY/ CORRECTING A MISTAKE. *Laker Airways Ltd v Department of Trade* [1977] QB 643, 728D-F (claimants as "victims of a change of government policy. This often happens. Estoppel cannot be allowed to hinder the formation of government policy"), 708G-H ("far-reaching constitutional implications ... [if], in the event of a change of government, a new government might ... find itself precluded in whole or in part from implementing a change of policy which it had included in its election programme"); <40.1.5> (defendant changing its policy); *Rootkin v Kent County Council* [1981] 1 WLR 1186 (no estoppel because entitled to correct a mistake); <40.2.1(D)> (legitimate expectation and correcting a mistake).

(C) OSTENSIBLE AUTHORITY. *Howell v Falmouth Boat Construction Co Ltd* [1951] AC 837, 845 (rejecting the suggestion that "whenever government officers, in their dealings with a subject, take on themselves to assume authority in a matter with which he is concerned, the subject is entitled to rely on their having the authority which they assume"); *R v Secretary of State for the Home Department, ex p Chung, Ku & Kuet* [1994] Imm AR 183 (Laws J), 188 (rejecting an "ostensible authority" argument in the context of an official having acted without authority; and see CA at [1995] QB 364); cf. *South Bucks District Council v Flanagan* [2002] EWCA Civ 690 [2002] 1 WLR 2601 at [18] (need for actual or ostensible authority for a representation said to form the basis of a legitimate expectation).

40.2.5 Relationship between estoppel and legitimate expectation.[59] *R v East Sussex County Council, ex p Reprotech (Pebsham) Ltd* [2002] UKHL 8 [2003] 1 WLR 348 at [34] (Lord Hoffmann: "There is of course an analogy between a private law estoppel and the public law concept of a legitimate expectation created by a public authority, the denial of which may amount to an abuse of power ... But it is no more than an analogy because remedies against public authorities also have to take into account the interests of the general public which the authority exists to promote"), [35] ("in this area, public law has already absorbed whatever is

---

[59] Nicholas Bamforth [1998] JR 196.

useful from the moral values which underlie the private law concept of estoppel and the time has come for it to stand upon its own two feet"), applied in *South Bucks District Council v Flanagan* [2002] EWCA Civ 690 [2002] 1 WLR 2601; *R (Zeqiri) v Secretary of State for the Home Department* [2002] UKHL 3 [2002] INLR 291 at [44] (Lord Hoffmann, discussing legitimate expectation based on an alleged representation: "The question is not whether it would have founded an estoppel in private law but the broader question of whether, as Simon Brown LJ said in [*Unilever*], a public authority acting contrary to the representation would be acting `with conspicuous unfairness' and in that sense abusing its power"); *Henry Boot Homes Ltd v Bassetlaw District Council* [2002] EWCA Civ 983 [2002] 4 PLR 108 (both legitimate expectation and estoppel only capable in exceptional circumstances to override planning requirements of the statutory code); *R v Northamptonshire County Council, ex p Commission for the New Towns* [1992] COD 123 (doctrine of estoppel not sufficient by itself, but supporting legitimate expectation); *R v Devon County Council, ex p Baker* [1995] 1 All ER 73, 88g (cases where legitimate expectation "is akin to an estoppel"); *R v Ministry for Agriculture Fisheries & Food, ex p Hamble Fisheries (Offshore) Ltd* [1995] 2 All ER 714, 725h (legitimate expectation not "another name for estoppel. It is precisely because public authorities have public duties to perform that they can no more be estopped from performing them than they can contract out of them"), but 731g (substantive legitimate expectation "is as near as public law is able to approach to estoppel"); *R v Jockey Club, ex p RAM Racecourses* [1993] 2 All ER 225, 236h ("many similarities with the principles of estoppel in private law").

40.2.6 **Relationship between estoppel and substantive unfairness/ abuse of power.** <54.1.14(C)>; *R v Inland Revenue Commissioners, ex p MFK Underwriting Agents Ltd* [1990] 1 WLR 1545, 1574B (considering use of the term "estoppel" in *R v Inland Revenue Commissioners, ex p Preston* [1985] AC 835); *R v Inland Revenue Commissioners, ex p Unilever Plc* [1996] STC 681, 695b (and below at [1994] STC 841, 852e-f), citing *R v Independent Television Commission, ex p TSW Broadcasting Ltd* 5th February 1992 unrep. ("The test in public law is fairness, not an adaptation of the law of contract or estoppel"; HL is at [1994] 2 LRC 414); *R v Ministry of Agriculture Fisheries & Food, ex p Cox* (1994) 6 Admin LR 421, 436G-437E (Ministry's own guidance proceeding upon same erroneous assumption as claimant, so "inequitable" to remove claimant's quota); *HTV Ltd v Price Commission* [1976] ICR 170, 185G-H (Lord Denning MR: "a public body, which is entrusted by Parliament with the exercise of powers for the public good, cannot fetter itself in the exercise of them. It cannot be estopped from doing its public duty. But that is subject to the qualification that it must not misuse its powers: and it is a misuse of power for it to act unfairly or unjustly towards a private citizen when there is no overriding public interest to warrant it"), cited in *R v Inland Revenue Commissioners, ex p Preston* [1985] AC 835, 865D (Lord Templeman); *Laker Airways Ltd v Department of Trade* [1977] QB 643, 707D-F (Crown can "be estopped when it is not properly exercising its powers, but is misusing them; and it does misuse them if it exercises them in circumstances which work injustice or unfairness to the individual without any countervailing benefit for the public"), 709A-E (Roskill LJ).

40.2.7 **Agreements and inalienability problems.** *R (DFS Furniture Co Ltd) v Commissioners of Customs and Excise* [2002] EWCA Civ 1708 (Customs and Excise entitled to exercise retrospective power to reclaim repaid VAT, having on the facts not reached an agreement settling a VAT appeal under the Value Added Tax Act 1994 s.85); *R (H) v Commissioners of Inland Revenue* [2002] EWHC 2164 (Admin) [2002] STC 1354 at [54] (Stanley Burnton J: "If a public authority does that which Parliament has enacted to be lawful, I do not think that that authority can by agreement render its action unlawful. On the other hand, if the result of the agreement is that the public authority acts in a way that is not protected by the statute, *ex hypothesi* the statute cannot protect it from liability if the agreement is ineffective").

> **P41 Legitimate expectation.** Promises or practices may raise
> expectations incapable of unfair or unreasonable dishonour.

41.1 The role of legitimate expectation
41.2 Basic anatomy of a legitimate expectation

41.1 The role of legitimate expectation.[60] Just as proportionality protects certain rights, legitimate expectation protects certain expectations. It does so by identifying action which is procedurally or substantively unfair.[61]

41.1.1 Legitimate expectation: from catch-phrase to principle. *Behluli v Secretary of State for the Home Department* [1998] Imm AR 407, 415 (Beldam LJ: "Although legitimate expectation may in the past have been categorised as a catchphrase not to be elevated into a principle, or as an easy cover for a general complaint about unfairness, it has nevertheless achieved an important place in developing the law of administrative fairness. It is an expectation which, although not amounting to an enforceable legal right, is founded on a reasonable assumption which is capable of being protected in public law. It enables a citizen to challenge a decision which deprives him of an expectation founded on a reasonable basis that his claim would be dealt with in a particular way"); *Surendra Jessa Chundawadra v Immigration Appeal Tribunal* [1988] Imm AR 161, 169 (legitimate expectation a "phrase ... first used by Lord Denning in *Schmidt v Secretary of State for Home Affairs* [1969] 2 Ch 149"), 174 ("a feature of our law since [then]"); *In re Findlay* [1985] AC 318, 338D (Lord Scarman: "The doctrine of legitimate expectation has an important place in the developing law of judicial review"); *Lloyd v McMahon* [1987] AC 625, 714F (Lord Templeman, rejecting the argument "that a legitimate expectation ... is an objective fundamental right which, if not afforded, results in a breach of law or breach of natural justice which invalidates any decision": "This extravagant language does not tempt me to elevate a catch-phrase into a principle. The true principle is that the auditor, like any other decision-maker, must act fairly"); *R v London Borough of Camden, ex p Hughes* [1994] COD 253 (legitimate expectation as "an easy cover for a general complaint of unfairness").

41.1.2 Generalised references to legitimate expectation.
(A) EXPECTATIONS COMPARED/CONTRASTED WITH RIGHTS. *Council of Civil Service Unions v Minister for the Civil Service* [1985] AC 374, 412B-C (civil servant having no employment "right enforceable by him in private law; at most it can only be a legitimate expectation"), 401A (albeit "no legal right" in private law, individual "may have a legitimate expectation of receiving [a] benefit or privilege, and, if so, the courts will protect his expectation by judicial review as a matter of public law"), 411G (fairness applying "where the decision is one which does not alter rights or obligations enforceable in private law but only deprives a person of legitimate expectations"), *Attorney-General of Hong Kong v Ng Yuen Shiu* [1983] 2 AC 629, 636F ("legitimate expectations" as "including expectations which go beyond enforceable legal rights"); *Anisminic Ltd v Foreign Compensation Commission* [1969] 2 AC 147, 172A ("The effect of the Order was to confer legal rights on persons"), 173D (previously

---

[60] Rabinder Singh & Karen Steyn [1996] JR 17, [1997] JR 33; Michael Fordham [2000] JR 188, [2001] JR 262; Karen Steyn [2001] JR 244; Philip Sales [2006] JR 186; Mark Elliott [2006] JR 281; Ashley Underwood QC [2006] JR 294.

[61] This paragraph in a previous edition was cited in *Mastercard UK Members Forum Ltd v Office of Fair Trading* [2006] CAT 14 at [36].

they had only "a hope or expectation").
(B) EXPECTATIONS AND REVIEWABILITY. <34.2.10(B)>.
(C) EXPECTATIONS AND STANDING. *In re Findlay* [1985] AC 318, 338D-E (Lord Scarman: "a legitimate expectation can provide a sufficient interest to enable one who cannot point to the existence of a substantive right to obtain the [permission] of the court to apply for judicial review"); *R v London Borough of Camden, ex p Hughes* [1994] COD 253 (legitimate expectation relevant to whether standing to complain of a failure to consult); *R v Secretary of State for Transport, ex p Greater London Council* [1986] QB 556, 587D (expectations entitling claimant to seek judicial review).

41.1.3 Legitimate expectation: Simon Brown LJ's categories. *R v Devon County Council, ex p Baker* [1995] 1 All ER 73, 88d (Simon Brown LJ, identifying "in broad categories, various of the distinct senses in which the phrase `legitimate expectation' is ... used"), 88e ("(1) Sometimes the phrase is used to denote a substantive right: an entitlement that the claimant asserts cannot be denied him"), 88j-89a ("(2) Perhaps more conventionally the concept of legitimate expectation is used to refer to the claimant's interest in some ultimate benefit ... [which] interest ... is one that the law holds protected by the requirements of procedural fairness ... [and] rational grounds for any adverse decision"), 89b-c ("(3) Frequently, however, the concept of legitimate expectation is used to refer to the fair procedure itself. In other words it is contended that the claimant has a legitimate expectation that the public body will act fairly towards him"), 89e-g ("(4) The final category of legitimate expectation encompasses those cases in which it is held that a particular procedure, not otherwise required by law in the protection of an interest, must be followed consequent upon some specific promise or practice"), discussed in *R (Bhatt Murphy) v Independent Assessor* [2008] EWCA Civ 755.

41.1.4 Legitimate expectation as a general principle of EC law. *R v Ministry for Agriculture Fisheries & Food, ex p Hamble Fisheries (Offshore) Ltd* [1995] 2 All ER 714, 726a-b); *Milk Marketing Board of England and Wales v Tom Parker Farms Ltd* [1999] EuLR 154, 164F-G ("the purpose of the principle of protection of legitimate expectations is the avoidance of prejudice to a party who has justifiably relied on the continuance of the other party's anterior position but where the latter party has changed that anterior position to the detriment of the other"); <41.1.16> (legitimate expectation and damages).

41.1.5 Procedural legitimate expectation. <60.1.11>.

41.1.6 Substantive legitimate expectation. <54.2>.

41.1.7 Legitimate expectation: the international instrument problem. *R v Secretary of State for the Home Department, ex p Ahmed* [1999] Imm AR 22, 40 (legitimate expectation that Secretary of State would not, without reason, act inconsistently with ratified Convention); *R v Uxbridge Magistrates' Court, ex p Adimi* [2001] QB 667, 686D, 690D-691D (treating ratification of UN Convention on Refugees as capable of giving rise to legitimate expectation that its provisions would be followed); *R (European Roma Rights Centre) v Immigration Officer at Prague Airport* [2003] EWCA Civ 666 [2004] QB 811 (CA) at [51] (*Adimi* "superficial" and "suspect", not least because overlooking *Chundawadra* [1988] Imm AR 161 and *Behluli* [1998] Imm AR 407), [100] ("we must not be seduced by humanitarian claims to a spurious acceptance of a false source of law") (HL is [2004] UKHL 55 [2005] 2 AC 1); *Higgs v Minister of National Security* [2000] 2 AC 228, 241E-G ("the existence of [an unincorporated] treaty may give rise to a legitimate expectation on the part of citizens that the government, in its acts affecting them, will observe the terms of the treaty ... [But] the legal effect of creating such a legitimate expectation is purely procedural. The executive cannot depart from the expected course of conduct unless it has given notice that [it] intends to do so and has given the person affected an opportunity to make representations"); *R v Asfaw* [2008] UKHL 31 [2008] 2 WLR 1178 at [30] (where partially-effective statutory incorporation, no "legitimate expectation of being treated otherwise than in accordance with the ... Act").

41.1.8 Legitimate expectation: the prisoner policy cases. *In re Findlay* [1985] AC 318, 338 (legitimate expectation merely to have case considered under current policy); *R v Secretary of State for the Home Department, ex p Hargreaves* [1997] 1 WLR 906[62] (whether defendant entitled to change policy involving *Wednesbury* test); *R v Secretary of State for the Home Department, ex p Pierson* [1998] AC 539, 590G-591A (identifying the "controversial" question of legitimate expectation having "substantive effect"); *R v Secretary of State for the Home Department, ex p Hindley* [2001] 1 AC 410, 419B (leaving open whether *Findlay* still good law).

41.1.9 Legitimate expectation: inalienability problems. <40.2.1>.

41.1.10 Legitimate expectation as a relevancy. <56.1.8>.

41.1.11 Legitimate expectation not necessary.
(A) STANDING. See eg. *R v Secretary of State for Foreign & Commonwealth Affairs, ex p Rees-Mogg* [1994] QB 552, 562A; *R v Secretary of State for Foreign and Commonwealth Affairs, ex p World Development Movement Ltd* [1995] 1 WLR 386, 395G-396A.
(B) PROCEDURAL GROUNDS. *R (Machi) v Legal Services Commission* [2001] EWCA Civ 2010 [2002] 1 WLR 983 at [31] (referring to an issue "of procedural fairness" which "gains nothing by being cast in terms of legitimate expectation"); *R v Birmingham City Council, ex p Dredger* (1994) 6 Admin LR 553, 566H-572C (treating as independent questions, whether a right of consultation via (a) legitimate expectation or (b) procedural fairness); *R v Secretary of State for Education, ex p London Borough of Southwark* [1995] ELR 308, 320F (there are "plainly circumstances beyond those where there was a clear promise or practice of consultation ... in which principle requires that a party affected by a forthcoming decision should be told about the decision-maker's provisional view, and thus consulted"); *R v BBC, ex p David Kelly* [1996] COD 58 (no duty to consult because no legitimate expectation); *R v Secretary of State for the Home Department, ex p Duggan* [1994] 3 All ER 277 (legitimate expectation argument rejected, but natural justice argument accepted).
(C) SUBSTANTIVE GROUNDS. *R v Secretary of State for the Home Department, ex p Pierson* [1998] AC 539, 590G-591A (substantive fairness applicable independently of legitimate expectation); *R v Inland Revenue Commissioners, ex p Unilever Plc* [1996] STC 681 (substantive unfairness); <P57> (unreasonableness); <32.3> (anxious scrutiny).

41.1.12 Legitimate expectation limited by the law.
(A) YIELDING TO PRIMARY LEGISLATION. *R v Department for Education and Employment, ex p Begbie* [2000] 1 WLR 1115, 1125D ("any expectation must yield to the terms of the statute under which the Secretary of State is required to act"), 1129E (legitimate expectation would mean requiring Secretary of State to act inconsistently with statute); *R v Commissioners of Customs and Excise, ex p Kay and Co* [1996] STC 1500, 1522h, 1528b (clear primary legislation could override legitimate expectation/ substantive unfairness); *R v Director of Public Prosecutions, ex p Kebilene* [2000] 2 AC 326, 368E (legitimate expectation rejected as contrary to "clear statutory intent" and "contradicted by the language of the statute"); *R v Environment Agency, ex p Anglian Water Services Ltd* [2002] EWCA Civ 5 at [33] (legitimate expectation could not predispose defendant to an outcome, given statutory duty to decide a

---

[62] Kate Markus & Martin Westgate [1997] JR 220.

dispute even-handedly), [32] (result compelled by proper interpretation of the Act); *R (Aggregate Industries UK Ltd) v English Nature* [2002] EWHC 908 (Admin) [2003] Env LR 83 at [117] ("Any legitimate expectation must yield to the terms of any statute"; defendant "cannot estop itself from discharging its statutory functions in the public interest").

(B) YIELDING TO SECONDARY LEGISLATION. *R v Staffordshire Moorlands District Council, ex p Bartlam* (1999) 77 P & CR 210 (disappointment of the legitimate expectation could not give the claimant "a right, in effect, to override the provisions of the [Order]")

(C) STATING THE LAW. *R (Beale) v Camden London Borough Council* [2004] EWHC 6 (Admin) [2004] LGR 291 at [22] ("Statements by ministers as to what the law is are no more determinative of the citizen's rights than similar statements by anyone else... If it is correct it adds nothing: if it is incorrect it is for present purposes irrelevant").

(D) LEGITIMATE EXPECTATION OF UNLAWFUL ACT. *R (AP) v Leeds Youth Court* [2001] EWHC Admin 215 (no legitimate expectation arising from magistrates' order that would dismiss prosecution in circumstances where no power to do so: "There cannot be a legitimate expectation that a court will act illegally"); *R (Theophilus) v London Borough of Lewisham* [2002] EWHC 1371 (Admin) [2002] 3 All ER 851 at [17] (no legitimate expectation if no power to provide student support); <40.2.1(B)> (legitimate expectation and lack of power/authority).

41.1.13 Legitimate expectation: whether other special limits.

(A) PROMISES IN PARLIAMENT? *R (Wheeler) v Office of the Prime Minister* [2008] EWHC 1409 (Admin) at [53] (whether legitimate expectation capable of being based on statements in Parliament); *R (O'Callaghan) v Charity Commission* [2007] EWHC 2491 (Admin) (legitimate expectation of consultation from Minister's promise in Parliament); *Pepper v Hart* [1993] AC 593, 616G (asking "whether it could possibly be right to give effect to taxing legislation in such a way as to impose a tax which the Financial Secretary to the Treasury, during the passage of the Bill containing the relevant provision, had, in effect, assured the House of Commons it was not intended to impose"); *R (Westminster City Council) v National Asylum Support Service* [2002] UKHL 38 [2002] 1 WLR 2956 at [6] ("If exceptionally there is found in Explanatory Notes a clear assurance by the executive to Parliament about the meaning of a clause, or the circumstances in which a power will or will not be used, that assurance may in principle be admitted against the executive in proceedings in which the executive places a contrary contention before a court. This reflects the actual decision in *Pepper v Hart*"); *Wilson v First County Trust Ltd* [2003] UKHL 40 [2004] 1 AC 816 at [113] (Lord Hope, referring to the purpose of *Pepper v Hart* as being "to prevent the executive seeking to place a meaning on words used in legislation which is different from that which ministers attributed to those words when promoting the legislation in Parliament"); *Wilson v First County Trust Ltd* [2003] UKHL 40 [2004] 1 AC 816 at [60] (having regard to Hansard on judicial review of ministerial decisions not "questioning" what said in Parliament, so not incompatible with Bill of Rights); *Thoburn v Sunderland City Council* [2002] EWHC 195 (Admin) [2003] QB 151 at [76] (no legitimate expectation could arise solely from a statement in Parliament giving false impression as to effect of a Bill, since that would infringe the Bill of Rights); *R v Director of Public Prosecutions, ex p Kebilene* [2000] 2 AC 326 (DC), 339F ("hesitant to hold that a legitimate expectation could be founded on answers given in Parliament to often very general questions: to do so is to invest assertions by the executive with a quasi-legislative authority, which could involve an undesirable blurring of the distinct functions of the legislature and the executive").

(B) LEGITIMATE EXPECTATION TO ATTACK DELEGATED LEGISLATION? *R v Secretary of State for Health, ex p United States Tobacco International Inc* [1992] QB 353 (statutory instrument quashed for procedural unfairness); *R v Secretary of State for the Environment, ex p National & Local Government Officers' Association* (1993) 5 Admin LR 785, 804E ("doubtful whether, save perhaps in exceptional cases, the principle of legitimate expectation can be invoked to invalidate either primary or secondary legislation which is put

before Parliament"); *R v Secretary of State for the Environment, ex p British Telecommunications Plc* The Independent 5th September 1991 (rejecting legitimate expectation challenge to subordinate legislation).
(C) EXPECTATIONS OF THE PUBLIC AT LARGE? *R v Department for Education and Employment, ex p Begbie* [2000] 1 WLR 1115, 1133E ("no difficulty with the proposition that in cases where government has made known how it intends to exercise powers which affect the public at large it may be held to its word irrespective of whether the [claimant] had been relying specifically upon it. The legitimate expectation in such a case is that government will behave towards its citizens as it says it will"), approved in *R (Wagstaff) v Secretary of State for Health* [2001] 1 WLR 292, 314C; *R v Secretary of State for the Home Department, ex p Fire Brigades Union* [1995] 2 AC 513, 545H (suggesting "the doctrine of legitimate expectation cannot reasonably be extended to the public at large, as opposed to particular individuals or bodies who are directly affected by certain executive action"), 553D-F (legitimate expectation of victims of crime); *R v Secretary of State for Wales, ex p Emery* [1998] 4 All ER 367, 374j (legitimate expectation "cannot reasonably be extended to the public at large"); <41.1.7> (legitimate expectation and international instruments); *R (Bhatt Murphy) v Independent Assessor* [2008] EWCA Civ 755 at [46] (substantive legitimate expectation likely to be based on representation to small group).

41.1.14 **Legitimate expectation: promise by a different body.**[63] *R (BAPIO Action Ltd) v Secretary of State for the Home Department* [2008] UKHL 27 [2008] 2 WLR 1073 at [60] (Home Secretary's practice giving rise to a legitimate expectation infringed by Health Secretary); *R (O'Callaghan) v Charity Commission* [2007] EWHC 2491 (Admin) (Charity Commission consultation duty arising from promise by Minister in Parliament); *R (Bloggs 61) v Secretary of State for the Home Department* [2003] EWCA Civ 686 [2003] 1 WLR 2724 (unauthorised police representations not capable of founding a legitimate expectation as against prison service); *R (H) v Guildford Youth Court* [2008] EWHC 506 (Admin) (prosecution breaching legitimate expectation engendered by police promise); *Jones v Whalley* [2006] UKHL 41 [2006] 3 WLR 179 (police no-prosecution promise meaning private prosecution an abuse of process); *R v Director of Public Prosecutions, ex p Kebilene* [2000] 2 AC 326 (DC), 339E (ministerial statements not founding legitimate expectation concerning DPP's future decisions); *R v Lord Saville of Newdigate, ex p A* [2000] 1 WLR 1855 at [68(6)] (implications for Saville inquiry of statements made by Widgery inquiry); *R v Servite Houses and Wandsworth London Borough Council, ex p Goldsmith* (2000) 3 CCLR 325, 350B (promise made by service provider not founding legitimate expectation against local authority); *R (National Association of Guardians Ad Litem and Reporting Officers) v Children and Family Court Advisory and Support Service* [2001] EWHC Admin 693 [2002] 1 FLR 255 (promise by "project team" relevant to fairness by support service); *R (Pepushi) v Crown Prosecution Service* [2004] EWHC 798 (Admin) [2004] INLR 638 at [38] (CPS not bound by any legitimate expectation from ratification of Refugee Convention); *Rowland v Environment Agency* [2003] EWCA Civ 1885 [2005] Ch 1 (legitimate expectation from practice of statutory predecessors); *R (Bancoult) v Secretary of State for Foreign & Commonwealth Affairs* [2007] EWCA Civ 498 [2008] QB 365 (legitimate expectation created by predecessor in office).

41.1.15 **Legitimate expectation: related principles.** <54.1.14> (estoppel and public authorities); <40.2.3> (caution and estoppel); <40.2.5> (estoppel and legitimate expectation); <63.1.4> (abuse of process); *R v Horseferry Road Magistrates' Court, ex p Bennett* [1994] 1 AC 42, 61F ("there is a clear public interest to be observed in holding officials of the state to promises made by them in full understanding of what is entailed"), 74D-E (approving *R v*

---

[63] Harini Iyengar [2003] JR 215.

Croydon Justices, ex p Dean [1993] QB 769); *Attorney-General of Trinidad and Tobago v Phillip* [1995] 1 AC 396, 412E-F ("it is important that the state should not be able to resile from the terms of [a] pardon except in the most limited of circumstances"), 417D-F; <P54> (substantive unfairness).

41.1.16 Legitimate expectation and damages. *CNTA v Commission* [1975] ECR 533 (compensation in EU law for breach of a legitimate expectation); *R (Quark Fishing Ltd) v Secretary of State for Foreign and Commonwealth Affairs* [2003] EWHC 1743 (Admin) at [42] (Collins J, rejecting the suggestion of a "novel" claim for "breach of common law rights", being a hopeless "attempt to elevate a claimed legitimate expectation to become a right at common law"); *R (Nurse Prescribers Ltd) v Secretary of State for Health* [2004] EWHC 403 (Admin) at [82] (compensation "not available directly in judicial review proceedings arising out of a claim for disappointment of a legitimate expectation"); *R v Commissioners of Customs and Excise, ex p F & I Services Ltd* [2001] EWCA Civ 762 at [72] (Sedley LJ: "the unfairness which a change of policy may work on those who have relied on the earlier policy can often be adequately mitigated by ... compensating them in money. The point, however, is that such a payment of money is not an anticipatory payment of damages: it is a practical means of eliminating unfairness"); *R v Birmingham City Council, ex p L* [2000] ELR 543 at [18] (if legitimate expectation had arisen, fact that defendant had offered compensation for expense caused would have made a finding of unfairness unlikely); *R (Bibi) v Newham London Borough Council* [2001] EWCA Civ 607 [2002] 1 WLR 237 at [56] ("A further element for the Authority to bear in mind is the possibility of monetary compensation or assistance"; "a legitimate expectation may in some cases be appropriately taken into account by such a payment"); *Rowland v Environment Agency* [2003] EWCA Civ 1885 [2005] Ch 1 at [119] (referring to Professor Craig's suggestion of compensation to person whose legitimate expectation defeasible because of objection to allowing an ultra vires representation to be binding).

41.1.17 Codified legitimate expectation: reflected in instrument/policy. *R v Commissioners of Customs and Excise, ex p British Sky Broadcasting Group* [2001] EWHC Admin 127 [2001] STC 437 at [5]-[6] (describing the "Sheldon principle", a 1978 extra-statutory concession that: "If a Customs and Excise officer, with the full facts before him, has given a clear and unequivocal ruling on VAT in writing or, knowing the full facts, has misled a registered person to his detriment, any assessment of VAT due will be based on the correct ruling from the date the error was brought to the registered person's attention").

41.1.18 Legitimate expectation involves hard-edged questions. <P16> (hard-edged questions); *R (Lichfield Securities Ltd) v Lichfield District Council* [2001] EWCA Civ 304 [2001] 3 PLR 33 at [19] (Sedley LJ: "legitimate expectation is an aspect of fairness and ... fairness is a matter of law for the court").

41.1.19 Reasons and dishonour of legitimate expectation. <62.2.9(D)>.

41.2 Basic anatomy of a legitimate expectation.The necessary characteristics for a legitimate expectation depend on the context and category being considered. Conventional hallmarks are a promise or practice, engendering an expected advantage, whether procedural or substantive.

41.2.1 Words and acts: promises and practices. *HMB Holdings Ltd v Antigua and Barbuda* [2007] UKPC 37 at [31] (legitimate expectation claim fails "if the public body has done nothing or said nothing which can legitimately have generated the expectation that is contended for"); *R (Bhatt Murphy) v Independent Assessor* [2008] EWCA Civ 755 at [29] (paradigm case of procedural legitimate expectation is where promise or practice of procedural step), [33] (substantive legitimate expectation needing "a promise or practice of present and future substantive policy"); *Council of Civil Service Unions v Minister for the Civil Service* [1985] AC 374, 401B ("Legitimate ... expectation may arise either from an express promise given on behalf of a public authority or from the existence of a regular practice which the claimant can reasonably expect to continue"); *R v Secretary of State for Education, ex p S* [1994] ELR 252, 263B (although "growth in this area of the law has not ... ceased", currently "based either on practice or on promise"); *R v Secretary of State for Education, ex p London Borough of Southwark* [1995] ELR 308, 322H (possible third category: decision-maker maintaining a substantive policy as to how it will act); *R (Begum) v Tower Hamlets London Borough Council* [2006] EWCA Civ 733 [2006] LGR 674 at [45] ("whether or not there is a relevant legitimate expectation depends on all the circumstances of the particular case").

41.2.2 Promises/representations: illustrations. *R (HSMP Forum Ltd) v Secretary of State for the Home Department* [2008] EWHC 664 (Admin) at [52] (clear representation read in context), [53] (absence of any qualification); *R (Bancoult) v Secretary of State for Foreign & Commonwealth Affairs* [2007] EWCA Civ 498 [2008] QB 365 (representations that Chagossians would be permitted to return); *R (H) v Guildford Youth Court* [2008] EWHC 506 (Admin) (police promise to deal by final warning); *R (Harrington) v Bromley Magistrates Court* [2007] EWHC 2896 (Admin) at [14] (unequivocal indication by magistrates as to mode of sentencing); *R (Greenpeace Ltd) v Secretary of State for Trade and Industry* [2007] EWHC 311 (Admin) [2007] Env LR 623 (promise of fullest public consultation); *R v Swale Borough Council & Medway Ports Authority, ex p Royal Society for the Protection of Birds* (1990) 2 Admin LR 790 (promise of consultation); *R v London Borough of Tower Hamlets, ex p Tower Hamlets Combined Traders Association* [1994] COD 325 (promise must be made with authority); *R v Nottingham Magistrates' Court, ex p Davidson* [1999] COD 405 (court giving indication of sentence); *R (Ganidagli) v Secretary of State for the Home Department* [2001] EWHC Admin 70 (representation that asylum seeker's witness statement would stand as primary facts); *R (Zeqiri) v Secretary of State for the Home Department* [2002] UKHL 3 [2002] INLR 291 (no sufficiently clear representation of general applicability of test case).

41.2.3 Practices: illustrations. *R (BAPIO Action Ltd) v Secretary of State for the Home Department* [2008] UKHL 27 [2008] 2 WLR 1073 at [60] (immigration rules and practice giving rise to a legitimate expectation infringed by DoH guidance); *R (Swords) v Secretary of State for Communities and Local Government* [2007] EWCA Civ 795 [2007] LGR 757 at [14] (legitimate expectation of consultation arising from practice under DPM Manual); *R (Abbasi) v Secretary of State for Foreign and Commonwealth Affairs* [2002] EWCA Civ 1598 [2003] UKHRR 76 (legitimate expectation, arising from Government "practice", that consideration would be given to diplomatic intervention), at [82] (legitimate expectation "a well-established and flexible means for giving legal effect to a settled policy or practice for the exercise of an administrative discretion"); *Rowland v Environment Agency* [2003] EWCA Civ 1885 [2005] Ch 1 at [68(1)] (practice by navigation authorities), [73] ("regular and consistent practice" which "conduct" to "any objective observer" was "representing" as to nature of rights of navigation); *Guerra v Baptiste* [1996] 1 AC 397, 419C-F ("settled practice"); *R v Secretary of State for the Home Department, ex p McCartney* [1994] COD 528 ("declared policy"); *R (Corby District Council) v Secretary of State for Communities and Local Government* [2007] EWHC 1873 (Admin) [2008] LGR 109 (scheme as published).

41.2.4 Legitimate expectation: three basic questions. *R (Bibi) v Newham London Borough Council* [2001] EWCA Civ 607 [2002] 1 WLR 237 at [19] (Schiemann LJ: "In all legitimate expectation cases, whether substantive or procedural, three practical questions arise. The first question is to what has the public authority, whether by practice or by promise, committed itself;

423

the second is whether the authority has acted or proposes to act unlawfully in relation to its commitment; the third is what the court should do"); applied in *R (National Association of Guardians Ad Litem and Reporting Officers) v Children and Family Court Advisory and Support Service* [2001] EWHC Admin 693 [2002] 1 FLR 255 at [44].

41.2.5 Basic hallmarks: reliance on an unqualified representation. *R v Jockey Club, ex p RAM Racecourses* [1993] 2 All ER 225, 236h-237b (referring to: "(1) A clear and unambiguous representation... (2) That since the [claimant] was not a person to whom any representation was directly made it was within the class of persons who are entitled to rely upon it; or at any rate that it was reasonable for the [claimant] to rely upon it without more... (3) That it did so rely upon it. (4) That it did so to its detriment... (5) That there is no overriding interest arising from [the defendant's] duties and responsibilities"); *R v Inland Revenue Commissioners, ex p Unilever Plc* [1996] STC 681, 693c-d (referring to: "first, that the [claimant] ... must have put all his cards face upwards on the table, second, that the body concerned ... made a representation which was clear, unambiguous and devoid of relevant qualification, third, that the [claimant] was within the class of people to whom the representation was made or that it was otherwise reasonable for him to rely upon it, and fourth, that the [claimant] did indeed rely upon it to his detriment"); *R v Inland Revenue Commissioners, ex p MFK Underwriting Agents Ltd* [1990] 1 WLR 1545, 1569E-1570B (basic hallmarks discussed).

41.2.6 No rigid preconditions. *R v Inland Revenue Commissioners, ex p Unilever Plc* [1996] STC 681, 690f (Sir Thomas Bingham MR: "The categories of unfairness are not closed, and precedent should act as a guide not a cage"), 695j (Simon Brown LJ: "rare indeed will be the case when a fairness challenge will succeed outside the *MFK* parameters"); *Rowland v Environment Agency* [2003] EWCA Civ 1885 [2005] Ch 1 at [68(2)] ("It is not always a condition for a legitimate expectation to arise that there should be a clear, unambiguous and unqualified representation by the public authority ...: the test is whether the public authority has acted so unfairly that its conduct amounts to an abuse of power"); *R (Bibi) v Newham London Borough Council* [2001] EWCA Civ 607 [2002] 1 WLR 237 at [27].

41.2.7 Whether a clear representation. *R (Bancoult) v Secretary of State for Foreign & Commonwealth Affairs* [2007] EWCA Civ 498 [2008] QB 365 at [74] (clear public statement); *R (Zeqiri) v Secretary of State for the Home Department* [2002] UKHL 3 [2002] INLR 291 at [44] (degree of clarity of representation capable of depending on the circumstances, since "an alleged representation must be construed in the context in which it is made"), [54] (here, "no conduct which amounted within its context to a sufficiently clear representation"), [64] (statement not clear and unambiguous); *R (Theophilus) v London Borough of Lewisham* [2002] EWHC 1371 (Admin) [2002] 3 All ER 851 at [16] ("clear and unambiguous implication" from letters"); *R (Wheeler) v Office of the Prime Minister* [2008] EWHC 1409 (Admin) at [39] (need for precision where relying on implied representation); *R v Ministry of Defence, ex p Walker* [2000] 1 WLR 806 ("no express representation"); *R (British Civilian Internees - Far Eastern Region) v Secretary of State for Defence* [2003] EWCA Civ 473 [2003] QB 1397 at [62], [67] (no clear and unequivocal representation), [72]-[73] (need an "exceptional case" for legitimate expectation or conspicuous unfairness to succeed without a clear and unequivocal representation); *R (C) v Brent, Kensington and Chelsea and Westminster Mental Health NHS Trust* [2002] EWHC 181 (Admin) (2003) 6 CCLR 335 at [7] (assurance must be "clear and unequivocal"); *R v Inland Revenue Commissioners, ex p Unilever Plc* [1996] STC 681, 694h, 690a-f (absence of a clear and unambiguous representation not fatal); *R v Secretary of State for Wales, ex p Emery* [1998] 4 All ER 367, 374g-375d (emphasising need for "an express promise, representation or undertaking"); *R v Lord Chancellor, ex p Hibbit & Saunders* [1993] COD 326 (clear and unambiguous representation that no reduced bids would be allowed); *R v Secretary of State for the Home Department, ex p Hargreaves* [1997] 1 WLR 906, 922D-H (documents not sufficient basis for a legitimate expectation); *R v Lambeth London Borough Council, ex p N* [1996] ELR 299, 311C (no clear and unambiguous promise, express or implied); *R v O'Kane and Clarke, ex p Northern Bank Ltd* [1996] STC 1249, 1267h-j (Revenue offering comfort but not assurances); *R v Commissioners of Customs and Excise, ex p Kay and Co* [1996] STC 1500, 1527f-j ("in all the circumstances" representations interpreted as being "clear"); *R v Nottingham Magistrates' Court, ex p Davidson* [1999] COD 405 (sufficiently unqualified indication as to the sentence which court would or would not pass); *R v Rochdale Metropolitan Borough Council, ex p Schemet* [1994] ELR 89, 108H-109E (although legitimate expectation is of consultation, there need not "be shown to have existed either a practice of consultation or a promise of consultation"); *R v Secretary of State for Transport, ex p Richmond upon Thames London Borough Council (No.4)* [1996] 1 WLR 1460, 1470C-G (promise not necessary for *Baker* category 2: interest in a benefit giving rise to right to invoke basic principles of fairness and reasonableness); *R v Falmouth and Truro Port Health Authority, ex p South West Water Ltd* [2001] QB 445, 459B ("Once one accepts ... that consultation was `not otherwise required by law', then only the clearest of assurances can give rise to its legitimate expectation"); *R v Birmingham City Council, ex p L* [2000] ELR 543 at [16] (treating clear and unambiguous representation as a "prerequisite"); *R (Montana) v Secretary of State for the Home Department* [2001] 1 WLR 552, at [14] (no clear and unambiguous representation); *R (Structadene Ltd) v Hackney London Borough Council* [2001] 2 All ER 225, 236b (council merely giving information, not a representation); *R (Tunbridge Wells Borough Council) v Sevenoaks Magistrates' Court* [2001] EWHC Admin 897 [2002] 3 PLR 25 at [41] ("in principle, an implicit promise may be sufficient" but "the less explicit the promise, the less likely it will be that the court's sense of propriety and justice will be offended"); *R (White) v Barking Magistrates' Court* [2004] EWHC 417 (Admin) at [15] (magistrates' act of adjourning for pre-sentence report sufficient to give rise to legitimate expectation that they had accepted sentencing jurisdiction and would not remit to the crown court for sentence); *R (Ooi) v Secretary of State for the Home Department* [2007] EWHC 3221 (Admin) (extended qualification periods for work permit holders not breaching any legitimate expectation).

41.2.8 Whether preceded by full disclosure from claimant. *R v Inland Revenue Commissioners, ex p MFK Underwriting Agents Ltd* [1990] 1 WLR 1545, 1569E-G, 1570A-B and 1575B-C (person seeking assurance must make full disclosure); *R v Inland Revenue Commissioners, ex p Matrix-Securities Ltd* [1994] 1 WLR 334 <41.2.5>, 346C (Lord Templeman: "The [solicitors'] letter ... was inaccurate and misleading"), 356A (Lord Jauncey: "a piece of information essential to the deliberations required of the revenue by the taxpayer was not furnished to them") and see 352B-F, 354H, 356F-G and 358A; cf. *R v Secretary of State for the Home Department, ex p Hindley* [2001] 1 AC 410, 418F-H (not unlawful to increase tariff where previously set in ignorance of all relevant offending); *Rowland v Environment Agency* [2003] EWCA Civ 1885 [2005] Ch 1 at [68(3)]) ("whether there has been such a failure of disclosure by a party as to disentitle him from having a legitimate expectation must depend on the particular circumstances of the case").

41.2.9 Whether communication/knowledge.
(A) COMMUNICATION/KNOWLEDGE NECESSARY. *R (Weaver) v London & Quadrant Housing Trust* [2008] EWHC 1377 (Admin) at [86] (fatal here that no knowledge of representation); *R v Secretary of State for the Home Department, ex p Hindley* [2001] 1 AC 410, 419B-C (no legitimate expectation of 30 year tariff, because not communicated, so no knowledge or assurance); *R v Ministry of Defence, ex p Walker* [2000] 1 WLR 806 (no legitimate expectation frustrated where previous policy had not been communicated to the claimant); *R v Secretary of State for National Heritage, ex p J Paul Getty Trust* [1997] EuLR 407, 414B, 418A-C (statement could not give rise to a legitimate expectation on the part of the Trust, who had been unaware of it when it was made).

(B) COMMUNICATION/KNOWLEDGE UNNECESSARY.[64] *R (Rashid) v Secretary of State for the Home Department* [2005] EWCA Civ 744 [2005] INLR 550 at [25] (legitimate expectation of application of asylum policy albeit no knowledge); *R (Mugisha) v Secretary of State for the Home Department* [2005] EWHC 2720 (Admin) [2006] INLR 335 at [34] (knowledge of promise or practice not necessary); *R (M) v Commissioner of Police of the Metropolis* [2001] EWHC Admin 553 (legitimate expectation could arise even though claimants unaware of policy); *R v Secretary of State for the Home Department, ex p Ahmed* [1999] Imm AR 22, 40 (communication and knowledge not fatal to legitimate expectation based on ratified Convention); *Minister For Immigration and Ethnic Affairs v Teoh* [1995] 3 LRC 1 (knowledge not necessary for legitimate expectation from ratified Convention); *R (Bhatt Murphy) v Independent Assessor* [2008] EWCA Civ 755 at [30] ("significant difficulties" in imposing requirements of knowledge or reliance).

(C) INDIRECT COMMUNICATION. *R v Commissioners of Customs and Excise, ex p Kay and Co* [1996] STC 1500, 1527j-1528b (sufficient that representation made to associations of opticians, intended to be and in fact relied upon by individual opticians); *R (Hashmi) v Secretary of State for the Home Department* [2002] EWCA Civ 728 [2002] INLR 377 (letter to MP acting on claimant family's behalf, treated as proper notification of formal decision).

41.2.10 **Whether reliance.** *R v Department for Education and Employment, ex p Begbie* [2000] 1 WLR 1115, 1124B-D (although not always necessary, but "wrong to understate the significance of reliance"); *Francisco Javier Jaramillo-Silva v Secretary of State for the Home Department* [1994] Imm AR 352, 357 ("reliance and detriment as such are not necessarily required in every legitimate expectation case"); *R v Barking and Dagenham London Borough Council, ex p Lloyd* [2001] LGR 86 (Keene J) at [36] (reliance "normally ... highly relevant"); *R (National Association of Guardians Ad Litem and Reporting Officers) v Children and Family Court Advisory and Support Service* [2001] EWHC Admin 693 [2002] 1 FLR 255 at [45] (procedural legitimate expectation despite lack of reliance); *R v Commissioners of Customs and Excise, ex p Kay and Co* [1996] STC 1500, 1527j-1528b (clear representation made to associations of opticians, intended to be and in fact relied upon by individual opticians); *R v Falmouth and Truro Port Health Authority, ex p South West Water Ltd* [2001] QB 445, 459H-460A ("I do not accept that detrimental reliance on the assurance given is necessary to make good a legitimate expectation challenge in the present [procedural] category of case"), applied in *R (Structadene Ltd) v Hackney London Borough Council* [2001] 2 All ER 225, 236d; *Attorney-General of Hong Kong v Ng Yuen Shiu* [1983] 2 AC 629, 635B-C (absence of reliance not fatal); *R v Secretary of State for Wales, ex p Emery* [1998] 4 All ER 467, 374g-375d (indicating need for knowledge and reliance); *R v Secretary of State for the Home Department, ex p Popatia* [2000] INLR 587 at [82] (Sullivan J: "Whilst reliance is not essential, lack of reliance will often be relevant in deciding whether or not it would be fair and/or in the interests of good administration to correct a mistake"); *R (Joseph) v Secretary of State for the Home Department* 19th April 2002 unrep. at [16] (defendant entitled here to correct his mistake), [17] (at least absent detrimental reliance); *Downderry Construction Ltd v Secretary of State for Transport, Local Government and the Regions* [2002] EWHC 02 (Admin) at [32] (explaining that for the purposes of the related doctrine of estoppel, reliance need not be "reasonable").

41.2.11 **Whether detriment/prejudice.** *R (Bamber) v Revenue & Customs Commissioners* [2007] EWHC 798 (Admin) at [21] (emphasising that net detriment not significant); *Harley Development Inc v Commissioner of Inland Revenue* [1996] 1 WLR 727, 733G, 734B; *R v Lambeth London Borough Council, ex p N* [1996] ELR 299, 311C (Latham J: "I cannot see any way in which the school relied on any promise to its detriment"); *R (Bibi) v Newham London*

---

[64] Mark Elliott [2005] JR 281.

Borough Council [2001] EWCA Civ 607 [2002] 1 WLR 237 at [31] ("the significance of reliance and of consequent detriment is factual, not legal... In a strong case, no doubt, there will be both reliance and detriment; but it does not follow that reliance (that is, credence) without measurable detriment cannot render it unfair to thwart a legitimate expectation"), [55] (wrong to "disregard the legitimate expectation because no concrete detriment can be shown").

41.2.12 **Whether actual or ostensible authority.** *South Bucks District Council v Flanagan* [2002] EWCA Civ 690 [2002] 1 WLR 2601 at [18] ("Legitimate expectation involves notions of fairness and unless the person making the representation has actual or ostensible authority to speak on behalf of the public body, there is no reason why the recipient of the representation should be allowed to hold the public body to the terms of the representation. He might subjectively have acquired the expectation, but it would not be a legitimate one, that is to say it would not be one to which he was entitled"); *Rowland v Environment Agency* [2002] EWHC 2785 (Ch) [2003] Ch 581 at [68] ("The public body can only be bound by acts and statements of its employees and agents if and to the extent that they had actual or ostensible authority to bind the public body by their acts and statements", endorsed by CA [2003] EWCA Civ 1885 [2005] Ch 1 at [67]).

41.2.13 **Focusing on the `legitimacy' of the expectation.** *R v North and East Devon Health Authority, ex p Coughlan* [2001] QB 213 at [57(c)] (fairness/justification test <54.2.5> arising in cases where "once the legitimacy of the expectation is established, the court will have the task of weighing the requirements of fairness against any overriding interest relied upon for the change of policy"), [73] (rationality review is "not because the expectation is substantive but because it lacks legitimacy"); *R v Department for Education and Employment, ex p Begbie* [2000] 1 WLR 1115, 1125C-D ("No doubt statements such as those made ... did give rise to an expectation ... But the question for the court is whether those statements give rise to a legitimate expectation, in the sense of an expectation which will be protected by law"); *R v South Somerset District Council, ex p DJB (Group) Ltd* (1989) 1 Admin LR 11, 18E (cannot have been legitimate to expect, as a result of council's policy, that would be able to break the law without being prosecuted); *R v Gaming Board of Great Britain, ex p Kingsley* [1996] COD 178 and 241 (at 241) (doctrine of legitimate expectation based on considerations of fairness, even where benefit claimed not procedural, and should not be invoked to confer an unmerited or improper benefit); *R v Westminster City Council, ex p Dinev* 24th October 2000 unrep. (expectation lacking legitimacy where claimants had been trading unlawfully).

41.2.14 **Legitimate expectation: an objective approach.** *R v Secretary of State for the Home Department, ex p Ahmed* [1999] Imm AR 22, 40 (Hobhouse LJ: "The principle of legitimate expectation in English law is a principle of fairness in the decision-making process... In the present context, it is a wholly objective concept and is not based upon any actual state of knowledge of individual immigrants or would be immigrants"; "the application of the principle must be based upon some objectively identifiable legitimate expectation as to how decisions will be made and discretions exercised"); *R v Department for Education and Employment, ex p Begbie* [2000] 1 WLR 1115, 1130B (Laws LJ, speaking, in the context of legitimate expectation, of "objective concepts"); *R v Barking and Dagenham London Borough Council, ex p Lloyd* [2001] LGR 86 (Keene J) at [35] ("statements made on behalf of a public body ought to be interpreted on an objective basis and not in the light of evidence as to what the maker of the statement intended"; CA is at (2001) 4 CCLR 196); *R (National Association of Guardians Ad Litem and Reporting Officers) v Children and Family Court Advisory and Support Service* [2001] EWHC Admin 693 [2002] 1 FLR 255 at [44] ("The question [to what has the public authority committed itself] has to be looked at objectively and not through either [the claimant's] eyes or the eyes of [the defendant]").

| **P42 Onus.** The burden of proof is generally on the claimant. |

42.1 Onus generally on the claimant
42.2 Onus on the defendant in particular contexts

42.1 **Onus generally on the claimant.**In judicial review it is generally for the claimant to prove grounds for intervention, not for the defendant to disprove them.

42.1.1 **Claimant's onus/burden.** *Standard Commercial property Securities Ltd v Glasgow City Council* [2006] UKHL 50 at [61] (onus on claimant to show ultra vires or unreasonableness); *R (Ireneschild) v Lambeth London Borough Council* [2007] EWCA Civ 234 [2007] LGR 619 at [45] (onus on claimant to show failure to take account of relevancy); *R (Wheeler) v Office of the Prime Minister* [2008] EWHC 1409 (Admin) at [38] (claimant having "failed to satisfy us, as he must do" that breach of legitimate expectation); *R v Inland Revenue Commissioners, ex p Rossminster* [1980] AC 952, 1026H (claimant "has to satisfy the court that he has a case"), 1014A (claimants having "failed to establish" unlawfulness); *R v Birmingham City Council, ex p O* [1983] 1 AC 578, 597C-D ("the onus is on the [claimants] to establish that the local authority reached a decision that no reasonable authority could have approved").

42.1.2 **Defendant getting benefit of the doubt.** *R v Oxfordshire Local Valuation Panel, ex p Oxford City Council* (1981) 79 LGR 432, 440 (Woolf J: "In so far as there is a conflict between [the accounts] of what occurred ..., this court, only having the affidavits before it, cannot resolve that dispute. The position is well established that as the [claimants] have the onus of proof placed upon them to establish their case, in those circumstances the proper course to adopt is to act on the evidence given on behalf of the [defendants]... in so far as it is impossible from the internal evidence to come to any conclusion as to which account is the more credible"); *R v Governors of the Bishop Challoner Roman Catholic Comprehensive Girls' School, ex p Choudhury* [1992] 2 AC 182, 197E ("It is essential that in exercising the very important jurisdiction to grant judicial review, the court should not intervene just because the reasons given, if strictly construed, *may* disclose an error of law. The jurisdiction to quash a decision only exists when there has *in fact* been an error of law"); *R v Immigration Appeal Tribunal, ex p Khan (Mahmud)* [1983] 1 QB 790, 795G; *R v Secretary of State for the Home Department, ex p Cox* (1993) 5 Admin LR 17, 26F; *R v Secretary of State for the Home Department, ex p Frederick Kitoko-Vetukala* [1994] Imm AR 377, 379; *R v Local Government Boundary Commission, ex p Somerset, Avon & Cleveland County Councils* [1994] COD 517 (see transcript) ("We would not accept that the Commission had overlooked any aspects of the problem... unless it was plain that they had").

42.1.3 **Presumptions of validity.**[65]
(A) PRIMARY LEGISLATION. *R v Secretary of State for Transport, ex p Factortame Ltd* [1990] 2 AC 85, 142G (Lord Bridge: "the presumption that an Act of Parliament is compatible with Community law unless and until declared to be incompatible must be at least as strong as the presumption that delegated legislation is valid unless and until declared invalid"), 143B.
(B) DELEGATED LEGISLATION. *McEldowney v Forde* [1971] AC 632, 655F (Lord Pearson: "the presumption of regularity (omnia praesumuntur rite esse acta) applies and the regulation is assumed prima facie to be intra vires"), 649A ("the task of a subject who endeavours to challenge the validity of ... a regulation is a heavy one"), 661A ("the onus lies upon the party challenging the subordinate legislation to establish its invalidity"); *Hoffmann-La Roche (F) &*

---

[65] This paragraph in a previous edition was cited in *Wong Kei Kwong v Principal Assistant Secretary for the Civil Service* [2008] 2 HKC 555 at [46] (Saunders J).

Co AG v Secretary of State for Trade and Industry [1975] AC 295, 366E-F, 368A; *Percy v Hall* [1997] QB 924 (byelaws); *Boddington v British Transport Police* [1999] 2 AC 143, 155B-C (subordinate legislation presumed lawful until pronounced otherwise).
(C) DECISION-MAKING. *Standard Commercial Property Securities Ltd v Glasgow City Council* [2006] UKHL 50 at [74] (presumption of regularity applicable to vires of contract); *R v Inland Revenue Commissioners, ex p T.C.Coombs & Co* [1991] 2 AC 283, 299H ("where acts are of an official nature, or require the concurrence of official persons, a presumption arises in favour of their due execution"); *R v Inland Revenue Commissioners, ex p Rossminster* [1980] AC 952, 1013F-H ("Where Parliament has designated a public officer as decision-maker for a particular class of decisions the High Court ... must proceed on the presumption omnia praesumuntur rite esse acta until that presumption can be displaced by the [claimant] for review - upon whom the onus lies of doing so"); *A v B Bank (Governor and Company of the Bank of England Intervening)* [1993] QB 311, 326D-327G (Bank of England's acts attracting presumption of regularity); *Stancliffe Stone Co Ltd v Peak District National Park Authority* [2005] EWCA Civ 747 [2006] Env LR 158 at [47]-[48] (presumption of regularity "an evidential presumption" not an aid to construction where all facts known); *R (Sarkisian) v Immigration Appeal Tribunal* [2001] Imm AR 676 at [18] (court entitled to assume that expert tribunal understands "how it should perform its functions [and] what matters the relevant statute requires it to take into account").

42.1.4 Claimant's burden: disclosure, further information and cross-examination.<17.4>.

42.1.5 Standard of proof. *R v Secretary of State for the Home Department, ex p Khawaja* [1984] AC 74, 112E (Lord Scarman: "As judicial review ... is a civil proceeding, it would appear to be right ... to apply the civil standard of proof").

42.2 Onus on the defendant in particular contexts The claimant's onus is counterbalanced by increasingly expecting defendants to explain themselves and disclose documents. In some situations, as where fundamental rights are concerned, the balance is struck in a more vigilant way and the defendant body is called upon to justify the legal propriety of its action.

42.2.1 Defendant's duty of candour/reasons. <10.4> (duty of candour); <P62> (duty to give reasons).

42.2.2 Defendant's onus and fundamental rights/justification. <37.1.10> (proportionality/ HRA onus on defendant); *Eshugbayi Eleko v Government of Nigeria* [1931] AC 662, 670 ("no member of the executive can interfere with the liberty or property of a British subject except on the condition that he can support the legality of his action before a court of justice"), applied in *Boddington v British Transport Police* [1999] 2 AC 143, 173F; *R v Secretary of State for the Home Department, ex p Khawaja* [1984] AC 74, 112B ("in cases where the exercise of executive discretion interferes with liberty or property rights ... the burden of justifying the legality of the decision [is] ... upon the executive"); *R (Watkins-Singh) v Aberdare Girls High School Governors* [2008] EWHC 1865 (Admin) at [74] & [90] (defendant's onus as to justification of indirect discrimination); *R (Isiko) v Secretary of State for the Home Department* [2001] UKHRR 385 at [31] (the decision-maker must "demonstrate ... that his proposed action does not in truth interfere with the right"); *R v Secretary of State for the Home Department, ex p Norney* (1995) 7 Admin LR 861, 872G (in order to be lawful, policy infringing human rights "needs to be supported by cogent and compelling reasons"); *R (L) v Manchester City Council* [2001] EWHC Admin 707 (2002) 5 CCLR 268 at [92] ("Once an interference or failure to meet a positive obligation is shown, the burden of proof shifts to the defendant to show relevant and sufficient reason for its conduct. So it is for [the defendant] to prove justification"); *Chesterfield Properties Plc v Secretary of State for the Environment* [1998] JPL 568, 579 (Laws J: "Where

429

an administrative decision abrogates or diminishes a constitutional or fundamental right, *Wednesbury* requires that the decision-maker provide a substantial justification in the public interest for doing so"), 580 ("it must ... be demonstrated that [the decision-maker] has concluded that there exists a substantial public interest or interests outweighing the [claimant]'s rights"); *R v A Local Authority, ex p LM* [2000] 1 FLR 612, 626B (defendants' evidence "comes anywhere near demonstrating a pressing need"); *R v Oldham Justices, ex p Cawley* [1997] QB 1, 19B (in practice, judicial review like habeas corpus as to onus); *Abdul Sheikh v Secretary of State for the Home Department* [2001] INLR 98 at [8]-[9] (whether habeas corpus or judicial review, detainer having to show legal justification for detention); *R v Secretary of State for the Home Department, ex p Bugdaycay* [1987] AC 514, 537H-538A (court's "special responsibility", and sufficient that not clear that Secretary of State "took into account or adequately resolved" relevant matters); *R v Radio Authority, ex p Bull* [1998] QB 294 (treating onus as remaining on claimant, although decision restricting freedom of communication); *R v Secretary of State for Transport, ex p de Rothschild* [1989] 1 All ER 933 (where compulsory purchase order, no formal onus but need that "sufficient reasons are adduced affirmatively to justify it on its merits"); *R v Stoke-on-Trent Crown Court, ex p Marsden* [1999] COD 114 (decisions affecting liberty needing material to show that the decision was based on good and sufficient cause); *R v Lord Saville, ex p A* 17th June 1999 unrep. ("In effect the burden is on those who seek to uphold the decision"); *R (E) v JFS Governing Body* [2008] EWHC 1535 (Admin) at [184] (onus on defendant to justify indirect discrimination); *R (Suryananda) v Welsh Ministers* [2007] EWCA Civ 893 at [69] ("the burden of establishing a justifiable interference with the rights under Article 9(1) lay on the Minister").

42.2.3 Grant of permission means response called for. *R v Civil Service Appeal Board, ex p Cunningham* [1991] 4 All ER 310, 315j (Lord Donaldson MR: "the fact that [permission] has been granted calls for some reply from the [defendant]"); *R v Lancashire County Council, ex p Huddleston* [1986] 2 All ER 941, 945b ("if and when the [claimant] can satisfy a judge of the public law court that the facts disclosed by her are sufficient to entitle her to apply for judicial review ... [t]hen it becomes the duty of the [defendant] to make full and fair disclosure"); *R v Lambeth London Borough Council, ex p Mahmood* The Times 23rd February 1994; *R v Huntingdon Magistrates' Court, ex p Percy* [1994] COD 323 and *R v Aldershot Justices, ex p Rushmoor Borough Council* [1996] COD 21 (order for costs against defendants because of failure to take grant of permission sufficiently seriously).

42.2.4 Inferences against defendants. <62.2.8> (inferences from unreasoned decisions); *R v Manchester Metropolitan University, ex p Nolan* [1994] ELR 380, 391H (inferring that certain material was not before board of examiners); *R v Governors of the Hasmonean High School, ex p N & E* [1994] ELR 343, 355A-B, 350B-C, 352D; *R v Warwickshire County Council, ex p Collymore* [1995] ELR 217, 227D-H (inference that policy inflexibly applied); *R v Brent London Borough Council, ex p Bariise* (1999) 31 HLR 50, 58 (where something "so startling that one would not expect it to pass without individual comment, the Court may be justified in drawing the inference that it has not received any or sufficient consideration").

42.2.5 Defendant's onus/burden: other contexts.
(A) "DEPARTURE" CONTEXTS. <62.2.9>.
(B) SEVERABILITY. <43.1.8>.
(C) MATERIALITY/PREJUDICE/FUTILITY. <P4> (materiality); *R (Lichfield Securities Ltd) v Lichfield District Council* [2001] EWCA Civ 304 [2001] 3 PLR 33 at [26] ("it is for a public authority ... to establish that no harm has in practice resulted from its failure to act fairly"); *R v Governors of the Sheffield Hallam University, ex p R* [1995] ELR 267, 284D-E ("if a party in breach of proper procedure is to escape the ordinary consequence by asserting that nothing has been lost by the breach, it is for that party to demonstrate it"); *R v Birmingham City*

Council, ex p Dredger (1994) 6 Admin LR 553, 577 ("not persuaded" by defendant that remedy "would achieve little advantage"); *R v Leicester City Justices, ex p Barrow* [1991] 2 QB 260, 290D-E (decision quashed where position unclear as to whether unfairness caused prejudice); *R v London Borough of Camden, ex p Paddock* [1995] COD 130 (see transcript) ("the onus [is] on the decision-maker to satisfy the court that the irregularity in the event made no difference"); *R v Southwark London Borough Council, ex p Ryder* (1996) 28 HLR 56, 67 (Dyson J, as to considering an irrelevancy: "In the absence of details as to how and why she took it into account, I am driven to conclude that she may well have relied upon it in a material sense").

(D) MATTERS CALLING FOR AN EXPLANATION. *Engineers & Managers Association v Advisory Conciliation & Arbitration Service* [1980] 1 WLR 302, 310F ("such extraordinary delay as occurred here called for a clear and convincing explanation"); *R v Dorking Justices, ex p Harrington* [1984] AC 743, 749D-E ("no explanation has been vouchsafed of the reasons for what can only be regarded as this remarkable action"; "in the absence of some explanation - none is readily apparent - it is clear that their action was both wrong and unjudicial"); *R v Islington London Borough Council, ex p Rixon* [1997] ELR 66 (up to defendant to demonstrate good reason for any failure to comply with statutory guidance); *R v Chief Constable of Devon and Cornwall, ex p Hay* [1996] 2 All ER 711, 725g-h ("the only person who can describe his process of reasoning is the chief constable himself, and I do not consider that he has satisfactorily done so").

(E) OTHER. *R (Lichfield Securities Ltd) v Lichfield District Council* [2001] EWCA Civ 304 [2001] 3 PLR 33 at [26] (Sedley LJ: "it is for [the] public authority to make out any case that the remedy for its own unfairness lay in the [claimant's] hands"); *R v Highbury Corner Magistrates' Court, ex p Tawfick* [1994] COD 106 (defendant failing to show good grounds justifying impugned decision); *R v Camden London Borough Council, ex p Adair* (1997) 29 HLR 236 (no direct evidence that defendant's homelessness unit having made inquiries of district housing office); *R v Liverpool City Magistrates Court, ex p Banwell* [1998] COD 144 (judicial review granted where possible to read the decision-letter as reflecting a permissible approach, but not the only interpretation); *R v North West Lancashire Health Authority, ex p A* [2000] 1 WLR 977, 999E (in adopting the policy, authority not having "demonstrated that degree of rational consideration that can reasonably be expected of it"); *R v Flintshire County Council, ex p Armstrong-Braun* [2001] EWCA Civ 345 [2001] LGR 344 at [67] ("[The] evidence falls far short of demonstrating that ... proper considerations were before members").

42.2.6 **Standard of proof.** *R v Secretary of State for the Home Department, ex p Khawaja* [1984] AC 74, 114B-C (applying "the civil standard flexibly applied" in a case where "the burden lies on the executive to justify the exercise of a power of detention"); *R v Horseferry Road Magistrates' Court, ex p Bennett (No.2)* The Times 1st April 1994 (high balance of probabilities).

<table>
<tr><td>

P43 Severance. A measure may be partially upheld if, shorn of vitiated parts, the substantial purpose and effect remain intact.

</td></tr>
</table>

43.1 Severability

43.1 **Severability.**[66] A successfully impugned measure (enactment, rule or decision) may not be unlawful in its entirety. It may be possible for the offending parts to be struck down, and the rest upheld.

43.1.1 **Substantial severability in action.** *DPP v Hutchinson* [1990] 2 AC 783, 804F (Lord Bridge: "A legislative instrument is substantially severable if the substance of what remains after severance is essentially unchanged in its legislative purpose, operation and effect"), 813D-F (need "to ask whether the legislative instrument: `with the invalid portions omitted would be substantially a different law as to the subject matter dealt with by what remains from what it would be with the omitted portions forming part of it'"); *R v Inland Revenue Commissioners, ex p Woolwich Equitable Building Society* [1990] 1 WLR 1400, 1418D-E (discussing substantial severability); *R v Secretary of State for the Home Department, ex p Pierson* [1998] AC 539, 592A-D (substantial severability preferable to "the blunt remedy of total lawfulness or total unlawfulness. The domain of public law is practical affairs. Sometimes severance is the only sensible course"); *Commissioner of Police v Skip Patrick Davis* [1994] 1 AC 283, 299A-B (using substantial severability "since reading the subsection as applicable only to convictions on information would plainly effect no change in the substantial purpose and effect of the subsection"); *Bugg v DPP* [1993] QB 473, 503H; *Credit Suisse v Allerdale Borough Council* [1997] QB 306, 335C-G, 361H; *R v Institute of Chartered Accountants of England and Wales, ex p Taher Nawaz* 25th April 1997 unrep. (insofar as excessive power of delegation contained in byelaw, permissible for it to be substantially severed).

43.1.2 **Limits of substantial severability.** *DPP v Hutchinson* [1990] 2 AC 783, 804B-C (Court having "no jurisdiction to modify or adapt the law to bring it within the scope of the law-maker's power"); *R v Inland Revenue Commissioners, ex p Woolwich Equitable Building Society* [1990] 1 WLR 1400, 1419B ("It is ... no part of the court's function to legislate in this way"); *R v Secretary of State for Trade and Industry, ex p Thomson Holidays Ltd* The Times 12th January 2000 (wrong to "produce an order ... as to whose terms there had been no consultation pursuant to [the statute]"); *R (Middlebrook Mushrooms Ltd) v Agricultural Wages Board of England and Wales* [2004] EWHC 1447 (Admin) at [90]-[93] (discussing partial quashing/ severance in context of whether instrument should be the subject of further consultation); *R (Association of Pharmaceutical Importers) v Secretary of State for Health* [2001] EWCA Civ 1986 [2002] EuLR 197 (judicial review refused because not possible to sever the offending chapter of the pharmaceutical price regulation scheme, with which the claimant's complaints were concerned).

43.1.3 **Scope of the severability doctrine.**
(A) PRIMARY LEGISLATION. *Commissioner of Police v Skip Patrick Davis* [1994] 1 AC 283 (primary legislation partially void for inconsistency with written constitution); *Independent Jamaica Council for Human Rights (1998) Ltd v Marshall-Burnett* [2005] UKPC 3 [2005] 2 AC 356 at [22] (applying *Attorney General for Alberta v Attorney General for Canada* [1947] AC 503, 518: "The real question is whether what remains is so inextricably bound up with the part declared invalid that what remains cannot independently survive or, as it has sometimes been

---

[66] This paragraph in a previous edition was cited in *R (Secretary of State for the Home Department) v Mental Health Review Tribunal* [2005] EWCA Civ 1616 at [10].

put whether on a fair review of the whole matter it can be assumed that the legislature would have enacted what survives without enacting the part that is ultra vires at all").
(B) DELEGATED LEGISLATION. *DPP v Hutchinson* [1990] 2 AC 783; *R v Inland Revenue Commissioners, ex p Woolwich Equitable Building Society* [1990] 1 WLR 1400.
(C) POLICY. *R v Secretary of State for the Home Department, ex p Pierson* [1998] AC 539, 592A-D (using substantial severability in relation to the lawfulness of a policy); *R v Rochdale Metropolitan Borough Council, ex p Schemet* [1994] ELR 89, 106G (severance approach in relation to a partially unlawful policy).
(D) OTHER. *R v Secretary of State for Transport, ex p Greater London Council* [1986] QB 556, 578C-579D ("in principle and in appropriate proceedings, the court may hold to be unlawful part of an administrative order or decision having effect in public law while holding valid the remainder of the order or decision"); *R v Inner London Crown Court, ex p Sitki* [1994] COD 342 (entire liquor licence invalid, where not possible to sever unlawful condition); *R v Berkshire County Council, ex p Wokingham District Council* [1995] COD 364 (no power to sever a planning application into county and district matters); *Credit Suisse v Allerdale Borough Council* [1997] QB 306, 335C-G and 361H (applying substantial severability test to ultra vires contract).

43.1.4 **Role of textual severability.** *DPP v Hutchinson* [1990] 2 AC 783, 804F ("A legislative instrument is textually severable if a clause, a sentence, a phrase or a single word may be disregarded, as exceeding the law-maker's power, and what remains of the text is still grammatical and coherent"), 811D-E ("The test of textual severability has the great merit of simplicity and certainty"), 811F-G (first question is whether "textual severance is possible"); *Jersey Fishermen's Association Ltd v States of Guernsey* [2007] UKPC 30 at [60] (invalid Ordinance capable of textual severance, so substantial severance not necessary).

43.1.5 **Reading down/reading in: interpretation to allow validity.** <46.3>.

43.1.6 **Partial quashing.** *R v Secretary of State for the Environment, ex p Lancashire County Council* [1994] 4 All ER 165 (quashing offending passage in policy guidance); *R v Pateley Bridge Justices, ex p Percy* [1994] COD 453 (quashing sentence for contempt and substituting lesser sentence); *R v London Borough of Southwark, ex p Dagou* (1996) 28 HLR 72, 81-82 (power to sever decision document, quashing part only); *R (Guiney) v Greenwich London Borough Council* [2008] EWHC 2012 (Admin) (partial quashing not possible where sole aspect of planning permission complained of was key element of overall package); *R v Exeter Crown Court, ex p Chennery* [1996] COD 207 (Court quashing sentence of 18 months and substituting one of 12 months); *R v London Borough of Tower Hamlets, ex p Tower Hamlets Combined Traders Association* [1994] COD 325 (quashing street trading charges only to the extent excessive); *R v Secretary of State for Transport, ex p Greater London Council* [1986] QB 556, 580H-581C (suggesting that quashing order (certiorari) may sometimes be available to quash part only of a `direction'); *R v Belmarsh Magistrates Court, ex p Gilligan* [1998] 1 Cr App R 14 (quashing committal as to certain offences but not others); *R v Snaresbrook Crown Court, ex p Patel* [2000] COD 255 (quashing that part of crown court order denying defendant's costs order); *R v London (North) Industrial Tribunal, ex p Associated Newspapers Ltd* [1998] ICR 1212, 1230A-B (partially quashing a reporting restriction order); *R v Southwark Coroner's Court, ex p Epsom Health Care NHS Trust* [1995] COD 92 (quashing part of coroner's verdict, there being a public interest in leaving the central finding in place); *R v Inner South London Coroner, ex p Kendall* [1988] 1 WLR 1186, 1193A-1194B (quashing coroner's verdict, and remitting for new conclusion, but not quashing the inquest in its entirety; the jurisdiction to adopt such a response being "consistent ... with this court's increasing flexibility of response and remedy in the ever-developing field of judicial review"); *R (Middlebrook Mushrooms Ltd) v Agricultural Wages Board of England and Wales* [2004] EWHC 1447 (Admin) at [90]-[93]

(discussing partial quashing/severance in context of whether instrument should be the subject of further consultation); cf. *R v Old Street Magistrates Court, ex p Spencer* The Times 8th November 1994 (remitting the matter, but commenting that a partial quashing of the order would have been a more suitable response, had such a power existed).

43.1.7 Severance: other similar techniques.
(A) SUBSTITUTIONARY REMEDY: COURT RETAKING THE DECISION. <24.4.2>.
(B) INVALID ONLY AGAINST CLAIMANT. *Agricultural, Horticultural & Forestry Industry Training Board v Aylesbury Mushrooms Ltd* [1972] 1 WLR 190 (where failure to consult one body, Court holding that Order invalid but only as against them).
(C) VALID INSOFAR AS NOT AN EXCESS. *Thames Water Authority v Elmbridge Borough Council* [1983] QB 570 (council resolution valid insofar as not an excess of power); *DPP v Hutchinson* [1990] 2 AC 783, 808H-809A (referring to Australian Acts Interpretation Act 1901-1973 s.15A, whereby enactment "shall nevertheless be a valid enactment to the extent to which it is not in excess of ... power"); <43.1.6> (partial quashing).
(D) INVALIDITY CAPABLE OF CURE. *R (National Association of Health Stores) v Secretary of State for Health* [2005] EWCA Civ 154 (absence of required exemption could be, and had now been, cured by amendment to the regulations).

43.1.8 Onus of proof and severability. *R v Inner London Crown Court, ex p Sitki* [1994] COD 342 (onus lying on party seeking to uphold the `valid portion').

```
┌────────────────────────────────────────────────────────────────────┐
│     P44 Nullity. It can be helpful to regard a flawed act as a nullity.  │
└────────────────────────────────────────────────────────────────────┘
```

44.1 Invalidity labels
44.2 Flaws constituting "nullity"
44.3 Purpose/effect of "nullity"

44.1 Invalidity labels Various terms have been used to describe flawed (or fundamentally-flawed) decisions and measures, generally to help explain the consequences. A favoured term is "nullity". However, in the flexible and contextual world of judicial review, the true focus is always on the specific unlawfulness and consequences, in the particular context and circumstances.

44.1.1 **Disfavouring "void"/"voidable".** *Chief Constable of the North Wales Police v Evans* [1982] 1 WLR 1155, 1163A-B (Lord Hailsham, describing the "difficulty in applying the language of `void' and `voidable' (appropriate enough in situations of contract or of alleged nullity of marriage) to administrative decisions which give rise to practical and legal consequences which cannot be reversed"); *R v Secretary of State for the Home Department, ex p Khawaja* [1984] AC 74, 118C ("these transplants from the field of contract do not readily take root in the field of public law"); *R v Secretary of State for the Home Department, ex p Malhi* [1991] 1 QB 194, 208C-D ("with the current rapid development of the law of judicial review the distinction between `void' and `voidable' is now in some fields becoming obsolescent"); *R v Hendon Justices, ex p Director of Public Prosecutions* [1994] QB 167, 174A-B ("the void and voidable distinction is ordinarily no more than a convenient nomenclature to distinguish decisions all of which are outwith the conferred power, but some of which will and some of which will not have an ostensible effect until their character is judicially decided"); *Hoffmann-La Roche (F) & Co AG v Secretary of State for Trade and Industry* [1975] AC 295, 366A-B ("it leads to confusion to use such terms", being "ill-adapted to the field of public law"); *Credit Suisse v Allerdale Borough Council* [1997] QB 306, 337E-338C; *McLaughlin v Governor of the Cayman Islands* [2007] UKPC 50 [2007] 1 WLR 2839 (use of "void" apt, but different expressions not affecting outcome).

44.1.2 **"Jurisdictional" errors.** <P47>.

44.1.3 **"Nullity".** <44.2.1>.

44.1.4 **Focusing on legality and legal impact.**[67] *Bugg v DPP* [1993] QB 473, 491H-492A (describing the "movement away from seeking to categorise unlawful administrative action into different compartments, each with their separate label, such as void or voidable or ultra vires or nullity, and instead to emphasise the grounds upon which a court can intervene and to require that intervention before an administrative action will be categorised as invalid"); *Percy v Hall* [1997] QB 924, 950H-952D (Schiemann LJ, pointing out the need for flexibility in considering impact of court's decision that an enactment is invalid); <60.4.3>.

44.1.5 **"Mandatory"/"directory" procedural requirements.** <31.6.6>; <60.4.3>.

44.1.6 **"Target" duties.** <39.3.3>.

44.1.7 **Other.** *Independent Publishing Co Ltd v Attorney General of Trinidad and Tobago* [2004] UKPC 26 [2005] 1 AC 190 at [93] (PC, disapproving use of distinction between

---

[67] Robert Swerling [1997] JR 94.

fundamental breaches of natural justice and mere procedural irregularities or errors of law, in context of constitutional redress where right of appeal).

44.2 Flaws constituting "nullity". The impression given is that "nullity" is a label reserved for very serious vitiating flaws. But it does seem that, at some time or another, for some reason or another, each and every ground for judicial review has been treated as producing a flawed decision or measure which is a "nullity".

44.2.1 **"Nullity".** *Secretary of State for the Home Department v JJ* [2007] UKHL 45 [2008] 1 AC 385 at [27] (Lord Bingham: "An administrative order made without power to make it is, on well-known principles, a nullity"); *Seal v Chief Constable South Wales Police* [2007] UKHL 31 [2007] 1 WLR 1910 (civil proceedings a nullity where statutory precondition of leave of the court absent); *Boddington v British Transport Police* [1999] 2 AC 143; *R (Shrewsbury and Atcham Borough Council) v Secretary of State for Communities and Local Government* [2008] EWCA Civ 148 [2008] 3 All ER 548 at [57]-[58] (nullity inapt in relation to merely preparatory acts).

44.2.2 **All grounds as nullities.** *Anisminic Ltd v Foreign Compensation Commission* [1969] 2 AC 147, 171B-E (Lord Reid: "It has sometimes been said that it is only where a tribunal acts without jurisdiction that its decision is a nullity. But ... there are many cases where, although the tribunal had jurisdiction to enter on the inquiry, it has done or failed to do something in the course of the inquiry which is of such a nature that its decision is a nullity. It may have given its decision in bad faith. It may have made a decision which it had no power to make. It may have failed in the course of the inquiry to comply with the requirements of natural justice. It may in perfect good faith have misconstrued the provisions giving it power to act so that it failed to deal with the question remitted to it and decided some question which was not remitted to it. It may have refused to take into account something which it was required to take into account. Or it may have based its decision on some matter which, under the provisions setting it up, it had no right to take into account"); <P47>; *Credit Suisse v Allerdale Borough Council* [1997] QB 306, 340G (nullity wherever declared ultra vires), 343D (Lord Reid's categories in *Anisminic*), 352C (all grounds for judicial review to be treated as ultra vires); *R (Director of Public Prosecutions) v Birmingham City Justices* [2003] EWHC 2352 (Admin) at [37] (Crane J: "in the light of the case of *Boddington* [1999] 2 AC 143, whether the decision is what in former times would have been called a nullity, or a breach of the rules of natural justice, or simply a decision which was *Wednesbury* unreasonable and hence unlawful, the conclusion is the same, namely: the decision is unlawful").

44.2.3 **Nullity and particular grounds for judicial review.**
(A) JURISDICTIONAL ERROR. <P47>; *Ridge v Baldwin* [1964] AC 40, 141 ("If there is no jurisdiction, the decision is a nullity"); *South East Asia Fire Bricks v Non-Metallic Mineral Products Manufacturing Employers Union* [1981] AC 363, 370C-E; *R v Brent Justices, ex p Ward*[1993] COD 17 (re-committal following discharge of probation order a nullity); cf. *Gardi v Secretary of State for the Home Department (No.2)* [2002] EWCA Civ 1560 [2002] 1 WLR 3282 (decision of the Court of Appeal declared to be a "nullity" where the appeal from an adjudicator sitting in Scotland should have been to the Court of Session).
(B) ERROR OF LAW. <P48>; *In re A Company* [1981] AC 374, 383C ("The break-through made by *Anisminic* [1969] 2 AC 147 was that, as respects administrative tribunals and authorities, [any] error of law that could be shown to have been made by them in the course of reaching their decision on matters of fact or of administrative policy would result in their having asked themselves the wrong question with the result that the decision they reached would be a nullity").
(C) BAD FAITH. <52.1>; <44.2.2> (Lord Reid's list).

(D) PROCEDURAL UNFAIRNESS. *Attorney-General v Ryan* [1980] AC 718, 727D ("the Minister ... is required to observe the principles of natural justice ... and, if he fails to do so, his purported decision is a nullity"); *R v Secretary of State for the Home Department, ex p Fayed* [1998] 1 WLR 763, 771B-773B ("nullity" would include "not only the misinterpretation of legislation ... [but] any other error which would justify the intervention of the court on judicial review including a breach of the requirements of fairness"); *Ridge v Baldwin* [1964] AC 40, 139-141 (using "nullity" for certain breaches of natural justice), 171 (Lord Reid's list <44.2.2>); *South East Asia Fire Bricks v Non-Metallic Mineral Products Manufacturing Employers Union* [1981] AC 363, 370D-E ("a nullity for some reason such as breach of the rules of natural justice").

(E) PROCEDURAL ULTRA VIRES. <60.4>; *Boddington v British Transport Police* [1999] 2 AC 143, 158D-E, 159B-F, 170D (rejecting supposed distinction between substantive and procedural invalidity); *Grunwick Processing Laboratories Ltd v Advisory Conciliation & Arbitration Service* [1978] AC 655 ("null and void"); cf. *R v Secretary of State for Social Services, ex p Association of Metropolitan Authorities* [1986] 1 WLR 1, 14G-15C; *R v Wicks* [1998] AC 92 (alleged invalidity of enforcement notice on basis of a procedural impropriety not a ground for defence to criminal proceedings); *R v Seisdon Justices, ex p Dougan* [1982] 1 WLR 1476 (conviction a nullity where no notice); <60.4.3> (whether intended vitiating consequence).

(F) OTHER. *Fayed* <44.2.3(D)>; *R v Manchester Metropolitan University, ex p Nolan* [1994] ELR 380, 395B-C (failure to take relevant material into account "will ordinarily vitiate the material proceedings and nullify the decision"); *R v Seisdon Justices, ex p Dougan* [1982] 1 WLR 1476, 1482H-1482A (failure to consider proof of service before convicting defendant in his absence rendering the conviction a nullity); *Vine v National Dock Labour Board* [1957] AC 488 (improper delegation as nullity), 500, 504 ("nullity"); *R v Horseferry Road Magistrates Court, ex p Director of Public Prosecutions* [1997] COD 172, 173 (failure of stipendiary to discharge statutory duty rendered proceedings a nullity).

44.3 **Purpose/effect of "nullity".** Asking whether a public body's act is a "nullity" is generally so as to identify its legal consequences, for example as to whether: (1) judicial review is available; (2) the act can be ignored or needs to be challenged; and (3) the act infects (or is cured by) a subsequent act.

44.3.1 **Nullity and judicial review of acquittal.** <35.1.7>.

44.3.2 **Nullity and ouster.** <P28> (ouster).
(A) OUSTER DOES NOT APPLY TO A NULLITY. <28.1.9>.
(B) NULLITY AND PART-REVIEWABILITY OF CROWN COURT. <32.1.5(A)>.

44.3.3 **Nullity: whether defect curable by or infecting later decision.** [68] *Calvin v Carr* [1980] AC 574, 589G-590B (decision appealable even if a nullity for breach of natural justice) *Vine v National Dock Labour Board* [1957] AC 488, 499 (non-delegable decision cannot be cured by appeal); *R v Oxford Regional Mental Health Review Tribunal, ex p Secretary of State for the Home Department* [1988] AC 120, 126D-E (Lord Bridge: "Such a fundamental flaw as vitiated the proceedings leading to [the] decision must surely call for a complete rehearing de novo"); *Hoffmann-La Roche (F) & Co AG v Secretary of State for Trade and Industry* [1975] AC 295, 353D-E (Minister not acting ultra vires because of invalidity of report before him); *R v Secretary of State for the Home Department, ex p Naheed Ejaz* [1994] QB 496, 501E-F (whether naturalisation infected by husband's want of citizenship); <36.4> (curing procedural

---

[68] Nigel Pleming QC & Adam Robb [1999] JR 248.

unfairness); *Boddington v British Transport Police* [1999] 2 AC 143 (leaving open difficult questions as to whether invalid administrative measures and acts capable of having legal consequences during period prior to court's recognition of them as invalid); *R v Central London County Court, ex p London* [1999] QB 1260, 1278B-E[69] (applying the analysis of Dr Forsyth, referred to in *Boddington*, as to whether second actor having legal power to act notwithstanding the invalidity of the first act); *Attorney General's Reference No.2 of 2001* [2003] UKHL 68 [2004] 2 AC 72 (effect of breach of Art 6 right to prosecution within a reasonable time on lawfulness of subsequent criminal trial); *R (H) v Ashworth Hospital Authority* [2002] EWCA Civ 923 [2003] 1 WLR 127 at [46] (if discharge order quashed, "it will be treated as never having had any legal effect at all").

44.3.4 Nullity: need to challenge, or safe to disregard? *Smith v East Elloe Rural District Council* [1956] AC 736, 769-770 ("Unless the necessary proceedings are taken at law to establish the cause of invalidity and to get [an order] quashed or otherwise upset; it will remain as effective for its ostensible purpose as the most impeccable of orders"); *London & Clydeside Estates Ltd v Aberdeen District Council* [1980] 1 WLR 182, 203A-B ("A decision or other act of a more or less formal character may be invalid and subject to being so declared in court of law and yet have some legal effect or existence prior to such declaration"), 189G-H (leaving aside "cases in which a fundamental obligation may have been so outrageously and flagrantly ignored or defied that the subject may safely ignore what has been done", "in a very great number of cases, it may be in a majority of them, it may be necessary ... to go to the court for declaration of his rights, the grant of which may well be discretionary"); *R v Restormel Borough Council, ex p Corbett* [2001] EWCA Civ 330 [2001] 1 PLR 108 at [15] ("people rely, and are entitled to rely, upon decisions of public authorities as being lawful until such time as they are quashed"); *R (H) v Ashworth Hospital Authority* [2002] EWCA Civ 923 [2003] 1 WLR 127 at [56] (health professionals not entitled to readmit a patient following a mental health appeal tribunal discharge order which they regarded as flawed, unless and until that order were quashed by a court); *Hoffmann-La Roche (F) & Co AG v Secretary of State for Trade and Industry* [1975] AC 295, 365F ("Unless there is such a challenge and, if there is, until it has been upheld by a judgment of the court, the validity of the statutory instrument and the legality of acts done pursuant to the law declared by it are presumed"), 366D-E (if persons having standing do not challenge, then "the presumption of validity prevails"); *Percy v Hall* [1997] QB 924 (byelaws apparently valid and so constables entitled to enforce); *R v Lincoln City Council, ex p Wickes Building Supplies Ltd* (1994) 92 LGR 215, 223 (need to challenge primary legislation); <27.3.11> (defendant exception/ collateral challenge); *R v Secretary of State for the Home Department, ex p Fire Brigades Union* [1995] 2 AC 513, 551E-F (even if decision not to implement statutory scheme a "nullity", Secretary of State's attempt unlawfully to bind himself in this way unlawful); *R v Clerk to Liverpool Justices, ex p Abiaka* The Times 6th May 1999 (magistrates' clerk having no power to treat magistrates' order as a nullity; required instead to refer it back to the magistrates for reconsideration by them or a superior court); *R v Peak District National Park Authority, ex p Bleaklow Industries Ltd* [1999] Env LR D28 (quashing order appropriate because, although the impugned planning determination a nullity, it should not be left in the hope that people would realise this).

44.3.5 Nullity and remedy. *R v Dorking Justices, ex p Harrington* [1984] AC 743, 753B-C (quashing order not appropriate where "orders were a nullity"; mandatory order the proper remedy); *R v Horseferry Road Magistrates Court, ex p Director of Public Prosecutions* [1997] COD 172, 174 (mandatory order made); *Anisminic Ltd v Foreign Compensation Commission* [1969] 2 AC 147, 196B (Lord Pearce: "Where a decision is found to be in excess of or without

---

[69] Andrew Parsons & Gerard Clarke [1999] JR 260.

jurisdiction, there is strictly no need to quash it, since it is a nullity"); *Percy v Hall* [1997] QB 924 (even if byelaw substantially invalid (for uncertainty), arresting officers would have been entitled to defence of lawful justification in action for damages alleging wrongful arrest and false imprisonment).

C. GROUNDS FOR JUDICIAL REVIEW

public law wrongs justifying the Court's intervention

P45 Classifying grounds
P46 Ultra vires
P47 Jurisdictional error
P48 Error of law
P49 Error of fact
P50 Abdication/fetter
P51 Insufficient inquiry
P52 Bad faith/improper motive
P53 Frustrating the legislative purpose
P54 Substantive unfairness
P55 Inconsistency
P56 Relevancy/irrelevancy
P57 Unreasonableness
P58 Proportionality
P59 HRA-violation
P60 Procedural unfairness
P61 Bias
P62 Reasons
P63 External wrongs

<1.1> means "see para 1.1"

> **P45 Classifying grounds.** Inapt for rigid categorisation, grounds fit broadly within unlawfulness, unreasonableness and unfairness.

45.1 The conventional threefold division
45.2 Root concepts and unifying themes
45.3 Reviewing discretion: *Wednesbury* and abuse of power
45.4 Overlapping grounds and interchangeable labels

45.1 The conventional threefold division. The most popular classification is the threefold division into illegality (unlawfulness), irrationality (unreasonableness) and procedural impropriety (unfairness). These heads are neither exhaustive nor mutually exclusive. The classification is valuable, resting on two important distinctions: one between substance (unlawfulness and unreasonableness) and procedure (procedural unfairness); the other between hard-edged questions (unlawfulness and unfairness) and soft questions (unreasonableness).

45.1.1 **The *GCHQ* threefold division.** *Council of Civil Service Unions v Minister for the Civil Service* [1985] AC 374, 410D-411B (Lord Diplock: "one can conveniently classify under three heads the grounds upon which administrative action is subject to control by judicial review. The first ground I would call `illegality', the second `irrationality' and the third `procedural impropriety'. That is not to say that further development on a case by case basis may not in course of time add further grounds... By `illegality' as a ground for judicial review I mean that the decision-maker must understand correctly the law that regulates his decision-making power and must give effect to it... By `irrationality' I mean what can by now be succinctly referred to as `*Wednesbury* unreasonableness'... It applies to a decision which is so outrageous in its defiance of logic or of accepted moral standards that no sensible person who had applied his mind to the question to be decided could have arrived at it... I have described the third head as `procedural impropriety' rather than failure to observe basic rules of natural justice or failure to act with procedural fairness towards the person who will be affected by the decision. This is because susceptibility to judicial review under this head covers also failure by an administrative tribunal to observe procedural rules that are expressly laid down in the legislative instrument by which its jurisdiction is conferred"), 414E-H (Lord Roskill), 415B-C (describing "the great advantage of making clear the differences between each ground"); *R (Q) v Secretary of State for the Home Department* [2003] EWCA Civ 364 [2004] QB 36 at [112] ("Starting from the received checklist of justiciable errors set out by Lord Diplock in the *CCSU* case [1985] AC 374, the courts (as Lord Diplock himself anticipated they would) have developed an issue-sensitive scale of intervention to enable them to perform their constitutional function"); *Wheeler v Leicester City Council* [1985] AC 1054, 1078B-C (Lord Roskill: "Those three heads are not exhaustive, and as Lord Diplock pointed out, further grounds may hereafter require to be added. Nor are they necessarily mutually exclusive"); *R v Secretary of State for the Environment, ex p Nottinghamshire County Council* [1986] AC 240, 249D-E (a "valuable ... but certainly not exhaustive analysis"); *R v Secretary of State for the Home Department, ex p Brind* [1991] 1 AC 696, 750D (applying the "triple categorisation"); *R v Secretary of State for the Home Department, ex p Launder* [1997] 1 WLR 839, 856G.

45.1.2 **Important not to fetter the developing law.** *R v Panel on Take-overs and Mergers, ex p Guinness Plc* [1990] 1 QB 146, 160A-C (Lord Donaldson MR, referring to Lord Diplock in *GCHQ* as having "formulated the currently accepted categorisations in an attempt to rid the courts of shackles bred of the technicalities surrounding the old prerogative writs. But he added ... that further development on a case by case basis might add further grounds. In the context of the present appeal he might have considered an innominate ground formed of an amalgam of his own grounds with perhaps added elements ... for he would surely have joined in deploring any use of his own categorisation as a fetter on the continuous development of the new `public law court'"); *R v Secretary of State for the Environment, ex p Greater London Council* 3rd April 1985 unrep. (Mustill LJ, speaking against "the assumption that unless a particular case can be forced into one of the categories on the list, there is no power to give [a remedy], thus stunting the free growth of this developing area of law").

45.1.3 **Other broad summaries.** <45.2.1>, <45.4.2> (ultra vires as a single head); *R (Corner House Research) v Director of the Serious Fraud Office* [2008] UKHL 60 [2008] 3 WLR 568 at [32] (Lord Bingham: "the Director ... must seek to exercise his powers so as to promote the statutory purpose for which he is given them. He must direct himself correctly in law. He must act lawfully. He must do his best to exercise an objective judgment on the relevant material available to him. He must exercise his powers in good faith, uninfluenced by any ulterior motive, predilection or prejudice"); *R v Inland Revenue Commissioners, ex p Preston* [1985] AC 835, 862C ("Judicial review is available where a decision-making authority exceeds its powers, commits an error of law, commits a breach of natural justice, reaches a decision which no reasonable tribunal could have reached, or abuses its powers"); *R v Hillingdon London Borough Council, ex p Puhlhofer* [1986] AC 484, 518C-D (council "susceptible to judicial review where they have misconstrued the Act, or abused their powers or otherwise acted perversely"); *Engineers & Managers Association v Advisory Conciliation & Arbitration Service* [1980] 1 WLR 302, 318F (whether shown to have "misdirected itself in law, or to have failed to observe the requirements of natural justice, or to have failed to consider relevant matters; or to have conducted the reference in a way in which no reasonable advisory conciliation or arbitration service, paying due regard to the statute, could have conducted it").

45.1.4 **Codified formulations.**
(A) EC TREATY ART 230. Article 230 of the EC Treaty describes grounds for intervention by the ECJ with acts of the EC executive ("on grounds of lack of competence, infringement of an essential procedural requirement, infringement of this Treaty or of any rule of law relating to its application, or misuse of powers"), referred to in *R (Alconbury Developments Ltd) v Secretary of State for the Environment Transport and the Regions* [2001] UKHL 23 [2003] 2 AC 295 at [50] (suggesting that domestic grounds for judicial review reflected in article 230).
(B) COE:COM R(80)2. Recommendation No.R(80)2 of the Committee of Ministers of the Council of Europe 11th March 1980 ("Basic principles" requiring that an "administrative authority, when exercising a discretionary power: (1) does not pursue a purpose other than that for which the power has been conferred; (2) observes objectivity and impartiality, taking into account only the factors relevant to the particular case; (3) observes the principle of equality before the law by avoiding unfair discrimination; (4) maintains a proper balance between any adverse effects which its decision may have on the rights, liberties or interests of persons and the purpose which it pursues; (5) takes its decision within a time which is reasonable having regard to the matter at stake; (6) applies any general administrative guidelines in a consistent manner while at the same time taking account of the particular circumstances of each case; ... (7) Any general administrative guidelines which govern the exercise of a discretionary power are: (i) made public; or (ii) communicated in an appropriate manner and to the extent that is necessary to the person concerned, at his request, be it before or after the taking of the act concerning him; (8) Where an administrative authority, in exercising a discretionary power, departs from a general administrative guideline in such a manner as to affect adversely the rights, liberties or interests of a person concerned, the latter is informed of the reasons for this decision. This is done either by stating the reasons in the act or by communicating them, at his request, to the person concerned in writing within a reasonable time; ... (11) A court or other independent body which controls the exercise of a discretionary power has such powers of obtaining information as are necessary for the exercise of its function"), described in *R v Secretary of State for Transport, ex p Pegasus Holdings (London) Ltd* [1988] 1 WLR 990,

1001E-F <58.1.7>.
(C) OTHER. Barbados: Administrative Justice Act (see *C.O. Williams Construction v Donald George Blackman* [1995] 1 WLR 102, 105D-F) s.4 (grounds "include the following: (a) that an administrative act or omission was in any way unauthorised or contrary to law; (b) excess of jurisdiction; (c) failure to satisfy or observe conditions or procedures required by law; (d) breach of the principles of natural justice; (e) unreasonable or irregular or improper exercise of discretion; (f) abuse of power; (g) fraud, bad faith, improper purposes or irrelevant considerations; (h) acting on instructions from an unauthorised person; (i) conflict with the policy of an Act of Parliament; (j) error of law, whether or not apparent on the face of the record; (k) absence of evidence on which a finding or assumption of fact could reasonably be based; and (l) breach of or omission to perform a duty"); Australia: Administrative Decisions (Judicial Review) Act 1977 s.5).

45.2 Root concepts and unifying themes. Academic commentators have long debated whether the conceptual basis for all judicial review grounds is the principle of "ultra vires", so that Courts are merely holding public bodies to Parliament's intent. In truth, whether or not there is a statutory scheme, judicial review involves Courts articulating common law standards, invoking various helpful themes and concepts.

45.2.1 **Whether ultra vires is a unifying theme.** *R v Hull University Visitor, ex p Page* [1993] AC 682, 701E (Lord Browne-Wilkinson: "If the decision maker exercises his powers outside the jurisdiction conferred, in a manner which is procedurally irregular or is *Wednesbury* unreasonable, he is acting ultra vires his powers and therefore unlawfully"); *Boddington v British Transport Police* [1999] 2 AC 143, 164B (Lord Browne-Wilkinson: "I adhere to my view that the juristic basis of judicial review is the doctrine of ultra vires"), 171F-172A (Lord Steyn: "Leaving to one side the separate topic of judicial review of non-legal powers exercised by non statutory bodies, I see no reason to depart from the orthodox view that ultra vires is 'the central principle of administrative law'"); *R v Wicks* [1998] AC 92, 105C-D ("The greatly widened supervisory role now exercised by the court emerged largely from a much expanded application of the concept of ultra vires"); *Credit Suisse v Allerdale Borough Council* [1997] QB 306, 352C ("The essence of the modern law of judicial review is that decisions which involve illegality, irrationality or procedural impropriety ... are treated as ultra vires"); *R (Bancoult) v Secretary of State for Foreign & Commonwealth Affairs* [2007] EWCA Civ 498 [2008] QB 365 at [59]-[61] (unhelpful to treat ultra vires as the underpinning, at least for prerogative power); <45.4.2> (all grounds as ultra vires/unlawfulness); Forsyth (ed), *Judicial Review and the Constitution* (Hart Publishing, 2000), collecting together divergent views of commentators.

45.2.2 **Common law standards.** <7.6> (natural justice); <7.7> (unreasonableness); <7.5.1> (constitutional rights); <7.6.4> (natural justice having a common law source).

45.2.3 **Abuse of power as a root concept.**[1] *R v Department for Education and Employment, ex p Begbie* [2000] 1 WLR 1115, 1129F-G (Laws LJ: "Abuse of power has become, or is fast becoming, the root concept which governs and conditions our general principles of public law"); *R (Bancoult) v Secretary of State for Foreign & Commonwealth Affairs* [2007] EWCA Civ 498 [2008] QB 365 (abuse of prerogative power) at [60] (Sedley LJ: "Power may be abused in a variety of ways, of which acting beyond the limits of the power is one, acting irrationally is

---

[1] This subparagraph in a previous edition was cited in *R (Bancoult) v Secretary of State for Foreign and Commonwealth Affairs* [2007] EWCA Civ 498 [2008] QB 365 at [60].

another, acting for an improper purpose is a third and acting so as to frustrate a legitimate expectation is a fourth; and there are more, both procedural and substantive. Very commonly they run into one another"); <12.1.14> (the rule of law and preventing abuse of power); *R v Secretary of State for the Environment, ex p Nottinghamshire County Council* [1986] AC 240, 249C-D ("The ground upon which the courts will review the exercise of an administrative discretion by a public officer is abuse of power"); *R v Inland Revenue Commissioners, ex p Preston* [1985] AC 835, 862C ("Judicial review is available where a decision-making authority ... abuses its powers"); *R v Secretary of State for the Home Department, ex p Brind* [1991] 1 AC 696, 751B ("judicial review [is] a remedy invented by the judges to restrain the excess or abuse of power"), 765E (unreasonableness as "a branch of the abuse, or misuse, of power"); *R (Zeqiri) v Secretary of State for the Home Department* [2002] UKHL 3 [2002] INLR 291 at [44] (legitimate expectation as a "particular form of the more general concept of abuse of power"); <45.3.3> (abuse of power and review of discretion); *R (S) v Secretary of State for the Home Department* [2007] EWCA Civ 546 at [39]-[40] (abuse of power as a general concept but not a "magic ingredient, able to achieve remedial results which other forms of illegality cannot match"), [43] (depending on unfairness not "flagrancy of the administrative failing"); *R v Secretary of State for the Home Department, ex p Fire Brigades Union* [1995] 2 AC 513, 554A-G (decision "unlawful and an abuse of the prerogative power"); <45.3.3> (review of discretion: abuse of power).

45.2.4 Fairness as a root concept. *R (Anufrijeva) v Secretary of State for the Home Department* [2003] UKHL 36 [2004] 1 AC 604 at [30] (Lord Steyn: "fairness is the guiding principle of our public law").

45.2.5 The reasonable observer as a general theme. <61.3.4> (bias and the fair-minded and informed observer); *R v Secretary of State for the Home Department, ex p Q* [2000] UKHRR 386, 393F-H (real danger test a realistic and sensible way of evaluating whether any threat to constitutional right to a fair trial, so as to justify intervention); *R v Chelsea College of Art and Design, ex p Nash* [2000] ELR 686 at [48] (applying this test in the context of procedural irregularity: "Would a reasonable person, viewing the matter objectively and knowing all the facts which are known to the Court, consider that there was a risk that the procedure adopted by the tribunal in question resulted in injustice or unfairness?"); *Sheridan v Stanley Cole (Wainfleet) Ltd* [2003] EWCA Civ 1046 [2003] 4 All ER 1181 at [32] (fair-minded observer test applicable to Art 6 question of whether fair hearing); *R (Carson) v Secretary of State for Work and Pensions* [2003] EWCA Civ 797 [2003] 3 All ER 577 at [61] (use of "rational and fair-minded person" as to whether comparable circumstances calling for positive justification under HRA/ECHR Art 14; HL is at [2005] UKHL 37 [2006] 1 AC 173).

45.2.6 The need for objective standards. *R v Department for Education and Employment, ex p Begbie* [2000] 1 WLR 1115, 1130B (Laws LJ: "Fairness and reasonableness (and their contraries) are objective concepts; otherwise there would be no public law, or if there were it would be palm tree justice"); <14.3.1> (nothing personal and objective standards).

45.3 Reviewing discretion: *Wednesbury* and "abuse of power". Judicial review of discretionary powers was traditionally sub-classified under *Wednesbury* principles, but modern standards are dynamic and adapted to the context.

45.3.1 The *Wednesbury* principles.
(A) RELEVANCIES/IRRELEVANCIES AND UNREASONABLENESS. *Associated Provincial Picture Houses Ltd v Wednesbury Corporation* [1948] 1 KB 223, 233-234 (Lord Greene MR: "The court is entitled to investigate the action of the local authority with a view to seeing whether they have taken into account matters which they ought not to take into account,

or, conversely, have refused to take into account or neglected to take into account matters which they ought to take into account... [or whether] "they have nevertheless come to a conclusion so unreasonable that no reasonable authority could ever have come to it"); *R v Secretary of State for Trade and Industry, ex p Lonrho Plc* [1989] 1 WLR 525, 533D; *R v Secretary of State for the Home Department, ex p Brind* [1991] 1 AC 696, 751D.

(B) INCLUDING ERROR OF LAW.*Associated Provincial Picture Houses Ltd v Wednesbury Corporation* [1948] 1 KB 223, 229 ("a person entrusted with a discretion must, so to speak, direct himself properly in law"); *Bromley London Borough Council v Greater London Council* [1983] 1 AC 768, 821A-B (*Wednesbury* principle including "decisions reached in the exercise of a statutory discretion that are unlawful because it can be shown that in reaching the decision the body exercising the discretion has acted on an erroneous view of the applicable law").

(C) *WEDNESBURY* UNREASONABLENESS.*R v Tower Hamlets London Borough Council, ex p Chetnik Developments Ltd* [1988] AC 858, 873C (*Wednesbury* as "the classic exposition of the principle of reasonableness in relation to the exercise of administrative discretions"); *R v Secretary of State for the Environment, ex p Hammersmith & Fulham London Borough Council* [1991] 1 AC 521, 595C-D ("the classic statement of the basis for a challenge to an administrative decision on the ground of irrationality"); *Gillick v West Norfolk and Wisbech Area Health Authority* [1986] AC 112, 177E ("exercising a statutory discretion in a wholly unreasonable way" as "the classical 'Wednesbury' case for judicial review"); *R v Secretary of State for Trade and Industry, ex p Lonrho Plc* [1989] 1 WLR 525, 533D (Lord Keith: "not unreasonable, in the *Wednesbury* sense"); cf. *R v Secretary of State for the Home Department, ex p Onibiyo* [1996] QB 768, 785D (Sir Thomas Bingham MR, referring to "challenge on any *Wednesbury* ground, of which irrationality is only one").

(D) *WEDNESBURY* AS A FAMILIAR REFERENCE-POINT. *Holgate-Mohammed v Duke* [1984] AC 437, 443B ("too familiar to call for repetitious citation"); *R v Secretary of State for the Home Department, ex p Benwell* [1985] QB 554, 568A-B (Hodgson J: "In this jurisdiction everyone by now knows Lord Greene MR's summation of the *Wednesbury* principles by heart and, as has happened to *Donoghue v Stevenson* [1932] AC 562, no one now even opens the report of the *Wednesbury* case"); *Mercury Energy Ltd v Electricity Corporation of New Zealand Ltd* [1994] 1 WLR 521, 526H ("the definitive judgment"); *John Dee Limited v Customs and Excise Commissioners* The Times 17th February 1995 (Turner J) ("oft cited, but now seldom studied").

45.3.2 **Limits of *Wednesbury.*** *R v Secretary of State for the Environment, ex p Nottinghamshire County Council* [1986] AC 240, 249B-C (Lord Scarman: "'*Wednesbury* principles' is a convenient legal 'shorthand'" but not to "be treated as a complete, exhaustive, definitive statement of the law"); *Secretary of State for Education and Science v Tameside Metropolitan Borough Council* [1977] AC 1014, 1047F-G ("there is no universal rule as to the principles on which the exercise of a discretion may be reviewed: each statute or type of statute must be individually looked at"); *Congreve v Home Office* [1976] QB 629, 657C (Roskill LJ, referring to "what was authoritatively laid down in" *Wednesbury* and *Padfield*: "the law does not stand still, and those cases, while stating the relevant principles, leave open their application to the particular facts of particular cases which from time to time come before the courts").

45.3.3 **Review of discretion: abuse of power.** *R v Secretary of State for the Environment, ex p Nottinghamshire County Council* [1986] AC 240, 249C-D (Lord Scarman: "The ground upon which the courts will review the exercise of an administrative discretion by a public officer is abuse of power. Power can be abused in a number of ways: by a mistake of law in misconstruing the limits imposed by statute (or by common law in the case of a common law power) upon the scope of the power; by procedural irregularity; by unreasonableness in the *Wednesbury* sense; or by bad faith or an improper motive in its exercise"), applied in *R v Hillingdon London Borough Council, ex p Puhlhofer* [1986] AC 484, 518D (Lord Brightman: "The ground upon which the courts will review the exercise of an administrative discretion is abuse of power - eg. bad faith, a mistake in construing the limits of the power, a procedural irregularity, or unreasonableness"); *R v Inland Revenue Commissioners, ex p Preston* [1985] AC 835, 862C (judicial review where defendant "abuses its powers"); *Gillick v West Norfolk and Wisbech Area Health Authority* [1986] AC 112, 192C-D (whether defendant has "stepped beyond the proper limits of its power"); *R v Hull University Visitor, ex p Page* [1993] AC 682, 693G-H ("abuse of power" a concept distinct from mere error of law).

45.4 **Overlapping grounds and interchangeable labels.**[2] Like all judicial review principles, the grounds for judicial review are extremely flexible. Grounds have blurred edges and overlap, so that the `flaw' which justifies the Court's interference may be described in several different ways.

45.4.1 **Grounds merging into one another.** *Boddington v British Transport Police* [1999] 2 AC 143, 152E-F (Lord Irvine LC: "the various grounds for judicial review run together. The exercise of a power for an improper purpose may involve taking irrelevant considerations into account, or ignoring relevant considerations; and either may lead to an irrational result. The failure to grant a person affected by a decision a hearing, in breach of principles of procedural fairness, may result in a failure to take into account relevant considerations"), 170E ("the taking into account by a decision maker of extraneous considerations is variously treated as substantive or procedural"); *R v Secretary of State for the Home Department, ex p Oladehinde* [1991] 1 AC 254 (CA), 280E (Lord Donaldson MR: "it would be a mistake to approach the judicial review jurisdiction as if it consisted of a series of entirely separate boxes into which judges dipped as occasion demanded. It is rather a rich tapestry of many strands, which cross, re-cross and blend to produce justice"); *Wheeler v Leicester City Council* [1985] AC 1054, 1078B-C (classic threefold division not "necessarily mutually exclusive").

45.4.2 **All grounds as ultra vires/unlawfulness.** <45.2.1> (whether ultra vires underpins all grounds); *E v Secretary of State for the Home Department* [2004] EWCA Civ 49 [2004] QB 1044 (immigration appeal on basis of "error of law" reflecting all judicial review grounds), [42] (referring to judicial review and appeal on a point of law: "it has become a generally safe working rule that the substantive grounds for intervention are identical"); *Begum (Nipa) v Tower Hamlets London Borough Council* [2000] 1 WLR 306, 312G-313F, 327B (statutory appeal to county court "on any point of law arising from [the decision]" including all judicial review grounds), applied in *Begum v Tower Hamlets London Borough Council* [2003] UKHL 5 [2003] 2 AC 430 at [7] (Lord Bingham), [17] (Lord Hoffmann), [98] (Lord Millett); *S v Special Educational Needs Tribunal* [1995] 1 WLR 1627 (treating all orthodox judicial review grounds as questions of "law"); *Stefan v General Medical Council (No.2)* [2002] UKPC 10 at [6] ("question of law" including sufficiency of evidence and unfairness); *R (Director of Public Prosecutions) v Birmingham City Justices* [2003] EWHC 2352 (Admin) at [37] ("whether the decision is what in former times would have been called a nullity, or a breach of the rules of natural justice, or simply a decision which was *Wednesbury* unreasonable and hence unlawful, the conclusion is the same, namely: the decision is unlawful"); *Padfield v Minister of Agriculture Fisheries & Food* [1968] AC 997, 1058B-G (judicial review "will only issue if he acts unlawfully"); *Anisminic Ltd v Foreign Compensation Commission* [1969] 2 AC 147, 195B-C (wide concept of "lack of jurisdiction"); <47.1> (jurisdiction/jurisdictional error as a flexi-principle); <44.2.2> (Lord Reid's list of nullities).

---

[2] This paragraph from a previous edition was cited in *Boddington v British Transport Police* [1999] 2 AC 143, 170E (Lord Steyn).

45.4.3 **Overlap between unlawfulness and unreasonableness.** *R v Hendon Justices, ex p Director of Public Prosecutions* [1994] QB 167, 173F-G ("It is implicit in the enactment that a conferred power is not to be exercised unreasonably... If it is, then the exercise is outwith the conferred power and can be characterised as `illegal', `void' or a `nullity'"); *Bromley London Borough Council v Greater London Council* [1983] 1 AC 768, 821H (treating "the question of discretion" as "inseparable from the question of construction"), 836F-G (here "two ways of making the same point"); *Chief Adjudication Officer v Foster* [1993] AC 754, 765B-D (citing the observation from the CA that "One reason at least for setting aside subordinate legislation upon grounds of `Wednesbury unreasonableness' ... would be that Parliament never intended the regulation-making power to be exercised in that way. That is really indistinguishable from a question of `existence' or `vires'"); *Gillick v West Norfolk and Wisbech Area Health Authority* [1986] AC 112, 177E (Lord Scarman, characterising the challenge as "exercising a statutory discretion in a wholly unreasonable way"), 163E (Lord Fraser, commenting that the challenge "amounts to an assertion that the Secretary of State for Health and Social Security has acted illegally, in the sense of ultra vires"); *Engineers & Managers Association v Advisory Conciliation & Arbitration Service* [1980] 1 WLR 302 (approached in terms of irrationality (Lord Scarman at 318G), "ultra vires" (Lord Scarman at 318E), misdirection (Lord Diplock at 309A) and frustrating the policy of the Act (Lord Diplock at 306D)); *R v Dyfed County Council, ex p Manson* [1995] Env LR 83, 99, 102 (whether byelaw wholly unreasonable and so ultra vires); *Associated Provincial Picture Houses Ltd v Wednesbury Corporation* [1948] 1 KB 223, 229 (using `unreasonable' "in a rather comprehensive sense" including that "a person entrusted with a discretion must, so to speak, direct himself properly in law"); *R v Secretary of State for the Environment, ex p Nottinghamshire County Council* [1986] AC 240, 249B-C (referring to *Wednesbury* principles as describing "the circumstances in which the courts will intervene to quash as being illegal the exercise of an administrative discretion"); *R v Secretary of State for Trade and Industry, ex p Lonrho Plc* [1989] 1 WLR 525, 533F ("The exercise by the Secretary of State of his discretion ... can only be quashed by the court if the court is satisfied that the Secretary of State acted unlawfully"); *R v Secretary of State for the Home Department, ex p Brind* [1991] 1 AC 696, 755A and 757H ("The issue ... is whether [the defendant] has exceeded his discretionary powers, thus acting ultra vires and therefore unlawfully"), 757H ("If no reasonable minister properly directing himself would have reached the impugned decision, the minister has exceeded his powers and thus acted unlawfully"); *R v St Albans Crown Court, ex p Cinnamond* [1981] QB 480, 484C, F-G (whether `excess of jurisdiction' involves asking *Wednesbury* question, whether "no reasonable authority could have reached this decision without a self-misdirection"); *R v Sunderland City Council ex p Redezeus Ltd* (1995) 27 HLR 477 (having regard to matters beyond those set out in statute means acted beyond statutory powers); *Holgate-Mohammed v Duke* [1984] AC 437, 446C (referring to "an exercise of discretion that was ultra vires under *Wednesbury* principles because he took into consideration an irrelevant matter"); *R v Legal Aid Board, ex p Clark* (1994) 6 Admin LR 153; *R v Immigration Appeal Tribunal, ex p Singh (Bakhtaur)* [1986] 1 WLR 910, 919B-D (decision made without taking account of relevancy would be not "not in accordance with the law"); *R v Secretary of State for the Environment, ex p Hammersmith & Fulham London Borough Council* [1991] 1 AC 521, 597D-F (Lord Bridge: "If the court concludes, as the House did in the *Padfield* case [1968] AC 997, that a minister's exercise of a statutory discretion has been such as to frustrate the policy of the statute, that conclusion rests upon the view taken by the court of the true construction of the statute which the exercise of the discretion in question is then held to have contravened. The administrative action or inaction is then condemned on the ground of illegality. Similarly, if there are matters which, on the true construction of the statute conferring discretion, the person exercising the discretion must take into account and others which he may not take into account, disregard of those legally relevant matters or regard of those legally irrelevant matters will lay the decision open to review on the ground of illegality"); *R v Secretary of State for the Home Department, ex p Fire Brigades Union* [1995] 2 AC 513,

571E (whether regarded "as an abuse of the power which he was given... or as the exercise of a power which he has not been given, does not matter. The result is the same either way").

45.4.4 Overlap between unlawfulness and unfairness. *Fairmount Investments Ltd v Secretary of State for the Environment* [1976] 1 WLR 1255, 1263D-E (if order made in breach of "natural justice it may equally be said that the order is not within the powers of the Act and that a requirement of the Act has not been complied with. For it is to be implied, unless the contrary appears, that Parliament does not authorise by the Act the exercise of powers in breach of the principles of natural justice, and that Parliament does by the Act require, in the particular procedures, compliance with those principles"); <47.1.5> (natural justice as jurisdictional error); *R v Secretary of State for the Environment, ex p Davidson* (1990) 2 Admin LR 94, 95H-96A (breach of natural justice as "error of law"); *In re Medicaments and Related Classes of Goods (No.2)* [2001] 1 WLR 700 at [7] (bias as question of law); *Independent Publishing Co Ltd v Attorney General of Trinidad and Tobago* [2004] UKPC 26 [2005] 1 AC 190 at [91] (explaining that an "error of law" caused "the unfairness of the hearing"); *R v Inland Revenue Commissioners, ex p Preston* [1985] AC 835, 866F-G, 866F (Lord Templeman, speaking of *HTV Ltd v Price Commission* [1976] ICR 170: "If the Price Commission had not misconstrued the code, they would not have acted `inconsistently and unfairly'"); *Gillies v Secretary of State for Work and Pensions* [2006] UKHL 2 [2006] 1 WLR 781 at [6] ("whether a tribunal was properly constituted or was acting in breach of the principles of natural justice is essentially a question of law").

45.4.5 Overlap between unreasonableness and unfairness. *R (Khatun) v London Borough of Newham* [2004] EWCA Civ 55 [2005] QB 37 at [27] (Laws LJ: "it is not always useful to assess the merits of public law claims by making distinctions such as that between rights of procedural fairness and the discipline of sound reasoning. These two goods often run into one another, and austere legalisms may stunt rather than prosper the principled development of the law"); *R v Secretary of State for the Home Department, ex p Asif Mahmood Khan* [1984] 1 WLR 1337, 1352D (Dunn LJ: "an unfair action can seldom be a reasonable one"); *R v Chief Constable of the West Midlands Police, ex p Carroll* (1995) 7 Admin LR 45, 54E-F (agreeing "with both those ways of putting the matter"); *Ceylon University v Fernando* [1960] 1 WLR 223, 236 (whether action, in the "exercise of the wide discretion as to procedure ... sufficiently complied with the requirements of natural justice); *R v Lord Saville of Newdigate, ex p A* [2000] 1 WLR 1855 at [39] and [44] (possible to view question of unjustified refusal of anonymity as unreasonableness or unfairness); *British Oxygen Co Ltd v Board of Trade* [1971] AC 610, 625D-E (policy unobjectionable "provided the authority is always willing to listen to anyone with something new to say"); *R v London Borough of Newham, ex p Ajayi* (1996) 28 HLR 25, 29 (failure to explore certain matters as unfairness); *R v Secretary of State for the Environment, ex p Kirkstall Valley Campaign Ltd* [1996] 3 All ER 304, 324f-g ("the maxim audi alteram partem is ... one application of the wider principle that all relevant matters must be taken into account"); *Chief Constable of the North Wales Police v Evans* [1982] 1 WLR 1155, 1162H (Lord Hailsham: "he took into account matters which were never put to the [claimant] in connection with the relevant inquiry"); *R v Lambeth London Borough Council, ex p N* [1996] ELR 299 (function of adequate consultation as ensuring provision of the necessary material to make a proper and reasoned final decision); *Ceylon University v Fernando* [1960] 1 WLR 223, 232 (natural justice including absence of bad faith); *R v Criminal Injuries Compensation Board, ex p A* [1999] 2 AC 330, 345C (error of fact characterised here as "a breach of the rules of natural justice and constituted unfairness"); *R v Inland Revenue Commissioners, ex p Preston* [1985] AC 835, 864H (referring to "cases in which the court has granted judicial review on grounds of `unfairness' amounting to abuse of power" where "there has been some proven element of improper motive").

45.4.6 **Overlap between aspects of unlawfulness.** *Bromley London Borough Council v Greater London Council* [1983] 1 AC 768, 836D (ultra vires argument involving GLC having "misdirected itself in law" and "having proceeded upon an error of law"); *Chief Adjudication Officer v Foster* [1993] AC 754, 766H-767A (where ultra vires for "substantial invalidity", at any rate), 766F-G; <47.3> (error of law as jurisdictional error); <47.1> (link between jurisdictional error and ultra vires).

45.4.7 **Overlap between aspects of unreasonableness.** *R v Secretary of State for the Home Department, ex p Brind* [1991] 1 AC 696, 765E (" *Wednesbury* unreasonableness is a branch of the abuse, or misuse, of power"); *R v Tower Hamlets London Borough Council, ex p Chetnik Developments Ltd* [1988] AC 858, 873C ("common derivation" of "irrelevance and irrationality"); *Associated Provincial Picture Houses Ltd v Wednesbury Corporation* [1948] 1 KB 223, 229 (unreasonableness and irrelevancy: "all these things run into one another"); *R v Local Government Commission for England, ex p North Yorkshire County Council* 11th March 1994 unrep. (whether LGC ignored option of the status quo essentially a complaint that they "approached their task with closed minds"); *R v London Borough of Lambeth, ex p G* [1994] ELR 207, 218E (discretion "not exercised consistently with the statutory provisions" was "unreasonable in the *Wednesbury* sense").

> **P46 Ultra vires.** A body must not exceed its received powers
> or rules of higher authority, as properly interpreted.

46.1 Basic meanings of ultra vires
46.2 Rights-violation as ultra vires: the principle of legality
46.3 Interpretation to allow validity: reading down/reading in

46.1 Basic meanings of ultra vires. Ultra vires, a principle borrowed from company law, involves a body acting beyond its prescribed powers. There is a basic legal hierarchy comprising (1) EC legislation, (2) primary legislation, (3) rules (including subordinate legislation) and (4) decision-making. Ultra vires can connote any of these which is incompatible with limits imposed by any superior source in the hierarchy. Ultra vires can also be used in other ways, including as an all-embracing concept.

46.1.1 **Ultra vires: in a nutshell.** *R (Bancoult) v Secretary of State for Foreign & Commonwealth Affairs* [2007] EWCA Civ 498 [2008] QB 365 at [59] (Sedley LJ: "The concept of ultra vires acts was borrowed during the 19th century by public law from company law, where powers are spelt out in articles of association and acts can be measured against them. The same is frequently the case in public law: hence the transferability of the concept"; ultra vires inapt where "no empowering statute or measure"); *Attorney General's Reference No.2 of 2001* [2003] UKHL 68 [2004] 2 AC 72 at [125] ("An ultra vires act by a public authority is unlawful"); *R v Secretary of State for Trade and Industry, ex p Thomson Holidays Ltd* The Times 12th January 2000 ("ultra vires" as "a perfectly respectable shorthand to identify that legal defect or vice which consists in the making of a subordinate instrument which is not authorised by the text of its supposed parent in main legislation, given the correct construction of both measures"); *R (Bancoult) v Secretary of State for the Foreign and Commonwealth Office* [2001] QB 1067 at [46] ("elementary" that a body "created by a measure passed by a body which is legally prior to it must act within the confines of the power thereby conferred").

46.1.2 **Whether action incompatible with higher legal authority: illustrations.**
(A) WHETHER STATUTE INCOMPATIBLE WITH EC LAW. <8.3.1(A)>.
(B) WHETHER RULE INCOMPATIBLE WITH EC LAW. <8.3.1(B)>.
(C) WHETHER DECISION INCOMPATIBLE WITH EC LAW.*R (Min Min) v Secretary of State for the Home Department* [2008] EWHC 1604 (Admin) (refusal of permission to work breaching EC Directive); *R (Actis SA) v Secretary of State for Communities & Local Government* [2007] EWHC 2417 (Admin) (modified technical regulation unlawful for non-notification under the EC Directive); *R v Secretary of State for the Environment, ex p Royal Society for the Protection of Birds* [1997] QB 206 (economic-based exclusion from designated special protection area for wild birds incompatible with EC Directive); *R v Chief Constable of Sussex, ex p International Traders' Ferry Ltd* [1999] 2 AC 418 (restricted policing not incompatible with export rights under EC Treaty Art 29); *Berkeley v Secretary of State for the Environment* [2001] 2 AC 603 (planning decision incompatible with EC environmental assessment requirements).
(D) WHETHER RULE INCOMPATIBLE WITH STATUTE. <34.3.5> (judicial review of delegated legislation); *R (Bewry) v Secretary of State for the Home Department* [2007] EWHC 2711 (Admin) (whether amended Prison Rule ultra vires the Prison Act 1952); *Hoffmann-La Roche (F) & Co AG v Secretary of State for Trade and Industry* [1975] AC 295, 349B-C ("any order made must ... be within the mandate given by Parliament"); *R v Secretary of State for Social Security, ex p Joint Council for the Welfare of Immigrants* [1997] 1 WLR 275, 292D (asking whether the Regulations "contravene the express or implied requirements of a statute").
(E) WHETHER DECISION INCOMPATIBLE WITH STATUTE.*R (Corporation of London) v Secretary of State for Environment, Food and Rural Affairs* [2006] UKHL 30 [2006] 1 WLR

1721 (whether consent beyond scope of statutory power); *R (Risk Management Partners Ltd) v Brent London Borough Council* [2008] EWHC 692 (Admin) [2008] LGR 331 (participation in mutual insurance company ultra vires the Local Government Act 1972); *R (Looe Fuels Ltd) v Looe Harbour Commissioners* [2007] EWHC 1141 (Admin) (Harbour Commissioners having no power to buy and sell fuel for harbour-using vessels).

(F) WHETHER DECISION INCOMPATIBLE WITH RULE. *R (D) v Secretary of State for the Home Department* [2006] EWHC 980 (Admin) (breach of Detention Centre Rules in failing to conduct medical examination within 24 hours); *R v Oxford Regional Mental Health Review Tribunal, ex p Secretary of State for the Home Department* [1988] AC 120 (discharge breaching MHRT rules); *R v Immigration Appeal Tribunal, ex p Singh (Bakhtaur)* [1986] 1 WLR 910 (misinterpretation of immigration rules as to relevant circumstances); *R v Board of Visitors of Dartmoor Prison, ex p Smith* [1987] QB 106 (decision incompatible with Prison Rules).

46.1.3 Incompatibility with a related statute. *Apple Fields Ltd v New Zealand Apple & Pear Marketing Board* [1991] 1 AC 344 (levy imposed under fruit marketing statute a breach of the competition guarantee in commerce legislation); *R v Secretary of State for Social Security, ex p Joint Council for the Welfare of Immigrants* [1997] 1 WLR 275 (whether regulations inconsistent with rights reflected in subsequent Act), 293E (Waite LJ: "Subsidiary legislation must not only be within the vires of the enabling statute but must also be drawn as not to conflict with statutory rights already enacted by other primary legislation").

46.1.4 Uncertainty as ultra vires. *R (L) v Secretary of State for the Home Department* [2003] EWCA Civ 25 [2003] 1 WLR 1230 at [17] ("legal certainty is an aspect of the rule of law"), [25] ("It is an aspect of the rule of law that individuals and those advising them, since they will be presumed to know the law, should have access to it in authentic form"); *Percy v Hall* [1997] QB 924, 941c (Simon Brown LJ, asking whether byelaw "so uncertain in its language as to have no ascertainable meaning, or so unclear in its effect as to be incapable of certain application in any case"); *R v Director General of Telecommunications, ex p British Telecommunications Plc* 20th December 1996 unrep. (although licence condition involving some uncertainty, not so unclear as to be void); *R v Bristol City Council, ex p Anderson* (2000) 79 P & CR 358, 360 (planning condition only void for uncertainty if words can be given no sensible meaning); <55.1.19> (uncertainty); <12.1.12> (the rule of law and certainty); *McEldowney v Forde* [1971] AC 632, 643F (whether regulation "too vague and so arbitrary" to be "a legitimate and valid exercise of the Minister's power [conferred] on him by statute"); <57.3.4> (uncertainty as unreasonableness).

46.1.5 Delay as ultra vires/breach of statutory duty. *Lafarge Redland Aggregates Ltd v Scottish Ministers* [2000] 4 PLR 151 (serious delay in determining planning matter constituting a breach of statutory duty); *R v Gloucestershire County Council, ex p P* [1994] ELR 334, 337F (whether delay constituted a breach of statutory duty and/or was unreasonable); *R v Chief Constable of Northumbria Police, ex p Charlton* The Times 6th May 1994 (having certified the claimant as permanently disabled, no power to delay his retirement); *R v Secretary of State for Social Security, ex p Sutherland* [1997] COD 222 (no power to amend regulation so as to) withhold benefit pending appeal in related case); <59.5.11> (HRA:ECHR Art 6 right to a hearing "within a reasonable time").

46.1.6 Procedural ultra vires. <60.4>.

46.1.7 Criminality as ultra vires. *R (Smeaton) v Secretary of State for Health* [2002] EWHC 886 (Admin) [2002] 2 FLR 146 at [67] (order would be ultra vires if purporting to permit a criminal offence, because "Parliament is assumed not to have intended that statutory powers should be used to facilitate the commission of criminal offences").

46.1.8 **Whether ultra vires the sole underpinning for review grounds.** <45.2.1> (ultra vires as a sole underpinning: the academic debate); <45.4.2> (all grounds as ultra vires/unlawfulness).

46.2 Rights-violation as ultra vires: the principle of legality Prior to the Human Rights Act there had evolved the principle of legality. It operated so that general powers, however widely drawn, were construed as not permitting a breach of fundamental rights. This internal inhibition is the common law analogue to s.3 of the HRA. Under the currently perceived constitution, the principle is said to allow rights violations in cases of plain statutory words or necessary implication.

46.2.1 **The principle of legality.** <7.3>; *R v Secretary of State for the Home Department, ex p Pierson* [1998] AC 539, 575D (Lord Browne-Wilkinson: "A power conferred by Parliament in general terms is not to be taken to authorise the doing of acts by the donee of the power which adversely affect the legal rights of the citizen or the basic principles on which the law of the United Kingdom is based unless the statute conferring the power makes it clear that such was the intention of Parliament"); *R v Governor of Frankland Prison, ex p Russell* [2000] 1 WLR 2027 at [11] ("in the absence of express words or necessary implications to the contrary, even the most general words in an Act of Parliament and in subordinate legislation must be presumed to be intended to be subject to the basic rights of the individual"; also "Where the question arises as to [the] extent to which a power is impliedly conferred by statute to interfere with fundamental rights, there must be established a self-evident and pressing need for that power and the interference must be the minimum necessary to fulfil that need"); *R v Secretary of State for the Home Department, ex p Simms* [2000] 2 AC 115, 130D-G (Lord Steyn), 131E-G (Lord Hoffmann, referring to "Parliamentary sovereignty means that Parliament can, if it chooses, legislate contrary to fundamental principles of human rights. The Human Rights Act 1998 will not detract from this power. The constraints upon its exercise by Parliament are ultimately political, not legal. But the principle of legality means that Parliament must squarely confront what it is doing and accept the political cost. Fundamental rights cannot be overridden by general or ambiguous words... In the absence of express language or necessary implication to the contrary, the courts therefore presume that even the most general words were intended to be subject to the basic rights of the individual. In this way the courts of the United Kingdom, though acknowledging the sovereignty of Parliament, apply principles of constitutionality little different from those which exist in countries where the power of the legislature is expressly limited by a constitutional document").

46.2.2 **The principle of legality in action.**[3] *Raymond v Honey* [1983] 1 AC 1 (prison rules and standing orders ultra vires the Prison Act, insofar as fettering prisoner's right to communicate by letter with solicitor and the court); *R v Secretary of State for the Home Department, ex p Anderson* [1984] QB 778 (standing orders ultra vires since preventing access to legal advice in context of internal complaint); *R v Secretary of State for the Home Department, ex p Leech* [1994] QB 198 (prison rule enabling governor to read legal correspondence, ultra vires given incompatibility with right of access to the Court); *R v Lord Chancellor, ex p Witham* [1998] QB 575[4] (court fees Order ultra vires insofar as interfering with constitutional right of access to the Courts); *R v Secretary of State for Social Security, ex p Joint Council for the Welfare of Immigrants* [1997] 1 WLR 275 (asylum benefit-removing regulations ultra vires as incompatible

---

[3] Daniel Beard [1997] JR 166.

[4] Thomas Poole [2000] JR 33.

with basic humanity); 292B-F; *R v Secretary of State for the Home Department, ex p Pierson* [1998] AC 539 (whether decision unlawful as contrary to fundamental right against retrospective increase of penal sanction); *R v Secretary of State for the Home Department, ex p Simms* [2000] 2 AC 115, 130C (insofar as standing orders to be construed as permitting restriction with freedom of expression, ultra vires under the principle in *Leech* because no pressing social need); *R v Secretary of State for the Home Department, ex p Q* [2000] UKHRR 386, 398F-399F (applying *Witham* in the context of discretionary decisions, as to whether to move a prisoner, said to threaten the right to a fair trial); *General Mediterranean Holdings SA v Patel* [2000] 1 WLR 272 (general words delegating a power to legislate not sufficient to encroach fundamental right of legal professional privilege); *R v Immigration Appeal Tribunal, ex p Saleem* [2000] Imm AR 814 (immigration rule ultra vires because enabling Act not to be construed as impliedly authorising a rule interfering with fundamental right of access to immigration tribunals); *R v Secretary of State for the Home Department, ex p Daly* [2001] UKHL 26 [2001] 2 AC 532 (blanket policy of searching prisoners' legal correspondence in their absence ultra vires by reference to the common law principle of legality); *R (Morgan Grenfell & Co Ltd) v Inland Revenue Commissioners* [2002] UKHL 21 [2003] 1 AC 563 (Revenue notice requiring the bank to disclose Counsel's instructions and advice ultra vires, given violation of fundamental human right of legal professional privilege) at [8], [44].

46.2.3 Principle of legality as common law proportionality. *A v Secretary of State for the Home Department* [2004] EWCA Civ 1123 at [233]-[234] (Laws LJ: "The principle is in essence that of proportionality, which the common law has made its own. It is that the courts will expect the legislature to interfere with fundamental constitutional rights to the minimum extent necessary to fulfil the State's duty to safeguard its citizens and its own integrity. If it is perceived that that is not done, the courts will tend to confine and restrict the legislation's interference with constitutional rights, so far as they may do so consistently with Parliament's ultimate legislative supremacy") (HL is [2005] UKHL 71 [2006] 2 AC 221).

46.2.4 Whether the principle of legality yields to "necessary implication". *R v Lord Chancellor, ex p Lightfoot* [2000] QB 597 (necessary implication sufficient to override any fundamental right; identifying irresistible inference from legislative history); *R (Morgan Grenfell & Co Ltd) v Inland Revenue Commissioners* [2002] UKHL 21 [2003] 1 AC 563 (necessary implication treated as sufficient); *R v Secretary of State for the Home Department, ex p Pierson* [1998] AC 539, 575B-C (querying whether necessary implication would suffice); *R (Bancoult) v Secretary of State for the Foreign and Commonwealth Office* [2001] QB 1067 at [38] (referring to this as involving "some controversy"); <7.1.4> (necessary implication).

46.2.5 The broader potential of "the principle of legality". <7.3.2>.

46.3 Interpretation to allow validity: reading down/in Deciding whether one measure is compatible with a prior (superior) measure involves interpreting both. The Court may strive to uphold as valid the inferior measure by interpreting it in a particular way, to secure compatibility with the superior measure properly interpreted. It is like trimming the spread of the impugned measure, to fit the legal shadow cast by the superior source of law.

46.3.1 Meaning and validity: the choice. *R v Secretary of State for the Home Department, ex p Anderson* [1984] QB 778, 790H-791A (since Prison Rules clashing with basic constitutional right, they "must either be interpreted accordingly ... or ... regarded as ultra vires"); *Raymond v Honey* [1983] 1 AC 1, 13B (Lord Wilberforce: interpretation of rules narrow, so rules valid but decision under rules ultra vires); *R v Secretary of State for the Home Department, ex p Simms* [2000] 2 AC 115, 130C-G (although prison standing orders unambiguously allowing restriction of freedom of expression, on which basis would be ultra vires as inconsistent with fundamental rights, construed narrowly in accordance with the principle of legality); *McEldowney v Forde* [1971] AC 632 (majority in HL identifying a narrow meaning and so a valid measure; minority identifying a wide meaning and therefore an invalid measure).

46.3.2 **Construction to allow validity.** *R (Amicus - MSF Section) v Secretary of State for Trade and Industry* [2004] EWHC 860 (Admin) [2004] ELR 311 at [59] (in challenge to regulations as being incompatible with EC Directive, court "should construe the Regulations purposively so as to conform so far as possible with the Directive", applying *Pickstone v Freemans Plc* [1989] AC 66 and *Litster v Forth Dry Dock & Engineering Co Ltd* [1990] 1 AC 546); *DPP v Hutchinson* [1990] 2 AC 783, 818H (Lord Lowry: "when construing legislation the validity of which is under challenge, the first duty of the court, in obedience to the principle that a law should, whenever possible, be interpreted ut res magis valeat quam pereat, is to see whether the impugned provision can reasonably bear a construction which renders it valid"); *McEldowney v Forde* [1971] AC 632, 657G (Lord Pearson: "it should if possible be so construed as to have sufficient certainty to be valid - ut res magis valeat quam pereat"); *R v Croydon Crown Court, ex p Lewis* The Times 29th March 1994 (in deciding their meaning, Regulations to be construed so as not to be ultra vires the enabling Act); cf. *Roodal v The State* [2003] UKPC 78 [2005] 1 AC 328 at [26] ("the first stage is to determine whether [the statute] ... can be modified ... by reading down, reading in, or severance, so as to render the words of the statute in conformity with the Constitution").

46.3.3 **Reading down.** *R v Keogh* [2007] EWCA Crim 528 [2007] 1 WLR 1500 at [33] (reverse burden of proof read down under HRA s.3); *R v Secretary of State for the Home Department, ex p Simms* [2000] 2 AC 115, 130C-G (prison standing orders construed narrowly in accordance with the principle of legality); *R v Institute of Chartered Accountants of England and Wales, ex p Taher Nawaz* [1997] COD 111 (Sedley J) and 25th April 1997 unrep. (CA) (permissible for byelaw to be substantially severed/ `read down'); *R (McCormick) v Liverpool City Magistrates' Court* [2001] 2 All ER 705 at [60] (no need to strike down regulation since capable of taking effect lawfully, by proper construction); *Director of Public Prosecutions v Mollison (No.2)* [2003] UKPC 6 [2003] 2 AC 411 at [17] (PC substituting "the Court's pleasure" for "Her Majesty's pleasure" in Jamaican statute to ensure constitutional compatibility).

46.3.4 **Reading in.** *Elloy De Freitas v Permanent Secretary of Ministry of Agriculture Fisheries Lands and Housing* [1999] AC 69, 77H ("it may be justifiable on occasion to imply words into a statute where there is an ambiguity or an omission and the implied words are necessary to remedy such a defect").

46.3.5 **HRA s.3 as a form of reading down/reading in.** <9.3> (the HRA s.3 rule of interpretation); *R v A (No.2)* [2001] UKHL 25 [2002] 1 AC 45 at [25] (referring to the argument that the statute be "read down ... in accordance with section 3 of the Human Rights Act 1998 [to] be given effect in a way that was compatible with [the ECHR]"), [44] ("The techniques to be used will not only involve the reading down of express language in a statute but also the implication of provisions"); *R v Lambert* [2001] UKHL 37 [2002] 2 AC 545 at [81] (may be necessary under s.3 to "read down" or "read in"); *Sheldrake v Director of Public Prosecutions* [2004] UKHL 43 [2005] 1 AC 264 (s.3 reading down of legal reverse burden as evidential only); *Bellinger v Bellinger* [2003] UKHL 21 [2003] 2 AC 467 at [78] (Lord Hobhouse); *Rushbridger v HM Attorney-General* [2003] UKHL 38 [2004] 1 AC 357 at [40] (Lord Scott: "the section would now be `read down' as required by section 3 of the HRA"); *Attorney General's Reference (No.1 of 2004)* [2004] EWCA Crim 1025 [2004] 1 WLR 2111 at [51] (CA describing HRA s.3 as "reading down", as where legal reverse-burden needing to be read as evidential burden so as to ensure Art 6-compatibility).

46.3.6 Partial validity: severance and other techniques. <P43> (severance); <43.1.7> (other similar techniques).

> **P47 Jurisdictional error.** A body must understand
> the scope and limits of its jurisdiction.

47.1 Jurisdiction/jurisdictional error as a flexi-principle
47.2 Jurisdictional error as hard-edged review (correctness)
47.3 Error of law and jurisdictional error

47.1 Jurisdiction/jurisdictional error as a flexi-principle. The elusive terms "jurisdiction" and "jurisdictional error" can be used in different ways, in particular to mean: (1) ultra vires (acting without power); (2) an aspect of unlawfulness (misperceiving the limits of power); or (3) a vitiating legal flaw (producing a "nullity"). The continuing utility of "jurisdictional error" is questionable given the potential for confusion and since other tools exist for doing all these jobs.

47.1.1 **Jurisdiction: shades of meaning.** *In re McC (A Minor)* [1985] AC 528, 536B-C (Lord Bridge: "There are many words in common usage in the law which have no precise or constant meaning. But few, I think, have been used with so many different shades of meaning in different contexts or have so freely acquired new meanings with the development of the law as the word jurisdiction"); *R v Manchester City Magistrates' Court, ex p Davies* [1989] QB 631, 648D-E (Sir Roger Ormrod, describing "jurisdiction" as "a notoriously difficult word to construe ... often used by lawyers as a synonym for `power'"); *Anisminic Ltd v Foreign Compensation Commission* [1969] 2 AC 147, 207A and 208E (Lord Wilberforce, favouring "non technical terms, avoiding for the moment such words as `jurisdiction', `error' and `nullity' which create many problems", rather than "strained distinctions between facts which the tribunal might legitimately find and others (called `jurisdictional') which it might not"); *R v Bedwellty Justices, ex p Williams* [1997] AC 225, 232E ("`jurisdiction' ... is a term used in a number of different senses, and possibly its popularity and convenience are partly due to its very ambiguity"); *Neill v North Antrim Magistrates' Court* [1992] 1 WLR 1220, 1233C-D (querying "what if anything remains" of "the distinction between the assumption of a jurisdiction which does not exist and an error in the exercise of a jurisdiction which does exist").

47.1.2 **Jurisdictional error: wide meaning.** <47.1.2>; <47.3.2> (the language of *Anisminic*: wide sense of jurisdictional error); *In re McC (A Minor)* [1985] AC 528, 542F-G (referring to *Anisminic* and "the extended concept of acting without jurisdiction or in excess of jurisdiction which that landmark decision of your Lordships' House introduced"); *R v Governor of Pentonville Prison, ex p Sotiriadis* [1975] AC 1, 30D-F ("in extradition cases, the courts have assimilated such an error of law to acting in excess of jurisdiction").

47.1.3 **Jurisdictional error: narrow meaning.** *R (Strickson) v Preston County Court* [2007] EWCA Civ 1132 at [26] (Laws LJ, describing the "narrower pre-*Anisminic* sense of jurisdiction" as referring to the decision-maker's "right to embark upon the question in hand at all: what might be called the condition precedent for its having any jurisdiction in the matter"), [32] ("where the court embarks upon an enquiry which it lacks all power to deal with, or fails altogether to enquire or adjudicate upon a matter which it was its unequivocal duty to address"); *Anisminic Ltd v Foreign Compensation Commission* [1969] 2 AC 147, 171B-C ("the narrow and original sense of the tribunal being entitled to enter on the inquiry in question"); *R v Hull University Visitor, ex p Page* [1993] AC 682, 704F (referring to a decision "within" or "outside" the Visitor's jurisdiction "in the narrow sense"); *In re McC (A Minor)* [1985] AC 528 (magistrates' statutory liability in damages restricted to jurisdictional error in narrow sense), 546G-H (Lord Bridge); *Chen v Government of Romania* [2007] EWHC 520 (Admin) [2008] 1 All ER 851 at [62]-[63] (acting beyond the question which had been remitted); *Lesotho Highlands Development Authority v Impregilo SpA* [2005] UKHL 43 [2006] 1 AC 221 (error of law by arbitrator not "an excess of power" triggering statutory entitlement to have award quashed by court); <32.2.10(A)> (judicial review of county court decisions on permission to appeal); <48.2> (error of law: restricted categories).

47.1.4 **Jurisdiction: particular aspects of unlawfulness.**
(A) WRONGLY ASSERTING/EXERCISING JURISDICTION. *R (Britannic Asset Management Ltd) v Pensions Ombudsman* [2002] EWCA Civ 1405 [2002] 4 All ER 860 (pensions ombudsman wrong to treat claimant as administrators of pensions scheme and so to hear a complaint against them); *Baldock v Webster* [2005] EWCA Civ 1869 [2006] QB 315 (whether to set aside order of recorder unknowingly hearing High Court matter without being duly authorised); *R v Secretary of State for Health, ex p Barratt* [1994] COD 406 (erroneous decision that jurisdiction to entertain appeal by father purporting to act on behalf of non-consenting daughter who had reached 18); *R v Broadcasting Complaints Commission, ex p British Broadcasting Corporation* (1994) 6 Admin LR 714, 724C (erroneous conclusion that jurisdiction to entertain researcher's complaint).
(B) WRONGLY DECLINING JURISDICTION. *R (Gashi) v Chief Immigration Adjudicator* The Times 12th November 2001 (erroneous refusal to entertain a review of a special adjudicator's asylum decision, following provision of a non-competent interpreter); *R v Dorking Justices, ex p Harrington* [1984] AC 743, 753B-754A ("the duty of adjudging was declined"; "they were declining to adjudicate upon a matter upon which it was their duty to adjudicate and thus was a nullity"); *In re Wilson* [1985] AC 750 (refusing to hear application for variation); *R v Comptroller-General of Patents Designs & Trade Marks, ex p Gist-Brocades* [1986] 1 WLR 51 (refusing to entertain prospective application); <24.4.5(D)> (mandatory order and wrongly declining jurisdiction).
(C) CONDITIONS PRECEDENT TO JURISDICTION. *Anisminic Ltd v Foreign Compensation Commission* [1969] 2 AC 147, 195B-C (Lord Pearce: "Lack of jurisdiction may arise in various ways. There may be an absence of those formalities or things which are conditions precedent to the tribunal having any jurisdiction to embark on an inquiry"); *R v Manchester Stipendiary Magistrate, ex p Hill* [1983] 1 AC 328, 344C and 345E ("it is the laying of an information ... which is the foundation of the magistrates' court's jurisdiction to try an information summarily"; a "condition precedent"); *In re McC (A Minor)* [1985] AC 528, 546D-E and 552D ("statutory condition precedent"); *R v Horseferry Road Magistrates' Court, ex p Bennett* [1994] 1 AC 42, 80G-81A ("a condition precedent to jurisdiction was omitted"); *R v Manchester City Magistrates' Court, ex p Davies* [1989] QB 631 (means inquiry a condition precedent to committal of ratepayer to prison); *R v Southampton Crown Court, ex p Roddie* [1991] 1 WLR 303 (whether prosecution had acted with "all due expedition" a condition precedent to be viewed objectively).
(D) LACKING THE REQUISITE STATUS/AUTHORITY. *Kanda v Government of Malaya* [1962] AC 322 (Commissioner lacking requisite status); *R v Central Criminal Court, ex p Francis & Francis* [1989] AC 346, 368D-F and 382B (recorder lacking status to make order); *Anisminic Ltd v Foreign Compensation Commission* [1969] 2 AC 147, 170B-C (describing the situation where statute "provides that a certain order may be made by a person who holds a specified qualification or appointment"); *R (Queen Mary University of London) v Higher Education Funding Council for England* [2008] EWHC 1472 (Admin) at [39] (decision taken by person not authorised to do so).
(E) IMPROPER DELEGATION MEANS LACK OF JURISDICTION. *Vine v National Dock Labour Board* [1957] AC 488, 510 ("action taken by a delegated authority when there was no power to delegate [goes] to the root of the jurisdiction"); *Barnard v National Dock Labour Board* [1953] 2 QB 18, 38 ("The local board had no jurisdiction to delegate; the port manager had no jurisdiction to adjudicate; each purported so to do").

(F) BODY BECOMING FUNCTUS OFFICIO.[5] *R v Parliamentary Commissioner for Administration, ex p Dyer* [1994] 1 WLR 621, 629F (Parliamentary Ombudsman "clearly correct" that having reported to the MP in question "he was functus officio and unable to re-open the investigation without a further referral"); *R v Dorset Police Authority, ex p Vaughan* [1995] COD 153 (no power to reconsider decision which Regulations stated was "final"); *R v Parole Board, ex p Robinson* 29th July 1999 unrep. (Discretionary Lifer Panel functus having decided to direct release of prisoner); *Aparau v Iceland Frozen Foods Plc* [2000] 1 All ER 228, 235j-236a (industrial tribunal, like any other, exhausted its jurisdiction having delivered a final dispositive decision, subject only to the limited power of review under the statutory framework).

47.1.5 **"Jurisdiction" and general grounds for intervention.** *Neill v North Antrim Magistrates' Court* [1992] 1 WLR 1220, 1233C (no judicial review for "a mistake within their jurisdiction"); *Ridge v Baldwin* [1964] AC 40, 136 (distinguishing between "a want of jurisdiction as opposed to a failure to follow a procedural requirement"); *In re A Company* [1981] AC 374, 382G-H (*Anisminic* "a legal landmark; it has made possible the rapid development in England of a rational and comprehensive system of administrative law on the foundation of the concept of ultra vires"); <47.3> (error of law as jurisdictional error); *Anisminic Ltd v Foreign Compensation Commission* [1969] 2 AC 147, 198F-G ("an inferior tribunal which properly embarks on an inquiry may go outside its jurisdiction if, in the course of that inquiry, it rejects a consideration which it was told to have in mind"); *In re McC (A Minor)* [1985] AC 528, 546H-547B (magistrates "would, of course, be acting `without jurisdiction or in excess of jurisdiction' ... if, in the course of hearing a case within their jurisdiction they were guilty of some gross and obvious irregularity of procedure"); *R v Diggines, ex p Rahmani* [1985] QB 1109 (CA) (decision made contrary to rules of natural justice outside tribunal's jurisdiction); *Attorney-General v Ryan* [1980] AC 718, 730E ("It has long been settled law that a decision affecting the legal rights of an individual which is arrived at by a procedure which offends against the principles of natural justice is outside the jurisdiction of the decision-making authority"); <44.2.3(D)> (procedural unfairness as nullity); *R v Governor of Brixton Prison, ex p Armah* [1968] AC 192, 237G-238A (concept of jurisdiction capable of extending "to include inquiry as to whether there was any evidence to warrant a decision. This may have involved giving a somewhat extended or liberal interpretation to the concept of jurisdiction"); <49.1> (precedent fact).

47.1.6 **Jurisdiction: other uses.** <28.1.9> (nullity/ jurisdictional error and ouster); *In re McC (A Minor)* [1985] AC 528 (statutory liability of magistrates in damages); <32.1.5(A)> (reviewability of crown court).

47.2 Jurisdictional error as hard-edged review (correctness)

One use of "jurisdictional" has been to identify a hard-edged question which is reviewable by applying a correctness standard. The idea is that a question (whether fact or law) as to where the body's legal boundary ("jurisdiction") lies cannot be determined by itself but must be delineated by the Court.

47.2.1 **Public body cannot decide its own limits.** *R v Shoreditch Assessment Committee, ex p Morgan* [1910] 2 KB 859, 880 (Farwell LJ: "No tribunal of inferior jurisdiction can by its own decision finally decide on the question of the existence or extent of such jurisdiction: such question is always subject to review by the High Court, which does not permit the inferior tribunal either to usurp a jurisdiction which it does not possess, whether at all or to the extent

---

[5] Ben Collins [2001] JR 61.

claimed, or to refuse to exercise a jurisdiction which it has and ought to exercise"), cited in *Anisminic Ltd v Foreign Compensation Commission* [1969] 2 AC 147, 197E & 209A; *R v Northern & Yorks Regional Health Authority, ex p Trivedi* [1995] 1 WLR 961, 974A ("The jurisdiction of the appeal unit ... is statutory and cannot be extended by agreement"); cf. *Tan Te Lam v Superintendent of Tai A Chau Detention Centre* [1997] AC 97, 113G ("Their Lordships do not exclude the possibility that, by clear words, the legislature can confer power on the executive to determine its own jurisdiction").

47.2.2 **Body must identify its boundaries correctly.** *Anisminic Ltd v Foreign Compensation Commission* [1969] 2 AC 147, 174B-D ("It cannot be for the commission to determine the limits of its powers. Of course if one party submits to a tribunal that its powers are wider than in fact they are, then the tribunal must deal with that submission. But if they reach a wrong conclusion as to the width of their powers, the court must be able to correct that - not because the tribunal has made an error of law, but because as a result of making an error of law they have dealt with and based their decision on a matter with which, on a true construction of their powers, they had no right to deal"); *R v Fulham, Hammersmith & Kensington Rent Tribunal, ex p Zerek* [1951] 2 KB 1, 10; *R v Croydon & South West London Rent Tribunal, ex p Ryzewska* [1977] QB 876; *R v Croydon & South West London Rent Tribunal, ex p Ryzewska* [1977] QB 876, 879F-G, 881B-C; *R v Kensington & Chelsea (Royal) London Borough Rent Officer, ex p Noel* [1978] QB 1, 6C-D, 9A-B; *R v City of Liverpool Justices, ex p Knibb and Others* [1991] COD 53.

47.2.3 **Jurisdiction and two-tiered review.** <16.6.4> (two-tiered review); *Anisminic Ltd v Foreign Compensation Commission* [1969] 2 AC 147, 210D-E (recognising the need to "distinguish between doing something which is not in the tribunal's area and doing something wrong within that area - a crucial distinction which the court has to make"); *R v Governor of Brixton Prison, ex p Schtraks* [1964] AC 556, 585-586; *Holgate-Mohammed v Duke* [1984] AC 437; *White & Collins v Minister of Health* [1939] 2 KB 838.

47.2.4 **Precedent fact.** <49.1>.

47.3 **Error of law and jurisdictional error.**The orthodoxy once was that an error of law needed to be "jurisdictional" (or else on the face of the record) to be correctable. After *Anisminic*, any error of law is correctable. Not because such an error is, but because it no longer needs to be, "jurisdictional".

47.3.1 **Pre-*Anisminic*.** *R v Northumberland Compensation Appeal Tribunal, ex p Shaw* [1952] 1 KB 338, 346 (Denning LJ: "the Court of King's Bench can intervene to prevent a statutory tribunal from exceeding the jurisdiction which Parliament has conferred on it; but it is quite another thing to say that the King's Bench can intervene when a tribunal makes a mistake of law. A tribunal may often decide a point of law wrongly whilst keeping well within its jurisdiction"); *R v Governor of Brixton Prison, ex p Armah* [1968] AC 192, 234 ("If a magistrate or any other tribunal has jurisdiction to enter on the inquiry and to decide a particular issue, and there is no irregularity in the procedure, he does not destroy his jurisdiction by reaching a wrong decision. If he has jurisdiction to go right he has jurisdiction to go wrong. Neither an error in fact nor an error in law will destroy his jurisdiction"); <48.2.4> (error of law on the face of the record); *Anisminic Ltd v Foreign Compensation Commission* [1969] 2 AC 147, 199D-E (discussing "the difficult question of how far, if at all, the court could take cognisance of an error that was not manifest on the record. That problem did not arise in cases of excess or lack of jurisdiction since there the court for obvious reasons did not confine itself to the record. It looked into all relevant circumstances to see whether jurisdiction did or did not exist").

47.3.2 *Anisminic*. *Anisminic Ltd v Foreign Compensation Commission* [1969] 2 AC 147, 174A-D (Lord Reid: "the commission made an inquiry which the Order did not empower them to make, and they based their decision on a matter which they had no right to take into account. If one uses the word `jurisdiction' in its wider sense, they went beyond their jurisdiction in considering this matter ... It cannot be for the commission to determine the limits of its powers"; "if they reach a wrong conclusion as to the width of their powers, the court must be able to correct that - not because the tribunal has made an error of law, but because as a result of making an error of law they have dealt with and based their decision on a matter with which, on a true construction of their powers, they had no right to deal"); <44.2.2>.

47.3.3 **Interpreting *Anisminic*: error of law suffices.** *O'Reilly v Mackman* [1983] 2 AC 237, 283E-F (Lord Diplock: "the full consequences of the *Anisminic* case, in introducing the concept that if a statutory decision-making authority asks itself the wrong question it acts without jurisdiction, have been virtually to abolish the distinction between errors within jurisdiction that rendered voidable a decision that remained valid until quashed, and errors that went to jurisdiction and rendered a decision void ab initio provided that its validity was challenged timeously in the High Court by an appropriate procedure"); *In re A Company* [1981] AC 374, 383C (Lord Diplock: "The break-through made by *Anisminic* [1969] 2 AC 147 was that, as respects administrative tribunals and authorities, the old distinction between errors of law that went to jurisdiction and errors of law that did not, was for practical purposes abolished"); *Palacegate Properties Ltd v Camden London Borough Council* [2000] 4 PLR 59, 78B (effect of *Anisminic* is: "Any distinction between errors of law within and without jurisdiction has been abolished for the purpose of ascertaining and confining the limits of the legal powers enjoyed by public authorities, so that a decision of such an authority may fall to be quashed by judicial review for any error of law"); <P48> (error of law); <32.2.10(A)> (judicial review of county court decisions on permission to appeal).

48.1 Error of law/misdirection in law
48.2 Error of law: restricted categories

48.1 Error of law/misdirection in law. The judicial review Court will correct mistakes of law. Questions of judgment, discretion, policy and fact are primarily for the public body to decide, but questions of law are for redetermination by the reviewing Court, falling within its expertise. That promotes lawfulness and consistency. One challenge is characterising what is a question of "law", which is itself a matter decided by the reviewing Court.

48.1.1 Judicial review for error of law. *R (Q) v Secretary of State for the Home Department* [2003] EWCA Civ 364 [2004] QB 36 at [112] ("courts of judicial review have been competent since the decision in *Anisminic* [1969] 2 AC 147 to correct any error of law whether or not it goes to jurisdiction; and since the coming into effect of the Human Rights Act 1998, errors of law have included failures by the state to act compatibly with the Convention"); *Council of Civil Service Unions v Minister for the Civil Service* [1985] AC 374, 410F ("the decision-maker must understand correctly the law that regulates his decision-making power and must give effect to it. Whether he has or not is par excellence a justiciable question to be decided, in the event of dispute, by those persons, the judges, by whom the judicial power of the state is exercisable").

48.1.2 Questions of law as hard-edged questions. <16.3>.

48.1.3 The fact/law distinction. <13.2.2>.

48.1.4 The meaning of "ordinary words": whether a question of law. *Cozens v Brutus* [1973] AC 854, 861 ("The meaning of an ordinary word of the English language is not a question of law. The proper construction of a statute is a question of law"); *Moyna v Secretary of State for Work and Pensions* [2003] UKHL 44 [2003] 1 WLR 1929 at [24] (Lord Hoffmann, explaining *Cozens v Brutus*: "The meaning of an English word is not a question of law because it does not in itself have any legal significance. It is the meaning to be ascribed to the intention of the notional legislator in using that word which is a statement of law. It is because of the nature of language that, in trying to ascertain the legislator's meaning, it is seldom helpful to make additions or substitutions in the actual language he has used"), [25] ("the question of whether the facts as found or admitted fall one side or the other of some conceptual line drawn by the law is a question of fact"), [27] ("it may be said that there are two kinds of questions of fact: there are questions of fact; and there are questions of law as to which lawyers have decided that it would be inexpedient for an appellate tribunal to have to form an independent judgment"; "the degree to which an appellate court will be willing to substitute its own judgment ... will vary with the nature of the question"); *R (Cherwell District Council) v First Secretary of State* [2004] EWCA Civ 1420 [2005] 1 WLR 1128 at [57] (applying *Moyna*), *Pabari v Secretary of State for Work and Pensions* [2004] EWCA Civ 1480 [2005] 1 All ER 287 at [32] (applying *Moyna*); *R v Barnet London Borough Council, ex p Nilish Shah* [1983] 2 AC 309, 341A-C ("the meaning to be attributed to enacted words is a question of law"); *R v Radio Authority, ex p Bull* [1998] QB 294, 304E ("Words can take their meaning from their context... The courts exercising their supervisory jurisdiction have the responsibility for providing guidance where it is practical to do so"); *R (Goodman) v London Borough of Lewisham* [2003] EWCA Civ 140 [2003] Env LR 644 at [8] (a determination, "however fact-sensitive", "is not simply a finding of fact, nor of discretionary judgment", but: "Rather, it involves the application of the authority's understanding of the meaning in law of the expression used in the Regulation. If the authority reaches an understanding of those expressions that is wrong as a matter of law, then the court must correct that error: and in determining the meaning of the statutory expressions the concept of reasonable judgement as embodied in *Wednesbury* simply has no part to play").

48.1.5 Misdirection in law/error of law. *R v Barnet London Borough Council, ex p Nilish Shah* [1983] 2 AC 309, 350D ("an administrative or executive authority entrusted with the exercise of a discretion must direct itself properly in law"); *R (N) v Lambeth London Borough Council* [2006] EWHC 3427 (Admin) (failure to ask the right question); *R (Donnachie) v Cardiff Magistrates Court* [2007] EWHC 1846 (Admin) [2007] 1 WLR 3085 (error of law in concluding prosecutions not time-barred); *R (M) v Suffolk County Council* [2006] EWHC 2366 (Admin) [2007] ELR 158 (error of law as to whether care plan costs precluded); *R (Paul) v Coroner of the Queen's Household* [2007] EWHC 408 (Admin) [2008] QB 172 at [40] (error of law in not summoning inquest jury); *R (Hampstead Heath Winter Swimming Club) v Corporation of London* [2005] EWHC 713 (Admin) [2005] 1 WLR 2930 (error of law as to own liability to prosecution); *R (A) v Secretary of State for the Home Department* [2002] EWHC 1618 (Admin) [2003] 1 WLR 330 at [49] (policy based on error of law); <39.2.1> (duty to understand the nature of the power); <48.1.6> (material misdirection); *R v Canterbury City Council, ex p Springimage Ltd* [1993] 3 PLR 58 (planning committee misled by misdirection in law by director of planning); *R (Bodycote HIP Ltd) V HM Coroner for Herefordshire* [2008] EWHC 164 (Admin) (coroner's misdirection of jury); <8.3.3> (misdirection as to EC law); <6.2.8(B)> (misdirection as to policy guidance); *R (Sullivan) v Warwick District Council* [2003] EWHC 606 (Admin) [2003] 2 PLR 56 (misdirection by statutory consultee vitiating its advice, but remedy declined because same decision would have been reached anyway); <60.6.9> (error of approach by consultee/adviser).

48.1.6 Need[6] for material error of law/material misdirection.[7] *R v Hull University Visitor, ex p Page* [1993] AC 682, 702C-D (need for "an error in the actual making of the decision which affected the decision itself ... what must be shown is a relevant error of law, ie., an error in the actual making of the decision which affected the decision itself"), applied in *R v Governor of Brixton Prison, ex p Levin* [1997] AC 741, 749A; *R (British Board of Film Classification) v Video Appeals Committee* [2008] EWHC 203 (Admin) [2008] 1 WLR 1658 at [27] (court not able to be "confident" that committee had not "allowed itself to be influenced by its erroneous self-directions"); *R v Wolverhampton Coroner, ex p McCurbin* [1990] 1 WLR 719, 730H-731A ("the misdirection has not affected the outcome in any way"); *R (Gillan) v Winchester Crown Court* [2007] EWHC 380 (Admin) [2007] 1 WLR 2214 at [31] (error of law but decision correct); *Kalra v Secretary of State for the Environment* [1996] 1 PLR 37, 45A (whether it can "be safely said that the inspector would inevitably have reached the same decision if she had correctly directed herself in law"); *R v King's Lynn Justices, ex p Holland* [1993] 1 WLR 324, 328E (decision would have been the same); *Doughty v General Dental Council* [1988] AC 164, 171F-G ("satisfied that the misdirection ... neither prejudiced the [appellant] nor caused any miscarriage of justice"); *R v Boundary Commission for England, ex p Foot* [1983] QB 600, 646D-F ("no sufficient grounds for thinking that ... this misdirection in the event affected his ultimate conclusion in any way"); *R v Vale of Glamorgan Borough Council, ex p James* [1996] Env LR 102, 115-116 (asking whether decision would inevitably have been the same despite alleged misdirection); *R v Broadcasting Complaints Commission, ex p Owen* [1985] QB 1153, 1177B <4.2.2>; *R (Warren) v Mental Health Review Tribunal*

---

[6] This paragraph in a previous edition was cited in *R (B) v Secretary of State for the Home Department* [2002] EWHC Admin 854 at [23]; also *Victoria Pre-Cast Pty Ltd v Papazis* [2003] VSC 208; *R v Arbitration Tribunal, ex p Fiji Island Trade & Investment Bureau* [2005] FJHC 175.

[7] Christopher Knight [2008] JR 111.

London North and East Region [2002] EWHC 811 (Admin) at [17] ("In view of the medical evidence before the tribunal ... the error as to the legal status of the claimant was not material to the decision"); *R (Sullivan) v Warwick District Council* [2003] EWHC 606 (Admin) [2003] 2 PLR 56 at [97] (misdirection by statutory consultee vitiating its advice, but remedy declined because "precisely the same decision would have been reached had the full position been understood").

48.2 **Error of law: restricted categories.**[8] Although as a result of the landmark*Anisminic* case judicial review is generally available to correct a material error of law, there are said to be categories of case where only the narrower (pre*Anisminic*) errors going to "jurisdiction" or "on the face of the record" will suffice. That was once, but is no longer, said to apply to courts of law.

48.2.1 **Visitors etc: error of law insufficient.** <32.4.3>; *R v Hull University Visitor, ex p Page* [1993] AC 682, 704F (Lord Browne-Wilkinson: "judicial review does not lie to impeach the decisions of a visitor taken within his jurisdiction (in the narrow sense) on questions of either fact or law. Judicial review does lie to the visitor in cases where he has acted outside his jurisdiction (in the narrow sense) or abused his powers or acted in breach of the rules of natural justice"); *R v Visitors to the Inns of Court, ex p Calder & Persaud* [1994] QB 1, 40F (applying the "limited judicial review jurisdiction" in *Page*); *R v Edmundsbury and Ipswich Diocese (Chancellor), ex p White* [1948] 1 KB 195, 220-221; *R v Chief Rabbi, ex p Wachmann* [1992] 1 WLR 1036, 1042H; *R v Charity Commissioners for England and Wales, ex p Baldwin* (2001) 33 HLR 538 (Charity Commissioners reviewable for error of law only in narrow "jurisdictional" sense, applying *Page*).

48.2.2 *Anisminic* **and courts of law.** *R (Sivasubramaniam) v Wandsworth County Court* [2002] EWCA Civ 1738 [2003] 1 WLR 475 at [42] (referring to *Re A Company* (below) as authority for there being "no presumption that an ouster provision did not mean what it said when applied to a court of law"; but "not ... treated as authority for the proposition that judicial review of a court will not lie where the court has made an error of law"); *In re A Company* [1981] AC 374, 382G-383D (Lord Diplock, describing *Anisminic* as being "concerned only with decisions of administrative tribunals"), 383E-H (contrasting the position of "a court of law"); *O'Reilly v Mackman* [1983] 2 AC 237, 278D-F (*Anisminic* as having "liberated English public law from the fetters that the courts had theretofore imposed upon themselves so far as determinations of inferior courts and statutory tribunals were concerned"); *R v Greater Manchester Coroner, ex p Tal* [1985] QB 67, 82G-H ("as a matter of principle, the *Anisminic* principle applies to inferior courts as well as inferior tribunals"); *R v Hull University Visitor, ex p Page* [1993] AC 682, 693B-D (*Anisminic* applying to inferior courts); *R v Bedwellty Justices, ex p Williams* [1997] AC 225, 233C-D (judicial review of magistrates available for error of law); *Pearlman v Keepers & Governors of Harrow School* [1979] QB 56.

48.2.3 **Error of law going to "jurisdiction".** <47.3>.

48.2.4 **Error of law on the face of the record.** *O'Reilly v Mackman* [1983] 2 AC 237, 277C and E (Lord Diplock, describing the breakthrough in *R v Northumberland Compensation Appeal Tribunal, ex p Shaw* [1952] 1 KB 338: "What was there re-discovered was" judicial review "not only on the ground the it had acted outwith its jurisdiction but also on the ground that it was apparent upon the face of its written determination that it had made a mistake as to

---

[8] This paragraph in a previous edition was cited in *Re Belfast City Council* [2008] NIQB 13 at [23].

the applicable law"); *R v Patents Appeal Tribunal, ex p Beecham Group Ltd* [1974] AC 646 (error of law on the face of the record by the Patents Appeal Tribunal); *R v Medical Appeal Tribunal, ex p Gilmore* [1957] 1 QB 574 (judicial review for error of law on the face of the record by the Medical Appeal Tribunal, not ousted by statutory finality clause); *R v Governor of Brixton Prison, ex p Armah* [1968] AC 192, 253F-G (power "to correct any error of law provided that it is able to see that the error has occurred", but "difficult questions may arise as to whether an error appears on the face of the record and as to what are the documents which compose the record"); *R v Knightsbridge Crown Court, ex p International Sporting Club (London) Ltd* [1982] 1 QB 304 (broad approach to what constituting "the record", including oral judgment); <47.3.1> (jurisdictional error avoiding problems with the "record"); *R v Hull University Visitor, ex p Page* [1993] AC 682, 701F-G ("the decision in *Anisminic* ... rendered obsolete the distinction between errors of law on the face of the record and other errors of law by extending the doctrine of ultra vires"); *Boddington v British Transport Police* [1999] 2 AC 143, 154C (*Anisminic* "made obsolete the historic distinction between errors of law on the face of the record and other errors of law. It did so by extending the doctrine of ultra vires, so that any misdirection in law would render the relevant decision ultra vires and a nullity").

> **P49 Error of fact.** A body must not make errors of precedent fact, fundamental factual errors or findings unsupported by evidence.

49.1 Precedent fact
49.2 Fundamental error of fact

49.1 Precedent fact. The Court will intervene to correct an erroneous conclusion on a question of precedent (or antecedent) fact, having examined any relevant (including fresh) material, and deciding the question for itself. The logic of precedent fact questions, which are rare and elusive, is of an objective factual question whose existence is needed to "trigger" the public body's proper function.

49.1.1 **Precedent fact as a well-established doctrine.** *Eshugbayi Eleko v Government of Nigeria* [1931] AC 662, 669 (Lord Atkin, describing "three conditions precedent to any authority to make an order of withdrawal, and their existence can and must be investigated by the Court whenever the validity of the order or a deportation order founded on it is the subject of contest in judicial proceedings"); *Liversidge v Sir John Anderson* [1942] AC 206, 273 (Lord Wright, referring to *Eleko*: "It was a question of the extent of the authority given by the ordinance. That depended on specific facts, capable of proof or disproof in a court of law, and unless these facts existed, there was no room for executive discretion").

49.1.2 **Precedent fact as hard-edged review.** <16.2>.

49.1.3 **Precedent fact in action.**
(A) PRECEDENT FACT. *R v Secretary of State for the Home Department, ex p Khawaja* [1984] AC 74 ("illegal entrant" is a precedent fact); *R (Lim) v Secretary of State for the Home Department* [2006] EWHC 3004 (Admin) at [22] (breach of condition on leave to remain as precedent fact); *Tan Te Lam v Superintendent of Tai A Chau Detention Centre* [1997] AC 97, 112C-114E (detention "pending removal" as jurisdictional question for the Court); *R v Secretary of State for the Environment Transport and the Regions, ex p Alliance Against the Birmingham Northern Relief Road* [1999] Env LR 447, 466-467 ("information relating to the environment", and commercial confidentiality as objective questions of fact for the Court); *London Borough of Islington v Camp* (1999) [2004] LGR 58, 67e (whether councillor "disqualified" a precedent fact); *R v Commissioners of Customs and Excise, ex p Lunn Poly Ltd* [1999] EuLR 653, 661A-662C ("state aid" a precedent fact); *R (Britannic Asset Management Ltd) v Pensions Ombudsman* [2002] EWHC 441 (Admin) at [10] ("administrators of the pension scheme" as "jurisdictional or precedent fact") (CA is [2002] EWCA Civ 1405 [2002] 4 All ER 860).
(B) NOT A PRECEDENT FACT. *R (M) v Lambeth London Borough Council* [2008] EWHC 1364 (Admin) at [146] (asylum-seeker's age not a precedent fact); *R (Queen Mary University of London) v Higher Education Funding Council for England* [2008] EWHC 1472 (Admin) at [22] (whether breach of grant conditions not precedent fact); *WM (DRC) v Secretary of State for the Home Department* [2006] EWCA Civ 1495 at [9] ("fresh claim" not a precedent fact); *R v Secretary of State for Employment, ex p National Association of Colliery Overmen, Deputies & Shotfirers* [1994] COD 218 (seldom that matters of fact will fall within the `precedent fact' category); *R v Secretary of State for the Home Department, ex p Bugdaycay* [1987] AC 514, 522G-523B ("refugee" not a precedent fact); *Barnard v Gorman* [1941] AC 378 ("offender" not a precedent fact); *R (Jones) v Mansfield District Council* [2003] EWCA Civ 1408 [2004] Env LR 391 at [17] ("likely significant effects on the environment" not a precedent fact).

49.1.4 **Precedent fact: other aspects.**

(A) PART OF JURISDICTIONAL ERROR. <P47>.
(B) STATUTORY FORMULAE. <39.3.6>.
(C) SPECIAL QUESTIONS UNDER COMMUNITY LAW. <49.2.14>.

49.2 Fundamental error of fact. Judicial review judges have traditionally been cautious about fact-based challenges. Factual questions are primarily entrusted to the public body and their reinvestigation would expand the Courts' case-load and function. The Court can however intervene in a case of unsupported or unsustainable factual conclusions, or unfairness through ignorance or disregard of an established and material fact.[10]

49.2.1 Error of fact. <13.2> (fact and judicial restraint); *Adan v Newham London Borough Council* [2001] EWCA Civ 1916 [2002] 1 WLR 2120 at [41] ("a court of supervisory jurisdiction does not, without more, have the power to substitute its own view of the primary facts for the view reasonably adopted by the body to whom the fact-finding power has been entrusted"), [35]-[36] (no power to interfere in "cases in which complaint is made that an administrative decision-maker got the facts wrong by preferring one version of the facts to another when it could reasonably have accepted either version"); *R v London Residuary Body, ex p Inner London Education Authority* (1987) [1998] JR 238, 240 ("a mistake as to fact can vitiate a decision as where the fact is a condition precedent to an exercise of jurisdiction, or where the fact is the only evidential basis for a decision or where the fact was as to a matter which expressly or impliedly had to be taken into account. Outside those categories we do not accept that a decision can be flawed in this court, which is not an appellate tribunal, upon the ground of mistake of fact"); *South Glamorgan County Council v L and M* [1996] ELR 400, 411F-412H (error of fact not a ground for judicial review; applying *ILEA*); *Wandsworth London Borough Council v A* [2000] 1 WLR 1246, 1255H-1256B ("While there may, possibly, be special considerations that apply in the more formalised area of planning inquiries ...; and while the duty of `anxious scrutiny' imposed in asylum cases ... renders those cases an uncertain guide for other areas of public law; nonetheless ... there is still no general right to challenge the decision of a public body on an issue of fact alone"); *R v Secretary of State for Education, ex p S* [1995] ELR 71, 82E, 83B (despite a "gross factual error", decision not shown to be "other than one reached within the proper exercise of the Minister's discretion").

49.2.2 Unfair disregard of an established and relevant fact. *E v Secretary of State for the Home Department* [2004] EWCA Civ 49 [2004] QB 1044 (considering error of fact as a ground of appeal for "error of law") at [42] (appeal for "error of law" treated as identical to grounds for judicial review), [66] ("a mistake of fact giving rise to unfairness ... at least in those statutory contexts where the parties share an interest in co-operating to achieve the correct result"; "the ordinary requirements for a finding of unfairness are ... First, there must have been a mistake as to an existing fact, including a mistake as to the availability of evidence on a particular matter. Secondly, the fact or evidence must have been `established', in the sense that it was uncontentious and objectively verifiable. Thirdly, the appellant (or his advisers) must not have been responsible for the mistake. Fourthly, the mistake must have played a material (not

---

[9] Marie Demetriou & Stephen Houseman [1997] JR 27; Michael Kent QC [1999] JR 239; David Blundell [2004] JR 36; Martha Grekos [2004] JR 184.

[10] This paragraph in a previous edition was cited in *E v Secretary of State for the Home Department* [2004] EWCA Civ 49 [2004] QB 1044 at [51]; also *R (S) v Secretary of State for the Home Department* [2007] EWHC 426 (Admin) at [11].

necessarily decisive) part in the Tribunal's reasoning"), [91(ii)] ("unfairness resulting from 'misunderstanding or ignorance of an established and relevant fact'"); *Montes v Secretary of State for the Home Department* [2004] EWCA Civ 404 [2004] Imm AR 250 at [21] (describing the principle in *E* as "closely and carefully circumscribed"); *R (Assura Pharmacy Ltd) v NHS Litigation Authority* [2008] EWHC 289 (Admin) at [118] (applying *E*); *Secretary of State for Education and Science v Tameside Metropolitan Borough Council* [1977] AC 1014, 1031-1032 ("misunderstanding or ignorance of an established and relevant fact"); *R v Criminal Injuries Compensation Board, ex p A* [1999] 2 AC 330, 344G-345C (approving the principles of "misunderstanding or ignorance of an established and relevant fact" and "taking into account of a mistaken fact"); *R (Alconbury Developments Ltd) v Secretary of State for the Environment Transport and the Regions* [2001] UKHL 23 [2003] 2 AC 295 at [53] ("the court had jurisdiction to quash for a misunderstanding or ignorance of an established and relevant fact"), [61]-[62] and [169] (review for error of fact); *Begum v Tower Hamlets London Borough Council* [2003] UKHL 5 [2003] 2 AC 430 at [7] (judicial review where "the decision-maker is shown to have misunderstood or been ignorant of an established and relevant fact"); *R (Green) v Financial Ombudsman Service Ltd* [2003] EWHC 338 (Admin) at [60] (asking whether decision-maker shown to have misunderstood or been ignorant of an established and relevant fact); *R (Meredith) v Merthyr Tydfil County Borough Council* [2002] EWHC 634 (Admin) at [31] ("now a recognised head of judicial review in English law that a decision could be invalidated if the decision maker acted upon an incorrect basis of fact"), [32] ("the head of review is now sufficiently well established for me to rely upon it"); *R (McLellan) v Bracknell Forest Borough Council* [2001] EWCA Civ 1510 [2002] QB 1129 at [64] ("material error of fact").

49.2.3 Fundamental factual error: further cases. *R (MH) v Bedfordshire County Council* [2007] EWHC 2435 (Admin) [2008] ELR 191 at [51] (decision vitiated by error of material fact); *R (Ali) v Secretary of State for the Home Department* [2007] EWHC 1983 (Admin) at [24] ("decision maker reached a decision on a material misunderstanding of the true facts"), [26] ("failure to have regard to the proper factual situation"); *R (Omar) v Chief Constable of Bedfordshire Constabulary* [2002] EWHC 3060 (Admin) at [40] ("Although the jurisprudence is developing, mistake of fact can amount to a ground for applying for judicial review"; "I am satisfied that the decision was taken on an incorrect basis of fact, on the material then available to the police. That kind of error permits this court to intervene"); *R v Parliamentary Commissioner for Administration, ex p Balchin* [1998] 1 PLR 1, 15B-C (Sedley J: error of fact "reviewable if crucial to the decision", referring to *ILEA*); *R v North Somerset District Council, ex p Cadbury Garden Centre Ltd* The Times 22nd November 2000 (planning decision treated as flawed because made on a factually unsound basis); *R v Chief Registrar of Friendly Societies, ex p New Cross Building Society* [1984] QB 227, 273E-F (Slade LJ: "If the society were in a position to prove by compelling evidence that a particular finding of crucial fact by the chief registrar was clearly wrong, this might give the court power to intervene"); *R v Hertfordshire County Council, ex p Cheung* The Times 4th April 1986 (see transcript) (Sir John Donaldson MR, suggesting that it could be appropriate to quash a recommendation if shown to have been "reached by the application of a policy which was flawed by an error of fact").

49.2.4 Whether error of fact was material. *E v Secretary of State for the Home Department* [2004] EWCA Civ 49 [2004] QB 1044 at [63] (treating as a necessary ingredient that "(v) The mistaken impression played a material part in the reasoning"); *R (Mitchell) v Secretary of State for the Home Department* [2008] EWHC 1370 (Admin) at [16] (error of fact but not decisive); *Simplex v Secretary of State for the Environment* (1989) 57 P & CR 306 (whether factual error more than merely insubstantial); *R v Independent Television Commission, ex p Virgin Television Limited* [1996] EMLR 318 ("if [the] decision was truly based on erroneous fact, then the decision itself was flawed. But, as Lord Templeman made clear in *TSW*, mistakes of fact may be made provided that the mistakes are not grave enough to undermine the basis of a multi-faceted decision"); *R v Department of Health & Social Security, ex p Scotia Pharmaceuticals Ltd* 23rd July 1993 unrep. (error of fact by pharmaceutical adviser, but established that would have made no difference; therefore "it would be pointless to remit the application for a redetermination").

49.2.5 Error of fact and fresh evidence. <17.2.5(C)> (fresh evidence and error of fact); *R (Gorlov) v Institute of Chartered Accountants in England and Wales* [2002] EWHC 2202 (Admin) at [69] (wrong to use judicial review "to quash a decision in order to introduce fresh evidence").

49.2.6 Unsustainable conclusion of fact as error of law. *Edwards v Bairstow* [1956] AC 14, 36 (Lord Radcliffe: "it may be that the facts found are such that no person acting judicially and properly instructed as to the relevant law could have come to the determination under appeal. In those circumstances ... the court must intervene. It has no option but to assume that there has been some misconception of the law and that this has been responsible for the determination. So ... there has been error in point of law"); *Begum v Tower Hamlets London Borough Council* [2003] UKHL 5 [2003] 2 AC 430 at [99] (Lord Millett: "A decision may be quashed if it is based on a finding of fact or inference from the facts which is perverse or irrational; or there was no evidence to support it; or it was made by reference to irrelevant factors or without regard to relevant factors. It is not necessary to identify a specific error of law; if the decision cannot be supported the court will infer that the decision-making authority misunderstood or overlooked relevant evidence or misdirected itself in law. The court cannot substitute its own findings of fact for those of the decision-making authority if there was evidence to support them; and questions as to the weight to be given to a particular piece of evidence and the credibility of witnesses are for the decision-making authority and not the court. But these are the only significant limitations on the court's jurisdiction, and they are not very different from the limitations which practical considerations impose on an appellate court with full jurisdiction to entertain appeals on fact or law but which deals with them on the papers only and without hearing oral evidence"); *Stefan v General Medical Council (No.2)* [2002] UKPC 10 at [6] (appeal on "a question of law", where: "it is within the appellate jurisdiction of the Board to consider whether there is any or sufficient evidence to support a material finding. A clearly erroneous finding may disclose an error of law warranting interference. And a material misunderstanding of the evidence may amount to an error of law"); *R v Medicines Control Agency, ex p Pharma Nord Ltd* (1998) 10 Admin LR 646, 659C (questions of fact become questions of law "where the application of the statutory language to the facts as a matter of law requires only one answer", so that "only one conclusion is possible on the facts"); *R v North West Suffolk (Mildenhall) Magistrates Court, ex p Forest Heath District Council* [1998] Env LR 9, 18 ("It is obviously perverse and an error of law to make a finding of fact for which there is no evidential foundation"); *R (Alconbury Developments Ltd) v Secretary of State for the Environment Transport and the Regions* [2001] UKHL 23 [2003] 2 AC 295 at [61] (Lord Nolan, referring to *Edwards v Bairstow*); *South Glamorgan County Council v L and M* [1996] ELR 400 (warning against artificial attempts to extend jurisdiction to correct errors of law by contending that factual errors so flawed as to amount to error of law); *Hemns v Wheeler* [1948] 2 KB 61, 66 ("it is always a question of law... whether there was evidence to support ... findings of fact and whether the inferences ... drawn are possible inferences from the facts as found").

49.2.7 Unsustainable conclusion of fact as unreasonableness. *Council of Civil Service Unions v Minister for the Civil Service* [1985] AC 374, 410G-411A (no need for "ingenious" *Edwards v Bairstow* solution of inferred mistake of law: "'Irrationality' by now can stand upon its own feet"); *R v Housing Benefit Review Board of the London Borough of Sutton, ex p Keegan* (1995) 27 HLR 92, 100 (conclusion "was arrived at in the teeth of the evidence and was accordingly

Wednesbury unreasonable"); *R (Asif Javed) v Secretary of State for the Home Department* [2001] EWCA Civ 789 [2002] QB 129 at [73] (Secretary of State's conclusion unreasonable); *R v Monopolies & Mergers Commission, ex p South Yorkshire Transport Ltd* [1993] 1 WLR 23, 32H-33A (whether "the decision is so aberrant that it cannot be classed as rational"); *R v Inland Revenue Commissioners, ex p Preston* [1985] AC 835, 862F; cf. *Mugesera v Canada (No.2)* [2005] SCC 40 [2006] 1 LRC 542 at [38] (Supreme Court of Canada applying reasonableness standard to judicial review of factual errors by immigration tribunal).

49.2.8 **Decision unsupported by evidence (of probative value).** *Office of Fair Trading v IBA Health Ltd* [2004] EWCA Civ 142 [2004] 4 All ER 1103 at [93] (Carnwath LJ, referring to the judicial review principle as asking "whether there was adequate material to support [the defendant's] conclusion"); *Reid v Secretary of State for Scotland* [1999] 2 AC 512, 541G-G (Lord Clyde, referring to the test as whether decision "erroneous in respect of a legal deficiency, as for example, through the absence of evidence, or of sufficient evidence, to support it"), 542C (whether "there was truly no evidence to support the conclusion which was reached"); *R (Beresford) v Sunderland City Council* [2003] UKHL 60 [2004] 1 AC 889 (council erring in law in reaching conclusion that public use of land was under implied licence, such a conclusion being unsupported by evidence), [1] (issue being whether error of law), [8] ("there was nothing in the material before the council to support [its] conclusion"), [51] ("not ... a correct evidentiary conclusion"), [60] (facts not such as "justifies" inference drawn), [83] (no "evidence ... justifying the conclusion"); *Din (Taj) v Wandsworth London Borough Council* [1983] 1 AC 657, 664H (Lord Wilberforce, referring to judicial review "for error in law including no doubt absence of any material on which the decision could reasonably be reached"); *Mahon v Air New Zealand Ltd* [1984] AC 808, 820G-H (Lord Diplock, referring to a principle of "natural justice" that an investigative decision-maker "must base his decision upon evidence that has some probative value"); *Attorney-General v Ryan* [1980] AC 718, 732G (Minister's need to be "satisfied upon evidential material of probative value"), 733A (referring to findings of fact "base[d] upon proper evidential material"); *R v Hillingdon London Borough Council, ex p Islam (Tafazzul)* [1983] 1 AC 688, 708D-G (conclusion "not supported by the facts"), 717G ("no evidence to support the panel's decision"); *Bryan v United Kingdom* [1996] 1 PLR 47, 59H (statutory review available "if the evidence relied on by the inspector was not capable of supporting a finding of fact"); *R v West London Coroner, ex p Gray* [1988] QB 467, 479H-480A (Watkins LJ: "The development of judicial review to its present state with its devotion to, amongst other things, natural justice, cannot possibly allow verdicts by juries at inquests to stand which are based upon no or wholly insufficient evidence").

49.2.9 **Primary and secondary facts.** *R (Higham) v University of Plymouth* [2005] EWHC 1492 (Admin) [2005] ELR 547 at [32] (Stanley Burnton J, referring to findings of fact: "Such a finding, like all findings of fact, are susceptible of judicial review. In the case of a finding of primary fact, the test is whether there was evidence on the basis of which the decision maker could reasonably have made the finding. In the case of a finding of a secondary fact, the test is whether the primary facts found justified the secondary finding. The more serious the secondary fact, the more cogent must be the primary facts that lead to the secondary finding").

49.2.10 **Judicial review for lack of evidence: further examples.** *R (Daniel Thwaites Plc) v Wirral Borough Magistrates Court* [2008] EWHC 838 (Admin) at [63] (conclusion "without proper evidence"); *R (Martin) v Harrow Crown Court* [2007] EWHC 3193 (Admin) ("no evidence on which the court could properly [so] conclude"); *R (Kenny) v Leeds Magistrates Court* [2003] EWHC 2963 (Admin) [2004] 1 All ER 1333 at [56] (absence of necessary "evidential basis"); *R (Price) v Carmarthenshire County Council* [2003] EWHC 42 (Admin) at [23] (conclusion reached "without there being a proper evidential basis for doing so"); *R v Mildenhall Magistrates Court, ex p Forest Heath District Council* The Times 16th May 1997 (absence of evidential foundation constituting an error of law); *R v Governor of Pentonville Prison, ex p Sotiriadis* [1975] AC 1, 30E-F ("*no* evidence before the magistrate"); *Secretary of State for Social Security v Tait* [1995] COD 440 (absence of any reliable evidence treated as a matter of law); *R v Secretary of State for the Home Department, ex p Abdi* [1996] 1 WLR 298, 315E-F (statement as to knowledge and experience "is at least *some* evidence in support of the Secretary of State's certificate"); *R v Croydon London Borough Council, ex p Graham* (1994) 26 HLR 286, 291 (council's conclusion "was not justified by the facts on which the council appear to have relied"); *R v Governor of Belmarsh Prison, ex p Francis* [1995] 1 WLR 1121, 1126F-G ("evidence upon which a reasonable magistrate properly directing himself in law could commit"); *R v Camden London Borough Council, ex p Cran* (1996) 94 LGR 8, 38 (whether the decision was "on the basis of data which was manifestly grossly insufficient"); *R v Secretary of State for the Home Department, ex p Zakrocki* (1998) 1 CCLR 374 (no evidential basis for assertion); *R v Hampshire County Council, ex p H* [1999] 2 FLR 359, 366B (insufficient material upon which to base decision); *R (Cheltenham Builders Ltd) v South Gloucestershire District Council* [2003] EWHC 2803 (Admin) [2004] 4 PLR 95 at [32] ("no possible basis on which the committee could reasonably have concluded" that the statutory test was met); *Re T (Judicial Review: Local Authority Decisions Concerning Child in Need)* [2003] EWHC 2515 (Admin) [2004] 1 FLR 601 at [135] (Wall J: "the decision ... was made on inadequate information").

49.2.11 Judicial review of committals for insufficiency of evidence. *R v Bedwellty Justices, ex p Williams* [1997] AC 225, 237C-E (judicial review available where "committal based solely on inadmissible evidence" or "based solely on evidence not reasonably capable of supporting it"); *R v Dorset Magistrates Court, ex p Cox* [1997] COD 86 (judicial review of a committal needing substantial error leading to demonstrable injustice); *R v Belmarsh Magistrates Court, ex p Gilligan* [1998] 1 Cr App R 14 (whether error having substantial adverse consequences and/or whether evidence to justify the decision); *R v Whitehaven Justices, ex p Thompson* [1999] COD 15 (judicial review only appropriate in the very clearest of cases); *R (O'Shea) v Coventry Magistrates Court* [2004] EWHC 905 (Admin) (sufficient evidence to commit for crown court trial).

49.2.12 Misapprehension of fact as relevancy/irrelevancy. *Cheshire County Council v Secretary of State for the Environment* [1995] Env LR 316, 330-332 ("if there was an error in the factual background of which the Secretary of State should have been aware, then his decision would have failed to take into account the correct factual background [and would be liable to be quashed]"); *R v Housing Benefit Review Board of the London Borough of Sutton, ex p Keegan* (1995) 27 HLR 92, 100 (conclusion "was arrived at in the teeth of the evidence and was accordingly *Wednesbury* unreasonable... If I am wrong in this regard, I should make it plain that I am satisfied that a consideration of the findings of fact and the Board's reasons for their decision indicate a failure to take properly into account the effect of [the claimant's statement]"); *R v Secretary of State for Education, ex p E* [1996] ELR 312, 324B-C (assumptions about claimant and her family's religious observance, and nature of the Jewish faith, "were wrong assumptions upon which the [defendant] acted and as such her decision is flawed in law", "the decision was taken by taking into account matters which should not have been taken into account and, as such, the decision ... is irrational"); *South Glamorgan County Council v L and M* [1996] ELR 400, 411F-412H (not enough that factual mistake in relation to a matter which body was entitled to take into account).

49.2.13 Fundamental error of fact: other approaches. *R v Immigration Officer, ex p Quaquah* [2000] INLR 196, 205F ("The Secretary of State misdirected himself on the facts, as to the reason why the [claimant] should not be granted exceptional leave to remain in connection with his outstanding litigation"); *Simplex GE (Holdings) v Secretary of State for the Environment*

(1989) 57 P & CR 306 (where factual mistake in reaching planning decision, decision ultra vires unless error insignificant or insubstantial or court satisfied that same decision would have been reached on other valid reasons given); *Secretary of State for Education and Science v Tameside Metropolitan Borough Council* [1977] AC 1014, 1047F-G (Lord Wilberforce, referring to judicial review where the Minister acted "upon an incorrect basis of fact"); *R v Secretary of State for Health, ex p London Borough of Hackney* 25th April 1994 unrep. (Leggatt LJ, concluding that the reference in *Tameside* to "incorrect basis of fact" is not "of universal application"); *R v Camden London Borough Council, ex p Aranda* (1998) 30 HLR 76, 84 (council's decision illogical); *R v Immigration Appeal Tribunal, ex p Amin* [1992] Imm AR 367, 374 (Schiemann J: "In my judgment adjudicators should indicate with some clarity in their decisions: (1) what evidence they accept; (2) what evidence they reject; (3) whether there is any evidence as to which they cannot make up their minds whether or not they accept it; (4) what, if any, evidence they regard as irrelevant"); *R v Immigration Appeal Tribunal, ex p Sardar Ahmed* [1999] INLR 473, 477E-F (failure to make relevant general findings); *R v East Devon Borough Council Housing Benefit Review Board, ex p Preston* (1999) 31 HLR 936 (duty to make and explain findings as to whether and why evidence accepted); <51.2.3> (failure to grapple with relevant material); *T v Secretary of State for the Home Department* [1995] 1 WLR 545 (CA), 559F-G ("Given the tribunal's findings of fact, this court is as well able as the tribunal to form a judgment upon the sole issue arising... [whether crimes were 'non-political']"; and see HL at [1996] AC 742).

49.2.14 EC challenge drawing Court into legitimate fact-finding role. *R v Minister of Agriculture Fisheries & Food, ex p Bell Lines Ltd* [1984] 2 CMLR 502, 511 (Forbes J, explaining that where the domestic court is called upon to apply test "whether and to what extent the detailed measures of control are capable of constituting an impermissible restriction on intra-Community trade", it is "plain that this court is, some may think unfortunately but nevertheless ineluctably, being drawn into the business of fact-finding"); *R v Medicines Control Agency, ex p Pharma Nord Ltd* (1998) 10 Admin LR 646, 654D-655D, 658G-659A (whether question of product being a "medicine" for the purposes of an EC Directive a question of fact to be determined by the Court, whereby "the court itself would have to retake the critical decision", but not appropriate as a matter of discretion to order such an exercise here); *R v Secretary of State for the Environment Transport and the Regions, ex p Alliance Against the Birmingham Northern Relief Road* [1999] Env LR 447, 466-467 (whether "information relating to the environment" and whether exceptions apply, under Regulations implementing an EC Directive, objective questions of fact for the Court to decide); *Upjohn Ltd v Licensing Authority established by the Medicines Act 1968* [1999] 1 WLR 927 (EC law not requiring that court reviewing decision of Licensing Authority should substitute its view for that of the Authority); *SIAC Construction Ltd v Mayo County Council* [1999] EuLR 535 (approach to whether decision ultra vires the relevant Regulations no different in principle in a case where the Regulations had their source in EC law; neither Directive nor Regulations contemplating a review on the merits); *R v Commissioners of Customs and Excise, ex p Lunn Poly Ltd* [1999] EuLR 653, 661A, 662B-C (whether measure is a "state aid" for the purposes of EC Treaty Art 93(3) being a precedent fact for the Court to decide for itself); *Royal Society for the Protection of Birds v Secretary of State for Scotland* The Times 14th December 1999 (declining to decide factual questions at the substance of a challenge based on the Birds Directive).

49.2.15 Duty to reconsider where error of fact. *R v Newham London Borough Council, ex p Begum* (1996) 28 HLR 646, 656 (Stephen Richards: although error of fact not "a sufficient basis for quashing the decision ... Nevertheless the decision cried out for review when the error, on so important a matter, was drawn to the council's attention by the [claimant]'s solicitors ... A failure to reconsider the decision in those circumstances would in my judgment have been unlawful"); *R v Inner London North Coroner, ex p Touche* [2001] EWCA Civ 383 [2001] QB

1206 at [36] (although decision was originally correct, coroner should have changed his mind on information subsequently brought to his attention).

49.2.16 Power to reopen decision where error of fact. <6.1.7> (power to reconsider); *R v Bradford Crown Court, ex p Crossling* [2000] COD 107 (where Crown Court having refused to extend custody time limit on basis of fundamental misapprehension of fact, proper for prosecution to make fresh application to the Crown Court); *Porteous v West Dorset District Council* [2004] EWCA Civ 244 [2004] LGR 577 at [9] (housing authority "entitled to revisit and change an earlier decision [which] resulted from a fundamental mistake of fact").

49.2.17 Unjustified departure from another body's findings. <55.2.3>.

> **P50 Abdication/fetter.** A body must not surrender its function, as by: (a) acting under dictation; (b) improperly delegating its powers; or (c) operating an inflexible policy.

50.1 Basic duty not to abdicate/fetter
50.2 Acting under dictation
50.3 Improper delegation
50.4 Fetter by inflexible policy

50.1 Basic duty not to abdicate/fetter. A public body's basic statutory functions, powers and duties are inalienable. It must "own" its functions and actions. Bodies are not entitled to surrender or ignore their powers and duties, nor "fetter" their discretion, by over-committing themselves to a particular course or approach.

50.1.1 **Inalienability.** <P40>.

50.1.2 **Not entitled to abdicate/surrender power.** *R (S) v Secretary of State for the Home Department* [2007] EWCA Civ 546 at [50] ("A public authority may not adopt a policy which precludes it from considering individual cases on their merits, nor may it allow its treatment of applications to be dictated by agreement with another government body"); *R (Corner House Research) v Director of the Serious Fraud Office* [2008] UKHL 60 [2008] 3 WLR 568 (no surrender of judgment by DSFO); *R v Secretary of State for the Home Department, ex p Fire Brigades Union* [1995] 2 AC 513, 551D-E (Secretary of State "cannot lawfully surrender or release the [statutory] power contained ... so as to purport to exclude its future exercise either by himself or by his successors").

50.1.3 **Delay as abdication of function.** *Engineers & Managers Association v Advisory Conciliation & Arbitration Service* [1980] 1 WLR 302 (indefinite delay as abdication of power); *R (S) v Secretary of State for the Home Department* [2007] EWCA Civ 546 at [50] (unlawful "to defer a whole class of applications without good reasons"); *R v Secretary of State for the Home Department, ex p Fire Brigades Union* [1995] 2 AC 513 (unlawful decision not to bring statute into force); *R v Commissioners of Customs and Excise, ex p Kay and Co* [1996] STC 1500 (unlawful to defer statutory duty to repay VAT); <53.1.7> (delay as frustrating the legislative purpose).

50.1.4 **Not entitled to ignore a duty.** <P39> (discretion/duty); *R v Commissioners of Customs and Excise, ex p Kay and Co* [1996] STC 1500 (not entitled to defer payment where statutory duty to make it and no room for a general power to delay/defer); *R v Secretary of State for the Environment Transport and the Regions, ex p Watson* 21st July 1998 unrep. (Minister not entitled, on grounds of inconvenience, to dispense with a statutory requirement and process applications in the face of a statutory prohibition).

50.1.5 **Policy adopted must not conflict with duty.** *R v Shadow Education Committee of Greenwich London Borough Council, ex p Governors of John Ball Primary School* (1989) 88 LGR 589 (discussed in *R v Governors of the Bishop Challoner Roman Catholic Comprehensive Girls' School, ex p Choudhury* [1992] 2 AC 182 at 194D-E); *R v Lewisham Borough Council, ex p P* [1991] 1 WLR 308, 313C-D (policy precluding necessary balancing act); cf. *R v Chief Constable of South Wales, ex p Merrick* [1994] 1 WLR 663, 678G (policy unlawful insofar as it conflicted with basic common law rights).

50.1.6 **Not "fettering" the discretion.** *R v Secretary of State for the Home Department, ex p Venables* [1998] AC 407, 496G-497C ("the person on whom the power is conferred cannot fetter the future exercise of his discretion by committing himself now as to the way in which he will exercise his power in the future... By the same token, the person on whom the power has been conferred cannot fetter the way he will use that power by ruling out of consideration on the future exercise of that power factors which may then be relevant to such exercise"); <50.4> (fetter by inflexible policy);*R (Kilby) v Basildon District Council* [2007] EWCA Civ 479 [2007] HLR 586 (fetter by secure tenancy term); *R v Gaming Board of Great Britain, ex p Kingsley* [1996] COD 241 (improper to fetter self not to take account of relevancies); <30.4.1> (manifesto promises/ whip system).

50.2 **Acting under dictation.**[11] A public body must not surrender its independent judgment to a third party. Nor must one public body bring about the surrender of another public body's independent judgment.

50.2.1 **Abdication: acting as a "puppet".**[12] *Lavender (H) & Son Ltd v Minister of Housing and Local Government* [1970] 1 WLR 1231 (unlawful fetter for Minister of Housing to make the views of the Minister of Agriculture the sole material consideration); *R v Chief Constable Thames Valley Police, ex p Police Complaints Authority* [1996] COD 324 (unlawful fetter for PCA to treat decision of DPP as in effect binding); *R v Secretary of State for Trade and Industry, ex p Lonrho Plc* [1989] 1 WLR 525, 538C (discretion "must be exercised by him" and "not at the dictation of another Minister or body"); *R v Police Complaints Board, ex p Madden* [1983] 1 WLR 447 (fetter by erroneously treating policy guidance as binding); *R v Brent London Borough Council, ex p Macwan* (1994) 26 HLR 528 (not unlawful for council to decline to comply with Secretary of State's `guidance'); *R v Surrey County Council, ex p G and H* [1995] COD 50 (parents not entitled to dictate form of educational assessment); *R v Teignmouth District Council, ex p Teignmouth Quay Co Ltd* [1995] 2 PLR 1, 8C-D (council must not abdicate function of deciding whether breach of planning control to third parties); *R v Parole Board, ex p Watson* [1996] 1 WLR 906, 916F (Parole Board having to make up its own mind, not simply review Secretary of State's reasons for revocation of parole);*R v Birmingham City Justice, ex p Chris Foreign Foods (Wholesalers) Ltd* [1970] 1 WLR 1428 (magistrate's conduct in retiring "to take advice" from two officials calling into question whether decision taken was really his); *R v Secretary of State for Health, ex p Willan* 2nd February 1996 unrep. (entitled to consult on a preferred option of another body); *R v Tandridge District Council, ex p Al Fayed* [1999] 1 PLR 104, 110D-F (right to give great weight to advice of expert bodies on technical matters; no abdication providing that not treating decision as conclusively determined by those bodies) (CA is at [2000] 1 PLR 58); *R v Secretary of State for the Home Department, ex p Dinc* [1999] INLR 256, 262C-E (Secretary of State required to make up own mind as to deportation, in light of a recommendation by the crown court); *R (Barry) v Liverpool City Council* [2001] EWCA Civ 384 [2001] LGR 361 at [26] and [41] (although licensing authority treating police clearance as a requirement, decision not unlawfully delegated to police); *R (S) v London Borough of Brent* [2002] EWCA Civ 693 [2002] ELR 556 (no unlawful fetter in Secretary of State's statutory guidance having provided that pupil exclusion order made in accordance with a published discipline policy should "normally" be upheld).

50.2.2 **Abdication: "rubber-stamping".** *R (L) v Secretary of State for the Home Department* [2003] EWCA Civ 25 [2003] 1 WLR 1230 at [67] (Secretary of State would be acting

---

[11] This paragraph in a previous edition was cited in *R (Corner House) v Director of the Serious Fraud Office* [2008] EWHC 714 (Admin) at [68].

[12] Jason Braier [2005] JR 216.

unlawfully were he to "rubber stamp" Czech asylum applications as clearly unfounded, there being a duty to consider on an individual basis whether the claim is bound to fail); *R v South Somerset District Council, ex p DJB (Group) Ltd* (1989) 1 Admin LR 11 (no "mindless rubber stamping" here of committee's decision); *R v Metropolitan Borough of Sefton, ex p Healiss* (1995) 27 HLR 34 (duty to consider whether claimant homeless; not simply to rely on earlier refusal of housing transfer application); *R v Secretary of State for the Home Department, ex p Oladehinde* [1991] 1 AC 254, 301F-G (rejecting submission "that the decision to deport was taken by the immigration officers concerned and not by the inspectors"); *R v Special Adjudicator, ex p Paulino* [1996] Imm AR 122 (adjudicator needing to make up own mind as to whether agreeing with Secretary of State's certification); *R v Secretary of State for the Home Department, ex p Abdi* [1996] 1 WLR 298, 304H, 314C (adjudicator's position where Secretary of State satisfied that safe third country); *Gateshead Metropolitan Borough Council v Secretary of State for the Environment* [1994] 1 PLR 85, 96E (extent to which Secretary of State entitled to leave pollution control matters to Pollution Inspectorate).

50.2.3 Bringing about abdication: acting as a "puppeteer". *R (Girling) v Parole Board* [2006] EWCA Civ 1779 [2007] QB 783 (Secretary of State's directions merely suggestions so as not to compromise independence of parole board); *Laker Airways Ltd v Department of Trade* [1977] QB 643 (guidance ultra vires as cutting across the statute and requiring CAA to revoke licence); *R v Police Complaints Board, ex p Madden* [1983] 1 WLR 447 (received guidance could not lawfully bind); *R v Worthing Borough Council, ex p Burch* (1985) 50 P & CR 53 (circular unlawful as having practical effect of constraining local authority); *R v Port Talbot Borough Council, ex p Jones* [1988] 2 All ER 207 (borough housing officer unlawfully "dominated" by tenancy committee chairman); *R v Secretary of State for the Environment, ex p Lancashire County Council* [1994] 4 All ER 165 (Ministerial policy fettering the Local Government Commission); *R v City of Sunderland, ex p Baumber* [1996] COD 211 (educational psychologists' discretion to consult under regulations improperly fettered by instructions issued to them by employer authority); *R (United Kingdom Renderers Association Ltd) v Secretary of State for the Environment, Transport and the Regions* [2002] EWCA Civ 749 [2003] Env LR 178 (Secretary of State's guidance recommending that local authorities impose a general licence condition not unlawful).

50.3 Improper delegation.[13] Although there are sound practical reasons for a degree of shared or transferred responsibility (eg. between a Minister and departmental officials), a public body may not "give away" its key functions to another body. What is permissible depends on any statutory scheme, the relevant function and the particular context.

50.3.1 Ministerial departmental responsibility: the *Carltona* principle. *R v Secretary of State for the Home Department, ex p Oladehinde* [1991] 1 AC 254, 300A-B (Lord Griffiths: "It is obvious that the Secretary of State cannot personally take every decision ... The decision must be taken by a person of suitable seniority in the Home Office for whom the Home Secretary accepts responsibility. This devolution of responsibility was recognised as a practical necessity in the administration of government by the Court of Appeal in *Carltona Ltd v Works Commissioners* [1943] 2 All ER 560 and has come to be known as the *Carltona* principle"); *Director of Public Prosecutions v Haw* [2007] EWHC 1931 (Admin) [2008] 1 WLR 379 at [33] (*Carltona* in effect applicable to MPC); *R (National Association of Health Stores) v Secretary*

---

[13] Claire Weir [1998] JR 211; Stephen Bailey [2005] JR 84.

of State for Health [2005] EWCA Civ 154[14] at [24] (*Carltona* means act of duly authorised civil servant is act of the Minister).

50.3.2 **Local government departmental responsibility.** *R (S & B) v Independent Appeal Panel of Birmingham City Council* [2006] EWHC 2369 (Admin) [2007] ELR 57 at [49] (*Carltona* applicable to central not local government); *R v Birmingham City Council, ex p O* [1983] 1 AC 578, 586E-F (Lord Brightman: "It is an inevitable feature of local government today that there must be delegation of the multifarious functions of a local authority among numerous committees, sub-committees and individual officers. No local authority could function efficiently otherwise. Section 101 of the Local Government Act 1972 provides for this delegation in general terms"); *R v Southwark London Borough Council, ex p Bannerman* (1990) 2 Admin LR 381 (commonplace in both central and local government for decision to be taken in name of person who is not in meaningful sense the decision-maker).

50.3.3 **Delegation: permissible steps.** *Director of Public Prosecutions v Haw* [2007] EWHC 1931 (Admin) [2008] 1 WLR 379 at [33] (implied power to delegate where responsibilities of statutory office mean delegation inevitable); *R (Ealing London Borough Council) v Audit Commission for England and Wales* [2005] EWCA Civ 556 (2005) 8 CCLR 317 at [27] (Audit Commission entitled to adopt weighting scores by commission for social care inspection); *R v Secretary of State for the Home Department, ex p Oladehinde* [1991] 1 AC 254, 295G (permissible deployment of immigration inspectors); *R v Secretary of State for the Home Department, ex p Doody* [1994] 1 AC 531, 566F-567B (permissible tariff-delegation to junior minister); *R v Secretary of State for the Home Department, ex p Harshad Jashbhai Patel* (1995) 7 Admin LR 56, 62G-64G (statutory power to delegate); *R v Managers of South Western Hospital, ex p M* [1993] QB 683, 699C-G (consultation via the medium of an "agent" or "delegate").

50.3.4 **Delegation: impermissible steps.** *Vine v National Dock Labour Board* [1957] AC 488, 506 (invalid delegation of employment termination); *R v Tower Hamlets London Borough Council, ex p Khalique* (1994) 26 HLR 517, 525 (policy-making by unaccountable group of councillors and officers "a grave abuse of power", "the antithesis of ... democracy and openness"); *R (Tamil Information Centre) v Secretary of State for the Home Department* The Times 30th October 2002 (Authorisation an "impermissible delegation" of judgment statutorily-required of Minister personally); *R v Secretary of State for the Environment, ex p Hillingdon London Borough Council* [1986] 1 WLR 807 (invalid standing order delegating to committee chairman rather than committee); *R v Director of Public Prosecutions, ex p Association of First Division Civil Servants* (1988) 138 NLJ 158 (unlawful to delegate statutory screening of summary offences to non-qualified lawyers); *R v Secretary of State for Education, ex p Prior* [1994] ELR 231 (governors wrongly delegated disciplinary function to staff committee); *R v Servite Houses and Wandsworth London Borough Council, ex p Goldsmith* (2000) 3 CCLR 325, 339H (non-delegability meaning housing association not the council's agent in residential home arrangement, housing association not the council's agent); *R (Selter Associates Ltd) v Leicestershire County Council* [2005] EWHC 2615 (Admin) (order not lawfully made under delegated powers because precondition not met).

50.3.5 **Delegability: striking a balance.** *R (Ealing London Borough Council) v Audit Commission for England and Wales* [2005] EWCA Civ 556 (2005) 8 CCLR 317 at [27] (entitled to adopt, as its own, weighting scores of social care inspection body); *R (Varma) v Duke of Kent* [2004] EWHC 1705 (Admin) [2004] ELR 616 (University Visitor entitled to

---

[14] Iain Steele [2005] JR 232.

appoint a commissary to hold appeal hearing and give advice, provided that ultimate decision taken by Visitor); *R v North Thames Regional Health Authority and Chelsea & Westminster NHS Trust, ex p L* [1996] Med LR 385 (NHS Trust able "to make arrangements for elements or stages of the disciplinary process to be conducted by persons not holding office in the Trust; but it is the Trust alone as a public body and employer which has the power and duty to evaluate the findings of the inquiry and to decide what disciplinary step if any to take"); *R v Hertsmere Borough Council, ex p Woolgar* (1995) 27 HLR 703 (although impermissible to delegate decision-making duties, council entitled to delegate powers of investigation); *R v Solihull Metropolitan Borough Council Housing Benefits Review Board, ex p Simpson* (1994) 92 LGR 719, 727 (Regulations imposing a `personal obligation' on Chairman to bring into existence his record of the decision, but not requiring him physically to make the written record); *R v Chorley Borough Council, ex p Bound* (1996) 28 HLR 791 (sufficient that letter containing reasons verbally approved); *R v University of Cambridge, ex p Evans* [1998] ELR 515, 518C-520G (asking whether the control preserved was close enough for the decision to be identifiable as that of the delegating authority); *R v St Edmundsbury Council, ex p Walton* (1999) 11 Admin LR 648 (not entitled to entrust important function to officer unless by formal delegation); *R v Institute of Chartered Accountants of England and Wales, ex p Taher Nawaz* 25th April 1997 unrep. (insofar as byelaw containing excessive delegation of power, use of substantial severability and implied duty to act rationally to limit its effect).

50.3.6 Improper delegation and prejudice. *R v West Dorset District Council, ex p Gerrard* (1995) 27 HLR 150, 161, 165 (sufficient that decision might be different if addressed by the council itself, rather than the housing association to whom it had unlawfully delegated its function); *R v Oxfordshire County Council, ex p P* [1996] ELR 153, 159E-H.

50.3.7 Unreasonable delegation. *R v Institute of Chartered Accountants of England and Wales, ex p Taher Nawaz* 25th April 1997 unrep. (power to delegate should be construed as constrained by a duty not to exercise it in an irrational manner, or modified to that effect under the doctrine of substantial severability); *R v Secretary of State for the Home Department, ex p Doody* [1994] 1 AC 531, 566F-G (leaving open whether "there is another constraint as regards the degree of delegation, in the shape of a possible exposure to attack on the ground of irrationality").

50.3.8 Lack of delegation as ultra vires. *R (S & B) v Independent Appeal Panel of Birmingham City Council* [2006] EWHC 2369 (Admin) [2007] ELR 57 (decision ultra vires because made by department to whom power had not been delegated).

50.4 Fetter by inflexible policy.[15] A public body vested with discretionary powers should not operate a policy the nature or application of which is overrigid so as automatically to determine the outcome, thus evidencing a closed mind.

50.4.1 Individual examination in light of a lawful policy. *In re Findlay* [1985] AC 318, 338E-F (prisoner's entitlement "that his case will be examined individually in the light of whatever policy the Secretary of State sees fit to adopt provided always that the adopted policy is a lawful exercise of the discretion conferred upon him by the statute").

50.4.2 Legitimacy/need for a policy. *R (Walmsley) v Lane* [2005] EWCA Civ 1540 [2006] LGR 280 at [55] (public authority "risks being castigated for inconsistency if it does not have

---

[15] This paragraph in a previous edition was cited in *Linky Chance Ltd v Commissioner for Television and Entertainment Licensing* [2006] HKCU 2086 at [40].

a policy"); *R v North West Lancashire Health Authority, ex p A* [2000] 1 WLR 977, 991G ("proper for an Authority to adopt a general policy for the exercise of such an administrative discretion, to allow for exceptions from it in `exceptional circumstances' and to leave those circumstances undefined"); *British Oxygen Co Ltd v Board of Trade* [1971] AC 610, 625D-E (policy appropriate where dealing "with a multitude of similar applications"), 631A-C ("both reasonable and right that the Board should make known to those interested the policy it was going to follow"); *R v Secretary of State for the Home Department, ex p Venables* [1998] AC 407 (CA), 432G (wide discretion "which calls out for the development of policy as to the way it will in general be exercised. This would assist in providing consistency and certainty which are highly desirable in an area involving the administration of justice where fairness is particularly important"); *In re Findlay* [1985] AC 318, 335D-H ("the complexities are such that an approach based on a carefully formulated policy could be said to be called for"); *R v Governors of the Bishop Challoner Roman Catholic Comprehensive Girls' School, ex p Choudhury* [1992] 2 AC 182, 193E ("it is absolutely necessary that the school should have an admissions policy of some kind"); *R v Legal Aid Board, ex p Duncan* [2000] COD 159 (see transcript at [581]) (not irrational to launch scheme without spelling out principles on which would exercise discretion, but transparency desirable and so defendant asked to explain the principles); *R (Grogan) v Bexley NHS Care Trust* [2006] EWHC 44 (Admin) [2006] LGR 491 at [91], [94] (need for certainty, criteria too vague here); *R (Watkins-Singh) v Aberdare Girls High School Governors* [2008] EWHC 1865 (Admin) (breach of statutory duty to have a policy for promoting race equality); <55.1.14(C)> (need for a policy).

50.4.3 Policy must have a properly evaluated starting-point. *R v North West Lancashire Health Authority, ex p A* [2000] 1 WLR 977 (policy regarding funding of treatment of transsexuals unlawful because starting-point failed to evaluate transsexualism as an illness), 992G ("it is important that the starting point against which the exceptional circumstances have to be rated is properly evaluated"), 999E (in adopting the policy, authority not having "demonstrated that degree of rational consideration that can reasonably be expected of it"); <57.4.6> (unreasonable policy).

50.4.4 Duty not to adopt an unduly rigid policy. *R v Secretary of State for the Home Department, ex p Venables* [1998] AC 407, 496G-497C (Lord Browne-Wilkinson: "When Parliament confers a discretionary power ... the person on whom the power is conferred [is not precluded] from developing and applying a policy as to the approach which he will adopt in the generality of cases... But the position is different if the policy adopted is such as to preclude the person on whom the power is conferred from departing from the policy or from taking into account circumstances which are relevant to the particular case in relation to which the discretion is being exercised. If such an inflexible and invariable policy is adopted, both the policy and the decisions taken pursuant to it will be unlawful"); *R v Secretary of State for the Environment, ex p Brent London Borough Council* [1982] QB 593, 643G-H ("[The Minister is] entitled to have well in his mind his policy. To this extent the reference to keeping an open mind does not mean an empty mind. His mind must be kept `ajar'").

50.4.5 The policy must not automatically determine the outcome. *R v Hampshire County Council, ex p W* [1994] ELR 460, 476B (Sedley J: "What is required by the law is that, without falling into arbitrariness decision-makers must remember that a policy is a means of securing a consistent approach to individual cases, each of which is likely to differ from others. Each case must be considered, therefore in the light of the policy but not so that the policy automatically determines the outcome"); *R v Windsor Licensing Justices, ex p Hodes* [1983] 1 WLR 685, 693E ("licensing justices must exercise their discretion in each case that comes before them and cannot properly determine an application simply by reference to a pre-ordained policy relating to applications of a particular class, without reference to the particular facts of the application before them"); *R v Secretary of State for Education and Employment, ex p P* [2000] ELR 300, 305A ("the Secretary of State applied his policy without considering whether the individual circumstances ... justified a departure from it").

50.4.6 **Allowing the chance to persuade.** *Council of Civil Service Unions v Minister for the Civil Service* [1985] AC 374, 415F-G (Lord Roskill: "The principle [of legitimate expectation] may [include] ... an expectation of being allowed time to make representations especially where the aggrieved party is seeking to persuade an authority to depart from a lawfully established policy adopted in connection with the exercise of a particular power because of some suggested exceptional reasons justifying such a departure"); *R v Secretary of State for the Environment, ex p Oxford City Council* 28th February 1998 unrep. (entitled to decide that if any change to be made must be by way of change to the general policy rather than individual exception from it, provided that mind `ajar' and willing to listen to representations in support of request for an exception); *R (H) v Ashworth Hospital Authority* [2001] EWHC Admin 872 [2002] 1 FCR 206 at [136] (no fetter because of willingness to listen to arguments "urging a change of policy"); <60.5> (basic right to be heard).

50.4.7 **Consistency and non-rigidity: conflicting imperatives.** *R v Ministry for Agriculture Fisheries & Food, ex p Hamble Fisheries (Offshore) Ltd* [1995] 2 All ER 714, 722a-c (Sedley J, describing the "two conflicting imperatives of public law: the first is that while a policy may be adopted for the exercise of a discretion, it must not be applied with a rigidity which excludes consideration of possible departure in individual cases...; the second is that a discretionary public law power must not be exercised arbitrarily or with partiality as between individuals or classes potentially affected by it... The line between individual consideration and inconsistency, slender enough in theory, can be imperceptible in practice"), 722j (policy formulated together with exceptions "a legitimate method of resolving the potential conflict between the two principles"), revisited in *R v Lambeth London Borough Council, ex p Njomo* (1996) 28 HLR 737; *R (Assisted Reproduction and Gynaecology Centre) v Human Fertilisation and Embryology Authority* [2002] EWCA Civ 20 [2003] 1 FCR 266 at [54] ("It is one thing for a decision-maker to decide in advance that no applications of a particular kind are going to succeed. It is another to reach a reasoned decision which no doubt would - and arguably should - be reached again [on] similar facts. To call the latter a fettering of discretion is to damn the [defendant] if it attempts to achieve consistency from case to case and to damn it if it does not").

50.4.8 **Rigidity lawful.** *R (Nicholds) v Security Industry Authority* [2006] EWHC 1792 (Admin) [2007] 1 WLR 2067 at [60]-[61] (fetter principle inapplicable where exercising a rule-making power or where allowing exceptions would conflict with legislative aim); *R (Elias) v Secretary of State for Defence* [2006] EWCA Civ 1293 [2006] 1 WLR 3213 at [191] (fetter principle inapplicable to prerogative power); *R (S) v Chief Constable of South Yorkshire* [2004] UKHL 39 [2004] 1 WLR 2196 at [60] (blanket policy to retain DNA and fingerprint samples of those investigated by the police lawful, because "unrealistic and impractical" to consider each case individually); *R v Secretary of State for the Home Department, ex p Hepworth* [1998] COD 146 (acc transcript) (fixed criteria permissible for "a clear system for incentives within the prison"); *R (P) v Secretary of State for the Home Department* 17th May 2002 unrep. at [34] (lawful to have a "policy without exception" for "prisoners whose escape would expose the public to real and significant dangers"), [38] (still need individual consideration of escape potential of individual prisoners); *R (Ealing London Borough Council) v Audit Commission for England and Wales* [2005] EWCA Civ 556 (2005) 8 CCLR 317 at [17] (entitled to have absolute or binding rules).

50.4.9 **Whether overrigid policy: further illustrations.** *R (British Beer and Pub Association) v Canterbury City Council* [2005] EWHC 1318 (Admin) [2006] LGR 596 (overprescriptive liquor licensing policy); *R (Stephenson) v Stockton-on-Tees Borough Council* [2005] EWCA Civ 960 [2006] LGR 135 at [21] (applying family member rule without considering whether to exercise discretion to make an exception); *Lindsay v Commissioners of Customs and Excise* [2002] EWCA Civ 267 [2002] 1 WLR 1766 (blanket policy not permitting consideration of proportionality of penalty); *R v Army Board of the Defence Council, ex p Anderson* [1992] QB 169, 188E ("inflexible policy not to hold oral hearings"); *R v Warwickshire County Council, ex p Collymore* [1995] ELR 217 (on facts, operation of policy shown to be inflexible); *R v Nottingham City Council, ex p Howitt* [1999] COD 530 (inflexibility not shown on the facts); *R v North Yorkshire County Council, ex p Hargreaves (No.2)* (1998) 1 CCLR 331 (policy to pay only additional holiday costs an impermissible fetter); *R v Westminster City Council, ex p Hussain* (1999) 31 HLR 645 (policy that persons in claimant's position suspended for 2 years from receiving further housing offer an unreasonable fetter); *R (P and Q) v Secretary of State for the Home Department* [2001] EWCA Civ 1151 [2001] 1 WLR 2002 at [100]-[101] (policy of separating incarcerated mothers from their children after 18 months needing "greater flexibility" than limited exceptions of "a few weeks").

50.4.10 Substance and not form: practical operation of the policy.
(A) POLICY FLEXIBLE IN FORM BUT RIGID IN PRACTICE. *R v Warwickshire County Council, ex p Collymore* [1995] ELR 217, 223D-E (looking at statistics so as to conclude that policy in fact implemented inflexibly), 227B-H; *R v Lambeth London Borough Council, ex p Njomo* (1996) 28 HLR 737 (policy rigidly applied in the present case, because stated exceptions treated as exhaustive); *R v Southwark London Borough Council, ex p Melak* (1997) 29 HLR 223 (policy lawful but too rigidly applied); *R (P) v Secretary of State for the Home Department* 17th May 2002 unrep. at [34] (distinguishing "between the existence of a lawful policy and the question whether such policy has been lawfully implemented"), [21]; *R v North Derbyshire Health Authority, ex p Fisher* (1998) 10 Admin LR 27, 47A-D (rejecting authority's unsubstantiated assertion that it operated special cases criteria); *R v North West Lancashire Health Authority, ex p A* [2000] 1 WLR 977, 993H ("the stance of the Authority, coupled with the near uniformity of its reasons for rejecting each of the [claimants'] requests for funding was not a genuine application of a policy subject to individually determined exceptions"); *R v London Borough of Bexley, ex p Jones* [1995] ELR 42, 55 (defendants "effectually disabled themselves from considering individual cases"; "there has been no convincing evidence that at any material time they had an exceptions procedure worth the name. There is no indication that there was a genuine willingness to consider individual cases").
(B) POLICY RIGID IN FORM BUT FLEXIBLE IN PRACTICE. *R v Secretary of State for the Home Department, ex p Hindley* [2001] 1 AC 410, 417D-E (accepting assurances that Home Secretary prepared to reconsider life tariffs even absent the "exceptional progress" threshold referred to in the stated policy).
(C) POLICY IMPERMISSIBLE DESPITE ROOM FOR EXCEPTIONS. *R v Secretary of State for the Home Department, ex p Simms* [2000] 2 AC 115 (`blanket' policy held to be unlawful notwithstanding some room for exceptions in "wholly exceptional circumstances"), 124G; *R (Sacupima) v Newham London Borough Council* [2001] 1 WLR 563 (housing policy providing for exceptions which were insufficiently flexible to permit all relevant matters to be addressed); *R v Immigration Officer, ex p Quaquah* [2000] INLR 196, 205C (Home Secretary not entitled to operate "presumption" against the grant of exceptional leave to remain, but obliged to consider each case on its intrinsic merits); *R v Lambeth London Borough Council, ex p Njomo* (1996) 28 HLR 737, 744-745 (although policy with built-in exceptions not unlawful, applied too rigidly because exceptions treated as exhaustive); *R v Secretary of State for the Home Department, ex p Hindley* [2001] 1 AC 410, 417A-E (not sufficient that policy allowed reconsideration where "exceptional progress"; Court requiring assurances that Home Secretary prepared to reconsider generally); *R (Cannan) v Governor of HMP Full Sutton* [2003] EWCA Civ 1480 (test for exceptions too restrictive to be ECHR-compliant).

P51 Insufficient inquiry. A body must sufficiently acquaint itself with relevant information, fairly presented and properly addressed.

51.1 Duty of sufficient inquiry
51.2 Whether material fairly presented/properly addressed

51.1 Duty of sufficient inquiry. A public body has a basic duty to take reasonable steps to acquaint itself with relevant material.

51.1.1 The *Tameside* duty. *Secretary of State for Education and Science v Tameside Metropolitan Borough Council* [1977] AC 1014, 1065B (Lord Diplock: "the question for the court is, did the Secretary of State ask himself the right question and take reasonable steps to acquaint himself with the relevant information to enable him to answer it correctly?"); *R (DF) v Chief Constable of Norfolk Police* [2002] EWHC 1738 (Admin) at [45] ("a decision-maker has an obligation to equip himself with the information necessary to take an informed decision"); *R v Lincolnshire County Council and Wealden District Council, ex p Atkinson, Wales and Stratford* (1996) 8 Admin LR 529, 543C (referring to the *Tameside* duty as an "elementary duty"); *R v Camden London Borough Council, ex p H* [1996] ELR 360 (duty to make sufficient inquiries; specifically, having decided to resolve certain factual issues, duty to carry out investigations in that regard in a thorough and balanced way); *R v Wolverhampton Municipal Borough Council, ex p Dunne* (1997) 29 HLR 745 (duty to have regard to certain relevant considerations giving rise to further duty to conduct appropriate inquiries); *R v Secretary of State for the Home Department, ex p Iyadurai* [1998] Imm AR 470, 475 (Lord Woolf MR, asking: "whether the Secretary of State has (i) taken adequate steps to inform himself of the position ... (ii) properly considered the information which is available to him and (iii) come to an opinion which is consistent with that information, recognising that it is his responsibility to evaluate the material which is available to him"); <49.2.8> (whether sufficient evidential basis for decision).

51.1.2 Duty of inquiry: eliciting views. *R v Secretary of State for Education, ex p London Borough of Southwark* [1995] ELR 308, 323C (Laws J: "the decision-maker must call his own attention to considerations relevant to his decision, a duty which in practice may require him to consult outside bodies"); *R v Camden London Borough Council, ex p Adair* (1997) 29 HLR 236 (duty to make inquiries of another appropriate department); cf. *R (Anglian Water Services Ltd) v Environment Agency* [2003] EWHC 1506 (Admin) [2004] Env LR 287 at [36] (Environment Agency "were not under any obligation to seek independent advice. Its role under the statutory scheme was to resolve the dispute that had arisen ... It was fully entitled to consider the material submitted on both sides ... and to arrive at the decision"); *R (Khatun) v London Borough of Newham* [2004] EWCA Civ 55 [2005] QB 37 at [27] (Laws LJ: "the decision-maker's duty to have regard to relevant considerations may require him to take into account the affected person's views about the subject-matter"); <60.6.9> (consultee/adviser misinformed); <60.6.5> (consultation requirement of adequate information).

51.1.3 Statutory duty of inquiry. *R v Barnet London Borough Council, ex p Babalola* (1996) 28 HLR 196 (flawed finding of intentional homelessness, since council having made no finding as to whether accepting complaints of violence and placing on claimant burden of substantiating them, so that failing in statutory duty to make inquiries and satisfy itself); *R v Brent London Borough Council, ex p Baruwa* (1997) 29 HLR 915, 928 (considering local authorities' duty to make inquiries under Housing Act 1985 s.62: "the authority is under no obligation to investigate every detail and every inconsistency ... How much they investigate will be a matter for their appreciation and will depend on the person with whom they were dealing").

51.1.4 **Situations where no duty of independent inquiry.** *R (Anglian Water Services Ltd) v Environment Agency* [2003] EWHC 1506 (Admin) [2004] Env LR 287 at [36] (Environment Agency's "role under the statutory scheme was to resolve the dispute that had arisen ... It was fully entitled to consider the material submitted on both sides ... and to arrive at the decision"); *R v Criminal Injuries Compensation Board, ex p Milton* [1996] COD 264 (CICB under no duty to make inquiries or seek evidence of its own initiative); *R v Sedgemoor District Council, ex p McCarthy* (1996) 28 HLR 607 (no duty to inquire into matter where no reasonable grounds for believing it to be a live issue); <60.8.8> (whether a right of proactivity or assistance by the decision-making body).

51.1.5 **Sufficiency of inquiry primarily a matter for the decision-maker.** *R (Khatun) v London Borough of Newham* [2004] EWCA Civ 55 [2005] QB 37 at [35] (Laws LJ: "it is for the decision-maker and not the court, subject ... to *Wednesbury* review, to decide upon the manner and intensity of enquiry to be undertaken into any relevant factor accepted or demonstrated as such", referring to observations of Schiemann J (from *Costello* p.309) as to whether "no reasonable council possessed of [this] material could suppose that the inquiries they had made were sufficient", and Neill LJ (from *Bayani* p.415) that: "The court should not intervene merely because it considers that further inquiries would have been sensible or desirable. It should intervene only if no reasonable housing authority could have been satisfied on the basis of the inquiries made"); *R (Kanssen) v Secretary of State for the Environment, Food and Rural Affairs* [2005] EWHC 1024 (Admin) at [35] (whether no reasonable council could suppose that it had made sufficient inquiries).

51.1.6 **Whether sufficiency of inquiry: illustrations.**
(A) INADEQUATE. *R (Q) v Secretary of State for the Home Department* [2003] EWCA Civ 364 [2004] QB 36 at [90] (unfairness because questions asked not enabling the interviewer "to have a sufficiently full picture for a fair decision to be made"); *R v Ealing London Borough Council, ex p C* (2000) 3 CCLR 122, 130I (council failing to take reasonable steps to enable it to answer the question); *R v Secretary of State for the Home Department, ex p Venables* [1998] AC 407 (CA), 453F ("essential" to be "fully informed of all the material facts and circumstances"), 455G ("did not adequately inform himself of the full facts and circumstances of the case"), 456E-F ("not clear ... that he took any steps to inform himself of the relevant facts"), 466G ("The wider the discretion conferred on the Secretary of State the more important it must be that he has all relevant material to enable him properly to exercise it"); *R v Kensington and Chelsea Royal London Borough Council, ex p Silchenstedt* (1997) 29 HLR 728 (failure to conduct adequate inquiries); *R v Secretary of State for the Home Department, ex p Gashi* [1999] INLR 276 (failure of duty of inquiry, where striking statistics calling for an explanation), 306D-F (duty, in an anxious scrutiny context, to pursue any aspect of the evidence calling for an explanation); *R (Ramda) v Secretary of State for the Home Department* [2002] EWHC 1278 (Admin) at [23]-[24] (situation where "the adequacy of the total inquiry" was defective); *Naraynsingh v Commissioner of Police* [2004] UKPC 20 at [21] ("substantially more in the way of investigation was required than was undertaken here"), [23] ("a fair procedure demanded that further inquiries be made"); *R (Ford) v Leasehold Valuation Tribunal* [2005] EWHC 503 (Admin) (apparent conflict between lease and freehold raised a significant doubt calling for further inquiries).
(B) ADEQUATE. *R (National Association of Health Stores) v Secretary of State for Health* [2005] EWCA Civ 154 at [62] (decision-making Minister not having imputed knowledge from officials but only what they imparted, nevertheless knew "enough to enable him to make an informed judgment"); *R v Solihull Borough Council, ex p W* [1997] ELR 489, 499A-C (authorities' decisions to exclude pupil not flawed for failure to take reasonable steps to acquaint themselves with relevant information); *R v Secretary of State for the Home Department, ex p Elshani* [1999] INLR 265, 273C-E (mere fact that appraisal continuing at time of decision does

not establish failure to take reasonable steps to acquaint self with facts); *R (Hossack) v Kettering Borough Council* [2003] EWHC 1929 (Admin) at [47] ("the extent of the investigation carried out ... was ... sufficient to enable the council reasonably to proceed to a decision").

51.1.7 **Impact assessment.** *R (C) v Secretary of State for Justice* [2008] EWCA Civ 882 at [49] (importance of race equality impact assessment to comply with Race Relations Act 1976 s.71); *R (Watkins-Singh) v Aberdare Girls High School Governors* [2008] EWHC 1865 (Admin) (breach of statutory impact assessment duty); *R (Kaur) v Ealing London Borough Council* [2008] EWHC 2062 (Admin) (breach of impact assessment duty); *Berkeley v Secretary of State for the Environment* [2001] 2 AC 603 (environmental impact assessment).

51.2 **Whether material fairly presented/properly addressed** Public bodies and staff who assist them should ensure that relevant material, including views of consultees, are fairly and adequately presented to the decision-makers. They in turn should ensure that the material is properly considered and addressed.

51.2.1 **Inadequate presentation of material to the decision-maker.**[16] *R (Georgiou) v London Borough of Enfield* [2004] EWHC 779 (Admin) [2004] LGR 497 at [94] (deficiencies in officers' report meaning "the committee was not made sufficiently aware of relevant information and that its decision was flawed in consequence"), [85] ("the report to members was materially deficient and misleading. It resulted in the committee proceeding on a mistaken factual basis and failing to have proper regard to a material consideration"); *R (Saunders) v Tendring District Council* [2003] EWHC 2977 (Admin) (officers' report misleading in ignoring council's own objections in previously refusing planning permission for same development); *R v Camden London Borough Council, ex p Cran* (1996) 94 LGR 8, 73 ("affected citizens and representative organisations are entitled to expect objectivity in those whose duty it is to convey to decision makers what they have suggested"); *R v Powys County Council, ex p Andrews* [1997] Env LR 170, 182 (*Cran* a case about accuracy of communication of consultees' views, not general need for open-mindedness by officers, of the kind needed from decision-makers to whom officers reported); *James D'Avila v Tom Sawyer* 22nd March 1996 unrep. (exaggerated and misleading report preventing decision-maker from being able to give the matter fair and proper consideration); *R v Advertising Standards Authority Ltd, ex p the Insurance Service Plc* (1990) 2 Admin LR 77, 92B-93A (facts not accurately placed before decision-making committee by secretariat which had investigated complaint); *R v South Glamorgan County Council, ex p Harding* [1998] COD 243 (incumbent on officer reporting to lay the whole story out to the committee so that members could make a properly informed decision; case not fairly presented to the decision-maker); *R v Bacon's City Technology College, ex p W* [1998] ELR 488, 498G ("the summary report put before the governors was one-sided"); *R (Morley) v Nottinghamshire Healthcare NHS Trust* [2002] EWCA Civ 1728 [2003] 1 All ER 784 at [39]-[41] (responsible medical officer reporting to Secretary of State required to make proper inquiries and form a clinical judgment, but not required to notify the Secretary of State of alternative medical views); *R (Quark Fishing Ltd) v Secretary of State for Foreign and Commonwealth Affairs* [2002] EWCA Civ 1409 (material on which licence refusal direction made not giving an accurate and fair picture of the claimant's compliance record); *R (Bedford) v London Borough of Islington* [2002] EWHC 2044 (Admin) [2003] Env LR 463 at [113] (planning officers' reports not unfair); cf. *R v Independent Television Commission, ex p TSW Broadcasting Ltd* [1994] 2 LRC 414 (HL expressing caution as to impugning a decision by reference to criticising staff report).

---

[16] Jason Braier [2005] JR 156.

51.2.2 **Presentation of material to a consultee.** *R v Tandridge District Council, ex p Al Fayed* [2000] 1 PLR 58, 61D-G (treating there as having been a procedural impropriety where claimant's objection not put to specialist body whom the defendant was consulting).

51.2.3 **Conscientious consideration: duty to grapple with material.** *R v Secretary of State for the Home Department, ex p Iyadurai* [1998] Imm AR 470, 475 (Lord Woolf MR, asking "whether the Secretary of State has ... (ii) properly considered the information which is available to him and (iii) come to an opinion which is consistent with that information, recognising that it is his responsibility to evaluate the material which is available to him"); <60.6.7> (consultation: conscientious consideration); *R v Doncaster Metropolitan Borough Council, ex p Nortrop* (1996) 28 HLR 862, 874 (referring to the "duty to explore all the material evidence before it"); *O'Reilly v Coventry Coroner* [1996] COD 268 (where unresolved documentary inconsistencies, "insufficiency of inquiry" by coroner); *R v Secretary of State for the Home Department, ex p Ajayi* 12th May 1994 unrep. (duty to balance the relevant factors, not just have them in mind); *R v Burton upon Trent Justices, ex p Hussain* (1997) 9 Admin LR 233, 237D-H (magistrates' duty, on taxi licensing appeal, to make findings of fact); *R v Secretary of State for the Environment, ex p West Wiltshire District Council* [1996] Env LR 312 (no proper finding on crucial question of fact); <P56> (relevancy/irrelevancy duty); *R v Director of Public Prosecutions, ex p Treadaway* The Times 31st October 1997 (a civil court having found the alleged conduct proven, a most careful analysis of that decision by the DPP was required if a prosecution was not to be undertaken); *R v General Medical Council, ex p Salvi* The Times 24th February 1998 (see transcript) (given the nature of the issue of judgment, mere fact that deliberations only 5 minutes long not justifying conclusion that case was not given adequate consideration); *Dyason v Secretary of State for the Environment* [1998] 2 PLR 54 (informality of planning inspector's hearing indicating insufficiently thorough examination of the issues, so as not to constitute a fair hearing); *R v Legal Aid Area No.1 (London) Appeal Committee, ex p McCormick* [2000] 1 WLR 1804, 1813G-1814E (in deciding on sanction, committee obliged to decide whether claimant culpable); *R v Birmingham City Council, ex p Killigrew* (2000) 3 CCLR 109, 117G-118F ("no proper analysis", "no proper consideration"); *R v Ealing London Borough Council, ex p C* (2000) 3 CCLR 122, 130G ("no analysis" of relevant problems); *R v Lambeth London Borough Council, ex p K* (2000) 3 CCLR 141, 149H ("failure by the council to go through the logical and required process" required), 150D (insufficient "clarity of approach").

51.2.4 **Material considered by departmental official.** <50.3.1> (*Carltona* principle); *R (National Association of Health Stores) v Secretary of State for Health* [2005] EWCA Civ 154 (*Carltona* not meaning information known to officials imputed to Minister, where decision taken by Minister personally).

51.2.5 **Adequacy of reasons.** <62.3>.

> **P52 Bad faith/improper motive.** A body must not act
> in bad faith or have an improper object or purpose.

52.1 Bad faith
52.2 Improper motive

52.1 Bad faith. Judicial review will lie where a decision-maker is shown to have acted in bad faith. This is a strong accusation not lightly to be alleged and which is difficult to prove. It is also usually unnecessary given more familiar alternatives, such as bias and improper motive.

52.1.1 Good faith as a basic duty. *Associated Provincial Picture Houses Ltd v Wednesbury Corporation* [1948] 1 KB 223, 229 (Lord Greene MR: "Bad faith, dishonesty - those of course, stand by themselves"); *Smith v East Elloe Rural District Council* [1956] AC 736, 762 ("bad faith stands in a class by itself"); *Board of Education v Rice* [1911] AC 179, 182 ("they must act in good faith ... for that is a duty lying upon everyone who decides anything"); *R v Secretary of State for the Home Department, ex p Fire Brigades Union* [1995] 2 AC 513, 563H ("good faith ... is an indispensable element of the lawful exercise of ... any ... statutory discretion"); *Holgate-Mohammed v Duke* [1984] AC 437, 443D ("The first of the *Wednesbury* principles is that the discretion must be exercised in good faith"); *British Oxygen Co Ltd v Board of Trade* [1971] AC 610, 624F-G (describing as the first of "two general grounds on which the exercise of an unqualified discretion can be attacked": "It must not be exercised in bad faith"); *Nakkuda Ali v Jayaratne* [1951] AC 66, 77 (Lord Radcliffe: "No doubt he must not exercise the power in bad faith: but the field in which this kind of question arises is such that the reservation for the case of bad faith is hardly more than a formality").

52.1.2 Bad faith in action. *R v Derbyshire County Council, ex p Times Supplements Ltd* (1991) 3 Admin LR 241, 253A (Watkins LJ: "[this] decision-making ... can only in the circumstances have been activated in my view by bad faith or, in a word, vindictiveness. It was thus an abuse of power contrary to the public good"); *Watkins v Secretary of State for the Home Department* [2006] UKHL 17 [2006] 2 AC 395 (failed misfeasance claim arising out of prison officers opening legally privileged correspondence in bad faith).

52.1.3 Bad faith applying to delegated legislation/rules. *McEldowney v Forde* [1971] AC 632, 649E-F (describing the discretion to make "regulations for the preservation of peace and the maintenance of order", as capable of interference "if the Minister is shown to have gone outside the four corners of the Act or has acted in bad faith"); *Kruse v Johnson* [1898] 2 QB 91, 99 <13.5.4(A)>; *Bugg v DPP* [1993] QB 473, 500G (considering bad faith on part of maker of byelaws).

52.1.4 Bad faith as part of "natural justice". *Byrne v Kinematograph Renters Society Ltd* [1958] 1 WLR 762, 784 (Harman J: "What then are the requirements of natural justice in a case of this kind? First, I think that the person accused should know the nature of the accusation made; secondly, that he should be given an opportunity to state his case; and, thirdly, of course, that the tribunal should act in good faith. I do not myself think that there really is anything more"), cited in *Ceylon University v Fernando* [1960] 1 WLR 223, 232).

52.1.5 Need to particularise and prove bad faith. *Cannock Chase District Council v Kelly* [1978] 1 WLR 1 (defendant to possession proceedings failing to particularise and prove that notice to quit served in bad faith); *R (Amraf Training Plc) v Secretary of State for Education and Employment* The Times 28th June 2001 (need clear pleading and cogent evidence when alleging victimisation).

52.1.6 **Bad faith as nullity.** <44.2.2>.

52.1.7 **Bad faith and resolving disputed facts.** <17.3.11>.

52.2 Improper motive. Judicial review will lie where the decision-maker was motivated by some aim or purpose regarded by the law as illegitimate. This negative obligation (not to have an improper purpose) fits alongside the*Padfield* positive obligation (to promote the legislative purpose).

52.2.1 **Improper motive as a ground for judicial review.** *R v Secretary of State for the Environment, ex p Nottinghamshire County Council* [1986] AC 240, 250B (Lord Scarman, describing *Wheeler v Leicester City Council* [1985] AC 1054 as "a striking illustration on its facts of circumstances in which the courts may intervene on the ground of abuse of power arising from an improper motive in its exercise"); *R v Inland Revenue Commissioners, ex p Preston* [1985] AC 835, 864H-865B (Lord Templeman, referring to these three cases as improper motive cases: *Padfield v Minister of Agriculture Fisheries & Food* [1968] AC 997 (the fear of a "politically embarrassing" situation); *Congreve v Home Office* [1976] QB 629 (disapproval of lawful conduct); *Laker Airways Ltd v Department of Trade* [1977] QB 643 ("the ulterior motive of making it impossible ... to pursue a course of which the Minister disapproved").

52.2.2 **Punishing one who has done no wrong.** *Congreve v Home Office* [1976] QB 629, 651A-C ("when the licensee has done nothing wrong at all, I do not think the Minister can lawfully revoke the licence, at any rate, not without offering him his money back, and not even then except for good cause"); *Wheeler v Leicester City Council* [1985] AC 1054, 1081C ("this use by the council of its statutory powers was a misuse of power. The council could not properly seek to use its statutory powers of management or any other statutory powers for the purposes of punishing the club when the club had done no wrong"); *R v Secretary of State for Trade, ex p Perestrello* [1981] QB 19, 35F-G (use of power, "not for the purposes for which the power was given, but, for example, to punish someone"); *R v Lewisham Borough Council, ex p Shell* [1988] 1 All ER 938, 952d-e (pressure on Shell to withdraw from South Africa, when Shell not "acting in any way unlawfully"); *R v Greenwich London Borough Council, ex p Lovelace* [1991] 1 WLR 506 (no evidence that councillors removed from committee as punishment for opposition); *R v Secretary of State for the Environment, ex p Haringey London Borough Council* (1994) 92 LGR 538 (Secretary of State entitled to make direction barring council from collecting refuse because it had distorted competition between tenderers; intention to "make an example" of the council not an improper motive).

52.2.3 **Whether "political" motives improper.** *Magill v Porter* [2001] UKHL 67 [2002] 2 AC 357 (misuse of power to designate council houses for sale to pursue electoral advantage), at [19(5)] (Lord Bingham, discussing the principle that "powers conferred on a local authority may not lawfully be exercised to promote the electoral advantage of a political party"); *Padfield v Minister of Agriculture Fisheries & Food* [1968] AC 997, 1058F-G (the "reasons for refusing an investigation ... must not be based on political considerations which as Farwell LJ said in *R v Board of Education* [1910] 2 KB 165, 181 are pre eminently extraneous"), 1061F ("This fear of parliamentary trouble ... if an inquiry were ordered and its possible results is alone sufficient to vitiate the Minister's decision which ... can never validly turn on purely political considerations"), 1032E ("to refuse to refer a complaint because, if he did so, he might later find himself in an embarrassing situation, ... would plainly be a bad reason"); *R v London Borough of Ealing, ex p Times Newspapers Ltd* [1987] IRLR 129 (local authorities' decision to ban Murdoch newspapers from public libraries ultra vires and an abuse of power, being inspired by political views); *R v Secretary of State for the Home Department, ex p Launder* [1997] 1 WLR 839, 868B-D (suggesting decision would have been open to challenge if "based wholly on political policy considerations"); *R v Secretary of State for Foreign and Commonwealth Affairs, ex p World Development Movement Ltd* [1995] 1 WLR 386, 398C-D ("a political purpose can taint a decision with impropriety"); *R v Southwark London Borough Council, ex p Udu* (1996) 8 Admin LR 25 (council a political body, entitled to reach a political decision not to give grants to students at private institutions); *R v Leeds City Council, ex p Cobleigh* [1997] COD 69 (political considerations do not necessarily flaw a local authority's decisions); *R v Local Commissioner for Administration in North and North East England, ex p Liverpool City Council* [2001] 1 All ER 462 at [36] (party political influence decisive in consideration of planning application, meaning that immaterial consideration taken into account).

52.2.4 **Other examples of improper motive/purpose.** *R v Walsall Justices, ex p W* [1990] 1 QB 253, 260E-H (improper to adjourn case because of imminent change in the law which magistrates regarding as more just); *R v Hendon Justices, ex p Director of Public Prosecutions* [1994] QB 167, 174E-F (improper to dismiss informations because of irritation at CPS inefficiency); *Board of Education v Rice* [1911] AC 179, 186 (Earl of Halsbury: "hostility to the Church schools"); *Municipal Council of Sydney v Campbell* [1925] AC 339 (land-acquisition for re-sale at a profit an improper use of statutory power to acquire land for improving the city); *R v Hillingdon London Borough Council, ex p Royco Homes Ltd* [1974] QB 720 (ulterior object for planning condition requiring properties to be let to persons on the council's waiting list); *R v Wellingborough Magistrates Court, ex p Francois* [1994] COD 462 (impropriety where prosecutor in a hurry to finish the case); *In re Arrows Ltd (No.4)* [1995] 2 AC 75, 107E ("it was an improper exercise of ... discretion... to seek to prevent the use by the Serious Fraud Office of those transcripts in the criminal proceedings"); *R v Maidstone Crown Court, ex p Hollstein* [1995] 3 All ER 503 and *R v Maidstone Crown Court, ex p Clark* [1995] 1 WLR 831, 836E (impermissible to use arraignment to foil right to bail); *R v National Rivers Authority, ex p Haughey* (1996) 8 Admin LR 567 (NRA not entitled to use its licensing powers to enforce its side of an argument); *R v Secretary of State for the Home Department, ex p Adams* [1995] All ER (EC) 177 (where Secretary of State entitled to withhold reasons need exceptional case to intervene on improper motive grounds); *R v Inner London Crown Court, ex p B* [1996] COD 17 (sentencing judge's decision to lift restriction on naming of a young offender, general deterrence (cf. simply ensuring wider publicity) a permissible objective); *St George's Healthcare NHS Trust v S* [1999] Fam 26 (improper to use Mental Health Act to protect the unborn child from mother's exercise of right to refuse medical intervention); *R v Inland Revenue Commissioners, ex p Preston* [1985] AC 835, 870D ("would have been inspired by an improper motive and would have constituted an abuse of power" to have "deliberately waited from 1979 until 1982 in order that the claims of the appellant might be time barred").

52.2.5 **Link between improper motive and** *Padfield.* <P53> (*Padfield* principle); *R v Inland Revenue Commissioners, ex p Preston* [1985] AC 835, 865B (Lord Templeman, describing improper motive cases as cases where "judicial review was granted because the Ministers acted 'unfairly' when they abused their powers by exercising or declining to exercise those powers in order to achieve objectives which were not the objectives for which the powers had been conferred"); *R v Maidstone Crown Court, ex p Clark* [1995] 1 WLR 831 (arraignment to defeat the statutory protections of the right to bail not a proper use of the power), 836D-G; *R v Wilson, ex p Williamson* [1996] COD 42 (*Padfield*-type challenge succeeding, but clear that no question of improper motive); *Stewart v Perth and Kinross Council* [2004] UKHL 16 at [28] (Lord Hope: "the discretion which is vested in the licensing authority is not unlimited. The authority is not at liberty to use it for an ulterior object, however desirable that object may seem to it to be in the public interest").

52.2.6 **The approach to mixed purposes/mixed motives.** <4.2.2> (materiality and mixed/separable reasons); *R (Richards) v Pembrokeshire County Council* [2004] EWCA Civ 1000 [2005] LGR 105 at [44] (traffic control directions unlawful where statutorily-prescribed harbour-management purpose was their "collateral consequence" but not "one of their main purposes"); *Porter v Magill* (1998) 96 LGR 157 (DC), 167d-f (where several purposes, sufficient that "true and dominant purpose" is lawful, even though incidental unlawful purpose; where two purposes, decision vitiated if ultra vires purpose "a major purpose"), also HL at [2001] UKHL 67 [2002] 2 AC 357 (drawing a distinction between an exercise of power for a legitimate purpose, in the hope of electoral advantage, and action to promote electoral advantage); *R v Crown Court at Southwark, ex p Bowles* [1998] AC 641, 651F-G (statutory purpose for use of power must be true and dominant purpose); *R v Inner London Education Authority, ex p Westminster City Council* [1986] 1 WLR 28, 49H (sufficient that improper purpose "materially influenced" the relevant decision); *R v Broadcasting Complaints Commission, ex p Owen* [1985] QB 1153, 1176G-1177C (mixed purposes); *R v Lewisham Borough Council, ex p Shell* [1988] 1 All ER 938, 952f (impermissible motive "inextricably mixed up with [permissible] ... and this extraneous and impermissible purpose has the effect of vitiating the decision as a whole"); *Earl Fitwilliam's Wentworth Estates Co Ltd v Minister of Town and Country Planning* [1951] 2 KB 284, 307 ("the law always has regard to the dominant purpose"); *In re K (A Child) (Secure Accommodation Order: Right to Liberty)* [2001] Fam 377 at [64] (sufficient for detention justified under ECHR Art 5(1)(d) as detention "for the purpose of educational supervision", that such supervision "one of the purposes" of the detention).

P53 Frustrating the legislative purpose. A body must act so as to promote the purpose for which the power was conferred.

53.1 Duty to promote the legislative purpose

53.1 Duty to promote the legislative purpose. Statutes are interpreted by reference to their purpose, and statutory powers must be exercised for the purpose for which they were conferred. Public authorities are required to promote, and not to frustrate, the legislative purpose.

53.1.1 Power must be exercised for purposes for which conferred. <39.1.2>; also <29.2> (legislative purpose and judicial review); <29.1.1> (purposive approach to statutory interpretation).

53.1.2 *Padfield*: the duty to promote the legislative purpose. *Langley v Liverpool City Council* [2005] EWCA Civ 1173 [2006] 1 WLR 375 at [33] ("discretionary statutory powers must be exercised to promote the policy and objects of the statute"); *Padfield v Minister of Agriculture Fisheries & Food* [1968] AC 997, 1030B-D (Lord Reid: "Parliament must have conferred the discretion with the intention that it should be used to promote the policy and objects of the Act, the policy and objects of the Act must be determined by construing the Act as a whole and construction is always a matter of law for the court"; "if the Minister, by reason of his having misconstrued the Act or for some other reason, so uses his discretion as to thwart or run counter to the policy and objects of the Act, then ... persons aggrieved [are] entitled to the protection of the court"), 1060G ("the executive ... must act lawfully and that is a matter to be determined by looking at the Act and its scope and object in conferring a discretion upon the Minister"); *R v Braintree District Council, ex p Halls* (2000) 32 HLR 770, 779 ("It is very securely established that a public decision-maker may only use statutory power conferred on him to further the policy; and objects of the Act"); *R v Secretary of State for the Home Department, ex p Brind* [1991] 1 AC 696, 756G ("the discretion ... must be used only to advance the purposes for which it was conferred. It has accordingly to be used to promote the policy and objects of the Act"); *R (Hooper) v Secretary of State for Work and Pensions* [2005] UKHL 29 [2005] 1 WLR 1681 at [123] (abuse of power to exercise it "inconsistently with Parliament's clearly expressed will"); *R (Walker) v Secretary of State for Justice* [2008] EWCA Civ 30 [2008] 3 All ER 104 at [41] (failure to fund adequate offending behaviour courses in prisons breaching *Padfield* principle); *R (W) v Commissioner of Police for the Metropolis* [2006] EWCA Civ 458 [2007] QB 399 at [35] (*Padfield* principle meaning police power not a curfew power, but needing to be exercised to protect from or prevent anti-social behaviour); *R v Maidstone Crown Court, ex p Hollstein* [1995] 3 All ER 503 (arraignment foiling the plain spirit of the Bail Act); *R v London Borough of Lambeth, ex p Ghous* [1993] COD 302 (policy thwarting legislative principle of parental choice); *R v Secretary of State for the Home Department, ex p Fire Brigades Union* [1995] 2 AC 513, 552D (wrong to use prerogative powers "so as to frustrate the will of Parliament expressed in a statute"); *R v Warwickshire County Council, ex p Williams* [1995] ELR 326, 331F (duty not to "use its discretion as to thwart or run counter to the policy and objects of the Act"); *R v Secretary of State for the Home Department, ex p Yousaf* [2000] 3 All ER 649 at [48] (importance of the *Padfield* principle); *R v J* [2004] UKHL 42 [2005] 1 AC 562 at [38] (CPS having acted so as to "circumvent the intent of Parliament").

53.1.3 COE:COM R(80)2. Recommendation No.R(80)2 of the Committee of Ministers (adopted 11 March 1980) <45.1.4(B)> (including in the "Basic principles": "An administrative authority, when exercising a discretionary power: (1) does not pursue a purpose other than that for which the power has been conferred").

53.1.4 **Express statutory purpose.** *McEldowney v Forde* [1971] AC 632, 655C ("If regulations purporting to be made under this power could be shown to have been made otherwise than for the specified purposes ... they could be held to be ultra vires"); *R v Secretary of State for Foreign Affairs, ex p World Development Movement Ltd* [1995] 1 WLR 386 (exercise of power not falling within express statutory purpose); *UK Waste Management Ltd v West Lancashire District Council* The Times 5th April 1996 (power to make road order "for the purpose of carrying out an experimental scheme of traffic control" not to be used for sole purpose of banning heavy goods vehicles); *R v Secretary of State for Employment, ex p National Association of Colliery Overmen, Deputies & Shotfirers* [1994] COD 218 ("designed etc" treated as an express purpose, not an ascertainable result or a condition precedent); *Fawcett Properties Ltd v Chertsey Urban District Council* [1961] AC 636 (whether genuine planning purpose).

53.1.5 *Padfield* **challenge to delegated legislation/rules.** *R v Secretary of State for the Environment, Transport and the Regions, ex p Spath Holme* [2001] 2 AC 349 (whether Order ultra vires because made for a purpose different from that for which Parliament intended to confer the power); *R v Secretary of State for the Home Department, ex p National Association of Probation Officers* [1996] COD 399; *R v London Boroughs Transport Committee, ex p Freight Transport Association Ltd* [1991] 1 WLR 828, 836F-H (*Padfield* treated as available to attack Order and licence condition); *R v Secretary of State for the Environment, ex p Brent London Borough Council* [1982] QB 593, 636B-D; *R v Life Assurance & Unit Trust Regulatory Organisation, ex p Kendall* [1994] COD 169 (whether Lautro rule within statutory purposes).

53.1.6 **Decision frustrating the purpose of secondary legislation.** *R (Saadat) v Rent Service* [2001] EWCA Civ 1559 [2002] HLR 613 (decision offending the purpose of a housing benefit Order) at [15] (decision "contrary to the meaning and purposes of the Order").

53.1.7 **Delay as frustrating the legislative purpose.** *R v Tower Hamlets London Borough Council, ex p Khalique* (1994) 26 HLR 517, 522 (council entitled to provide temporary accommodation "so long as the entitlement to settled accommodation is not so deferred as to frustrate the purpose of the legislation and the rights which it gives to individuals, nor deferred or withheld for some improper or illicit reason").

53.1.8 **Proper purpose but not permitted mode.** *R v Secretary of State for Transport, ex p Richmond-upon-Thames London Borough Council* [1994] 1 WLR 74, 89D-E (no answer that purpose was proper if the means chosen was not one of "the permitted modes").

53.1.9 **Cutting across the legislative scheme.** *R v Sefton Metropolitan Borough Council, ex p Help The Aged* [1997] 4 All ER 532, 543g-h (means threshold adopted in council's policy unlawful since conflicting with threshold adopted in regulations); *Laker Airways Ltd v Department of Trade* [1977] QB 643 (judicial review of statutory "guidance" for cutting across the main purpose of the Act); *R v Liverpool City Council, ex p Baby Products Association* [2000] LGR 171 (no power to issue press release where would circumvent detailed statutory code as to enforcement action).

53.1.10 *Padfield* **and other principles.** *R v Managers of South Western Hospital, ex p M* [1993] QB 683, 696E (Laws J: "Elementarily, the public law safeguards enshrined in *Wednesbury* and *Padfield* rules apply to all exercises of administrative power..."); *R v General Medical Council, ex p Virik* [1996] ICR 433, 462F-G (CA interpreting judge's references to *Wednesbury* as inextricably linked to conclusions on statutory construction and *Padfield*); *Chertsey Urban District Council v Mixnam's Properties Ltd* [1965] AC 735, 761A-B (Lord Guest, describing as "ultra vires": "whether the provisions ... can be said to be fairly and reasonably related to the scope and object of the Act").

53.1.11 **Mixed motives/mixed purposes.** <52.2.6> (mixed motives/purposes); <4.2.2> (materiality and mixed/separable reasons).

P54 Substantive unfairness. A body must not act
conspicuously unfairly, nor so unfairly as to abuse its power,
nor in unjustified breach of a legitimate expectation.

54.1 Substantive unfairness
54.2 Unjustified breach of a substantive legitimate expectation

54.1 Substantive unfairness. Though once associated with procedure, fairness is also a substantive standard linked to abuse of power and legitimate expectation. Whether conduct is conspicuously unfair or an abuse of power depends ultimately on whether, in all the circumstances, strong disapproval is called for.

54.1.1 **Fairness beyond process.** *E v Secretary of State for the Home Department* [2004] EWCA Civ 49 [2004] QB 1044 at [65] (fairness test for misunderstanding or ignorance of a relevant fact); *R v North and East Devon Health Authority, ex p Coughlan* [2001] QB 213 (fairness test for justification in breaching a substantive legitimate expectation); *R v Secretary of State for the Home Department, ex p Hindley* [2000] 1 QB 152 (CA), 163D (Lord Woolf MR: "The principle of due process is not confined to procedure. It can have effect on the substance of what is happening in carrying out the sentence"), 164B ("it can result in substantive benefits"); <60.1.7> (due process): <7.6> (basic fairness as a constitutional fundamental); <7.3.3(A)> (basic fairness and the principle of legality); <49.2.2> (disregard of an established and relevant fact as unfairness).

54.1.2 **The rule of law and minimum standards of substantive fairness.** *R v Secretary of State for the Home Department, ex p Pierson* [1998] AC 539, 591A (Lord Steyn: "The rule of law in its wider sense has procedural and substantive effect"), 591F (Lord Steyn: "the rule of law enforces minimum standards of fairness, both substantive and procedural"), 603C (Lord Hope, referring to the Secretary of State as "bound by considerations of substantive fairness ... the presumption must be that he will exercise his powers in a manner which is fair in all the circumstances. What fairness demands depends on the context in which the power is being exercised"); *R v Secretary of State for the Home Department, ex p Hindley* [2001] 1 AC 410, 418D-H (not substantively unfair to replace fixed tariff with whole life tariff).

54.1.3 **Substantive unfairness in action.**
(A) UNFAIR. *R (S) v Secretary of State for the Home Department* [2007] EWCA Civ 546 (arbitrary deferral of old asylum cases to meet target for new ones); *R (British Medical Association) v Secretary of State for Health* [2008] EWHC 599 (Admin) at [12], [27] (retrospective alteration of pensionable earnings method); *R (Bancoult) v Secretary of State for Foreign & Commonwealth Affairs* [2007] EWCA Civ 498 [2008] QB 365 (unfair Orders excluding Chagossians from returning home); *R v Inland Revenue Commissioners, ex p Unilever Plc* [1996] STC 681 (unfair changed practice refusing late tax returns); *R v National Lottery Commission, ex p Camelot Group Plc* [2001] EMLR 3 (allowing one bidder only to allay concerns); *R v Secretary of State for the Home Department, ex p Asif Mahmood Khan* [1984] 1 WLR 1337 (unfair to refuse entry other than by reference to stated criteria); *R (Rashid) v Secretary of State for the Home Department* [2005] EWCA Civ 744 [2005] INLR 550 (unfair non-application of asylum policy to claimant); *R (TB) v Secretary of State for the Home Department* [2007] EWHC 3381 (Admin) at [19], [24] (substantively unfair and an abuse of process for Secretary of State to deny asylum on a ground not raised during the AIT appeal).
(B) NOT UNFAIR. *R v Inland Revenue Commissioners, ex p Matrix-Securities Ltd* [1994] 1 WLR 334 (Revenue withdrawal of tax clearance not substantively unfair in all the circumstances); *R v Inland Revenue Commissioners, ex p Preston* [1985] AC 835 (no substantive unfairness to reassess tax, in the light of earlier correspondence and delay); *R v*

Secretary of State for the Home Department, ex p Hargreaves [1997] 1 WLR 906 (not substantively unfair to amend prisoner compact delaying home leave eligibility); *R v Ministry for Agriculture Fisheries & Food, ex p Hamble Fisheries (Offshore) Ltd* [1995] 2 All ER 714 (change of policy as to transfer of fish quota not substantively unfair); *R v Commissioners of Customs and Excise, ex p British Sky Broadcasting Group* [2001] EWHC Admin 127 [2001] STC 437 (not unfair to treat taxpayers differently, where perceived (albeit incorrectly) a difference between them).

54.1.4 **Substantive fairness: Lord Scarman's contribution.** *HTV Ltd v Price Commission* [1976] ICR 170, 189A-B & E (Scarman LJ: "Agencies, such as the Price Commission, must act fairly. If they do not, the High Court may intervene either by prerogative order to prohibit, quash or direct a determination as may be appropriate"); *R v Inland Revenue Commissioners, ex p National Federation of Self-Employed and Small Businesses Ltd* [1982] AC 617, 651E-G (Lord Scarman, recognising "a legal duty owed by the revenue to the general body of the taxpayers to treat taxpayers fairly; to use their discretionary powers so that, subject to the requirements of good management, discrimination between one group of taxpayers and another does not arise; to ensure that there are no favourites and no sacrificial victims"), 652H-653A ("a legal duty of fairness is owed by the revenue to the general body of taxpayers"); *R v Inland Revenue Commissioners, ex p Preston* [1985] AC 835, 851D-E (Lord Scarman: "the principle of fairness has an important place in the law of judicial review").

54.1.5 **No universal formula.** *R (Bibi) v Newham London Borough Council* [2001] EWCA Civ 607 [2002] 1 WLR 237 at [25] (Schiemann LJ, in the context of legitimate expectation: "Several attempts have been made to find a formulation which will provide a test for all cases. However, history shows that wide-ranging formulations, while capable of producing a just result in the individual case, are seen later to have needlessly constricted the development of the law").

54.1.6 **Conduct so unfair as to be an abuse of power.**[17] *R (S) v Secretary of State for the Home Department* [2007] EWCA Civ 546 (abuse of power to defer old asylum cases); *R v Inland Revenue Commissioners, ex p Preston* [1985] AC 835, 853A ("unfairness amounting to an abuse of power"), 867B-C; *R v Inland Revenue Commissioners, ex p Unilever Plc* [1996] STC 681, 695a ("Unfairness amounting to an abuse of power" as "conspicuous unfairness"); *R v Inland Revenue Commissioners, ex p Matrix-Securities Ltd* [1994] 1 WLR 334, 351D-E (whether "contrary to the spirit of fair dealing, which should inspire the whole of public life"); *R v Commissioners of Customs and Excise, ex p Kay and Co* [1996] STC 1500 (policy deferring VAT repayments pending retrospective legislation so unfair as to be an abuse of power); *R v Inspector of Taxes, Reading, ex p Fulford-Dobson* [1987] QB 978, 993C-D (whether unfairly moving the goalposts); *R (Thompson) v Fletcher (HM Inspector of Taxes)* [2002] EWHC 1447 (Ch) [2002] EWHC 1448 (Admin) [2002] STC 1149 (withdrawal of tax relief not so unfair as to be an abuse of power); *R (Bancoult) v Secretary of State for Foreign & Commonwealth Affairs* [2007] EWCA Civ 498 [2008] QB 365 at [67] and [123] (Orders an abuse of power because no proper regard to interests of relevant population).

54.1.7 **Departing from conduct equivalent to contract/representation.** *R v Inland Revenue Commissioners, ex p Preston* [1985] AC 835, 866H-867C (Lord Templeman, describing the entitlement "to judicial review of a decision taken by the commissioners if that decision is unfair to the appellant because the conduct of the commissioners is equivalent to a breach of contract

---

[17] This subparagraph in a previous edition was cited in *R v Somerset County Council, ex p Prospects Care Services* [2000] 1 FLR 636.

or a breach of representation. Such a decision falls within the ambit of an abuse of power"), 865H (explaining *Robertson v Minister of Pensions* [1949] 1 QB 227; *Wells v Minister of Housing & Local Government* [1967] 1 WLR 1000 and *Lever Finance Ltd v Westminster (City) London Borough Council* [1971] 1 QB 222 as cases where: "the authorities acted in a manner for which, if the authorities had not been emanations of the Crown, the [claimants] would have enjoyed a remedy by way of damages or an injunction for breach of contract or breach of representations"); *R (Zeqiri) v Secretary of State for the Home Department* [2002] UKHL 3 [2002] INLR 291 at [44] (Lord Hoffmann: "It is well established that conduct by an officer of state equivalent to a breach of contract or breach of representation may be an abuse of power for which judicial review is the appropriate remedy... This particular form of the more general concept of abuse of power has been characterised as the denial of a legitimate expectation"); *R v Commissioners of Customs and Excise, ex p Kay and Co* [1996] STC 1500 (clear statement recognising entitlement to VAT repayments), 1523a-1528e; *R v Secretary of State for the Home Department, ex p Golam Mowla* [1992] 1 WLR 70 (visa-exempt passport stamps not constituting representations of entitlement to enter, beyond the terms of the statutory scheme), 85H-86A; *Harley Development Inc v Commissioner of Inland Revenue* [1996] 1 WLR 727 (no representation or reliance); *R v Inland Revenue Commissioners, ex p Allen* [1997] STC 1141 (no assurance or representation that claimant would remain free from prosecution; *R (DFS Furniture Co Ltd) v Commissioners of Customs and Excise* [2002] EWHC 807 (Admin) (Customs and Excise entitled to exercise retrospective power to reclaim repaid VAT, having on the facts not reached an agreement settling a VAT appeal).

54.1.8 Substantive unfairness in all the circumstances. *R v Inland Revenue Commissioners, ex p Matrix-Securities Ltd* [1994] 1 WLR 334, 358F (approaching substantive unfairness on a "broader front ... taking into account all aspects of the exchanges between the appellants and the authorities"); *R v Secretary of State for the Home Department, ex p Pierson* [1998] AC 539, 603C (applying "the presumption ... that [the Secretary of State] will exercise his powers in a manner which is fair in all the circumstances. What fairness demands depends on the context in which the power is being exercised"); *R v National Lottery Commission, ex p Camelot Group Plc* [2001] EMLR 3 (looking at all the circumstances); *R (Bamber) v Revenue & Customs Commissioners* [2007] EWHC 798 (Admin) at [20] (due weight given to what Revenue responsibly evaluated as fair).

54.1.9 Conspicuous unfairness. *R (Actis SA) v Secretary of State for Communities & Local Government* [2007] EWHC 2417 (Admin) at [139]-[140], [146] (conspicuous unfairness in changing technical regulation); *R (Mugisha) v Secretary of State for the Home Department* [2005] EWHC 2720 (Admin) [2006] INLR 335 at [37] (conspicuously unfair to refuse exceptional leave to remain under policy applicable had nationality not been incorrectly denied); *R (A) v Secretary of State for the Home Department* [2006] EWHC 526 (Admin) [2006] Imm AR 477 (conspicuously unfair where previous wrongful refusal of leave to remain under the then Iraq asylum policy); *R (HSMP Forum Ltd) v Secretary of State for the Home Department* [2008] EWHC 664 (Admin) at [61] (conspicuous unfairness in rule change); *R v Inland Revenue Commissioners, ex p Unilever Plc* [1996] STC 681, 695a ("conspicuous unfairness" as abuse of power); *R v National Lottery Commission, ex p Camelot Group Plc* [2001] EMLR 3 (conspicuous unfairness); *R (International Transport Roth GmbH) v Secretary of State for the Home Department* [2002] EWCA Civ 158 [2003] QB 728 at [26]-[27] (approach to HRA:ECHR Art 1P by asking whether scheme "plainly unfair"), [59] ("conspicuously unfair").

54.1.10 Substantive unfairness and the forbidden substitutionary approach. *Council of Civil Service Unions v Minister for the Civil Service* [1985] AC 374, 414H-415A (Lord Roskill: "the duty to act fairly ... must not ... be misunderstood or misused. It is not for the courts to determine whether a particular policy or particular decisions taken in fulfillment of that policy are fair"); *R v Commissioners of Customs and Excise, ex p British Sky Broadcasting Group* [2001] EWHC Admin 127 [2001] STC 437 at [8]-[10] (Elias J: "the threshold of unfairness amounting to an abuse of power is a high one, and ... the court must be careful not to interfere simply because a decision can be justifiably subject to some criticism"); *R (Bibi) v Newham London Borough Council* [2001] EWCA Civ 607 [2002] 1 WLR 237 at [41] (Schiemann LJ: "The court, even where it finds that the [claimant] has a legitimate expectation of some benefit, will not order the authority to honour its promise where to do so would be to assume the powers of the executive").

54.1.11 **Substantive unfairness and inalienability.** <P40> (inalienability); *R v Commissioners of Customs and Excise, ex p F & I Services Ltd* [2001] EWCA Civ 762 (no legitimate expectation that tax authorities will administer the tax scheme in a way which is contrary to law; no breach of legitimate expectation above having fair notice of change and not being made liable retrospectively for back tax); *R v Inland Revenue Commissioners, ex p Preston* [1985] AC 835, 864G (Lord Templeman: "The court can only intervene by judicial review to direct the commissioners to abstain from performing their statutory duties or from exercising their statutory powers if the court is satisfied that `the unfairness' of which the [claimant] complains renders the insistence by the commissioners on performing their duties or exercising their powers an abuse of power by the commissioners"); *HTV Ltd v Price Commission* [1976] ICR 170, 185 ("a public body, which is entrusted by Parliament with the exercise of powers for the public good, cannot fetter itself in the exercise of them. It cannot be estopped from doing its public duty. But that is subject to the qualification that it must not misuse its powers: and it is a misuse of power for it to act unfairly or unjustly towards a private citizen when there is no overriding public interest to warrant it"); *R v Croydon Justices, ex p Dean* [1993] QB 769, 776H-778G (police conduct could mean prosecution an abuse of process, notwithstanding entitlement and duty to prosecute, and absence of authority to give promises not to do so); *Francisco Javier Jaramillo-Silva v Secretary of State for the Home Department* [1994] Imm AR 352 (not unfair to correct a mistake as to right to appeal).

54.1.12 **Overlap with substantive legitimate expectation.** <54.2> (substantive legitimate expectation); *R v East Sussex County Council, ex p Reprotech (Pebsham) Ltd* [2002] UKHL 8 [2003] 1 WLR 348 at [34] (Lord Hoffmann, linking legitimate expectation and unfair abuse of power, in referring to "the public law concept of a legitimate expectation created by a public authority, the denial of which may amount to an abuse of power"); *R v Secretary of State for the Home Department, ex p Pierson* [1998] AC 539, 590H (substantive unfairness and legitimate expectation treated as separate: not necessary to decide whether legitimate expectation has substantive effect), 591F (rule of law enforces minimum standards of fairness, procedural and substantive); *R v Ministry of Defence, ex p Walker* [2000] 1 WLR 806 (HL analysing substantive fairness argument in terms of legitimate expectation); *R v Secretary of State for the Home Department, ex p Bobby Gangadia* [1994] Imm AR 341, 344 (treating the contract/representation principle <54.1.7> as part of legitimate expectation); *R v Commissioners of Customs and Excise, ex p Kay and Co* [1996] STC 1500, 1523a (treating legitimate expectation/ abuse of power and unfairness together).

54.1.13 **Link between substantive unfairness and other related concepts.** <57.3.3> (oppression); <45.4> (overlapping grounds); <P55> (inconsistency).

54.1.14 **Estoppel and public bodies.**
(A) CAUTION AND ESTOPPEL. <40.2.3>.
(B) ESTOPPEL AVAILABLE IN PRINCIPLE. *Downderry Construction Ltd v Secretary of State for Transport, Local Government and the Regions* [2002] EWHC 02 (Admin) at [19] ("estoppel is available in principle in the present [planning] context, by way of exception to the

normal rule that a public authority cannot be estopped in the exercise of its statutory functions", referring to *Western Fish Products Ltd v Penwith District Council* [1981] 2 All ER 204); *London Borough of Tower Hamlets v Sherwood* [2002] EWCA Civ 229 (council estopped from revoking permission for kiosks at Tower Hill, having been refurbished in the expectation of being permitted to continue to trade) at [68] (Chadwick LJ, applying the principle that it is "not ... open to a person who has encouraged another to go onto his land and expend money in the expectation that he would be allowed to remain for an indefinite but lengthy period ... to revoke that permission for no reason other than that he has had a change of mind");   *R v Caradon District Council, ex p Knott* [2000] 3 PLR 1 (council estopped from taking planning enforcement action, by means of (a) estoppel by representation; (b) issue estoppel; and/or (c) estoppel by convention).

(C) ESTOPPEL AND ABUSE OF POWER. <40.2.6>; *R (Anufrijeva) v Secretary of State for the Home Department* [2003] UKHL 36 [2004] 1 AC 604 at [35] (Lord Steyn, relying on the proposition that: "While generally an estoppel cannot operate against the Crown, it can be estopped when it is abusing its powers", referring to *HTV*, *Preston* and *Laker*).

(D) ESTOPPEL, STATUTORY DUTY AND FAIRNESS. *Buckinghamshire County Council v Secretary of State for the Environment, Transport and the Regions* [2001] 1 PLR 38, 55H-56B ("It is well established that no authority can be estopped from exercising their statutory duty, at least subject to the principles of fairness explained in *R v North and East Devon Health Authority, ex p Coughlan* [2001] QB 213. That apart, I see no reason why, in principle, estoppel cannot apply in the context of planning control").

(E) ESTOPPEL AND ACCRUED RIGHTS. *Buckinghamshire County Council v Secretary of State for the Environment, Transport and the Regions* [2001] 1 PLR 38, 56A-B ("estoppel cannot apply in the context of planning control"; "estoppel cannot itself directly override or alter accrued rights under the statute, such as planning permission or a lawful use certificate").

(F) ESTOPPEL AND (WAIVING) PROCEDURAL REQUIREMENTS. *Wells v Minister of Housing & Local Government* [1967] 1 WLR 1000 (planning authority could not be estopped from doing its public duty, but could be estopped from relying on procedural technicalities; but no positive statement there that no planning permission necessary);   *Western Fish Products Ltd v Penwith District Council* [1981] 2 All ER 204 (whether waiver of procedural requirements); *R v Secretary of State for the Home Department, ex p Khan* [1980] 1 WLR 569 (waiver of eligibility requirements).

(G) ESTOPPEL BY REPRESENTATION. *Downderry Construction Ltd v Secretary of State for Transport, Local Government and the Regions* [2002] EWHC 02 (Admin) at [22] (Richards J, recording the elements of estoppel by representation, approving this passage from Wilken and Villers, Waiver, Variation and Estoppel: "First, A makes a false representation of fact to B or to a group of which B was a member. Secondly, in making the representation, A intended or knew that it was likely to be acted upon. Thirdly, B, believing the representation, acts to its detriment in reliance on the representation. Fourthly, A subsequently seeks to deny the truth of the representation. Fifthly, no defence to estoppel can be raised by A"), [24] ("necessary to establish not only that the officer was acting within the scope of his ostensible authority but also that the person dealing with him was justified in thinking that what he said would bind the planning authority", referring to *Lever Finance Ltd v Westminster London Borough Council* [1971] 1 QB 222).

(H) ESTOPPEL BY CONVENTION. *Downderry Construction Ltd v Secretary of State for Transport, Local Government and the Regions* [2002] EWHC 02 (Admin) at [47] (estoppel by convention "requires that the parties have a shared assumption of fact or law on the basis of which they have regulated their dealings and that it would be unjust or unconscionable to allow one of the parties to resile from the shared assumption").

(I) ISSUE ESTOPPEL ETC. <2.5.12>.

(J) RELATIONSHIP BETWEEN ESTOPPEL AND FAIRNESS. <40.2.5> (estoppel and legitimate expectation); <40.2.6> (estoppel and substantive unfairness).

(K) ESTOPPEL: INALIENABILITY PROBLEMS. <40.2>.

(L) OTHER. *Robertson v Minister of Pensions* [1949] 1 KB 227, 231-232; *Lever Finance Ltd v Westminster (City) London Borough Council* [1971] 1 QB 222; *Re Selectmove Ltd* [1995] 2 All ER 531, 539a-e (estoppel treated as available against the Inland Revenue in proceedings based on non-payment of taxes); *Southwark London Borough Council v Logan* (1996) 8 Admin LR 315, 321H-324B (whether proprietary estoppel as a result of council officer's representation); *Nahar v Social Security Commissioners* [2001] EWHC Admin 1049 [2002] 2 FCR 442 at [64]-[67] (discussing the principle in *Robertson*) (CA is at [2002] EWCA Civ 859); *Dunn v Bradford Metropolitan District Council* [2002] EWCA Civ 1137 [2003] HLR 154 at [44] (council not estopped here from defending claim for damages alleging breach of repairing covenants, by alleging that the tenancy had earlier been determined, it not being unconscionable so to allege); *R v East Sussex County Council, ex p Reprotech (Pebsham) Ltd* [2002] UKHL 8 [2003] 1 WLR 348 at [31] (Lord Hoffmann, discussing *Wells* and referring to the situation of a "letter ... intended to be a decision having immediate legal consequences"); *Milk Marketing Board of England and Wales v Tom Parker Farms Ltd* [1999] EuLR 154, 166H (need unequivocal expression).

54.1.15 **Holding the defendant to its binding determinations.** *Re No.56 Denton Road, Twickenham* [1953] Ch 51, 56 (Vaisey J: "[W]here Parliament confers upon a body such as the War Damage Commission the duty of deciding or determining any question, the deciding or determining of which affects the rights of the subject, such decision or determination made and communicated in terms which are not expressly preliminary or provisional is final and conclusive, and cannot in the absence of express statutory power or the consent of the person or persons affected be altered or withdrawn by that body"), applied in *R v Ministry of Agriculture Fisheries & Food, ex p Cox* (1994) 6 Admin LR 421, 435F-436E and in *R v Parole Board, ex p Robinson* 29th July 1999 unrep. (decision of Discretionary Lifer Panel binding and not capable of being overturned); *Wells v Minister of Housing & Local Government* [1967] 1 WLR 1000; *R v British Advertising Clearance Centre, ex p Swiftcall Ltd* 16th November 1995 unrep. (effect of approval not a binding decision precluding revocation, but a relevant consideration requiring a good reason for such a course); *Nahar v Social Security Commissioners* [2001] EWHC Admin 1049 [2002] 2 FCR 442 at [64]-[67] (CA is at [2002] EWCA Civ 859); *R (Hashmi) v Secretary of State for the Home Department* [2002] EWCA Civ 728 [2002] INLR 377 (Home Office letter, referring to decision to grant indefinite leave to remain, constituting a "notice in writing" under the Immigration Act 1971 s.4(1)).

54.2 **Unjustified breach of a substantive legitimate expectation.** One species of substantive unfairness is where the defendant body has unjustifiedly (or perhaps unreasonably) departed from a legitimate expectation of a substantive benefit, engendered by a previous relevant act such as a promise or practice.

54.2.1 **Legitimate expectation.** <41.1> (role of legitimate expectation); <41.2> (anatomy of a legitimate expectation).

54.2.2 **Breach of substantive substantive legitimate expectation (SLE).** *R v North and East Devon Health Authority, ex p Coughlan* [2001] QB 213 (breach of SLE of residential home for life); *R (BAPIO Action Ltd) v Secretary of State for the Home Department* [2008] UKHL 27 [2008] 2 WLR 1073 at [60] (DoH guidance infringing SLE engendered by immigration rules and practice); *R (Rashid) v Secretary of State for the Home Department* [2005] EWCA Civ 744 [2005] INLR 550 at [25] (breach of SLE of application of asylum policy); *R (Corby District Council) v Secretary of State for Communities and Local Government* [2007] EWHC 1873 (Admin) [2008] LGR 109 at [44], [53] (unjustified departure from SLE engendered by local

499

government scheme as published); *R (Staff Side of the Police Negotiating Board) v Secretary of State for the Home Department* [2008] EWHC 1173 (Admin) at [65] (Secretary of State complying with legitimate expectation not to reject recommendations without careful consideration).

54.2.3 The evolution of substantive legitimate expectation. *Breen v Amalgamated Engineering Union* [1971] 2 QB 175, 191F (Lord Denning MR, dissenting, referring to the claimant as having had "a legitimate expectation that he would be approved by the district committee, unless there were good reasons against him"); *R v Secretary of State for the Home Department, ex p Asif Mahmood Khan* [1984] 1 WLR 1337 (legitimate expectation that entry would be decided against criteria in Secretary of State's circular; impermissible to change the policy without giving a hearing to those affected, and only then if the overriding public interest demanded such a change); *R v Secretary of State for the Home Department, ex p Ruddock* [1987] 1 WLR 1482, 1497A-B (Taylor J: "the doctrine of legitimate expectation in essence imposes a duty to act fairly. Whilst most of the cases are concerned ... with a right to be heard, I do not think the doctrine is so confined. Indeed, in a case where ex hypothesi there is no right to be heard, it may be thought the more important to fair dealing that a promise or undertaking given by a minister as to how he will proceed should be kept"); *R v Ministry for Agriculture Fisheries & Food, ex p Hamble Fisheries (Offshore) Ltd* [1995] 2 All ER 714, 723c-724e (Sedley J, legitimate expectation capable of being substantive, and that "the same principle of fairness in my judgment governs both" procedural and substantive legitimate expectations), 731f-g; *Coughlan* (below); *R v East Sussex County Council, ex p Reprotech (Pebsham) Ltd* [2002] UKHL 8 [2003] 1 WLR 348 at [34] (Lord Hoffmann, referring to "the public law concept of a legitimate expectation created by a public authority, the denial of which may amount to an abuse of power").

54.2.4 Substantive legitimate expectation: reasonableness test. *R v North and East Devon Health Authority, ex p Coughlan* [2001] QB 213, at [57(a)] (describing the category of cases where "the court is confined to reviewing the decision on *Wednesbury* grounds"), [71] (here, the principle of legitimate expectation can "operate as an aspect of good administration, qualifying the intrinsic rationality of policy choices"), [73] (ultimately, "the individual can claim no higher expectation than to have his individual circumstances considered by the decision-maker in the light of the policy then in force"), [76] (fairness requires no more than this); *R v Secretary of State for the Home Department, ex p Hargreaves* [1997] 1 WLR 906, 921E (Hirst LJ: "*Wednesbury* provides the correct test"), 924H (Pill LJ: "The court can quash the decision only if, in relation to the expectation and in all the circumstances, the decision to apply the new policy in the particular case was unreasonable in the *Wednesbury* sense"); *R (Carvill) v Commissioners of Inland Revenue* [2002] EWHC 1488 (Ch) [2002] STC 1167 at [33] (Hart J, commenting that no material difference between *Unilever* and the *Brind* irrationality test), [34] (approaching the matter in a way "so as to echo the test of irrationality applicable to a judicial review claim").

54.2.5 Substantive legitimate expectation: justification/fairness test.[18] *R v North and East Devon Health Authority, ex p Coughlan* [2001] QB 213, at [57(c)] (cases where "once the legitimacy of the expectation is established, the court will have the task of weighing the requirements of fairness against any overriding interest relied upon for the change of policy"), [89] (whether decision involved an "overriding public interest which justified it"); *R (Bancoult) v Secretary of State for Foreign & Commonwealth Affairs* [2007] EWCA Civ 498 [2008] QB 365 at [73], [76], [100], [120]-[121] (justification test applied to Orders in Council); *R (HSMP*

---

[18] Mark Elliott [2000] JR 27.

Forum Ltd) v Secretary of State for the Home Department [2008] EWHC 664 (Admin) at [61] (no sufficient public interest to outweigh the unfairness); *R (Charlton) v Secretary of State for Education and Skills* [2005] EWHC 1378 (Admin) [2005] 2 FCR 603 at [161] (pressing public interest test shown here); *R (Barker) v Waverley Borough Council* [2001] ACD 344 (applying justification test test where planning condition having stood for many years and now varied); *R v Commissioners of Customs and Excise, ex p Greenwich Property Ltd* [2001] EWHC Admin 230 [2001] STC 618 (applying justification test where Customs and Excise had approved a concession on which claimant had relied); *R (Bath) v North Somerset Council* [2008] EWHC 630 (Admin) at [39]-[41] (justification test met here).

54.2.6 **Reasonableness or justification: selecting the appropriate test.** *R v North and East Devon Health Authority, ex p Coughlan* [2001] QB 213 at [59] (deciding whether case falls into reasonableness or justification category is a "difficult task" in "what is still a developing field of law"), [56] (needing "a detailed examination of the precise terms of the promise or representation made, the circumstances in which the promise was made and the nature of the statutory or other discretion"), [59] (most justification cases are "likely in the nature of things to be cases where the expectation is confined to one person or a few people, giving the promise or representation the character of a contract"); *R v Department for Education and Employment, ex p Begbie* [2000] 1 WLR 1115, 1130F (Laws LJ: "The facts of the case, viewed always in their statutory context, will steer the court to a more or less intrusive quality of review"); *R (Q) v Secretary of State for the Home Department* [2003] EWCA Civ 364 [2004] QB 36 at [112] ("an issue-sensitive scale of intervention"); *R (Barker) v Waverley Borough Council* [2001] ACD 344 (choosing justification test); *R v Commissioners of Customs and Excise, ex p Greenwich Property Ltd* [2001] EWHC Admin 230 [2001] STC 618 (applying justification test); *R (Bodimeade) v Camden London Borough Council* [2001] EWHC Admin 271 (2001) 4 CCLR 246 at [30] (Court explaining choice of justification test in context of promise of a "home for life"); *R (Collins) v Lincolnshire Health Authority* [2001] EWHC Admin 685 (2001) 4 CCLR 429 at [48]-[52] (justification test applied in "home for life" case).

54.2.7 **Substantive legitimate expectation: other important aspects.**
(A) TENSIONS IN THE LAW. Especially <41.1.7> to <41.1.14>.
(B) INALIENABILITY PROBLEMS. <40.2>.
(C) SPECIAL LIMITS OF LEGITIMATE EXPECTATION. <41.1.13>.
(D) ESTOPPEL AND PUBLIC BODIES. <54.1.14>.

> **P55 Inconsistency.** A body should ensure equal treatment, certainty of approach and no legally relevant unjustified departures.

> 55.1 Equal treatment, non-arbitrariness and certainty
> 55.2 Unjustified departure

55.1 Equal treatment, non-arbitrariness and certainty[19] Consistency is a principle of good administration. Judicial review may lie because treatment is unjustifiedly unfavourable compared with action in relevantly like cases (or prior treatment in the same case), or because it unjustifiedly fails to distinguish other unlike cases. Consistency links with freedom from arbitrariness, each of which also links with (and is promoted by) adequate certainty of approach.

55.1.1 **Equality/equal treatment in EC law.** <8.1.7>; *R (Partridge Farms Ltd) v Secretary of State for Environment, Food & Rural Affairs* [2008] EWHC 1645 (Admin) (Order breaching EC principle of equality).

55.1.2 **Non-discrimination under HRA:ECHR Art 14.** <59.8>; *AL (Serbia) v Secretary of State for the Home Department* [2008] UKHL 42 [2008] 1 WLR 1434 at [42] (common law principle of equal treatment adding little to Art 14 where engaged).

55.1.3 **Statutory equality duties/non-discrimination guarantees.[20]** *R (C) v Secretary of State for Justice* [2008] EWCA Civ 882 (regulations quashed for breach of duty to conduct disability impact assessment); *R (Kaur) v Ealing London Borough Council* [2008] EWHC 2062 (Admin) (funding decision quashed for absence of full race equality impact assessment); *R (Elias) v Secretary of State for Defence* [2006] EWCA Civ 1293 [2006] 1 WLR 3213 (adoption of exclusionary criterion in ex gratia compensation scheme breaching the Race Relations Act 1976); *R (Watkins-Singh) v Aberdare Girls High School Governors* [2008] EWHC 1865 (Admin) (refusal of exemption for Sikh kara bangle breaching statutory race and religion equality duties); *R (E) v JFS Governing Body* [2008] EWHC 1535 (Admin) (non-compliance with race equality duties, but declaration only); *R (European Roma Rights Centre) v Immigration Officer at Prague Airport* [2004] UKHL 55 [2005] 2 AC 1 (immigration practice at Prague Airport incompatible with the Race Relations Act); *R (Al Rawi) v Secretary of State for Foreign and Commonwealth Affairs* [2006] EWCA Civ 1279 [2008] QB 289 (no race discrimination in refusal of diplomatic assistance for non-nationals in Guantanamo Bay); *R v Birmingham City Council, ex p Equal Opportunities Commission* [1989] 1 AC 1155 (sex discrimination and school places); *R v Powys County Council, ex p Hambidge (No.2)* [2000] LGR 564 (whether council home care charges in breach of the Disability Discrimination Act 1995).

55.1.4 **Statutory duty to act equitably/preferentially.** *Waikato Regional Airport Ltd v Attorney General* [2003] UKPC 50 (applying a statutory duty to "take all reasonable steps to ensure [costs] ... recovered in accordance with the principles of equity and efficiency", because of failure to levy charges equitably between different airports); *R (A) v Lambeth London Borough Council* [2002] EWCA Civ 1084 [2002] HLR 998 (council's housing allocation policy not complying with statutory duty to afford "reasonable preference" to particular groups, because giving equal preference to non-listed groups).

---

[19] Dinah Rose [2006] JR 19.

[20] John Halford [2007] JR 89; Laura West [2008] JR 41; Karon Monaghan QC [2008] JR 78.

55.1.5 **Consistency as an administrative law principle.**[21] *R (O'Brien) v Independent Assessor* [2007] UKHL 10 [2007] 2 AC 312 at [30] ("It is generally desirable that decision-makers, whether administrative or judicial, should act in a broadly consistent manner", but not required to follow previous decisions if considered erroneous); *N v Secretary of State for the Home Department* [2005] UKHL 31 [2005] 2 AC 296 at [9] ("in principle the law should seek to treat like cases alike. A similar principle applies to the exercise of administrative discretions"); *Secretary of State for Defence v Percy* [1999] 1 All ER 732, 742b ("the principles of public law ... include principles of ... equality before the law"); *R v Secretary of State for the Home Department, ex p Urmaza* [1996] COD 479 (legal principle of consistency in the exercise of public law powers); *R (G) v Barnet London Borough Council* [2003] UKHL 57 [2004] 2 AC 208 at [46] ("Like cases must be treated alike"); *R v Hertfordshire County Council, ex p Cheung* The Times 4th April 1986 (see transcript) (Sir John Donaldson MR: "it is a cardinal principle of good public administration that all persons who are in a similar position shall be treated similarly"; "prima facie good public administration would require that all 1978 class students should be treated alike"); *R (Mullen) v Secretary of State for the Home Department* [2004] UKHL 18 [2005] 1 AC 1 at [12] (Lord Bingham, describing the Secretary of State's public law responsibilities in administering an ex gratia scheme as being to act "fairly, rationally, consistently and in a manner that does not defeat substantive legitimate expectations"); *R (Middlebrook Mushrooms Ltd) v Agricultural Wages Board of England and Wales* [2004] EWHC 1447 (Admin) at [74] ("the Board had no lawful justification for the exclusion of mushroom pickers from the MHW rate. `It is a cardinal principle of public administration that all persons in a similar position should be treated similarly' (Lord Donaldson in [*Cheung*]) ... This principle was infringed. The exclusion of manual harvesters of mushrooms from the MHW category was *Wednesbury* unreasonable and unlawful"); <8.1.7> (equal treatment as a general principle of EC law); Recommendation No.R(80)2 of the Committee of Ministers (adopted 11 March 1980) <45.1.4(B)> (referring to "Basic principles" as including that "An administrative authority, when exercising a discretionary power: ... observes the principle of equality before the law by avoiding unfair discrimination").

55.1.6 **Non-arbitrariness.** *R (S) v Secretary of State for the Home Department* [2007] EWCA Civ 546 at [52] (arbitrary deferral of older asylum cases an arbitrary decision); *R v Secretary of State for the Home Department, ex p Urmaza* [1996] COD 479 (describing the principle of consistency and avoidance of arbitrariness); *R v Ministry for Agriculture Fisheries & Food, ex p Hamble Fisheries (Offshore) Ltd* [1995] 2 All ER 714, 722a-c (an "imperative of public law", that "a discretionary public law power must not be exercised arbitrarily or with partiality as between individuals or classes potentially affected by it"); *R v MAFF, ex parte First City Trading* [1997] 1 CMLR 250 at [69] (irrationality and proportionality as "the imposition of compulsory standards on decision-makers so as to secure the repudiation of arbitrary power").

55.1.7 **Inconsistency as unfairness/abuse of power.** *R v Special Adjudicator, ex p Kandasamy* [1994] Imm AR 333 (not unfair to approach claimant's case differently from that of fellow traveller), 340 (Hidden J, suggesting that "consistency as such is not a principle of administrative law; the governing principle is whether there has been unfairness such as to amount to an abuse of power").

55.1.8 **Partial and unequal measures.** *Kruse v Johnson* [1898] 2 QB 91 (DC), 99 (byelaw would be unlawful if "partial or unequal in its operation"); *R v Immigration Appeal Tribunal, ex p Manshoora Begum* [1986] Imm AR 385 (judicial review granted where decision based on immigration rule which satisfied *Kruse* test, being "`partial and unequal' in its operation as

---

[21] Karen Steyn [1997] JR 22.

between different classes").

55.1.9 Equality/equal treatment/non-discrimination. *R (Zeqiri) v Secretary of State for the Home Department* [2002] UKHL 3 [2002] INLR 291 at [56] (Lord Hoffmann: "it would be unfair of the Secretary of State not to treat like cases alike in the sense of discriminating against someone upon [inadequate] grounds"; however, "it would unduly restrict his discretion if he could not make an ex gratia concession on the ground of a general public interest in the fair and efficient administration of the immigration law"); *Matadeen v Pointu* [1999] 1 AC 98, 109C-111G, 118F (PC concluding that no general constitutional principle of equality/ freedom from discrimination; recognising general common law principle of equality; whether justification for the inequality a question entrusted to the decision-maker, subject to orthodox review); *R (Gurung) v Ministry of Defence* [2002] EWHC 2463 (Admin) at [35]-[39] (*Matadeen* "leaves intact the common law principle of equality"; exclusion from compensation unreasonable by reference to common law principle of equality); *R (British Civilian Internees - Far Eastern Region) v Secretary of State for Defence* [2003] EWCA Civ 473 [2003] QB 1397 at [85]-[86] (leaving open "whether there is a free-standing principle of equality in English domestic law", or whether merely part of the *Wednesbury* principle); *R (Kelsall) v Secretary of State for the Environment, Food and Rural Affairs* [2003] EWHC 459 (Admin) at [63] (compensation provisions "operate unfairly as between different farmers and generally; they fail to take account of the different values of premium breeds and thus discriminate ... without justification; and they produce arbitrary effects. Reasons have been put forward to justify provisions of the order that do not bear scrutiny and are irrational"); *R v Secretary of State for Trade and Industry, ex p BT3G Ltd* [2001] EWCA Civ 1448 [2001] EuLR 822 (CA asking whether difference in treatment between licence bidders objectively justified, so as not to be discriminatory under English public law); *R v Immigration Appeal Tribunal, ex p Jeyeanthan* [1998] Imm AR 369 (Sedley J), 374 (referring in the context of immigration appeals notices to the "principle of equality before the law" as being "jeopardised if the state as appellant is placed or is allowed to place itself in a materially different position from any other appellant"; CA is at [2000] 1 WLR 354); *R (L) v Manchester City Council* [2001] EWHC Admin 707 (2002) 5 CCLR 268 at [78(4)] (effect of policy "is fundamentally discriminatory"); *Ghaidan v Godin-Mendoza* [2004] UKHL 30 [2004] 2 AC 557 at [132] (Baroness Hale: "a guarantee of equal treatment is ... essential to democracy"); *R (Middlebrook Mushrooms Ltd) v Agricultural Wages Board of England and Wales* [2004] EWHC 1447 (Admin) at [74] (exclusion a breach of the "cardinal principle of public administration that all persons in a similar position should be treated similarly" and so "unreasonable and unlawful").

55.1.10 Equal treatment: illustrations. *R (Ali) v Birmingham City Council* [2008] EWCA Civ 48 at [45] (housing policy unlawful because unjustified distinction between categories of homeless both owed the same statutory duty); *R (Abbey Mine Ltd) v Coal Authority* [2008] EWCA Civ 353 at [34] (duty of evenhandedness between rival licence bidders); *R (Hill) v Secretary of State for the Home Department* [2007] EWHC 2164 (Admin) (Secretary of State breaching duty to "have an even-handed approach to the exercise of [his] discretion", because practice of (a) accepting adverse recommendations of Parole Board while (b) actively questioning favourable ones); *Manzeke v Secretary of State for the Home Department* [1997] Imm AR 524, 529 ("Consistency in the treatment of asylum seekers is important in so far as objective considerations, not directly affected by the circumstances of the individual asylum seeker, are involved"); *Secretary of State for the Home Department v Mohammed Yasin* [1995] Imm AR 118, 120-121 ("of course decisions should be consistent. There should be a consistent application of principle and a consistent application of rules... But situations are never precisely similar"); *Firmin Gnali v Immigration Appeal Tribunal* [1998] Imm AR 331, 336 (apparently inconsistent decisions "may stem from error" and "engender a sense of grievance"); *R v Secretary of State for the Home Department, ex p Namusisi* [1994] Imm AR 399, 401 (need for "fairness as between applicants"); *Shirazi v Secretary of State for the Home Department* [2003] EWCA Civ 1562 [2004] INLR 92 at [29] (albeit "not a ground of appeal ... that another tribunal *has* reached a different conclusion on very similar facts ... it has to be a matter of concern that the same political and legal situation ... is being evaluated differently by different tribunals"; "inconsistency on such questions works against legal certainty"); *R v Director General of Electricity Supply, ex p Scottish Power Plc* 3rd February 1997 unrep. (no valid or rational basis for treating electricity supply companies differently); *R v Cheshire Justices, ex p Sinnott* The Times 26th October 1994 (quashing drink-driving convictions as likely to give rise to grievance where acquittals in materially identical cases); <50.4.2> (lawfulness of adopting a policy, in the interests of consistency); *R v Secretary of State for Trade and Industry, ex p McCormick* [1998] COD 160 (lawful not to apply similar policy to directors' disqualification proceedings as to criminal proceedings); *R v Secretary of State for the Environment, ex p Oxford City Council* 28th February 1998 unrep. (Secretary of State entitled to refuse to make individual exception, given principle of consistency); *North Wiltshire District Council v Secretary of State for the Environment* [1992] PLR 113 (because of importance of fostering consistency, planning inspector should make clear why departing from a previous decision); *R v Secretary of State for Defence, ex p Wilkins* The Times 26th July 2000 at [55] ("if there had been an erroneous departure from the rules in the past, the Ministry was not under any obligation to repeat those errors in a wish to be consistent") *R (L) v Manchester City Council* [2001] EWHC Admin 707 (2002) 5 CCLR 268 (arbitrary and inconsistent to set foster carer payments at lower level for relatives and friends than for other carers); *R v Secretary of State for the Home Department, ex p Northumbria Police Authority* (1993) 5 Admin LR 489, 504C-E ("Undoubtedly... the decisions on these applications were wholly inconsistent with the decision on the application against Derbyshire ... [but] there is no evidence that it amounted to any sort of an abuse of discretion").

55.1.11 Inconsistency as unlawfulness. *R (Aweys) v Birmingham City Council* [2007] EWHC 52 (Admin) [2007] HLR 394 at [27] (housing allocation policy unlawful where impossible to justify distinctions drawn between priority categories); *R v Preston Supplementary Benefits Appeal Tribunal, ex p Moore* [1975] 1 WLR 624, 632A-B; *R v National Security Commissioner, ex p Stratton* [1979] QB 361, 369A-C, 374D-E; *Presho v Insurance Officer* [1984] 1 AC 310, 319B; *Cartlidge v Chief Adjudication Officer* [1986] QB 360, 377E-G.

55.1.12 Inconsistency as unreasonableness. *R v Director General of Electricity Supply, ex p Scottish Power Plc* 3rd February 1997 unrep. (no valid or rational basis for treating electricity supply companies differently); *R (Middlebrook Mushrooms Ltd) v Agricultural Wages Board of England and Wales* [2004] EWHC 1447 (Admin) at [74] ("`It is a cardinal principle of public administration that all persons in a similar position should be treated similarly'... This principle was infringed. The exclusion ... was *Wednesbury* unreasonable and unlawful"); *R v Birmingham City Council, ex p Sheptonhurst Ltd* [1990] 1 All ER 1026 (where sex shop licence granted previously, need for rational explanation of why inappropriate to grant renewal); *L v Salford City Council* [1998] ELR 28, 35E (conclusion of fact "neither inconsistent nor perverse"); *Matadeen* <55.1.9>.

55.1.13 Interests of consistency/previous decisions as a relevancy.
(A) PRIOR ACTION IN SAME CASE. *R (Watson) v Dartford Magistrates Court* [2005] EWHC 905 (Admin) (magistrates only entitled to revoke earlier order refusing adjournment where "change of circumstances"); *R (Chisnell) v Richmond Upon Thames London Borough Council* [2005] EWHC 134 (Admin) at [19]-[20] (previous planning decisions in respect of same site relevant considerations; need to recognise importance of consistency and give reasons for departure); *R v Secretary of State for the Home Department, ex p Golam Mowla* [1992] 1 WLR 70 (unreasonable to disregard "the facts as to the passport holder's previous leaves to enter

and remain in the United Kingdom, and his or her conduct and history while in the United Kingdom"); *R (Saunders) v Tendring District Council* [2003] EWHC 2977 (Admin) at [62] (officer's report seriously misleading because did not present members with proper opportunity to consider whether still adhered to earlier objections, and if not why not); *R v Birmingham City Council, ex p Sheptonhurst Ltd* [1990] 1 All ER 1026, 1035j ("when considering an application for renewal the local authority has to give due weight to the fact that a licence was granted in the previous year and indeed for however many years before that"); *Secretary of State for the Home Department v AF* [2008] EWCA Civ 117 (previous findings in control order proceedings not binding in later hearing).

(B) ACTION IN SIMILAR CASES. *R (O'Brien) v Independent Assessor* [2007] UKHL 10 [2007] 2 AC 312 at [30] (no duty to follow previous decisions if considered erroneous); *R (N) v Independent Appeal Panel of Barking and Dagenham London Borough Council* [2008] EWHC 390 (Admin) at [20] (previous related decision not a relevancy); *R (Rank) v East Cambridgeshire District Council* [2002] EWHC 2081 (Admin) at [11] (previous decision on similar planning application on same site a relevant consideration), [16] ("The potential relevance arises because consistency is desirable and inconsistency may occur if the authority fails to have regard to a previous decision"); *R v Secretary of State for the Home Department, ex p Walsh* The Times 18th December 1991 (DC) (in setting tariff, length of terms served by claimant's co-defendants a relevancy) (CA is at (1993) 5 Admin LR 138).

55.1.14 **Policy guidance and equal treatment.**

(A) POLICY PROMOTES CONSISTENCY. <50.4.2> (policy guidance promotes consistency).

(B) PROPER TO HAVE A POLICY. *R (Alconbury Developments Ltd) v Secretary of State for the Environment Transport and the Regions* [2001] UKHL 23 [2003] 2 AC 295 at [143] (Lord Clyde: "The formulation of policies is a perfectly proper course for the provision of guidance in the exercise of an administrative discretion. Indeed policies are an essential element in securing the coherent and consistent performance of administrative functions... Provided that the policy is not regarded as binding and the authority still retains a free exercise of discretion the policy may serve the useful purpose of giving a reasonable guidance both to applicants and decision-makers"); *R (S) v London Borough of Brent* [2002] EWCA Civ 693 [2002] ELR 556 at [16] ("the promotion of consistency is a necessary purpose of guidance"); *R v Secretary of State for the Home Department, ex p Urmaza* [1996] COD 479 (decision-maker can be held in public law to his policy, with departure requiring the articulation of a good reason, given (i) the principle of consistency (and avoidance of arbitrariness), (ii) the duty to have regard to relevancies, (iii) the avoidance of over-rigidity, and (iv) the need to give effect to legitimate expectations).

(C) NEED FOR A POLICY/DUTY TO HAVE A POLICY. *R (Refugee Legal Centre) v Secretary of State for the Home Department* [2004] EWCA Civ 1481 [2005] 1 WLR 2219 (considering fairness of fast-track asylum process) at [18] (asylum system needing "a clearly stated procedure - in public law, a policy - which recognises that it will be unfair not to enlarge the standard timetable in a variety of instances"); *R (Teleos Plc) v Customs and Excise Commissioners* [2005] EWCA Civ 200 [2005] 1 WLR 3007 at [24] ("the Commissioners should make a clear statement of their policy and they should publish the criteria by which they exercise the discretion to make interim payments"); *B v Secretary of State for Work and Pensions* [2005] EWCA Civ 929 [2005] 1 WLR 3796 at [43] (Sedley LJ: "It is axiomatic in modern government that a lawful policy is necessary if an executive discretion of the significance of the one now under consideration is to be exercised, as public law requires it to be exercised, consistently from case to case but adaptably to the facts of individual cases"); <50.4.2> (need for a policy).

(D) DUTY TO PUBLISH POLICY GUIDANCE. <6.2.11>.

(E) DUTY TO FOLLOW POLICY. <6.2> (holding a decision-maker to policy guidance).

55.1.15 Equal treatment in taxation matters. *R v Commissioners of Customs and Excise, ex p British Sky Broadcasting Group* [2001] EWHC Admin 127 [2001] STC 437 at [6]-[8] (common ground that if Customs and Excise considered companies to be in an identical position and decided to treat one less favourably as a test case, would be a breach of the duty to act fairly), [33] (can be unfair disparate treatment where complaint is that `others too' should have been treated in the same way), [35] (preferring view that taxpayer could in an appropriate case recover tax paid); *R v Inland Revenue Commissioners, ex p National Federation of Self-Employed and Small Businesses Ltd* [1982] AC 617, 651E-G (referring to the "legal duty owed by the revenue to the general body of the taxpayers to treat taxpayers fairly; to use their discretionary powers so that, subject to the requirements of good management, discrimination between one group of taxpayers and another does not arise; to ensure that there are no favourites and no sacrificial victims"); *R v Inland Revenue Commissioners, ex p Unilever Plc* [1996] STC 681, 692 (treatment "may be unfair if other taxpayers similarly placed have been treated differently").

55.1.16 Failure to discriminate/treat different cases differently. *R v Secretary of State for the Home Department, ex p Mersin* [2000] INLR 511, 522E ("In this case the [defendant] ought to have treated the [claimant] and those in a similar position differently to other categories of cases"); *R v Tower Hamlets London Borough Council, ex p Uddin* (2000) 32 HLR 391, 403 (housing transfer points scheme irrational because failing to distinguish between households with markedly different needs); *R (Kaur) v Ealing London Borough Council* [2008] EWHC 2062 (Admin) at [52] (unlike cases must be treated differently).

55.1.17 Policy must not be over-rigid. <50.4>; *R v Hampshire County Council, ex p W* [1994] ELR 460, 476B (Sedley J: "What is required by the law is that, without falling into arbitrariness decision-makers must remember that a policy is a means of securing a consistent approach to individual cases, each of which is likely to differ from others. Each case must be considered therefore in the light of the policy, but not so that the policy automatically determines the outcome").

55.1.18 Arbitrariness/inequality: other illustrations. *R v Bradford Metropolitan Borough Council, ex p Sikander Ali* [1994] ELR 299, 308E (Jowitt J: "I accept that a criterion so nebulous as to be unlikely to produce any result other than one which was quixotic, or arbitrary or whimsical would be *Wednesbury* unreasonable"); *Chertsey Urban District Council v Mixnam's Properties Ltd* [1965] AC 735, 753E-G (referring to "arbitrariness" as an application of "the general rule that subordinate legislation, to be valid, must be shown to be within the powers conferred by the statute"); *R (Saadi) v Secretary of State for the Home Department* [2001] EWCA Civ 1512 [2002] 1 WLR 356 (CA) at [29] ("the fact that there is limited room at Oakington [the detention centre], so that not all who would qualify to go there can be accommodated, does not result in arbitrariness"); *R v Governor of Frankland Prison, ex p Russell* [2000] 1 WLR 2027 (policy of restricting prisoners to one meal a day an unjustified interference with fundamental rights), at [18] ("The limitation of the provision to one meal a day is arbitrary and operates irrespective of the impact on the individual prisoner").

55.1.19 Uncertainty.[22] *Secretary of State for Defence v Percy* [1999] 1 All ER 732, 742b ("the principles of public law ... include principles of legal certainty"); <59.1.4> (uncertainty under ECHR/HRA); *McEldowney v Forde* [1971] AC 632, 643F (asking whether regulation "too vague and so arbitrary as to be wholly unreasonable"); *R (Grogan) v Bexley NHS Care Trust* [2006] EWHC 44 (Admin) [2006] LGR 491 at [94], [100] (decision unlawful because made by

---

[22] Richard Moules [2007] JR 104.

reference to vague policy criteria); *R (C) v Lambeth London Borough Council* [2008] EWHC 1230 at [42] (elements "so vague as to not be able to constitute a [pathway] plan"); <46.1.4> (uncertainty as ultra vires); <57.3.4> (uncertainty as unreasonableness); <12.1.12> (the rule of law and certainty).

55.2 Unjustified departure. There are a number of situations where the "departure" from a legally relevant position will require a good reason or cogent justification. They include departure from: (1) conduct engendering a legitimate expectation; (2) policy guidance; (3) another body's findings; (4) action in other like cases; and (5) prior action in the same case.

55.2.1 Departure from conduct engendering legitimate expectation. <P41> (legitimate expectation); <54.2> (substantive legitimate expectation); <60.1.11> (procedural legitimate expectation).

55.2.2 Departure from policy guidance. <6.2>.

55.2.3 Unjustified departure from another body's findings.[23]
(A) DEPARTURE REQUIRES JUSTIFICATION.*R (Bradley) v Secretary of State for Work and Pensions* [2008] EWCA Civ 36 [2008] 3 All ER 1116 at [91] (although non-binding, Secretary of State needing good reason for rejecting ombudsman's findings, beyond restatement of own otherwise rational view); *R (Viggers) v Pensions Appeal Tribunal* [2006] EWHC 1066 (Admin) (need to spell out reasons for disagreeing with views of Veterans Agency Medical Services); *R (IT) v Secretary of State for Justice* [2008] EWHC 1707 (Admin) (no new basis for Secretary of State to recall patient following discharge decision of mental health review tribunal); *R v Avon County Council, ex p M* [1994] 2 FLR 1006, 1019F-1020D (council not entitled to depart from review panel "without a substantial reason and without having given that recommendation the weight it required"); *Jafar Danaie v Secretary of State for the Home Department* [1998] Imm AR 84 (Home Secretary could not rationally reject adjudicator's favourable credibility findings, unless demonstrably irrational or ignored relevancies, or fresh material); *R v Secretary of State for the Home Department, ex p Linda Boafo* [2002] EWCA Civ 44 [2002] 1 WLR 1919 (adjudicator's decision binding under statutory scheme); *R (TB (Jamaica)) v Secretary of State for the Home Department* [2008] EWCA Civ 977 (Secretary of State not entitled to deny refugee status on basis that could have been raised in AIT); *R v Warwickshire County Council, ex p Powergen Plc* [1997] 3 PLR 62 (irrational for council not to apply planning inspector's conclusion as to road safety objections); *R (Mayor of London) v Enfield London Borough Council* [2008] EWCA Civ 202 [2008] LGR 615 at [29] (unreasonable to depart from planning appeal adjudication on same issue absent an additional reason of substance); *R v Cardiff County Council, ex p Sears Group Properties Ltd* [1998] 3 PLR 55, 65F (whether sufficient change in circumstances); *R v Hampshire County Council, ex p H* [1999] 2 FLR 359, 370C (appeal panel views to be properly respected); *R (T) v Enfield London Borough Council* [2004] EWHC 2297 (Admin) [2005] 3 FCR 55 (failure to take account of available views of consultant paediatrician and child guidance team); *George Wimpey UK Ltd v First Secretary of State* [2004] EWHC 2419 (Admin) at [39] (no adequate reasons for departing from planning inspector's recommendations); *R v Cardiff County Council, ex p Sears Group Properties Ltd* [1998] 3 PLR 55, 64B-F ("where a formal decision has been made on a particular subject-matter or issue affecting private rights by a competent public authority, that decision will be regarded as binding on other authorities directly involved, unless and until circumstances change in a way that can be reasonably found to undermine the basis of the

---

[23] Caroline Neenan [2000] JR 36.

original decision").

(B) SPECIAL SITUATIONS. *R (Staff Side of the Police Negotiating Board) v Secretary of State for the Home Department* [2008] EWHC 1173 (Admin) at [11] (statutory duty to "take into consideration" recommendations of tribunal), [42] (duty only to have regard to pay recommendations); *R (Nejad) v Secretary of State for the Home Department* [2004] EWCA Civ 33 (Secretary of State needing "good reason" to depart from "judicial expression of view" by LCJ as to tariff); *R (Von Brandenburg) v East London and The City Mental Health NHS Trust* [2003] UKHL 58 [2004] 2 AC 280 (approved social worker entitled to seek compulsory mental health detention on new information, despite mental health review tribunal's decision ordering discharge); *M v Secretary of State for the Home Department* [2003] EWCA Civ 146 [2003] 1 WLR 1980 (Secretary of State obliged to explain why taking different view from criminal court which had declined to recommend deportation); *R (Brent London Borough Council) v Fed 2000* [2005] EWHC 2679 (Admin) [2006] ELR 169 (statutory duty to implement school organisation committee's approval decision); *R v Secretary of State for Trade and Industry, ex p Thomson Holidays Ltd* The Times 12th January 2000 (Secretary of State acting ultra vires in responding to MMC report by reference to his own findings of fact rather than those made by the MMC); *R (Bantamagbari) v City of Westminster* [2003] EWHC 1350 (Admin) at [7], [24] (intentional homelessness a question for notifying authority, so that notified authority not entitled to depart unless by seeking judicial review).

(C) ENTITLED TO DEPART. *R (M) v Lambeth London Borough Council* [2008] EWHC 1364 (Admin) at [163] (council having good and sound reasons to depart from AIT's finding as to age); *R (Banfield) v Secretary of State for Justice* [2007] EWHC 2605 (Admin) at [28] (Secretary of State entitled to depart from parole board recommendation); *R v Secretary of State for the Home Department, ex p Harry* [1998] 1 WLR 1737 (where Mental Health Review Tribunal's recommendations leaving Secretary of State in doubt, entitled to look to Advisory Board for assistance); *R (SmithKline Beecham) v Advertising Standards Authority* 17th January 2001 unrep. (British Dental Association approval of advertisement not binding; ASA entitled to depart from it in the circumstances); *R v Secretary of State for the Home Department, ex p Doody* [1994] 1 AC 531, 557H-559C (Home Secretary, in consulting the trial judge and Lord Chief Justice as to setting the penal `tariff' for life prisoners, not obliged to follow the recommendation of those judges); *R (Akhtar) v Secretary of State for the Home Department* [2001] EWHC Admin 38 at [23]-[24] (*Danaie/Powergen* principle not preventing Secretary of State from general recall of prisoner in breach of licence, despite magistrates' decision of limited recall); *Nahar v Social Security Commissioners* [2001] EWHC Admin 1049 [2002] 2 FCR 442 (no issue estoppel or legitimate expectation on social security commissioners to uphold validity of marriage where previously upheld by immigration adjudicators) (CA is at [2002] EWCA Civ 859); *R (Bhoti) v Secretary of State for the Home Department* [2003] EWHC 1628 (Admin) (police disciplinary tribunal) at [12] ("plain ... that the Secretary of State has power to reverse a Tribunal on questions of fact", referring to *R v Secretary of State for the Home Department, ex p Barr* (1995) 7 Admin LR 157, 170); *R (A) v National Probation Service* [2003] EWHC 2910 (Admin) (2004) 7 CCLR 335 at [27]-[28] (probation service entitled to form own assessment of risk, departing from parole board's view); *R (Johnson) v Reading Borough Council* [2004] EWHC 765 (Admin) at [64] (councillors entitled to depart from recommendation in report commissioned by them, being entitled to regard the report on focusing on one area of the city); <60.6.9> (error of approach by consultee/adviser).

55.2.4 Departure from action taken in other like cases.

(A) OTHER DECISION AS A RELEVANCY. <55.1.13(B)> (other decision as a relevancy: other similar cases).

(B) DEPARTURE FROM PREVIOUS INTERPRETATION/APPLICATION.*HTV Ltd v Price Commission* [1976] ICR 170, 185E-H (Lord Denning MR: "It is ... the duty of the Price Commission to act with fairness and consistency in their dealings with manufacturers and traders. Allowing that it is primarily for them to interpret and apply the code, nevertheless if they regularly interpret the words of the code in a particular sense - or regularly apply the code in a particular way - they should continue to interpret it and apply it in the same way thereafter unless there is good cause for departing from it. At any rate they should not depart from it in any case where they have, by their conduct, led the manufacturer or trader to believe that he can safely act on that interpretation of the code or on that method of applying it, and he does so act on it. It is not permissible for them to depart from their previous interpretation and application where it would not be fair or just to do so"), 192A-G; *R (Adriano) v Surrey County Council* [2002] EWHC 2471 (Admin) [2003] Env LR 559 at [28] (unfair and unreasonable here to depart from the interpretation of a policy, having previously formally rejected the very interpretation now adopted).

(C) DEPARTURE FROM OTHER SIMILAR CASES.*JJ Gallagher Ltd v Secretary of State for Transport, Local Government and the Regions* [2002] EWHC 1812 (Admin) [2002] 4 PLR 32 at [56] (where apparent inconsistency between grant of planning permission in one case and its refusal in another, need for an explanation); *R v Department of Health, ex p Misra* [1996] 1 FLR 128, 133 (divergent decisions "require the court to consider with the greatest care how such a result can be justified as a matter of law"); *R v Special Adjudicator, ex p Turus* [1996] Imm AR 388, 413 (where adjudicator departing from determination on same or similar facts, obliged to give clear and cogent reasons for so doing); *R (X) v Y School* [2007] EWHC 298 (Admin) [2007] ELR 278 at [136] (times having moved on since previous policy applied to claimant's siblings).

55.2.5 Departure from prior action in the same case. <55.1.13(A)> (other decision as a relevancy: same case); *R (Carvill) v Commissioners of Inland Revenue* [2003] EWHC 1852 (Admin) (not irrational, unfair or an abuse of power to repay tax where final judicial determination in earlier years unchallenged, albeit that successfully challenged in later years); <55.2.3> (departure from factual findings of another body); <54.1.15> (binding determinations); *R v Aylesbury Vale District Council, ex p Chaplin* [1997] 3 PLR 55 (considering whether departure from earlier decision unlawful in the absence of an explanation; here, good and obvious reason for the later decision); *R v East Hertfordshire District Council, ex p Beckham* [1998] JPL 55, 59 (Lightman J: "Where a decision of the council is made to reverse a position taken twice in so recent a period, fairness and good administration require that the reasoning advanced by the council should be clear and unambiguous; it should not be contradictory, unsatisfactory or pregnant with possibilities of error"); *R v Mendip District Council, ex p Fabre* [2000] COD 372 (where background well-known to decision-makers, planning officer not obliged specifically to mention in his report that planning permission previously refused);*R v Secretary of State for Education, ex p C* [1996] ELR 93 (not necessary irrational for same decision-maker to assess same case differently at different times); *R v Bradford Crown Court, ex p Crossling* [2000] COD 107 (not an abuse of process for prosecution to make fresh application to Crown Court to extend custody time limit, where previously refused on basis of fundamental misapprehension of fact); *R (C) v Sunderland Youth Court* [2003] EWHC 2385 (Admin) (unlawful for court to make anti-social behaviour order, having declined one at an earlier hearing, without clearly explaining basis for doing so); *R v Inland Revenue Commissioners, ex p Unilever Plc* [1996] STC 681 (unfair abuse of power because of prior treatment of late returns); *R v Chief Constable of West Yorkshire, ex p Wilkinson* [2002] EWHC 2353 (Admin) at [74] ("Inconsistency is not necessarily to be equated with irrationality, but if a decision is reached in a particular case which cannot stand as a matter of consistency with another decision reached in the same case, then that should ... be taken into consideration in deciding whether the decisions under attack are decisions properly open to be made and not irrational"); *R v Secretary of State for the Home Department, ex p Golam Mowla* [1992] 1 WLR 70 ("clearly ... desirable that so far as possible decisions made on the same facts about an applicant for entry or for leave to remain for an extended period should be consistent with each other").

> **P56 Relevancy/irrelevancy.** A body must have regard
> to all, and to only, legally relevant considerations.

56.1 The relevancy/irrelevancy principle
56.2 Obligatory and discretionary relevance
56.3 Relevance and weight

56.1 The relevancy/irrelevancy principle.

A public body should take into account all relevant considerations and no irrelevant ones. A material failure to do so is a common ground for judicial review.

56.1.1 **Relevancy/irrelevancy principle: in a nutshell.** *In Re Duffy* [2008] UKHL 4 at [53] (Lord Carswell: "the Secretary of State was bound to have regard to the proper factors, and not to have regard to any other improper factors, in reaching his decision"); *R (Alconbury Developments Ltd) v Secretary of State for the Environment Transport and the Regions* [2001] UKHL 23 [2003] 2 AC 295 at [50] (Lord Slynn: "if the Secretary of State ... takes into account matters irrelevant to his decision or refuses or fails to take account of matters relevant to his decision ... the court may set his decision aside"); *R v Secretary of State for Trade and Industry, ex p Lonrho Plc* [1989] 1 WLR 525, 533D (Lord Keith: "the discretion ... must be exercised ... by reference to relevant and not irrelevant considerations"); *R v Director General of Telecommunications, ex p Cellcom Ltd* [1999] COD 105 (see transcript) (Lightman J: "The Court may interfere if the Director has taken into account an irrelevant consideration or has failed to take into account a relevant consideration"); COE:COM No.R(80)2 of the Committee of Ministers (adopted 11 March 1980) <45.1.4(B)> (describing the "basic principle" that an "administrative authority, when exercising a discretionary power ... tak[es] into account only the factors relevant to the particular case").

56.1.2 **Decision vitiated by disregarding of relevancy.** *R (McCarthy) v Basildon District Council* [2008] EWHC 987 (Admin) at [40] & [66] (position of individual families); *R (Assura Pharmacy Ltd) v NHS Litigation Authority* [2008] EWHC 289 (Admin) at [79]-[80] (choice); *R (BMW AG) v Revenue & Customs Commissioners* [2008] EWHC 712 (Admin) at [105] (financial implications); *R (Murphy) v Salford Primary Care Trust* [2008] EWHC 1908 (Admin) at [31] (failure to look at the circumstances in the round); *R (Mersey Care NHS Trust) v Mental Health Review Tribunal* [2004] EWHC 1749 (Admin) [2005] 1 WLR 2469 at [72] (security considerations); *R (T) v Enfield London Borough Council* [2004] EWHC 2297 (Admin) [2005] 3 FCR 55 (views of consultant and child guidance team); *R v Director of Public Prosecutions, ex p Manning* [2001] QB 330 at [42] (relevancies in deciding whether to prosecute); *R v Flintshire County Council, ex p Armstrong-Braun* [2001] EWCA Civ 345 [2001] LGR 344 (democratic implications); *R (Ashbrook) v East Sussex County Council* [2002] EWCA Civ 1701 [2003] 1 PLR 66 (deliberate obstruction giving rise to the problem); *R (Watford Grammar School for Girls) v Adjudicator for Schools* [2003] EWHC 2480 (Admin) [2004] ELR 40 at [82] & [85] (failure to appreciate "other possible ways of achieving the result which he considered to be desirable").

56.1.3 **Decision vitiated by considering an irrelevancy.** *R (Campbell) v General Medical Council* [2005] EWCA Civ 250 [2005] 1 WLR 3488 (mitigation matters irrelevant to whether professional misconduct); *R (Stace) v Milton Keynes Magistrates Court* [2006] EWHC 1049 (Admin) at [97] (community rehabilitation order irrelevant to driving licence revocation); *R v Secretary of State for Education, ex p E* [1996] ELR 312 (mistaken assumptions about the Jewish faith); *R v Crown Court at Portsmouth, ex p Thomas* [1994] COD 373 (previous convictions irrelevant to whether to state a case); *R v Secretary of State for the Environment, ex p Royal Society for the Protection of Birds* [1997] QB 206 (economic considerations irrelevant to designating special protection area).

56.1.4 **Anxious scrutiny and relevancy/irrelevancy.** <32.3> (anxious scrutiny); *R v Secretary of State for the Home Department, ex p Brind* [1991] 1 AC 696, 757B-C (Lord Ackner, considering whether "the minister failed to call his attention to matters which he was bound to consider, nor that he included in his considerations matters which were irrelevant": "In a field which concerns a fundamental human right ... close scrutiny must be given to the reasons provided as justification for interference with that right"); *R v Secretary of State for the Home Department, ex p Bugdaycay* [1987] AC 514, 534A ("Since the decisions ... appear to have been made without taking [the degree of danger] into account, they cannot, in my opinion, now stand").

56.1.5 **Fundamental rights/effect on rights as a relevant consideration.** *R v Immigration Officer, ex p Quaquah* [2000] INLR 196, 202G-H (applying the "proposition" that "where his decision touches convention rights the Secretary of State (or other decision-maker) must consider and decide whether in his view the Convention right in issue has been violated"); *R v Flintshire County Council, ex p Armstrong-Braun* [2001] EWCA Civ 345 [2001] LGR 344 at [37] (impact of decision on councillor's ability to raise matters in discussion should have been given "most anxious consideration"); *R v Human Fertilisation and Embryology Authority, ex p Blood* [1999] Fam 151 (judicial review granted for failure to take account of EC Treaty rights affected by decision); *R v Secretary of State for Education and Employment, ex p Liverpool Hope University College* [2001] EWCA Civ 362 [2001] ELR 552 at [81]-[83] (if rights not specifically mentioned court can look at content of decision to see whether requirements of EC law nevertheless met); *R (Fuller) v Chief Constable of Dorset Constabulary* [2001] EWHC Admin 1057 [2003] QB 480 at [67] ("a local authority must consider the Convention rights of trespassers living on their land and their human needs generally when deciding whether or not to enforce its right to possession of that land"); *R (Richards) v Pembrokeshire County Council* [2004] EWCA Civ 1000 [2005] LGR 105 at [69]-[70] (Directions unlawful because council having failed adequately to consider relevancy, namely that they might invade claimants' property rights without compensation or adequate justification); *R (Goldsmith) v London Borough of Wandsworth* [2004] EWCA Civ 1170 (2004) 7 CCLR 472 at [91] (decision flawed for failure to address claimant's HRA:ECHR Art 8 rights); <6.3.11> (international law as a relevancy); <58.4.1> (focus on outcome not reasoning process).

56.1.6 **Materiality and relevancy/irrelevancy.**
(A) RELEVANCY. *R (Assura Pharmacy Ltd) v NHS Litigation Authority* [2008] EWHC 289 (Admin) at [83] (appropriate to grant judicial review where unable to say would inevitably have exercised discretion the same way); *R v Parliamentary Commissioner for Administration, ex p Balchin* [1998] 1 PLR 1, 15C ("test" is "whether a consideration has been omitted which, had account been taken of it, might have caused the decision maker to reach a different conclusion"); *R (Hampson) v Wigan Metropolitan Borough Council* [2005] EWHC 1656 (Admin) (omitted reference to development plan would not have affected outcome); *R v Thurrock Borough Council, ex p Tesco Stores Ltd* [1993] 3 PLR 114, 124D ("not ... a matter which stood any chance of persuading the authority to change their mind"); *R v Royal Borough of Kensington and Chelsea, ex p Kassam* (1994) 26 HLR 455, 465 ("the authority might - and that is all that is necessary - have reached a different decision, had it had fully in mind the true position"); *A v Kirklees Metropolitan Borough Council* [2001] EWCA Civ 582 [2001] ELR 657 at [17] ("the objective question whether the evidence was capable of having made a difference"); *R (Mount Cook Land Ltd) v Westminster City Council* [2003] EWCA Civ 1346 [2004] 1 PLR 29 at [37] ("no conceivable basis upon which [the claimant's] proposals could have caused the Council to reach a different decision").
(B) IRRELEVANCY. *R v Swansea City Council, ex p Elitestone Ltd* [1993] 2 PLR 65, 73F ("it

is not ... credible that the committee's decision would have been different" if matter had "not been put before them"); *R v Wandsworth London Borough Council, ex p Onwudiwe* [1994] COD 229 (see transcript) (impossible to conclude that authority's decision would have been `in the least bit different had it not considered the irrelevancy); *Kwaku Boateng Kwapong v Secretary of State for the Home Department* [1994] Imm AR 207, 214 (no suggestion "that it formed part of the basis for the decision"); *R v London Borough of Newham, ex p Dawson* (1994) 26 HLR 747, 759 ("the most likely inference is that ... the rent issue played no further part in the decision"); *R v Secretary of State for the Environment, ex p Kingston upon Hull City Council* [1996] Env LR 248, 263 (irrelevant consideration played a major role in the decision); *R v Secretary of State for Wales, ex p Kennedy* [1996] 1 PLR 97, 101G ("any established irrelevancy would certainly not be of a quality to vitiate the validity of the inspector's overall conclusion"); *R v Wolverhampton Coroner, ex p McCurbin* [1990] 1 WLR 719 (coroner's reference to manslaughter had introduced an irrelevant matter, but clear that this had no bearing on the outcome); *R v Secretary of State for Health, ex p Eastside Cheese Company* [1999] EuLR 968, 983C-D ("the department would in all probability have reached the same decision, if indeed it was not bound to do so, whether or not account had been taken of the matters which the judge held to be irrelevant"); *R v Investors Compensation Scheme Ltd, ex p Bowden* [1996] 1 AC 261, 281E ("very much a subsidiary reason").

56.1.7 Relevancy/irrelevancy in the real world. *R v London County Council, ex p London and Provincial Electric Theatres Ltd* [1915] 2 KB 466, 490 (Pickford LJ: "probably hardly any decision of a body like the London county council dealing with these matters could stand if every statement which a member made in debate were to be taken as a ground of the decision"; "there are probably few debates in which some one does not suggest as a ground for decision something which is not a proper ground; and to say that, because somebody in debate has put forward an improper ground, the decision ought to be set aside as being founded on that particular ground is wrong"), applied in *R v Exeter City District Council, ex p JL Thomas & Co* [1991] 1 QB 471, 484; *R v Chief Registrar of Friendly Societies, ex p New Cross Building Society* [1984] QB 227, 260G-261A ("In a decision involving the weighing of many complex factors it will always be possible to point to some factors which should arguably have been taken into account or left out of account"); *R v Westminster City Council, ex p Monahan* [1990] 1 QB 87, 111C-F ("Financial constraints on the economic viability of a desirable planning development are unavoidable facts of life in an imperfect world. It would be unreal and contrary to common sense to insist that they must be excluded from the range of considerations which may properly be regarded as material in determining planning applications"); *R (L (A Minor)) v Governors of J School* [2003] UKHL 9 [2003] 2 AC 633 (significance of threat of industrial action to mode of school reinstatement).

56.1.8 Legitimate expectation as a relevancy.[24] *R (Bibi) v Newham London Borough Council* [2001] EWCA Civ 607 [2002] 1 WLR 237 at [49] (Schiemann LJ: "The Authority in its decision making process has simply not acknowledged that the promises were a relevant consideration in coming to a conclusion"; "that is an error of law"), [51] ("The law requires that any legitimate expectation be properly taken into account in the decision making process"); *R (Bodimeade) v Camden London Borough Council* [2001] EWHC Admin 271 (2001) 4 CCLR 246 at [32] (decision quashed because legitimate expectation "never considered"); *R (Theophilus) v London Borough of Lewisham* [2002] EWHC 1371 (Admin) [2002] 3 All ER 851 at [26] (failure to take account of breach of promise, applying *Bibi*); *R (Ibrahim) v London Borough of Redbridge* [2002] EWHC 2756 (Admin) at [11] (council having discharged its obligation "to take the expectation into account"); *R (Bloggs 61) v Secretary of State for the*

---

[24] David Pievsky [2003] JR 144.

Home Department [2003] EWCA Civ 686 [2003] 1 WLR 2724 at [75] (depending on the circumstances, even an unauthorised promise could be a relevant consideration); *R v British Advertising Clearance Centre, ex p Swiftcall Ltd* 16th November 1995 unrep. (legitimate expectation from prior approval a relevant consideration requiring a good reason for such a course); *R v Merton, Sutton and Wandsworth Health Authority, ex p Perry* (2000) 3 CCLR 378 at [80] (council should have formally considered previous promise of a home for life); *R v Isleworth Crown Court, ex p Irvin* The Times 5th December 1991 (on Crown Court appeal against sentence, wrong to ignore expectation given to the claimant by the justices), applied in *R v Truro Crown Court, ex p Warren* [1993] COD 294; *R v Shropshire County Council, ex p Jones* [1997] COD 116 (should have given more attention to the expectation of a discretionary grant); *R v Commissioners of Customs and Excise, ex p Kay and Co* [1996] STC 1500, 1528c (in exercising statutory discretion "the commissioners would almost certainly have to take into account the existence of their representations"); *R v Lord Saville of Newdigate, ex p B* The Times 15th April 1999 (legitimate expectation arising from assurance given by Widgery inquiry (1972) was a consideration which could not be ignored by the Saville inquiry (1999), but had to be taken into account and given appropriate weight); *R v North and East Devon Health Authority, ex p Coughlan* [2001] QB 213, at [57(a)] (reasonableness category of substantive legitimate expectation), [58] (ask "whether the public body has given proper weight to the implications of not fulfilling the promise"), [73] (must "take into account all relevant matters which here will include the promise or other conduct giving rise to the expectation"); *R (Abbasi) v Secretary of State for Foreign and Commonwealth Affairs* [2002] EWCA Civ 1598 [2003] UKHRR 76 at [82] ("The expectation is not that the policy or practice will necessarily remain unchanged ... However, so long as it remains unchanged, the subject is entitled to have it properly taken into account in considering his individual case"); *Rowland v Environment Agency* [2003] EWCA Civ 1885 [2005] Ch 1 at [153] and [155] (legitimate expectation arising from previous practice a matter to be taken into account); <56.1.10(B)> (legitimate expectation of a relevancy).

56.1.9 **Whether limited resources are relevant.** *R (G) v Barnet London Borough Council* [2003] UKHL 57 [2004] 2 AC 208 at [35] (Lord Nicholls: "Ordinarily cost, where relevant, will be a matter to be taken into account by a local authority when considering its response to an assessed need rather than at the stage of assessment"); *R v East Sussex County Council, ex p Tandy* [1998] AC 714 (resources not relevant to statutory duty to assess "suitable" education provision); *R (Conville) v Richmond upon Thames London Borough Council* [2006] EWCA Civ 718 [2006] 1 WLR 2808 at [36] (resources not capable of diluting duty to give reasonable opportunity of securing housing); *R v Gloucestershire County Council, ex p Barry* [1997] AC 584[25] (resources relevant to statutory duty to assess what "necessary" to meet "needs"); *R v Sefton Metropolitan Borough Council, ex p Help The Aged* [1997] 4 All ER 532 (resources relevant to statutory duty to assess whether "need of care and attention"); *R (Batantu) v Islington London Borough Council* (2001) 33 HLR 871 (having decided need, resources not relevant basis for failing to fulfil it); *R v Norfolk County Council, ex p Thorpe* (1998) 96 LGR 597 (resources relevant to statutory duty to provide footways where "necessary or desirable" for pedestrian safety); *R v Bristol City Council, ex p Penfold* (1998) 1 CCLR 315 (resources not relevant to decision whether or not to conduct community care assessment); *R v Birmingham City Council, ex p Mohammed* [1999] 1 WLR 33 (resources not relevant to decision whether to provide a disabled facilities grant); *R (Khan) v London Borough of Newham* [2001] EWHC Admin 589 (where housing duty, limited resources not relevant to court's decision whether to make a mandatory order); <31.2.3> (circumstances where limited resources); cf. *R (Noorkoiv) v Secretary of State for the Home Department* [2002] EWCA Civ 770 [2002] 1 WLR 3284 (lack

---

[25] Ben Rayment [1996] JR 222, [1997] JR 158; Luke Clements [1997] JR 162.

of resources not an answer to breach of Human Rights Act:ECHR Art 5(4)); *R (Spink) v Wandsworth London Borough Council* [2005] EWCA Civ 302 [2005] 1 WLR 2884 (parental resources relevant in deciding whether necessary to provide aids and adaptations for disabled children).

56.1.10 Other aspects of relevancy/irrelevancy.
(A) POLICY GUIDANCE AND RELEVANCY. <6.2>; *Jordan Abiodun Iye v Secretary of State for the Home Department* [1994] Imm AR 63, 66 ("If it became clear a particular officer had disregarded the guidance, that would be a valid reason for saying the decision was wrongly made"); *R v Wolverhampton Municipal Borough Council, ex p Dunne* (1997) 29 HLR 745 (Secretary of State's guidance identifying material considerations to which council obliged to have regard).
(B) LEGITIMATE EXPECTATION OF A RELEVANCY. *R (Quark Fishing Ltd) v Secretary of State for Foreign and Commonwealth Affairs* [2002] EWCA Civ 1409 at [60] ("by past practice a legitimate expectation had been generated that loyalty [to the fishery] would be taken into account"); <6.2.6> (policy guidance giving rise to a legitimate expectation (including of criteria or matters to be considered)).
(C) CONSISTENCY: PREVIOUS DECISIONS AS A RELEVANCY. <55.1.13>.
(D) LINK BETWEEN RELEVANCY AND PROCEDURAL FAIRNESS. *R v Hampshire County Council, ex p K* [1990] 2 QB 71, 78G (fair procedure meaning: "Whatever their eventual decision, they would at least have had before them the material upon which to base a fully informed and judicial exercise of the discretion").
(F) SUFFICIENCY OF INQUIRY. <P51>.

56.2 Obligatory and discretionary relevance. The law strikes a balance as to when the Court should substitute its own judgment on questions of relevancy. One distinction is between matters whose relevance is (1) dictated by the Court applying a hard-edged correctness review or (2) chosen by the public body subject to a soft reasonableness review.

56.2.1 Obligatory and discretionary relevance: *Creednz.* *In re Findlay* [1985] AC 318, 333H-334C, approving *Creednz Inc v Governor-General* [1981] 1 NZLR 172, 183 (court intervenes "when the statute expressly or impliedly identifies considerations required to be taken into account by the authority as a matter of legal obligation" or matter "obviously material"); *R (Hurst) v London Northern District Coroner* [2007] UKHL 13 [2007] 2 AC 189 at [57] (referring to *Creednz*); *R (Corner House Research) v Director of the Serious Fraud Office* [2008] UKHL 60 [2008] 3 WLR 568 at [40] (Lord Bingham: "A discretionary decision is not ... vitiated by a failure to take into account a consideration which the decision-maker is not obliged by the law or the facts to take into account, even if he may properly do so"); *R (Al Rawi) v Secretary of State for Foreign and Commonwealth Affairs* [2006] EWCA Civ 1279 [2008] QB 289 at [131] ("what is and what is not a relevant consideration for a public decision-maker to have in mind is (absent a statutory code of compulsory considerations) for the decision-maker, not the court, to decide"); *R (National Association of Health Stores) v Secretary of State for Health* [2005] EWCA Civ 154 at [63], [75] (applying *Creednz*); *R (Greenpeace Ltd) v Secretary of State for the Environment, Food and Rural Affairs* [2005] EWCA Civ 1656 [2006] Env LR 627 at [26] ("the decision-maker is generally the master of the matters he will treat as relevant and the depth or detail into which he will go"); *R (Coghlan) v Chief Constable of Greater Manchester Police* [2004] EWHC 2801 (Admin) [2005] 2 All ER 890 at [48] (applying *Creednz*), [54] (non-statutory guidance "so obviously material" that disregarding it "would not be in accordance with the intention of the statutory scheme").

56.2.2 Discretionary relevance: primarily a matter for the decision-maker. *R (Khatun) v*

515

London Borough of Newham [2004] EWCA Civ 55 [2005] QB 37 at [35] ("where a statute conferring discretionary power provides no lexicon of the matters to be treated as relevant by the decision-maker, then it is for the decision-maker and not the court to conclude what is relevant subject only to *Wednesbury* review"); *R (Adlard) v Secretary of State for the Environment, Transport and the Regions* [2002] EWCA Civ 735 [2002] 1 WLR 2515 at [41] (considerations "of the kind which the Secretary of State can have regard to or not as he chooses"); *R (Jones) v North Warwickshire Borough Council* [2001] EWCA Civ 315 at [20] ("decision-maker must decide for himself what he will take into account. In doing so he must obviously be guided by the policy and objects of the governing statute"); *R (Ireneschild) v Lambeth London Borough Council* [2007] EWCA Civ 234 [2007] LGR 619 at [41], [77] (report obviously relevant); *R (Manchester City Council) v Secretary of State for Environment, Food & Rural Affairs* [2007] EWHC 3167 (Admin) (entitled to have regard to public petition regarding public right of way).

56.2.3 Obligatory relevance: significance of the statute. *Associated Provincial Picture Houses Ltd v Wednesbury Corporation* [1948] 1 KB 223, 228 (Lord Greene MR: "If, in the statute conferring the discretion, there is to be found expressly or by implication matters which the authority exercising the discretion ought to have regard to, then in exercising the discretion it must have regard to those matters ... if the nature of the subject matter and the general interpretation of the Act make it clear that certain matters would not be germane to the matter in question, the authority must disregard those irrelevant collateral matters"); *Secretary of State for Education and Science v Tameside Metropolitan Borough Council* [1977] AC 1014, 1064H-1065B (asking whether Secretary of State "had directed himself properly in law and had in consequence taken into consideration the matters which upon the true construction of the Act he ought to have considered and excluded from his consideration matters that were irrelevant to what he had to consider"); *R (Baker) v Secretary of State for Communities and Local Government* [2008] EWCA Civ 141 [2008] LGR 239 (statutory duty to have "due regard" to prescribed race equality matters); *R (Chavda) v Harrow London Borough Council* [2007] EWHC 3064 (Admin) [2008] LGR 657 (failure of statutory duty to have "due regard" to disability equality issues); *Tesco Stores Ltd v Secretary of State for the Environment* [1995] 1 WLR 759 ("material" considerations under Town and Country Planning Act 1990 s.70(2)); *R v Wandsworth London Borough Council, ex p Hawthorne* [1994] 1 WLR 1442, 1448D (statutory duty to have regard to Code of Guidance); <6.2.2> (policy guidance: statutorily-prescribed duty); *R v Oadby and Wigston Borough Council, ex p Dickman* (1996) 28 HLR 806, 817 (regulations setting out "the only factors that are relevant"); *R v Secretary of State for the Environment, ex p Lancashire County Council* [1994] 4 All ER 165, 174e (unlawful for guidance to supply further criterion to those already in statute); *R v Sunderland City Council ex p Redezeus Ltd* (1995) 27 HLR 477 (statute setting out only matters to which regard could be had); *R v Licensing Authority of the Department of Health, ex p Scotia Pharmaceuticals* [1995] 3 CMLR 657 (EC Directive laying down information required to be submitted and considered).

56.2.4 Discretionary relevance: whether reasonable choice of relevancies. *R v Secretary of State for Transport, ex p Richmond-upon-Thames London Borough Council* [1994] 1 WLR 74, 95C (Laws J: "in a case where the statute itself does not specify the considerations to be taken into account in arriving at a discretionary decision, it will be for the decision-making body to decide what is and what is not a relevant consideration, and this decision will itself only be subject to review on *Wednesbury* grounds"); *R (Metropolitan Borough of Wirral) v Chief Schools Adjudicator* [2001] ELR 574 at [53] (obligation to "consider those consequences which the reasonable decision-maker, fulfilling that particular statutory duty, would realise were necessary or fundamental considerations arising as part and parcel of his very determination"); *R v Lambeth London Borough Council, ex p Njomo* (1996) 28 HLR 737, 743 (rent arrears among those "considerations which can in the decision-maker's own discretion lawfully be taken into account"); *R v Gaming Board of Great Britain, ex p Kingsley* [1996] COD 178 (assessment of relevancies for defendant's expertise, providing that had regard to statutory purpose and matters related to statutory test, and subject to *Wednesbury*); *R v Secretary of State for the Home Department, ex p Mehari* [1994] QB 474, 492F-G (credibility findings not logically relevant to whether France a safe third country); *The Bath Society v Secretary of State for the Environment* [1991] 1 WLR 1303, 1311B-F (so obviously material that unreasonable not to consider); *R v Parliamentary Commissioner for Administration, ex p Balchin* [1998] 1 PLR 1, 15D (consideration "one to which the law requires the decision maker to have regard" because it "is squarely presented by the very facts established by the Commissioner's own thorough investigation"); *R v Panel on Take-overs and Mergers, ex p Guinness Plc* [1990] 1 QB 146 at 159D (referring to "considerations which on any view must have been irrelevant or ... relevant"), applied in *R (C) v Lewisham London Borough Council* [2003] EWCA Civ 927 [2003] 3 All ER 1277 at [48].

56.2.5 **Relevancies and objectives.** <56.3.6>.

56.3 **Relevance and weight.**Another way of striking a balance, as to when the Court should substitute its own judgment regarding relevancy and irrelevancy, is by distinguishing between (1) relevance (a hard-edged question capable of hard-edged review) and (2) weight (a soft question for reasonableness review).

56.3.1 **Relevancy as law, weight as discretion.** *Tesco Stores Ltd v Secretary of State for the Environment* [1995] 1 WLR 759, 764G-H (Lord Keith: "It is for the courts ... to decide what is a relevant consideration. If the decision maker wrongly takes the view that some consideration is not relevant, and therefore has no regard to it, his decision cannot stand and he must be required to think again. But it is entirely for the decision maker to attribute to the relevant considerations such weight as he thinks fit, and the courts will not interfere unless he has acted unreasonably in the *Wednesbury* sense"), 770B ("regard must be had to [the material consideration]... But the extent, if any, to which it should affect the decision is a matter entirely within the discretion of the decision maker"), 780F-H (Lord Hoffmann: "The law has always made a clear distinction between the question of whether something is a material consideration and the weight which it should be given. The former is a question of law and the latter is a question of planning judgment"); *R v Secretary of State for Transport, ex p Owen* The Times 13th November 1995 (relevancy as a matter of law).

56.3.2 **Weight as a matter for the decision-maker.** *R (Staff Side of the Police Negotiating Board) v Secretary of State for the Home Department* [2008] EWHC 1173 (Admin) at [66] ("So long as they are relevant factors, the judgment as to how much weight should be attached to them is a matter for the Secretary of State"); *City of Edinburgh Council v Secretary of State for Scotland* [1997] 1 WLR 1447, 1458G-H (Lord Clyde: "the assessment of the facts and the weighing of the considerations [are left] in the hands of the decision-maker. It is for him to assess the relative weight to be given to all the material considerations"); *R (Swords) v Secretary of State for Communities and Local Government* [2007] EWCA Civ 795 [2007] LGR 757 at [52] (entitled to take account but decide to give no weight); *R (Manchester City Council) v Secretary of State for Environment, Food & Rural Affairs* [2007] EWHC 3167 (Admin) ("weight ... entirely a matter for the inspector's expert judgment"); *R v Secretary of State for the Home Department, ex p Bulger* [2001] EWHC Admin 119 at [36] ("Weight is a matter for the decision maker"), [50] ("A submission that undue or insufficient weight has been given to a relevant factor does not raise any arguable error of law"); *R v Somerset County Council, ex p Fewings* [1995] 1 WLR 1037, 1050E ("its weight in the overall balance was exclusively [for the defendant]"); *Seddon Properties Ltd v Secretary of State for the Environment* (1981) 42 P & CR 26, 28 ("the courts will not entertain a submission that he gave undue weight to one argument or failed to give any weight at all to another"); *R v British Broadcasting Corporation, ex p Referendum Party* (1997) 9 Admin LR 553, 567H (weight a matter for the BBC/ITC, provided not irrational).

56.3.3 Special/statutory weight. *R v City of Westminster Housing Benefit Review Board, ex p Mehanne* [2001] UKHL 11 [2001] 1 WLR 539 at [13] ("having regard in particular" in statute meaning "[t]hat factor is singled out for special mention and is thereby given the status of a mandatory consideration which carries the most weight"); cf. *R (Manchester City Council) v Secretary of State for Environment, Food & Rural Affairs* [2007] EWHC 3167 (Admin) ("in particular" meaning mandatory relevancy not "enhanced" weight); *R v Video Appeals Committee of the British Board of Film Classification, ex p British Board of Film Classification* [2000] COD 239 (statutory duty requiring "special regard" to be had to harm, "among the other relevant factors"); *R (D) v Secretary of State for the Home Department* [2003] EWHC 155 (Admin) [2003] 1 FLR 979 at [16] (judge describing the duty to "accord primary consideration to the best interests of the child"); <56.2.3> (statutory "due regard" duties).

56.3.4 Wrongly giving too little weight. *Tesco Stores Ltd v Secretary of State for the Environment* [1995] 1 WLR 759, 784B-D ("if the decision to give that consideration no weight is based on rational planning grounds, then the planning authority is entitled to ignore it"); *R v Mid-Hertfordshire Justices, ex p Cox* (1996) 8 Admin LR 409, 413H (magistrates "simply failed to give any weight whatever to the evidence of [the claimant's] changed circumstances"); *R v Secretary of State for the Environment, ex p Torridge District Council* [1997] Env LR 557 (wrongly treating one matter as the sole material consideration, to the exclusion of others); *Secretary of State for Education and Science v Tameside Metropolitan Borough Council* [1977] AC 1014, 1048C-D (asking "whether the Secretary of State has given sufficient, or any, weight to this particular factor in the exercise of his judgment"); *R v Avon County Council, ex p M* [1994] 2 FLR 1006, 1019G-1020D (failure to give "sufficient weight" to recommendation by review panel); *R v Secretary of State for the Home Department, ex p Yousaf* [2000] 3 All ER 649 at [51] (defendant "dismissive of this potentially relevant element in a way which the material before him did not justify"); *R (Von Brandenburg) v East London and The City Mental Health NHS Trust* [2001] EWCA Civ 239 [2002] QB 235 (CA) at [41] (Sedley LJ: "The principle that the weight to be given to such facts is a matter for the decision-maker, moreover, does not mean that the latter is free to dismiss or marginalise things to which the structure and policy of the Act attach obvious importance") (HL is at [2003] UKHL 58 [2004] 2 AC 280); *R v Secretary of State for Trade and Industry, ex p BT3G Ltd* [2001] EuLR 325 (Silber J) at [187] ("Courts have ... been willing to strike down as unreasonable decisions where manifestly excessive or manifestly inadequate weight has been accorded to a relevant consideration") (CA is [2001] EWCA Civ 1448 [2001] EuLR 822): <56.3.3> (special/statutory weight); *R v Manchester Crown Court, ex p McDonald* [1999] 1 WLR 841, 846E (defendant court had to be careful to give full weight to overriding purposes of relevant statutory provisions); <55.2.3> (duty to give full weight to another body's findings).

56.3.5 Wrongly giving too much weight. *R v Waltham Forest London Borough Council, ex p Baxter* [1988] QB 419, 428G (entitled to have regard to party loyalty, but not by blindly allowing it to dominate); *R v Governors of the Hasmonean High School, ex p N & E* [1994] ELR 343, 352D, 355B and 356C (whether factor taken into consideration to an unacceptable degree); *R v South Gloucestershire Housing Benefit Review Board, ex p Dadds* (1997) 29 HLR 700, 707 (decision-makers having concentrated on certain relevant factors so heavily that their decision irrational); *R v Local Commissioner for Administration in North and North East England, ex p Liverpool City Council* [2001] 1 All ER 462 at [36] (allowing party political influence to be decisive); *R v Secretary of State for Trade and Industry, ex p BT3G Ltd* [2001] EuLR 325 (Silber J) at [187] ("Courts have ... been willing to strike down as unreasonable decisions where manifestly excessive or manifestly inadequate weight has been accorded to a relevant consideration") (CA is [2001] EWCA Civ 1448 [2001] EuLR 822); <P50> (abdication/fetter); *R v Secretary of State for the Home Department, ex p Benson* 9th November 1988 unrep. ("if in the view of the court the weight to be attached to the two incidents is so small that they ought to be disregarded altogether, then it is our duty to say so"); *R v Liverpool Crown Court, ex p Luxury Leisure Ltd* [1999] LGR 345, 351g & 353e (public objections which are demonstrably misinformed would carry no weight and would require to be ignored); *R (Mount Cook Land Ltd) v Westminster City Council* [2003] EWCA Civ 1346 [2004] 1 PLR 29 at [33] (Auld LJ: although relevance (materiality) and weight "essentially matters of planning judgment", court not "shy in an appropriate case of concluding that it would have been irrational of a decision-maker to have had regard to an alternative proposal as a material consideration or that, even if possibly he should have done so, to have given it any or any sufficient weight").

56.3.6 **Relevancies and objectives.** *R v Daventry District Council, ex p Thornby Farms Ltd* [2002] EWCA Civ 31 [2003] QB 503 (considering statutorily-required "relevant objectives") at [53] ("An objective ... is something different from a material consideration... An objective which is obligatory must always be kept in mind when making a decision even while the decision maker has regard to other material considerations"); *R v East Sussex County Council, ex p Tandy* [1998] AC 714 (CA, rejecting argument that relevancy (resources) had been given such weight as to constitute a predominant ulterior purpose); [26] *R (Blewett) v Derbyshire County Council* [2004] EWCA Civ 1508 [2004] Env LR 293 at [91] (duty in having regard to EC law objectives considered in terms of appropriate "weight").

56.3.7 **Weight and fundamental rights.** *R v Secretary of State for the Home Department, ex p Daly* [2001] UKHL 26 [2001] 2 AC 532 at [27] (Lord Steyn, referring to the HRA: "the proportionality test may go further than the traditional grounds of review inasmuch as it may require attention to be directed to the relative weight accorded to interests and considerations"); *Chesterfield Properties Plc v Secretary of State for the Environment* [1998] JPL 568, 579-580 (Laws J: "where what may be called a fundamental or constitutional right is threatened by an administrative decision of the state ... the decision-maker must give a high place to the right in question. He cannot treat it merely as something to be taken into account, akin to any other relevant consideration; he must recognise it as a value to be kept, unless in his judgment there is a greater value that justifies its loss"; "where a constitutional right is involved, the law presumes it to carry substantial force. Only another interest, a public interest, of greater force may override it"); <32.3> (anxious scrutiny); *R v Lord Saville of Newdigate, ex p A* [2000] 1 WLR 1855 at [68(1)] ("The tribunal has failed to attach sufficient significance to the fact that" it would be satisfying requirements of public confidence); <37.1.8> (HRA proportionality); *R (Samaroo) v Secretary of State for the Home Department* [2001] EWCA Civ 1139 [2001] UKHRR 1150 at [39] (Dyson LJ: "The court will interfere with the weight accorded by the decision-maker if, despite an allowance for the appropriate margin of discretion, it concludes that the weight accorded was unfair and unreasonable. In this respect, the level of scrutiny is undoubtedly more intense than it is when a decision is subject to review on traditional *Wednesbury* grounds, where the court usually refuses to examine the weight accorded by the decision-maker to the various relevant factors").

---

[26] Tim Kerr [1997] JR 216.

P57 Unreasonableness. A body must not act unreasonably.

57.1 The unreasonableness principle
57.2 High threshold epithets
57.3 Species of unreasonableness
57.4 Unreasonableness in action

57.1 The unreasonableness principle. Unreasonableness ("irrationality") means a public authority has acted in a way which is not reasonably open to it. This principle involves judicial interference with those questions of substance having built-in latitude: such as judgment, discretion and policy. That generally means a strong and clear case is needed, though this is contextual test.

57.1.1 **The unreasonableness test.**[27] *Boddington v British Transport Police* [1999] 2 AC 143, 175H (Lord Steyn: whether decision "within the range of reasonable decisions open to a decision maker"); *R (Corner House Research) v Director of the Serious Fraud Office* [2008] UKHL 60 [2008] 3 WLR 568 at [38] (Lord Bingham, asking whether "a decision outside the lawful bounds of the discretion"); *In Re Duffy* [2008] UKHL 4 at [28] (Lord Bingham: "the decision ... was one which a reasonable Secretary of State could not have made if properly directing himself in law, if seised of the relevant facts and if taking account of considerations which, in this context, he was bound to take into account"); *R v Chief Constable of Sussex, ex p International Trader's Ferry Ltd* [1999] 2 AC 418, 452B-F (Lord Cooke: "in *Tameside* [[1977] AC 1014] ... the simple test used throughout was whether the decision in question was one which a reasonable authority could reach. The converse was described ... as 'conduct which no sensible authority acting with due appreciation of its responsibilities would have decided to adopt'. These unexaggerated criteria give the administrator ample and rightful rein, consistently with the constitutional separation of powers"); *R v Secretary of State for the Home Department, ex p Brind* [1991] 1 AC 696, 749A-B (Lord Bridge: "whether a reasonable Secretary of State, on the material before him, could reasonably make that ... judgment"); *Office of Fair Trading v IBA Health Ltd* [2004] EWCA Civ 142 [2004] 4 All ER 1103 at [100] (Carnwath LJ, favouring a "reasonableness" approach where context not one involving policy or political judgment); *Mohammed Jafar v Secretary of State for the Home Department* [1994] Imm AR 497, 500 (preferring "unreasonableness" to "perversity"); *R (A) v Lambeth London Borough Council* [2001] EWCA Civ 1624 (2001) 4 CCLR 486 (CA) at [43] (Laws LJ, referring to the unreasonableness principle as "the rule of reason") (HL is *R (G) v Barnet London Borough Council* [2003] UKHL 57 [2004] 2 AC 208); *R (Wells) v Parole Board* [2007] EWHC 1835 (Admin) [2008] 1 All ER 138 at [38] (*Wednesbury* unreasonableness "a somewhat old-fashioned legal construct"); *R (Pinnington) v Chief Constable of Thames Valley* [2008] EWHC 1870 (Admin) at [47] (the "straightforward *Wednesbury* test": "whether the opinion formed ... was reasonably open to him"); <7.7> (basic reasonableness).

57.1.2 **Unreasonableness: a strong requirement.** *Secretary of State for Education and Science v Tameside Metropolitan Borough Council* [1977] AC 1014, 1074H-1075C (Lord Russell: "it is quite unacceptable ... to proceed from 'wrong' to 'unreasonable'... History is replete with genuine accusations of unreasonableness when all that is involved is disagreement, perhaps passionate, between reasonable people"; "'unreasonably' is a very strong word indeed, the strength of which may easily fail to be recognised"); *In re W (An Infant)* [1971] AC 682, 700D-E (Lord Hailsham: "Two reasonable [persons] can perfectly reasonably come to opposite

---

[27] Jeffrey Jowell QC [1997] JR 75; Andrew Le Sueur [2005] JR 32; Richard Clayton QC & Karim Ghaly [2007] JR 210.

conclusions on the same set of facts without forfeiting their title to be regarded as reasonable... Not every reasonable exercise of judgment is right, and not every mistaken exercise of judgment is unreasonable"), cited in *Tameside* at 1070H; cf. <57.4.1> (high threshold but not unattainable); *Huang v Secretary of State for the Home Department* [2005] EWCA Civ 105 [2006] QB 1 at [28] (*Wednesbury* "largely remote from the merits of the decision under review", applying "relatively undemanding standards") (HL is [2007] UKHL 11 [2007] 2 AC 167); cf. *R (Dart Harbour and Navigation Authority) v Secretary of State for Transport, Local Government and the Regions* [2003] EWHC 1494 (Admin) at [29] (Lightman J, referring to statutory "reasonableness" test as a "straightforward reconsideration ... in the light of the full facts of the reasonableness of the Authority's decision").

57.1.3 **Unreasonableness as a sliding scale/spectrum.** *R v Department for Education and Employment, ex p Begbie* [2000] 1 WLR 1115, 1130B (Laws LJ, describing "reasonableness" as "a spectrum, not a single point": "the *Wednesbury* principle itself constitutes a sliding scale of review, more or less intrusive according to the nature and gravity of what is at stake"); *R (Asif Javed) v Secretary of State for the Home Department* [2001] EWCA Civ 789 [2002] QB 129 at [49] (Lord Phillips MR: "The extent to which the exercise of a statutory power is in practice open to judicial review on the ground of irrationality will depend critically on the nature and purpose of the enabling legislation"); *Sheffield City Council v Smart* [2002] EWCA Civ 4 [2002] HLR 639 at [42] ("the intensity of judicial review varies with the subject-matter").

57.1.4 **Reasonableness waiting to be joined by proportionality.** <58.1>.

57.1.5 **Reasonableness as an objective matter.** *R v Department for Education and Employment, ex p Begbie* [2000] 1 WLR 1115, 1130B (describing reasonableness as an "objective concept[]: otherwise there would be no public law, or if there were it would be palm tree justice"); *Secretary of State for Education and Science v Tameside Metropolitan Borough Council* [1977] AC 1014, 1054B-C (Viscount Dilhorne, question of reasonableness "had to be viewed objectively");*R v Boundary Commission for England, ex p Foot* [1983] QB 600, 626E-627A (an "objective standard"); *In re W (An Infant)* [1971] AC 682, 718B (Lord Hodson: "The test of unreasonableness is objective"), 699H-700A (Lord Hailsham: "unreasonableness can include anything which can objectively be adjudged to be unreasonable"); cf. *R v Secretary of State for the Home Department, ex p Brind* [1991] 1 AC 696, 757H-758B (wrong to intervene by asking whether the decision was the single "objectively reasonable decision"), 766B ("on the subject of reasonableness, there is bound to be a subjective element in the decision. There is no objective standard in either case which would allow the result to be foretold with certainty").

57.2 **High threshold epithets.**Many colourful phrases have been used to explain that only in a strong case will Courts intervene on grounds of unreasonableness. They warn against the forbidden substitutionary method. But there are dangers in setting the bar too high, affording widespread immunity from substantive review.

57.2.1 **"Perversity"/"perverse".** In the HL alone, see eg. *Reid v Secretary of State for Scotland* [1999] 2 AC 512, 541G, 542C; *United Kingdom Association of Professional Engineers v Advisory Conciliation & Arbitration Service* [1981] AC 424, 444D; *R v Hillingdon London Borough Council, ex p Puhlhofer* [1986] AC 484, 518C; *R v Secretary of State for Trade and Industry, ex p Lonrho Plc* [1989] 1 WLR 525, 534D; *R v Secretary of State for the Home Department, ex p Brind* [1991] 1 AC 696, 751D, 757H.

57.2.2 **"Outrageous defiance of logic or morality".** *Council of Civil Service Unions v Minister for the Civil Service* [1985] AC 374, 410G-H (Lord Diplock: "By `irrationality' I mean what can by now be succinctly referred to as `*Wednesbury* unreasonableness' ... It applies to a decision which is so outrageous in its defiance of logic or of accepted moral standards that no sensible person who had applied his mind to the question to be decided could have arrived at it"), applied in *AA (Uganda) v Secretary of State for the Home Department* [2008] EWCA Civ 579 at [41].

57.2.3 Decision-maker "taking leave of its senses". *R v Secretary of State for the Environment, ex p Nottinghamshire County Council* [1986] AC 240 (a modified review case <32.4.9>), 247H & 248C-D (Lord Scarman, referring to guidance with consequences "so absurd that he must have taken leave of his senses"; "a pattern of perversity or an absurdity of such proportions that the guidance could not have been framed by a bona fide exercise of political judgment on the part of the Secretary of State"); *O'Connor v Chief Adjudication Officer* [1999] 1 FLR 1200, 1210F-H ("It is wrong to deduce from [the] dicta a notion of `extreme' irrationality. Good old *Wednesbury* irrationality is about as an extreme form of irrationality as there is").

57.2.4 The need for "something overwhelming". *Associated Provincial Picture Houses Ltd v Wednesbury Corporation* [1948] 1 KB 223, 230 (Lord Greene MR: "if a decision on a competent matter is so unreasonable that no reasonable authority could ever have come to it, then the courts can interfere... but to prove a case of that kind would require something overwhelming"), cited eg. in *Avon County Council v Buscott* [1988] QB 656, 664H.

57.2.5 Other high threshold formulations. *Bromley London Borough Council v Greater London Council* [1983] 1 AC 768, 821B (Lord Diplock: "decisions that, looked at objectively, are so devoid of any plausible justification that no reasonable body of persons could have reached them"); *R v Hillingdon London Borough Council, ex p Puhlhofer* [1986] AC 484, 518C-D (Lord Brightman: "unreasonableness in the *Wednesbury* sense - unreasonableness verging on an absurdity"); *Associated Provincial Picture Houses Ltd v Wednesbury Corporation* [1948] 1 KB 223, 229 ("something so absurd that no sensible person could ever dream that it lay within the powers of the authority"); *R v Secretary of State for the Environment, Transport and the Regions, ex p Wheeler* [2000] 3 PLR 98, 109E (for decision to be intrinsically perverse must defy comprehension); *R v Bradford Metropolitan Borough Council, ex p Sikander Ali* [1994] ELR 299, 308E ("a criterion so nebulous as to be unlikely to produce any result other than one which was quixotic, or arbitrary or whimsical would be *Wednesbury* unreasonable"); *R v Ministry of Defence, ex p Smith* [1996] QB 517, 558C ("The threshold of irrationality is a high one"); *R v Inland Revenue Commissioners, ex p Unilever Plc* [1996] STC 681, 692d ("The threshold of public law irrationality is notoriously high"); *R v Lord Chancellor, ex p Maxwell* [1997] 1 WLR 104, 109B ("In making such a challenge, the [claimant] has a mountain to climb"), 109E ("Decisions so unreasonable as to warrant interference jump off the page at you"); <57.1.2> (unreasonableness: a strong requirement).

57.2.6 The unreasonableness threshold and the forbidden substitutionary approach.<15.1> (forbidden substitutionary approach); *R v Secretary of State for the Home Department, ex p Brind* [1991] 1 AC 696, 757F-G (Lord Ackner, explaining that the "standard of unreasonableness ... has to be expressed in terms that confine the jurisdiction exercised by the judiciary to a supervisory, as opposed to an appellate, jurisdiction"), 765D (Lord Lowry, referring to "colourful statements [which] emphasize the legal principle that judicial review of administrative action is a supervisory and not an appellate jurisdiction"); *R (Khatun) v London Borough of Newham* [2004] EWCA Civ 55 [2005] QB 37 at [40] ("the court has no role to impose what it perceives as ideal solutions under cover of the *Wednesbury* principle's application").

57.2.7 Extreme language is not helpful: the Cooke observation. *R v Chief Constable of Sussex, ex p International Trader's Ferry Ltd* [1999] 2 AC 418, 452B-F (Lord Cooke, explaining the weaknesses of the *Wednesbury* case and its formulation of the test, preferring to avoid "admonitory circumlocutions" or "needless complexity"; preferring "unexaggerated criteria [which] give the administrator ample and rightful rein, consistently with the constitutional separation of powers"); *R v Secretary of State for the Home Department, ex p Daly* [2001] UKHL 26 [2001] 2 AC 532 at [32] (Lord Cooke: "I think that the day will come when it will be more widely recognised that [*Wednesbury*] was an unfortunately retrogressive decision in English administrative law, insofar as it suggested that there are degrees of unreasonableness and that only a very extreme degree can bring an administrative decision within the legitimate scope of judicial invalidation. The depth of judicial review and the deference due to administrative discretion vary with the subject matter. It may well be, however, that the law can never be satisfied in any administrative field merely by a finding that the decision under review is not capricious or absurd"), cited with approval in *R (Farrakhan) v Secretary of State for the Home Department* [2002] EWCA Civ 606 [2002] QB 1391 at [66] (suggesting "that it [is] not merely in cases involving fundamental rights that the *Wednesbury* test should be replaced with a more flexible approach"); also Lord Cooke, `Damnosa Hereditas' in Andenas and Fairgrieve, *Judicial Review in International Perspective* (Kluwer, 2000) p.242 (lamenting English law of reasonableness as previously failing to have "lived up to its potential").

57.3 Species of unreasonableness. Reasonableness is a general test, but it includes sub-categories or indicators of action apt to be characterised as unreasonable.

57.3.1 Illogical. *R v Parliamentary Commissioner for Administration, ex p Balchin* [1998] 1 PLR 1, 13E-F (the claimant "does not have to demonstrate ... a decision so bizarre that its author must be regarded as temporarily unhinged. What the not very apposite term `irrationality' generally means in this branch of the law is a decision which does not add up - in which, in other words, there is an error of reasoning which robs the decision of logic"); *R (A) v Liverpool City Council* [2007] EWHC 1477 (Admin) at [39] ("the defendant's approach ... lacks logic to such a degree as to be unreasonable"); *R v Camden London Borough Council, ex p Aranda* (1998) 30 HLR 76, 84 (interfering because council's decision illogical); *R v Stockport Justices, ex p Conlon* [1997] 2 All ER 204 (rejection of supervision order was illogical in the circumstances); *R v Secretary of State for the Home Department, ex p Freeman* 2nd June 1998 unrep. ("illogical, and therefore lacking in rationality" for Home Secretary to rely on same factors as now justifying detention when they were present at the time of earlier decisions to release on licence); *R (Interbrew SA) v Competition Commission* [2001] EWHC Admin 367 (Moses J, commenting that the court can intervene "if the reasons make no sense and are without foundation"; ie. asking whether they "stack up"); *R (Norwich and Peterborough Building Society) v Financial Ombudsman Service Ltd* [2002] EWHC 2379 (Admin) at [59] (whether decision does not "add up", referring to *Balchin*).

57.3.2 Not sensible. *HMB Holdings Ltd v Antigua and Barbuda* [2007] UKPC 37 at [31] ("The test of irrationality will be satisfied" where decision "which no sensible person who had applied his mind to the question to be decided could have arrived at"); *Secretary of State for Education and Science v Tameside Metropolitan Borough Council* [1977] AC 1014, 1064E-F ("conduct which no sensible authority acting with due appreciation of its responsibilities would have decided to adopt").

57.3.3 Oppressive. *R (Khatun) v London Borough of Newham* [2004] EWCA Civ 55 [2005] QB 37 at [41] (Laws LJ: "Clearly a public body may choose to deploy powers it enjoys under statute in so draconian a fashion that the hardship suffered by affected individuals in consequence will justify the court in condemning the exercise as irrational or perverse... It may well be that the court's decision in such cases they would more aptly be articulated in terms of the proportionality principle... At all events it is plain that oppressive decisions may be held repugnant to compulsory public law standards"), [45] (not oppressive to require homeless applicants to accept housing without first viewing it); *R (Barry) v Liverpool City Council* [2001] EWCA Civ 384 [2001] LGR 361 at [16]-[18] (asking whether licence conditions "oppressive" and so unreasonable); <58.2.5> (oppression and proportionality).

57.3.4 Uncertainty as unreasonableness. *R v Blackpool Borough Council, ex p Red Cab Taxis Ltd* [1994] COD 513 (obscurely-worded condition *Wednesbury* unreasonable); *R v Newcastle-upon-Tyne City Council, ex p Dixon* (1995) 92 LGR 168, 174-178, 179; *R v Bradford Metropolitan Borough Council, ex p Sikander Ali* [1994] ELR 299, 308G (asking whether "this particular criterion is of so uncertain a nature as to be incapable of providing any meaningful answer which is other than arbitrary"); <55.1.19> (uncertainty); <12.1.12> (the rule of law and certainty); <46.1.4> (uncertainty as ultra vires).

57.3.5 Delay as unreasonableness/unreasonable delay. *R (M) v Criminal Injuries Compensation Authority* [2002] EWHC 2646 (Admin) at [39] (unreasonable delay in dealing with compensation claim); *R (AA (Afghanistan)) v Secretary of State for the Home Department* [2006] EWCA Civ 1550 at [21] (deplorable and unexplained delay, but removal nevertheless reasonable); *R v Children and Family Court Advisory and Support Service* [2003] EWHC 235 (Admin) [2003] 1 FLR 953 at [91(3)] (delay "controlled by the application of established public law principles (which include the *Wednesbury* test)"); *R v Gloucestershire County Council, ex p P* [1994] ELR 334, 337F (whether delay constituted a breach of statutory duty and/or was unreasonable), 338D, 340B-D (delay not "reprehensible"); *R v Merton London Borough Council, ex p Sembi* (2000) 32 HLR 439 (whether unreasonable delay so that no discharge of statutory duty); *R v Secretary of State for the Home Department, ex p Mersin* [2000] INLR 511 (unreasonable delay in granting refugee status and leave to remain, following successful asylum appeal); *R v Secretary of State for the Home Department, ex p Paulo* [2001] Imm AR 645 (regrettable managerial delays in asylum benefits but declaratory orders inapt); *R (J) v Newham London Borough Council* [2001] EWHC Admin 992 (2002) 5 CCLR 302 (irrational to postpone Children Act assessments because of intended housing transfer); *R v Cambridge County Council, ex p Leach* [1998] COD 101 (whether discharge of statutory duties culpably slow); *R (Uddin) v Asylum and Immigration Tribunal* [2006] EWHC 2127 (Admin) (lodging and listing time-frame not unreasonable); <58.1.8> (delay as lack of proportionality).

57.3.6 Conspicuous unfairness. <54.1.9>.

57.3.7 Inconsistency. <P55>.

57.3.8 Disproportionality. <P58>.

57.4 Unreasonableness in action.[28] The reasonableness principle is: (1) a safety-net ensuring that policy, judgment and discretion are not above the law; (2) a flexible standard capable of enhanced or relaxed scrutiny; (3) a broad principle to nurture and stabilize emergent species of public law wrong; and (4) a meaningful standard used successfully, where appropriate, in everyday cases.

57.4.1 A high threshold, but not unattainable. *R v Director of Public Prosecutions, ex p*

---

[28] Richard Leiper [1999] JR 244.

Manning [2001] QB 330, at [23] (Court slow to interfere but "the standard of review should not be set too high, since judicial review is the only means by which the citizen can seek redress against a decision not to prosecute and if the test were too exacting an effective remedy would be denied"); *R (International Transport Roth GmbH) v Secretary of State for the Home Department* [2002] EWCA Civ 158 [2003] QB 728 at [54] ("Constitutional dangers exist no less in too little judicial activism as in too much").

57.4.2 Unreasonableness in action: recent illustrations. *R (Paul-Coker) v Southwark London Borough Council* [2006] EWHC 497 (Admin) [2006] HLR 573 at [51] (unreasonable interim housing refusal); *R (LH) v Lambeth London Borough Council* [2006] EWHC 1190 (Admin) [2006] 2 FCR 348 at [66] (irrational to decide against residential care assessment); *R (Slator) v Bow Street Magistrates Court* [2006] EWHC 2628 (Admin) (unreasonable refusal to adjourn); *R (Rogers) v Swindon NHS Primary Care Trust* [2006] EWCA Civ 392 [2006] 1 WLR 2649 at [82] (unreasonable approach to cancer drug availability); *R (Hampshire County Council) v Independent Appeal Panel for Hampshire* [2006] EWHC 2460 (Admin) [2007] ELR 266 (perverse appeal panel decision); *AM (Serbia) v Secretary of State for the Home Department* [2007] EWCA Civ 16 at [29] (unreasonable AIT Procedure Rule); *R (A) v Liverpool City Council* [2007] EWHC 1477 (Admin) (unreasonable decision as to asylum-seeker's age); *R (Wells) v Parole Board* [2007] EWHC 1835 (Admin) [2008] 1 All ER 138 at [48] (unreasonable to detain for lack of progress while denying opportunity for such progress); *R (Otley) v Barking and Dagenham NHS Primary Care Trust* [2007] EWHC 1927 (Admin) (unreasonable to refuse cancer drug); *R (Bicknell) v HM Coroner for Birmingham* [2007] EWHC 2547 (Admin) at [26] (unreasonable refusal to hold an inquest); *R (Bashir) v Secretary of State for the Home Department* [2007] EWHC 3017 (Admin) at [22] (unreasonable to detain claimant pending removal); *R (Gwynn) v General Medical Council* [2007] EWHC 3145 (Admin) (unreasonable to proceed after long lapse of time); *R (Director of Public Prosecutions) v North & East Hertfordshire Justices* [2008] EWHC 103 (Admin) at [27] (unreasonable refusal to adjourn); *R (Davies) v Child Support Agency* [2008] EWHC 334 (Admin) at [14] (irrational not to disclose documents ordered by appeal tribunal); *R (Latham) v Northampton Magistrates Court* [2008] EWHC 245 (Admin) (unreasonable to issue summons); *R (Doughty) v Ely Magistrates Court* [2008] EWHC 522 (Admin) at [20] (no reasonable basis to exclude former policeman as expert witness); *R (Mayor of London) v Enfield London Borough Council* [2008] EWCA Civ 202 [2008] LGR 615 at [29] (irrational not to withdraw waste-management direction in light of Secretary of State's planning decision); *R (Dennis) v Independent Police Complaints Commission* [2008] EWHC 1158 (Admin) at [32] (unreasonable decision); *In Re Duffy* [2008] UKHL 4 at [28], [53] (unreasonable appointment of hardliners to Parades Commission); *R (Kaur) v Ealing London Borough Council* [2008] EWHC 2062 (Admin) at [46] (perverse conclusion of no correlation between domestic violence and ethnicity).

57.4.3 Unreasonableness is contextual. *Secretary of State for Education and Science v Tameside Metropolitan Borough Council* [1977] AC 1014, 1047G (Lord Wilberforce: "there is no universal rule as to the principles on which the exercise of a discretion may be reviewed: each statute or type of statute must be individually looked at"); *R v Teignmouth District Council, ex p Teignmouth Quay Co Ltd* [1995] 2 PLR 1, 10D ("The question whether to quash this decision is not answered simply by asking whether the council behaved `unreasonably' in the general sense", but "whether they behaved `unreasonably' in the way they purported to exercise the powers granted and limited by statute"); <57.1.3> (unreasonableness as a sliding scale).

57.4.4 Unreasonableness and fundamental rights: anxious scrutiny. <32.3>.

57.4.5 Unreasonable rules/regulations/orders. *R v Immigration Appeal Tribunal, ex p Manshoora Begum* [1986] Imm AR 385, 394 (immigration rule partial and unequal in its operation, manifestly unjust and unreasonable); *AM (Serbia) v Secretary of State for the Home Department* [2007] EWCA Civ 16 at [29] (unreasonable AIT Procedure Rule); *O'Connor v Chief Adjudication Officer* [1999] 1 FLR 1200, 1210F-H (Auld LJ: "Irrationality is a separate ground for challenging subsidiary legislation"); *McEldowney v Forde* [1971] AC 632, 643F (asking whether regulation "too vague and so arbitrary as to be wholly unreasonable"); cf. *Adams v Lord Advocate* [2002] UKHRR 1189 at [62]-[64] (irrationality not available as a ground of challenge to an enactment of the Scottish Parliament); <32.4.8> (whether modified review of Westminster-approved matters).

57.4.6 **Unreasonable policy.** *R (Rogers) v Swindon NHS Primary Care Trust* [2006] EWCA Civ 392 [2006] 1 WLR 2649 at [82] (cancer drug availability policy unreasonable); *R v London Borough of Lambeth, ex p Ashley* (1997) 29 HLR 385 (housing allocation points scheme illogical and irrational); *R v Tower Hamlets London Borough Council, ex p Uddin* (2000) 32 HLR 391, 403 (housing transfer points scheme irrational); *R v North Derbyshire Health Authority, ex p Fisher* (1998) 10 Admin LR 27, 43G (policy "unsustainable"), 46H (being a conclusion of "*Wednesbury* unreasonableness"); *R v Islington London Borough Council, ex p Reilly* (1999) 31 HLR 651 (policy unreasonable because incapable of producing a fair assessment of relative housing needs); <50.4.3> (policy must have properly evaluated starting-point).

57.4.7 **Reasonableness following choice.** *R v Secretary of State for the Home Department, ex p McCartney* [1994] COD 528 (having exercised the power to consult the Lord Chief Justice, unreasonable to reject his recommendation); *R v London Borough of Newham, ex p Gentle* (1994) 26 HLR 466, 471 (no duty to operate appeal mechanism, but having chosen to do so, duty not to operate an irrational/unfair policy); cf. <60.1.20> (fairness following choice).

57.4.8 **Whether to prefer ultra vires rather than unreasonableness.** *Bromley London Borough Council v Greater London Council* [1983] 1 AC 768, 820D-E, 830F-G, 835F (preferring to identify ultra vires rather than unreasonableness); *Gillick v West Norfolk and Wisbech Area Health Authority* [1986] AC 112, 192F-H ("there is no specific statutory background by reference to which the appropriate *Wednesbury* questions could be formulated"); *R v Inner London Education Authority, ex p Brunyate* [1989] 1 WLR 542, 549E-F (Lord Bridge: "I do not believe that this is a matter of reasonableness. The true view, in my opinion, is that [it] ... is an unlawful exercise of the power conferred"); *Chertsey Urban District Council v Mixnam's Properties Ltd* [1965] AC 735, 753E-G (describing unreasonableness of subordinate legislation a a particular application of "the general rule that subordinate legislation, to be valid, must be shown to be within the powers conferred by the statute").

57.4.9 **Relationship between unreasonableness and other (emergent) grounds.**
(A) ERROR OF FACT AS UNREASONABLENESS. <49.2.7>.
(B) PROPORTIONALITY AS UNREASONABLENESS. <58.2>.
(C) ABSENCE OF REASONS AS UNREASONABLENESS. <62.2.9>.
(D) INCONSISTENCY AS UNREASONABLENESS. <55.1.12>.

> **P58 Proportionality.** Certain contexts require a body's response to be appropriate and necessary to achieve a legitimate aim.

58.1 Proportionality and the common law
58.2 Proportionality as part of reasonableness
58.3 Common law proportionality: rights and penalties
58.4 Proportionality and scrutiny of evidence/reasoning
58.5 Latitude and intensity of review

58.1 Proportionality and the common law. Proportionality provides a disciplined framework for substantive review. It has been applied to test the justification for interferences with EC, HRA and common law rights, and the imposition of sanctions. Its wider application is an open question. As a principle to complement reasonableness it offers much: a focused analysis, variable standards of scrutiny, and an in-built recognition of latitude.

58.1.1 Proportionality template. <P37>.

58.1.2 Proportionality and EC/HRA. <37.1.7> (proportionality and EC law); <37.1.8> (proportionality and the HRA); <P59> (HRA-violation).

58.1.3 Common law proportionality?[29] *Somerville v Scottish Ministers* [2007] UKHL 44 [2007] 1 WLR 2734 at [55]-[56], [82], [147], [198] (HL leaving open whether proportionality an independent ground for judicial review); *R (British Civilian Internees - Far Eastern Region) v Secretary of State for Defence* [2003] EWCA Civ 473 [2003] QB 1397 at [32]-[37] (proportionality not yet available as a separate ground of review absent EC law or ECHR rights), [37] ("this is a step which can only be taken by the House of Lords"); *R (Medway Council) v Secretary of State for Transport* [2002] EWHC 2516 (Admin) at [47] (Maurice Kay J: "the greater intensity of review which is required by the proportionality test does not arise in domestic law where there is no engagement of a Convention right and no fundamental right is in play. The test remains *Wednesbury*"); *R (Isle of Anglesey County Council) v Secretary of State for Work and Pensions* [2003] EWHC 2518 (Admin) [2004] LGR 614 at [25] (proportionality of recoupment of overpaid housing benefit tested by reference to *Wednesbury* test); *Kataria v Essex Strategic Health Authority* [2004] EWHC 641 (Admin) [2004] 3 All ER 572 at [74]-[75] (treating proportionality as a doctrine applicable only where decision interferes with fundamental right), [76] (little difference between reasonableness and proportionality).

58.1.4 Common law proportionality: the Diplock prophesy. *Council of Civil Service Unions v Minister for the Civil Service* [1985] AC 374, 410E (Lord Diplock, contemplating "the possible adoption in the future of the principle of `proportionality'"); *R v Secretary of State for the Home Department, ex p Brind* [1991] 1 AC 696, 750D-F (Lord Roskill: "the present is not a case in which the first step can be taken... [b]ut so to hold in the present case is not to exclude the possible future development of the law in this respect, a possibility which has already been canvassed in some academic writings"), 749H (referring to "possible future development of the law"); *R v Secretary of State for Trade, ex p Vardy* [1993] ICR 720, 760E-F (not necessary here to "follow Lord Diplock's suggestion").

---

[29] Andrew Sharland [1997] JR 225; Michael Fordham [2002] JR 110; Kate Olley [2004] JR 197; Christopher Knight [2007] JR 117.

58.1.5 **Common law proportionality: the Slynn endorsement.** *R (Alconbury Developments Ltd) v Secretary of State for the Environment Transport and the Regions* [2001] UKHL 23 [2003] 2 AC 295 at [51] (Lord Slynn, referring to EC law proportionality and *Wednesbury*: "the difference in practice is not as great as is sometimes supposed. The cautious approach of the European Court of Justice in applying the principle is shown inter alia by the margin of appreciation it accords to the institutions of the Community in making economic assessments. I consider that even without reference to the Human Rights Act 1998 the time has come to recognise that this principle is part of English administrative law, not only when judges are dealing with Community acts but also when they are dealing with acts subject to domestic law. Trying to keep the *Wednesbury* principle and proportionality in separate compartments seems to me to be unnecessary and confusing"), [169] (Lord Clyde, noting "the recognition of the idea of proportionality"); *R (Tucker) v Secretary of State for Social Security* [2001] EWCA Civ 1646 [2002] HLR 500 at [25]-[26] (Court considering whether housing benefit regulation infringing "proportionality" at common law, under the head of "irrationality", by reference to Lord Slynn's observation in *Alconbury*).

58.1.6 **Common law proportionality: other observations.** *Reid v Secretary of State for Scotland* [1999] 2 AC 512, 541G (Lord Clyde, referring to whether decision "found to be perverse, or irrational, or grossly disproportionate to what was required"); *R v Secretary of State for the Home Department, ex p Hindley* [2001] 1 AC 410, 419H-420D (asking whether tariff disproportionate); *R v Manchester Metropolitan University, ex p Nolan* [1994] ELR 380, 395D (Sedley J, proceeding on the basis "that proportionality is potentially available today as a discrete head of challenge in appropriate cases"); *R v Coventry City Council, ex p Phoenix Aviation* [1995] 3 All ER 37, 63c (council's resolution to ban Phoenix "was wholly disproportionate to the security risk presented at that time"); *R v Secretary of State for the Home Department, ex p Simms* [2000] 2 AC 115, 142G (Lord Hobhouse, describing a policy as being "both unreasonable and disproportionate and cannot be justified as a permissible restraint upon the rights of the prisoner"); *R v Plymouth City Council, ex p Plymouth & South Devon Cooperative Society Ltd* [1993] 2 PLR 75, 88A-B (status of proportionality as an instrument of English judicial review uncertain); *R v Secretary of State for the Environment, ex p National & Local Government Officers' Association* (1993) 5 Admin LR 785, 799E, 800E-801C (proportionality not yet available in a challenge to a decision of the Secretary of State, albeit countenancing the possibility of it being available against other subordinate bodies); *R v Secretary of State for the Home Department, ex p Fayed* [2001] Imm AR 134 at [40] and [91] (not necessary to decide whether separate ground of review); *R (Lambeth London Borough Council) v Secretary of State for Work and Pensions* [2005] EWHC 637 (Admin) [2005] LGR 764 at [48] ("Perversity is the applicable criterion for unlawfulness, rather than disproportionality, since no Convention right is engaged").

58.1.7 **Proportionality under COE:COM R(80)2.** <45.1.4(B)>; *R v Secretary of State for Transport, ex p Pegasus Holdings (London) Ltd* [1988] 1 WLR 990, 1001E-F (Schiemann J: "It would, perhaps, be difficult for anyone appearing for the Government to take issue on the principle of proportionality being applied by administrative authorities, bearing in mind Recommendation No.R(80)2 of the Committee of Ministers Concerning the Exercise of Discretionary Powers by Administrative Authorities that was adopted by the Committee of Ministers of the Council of Europe on 11 March 1980 and that recommends governments of member states to be guided in their law and administrative practice by the principles annexed to that recommendation, one of which basic principles is that an administrative authority when exercising a discretionary power should maintain a proper balance between any adverse effects that its decision may have on the rights, liberties or interests of persons and the purpose that it pursues").

58.1.8 **Delay as lack of proportionality.** *R (UK Tradecorp Ltd) v Customs and Excise Commissioners* [2004] EWHC 2515 (Admin) (considering legality of delay in investigating VAT refund by reference to the concept of proportionality).

58.2 **Proportionality as part of reasonableness.**Whether or not an independent head of review, lack of proportionality is a strong indicator of unreasonableness.

58.2.1 **Proportionality as a facet of reasonableness.** *R v Secretary of State for the Home Department, ex p Brind* [1991] 1 AC 696, 759D (asking whether "the Secretary of State has used a sledgehammer to crack a nut" as "a picturesque way of describing the *Wednesbury* 'irrational' test"), 762D-E ("Clearly a decision by a minister which suffers from a total lack of proportionality will qualify for the *Wednesbury* unreasonable epithet. It is, ex hypothesi, a decision which no reasonable minister could make"); *R v General Medical Council ex p Colman* [1990] 1 All ER 489, 503j-504e (proportionality not "an independent head of review" but "an aspect of the submission based on *Wednesbury* unreasonableness"); *R v Secretary of State for the Environment, ex p Nottinghamshire County Council* [1986] AC 240, 246H (Lord Scarman, referring to the argument that guidance was "so disproportionately disadvantageous ... that it is a perversely unreasonable exercise of the power conferred by the statute"); *R v Secretary of State for Transport, ex p Pegasus Holdings (London) Ltd* [1988] 1 WLR 990, 1001C-H, 1002D-E; *R v St Albans Crown Court, ex p Cinnamond* [1981] QB 480, 484F-G (testing the proportionality of penalty by asking the *Wednesbury* question); *R v Brent London Borough Council, ex p Assegai* The Times 18th June 1987 (response clearly out of proportion to allegations against the claimant providing a clear indication of *Wednesbury* unreasonableness); *R v Secretary of State for Health, ex p United States Tobacco International Inc* [1992] QB 353, 366G (counsel accepting "for the purposes of this case ... that proportionality should be considered simply as a facet of irrationality"); *R v Secretary of State for Health, ex p Hickey* [1992] COD 482 (whether doctor's remuneration so excessive as to be outside range of lawful decisions); *R v Secretary of State for the Home Department, ex p Cox* (1993) 5 Admin LR 17, 27G ("accepted that in English law [proportionality] is a matter which can be considered as an indication of unreasonableness"); *R v O'Kane and Clarke, ex p Northern Bank Ltd* [1996] STC 1249, 1269j (statutory notices "grossly oppressive and unfair and thus 'irrational' within the meaning of that term in the field of judicial review"); *R v University of Central England, ex p Iqbal Sandhu* [1999] ELR 121, 132H-133E (award of no marks for late dissertation not disproportionate, because no irrationality or error of law).

58.2.2 **Proportionality more exacting than *Wednesbury*.**[30] *R v MAFF, ex parte First City Trading* [1997] 1 CMLR 250 at [68]-[69] (Laws J: "The difference between *Wednesbury* and European review is that in the former case the legal limits lie further back. I think there are two factors. First, the limits of domestic review are not, as the law presently stands, constrained by the doctrine of proportionality. Secondly, at least as regards a requirement such as that of objective justification in an equal treatment case, the European rule requires the decision-maker to provide a fully reasoned case"; "*Wednesbury* and European review are different models – one looser, one tighter – of the same juridical concept, which is the imposition of compulsory standards on decision-makers so as to secure the repudiation of arbitrary power"); *R v Secretary of State for Health, ex p Eastside Cheese Company* [1999] EuLR 968 (test on EC Art 36 being whether exercise of power "had been objectively justified and had been shown not to be disproportionate... The test is more demanding than that of 'manifest error' and is also more demanding than that of *Wednesbury* unreasonableness"); *Daly* <58.3.3>.

---

[30] Claire Weir [1999] JR 263.

58.2.3 **Proportionality and reasonableness often yielding the same result.** *R v Chief Constable of Sussex, ex p International Trader's Ferry Ltd* [1999] 2 AC 418, 439E-F (Lord Slynn: "the distinction between the two tests in practice is in any event much less than is sometimes suggested. The cautious way in which the European Court usually applies this test, recognising the importance of respecting the national authority's margin of appreciation, may mean that whichever test is adopted, and even allowing for a difference in onus, the result is the same"), 1288G-H (Lord Cooke: "on the particular facts of this case the European concepts of proportionality and margin of appreciation produce the same result as what are commonly called the *Wednesbury* principles. Indeed in many cases that is likely to be so"); *R (British Civilian Internees - Far Eastern Region) v Secretary of State for Defence* [2003] EWCA Civ 473 [2003] QB 1397 at [40] ("Just as in satisfying the requirements of proportionality, so too in meeting the *Wednesbury* test, the measures designed to further the objective must be rationally connected to it"); *R v Secretary of State for the Home Department, ex p Fayed* [2001] Imm AR 134 at [40] ("In simple language, what is said is that the decision was so out of proportion, or, in simpler language still, so much of an over-reaction, to the unimportance of the facts relied on that no sensible person could have made it. The case having been put that way, the substance of it, as [counsel] has accepted, can be seen to be conventional irrationality"), [91] ("there will be very few cases where a decision which would otherwise be regarded as rational is struck down because it is found to be disproportionate").

58.2.4 **Abuse of power and proportionality.** *R v Department for Education and Employment, ex p Begbie* [2000] 1 WLR 1115, 1129F-G (Laws LJ: "Abuse of power has become, or is fast becoming, the root concept which governs and conditions our general principles of public law. It may be said to be the rationale of the doctrines enshrined in [*Wednesbury*] [1948] 1 KB 223 and [*Padfield*] [1968] AC 997, of illegality as a ground of challenge, of the requirement of proportionality, and of the court's insistence on procedural fairness").

58.2.5 **Oppression and proportionality.** *R (Khatun) v London Borough of Newham* [2004] EWCA Civ 55 [2005] QB 37 at [41] (Laws LJ: "a public body may choose to deploy powers it enjoys under statute in so draconian a fashion that the hardship suffered by affected individuals in consequence will justify the court in condemning the exercise as irrational or perverse... It may well be that the court's decision in such cases today would more aptly be articulated in terms of the proportionality principle"); *R v Eastbourne Magistrates' Court, ex p Hall* [1993] COD 140 (poll-tax default committal decision harsh and oppressive and as such lacking in proportionality).

58.2.6 **Common law unsuitability.** <P37> (proportionality template); *R (Wandsworth London Borough Council) v Schools Adjudicator* [2003] EWHC 2969 (Admin) [2004] ELR 274 (Schools Adjudicator's decision imposing reduced intakes of high-ability children unreasonable), [73] (Goldring J: "the remedy chosen was not rationally capable of correcting the unfairness"); *R (British Civilian Internees - Far Eastern Region) v Secretary of State for Defence* [2003] EWCA Civ 473 [2003] QB 1397 at [40] ("Just as in satisfying the requirements of proportionality, so too in meeting the *Wednesbury* test, the measures designed to further the objective must be rationally connected to it"); *R v Islington London Borough Council, ex p Reilly* (1999) 31 HLR 651 (housing policy unreasonable because "incapable of producing a fair assessment of [claimants'] respective housing needs").

58.2.7 **Common law necessity/least intrusive alternative.** *R (Corner House Research) v Director of the Serious Fraud Office* [2008] UKHL 60 [2008] 3 WLR 568 at [38] (question is not whether no alternative course was open to the decision-maker, but whether decision was within the lawful bounds of discretion); *Dad v General Dental Council* [2000] 1 WLR 1538, 1543A (professional conduct committee required to balance the nature and gravity of the offences and their bearing on the appellant's fitness to practise against the need for the imposition of the penalty and its consequences; should have explored whether possibility of rehabilitation by postponing the effect of the order); *R v London (North) Industrial Tribunal, ex p Associated Newspapers Ltd* [1998] ICR 1212 (reporting restriction orders required to extend so far and no further than what was necessary); *R (W) v Governors of B School* [2001] LGR 561 (CA) at [29] (statutory scheme as to reinstatement of pupil to implement decision of panel having the effect that: "the governors are required to act proportionately to any threat of industrial action. That is, they should consider what is the *least* derogation from the pupil's full reintegration into the school that must be conceded so as to secure the protection of the other pupils' interests... What constitutes such minimal derogation is for their primary judgment; the court exercises a secondary judgment on judicial review") (HL is *R (L (A Minor)) v Governors of J School* [2003] UKHL 9 [2003] 2 AC 633); *R (Yumsak) v Enfield London Borough Council* [2002] EWHC 280 (Admin) [2003] HLR 1 at [32] (asylum housing dispersal decision unreasonable where "no evidence that there was no suitable and cost-effective alternative temporary accommodation in or closer to Enfield"); *R (Watford Grammar School for Girls) v Adjudicator for Schools* [2003] EWHC 2480 (Admin) [2004] ELR 40 at [82] (Collins J, finding that schools adjudicator should have "appreciated that there were other possible ways of achieving the result which he considered to be desirable"), [85] (thus, he "fail[ed] to have regard to material considerations").

58.3 **Common law proportionality: rights and penalties**Beyond EC and HRA rights, the two contexts where the Courts seem most at home with overt use of proportionality reasoning is where the case involves (1) a fundamental common law right or (2) some penalty or sanction.

58.3.1 **Common law proportionality: protecting basic (constitutional) rights.** <7.5.1> (constitutional rights); <7.3> and <46.2> (the common law principle of legality); <46.2.3> (principle of legality as common law proportionality); <32.3> (anxious scrutiny: common law principles of justification); *R v Secretary of State for the Home Department, ex p Simms* [2000] 2 AC 115, 131H-132A (Lord Hoffmann, explaining that since "much of the Convention reflects the common law", "the adoption of the text as part of domestic law [by the Human Rights Act 1998] is unlikely to involve radical change in our notions of fundamental human rights"); *R v Secretary of State for the Home Department, ex p Brind* [1991] 1 AC 696, 751E-F (Lord Templeman: "the courts cannot escape from asking themselves whether a reasonable Secretary of State, on the material before him, could reasonably conclude that the interference with freedom of expression which he determined to impose was justifiable. In terms of the [European] Convention [on Human Rights], as construed by the European Court, the interference with freedom of expression must be necessary and proportionate to the damage which the restriction is designed to prevent"); *R v Secretary of State for the Home Department, ex p Pegg* [1995] COD 84 (Steyn LJ, leaving open whether proportionality available as a self-standing ground in cases involving liberty); *R v Secretary of State for the Home Department, ex p McQuillan* [1995] 4 All ER 400, 423a (Sedley J, raising the question whether common law anxious scrutiny "in itself is a doctrine of proportionality" and commenting that "if it is, the House of Lords has long since contemplated its arrival with equanimity"); *R v Lord Saville of Newdigate, ex p A* [2000] 1 WLR 1855 at [37] ("it is unreasonable to reach a decision which contravenes or could contravene human rights unless there are sufficiently significant countervailing considerations. In other words it is not open to the decision-maker to risk interfering with fundamental rights in the absence of compelling justification"); *R v Secretary of State for the Home Department, ex p Turgut* [2001] 1 All ER 719 (Simon Brown LJ, commenting that judicial review needing to test whether measure "answers a pressing social need or is proportionate to the aims pursued"); *R v Governor of Frankland Prison, ex p Russell*

[2000] 1 WLR 2027 (policy restricting prisoners to one meal a day falling foul of test whereby "there must be established a self-evident and pressing need for [the] power and the interference must be the minimum necessary to fulfil that need", because arbitrary and unjustified); *R v Secretary of State for the Home Department, ex p Daly* [2001] UKHL 26 [2001] 2 AC 532 at [21] ("degree of intrusion ... greater than is justified by the objectives the policy is intended to serve, and so violates the common law rights of prisoners"), [23] (common law and HRA yielding same result here).

58.3.2 **Common law rights: no prescriptive instrument of codified rights.** *R v Secretary of State for the Home Department, ex p Simms* [2000] 2 AC 115, 131G-132B (Lord Hoffmann, referring to the change whereby "the principles of fundamental human rights which exist at common law will be supplemented by a specific text, namely the European Convention on Human Rights and Fundamental Freedoms"); *R (Mahmood) v Secretary of State for the Home Department* [2001] 1 WLR 840 at [39]-[40] (Lord Phillips MR, explaining why common law test of justification "requires modification where a decision is reviewed that was required, pursuant to the 1998 Act, to comply with the Convention. In such circumstances the Court can no longer uphold the decision on the general ground that there was `substantial justification' for interference with human rights. Interference with human rights can only be justified to the extent permitted by the Convention itself").

58.3.3 **Proportionality more sophisticated than anxious scrutiny.**<32.3> (anxious scrutiny); *R v Secretary of State for the Home Department, ex p Daly* [2001] UKHL 26 [2001] 2 AC 532 at [27] (Lord Steyn, referring to proportionality principles as "more precise and more sophisticated than the traditional grounds of review... The starting point is that there is an overlap between the traditional grounds of review and the approach of proportionality. Most cases would be decided in the same way whichever approach is adopted. But the intensity of review is somewhat greater under the proportionality approach. Making due allowance for important structural differences between various convention rights, which I do not propose to discuss, a few generalisations are perhaps permissible. I would mention three concrete differences without suggesting that my statement is exhaustive. First, the doctrine of proportionality may require the reviewing court to assess the balance which the decision maker has struck, not merely whether it is within the range of rational or reasonable decisions. Secondly, the proportionality test may go further than the traditional grounds of review inasmuch as it may require attention to be directed to the relative weight accorded to interests and considerations. Thirdly, even the heightened scrutiny test developed in *R v Ministry of Defence, ex p Smith* [1996] QB 517, 554 is not necessarily appropriate to the protection of human rights [in the light of *Smith and Grady v United Kingdom* (1999) 29 EHRR 493]"); *R (Wilkinson) v Responsible Medical Officer Broadmoor Hospital* [2001] EWCA Civ 1545 [2002] 1 WLR 419 at [27] (HRA proportionality not the same as the *Smith* test), also at [53] and [83].

58.3.4 **Proportionality and penalties/sanctions.** *Ghosh v General Medical Council* [2001] UKPC 29 [2001] 1 WLR 1915 at [34] (in disciplinary appeal, court can decide "whether the sanction ... was appropriate and necessary in the public interest or was excessive and disproportionate"); *Dad v General Dental Council* [2000] 1 WLR 1538 (consequences of penalty so severe compared to nature and gravity of the offences that penalty could reasonably be said to be wrong and unjustified); *Sanders v Kingston (No.2)* [2005] EWHC 2132 (Admin) [2006] LGR 111 (disqualification of local councillor disproportionate and manifestly excessive); *R v Snaresbrook Crown Court, ex p Patel* [2000] COD 255 (whether sentence so clearly outside the bounds of the lower court's sentencing discretion as to be indicative of legal error); *R v St Albans Crown Court, ex p Cinnamond* [1981] QB 480, 485D ("so great a disparity with the normal range as to constitute an error of law"); *R v Eastbourne Magistrates' Court, ex p Hall* [1993] COD 140 (poll-tax default committal harsh and oppressive and as such lacking in proportionality); *R v Highbury Corner Justices, ex p Uchendu* The Times 28th January 1994 (penalty not imposed with due regard to the principle of proportionality in sentencing); *R v London Metal Exchange Ltd, ex p Albatros Warehousing BV* 31st March 2000 unrep. at [54]-[57] (fine not grossly disproportionate); *R v Northallerton Magistrates Court, ex p Dove* [1999] COD 284 (prosecution costs order grossly disproportionate to level of fine imposed); *Lindsay v Commissioners of Customs and Excise* [2002] EWCA Civ 267 [2002] 1 WLR 1766 (forfeiture of cars involved in tobacco smuggling disproportionate by reference to Art 1P); *R v Secretary of State for the Home Department, ex p Benwell* [1985] QB 554, 569A (Hodgson J: "in an extreme case an administrative or quasi-judicial penalty can be successfully attacked on the ground that it was so disproportionate to the offence as to be perverse"); *R v Ramsgate Magistrates' Court and Thanet District Council, ex p Haddow* (1993) 5 Admin LR 359, 363B (asking whether decision "astonishing, truly astonishing or so widely disproportionate that no reasonable bench of justices could arrive at it. In other words, the real question here is that of *Wednesbury* reasonableness"); *R v Secretary of State for the Home Department, ex p Chapman* The Times 25th October 1994 (discretionary lifer's tariff far exceeding any equivalent fixed-term sentence so that no reasonable Home Secretary could have allowed it to stand); *R v Truro Crown Court, ex p Adair* [1997] COD 296 (suggesting "more helpful to ask the question whether the sentence or order in question falls clearly outside the broad area of the lower court's sentencing discretion"); *R (A) v Head Teacher of P School* [2001] EWHC Admin 721 [2002] ELR 244 at [41] (in excluding pupil, "the headteacher acted in a manifestly unreasonable and disproportionate manner").

58.4 Proportionality and scrutiny of evidence/reasoning.[31] The template of proportionality poses questions which a public authority should address for itself. Such a discipline would assist in demonstrating justification, and earning the latitude for which the public body will look to the Court. However, what may ultimately matter is the outcome and not the reasoning process.

58.4.1 Focus on outcome not reasoning process. *R (SB) v Headteacher and Governors of Denbigh High School* [2006] UKHL 15 [2007] 1 AC 100 at [29] (HRA focus not "on whether a challenged decision or action is the product of a defective decision-making process, but on whether, in the case under consideration, the applicant's Convention rights have been violated"), [31] ("what matters in any case is the practical outcome, not the quality of the decision-making process that led to it"), [68]; *Belfast City Council v Miss Behavin' Ltd* [2007] UKHL 19 [2007] 1 WLR 1420 (where decision not violating rights, no duty to address them), [13]-[14], [23] (Lord Rodger: "if the refusal did not interfere disproportionately with the ... right to freedom of expression, then it was lawful ... whether or not the council had deliberated on that right before refusing"); <56.1.5> (fundamental rights as relevancy).

58.4.2 Proportionality inquiry for the public authority. <51.1> (duty of inquiry).

58.4.3 Relevance of deficient proportionality reasoning. *R (Suryananda) v Welsh Ministers* [2007] EWCA Civ 893 at [67] ("the task of a challenge is made more difficult if the decision maker has conscientiously paid proper attention to the human rights considerations"); *R (Elias) v Secretary of State for Defence* [2006] EWCA Civ 1293 [2006] 1 WLR 3213 at [130] ("legal and practical difficulties" in advancing justification that "was not even considered when the ... criteria were adopted"); *R (D) v Secretary of State for the Home Department* [2003] EWHC 155

---

[31] Richard Gordon QC [2006] JR 136; Mohammad Mazher Idriss [2006] JR 239; Christopher Knight [2007] JR 221.

(Admin) [2003] 1 FLR 979 at [23] ("the decision ... was made without proper consideration by the decision-maker of highly relevant proportionality issues and, in these circumstances, the decision never reached the point of refinement at which the judicial obligation of deference crystallised"); *R (Madden) v Bury Metropolitan Borough Council* [2002] EWHC 1882 (Admin) (2002) 5 CCLR 622 at [68]-[70] (failure to consider Art 8 and justification); *R (Jarrett) v Legal Services Commission* [2001] EWHC Admin 389 (failure to approach decision on correct (Art 6) basis); *Lindsay v Commissioners of Customs and Excise* [2002] EWCA Civ 267 [2002] 1 WLR 1766 at [2.53] (policy unlawful because prevented consideration of proportionality, a material consideration); *R (Gunter) v South Western Staffordshire Primary Care Trust* [2005] EWHC 1894 (Admin) (2006) 9 CCLR 121 at [21] (residential home closure remitted where Art 8 not properly appreciated and considered); *R v Human Fertilisation and Embryology Authority, ex p Blood* [1999] Fam 151, 184G (decision remitted where failed to appreciate EC right impeded and justification needed); *Machado v Secretary of State for the Home Department* [2005] EWCA Civ 597 [2006] INLR 69 (appeal remitted to IAT where failure properly to approach proportionality); *R (Clays Lane Housing Cooperative Ltd) v Housing Corporation* [2004] EWCA Civ 1658 [2005] 1 WLR 2229 at [28] (defendant not consciously and specifically applying correct proportionality test, but "entirely satisfied" would have come to same conclusion had it done so); *R (Samaroo) v Secretary of State for the Home Department* [2001] EWCA Civ 1139 [2001] UKHRR 1150 at [19] (inquiry as to "whether the legitimate aim can be achieved by means that do not interfere, or interfere so much, with a person's rights under the Convention" being an "inquiry [which] must be undertaken by the decision-maker in the first place").

58.4.4 **Unassisted court strikes its own balance.** *Belfast City Council v Miss Behavin' Ltd* [2007] UKHL 19 [2007] 1 WLR 1420 at [31] (Baroness Hale: where human rights not addressed by decision-maker, court decides for itself whether rights infringed), [37] (court striking balance for itself if decision-maker has not balanced rights and interests), [47] (Lord Mance), [92] (Lord Neuberger), [27] (Lord Rodger).

58.4.5 **Whether proportionality built-into statutory scheme.** *Huang v Secretary of State for the Home Department* [2007] UKHL 11 [2007] 2 AC 167 (proportionality balance to be struck by immigration judge; not already struck by the immigration rules); *Belfast City Council v Miss Behavin' Ltd* [2007] UKHL 19 [2007] 1 WLR 1420 at [37], [41], [87] (legislation not taken as striking the balance); *Kay v Lambeth London Borough Council* [2006] UKHL 10 [2006] 2 AC 465 at [35] (statutory scheme "likely to satisfy the article 8(2) requirement of proportionality", being "a democratic solution to the problems inherent in housing allocation"), [180] (proper application of the statute supplying Art 8(2) justification), considered in *Doherty v Birmingham City Council* [2008] UKHL 57 [2008] 3 WLR 636; *R (London and Continental Stations and Property Ltd) v Rail Regulator* [2003] EWHC 2607 (Admin) at [44] ("the statutory procedure ... itself requires a balancing exercise between the public interest and [the claimant]'s rights"; compliance with statutory "obligation on the Regulator to exercise his functions in the manner best calculated to impose the minimum of restrictions consistent with the performance of his functions ... ensures that he strikes a fair balance"); *Lough v First Secretary of State* [2004] EWCA Civ 905 [2004] 1 WLR 2557 at [45]-[46] (planning process striking an appropriate balance), [49] ("The concept of proportionality is inherent in the approach to decision making in planning law"), [50] (decision not unlawful by failure to refer to proportionality); *R (X) v Chief Constable of West Midlands Police* [2004] EWCA Civ 1068 [2005] 1 WLR 65 at [41] ("the statute meets the requirements of article 8(2)").

58.4.6 **Evidence to justify legislation.** <17.1.5> (evidence and HRA justification/ proportionality).

58.5 Latitude and intensity of review.[32] Hand in hand with proportionality principles is a concept of latitude which recognises that the Court does not become the primary decision-maker on matters of policy, judgment and discretion. Its width (and the intensity of review) vary depending on the context and circumstances. Since the Strasbourg (ECHR) concept (the "margin of appreciation") includes an inapt international deference, HRA review has its own (the "discretionary area of judgment"). Latitude should not be overstated: Courts retain the responsibility of deciding whether a response is proportionate.

58.5.1 Latitude and EC law proportionality. *R v Secretary of State for the Home Department, ex p Arthur H Cox Ltd* [1999] EuLR 677, 697F-H (although not to be equated with *Wednesbury*, nevertheless wide margin of appreciation in the present context); *R v Secretary of State for the Home Department, ex p International Lottery in Liechtenstein Foundation* [1999] EuLR 905, 923E (UK free to determine whether necessary to restrict lotteries), 926D (national authorities having wide regulatory margin of evaluation in any case); *Upjohn Ltd v Licensing Authority established by the Medicines Act 1968* [1999] 1 WLR 927 at [34] ("where a Community authority is called on, in the performance of its duties, to make complex assessments, it enjoys a wide measure of discretion"); *R v Secretary of State for the Home Department, ex p Hoverspeed* [1999] EuLR 595, 614D ("scope for a significant margin of appreciation"); *R v Ministry of Agriculture Fisheries and Food, ex p Astonquest* [2000] EuLR 371, 384C-D ("The margin of appreciation depends on the character of the decision which the national decision-maker has to make"; "the size of the target area varies according to the circumstances"); *R v Secretary of State for the Home Department, ex p International Lottery in Liechtenstein Foundation* [1999] EuLR 905, 926D-G (in circumstances where very wide margin of appreciation, appropriate test whether value judgments appear "manifestly unreasonable"); *R v Secretary of State for Employment, ex p Seymour-Smith* [1999] 2 AC 554 (ECJ) at [75] (social policy involving "broad margin of discretion"), applied in *R v Secretary of State for Employment, ex p Seymour-Smith (No.2)* [2000] 1 WLR 435, 450E-F ("governments are to be afforded a broad measure of discretion"), 452C ("broad measure of discretion").

58.5.2 Beware the Strasbourg "margin of appreciation" (MOA).
(A) MOA INCLUDES INTERNATIONAL DEFERENCE. *R v Director of Public Prosecutions, ex p Kebilene* [2000] 2 AC 326, 380E-381A (Lord Hope, explaining the Strasbourg MOA as based on the insight "that, by reason of their direct and continuous contact with the vital forces of their countries, the national authorities are in principle better placed to evaluate local needs and conditions than an international court ... This doctrine is an integral part of the supervisory jurisdiction which is exercised over state conduct by the international court"); *Huang v Secretary of State for the Home Department* [2005] EWCA Civ 105 [2006] QB 1 (CA) at [46] (MOA "a doctrine by which, as an international tribunal, it accords a margin of appreciation upon human rights questions to the state authorities out of respect for their closer knowledge of national conditions"); *Sheffield City Council v Smart* [2002] EWCA Civ 4 [2002] HLR 639 at [42] (MOA "to reflect the necessary distance from which an international tribunal must view the affairs of a nation State subject to its jurisdiction"), *R (Mahmood) v Secretary of State for*

---

[32] This paragraph from a previous edition was cited in *R (ProLife Alliance) v British Broadcasting Corporation* [2003] UKHL 23 [2004] 1 AC 185 at [138] (Lord Walker); also in *Tweed v Parades Commission for Northern Ireland* [2006] UKHL 5 [2007] 1 AC 650 at [36] (Lord Carswell); *Re The Christian Institute* [2007] NIQB 66 at [82]; *Langley v Liverpool City Council* [2005] EWCA Civ 1173 [2006] 2 All ER 202 at [58].

the Home Department [2001] 1 WLR 840 at [31] ("a self-denying ordinance adopted by an international court").

(B) WRONG TO READ-ACROSS MOA INTO HRA REVIEW. *In re G (Adoption: Unmarried Couple)* [2008] UKHL 38 [2008] 3 WLR 76 (HL finding HRA violation albeit ECtHR would uphold as within MOA) at [32] (MOA as international deference), [118]; *R (ProLife Alliance) v British Broadcasting Corporation* [2003] UKHL 23 [2004] 1 AC 185 at [132] (MOA confusing and inapposite); *Brown v Stott (Procurator Fiscal, Dunfermline)* [2003] 1 AC 681, 703C (Lord Bingham: "While a national court does not accord the margin of appreciation recognised by the European Court as a supra-national court, it will give weight to the decisions of a representative legislature and a democratic government within the discretionary area of judgment accorded to those bodies"), 710H-711A (Lord Steyn, describing MOA as a "principle ... logically not applicable to domestic courts"); *Knight v Nicholls* [2004] EWCA Civ 68 [2004] 1 WLR 1653 at [38] (MOA not belonging part of domestic jurisprudence); *Evans v Amicus Healthcare Ltd* [2004] EWCA Civ 727 [2005] Fam 1 at [63] (MOA "has no direct relevance to the process by which a court adjudicates, within a state, on the compatibility of a measure"); *R (International Transport Roth GmbH) v Secretary of State for the Home Department* [2002] EWCA Civ 158 [2003] QB 728 at [81] ("We do not apply the Strasbourg margin of appreciation, because we are a domestic, not an international tribunal").

(C) MOA HELPFULLY INDICATES LATITUDE. *Montgomery v Her Majesty's Advocate and the Advocate General for Scotland* [2003] 1 AC 641, 650E (Lord Hoffmann: "The doctrine of a `margin of appreciation' exists to enable the concepts in the Convention to be given somewhat different content in the various contracting states, according to their respective histories and cultures"); *R (Countryside Alliance) v Attorney General* [2007] UKHL 52 [2008] 1 AC 719 at [126] (wrong to second-guess Parliament where the Court "can reasonably predict that Strasbourg would regard the matter as within the margin of appreciation left to the member states"); *R (Trailer and Marina (Leven) Ltd) v Secretary of State for the Environment, Food and Rural Affairs* [2004] EWHC 153 (Admin) [2004] Env LR 828 at [63] (Ouseley J: "the width of the margin of appreciation accorded in such cases by the ECtHR is an indication of the appropriate width of the area of discretionary judgement") (CA is [2004] EWCA Civ 1580 [2005] 1 WLR 1267); *R v Stratford Justices, ex p Imbert* [1999] 2 Cr App R 276 (wrong to "apply or have recourse to the doctrine of the margin of appreciation as implemented by the Strasbourg Court", but right to "recognise the impact of that doctrine upon the Strasbourg Court's analysis of the meaning and implications of the broad terms of the Convention provisions").

(D) MOA UNDERLINES NATIONAL COURT VIGILANCE. *A v Secretary of State for the Home Department* [2004] UKHL 56 [2005] 2 AC 68 at [131] (Lord Hope: "When the European Court talks about affording a margin of appreciation to the assessment of the British Government it assumes that its assessment will at the national level receive closer scrutiny"), [176] (Lord Rodger: "the considerable deference which the European Court of Human Rights shows to the views of the national authorities in such matters really presupposes that the national courts will police those limits").

58.5.3 **HRA latitude.**[33] *A v Secretary of State for the Home Department* [2004] UKHL 56 [2005] 2 AC 68 at [80] (Lord Nicholls, referring to "latitude"); *R (Williamson) v Secretary of State for Education and Employment* [2005] UKHL 15 [2005] 2 AC 246 at [51] (Lord Nicholls: "The legislature is to be accorded a considerable degree of latitude"); *R (Mahmood) v Secretary of State for the Home Department* [2001] 1 WLR 840 at [33] (Laws LJ: "there must be a

---

[33] Mark Elliott [2001] JR 166 & [2002] JR 97; Sadat Sayeed [2005] JR 111; Lord Justice Dyson [2006] JR 103; Richard Clayton QC [2006] JR 109; Michael Beloff QC [2006] JR 213.

principled distance between the court's adjudication in a case such as this and the Secretary of State's decision, based on his perception of the case's merits"); *Wilson v First County Trust Ltd* [2003] UKHL 40 [2004] 1 AC 816 at [110] (HRA leaving "effect ... on the relationship between the courts and Parliament ... to be worked out in accordance with familiar constitutional principles"); *Ghosh v General Medical Council* [2001] UKPC 29 [2001] 1 WLR 1915 at [34] (in disciplinary appeal, court would accord "an appropriate measure of respect to the judgment of the [GMC]"); *R (International Transport Roth GmbH) v Secretary of State for the Home Department* [2002] EWCA Civ 158 [2003] QB 728 at [26] ("a high degree of deference due by the court to Parliament"), [76] (Laws LJ: "a proper degree of deference"), [137] (Jonathan Parker LJ).

58.5.4 Respect for Parliament's views. *R (Countryside Alliance) v Attorney General* [2007] UKHL 52 [2008] 1 AC 719 at [45] (pre-eminently a case where respect to be shown to what Commons decided), [132]; *R (Animal Defenders International) v Secretary of State for Culture Media and Sport* [2008] UKHL 15 [2008] 2 WLR 781 (giving great weight to Parliament's views); *Wilson v First County Trust Ltd* [2003] UKHL 40 [2004] 1 AC 816 at [70] ("Assessment of the advantages and disadvantages of the various legislative alternatives is primarily a matter for Parliament... The readiness of a court to depart from the views of the legislature depends upon the circumstances, one of which is the subject matter of the legislation"); *Brown v Stott (Procurator Fiscal, Dunfermline)* [2003] 1 AC 681, 711A ("national courts may accord to the decisions of national legislatures some deference *where the context justifies it*"); *R v Lichniak* [2002] UKHL 47 [2003] 1 AC 903 at [14] ("a degree of deference is due to the judgment of a democratic assembly on how a particular social problem is best tackled"); *Marcic v Thames Water Utilities Ltd* [2003] UKHL 66 [2004] 2 AC 42 at [71] (a broad discretion); *Ghaidan v Godin-Mendoza* [2004] UKHL 30 [2004] 2 AC 557 at [19] ("National housing policy is a field where the court will be less ready to intervene"); *R v A (No.2)* [2001] UKHL 25 [2002] 1 AC 45 at [36] ("when the question arises whether in the criminal statute in question Parliament adopted a legislative scheme which makes an excessive inroad into the right to a fair trial the court is qualified to make its own judgment and must do so"); *R v Johnstone* [2003] UKHL 28 [2003] 1 WLR 1736 at [51] ("Parliament, not the court, is charged with the primary responsibility for deciding, as a matter of policy, what should be the constituent elements of a criminal offence"); *R (Carson) v Secretary of State for Work and Pensions* [2005] UKHL 37 [2006] 1 AC 173 at [25] ("very much a case in which Parliament is entitled to decide whether the differences justify a difference in treatment"), [45], [80]; *R (Williamson) v Secretary of State for Education and Employment* [2005] UKHL 15 [2005] 2 AC 246 at [51] ("broad social policy ... pre-eminently well suited for decision by Parliament"); *Campbell v MGN Ltd (No.2)* [2005] UKHL 61 [2005] 1 WLR 3394 at [26] (Parliament entitled to have "a general rule in order to enable the scheme to work in a practical and effective way").

58.5.5 The "discretionary area of judgment". *R v Director of Public Prosecutions, ex p Kebilene* [2000] 2 AC 326, 381B-D (Lord Hope: "In some circumstances it will be appropriate for the courts to recognise that there is an area of judgment within which the judiciary will defer, on democratic grounds, to the considered opinion of the elected body or person whose act or decision is said to be incompatible with the Convention. This point is well made [by Lester and Pannick] where the area in which these choices may arise is conveniently and appropriately described as the `discretionary area of judgment'"); *R (Samaroo) v Secretary of State for the Home Department* [2001] EWCA Civ 1139 [2001] UKHRR 1150 at [35] (applying the discretionary area of judgment); *Brown v Stott (Procurator Fiscal, Dunfermline)* [2003] 1 AC 681, 703D (Lord Bingham: "While a national court does not accord the margin of appreciation recognised by the European Court as a supra-national court, it will give weight to the decisions of a representative legislature and a democratic government within the discretionary area of judgment accorded to those bodies"); *R (Asif Javed) v Secretary of State for the Home*

Department [2001] EWCA Civ 789 [2002] QB 129 at [54] (wide discretionary area of judgment when deciding whether to designate a country for asylum certification purposes); *Adams v Lord Advocate* [2002] UKHRR 1189 at [92] ("discretionary area of judgment" treated as "the most correct and helpful expression in considering the extent to which this court will defer to the Scottish Parliament, whose act is said to be incompatible with the Convention"); *R (ProLife Alliance) v British Broadcasting Corporation* [2003] UKHL 23 [2004] 1 AC 185 at [132] (Lord Walker, using the concept of the "discretionary area of judgment"); *Evans v Amicus Healthcare Ltd* [2004] EWCA Civ 727 [2005] Fam 1 at [63] (explaining why "discretionary area of judgment" a better phrase than "margin of discretion").

58.5.6 A test of "objective justification". *Tweed v Parades Commission for Northern Ireland* [2006] UKHL 53 [2007] 1 AC 650 at [55] (Lord Brown, identifying as "the critical question in any proportionality case": "whether the interference with the right in question is objectively justified"); *R (S) v Chief Constable of South Yorkshire* [2004] UKHL 39 [2004] 1 WLR 2196 at [40] (need for "objective justification" under HRA:ECHR Art 8); *R (L) v Manchester City Council* [2001] EWHC Admin 707 (2002) 5 CCLR 268 at [93] ("an interference by a public body with a fundamental right requires a substantial objective justification"); *R (Isiko) v Secretary of State for the Home Department* [2001] UKHRR 385 at [31] ("a substantial objective justification for the interference"); *R (J and P) v West Sussex County Council* [2002] EWHC 1143 (Admin) [2002] 2 FLR 1192 at [15] ("substantial justification", meaning "real and cogent evidence of a pressing need").

58.5.7 A test of "a fair balance". *R (Razgar) v Secretary of State for the Home Department* [2004] UKHL 27 [2004] 2 AC 368 at [20] (Lord Bingham, explaining that proportionality "must always involve the striking of a fair balance between the rights of the individual and the interests of the community which is inherent in the whole of the Convention"); *Brown v Stott (Procurator Fiscal, Dunfermline)* [2003] 1 AC 681, 704F, 720E; *R (ProLife Alliance) v British Broadcasting Corporation* [2003] UKHL 23 [2004] 1 AC 185 at [137]; *McIntosh v Lord Advocate* [2001] UKPC D1 [2003] 1 AC 1078 at [30], [45]; *In Re Officer L* [2007] UKHL 36 [2007] 1 WLR 2135 at [21] (fair balance in Art 2 context); *R v A (No.2)* [2001] UKHL 25 [2002] 1 AC 45 at [91] (Lord Hope: "The principle of proportionality directs attention to the question whether a fair balance has been struck between the general interest of the community and the protection of the individual"); *R v Director of Public Prosecutions, ex p Kebilene* [2000] 2 AC 326, 384D-G; *Marcic v Thames Water Utilities Ltd* [2003] UKHL 66 [2004] 2 AC 42 (applying "fair balance" test in analysing statutory scheme as ECHR-compatible); *R (Ponting) v Governor of HMP Whitemoor* [2002] EWCA Civ 224 ("fair balance" test applied); *R (Baiai) v Secretary of State for the Home Department* [2008] UKHL 53 [2008] 3 WLR 549 at [24] (fair balance test inapt in considering proportionality of immigration marriage-approval provision).

58.5.8 A test of a "margin of discretion". *R (Al Rawi) v Secretary of State for Foreign and Commonwealth Affairs* [2006] EWCA Civ 1279 [2008] QB 289 at [148] ("broad margin of discretion" as to foreign relations); *R (Forbes) v Secretary of State for the Home Department* [2006] EWCA Civ 962 [2006] 1 WLR 3075 at [18] (wide "margin of discretion"); *Marcic v Thames Water Utilities Ltd* [2003] UKHL 66 [2004] 2 AC 42 at [71] ("broad margin of discretion"); *A v Secretary of State for the Home Department* [2004] UKHL 56 [2005] 2 AC 68 at [107]; *R (Blewett) v Derbyshire County Council* [2004] EWCA Civ 1508 [2004] Env LR 293 at [85] ("margin of discretion" used in EC law context).

58.5.9 Variable latitude/intensity: proportionality as a flexi-principle. <31.6.5> (HRA/ECHR as a flexi-principle); *A v Secretary of State for the Home Department* [2004] UKHL 56 [2005] 2 AC 68 at [39] (Lord Bingham: "while any decision made by a representative democratic body must of course command respect, the degree of respect will be conditioned by the nature of the decision"), [29] ("The more purely political (in a broad or narrow sense) a question is, the more appropriate it will be for political resolution and the less likely it is to be an appropriate matter for judicial decision ... Conversely, the greater the legal content of any issue, the greater the potential role of the court"), [80] (Lord Nicholls: "The latitude will vary according to the subject matter under consideration, the importance of the human right in question, and the extent of the encroachment upon that right"); *R (Mahmood) v Secretary of State for the Home Department* [2001] 1 WLR 840 at [18] ("the intensity of review in a public law case will depend on the subject matter in hand"), endorsed in *R v Secretary of State for the Home Department, ex p Daly* [2001] UKHL 26 [2001] 2 AC 532 at [28]; *R (Carson) v Secretary of State for Work and Pensions* [2005] UKHL 37 [2006] 1 AC 173 at [17] (Lord Hoffmann, distinguishing between cases where "the right to respect for the individuality of a human being is at stake" and where "merely a question of general social policy"); *R (British American Tobacco) v Secretary of State for Health* [2004] EWHC 2493 (Admin) at [27] (protection of public health as an area "in which the court must be particularly wary of imposing its own value judgments upon a legislative scheme"); *R (Countryside Alliance) v Attorney General* [2007] UKHL 52 [2008] 1 AC 719 (wide latitude in EC/HRA challenge to Hunting Act); *R (Mabanaft Ltd) v Secretary of State for Trade and Industry* [2008] EWHC 1052 (Admin) at [72] (wide margin in implementing EC compulsory oil stocks duties); *R (Wilson) v Wychavon District Council* [2007] EWCA Civ 52 [2007] QB 801 at [44]-[51] (discussing width of discretionary area of judgment).

58.5.10 **Proportionality raises a question for the Court.** *R (Baiai) v Secretary of State for the Home Department* [2008] UKHL 53 [2008] 3 WLR 549 at [25] (Lord Bingham: "the court cannot abdicate its function of deciding whether as a matter of law the [statutory] scheme, as promulgated and operated, violate[s] the ... [Convention] right"); *A v Secretary of State for the Home Department* [2004] UKHL 56 [2005] 2 AC 68 at [40] (Lord Bingham: "domestic courts must themselves form a judgment whether a Convention right has been breached"); *B v Secretary of State for the Home Department* [2000] UKIIRR 498, 502D ("the question whether deportation constitutes a proportionate response to the appellant's offending" as "a question of law" which "has to be answered afresh"); *Huang v Secretary of State for the Home Department* [2007] UKHL 11 [2007] 2 AC 167 (immigration judge needing to strike proportionality balance as a primary judgment); *R v Secretary of State for the Home Department, ex p Daly* [2001] UKHL 26 [2001] 2 AC 532 at [23] (Lord Bingham: "domestic courts must themselves form a judgment whether a convention right has been breached (conducting such inquiry as is necessary to form that judgment)"); *R (Gillan) v Commissioner of Police of the Metropolis* [2004] EWCA Civ 1067 [2005] QB 388 at [35] ("What action is or is not proportionate is ... very much an issue for the judgment of the court"; "the ultimate determination of what is or is not proportionate ... rests with the court") (HL is [2006] UKHL 12 [2006] 2 AC 307); *Wilson v First County Trust Ltd* [2003] UKHL 40 [2004] 1 AC 816 at [141] (Lord Hobhouse: "Whether a particular statutory provision offends against any of the `Convention rights' is an objective question to be answered having regard to all relevant evidence"), [116] (Lord Hope, referring to the court "forming its own view ... as to whether or not the legislation is compatible"); *R (SB) v Headteacher and Governors of Denbigh High School* [2006] UKHL 15 [2007] 1 AC 100 at [30] (Lord Bingham: "The domestic court must now make a value judgment, an evaluation, by reference to the circumstances prevailing at the relevant time ... Proportionality must be judged objectively, by the court"); *R (T) v Secretary of State for the Home Department* [2003] EWCA Civ 1285 [2003] UKHRR 1321 at [19] ("Once the facts are known, the question of whether they bring the applicant actually or imminently within the protection of Article 3 is one which [Counsel] accepts can be answered by the court - assuming that viable grounds of challenge have been shown - without deference to the initial decision-maker"); *R v Johnstone* [2003] UKHL 28 [2003] 1 WLR 1736 at [51] ("the court's role is one of review. Parliament, not the court, is charged with the primary responsibility for deciding, as a matter of policy, what should be the constituent elements of a criminal offence").

59.1 Testing for an HRA-violation
59.2 Article 2: life
59.3 Article 3: cruelty
59.4 Article 5: liberty
59.5 Article 6: fair-hearing
59.6 Article 8: privacy
59.7 Article 10: expression
59.8 Article 14: non-discrimination
59.9 Article 1P: property-interference
59.10 Further Convention rights and provisions

59.1 Testing for an HRA-violation. Whether an HRA:ECHR right has been violated depends on whether: (1) the right applies, is engaged and is interfered with; and (2) such interference can be justified by reference to (a) the relevant HRA:ECHR Article and (b) applicable principles enunciated in the case-law.

59.1.1 The HRA <64.7>. <P9>.

59.1.2 The HRA and authority/precedent. <11.1.9>.

59.1.3 Importance of the express terms of the codified Convention rights. <9.2> (codified Convention rights); <9.2.3> (meaning of Convention rights under the HRA); *R (Mahmood) v Secretary of State for the Home Department* [2001] 1 WLR 840 at [39] (Lord Phillips MR: "Interference with human rights can only be justified to the extent permitted by the Convention itself. Some articles of the Convention brook no interference with the rights enshrined within them. Other articles qualify the rights, or permit interference with them"); *R v Secretary of State for the Home Department, ex p Daly* [2001] UKHL 26 [2001] 2 AC 532 at [27] (Lord Steyn, recognising the need to make "due allowance for important structural differences between various convention rights"); <37.1.6> (codified justification).

59.1.4 Legality/certainty: "prescribed by law" etc. See especially Art 2 (right to life: death penalty must be "provided by law"); Art 5 (right to liberty/freedom from imprisonment: deprivation of liberty must be "in accordance with a procedure prescribed by law"); Art 6 (fair hearing: independent and impartial tribunal must be "established by law"); Art 8 (privacy: interference must be "in accordance with the law"); Art 9 (freedom of religion: limitations must be "prescribed by law"); Art 10 (freedom of expression: restrictions must be "prescribed by law"); Art 11 (freedom of association: restrictions must be "prescribed by law"); Art 1P (protection of property: deprivation must be "subject to the conditions provided for by law"); *R (S) v Chief Constable of South Yorkshire* [2004] UKHL 39 [2004] 1 WLR 2196 at [36] (discretion to retain fingerprints and DNA sufficiently provided for by law); *Director of Public Prosecutions v Haw* [2007] EWHC 1931 (Admin) [2008] 1 WLR 379 at [43] (condition unworkable and so not prescribed by law); *R (Munjaz) v Mersey Care NHS Trust* [2005] UKHL 58 [2006] 2 AC 148 at [34] (sufficient that governed by guidance and policy, albeit hospital entitled to depart); *R v Shayler* [2002] UKHL 11 [2003] 1 AC 247 at [24] (statutory restriction on free speech "prescribed with complete clarity"), [56] (legal basis for interference, being both accessible and non-arbitrary); *R v Rimmington* [2005] UKHL 63 [2006] 1 AC 459 at [35]-[36] (common law offence of public nuisance sufficiently clear and predictable for HRA:ECHR Art 7 purposes); *R (Gillan) v Commissioner of Police of the Metropolis* [2006] UKHL 12 [2006] 2 AC 307 at [34]-[35], [56] (stop and search power prescribed by law, albeit statutory authorisation not published); *R v P* [2002] 1 AC 146, 469E-471F (discussing "in accordance with the law", as to admissibility of telephone interception evidence); *R (L) v Secretary of State for the Home Department* [2003] EWCA Civ 25 [2003] 1 WLR 1230 at [17] (need for legislation to be published); *R (Nilsen) v Governor of HMP Full Sutton* [2004] EWCA Civ 1540 [2005] 1 WLR 1028 at [32] (standing order, under which prisoner autobiography manuscript seized, sufficiently certain); *R (Northern Cyprus Tourism Centre Ltd) v Transport for London* [2005] EWHC 1698 (Admin) [2005] UKHRR 1231 at [86] (refusal of tourism adverts insufficiently foreseeable to be "in accordance with law"); *Langley v Liverpool City Council* [2005] EWCA Civ 1173 [2006] 1 WLR 375 at [52] (violation of Art 8 since not "in accordance with law" where act interfering with family life and not compatible with domestic law); *A v Head Teacher and Governors of Lord Grey School* [2006] UKHL 14 [2006] 2 AC 363 at [61] (incompatibility with domestic law only a breach of a Convention right if Convention right removed).

59.1.5 "Necessary"/"necessary in a democratic society"/"pressing need". See especially Art 2 (deprivation of right to life: use of force to defend from violence must be "no more than absolutely necessary"); Art 5 (right to liberty/freedom from imprisonment: deprivation of liberty "when it is reasonably considered necessary" to prevent offence); Art 6 (fair hearing: exclusion of press/public where "in the interest of morals, public order or national security in a democratic society" or where "strictly necessary in the opinion of the court in special circumstances where publicity would prejudice the interests of justice"); Art 8 (privacy: interference must be "necessary in a democratic society in the interests of national security, public safety or the economic well-being of the country, for the prevention of disorder or crime, for the protection of health or morals, or for the protection of the rights and freedoms of others"); Art 9 (freedom of religion: limitations must be "necessary in a democratic society in the interests of public safety, for the protection of public order, health or morals, or for the protection of the rights and freedoms of others"); Art 10 (freedom of expression: restrictions must be "necessary in a democratic society, in the interests of national security, territorial integrity or public safety, for the prevention of disorder or crime, for the protection of health or morals, for the protection of the reputation or rights of others, for preventing the disclosure of information received in confidence, or for maintaining the authority and impartiality of the judiciary"); Art 11 (freedom of association: restrictions must be "necessary in a democratic society in the interests of national security or public safety, for the prevention of disorder or crime, for the protection of health or morals or for the protection of the rights and freedoms of others"); Art 1P (protection of property: deprivation must be "in the public interest" and state control on use must be "to enforce such laws as it deems necessary to control the use of property in accordance with the general interest or to secure the payment of taxes or other contributions or penalties"); *R (Clays Lane Housing Cooperative Ltd) v Housing Corporation* [2004] EWCA Civ 1658 [2005] 1 WLR 2229 ("necessary" not meaning "strict necessity" in Art 1P context); *R (McLellan) v Bracknell Forest Borough Council* [2001] EWCA Civ 1510 [2002] QB 1129 at [45] ("necessary in a democratic society" meaning: "(a) that the reasons given to justify the interference must be relevant and sufficient; (b) that the interference must correspond to a pressing social need; and (c) that the interference must be proportionate to the aim pursued"); *R v Shayler* [2002] UKHL 11 [2003] 1 AC 247 at [59] (pressing social need); *R (MWH & H Ward Estates Ltd) v Monmouthshire County Council* [2002] EWCA Civ 1915 at [31] ("pressing social need" not the appropriate test for Art 1P).

59.1.6 HRA proportionality. <P37> (proportionality template); <37.1.8> (proportionality and the HRA).

59.1.7 HRA suitability. *Aston Cantlow and Wilmcote with Billesley Parochial Church Council v Wallbank* [2001] EWCA Civ 713 [2002] Ch 51 at [51] ("Proportionality ... calls for consideration of the appropriateness of the measure to the need which it is designed to meet") (HL is at [2003] UKHL 37 [2004] 1 AC 546); *A v Secretary of State for the Home Department* [2004] UKHL 56 [2005] 2 AC 68 (detention of non-nationals without trial not rationally linked to security threat, since UK nationals posing such a threat not so detained).

59.2 Article 2: life.[34] There can be a violation of Article 2 where public authorities have (1) taken life, (2) failed to safeguard life or (3) failed to ensure a sufficient investigation into death.

59.2.1 Article 2: the right to life. See HRA Sch 1 Art 2 (HRA:ECHR Art 2) ("1. Everyone's right to life shall be protected by law. No one shall be deprived of his life intentionally save in the execution of a sentence of a court following his conviction of a crime for which this penalty is provided by law. 2. Deprivation of life shall not be regarded as inflicted in contravention of this Article when it results from the use of force which is no more than absolutely necessary: (a) in defence of any person from unlawful violence; (b) in order to effect a lawful arrest or to prevent the escape of a person lawfully detained; (c) in action lawfully taken for the purpose of quelling a riot or insurrection"); *R (Middleton) v West Somerset Coroner* [2004] UKHL 10 [2004] 2 AC 182 at [2]-[3] (Lord Bingham, summarising Art 2 principles), [5] ("Compliance with the [Art 2] substantive obligations ... must rank among the highest priorities of a modern democratic state governed by the rule of law. Any violation or potential violation must be treated with great seriousness").

59.2.2 Article 2: state use of lethal force.[35] *R (Middleton) v West Somerset Coroner* [2004] UKHL 10 [2004] 2 AC 182 at [2] (referring to the Art 2 "substantive obligation[] not to take life without justification"); *R (A) v Lord Saville of Newdigate* [2001] EWCA Civ 2048 [2002] 1 WLR 1249 at [10]-[11] (Art 2 engaged in relation to Bloody Sunday inquiry, arising out of deaths at the hands of the state); *McCann v United Kingdom* (1995) 21 EHRR 97 (Art 2 violation where IRA terrorists killed by SAS officers on Gibraltar).

59.2.3 Article 2: safeguarding duty. *R (Middleton) v West Somerset Coroner* [2004] UKHL 10 [2004] 2 AC 182 at [2] (Art 2 "substantive obligation[] to establish a framework of laws, precautions, procedures and means of enforcement which will, to the greatest extent reasonably practicable, protect life"); *In Re Officer L* [2007] UKHL 36 [2007] 1 WLR 2135 (public inquiry witness anonymity and real and immediate risk to life); *Savage v South East Partnership NHS Foundation Trust* [2007] EWCA Civ 1375 [2008] 1 WLR 1667 (Art 2 duty to protect mental health detainee from foreseeable self-harm); *Van Colle v Hertfordshire Chief Constable* [2008] UKHL 50 [2008] 3 WLR 593 (Art 2 violation where failure of witness protection); *R (Burke) v General Medical Council* [2005] EWCA Civ 1003 [2006] QB 273 at [38]-[39] (application of Art 2 to artificial nutrition in medical context); *R (T) v Mental Health Review Tribunal* [2002] EWHC 247 (Admin) (any danger to claimant's life from discharge of ex-partner too remote to engage Art 2); *R (H) v Ashworth Hospital Authority* [2001] EWHC Admin 872 [2002] 1 FCR 206 ("no condoms" policy not a breach of Art 2).

59.2.4 Article 2: procedural duty (state investigation).[36] *R (Middleton) v West Somerset*

---

[34] Robert Weekes [2005] JR 19.

[35] Thomas A Cross [2006] JR 180.

[36] Sarabjit Singh [2004] JR 147.

Coroner [2004] UKHL 10 [2004] 2 AC 182 (coroners' statutory function of investigating "how" death occurred must extend to "by what means and in what circumstances", in order to be Art 2-compatible), at [3] (duty to investigate a death "occurring in circumstances in which it appears that [the Art 2] substantive obligations has been, or may have been, violated and it appears that agents of the state are, or may be, in some way implicated"); *R (L (A Patient) v Secretary of State for the Home Department* [2007] EWCA Civ 767 [2008] 1 WLR 158 (duty to investigate serious injury sustained by suicide attempt in state custody); *In re McKerr* [2004] UKHL 12 [2004] 1 WLR 807 (no duty in relation to pre-2.10.00 death); *R (Green) v Police Complaints Authority* [2004] UKHL 6 [2004] 1 WLR 725 at [11] (independent investigation where cyclist alleged police drove at him with intent to kill); *R (Gentle) v Prime Minister* [2008] UKHL 20 [2008] 2 WLR 879 (no duty to investigate approach to legality of Iraq war in which British soldiers killed); *R (Khan) v Secretary of State for the Health* [2003] EWCA Civ 1129 [2004] 1 WLR 971 (need for inquest with victim's family having funded legal representation); *R (Scholes) v Secretary of State for the Home Department* [2006] EWCA Civ 1343 [2006] HRLR 1391 (thorough inquest and remedial willingness sufficing); *R (Takoushis) v Inner North London Coroner* [2005] EWCA Civ 1140 [2006] 1 WLR 461 (coroner needing to investigate hospital's system); *R (D) v Secretary of State for the Home Department* [2006] EWCA Civ 143 [2006] 3 All ER 946 (inquiry to be in public and with funded family attendance).

59.3 **Article 3: cruelty.**[37] There can be a violation of Article 3 where public authorities engage in, or fail to protect against or respond to, serious harm.

59.3.1 **Article 3: torture, inhuman and degrading treatment.** See HRA:ECHR Art 3 ("No one shall be subjected to torture or to inhuman or degrading treatment or punishment").

59.3.2 **Article 3: positive obligation (safeguarding).** *R (Limbuela) v Secretary of State for the Home Department* [2005] UKHL 66 [2006] 1 AC 396 (positive Art 3 obligation and asylum welfare); *R (Pretty) v Director of Public Prosecutions* [2001] UKHL 61 [2002] 1 AC 800 (Art 3 not bearing on right to live or die); *R (Gezer) v Secretary of State for the Home Department* [2004] EWCA Civ 1730 [2005] Imm AR 131 (no duty to investigate individual housing conditions before making asylum dispersal decision).

59.3.3 **Article 3: procedural duty (state investigation).** *R (Green) v Police Complaints Authority* [2004] UKHL 6 [2004] 1 WLR 725 (Police Complaints Authority satisfying duty of state investigation arising under Art 3 as well as Art 2); *R (Spinks) v Secretary of State for the Home Department* [2005] EWCA Civ 275 at [30] (Art 3 procedural duty discussed), [31], [53] (investigative duty applicable only to past violations; duty as to continuing violations being to ensure their termination).

59.3.4 **Article 3: illustrations.** *R (Graham) v Secretary of State for Justice* [2007] EWHC 2940 (Admin) (handcuffing of prisoner during outpatient chemotherapy violating Art 3 in the circumstances); *R (Ullah) v Secretary of State for the Home Department* [2004] UKHL 26 [2004] 2 AC 323 (applicability of Art 3 to immigration removals where ill-treatment suffered in receiving state an exceptional extension of the ECHR); *R (Bagdanavicius) v Secretary of State for the Home Department* [2005] UKHL 38 [2005] 2 AC 668 (real risk of Art 3 ill-treatment in receiving state and state agents implicated or insufficiency of protection); *N v Secretary of State for the Home Department* [2005] UKHL 31 [2005] 2 AC 296 (removal of AIDS-sufferer not violating Art 3 unless critical condition and compelling humanitarian

---

[37] David Pievsky [2005] JR 169.

reasons); *R v Governor of Frankland Prison, ex p Russell* [2000] 1 WLR 2027 (limit of one meal per day violating prisoners' Art 3 rights of freedom from inhuman and degrading treatment); *R v Lichniak* [2002] UKHL 47 [2003] 1 AC 903 (mandatory life sentence not incompatible with Art 3); *Napier v Scottish Ministers* [2004] UKHRR 881 (slopping out prison regime violating Art 3); *R (Munjaz) v Mersey Care NHS Trust* [2005] UKHL 58 [2006] 2 AC 148 (seclusion policy not violating Art 3); *R (Limbuela) v Secretary of State for the Home Department* [2005] UKHL 66 [2006] 1 AC 396 (withholding of welfare benefits from asylum-seekers violating Art 3 where left on the streets, seriously hungry and unable to satisfy basic hygiene needs); *R (JB) v Haddock* [2006] EWCA Civ 961 [2006] HRLR 1237 (Art 3 and forced medical treatment); *R (Pretty) v Director of Public Prosecutions* [2001] UKHL 61 [2002] 1 AC 800 (no breach of Art 3 in declining to rule out prosecution for assisted suicide; Art 3 not bearing on right to live or die); *R (C) v Secretary of State for Justice* [2008] EWCA Civ 882 at [79] (Secure Training Centre restraint rules violating Art 3).

59.4 Article 5: liberty.[38] Article 5 is violated where deprivation of liberty cannot be justified as prescribed permissible detention.

59.4.1 Article 5: right to liberty. See HRA:ECHR Art 5 ("1. Everyone has the right to liberty and security of person. No one shall be deprived of his liberty save in the following cases and in accordance with a procedure prescribed by law: (a) the lawful detention of a person after conviction by a competent court; (b) the lawful arrest or detention of a person for non-compliance with the lawful order of a court or in order to secure the fulfilment of any obligation prescribed by law; (c) the lawful arrest or detention of a person effected for the purpose of bringing him before the competent legal authority on reasonable suspicion of having committed an offence or when it is reasonably considered necessary to prevent his committing an offence or fleeing after having done so; (d) the detention of a minor by lawful order for the purpose of educational supervision or his lawful detention for the purpose of bringing him before the competent legal authority; (e) the lawful detention of persons for the prevention of the spreading of infectious diseases, of persons of unsound mind, alcoholics or drugs addicts or vagrants; (f) the lawful arrest or detention of a person to prevent his effecting an unauthorised entry into the country or of a person against whom action is being taken with a view to deportation or extradition. 2. Everyone who is arrested shall be informed promptly, in a language which he understands, of the reasons for his arrest and of any charge against him. 3. Everyone arrested or detained in accordance with the provisions of paragraph 1(c) of this Article shall be brought promptly before a judge or other officer authorised by law to exercise judicial power and shall be entitled to trial within a reasonable time or to release pending trial. Release may be conditioned by guarantees to appear for trial. 4. Everyone who is deprived of his liberty by arrest or detention shall be entitled to take proceedings by which the lawfulness of his detention shall be decided speedily by a court and his release ordered if the detention is not lawful. 5. Everyone who has been the victim of arrest or detention in contravention of the provisions of this Article shall have an enforceable right to compensation"). See HRA s.14 <64.7> (designated derogations), Schedule 3 Part I (the 1988 and 1989 notifications, in relation to statutory powers of detention of suspected terrorists) and section 16 (period for which designated derogations have effect); also ECHR Art 15 and HRA s.14(6).

59.4.2 Article 5: "deprivation of liberty". *R (Gillan) v Commissioner of Police of the Metropolis* [2006] UKHL 12 [2006] 2 AC 307 at [25] (stop and search not a deprivation of liberty, absent special circumstances); *Secretary of State for the Home Department v JJ* [2007]

---

[38] Parishil Patel [2005] JR 303.

UKHL 45 [2008] 1 AC 385 (confinement to a flat 18 hours a day a deprivation of liberty); *Austin v Metropolitan Police Commissioner* [2007] EWCA Civ 989 [2008] QB 660 (May Day protest containment not a deprivation of liberty).

59.4.3 Article 5: mental health illustrations. *R (H) v Secretary of State for the Home Department* [2003] UKHL 59 [2004] 2 AC 253 (mental health review tribunal having power to review its decision where discharge conditions proving unsustainable, and failure breaching Art 5(4), but not rendering detention unlawful under Art 5(1)(e)); *R (H) v Secretary of State for Health* [2005] UKHL 60 [2006] 1 AC 441 (statutory scheme regarding incompetent patient's access to MHRT or county court, where next of kin displacement sought, capable of operating Art 5(4)-compatibly); *Anderson v Scottish Ministers* [2001] UKPC D5 [2003] 2 AC 602 (treatment not a requirement of mental health detention under Art 5(1)(e)); *R (Munjaz) v Mersey Care NHS Trust* [2005] UKHL 58 [2006] 2 AC 148 (seclusion policy Art 5-compatible); *R (D) v Secretary of State for the Home Department* [2002] EWHC 2805 (Admin) [2003] 1 WLR 1315 (Mental Health Act incompatible with Art 5 because discretionary lifer having served tariff period and detained on mental health grounds not having a legal right of access to parole board); *R (A) v Secretary of State for the Home Department* [2002] EWHC 1618 (Admin) [2003] 1 WLR 330 at [71] (unreasonable delay in Mental Health Act case, breaching Art 5(4)); *R (S) v Mental Health Review Tribunal* [2002] EWHC 2522 (Admin) (mandatory examination by medical mental health tribunal member not incompatible with Art 5(4)); *R (H) v Nottinghamshire Healthcare National Health Service Trust* [2001] EWHC Admin 1037 (2002) 5 CCLR 62 (mental health review tribunal supervision orders compatible with Art 5(1)(a), notwithstanding delay where psychiatrists unwilling to supervise patient on discharge); *R (A) v Harrow Crown Court* [2003] EWHC 2020 (Admin) (although crown court mental health detention order made without power, detention under invalid order compatible with Art 5 because procedure followed was "prescribed by law"); *R (KB) v Mental Health Review Tribunal* [2002] EWHC 639 (Admin) (2002) 5 CCLR 458 (delays in holding mental health review hearings inconsistent with HRA:ECHR Art 5(4)); *R (W) v Doncaster Metropolitan Borough Council* [2004] EWCA Civ 378 [2004] LGR 743 (despite delays in making suitable arrangements as required in MHRT-directed conditional discharge, given continued mental disorder continuing detention Art 5-compatible).

59.4.4 Article 5: immigration illustrations. *A v Secretary of State for the Home Department* [2004] UKHL 56 [2005] 2 AC 68 (derogation from Art 5, where non-nationals detained without trial on security grounds, not strictly necessary under Art 15); *R (Saadi) v Secretary of State for the Home Department* [2002] UKHL 41 [2002] 1 WLR 3131 (detention of asylum-seekers for short period pending decision-making compatible with Art 5(1)(f)); *R (D) v Secretary of State for the Home Department* [2006] EWHC 980 (Admin) (damages under Art 5 where failure to conduct medical examination and claimant would probably have been released); *R (I) v Secretary of State for the Home Department* [2002] EWCA Civ 888 [2003] INLR 196 (continued detention of failed asylum-seeker whose removal to Afghanistan could not presently be achieved infringing Art 5 on the facts); *R (Nadarajah) v Secretary of State for the Home Department* [2003] EWCA Civ 1768 [2004] INLR 139 (detention of asylum seekers unlawful by reference to Art 5(1)(f), where Secretary of State's policy not sufficiently known to be accessible or foreseeable); cf.*Naidike v Attorney-General of Trinidad and Tobago* [2004] UKPC 49 [2005] 1 AC 538 (detention unlawful where not preceded by necessary ministerial order).

59.4.5 Article 5: parole/release/recall illustrations. *In Re D* [2008] UKHL 33 [2008] 1 WLR 1499 at [35] (no undue delay by Life Sentence Review Commissioners violating Art 5(4)); *R (Cawley) v Parole Board* [2007] EWHC 2649 (Admin) (parole delay breaching Art 5(4)); *R*

(Brooke) v Parole Board [2008] EWCA Civ 29 [2008] 3 All ER 289[39] (Secretary of State's relationship with Parole Board compromising its independence); *R (Black) v Secretary of State for Justice* [2008] EWCA Civ 359 (Art 5(4) applicable to determinate sentence releases); *R v Lichniak* [2002] UKHL 47 [2003] 1 AC 903 (mandatory life sentence not incompatible with Art 5); *R (Giles) v Parole Board* [2003] UKHL 42 [2004] 1 AC 1 (no need for periodic review of protective element of extended sentence); *R (West) v Parole Board* [2005] UKHL 1 [2005] 1 WLR 350 at [37] (parole board oral hearings); *R (Roberts) v Parole Board* [2005] UKHL 45 [2005] 2 AC 738 (use of special advocate); *R (Girling) v Parole Board* [2006] EWCA Civ 1779 [2007] QB 783 (Secretary of State's "directions" to parole board merely suggestions so compatible with Art 5(4) independence); *R (Johnson) v Secretary of State for the Home Department* [2007] EWCA Civ 427 [2007] 1 WLR 1990 (Art 5(4) applicable to long-term determinate sentence parole delay); *R (Mason) v Ministry of Justice* [2008] EWHC 1787 (QB) (Art 5(4) not applicable to home detention curfew during sentence).

59.4.6 Article 5: other treatment of prisoners/detainees illustrations. *R (Al-Jedda) v Secretary of State for Defence* [2007] UKHL 58 [2008] 1 AC 332 (HRA:ECHR Art 5 qualified by UN Security Council Resolution, regarding detention in postwar Iraq); *R (Manjit Singh Sunder) v Secretary of State for the Home Department* [2001] EWHC Admin 252 at [23] (reclassification of prisoner not engaging Art 5 since deprivation of liberty was the sentence of the criminal court); *R (Cawser) v Secretary of State for the Home Department* [2003] EWCA Civ 1522 [2004] UKHRR 101 (no breach of Art 5(1)(a) in failing to ensure sex offender treatment programme place in time for claimant's tariff expiry).

59.4.7 Article 5: criminal process illustrations. *R (Wardle) v Crown Court at Leeds* [2001] UKHL 12 [2002] 1 AC 754 (custody time limits regulations not arbitrary detention incompatible with Art 5); *R (Director of Public Prosecutions) v Havering Magistrates' Court* [2001] 1 WLR 805 (no Art 5 breach where proceedings for breach of bail conditions without oral evidence and cross-examination); *R (O) v Harrow Crown Court* [2006] UKHL 42 [2006] 3 WLR 195 ("exceptional circumstances" test for bail in certain cases not incompatible with Art 5(3), if read down as imposing only an evidential burden); *Austin v Commissioner of Police of the Metropolis* [2005] EWHC 480 (QB) [2005] UKHRR 1039 (police containment not violating Art 5(1)(c)); *R (Gillan) v Commissioner of Police of the Metropolis* [2006] UKHL 12 [2006] 2 AC 307 (stop and search not violating Art 5).

59.4.8 Article 5: other illustrations. *R v Secretary of State for the Home Department, ex p Chahal (No.2)* [2000] UKHRR 215 (Art 5 in context of national security); *In re K (A Child) (Secure Accommodation Order: Right to Liberty)* [2001] Fam 377 (secure accommodation order to protect child and others lawful as being within Art 5(1)(d): "for the purpose of educational supervision"); *R (Conlon) v Secretary of State for the Home Department* [2001] ACD 296 (no unlawful detention albeit that appeal against conviction successful); *R (Kashamu) v Governor of Brixton Prison* [2001] EWHC Admin 980 [2002] QB 887 (magistrates' jurisdiction to review legality of extradition detention, satisfying Art 5(4)).

59.5 Article 6: fair-hearing.[40] Article 6 violations occur where, viewed overall, the state has

---

[39] Christopher Knight [2008] JR 46.

[40] James Maurici & Sasha Blackmore [2007] JR 56; Sir Stephen Richards [1999] JR 106; Daniel Lightman [1999] JR 54, [2000] JR 111; Monica Carss-Frisk [2000] JR 198; Philip Sales [2001] JR 236 and [2005] JR 52; James Maurici [2003] JR 21; Angela Grunberg [2003] JR 46; Jonathan Cooper [2006]

failed to secure adequate guarantees of civil and criminal due process, embracing a fair and independent civil hearing or criminal trial.

59.5.1 **Article 6(1): fair-hearing (civil protections).** See HRA:ECHR Art 6(1) ("In the determination of his civil rights and obligations or of any criminal charge against him, everyone is entitled to a fair and public hearing within a reasonable time by an independent and impartial tribunal established by law. Judgment shall be pronounced publicly but the press and public may be excluded from all or part of the trial in the interest of morals, public order or national security in a democratic society, where the interests of juveniles or the protection of the private life of the parties so require, or to the extent strictly necessary in the opinion of the court in special circumstances where publicity would prejudice the interests of justice"); *HM Advocate v R* [2002] UKPC D3 [2004] 1 AC 462 at [8] (Art 6(1) containing "three separate, distinct, and independent guarantees").

59.5.2 **Article 6(2)-(3): fair-trial (criminal protections)**. See HRA:ECHR Art 6(2) ("Everyone charged with a criminal offence shall be presumed innocent until proved guilty according to law") and Art 6(3) ("Everyone charged with a criminal offence has the following minimum rights: (a) to be informed promptly, in a language which he understands and in detail, of the nature and cause of the accusation against him; (b) to have adequate time and facilities for the preparation of his defence; (c) to defend himself in person or through legal assistance of his own choosing or, if he has not sufficient means to pay for legal assistance, to be given it free when the interests of justice so require; (d) to examine or have examined witnesses against him and to obtain the attendance and examination of witnesses on his behalf under the same conditions as witnesses against him; (e) to have the free assistance of an interpreter if he cannot understand or speak the language used in court").

59.5.3 **Article 6: classification as civil or criminal.** *Secretary of State for the Home Department v MB* [2007] UKHL 46 [2008] 1 AC 440 (control orders civil not criminal); *R (Greenfield) v Secretary of State for the Home Department* [2005] UKHL 14 [2005] 1 WLR 673 (prison disciplinary offence a criminal charge); *R v Benjafield; R v Rezvi* [2002] UKHL 1 & 2 [2003] 1 AC 1099 (confiscation orders not a new criminal charge); *Magill v Porter* [2001] UKHL 67 [2002] 2 AC 357 at [83]-[86] (district auditor surcharge not a criminal charge for Art 6 purposes); *R v H* [2003] UKHL 1 [2003] 1 WLR 411 (jury procedure for dealing with defendant unfit to stand trial not the determination of a criminal charge because could not culminate in a penal sanction); *R (R) v Durham Constabulary* [2005] UKHL 21 [2005] 1 WLR 1184 (warning under Crime and Disorder Act 1998 not determination of a criminal charge); *R (McCann) v Crown Court at Manchester* [2002] UKHL 39 [2003] 1 AC 787 (ASBOs civil not criminal); *McIntosh v Lord Advocate* [2001] UKPC D1 [2003] 1 AC 1078 (in confiscation order proceedings, defendant not charged with a criminal offence).

59.5.4 **Article 6: criminal cases and protections.**
(A) SUFFICIENT SAFEGUARDS. *Montgomery v Her Majesty's Advocate and the Advocate General for Scotland* [2003] 1 AC 641, 673C (need for "'sufficient' guarantees or safeguards and for the exclusion of any 'legitimate doubt'").
(B) FAIR TRIAL (CRIMINAL). *R (Greenfield) v Secretary of State for the Home Department* [2005] UKHL 14 [2005] 1 WLR 673 (violation of Art 6 (criminal) where prison disciplinary finding without legal representation); *R v H* [2004] UKHL 3 [2004] 2 AC 134 (Art 6-compliance in the context of prosecution disclosure, public interest immunity and use of special

JR 78; Jonny Landau [2007] JR 261.

counsel); *R v A (No.2)* [2001] UKHL 25 [2002] 1 AC 45 (construing statutory restrictions on evidential admissibility to protect fair trial right); *McLean v Buchanan* [2001] UKPC D3 [2001] 1 WLR 2425 (fixed fee payments for criminal defence work not preventing effective legal assistance under Art 6(3)); *R v P* [2002] 1 AC 146 (fair hearing test in Art 6 and admissibility of telephone intercept evidence); *R (D) v Camberwell Green Youth Court* [2005] UKHL 4 [2005] 1 WLR 393 (special measures directions compatible with Art 6 (criminal) fair trial); *Montgomery v Her Majesty's Advocate and the Advocate General for Scotland* [2003] 1 AC 641 (Art 6 and whether pre-trial publicity preventing fair trial).

(C) PRESUMPTION OF INNOCENCE/REVERSE ONUS OF PROOF.*Sheldrake v Director of Public Prosecutions* [2004] UKHL 43 [2005] 1 AC 264 (disproportionate legal reverse-burden read as evidential only under HRA s.3), [21]; *R v Lambert* [2001] UKHL 37 [2002] 2 AC 545 (whether objective justification for imposing burden of proof as to certain defences on the accused); *R v Johnstone* [2003] UKHL 28 [2003] 1 WLR 1736 (Art 6 and presumption of innocence/reverse burden of proof in context of prosecution under Trade Marks Act 1994 s.92); *R v Keogh* [2007] EWCA Crim 528 [2007] 1 WLR 1500 (reverse burden of proof read down for Art 6(2) compatibility); *R (Griffin) v Richmond Magistrates Court* [2008] EWHC 84 (Admin) [2008] 1 WLR 1525 at [29] (legal reverse-burden Art 6-compatible).

(D) SELF-INCRIMINATION/RIGHT TO SILENCE. *Brown v Stott (Procurator Fiscal, Dunfermline)* [2003] 1 AC 681 (provision permitting use of confession made under compulsion not disproportionate interference with privilege against self-incrimination, being a right implied within Art 6); *R (Bright) v Central Criminal Court* [2001] 1 WLR 662 (privilege against self-incrimination, an aspect of Art 6; interference authorised by necessary implication in the statute); *Attorney-General's Reference (No.7 of 2000)* [2001] EWCA Crim 888 [2001] 1 WLR 1879 (not a breach of Art 6 to use compulsorily-obtained insolvency documentation for the purposes of criminal prosecution); *R v Kansal (No.2)* [2001] EWCA Crim 1260 [2001] 3 WLR 751 (CA) (use of bankruptcy examination a breach of Art 6; HL is [2001] UKHL 62 [2002] 2 AC 69); *R v Dimsey; R v Allen* [2001] UKHL 46 & 45 [2002] 1 AC 509 (convictions for failure to declare income to the revenue not a breach of Art 6 self-incrimination protection); *R v Kearns* [2002] EWCA Crim 748 [2002] 1 WLR 2815 (bankruptcy offence of failing to account a justified and proportionate restriction of the right to silence and non-self-incrimination).

(E) SENTENCING/TARIFF FUNCTIONS. *R (Anderson) v Secretary of State for the Home Department* [2002] UKHL 46 [2003] 1 AC 837 (mandatory tariff-setting a judicial sentencing function and so incompatible with Art 6 for Secretary of State to undertake it).

59.5.5 **Article 6: "determination of civil rights or obligations".**

(A) DOCRO: EXAMPLES. *R (Wright) v Secretary of State for Health* [2007] EWCA Civ 999 [2008] QB 422 (interim listing as unsuitable care worker); *Sheffield City Council v Smart* [2002] EWCA Civ 4 [2002] HLR 639 (bringing a non-secure council tenancy to an end); *Adan v Newham London Borough Council* [2001] EWCA Civ 1916 [2002] 1 WLR 2120 at [9] (housing decision); *R (Chief Constable of Lancashire) v Preston Crown Court* [2001] EWHC Admin 928 [2002] 1 WLR 1332 at [17] (liquor licensing decision); *R (Husain) v Asylum Support Adjudicator* [2001] EWHC Admin 852 (termination of asylum support); *R (Reeson) v Dorset County Council* [2002] EWCA Civ 1812 [2003] UKHRR 353 (decision as to liability to contribute to residential care); *Friends Provident Life and Pensions Ltd v Secretary of State for Transport, Local Government and Regions* [2001] EWHC Admin 820 [2002] 1 WLR 1450 at [70] (planning decision determining objector's civil rights or obligations); *R (Thompson) v Law Society* [2004] EWCA Civ 167 [2004] 1 WLR 2522 at [80] (professional disciplinary proceedings).

(B) NO DOCRO: EXAMPLES. *R (Kehoe) v Secretary of State for Work and Pensions* [2005] UKHL 48 [2006] 1 AC 42 (enforcement of maintenance arrears); *R (M) v Lambeth London Borough Council* [2008] EWHC 1364 (Admin) (determination of asylum-seeker's age); *R (M) v Secretary of State for Constitutional Affairs* [2004] EWCA Civ 312 [2004] 1 WLR 2298 at

[39(5)] (interim ASBO); *R v Richmond upon Thames London Borough Council, ex p JC* [2001] ELR 21 at [59] (primary school admissions decision); *R (Ullah) v Secretary of State for the Home Department* [2003] EWCA Civ 1366 at [20] (immigration decisions); *R (Tawfick) v Secretary of State for the Home Department* [2001] ACD 171 (refusal of ex gratia compensation); *R (Mitchell) v Horsham District Council* [2003] EWHC 234 (Admin) at [33] (enforcement action to remove unauthorised gypsy caravans).
(C) OTHER. *Begum v Tower Hamlets London Borough Council* [2003] UKHL 5 [2003] 2 AC 430 (leaving open whether homelessness decision a DOCRO); *R (S) v London Borough of Brent* [2002] EWCA Civ 693 [2002] ELR 556 at [30] (treating school exclusion decision as a DOCRO); *R (Aggregate Industries UK Ltd) v English Nature* [2002] EWHC 908 (Admin) [2003] Env LR 83 at [71] (Art 6 not engaged by formulation and presentation of development plan policies), [73] (Art 6 engaged by process of notification and confirmation of site of special scientific interest on claimant's land); *R (Harrison) v Secretary of State for the Home Department* [2003] EWCA Civ 432 [2003] INLR 284 (doubting whether citizenship decisions capable of constituting DOCRO).

59.5.6 Article 6: independent and impartial tribunal. *R (Anderson) v Secretary of State for the Home Department* [2002] UKHL 46 [2003] 1 AC 837 (Secretary of State not an independent and impartial tribunal in setting mandatory lifer tariffs); *Starrs and Chalmers v Procurator Fiscal, Linlithgow* [2000] HRLR 191 (Scottish temporary sheriffs not an independent tribunal under Art 6, because of power of recall by Secretary of State); *R v Spear* [2002] UKHL 31 [2003] 1 AC 734 (military Court Martial having sufficient independence and impartiality despite practice of having permanent presidents); *R (Gilboy) v Liverpool City Council* [2008] EWCA Civ 751 [2008] LGR 521 (council's internal review Art 6-compatible); *R (Chief Constable of Lancashire) v Preston Crown Court* [2001] EWHC Admin 928 [2002] 1 WLR 1332 (crown court rules requiring licensing justices to sit on crown court appeal Art 6-incompatible); *Coppard v Customs and Excise Commissioners* [2003] EWCA Civ 511 [2003] QB 1428 (High Court a tribunal "established by law" albeit judge not authorised to sit as High Court judge); *R v Abdroikov* [2007] UKHL 37 [2007] 1 WLR 2679 (Art 6 incompatibility where serving police officer on jury in criminal trial involving conflict of evidence between police and accused); *Hoekstra v HM Advocate* [2000] UKHRR 578 (infringement of Art 6 where judge had written newspaper articles criticising the ECHR); *R (Husain) v Asylum Support Adjudicator* [2001] EWHC Admin 852 (asylum support adjudicators independent); *R (Bono) v Harlow District Council* [2002] EWHC 423 (Admin) [2002] 1 WLR 2475 (council's housing benefit decision not independent and impartial but judicial review remedying the deficiency); *R (Bibi) v Housing Benefit Review Board of Rochdale Metropolitan Borough Council* [2001] EWHC Admin 967 (housing benefit review board not infringing Art 6 despite being composed of councillors, applying *McLellan* and *Bewry*); *R (Aggregate Industries UK Ltd) v English Nature* [2002] EWHC 908 (Admin) [2003] Env LR 83 at [93] (English Nature's position in confirming its own recommendation "sufficiently akin to that of a party to the dispute for it to lack the necessary appearance of independence and impartiality"); *Sadler v General Medical Council* [2003] UKPC 59 [2003] 1 WLR 2259 (GMC's Committee on Professional Performance an independent and impartial tribunal).

59.5.7 Article 6: judicial review/appeal ("full jurisdiction") suffices.[41] *R (Alconbury Developments Ltd) v Secretary of State for the Environment Transport and the Regions* [2001] UKHL 23 [2003] 2 AC 295 (Secretary of State not independent and impartial, but planning system together with judicial review compliant with Art 6); *Begum v Tower Hamlets London Borough Council* [2003] UKHL 5 [2003] 2 AC 430 (council employee not an independent and

---

[41] Richard Clayton QC & Vikram Sachdeva [2003] JR 90; John Howell QC [2007] JR 9.

impartial tribunal, but judicial review-type appeal sufficient "full jurisdiction" in the context of homeless decisions being an "administrative" function statutorily entrusted to the local authority); *Magill v Porter* [2001] UKHL 67 [2002] 2 AC 357 (no breach of Art 6 as to independence and impartiality given combined procedures of district auditor and Divisional Court on appeal); *R (Bono) v Harlow District Council* [2002] EWHC 423 (Admin) [2002] 1 WLR 2475 (council's housing benefit decision not independent and impartial but judicial review remedying the deficiency where sufficient control in respect of issues of primary fact); *R (Q) v Secretary of State for the Home Department* [2003] EWCA Civ 364 [2004] QB 36 at [116]-[117] (provided that fair system of questioning of asylum-seekers in relation to welfare benefits, availability of judicial review would ensure compliance with Art 6); *R (Thompson) v Law Society* [2004] EWCA Civ 167 [2004] 1 WLR 2522 at [100] (if Office for Supervision of Solicitors had been determining a civil right or obligation, judicial review would secure Art 6-compatibility).

59.5.8 **Article 6: fair hearing.** *Secretary of State for the Home Department v MB* [2007] UKHL 46 [2008] 1 AC 440 at [29] (control orders and individuals' Art 6 right to be told case against them); *Magill v Porter* [2001] UKHL 67 [2002] 2 AC 357 at [87] (the "rights to a fair hearing, to a public hearing and to a hearing within a reasonable time"); *R v Mirza* [2004] UKHL 2 [2004] 1 AC 1118 (rule regarding non-investigation into jury deliberations Art 6-compatible); *R (Wright) v Secretary of State for Health* [2007] EWCA Civ 999 [2008] QB 422 (right to make representations prior to listing as unsuitable care worker).

59.5.9 **Article 6: public hearing/judgment in public.** *R (Pelling) v Bow County Court* [2001] UKHRR 165 (CPR rule allowing hearings to be in private not incompatible with Art 6); *Clark v Kelly* [2003] UKPC D1 [2004] 1 AC 681 (criminal trial before the Scottish District Court a "public hearing", since clerk's advice given in private was provisional and ventilated in open court); *In re Trusts of X Charity* [2003] EWHC 257 (Ch) [2003] 1 WLR 2751 (no breach of Art 6 here for court's judgment to be given in private); *Department for Economics, Policy and Development of City of Moscow v Bankers Trust Co* [2004] EWCA Civ 314 [2005] QB 207 (considering Art 6 public hearing requirement in context of High Court challenge to arbitration); *Pelling v Bruce-Williams* [2004] EWCA Civ 845 [2004] Fam 155 (considering Art 6-compatibility of provisions regarding whether family residency hearings in public and whether details publishable; compatible with Art 6 provided that balancing exercise considered in each case); *R (Bannatyne) v Independent Adjudicator* [2004] EWHC 1921 (Admin) (disciplinary prison matter not violating Art 6 despite no public hearing, it being contrary to the public interest to require all such hearings to be in public); *R (Mersey Care NHS Trust) v Mental Health Review Tribunal* [2004] EWHC 1749 (Admin) [2005] 1 WLR 2469 (erroneous for mental health review tribunal to have decided to conduct review hearing in public here); *R (Dudson) v Secretary of State for the Home Department* [2005] UKHL 52 [2006] 1 AC 245 (tariff resetting not requiring oral hearings for Art 6-compatibility here); *R (Hammond) v Secretary of State for the Home Department* [2005] UKHL 69 [2006] 1 AC 603 (Art 6 requiring statutory implied condition allowing oral hearing of tariff-reconsideration in an appropriate case); *R (Morgan Grenfell & Co Ltd) v Inland Revenue Commissioners* [2001] EWCA Civ 329 [2003] 1 AC 563 (CA) at [50] ("the possibility of an oral hearing is excluded by the nature of the process in question") (HL is at [2002] UKHL 21 [2003] 1 AC 563).

59.5.10 **Article 6: equality of arms.** *R v Secretary of State for the Environment, ex p Challenger* [2001] Env LR 209 (court not persuaded that "inequality of arms" under Art 6 where claimant not having financial resources for representation at rail public inquiry); *R (Shields) v Crown Court at Liverpool* [2001] EWHC Admin 90 [2001] UKHRR 610 (question whether refusal of legal aid for a co-defendant to have Leading Counsel incompatible with Art 6 being a question for the Court of Appeal Criminal Division in deciding whether there had been a fair trial); *R (Fleurose) v Securities and Futures Authority* [2001] EWHC Admin 292 (Administrative Court) (no absolute right of legal representation) (CA is [2001] EWCA Civ 2015); *McLean v Buchanan* [2001] UKPC D3 [2001] 1 WLR 2425 at [39] (considering equality of arms in context of fixed legal aid fees); *R (Jarrett) v Legal Services Commission* [2001] EWHC Admin 389 (whether withholding of legal aid incompatible with Art 6); *Pine v Law Society* [2001] EWCA Civ 1574 [2002] UKHRR 81 (no breach of Art 6 on the facts, where solicitor's impecuniosity prevented him from attending or being represented at Solicitor's Disciplinary Tribunal).

59.5.11 **Article 6: hearing within a reasonable time.** *Attorney General's Reference No.2 of 2001* [2003] UKHL 68 [2004] 2 AC 72 (consequences of Art 6 delay on whether trial unfair); *Magill v Porter* [2001] UKHL 67 [2002] 2 AC 357 at [108]-[109] (whether "time taken to determine the person's rights and obligations was unreasonable"); *Procurator Fiscal, Linlithgow v Watson* [2002] UKPC D1 [2004] 1 AC 379 (delay in prosecution incompatible with Art 6 "reasonable time" requirement); *HM Advocate v R* [2002] UKPC D3 [2004] 1 AC 462 (unreasonable delay rendering continuance of prosecution incompatible with Art 6); *R (Lloyd) v Bow Street Magistrates Court* [2003] EWHC 2294 (Admin) (breach of right to have enforcement proceedings determined within a reasonable time); *In re Saggar (Confiscation Order: Delay)* [2005] EWCA Civ 174 [2005] 1 WLR 2693 (reasonable time requirement engaged by application for confiscation order increase certification); *R (Stone) v Plymouth Magistrates' Court* [2007] EWHC 2519 (Admin) (13 years' delay in enforcing confiscation order).

59.5.12 **Article 6: access to court.** *Matthews v Ministry of Defence* [2003] UKHL 4 [2003] 1 AC 1163 (Crown immunity from tort action a substantive legal provision so not engaging Art 6 right of access to a court); *R (Kehoe) v Secretary of State for Work and Pensions* [2005] UKHL 48 [2006] 1 AC 42 (non-enforceability of maintenance by carer parent not incompatible with Art 6 access to court, since no domestic law substantive right being determined); *Wilson v First County Trust Ltd* [2003] UKHL 40 [2004] 1 AC 816 (statutory unenforceability of consumer credit agreement a substantive bar, not a procedural bar on access to a court); *R (Ponting) v Governor of HMP Whitemoor* [2002] EWCA Civ 224 (restricted access by dyslexic litigant prisoner to a computer striking a fair balance and not breaching Art 6 access to a court); *Heath v Metropolitan Police Commissioner* [2004] EWCA Civ 493 (immunity of Police Disciplinary Board as a judicial body from sex discrimination complaint not an Art 6 violation); *R (Alliss) v Legal Services Commission* [2002] EWHC 2079 (Admin) at [44] (late withdrawal of legal aid a denial of effective access to the court in breach of Art 6); *Jones v Ministry of Interior of Saudi Arabia* [2006] UKHL 26 [2007] 1 AC 270 (Art 6-compatibility of state immunity in tort claims based on foreign state torture abroad).

59.5.13 **Article 6: other.** *Hubbard v Lambeth Southwark and Lewisham Health Authority* The Times 8th October 2001 (pre-trial meeting of experts not incompatible with Art 6); *St Brice v Southwark London Borough Council* [2001] EWCA Civ 1138 [2002] 1 WLR 1537 (enforcement of possession order without any further judicial determination compatible with Art 6); *R (Cannan) v Governor of HMP Full Sutton* [2003] EWCA Civ 1480 (prison "prior clearance" policy for receipt of legal documents Art 6-incompatible); *R (Aru) v Chief Constable of Merseyside* [2004] EWCA Civ 199 [2004] 1 WLR 1697 at [12] ("Art 6 does not confer a right of appeal"); *A v Secretary of State for the Home Department* [2005] UKHL 71 [2006] 2 AC 221 at [26] (use of torture-induced evidence in domestic court incompatible with Art 6); <31.4.3> (waiver); *Millar v Procurator Fiscal* [2001] UKPC D4 [2002] 1 WLR 1615 (in context of right to an independent and impartial tribunal, waiver needing voluntary, informed and unequivocal election); <62.2.8(B)> (reasons and Art 6).

59.5.14 **Relationship between the common law and Article 6.**[42] *R (Murungaru) v Secretary of State for the Home Department* [2008] EWCA Civ 1015 at [25]-[26] (ECHR not needed here, where common law due process sufficient); *R v Legal Aid Board, ex p Duncan* [2000] COD 159 (see transcript at [457]) ("The position in the law of England and Wales is in line with the jurisprudence of the European Court of Human Rights", referring to *Ashingdane v United Kingdom* (1985) 7 EHRR 528 at [57] and *R v Lord Chancellor, ex p Witham* [1998] QB 575, 585B); *R v Secretary of State for the Home Department, ex p Abid Jamil* [2000] Imm AR 51, 55 (Tucker J: "I am bound to say that in my view the portions of [Art 6] which apply to the present case do no more than reflect what has been part of the common law of England for many years, and add nothing to our already established practices. Of course a person is entitled to a fair hearing. That principle applies whether or not the Convention is incorporated"); *R v Cambridge University, ex p Beg* (1999) 11 Admin LR 505, 512g ("for present purposes I do not see any distinction between the right to a fair trial under the rules of natural justice at Common Law and the right to a fair trial under art 6 of the Convention which will be directly conferred when the Human Rights Act 1998 is brought into force in due course"); *R (Beeson) v Dorset County Council* [2002] EWCA Civ 1812 [2003] UKHRR 353 (Court of Appeal achieving a parallel between Art 6 and the common law by means of (a) a broad approach to whether there is a "determination of a civil right or obligation", so that Article 6 is engaged; but (b) respect for the statutory scheme applied fairly and reasonably, together with the check of judicial review); *Nwabueze v General Medical Council* [2000] 1 WLR 1760, 1775F (PC describing common law requirement of disclosure of advice to GMC, for comment by parties; "In this respect the requirements of the common law would appear to be at one with those of article 6 of the Convention"); *R v Secretary of State for the Home Department, ex p Q* [2000] UKHRR 386 (allocation to a particular prison not an infringement of right to a fair trial at common law, being the same for these purposes as Art 6); *R (Bright) v Central Criminal Court* [2001] 1 WLR 662, 679E (Judge LJ: "by now we surely fully appreciate that the principles to be found in articles 6 and 10 of the European Convention are bred in the bone of the common law"); *R v Looseley* [2001] UKHL 53 [2001] 1 WLR 2060 (no appreciable difference between well-established English law as to excluding evidence or staying criminal proceedings as an abuse of process and the right to a fair hearing under HRA:ECHR Art 6); *R (Bewry) v Norwich City Council* [2001] EWHC Admin 657 [2002] HRLR 21 (immaterial that decision pre-October 2000, because common law matching HRA:ECHR Art 6 as to independent and impartial tribunal); *R (Wooder) v Feggetter* [2002] EWCA Civ 554 [2003] QB 219 at [46] ("the common law sets high standards of due process in non-judicial settings to which the European Court of Human Rights at Strasbourg declines to apply article 6").

59.5.15 **Article 6 as a flexi-principle.** *R v Spear* [2001] EWCA Crim 3 [2001] QB 804 (CA) at [35] ("There is as we understand it no jurisprudence to show that the `guarantees' referred to in *Findlay's* case 24 EHRR 211, 244 and elsewhere must as a matter of law be formal, in some way cast in stone. Indeed the terms of paragraph 67 of the judgment in *Incal's* case 29 EHRR 449, 485-486 ... clearly imply the contrary. This is with respect no surprise: were it otherwise, the benign and flexible *principles* underlying article 6 would be turned into constricting inflexible *rules*, and the doing of justice would be ill-served") (HL is [2002] UKHL 31 [2003] 1 AC 734); *Begum v Tower Hamlets London Borough Council* [2003] UKHL 5 [2003] 2 AC 430 (approaching the Art 6 requirements of independence as being contextual, with judicial review readily ensuring compatibility in the context of an "administrative" decision-making context); *R (Vetterlein) v Hampshire County Council* [2001] EWHC Admin 560 [2002] Env LR 198 at [68] (Sullivan J: "A `fair' hearing does not necessarily require an oral hearing, much less does it require that there should be an opportunity to cross-examine.

---

[42] Martin Westgate [2006] JR 57.

Whether a particular procedure is 'fair' will depend upon all the circumstances, including the nature of the claimant's interest, the seriousness of the matter for him and the nature of any matters in dispute"); *R (M) v Commissioner of Police of the Metropolis* [2001] EWHC Admin 553 (Art 6 not a straitjacket, but operation depending on precise facts); *Pine v Law Society* [2001] EWCA Civ 1574 [2002] UKHRR 81 (whether inability to attend disciplinary tribunal because of impecuniosity involving a breach of Art 6 turning on the particular facts); *R (Fleurose) v Securities and Futures Authority* [2001] EWCA Civ 2015 at [14] (Schiemann LJ, speaking in the context of Art 6: "What fairness requires will vary from case to case"); *R (International Transport Roth GmbH) v Secretary of State for the Home Department* [2002] EWCA Civ 158 [2003] QB 728 at [84] (Laws LJ, referring to Art 6 as not being "absolute" in the sense of involving "uniform requirements"), [148] (referring to a "flexible interpretation", not a "straitjacket").

59.6 **Article 8: privacy.**[43] Violation of Article 8 involves public authorities unjustifiedly interfering with, or failing to protect against interference with, the basic right to respect for private and family life and home.

59.6.1 **Article 8: Right of respect for home, private and family life.** See HRA:ECHR Art 8 ("1. Everyone has the right to respect for his private and family life, his home and his correspondence. 2. There shall be no interference by a public authority with the exercise of this right except such as is in accordance with the law and is necessary in a democratic society in the interests of national security, public safety or the economic well-being of the country, for the prevention of disorder or crime, for the protection of health or morals, or for the protection of the rights and freedoms of others").

59.6.2 **Article 8: positive obligation.** *Anufrijeva v Southwark London Borough Council* [2003] EWCA Civ 1406 [2004] QB 1124 at [16] (Art 8 positive obligation often involving duty to introduce and operate a legislative/administrative scheme to protect private and family life); *R (Howard League for Penal Reform) v Secretary of State for the Home Department* [2002] EWHC 2497 (Admin) [2003] 1 FLR 484 at [66] (Art 8 imposing positive obligations on prison authorities); *R (Painter) v Carmarthenshire County Council Housing Benefit Review Board* [2001] EWHC Admin 308 [2002] HLR 447 at [16] (no positive obligation to provide welfare benefits for housing or protection of family life); *R (Ali) v Birmingham City Council* [2002] EWHC 1511 (Admin) [2002] HLR 913 at [77] (no positive obligation under Art 8 to provide accommodation).

59.6.3 **Article 8: procedural obligations.** *R (B) v Stafford Combined Court* [2006] EWHC 1645 (Admin) [2007] 1 WLR 1524 (disclosure of witness health records to criminal accused violating Art 8 because insufficient procedural safeguards); *CF v Secretary of State for the Home Department* [2004] EWHC 111 (Fam) [2004] 1 FCR 577 (unlawful decision to separate mother and child in prison) at [157] (Art 8 affording significant procedural safeguards, so that administrative decision-making requiring that parents' views be known and taken into account), [158] (equally applicable to child), [170] (here, child's interests not properly represented).

59.6.4 **Article 8: immigration illustrations.** *R v Secretary of State for the Home Department, ex p Arman Ali* [2000] Imm AR 134 (refusal of entry clearance preventing family from living together, a breach of Art 8); *R (Razgar) v Secretary of State for the Home Department* [2004] UKHL 27 [2004] 2 AC 368 (whether Art 8 engaged by mental health ill-effects of removal); *Z*

---

[43] Suzanne Lambert, Andrea Lindsay-Strugo & Jonathan Lewis [2008] JR 29.

v Secretary of State for the Home Department [2002] EWCA Civ 952 (decision to return homosexual asylum-seekers to face Zimbabwean sodomy laws an infringement of Art 8); *R (Harris) v Secretary of State for the Home Department* [2001] INLR 584 at [32] (refusal of leave to re-enter following brief visit to dying father abroad an unjustified interference with Art 8); *R (Montana) v Secretary of State for the Home Department* [2001] 1 WLR 552 (refusal to register a father's illegitimate son as a British citizen not an interference with family life); *R (Blackwood) v Secretary of State for the Home Department* [2003] EWHC 98 (Admin) [2003] HLR 638 (dispersal of claimant asylum-seeker disproportionate interference with physical and psychological integrity); *Anufrijeva v Southwark London Borough Council* [2003] EWCA Civ 1406 [2004] QB 1124 (whether mishandling of asylum claim breaching Art 8 because of damage to mental health); *R (Kpandang) v Secretary of State for the Home Department* [2004] EWHC 2130 (Admin) at [64] (short fast-track detention of asylum-seeker with UK family life necessary and proportionate).

59.6.5 Article 8: prisoner/detention illustrations. *R (G) v Nottinghamshire Healthcare NHS Trust* [2008] EWHC 1096 (Admin) (implementation of smoking ban in mental health detention unit Art 8-compatible); *R v Secretary of State for the Home Department, ex p Daly* [2001] UKHL 26 [2001] 2 AC 532 (blanket policy of searching legal correspondence in prisoners' absence violating ECHR Art 8); *R (Shaheen) v Secretary of State for Justice* [2008] EWHC 1195 (Admin) at [42] (refusal to consent to transfer of prisoner to home country fair and proportionate); *R (P and Q) v Secretary of State for the Home Department* [2001] EWCA Civ 1151 [2001] 1 WLR 2002 (policy of only permitting babies to remain with incarcerated mothers until 18 months old an impairment of family life but justified in the interests of punishment and prison management; but not to be applied rigidly); *R (N) v Ashworth Special Hospital Authority* [2001] EWHC Admin 339 [2001] HRLR 1010 (random monitoring of phone calls proportionate and compatible with Art 8); *R (H) v Ashworth Hospital Authority* [2001] EWHC Admin 872 [2002] 1 FCR 206 ('no condoms' policy not a breach of Art 8); *R (E) v Ashworth Hospital Authority* [2001] EWHC Admin 1089 (restriction on cross-dressing at mental institution necessary and proportionate, giving due weight to the views of the responsible experts); *R (Banks) v Governor of Wakefield Prison* [2001] EWHC Admin 917 [2002] 1 FCR 445 (uncle-nephew relationship not engaging Art 8 where policy preventing visit to uncle in prison); *R (D) v Secretary of State for the Home Department* [2003] EWHC 155 (Admin) [2003] 1 FLR 979 (separating misbehaving mother from child in prison mother and baby unit incompatible with Art 8 because of failure to address proportionality); *R (Szuluk) v Governor HM Prison Full Sutton* [2004] EWHC 514 (Admin) (disproportionate insistence that prison medical officer check correspondence between prisoner, having life-threatening medical condition, and his external medical advisers); *Napier v Scottish Ministers* [2004] UKHRR 881 (slopping out regime at Glasgow prison violating Art 8); *R (C) v Secretary of State for Justice* [2008] EWCA Civ 882 at [82] (Secure Training Centre restraint rules violating Art 8).

59.6.6 Article 8: data/information/publicity illustrations.[44] *R (Wood) v Metropolitan Police Commissioner* [2008] EWHC 1105 (Admin) at [60] (taking and retention of photos of protester attending arms company AGM not interfering with Art 8 rights), *R (S) v Chief Constable of South Yorkshire* [2004] UKIIL 39 [2004] 1 WLR 2196 (police retention of fingerprint and DNA information of acquitted defendants Art 8-compatible); *R (Hafner) v Westminster Magistrates Court* [2008] EWHC 524 (Admin) (obtaining of evidence Art 8-incompatible); *R (Robertson) v Secretary of State* [2003] EWHC 1760 (Admin) (restricted sale of electoral register Art 8-compatible); *R (S) v Swindon Borough Council* [2001] LGR 318 (investigation and disclosure of information justified despite acquittal on child abuse charges); *R (Forbes) v Secretary of*

---

[44] Nusrat Zar [2001] JR 161.

State for the Home Department [2006] EWCA Civ 962 [2006] 1 WLR 3075 (sex offence statutory notification requirements Art 8-compatible); *R (X) v Chief Constable of West Midlands Police* [2004] EWCA Civ 1068 [2005] 1 WLR 65 (disclosure of contents of Enhanced Criminal Record Certificate to a potential employer compatible with Art 8); *R (B) v Stafford Combined Court* [2006] EWHC 1645 (Admin) [2007] 1 WLR 1524 (disclosure of witness health records to criminal accused violating Art 8 because insufficient procedural safeguards); *R (Stone) v South East Coast Strategic Health Authority* [2006] EWHC 1668 (Admin) [2007] UKHRR 137 (publication justified of independent report into murderer's pre-crime care and treatment); *R (Ellis) v Chief Constable of Essex police* [2003] EWHC 1321 (Admin) [2003] 2 FLR 566 (Offender Naming Scheme); *In Re S (A Child) (Identification: Restrictions on Publication)* [2004] UKHL 47 [2005] 1 AC 593 (reporting of identity of mother convicted of murder justified); *R (S) v Plymouth City Council* [2002] EWCA Civ 388 [2002] 1 WLR 2583 (mother entitled to disclosure of confidential information about her child from local authority guardian).

59.6.7 Article 8: housing illustrations. *Doherty v Birmingham City Council* [2008] UKHL 57 [2008] 3 WLR 636 (whether Art 8 available as defence to possession proceedings against gypsies having no possessory entitlement); *Poplar Housing and Regeneration Community Association Ltd v Donoghue* [2001] EWCA Civ 595 [2002] QB 48 (mandatory statutory possession of assured shorthold tenancies proportionate); *St Brice v Southwark London Borough Council* [2001] EWCA Civ 1138 [2002] 1 WLR 1537 (enforcement of possession order without any further judicial determination compatible with Art 8); *Sheffield City Council v Smart* [2002] EWCA Civ 4 [2002] HLR 639 (possession of non-secure council housing compatible with Art 8(2)); *R (McLellan) v Bracknell Forest Borough Council* [2001] EWCA Civ 1510 [2002] QB 1129 (eviction of introductory tenant compatible with Art 8); *Anufrijeva v Southwark London Borough Council* [2003] EWCA Civ 1406 [2004] QB 1124 (inadequate accommodation not breaching Art 8 unless seriously inhibiting family life); *Lee v Leeds City Council* [2002] EWCA Civ 6 [2002] HLR 367 (Art 8 not imposing a general duty on council landlord to remedy damp from design defects in housing stock); *R (C) v Brent, Kensington and Chelsea and Westminster Mental Health NHS Trust* [2002] EWHC 181 (Admin) (2003) 6 CCLR 335 (decision to move long-term psychiatric patients to another home justified); *R (Price) v Carmarthenshire County Council* [2003] EWHC 42 (Admin) (council breaching Art 8 where housing decision based on unjustified dismissal of claimant gypsy's cultural aversion to conventional housing); *R (Yumsak) v Enfield London Borough Council* [2002] EWHC 280 (Admin) [2003] HLR 1 at [33] (dispersal housing of asylum-seeker breaching Art 8); *Chichester District Council v First Secretary of State* [2004] EWCA Civ 1248 [2005] 1 WLR 279 (planning enforcement notices violating gypsies' Art 8 rights).

59.6.8 Article 8: other illustrations. *Anufrijeva v Southwark London Borough Council* [2003] EWCA Civ 1406 [2004] QB 1124 (Art 8 and serious maladministration regarding provision of welfare support); *R (G) v Nottingham City Council* [2008] EWHC 400 (Admin) (Art 8-incompatible separation of mother and baby); *R (Countryside Alliance) v Attorney General* [2007] UKHL 52 [2008] 1 AC 719 (Art 8 not engaged by hunting ban); *R (Pretty) v Director of Public Prosecutions* [2001] UKHL 61 [2002] 1 AC 800 (Art 8 not engaged by question of assisted suicide); *R v P* [2002] 1 AC 146 (admissibility of telephone intercept evidence not a breach of Art 8); *Marcic v Thames Water Utilities Ltd* [2003] UKHL 66 [2004] 2 AC 42 (statutory sewerage scheme Art 8-compatible); *R (JB) v Haddock* [2006] EWCA Civ 961 [2006] HRLR 1237 (Art 8 and forced medical treatment); *Re B (A Minor)* [2001] UKHL 70 [2002] 1 WLR 258 (Art 8 and adoption orders); *R (Denson) v Child Support Agency* [2002] EWHC 154 (Admin) [2002] 1 FCR 460 (operation of Child Support Act Art 8-compatible); *R (Medway Council) v Secretary of State for Transport* [2002] EWHC 2516 (Admin) at [41] (Art 8 not engaged by consultation regarding airport runway capacity).

59.7 Article 10: expression. Article 10 is violated where freedom of expression and communication is unjustifiedly interfered with or inadequately protected by public authorities.

59.7.1 Article 10: Freedom of expression (speech). See HRA:ECHR Art 10 ("1. Everyone has the right to freedom of expression. This right shall include freedom to hold opinions and to receive and impart information and ideas without interference by public authority and regardless of frontiers. This Article shall not prevent States from requiring the licensing of broadcasting, television or cinema enterprises. 2. The exercise of these freedoms, since it carries with it duties and responsibilities, may be subject to such formalities, conditions, restrictions or penalties as are prescribed by law and are necessary in a democratic society, in the interests of national security, territorial integrity or public safety, for the prevention of disorder or crime, for the protection of health or morals, for the protection of the reputation or rights of others, for preventing the disclosure of information received in confidence, or for maintaining the authority and impartiality of the judiciary").

59.7.2 Article 10: media illustrations. *R (Malik) v Manchester Crown Court* [2008] EWHC 1362 (Admin) (unduly wide production order requiring journalist to reveal source material); *R (ProLife Alliance) v British Broadcasting Corporation* [2003] UKHL 23 [2004] 1 AC 185 (BBC's refusal to broadcast a party election broadcast on grounds of taste and decency not an unjustified interference with freedom of political speech, given the admitted legitimacy of a power to prevent the broadcast of "offensive material"); *R (Northern Cyprus Tourism Centre Ltd) v Transport for London* [2005] EWHC 1698 (Admin) [2005] UKHRR 1231 (refusal of Northern Cyprus adverts on London buses a breach of Art 10); *Ashworth Hospital Authority v MGN Ltd* [2002] UKHL 29 [2002] 1 WLR 2033 (circumstances to justify necessity for an order requiring newspaper to disclose identify of intermediary, in order to identify original source releasing medical information in breach of confidence); *Ex p Telegraph Group Plc* [2001] EWCA Crim 1075 [2001] 1 WLR 1983 (approach to reporting restrictions regarding criminal trial); *Ashdown v Telegraph Group Ltd* [2001] EWCA Civ 1142 [2002] Ch 149 (relationship between Art 10 and copyright legislation); *A v B* [2001] 1 WLR 2341 (freedom of expression and privacy in context of injunction to prevent `kiss and tell' publication); *Campbell v MGN Ltd* [2004] UKHL 22 [2004] 2 AC 457 (HL considering interrelationship between Art 10 and Art 8).

59.7.3 Article 10: inquiry illustrations.[45] *R (Wagstaff) v Secretary of State for Health* [2001] 1 WLR 292 (justification for prohibition on reporting of Shipman inquiry not "persuasive"); *R (Persey) v Secretary of State for the Environment, Food and Rural Affairs* [2002] EWHC 371 (Admin) [2003] QB 794 (decision to have closed inquiries into foot and mouth crisis not engaging Art 10; in any event no duty to have inquiry in public); *R (Howard) v Secretary of State for Health* [2002] EWHC 396 (Admin) [2003] QB 830 (compatible with Art 10 for inquiries into misconduct by doctors to be in private).

59.7.4 Article 10: prisoner/detainee illustrations. *R (Nilsen) v Governor of HMP Full Sutton* [2004] EWCA Civ 1540 [2005] 1 WLR 1028 (confiscation of notorious prisoner's autobiographical manuscript proportionate); *R (Hirst) v Secretary of State for the Home Department* [2002] EWHC 602 (Admin) [2002] 1 WLR 2929 (blanket ban on prisoner contact with the media by phone unjustified, not being necessary in a democratic society); *R (A) v Secretary of State for the Home Department* [2003] EWHC 2846 (Admin) [2004] HRLR 344

---

[45] Simon McKay [2002] JR 260; Philip Sales [2004] JR 173; Tim Buley [2004] JR 293.

(policy of requiring journalists' interviews with asylum-seekers' detained as suspected terrorists to be tape-recorded and within earshot of officials Art 10-compatible being required to safeguard national security and prison order/discipline).

59.7.5 **Article 10: commercial expression illustrations.** *R (Matthias Rath BV) v Advertising Standards Authority Ltd* [2001] HRLR 436 (to the extent that ASA interfering with claimant's freedom of speech, Code of Practice prescribed by law and satisfying necessity test);*R (British American Tobacco) v Secretary of State for Health* [2004] EWHC 2493 (Admin) (reach of exception to tobacco advertising ban justified and proportionate); cf. *Cable and Wireless (Dominica) Ltd v Marpin Telecoms and Broadcasting Co Ltd* [2001] 1 WLR 1123 (phone service monopoly interfering with competitors constitutional rights of freedom of expression and so required justification); *Douglas v Hello! Ltd (No.3)* [2005] EWCA Civ 595 [2006] QB 125 (balancing Art 8 and Art 10 in context of media photos and privacy).

59.7.6 **Article 10: other illustrations.** *Attorney General v Scotcher* [2005] UKHL 36 [2005] 1 WLR 1867 (statutory confidentiality of jury room deliberations Art 10-compatible, since allowing bona fide disclosures to court authorities); *R v Shayler* [2002] UKHL 11 [2003] 1 AC 247 (Official Secrets Act restrictions on any public immunity defence Art 10-compatible given other whistleblowing safeguards); *Percy v Director of Public Prosecutions* [2001] EWHC Admin 1125 (conviction for insulting behaviour in denigrating the US flag violating Art 10); *Campbell v MGN Ltd (No.2)* [2005] UKHL 61 [2005] 1 WLR 3394 (statutory rule allowing CFAs Art 10-compatible); cf. *Panday v Gordon* [2005] UKPC 36 [2006] 1 AC 427 (political free speech not overriding common law of defamation).

59.7.7 **Effect of remedy on freedom of expression.** <9.4.7>.

59.8 **Article 14: non-discrimination** A violation of Article 14 arises where, in a case falling within the ambit of another Convention right, there is an unjustified inequality of treatment, on some status-related basis, of persons in relevantly comparable positions.

59.8.1 **Article 14: Prohibition of discrimination.**[46] See HRA:ECHR Art 14 ("The enjoyment of the rights and freedoms set forth in this Convention shall be secured without discrimination on any ground such as sex, race, colour, language, religion, political or other opinion, national or social origin, association with a national minority, property, birth or other status"); *Ghaidan v Godin-Mendoza* [2004] UKHL 30 [2004] 2 AC 557 at [9] (Lord Nicholls, explaining the importance of Art 14).

59.8.2 **Article 14: the structured approach.** *Michalak v London Borough of Wandsworth* [2002] EWCA Civ 271 [2003] 1 WLR 617 at [20] (posing "four questions": "(i) Do the facts fall within the ambit of one or more of the substantive Convention provisions ...? (ii) If so, was there different treatment as respects that right between the complainant on the one hand and other persons put forward for comparison (`the chosen comparators') on the other? (iii) Were the chosen comparators in an analogous situation to the complainant's situation? (iv) If so, did the difference in treatment have an objective and reasonable justification: in other words, did it pursue a legitimate aim and did the differential treatment bear a reasonable relationship of proportionality to the aims sought to be achieved?"); *R (Carson) v Secretary of State for Work and Pensions* [2002] EWHC 978 (Admin) [2002] 3 All ER 994 (High Court) at [52] (Stanley Burnton J, adding "a fifth question": "is the basis for the different treatment of the complainant

---

[46] Corinna Ferguson [2008] JR 71.

as against that of the chosen comparators based on `any ground such as sex, race, colour, language ... or other status' within the meaning of Article 14?"); *Ghaidan v Godin-Mendoza* [2004] UKHL 30 [2004] 2 AC 557 at [133]-[134] (recognising the five *Michalak* questions); *R (S) v Chief Constable of South Yorkshire* [2004] UKHL 39 [2004] 1 WLR 2196 at [42] (Lord Steyn, recognising the five questions); *A v Secretary of State for the Home Department* [2004] UKHL 56 [2005] 2 AC 68 at [50] (applying *S* at [42]); *R (Carson) v Secretary of State for Work and Pensions* [2005] UKHL 37 [2006] 1 AC 173 at [29] (Lord Hoffmann, "not sure" that the *Michalak* questions "always helpful as a framework for reasoning"), [33] (here, "better not to use the *Michalak* framework"), [43] (Lord Rodger: inappropriate to "go mechanically through a series of questions"), [64] (Lord Walker: "the *Michalak* catechism, even in a corrected form, is not always the best approach"), [97] (Lord Carswell: "a broader and simpler approach to discrimination is required"); *R (Purja) v Ministry of Defence* [2003] EWCA Civ 1345 [2004] 1 WLR 289 at [47] (commenting that *Michalak* "structured approach" in the present case "not merely inconvenient, but positively misleading", referring to the "acute" difficulty of "separating out the individual *Michalak* questions").

59.8.3 Article 14: "within the ambit" of a Convention right. *Gallagher v Church of Jesus Christ of Latter-Day Saints* [2008] UKHL 56 [2008] 1 WLR 1852 at [13] & [31] (inapplicability of tax advantage not within the ambit of Art 9 for Art 14 purposes); *R (Clift) v Secretary of State for the Home Department* [2006] UKHL 54 [2007] 1 AC 484 at [13] (ambit connoting a situation where "a personal interest close to the core of such a right is infringed"); *R (Purja) v Ministry of Defence* [2003] EWCA Civ 1345 [2004] 1 WLR 289 at [42] (pension provision "within the ambit" of Art 1P (for Art 14 purposes) albeit a non-contributory benefit); *R (Morris) v Westminster City Council* [2005] EWCA Civ 1184 [2006] 1 WLR 505 (priority housing need of family falling within Art 8 ambit); *M v Secretary of State for Work and Pensions* [2006] UKHL 11 [2006] 2 AC 91 (legislation paying non-resident parent more child support when in homosexual not heterosexual relationship, not within the ambit of Art 8 or Art 1P); *R (Erskine) v Lambeth London Borough Council* [2003] EWHC 2479 (Admin) (statutory scheme regarding accommodation unfit for human habitation not sufficient link with Art 8); *R (Douglas) v North Tyneside Metropolitan Borough Council* [2003] EWCA Civ 1847 [2004] 1 WLR 2363 at [60] (student loan arrangements not within the ambit of Art 2P); *Secretary of State for Defence v Hopkins* [2004] EWHC 299 (Admin) (pension allowance requirement of pre-service cohabitation not within the ambit of Art 8 or Art 1P); *B v Secretary of State for Work and Pensions* [2005] EWCA Civ 929 [2005] 1 WLR 3796 at [22] (recovery of overpaid benefits not within the ambit of Art 1P); *R (British Civilian Internees - Far Eastern Region) v Secretary of State for Defence* [2003] EWCA Civ 473 [2003] QB 1397 at [82] (unfounded ex gratia compensation claims outside the scope of Art 1P); *X v Y* [2004] EWCA Civ 662 [2004] UKHRR 1172 (employee dismissal relying on criminal conduct in public place not within the ambit of Art 8).

59.8.4 Article 14: whether treatment based on "status". *AL (Serbia) v Secretary of State for the Home Department* [2008] UKHL 42 [2008] 1 WLR 1434 (persons who entered UK as unaccompanied minors having `status'); *R (Carson) v Secretary of State for Work and Pensions* [2005] UKHL 37 [2006] 1 AC 173 at [13] (residence assumed to be a "personal characteristic" so as to constitute a status), [52] (residence and age constituting status); *R (Countryside Alliance) v Attorney General* [2007] UKHL 52 [2008] 1 AC 719 at [24], [64], [130], [145] (no personal characteristic); *In re G (Adoption: Unmarried Couple)* [2008] UKHL 38 [2008] 3 WLR 76 (being unmarried a status); *R (RJM) v Secretary of State for Work and Pensions* [2007] EWCA Civ 614 [2007] 1 WLR 3067 at [46] (homelessness not a personal characteristic); *R (T) v Secretary of State for Health* [2002] EWHC 1887 (Admin) (2003) 6 CCLR 277 at [86] (status as asylum-seekers); *R (S) v Chief Constable of South Yorkshire* [2004] UKHL 39 [2004] 1 WLR 2196 (no "status" where persons previously the subject of police investigation); *In re Malcolm*

[2004] EWCA Civ 1748 [2005] 1 WLR 1238 at [27] (employed/self-employed not a status); *Lancashire County Council v Taylor* [2005] EWCA Civ 284 [2005] 1 WLR 266 at [49] (character of tenants' covenants not a status).

59.8.5 Article 14: whether "relevantly comparable" categories. *A v Secretary of State for the Home Department* [2004] UKHL 56 [2005] 2 AC 68 at [53] (non-nationals and UK nationals posing terrorist threat constituting analogous groups); *R (Purja) v Ministry of Defence* [2003] EWCA Civ 1345 [2004] 1 WLR 289 (differential treatment of ex-Gurkha (compared to other) members of the British army not Art 14-incompatible, the two groups not being in an analogous or relevantly comparable position), at [60], [65], [85], [87]; *Malcolm v Benedict Mackenzie* [2004] EWHC 339 (Ch) [2004] 1 WLR 1803 (retirement annuity contract and occupational pension not sufficiently similar for purposes of Art 14 with Art 1P); *R (Waite) v Hammersmith and Fulham London Borough Council* [2002] EWCA Civ 482 [2003] HLR 24 (housing benefit discrimination between different types of prison detainee compatible with Art 14, there being no sufficient analogy between convicted and remand prisoners); *R (Smith) v London Borough of Barking and Dagenham* [2002] EWHC 2400 (Admin) at [11] (gypsy caravan site occupants and conventional council tenants in sufficiently analogous situation to be Art 14 comparators); *Francis v Secretary of State for Work and Pensions* [2005] EWCA Civ 1303 [2006] 1 WLR 3202 at [19] (residence order and adoption order parents in relevantly similar situation).

59.8.6 Article 14: whether differential treatment. *Ghaidan v Godin-Mendoza* [2004] UKHL 30 [2004] 2 AC 557 (housing legislation treating homosexual surviving partners less favourably than heterosexual ones); *R (Roberts) v Parole Board* [2003] EWHC 3120 (Admin) [2004] 2 All ER 776 (no differential treatment as between mandatory and discretionary lifers, since same course (specially-appointed advocate) would have been available in a discretionary lifer case) (HL is at [2005] UKHL 45 [2005] 2 AC 738); *R (Amicus - MSF Section) v Secretary of State for Trade and Industry* [2004] EWHC 860 (Admin) [2004] ELR 311 at [199] (regulations producing no difference in treatment but rather conferring certain rights not to be discriminated against).

59.8.7 Article 14: whether justified. *In re G (Adoption: Unmarried Couple)* [2008] UKHL 38 [2008] 3 WLR 76 (bar on adoption by unmarried couples an unjustified bright line rule); *AL (Serbia) v Secretary of State for the Home Department* [2008] UKHL 42 [2008] 1 WLR 1434 (differential approach to indefinite leave to remain of those who entered UK as unaccompanied minors justified); *R (Clift) v Secretary of State for the Home Department* [2006] UKHL 54 [2007] 1 AC 484 (lack of objective justification for statutory disentitlement to parole board review of long-term prisoners liable to deportation); *Ghaidan v Godin-Mendoza* [2004] UKHL 30 [2004] 2 AC 557 (less favourable treatment of homosexual former partners lacking any rational or fair basis); *M v Secretary of State for Work and Pensions* [2006] UKHL 11 [2006] 2 AC 91 (former unequal treatment for homosexual and heterosexual relationships for child support justified where law and social values were in state of transition); *R (Morris) v Westminster City Council* [2005] EWCA Civ 1184 [2006] 1 WLR 505 at [48] (not a logical or proportionate response to problems of benefit tourism and unlawful migration); *R (Carson) v Secretary of State for Work and Pensions* [2005] UKHL 37 [2006] 1 AC 173 at [41] (justification from "need for legal certainty and a workable rule"); *AL (Serbia) v Secretary of State for the Home Department* [2006] EWCA Civ 1619 [2007] HRLR 143 (family amnesty policy discriminating against unaccompanied minors but justified); *R (Wilson) v Wychavon District Council* [2007] EWCA Civ 52 [2007] QB 801 at [73] (justified bright line rule); *R (Gurung) v Ministry of Defence* [2008] EWHC 1496 (Admin) at [77] (backdated pension cut-off justified and proportionate).

59.8.8 **Article 14: illustrations.**
(A) VIOLATION. *A v Secretary of State for the Home Department* [2004] UKHL 56 [2005] 2 AC 68 (derogation and detention without trial violating Art 14 (with Art 5) because targeting non-nationals only: unjustified discrimination on nationality grounds); *R (Wilkinson) v Commissioners of Inland Revenue* [2005] UKHL 30 [2005] 1 WLR 1718 (widow's bereavement allowance discriminatory); *Bellinger v Bellinger* [2003] UKHL 21 [2003] 2 AC 467 (statutory requirement that marriage be between male and female declared incompatible with Art 14 read with Art 8); *R (Morris) v Westminster City Council* [2005] EWCA Civ 1184 [2006] 1 WLR 505 (statutory disentitlement to priority housing need based on dependent child's immigration control status constituting unjustified discrimination based on national origin); *R (L) v Manchester City Council* [2001] EWHC Admin 707 (2002) 5 CCLR 268 (breach of Art 14 where short-term foster carer payments set at lower level for relatives/friends than other foster carers); *R (Middlebrook Mushrooms Ltd) v Agricultural Wages Board of England and Wales* [2004] EWHC 1447 (Admin) at [85] (exclusion of mushroom pickers from reduced minimum wage for manual harvest workers an unjustified inequality of treatment of their employers, in breach of HRA:ECHR Art 14 with Art 1P); *Francis v Secretary of State for Work and Pensions* [2005] EWCA Civ 1303 [2006] 1 WLR 3202 (maternity grant for adoption order not residence order parents violating Art 14 with Art 8).
(B) NO VIOLATION. *R (Hooper) v Secretary of State for Work and Pensions* [2005] UKHL 29 [2005] 1 WLR 1681 (previous payments of widows pension justified; s.6(2) defence regarding widows payments and widowed mothers allowance); *Wilkinson v Kitzinger* [2006] EWHC 2022 (Fam) [2006] HRLR 1141 at [122] (non-recognition of same-sex partnerships as marriage justified difference in treatment); *R (Pretty) v Director of Public Prosecutions* [2001] UKHL 61 [2002] 1 AC 800 (Art 14 not engaged in refusing to rule out prosecution for assisted suicide, and no discrimination); *R (Gangera) v Hounslow London Borough Council* [2003] EWHC 794 (Admin) [2003] HLR 1028 (rules limiting succession to a secure tenancy to a single assignment not a breach of Art 14 with Art 8).

59.9 **Article 1P: property-interference.** Violation of Article 1P arises where there is a deprivation of property or control of its use, and public authorities are unable to justify their action (or relevant inaction).

59.9.1 **Using the shorthand "1P".** For "Article 1P" to describe ECHR Art 1 Protocol I: *R (Carson) v Secretary of State for Work and Pensions* [2003] EWCA Civ 797 [2003] 3 All ER 577 (CA) at [1]; *R (Purja) v Ministry of Defence* [2003] EWCA Civ 1345 [2004] 1 WLR 289.

59.9.2 **Article 1P (Article 1 Protocol I): protection of property.**[47] See HRA:ECHR Art 1P ("Every natural or legal person is entitled to the peaceful enjoyment of his possessions. No one shall be deprived of his possessions except in the public interest and subject to the conditions provided for by law and by the general principles of international law. The preceding provisions shall not, however, in any way impair the right of a State to enforce such laws as it deems necessary to control the use of property in accordance with the general interest or to secure the payment of taxes or other contributions or penalties").

59.9.3 **Article 1P illustrations.** *R (Countryside Alliance) v Attorney General* [2007] UKHL 52 [2008] 1 AC 719 (Hunting Act Art 1P-compatible); *Belfast City Council v Miss Behavin' Ltd* [2007] UKHL 19 [2007] 1 WLR 1420 (refusal of sex shop licence not violating Art 1P); *Wilson v First County Trust Ltd* [2003] UKHL 40 [2004] 1 AC 816 (automatic unenforceability of non-

---

[47] Philip Sales [2006] JR 141.

compliant consumer credit agreement compatible with Art 1P); *R (Federation of Tour Operators) v HM Treasury* [2008] EWCA Civ 752 (increased air passenger duty not an individual and excessive burden on tour operators); *R (RJM) v Secretary of State for Work and Pensions* [2007] EWCA Civ 614 [2007] 1 WLR 3067 (non-contributory benefit a possession); *R (International Transport Roth GmbH) v Secretary of State for the Home Department* [2002] EWCA Civ 158 [2003] QB 728 (immigration carrier vehicle detention violating Art 1P); *Lindsay v Commissioners of Customs and Excise* [2002] EWCA Civ 267 [2002] 1 WLR 1766 (confiscation of tobacco-smuggling cars disproportionate under Art 1P); *Marcic v Thames Water Utilities Ltd* [2003] UKHL 66 [2004] 2 AC 42 (statutory sewerage remedies Art 1P-compatible); *R (Kelsall) v Secretary of State for the Environment, Food and Rural Affairs* [2003] EWHC 459 (Admin) at [62] (fur farmer compensation scheme Art 1P-incompatible); *R (London and Continental Stations and Property Ltd) v Rail Regulator* [2003] EWHC 2607 (Admin) (statutory direction not an excessive burden); *R (Fisher) v English Nature* [2004] EWCA Civ 663 [2005] 1 WLR 147 (no Art 1P violation in notifying site of special scientific interest); *R (Clays Lane Housing Cooperative Ltd) v Housing Corporation* [2004] EWCA Civ 1658 [2005] 1 WLR 2229 (compulsory transfer of housing stock not an Art 1P violation); *Rowland v Environment Agency* [2003] EWCA Civ 1885 [2005] Ch 1 (legitimate expectation an Art 1P possession, but interference justified and proportionate); *R (Smith) v Secretary of State for Defence* [2004] EWHC 1797 (Admin) [2005] 1 FLR 97 at [27] (pension-sharing legislation defining, rather than interfering with, claimant's welfare possession); *R (Trailer and Marina (Leven) Ltd) v Secretary of State for the Environment, Food and Rural Affairs* [2004] EWCA Civ 1580 [2005] 1 WLR 1267 (restricted compensation for affected landowners in nature conservation legislation not manifestly disproportionate); *R (Malik) v Waltham Forest Primary Care Trust* [2007] EWCA Civ 265 [2007] 1 WLR 2092 (right to practise in NHS from inclusion in list not a possession); *R (Murungaru) v Secretary of State for the Home Department* [2008] EWCA Civ 1015 (contractual rights not property rights here), [34] (withdrawal of visa an immigration control matter, not a property interference).

59.10 **Further Convention rights and provisions.**The HRA guarantees protection against violation of other important listed Convention rights, ranging from slavery (Article 4) to the right to vote (Article 3P). There are also ancillary ECHR provisions which inform issues of HRA-violation, whether because (1) the HRA says so (eg. HRA s.1 referring to Articles 16-18) or (2) the very domestication of Convention rights so suggests (eg. Articles 1, 13 and 15).

59.10.1 **Article 4: freedom from slavery/forced labour.**[48] See HRA:ECHR Art 4 ("1. No one shall be held in slavery or servitude. 2. No one shall be required to perform forced or compulsory labour. 3. For the purpose of this Article the term `forced or compulsory labour' shall not include: (a) any work required to be done in the ordinary course of detention imposed according to the provisions of Article 5 of this Convention or during conditional release from such detention; (b) any service of a military character or, in the case of conscientious objectors in countries where they are recognised, service exacted instead of compulsory military service; (c) any service exacted in case of an emergency or calamity threatening the life or well-being of the community; (d) any work or service which forms part of normal civic obligations"); *R (Ali) v Immigration Appeal Tribunal* [2004] EWHC 98 (Admin) (adjudicator was entitled to characterise feared ill-treatment at the hands of a Somali dominant clan as protectionist social patronage and not constituting slavery under Art 4).

---

[48] Zoe Leventhal [2005] JR 237.

59.10.2 **Article 7: no punishment without law.**[49] See HRA:ECHR Art 7 ("1. No one shall be held guilty of any criminal offence on account of any act or omission which did not constitute a criminal offence under national or international law at the time when it was committed. Nor shall a heavier penalty be imposed than the one that was applicable at the time the criminal offence was committed. 2. This Article shall not prejudice the trial and punishment of any person for any act or omission which, at the time when it was committed, was criminal according to the general principles of law recognised by civilised nations"); *R (Uttley) v Secretary of State for the Home Department* [2004] UKHL 38 [2004] 1 WLR 2278 (statutory licence provisions post-dating relevant offence Art 7-compatible); *Togher v Revenue and Customs Prosecution Office* [2007] EWCA Civ 686 [2008] QB 476 (confiscation enforcement Art 7-incompatible but Act incapable of compatible interpretation); *R v Field* [2002] EWCA Crim 2913 [2003] 1 WLR 882 (disqualification orders applicable to offences predating the statutory power without offending Art 7, being preventative not punitive); *Gough v Chief Constable of Derbyshire* [2002] EWCA Civ 351 [2002] QB 1213 (football banning orders compatible with Art 7); *R (McFetrich v Secretary of State for the Home Department* [2003] EWHC 1542 (Admin) [2003] 4 All ER 1093 (setting of tariff by reference to English judge not Art 7-incompatible in the case of a prisoner transferred from Scotland to England); *R v R* [2003] EWCA Crim 2199 [2004] 1 WLR 490 (statutory power to extend licence period to whole sentence preventative and so exercisable when sentencing for an offence predating the power, despite Art 7); *R v C* [2004] EWCA Crim 292 [2004] 1 WLR 2098 (conviction for marital rape, committed prior to Courts' recognition of such an offence, not Art 7-incompatible); *R v Rimmington* [2005] UKHL 63 [2006] 1 AC 459 at [35]-[36] (common law offence of public nuisance sufficiently clear and predictable for Art 7 purposes).

59.10.3 **Article 9: Freedom of thought, conscience and religion.**[50] See HRA:ECHR Art 9 ("1. Everyone has the right to freedom of thought, conscience and religion; this right includes freedom to change his religion or belief and freedom, either alone or in community with others and in public or private, to manifest his religion or belief, in worship, teaching, practice and observance. 2. Freedom to manifest one's religion or beliefs shall be subject only to such limitations as are prescribed by law and are necessary in a democratic society in the interests of public safety, for the protection of public order, health or morals, or for the protection of the rights and freedoms of others"); HRA s.13 ("(1) If a court's determination of any question arising under this Act might affect the exercise by a religious organisation (itself or its members collectively) of the Convention right to freedom of thought, conscience and religion, it must have particular regard to the importance of that right. (2) In this section `court' includes a tribunal"); *R (Williamson) v Secretary of State for Education and Employment* [2002] EWCA Civ 1926 [2003] QB 1300 (CA) at [48], [181], [313] (doubting whether Christian school a "religious organisation", and considering whether s.13 materially adding to Art 9); *R (Amicus - MSF Section) v Secretary of State for Trade and Industry* [2004] EWHC 860 (Admin) [2004] ELR 311 at [41] (duty to have regard, but no greater weight than ECHR Art 9 rights); *R (Williamson) v Secretary of State for Education and Employment* [2005] UKHL 15 [2005] 2 AC 246 (statutory prohibition on corporal punishment, preventing disciplinary measures at Christian school administered in the name of biblical observance, a justified interference with Art 9); *R (SB) v Headteacher and Governors of Denbigh High School* [2006] UKHL 15 [2007] 1 AC 100 (school uniform policy barring jilbab compatible with Art 9 because other schools available and justified in any event); *R (Playfoot) v Governing Body of Millais School* [2007] EWHC 1698 (Admin) [2007] 3 FCR 754 (chastity ring not a manifestation of belief); *R (Ullah)*

---

[49] Sarah Hannett [2007] JR 112.

[50] Thomas Cross & John Beckett [2007] JR 75; Alexander Horne [2008] JR 101.

v Secretary of State for the Home Department [2004] UKHL 26 [2004] 2 AC 323 (Art 9 capable of being engaged by immigration removal to country where flagrant denial of religious freedoms); *Copsey v WWB Devon Clays Ltd* [2005] EWCA Civ 932 [2005] HRLR 1136 (not unfair dismissal where religion-based refusal to abide by working arrangements); *Khan v RAF Summary Appeal Court* [2004] EWHC 2230 (Admin) [2004] HRLR 1212 (no manifestation of conscientious objection until military authorities formally informed); *R (Suryananda) v Welsh Ministers* [2007] EWCA Civ 893 (slaughter of temple bullock Art 9-compatible being necessary and proportionate).

59.10.4 **Article 11: Freedom of assembly and association.** See HRA:ECHR Art 11 ("1. Everyone has the right to freedom of peaceful assembly and to freedom of association with others, including the right to form and to join trade unions for the protection of his interests. 2. No restrictions shall be placed on the exercise of these rights other than such as are prescribed by law and are necessary in a democratic society in the interests of national security or public safety, for the prevention of disorder or crime, for the protection of health or morals or for the protection of the rights and freedoms of others. This Article shall not prevent the imposition of lawful restrictions on the exercise of these rights by members of the armed forces, of the police or of the administration of the State"); *R (Laporte) v Chief Constable of Gloucestershire* [2006] UKHL 55 [2007] 2 AC 105 (preventing attendance at anti-war demonstration violating Art 11); *R (L) v Governors of J School* [2001] EWHC Admin 318 [2001] ELR 411 at [35] (separation of one pupil from others not engaging Art 11); *R (National Union of Journalists) v Central Arbitration Committee* [2004] EWHC 2612 (Admin) (rejection of union recognition not violating Art 11); *R (Countryside Alliance) v Attorney General* [2007] UKHL 52 [2008] 1 AC 719 (Art 11 not engaged by hunting ban); *R (Staff Side of the Police Negotiating Board) v Secretary of State for the Home Department* [2008] EWHC 1173 (Admin) at [49] (albeit police precluded from union membership, Art 11 not requiring Secretary of State to accept tribunal's pay recommendations).

59.10.5 **Article 12: Right to marry.** See HRA:ECHR Art 12 ("Men and women of marriageable age have the right to marry and to found a family, according to the national laws governing the exercise of this right"); *R (Baiai) v Secretary of State for the Home Department* [2008] UKHL 53 [2008] 3 WLR 549 (certified approval of all immigration control marriages violating Art 12); *R (Mellor) v Secretary of State for the Home Department* [2001] EWCA Civ 472 [2002] QB 13 (refusal to allow prisoner access to artificial insemination compatible with Art 12); *Wilkinson v Kitzinger* [2006] EWHC 2022 (Fam) [2006] HRLR 1141 (Art 12 inapplicable to statutory non-recognition of same-sex civil partnership as marriage).

59.10.6 **Article 2P (Article 2 Protocol I): Right to education.** See HRA:ECHR Art 2P ("No person shall be denied the right to education. In the exercise of any functions which it assumes in relation to education and to teaching, the State shall respect the right of parents to ensure such education and teaching in conformity with their own religious and philosophical convictions"); HRA s.15 (designated reservations), Schedule 3 Part II (UK reservation of 20th March 1952: "declar[ing] that, in view of certain provisions of the Education Acts in the United Kingdom, the principle affirmed in the second sentence of Article 2 is accepted by the United Kingdom only so far as it is compatible with the provision of efficient instruction and training, and the avoidance of unreasonable public expenditure") and section 17 (periodic review of designated reservations); *R (Williamson) v Secretary of State for Education and Employment* [2005] UKHL 15 [2005] 2 AC 246 at [36] (education under Art 2P "wide enough to include the manner in which discipline is maintained in a school"); *A v Head Teacher and Governors of Lord Grey School* [2006] UKHL 14 [2006] 2 AC 363 (exclusion from school not a violation, Art 2P being concerned with non-discriminatory access to state education, not attendance at a particular school); *R (SB) v Headteacher and Governors of Denbigh High School* [2006] UKHL

15 [2007] 1 AC 100 (school uniform policy barring jilbab compatible with Art 2P); *R (K) v London Borough of Newham* [2002] EWHC 405 (Admin) [2002] ELR 390 (school admissions decision unlawful because of failure to elicit and give due weight to genuine religious conviction on which parental choice based) at [29] (Collins J: "since the coming into effect of the Human Rights Act 1998, the religious conviction of a parent is something to which due weight must be given in considering admission to a particular school"); *R v Department for Education and Employment, ex p Begbie* [2000] 1 WLR 1115, 1128F-1129B (no breach of Art 2 Protocol I where removal of scheme for assisted places in private schools); *R v Carmarthenshire County Council, ex p White* [2001] ELR 172 at [55] (in a school transport case, no material difference between Art 2 of Protocol I); *R v Birmingham City Council, ex p Youngson* [2001] LGR 218 at [33] (refusal to fund place at residential dance school not an interference with the right to education under Art 2 Protocol I); *R (Holub) v Secretary of State for the Home Department* [2001] 1 WLR 1359 (Art 2 of Protocol I not engaged where removal under legitimate immigration control); *R (Khundakji) v Cardiff County Council* [2003] EWHC 436 (Admin) [2003] ELR 495 at [53] (Art 2P adding nothing to present case of school admissions refusal); *R (Douglas) v North Tyneside Metropolitan Borough Council* [2003] EWCA Civ 1847 [2004] 1 WLR 2363 (Art 2P applying to tertiary education, but not to student loan arrangements).

59.10.7 Article 3P (Article 3 of Protocol I): Right to free elections. See HRA:ECHR Art 3P ("The High Contracting Parties undertake to hold free elections at reasonable intervals by secret ballot, under conditions which will ensure the free expression of the opinion of the people in the choice of the legislature"); *R (Pearson) v Secretary of State for the Home Department* [2001] EWHC Admin 239 (statutory bar on prisoners voting compatible with Art 3P); *R (Robertson) v City of Wakefield Metropolitan Council* [2001] EWHC Admin 915 [2002] QB 1052 (practice of selling Electoral Register to commercial interests contravening Art 3P); *R (Robertson) v Secretary of State* [2003] EWHC 1760 (Admin) (no contravention of Art 3P where electoral register sold only for credit reference purposes and not direct marketing purposes, being a limited interference well within wide margin of appreciation); *Knight v Nicholls* [2004] EWCA Civ 68 [2004] 1 WLR 1653 at [29] (Tuckey LJ: "States have a wide margin as to how they fulfil the obligation under Article 3 of the First Protocol"); *R (Barclay) v Secretary of State for Justice* [2008] EWHC 1354 (Admin) (legislative reform for Sark Art 3P-compatible).

59.10.8 Protocol VI and the death penalty (Articles 1-2 Protocol VI). See Protocol VI Art 1 ("The death penalty shall be abolished. No one shall be condemned to such penalty or executed"), Art 2 ("A State may make provision in its law for the death penalty in respect of acts committed in time of war or of imminent threat of war; such penalty shall be applied only in the instances laid down in the law and in accordance with its provisions. The State shall communicate to the Secretary General of the Council of Europe the relevant provisions of that law"); *St John v United States of America* [2001] EWHC Admin 543 [2002] QB 613 (relevance of Protocol VI Art 1 in context of extradition to face the death penalty).

59.10.9 Additional restrictions: Articles 16-18 (codified). See HRA s.1(1) <9,2,3> (meaning of "Convention rights"); HRA:ECHR Art 16 ("Nothing in Articles 10, 11 and 14 shall be regarded as preventing the High Contracting Parties from imposing restrictions on the political activity of aliens"); *R (Farrakhan) v Secretary of State for the Home Department* [2002] EWCA Civ 606 [2002] QB 1391 at [70] (treating Art 16 as being "directed at permissible restrictions on the political rights of aliens in the host country and ... designed to preclude a discrimination challenge where less favourable treatment is accorded to aliens than others after admission"); Art 17 ("Nothing in this Convention may be interpreted as implying for any State, group or person any right to engage in any activity or perform any act aimed at the destruction of any of the rights and freedoms set forth herein or at their limitation to a greater extent than is provided for in the Convention"); Art 18 ("The restrictions permitted under this Convention to the said rights and freedoms shall not be applied for any purpose other than those for which they have been prescribed").

59.10.10 **Article 1 (uncodified): territoriality.**[51] <9.1.13>.

59.10.11 **Article 13 (uncodified): the right to an effective remedy.** See ECHR Art 13 ("Everyone whose rights and freedoms as set forth in this Convention are violated shall have an effective remedy before a national authority notwithstanding that the violation has been committed by persons acting in an official capacity"); *In re S (Care Order: Implementation of Care Plan)* [2002] UKHL 10 [2002] 2 AC 291 at [59] (failure to provide an effective remedy for breach of Art 8 not itself a breach of Art 8), [60] (Art 13 not a Convention right); *R (L) v Secretary of State for the Home Department* [2003] EWCA Civ 25 [2003] 1 WLR 1230 at [23] (where decisions made during period of non-promulgation of new legislation, commenting as to the possible engagement of Art 13 that it "is not scheduled to the Human Rights Act"); <32.3.14> (whether judicial review complies with Art 13).

59.10.12 **Article 15: the State's right of emergency derogation.** See ECHR Art 15 ("(1) In time of war or other public emergency threatening the life of the nation any High Contracting Party may take measures derogating from its obligations under this Convention to the extent strictly required by the exigencies of the situation, provided that such measures are not inconsistent with its other obligations under international law. (2) No derogation from Article 2, except in respect of deaths resulting from lawful acts of war, or from Articles 3, 4 (paragraph 1) and 7 shall be made under this provision. (3) Any High Contracting Party availing itself of this right of derogation shall keep the Secretary General of the Council of Europe fully informed of the measures which it has taken and the reasons therefor. It shall also inform the Secretary General of the Council of Europe when such measures have ceased to operate and the provisions of the Convention are again being fully executed"); HRA s.14 (derogations); *A v Secretary of State for the Home Department* [2004] UKHL 56 [2005] 2 AC 68 (Art 15 relevant in testing, and ultimately quashing, Derogation Order permitting detention without trial of non-nationals, as not being "strictly necessary"), [10] (Art 15 not scheduled to the HRA but dealt with by HRA s.14), cf. [146] (Lord Scott, describing Art 15 as not part of domestic law).

---

[51] Sarah Wilkinson [2004] JR 243.

> **P60 Procedural unfairness.** A body must adopt a fair
> procedure, giving those affected a fair and informed say.

60.1 The basic concept of fairness
60.2 Procedural fairness as a flexi-principle
60.3 Procedural fairness: supplementing the legislative scheme
60.4 Procedural ultra vires
60.5 The basic right to be heard
60.6 Adequate consultation
60.7 The basic right to be informed
60.8 Other rights of procedural fairness

60.1 The basic concept of fairness.[52] The common law imposes minimum standards of procedural fairness or due process (natural justice). This concept, and its twin pillar (the rule against bias), have been reinforced by the procedural guarantees in the Human Rights Act (HRA:ECHR Art 6).

60.1.1 **Natural justice as a fundamental principle.** <7.6.3>.

60.1.2 **Twin pillars: impartiality and fair hearing.** *Kanda v Government of Malaya* [1962] AC 322, 337 (Lord Denning: "The rule against bias is one thing. The right to be heard is another. Those two rules are the essential characteristics of what is often called natural justice. They are the twin pillars supporting it"); *O'Reilly v Mackman* [1983] 2 AC 237, 279F-G (Lord Diplock: "the two fundamental rights accorded to him by the rules of natural justice or fairness, viz. to have afforded to him a reasonable opportunity of learning what is alleged against him and of putting forward his own case in answer to it, and to the absence of personal bias against him on the part of the person by whom the decision falls to be made"); *Chief Constable of the North Wales Police v Evans* [1982] 1 WLR 1155, 1164H ("the rules of natural justice"); *R (D) v Independent Appeal Panel of Bromley London Borough Council* [2007] EWCA Civ 1010 [2008] LGR 267 at [6] (failure of "natural justice").

60.1.3 **Traditional link with decisions affecting rights/expectations.** *R v Secretary of State for the Environment, ex p Hammersmith & Fulham London Borough Council* [1991] 1 AC 521, 598D-G (Lord Bridge, referring to the existence of "a person whose `rights' in the broadest sense, are liable to be detrimentally affected by any action taken by the Secretary of State" as being "the necessary assumption on which to base an argument ... that the court must supplement the procedural requirements which the Act itself stipulates by implying additional requirements said to be necessary to ensure that the principles of natural justice are observed"); *Attorney-General v Ryan* [1980] AC 718, 727D ("the Minister was a person having legal authority to determine a question affecting the rights of individuals. This being so it is a necessary implication that he is required to observe the principles of natural justice when exercising that authority"); *Mahon v Air New Zealand Ltd* [1984] AC 808, 820H ("adversely affected"); *Pearlberg v Varty* [1972] 1 WLR 534, 546B-C (Viscount Dilhorne: "judicial determination affecting a person's rights and liabilities"); *R v Norfolk County Council, ex p M* [1989] QB 619, 628F-G; *Public Disclosure Commission v Isaacs* [1988] 1 WLR 1043 (decision to reject claimant's complaint not adverse to him, so no duty to allow opportunity comment on material being taken into account).

---

[52] This paragraph in a previous edition was cited in *Abrahaem v General Medical Council* [2008] EWHC 183 (Admin) at [41].

60.1.4 Traditional link with being "condemned". *General Medical Council v Spackman* [1943] AC 627, 636 (Viscount Simon LC: "the accused should not be condemned without being first given a fair chance of exculpation"); *O'Reilly v Mackman* [1983] 2 AC 237, 276B-C (Lord Diplock: "the requirement that a person who is charged with having done something which, if proved to the satisfaction of a statutory tribunal, has consequences that will, or may, affect him adversely, should be given a fair opportunity of hearing what is alleged against him and of presenting his own case, is so fundamental to any civilised legal system that it is to be presumed that Parliament intended that a failure to observe it should render null and void any decision reached in breach of this requirement"); *Furnell v Whangarei High Schools Board* [1973] AC 660, 682D (Lord Morris: "One of the principles of natural justice is that a man should not be condemned unheard. But the sub-committee do not condemn. Nor do they criticise"); *Ridge v Baldwin* [1964] AC 40, 113-114 (Lord Morris: "It is well established that the essential requirements of natural justice at least include that before someone is condemned he is to have an opportunity of defending himself, and in order that he may do so that he is to be made aware of the charges or allegations or suggestions which he has to meet... [H]ere is something which is basic to our system: the importance of upholding it far transcends the significance of any particular case").

60.1.5 The *McInnes* categories: forfeiture, application, expectation. *McInnes v Onslow Fane* [1978] 1 WLR 1520, 1529A-C (Sir Robert Megarry V-C, distinguishing between three situations: "First, there are what may be called the forfeiture cases. In these, there is a decision which takes away some existing right or position, as where a member of an organisation is expelled or a licence is revoked. Second, at the other extreme there are what may be called the application cases. These are cases where the decision merely refuses to grant the applicant the right or position that he seeks, such as membership of the organisation, or a licence to do certain acts. Third, there is an intermediate category, which may be called the expectation cases, which differ from the application cases only in that the applicant has some legitimate expectation from what has already happened that his application will be granted. This head includes cases where an existing licence-holder applies for a renewal of his licence, or a person already elected or appointed to some position seeks confirmation from some confirming authority"); *Naidike v Attorney-General of Trinidad and Tobago* [2004] UKPC 49 [2005] 1 AC 538 at [24] ("between on the one extreme cases of forfeiture and on the other mere application cases there lies an intermediate category of cases where the applicant seeks the renewal or confirmation of some benefit ... which properly ought not to be denied him without good reason and without his having a chance to satisfy whatever concerns the decision maker may have"); *R (Quark Fishing Ltd) v Secretary of State for Foreign and Commonwealth Affairs* [2001] EWHC Admin 1174 (Administrative Court) at [67]-[68] (fairness applying even though an "application" case under the *McInnes* classification) (CA is at [2002] EWCA Civ 1409).

60.1.6 Duty to act fairly. *Council of Civil Service Unions v Minister for the Civil Service* [1985] AC 374, 414G-H (Lord Roskill, referring to: "what are often called `principles of natural justice'" as being a "phrase ... no doubt hallowed by time and much judicial repetition, but it is a phrase often widely misunderstood and therefore as often misused. That phrase perhaps might now be allowed to find a permanent resting-place and be better replaced by speaking of a duty to act fairly"), 399A-B (Lord Fraser: "subject to an implied obligation to act fairly. (Such an obligation is sometimes referred to as an obligation to obey the rules of natural justice, but that is a less appropriate description, at least when applied, as in the present case, to a power which is executive and not judicial)"); *R v Oxford Regional Mental Health Review Tribunal, ex p Secretary of State for the Home Department* [1988] AC 120, 126H (Lord Bridge: "[a] decision ... made in breach of the rules of natural justice, which in a word means unfairly"); *Cheall v Association of Professional Executive Clerical & Computer Staff* [1983] 2 AC 180, 190C-D (Lord Diplock, agreeing with the description of natural justice as "fair play in action"); *R v*

Independent Television Commission, ex p Virgin Television Limited [1996] EMLR 318 ("duty to be even-handed").

60.1.7 **"Due process".** *R (Murungaru) v Secretary of State for the Home Department* [2008] EWCA Civ 1015 at [26] & [39] (referring to "a common law due process claim"); *Neill v North Antrim Magistrates' Court* [1992] 1 WLR 1220, 1230D-E (Lord Mustill, identifying "what in the vocabulary of judicial review would be called a breach of natural justice... There has been a material irregularity in the conduct of the committal; or, if one prefers the transatlantic terminology, a want of due process"); *R v Secretary of State for the Home Department, ex p Hindley* [2000] 1 QB 152 (CA), 163B-164H (Lord Woolf MR, referring to the doctrine of "due process", having both procedural and substantive aspects); *R (Ramda) v Secretary of State for the Home Department* [2002] EWHC 1278 (Admin) at [8] (Sedley LJ, using the phrase "due process" to describe requirements of procedural fairness); *Higgs v Minister of National Security* [2000] 2 AC 228, 246A (referring to "the ordinary common law concept of due process" and its implication into the Constitution of the Bahamas as being "in accordance with law and general principles of fairness"); *R v London Borough of Camden, ex p Paddock* [1995] COD 130 (see transcript) (referring to "due process" and material irregularity); *R v Secretary of State for the Home Department, ex p Moon* (1996) 8 Admin LR 477, 485C (Sedley J, referring to "the safeguards of due process"); *R v Secretary of State for the Environment, ex p Kirkstall Valley Campaign Ltd* [1996] 3 All ER 304, 324f (Sedley J: "Since *Ridge v Baldwin*, although not without occasional deviations, public law has returned to the broad highway of due process across the full range of justiciable decision-making"); *Flannery v Halifax Estate Agencies Ltd* [2000] 1 WLR 377, 381G (courts' duty to give reasons "a function of due process, and therefore of justice"); *Thomas v Baptiste* [2000] 2 AC 1 (constitutional right of due process).

60.1.8 **Material irregularity.** *R v Number 8 Area Committee of the Legal Aid Board, ex p Megarry* [1994] PIQR 476 ("a procedural irregularity"); *De Four v The State* [1999] 1 WLR 1731, 1737H (trial judge's 30-minute time limit given to jury a material irregularity); *Neill v North Antrim Magistrates' Court* [1992] 1 WLR 1220, 1230D-1231H (Lord Mustill, contrasting "a bona fide but mistaken ruling on a procedural matter [where] the [claimant] has suffered real prejudice" with "a really substantial error leading to a demonstrable injustice"); <4.3.3> (prejudice and procedural flaws).

60.1.9 **Aspects of fairness.** *R v Secretary of State for the Environment, ex p Greater London Council* 3rd April 1985 unrep. (Mustill LJ, identifying these ways in which the decision there under review might be procedurally improper, namely "(i) Unfair behaviour towards persons affected by the decision; ... (ii) Failure to follow a procedure laid down by the legislation... (iii) Failure properly to marshall the evidence on which the decision should be based. For example, taking into account an immaterial factor or failing to take into account a material factor or failing to take reasonable steps to obtain the relevant information... (iv) Failure to approach the decision in the right spirit. For example, where the decision maker is actuated by bias, or where he is content to let the decision be made by chance").

60.1.10 **Systemic unfairness/unfair system.** *R (Refugee Legal Centre) v Secretary of State for the Home Department* [2004] EWCA Civ 1481 [2005] 1 WLR 2219 at [6] (asking whether fast-track system placing asylum-seekers at unacceptable risk of being processed unfairly), [7] ("Potential unfairness is susceptible to one of two forms of control which the law provides. One is access, retrospectively, to judicial review if due process has been violated. The other, of which this case is put forward as an example, is appropriate relief, following judicial intervention to obviate in advance a proven risk of injustice which goes beyond aberrant interviews or decisions and inheres in the system itself"), [8] ("three factors which the court will weigh: the individual interest at issue, the benefits to be derived from added procedural safeguards, and the costs to the administration of compliance"); *R (Dirshe) v Secretary of State for the Home Department* [2005] EWCA Civ 421 (absence of taping of asylum interviews a procedurally unfair system).

60.1.11 **Procedural legitimate expectation.** <P41> (legitimate expectation).
(A) THE CHANCE TO MEET CURRENT CRITERIA. *R v North and East Devon Health Authority, ex p Coughlan* [2001] QB 213 at [73] (referring to situations where "the individual can claim no higher expectation than to have his individual circumstances considered by the decision-maker in the light of the policy then in force"); *In re Findlay* [1985] AC 318, 338E-F ("the most that a convicted prisoner can legitimately expect is that his case will be examined individually in the light of whatever policy the Secretary of State sees fit to adopt provided always that the adopted policy is a lawful exercise of the discretion"); *Fisher v Minister of Public Safety and Immigration (No.2)* [2000] 1 AC 434, 447A-B (PC deciding, 3-2, that decision-maker entitled to act inconsistently with legitimate expectation created, provided adequate notice of this intention and opportunity for those affected to state their case).
(B) SPECIAL PROCEDURAL RIGHT. <41.1.3>.
(C) PROCEDURAL LEGITIMATE EXPECTATION: ILLUSTRATIONS.*R (Bhatt Murphy) v Independent Assessor* [2008] EWCA Civ 755 at [50] (defendant having a duty to consult where "without any promise, it has established a policy distinctly and substantially affecting a specific person or group who in the circumstances was in reason entitled to rely on its continuance and did so"); *R (Actis SA) v Secretary of State for Communities & Local Government* [2007] EWHC 2417 (Admin) at [136] & [155] (legitimate expectation of consultation before changes in technical regulation); *R (Greenpeace Ltd) v Secretary of State for Trade and Industry* [2007] EWHC 311 (Admin) [2007] Env LR 623 at [48], [54], [120] (promise of full public consultation); *R v North and East Devon Health Authority, ex p Coughlan* [2001] QB 213, at [57(b)] ("the court may decide that the promise or practice induces a legitimate expectation of, for example, being consulted before a particular decision is taken. Here it is uncontentious that the court itself will require *the opportunity for consultation* to be given unless there is an overriding reason to resile from it ... in which case the court will itself judge the adequacy of the reason advanced for the change of policy, taking into account what fairness requires"), [62] (court decides fairness); *Attorney-General of Hong Kong v Ng Yuen Shiu* [1983] 2 AC 629, 638G ("a public authority is bound by its undertakings as to the procedure it will follow, provided they do not conflict with its duty"); *R v Rochdale Metropolitan Borough Council, ex p Schemet* [1994] ELR 89, 106H-108E (previous practice of providing free transport giving rise to legitimate expectation of consultation prior to any change in policy); *R v Devon County Council, ex p Baker* [1995] 1 All ER 73 (legitimate expectation of consultation prior to closure of residential home); *R v Falmouth and Truro Port Health Authority, ex p South West Water Ltd* [2001] QB 445, 459B ("Once one accepts ... that consultation was `not otherwise required by law', then only the clearest of assurances can give rise to its legitimate expectation"); *R v Secretary of State for Education and Employment, ex p Amraf Training Plc* [2001] ELR 125 at [52] (Elias J: "the doctrine [of legitimate expectation] will only in very exceptional circumstances entitle a public authority to override procedural as opposed to substantive rights"); *R (Montpeliers & Trevors Association) v City of Westminster* [2005] EWHC 16 (Admin) [2006] LGR 304 at [44] (breach of legitimate expectation of consultation); *R (Haringey Consortium of Disabled People and Carers Association) v Haringey London Borough Council* (2002) 5 CCLR 422 at [48] (legitimate expectation of consultation, arising by virtue of general conditions in agreement); *Naidike v Attorney-General of Trinidad and Tobago* [2004] UKPC 49 [2005] 1 AC 538 at [24] (legitimate expectation that work permit renewal not refused without opportunity to address concerns).

60.1.12 **A unified fair appearances (fair-minded observer) test.** <45.2.5>.

60.1.13 **Standards of procedural fairness as a hard-edged question.** <16.5>.

60.1.14 **Procedural fairness: whether need for prejudice.** <4.3.3> (prejudice and procedural flaws); <60.1.8> (material irregularity); <60.4.4> (whether procedural ultra vires needs prejudice); *Boddington v British Transport Police* [1999] 2 AC 143, 174B-D (Lord Steyn, rejecting the proposition that in a case of procedural invalidity of a byelaw a claimant must "show that he has suffered substantial prejudice"); *General Medical Council v Spackman* [1943] AC 627, 644-645 ("If the principles of natural justice are violated in respect of any decision, it is, indeed, immaterial whether the same decision would have been arrived at in the absence of the departure from the essential principles of justice. The decision must be declared to be no decision"); *Ridge v Baldwin* [1964] AC 40, 128 (Lord Hodson: "I do not find that the answer put by counsel for the watch committee to your Lordships that the case was as plain as a pike-staff is an answer to the demand for natural justice"); *In re Evans* [1994] 1 WLR 1006, 1013D ("The accused is given an opportunity to make representations by himself or his counsel because no order for committal should be made against a person who has not been allowed to object and to state his reasons for objection, good or bad, relevant or irrelevant"); *Kanda v Government of Malaya* [1962] AC 322, 337 (Lord Denning: "It follows, of course, that the judge or whoever has to adjudicate must not hear evidence or receive representations from one side behind the back of the other. The court will not inquire whether the evidence or representations did work to his prejudice. Sufficient that they might do so. The court will not go into the likelihood of prejudice. The risk of it is enough"); *Chief Constable of the North Wales Police v Evans* [1982] 1 WLR 1155, 1161H (Lord Hailsham: "might ... have influenced the decision"); *R v Leicester City Justices, ex p Barrow* [1991] 2 QB 260, 290D-E (Lord Donaldson MR: "Any unfairness, whether apparent or actual and however inadvertent, strikes at the roots of justice. I cannot be sure that the [claimants] were not prejudiced and accordingly I have no doubt that the justices' order should be quashed"); *Malloch v Aberdeen Corporation* [1971] 1 WLR 1578, 1595B (need "something of substance which has been lost by the failure"); *R v London Borough of Camden, ex p Paddock* [1995] COD 130 (see transcript) (in certain cases of formal procedure "formality itself is a matter of substance", but that "beyond this class there must at least be a general, though rebuttable, presumption that departures from fair procedure matter"); *R v Inner West London Coroner, ex p Dallaglio* [1994] 4 All ER 139, 152d ("It is not necessary for the [claimants] to demonstrate a real possibility that the coroner's decision would have been different but for bias").

60.1.15 **Whether procedural unfairness "cured".** <36.4>.

60.1.16 **Blameless unfairness/objective unfairness.**
(A) OBJECTIVE UNFAIRNESS. *R v Criminal Injuries Compensation Board, ex p A* [1999] 2 AC 330, 345C-D (Lord Slynn: "what happened in these proceedings was a breach of the rules of natural justice and constituted unfairness. It does not seem to me to be necessary to find that anyone was at fault in order to arrive at this result. It is sufficient if objectively there is unfairness"); *R (Marsh) v Lincoln District Magistrates Court* [2003] EWHC 956 (Admin) at [45] (applying Lord Slynn's "simple statement of principle" in *A*); *E v Secretary of State for the Home Department* [2004] EWCA Civ 49 [2004] QB 1044 at [63] (describing *A* as a case which "turned, not on issues of fault or lack of fault on either side; it was sufficient that 'objectively' there was unfairness"), [65] (referring to "fault" as "not essential to the reasoning of the House").
(B) RELEVANCE OF CLAIMANT/ADVISER FAULT. *R v Secretary of State for the Home Department, ex p Al-Mehdawi* [1990] 1 AC 876 (HL treating factual unfairness as not sufficing because attributable to the fault of claimant's legal advisers); *Haile v Immigration Appeal Tribunal* [2001] EWCA Civ 663 [2002] Imm AR 170 at [26] (Simon Brown LJ: "I am [not] persuaded that the House of Lords' decision in *Al-Mehdawi* precludes this court having regard to the wider interests of justice here, not least given that this is an asylum case rather than a student leave case as was *Al-Mehdawi*. Aspects of that decision may in any event now need to

be reconsidered in the light of the House of Lords' speeches in *R v Criminal Injuries Compensation Board, ex p A* [1999] 2 AC 330"); *R (Mathialagan) v Southwark London Borough Council* [2004] EWCA Civ 1689 at [38] (applying *Al-Mehdawi*).
(C) BLAMELESS/OBJECTIVE UNFAIRNESS: OTHER CASES. *R (Maqsood) v Special Adjudicator* [2002] Imm AR 268 (decision of immigration appellate authorities could be unfair notwithstanding lack of fault by the decision-maker); *Khan v Secretary of State for the Home Department* [1987] Imm AR 543, 555 (Bingham LJ: "If a procedural mishap occurs as a result of a misunderstanding, confusion, failure of communication, or perhaps even inefficiency, and the result is to deny justice to the applicant, I should be very sorry to hold that the remedy of judicial review was not available"), applied in *R (Ganidagli) v Secretary of State for the Home Department* [2001] EWHC Admin 70 at [36]; *R (Tataw) v Immigration Appeal Tribunal* [2003] EWCA Civ 925 [2003] INLR 585 (justice requiring IAT decision to be quashed where erroneously, albeit blamelessly, treated asylum appeal as out of time); *R (Ford) v Leasehold Valuation Tribunal* [2005] EWHC 503 (Admin) at [45]-[46] (injustice where full material not before the tribunal); <14.3.3> (unfairness: nothing personal); *R (Pownall) v Flintshire Magistrates Court* [2004] EWHC 1289 (Admin) (blameless unfairness in inducing guilty plea by innocently misrepresenting that valid speed limit in force on stretch of road).

60.1.17 The procedure that was bargained for. *Modahl v British Athletic Federation* [2001] EWCA Civ 1447 [2002] 1 WLR 1192 at [61] ("where an apparently sensible appeal structure has been put in place, the court is entitled to approach the matter on the basis that the parties should have been taken [to] have agreed to accept what in the end is a fair decision"), [115] (Mance LJ); *Ceylon University v Fernando* [1960] 1 WLR 223, 233 ("he must be taken to have agreed, when he became a member of the university, to be bound by the statutes of the university"); *Furnell v Whangarei High Schools Board* [1973] AC 660, 683B ("a teacher knows that under the terms governing his employment if charges are made and are to be investigated a suspension `pending the determination of the matter' may take place"); *Calvin v Carr* [1980] AC 574, 594F (whether "the complainant has had a fair deal of the kind he bargained for"); *Hamlet v General Municipal Boilermakers & Allied Trades Union* [1987] 1 WLR 449, 456B (Harman J: "where a man has expressly agreed by contract to accept a tribunal containing certain persons, he cannot thereafter come bleating to the courts complaining of breach of natural justice when the contract is carried out exactly according to its terms").

60.1.18 Procedural fairness and waiver/failure to complain/request. <31.4.4> (procedural fairness and failure to complain/ request); <61.3.9> (apparent bias and waiver); *R v Visitors to the Inns of Court, ex p Calder & Persaud* [1994] QB 1, 57F-G (leaving open question of waiver of breach of natural justice); *Thomas v University of Bradford (No.2)* [1992] 1 All ER 964, 979b-j, 981f; *Modahl v British Athletic Federation Ltd* 28th July 1997 unrep. (CA) (whether waiver/ estoppel in relation to bias).

60.1.19 Fairness not best practice. *R v Secretary of State for the Home Department, ex p Doody* [1994] 1 AC 531, 560H-561A (Lord Mustill: "the [claimants] acknowledge that it is not enough for them to persuade the court that some procedure other than the one adopted by the decision-maker would be better or more fair. Rather, they must show that the procedure is actually unfair. The court must constantly bear in mind that it is to the decision maker, not the court, that Parliament has entrusted not only the making of the decision but also the choice as to how the decision is made"); *R v Devon County Council, ex p Baker* [1995] 1 All ER 73, 85c-d (Dillon LJ: "Obviously it could be said to be best practice, in modern thinking, that before an administrative decision is made there should be consultation in some form, with those who will clearly be adversely affected by the decision. But judicial review is not granted for a mere failure to follow best practice. It has to be shown that the failure to consult amounts to a failure by the local authority to discharge its admitted duty to act fairly"); *Hobbs v London Borough of Sutton*

(1994) 26 HLR 132, 147 ("It is obvious that in the field of administrative decision-making, there must be some compromise between what is administratively practical and what is ideally desirable"); *R v Wokingham District Council, ex p J* [1999] 2 FLR 1136, 1147B (although desirable not a requirement of natural justice that natural parent should have been permitted to make written representations to adoption panel); *R (Thompson) v Law Society* [2004] EWCA Civ 167 [2004] 1 WLR 2522 at [50] (applying *Doody*); <16.5.4> (room for some discretion as to procedure).

60.1.20 Fairness following choice.
(A) VOLUNTARY CONSULTATION MUST BE ADEQUATE. *R (Eisai Ltd) v National Institute for Health and Clinical Excellence* [2008] EWCA Civ 438 at [24] ("whether or not consultation is a legal requirement, if it is embarked upon it must be carried out properly"); *R (Wagstaff) v Secretary of State for Health* [2001] 1 WLR 292, 314G (ditto); *R (Medway Council) v Secretary of State for Transport* [2002] EWHC 2516 (Admin) at [28] ("it is axiomatic that consultation, whether it is a matter of obligation or undertaken voluntarily, requires fairness"); *R (Montpeliers & Trevors Association) v City of Westminster* [2005] EWHC 16 (Admin) [2006] LGR 304 at [21] ("If a local authority decides to embark upon a non-statutory process of consultation the applicable principles are no different from those which apply to statutory consultation"); *R (British Waterways Board) v First Secretary of State* [2006] EWHC 1019 (Admin) at [23] (having chosen to consult, should have enabled claimant to comment); *R (Royden) v Wirral Metropolitan Borough Council* [2002] EWHC 2484 (Admin) [2003] LGR 290 at [54] (having chosen to consult, must be adequate); *R (Capenhurst) v Leicester City Council* [2004] EWHC 2124 (Admin) (2004) 7 CCLR 557 at [18] ("irrespective of whether the council was obliged to consult ... it did in fact decide to consult ... [and] thereby was under an obligation to do so fairly").
(B) OTHER. <62.3.12> (having chosen to give reasons, obliged to give adequate reasons); *R v Secretary of State for the Home Department, ex p McCartney* [1994] COD 160 DC (having decided to take judicial advice, Minister obliged to allow prisoner to comment); *R v Life Assurance and Unit Trust Regulatory Organisation Ltd, ex p Tee* (1995) 7 Admin LR 289; *R v London Borough of Camden, ex p Paddock* [1995] COD 130 (see transcript) ("It cannot be right that a public decision-making body which is not obliged to accord a hearing may choose to do so but may then make a charade of it", referring to *Central Council for Education and Training in Social Work v Edwards* The Times 5th May 1978); *R v Inner West London Coroner, ex p Dallaglio* [1994] 4 All ER 139, 153e; *R v Governors of the Sheffield Hallam University, ex p R* [1995] ELR 267, 282-284 (university's failure to follow own procedures); *R v Bishop of Stafford, ex p Owen* [2001] ACD 83 (whether Bishop followed sufficiently closely the procedure he said he would); cf. *R v Kensington and Chelsea Royal London Borough Council, ex p Grillo* (1996) 28 HLR 94, 105-106 (emphasising fact that voluntary appeals procedure); cf. <57.4.7> (reasonableness following choice).

60.1.21 Fairness and interim decisions. <36.4.1> (fairness and rights of immediate recourse).

60.1.22 Delay as procedural unfairness. <60.8.2>.

60.1.23 Fairness as part of a test of substantive justification. <P54> (substantive fairness); <54.2.5> (substantial legitimate expectation: fairness/ justification test).

60.1.24 HRA:ECHR Art 6: Right to a fair and independent hearing. <59.5>.

60.1.25 The bias principle. <P61>.

60.2 **Procedural fairness as a flexi-principle.**[53] Natural justice has always been an entirely contextual principle. There are no rigid or universal rules as to what is needed in order to be procedurally fair. The content of the duty depends on the particular function and circumstances of the individual case.

60.2.1 **Natural justice as a flexi-principle: no tablets of stone.** *Lloyd v McMahon* [1987] AC 625, 702H (Lord Bridge: "the so-called rules of natural justice are not engraved on tablets of stone. To use the phrase which better expresses the underlying concept, what the requirements of fairness demand when any body, domestic, administrative or judicial, has to make a decision which will affect the rights of individuals depends on the character of the decision-making body, the kind of decision it has to make and the statutory or other framework in which it operates"); *Russell v Duke of Norfolk* [1949] 1 All ER 109, 118D-E (Tucker LJ: "There are, in my view, no words which are of universal application to every kind of inquiry and every kind of domestic tribunal. The requirements of natural justice must depend on the circumstances of the case, the nature of the inquiry, the rules under which the tribunal is acting, the subject-matter under consideration and so forth"), cited in *Ceylon University v Fernando* [1960] 1 WLR 223, 231; *Ridge v Baldwin* [1964] AC 40, 132; *Pearlberg v Varty* [1972] 1 WLR 534, 540E; *Rees v Crane* [1994] 2 AC 173, 192D-E.

60.2.2 **No precise prescriptions/rigid rules.** *Wiseman v Borneman* [1971] AC 297, 308H-309C (Lord Morris: "We often speak of the rules of natural justice. But there is nothing rigid or mechanical about them. What they comprehend has been analyzed and described in many authorities. But any analysis must bring into relief rather their spirit and their inspiration than any precision of definition or precision as to their application. We do not search for prescriptions which will lay down exactly what must, in various divergent situations, be done. The principles and procedures are to be applied which, in any particular situation or set of circumstances, are right and just and fair. Natural justice, it has been said, is only `fair play in action'. Nor do we wait for directions from Parliament. The common law has abundant riches: there may we find what Byles J called `the justice of the common law'", referring to *Cooper v Wandsworth Board of Works* (1863) 14 CBNS 180, 194); *Furnell v Whangarei High Schools Board* [1973] AC 660, 679G ("the requirements of natural justice must depend on the circumstances of each particular case and the subject matter under consideration"); *Sheridan v Stanley Cole (Wainfleet) Ltd* [2003] EWCA Civ 1046 [2003] 4 All ER 1181 at [33] (Ward LJ: "It is ... impossible to lay down a rigid rule as to where the boundaries of procedural irregularity lie, or when the principles of natural justice are to apply, or what makes a hearing unfair. Everything depends on the subject matter and the facts and circumstances of each case").

60.2.3 **Lord Mustill's principles of intuitive judgment.** *R v Secretary of State for the Home Department, ex p Doody* [1994] 1 AC 531, 560D-G (Lord Mustill: "What does fairness require in the present case? My Lords, I think it unnecessary to refer by name or to quote from, any of the often-cited authorities in which the courts have explained what is essentially an intuitive judgment. They are far too well known. From them, I derive that (1) where an Act of Parliament confers an administrative power there is a presumption that it will be exercised in a manner which is fair in all the circumstances. (2) The standards of fairness are not immutable. They may change with the passage of time, both in ... general and in their application to decisions of a particular type. (3) The principles of fairness are not to be applied by rote identically in every situation. What fairness demands is dependent on the context of the decision, and this is to be

---

[53] This paragraph in a previous edition was cited in *R v Bank of England, ex p Mellstrom* [1995] CLC 232.

taken into account in all its aspects. (4) An essential feature of the context is the statute which creates the discretion, as regards both its language and the shape of the legal and administrative system within which the decision is taken. (5) Fairness will very often require that a person who may be adversely affected by the decision will have an opportunity to make representations on his own behalf either before the decision is taken with a view to producing a favourable result; or after it is taken, with a view to procuring its modification; or both. (6) Since the person affected usually cannot make worthwhile representations without knowing what factors may weigh against his interests fairness will very often require that he is informed of the gist of the case which he has to answer").

60.2.4 **Lord Russell's fair crack of the whip.** *Fairmount Investments Ltd v Secretary of State for the Environment* [1976] 1 WLR 1255, 1265H-1266A (Lord Russell: "All cases in which principles of natural justice are invoked must depend on the particular circumstances of the cases. I am unable, my Lords, in the instant case, to generalise. I can only say that in my opinion, in the circumstances I have outlined, Fairmount has not had - in a phrase whose derivation neither I nor your Lordships could trace - a fair crack of the whip"), applied in *E v Secretary of State for the Home Department* [2004] EWCA Civ 49 [2004] QB 1044 at [65] (in considering whether error of fact rendering decision unfair).

60.2.5 **Procedural fairness as a flexi-principle: other.** *R (Eisai Ltd) v National Institute for Health and Clinical Excellence* [2008] EWCA Civ 438 at [27] ("What fairness requires depends on the context and the particular circumstances"); *Bushell v Secretary of State for the Environment* [1981] AC 75, 95D ("What is a fair procedure to be adopted at a particular inquiry will depend upon the nature of its subject matter"); *Council of Civil Service Unions v Minister for the Civil Service* [1985] AC 374, 411H ("what procedure will satisfy the public law requirement of procedural propriety depends upon the subject matter of the decision, the executive functions of the decision-maker ... and the particular circumstances in which the decision came to be made"), 415A-B ("Many features will come into play including the nature of the decision and the relationship of those involved on either side"); *Ceylon University v Fernando* [1960] 1 WLR 223, 231 (depends "on the facts and circumstances of the case in point"); *R v Norfolk County Council, ex p M* [1989] QB 619, 630A-B (Waite J: "Fairness is, and needs to be, a flexible concept, and circumstances are liable to vary widely as to the degree of advance notice or opportunity of objection or consultation which attention to fairness in particular cases requires"); *In re D (Minors) (Adoption Reports: Confidentiality)* [1996] AC 593, 609B ("the requirements of natural justice are not invariable, and ... circumstances must alter cases"); *R v Inland Revenue Commissioners, ex p Unilever Plc* [1996] STC 681, 690f ("The categories of unfairness are not closed, and precedent should act as a guide not a cage"); *R v Secretary of State for the Home Department, ex p Moon* (1996) 8 Admin LR 477, 480E-F ("The well attested flexibility of natural justice does not mean that the Court applies differential standards at will, but that the application of the principles (which, subject to known exceptions, are constant) is necessarily as various as the situations in which they are invoked"); *R (Wooder) v Feggetter* [2002] EWCA Civ 554 [2003] QB 219 at [42] ("lawyers seem to have manifested their classic learnt response to [the leading] cases [on the duty to give reasons] by treating the categories so far acknowledged in the reactive and exploratory growth of the common law as exhaustive. Rather than try to fit given shapes into pre-formed slots like toddlers in a playgroup ..., the courts have to continue the process of working out and refining, case by case, the relevant principles of fairness").

60.2.6 **ECHR Art 6 as a flexi-principle.** <59.5.15>.

60.3 Procedural fairness: supplementing the legislative scheme. Common law minimum standards of procedural fairness readily supplement a statutory scheme, even in situations of express and limited statutory protection.

60.3.1 Fairness supplying the legislative omission: the Byles principle. *Cooper v Wandsworth Board of Works* (1863) 14 CB (NS) 180, 194 (Byles J: "although there are no positive words in a statute requiring that the parties shall be heard, yet the justice of the common law will supply the omission of the legislature"); *R v Secretary of State for the Home Department, ex p Pierson* [1998] AC 539, 588H (Lord Steyn: "our public law is, of course, replete with ... instances of the common law so supplementing statutes"); *R (Khatun) v London Borough of Newham* [2004] EWCA Civ 55 [2005] QB 37 at [30] (Laws LJ, referring to those situations where "a right to be heard [can] be inserted or implied into the statutory scheme not by virtue of the statute's words, but by force of our public law standards of procedural fairness"), [31] ("the courts may in the name of fairness insist on the conferment upon affected persons of a right to be heard in the administration of a statutory scheme, itself silent as to such a right"); *R (Wooder) v Feggetter* [2002] EWCA Civ 554 [2003] QB 219 at [44] ("The process is not one of discerning implied terms but of adding necessary ones"); *R (S) v London Borough of Brent* [2002] EWCA Civ 693 [2002] ELR 556 at [14] ("the longstanding default principle that the common law will supplement such procedures to the extent necessary to ensure that they operate fairly"); *Chuan v Public Prosecutor* [1981] AC 648 (referring to the concept of "law" as meaning a system incorporating fundamental common law rules of natural justice); *Wiseman v Borneman* [1971] AC 297, 317G ("It is necessary to look at the [statutory] procedure in its setting and ask the question whether it operates unfairly ... to a point where the courts must supply the legislative omission").

60.3.2 Procedural fairness supplementing an express procedure. *Belfast City Council v Miss Behavin' Ltd* [2007] UKHL 19 [2007] 1 WLR 1420 at [8] (discretion to consider late objections, supplementing the statutory scheme to ensure fair and workable); *R (S) v London Borough of Brent* [2002] EWCA Civ 693 [2002] ELR 556 at [14] (asking whether any feature of statutory scheme "which blocks the application of the longstanding default principle that the common law will supplement such procedures to the extent necessary to ensure that they operate fairly"); *Lloyd v McMahon* [1987] AC 625, 702H-703A ("when a statute has conferred on any body the power to make decisions affecting individuals, the courts will not only require the procedure prescribed by the statute to be followed, but will readily imply so much and no more to be introduced by way of additional procedural safeguards as will ensure the attainment of fairness"); *R v Secretary of State for the Home Department, ex p Doody* [1994] 1 AC 531, 562A-B ("impossible to accept that these limited and fragmentary statutory rights demonstrate a Parliamentary intention to exclude all other aspects of fair treatment"); *Wiseman v Borneman* [1971] AC 297, 317G ("It is necessary to look at the procedure in its setting and ask the question whether it operates unfairly ... to a point where the courts must supply the legislative omission"); *Pearlberg v Varty* [1972] 1 WLR 534, 551A-B ("the legislature cannot be expected to specify everything that shall or shall not be done in order to comply with natural justice"); *Malloch v Aberdeen Corporation* [1971] 1 WLR 1578, 1582G-H (not difficult to imply the right to be heard); *R v Secretary of State for Education and Employment, ex p Morris* The Times 15th December 1995 (marked and explicable absence of consultation duty); *R v Secretary of State for the Home Department, ex p Abdi* [1996] 1 WLR 298, 314A, 315B-C (duty to disclose all material would be inconsistent with express duty to disclose certain material); *Stefan* <62.2.4(C)>; *R (McNally) v Secretary of State for Education* [2001] EWCA Civ 332 [2001] ELR 773 at [28] (despite statutory entitlement to attend hearing, "natural justice may make it so inappropriate"), [39] (using principle of legality to ensure wide statutory provisions read as consistent with natural justice).

60.3.3 **Procedural fairness supplementing rules/regulations.** *R v Wareham Magistrates' Court, ex p Seldon* [1988] 1 WLR 825 (natural justice supplementing the Magistrates Courts Rules 1981); *R (Bentley) v HM Coroner District of Avon* [2001] EWHC Admin 170 (although coroner's rules not requiring advance disclosure of documents, disclosure should have been made in fairness); *R (Gupta) v General Medical Council* The Times 16th October 2001 (fairness requiring steps beyond those set out in GMC disciplinary rules); *Stratford-on-Avon District Council & Secretary of State for the Environment v Bryant Homes Limited* 30th January 1995 unrep. (court "would be slow to accept that [the Rules] contain so comprehensive a code that there could be no breach of natural justice without a breach of the Rules"); *R v Ministry of Agriculture Fisheries and Food, ex p St Clere's Hall Farm* [1995] 3 CMLR 125, 136-137 (whether natural justice supplementing EC Regulations).

60.3.4 **Statutory exclusion of additional procedural fairness.**
(A) PLAIN WORDS/MEANING. *Wiseman v Borneman* [1971] AC 297, 318C ("the legislature may certainly exclude or limit the application of the general rules. But it has always been insisted that this must be done, clearly and expressly"); *R v Secretary of State for the Home Department, ex p Fayed* The Times 13th March 1996 (statute ruling out duty to give reasons, but not duty to disclose concerns so that claimants could make representations); *R v Secretary of State for the Home Department, ex p Abdi* [1996] 1 WLR 298, 314A ("this is not a case of mere omission. It is not a case of Parliament having left a gap which the courts can fill. [Counsel] argues that an implied obligation to disclose all relevant documents is wholly inconsistent with the express obligation to disclose specific documents as set out in Rule 5(6) of the Rules").
(B) DELIBERATE PROTECTIONS/OMISSIONS. *R v Secretary of State for the Environment, ex p Hammersmith & Fulham London Borough Council* [1991] 1 AC 521, 600E-F (reasons duty "plainly excluded by the very precise terms in which the statute lays down the relevant procedure to be followed); *Pearlberg v Varty* [1972] 1 WLR 534, 545E-G (Viscount Dilhorne: "the omission ... cannot ... be regarded as anything other than deliberate"); *Furnell v Whangarei High Schools Board* [1973] AC 660, 681G (omission "must have been deliberate since the regulations proceed with great particularity to specify when and how communication should be made to him and when and how he should make response"); *C v Special Educational Needs Tribunal* [1997] ELR 390, 402H-403A (regulations deliberately imposing duty to give reasons for refusing an appeal, and not for refusing a review); *R (Venture Projects Ltd) v Secretary of State for the Home Department* 20th October 2000 unrep. (common law duty to give reasons not arising where EC Directive required reasons for some decisions but not this type); *R (Morgan Grenfell & Co Ltd) v Inland Revenue Commissioners* [2001] EWCA Civ 329 [2003] 1 AC 563 (CA) at [50] ("the possibility of an oral hearing is excluded by the nature of the process in question") (HL is at [2002] UKHL 21 [2003] 1 AC 563).

60.3.5 **Is the statutory procedure fair?** This was the question posed in *Wiseman v Borneman* [1971] AC 297, 308G, 311G, 312D-E and 320E-F; *Furnell v Whangarei High Schools Board* [1973] AC 660 at 682F-683D; *Huntley v Attorney-General for Jamaica* [1995] 2 AC 1, 13B; *R v Bakewell Magistrates' Court, ex p Brewer* [1995] COD 98; also *Pearlberg v Varty* [1972] 1 WLR 534, 545E ("assume that what has been done is fair until the contrary is shown").

60.3.6 **Supplementing the Act and preserving legislative purpose.** *Wiseman v Borneman* [1971] AC 297, 308B-C ("the courts have, without objection from Parliament, supplemented procedure laid down in legislation where they have found that to be necessary for this purpose. But before this unusual kind of power is exercised it must be clear that the statutory procedure is insufficient to achieve justice and that to require additional steps would not frustrate the apparent purpose of the legislation"), cited with approval in *Pearlberg v Varty* [1972] 1 WLR 534, 545D and in *Century National Merchant Bank and Trust Co Ltd v Davies* [1998] AC 628,

638C-639D; *Ridge v Baldwin* [1964] AC 40, 141 ("Whether [the principles of natural justice]... are to be applied to any statutory procedure depends upon an implication to be drawn from the statute itself"); *Maynard v Osmond* [1977] QB 240; *R v Birmingham City Council, ex p Ferrero Ltd* [1993] 1 All ER 530, 543c-d ("To imply such a duty [to consult] would tend to frustrate the statutory purpose"); *R v Secretary of State for Education and Employment and the North East London Education Authority, ex p M* [1996] ELR 162, 208D ("The underlying statutory objectives of this new group of powers must not be stultified by an over-zealous super-imposition of common law procedural requirements"); *R v North Yorkshire Family Health Services Authority, ex p Wilson* (1996) 8 Admin LR 613, 623G (Regulations drawing distinction between 2 types of situation, one where consultation because prejudice to consultees in issue, the other without consultation because no reference to that issue; "That being the scheme of the Regulations, it is not open to me, judicially, to amend it").

60.3.7 Supplementing the Act with ad hoc/generalised duties. *R v Secretary of State for Wales, ex p Emery* [1998] 4 All ER 367, 376j-377a (Roch LJ: "When the court supplements a statutory procedure, the additional safeguard which the court requires will apply in every case"); *R v Wareham Magistrates' Court, ex p Seldon* [1988] 1 WLR 825, 832H-833A (McCullough J: "the question is not one of the implication into the provision under consideration of a rigid requirement applicable in every case. It is one of fairness. In some cases fairness will require steps to be taken which in other cases it will not require").

60.4 Procedural ultra vires. This hybrid principle concerns process obligations prescribed in a legally superior source. The Court considers the context and circumstances to decide what the consequence of non-compliance should be.

60.4.1 Procedural ultra vires alongside procedural unfairness. *Council of Civil Service Unions v Minister for the Civil Service* [1985] AC 374, 411A-B (Lord Diplock: "I have described the third head as 'procedural impropriety' rather than failure to observe basic rules of natural justice or failure to act with procedural fairness towards the person who will be affected by the decision. This is because susceptibility to judicial review under this head covers also failure by an administrative tribunal to observe procedural rules that are expressly laid down in the legislative instrument by which its jurisdiction is conferred, even where such failure does not involve any denial of natural justice"); *General Medical Council v Spackman* [1943] AC 627, 640 (statutory duty to make "due inquiry" described as "natural justice"); *Kanda v Government of Malaya* [1962] AC 322, 337-338.

60.4.2 Examples of express procedural duties. *R (Edwards) v Environment Agency* [2008] UKHL 22 (statutory EIA duty to consult); *R (Swords) v Secretary of State for Communities and Local Government* [2007] EWCA Civ 795 [2007] LGR 757 at [49] (duty to take account of leaseholders' views arising under DPM Manual); *R v Commission for Racial Equality, ex p Hillingdon London Borough Council* [1982] AC 779, 787G-H (statutory duty ensuring natural justice); *R v Oxford Regional Mental Health Review Tribunal, ex p Secretary of State for the Home Department* [1988] AC 120 (Home Secretary's right to be heard contained in the MHRT rules); *Save Britain's Heritage v Number 1 Poultry Ltd* [1991] 1 WLR 153 (statutory duty to give reasons); *Bradbury v Enfield London Borough Council* [1967] 1 WLR 1311 (notice requirements); *London & Clydeside Estates Ltd v Aberdeen District Council* [1980] 1 WLR 182 (right to be told of right of appeal); *R v Seisdon Justices, ex p Dougan* [1982] 1 WLR 1476 (notice); *R v Central Criminal Court, ex p Adegbesan* [1986] 1 WLR 1292 (information to accompany notices); *R v Bradford Metropolitan Borough Council, ex p Sikander Ali* [1994] ELR 299, 316C-D (duty to publish particulars of school admissions policy); *R v Governors of Astley High School, ex p Northumberland County Council* [1994] COD 27 (information); *R v*

Swansea City Council, ex p Elitestone Ltd [1993] 2 PLR 65 (published agenda); *R v Stoke City Council, ex p Highgate Projects* (1997) 29 HLR 271 (chairman's duties as to creation of record of decision); *Wang v Commissioner of Inland Revenue* [1994] 1 WLR 1286 (express duty not to delay); *R (Actis SA) v Secretary of State for Communities & Local Government* [2007] EWHC 2417 (Admin) (non-notification under EC Directive).

60.4.3 **Whether intended vitiating consequence.** *R v Soneji* [2005] UKHL 49 [2006] 1 AC 340 at [23] (emphasising "the consequences of non-compliance, and posing the question whether Parliament can fairly be taken to have intended total invalidity"); *R v Immigration Appeal Tribunal, ex p Jeyeanthan* [2000] 1 WLR 354, 358E-G (asking "what the legislator should be judged to have intended should be the consequence of the non-compliance"); *Secretary of State for the Home Department v E* [2007] UKHL 47 [2008] 1 AC 499 at [15] (statute not making compliance with duty a condition precedent to validity of control order); *Attorney-General's Reference (No.3 of 1999)* [2001] 2 AC 91, 117B, 120C (applying *Jeyeanthan*); *Wang v Commissioner of Inland Revenue* [1994] 1 WLR 1286, 1296 ("did the legislature intend that a failure to comply ... would ... render any decision ... null and void?"); *Charles v Judicial and Legal Service Commission* [2002] UKPC 34 [2003] 1 LRC 422 ("the regulations cannot have been framed with the intention that breaches of the kind in issue would deprive the Commission of jurisdiction to act"); *Robinson v Secretary of State for Northern Ireland* [2002] UKHL 32 at [13] (applying *Wang*); *Seal v Chief Constable South Wales Police* [2007] UKHL 31 [2007] 1 WLR 1910 at [7] (considering purpose of statutory precondition); *R v Clarke* [2008] UKHL 8 [2008] 1 WLR 338 (consequence of default meaning no valid trial on indictment); *R (Winchester College) v Hampshire County Council* [2007] EWHC 2786 (Admin) (non-complaint documents not vitiating rights of way application).

60.4.4 **Whether procedural ultra vires needs prejudice.** <4.3.3> (prejudice and procedural flaws); *London & Clydeside Estates Ltd v Aberdeen District Council* [1980] 1 WLR 182, 195B (Lord Fraser: "The validity of a certificate is not in my opinion dependent on whether the appellants were actually prejudiced by it or not"); *R v Board of Visitors of Dartmoor Prison, ex p Smith* [1987] QB 106, 125A-C (refusal to imply additional requirement of prejudice); *R v Camden London Borough Council, ex p Cran* (1996) 94 LGR 8, 75 (sufficient that significant risk that decision might have been different); *R v Westminster City Council, ex p Ermakov* [1996] 2 All ER 302 (failure to give reasons: prejudice unnecessary), 314f-h (distinguishing *Save Britain's Heritage*); *Westminster City Council v Cabaj* The Times 8th May 1996 (contractual right to a correctly constituted appeal panel not necessarily meaning dismissal unfair); *R v Department of Health, ex p Gandhi* [1991] 1 WLR 1053, 1068A-B (even though outcome may not have been any different, and delay, appropriate to make declaration that procedural requirements not followed); *R v Swansea City Council, ex p Elitestone Ltd* [1993] 2 PLR 65, 70B-C ("a requirement in the public interest which must be observed regardless of lack of prejudice to any specific individual... Parliament has enacted an inhibition and that inhibition must be observed"); *R v Bradford Metropolitan Borough Council, ex p Sikander Ali* [1994] ELR 299, 318C (claimant not "underinformed or in any way misled"); *R v Secretary of State for the Home Department, ex p Awuls Karni Butt* [1994] Imm AR 11, 13 (no prejudice from failure to complete examination, where induced by claimant's own conduct); *R v Westminster City Council, ex p Ermakov* [1996] 2 All ER 302 (rejecting argument that statutory duty to give reasons with decision merely procedural and prejudice necessary). *R v MacDonald (Inspector of Taxes), ex p Hutchinson and Co Ltd* [1998] STC 680, 686j-687b (effect of failure to comply with statutory duty to give summary of reasons "depends on the importance of the requirements in the context of the particular statutory scheme"; here, important protection in context of intrusive power, so failure normally provides grounds to set aside the decision, subject to discretion to refuse a remedy).

60.4.5 **Procedural ultra vires: other aspects.**
(A) PROCEDURAL INVALIDITY OF DELEGATED LEGISLATION. *Hoffmann-La Roche (F) & Co AG v Secretary of State for Trade and Industry* [1975] AC 295, 365C-D (Lord Diplock: "the courts have jurisdiction to declare [the Order] to be invalid if they are satisfied that in making it the Minister who did so acted outwith the legislative powers conferred upon him by the previous Act of Parliament under which the order purported to be made, and this is so whether the order is ultra vires by reason of its contents (patent defects) or by reason of defects in the procedure followed prior to its being made (latent defects)"); *R v Secretary of State for Health, ex p United States Tobacco International Inc* [1992] QB 353 (regulations quashed for failure to consult on scientific report on which based); *R v Secretary of State for Education and Employment, ex p National Union of Teachers* 14th July 2000 unrep. (statutory instrument unlawful for failure to consult); *Simmonds v Newell* [1953] 1 WLR 826; *R v Sheer Metalcraft Ltd* [1954] 1 QB 586; *R v Secretary of State for Social Services, ex p Association of Metropolitan Authorities* [1986] 1 WLR 1; *R v Secretary of State for Social Services, ex p Camden London Borough Council* [1987] 1 WLR 819.
(B) PROCEDURAL ULTRA VIRES AS NULLITY. <44.2.3(E)>.
(C) PROCEDURAL ULTRA VIRES UNDER COMMUNITY LAW *R v Department of Health & Social Security, ex p Scotia Pharmaceuticals Ltd* 23rd July 1993 unrep.; *R v Licensing Authority of the Department of Health, ex p Scotia Pharmaceuticals* [1995] 3 CMLR 657; *R v Secretary of State for the Home Department, ex p Gallagher* [1994] 3 CMLR 295, paras [28], [30], [42] and [1996] 1 CMLR 557.
(D) PROCEDURAL ULTRA VIRES AND FAILURE TO COMPLAIN. <31.4.5>.
(E) PROCEDURAL ULTRA VIRES AS A QUESTION FOR THE COURT. <16.5.3>.

60.5 **The basic right to be heard.** A fundamental aspect of procedural fairness is the duty to give relevant persons an opportunity to make representations, often by putting matters and allowing a chance to comment.

60.5.1 **The right to be heard: general.** *R v Secretary of State for the Home Department, ex p Doody* [1994] 1 AC 531, 560D-G (Lord Mustill: "Fairness will very often require that a person who may be adversely affected by the decision will have an opportunity to make representations on his own behalf either before the decision is taken with a view to producing a favourable result; or after it is taken, with a view to procuring its modification; or both"); *In re Hamilton; In re Forrest* [1981] AC 1038, 1045B-D (Lord Fraser: "One of the principles of natural justice is that a person is entitled to adequate notice and opportunity to be heard before any judicial order is pronounced against him, so that he, or someone acting on his behalf, may make such representations, if any, as he sees fit. That is the rule of audi alteram partem"); *Hoffmann-La Roche (F) & Co AG v Secretary of State for Trade and Industry* [1975] AC 295, 368D-E ("the commissioners ... must act fairly by giving to the person whose activities are being investigated a reasonable opportunity to put forward facts and arguments in justification of his conduct of these activities before they reach a conclusion which may affect him adversely").

60.5.2 **The right to be heard: illustrations.**
(A) COURT PROCEEDINGS. *R v Trafford Magistrates Court, ex p Riley [1995] COD 373 (court order for destruction of dangerous dog unlawful for failure to allow known owner the opportunity of being heard); R v Pateley Bridge Justices, ex p Percy* [1994] COD 453 (unfair not to allow the chance to apologise, in contempt proceedings); *R v Selby Justices, ex p Frame* [1992] QB 72, 82B-C (committal for contempt unfair for failure to allow representations); *R (Afzal) v Election Court* [2005] EWCA Civ 647 [2005] LGR 823 at [42] (election court did not allow fair opportunity to deal with identification issues).
(B) IMMIGRATION. *R (L) v Secretary of State for the Home Department* [2003] EWCA Civ

25 [2003] 1 WLR 1230 at [30] (Secretary of State required to give fair hearing before certifying human rights claim as clearly unfounded and removing asylum seeker; need to give fair opportunity to demonstrate an arguable case; but fast-track procedure giving fair and adequate opportunity); *R (Q) v Secretary of State for the Home Department* [2003] EWCA Civ 364 [2004] QB 36 at [90] (unfair process because of inadequate questioning of asylum-seekers in relation to denial of welfare entitlements).

(C) PRISONERS/DETAINEES. *R (D) v Secretary of State for the Home Department* [2003] EWHC 155 (Admin) [2003] 1 FLR 979 at [28] (detained mother should have been given an opportunity to make representations before being separated from her baby); *R (Morley) v Nottinghamshire Healthcare NHS Trust* [2002] EWCA Civ 1728 [2003] 1 All ER 784 at [47] (no duty on Secretary of State to hear representations on clinical judgment as to treatability of transferred detainee); *R (Palmer) v Secretary of State for the Home Department* [2004] EWHC 1817 (Admin) at [27] (no duty in fairness to hear representations in relation to determinate sentence prisoner re-categorisation decision), [28] (emphasising availability of appeal against decision); *R (Hirst) v Secretary of State for the Home Department* [2001] EWCA Civ 378 at [26] (before reclassifying discretionary lifer, should give reasons and allow representations); *R (SP) v Secretary of State for the Home Department* [2004] EWCA Civ 1750 (fairness requiring opportunity to make representations before segregation order made).

(D) SECRETARY OF STATE. *R v Secretary of State for Education and Employment, ex p McCarthy* The Times 24th July 1996 (withdrawal of approval for independent school for children with special needs unfair for failure to consult the proprietor); *R v Secretary of State for the Environment, ex p Brent London Borough Council* [1982] QB 593 (breach of natural justice for Minister to fix rate support policy and then not permit representations by local authorities); *R v Secretary of State for the Home Department, ex p Norgren* [2000] QB 817 (no duty to invite further representations in an extradition context); *R (Quark Fishing Ltd) v Secretary of State for Foreign and Commonwealth Affairs* [2002] EWCA Civ 1409 at [57] ("foreign policy issues are an area of government decision-making as regards which our public law principles of fairness will not impose a requirement upon the Secretary of State to invite representations from parties who may be affected by the decision"), [58] (representations should have been invited on the question of compliance record, that not being a matter of foreign policy).

(E) LOCAL AUTHORITY. *R (Khatun) v London Borough of Newham* [2004] EWCA Civ 55 [2005] QB 37 at [32] (homeless person having no right to be heard as to housing and its suitability, but only to take advantage of favourable decision if reached); *R v Broxtowe Borough Council, ex p Bradford* [2000] LGR 386 (tennis coach banned for alleged sex abuse should have been given the opportunity to answer the allegations); *R v Devon County Council, ex p O (Adoption)* [1997] 2 FLR 388 (before child removed from prospective adopters, they should have been consulted and given an opportunity to meet its concerns); *R v Norfolk County Council, ex p M* [1989] QB 619 (unfair entry onto child abuse register), 628G-H; *R (C) v Brent, Kensington and Chelsea and Westminster Mental Health NHS Trust* [2002] EWHC 181 (Admin) (2003) 6 CCLR 335 at [24] (no duty to consult residents before moving them out of what was always intended to be interim accommodation); *R v London Borough of Hackney, ex p Decordova* (1995) 27 HLR 108, 113 (Laws J: "If the authority is minded to make an adverse decision because it does not believe the account given by the [claimant], it has to give the [claimant] an opportunity to deal with it"); *R v Huntingdon District Council, ex p Cowan* [1984] 1 WLR 501 (claimant should have been given opportunity to respond to licensing objections); *R v Birmingham City Council, ex p Dredger* (1994) 6 Admin LR 553 (changed basis of calculating stall charges for market traders unfair given prior practice of consultation); *R v Enfield London Borough Council, ex p TF Unwin (Roydon) Ltd* (1989) 1 Admin LR 50 (unfairness in suspending company from list of preferred contractors); *R v Devon County Council, ex p Baker* [1995] 1 All ER 73 (decision to close residential homes for the elderly unfair for failure properly to consult); *R v Falmouth and Truro Port Health Authority, ex p South West Water Ltd* [2001]

QB 445, 458B-459C (no general duty to allow representations before serving nuisance abatement notice; since not otherwise required by law, "only the clearest of assurances can give rise to [a] legitimate expectation [of consultation]"); *R (A1 Veg Ltd) v Hounslow London Borough Council* [2003] EWHC 3112 (Admin) [2004] LGR 536 (unfair for council in allocating reduced market space not to raise factual matters for disabusement).

(F) ONE-PARTY HEARINGS AND INTERIM ORDERS.*R (Kenny) v Leeds Magistrates Court* [2003] EWHC 2963 (Admin) [2004] 1 All ER 1333 at [23] (Owen J: "nothing inherently unlawful in interim injunctions made without notice. The power to make such orders is a necessary weapon in the judicial armour, enabling the court to do justice in circumstances where it is necessary to act urgently to protect the interests of a party, or where it is necessary to act without notice to a prospective defendant in order to ensure that the order of the court is effective"); *Moat Housing Group - South Ltd v Harris* [2005] EWCA Civ 287 [2005] 3 WLR 691 at [72] ("to make an order without notice is to depart from the normal rules as to due process and warrants the existence of exceptional circumstances").

(G) OTHER ILLUSTRATIONS.*R (Hodgson) v South Wales Police Authority* [2008] EWHC 1183 (Admin) (compulsory retirement of police officer unlawful absent an opportunity to make representations); *R (Sporting Options plc) v Horserace Betting Levy Board* [2003] EWHC 1943 (Admin) at [148] ("fairness required consultation with those liable to be adversely affected by the imposition of a tax by a statutory body such as the Levy Board"); *R v Legal Aid Board, ex p Donn & Co (a Firm)* [1996] 3 All ER 1, 14e-15h (solicitors entitled to be heard before multi-party litigation contract awarded); *Lewis v Attorney-General of Jamaica* [2001] 2 AC 50 (procedural defects in considering prerogative of mercy); *R (R) v Health Service Commissioner* [2004] EWHC 1847 (Admin) at [179] (Health Service Commissioner owing duty to disclose report in draft for comment, to anyone criticised in it) *R (Singapore Medical Council) v General Medical Council* [2006] EWHC 3277 (Admin) (no duty to allow SMC to make representations before discontinuing against doctor complaints which SMC had previously upheld); *Century National Merchant Bank and Trust Co Ltd v Davies* [1998] AC 628, 639C-D (impracticable and contrary to the public interest for bank directors to be heard before ministerial intervention); *R (X) v Chief Constable of West Midlands Police* [2004] EWCA Civ 1068 [2005] 1 WLR 65 at [37] (no duty to allow representations before disclosing Enhanced Criminal Record to potential employer); *R (Tucker) v Director General of the National Crime Squad* [2003] EWCA Civ 2 (no duty to hear representations before terminating secondment to the National Crime Squad).

60.5.3 **Extent of the duty to hear: relevant/affected persons.** *R v Commission for Racial Equality, ex p Hillingdon London Borough Council* [1982] AC 779, 787F (Lord Diplock, describing the "presumption that Parliament intended that the administrative body should act fairly towards those persons who will be affected by their decision"); *Bushell v Secretary of State for the Environment* [1981] AC 75, 96E (Lord Diplock: "Fairness would suggest that [as well as objectors] supporters of the scheme should also be heard and would require that before a decision is made to modify a draft scheme those adversely affected by the modification should be given an opportunity of stating their reasons for objecting to it"); *Cheall v Association of Professional Executive Clerical & Computer Staff* [1983] 2 AC 180, 190B (Lord Diplock: "Decisions that resolve disputes between the parties to them, whether by litigation or some other adversarial dispute-resolving process, often have consequences which affect persons who are not parties to the dispute; but the legal concept of natural justice has never been extended to give such persons as well as the parties themselves rights to be heard by the decision-making tribunal before the decision is reached"); *R v Liverpool Corporation, ex p Liverpool Taxi Fleet Operators' Association* [1972] 2 QB 299, 307 ("duty to act fairly ... means that they should be ready to hear not only the particular applicant but also any other persons or bodies whose interests are affected"); *R v Camden London Borough Council, ex p H* [1996] ELR 360 (importance of obtaining information as to the victim's point of view); *R v City of London Magistrates, ex p Asif* [1996] STC 611 (applications for access orders as to bank documents relating to claimant should have been inter partes on notice to claimant, and bank); *R v Bow County Court, ex p Pelling* [1999] 1 WLR 1807 (reasons for refusal to allow litigant in person to have assistance of McKenzie friend should be given to the litigant in person).

60.5.4 **Claimant relying on duty to hear/consult a third party.** *R (C) v Secretary of State for Justice* [2008] EWCA Civ 882 (claimant relying on Secretary of State's failure to consult the Children's Commissioner); *R v North Yorkshire County Council, ex p M* [1989] QB 411, 418A-F (parents successfully relying on duty to consult guardian ad litem); *R (Chaston) v Devon County Council* [2007] EWHC 1209 (Admin) at [66] (unfair not to refer new material back to inspector who had conducted inquiry); *In re Findlay* [1985] AC 318, 333E-334C (prisoners relying on alleged duty to consult the Parole Board); *R v Manchester Crown Court, ex p Taylor* [1988] 1 WLR 705; *R v North West Thames Regional Health Authority, ex p Daniels (Rhys William)* [1994] COD 44; *R v Managers of South Western Hospital, ex p M* [1993] QB 683, 698D-700E (failure adequately to consult nearest relative); *R v Secretary of State for the Home Department, ex p McCartney* [1994] COD 528 (implied power, but not duty, to consult Lord Chief Justice); *R v Newham London Borough Council, ex p X* [1995] ELR 303, 304G, 305B-E (duty to hear representations from parents); *R v Wandsworth London Borough Council, ex p Beckwith (No.2)* The Times 5th June 1995 (duty to consult residents of other homes); but see *R v Wandsworth London Borough Council, ex p Beckwith* [1996] 1 WLR 60 (HL); *R v Tunbridge Wells Health Authority, ex p Goodridge* The Times 21st May 1988 (doctors granted judicial review of hospital closure for failure to consult CHC); *R v BBC, ex p David Kelly* [1996] COD 58; *R v Secretary of State for Education and Employment, ex p National Union of Teachers* 14th July 2000 unrep. (duty to refer the matter to the review body); *R (Edwards) v Environment Agency* [2004] EWHC 736 (Admin) [2004] 3 All ER 21 (claimant having standing to challenge decision even though not having participated in the consultation exercise alleged to have been flawed), [16] (sufficient that "affected by its outcome"); *R (Ghadami) v Harlow District Council* [2004] EWHC 1883 (Admin) [2005] LGR 24 (defective notification and advertisement of planning permission), [67] (judge "satisfied that none of those upon whom notices should have been served can have been unaware of the planning permission or denied the opportunity to submit representations"), [73] ("satisfied that the defect in the advertisement did not frustrate the relevant objective of giving the public an opportunity to make representations").

60.5.5 **Fair hearing: not a court model.** *Board of Education v Rice* [1911] AC 179, 182 (decision-making body not "bound to treat such a question as though it were a trial. They have no power to administer an oath, and need not examine witnesses. They can obtain information in any way they think best, always giving a fair opportunity to those who are parties in the controversy for correcting or contradicting any relevant statement prejudicial to their view"); *Local Government Board v Arlidge* [1915] AC 120, 134 (criticising the "fallacy of the judgment of the majority in the Court of Appeal ... [in] setting up the test of the procedure of a Court of justice"); *Bushell v Secretary of State for the Environment* [1981] AC 75, 95B-D (Lord Diplock, endorsing a "warning against applying to procedures involved in the making of administrative decisions concepts that are appropriate to the conduct of ordinary civil litigation between private parties. So rather than use such phrases as `natural justice' which may suggest that the prototype is only to be found in procedures followed by English courts of law, I prefer ... that [the inquiry] must be fair"), 97B-D ("To `over-judicialise' the inquiry by insisting on observance of the procedures of a court of justice which professional lawyers alone are competent to operate effectively in the interests of their clients would not be fair"); *Ceylon University v Fernando* [1960] 1 WLR 223, 234 ("the Vice-Chancellor was not bound to treat the matter as if it was a trial... but could obtain information about it in any way he thought best, [and] it was open to him, if he thought fit, to question witnesses without inviting the plaintiff to be present"); *R v Secretary of State for the Home Department, ex p Venables* [1998] AC 407, 503C-D ("Whilst it is right for the courts to ensure that in making his decision the Secretary of State acts in accordance with natural justice ... the court should be careful not to impose judicial procedures and attitudes on what Parliament has decided should be an executive function"); *Hoffmann-La Roche (F) & Co AG v Secretary of State for Trade and Industry* [1975] AC 295, 368C-D ("The adversary procedure followed in a court of law is not appropriate"); *Mahon v Air New Zealand Ltd* [1984] AC 808, 821A ("The technical rules of evidence applicable to civil or criminal litigation form no part of the rules of natural justice"); *R (B) v Merton London Borough Council* [2003] EWHC 1689 (Admin) [2003] 4 All ER 280 (considering local authority's approach whether unaccompanied asylum-seeker owed duty as being aged less than 18 years old) at [50] (wrong "to impose unrealistic and unnecessary burdens"; "Judicialisation of what are relatively straightforward decisions is to be avoided").

60.5.6 Whether to have a public inquiry. *R (Persimmon Homes (South East) Ltd) v Secretary of State for Transport* [2005] EWHC 96 (Admin) at [22] (fairness not requiring Secretary of State to have an extra-statutory public inquiry); <59.2.4> (HRA:ECHR Art 2 investigative duty); *R (Wagstaff) v Secretary of State for Health* [2001] 1 WLR 292 (irrational all the circumstances for the Shipman inquiry to sit in private and not in public).

60.5.7 The basic right to be informed. <60.7>.

60.6 Adequate consultation. Legal standards require that a consultation exercise (1) be conducted at a time when proposals are at a sufficiently formative stage, (2) with adequate information and time to allow a proper and informed response, and (3) leading to a conscientious and open-minded consideration of relevant matters.

60.6.1 Adequate consultation in a nutshell. *R v North and East Devon Health Authority, ex p Coughlan* [2001] QB 213, at [108] ("To be proper, consultation must be undertaken at a time when proposals are still at a formative stage; it must include sufficient reasons for particular proposals to allow those consulted to give intelligent consideration and an intelligent response; adequate time must be given for this purpose; and the product of consultation must be conscientiously taken into account when the ultimate decision is taken"); *R (Greenpeace Ltd) v Secretary of State for Trade and Industry* [2007] EWHC 311 (Admin) [2007] Env LR 623 at [59] (overriding need for fairness); *R (Medway Council) v Secretary of State for Transport* [2002] EWHC 2516 (Admin) at [28] (consultation must be "fair").

60.6.2 Trigger for consultation. *R (Bhatt Murphy) v Independent Assessor* [2008] EWCA Civ 755 (no legitimate expectation or exceptional circumstance to require consultation regarding changes to scheme for compensation); <60.1.11> (procedural legitimate expectation); <60.4.2> (express procedural duty).

60.6.3 Adequate consultation: the Sedley requirements.[54] *R v London Borough of Barnet, ex p B* [1994] ELR 357, 372G (referring to "the Sedley requirements"), 370H-371A (Auld LJ: "The classic statement of the basic requirements of consultation is that formulated by Mr Stephen Sedley QC, as he then was, in argument, and adopted by Hodgson J in his judgment, in *R v Brent London Borough Council, ex p Gunning* (1985) 84 LGR 168, and approved by Webster J in *R v Sutton London Borough Council, ex p Hamlet* [26th March 1986 unrep.]..., namely: 'First, ... consultation must be at a time when proposals are still at a formative stage. Secondly... the proposer must give sufficient reasons for any proposal to permit of intelligent consideration

---

[54] Kate Olley [2001] JR 99; Michael Fordham [2007] JR 187.

and response. Thirdly... adequate time must be given for consideration and response and, finally, fourthly... the product of consultation must be conscientiously taken into account in finalising any... proposals'"). See too the Cabinet Office Code of Practice on Written Consultation.

60.6.4 Consultation at a formative stage. *R (Montpeliers & Trevors Association) v City of Westminster* [2005] EWHC 16 (Admin) [2006] LGR 304 at [25] (consultation vitiated because an option of central significance had "already been excluded from further consideration"), [29] (fairness required consultation on all the various options); *R (Parents for Legal Action Ltd) v Northumberland County Council* [2006] EWHC 1081 (Admin) [2006] ELR 397 at [36] (phased consultation meaning unlawful exclusion of comments on impact on schools when identifying model of schooling); *R v North & East Devon Health Authority, ex p Pow* (1998) 1 CCLR 280 (duty to consult when proposal at a formative stage, not to wait until it had evolved into a definite solution); *Nichol v Gateshead Metropolitan Borough Council* (1988) 87 LGR 435, 451-456 (ability to choose a preferred option and reject others means that "formative stage" of proposal not yet arrived at); *R (Medway Council) v Secretary of State for Transport* [2002] EWHC 2516 (Admin) at [32] (unfair to exclude an option and deny the only real opportunity to present a case on it).

60.6.5 Sufficient explanation/notification. *R (Greenpeace Ltd) v Secretary of State for Trade and Industry* [2007] EWHC 311 (Admin) [2007] Env LR 623 (paper containing insufficient information to be adequate consultation) at [68] (thumbnail sketch of issues wholly inadequate), [116]; *R (Eisai Ltd) v National Institute for Health and Clinical Excellence* [2008] EWCA Civ 438 at [66] (unfair not to disclose fully-executable version of model); *R (Lloyd) v Dagenham London Borough Council* [2001] EWCA Civ 533 (2001) 4 CCLR 196 at [13] (need "candid disclosure of the reasons for what is proposed"); *R (Madden) v Bury Metropolitan Borough Council* [2002] EWHC 1882 (Admin) (2002) 5 CCLR 622 at [58] (no adequate and accurate summary of the true reasons), [60] (no indication of possible alternatives); *R v Secretary of State for Transport, ex p Richmond Upon Thames London Borough Council* [1995] Env LR 390, 405 (misleading consultation paper); *R v Lambeth London Borough Council, ex p N* [1996] ELR 299 (need to explain timetable and alternative arrangements); *R v Secretary of State for Education, ex p Bandtock* [2001] ELR 333 at [37] (claimant could have checked if something unclear); *R (Wainwright) v Richmond upon Thames London Borough Council* [2001] EWHC Admin 1090 (whether insufficiently widespread distribution of mailshot to local residents); *R (Beale) v Camden London Borough Council* [2004] EWHC 6 (Admin) [2004] LGR 291 at [19] (no need to articulate "both sides of the argument"); *R (Capenhurst) v Leicester City Council* [2004] EWHC 2124 (Admin) (2004) 7 CCLR 557 at [46] (need to explain criteria and key factors).

60.6.6 Adequate time. *R v Secretary of State for Education and Employment, ex p National Union of Teachers* 14th July 2000 unrep. (four days wholly insufficient); *R v Secretary of State for Wales, ex p Williams* [1997] ELR 100 (no duty to prolong consultation to allow comments on other people's comments); *R (Amvac Chemical UK Ltd) v Secretary of State for Environment, Food and Rural Affairs* [2001] EWHC Admin 1011 at [63] (despite urgency, period of notification too short prior to suspension of use of a pesticide).

60.6.7 Conscientious consideration. *R v London Borough of Barnet, ex p B* [1994] ELR 357, 375C (commenting, as to the fourth requirement, that "the important thing is that the council should have embarked upon the consultation process prepared to change course, if persuaded by it to do so"); *R (Smith) v East Kent Hospital NHS Trust* [2002] EWHC 2640 (Admin) (2003) 6 CCLR 251 at [61] (duty to take conscientiously into account, not "a duty not to make a decision without prior agreement or consensus of the consultees"); *R (Cummins) v London*

Borough of Camden [2001] EWHC Admin 111 at [256] ("The decision-making structure, the nature of the functions and the democratic accountability of Councillors permit, indeed must recognise, the legitimate potential for predisposition towards a particular decision"), applied in *R (Westminster City Council) v Mayor of London* [2002] EWHC 2440 (Admin) [2003] LGR 611 at [27] (adequate consultation as to Congestion Charging Scheme for London).

60.6.8 **Consultation: other matters.** *R (British Casino Association Ltd) v Secretary of State for Culture Media and Sport* [2007] EWHC 1312 (Admin) at [85] (leaving open whether consultation duty could arise in relation to delegated legislation); *R (Legal Remedy UK Ltd) v Secretary of State for Health* [2007] EWHC 1252 (Admin) at [135] (sufficient to consult with representative organisations); *R (Medway Council) v Secretary of State for Transport* [2002] EWHC 2516 (Admin) (unreasonable or unfair to exclude one airport from consultation on regional runway capacity); *R (Smith) v East Kent Hospital NHS Trust* [2002] EWHC 2640 (Admin) (2003) 6 CCLR 251 at [45] (no duty to reconsult unless "fundamental difference between the proposals consulted on and those which the consulting party subsequently wishes to adopt"), [57] (no duty to consult further on amended proposal emerging in the consultation process itself); *R (Carton) v Coventry City Council* (2001) 4 CCLR 41, 44C-E (further consultation required where fundamental change).

60.6.9 **Error of approach by consultee/adviser.** *R (Cathco Property Holdings Ltd) v Cygnor Gwynedd Council* [2008] EWHC 1462 (Admin) at [77] (planning committee misled by planning officer's erroneous advice); *R (Morris) v Trafford Healthcare NHS Trust* [2006] EWHC 2334 (Admin) (2006) 9 CCLR 648 at [60] (wrongly relying on expert report where expert had been misinformed); *R v Secretary of State for Education and Employment, ex p Portsmouth Football Club Ltd* [1998] COD 142 (consulted bodies had wrongly treated Secretary of State's policy as though rigid criteria); *R (Smith) v Secretary of State for the Home Department* [2004] EWCA Civ 99 [2004] QB 1341 at [14] (any procedural or substantive shortcomings in the tariff decision of the Lord Chief Justice could be laid at the Secretary of State's door "on the ground that he had acted on the advice of the Lord Chief Justice") (HL is [2005] UKHL 51 [2006] 1 AC 159); *R (Goldsmith) v London Borough of Wandsworth* [2004] EWCA Civ 1170 (2004) 7 CCLR 472 (council's decision to terminate residential placement vitiated by flaws by Care Panel whose recommendations it adopted, where Panel had failed to keep minutes, give reasons, take account of a relevant care assessment and allow claimant's daughter to attend a meeting); <63.1.5> (external unfairness).

60.6.10 **Consultation: further illustrations.** *R v Secretary of State for Social Services, ex p Association of Metropolitan Authorities* [1986] 1 WLR 1 ("In any context the essence of consultation is the communication of a genuine invitation to give advice and a genuine receipt of that advice"); *R v Secretary of State for Trade and Industry, ex p UNISON* [1996] ICR 1003, 1015F (Otton LJ: "Under our domestic law fair consultation involves giving the body consulted a fair and proper opportunity to understand fully the matters about which it is being consulted and to express its views on those subjects, with the consultor thereafter considering those views properly and genuinely"); *R v Birmingham City Council, ex p Dredger* (1994) 6 Admin LR 553, 572D-573H; *R v Secretary of State for Health, ex p London Borough of Hackney* 25th April 1994 and 29th July 1994 unrep.; *R v Kingston & Richmond Health Authority, ex p Paxman* [1995] COD 410 (consultation ill-timed, ill-defined and inadequate); *R v Secretary of State for Education and Employment and the North East London Education Authority, ex p M* [1996] ELR 162, 206A-210D (despite "striking omission" of any statutory requirement to consult the court could not accept that no duty to consult arose; but such an omission was relevant when considering the extent to which consultation was demanded).

60.7 **The basic right to be informed.**Hand in hand with the right to be heard is a right to be given sufficient information to enable proper representations. This allows representations to be properly informed and avoids unfair secrecy or the relevant person later being unfairly taken by surprise.

60.7.1 **Codified rights to information.** <17.4.2>.

60.7.2 **Being heard and being told: the vital link.** <60.5> (the basic right to be heard).
(A) LISTEN MEANS TELL. *R (Ramda) v Secretary of State for the Home Department* [2002] EWHC 1278 (Admin) at [25] (Sedley LJ: "[The Home Secretary] must not rely on potentially influential material which is withheld from the individual affected. This is a simple corollary of Lord Loreburn's axiom that the duty to listen fairly to both sides lies upon everyone who decides anything (*Board of Education v Rice* [1911] AC 179) and of Lord Denning's dictum that if the right to be heard is to be worth anything it must carry a right in the accused man to know the case against him (*Kanda v Government of Malaya* [1962] AC 322)"); *Malloch v Aberdeen Corporation* [1971] 1 WLR 1578, 1588F (Lord Morris (dissenting in the result): "What would be the point of giving someone a right to be heard while denying to him any knowledge as to what he was to be heard about?"); *Kanda v Government of Malaya* [1962] AC 322, 337 (Lord Denning: "If the right to be heard is to be a real right which is worth anything, it must carry with it a right in the accused man to know the case which is made against him. He must know what evidence has been given and what statements have been made affecting him: and then he must be given a fair opportunity to correct or contradict them"); *R v Commission for Racial Equality, ex p Hillingdon London Borough Council* [1982] AC 779, 787H-788A ("The right of a person to be heard in support of his objection to a proposal to embark upon an investigation of his activities cannot be exercised effectively unless that person is informed with reasonable specificity what are the kinds of acts to which the proposed investigation is to be directed and confined"); *Ridge v Baldwin* [1964] AC 40, 113-114 ("the essential requirements of natural justice at least include that before someone is condemned he is to have an opportunity of defending himself, and in order that he may do so that he is to be made aware of the charges or allegations or suggestions which he has to meet"; "here is something which is basic to our system: the importance of upholding it far transcends the significance of any particular case"); *O'Reilly v Mackman* [1983] 2 AC 237, 279G ("a reasonable opportunity of learning what is alleged against him and of putting forward his own case in answer to it"); *De Verteuil v Knaggs* [1918] AC 557, 560 ("a duty of giving to any person against whom the complaint is made a fair opportunity to make any relevant statement which he may desire to bring forward and a fair opportunity to correct or controvert any relevant statement brought forward to his prejudice"); *In re D (Minors) (Adoption Reports: Confidentiality)* [1996] AC 593, 603H-604A ("it is a first principle of fairness that each party to a judicial process shall have an opportunity to answer by evidence and argument any adverse material which the tribunal may take into account when forming its opinion. This principle is lame if the party does not know the substance of what is said against him (or her), for what he does not know he cannot answer"); *R v Secretary of State for the Home Department, ex p Murat Akdogan* [1995] Imm AR 176, 179-181 (not enough simply to ask whether person concerned wants to say/add anything), applying *R v Secretary of State for the Home Department, ex p Sittampalam Thirukumar* [1989] Imm AR 402, 414 ("if the opportunity to make representations is to be meaningful the mind of the applicant must be directed to the considerations which will, as matters stand, defeat the application"); *R v P Borough Council, ex p S* [1999] Fam 188, 220C ("One of the basic requirements of procedural fairness is that the decision-maker must disclose to the person affected, in advance of the decision, information of relevance to the decision so that the person affected has an opportunity to controvert it or to comment on it"); *R v Secretary of State for the Home Department, ex p Kingdom of Belgium* 15th February 2000 unrep. (since

requesting states being consulted, fairness also requiring disclosure of Pinochet medical document).
(B) TELL MEANS LISTEN: DISCLOSURE/NOTIFICATION MEANS DUTY TO LISTEN. *Ceylon University v Fernando* [1960] 1 WLR 223, 234 (Lord Jenkins: "the vital condition... that a fair opportunity must have been given to the plaintiff to correct or contradict any relevant statement to his prejudice"); *R v North Yorkshire County Council, ex p M* [1989] QB 411, 418D-E ("duty on the part of the local authority, not only to disclose proposals for change in relation to the child, but also to listen to the views of the guardian ad litem"); *R v Devon County Council, ex p Baker* [1995] 1 All ER 73, 83c-d; *Wiseman v Borneman* [1971] AC 297, 315D-E ("to give the taxpayer the right to see the counter-statement would be useless unless he were also allowed to comment upon it and have his comments taken into consideration by the tribunal"), 308D (Lord Reid), 312B-C (Lord Guest); *R (Wainwright) v Richmond upon Thames London Borough Council* [2001] EWHC Admin 1090 at [6] (purpose of notification of the public of proposal means council having duty to consider representations made in response to notification).

60.7.3 **The right not to be unfairly taken by surprise.** *R (Anufrijeva) v Secretary of State for the Home Department* [2003] UKHL 36 [2004] 1 AC 604 at [30] (Lord Steyn: "In our system of law surprise is regarded as the enemy of justice"); *Fairmount Investments Ltd v Secretary of State for the Environment* [1976] 1 WLR 1255, 1266D-E ("taken by surprise in a relevantly unfair way by the conclusions of the inspector accepted by the Secretary of State"); *Hadmor Productions Ltd v Hamilton* [1983] 1 AC 191, 233B-C ("one of the most fundamental rules of natural justice: the right of each to be informed of any point adverse to him that is going to be relied upon by the judge and to be given an opportunity of stating what his answer to it is"); *R v Birmingham City Justice, ex p Chris Foreign Foods (Wholesalers) Ltd* [1970] 1 WLR 1428 (unfair for magistrate to retire to take private advice from local authority officials); *R v Chance, ex p Coopers & Lybrand* (1995) 7 Admin LR 821, 835H ("surprise is the enemy of justice"); *R v Secretary of State for Education, ex p E* [1996] ELR 312 (Secretary of State introducing new point, without communicating it and allowing representations); *R v Immigration Appeal Tribunal, ex p Sui Rong Suen* [1997] Imm AR 355, 363 ("It is normally incumbent upon an adjudicator or Tribunal, which is going to refer to an authority or a proposition of law which has not been put to an appellant to cause that to be done before the decision is finally reached. Sometimes it may happen that an adjudicating body discovers a relevant authority after the argument has been heard. If so, and if it might be determinative and need argument, there should be a reconvening of the hearing or, at the very least, an opportunity given for submissions to be made in writing"); *R v Criminal Injuries Compensation Board, ex p K* [1999] QB 1131, 1141E (board under no duty to warn claimant's counsel of intention to take particular point at hearing); *R (Interbrew SA) v Competition Commission* [2001] EWHC Admin 367 (no fair opportunity to deal with crucial point of concern); *R (Persaud) v University of Cambridge* [2001] EWCA Civ 534 [2001] ELR 480 at [38]-[39] (failure to put material questions to claimant).

60.7.4 **Whether a right to be told.** *Secretary of State for the Home Department v MB* [2007] UKHL 46 [2008] 1 AC 440 at [29] (control orders and entitlement to be told case against them); *Belfast City Council v Miss Behavin' Ltd* [2007] UKHL 19 [2007] 1 WLR 1420 at [8], [74] (licence applicant entitled to have late objections fairly put); *Ward v Police Service of Northern Ireland* [2007] UKHL 50 [2007] 1 WLR 3013 (claimant lawfully excluded from closed part of hearing); *R (Abbey Mine Ltd) v Coal Authority* [2008] EWCA Civ 353 at [31]-[32] (licence bidder entitled to be told concerns regarding bid, but not details of rival bidder's case); *R (D) v Independent Appeal Panel of Bromley London Borough Council* [2007] EWCA Civ 1010 [2008] LGR 267 (parents entitled to be told case needing to meet on reinstatement); *R (Benson) v Secretary of State for Justice* [2007] EWHC 2055 (Admin) (recalled prisoner not provided with information regarding alleged licence breach in sufficient detail to provide meaningful response); *R (Oyeyi-Effiong) v Bridge NDC Seven Sisters Partnership* [2007] EWHC 606 (Admin) [2007] LGR 669 at [55] (needing clear picture of misconduct case and nature of investigation); *R (Eisai Ltd) v National Institute for Health and Clinical Excellence* [2008] EWCA Civ 438 at [66] (unfair not to disclose fully-executable model); *R (Ireneschild) v Lambeth London Borough Council* [2007] EWCA Civ 234 [2007] LGR 619 at [70] (non-disclosure of internal assessment report not unfair); *R (Banks) v Secretary of State for the Environment, Food and Rural Affairs* [2004] EWHC 416 (Admin) at [95] (failure to explain "what concerns they had to answer"); *R v Secretary of State for the Home Department, ex p Fayed* [1998] 1 WLR 763[55] (citizenship applicant entitled to be told of Secretary of State's concerns); *R (Amvac Chemical UK Ltd) v Secretary of State for Environment, Food and Rural Affairs* [2001] EWHC Admin 1011 at [54]-[64] (despite urgency, failure to give fair and prompt warning and opportunity for comment); *R (Kent Pharmaceuticals Ltd) v Director of the Serious Fraud Office* [2004] EWCA Civ 1494 [2005] 1 WLR 1302 at [29] (owner of seized documents entitled to be told of intended disclosure to another government department).

60.7.5 **Whether a right to see documents/materials relied upon.** *R (Roberts) v Parole Board* [2005] UKHL 45 [2005] 2 AC 738 at [43] (Lord Woolf, referring to a "golden rule of full disclosure"); *R (Ramda) v Secretary of State for the Home Department* [2002] EWHC 1278 (Admin) at [25] (Secretary of State "must not rely on potentially influential material which is withheld from the individual affected"); *R (Edwards) v Environment Agency* [2006] EWCA Civ 877 [2007] Env LR 126 (CA) at [106] (unfair not to disclose internal expert report); *R v London Borough of Camden, ex p Paddock* [1995] COD 130 (see transcript) (describing as "fundamental", the "principle that a decision-making body should not see relevant material without giving those affected a chance to comment on it and, if they wish, to controvert it"); *R (Banks) v Secretary of State for the Environment, Food and Rural Affairs* [2004] EWHC 416 (Admin) (unfair failure to disclose test results), [104] ("Defra deliberately refused to disclose highly material information to the claimants"); *Wiseman v Borneman* [1971] AC 297, 320B-C ("the natural aversion against allowing a decision to be made on the basis of material he has not seen"); *Kanda v Government of Malaya* [1962] AC 322, 336 ("the hearing by the adjudicating officer was vitiated by his being furnished with [the] report without inspector Kanda being given any opportunity of correcting or contradicting it"); *Crompton v General Medical Council* [1981] 1 WLR 1435, 1441E ("observance of the rules of natural justice would have demanded that the psychiatric medical evidence upon which the committee proposed to act should be disclosed to the doctor and an opportunity given to him to answer it and adduce, if he so wished, expert psychiatric evidence on his own behalf to contradict it"); *R (O'Leary) v Chief Constable of the Merseyside Police* 9th February 2001 unrep. at [16] (unfair not to disclose and allow comment on departmental report relied on in imposing employment restrictions); *R v Hampshire County Council, ex p K* [1990] 2 QB 71 (duty in child abuse case to disclose to accused parents oral and written medical reports); *R v Bank of England, ex p Mellstrom* [1995] CLC 232, 240B-241E (whether breach of natural justice even though material not in fact relied upon); *R v Bromley Magistrates' Court, ex p Smith* [1995] 1 WLR 944, 947F-H (right to see unused material); *R v London Legal Aid Area Office Committee, ex p Ewing* [1997] COD 134 (no duty to disclose memorandum of guidance to decision-maker, regarding relevant legal principles); *R v Criminal Injuries Compensation Authority, ex p Leatherland* [2001] ACD 76 ("It is ... a requirement of fairness ... that a claimant who is appealing to the [Criminal Injuries Compensation] Appeals Panel should be provided, in advance of the day of the hearing, with access to the evidential material which the Authority, through its presenting officers, will be relying upon at the hearing of the appeal"); *R (Bentley) v HM Coroner District of Avon* [2001] EWHC Admin 170 (unfair

---

[55] Sarah-Jane Davies [1997] JR 17.

for coroner not to have made advance disclosure of witness statements); *R v Governors of Dunraven School, ex p B* [2000] ELR 156 (unfair for governors to have access to material to which accused pupil did not); *R (Bedford) v London Borough of Islington* [2002] EWHC 2044 (Admin) [2003] Env LR 463 at [102] (no unfairness here in non-disclosure of confidential document relating to planning application); *Sheridan v Stanley Cole (Wainfleet) Ltd* [2003] EWCA Civ 1046 [2003] 4 All ER 1181 (unfair for EAT not to allow chance to make representations on new authorities relied on, if central to its decision); *R (Green) v Police Complaints Authority* [2004] UKHL 6 [2004] 1 WLR 725 (Police Complaints Authority entitled to decline to disclose to the complainant confidential statements and documents relating to eye-witnesses, where disclosure was not necessary for the proper discharge of the PCA's functions).

60.7.6 **A right to sufficient information.** *Bushell v Secretary of State for the Environment* [1981] AC 75, 96C-D (Lord Diplock: "fairness requires that the objectors should ... be given sufficient information about the reasons relied on by the department as justifying the draft scheme to enable them to challenge the accuracy of any facts and the validity of any arguments upon which the departmental reasons are based"); *In re Pergamon Press Ltd* [1971] Ch 388, 400E-F; *Chiltern District Council v Keane* [1985] 1 WLR 619, 622A-B; *R v Secretary of State for Social Services, ex p Association of Metropolitan Authorities* [1986] 1 WLR 1, 4G; *R v Secretary of State for the Home Department, ex p Hickey (No.2)* [1995] 1 WLR 734, 742D-F, 743C-D, 744A-C; *R v Inland Revenue Commissioners, ex p Howmet* [1994] STC 413, 414d-j.

60.7.7 **Whether a right to disclosure of other persons' representations/material.** *R (Abbey Mine Ltd) v Coal Authority* [2008] EWCA Civ 353 at [31]-[32] (no entitlement to description of rival bidder's case); *R v Secretary of State for Health, ex p United States Tobacco International Inc* [1992] QB 353, 370F-G (not entitled to see other persons' representations); *Kanda v Government of Malaya* [1962] AC 322, 337 (entitled to "know what evidence has been given and what statements have been made affecting him"); *R v Secretary of State for Wales, ex p Williams* [1997] ELR 100 (no duty to prolong consultation to allow everybody to comment on everybody else's comments); *R (Green) v Police Complaints Authority* [2004] UKHL 6 [2004] 1 WLR 725 (no duty here to disclose eyewitness statements to victim); *R (Begum) v Tower Hamlets London Borough Council* [2002] EWHC 633 (Admin) [2003] HLR 70 at [34] (Stanley Burnton J, accepting in the context of a housing application that "when inquiries of third persons yield significant information inconsistent with that provided by the applicant, which will substantially affect the decision of the local authority, the local authority must put that information to the applicant and give him an opportunity to comment on it"); *R (Anglian Water Services Ltd) v Environment Agency* [2003] EWHC 1506 (Admin) [2004] Env LR 287 at [26] (unfair for Environment Agency not to disclose residents' representations for sewerage company to comment, where dispute as to whether to impose requirement to provide a public sewer).

60.7.8 **A right to pre-decision 'reasons'/impressions.** *R (Interbrew SA) v Competition Commission* [2001] EWHC Admin 367 (Moses J: "generally [the duty of fairness] will require the decision maker to identify in advance areas which are causing him concern in reaching the decision in question"); *R (Gupta) v General Medical Council* The Times 16th October 2001 (GMC should have given notice of impressions and fact that minded to impose interim suspension pending appeal); *Bushell v Secretary of State for the Environment* [1981] AC 75, 96C-D (Lord Diplock: "fairness requires that the objectors should have an opportunity of communicating to the minister the reasons for their objections to the scheme and the facts on which they are based... Fairness ... also requires that the objectors should be given sufficient information about the reasons relied on by the department as justifying the draft scheme to enable them to challenge the accuracy of any facts and the validity of any arguments upon which the departmental reasons are based"); *Mahon v Air New Zealand Ltd* [1984] AC 808,

821B ("the risk of the finding being made"); *R v Gaming Board for Great Britain, ex p Benaim & Khaida* [1970] 2 QB 417, 430H ("impressions"); *R v Secretary of State for the Home Department, ex p Fayed* [1998] 1 WLR 763, 776H (duty "to identify the subject of his concern in such terms as to enable the [claimant] to make such submissions as he can"); *R v Governor of Maidstone Prison, ex p Peries* [1998] COD 150 (non-category A prisoner entitled to post-decision reasons as to classification review, but not pre-decision impressions: given effect of decision and administrative burden); *R v Chief Constable of the North Wales Police, ex p AB* [1999] QB 396, 428B-F (before deciding whether pressing need justifying disclosure to the public of whereabouts of paedophiles, they should have been given the gist of what the police had learned and permitted to make representations on it); *R v Parliamentary Commissioner for Administration, ex p Dyer* [1994] 1 WLR 621, 628G-629E (no breach of natural justice for Parliamentary Ombudsman to disclose draft report to DSS but not to complainant); *Huntley v Attorney-General for Jamaica* [1995] 2 AC 1, 17C-E (due process in context of prerogative of mercy); *R v Pateley Bridge Justices, ex p Percy* [1994] COD 453 (risk of imprisonment, in contempt proceedings); *R v Governors of the Sheffield Hallam University, ex p R* [1995] ELR 267, 282-284 (right to "adequate prior warning" prior to expulsion); *R v Southwark London Borough Council, ex p Ryder* (1996) 28 HLR 56, 67 (failure to give opportunity to comment on decisive factor); *R (Q) v Secretary of State for the Home Department* [2003] EWCA Civ 364 [2004] QB 36 at [99] (failure to put relevant matters to asylum-seekers in relation to welfare benefits); *R (Varma) v Duke of Kent* [2004] EWHC 1705 (Admin) [2004] ELR 616 at [24] (Visitor should in fairness give student opportunity to make representations on commissary's advice).

60.7.9 **The right to the `gist'.**

(A) ENTITLEMENT. *R v Secretary of State for the Home Department, ex p Doody* [1994] 1 AC 531, 560F-G (Lord Mustill: "Since the person affected usually cannot make worthwhile representations without knowing what factors may weigh against his interests fairness will very often require that he is informed of the gist of the case which he has to answer"); *Re McClean* [2005] UKHL 46 [2005] UKHRR 826 (importance of giving gist in sentence review context); *R v Secretary of State for the Home Department, ex p Duggan* [1994] 3 All ER 277 (category A prisoner under security category review, right to see the gist); *R v Chief Constable of the North Wales Police, ex p AB* [1999] QB 396, 428B-F (paedophiles entitled to gist of the information held by police, before dissemination); *R v Secretary of State for the Home Department, ex p Harry* [1998] 1 WLR 1737 (restricted prisoner entitled to gist of information before Advisory Board).
(B) ADEQUACY. *R v Secretary of State for the Home Department, ex p Harry* [1998] 1 WLR 1737, 1748B-D ("When a fundamental right is in issue, a more expansive and informative summary may be called for. The detail required must depend on what (having regard to the importance of the issue at stake and of the contents of the document in question on that issue) fairness requires to enable the making of meaningful and focused representations"); *R (Lord v Secretary of State for the Home Department* [2003] EWHC 2073 (Admin) at [58] ("The essential vice in the gist is that it failed to reveal the divergence of opinion and that it failed to provide the gist of *each* of those divergent views").
(C) MORE THAN A GIST. *Lewis v Attorney-General of Jamaica* [2001] 2 AC 50 (condemned prisoner entitled to documents not merely the gist, in relation to prerogative of mercy); *R (Williams) v Secretary of State for the Home Department* [2002] EWCA Civ 498 [2002] 1 WLR 2264 at [32] (in exceptional case where favourable decision of Discretionary Lifer Panel, Category A Review Panel should have given prisoner an oral hearing and disclosure of full reports, not just gists)

60.7.10 **Practical limits of the duty to tell.** *Hoffmann-La Roche (F) & Co AG v Secretary of State for Trade and Industry* [1975] AC 295, 369D-E (Lord Diplock: "Even in judicial

proceedings in a court of law, once a fair hearing has been given to the rival cases presented by the parties the rules of natural justice do not require the decision maker to disclose what he is minded to decide so that the parties may have a further opportunity of criticising his mental processes before he reaches a final decision. If this were a rule of natural justice only the most talkative of judges would satisfy it and trial by jury would have to be abolished");*R v Secretary of State for Education, ex p S* [1995] ELR 71, 81G-H, 85F-G (Russell LJ: "There must come a time when finality has to be achieved"); *R (Ramda) v Secretary of State for the Home Department* [2002] EWHC 1278 (Admin) at [25] ("the Home Secretary is not required to be drawn into a never-ending dialogue"); *R v Secretary of State for Wales, ex p Williams* [1997] ELR 100 (no duty to prolong consultation to allow everybody to comment on everybody else's comments); *R v Secretary of State for the Home Department, ex p Al-Mehdawi* [1990] 1 AC 876 (sending notice of hearing sufficed); *Bolton Metropolitan District Council v Secretary of State for the Environment* [1995] 3 PLR 37, 42D (adequate reasons not meaning duty to refer to every material consideration; "otherwise his task would never be done"); *R v Secretary of State for Education and Employment, ex p M* [1996] ELR 162, 209E-F ("In short, there was much forewarning here of the possibility that this school was doomed. The writing was on the wall if only in pencil. If that was not to be inked in, however, those opposed knew from an early date that they had to marshall their opposition"); *R v Secretary of State for the Home Department, ex p McAvoy* [1998] 1 WLR 790 (category A prisoners entitled only to gist of reports relevant to category review, not full disclosure of material or names of sources); <60.7.9> (right to the gist); *In re Pergamon Press Ltd* [1971] Ch 388, 399H-400A (Lord Denning MR: "The inspectors can obtain information in any way they think best, but before they condemn or criticise a man, they must give him a fair opportunity for correcting or contradicting what is said against him. They need not quote chapter and verse. An outline of the charge will usually suffice"); *R v Bradford Metropolitan Borough Council, ex p Sikander Ali* [1994] ELR 299, 318B (Jowitt J: "The statutory requirement is to publish information about the policy to be followed in deciding admissions. That does not require that every nut and bolt of what is to be done has to be spelt out").

60.7.11 **Confidentiality and disclosure.**
(A) THE CONFIDENTIALITY BALANCE. *R v Secretary of State for the Home Department, ex p Kingdom of Belgium* 15th February 2000 unrep. (Simon Brown LJ, asking: "does the public interest in making the limited further disclosure now sought outweigh the remaining confidentiality in the report? That [depends] upon whether disclosure to the requesting states is required in the interests of fairness. If fairness demands disclosure, then to my mind disclosure clearly becomes the overriding public interest"); *R (Gunn-Russo) v Nugent Care Society* [2001] EWHC Admin 566 [2001] UKHRR 1320 (discussing the approach to fairness and confidentiality).
(B) DISCLOSURE FOR THE PROPER PERFORMANCE OF FUNCTIONS. *R v Chief Constable of the North Wales Police, ex p AB* [1999] QB 396, 409H-410C (Lord Bingham CJ (DC): "When, in the course of performing its public duties, a public body ... comes into possession of information relating to a member of the public, being information not generally available and potentially damaging to that member of the public if disclosed, the body ought not to disclose such information save for the purpose of and to the extent necessary for performance of its public duty or enabling some other public body to perform its public duty... The principle ... rests on a fundamental rule of good public administration, which the law must recognise and if necessary enforce"), 429D (Lord Woolf MR (CA): "the information having come into the police's possession to enable them to perform their functions, as a public body they were only entitled to use that information when this was reasonably required to enable them to properly carry out their functions"), applied in *R v Secretary of State for the Home Department, ex p Kingdom of Belgium* 15th February 2000 unrep. (fairness requiring disclosure and so necessary for performance of duty); *R (Green) v Police Complaints Authority* [2004] UKHL 6 [2004] 1

WLR 725 at [73] (Lord Rodger: "if disclosure were ... necessary for the proper discharge of the Authority's functions, then the statements would have to be disclosed, whether or not they were regarded as confidential. But it should be recognised that the [statutory] starting-point ... is that information provided to the Authority is to be kept confidential").
(C) OTHER CASES. *R v Gaming Board for Great Britain, ex p Benaim & Khaida* [1970] 2 QB 417, 431B-G (confidentiality means not entitled to sources); *R v Lewes Justices, ex p the Gaming Board of Great Britain* [1973] AC 388; *R v Joint Higher Committee on Surgical Training, ex p Milner* (1995) 7 Admin LR 454, 468F-470D (confidentiality of educational references not overridden by natural justice); *R v Poole Borough Council, ex p Cooper* (1995) 27 HLR 605, 612-613 ("If fairness demands disclosure to the homeless applicant of any material that might disadvantage, even marginally, his or her claim, the local authority must not do anything to put at risk the applicant's right to be treated fairly in being given the opportunity to deal with matters adverse to the application. A local authority which must know that, in acquiring information, it might be the recipient of material adverse to the applicant, must refrain from doing anything to induce such a situation. It cannot allow a third party, who supplies information, to affect adversely the relationship between the claimant to housing and the local housing authority"); *R v Secretary of State for the Home Department, ex p Gallagher* [1996] 1 CMLR 557 (person deported under the Prevention of Terrorism Act not entitled under EC law to know identity and status of person dealing with case); *R v London Beth Din (Court of the Chief Rabbi), ex p Michael Bloom* [1998] COD 131 (defendant entitled to balance interests by concluding that information provided in confidence should not be disclosed); *In re D (Minors) (Adoption Reports: Confidentiality)* [1996] AC 593 (as to confidentiality and substance of report); *Soden v Burns* [1996] 3 All ER 967 (effect of qualified duty of confidence attaching to information obtained under compulsory powers); *R v Secretary of State for the Home Department, ex p Mulkerrins* [1998] COD 235 (judicial review court having no power independently to assess in the interests of justice appropriateness of claim to withhold information as confidential); *R v Criminal Injuries Compensation Authority, ex p Leatherland* [2001] ACD 76 (confidentiality not a sufficient reason not to disclose evidence on which relying).

60.7.12 Claimant relying on duty to inform/disclose information to a third party. *Wilson v Environment Secretary* [1973] 1 WLR 1083, 1096D-1097A (claimants entitled to rely on deficient public notice because, whether or not themselves prevented from making representations, it was in their interests that other members of the public should have the opportunity to come forward and object); *R (Wainwright) v Richmond upon Thames London Borough Council* [2001] EWHC Admin 1090 at [47] ("it will only be in a rare or (at least) comparatively rare case that a claimant who has the opportunity of making detailed representations will be able to rely upon a failure to consult others"), [46] ("no evidence that the [claimant] was in fact deprived of any support or that other persons would have made any additional points"); *R v Secretary of State for the Home Department, ex p Abdi* [1996] 1 WLR 298 (whether Secretary of State having obligation to afford adequate and balanced information to adjudicator considering appeal); *R v Kent Police Authority, ex p Godden* [1971] 2 QB 662 (natural justice requiring that claimant's doctor, albeit not claimant himself, should have before him all the information to which the police authority's doctor had access); *R v Secretary of State for Education, ex p S* [1995] ELR 71 (considering whether additional material ought to have been disclosed to the claimant parents and the relevant LEA); *R v City of London Magistrates, ex p Asif* [1996] STC 611 (applications for access orders as to bank documents relating to claimant should have been inter partes on notice to claimant, and bank); *R v Commissioners of Inland Revenue, ex p Continental Shipping Ltd* [1996] STC 813 (remedy refused where failure to provide statutorily-required reasons but duty owed to individuals who had not complained and were not parties to the proceedings); <60.5.4> (claimant relying on duty to hear third party).

60.8 **Other rights of procedural fairness.**Procedural fairness can extend beyond the duty to listen and tell. Context and circumstances may require other procedural duties. Or the public body may have an important procedural *power*, with a basic duty properly to consider whether to exercise it.

60.8.1 **A right to time to prepare.** *Council of Civil Service Unions v Minister for the Civil Service* [1985] AC 374, 415F-G (describing situations involving "an expectation of being allowed time to make representations"); *R v Cheshire County Council, ex p C* [1998] ELR 66, 73G-74B (Sedley J, speaking of the exercise of the power to adjourn as "classically a free-standing public law obligation and justiciable as such"); *R v Kingston-Upon-Thames Justices, ex p Peter Martin* [1994] Imm AR 172, 178; *R v London Borough of Barnet, ex p B* [1994] ELR 357, 374H; *R v Devon County Council, ex p Baker* [1995] 1 All ER 73, 83c-d, 84j-85a, 86g-h, 91d-e; *R v Birmingham City Council, ex p Dredger* (1994) 6 Admin LR 553, 574H-576B; *R v Northern & Yorks Regional Health Authority, ex p Trivedi* [1995] 1 WLR 961, 975B; *R v Secretary of State for Social Services, ex p Association of Metropolitan Authorities* [1986] 1 WLR 1, 4E-H; *R v Governors of Haberdasher Aske's Hatcham Schools, ex p Inner London Education Authority* (1989) 1 Admin LR 22, 26A; *R v Legal Aid Board, ex p Duncan* [2000] COD 159 (transcript at [515]) ("the imposition of a timetable of some kind was both necessary and desirable"); <60.6.6> (basic consultation duty including affording adequate time).

60.8.2 **A right to a prompt resolution: delay as procedural unfairness.** *R v Lambeth London Borough Council, ex p Crookes* (1997) 29 HLR 28 (inordinate delay as procedural impropriety); *Goose v Wilson Sandford and Co* The Times 19th February 1998 (allowing a civil appeal, High Court's 20 month delay in giving judgment inexcusable; denial of justice and ultimately subversive of the rule of law); *R v Secretary of State for the Home Department, ex p Roberts* 7th July 1998 unrep. (delay in parole review inordinate and consonant neither with fairness nor good administration).

60.8.3 **A right to representation/assistance.** *R v Board of Visitors of HM Prison, The Maze, ex p Hone* [1988] AC 379, 392D (fairness may require legal representation before board of visitors); *R v Secretary of State for the Home Department, ex p Tarrant* [1985] QB 251, 278F (lawyer), 282E-F (friend/adviser); *R v Leicester City Justices, ex p Barrow* [1991] 2 QB 260, 284H-285A, 285G (right to reasonable assistance in presenting case, eg. McKenzie friend); *R v Secretary of State for the Home Department, ex p Lawson* [1994] Imm AR 58 (asylum-seeker having no right to legal representation during interview; but discretion as to whether to allow this); *R v Secretary of State for the Home Department, ex p Bostanci* [1999] Imm AR 411 (asylum seeker having no right to be accompanied at interview by an interpreter, but discretion; here, refusal irrational); *R (Wagstaff) v Secretary of State for Health* [2001] 1 WLR 292, 322F (vulnerability to challenge of tribunal decision refusing to provide lawyers for affected families); *R (S) v Knowsley NHS Primary Care Trust* [2006] EWHC 26 (Admin) at [101] (Trust should have allowed legal representation before deciding removal from NHS list).

60.8.4 **Whether a right to an oral/public hearing.** *Naraynsingh v Commissioner of Police* [2004] UKPC 20 at [19] (no obligation to hold an oral hearing in relation to revocation of firearms certificate); *R (Thompson) v Law Society* [2004] EWCA Civ 167 [2004] 1 WLR 2522 at [45] (CA recognising that could be circumstances where court would intervene at common law for unfair failure to hold an oral hearing), [51] (asking whether any "disputed issue of fact which was central to the Adjudication Panel's assessment" and "which could not fairly be resolved without hearing oral evidence and without an oral hearing"); *R v Camden London Borough Council, ex p Cran* (1996) 94 LGR 8, 39 (McCullough J, rejecting the idea "that consultation, *by definition*, requires dialogue, in the sense of face to face discussion rather than a mere exchange of written material"); *R v Department of Health, ex p Gandhi* [1991] 1 WLR 1053, 1063F ("An oral hearing should be held where, in all the circumstances, the issues cannot fairly be resolved otherwise"); *R v Solicitors Complaints Bureau, ex p Curtin* (1994) 6 Admin LR 657 (solicitor disciplinary decision not vitiated by lack of an oral hearing); *R v Criminal Injuries Compensation Board, ex p Dickson* [1997] 1 WLR 58 (entitlement to oral hearing under CICB scheme, as properly construed); *Hobbs v London Borough of Sutton* (1994) 26 HLR 132 (council not required to hold an oral hearing whenever good faith doubted in homelessness context); *R v City of London Magistrates, ex p Asif* [1996] STC 611 (access order applications should have been inter partes); *R v Parole Board, ex p Downing* [1997] COD 149 (no common law right to oral parole hearing, on the part of prisoners held at Her Majesty's pleasure); *R v Secretary of State for Trade and Industry, ex p Lonrho Plc* [1989] 1 WLR 525, 535G-H (Lord Keith: "Lonrho's arguments ... could be and were fully set forth and explained in written submissions of inordinate length to which oral representations added nothing"); *Storer v British Gas Plc* [2000] 1 WLR 1237 (decision of industrial tribunal quashed and remitted because not conducted in public, being a fundamental requirement reflected in a mandatory Regulation); *R (Morgan Grenfell & Co Ltd) v Inland Revenue Commissioners* [2001] EWCA Civ 329 [2003] 1 AC 563 (CA) at [50] ("the possibility of an oral hearing is excluded by the nature of the process in question") (HL is at [2002] UKHL 21 [2003] 1 AC 563); *R (Williams) v Secretary of State for the Home Department* [2002] EWCA Civ 498 [2002] 1 WLR 2264 at [32] (in exceptional case where favourable decision of Discretionary Lifer Panel, Category A Review Panel should have given prisoner an oral hearing); *R (West) v Parole Board* [2005] UKHL 1 [2005] 1 WLR 350 at [31], [35] (Parole Board should normally hold oral hearing in relation to licence revocation decision); *R (Jemchi) v Visitor of Brunel University* [2002] EWHC 2166 (Admin) [2003] ELR 125 (not unfair for University Visitor to proceed without an oral hearing).

60.8.5 **Whether a right to cross-examine.** *Bushell v Secretary of State for the Environment* [1981] AC 75, 116D (fairness requiring "that a party be given an opportunity of challenging by cross-examination witnesses called by another party on relevant issues"); *Ceylon University v Fernando* [1960] 1 WLR 223, 235; *R v Criminal Injuries Compensation Board, ex p Cobb* [1995] COD 126 (right to an adjournment to allow key witness to attend for cross-examination); *Re I and H (Contact: Right to Give Evidence)* [1998] 1 FLR 876 (breach of fundamental right to be heard for county court judge to deny applicant for parental contact order the right to cross-examine and give oral evidence); *R (S) v Knowsley NHS Primary Care Trust* [2006] EWHC 26 (Admin) at [91] (Trust should have allowed oral evidence and cross-examination in deciding removal from NHS list).

60.8.6 **The right to have material fairly/accurately presented.** <51.2>.

60.8.7 **The right to a stay pending related proceedings?**[56] *R v Panel on Takeovers and Mergers, ex p Fayed* [1992] BCC 524, 531E-F (Neill LJ: "the Court has power to intervene to prevent injustice where the continuation of one set of proceedings may prejudice the fairness of the trial of other proceedings ... But it is a power which has to be exercised with great care and only where there is a real risk of serious prejudice which may lead to injustice"), applied in *R v Institute of Chartered Accountants in England & Wales, ex p Brindle* 21st December 1993 unrep. (claim succeeding on the ground of real risk of serious prejudice); cf. *R v Chairman of the Regulatory Board of Lloyds Ltd, ex p Macmillan* The Times 14th December 1994, *R v Chance, ex p Coopers & Lybrand* (1995) 7 Admin LR 821, 829D-G, 832F-833D; *R v Executive Council of the Joint Disciplinary Scheme, ex p Hipps* 12th June 1996 unrep. (all of which

---

[56] Stephen Houseman [1999] JR 60; Tim Kerr [1999] JR 188.

applications failed and *Brindle* was distinguished as exceptional).

60.8.8 **Rights to proactivity/assistance by the decision-maker.** *R (O) v Independent Appeal Panel for Tower Hamlets London Borough Council* [2007] EWHC 1455 (Admin) [2007] ELR 468 (panel not obliged in fairness to raise question of hearing linked cases together); *Dennis v United Kingdom Central Council for Nursing* [1993] Med LR 252 (tribunal should explain its views on construction of relevant Act or rules, so that parties can decide what evidence to adduce); *R v Nature Conservancy Council, ex p Bolton Metropolitan Borough Council* [1995] Env LR 237, 256-257 (NCC should have corrected consultee's misapprehension); *R v Blundeston Board of Prison Visitors, ex p Fox-Taylor* [1982] 1 All ER 646 (unfair not to disclose existence of potential defence witness);*R v Criminal Injuries Compensation Board, ex p A* [1999] 2 AC 330, 347B ("unfairness in the failure to put the doctor's evidence before the board and if necessary to grant an adjournment for that purpose"); *R v Sefton Housing Benefit Review Board, ex p Brennan* (1997) 29 HLR 735 (Board should have informed claimant's representative that minded to reject his assertion, so that supportive evidence could be adduced); *R (Ford) v Leasehold Valuation Tribunal* [2005] EWHC 503 (Admin) (tribunal should have investigated doubt, to ensure no injustice to absent landlord); <31.4.2> (failed appeals: unpleaded grounds of appeal).

60.8.9 **Duty to consider exercising basic *powers* of procedural fairness.** <39.2.2> (duty to consider exercising the power); *R v Secretary of State for the Home Department, ex p Tarrant* [1985] QB 251 (boards of prison visitors acting unlawfully in concluding that no power to allow representation, when should have considered exercising the power); *R v Army Board of the Defence Council, ex p Anderson* [1992] QB 169 (Army Board should have considered whether to hold an oral hearing), 188D-F; *R (WB) v Leeds School Organisation Committee* [2002] EWHC 1927 (Admin) [2003] ELR 67 at [30] (school organisation committee having a power, but not a duty, to hear oral representations from objectors); *R v Clerkenwell Metropolitan Stipendiary Magistrate, ex p Telegraph Plc* [1993] QB 462 (wrongly concluding that no power to hear the press regarding reporting restrictions); *R v Bromley Licensing Justices, ex p Bromley Licensed Victuallers' Association* [1984] 1 WLR 585 (error in concluding that the police alone were entitled to object to applications for liquor licences), 590D-E; *R v Northern & Yorkshire Regional Health Authority, ex p Tescos Stores Ltd* [1996] COD 140 (error in concluding that no power to hear appeals together); *R v Secretary of State for the Home Department, ex p Vera Lawson* [1994] Imm AR 58, 60-61 (power to allow legal representation, and duty to consider exercising that power); *R v Guildford Crown Court, ex p Siderfin* [1990] 2 QB 683, 694E-H (no valid reason for not adjourning to allow claimant to be represented in conscientious objection appeal against refusal to excuse her from jury service); *R v Board of Visitors of Hull Prison, ex p St Germain (No.2)* [1979] 1 WLR 1401 (unfairness in refusing to exercise the discretion to allow an opportunity to (a) call witnesses; and/or (b) challenge hearsay evidence).

60.8.10 **Whether other procedural rights.** *R (Mapah) v Secretary of State for the Home Department* [2003] EWHC 306 (Admin) [2003] Imm AR 395 (fairness not requiring that Secretary of State make arrangements for asylum interviews to be tape-recorded); *Raji v General Medical Council* [2003] UKPC 24 [2003] 1 WLR 1052 (doctor's right to a decision and reasons on restoration before representations being made on suspension); *R (Tromans) v Cannock Chase District Council* [2004] EWCA Civ 1036 [2004] LGR 735 (unfair not to check accuracy of disputed recording of planning committee vote); *R (Goldsmith) v London Borough of Wandsworth* [2004] EWCA Civ 1170 (2004) 7 CCLR 472 at [68] (Panel wrongly failing to keep minutes of meetings); *Tangney v Governor of HMP Elmley* [2005] EWCA Civ 1009 [2005] HRLR 1220 (no common law right to disciplinary decision being an independent adjudication).

> **P61 Bias.** A body must not have a direct interest in the outcome of a decision, or show actual bias or a real possibility of bias.

61.1 Automatic disqualification
61.2 Actual bias
61.3 Apparent bias

61.1 Automatic disqualification.

Where a decision-maker is a party to the matter or has a direct interest (pecuniary or not) in its outcome in common with a party, this presumed bias is an automatic disqualification, absent waiver.

61.1.1 Automatic disqualification in a nutshell. *Davidson v Scottish Ministers* [2004] UKHL 34 [2004] HRLR 948 at [6] (Lord Bingham: "judicial tribunals established to resolve issues arising between citizen and citizen, or between the citizen and the state, should be independent and impartial. This means that such tribunals should be in a position to decide such issues on their legal and factual merits as they appear to the tribunal, uninfluenced by any interest, association or pressure extraneous to the case. Thus a judge will be disqualified from hearing a case (whether sitting alone, or as a member of a multiple tribunal) if he or she has a personal interest which is not negligible in the outcome, or is a friend or relation of a party or a witness, or is disabled by personal experience from bringing an objective judgment to bear on the case in question... What disqualifies the judge is the presence of some factor which could prevent the bringing of an objective judgment to bear, which could distort the judge's judgment"); *R v Bow Street Metropolitan Stipendiary Magistrate, ex p Pinochet Ugarte (No.2)* [2000] 1 AC 119, 132G-133C ("if a judge is in fact a party to the litigation or has a financial or proprietary interest in its outcome then [that fact] is sufficient to cause his automatic disqualification ... without any investigation into whether there was a likelihood or suspicion of bias"); *Locabail (UK) Ltd v Bayfield Properties Ltd* [2000] QB 451 (analysing the position as to disqualifying interests); *Laker Airways Inc v FLS Aerospace Ltd* [2000] 1 WLR 113, 118A-C.

61.1.2 Party. *R v Bow Street Metropolitan Stipendiary Magistrate, ex p Pinochet Ugarte (No.2)* [2000] 1 AC 119, 133B-G (judge who is a party to the suit automatically disqualified); *Meerabux v Attorney General of Belize* [2005] UKPC 12 [2005] 2 AC 513 at [24] (automatic disqualification where "active involvement in the institution of the particular proceedings").

61.1.3 Direct pecuniary interest. *R v Gough* [1993] AC 646, 661B-F (Lord Goff, referring to the situation "where a person sitting in a judicial capacity has a pecuniary interest in the outcome of the proceedings": "The nature of the interest is such that public confidence in the administration of justice requires that the decision should not stand"); *Dimes v Proprietors of Grand Junction Canal* (1852) 3 HL Cas 759 (setting aside decision where Lord Chancellor had an interest).

61.1.4 Other direct interest. *R v Bow Street Metropolitan Stipendiary Magistrate, ex p Pinochet Ugarte (No.2)* [2000] 1 AC 119, 135E ("there must be a rule which automatically disqualifies a judge who is involved, whether personally or as a director of a company, in promoting the same causes in the same organisation as is a party to the suit"), 138B (Lord Goff, emphasising close connection with a party), 143C (Lord Hope, referring to duration and proximity of link), 145D (Lord Hutton, referring to strong commitment to some cause or belief); *Meerabux v Attorney General of Belize* [2005] UKPC 12 [2005] 2 AC 513 (no automatic disqualification preventing member of Bar Association sitting on disciplinary council considering complaints against judge), at [24] (not sufficient that "mere membership of an association by which proceedings are brought"), [22] (suggesting *Pinochet* perhaps best seen as apparent bias case); *R (Bennion) v Chief Constable of Merseyside Police* [2001] EWCA Civ

638 (chief constable not automatically disqualified from hearing disciplinary matter against officer having named him as defendant in sex discrimination proceedings); *Jones v DAS Legal Expenses Insurance Co Ltd* [2003] EWCA Civ 1071 (no presumed bias from fact that chairman of employment tribunal married to a barrister who undertook work for the employer) at [18] (no presumed bias if judge not having "the relevant interest in the party whose cause is before him"); *In re P (A Barrister)* [2005] 1 WLR 3019 (automatic disqualification, of member of Bar Council's prosecutorial Professional Conduct and Complaints Committee, from sitting on disciplinary panel of Visitors of Inns).

61.1.5 **Automatic disqualification: other.** *Locabail (UK) Ltd v Bayfield Properties Ltd* [2000] QB 451 at [10] (de minimis exception to automatic disqualification rule, where potential effect of judge's interest so small as to be incapable of affecting decision one way or the other); *R v London Metal Exchange Ltd, ex p Albatros Warehousing BV* 31st March 2000 unrep. at [35] (financial gain to committee from imposing fine too remote and within de minimis principle); *R v Secretary of State for the Environment, ex p Kirkstall Valley Campaign Ltd* [1996] 3 All ER 304, 325b-c ("the principle that a person is disqualified from participation in a decision if there is a real danger that he or she will be influenced by a pecuniary or personal interest in the outcome, is of general application in public law and is not limited to judicial or quasi-judicial bodies or proceedings"); *R v Holderness Borough Council, ex p James Robert Developments Ltd* [1993] 1 PLR 108 (no direct pecuniary interest in planning decision where councillor a rival builder); *R v Kirklees Metropolitan Borough Council, ex p Beaumont* [2001] ELR 204 (councillors disqualified from voting because governors of a school which stood to benefit from decision to close another school); *R (Richardson) v North Yorks County Council* [2003] EWCA Civ 1860 [2004] 1 WLR 1920 (councillors' duty to withdraw under Code of Conduct where having a prejudicial interest).

61.1.6 **Automatic disqualification and waiver etc.** *R v Bow Street Metropolitan Stipendiary Magistrate, ex p Pinochet Ugarte (No.2)* [2000] 1 AC 119, 133C (disqualification unless sufficient disclosure made), 141A ("the parties to the suit may waive the objection"); *Locabail (UK) Ltd v Bayfield Properties Ltd* [2000] QB 451 at [15] & [26] (waiver must be clear and unequivocal and based on full knowledge of relevant facts); *R v Secretary of State for the Home Department, ex p Fayed* [2001] Imm AR 134 at [86] and [111] (actual bias incapable of waiver) [89] and [120] (apparent bias waived here); *R v London Metal Exchange Ltd, ex p Albatros Warehousing BV* 31st March 2000 unrep. at [35]-[36] (claimant's "clear and unequivocal agreement" to procedures and participation of committee member); *Jones v DAS Legal Expenses Insurance Co Ltd* [2003] EWCA Civ 1071 at [30] (CA accepting that presumed bias capable of waiver, as here); *David Eves v Hambros Bank (Jersey) Ltd* [1996] 1 WLR 251, 256C-D (administration of justice not to be "frustrated by technical objections to proceedings in which [the claimant] has no legal interest").

61.2 **Actual bias.** Actual bias is a conclusive vitiating factor. The shortage of relevant cases reflects the fact that actual bias is rare, difficult to prove and largely redundant given grounds of bad faith, improper motive and apparent bias.

61.2.1 **Actual bias.** *R v Gough* [1993] AC 646, 661G (Lord Goff: "if actual bias is proved, that is an end of the case; the person concerned must be disqualified"); *In re Medicaments and Related Classes of Goods (No.2)* [2001] 1 WLR 700 at [38] (actual bias explained as meaning decision-maker either (a) influenced by partiality or prejudice or (b) actually prejudiced); *R v Inner West London Coroner, ex p Dallaglio* [1994] 4 All ER 139, 151j, 162a-b (actual and conscious bias); *O'Reilly v Mackman* [1983] 2 AC 237, 276E (need for prison visitors to "enter upon the inquiry without any pre-conceived personal bias against the prisoner"); *Locabail (UK)*

Ltd v Bayfield Properties Ltd [2000] QB 451 at [3] (actual bias cases rare, partly because difficult to prove); *Laker Airways Inc v FLS Aerospace Ltd* [2000] 1 WLR 113, 117H ("actual bias will of course always disqualify a person from sitting in judgment"); *R v Secretary of State for the Home Department, ex p Fayed* [2001] Imm AR 134 (court rejecting argument that Home Secretary was actually biased, having prejudged a nationality decision).

61.2.2 **Bad faith.** <52.1>.

61.2.3 **Improper motive.** <52.2>.

61.2.4 **Actual bias and waiver.** *R v Secretary of State for the Home Department, ex p Fayed* [2001] Imm AR 134 at [86] (suggesting that "there may be cases of actual bias being shown which in the public interest the courts will say cannot be waived"), [111].

61.3 **Apparent bias.**[57] The law on apparent bias asks whether the ascertained relevant circumstances would lead a fair-minded and informed observer to conclude that there was a real possibility that the decision-maker was biased. Appearances matter and justice must be seen to be done.

61.3.1 **The "real possibility" test.** *Magill v Porter* [2001] UKHL 67 [2002] 2 AC 357 at [103] (Lord Hope: "The question is whether the fair-minded and informed observer, having considered the facts, would conclude that there was a real possibility that the tribunal was biased"); applied in *R v Abdroikov* [2007] UKHL 37 [2007] 1 WLR 2679 at [15]; *Lawal v Northern Spirit Ltd* [2003] UKHL 35 [2004] 1 All ER 187 at [20] ("One starts by identifying the circumstances which are said to give rise to bias"), [21] ("The principle [then] to be applied is ... whether a fair minded and informed observer, having considered the given facts, would conclude that there was a real possibility that the tribunal was biased"); *Davidson v Scottish Ministers* [2004] UKHL 34 [2004] HRLR 948 at [7]; *R (Al-Hasan) v Secretary of State for the Home Department* [2005] UKHL 13 [2005] 1 WLR 688 at [30]; cf. *R (Mahfouz) v General Medical Council* [2004] EWCA Civ 233 at [33] (Carnwath LJ, suggesting that the test in *Montgomery v HM Advocate* [2003] 1 AC 641, 667G (whether risk of prejudice so grave that no direction could reasonably be expected to remove it) preferable to apparent bias approach where issue is prejudicial effect of inadmissible material on an otherwise impartial tribunal).

61.3.2 **Whether apparent bias: examples.**
(A) APPARENT BIAS. *R v Abdroikov* [2007] UKHL 37 [2007] 1 WLR 2679 (jury including serving officer, in a criminal trial involving conflict of evidence between police and accused); *R (Al-Hasan) v Secretary of State for the Home Department* [2005] UKHL 13 [2005] 1 WLR 688 (deputy governor conducting disciplinary hearing on charge of disobeying order given in his presence); *Lawal v Northern Spirit Ltd* [2003] UKHL 35 [2004] 1 All ER 187 (EAT hearing involved Counsel for a party and a lay member of the tribunal, having previously sat together as a tribunal in an earlier case); *Davidson v Scottish Ministers* [2004] UKHL 34 [2004] HRLR 948 (Scottish appellate judge had previously stated views on the issue when acting as Lord Advocate in promoting the Scotland Bill); *El Faraghy v El Faraghy* [2007] EWCA Civ 1149 [2007] 3 FCR 711 (judge's racially offensive jokes in matrimonial proceedings); *R (Lewis) v*

---

[57] Ben Rayment [1996] JR 102, [1997] JR 107 & [2001] JR 93; Philip Havers QC and Owain Thomas [1999] JR 111; David Manknell [2001] JR 177; Saima Hanif [2005] JR 78; James Maurici [2007] JR 251.

Redcar & Cleveland Borough Council [2008] EWCA Civ 746 (whether apparent bias in the sense of predetermination by planning committee); *R (Ghadami) v Harlow District Council* [2004] EWHC 1883 (Admin) [2005] LGR 24 (planning committee's chairman's closeness to developers); *R (A1 Veg Ltd) v Hounslow London Borough Council* [2003] EWHC 3112 (Admin) [2004] LGR 536 at [83] (competition for market space and tenants' association involved in process, including in making adverse comments on competitors with no opportunity of rebuttal); *R (Morris) v Woolwich Magistrates Court* [2005] EWHC 781 (Admin) (district judge dealing with assault on court staff arising in connection with proceedings before him); *AWG Group Ltd v Morrison* [2006] EWCA Civ 6 [2006] 1 WLR 1163 (judge personally knew proposed witness). (B) NO APPARENT BIAS. *Magill v Porter* [2001] UKHL 67 [2002] 2 AC 357 at [105] (no real possibility of bias in district auditor holding press conference to state provisional views publicly); *R (Paul) v Coroner of the Queen's Household* [2007] EWHC 408 (Admin) [2008] QB 172 at [65] (no apparent bias from coroner's support of publication of police report); *National Assembly for Wales v Condron* [2006] EWCA Civ 1573 [2007] LGR 87 (no apparent bias from planning chair's predisposition); *R (Port Regis School Ltd) v North Dorset District Council* [2006] EWHC 742 (Admin) [2006] LGR 696 (no apparent bias from freemason councillors' participation in planning development benefiting Masonic lodge); *Feld v Barnet London Borough Council* [2004] EWCA Civ 1307 [2005] HLR 111 (no apparent bias where reviewing officer conducting review of sequential housing decisions); *AMEC Capital Projects Ltd v Whitefriars City Estates Ltd* [2004] EWCA Civ 1418 [2005] 1 All ER 723 (no apparent bias where building contract adjudicator had made previous ruling); *R (PD) v West Midlands and North West Mental Health Review Tribunal* [2004] EWCA Civ 311 (no appearance of bias in MHRT medical member being employed by the detaining NHS trust); *Meerabux v Attorney General of Belize* [2005] UKPC 12 [2005] 2 AC 513 (no apparent bias where Bar Association member sitting on disciplinary council hearing complaints against judge); *Gillies v Secretary of State for Work and Pensions* [2006] UKHL 2 [2006] 1 WLR 781 (no apparent bias where disability appeal tribunal included doctor who had reported as examining medical practitioner in other cases); *Prince Jeffri Bolkiah v Brunei Darussalam* [2007] UKPC 62 (no apparent bias preventing Chief Justice from hearing proceedings brought by Government against Prince).

61.3.3 **Real possibility test mirrors Art 6 independent and impartial tribunal.** <59.5.6> (Art 6: independent and impartial tribunal); *Magill v Porter* [2001] UKHL 67 [2002] 2 AC 357 at [103] (unified common law and Art 6 test); *R v Abdroikov* [2007] UKHL 37 [2007] 1 WLR 2679 at [17] (apparent bias at common law and Art 6); *Davidson v Scottish Ministers* [2004] UKHL 34 [2004] HRLR 948 at [47] ("The word `bias' is used as a convenient shorthand"; but "the essence of it is captured in the Convention concept of impartiality").

61.3.4 **The fair-minded and informed observer.** <61.3.1> (the real possibility test); <45.2.5> (hypothetical observer: more general application); *Taylor v Lawrence* [2002] EWCA Civ 90 [2003] QB 528 at [61]-[63] (CA emphasising the crucial importance of the hypothetical observer being an "informed" one); *Lawal v Northern Spirit Ltd* [2003] UKHL 35 [2004] 1 All ER 187 at [14] ("the fair-minded and informed observer" taken to "adopt a balanced approach ... `neither complacent nor unduly sensitive or suspicious'"); *R (Port Regis School Ltd) v North Dorset District Council* [2006] EWHC 742 (Admin) [2006] LGR 696 (knowledge of limited nature of freemasons' mutual support obligations); *Reza v General Medical Council* [1991] 2 AC 182, 194B ("someone familiar with the procedure of the committee"); *Meerabux v Attorney General of Belize* [2005] UKPC 12 [2005] 2 AC 513 at [25] (knowledge of "all the facts which put ... membership of the Bar Association into its proper context"); *R (Lewis) v Redcar & Cleveland Borough Council* [2008] EWCA Civ 746 at [68] (court's own judgment applicable where planning decision and apparent bias in the sense of predetermination).

61.3.5 **Appearances/public confidence: justice seen to be done.** *Davidson v Scottish Ministers*

[2004] UKHL 34 [2004] HRLR 948 at [7] (Lord Bingham: "It has ... been accepted for many years that justice must not only be done but must also be seen to be done"), [46] (Lord Hope); *Lawal v Northern Spirit Ltd* [2003] UKHL 35 [2004] 1 All ER 187 at [14] (Lord Steyn, referring to the *Porter* test as having "at its core the need for 'the confidence which must be inspired by the courts in a democratic society'"), [22]; *Modahl v British Athletic Federation* [2001] EWCA Civ 1447 [2002] 1 WLR 1192 at [66] (appearance of fairness "clearly an appropriate concept ... for the supervision of public bodies").

61.3.6 **Materiality and apparent bias: operative bias.** *R (Al-Hasan) v Secretary of State for the Home Department* [2005] UKHL 13 [2005] 1 WLR 688 at [43] (Lord Brown: "once proceedings have been successfully impugned for want of independence and impartiality on the part of the tribunal, the decision itself must necessarily be regarded as tainted by unfairness and so cannot be permitted to stand"); cf. *Modahl v British Athletic Federation* [2001] EWCA Civ 1447 [2002] 1 WLR 1192 (no material apparent bias); *Locabail (UK) Ltd v Bayfield Properties Ltd* [2000] QB 451 at [18] (relevant to ask whether decision-maker aware of matter relied on as appearing to undermine his impartiality); *R v Secretary of State for the Environment, ex p Kirkstall Valley Campaign Ltd* [1996] 3 All ER 304, 337a-h (at the relevant moment, "the ground of bias was no longer operative"); *In re Medicaments and Related Classes of Goods (No.2)* [2001] 1 WLR 700 at [99] (real danger of bias by one member of Restrictive Practices Court infecting all 3 members).

61.3.7 **Apparent bias and function/necessity/reality.** *Meerabux v Attorney General of Belize* [2005] UKPC 12 [2005] 2 AC 513 at [28] (since Constitution envisaging Chair of disciplinary council would be Bar Association member, "conclusive" indication that not a ground of disqualification); *R v Secretary of State for Trade, ex p Perestrello* [1981] QB 19, 35A-C (predisposition or suspicion part of "performing their functions properly" where "acting in a policing role"); *R (Lewis) v Redcar & Cleveland Borough Council* [2008] EWCA Civ 746 at [89] (planning committee entitled to have a predisposition); *R v Board of Visitors of Frankland Prison, ex p Lewis* [1986] 1 WLR 130 (inevitable that members of Board of Prison Visitors having background information; here from sitting on Parole Board); *R v Doncaster Metropolitan Borough Council, ex p Nortrop* (1996) 28 HLR 862, 875 ("inevitable that councillors in carrying on their duties for local authorities may from time to time decide cases which relate to the same person in their local authority area"); *R v Bristol Crown Court, ex p Cooper* [1990] 1 WLR 1031 (magistrate required to have knowledge of licensing policy); *Nwabueze v General Medical Council* [2000] 1 WLR 1760, 1771D-E ("It is in the public interest that those who serve as lay members on disciplinary bodies of this kind should be well-informed and have experience of working in the area"); *R (PD) v West Midlands and North West Mental Health Review Tribunal* [2004] EWCA Civ 311 (no apparent bias or Art 6 violation where MHRT medical member employed by the NHS Trust responsible for the detaining hospital), [11] ("The Strasbourg Court does not lose sight of practical realities when applying the Convention").

61.3.8 **Apparent bias and witness statement evidence.** *R (Georgiou) v London Borough of Enfield* [2004] EWHC 779 (Admin) [2004] LGR 497 at [36] (Richards J: "Having regard to the objective nature of the question of apparent bias, I do not think that any significant weight is to be attached to the members' own witness statements in which they state that they did approach the planning decision with open minds", referring to *Magill v Porter* [2001] UKHL 67 [2002] 2 AC 357 at [104]); *R (A1 Veg Ltd) v Hounslow London Borough Council* [2003] EWHC 3112 (Admin) [2004] LGR 536 at [79]; <17.3.6(D)> (statements of decision-makers relating to bias).

61.3.9 **Apparent bias and waiver.** *Amjad v Steadman-Byrne* [2007] EWCA Civ 625 [2007]

1 WLR 2484 at [17] (apparent bias should be raised with tribunal at the time not after adverse outcome); *R v Secretary of State for the Home Department, ex p Fayed* [2001] Imm AR 134 at [85] ("with all the relevant knowledge at his disposal the appellant clearly and unequivocally waived any right he may have had to object to the Home Secretary deciding his application"), [120]; *Smith v Kvaerner Cementations Foundation Ltd* [2006] EWCA Civ 242 [2007] 1 WLR 370 (no waiver where party did not have all relevant information explained and had been encouraged not to object); *R (A1 Veg Ltd) v Hounslow London Borough Council* [2003] EWHC 3112 (Admin) [2004] LGR 536 at [89] (not "full knowledge" or "clear and unequivocal" waiver); <31.4.3>.

61.3.10 Apparent bias: the previous law. *R v Gough* [1993] AC 646, 670F (asking "whether, having regard to [the] circumstances, there was a real danger of bias"); *R v Secretary of State for the Environment, ex p Kirkstall Valley Campaign Ltd* [1996] 3 All ER 304, 325g-h (*Gough* test to be "uniformly applied"); *Doherty v McGlennan* 1997 SLT 444 (adoption of reasonable suspicion test in Scotland); *Locabail (UK) Ltd v Bayfield Properties Ltd* [2000] QB 451 at [17] (surveying the comparative case-law); *Roylance v General Medical Council (No.2)* [2000] 1 AC 311, 319F-H (different formulations but essentially the same concept); *R v Bow Street Metropolitan Stipendiary Magistrate, ex p Pinochet Ugarte (No.2)* [2000] 1 AC 119, 142F-G (different tests likely in practice to yield the same result).

P62 Reasons. Bodies are often required to give (adequate) reasons.

62.1 Importance of reasons in the developing law
62.2 Judicial review for failure to give reasons
62.3 Adequacy of reasons
62.4 Timing of reasons
62.5 Remedy for lack/insufficiency of reasons

62.1 Importance of reasons in the developing law. Administrative law recognises the strong principled basis for requiring public authorities adequately to explain why they acted. The discipline of express reasoning assists the claimant, the Court and the defendant body itself. The conventional approach has been that there is no general duty, but with a vast number of incrementally-recognised exceptional cases where a duty arises. The alternative view, yet to be fully embraced, is that there is in truth a general duty, but with a moderate number of incrementally-recognised exceptional cases where no duty arises.

62.1.1 **No general common law duty.***Stefan v General Medical Council* [1999] 1 WLR 1293, 1300G ("the established position of the common law [is] that there is no general duty, universally imposed on all decision-makers"), 1301A-B (not "an appropriate opportunity to explore the possibility of ... a departure"); *R v Secretary of State for the Home Department, ex p Doody* [1994] 1 AC 531, 564E-F ("the law does not at present recognise a general duty to give reasons for an administrative decision. Nevertheless, it is equally beyond question that such a duty may in appropriate circumstances be implied"); *Rey v Government of Switzerland* [1999] 1 AC 54, 66B-C (Lord Steyn); *R v Kensington and Chelsea Royal London Borough Council, ex p Grillo* (1996) 28 HLR 94, 105 (at present no "general obligation on administrative authorities to give reasons for their decisions"); JUSTICE Report, *Administration Under Law* (1971) at p.23 ("No single factor has inhibited the development of English administrative law as seriously as the absence of any general obligation upon public authorities to give reasons for their decisions").

62.1.2 **Momentum towards a general duty.**[58] *North Range Shipping Ltd v Seatrans Shipping Corp* [2002] EWCA Civ 405 [2002] 1 WLR 2397 at [15] ("the trend of the law has been towards an increased recognition of the duty to give reasons"); *Stefan v General Medical Council* [1999] 1 WLR 1293, 1301A-B ("There is certainly a strong argument for the view that what were once seen as exceptions to a rule may now be becoming examples of the norm, and the cases where reasons are not required may be taking on the appearance of exceptions"), 1300G ("The trend of the law has been towards an increased recognition of the duty upon decision-makers of many kinds to give reasons. This trend is consistent with current developments towards an increased openness in matters of government and administration. But the trend is proceeding on a case by case basis"); *R v Kensington and Chelsea Royal London Borough Council, ex p Grillo* (1996) 28 HLR 94, 105 (Neill LJ: "There may come a time when English law does impose a general obligation on administrative authorities to give reasons for their decisions"); *R (Wooder) v Feggetter* [2002] EWCA Civ 554 [2003] QB 219 at [39] (Sedley LJ, referring to academic analysis as demonstrating "the distance still to be travelled in this regard between the present state of English authority and a principled framework of public decision-making"), [41] (questioning whether *Institute of Dental Surgery* "would necessarily be decided in the same way today"); *R v Higher Education Funding Council, ex p Institute of Dental Surgery* [1994] 1 WLR 242, 259A-B ("There are certainly good arguments of public law and of public administration in favour of such a rule, but it is axiomatically not, or not yet, part

---

[58] Thomas de la Mare [1996] JR 88; David Toube [1997] JR 68.

of our law. It remains to be seen what the `continuing momentum in administrative law towards openness of decision-making' ... will bring"); *R v Secretary of State for Education, ex p G* [1995] ELR 58, 67E-F ("whilst there is a spectrum of factual situations ranging from those where no reasons are required at all on the one hand, to those where the circumstances are such as to cry out for full and detailed reasons, the general approach has been to require there to be sufficient reasons to be given to determine whether or not the decision-maker has asked the right question and approached it in an apparently rational way"); *R v London Borough of Lambeth, ex p Walters* (1994) 26 HLR 170, 178 (Sir Louis Blom-Cooper QC: "It seems to me that English law has now arrived at the point where there is at least a general duty to give reasons whenever the statutorily-impregnated administrative process is infused with the concept of fair treatment to those potentially affected by administrative action"), but see *Grillo* at 104-106 and *R v London Borough of Islington, ex p Hinds* (1995) 27 HLR 65 (cf. CA at (1996) 28 HLR 302); *R v Aylesbury Vale District Council, ex p Chaplin* The Times 23rd July 1996 (Keene J, criticising the ill-defined incremental exceptions from the decision-maker's point of view); *R v Ministry of Defence, ex p Murray* [1998] COD 134 (no general duty to give reasons, but a perceptible trend towards openness in administrative decision-making); *R v Secretary of State for Health, ex p Scherer* [1998] EuLR 1, 16G-H (Judge J referring to the requirements "already well understood in judicial review proceedings, that administrative authorities should normally provide an account of the reasons for their decisions"); *R v Director of Public Prosecutions, ex p Manning* [2001] QB 330, at [33] ("wrong in principle to require the citizen to make a complaint of unlawfulness against the [DPP] in order to obtain a response which good administrative practice would in the ordinary course require").

62.1.3 Reform. Justice/All Souls Report, *Administrative Justice: Some Necessary Reforms* (1988) at p.72 (advocating a general (statutory) duty to give reasons); Donoughmore Committee (Report of the Committee on Ministers' Powers (1932) Cmd 4060) at p.100 ("Any party affected by a decision should be informed of the reasons on which the decision is based ... in the form of a reasoned document ... (which) should state the conclusions as to the facts and to any points of law which have emerged").

62.1.4 The importance of transparency: defendant's duty of candour/cooperation.<10.4>.

62.1.5 Practical importance of disclosing the reasons.[59] *Board of Education v Rice* [1911] AC 179, 185 (misdirection apparent from document "which purports to be their decision"); *Edwards v Bairstow* [1956] AC 14, 36 (reasoning setting out facts found and determination, revealing irrationality constituting error of law); *Kanda v Government of Malaya* [1962] AC 322, 335-336 (report, wrongly relied on, only coming to light on 4th day of trial); *Ridge v Baldwin* [1964] AC 40, 110 and 137 (grounds relied upon triggering the applicability of natural justice); *Padfield v Minister of Agriculture Fisheries & Food* [1968] AC 997, 1031D, 1049C; 1054A; 1058G and 1059F (reasons scrutinised and found to reveal unlawful approach); *Anisminic Ltd v Foreign Compensation Commission* [1969] 2 AC 147, 171G-H and 173H (error appearing from reasons voluntarily disclosed); *Secretary of State for Education and Science v Tameside Metropolitan Borough Council* [1977] AC 1014, 1065C (scrutiny of reasons revealing misdirection/irrelevancy); *R v Commission for Racial Equality, ex p Hillingdon London Borough Council* [1982] AC 779, 790F, 791E-F ("candid" admission showing ultra vires); *Chief Constable of the North Wales Police v Evans* [1982] 1 WLR 1155, 1161H, 1171F-G (written evidence showing that matters were considered but not put); *R v Barnet London*

---

[59] This and subsequent subparagraphs in a previous edition was cited in *Capital Rich Development Ltd v Town Planning Board* [2007] HKCU 90 at [97].

Borough Council, ex p Nilish Shah [1983] 2 AC 309 (authorities' explanation disclosing error of law); *R v Tower Hamlets London Borough Council, ex p Chetnik Developments Ltd* [1988] AC 858, 878E-H (reasons showing misdirection/irrelevancy). See too *R v Director of Public Prosecutions, ex p Manning* [2001] QB 330 (note showing that relevant matters not considered); *R v Director of Public Prosecutions, ex p Jones* 23rd March 2000 unrep. (although DPP reciting correct test, read as a whole reasons indicating had applied a different test); *R (Quark Fishing Ltd) v Secretary of State for Foreign and Commonwealth Affairs* [2002] EWCA Civ 1409 (unlawful approach becoming clear from documents disclosed following court order); *R (Kelsall) v Secretary of State for the Environment, Food and Rural Affairs* [2003] EWHC 459 (Admin) at [35] ("if [the] reasons do not bear scrutiny they add substance to the argument that the provisions of the Order are so flawed as to be irrational and unfair").

62.1.6 Judicial review disarmed, absent a reasons duty. *R v Nat Bell Liquors Ltd* [1922] 2 AC 128, 159 (absence of reasons for convictions "did not stint the jurisdiction of the Queen's Bench, or alter the actual law of certiorari": "What it did was to disarm its exercise"); *O'Reilly v Mackman* [1983] 2 AC 237, 277F-G (judicial review was "liable to be defeated by the decision-making body if it gave no reasons for its determination"); *In re A Company* [1981] AC 374, 383C-E (statutory duty to give reasons "facilitates the detection of errors of law by those tribunals and by administrative authorities, generally").

62.1.7 Purpose of reasons.
(A) GENERAL. *R v London Borough of Islington, ex p Hinds* (1995) 27 HLR 65, 75 (adequate reasons informing claimant, court and third parties, enhancing the machinery of government, public confidence and as a self-disciplining exercise); *English v Emery Reimbold and Strick Ltd* [2002] EWCA Civ 605 [2002] 1 WLR 2409 at [16] ("justice will not be done if it is not apparent to the parties why one has won and the other has lost"); *Cullen v Chief Constable of the Royal Ulster Constabulary* [2003] UKHL 39 [2003] 1 WLR 1763 at [7] (Lord Steyn: "First, they impose a discipline ... which may contribute to such [decisions] being considered with care. Secondly, reasons encourage transparency ... Thirdly, they assist the courts in performing their supervisory function if judicial review proceedings are launched"), [56] (Lord Millett).
(B) FOCUSING THE DECISION-MAKER'S MIND.[60] *R v Brent London Borough Council, ex p Baruwa* (1996) 28 HLR 361 (Roger Toulson QC), 373 ("when people who make decisions have to give their reasons it improves the decision making process, both from the point of view of the person making the decision and of the person who is going to be affected by it"; CA is at (1997) 29 HLR 915); *R v Ministry of Defence, ex p Murray* [1998] COD 134 (duty to give reasons concentrates the decision-maker's mind on the right questions and demonstrates that the issues have been conscientiously addressed); *Flannery v Halifax Estate Agencies Ltd* [2000] 1 WLR 377, 381G-H ("a requirement to give reasons concentrates the mind; if it is fulfilled, the resulting decision is much more likely to be soundly based on the evidence than if it is not"); *R (Chisnell) v Richmond Upon Thames London Borough Council* [2005] EWHC 134 (Admin) at [42] ("useful exercise for those who reach decisions to go through the intellectual exercise which the drafting of summary reasons involves").
(C) INFORMING THE PARTIES. *Union of Construction and Allied Trades Technicians v Brain* [1981] IRLR 225, 228 (to "tell the parties in broad terms why they lost or, as the case may be, won"); *R v University of Cambridge, ex p Evans* [1998] ELR 515, 520H-521B (tells claimants where to concentrate their efforts; may give rise to defects which can be corrected in future; demonstrates that "proper care has been taken"); *Flannery v Halifax Estate Agencies Ltd* [2000] 1 WLR 377, 381G-H ("fairness surely requires that the parties - especially the losing party - should be left in no doubt why they have won or lost").

---

[60] Michael Fordham [1998] JR 158.

(D) REVEALING WHETHER GROUNDS FOR CHALLENGE *R v Westminster City Council, ex p Ermakov* [1996] 2 All ER 302, 309f (reasons obligation imposed "so that the persons affected by the decision may know why they have won or lost and, in particular, may be able to judge whether the decision is valid and therefore unchallengeable, or invalid and therefore open to challenge"); *Save Britain's Heritage v Number 1 Poultry Ltd* [1991] 1 WLR 153, 166C (Lord Bridge: "[Reasons] should enable a person who is entitled to contest the decision to make a proper assessment as to whether the decision should be challenged"), 170H ("a salutary safeguard to enable interested parties to know that the decision has been taken on relevant and rational grounds and that any applicable statutory criteria have been observed"); *R v Secretary of State for the Home Department, ex p Doody* [1994] 1 AC 531, 565G-H ("important that there should be an effective means of detecting the kind of error which would entitle the court to intervene"); *R v Parole Board, ex p Lodomez* (1994) 26 BMLR 162 (reasons needing to be written and adequate, to assess whether grounds for challenge).

62.1.8 **Advantages/disadvantages of reasons.** *Stefan v General Medical Council* [1999] 1 WLR 1293, 1300D-F (advantages "in strengthening [the] process itself, in increasing the public confidence in it, and in the desirability of the disclosure of error where error exists... But there are also dangers and disadvantages in a universal requirement for reasons. It may impose an undesirable legalism into areas where a high degree of informality is appropriate and add to delay and expense"); *R v City of London Corporation, ex p Matson* [1997] 1 WLR 765, 783A-D (as to "the difficulty of articulating" reasons: experience shows that "the requirement to give reasons ... concentrated the minds on the proper issues involved in the decision making and imposed a very desirable discipline. The giving of reasons ensured that the decisions were based on proper objective grounds"); *R v Ministry of Defence, ex p Murray* [1998] COD 134 (inconvenience arguments overridden in context of court martial); *R v London Borough of Newham, ex p Dawson* (1994) 26 HLR 747, 759 ("unimpressed by the considerations advanced by the council, that the giving of reasons in cases such as this is unduly burdensome, or would create practical problems for a committee with diverse views"); *R (Wooder) v Feggetter* [2002] EWCA Civ 554 [2003] QB 219 at [27] (social justice benefit from reasons); <62.3.10> (reasons and resources).

62.1.9 **Reasons and lack of prejudice.** *Grant v Teacher's Appeal Tribunal* [2006] UKPC 59 at [35] ("no prejudice was caused ... by any deficiency in the Tribunal's reasons"); *Brabazon-Drenning v United Kingdom Central Council for Nursing Midwifery and Health Visiting* [2001] HRLR 91 (lack of reasons: "The fact that the appellant may not have been prejudiced ... is irrelevant"); *R v Immigration Appeal Tribunal, ex p Dhaliwal* [1994] Imm AR 387, 392 (for "a remedy based on the absence of proper reasoning, there should be some element of prejudice").

62.2 **Judicial review for failure to give reasons** Reasons duties generally arise: (1) where required in legislation, rules or policy; (2) where called for in fairness (or via a legitimate expectation); (3) through the rule of "reason" (reasonableness) where an unreasoned response may be unreasonable; or (4) under the duty of candour owed by a body under challenge.

62.2.1 **Duty to give reasons: courts and judges.** *Flannery v Halifax Estate Agencies Ltd* [2000] 1 WLR 377, 381B ("today's professional judge owes a general duty to give reasons", referring to *R v Crown Court at Harrow, ex p Dave* [1994] 1 WLR 98); *Eagil Trust Co Ltd v Pigott-Brown* [1985] 3 All ER 119, 122a ("A professional judge should, as a rule, give reasons for his decision"); *R v Bow County Court, ex p Pelling* [1999] 1 WLR 1807 (county court judge should give reasons for refusal to allow litigant in person to have assistance of McKenzie friend); *Anya v University of Oxford* [2001] EWCA Civ 405 [2001] ELR 711 at [12] (Human Rights Act:ECHR Art 6 jurisprudence requiring "that adequate and intelligible reasons must be given for judicial decisions"); *English v Emery Reimbold and Strick Ltd* [2002] EWCA Civ 605 [2002] 1 WLR 2409 (under HRA:ECHR Art 6, courts should give reasons for decisions on costs); *R (Tofik) v Immigration Appeal Tribunal* [2003] EWCA Civ 1138 at [17] (even if statutory duty to give reasons for refusal of leave to appeal not extending to reasons for refusing an extension of time, common law duty would have arisen).

62.2.2 **Body under a duty to give reasons: other examples.** *R (Cash) v Northamptonshire Coroner* [2007] EWHC 1354 (Admin) [2007] 4 All ER 903 at [45] (coroner should have given reasons); *R v City of London Corporation, ex p Matson* [1997] 1 WLR 765 (Court of Aldermen's decision not to confirm the election of an Alderman following favourable ward vote); *R v Civil Service Appeal Board, ex p Cunningham* [1991] 4 All ER 310 (CSAB's award of compensation); *R v Ministry of Defence, ex p Murray* [1998] COD 134 (court martial decision rejecting exemplary accused soldier's evidence); *Stefan v General Medical Council* [1999] 1 WLR 1293 (GMC health committee); *R v Director of Public Prosecutions, ex p Manning* [2001] QB 330, at [33] (DPP obliged to give reasons for not prosecuting where inquest jury had decided unlawful killing); *R (Wooder) v Feggetter* [2002] EWCA Civ 554 [2003] QB 219 (forcible medication needing written reasons); *R (Lin) v Barnet London Borough Council* [2007] EWCA Civ 132 [2007] HLR 440 (housing allocation policy inadequately reasoned).

62.2.3 **Body under no duty to give reasons: examples.** *R (Mathialagan) v Southwark London Borough Council* [2004] EWCA Civ 1689 at [25] (magistrates not always required to give reasons); *R v Kensington and Chelsea Royal London Borough Council, ex p Grillo* (1996) 28 HLR 94 (council's decision that accommodation offered was 'suitable', in voluntary appeals procedure); *R v Aylesbury Vale District Council, ex p Chaplin* [1997] 3 PLR 55 (no duty to give reasons for grant of planning permission); *Friends Provident Life and Pensions Ltd v Secretary of State for Transport, Local Government and Regions* [2001] EWHC Admin 820 [2002] 1 WLR 1450 at [103] (no general duty to give reasons for refusing to call-in a planning application); *Rey v Government of Switzerland* [1999] 1 AC 54, 66F-67A (no general duty on magistrates in extradition cases to give reasons in relation to factual disputes); *Dad v General Dental Council* [2000] 1 WLR 1538, 1541H (Professional Conduct Committee of GMC/ GDC under no general duty to give reasons); *Gupta v General Medical Council* [2001] UKPC 61 [2002] 1 WLR 1691 (in general, no duty to give reasons for disciplinary committee's findings of fact, although duty arising in respect of penalty); *R (Tucker) v Director General of the National Crime Squad* [2003] EWCA Civ 2 (no duty to give reasons in deciding to terminate police officer's secondment to the National Crime Squad); *R (Giles) v Fareham Borough Council* [2002] EWHC 2951 (Admin) [2003] HLR 524 at [12] (decision to defer housing application, reached following an extra-statutory review); *R (Hasan) v Secretary of State for Trade & Industry* [2007] EWHC 2630 (Admin) (no duty to publish reasons for arms exports decisions).

62.2.4 **Express/codified rights to reasons.**
(A) STATUTORY DUTY TO GIVE REASONS: EXAMPLES. *Grunwick Processing Laboratories Ltd v Advisory Conciliation & Arbitration Service* [1978] AC 655, 699E (express requirement for reasons); *R v Secretary of State for the Home Department, ex p Dannenberg* [1984] QB 766 (reasons required under EC Directive); *R (Midcounties Cooperative Ltd) v Forest of Dean District Council* [2007] EWHC 1714 (Admin) (planning permissions quashed for failure to give summary reasons as required by 1995 Order); *R v Immigration Appeal Tribunal, ex p Khan (Mahmud)* [1983] 1 QB 790 (IAT's statutory duty to give reasons); *R v Croydon London Borough Council, ex p Graham* (1994) 26 HLR 286 (Housing Act 1985 s.64); *R v Solihull Metropolitan Borough Council Housing Benefits Review Board, ex p Simpson* (1994) 92 LGR 719 (duty to give reasons under housing benefit regulations); *R v Westminster City Council, ex p Ermakov* [1996] 2 All ER 302 (homelessness decision involving statutory

duty to give reasons); *R v Commissioners of Inland Revenue, ex p Continental Shipping Ltd* [1996] STC 813 (tax notices statutorily requiring summary of reasons); *R v Parole Board, ex p Lodomez* (1994) 26 BMLR 162 (duty to give reasons under Parole Rules).
(B) STATUTE EXCLUDING REASONS DUTY. *R v Secretary of State for the Home Department, ex p Fayed* [1998] 1 WLR 763, 788D (rejecting argument that common law duty to give reasons could co-exist, where statutory duty to give reasons excluded); *R v Secretary of State for Social Services, ex p Connolly* [1986] 1 WLR 421.
(C) IMPLIED STATUTORY DUTY. *Stefan v General Medical Council* [1999] 1 WLR 1293, 1297C-D ("neither in the Act of 1983 nor in the Rules is any such express obligation to be found. In such a situation an obligation to give reasons may nevertheless be found to exist. This may arise through construction of the statutory provisions as a matter of implied intention. Alternatively it may be held to exist by operation of the common law as a matter of fairness").
(D) REASONS DUTY UNDER POLICY GUIDANCE. *R (Asha Foundation) v Millennium Commission* [2003] EWCA Civ 88 (reasons promised in guidance to grant applicants); *R v Governor of HM Prison Long Lartin, ex p Ross* The Times 9th June 1994 (reasons required under a Home Office Circular); *R v Bacon's City Technology College, ex p W* [1998] ELR 488, 494G-H (contrary to own internal memorandum for governors not to give reasons).

62.2.5 Duty to give reasons under EC law. *R v Secretary of State for the Home Department, ex p Dannenberg* [1984] QB 766 (duty to give reasons arising under EC Directive); *R v Secretary of State for Health, ex p Pfizer Ltd* (1999) 2 CCLR 270, 284I (breach of duty to give reasons under EC Directive).

62.2.6 Reasons required in fairness. *Save Britain's Heritage v Number 1 Poultry Ltd* [1991] 1 WLR 153, 170H-171A (Lord Bridge, referring to reasons as "the analogue in administrative law of the common law's requirement that justice should not only be done, but also be seen to be done"); *R v Secretary of State for the Home Department, ex p Duggan* [1994] 3 All ER 277, 287h ("the authorities show an ever-increasing variety of situations where, depending on the nature of the decision and the process by which it is reached, fairness requires that reasons be given"); *R v Burton upon Trent Justices, ex p Hussain* (1997) 9 Admin LR 233, 237G-H (failure to make findings of fact and give reasons amounting to "a denial of natural justice"); *R (Wooder) v Feggetter* [2002] EWCA Civ 554 [2003] QB 219 at [42] (Sedley LJ: "lawyers seem to have manifested their classic learnt response to [the leading] cases by treating the categories so far acknowledged in the reactive and exploratory growth of the common law as exhaustive. Rather than try to fit given shapes into pre-formed slots like toddlers in a playgroup ..., the courts have to continue the process of working out and refining, case by case, the relevant principles of fairness"); *R v Higher Education Funding Council, ex p Institute of Dental Surgery* [1994] 1 WLR 242, 258D-E (referring to a class of case, such as *R v Secretary of State for the Home Department, ex p Doody* [1994] 1 AC 531, "where the nature of the process itself calls in fairness for reasons to be given"); *R v Ministry of Defence, ex p Murray* [1998] COD 134 (reasons required where necessary to achieve justice); *Gupta v General Medical Council* [2001] UKPC 61 [2002] 1 WLR 1691 at [14] (referring to "cases where the principle of fairness may require the [GMC committee] to give reasons for their decision even on matters of fact").

62.2.7 Reasons and fundamental rights.
(A) COMMON LAW. *R v Secretary of State for the Home Department, ex p Doody* [1994] 1 AC 531 (reasons and liberty); *R v Director of Public Prosecutions, ex p Manning* [2001] QB 330, at [33] (duty to give reasons arising in unlawful killing case because of right to life); *R (Wooder) v Feggetter* [2002] EWCA Civ 554 [2003] QB 219 at [24], [38] (reasons required for decision forcibly to give medication); *R (Faulkner) v Secretary of State for the Home Department* [2005] EWHC 2567 (Admin) (reasons for immigration detention).
(B) HRA:ECHR ART 6. *Anya v University of Oxford* [2001] EWCA Civ 405 [2001] ELR 711

at [12] (Art 6 jurisprudence requiring "that adequate and intelligible reasons must be given for judicial decisions"); *North Range Shipping Ltd v Seatrans Shipping Corp* [2002] EWCA Civ 405 [2002] 1 WLR 2397 at [16]-[22], [28] (examining the Art 6 jurisprudence in relation to reasons); *Stefan v General Medical Council* [1999] 1 WLR 1293, 1301B-C (Art 6 "will require closer attention to be paid to the duty to give reasons, at least in relation to those cases where a person's civil rights and obligations are being determined"); *Gupta v General Medical Council* [2001] UKPC 61 [2002] 1 WLR 1691 (notwithstanding Art 6, no general duty to give reasons for disciplinary committee's findings of fact); *Moran v Director of Public Prosecutions* [2002] EWHC 89 (Admin) (still no duty to give reasons for rejecting submission of no case to answer, despite HRA); *R v City of London Corporation, ex p Matson* [1997] 1 WLR 765, 776A-C, 777E (unnecessary to decide whether Art 6 of the Convention applying); *R v Crown Court at Canterbury, ex p Howson-Ball* [2001] Env LR 639 (Art 6 supporting the conclusion that the decision should be quashed for inadequate reasons).

62.2.8 Reasons and decision aberrant/calling for explanation. *R v Higher Education Funding Council, ex p Institute of Dental Surgery* [1994] 1 WLR 242, 258B-E (need "an apparently inexplicable decision"), 261E-G ("so aberrant as in itself to call for an explanation"); *Padfield v Minister of Agriculture Fisheries & Food* [1968] AC 997, 1053G-1054A (Lord Pearce: "If all the prima facie reasons seem to point in favour of his taking a certain course to carry out the intentions of Parliament in respect of a power which it has given him in that regard, and he gives no reason whatever for taking a contrary course, the court may infer that he has no good reason and that he is not using the power given by Parliament to carry out its intentions"), 1061G-1062A (Lord Upjohn: "if he does not give any reason for his decision it may be, if circumstances warrant it, that a court may be at liberty to come to the conclusion that he had no good reason for reaching that conclusion and order a prerogative writ to issue accordingly"); *R (Quark Fishing Ltd) v Secretary of State for Foreign and Commonwealth Affairs* [2002] EWCA Civ 1409 at [50] ("If the court has not been given a true and comprehensive account, but has had to tease the truth out of late [disclosure], it may be appropriate to draw inferences against the Secretary of State upon points which remain obscure"), [62] (applying the *Padfield* inference to circumstances "where the Minister has given conflicting, or apparently conflicting, reasons": "I am not prepared to assume, or find as a fact in these proceedings, that the decision ... was taken on rational grounds having regard only to relevant considerations"); *R (Farrakhan) v Secretary of State for the Home Department* [2002] EWCA Civ 606 [2002] QB 1391 at [7] (declining to conclude "that, under established principles of judicial review, the absence of reasons gives rise to the inference that none exists"); *R v Secretary of State for Trade and Industry, ex p Lonrho Plc* [1989] 1 WLR 525, 539H-540B ("The only significance of the absence of reasons is that if all other known facts and circumstances appear to point overwhelmingly in favour of a different decision, the decision-maker, who has given no reasons, cannot complain if the court draws the inference that he had no rational reason for his decision"); *R v Inland Revenue Commissioners, ex p T.C.Coombs & Co* [1991] 2 AC 283, 300F, 302F ("No unfavourable inference can be drawn from the silence of the revenue because there is ... an obvious explanation for their silence"); *Bolton Metropolitan District Council v Secretary of State for the Environment* [1995] 3 PLR 37, 43G ("Since there is no obligation to refer to every material consideration, but only the main issues in dispute, the scope for drawing any inference will necessarily be limited to the main issues, and then only, as Lord Keith pointed out [in *Lonrho*], when `all other known facts and circumstances appear to point overwhelmingly' to a different decision"); *R v Secretary of State for Education, ex p Standish* The Times 15th November 1993 (failure to give reasons for his decision debarring a teacher from employment; judicial review granted for inferred irrationality); *R v Secretary of State for the Home Department, ex p Benjamin Yaw Amankwah* [1994] Imm AR 240 (deportation decision inconsistent with Secretary of State's policy and, absent reasons, unfair and perverse); *R v Secretary of State for the Home Department, ex p Pegg* [1995] COD 84 (in the absence of reasons, this decision unreasonable); *R v Number 8 Area Committee of the Legal Aid Board, ex p Megarry* [1994] PIQR 476 ("in the absence of reasoning as to why the committee found against the [claimant] on this point, the court can only conclude that they have not properly considered the points that were raised"); *R v Secretary of State for the Home Department, ex p Nelson* The Independent 2nd June 1994 (inadequate contemporaneous reasons meaning reviewing court "not satisfied that the material before the Secretary of State was properly considered before the decision was taken"); *R v Central Criminal Court, ex p Behbehani* [1994] COD 193 (absence of distinct reasons on single issue supporting conclusion that no material on which relevant conclusion could properly have been reached).

62.2.9 **"Departure" cases: good reason must be demonstrated.**
(A) REASONS REQUIRED WHERE INCONSISTENCY. <55.1.13> (reasons for departing from previous decision); <55.1.10> (unequal treatment).
(B) REASONS FOR DEPARTING FROM POLICY GUIDANCE. <6.2>;*Gransden v Secretary of State for the Environment* (1987) 54 P & CR 86 (Woolf J: "if it is going to depart from the policy, it must give clear reasons for ... doing so in order that the recipient of its decision will know why the decision is being made as an exception to the policy and the grounds upon which the decision is taken"), applied in *Horsham District Council v Secretary of State for the Environment* [1992] 1 PLR 81, 88C-G, 94F-G; *R v Islington London Borough Council, ex p Rixon* [1997] ELR 66 (duty to comply with statutory guidance unless good reason for departure, properly articulated).
(C) REASONS FOR DEPARTING FROM ANOTHER BODY'S FINDINGS. <55.2.3>.
(D) REASONS AND DISHONOUR OF LEGITIMATE EXPECTATION.*R (Bibi) v Newham London Borough Council* [2001] EWCA Civ 607 [2002] 1 WLR 237 at [59] ("In circumstances such as the present where the conduct of the Authority has given rise to a legitimate expectation then fairness requires that, if the Authority decides not to give effect to that expectation, the Authority articulate its reasons so that their propriety may be tested by the court if that is what the disappointed person requires").
(E) REASONS AND REJECTING/PREFERRING EVIDENCE.*R (I) v Secretary of State for the Home Department* [2005] EWHC 1025 (Admin) at [54] (no "sound basis" for rejecting expert reports); *R (H) v Ashworth Hospital Authority* [2002] EWCA Civ 923 [2003] 1 WLR 127 at [81] (tribunal should have explained reasons why preferred one expert to others); *R (C) v Merton London Borough Council* [2005] EWHC 1753 (Admin) [2005] 3 FCR 42 at [31] (council failing to give adequate reasons for rejecting expert evidence); *R (Beeson) v Dorset County Council* [2001] EWHC Admin 986 [2002] HRLR 368 (duty to give adequate reasons for rejecting claimant's evidence) (CA is [2002] EWCA Civ 1812 [2003] UKHRR 353); *R (Alliss) v Legal Services Commission* [2002] EWHC 2079 (Admin) at [65] (no need for LSC to give reasons for preferring on expert over another).
(F) REASONS AND OTHER DEPARTURES.*Pepys v London Transport* [1975] 1 WLR 234 (Lands Tribunal required to give reasons for departing from normal rule as to costs).

62.2.10 **Reasons required by the Court: defendant's duty of candour.**<10.4>.

62.2.11 **Power to give reasons.** *R v Secretary of State for the Home Department, ex p Fayed* [1998] 1 WLR 763 (statute excluding any duty to give reasons, but Secretary of State having a discretion to give reasons, although refusal here unimpeachable); <60.8.9> (duty to consider exercising the power).

62.2.12 **Reasons and failure to complain: whether claimant obliged to request reasons.** *R v Crown Court of Southwark ex p Samuel* [1995] COD 249 ("no application should be made to this court unless reasons have been asked for and refused"); *English v Emery Reimbold and Strick Ltd* [2002] EWCA Civ 605 [2002] 1 WLR 2409 at [25] (where appeal court considering

permission to appeal from a court, should consider remitting for further reasons) [61]; *Re B (Appeal: Lack of Reasons)* [2003] EWCA Civ 881 [2003] 2 FLR 1035 (applying *English v Emery Reimbold*, CA remitting case for judge to give additional reasons as to care order); *R v Burton upon Trent Justices, ex p Hussain* (1997) 9 Admin LR 233, 236F (reasons not requested), 237D-H (nevertheless, breach of natural justice not to make findings of fact and give reasons); *R v Crown Court at Stafford, ex p Wilf Gilbert (Staffs) Ltd* [1999] 2 All ER 955, 960a ("This is not a case where there has been a refusal of reasons because the reasons have not been sought"); *R v Lancashire County Council, ex p M* [1995] ELR 136, 139H (should have asked for reasons under the Tribunals and Inquiries Act 1992 s.10); Justice/All Souls Report, *Administrative Justice: Some Necessary Reforms* (1988) at p.72 (favouring "a statutory right to obtain reasons on demand").

62.3 Adequacy of reasons. The level of reasoning must, without needing to be over-elaborate, be adequately informative in the context and circumstances. Lawyers can assist a body in presenting its reasoning, but the reasons must always be those of the body and not the lawyer.

62.3.1 **Adequacy of reasons in a nutshell.** *R v Brent London Borough Council, ex p Baruwa* (1997) 29 HLR 915, 929 (Schiemann LJ: "where, as here, an authority is required to give reasons for its decision it is required to give reasons which are proper, adequate, and intelligible and enable the person affected to know why they have won or lost. That said, the law gives decision makers a certain latitude in how they express themselves and will recognise that not all those taking decisions find it easy in the time available to express themselves with judicial exactitude"); *South Bucks District Council v Porter (No.2)* [2004] UKHL 33 [2004] 1 WLR 1953 (as to reasons for planning decisions) at [36] (Lord Brown: "The reasons for a decision must be intelligible and they must be adequate. They must enable the reader to understand why the matter was decided as it was and what conclusions were reached on the 'principal important controversial issues', disclosing how any issue of law or fact was resolved. Reasons can be briefly stated, the degree of particularity required depending entirely on the nature of the issues falling for decision. The reasoning must not give rise to a substantial doubt as to whether the decision-maker erred in law, for example by misunderstanding some relevant policy or some other important matter or by failing to reach a rational decision on relevant grounds. But such adverse inference will not readily be drawn. The reasons need refer only to the main issues in the dispute, not to every material consideration. They should enable disappointed developers to assess their prospects of obtaining some alternative development permission, or, as the case may be, their unsuccessful opponents to understand how the policy or approach underlying the grant of permission may impact upon future such applications. Decision letters must be read in a straightforward manner, recognising that they are addressed to parties well aware of the issues involved and the arguments advanced. A reasons challenge will only succeed if the party aggrieved can satisfy the court that he has genuinely been substantially prejudiced by the failure to provide an adequately reasoned decision"); *R (Iran) v Secretary of State for the Home Department* [2005] EWCA Civ 982 [2005] Imm AR 535 (immigration reasons) at [90] ("A decision should not be set aside for inadequacy of reasons unless the adjudicator failed to identify and record the matters that were critical to his decision on material issues, in such a way that the IAT was unable to understand why he reached that decision").

62.3.2 **Drafting reasons: proper limits of the lawyer's function.** *R v Wandsworth London Borough Council, ex p Dodia* (1998) 30 HLR 562, 565-566 (Jowitt J: "there is a certain

---

[61] Katherine Olley [2007] JR 82.

knowledge required as to what matters should be dealt with in decision letters. Provided the distinction is clearly observed between the decision-maker's role which is to decide where the truth lies, to decide on the relevant facts and to provide the reasons for those decisions and any assistance given in formulating a decision letter in a way which deals with clarity with the decision and the reasons for it, I can see no objection to a decision-maker receiving advice in the drafting of the decision letter, provided, I stress, that division of labours is observed: the boundary between a decision-maker's function and his or her reasons for it and assistance then about how the decision letter should be drawn so that it can properly fulfil the duty under the Act to give reasons"); *R v Southwark London Borough Council, ex p Campisi* (1999) 31 HLR 560, 565 (speaking of a lack of "confidence that somebody actually sat back and seriously thought about it, as opposed to a lawyer afterwards reconstructing from various bits of mosaic to be found in various files, something which could have been a perfectly reasonable decision").

62.3.3 Adequacy of reasons and tribunals: the Burnton propositions. *R (Ashworth Hospital Authority) v Mental Health Review Tribunal for West Midlands and North West Region* [2001] EWHC Admin 901 (2002) 5 CCLR 36 (Administrative Court) at [77] (Stanley Burnton J, suggesting "the following propositions": "(a) proper adequate reasons must be given that deal with the substantial points that have been raised ...; (b) Reasons must be sufficient for the parties to know whether the tribunal made any error of law... (c) Where ... Parliament has required that a decision be given with written reasons, those reasons have to be adequate. They may be elucidated by subsequent evidence, but in general, inadequate written reasons cannot be saved by such evidence... (d) [the tribunal's] reasons must deal with the entirety of its decision... (e) It is unnecessary for a tribunal to set out the evidence and arguments before it or the facts found by it in detail ... (f) It is often difficult to explain why one witness is preferred to another. Generally speaking, a tribunal's decision will not be inadequately reasoned if it does not give such an explanation. (g) In assessing the adequacy of reasons, one must bear in mind that the decision will be considered by parties who know what the issues were ... (h) However, the reasons must sufficiently inform [the parties] as to the findings of the tribunal ... A tribunal must also bear in mind that its decision may have to be considered by those who were not present at or parties to the hearing ... (i) In considering the adequacy of reasons the Court is entitled to take into account the fact that the tribunal has a legally-qualified chairman, and [if] the reasons do not have to be given immediately ...") (CA is *R (H) v Ashworth Hospital Authority* [2002] EWCA Civ 923 [2003] 1 WLR 127).

62.3.4 Intelligible reasons dealing with the main points. *Bolton Metropolitan Borough Council v Secretary of State for the Environment* [1995] 3 PLR 37, 43C ("What the Secretary of State must do is to state his reasons in sufficient detail to enable the reader to know what conclusion he has reached on the `principal important controversial issues'"); *City of Edinburgh Council v Secretary of State for Scotland* [1997] 1 WLR 1447, 1465B-C ("It is necessary that an account should be given of the reasoning on the main issues which were in dispute sufficient to enable the parties and the court to understand that reasoning"); *Westminster City Council v Great Portland Estates Plc* [1985] AC 661, 673D (need for "proper, adequate, and intelligible" reasons); *R (Wheeler) v Assistant Commissioner of the Metropolitan Police* [2008] EWHC 439 (Admin) at [1.18] (failure to address the substantial points made by the person affected).

62.3.5 Adequacy depends on context. *R (Asha Foundation) v Millennium Commission* [2003] EWCA Civ 88 at [27] (Lord Woolf CJ: "The standard of reasons required depends upon the circumstances of the particular case. Where reasons are required to be given, the obligation is to give appropriate reasons having regard to the circumstances of the case"); *R (Shields) v Criminal Injuries Compensation Appeals Panel* [2001] ELR 164 at [30] ("the reasons were plain in the context of the case as it was argued"); *R v Immigration Appeal Tribunal, ex p Jebunisha Kharvaleb Patel* [1996] Imm AR 161, 167 ("the duty to give reasons require reasons

that are clear and adequate and deal with the substantial issues in the case. But ... what are good reasons in any particular case depend on the circumstances of the case"); *Flannery and Flannery v Halifax Estate Agencies Ltd* [2000] 1 WLR 377, 382A-C ("The extent of the duty, or rather the reach of what is required to fulfil it, depends on the subject matter"); *R v Criminal Injuries Compensation Board, ex p Aston* [1994] PIQR 460 (adequacy dependent upon the circumstances of the case).

62.3.6 **Reasoning inferred/incorporated from officer/staff report.** *R (Richardson) v North Yorks County Council* [2003] EWCA Civ 1860 [2004] 1 WLR 1920 at [35] (Simon Brown LJ, accepting that: "where a planning officer makes a recommendation which is followed by the members, the reasonable inference is that the members did so for the reasons advanced by the officer, unless of course there is some indication to the contrary"); *R (Heath & Hampstead Society) v Camden London Borough Council* [2008] EWCA Civ 193 [2008] 3 All ER 80 at [4] (officer's reasoning expressly incorporated in reasons for planning grant); *R (Hereford Waste Watchers Ltd) v Hereford Council* [2005] EWHC 191 (Admin) [2005] Env LR 586 at [13] (in adopting officer's recommendations, council taken to have approved reasons in his report); *R (Richards) v Pembrokeshire County Council* [2004] EWCA Civ 1000 [2005] LGR 105 at [40] (right to "refer to the Report, because it was the material document before the Council Cabinet which made the decision, and the Cabinet expressly gave as its reasons for adopting the Directions the reasons set out in the Report for its recommendations"); *R (Chisnell) v Richmond Upon Thames London Borough Council* [2005] EWHC 134 (Admin) at [42] (committee should generally identify own summary reasons, not simply make global reference to document).

62.3.7 **Standard form reasons/generalised incantations.** *R (London Fire and Emergency Planning Authority) v Secretary of State for Communities and Local Government* [2007] EWHC 1176 (Admin) [2007] LGR 591 at [64] (invocation of an uninformative formula suggesting absence or concealment of specific reasons); *R (Reading Borough Council) v Admissions Appeal Panel for Reading Borough Council* [2005] EWHC 2378 (Admin) [2006] ELR 186 at [13] (bare recitation of statutory grounds inadequate); *R v Mental Health Review Tribunal, ex p Clatworthy* [1985] 3 All ER 699 (insufficient to rehearse the circumstance in which a discharge could be granted); *R v Birmingham City Council, ex p B* [1999] ELR 305, 312E ("an appellant is entitled to know the basis for the decision beyond simply a ritual incantation of the [statutory] test"); *R v Camden London Borough Council, ex p Adair* (1997) 29 HLR 236, 247 (recitation of general formula, that all evidence taken into account and all inquiries made); *R v Northampton Borough Council, ex p Carpenter* [1993] COD 133 (not sufficient to refer to 'regard has been given to the general circumstances'); *R v Royal Borough of Kensington and Chelsea, ex p Kassam* (1994) 26 HLR 455, 462 ("'reasons' involves more than merely reciting the provision of the sections referring to the circumstances to which regard has to be paid"), 465; *Minister for Immigration and Ethnic Affairs v Wu Shan Liang* [1996] 4 LRC 156 (High Court of Australia), 164d-g (legality of use of incantation of formula depending on whether decision otherwise lawful or infected); *R (L) v Independent Appeal Panel of St Edward's College* [2001] EWHC Admin 108 [2001] ELR 542 at [38] (panel should not have used a standard form letter in the present case); *R (Asha Foundation) v Millennium Commission* [2003] EWCA Civ 88 (no duty to give reasons beyond saying preferred other options); *R (A1 Veg Ltd) v Hounslow London Borough Council* [2003] EWHC 3112 (Admin) [2004] LGR 536 at [131] (sufficient to say that market tenant unsuccessful after due consideration).

62.3.8 **Lawyers/non-lawyers and reasons.** *R v Governors of the Bishop Challoner Roman Catholic Comprehensive Girls' School, ex p Choudhury* [1992] 2 AC 182, 197E (Lord Browne-Wilkinson: "the court should not approach decisions and reasons given by committees of laymen expecting the same accuracy in the use of language which a lawyer might be expected to adopt"); *R (London Fire & Emergency Planning Authority) v Board of Medical Referees* [2007]

EWHC 2805 (Admin) (although "wrong to be too critical of the reasons given by a board that is not chaired by a lawyer", nevertheless reasons inadequate); *Save Britain's Heritage v Number 1 Poultry Ltd* [1991] 1 WLR 153, 165G (Lord Bridge, doubting "how far any willingness on the part of the courts to construe inspectors' decision letters benevolently is properly referable to their having been drafted without legal assistance. Even if it is, I do not think that the converse follows that a decision by the Secretary of State, because he has access to legal assistance in drafting decision letters, should on that account be subjected to more rigorous criticism in condemning flaws in the quality of the draftsmanship").

62.3.9 **Systematic analysis/logical sequence/working through.** *R v Richmond-upon-Thames London Borough Council, ex p T* (2001) 33 HLR 737 (statutory duty to set out material findings of fact, meaning that required to identify all relevant matters, to show they were considered whether or not outweighed by other matters or not supporting decision-maker's conclusion); *R v Mental Health Review Tribunal, ex p Pickering* [1986] 1 All ER 99 (failure to identify which of two alternative grounds were relied upon); *R v Immigration Appeal Tribunal, ex p Khan (Mahmud)* [1983] QB 790 (failure to set out the issue which the tribunal was deciding and a failure to set out the basis on which the decision had been reached); *R v Immigration Appeal Tribunal, ex p Amin* [1992] Imm AR 367, 374 (immigration judges needing to indicate "(1) what evidence they accept; (2) what evidence they reject; (3) whether there is any evidence as to which they cannot make up their mind, whether or not they accept it; (4) what, if any, evidence they regard as irrelevant"); *R (Bahrami) v Immigration Appeal Tribunal* [2003] EWHC 1453 (Admin) at [8] ("the determination should be sufficiently reasoned to enable a claimant, his advisers, and any appellate or reviewing body, to see why the claimant lost on a particular issue"); *R (Sivanesan) v Secretary of State for the Home Department* [2008] EWHC 1146 (Admin) at [30] ("essential to grapple" with "critical aspects"); *R v Immigration Appeal Tribunal, ex p Shahim Begum* The Times 15th February 1995 (failure to isolate separate issues); *R v Housing Benefit Review Board of South Tyneside Metropolitan Borough Council, ex p Tooley* [1996] COD 143 (decision letter should have summarised (a) the claimant's contentions, (b) the supporting evidence, (c) the council's conclusions and (d) the reasons for (c)); *R v A Special Adjudicator, ex p Hanif Ahmad* [1999] Imm AR 390, 399 (failure, in an asylum case and where decision reserved, to deal with the matters raised by the applicant; so that decision unreasoned and unreasonable); *R (Lowe) v Family Health Services Appeal Authority* [2001] EWCA Civ 128 (reasons inadequate because did not deal with question in correct "logical sequence"); *Curtis v London Rent Assessment Committee* [1999] QB 92, 118G-119C (rent assessment committee's duty to give reasons needing some "working through", ie. arithmetical explanation, of the assessment); *R v Parole Board, ex p Gordon* [2001] ACD 265 at [38] ("the balancing exercise they are required to carry out is so fundamental to the decision making process that they should make it plain that this has been done and to state broadly which factors they have taken into account"); *R v Crown Court at Canterbury, ex p Howson-Ball* [2001] Env LR 639, 646-647 (need for crown court to provide "some analysis" of the relevant matters).

62.3.10 **Reasons and resources.** *R (H) v Ashworth Hospital Authority* [2002] EWCA Civ 923 [2003] 1 WLR 127 at [76] (Dyson LJ: "If tribunals do not have the time and back-up resources that they need to discharge their statutory obligation to provide adequate reasons, then the time and resources must be found. I absolutely reject the submission that reasons which would be inadequate if sufficient resources were available may be treated as adequate simply because sufficient resources are not available. Either the reasons are adequate or they are not, and the sufficiency of resources is irrelevant to that question").

62.3.11 **"Departure" cases: duty to explain departure.** <62.2.9>.

62.3.12 **Adequacy and voluntary reasons.** *R v Criminal Injuries Compensation Board, ex p*

Cummins (1992) 4 Admin LR 747 (having chosen to give reasons, obliged to give adequate reasons); *R v Criminal Injuries Compensation Board, ex p Moore* [1999] 2 All ER 90 (Sedley J), 95j ("since reasons were given in the present case, it is not necessary to decide whether there was a legal obligation to give them. Once given; their adequacy falls to be tested by the same criteria as if they were obligatory"; CA is at [1999] COD 241); *R (Martin) v Legal Services Commission* [2007] EWHC 1786 (Admin) at [60] ("legal inadequacy of ... voluntary reasons" warranting quashing the decision).

62.3.13 Whether reasons should be in writing. *R v Parole Board, ex p Lodomez* (1994) 26 BMLR 162 (duty to give reasons under the Parole Rules meaning full reasons in writing); *R v Criminal Injuries Compensation Board, ex p Moore* [1999] COD 241 (whether reasons should be given in writing, where requested by the claimant); *R v London Borough of Islington, ex p Hinds* (1995) 27 HLR 65, 75 (commenting that: "Decisions are more likely to be correct if they are carefully considered and properly articulated. Writing brings clarity and precision to thought"); *R (Wooder) v Feggetter* [2002] EWCA Civ 554 [2003] QB 219 at [34] (declaration that certifying doctor administering compulsory medication to a competent non-consenting adult "should give in writing the reasons").

62.3.14 No need for lengthy reasons. *Stefan v General Medical Council* [1999] 1 WLR 1293, 1304B ("The extent and substance of the reasons must depend upon the circumstances. They need not be elaborate nor lengthy. But they should be such as to tell the parties in broad terms why the decision was reached"), 1301F ("there can clearly be circumstances where a quite minimal explanation will legitimately suffice"); *R (Alconbury Developments Ltd) v Secretary of State for the Environment Transport and the Regions* [2001] UKHL 23 [2003] 2 AC 295 at [170] (Lord Clyde: "What is required is that there should be a decision with reasons. Provided that these set out clearly the grounds on which the decision has been reached it does not seem to me necessary that all the thinking which lies behind it should also be made available"); *Save Britain's Heritage v Number 1 Poultry Ltd* [1991] 1 WLR 153, 164G (not required "to dot every `i' and cross every `t'"); *R v Civil Service Appeal Board, ex p Bruce* [1989] 2 All ER 907, 912a ("no obligation to go into lengthy reasoning, examining all points in detail, or anything of that sort"); *R v London Borough of Southwark, ex p Davies* (1994) 26 HLR 677, 680 (Laws J: "not necessary for the local authority to embark on a long diatribe"); *R (Hargrave) v Stroud District Council* [2002] EWCA Civ 1281 [2002] 3 PLR 115 at [13]-[14] (magistrates not required to give detailed reasons for conviction, even by reference to HRA:ECHR Art 6); *R (Leung) v Imperial College of Science, Technology and Medicine* [2002] EWHC 1358 (Admin) [2002] ELR 653 at [36] ("no need to deal with every point that has been raised"); *R v Governor of HM Prison Long Lartin, ex p Ross* 27th May 1994 unrep. (not required "to give chapter and verse"); *R v Lancashire County Council, ex p M* [1995] ELR 136, 139E-G ("broad grounds" in "standard form letter" sufficient); *R v Immigration Appeal Tribunal, ex p Mohammed Rashid* [1995] Imm AR 194, 196 ("not necessary for the [IAT] to spell out, in any detail, the basis on which it rejects any proposition of law put to it in the grounds of appeal"); *R v Immigration Appeal Tribunal, ex p Befikadi Minewuyelet Kassa* [1995] Imm AR 246, 247 (adjudicator not obliged "to take the matter sentence by sentence and reject or accept each part of the evidence"); *R v London Borough of Islington, ex p Hinds* (1996) 28 HLR 302 (adequate reasons should not mean imposing an unrealistic or impractical burden); *R v Criminal Injuries Compensation Board, ex p Cook* [1996] 1 WLR 1037, 1043A-F (no duty to deal with every material consideration), 1045B (no duty to demonstrate in reasoning that conclusion reached by appropriate process of reasoning).

62.3.15 Benevolent approach to reasons. <13.5.4(D)>.

62.3.16 Obvious reasons/informed audience.

(A) REASONS WERE OBVIOUS. *R v Bristol City Council, ex p Bailey and Bailey* (1995) 27 HLR 307, 317 (open hearing on simple issue: reasons obvious and therefore unnecessary); *R v Governors of St Gregory's RC Aided High School, ex p M* [1995] ELR 290, 298D-300A (sufficient that letter merely expression of ultimate decision; approach having been made plain during hearing); *R v Crown Court of Southwark ex p Samuel* [1995] COD 249 (merely stating the result might suffice in a straightforward case); *R v Wallace* The Times 31st December 1996 (ruling left the answer in no doubt); *R v Aylesbury Vale District Council, ex p Chaplin* [1997] 3 PLR 55, 60H, 61C (question under consideration clear and good and obvious reason for decision which was reached); *R v General Medical Council, ex p Salvi* The Times 24th February 1998 (see transcript) (relevant "question could sensibly and fairly be answered on the facts of this case by a simple `no'"); *R (Thompson) v Secretary of State for the Home Department* [2003] EWHC 538 (Admin) at [41] (where decision was an application of a stated policy: "The reason is the policy ... Therefore the reason for the decision is manifest"); cf. *R v London Borough of Lambeth, ex p Walters* (1994) 26 HLR 170, 175 ("the fact that the reasons are obvious, without the obvious being stated, does not absolve the local authority from its duty for stating the obvious"); *Pullum v Crown Prosecution Service* [2000] COD 206 (court obliged to give reasons, even though case a simple one).

(B) INFORMED AUDIENCE. *R (Roberts) v Secretary of State for Communities and Local Government* [2008] EWHC 677 (Admin) (reasons "must be read from the standpoint of an informed party"); *English v Emery Reimbold and Strick Ltd* [2002] EWCA Civ 605 [2002] 1 WLR 2409 at [118] ("an unsuccessful party should not seek to upset a judgment on the ground of inadequacy of reasons unless, despite the advantage of considering the judgment with knowledge of the evidence given and submissions made at the trial, that party is unable to understand why it is that the Judge has reached an adverse decision"); *North Range Shipping Ltd v Seatrans Shipping Corp* [2002] EWCA Civ 405 [2002] 1 WLR 2397 at [27] ("the judge's brief reasons are directed to a fully informed applicant"); *R (H) v Ashworth Hospital Authority* [2002] EWCA Civ 923 [2003] 1 WLR 127 at [79] ("I do not accept that the `informed audience' point can properly be relied on to justify as adequate a standard of reasoning in tribunals which would not be regarded as adequate in a judgment by a judge"); *R (Warren) v Mental Health Review Tribunal London North and East Region* [2002] EWHC 811 (Admin) at [15] (agreeing that: "Brevity is an administrative virtue, and elliptical reasons may be perfectly comprehensible when considered against the background of the arguments at the hearing").

62.3.17 **Reasons and prejudice.** <4.3.2>.

62.4 **Timing of reasons.** It is a vexed question whether and when absent or inadequate reasons can be remedied by fresh further reasons. It may seem artificial to review a decision without reference to a fuller explanation which is to hand. But it can be wrong in principle (and dangerous in practice) to allow the requisite focused-mind to be brought to bear only in defending a decision after the event.

62.4.1 **Opportunities to seek to give a fuller explanation.**
(A) ON REQUEST AT THE TIME OF THE DECISION. <62.2.12>.
(B) PRE-ACTION PROTOCOL: LETTER OF RESPONSE. <19.1.5>.
(C) ACKNOWLEDGMENT OF CLAIM FORM. <19.3>.
(D) POST-PERMISSION WRITTEN EVIDENCE. <22.1.3>.

62.4.2 **Reasons: limits of the lawyer's proper function.** <62.3.2>.

62.4.3 **Collective decision-making body.**
(A) BODY SPEAKS THROUGH STATED DECISION/RESOLUTION. *R v Carrick District*

Council, ex p Shelley [1996] Env LR 273, 283 (Carnwath J: "A Committee of this kind expresses itself by voting on a resolution and the minute then forms the public record of its decision. In normal circumstances, the decision can only be ascertained by reference to the terms of the resolution"), 284 ("It is the form of the resolution that provides the essential discipline for members when they come to vote. Furthermore, the public is entitled to know that the matter has been properly considered").

(B0 DANGERS OF INDIVIDUAL RATIONALISATION.*R (Young) v Oxford City Council* [2002] EWCA Civ 990 [2002] 3 PLR 86 at [20] (Pill LJ, describing "dangers in permitting a planning authority, whether by its committee chairman or a planning officer, providing an explanatory statement. The danger is that, even acting in good faith, the witness may attempt to rationalise a decision in such a way as to meet a question which has arisen upon the effect of the decision. Moreover, it will usually be impossible to assess the reasoning process of individual members and there are obvious dangers in speculating about them. It is therefore important that the decision-making process is made clear in the recorded decisions of the committee, together with the officers' report to committee and any record of the committee's decisions. Decisions recorded in the minutes should speak for themselves"); *Breen v Amalgamated Engineering Union* [1971] 2 QB 175, 192H ("not open to the individual members of that body, be they one or many, to give evidence to add to, vary or contradict the reasons which have been given authoritatively on behalf of all").

(C) WHETHER ELUCIDATION POSSIBLE.*R (Nash) v Chelsea College of Art and Design* [2001] EWHC Admin 538 (although desirable that all members of decision-making committee should subscribe to reasons subsequently put forward, not essential where court satisfied that they represent the true reasons); *R (Wall) v Brighton and Hove City Council* [2004] EWHC 2582 (Admin) [2004] 4 PLR 115 (failure to provide required summary of reasons not satisfactorily addressed by evincing reasons of individual members, but warranted collectively reconvening the planning committee in public session).

62.4.4 Proper later explanation/amplification. *Baxendale-Walker v Law Society* [2006] EWHC 643 (Admin) [2006] 3 All ER 675 at [28] (tribunal entitled to give reasons either at the time of the decision or later); *R (Swords) v Secretary of State for Communities and Local Government* [2007] EWCA Civ 795 [2007] LGR 757 at [47] (later reasons allowed); *Re L* [1994] ELR 16, 24A-B (since reasons now given, "no useful purpose would be served by quashing the decision now on the ground that it did not itself contain reasons"); *R v Northavon District Council, ex p Smith* [1994] 2 AC 402, 412A-B (affidavit explaining reasons); *R v Secretary of State for the Home Department, ex p Canbolat* [1997] Imm AR 281 (DC), 288 (Secretary of State entitled to communicate decision by means of common form decision-letter, but when challenged on appeal, obliged to give fuller reasons); *R v Brent London Borough Council, ex p Baruwa* (1997) 29 HLR 915, 929 ("affidavit ... by way of amplification of the reasons for the decision. Looking at such an affidavit is often a sensible course and saves the bother and expense of going back to the decision maker to make a new decision which will incorporate the material which appears in the affidavit"); *R v National Lottery Commission, ex p Camelot Group Plc* [2001] EMLR 3 at [81] (even if reasons required by the statute, proper to look at reasons provided in witness statement); *R v Secretary of State for the Environment, Transport and the Regions, ex p Alliance Against the Birmingham Northern Relief Road* 23rd March 1999 unrep. (witness statement admissible to show how decision was approached); *Office of Fair Trading v IBA Health Ltd* [2004] EWCA Civ 142 [2004] 4 All ER 1103 at [106] ("There is ... nothing unusual, particularly in a case which has to be dealt with in a relatively short timescale, for the stated reasons to be amplified by evidence before the court" albeit "the Court may need to be `circumspect' to ensure that this is not used as means of concealing or altering the true grounds of the decision"); *R (Gleaves) v Secretary of State for the Home Department* [2004] EWHC 2522 (Admin) at [31] (witness statement reasons admitted for prison disciplinary decision).

62.4.5 Later reasons supporting view that flawed approach. <62.1.5>; *R (London Fire and Emergency Planning Authority) v Secretary of State for Communities and Local Government* [2007] EWHC 1176 (Admin) [2007] LGR 591 at [67] (where expanded reasons disclose a defect, claimant entitled to rely on them because incompleteness concern inapplicable); *R v North West Lancashire Health Authority, ex p A* [2000] 1 WLR 977, 992E (finding unlawful approach adopted in authority's policy, by reference to further reasoning); *R v Director of Public Prosecutions, ex p Manning* [2001] QB 330 (judicial review granted because of deficiency in contemporaneous note disclosed later); *R (Nash) v Chelsea College of Art and Design* [2001] EWHC Admin 538 at [22] (chairman's later defective reasons would justify quashing of decision even if may not have been shared by other committee members), [28] (referring to *R v Legal Aid Area No.8 (Northern) Appeal Committee, ex p Angell* (1991) 3 Admin LR 189).

62.4.6 Resistance to retro-reasons. *R (Bancoult) v Secretary of State for Foreign & Commonwealth Affairs* [2007] EWCA Civ 498 [2008] QB 365 at [70] ("in principle a decision-maker who gives one set of reasons cannot, when challenged, come up with another set"); *R (London Fire and Emergency Planning Authority) v Secretary of State for Communities and Local Government* [2007] EWHC 1176 (Admin) [2007] LGR 591 at [66] (rejecting expanded reasons seeking to justify original decisions, provided much later and when under challenge, without the benefit of any contemporaneous record); *R (Hereford Waste Watchers Ltd) v Hereford Council* [2005] EWHC 191 (Admin) [2005] Env LR 586 at [48] ("the courts must be alive to ensure that there is no rewriting of history, even subconsciously... the truth can become refracted, even in the case of honest witnesses, through the prism of self justification. There will be a particular reluctance to permit a defendant to rely on subsequent reasons where they appear to cut against the grain of the original reasons"); *R (S) v London Borough of Brent* [2002] EWCA Civ 693 [2002] ELR 556 at [26] ("it is not ordinarily open to a decision-maker who is required to give reasons to respond to a challenge by giving different or better reasons"), [44]; *R (Goldsmith) v London Borough of Wandsworth* [2004] EWCA Civ 1170 (2004) 7 CCLR 472 at [91] ("the court has to look at the decision at the time it was made and at the manner in which it was communicated to the person or persons affected by it"); *R (D) v Secretary of State for the Home Department* [2003] EWHC 155 (Admin) [2003] 1 FLR 979 at [18] ("It is well established that the court should exercise caution before accepting reasons for a decision which were not articulated at the time of the decision but were only expressed later, in particular after the commencement of proceedings"), [19] (contemporaneous documents and surrounding facts supporting conclusion that proper consideration not given to the matter, despite witness statement to the contrary); *R v Secretary of State for the Home Department, ex p Chetta* [1996] COD 463 (see transcript) (given that one rationale for reasons is so that claimant knows whether decision challengeable, court criticising "Alice in Wonderland" situation where reasons only given after challenge brought); *R v Crown Court at Portsmouth, ex p Thomas* [1994] COD 373 (ex post facto rationalisation); *R v Secretary of State for the Environment, ex p Kingston upon Hull City Council* [1996] Env LR 248, 262 (preferring contemporaneous letter to letters "written after the event in response to the application for judicial review"); *R v Deputy Chief Constable of Thames Valley Police, ex p Cotton* [1989] COD 318 (preference for contemporaneous documents); *R v South West Thames Mental Health Review Tribunal, ex p Demetri* [1997] COD 445 (inadequate reasons not cured by subsequent affidavit by chairman of tribunal); *R v Haringey London Borough Council, ex p Norton* (1998) 1 CCLR 168, 174F ("need for very considerable caution before the admission of affidavit evidence which purports to supplement, amend or impugn a document enshrining a decision which on its face bears no mark of invalidity"); *R (T) v Independent Appeal Panel for Devon County Council* [2007] EWHC 763 (Admin) [2007] ELR 499 at [42] (new reasons contradicting decision letter); cf. *R (C) v Secretary of State for Justice* [2008] EWCA Civ 882 at [49] (where impact assessment should inform decision, wrong in principle to refuse judicial review by reference to assessment produced after the event, albeit in good faith, serving to validate the decision).

62.4.7 **Retro-reasons and statutory instrument.** *R (Bancoult) v Secretary of State for Foreign & Commonwealth Affairs* [2007] EWCA Civ 498 [2008] QB 365 at [70] (whether retro-reasons admissible in considering legality of Order in Council).

62.4.8 **Retro-reasons: the *Nash* principles.** *R (Nash) v Chelsea College of Art and Design* [2001] EWHC Admin 538 at [34] (Stanley Burnton J, setting out these propositions: "(i) Where there is a statutory duty to give reasons as part of the notification of the decision, so that ... `the adequacy of the reasons is itself made a condition of the legality of the decision', only in exceptional circumstances if at all will the Court accept subsequent evidence of the reasons. (ii) In other cases, the Court will be cautious about accepting late reasons. The relevant considerations include the following, which to a significant degree overlap: (a) Whether the new reasons are consistent with the original reasons. (b) Whether it is clear that the new reasons are indeed the original reasons of the whole committee. (c) Whether there is a real risk that the later reasons have been composed subsequently in order to support the tribunal's decision, or are a retrospective justification of the original decision. This consideration is really an aspect of (b). (d) The delay before the later reasons were put forward. (e) The circumstances in which the later reasons were put forward. In particular, reasons put forward after the commencement of proceedings must be treated especially carefully. Conversely, reasons put forward during correspondence in which the parties are seeking to elucidate the decision should be approached more tolerantly"); *R (B) v Merton London Borough Council* [2003] EWHC 1689 (Admin) [2003] 4 All ER 280 at [42] (Stanley Burnton J, explaining that *Nash* proposition (i) was too widely expressed: "Reasons that merely elucidate reasons given contemporaneously with a decision will normally be considered by the Court"); *R (Levy) v Environment Agency* [2002] EWHC 1663 (Admin) [2003] Env LR 245 at [83] (applying *Nash* to admit evidence); *R (Leung) v Imperial College of Science, Technology and Medicine* [2002] EWHC 1358 (Admin) [2002] ELR 653 at [29]-[30] (Silber J, applying the principles in *Nash*, but adding: "whether the decision-maker would have been expected to state in the decision document the reason that he or she is seeking to adduce later"; and "whether it would be just in all the circumstances to refuse to admit the subsequent reasons of the decision-maker"); *R (Medway Council) v Secretary of State for Transport* [2002] EWHC 2516 (Admin) at [7], [10] (applying *Nash*).

62.4.9 **Statutory reasons duties and retro-reasons.**[62] *R v Westminster City Council, ex p Ermakov* [1996] 2 All ER 302, 312e (Hutchison LJ: "(1) If the reasons given are insufficient to enable the court to consider the lawfulness of the decision, the decision itself will be unlawful; and (2) the court should, at the very least, be circumspect about allowing material gaps to be filled by affidavit evidence or otherwise"); *Hijazi v Kensington and Chelsea Royal London Borough Council* [2003] EWCA Civ 692 [2003] HLR 1113 at [31] (Dyson LJ, describing *Ermakov* as "a classic exposition of the relevant law"); *R (Metropolitan Borough of Wirral) v Chief Schools Adjudicator* [2001] ELR 574 at [58] (where "specific statutory duty ... to give an adjudication with reasons ... a subsequent witness statement is not permissible"); *R v Tynedale District Council, ex p Shield* (1990) 22 HLR 144 (court should not go behind decision letter because one purpose of statutory reasons requirement is to allow decision to be challenged); *R v Lambeth London Borough Council Housing Benefit Review Board, ex p Harrington* The Times 10th December 1996 (applying *Ermakov* to Housing Benefit Review Boards)); *R v Doncaster Metropolitan Borough Council, ex p Nortrop* (1996) 28 HLR 862, 874 (declining to look at supplementary affidavit reasons in the context of a statutory reasons duty); *Re P (Contact: Discretion)* [1998] 2 FLR 696, 701H (explaining, as to magistrates' statutory duty to state findings and reasons, not entitled later to supplement that written record); *R (Jackson) v Parole Board* [2003] EWHC 2437 (Admin) at [24]-[25] (Court entitled to accept Secretary of

---

[62] Richard McManus [1996] JR 156.

State's evidence that written reasons document was incorrect, where no statutory duty to give reasons at same time as decision and Secretary of State able to point to a contemporaneous document predating the misleading reasons document and which containing the true reasons); *Hijazi v Kensington and Chelsea Royal London Borough Council* [2003] EWCA Civ 692 [2003] HLR 1113 at [32] ("nothing objectionable in a decision-maker making a subsequent statement in which he identifies the material that he took into account in the course of the decision-making process"); *R (Richardson) v North Yorks County Council* [2003] EWCA Civ 1860 [2004] 1 WLR 1920 at [39] (situations where "the law regards it as acceptable to formulate and state the reasons for a decision subsequent to the decision itself"); *R v Northamptonshire County Council, ex p W* [1998] ELR 291, 299H-300E (amplificatory affidavit admissible because no shift in ground); *R (GB) v Oxfordshire County Council* [2001] EWCA Civ 1358 [2002] ELR 8 (generally not appropriate for statutory tribunal, required to give reasoned decisions, to respond to an appeal by purporting to amplify the reasons given); *R (Taylor) v Maidstone Crown Court* [2003] EWHC 2555 (Admin) at [9]-[11] (declining to take account of crown court's later reasons with its acknowledgment of the judicial review claim form).

62.4.10 **The *Ermakov* approach and common law duties/non-statutory reasons.**[63] *R v Secretary of State for the Home Department, ex p Lillycrop* 27th November 1996 unrep. (applying *Ermakov* as "the proper approach" where Parole Board's duty to give reasons arising by virtue of "the demands of natural justice and fairness"; "Accordingly we conclude that where evidence is proffered to elucidate correct or add to the reasons contained in the decision letter a Court should examine the proffered evidence with care, and should only act upon it with caution. In particular, a Court should not substitute the reasons contained in proffered evidence for the reasons advanced in a decision letter. To do so would unquestionably raise the perception, if not the reality, of subsequent rationalisation of a decision that had not been properly considered at the time"); *R v Secretary of State for the Home Department, ex p Freeman* 2nd June 1998 unrep. (applying *Lillicrop*); *R v Snaresbrook Crown Court, ex p Impact Management Ltd* 4th March 1999 unrep. (similar approach to *Ermakov* to crown court's duty to give reasons); *R (Richards) v Pembrokeshire County Council* [2004] EWCA Civ 1000 [2005] LGR 105 (adopting an *Ermakov* approach to question whether directions ultra vires because not made for the statutorily-prescribed purpose), [58] (primary source of reasons contemporaneous, and fresh evidence permissible only to explain an "ambiguity" in the reason and then only where "credible and authoritative"), [63] ("inappropriate as a matter of principle, unfair on the [claimants] and inconsistent with authority" to admit witness statement evidence "in order to afford new and arguably lawful grounds for the Directions, when the stated reasons for recommending and adopting the Directions are ultra vires"); *R v Bacon's City Technology College, ex p W* [1998] ELR 488, 495C-D (treating *Ermakov* principle as only applicable where duty to give reasons a statutory duty); *E Barke v Seetec Business Technology Centre Ltd* [2005] EWCA Civ 578 at [36] (treating *Ermakov* as concerned with statutory duty to give reasons at the same time as the decision).

62.4.11 **Later reasons must elucidate not contradict.** *Commissioners of Customs and Excise v Shah* 18th June 1999 unrep. ("It is only in an exceptional case that the Court should take into account post decision declarations, by the makers of them, as to the ... reasons for the decision, when the reasons given at the time and the subsequent explanations of them are in plain conflict"); *R v Director General of Electricity Supply, ex p London Electricity Plc* The Times 13th June 2000 ("very reluctant to accept that the points made in [the] witness statement were merely elucidation of the reasons that had been given... [They] seem to me to smack of ex post facto rationalisation having seen the grounds advanced by the [claimant] in its [claim form]");

---

[63] Abigail Schaeffer [2004] JR 151.

R v South Bank University, ex p Coggeran [2001] ELR 42, at [36] (evidence rightly rejected because deployed to alter or contradict the contemporaneous minutes); *R (G) v Legal Services Commission* [2004] EWHC 276 (Admin) at [52] (later reasoning acceptable, as involving no "material change of reason"); *R (I) v Independent Appeal Panel for G Technology College* [2005] EWHC 558 (Admin) [2005] ELR 490 at [11] (reasons in witness statement could not be relied on, as "they are contradictory of the previous reasons"); *Re C and P* [1992] COD 29 (in principle evidence not admissible to show that education appeal committee meant something different from what said in unambiguous reasons set out in decision letter); *R v Criminal Injuries Compensation Board, ex p B* 7th December 1998 unrep. (defendant not entitled to adduce evidence in CA to show that reasoning as presented to the High Court was incorrect).

62.5 **Remedy for lack/insufficiency of reasons.**[64] The remedy for breach of a reasons duty should normally be quashing the decision to be taken afresh, rather than ordering the giving of reasons. That reflects the self-disciplining rationale of reasons and avoids after-the-event "reconstruction".

62.5.1 **Analytical consequence of reasons breach.** *R v Higher Education Funding Council, ex p Institute of Dental Surgery* [1994] 1 WLR 242, 257F-258A (reasons obligation "an independent and enforceable legal obligation and hence a ground of nullity where it is violated"); *R v Immigration Appeal Tribunal, ex p Khan (Mahmud)* [1983] QB 790 (failure to give adequate reasons constituting an error of law); *Crake v Supplementary Benefits Commission* [1982] 1 All ER 498 (inadequate reasons treated as not being an error of law justifying allowing statutory appeal); *R v MacDonald (Inspector of Taxes), ex p Hutchinson and Co Ltd* [1998] STC 680, 686j-687b (in statutory context where reasons an important protection, failure normally provides grounds to set aside the decision); *Crean v Somerset County Council* [2002] ELR 152 at [89] (on statutory appeal quash and remit for fresh decision, where failure by tribunal to grapple with key points); *R (Gleaves) v Secretary of State for the Home Department* [2004] EWHC 2522 (Admin) at [34] (here, "the adequacy of the reasons is not of itself a condition of the legality of the decision"); *R (Faulkner) v Secretary of State for the Home Department* [2005] EWHC 2567 (Admin) [2006] INLR 502 (immigration detention unlawful because of failure to give reasons).

62.5.2 **Requiring a fresh decision.** *R v Westminster City Council, ex p Ermakov* [1996] 2 All ER 302 (in context of statutory duty to give reasons, where failure to give (accurate) reasons at time of decision, claimant prima facie entitled to have the decision quashed); *R v Ministry of Defence, ex p Murray* [1998] COD 134 (court martial decision quashed for inadequate reasons); *R v City of London Corporation, ex p Matson* [1997] 1 WLR 765, 777F (decision quashed and matter remitted for fresh decision together with reasons); *Stefan v General Medical Council* [1999] 1 WLR 1293, 1304F (GMC ordered to rehear and reconsider); *R v Number 8 Area Committee of the Legal Aid Board, ex p Megarry* [1994] PIQR 476 (decision quashed, inter alia for inadequate reasons); *R v London Borough of Southwark, ex p Dagou* (1996) 28 HLR 72, 82 (quashing order for breach of statutory duty to give reasons); *Re L (Residence. Justices' Reasons)* [1995] 2 FLR 445 (matter remitted for reconsideration by differently constituted bench); *Curtis v London Rent Assessment Committee* [1999] QB 92, 120G-121G (considering relationship between remedy and whether absence of reasons leading to inference of unlawfulness or unreasonableness); *R v Metropolitan Borough of Sefton, ex p Healiss* (1995) 27 HLR 34, 40 (decision quashed and remitted to be "considered again by the local authority,

---

[64] This paragraph in a previous edition was cited in *Sukhmander Singh v Permanent Secretary for Security* [2006] HKCU 1222 at [33].

when they can ensure at least that they make it plain that they have carried out all the necessary investigations and that they give all the proper reasons for whatever decision they do subsequently arrive at"); *R v Islington London Borough Council, ex p Okocha* (1998) 30 HLR 191, 202 (appropriate to quash decision; justice of the case requiring a fresh decision); *Flannery v Halifax Estate Agencies Ltd* [2000] 1 WLR 377, 381H (want of reasons as a self-standing ground of appeal), 379f-j (ordering new trial); *Cedeno v Logan* [2001] 1 WLR 86 (no prejudice to appeal despite lack of reasons, so conviction not quashed); *R (Nash) v Chelsea College of Art and Design* [2001] EWHC Admin 538 at [27] (referring to *R v Legal Aid Area No.8 (Northern) Appeal Committee, ex p Angell* (1991) 3 Admin LR 189 (below) and suggesting that it could not stand with *Matson* (above)); *R (Cleary) v Revenue & Customs Commissioners* [2008] EWHC 1987 (Admin) (inadequate reasons not justifying quashing decision in the circumstances); *R (Midcounties Cooperative Ltd) v Forest of Dean District Council* [2007] EWHC 1714 (Admin) (planning permissions quashed for breach of reasons duty).

62.5.3 **Ordering proper reasons.** *Flannery v Halifax Estate Agencies Ltd* [2000] 1 WLR 377, 383D (on appeal, "one alternative remedy to quashing the decision is to invite or require the court to give reasons"); *English v Emery Reimbold and Strick Ltd* [2002] EWCA Civ 605 [2002] 1 WLR 2409 at [25] (appeal court can adjourn permission to appeal and seek additional reasons); *R v Legal Aid Area No.8 (Northern) Committee, ex p Angell* (1991) 3 Admin LR 189, 207D (court could grant remedy of "requiring proper and adequate reasons"); *Adami v Ethical Standards Officer* [2005] EWCA Civ 1754 [2006] LGR 397 (permissibility of appellate court allowing appeal for inadequate reasons and remitting to specialist statutory tribunal for explanation or reconsideration).

> **P63 External wrongs.** Judicial review may occasionally lie against a
> blameless body, for a third party wrong or external injustice.

63.1 External wrongs

63.1 External wrongs. Usually, a judicial review claimant is relying on a wrong which, if made out, can squarely be laid at the defendant public authority's door. However, in some special cases the Court can intervene because something has gone wrong which is external and not attributable to the defendant at all.

63.1.1 The special nature of judicial review for external wrongs. *R v Burton upon Trent Magistrates Court, ex p Woolley* The Times 17th November 1994 (judicial review of magistrates' conviction for impropriety on the part of the prosecution, characterised as a "sui generis" jurisdiction beyond the conventional threefold classification of grounds for judicial review); *R v Guildford Magistrates' Court, ex p Healy* [1983] 1 WLR 108, 114A (judicial review for extradition abuse "may leave one wondering precisely how a justice in such circumstances can be said to have acted in excess of jurisdiction or made an error of law"); cf. habeas corpus (frequently directed to a blameless custodian).

63.1.2 Decision procured by fraud/collusion/perjury. *R v West Sussex Quarter Sessions, ex p Albert and Maud Johnson Trust Ltd* [1974] QB 24, 36D-E (quashing appropriate "where there is evidence that the decision of an inferior court has been obtained by the fraud of a party or by collusion ... [or] perjury"); *R v Knightsbridge Crown Court, ex p Goonatilleke* [1986] QB 1 (fraud by prosecutor vitiating conviction); *R v Wolverhampton Crown Court, ex p Crofts* [1983] 1 WLR 204 (witness's perjured evidence vitiating appeal decision).

63.1.3 Extradition abuse, vitiating domestic criminal proceedings.[65] *R v Horseferry Road Magistrates' Court, ex p Bennett* [1994] 1 AC 42, 64E (judicial review court having "power to inquire into the circumstances by which a person has been brought within the jurisdiction and if itself satisfied that it was in disregard of extradition procedures it may stay the prosecution and order the release of the accused"), 62B-C (based on the rule of law); *Panday v Virgil* [2008] UKPC 24 [2008] 3 WLR 296 (discussing *Bennett*); *R v Horseferry Road Magistrates' Court, ex p Bennett (No.2)* The Times 1st April 1994 (committal quashed for abuse of process); *R v Staines Magistrates' Court, ex p Westfallen* [1998] 1 WLR 652 (extradition abuse must be serious); *R v Mullen* [2000] QB 520 (allowing an appeal against conviction on *Bennett* grounds) and *R (Mullen) v Secretary of State for the Home Department* [2004] UKHL 18 [2005] 1 AC 1 (subsequent compensation claim); *In re Schmidt* [1995] 1 AC 339 (no inherent *Bennett*-type jurisdiction to stay proceedings for extradition to another state on grounds of abuse of process); *A v Secretary of State for the Home Department* [2005] UKHL 71 [2006] 2 AC 221 (HL discussing *Bennett* in context of exclusion of torture-induced evidence).

63.1.4 Proceedings vitiated by abuse of process. *R v Asfaw* [2008] UKHL 31 [2008] 2 WLR 1178 (prosecution in breach of Refugee Convention should have been stayed as an abuse of process); *Panday v Virgil* [2008] UKPC 24 [2008] 3 WLR 296 at [28] (abuse of process applicable where proceedings the result of abuse of executive power); *R v Croydon Justices, ex p Dean* [1993] QB 769 (judicial review to halt prosecution as an abuse of process, given earlier promises by police); *R v General Court-Martial at RAF Uxbridge, ex p Wright* (1999) 11 Admin LR 747 (dual role of Court Martial prosecutor not an abuse of process); *R (AP) v Leeds Youth Court* [2001] EWHC Admin 215 (discussing limits of magistrates' function in relation

---

[65] Emma Dixon [1997] JR 86.

to abuse of process); *R v Horseferry Road Magistrates Court, ex p Director of Public Prosecutions* [1999] COD 441 (types of abuse of process); *R v Milton Keynes Magistrates' Court, ex p Roberts* The Independent 26th October 1994 (asking whether conduct degrading the rule of law or manipulating the court's process so as to cause serious prejudice); *R v Maidstone Crown Court, ex p Clark* [1995] 1 WLR 831 (improper use of arraignment); *R v Leominster Magistrates Court, ex p Aston Manor Brewery Co* The Times 8th January 1997 (integrity of criminal proceedings compromised); *R (Salubi) v Bow Street Magistrates Court* [2002] EWHC 919 (Admin) [2002] 1 WLR 3073 at [20] (normally abuse of process in relation to prosecution should be resolved by the criminal courts); *R (TB) v Secretary of State for the Home Department* [2007] EWHC 3381 (Admin) at [19], [24] (abuse of process for Secretary of State to deny asylum on a ground not raised during the AIT appeal).

63.1.5 **External error/unfairness/impropriety.** *PJG v Child Support Agency* [2006] EWHC 423 (Fam) [2006] 2 FLR 857 (magistrates liability order quashed as being based on incorrect figures supplied by CSA); *R (Marsh) v Lincoln District Magistrates Court* [2003] EWHC 956 (Admin) (magistrates' decision vitiated by CSA failure to draw attention to crucially important fact), [34]-[38] (wrong to "define or delimit the ambit of what is, after all, a residual jurisdiction"; sufficient that "an irregularity producing an unjust or potentially unjust result"); *R v Criminal Injuries Compensation Board, ex p A* [1999] 2 AC 330, 347A-B (CICB's decision vitiated by police failure to put doctor's evidence before it); <60.1.16> (blameless unfairness); *R v Leyland Justices, ex p Hawthorn* [1979] QB 283 (magistrates conviction quashed for unfairness by prosecution); *R v Harrow Crown Court, ex p Dave* [1994] 1 WLR 98 (decision of Crown Court quashed for prosecution's failure to disclose witness's prior convictions for dishonesty); *R v Maidstone Crown Court, ex p Shanks & McEwan (Southern) Ltd* [1993] Env LR 340 (asking whether any "manipulation or misuse of the prosecution's powers"); *R v Thames Stipendiary Magistrate, ex p Bates* [1995] COD 6 (judicial review of conviction on grounds of misconduct by prosecution requires bad faith, gross irregularity or unjustifiable commencement of proceedings); *R v Bolton Justices, ex p Scally* [1991] 1 QB 537 (whether conduct `analogous to fraud'); <51.2> (whether material fairly presented); <60.6.9> (error of approach by consultee/adviser); *Bedfordshire County Council v Fitzpatrick Contractors Ltd* [2001] LGR 397 (abuse of power to award a contract if council knew that the successful tenderer had acted in bad faith); <52.1> (bad faith).

63.1.6 **External/fresh evidence.** <17.2.5(B)> (fresh evidence showing error as to precedent fact); <17.2.5(C)> (fresh evidence and misapprehension of fact); *In re Rapier, decd.* [1988] QB 26 (statutory grounds for quashing a coroner's verdict, where new evidence having subsequently come to light).

D. MATERIALS

key sources of rules and procedure (64.1–64.10)

64.1   Supreme Court Act 1981 s.31
64.2   Civil Procedure Rules Part 54(I)
64.3   Civil Procedure Rules Part 54 Practice Direction
64.4   Administrative Court Office Notes for Guidance
64.5   Judicial Review Pre-Action Protocol
64.6   Judicial Review Urgent Cases Procedure
64.7   Human Rights Act 1998
64.8   Form N461
64.9   Form N462
64.10 Form N463
64.11 A List of Articles

64.1 Supreme Court Act 1981 section 31

Application for judicial review.

31.—(1) An application to the High Court for one or more of the following forms of relief, namely—

(a) an order of mandamus, prohibition or certiorari;

(b) a declaration or injunction under subsection (2); or

(c) an injunction under section 30 restraining a person not entitled to do so from acting in an office to which that section applies,

shall be made in accordance with rules of court by a procedure to be known as an application for judicial review.

(2) A declaration may be made or an injunction granted under this subsection in any case where an application for judicial review, seeking that relief, has been made and the High Court considers that, having regard to—

(a) the nature of the matters in respect of which relief may be granted by orders of mandamus, prohibition or certiorari;

(b) the nature of the persons and bodies against whom relief may be granted by such orders; and

(c) all the circumstances of the case,

it would be just and convenient for the declaration to be made or the injunction to be granted, as the case may be.

(3) No application for judicial review shall be made unless the leave of the High Court has been obtained in accordance with rules of court; and the court shall not grant leave to make such an application unless it considers that the applicant has a sufficient interest in the matter to which the application relates.

(4) On an application for judicial review the High Court may award damages to the applicant if—

(a) he has joined with his application a claim for damages arising from any matter to which the application relates; and

(b) the court is satisfied that, if the claim had been made in an action begun by the applicant at the time of making his application, he would have been awarded damages.

(5) If, on an application for judicial review seeking an order of certiorari, the High Court quashes the decision to which the application relates, the High Court may remit the matter to the court, tribunal or authority concerned, with a direction to reconsider it and reach a decision in accordance with the findings of the High Court.

(6) Where the High Court considers that there has been undue delay in making an application for judicial review, the court may refuse to grant—

(a) leave for the making of the application; or

(b) any relief sought on the application,

if it considers that the granting of the relief sought would be likely to cause substantial hardship to, or substantially prejudice the rights of, any person or would be detrimental to good administration.

(7) Subsection (6) is without prejudice to any enactment or rule of court which has the effect of limiting the time within which an application for judicial review may be made.

64.2 Civil Procedure Rules Part 54(1)

Civil Procedure Rules Part 54

JUDICIAL REVIEW AND STATUTORY REVIEW

I JUDICIAL REVIEW

Scope and interpretation

54.1 (1) This Section of this Part contains rules about judicial review.

(2) In this Section—

(a) a 'claim for judicial review' means a claim to review the lawfulness of—

(i) an enactment; or

(ii) a decision, action or failure to act in relation to the exercise of a public function.

(b) revoked

(c) revoked

(d) revoked

(e) 'the judicial review procedure' means the Part 8 procedure as modified by this Section;

(f) 'interested party' means any person (other than the claimant and defendant) who is directly affected by the claim; and

(g) 'court' means the High Court, unless otherwise stated.

(Rule 8.1(6)(b) provides that a rule or practice direction may, in relation to a specified type of proceedings, disapply or modify any of the rules set out in Part 8 as they apply to those proceedings)

When this Section must be used

54.2 The judicial review procedure must be used in a claim for judicial review where the claimant is seeking—

(a) a mandatory order;

(b) a prohibiting order;

(c) a quashing order; or

(d) an injunction under section 30 of the Supreme Court Act 1981([1]) (restraining a person from acting in any office in which he is not entitled to act).

When this Section may be used

54.3 (1) The judicial review procedure may be used in a claim for judicial review where the claimant is seeking—

(a) a declaration; or

(b) an injunction (GL).

(Section 31(2) of the Supreme Court Act 1981 sets out the circumstances in which the court may grant a declaration or injunction in a claim for judicial review)

(Where the claimant is seeking a declaration or injunction in addition to one of the remedies listed in rule 54.2, the judicial review procedure must be used)

(2) A claim for judicial review may include a claim for damages, restitution or the recovery of a sum due but may not seek such a remedy alone.

(Section 31(4) of the Supreme Court Act sets out the circumstances in which the court may award damages, restitution or the recovery of a sum due on a claim for judicial review)

Permission required

54.4 The court's permission to proceed is required in a claim for judicial review whether started under this Section or transferred to the Administrative Court.

Time limit for filing claim form

54.5 (1) The claim form must be filed—

    (a) promptly; and
    (b) in any event not later than 3 months after the grounds to make the claim first arose.

(2) The time limit in this rule may not be extended by agreement between the parties.
(3) This rule does not apply when any other enactment specifies a shorter time limit for making the claim for judicial review.

Claim form

54.6 (1) In addition to the matters set out in rule 8.2 (contents of the claim form) the claimant must also state—

    (a) the name and address of any person he considers to be an interested party;
    (b) that he is requesting permission to proceed with a claim for judicial review; and
    (c) any remedy (including any interim remedy) he is claiming.

    (Part 25 sets out how to apply for an interim remedy)
(2) The claim form must be accompanied by the documents required by the relevant practice direction.

Service of claim form

54.7 The claim form must be served on—

    (a) the defendant; and
    (b) unless the court otherwise directs, any person the claimant considers to be an interested party,

within 7 days after the date of issue.

Acknowledgment of service

54.8 (1) Any person served with the claim form who wishes to take part in the judicial review must file an acknowledgment of service in the relevant practice form in accordance with the following provisions of this rule.
(2) Any acknowledgment of service must be—

(a) filed not more than 21 days after service of the claim form; and

(b) served on—

(i) the claimant; and

(ii) subject to any direction under rule 54.7(b), any other person named in the claim form,

as soon as practicable and, in any event, not later than 7 days after it is filed.

(3) The time limits under this rule may not be extended by agreement between the parties.

(4) The acknowledgment of service—

(a) must—

(i) where the person filing it intends to contest the claim, set out a summary of his grounds for doing so; and

(ii) state the name and address of any person the person filing it considers to be an interested party; and

(b) may include or be accompanied by an application for directions.

(5) Rule 10.3(2) does not apply.

Failure to file acknowledgment of service

54.9 (1) Where a person served with the claim form has failed to file an acknowledgment of service in accordance with rule 54.8, he—

(a) may not take part in a hearing to decide whether permission should be given unless the court allows him to do so; but

(b) provided he complies with rule 54.14 or any other direction of the court regarding the filing and service of—

(i) detailed grounds for contesting the claim or supporting it on additional grounds; and

(ii) any written evidence,

may take part in the hearing of the judicial review.

(2) Where that person takes part in the hearing of the judicial review, the court may take his failure to file an acknowledgment of service into account when deciding what order to make about costs.

(3) Rule 8.4 does not apply.

Permission given

54.10 (1) Where permission to proceed is given the court may also give directions.

(2) Directions under paragraph (1) may include a stay (GL) of proceedings to which the claim relates.

(Rule 3.7 provides a sanction for the non-payment of the fee payable when permission to proceed has been given)

Service of order giving or refusing permission

54.11 The court will serve—

    (a) the order giving or refusing permission; and

    (b) any directions,

on—

    (i) the claimant;

    (ii) the defendant; and

    (iii) any other person who filed an acknowledgment of service.

Permission decision without a hearing

54.12 (1) This rule applies where the court, without a hearing—

    (a) refuses permission to proceed; or

    (b) gives permission to proceed—

        (i) subject to conditions; or

        (ii) on certain grounds only.

    (2) The court will serve its reasons for making the decision when it serves the order giving or refusing permission in accordance with rule 54.11.

    (3) The claimant may not appeal but may request the decision to be reconsidered at a hearing.

    (4) A request under paragraph (3) must be filed within 7 days after service of the reasons under paragraph (2).

    (5) The claimant, defendant and any other person who has filed an acknowledgment of service will be given at least 2 days' notice of the hearing date.

Defendant etc. may not apply to set aside (GL)

54.13 Neither the defendant nor any other person served with the claim form may apply to set aside (GL) an order giving permission to proceed.

Response

54.14 (1) A defendant and any other person served with the claim form who wishes to contest the claim or support it on additional grounds must file and serve—

    (a) detailed grounds for contesting the claim or supporting it on additional grounds; and

    (b) any written evidence,

within 35 days after service of the order giving permission.

    (2) The following rules do not apply—

    (a) rule 8.5 (3) and 8.5 (4)(defendant to file and serve written evidence at the same time as acknowledgment of service); and

    (b) rule 8.5 (5) and 8.5(6) (claimant to file and serve any reply within 14 days).

Where claimant seeks to rely on additional grounds

54.15 The court's permission is required if a claimant seeks to rely on grounds other than those for which he has been given permission to proceed.

Evidence

54.16 (1) Rule 8.6 (1) does not apply.

(2) No written evidence may be relied on unless—

(a) it has been served in accordance with any—

(i) rule under this Section; or
(ii) direction of the court; or

(b) the court gives permission.

Court's powers to hear any person

54.17 (1) Any person may apply for permission—

(a) to file evidence; or
(b) make representations at the hearing of the judicial review.

(2) An application under paragraph (1) should be made promptly.

Judicial review may be decided without a hearing

54.18 The court may decide the claim for judicial review without a hearing where all the parties agree.

Court's powers in respect of quashing orders

54.19 (1) This rule applies where the court makes a quashing order in respect of the decision to which the claim relates.

(2) The court may—

(a)

(i) remit the matter to the decision-maker; and
(ii) direct it to reconsider the matter and reach a decision in accordance with the judgment of the court; or

(b) in so far as any enactment permits, substitute its own decision for the decision to which the claim relates.

(Section 31 of the Supreme Court Act 1981(²) enables the High Court, subject to certain conditions, to substitute its own decision for the decision in question.)

Transfer

54.20 The court may

(a) order a claim to continue as if it had not been started under this Section; and
(b) where it does so, give directions about the future management of the claim.

(Part 30 (transfer) applies to transfers to and from the Administrative Court)

III APPLICATIONS FOR STATUTORY REVIEW UNDER SECTION 103A OF THE NATIONALITY, IMMIGRATION AND ASYLUM ACT 2002

Scope and interpretation

54.28 (1) This Section of this Part contains rules about applications to the High Court under section 103A of the Nationality, Immigration and Asylum Act 2002([2]) for an order requiring the Asylum and Immigration Tribunal to reconsider its decision on an appeal.

(2) In this Section—

(a) 'the 2002 Act' means the Nationality, Immigration and Asylum Act 2002;

(b) 'the 2004 Act' means the Asylum and Immigration (Treatment of Claimants, etc.) Act 2004([4]);

(c) 'appellant' means the appellant in the proceedings before the Tribunal;

(d) 'applicant' means a person applying to the High Court under section 103A;

(e) 'asylum claim' has the meaning given in section 113(1) of the 2002 Act;

(ea) 'fast track case' means any case in relation to which an order made under section 26(8) of the 2004 Act provides that the time period for making an application under section 103A(1) of the 2002 Act or giving notification under paragraph 30(5) of Schedule 2 to the 2004 Act is less than 5 days;

(f) 'filter provision' means paragraph 30 of Schedule 2 to the 2004 Act;

(g) 'order for reconsideration' means an order under section 103A(1) requiring the Tribunal to reconsider its decision on an appeal;

(h) 'section 103A' means section 103A of the 2002 Act;

(i) 'Tribunal' means the Asylum and Immigration Tribunal.

(3) Any reference in this Section to a period of time specified in—

(a) section 103A(3) for making an application for an order under section 103A(1); or

(b) paragraph 30(5)(b) of Schedule 2 to the 2004 Act for giving notice under that paragraph,

includes a reference to that period as varied by any order under section 26(8) of the 2004 Act.

(4) Rule 2.8 applies to the calculation of the periods of time specified in—

(a) section 103A(3); and

(b) paragraph 30(5)(b) of Schedule 2 to the 2004 Act.

(5) Save as provided otherwise, the provisions of this Section apply to an application under section 103A regardless of whether the filter provision has effect in relation to that application.

Representation of applicants while filter provision has effect

54.28A(1) This rule applies during any period in which the filter provision has effect.

(2) An applicant may, for the purpose of taking any step under rule 54.29 or 54.30, be represented by any person permitted to provide him with immigration advice or immigration services under section 84 of the Immigration and Asylum Act 1999([5]).

(3) A representative acting for an applicant under paragraph (2) shall be regarded as the applicant's legal representative for the purpose of rule 22.1 (Documents to be verified by a statement of truth) regardless of whether he would otherwise be so regarded.

Service of documents on appellants within the jurisdiction

54.28B(1) In proceedings under this Section, rules 6.4(2) and 6.5(5) do not apply to the service of documents on an appellant who is within the jurisdiction.

(2) Where a representative is acting for an appellant who is within the jurisdiction, a document must be served on the appellant by—

(a) serving it on his representative; or

(b) serving it on the appellant personally or sending it to his address by first class post (or an alternative service which provides for delivery on the next working day),

but if the document is served on the appellant under sub-paragraph (b), a copy must also at the same time be sent to his representative.

Application for review

54.29 (1) Subject to paragraph (5), an application for an order for reconsideration must be made by filing an application notice—

(a) during a period in which the filter provision has effect, with the Tribunal at the address specified in the relevant practice direction; and

(b) at any other time, at the Administrative Court Office.

(2) During any period in which the filter provision does not have effect, the applicant must file with the application notice—

(a) the notice of the immigration, asylum or nationality decision to which the appeal related;

(b) any other document which was served on the appellant giving reasons for that decision;

(c) the grounds of appeal to the Tribunal;

(d) the Tribunal's determination on the appeal; and

(e) any other documents material to the application which were before the Tribunal.

(2A) During any period in which the filter provision has effect, the applicant must file with the application notice a list of the documents referred to in paragraph (2)(a) to (e).

(3) The applicant must also file with the application notice written submissions setting out—

(a) the grounds upon which it is contended that the Tribunal made an error of law which may have affected its decision; and

(b) reasons in support of those grounds.

(4) Where the applicant—

(a) was the respondent to the appeal; and

(b) was required to serve the Tribunal's determination on the appellant,

the application notice must contain a statement of the date on which, and the means by which, the determination was served.

(5) Where the applicant is in detention under the Immigration Acts, the application may be made either—

(a) in accordance with paragraphs (1) to (3); or

(b) by serving the documents specified in paragraphs (1) to (3) on the person having custody of him.

(6) Where an application is made in accordance with paragraph (5)(b), the person on whom the application notice is served must—

(a) endorse on the notice the date that it is served on him;
(b) give the applicant an acknowledgment in writing of receipt of the notice; and
(c) forward the notice and documents within 2 days

(i) during a period in which the filter provision has effect, to the Tribunal; and
(ii) at any other time, to the Administrative Court Office.

Application to extend time limit

54.30 An application to extend the time limit for making an application under section 103A(1) must—

(a) be made in the application notice;
(b) set out the grounds on which it is contended that the application notice could not reasonably practicably have been filed within the time limit; and
(c) be supported by written evidence verified by a statement of truth.

Procedure while filter provision has effect

54.31 (1) This rule applies during any period in which the filter provision has effect.
(2) Where the applicant receives notice from the Tribunal that it—

(a) does not propose to make an order for reconsideration; or
(b) does not propose to grant permission for the application to be made outside the relevant time limit,

and the applicant wishes the court to consider the application, the applicant must file a notice in writing at the Administrative Court Office in accordance with paragraph 30(5)(b) of Schedule 2 to the 2004 Act.

(2A) The applicant must file with the notice—

(a) a copy of the Tribunal's notification that it does not propose to make an order for reconsideration or does not propose to grant permission for the application to be made outside the relevant time limit (referred to in CPR rule 54.31(2));
(b) any other document which was served on the applicant by the Tribunal giving reasons for its decision in paragraph (a);
(c) written evidence in support of any application by the applicant seeking permission to make the application outside the relevant time limit, if applicable;
(d) a copy of the application for reconsideration under section 103A of the 2002 Act (Form AIT/103A), as submitted to the Tribunal (referred to in Rule 54.29(1)(a).

(3) Where the applicant—

(a) was the respondent to the appeal; and
(b) was required to serve the notice from the Tribunal mentioned in paragraph (2) on the appellant,

the notice filed in accordance with paragraph 30(5)(b) of Schedule 2 to the 2004 Act must contain a statement of the date on which, and the means by which, the notice from the Tribunal was served.

(4) A notice which is filed outside the period specified in paragraph 30(5)(b) must—

    (a) set out the grounds on which it is contended that the notice could not reasonably practicably have been filed within that period; and

    (b) be supported by written evidence verified by a statement of truth.

(5) If the applicant wishes to respond to the reasons given by the Tribunal for its decision that it—

    (a) does not propose to make an order for reconsideration; or

    (b) does not propose to grant permission for the application to be made outside the relevant time limit,

the notice filed in accordance with paragraph 30(5)(b) of Schedule 2 to the 2004 Act must be accompanied by written submissions setting out the grounds upon which the applicant disputes any of the reasons given by the Tribunal and giving reasons in support of those grounds.

Procedure in fast track cases while filter provision does not have effect

54.32 (1) This rule applies only during a period in which the filter provision does not have effect.

    (2) Where a party applies for an order for reconsideration in a fast track case—

        (a) the court will serve copies of the application notice and written submissions on the other party to the appeal; and

        (b) the other party to the appeal may file submissions in response to the application not later than 2 days after being served with the application.

Determination of the application by the Administrative Court

54.33 (1) This rule, and rules 54.34 and 54.35, apply to applications under section 103A which are determined by the Administrative Court.

    (2) The application will be considered by a single judge without a hearing.

    (3) Unless it orders otherwise, the court will not receive evidence which was not submitted to the Tribunal.

    (4) Subject to paragraph (5), where the court determines an application for an order for reconsideration, it may—

        (a) dismiss the application;

        (b) make an order requiring the Tribunal to reconsider its decision on the appeal under section 103A(1) of the 2002 Act; or

        (c) refer the appeal to the Court of Appeal under section 103C of the 2002 Act.

    (5) The court will only make an order requiring the Tribunal to reconsider its decision on an appeal if it thinks that—

        (a) the Tribunal may have made an error of law; and

        (b) there is a real possibility that the Tribunal would make a different decision on reconsidering the appeal (which may include making a different direction under section 87 of the 2002 Act).

    (6) Where the Court of Appeal has restored the application to the court under section 103C(2)(g) of the 2002 Act, the court may not refer the appeal to the Court of Appeal.

(7) The court's decision shall be final and there shall be no appeal from that decision or renewal of the application.

Service of order

54.34 (1) The court will send copies of its order to—

(a) the applicant and the other party to the appeal, except where paragraph (2) applies; and

(b) the Tribunal.

(2) Where the appellant is within the jurisdiction and the application relates, in whole or in part, to an asylum claim, the court will send a copy of its order to the Secretary of State.

(2A) Paragraph (2) does not apply in a fast track case.

(3) Where the court sends an order to the Secretary of State under paragraph (2), the Secretary of State must—

(a) serve the order on the appellant; and

(b) immediately after serving the order, notify—

(i) the court; and

(iii) where the order requires the Tribunal to reconsider its decision on the appeal, the Tribunal,

on what date and by what method the order was served.

(4) The Secretary of State must provide the notification required by paragraph (3)(b) no later than 28 days after the date on which the court sends him a copy of its order.

(5) If, 28 days after the date on which the court sends a copy of its order to the Secretary of State in accordance with paragraph (2), the Secretary of State has not provided the notification required by paragraph (3)(b)(i), the court may serve the order on the appellant.

(5A) Where the court serves an order for reconsideration under paragraph (5), it will notify the Tribunal of the date on which the order was served.

(6) If the court makes an order under section 103D(1) of the 2002 Act, it will send copies of that order to—

(a) the appellant's legal representative; and

(b) the Legal Services Commission.

(7) Where paragraph (2) applies, the court will not serve copies of an order under section 103D(1) of the 2002 Act until either—

(a) the Secretary of State has provided the notification required by paragraph (3)(b); or

(b) 28 days after the date on which the court sent a copy of its order to the Secretary of State,

whichever is the earlier.

Costs

54.35 The court shall make no order as to the costs of an application under this Section except, where appropriate, an order under section 103D(1) of the 2002 Act.

Continuing an application in circumstances in which it would otherwise be treated as abandoned

54.36 (1) This rule applies to an application under section 103A of the 2002 Act which—

    (a) would otherwise be treated as abandoned under section 104(4A) of the 2002 Act; but

    (b) meets the conditions set out in section 104(4B) or section 104(4C) of the 2002 Act.

(2) Where section 104(4A) of the 2002 Act applies and the applicant wishes to pursue the application, the applicant must file a notice at the Administrative Court Office—

    (a) where section 104(4B) of the 2002 Act applies, within 28 days of the date on which the applicant received notice of the grant of leave to enter or remain in the United Kingdom for a period exceeding 12 months; or

    (b) where section 104(4C) of the 2002 Act applies, within 28 days of the date on which the applicant received notice of the grant of leave to enter or remain in the United Kingdom.

(3) Where the applicant does not comply with the time limits specified in paragraph (2), the application will be treated as abandoned in accordance with section 104(4) of the 2002 Act.

(4) The applicant must serve the notice filed under paragraph (2) on the other party to the appeal.

(5) Where section 104(4B) of the 2002 Act applies, the notice filed under paragraph (2) must state—

    (a) the applicant's full name and date of birth;

    (b) the Administrative Court reference number;

    (c) the Home Office reference number, if applicable;

    (d) the date on which the applicant was granted leave to enter or remain in the United Kingdom for a period exceeding 12 months; and

    (e) that the applicant wishes to pursue the application insofar as it is brought on grounds relating to the Refugee Convention specified in section 84(1)(g) of the 2002 Act.

(6) Where section 104(4C) of the 2002 Act applies, the notice filed under paragraph (2) must state—

    (a) the applicant's full name and date of birth;

    (b) the Administrative Court reference number;

    (c) the Home Office reference number, if applicable;

    (d) the date on which the applicant was granted leave to enter or remain in the United Kingdom; and

    (e) that the applicant wishes to pursue the application insofar as it is brought on grounds relating to section 19B of the Race Relations Act 1976 specified in section 84(1)(b) of the 2002 Act.

(7) Where an applicant has filed a notice under paragraph (2) the court will notify the applicant of the date on which it received the notice.

(8) The court will send a copy of the notice issued under paragraph (7) to the other party to the appeal.

64.3 Civil Procedure Rules Part 54 Practice Direction

PRACTICE DIRECTION—JUDICIAL REVIEW

THIS PRACTICE DIRECTION SUPPLEMENTS PART 54

Contents of this Practice Direction

SECTION I—GENERAL PROVISIONS RELATING TO JUDICIAL REVIEW

1.1   In addition to Part 54 and this practice direction attention is drawn to:

- section 31 of the Supreme Court Act 1981; and
- the Human Rights Act 1998

THE COURT

2.1   Part 54 claims for judicial review are dealt with in the Administrative Court.

2.2   Where the claim is proceeding in the Administrative Court in London, documents must be filed at the Administrative Court Office, the Royal Courts of Justice, Strand, London, WC2A 2LL.

2.3   Where the claim is proceeding in the Administrative Court in Wales (see paragraph 3.1), documents must be filed at the Civil Justice Centre, 2 Park Street, Cardiff, CF10 1ET.

Urgent applications

2.4   Where urgency makes it necessary for the claim for judicial review to be made outside London or Cardiff, the Administrative Court Office in London should be consulted (if necessary, by telephone) prior to filing the claim form.

JUDICIAL REVIEW CLAIMS IN WALES

3.1   A claim for judicial review may be brought in the Administrative Court in Wales where the claim or any remedy sought involves:

(1) a devolution issue arising out of the Government of Wales Act 1998; or

(2) an issue concerning the National Assembly for Wales, the Welsh executive, or any Welsh public body (including a Welsh local authority) (whether or not it involves a devolution issue).

3.2   Such claims may also be brought in the Administrative Court at the Royal Courts of Justice

Rule 54.5—Time limit for filing claim form

4.1   Where the claim is for a quashing order in respect of a judgment, order or conviction, the date when the grounds to make the claim first arose, for the purposes of rule 54.5(1)(b), is the date of that judgment, order or conviction.

RULE 54.6—CLAIM FORM

Interested parties

5.1   Where the claim for judicial review relates to proceedings in a court or tribunal, any other parties to those proceedings must be named in the claim form as interested parties under rule 54.6(1)(a) (and therefore served with the claim form under rule 54.7(b)).

5.2   For example, in a claim by a defendant in a criminal case in the Magistrates or Crown Court for judicial review of a decision in that case, the prosecution must always be named as an interested party.

Human rights

5.3   Where the claimant is seeking to raise any issue under the Human Rights Act 1998, or seeks a remedy available under that Act, the claim form must include the information required by paragraph 15 of the practice direction supplementing Part 16.

Devolution issues

5.4   Where the claimant intends to raise a devolution issue, the claim form must:

   (1) specify that the applicant wishes to raise a devolution issue and identify the relevant provisions of the Government of Wales Act 1998, the Northern Ireland Act 1998 or the Scotland Act 1998; and

   (2) contain a summary of the facts, circumstances and points of law on the basis of which it is alleged that a devolution issue arises.

5.5   In this practice direction 'devolution issue' has the same meaning as in paragraph 1, schedule 8 to the Government of Wales Act 1998; paragraph 1, schedule 10 to the Northern Ireland Act 1998; and paragraph 1, schedule 6 of the Scotland Act 1998.

Claim form

5.6   The claim form must include or be accompanied by—

   (1) a detailed statement of the claimant's grounds for bringing the claim for judicial review;

   (2) a statement of the facts relied on;

   (3) any application to extend the time limit for filing the claim form;

   (4) any application for directions.

5.7   In addition, the claim form must be accompanied by

   (1) any written evidence in support of the claim or application to extend time;

   (2) a copy of any order that the claimant seeks to have quashed;

   (3) where the claim for judicial review relates to a decision of a court or tribunal, an approved copy of the reasons for reaching that decision;

   (4) copies of any documents on which the claimant proposes to rely;

   (5) copies of any relevant statutory material; and

   (6) a list of essential documents for advance reading by the court (with page references to the passages relied on).

5.8   Where it is not possible to file all the above documents, the claimant must indicate which documents have not been filed and the reasons why they are not currently available.

Bundle of documents

5.9   The claimant must file two copies of a paginated and indexed bundle containing all the documents referred to in paragraphs 5.6 and 5.7.

5.10   Attention is drawn to rules 8.5(1) and 8.5(7).

RULE 54.7—SERVICE OF CLAIM FORM

6.1   Except as required by rules 54.11 or 54.12(2), the Administrative Court will not serve documents and service must be effected by the parties.

6.2   Where the defendant or interested party to the claim for judicial review is the Asylum and Immigration Tribunal, the address for service of the claim form is the Asylum and Immigration Tribunal, Official Correspondence Unit, PO Box 6987, Leicester, LE1 6ZX or fax number 0116 249 4131.

       (Part 6 contains provisions about the service of claim forms.)

RULE 54.8—ACKNOWLEDGMENT OF SERVICE

7.1   Attention is drawn to rule 8.3(2) and the relevant practice direction and to rule 10.5.

RULE 54.10—PERMISSION GIVEN

Directions

8.1   Case management directions under rule 54.10(1) may include directions about serving the claim form and any evidence on other persons.

8.2   Where a claim is made under the Human Rights Act 1998, a direction may be made for giving notice to the Crown or joining the Crown as a party. Attention is drawn to rule 19.4A and paragraph 6 of the Practice Direction supplementing Section I of Part 19.

8.3   A direction may be made for the hearing of the claim for judicial review to be held outside London or Cardiff. Before making any such direction the judge will consult the judge in charge of the Administrative Court as to its feasibility.

Permission without a hearing

8.4   The court will generally, in the first instance, consider the question of permission without a hearing.

Permission hearing

8.5   Neither the defendant nor any other interested party need attend a hearing on the question of permission unless the court directs otherwise.

8.6   Where the defendant or any party does attend a hearing, the court will not generally make an order for costs against the claimant.

RULE 54.11—SERVICE OF ORDER GIVING OR REFUSING PERMISSION

9.1   An order refusing permission or giving it subject to conditions or on certain grounds only must set out or be accompanied by the court's reasons for coming to that decision.

RULE 54.14—RESPONSE

10.1 Where the party filing the detailed grounds intends to rely on documents not already filed, he must file a paginated bundle of those documents when he files the detailed grounds.

RULE 54.15—WHERE CLAIMANT SEEKS TO RELY ON ADDITIONAL GROUNDS

11.1 Where the claimant intends to apply to rely on additional grounds at the hearing of the claim for judicial review, he must give notice to the court and to any other person served with the claim form no later than 7 clear days before the hearing (or the warned date where appropriate).

RULE 54.16—EVIDENCE

12.1 Disclosure is not required unless the court orders otherwise.

RULE 54.17—COURT'S POWERS TO HEAR ANY PERSON

13.1 Where all the parties consent, the court may deal with an application under rule 54.17 without a hearing.

13.2 Where the court gives permission for a person to file evidence or make representations at the hearing of the claim for judicial review, it may do so on conditions and may give case management directions.

13.3 An application for permission should be made by letter to the Administrative Court office, identifying the claim, explaining who the applicant is and indicating why and in what form the applicant wants to participate in the hearing.

13.4 If the applicant is seeking a prospective order as to costs, the letter should say what kind of order and on what grounds.

13.5 Applications to intervene must be made at the earliest reasonable opportunity, since it will usually be essential not to delay the hearing.

RULE 54.20—TRANSFER

14.1 Attention is drawn to rule 30.5.

14.2 In deciding whether a claim is suitable for transfer to the Administrative Court, the court will consider whether it raises issues of public law to which Part 54 should apply.

Skeleton arguments

15.1 The claimant must file and serve a skeleton argument not less than 21 working days before the date of the hearing of the judicial review (or the warned date).

15.2 The defendant and any other party wishing to make representations at the hearing of the judicial review must file and serve a skeleton argument not less than 14 working days before the date of the hearing of the judicial review (or the warned date).

15.3 Skeleton arguments must contain:

(1) a time estimate for the complete hearing, including delivery of judgment;
(2) a list of issues;
(3) a list of the legal points to be taken (together with any relevant authorities with page references to the passages relied on);
(4) a chronology of events (with page references to the bundle of documents (see paragraph 16.1);

(5) a list of essential documents for the advance reading of the court (with page references to the passages relied on) (if different from that filed with the claim form) and a time estimate for that reading; and

(6) a list of persons referred to.

Bundle of documents to be filed

16.1   The claimant must file a paginated and indexed bundle of all relevant documents required for the hearing of the judicial review when he files his skeleton argument.

16.2   The bundle must also include those documents required by the defendant and any other party who is to make representations at the hearing.

Agreed final order

17.1   If the parties agree about the final order to be made in a claim for judicial review, the claimant must file at the court a document (with 2 copies) signed by all the parties setting out the terms of the proposed agreed order together with a short statement of the matters relied on as justifying the proposed agreed order and copies of any authorities or statutory provisions relied on.

17.2   The court will consider the documents referred to in paragraph 17.1 and will make the order if satisfied that the order should be made.

17.3   If the court is not satisfied that the order should be made, a hearing date will be set.

17.4   Where the agreement relates to an order for costs only, the parties need only file a document signed by all the parties setting out the terms of the proposed order.

SECTION II—APPLICATIONS FOR PERMISSION TO APPLY FOR JUDICIAL REVIEW IN IMMIGRATION AND ASYLUM CASES— CHALLENGING REMOVAL

18.1   (1)   This Section applies where—

(a)   a person has been served with a copy of directions for his removal from the United Kingdom by the Immigration and Nationality Directorate of the Home Office and notified that this Section applies; and

(b)   that person makes an application for permission to apply for judicial review before his removal takes effect.

(2)   This Section does not prevent a person from applying for judicial review after he has been removed.

(3)   The requirements contained in this Section of this Practice Direction are additional to those contained elsewhere in the Practice Direction.

18.2   (1)   A person who makes an application for permission to apply for judicial review must file a claim form and a copy at court, and the claim form must—

(a)   indicate on its face that this Section of the Practice Direction applies; and

(b)   be accompanied by—

(i)   a copy of the removal directions and the decision to which the application relates; and

(ii)   any document served with the removal directions including any document which contains the Immigration and Nationality Directorate's factual summary of the case; and

    (c) contain or be accompanied by the detailed statement of the claimant's grounds for bringing the claim for judicial review; or

    (d) if the claimant is unable to comply with paragraph (b) or (c), contain or be accompanied by a statement of the reasons why.

(2) The claimant must, immediately upon issue of the claim, send copies of the issued claim form and accompanying documents to the address specified by the Immigration and Nationality Directorate.

(Rule 54.7 also requires the defendant to be served with the claim form within 7 days of the date of issue. Rule 6.5(8) provides that service on a Government Department must be effected on the solicitor acting for that Department, which in the case of the Immigration and Nationality Directorate is the Treasury Solicitor. The address for the Treasury Solicitor may be found in the Annex to Part 66 of these Rules.)

18.3   Where the claimant has not complied with paragraph 18.2(1)(b) or (c) and has provided reasons why he is unable to comply, and the court has issued the claim form, the Administrative Court—

    (a) will refer the matter to a Judge for consideration as soon as practicable; and

    (b) will notify the parties that it has done so.

18.4   If, upon a refusal to grant permission to apply for judicial review, the Court indicates that the application is clearly without merit, that indication will be included in the order refusing permission.

64.4 Administrative Court Office Notes for Guidance

Administrative Court Guidance

Notes for guidance on applying for judicial review

January 2005

1 Introduction
2 What is Judicial Review?
3 What is the Pre-action protocol?
4 Where should I commence proceedings?
5 When should I lodge my application?
6 Fees
7 How do I apply for Judicial Review?
8 What do I do if my application is urgent?
9 Acknowledgements of Service
10 What happens if my application for permission is refused?
11 What happens if my application for permission is granted?
12 What happens when my case is ready for hearing?
13 What if I need to make an application for further orders after the grant of permission?
14 Can my application be determined without the need for a hearing?
15 What if the proceedings settle by consent prior to the hearing of my application?
16 What if I want to discontinue the proceedings at any stage?
17 Will I be responsible for costs?
18 What can I do if I am unhappy with the Judge's decision?
19 Where can I get advice about procedural matters?

Section 1

General Introduction

1   These notes are not intended to be exhaustive but are designed to offer an outline of the procedure to be followed when seeking to make an application for judicial review in the Administrative Court. For further details of the procedure to be followed you and your representatives/legal advisers should consult Part 54 of the Civil Procedure Rules (CPR) and the appropriate Practice Direction 54.

Section 2

What is judicial review?

2.1   Judicial review is the procedure by which you can seek to challenge the decision, action or failure to act of a public body such as a government department or a local authority or other body exercising a public law function. If you are challenging the decision of a court, the jurisdiction of judicial review extends only to decisions of inferior courts. It does not extend to decisions of the High Court or Court of Appeal. Judicial review must be used where you are seeking:

- a mandatory order (i.e. an order requiring the public body to do something and formerly known as an order of mandamus);

- a prohibiting order (i.e. an order preventing the public body from doing something and for merly known as an order of prohibition); or
- a quashing order (i.e. an order quashing the public body's decision and formerly known as an order of certiorari)
- a declaration

HRA Damages

2.2 Claims will generally be heard by a single Judge sitting in open Court at the Royal Courts of Justice in London. They may be heard by a Divisional Court (a court of two judges) where the Court so directs.

Section 3

What is the pre-action protocol?

3.1 Any claim for judicial review must indicate whether or not the protocol has been complied with. If the protocol has not been complied with, the reasons for failing to do so should be set out in the claim form.

3.2 The protocol sets out a code of good practice and contains the steps which parties should generally follow before making a claim for judicial review. The objective of the pre-action protocol is to avoid unnecessary litigation.

3.3 Before making your claim for judicial review, you should send a letter to the defendant. The purpose of this letter is to identify the issues in dispute and establish whether litigation can be avoided. The letter should contain the date and details of the decision, act or omission being challenged and a clear summary of the facts on which the claim is based. It should also contain the details of any relevant information that the claimant is seeking and an explanation of why this is considered relevant. A claim should not normally be made until the proposed reply date given in the letter before claim has passed, unless the circumstances of the case require more immediate action to be taken.

3.4 Defendants should normally respond to that letter within 14 days and sanctions may be imposed unless there are good reasons for not responding within that period.

NB—The protocol does not affect the time limit specified by CPR Part 54.5(1) namely that an application for permission to apply for judicial review must be made promptly and in any event not later than 3 months after the grounds upon which the claim is based first arose.

NB—You should seek advice as to whether the protocol is appropriate in the circumstances of your case. Use of the protocol will not be appropriate where the defendant does not have the legal power to change the decision being challenged. It also may not be appropriate in circumstances where the application is urgent.

NB—A letter before claim will not automatically stop the implementation of a disputed decision.

NB—Even in emergency cases, it is good practice to fax the draft claim form that you are intending to issue to the defendant. You will also normally be required to notify a defendant when you are seeking an interim order; i.e. an order giving some form of relief pending the final determination of the claim.

Section 4

Where should I commence proceedings?

4.1 Claims for judicial review under CPR Part 54 are dealt with in the Administrative Court. Where the claim is proceeding in the Administrative Court in London, documents must be filed at the Administrative Court Office, the Royal Courts of Justice, Strand, London, WC2A 2LL. Where the claim is proceeding in the Administrative Court in Wales (because it concerns (a) a devolution issue arising out of the Government of Wales Act 1998; or (b) an issue concerning the National Assembly for Wales, the Welsh executive, or any Welsh public body (including a Welsh local authority)) the documents may be filed at the Cardiff Civil Justice Centre, 2 Park Street, Cardiff CF10 1ET or at the Administrative Court Office, the Royal Courts of Justice, Strand, London, WC2A 2LL.

Can I get Legal Services Commission funding (Legal Aid) for my application?

4.2 Neither the Court nor the Administrative Court Office has power to grant funding (previously legal aid). The responsibility for the provision of public funding is held by the Legal Services Commission.

4.3 Further information on the type(s) of help available and the criteria for receiving that help may be found in the Legal Services Commission Manual Volume 3: "The Funding Code". This may be found on the Legal Services Commission website at http://www.legalservices.gov.uk/.

4.4 A list of contracted firms and Advice Agencies may be found on the Community Legal Services website at http://www.justask.org.uk/. The Legal Services Commission can also provide you with a list of solicitors in your area if you telephone them on 0845 608 1122.

Section 5

When should I lodge my application for permission to apply for judicial review?

5.1 The claim form must be filed promptly and in any event not later than three months after the grounds upon which the claim is based first arose (CPR Part 54.5).

5.2 The court has the power to extend the period for the lodging of an application for judicial review but will only do so where it is satisfied there are very good reasons for doing so.

NB—The time for the lodging of the application may not be extended by agreement between the parties.

NB—If you are seeking an extension of time for the lodging of your application, you must make the application in the claim form, setting out the grounds in support of that application to extend time (CPR Part 54.5).

Section 6

Is there a fee to pay and if so, when should I pay it?

6.1 A fee of £50.00 is payable when you lodge your application for permission to apply for Judicial Review. A further £180.00 is payable if you wish to pursue the claim after permission is granted (Civil Proceedings Fees Order 2004).

NB—If you are in receipt of certain types of benefits you may be entitled to exemption/remission of any fee due.

NB—Cheques should be made payable to HMCS. If you lodge your application at the court office in person, personal cheques must be supported by a cheque guarantee card presented at the time the application is lodged.

NB—An application for exemption/remission of fees must be made in writing to the Supreme Court Fees Office, Room E01, Royal Courts of Justice in advance of lodging the application for permission.

Section 7

How do I apply for judicial review?

7.1 Applications for permission to apply for judicial review must be made by claim form (Form N461).

7.2 The claim form must include or be accompanied by —

- a detailed statement of the claimant's grounds for bringing the claim for judicial review;
- a statement of the facts relied on;
- any application to extend the time limit for filing the claim form; and
- any application for directions.

7.3 Where you are seeking to raise any issue under the Human Rights Act 1998, or a remedy available under that Act, the claim form must include the information required by paragraph 16 of the Practice Direction supplementing Part 16 of the Civil Procedure Rules.

7.4 Where you intend to raise a devolution issue, the claim form must specify that you (a) wish to raise a devolution issue (b) identify the relevant provisions of the Government of Wales Act 1998, and (c) contain a summary of the facts, circumstances and points of law on the basis of which it is alleged that a devolution issue arises.

7.5 The claim form must also be accompanied by

- any written evidence in support of the claim or application to extend time;
- a copy of any order that you are seeking to have quashed;
- where the claim for judicial review relates to a decision of a court or tribunal, an approved copy of the reasons for reaching that decision;
- copies of any documents upon which you propose to rely;
- copies of any relevant statutory material;
- a list of essential documents for advance reading by the court (with page references to the passages relied upon). Where only part of a page needs to be read, that part should be indicated, by side-lining or in some other way, but not by highlighting.

NB—Where it is not possible for you to file all the above documents, you must indicate which documents have not been filed and the reasons why they are not currently available. The defendant and/or the interested party may seek an extension of time for the lodging of its acknowledgement of service pending receipt of the missing documents.

What documents do I need to lodge?

7.6 You must file the original claim form, together with a copy for the court's use, and a paginated and indexed bundle containing the documents referred to in paragraph 19 above (CPR Part 54.6 and the Practice Direction). Please ensure you paginate in consecutive page number order throughout your bundle. Also ensure that each page has a page number on it and provide an index, which lists the description of documents contained in your bundle together with their page reference numbers.

7.7 Please note that if your case is of a criminal nature then the Court will require you to lodge a further copy bundle.

7.8 You must also lodge sufficient additional copies of the claim form for the court to seal them (i.e. stamp them with the court seal) so that you can serve them on the defendant and any interested parties. The sealed copies will be returned to you so that you can serve them on the defendant and any interested parties.

7.9 If you are represented by solicitors they must also provide a paginated, indexed bundle of the relevant legislative provisions and statutory instruments required for the proper consideration of the application. If you are acting in person you should comply with this requirement if possible.

NB—Applications that do not comply with the requirements of CPR Part 54 and the Practice Direction will not be accepted, save in exceptional circumstances. In this context a matter will be regarded as exceptional where a decision is sought from the Court within 14 days of the lodging of the application. In such circumstances an undertaking will be required to provide compliance with the requirements of the CPR within a specified period.

NB—If the only reason given in support of urgency is the imminent expiry of the three month time limit for lodging an application, the papers will nonetheless be returned for compliance with Part 54 and the Practice Direction. In those circumstances you must seek an extension of time and provide reasons for the delay in lodging the papers in proper form.

Who should I serve my application on?

7.10 The sealed copy claim form (and accompanying documents) must be served on the defendant and any person that you consider to be an interested party (unless the court directs otherwise) within 7 days of the date of issue (i.e. the date shown on the court seal). The Administrative Court Office will not serve your claim on the defendant or any interested party.

NB—An interested party is a person who is likely to be directly affected by your judicial review application.

NB—Please note that under the provisions of the Crown Proceedings Act 1947 service must be upon the Department responsible for the Defendant.

NB—Where the claim for judicial review relates to proceedings in a court or tribunal, any other parties to those proceedings must be named in the claim form as interested parties and served with the claim form (CPR 54 PD.5). For example, in a claim by a defendant in a criminal case in the Magistrates' or Crown Court for judicial review of a decision in that case, the prosecution must always be named as an interested party.

7.11 You must lodge a Certificate of Service in Form N215 in the Administrative Court Office within 7 days of serving the defendant and other interested parties.

7.12 Rules of Court set out the following timetable under which the Court will presume service to have taken place. (See CPR 6.7).

Method	Deemed day of service
DX Delivering the document to or leaving it at a permitted address	The second day after it was left at the DX exchange
First class post	The day after it was delivered to or left at the permitted address
Fax (where service of fax is accepted by the recipient).	The second day after it was posted If it is transmitted on a business day before 4p.m, on that day or otherwise on the business day after the day on which it was transmitted
NB—The time for the lodging of the defendant and any interested party's acknowledgement of service commences from the date that the claim is deemed served upon them.	

Section 8

What do I do if my application is urgent?

8.1 If you want to make an application for your application for permission to be heard/considered by a Judge as a matter of urgency and/or seek an interim injunction, you must complete a Request for Urgent Consideration, Form N463, which can be obtained from the Court Office. The form sets out the reasons for urgency and the timescale sought for the consideration of the permission application, e.g. within 72 hours or sooner if necessary, and the date by which the substantive hearing should take place.

8.2 Where you are seeking an interim injunction, you must, in addition, provide a draft order; and the grounds for the injunction. You must serve the claim form, the draft order and the application for urgency on the defendant and interested parties (by FAX and by post), advising them of the application and informing them that they may make representations directly to the court in respect of your application.

8.3 A judge will consider the application within the time requested and may make such order as he considers appropriate.

NB—The judge may refuse your application for permission at this stage if he considers it appropriate, in the circumstances, to do so.

8.4 If the Judge directs that an oral hearing must take place within a specified time the Administrative Court will liaise with you and the representatives of the other parties to fix a permission hearing within the time period directed.

8.5 Where a manifestly inappropriate urgency application is made, consideration may, in appropriate cases, be given to making a wasted costs order.

Section 9

What is an acknowledgement of service?

9.1 Any person who has been served with the claim form and who wishes to take part in the judicial review should file an acknowledgment of service (Form N462) in the Administrative Court Office, within 21 days of the proceedings being served upon him.

NB—Whilst there is no requirement upon you to serve the defendant and any interested party with a Form N462 for completion by them, it is good practice to do so.

9.2 The acknowledgement of service must set out the summary of grounds for contesting the claim and the name and address of any person considered to be an interested party (who has not previously been identified and served as an interested party).

9.3 The acknowledgement of service must be served upon you and the interested parties no later than 7 days after it is filed with the court.

NB—Failure to file an acknowledgement of service renders it necessary for the party concerned to obtain the permission of the court to take part in any oral hearing of the application for permission.

What happens after the defendant and/or the interested party has lodged and acknowledgement of service?

9.4 Applications for permission to proceed with the claim for judicial review are considered by a single judge on the papers. The purpose of this procedure is to ensure that applications may be dealt with speedily and without unnecessary expense.

9.5 The papers will be forwarded to the judge by the Administrative Court Office upon receipt of the Acknowledgement of Service or at the expiry of the time limit for lodging such acknowledgement—whichever is earlier.

9.6 The judge's decision and the reasons for it (Form JRJ) will be served upon you, the defendant and any other person served with the claim form.

9.7 If the judge grants permission and you wish to pursue the claim, you must lodge a further fee of £180.00 (or a further certified fee remission/exemption form) with the Administrative Court Office within 7 days of service of the judge's decision upon you.

NB—If you do not lodge the additional fee, your file will be closed.

Section 10

What happens if my application for permission is refused or if permission is granted subject to conditions or in part only?

10.1 If permission is refused, or is granted subject to conditions or on certain grounds only, you may request a reconsideration of that decision at an oral hearing.

10.2 Request for an oral hearing must be made on the Notice of Renewal, Form 86b, (a copy of which will be sent to you at the same time as the judge's decision) and must be filed within 7 days after service of the notification of the judge's decision upon you (CPR Part 54.11 & 54.12).

651

10.3 Where the judge directs an oral hearing or you renew your application after refusal following consideration on paper, you may appear in person or be represented by an advocate (if you are legally represented). If you are not legally represented you may seek the court's permission to have someone speak on your behalf at the hearing.

NB—Any application for permission to have someone speak on your behalf should be made to the judge hearing the application who will make such decision as he considers appropriate in all of the circumstances.

10.4 Notice of the hearing is given to you, the defendant and any interested party by the Administrative Court List Office. An oral hearing is allocated a total of 30 minutes of court time. If it is considered that 30 minutes of court time is insufficient, you may provide a written estimate of the time required for the hearing and request a special fixture.

10.5 Neither the defendant nor any other interested party need attend a hearing on the question of permission unless the court directs otherwise.

Section 11

What happens after permission is granted?

11.1 On granting permission the court may make case management directions under CPR 54.10(1) for the progression of the case. Case management directions may include directions about serving the claim form and any evidence on other persons and directions as to expedition.

11.2 Where a claim is made under the Human Rights Act 1998, a direction may be made for the giving of notice to the Crown or joining the Crown as a party. In that regard you attention is drawn to the requirements of rule 19.4A and paragraph 6 of the Practice Direction supplementing Section I of Part 19.

11.3 A direction may be made for the hearing of the claim for judicial review to be held outside London or Cardiff.

When should the defendant/interested party lodge its evidence following the grant of permission?

11.4 A party upon whom a claim form has been served and who wishes to contest the claim (or support it on additional grounds) must, within 35 days of service of the order granting permission, file and serve on the Court and all of the other parties

- Detailed grounds for contesting the claim or supporting it on additional grounds and
- Any written evidence relied upon.

11.5 Any party who has done so may be represented at the hearing.

11.6 Where the party filing the detailed grounds intends to rely on documents not already filed, a paginated bundle of those documents must be filed at the Court when the detailed grounds are filed.

11.7 The Court has power to extend or abridge the time for lodging evidence.

Section 12

What happens when my case is ready for hearing?

12.1 When the time for lodging of evidence by the parties has expired, the case enters a warned list and all parties are informed of this by letter.

12.2 Where a direction has been given for expedition, the case will take priority over other cases waiting to be fixed and enters an expedited warned list.

What is the procedure for the listing of a case for hearing?

NB—The procedure is the same whether you act in p erson or are legally represented.

12.3 Where advocate's details have been placed on the court record, the parties will be contacted by the Administrative Court List Office in order to seek to agree a date for the hearing. You and advocate's clerks will be offered a range of dates and will have 48 hours to take up one of the dates offered. If the parties fail to contact the List Office within 48 hours, the List Office will fix the hearing on one of the dates offered without further notice and the parties will be notified of that fixture by letter. Where a hearing is listed in this way the hearing will only be vacated by the Administrative Court Office if both parties consent and good reason is provided for the need to vacate the fixture. Failing that, a formal application for adjournment must be made (on notice to all parties) to the Court.

What is the short warned list?

12.4 Whilst the Administrative Court usually gives fixed dates for hearings, there is also a need to short warn a number of cases to cover the large number of settlements that occur in the list. Parties in cases that are selected to be short warned will be notified that their case is likely to be listed from a specified date, and that they may be called into the list at less than a day's notice from that date. Approximately 6 cases are short warned for any specified week. If the case does not get on during that period, a date as soon as possible after that period will be fixed in consultation with the parties.

12.5 There are occasions when circumstances, outside the control of the List Office, may necessitate them having to vacate a hearing at very short notice. Sometimes this can be as late as 4.30pm the day before the case is listed. This could be as a result of a case unexpectedly overrunning, a judge becoming unavailable, or other reasons. The List Office will endeavour to re-fix the case on the next available date convenient to the parties.

What if I cannot attend at court on the date of the hearing?

12.6 There may be circumstances where you are unable to attend at court on the date fixed to hear your application, i.e. as a result of illness or accident. If you are unlikely to be able to attend court on the hearing date you must notify the List Office immediately in writing to seek an adjournment of the hearing, setting out the reasons why you are unable to attend Court. If illness is the cause of your inability to attend, a medical certificate should be provided. Your application for an adjournment will be considered by the Head of the Administrative Court Office. The views of the other parties to the proceedings will be sought and it is good practice to notify the parties of your intention to seek an adjournment of the hearing and ask them to notify the court of their views.

What is a skeleton argument and do I need to lodge one?

12.7 A skeleton argument is a document lodged with the court by a party prior to the substantive (or final) hearing of any application for judicial review.

12.8 Whilst there is no requirement for a litigant in person to lodge a skeleton argument there is nothing to prevent you from doing so if you wish and if you consider that it would assist the Court.

12.9   If you wish to lodge a skeleton argument you must file it with the Court and serve it on the other parties not less than 21 working days before the date of the hearing of the judicial review or the warned date, (i.e. where a case has been identified as likely to be listed the specified date is the warned date).

12.10 The defendant and any other party wishing to make representations at the hearing of the judicial review must file and serve a skeleton argument not less than 14 working days before the date of the hearing of the judicial review (or the warned date).

12.11 The skeleton argument must contain:

- A time estimate for the complete hearing, including delivery of judgment;
- A list of issues;
- A list of the legal points to be taken (together with any relevant authorities with page references to the passages relied on);
- A chronology of events (with page references to the bundle of documents);
- A list of essential documents for the advance reading of the court (with page references to the passages relied on) (if different from that filed with the claim form) and a time estimate for that reading; and
- A list of persons referred to.

What is a trial bundle and when should I lodge it?

12.12 You must file a paginated and indexed bundle of all relevant documents required for the hearing of the judicial review whether or not you file a skeleton argument. The bundle must be filed with the court and served on the other parties not less than 21 working days before the hearing.

NB—Two copies of the bundle are required by the Court when the application is to be heard by a Divisional Court

NB—The bundle must also include those documents required by the defendant and any other party who is to make representations at the hearing.

Section 13

What if I need to make an application to the court for further orders/directions after the grant of permission?

13.1   Where case management decisions or directions are sought after the consideration of the application to proceed, application should be made by way of an application under CPR Part 23.

Section 14

Can my application be determined without the need for a hearing?

14.1   The court may decide a claim for judicial review without a hearing where all parties agree (CPR Part 54.18).

Section 15

What do I need to do if the proceedings settle by consent prior to the substantive hearing of the application?

15.1 If you reach agreement with the other parties as to the terms of the final order to be made in your claim, you must file at the court a document (with 2 copies) signed by all the parties setting out the terms of the proposed agreed order.

NB—Where the draft order is lodged prior to the grant of permission it must be accompanied by the requisite fee (currently £50.00).

NB—If you agree with the other parties that a mandatory order etc. is required, the draft order should be accompanied by a short statement of the matters relied on as justifying the proposed agreed order and copies of any authorities or statutory provisions relied on. If settlement is reached before permission is considered, the draft consent order must include provision for permission to be granted.

NB—Such a statement is not normally required where the agreement as to disposal (usually by way of withdrawal of the application) requires an order for costs or a detailed assessment of the Claimant's Legal Services Commission costs—in those circumstances the parties should file a draft consent order setting out the terms of the proposed order signed by all the parties.

15.2 The court will consider the documents referred and will make the order if it is satisfied that the order should be made. If the court is not satisfied that the order should be made, the court will give directions and may direct that a hearing date be set for the matter to be considered further.

Section 16

What if I want to discontinue the proceedings at any stage?

Before service of the claim form etc on the other parties

16.1 If you have not yet served any of the parties with the sealed claim form and accompanying documents you may discontinue the proceedings by notifying the Court in writing of your intention to do so. The Court will accept a letter of withdrawal provided that you confirm in writing that you have not effected service on the parties.

After service of the claim form etc on the other parties

16.2 Discontinuance of a claim is governed by CPR Part 38. Discontinuance renders you liable for the costs incurred until the date of discontinuance.

16.3 There is a right to discontinue a claim at any time, except where:

- An interim injunction has been granted or an undertaking has been given—in those circumstances the permission of the court is required to discontinue the proceedings (an example of this would be where bail had been granted pending determination of the application for judicial review)
- Interim payment has been made by defendant—in those circumstances the consent of the defendant or the permission of the court is required to discontinue the proceedings
- There is more than one claimant—in those circumstances the consent of every other claimant or the permission of the court is required to discontinue the proceedings.

16.4 If you wish to discontinue the proceedings at any stage after the service of those proceedings upon the other parties you must file a Notice of Discontinuance in the requisite form (N279) at the Administrative Court Office and serve a copy on every other party.

16.5 A defendant may apply to set the Notice of Discontinuance aside, within 28 days of being served with it (CPR Part 38.4).

NB—If the parties require any other order for costs, then an order of the court setting out the terms of the order sought is required. A Notice of Discontinuance would not be appropriate in those circumstances.

Section 17

Will I be responsible for the costs of the defendant and/or the interested parties if my application is unsuccessful?

17.1 The general rule is that the party which loses a substantive claim for judicial review will be ordered to pay the costs. However the Judge considering the matter has discretion to deal with the issue of costs as he considers appropriate in all of the circumstances.

NB—Costs may be awarded in respect of an unsuccessful paper application and in respect of an unsuccessful renewed application (in court).

NB—Any application by the defendant for costs will normally be made in the Acknowledgment of Service.

Section 18

What can I do if I am unhappy with the Judge's decision?

Civil matters

Appeal after refusal of permission

18.1 If you are unhappy with the Court's decision in a civil matter you can appeal to the Court of Appeal Civil Division with the permission of the Court of Appeal (CPR Part 52.15) within 7 days of the decision. Application to the Court of Appeal must be made within 7 days of refusal of permission by the Administrative Court.

Appeal after substantive hearing

18.2 In substantive applications, permission to appeal may be sought from the Administrative Court when it determines the claim for judicial review. If an application for permission to appeal is not made at the conclusion of the case, the application for permission to appeal must be made to the Court of Appeal Civil Division within 14 days (CPR Part 52.3 & 52.4).

18.3 Guidance as to procedure should be sought from the Civil Appeals Office, Royal Courts of Justice, Strand, London, WC2A 2LL.

Criminal matters

Appeal after refusal of permission

18.4 There is no further remedy in the domestic courts after a refusal of permission by the Administrative Court.

Appeal after substantive hearing

18.5 The Administration of Justice Act 1960 provides:

> s.1(1)Subject to the provisions of this section, an appeal shall lie to the House of Lords, at the instance of the defendant or the prosecutor from any decision of the High Court in a criminal cause or matter; or
>
> (2)   No appeal shall lie under this section except with the leave of the Court below or of the House of Lords; and such leave shall not be granted unless it is certified by the court below that a point of law of general public importance is involved in the decision and it appears to that court or to the House of Lords, as the case may be, that the point is one which ought to be considered by that House."

18.6 If you are unhappy with the Court's decision in a substantive claim for judicial review in a criminal matter, you can appeal to the House of Lords but only with the leave of the Administrative Court or the House of Lords and such leave may only be granted if:

(a) The Administrative Court certifies that a point of law of general public importance is involved in its decision; and

(b) It appears to the Administrative Court or the House of Lords that the point is one which ought to be considered by the House of Lords.

Section 19

Where can I get advice about procedural matters?

19.1 If in doubt about any procedural matter you can contact the Administrative Court Office, telephone number: 020 7947 6205. Court staff cannot give legal advice.

Lynne Knapman
Head of the Administrative Court Office
The Administrative Court Office
Royal Courts of Justice
Strand
London WC2A 2LL

64.5 Judicial Review Pre-Action Protocol

PRE-ACTION PROTOCOL FOR JUDICIAL REVIEW

CONTENTS

INTRODUCTION

ANNEXES

A   LETTER BEFORE CLAIM
B   RESPONSE TO A LETTER BEFORE CLAIM
C   NOTES ON PUBLIC FUNDING FOR LEGAL COSTS IN JUDICIAL REVIEW

INTRODUCTION

This protocol applies to proceedings within England and Wales only. It does not affect the time limit specified by Rule 54.5(1) of the Civil Procedure Rules which requires that any claim form in an application for judicial review must be filed promptly and in any event not later than 3 months after the grounds to make the claim first arose.([1])

1   Judicial review allows people with a sufficient interest in a decision or action by a public body to ask a judge to review the lawfulness of:

   • an enactment; or
   • a decision, action or failure to act in relation to the exercise of a public function.([2])

2   Judicial review may be used where there is no right of appeal or where all avenues of appeal have been exhausted.

ALTERNATIVE DISPUTE RESOLUTION

3.1   The parties should consider whether some form of alternative dispute resolution procedure would be more suitable than litigation, and if so, endeavour to agree which form to adopt. Both the Claimant and Defendant may be required by the Court to provide evidence that alternative means of resolving their dispute were considered. The Courts take the view that litigation should be a last resort, and that claims should not be issued prematurely when a settlement is still actively being explored. Parties are warned that if the protocol is not followed (including this paragraph) then the Court must have regard to such conduct when determining costs. However, parties should also note that a claim for judicial review 'must be filed promptly and in any event not later than 3 months after the grounds to make the claim first arose'.

3.2   It is not practicable in this protocol to address in detail how the parties might decide which method to adopt to resolve their particular dispute. However, summarised below are some of the options for resolving disputes without litigation:

   • Discussion and negotiation.
   • Ombudsmen—the Parliamentary and Health Service and the Local Government Ombudsmen have discretion to deal with complaints relating to maladministration. The British and Irish Ombudsman Association provide information about Ombudsman schemes and other complaint handling bodies and this is available from their website at www.bioa.org.uk . Parties may wish to note that the Ombudsmen are not able to look into a complaint once court action has been commenced.

- Early neutral evaluation by an independent third party (for example, a lawyer experienced in the field of administrative law or an individual experienced in the subject matter of the claim).
- Mediation—a form of facilitated negotiation assisted by an independent neutral party.

3.3 The Legal Services Commission has published a booklet on 'Alternatives to Court', CLS Direct Information Leaflet 23 (www.clsdirect.org.uk/legalhelp/leaflet23.jsp), which lists a number of organisations that provide alternative dispute resolution services.

3.4 *It is expressly recognised that no party can or should be forced to mediate or enter into any form of ADR.*

4 **Judicial review may not be appropriate in every instance.**

Claimants are strongly advised to seek appropriate legal advice when considering such proceedings and, in particular, before adopting this protocol or making a claim. Although the Legal Services Commission will not normally grant full representation before a letter before claim has been sent and the proposed defendant given a reasonable time to respond, initial funding may be available, for eligible claimants, to cover the work necessary to write this. (See Annex C for more information.)

5 This protocol sets out a code of good practice and contains the steps which parties should generally follow before making a claim for judicial review.

6 This protocol does not impose a greater obligation on a public body to disclose documents or give reasons for its decision than that already provided for in statute or common law. However, where the court considers that a public body should have provided **relevant** documents and/or information, particularly where this failure is a breach of a statutory or common law requirement, it may impose sanctions.

This protocol will not be appropriate where the defendant does not have the legal power to change the decision being challenged, for example decisions issued by tribunals such as the Asylum and Immigration Tribunal.

This protocol will not be appropriate in urgent cases, for example, when directions have been set, or are in force, for the claimant's removal from the UK, or where there is an urgent need for an interim order to compel a public body to act where it has unlawfully refused to do so (for example, the failure of a local housing authority to secure interim accomodation for a homeless claimant) a claim should be made immediately. A letter before claim will not stop the implementation of a disputed decision in all instances.

7 All claimants will need to satisfy themselves whether they should follow the protocol, depending upon the circumstances of his or her case. Where the use of the protocol is appropriate, the court will normally expect all parties to have complied with it and will take into account compliance or non-compliance when giving directions for case management of proceedings or when making orders for costs.([2]) However, even in emergency cases, it is good practice to fax to the defendant the draft Claim Form which the claimant intends to issue. A claimant is also normally required to notify a defendant when an interim mandatory order is being sought.

THE LETTER BEFORE CLAIM

8 Before making a claim, the claimant should send a letter to the defendant. The purpose of this letter is to identify the issues in dispute and establish whether litigation can be avoided.

9   Claimants should normally use the suggested **standard format** for the letter outlined at Annex A.

10 The letter should contain **the date and details of the decision, act or omission being challenged and a clear summary of the facts** on which the claim is based. It should also contain the **details of any relevant information** that the claimant is seeking and an explanation of why this is considered relevant.

11 The letter should normally contain the **details of any interested parties**(<u>4</u>) known to the claimant. They should be sent a <u>**copy**</u> of the letter before claim <u>**for information**</u>. **Claimants are <u>strongly advised to seek appropriate legal advice</u> when considering such proceedings and, in particular, before sending the letter before claim to other interested parties or making a claim.**

12 A claim should not normally be made until the proposed reply date given in the letter before claim has passed, unless the circumstances of the case require more immediate action to be taken.

THE LETTER OF RESPONSE

13 Defendants should normally respond within 14 days using the **standard format** at Annex B. Failure to do so will be taken into account by the court and sanctions may be imposed unless there are good reasons.(<u>5</u>)

14 Where it is not possible to reply within the proposed time limit the defendant should send an interim reply and propose a reasonable extension. Where an extension is sought, reasons should be given and, where required, additional information requested. **<u>This will not affect the time limit for making a claim for judicial review</u>** (<u>6</u>)nor will it bind the claimant where he or she considers this to be unreasonable. However, where the court considers that a subsequent claim is made prematurely it may impose sanctions.

15 If the **claim is being conceded in full**, the reply should say so in clear and unambiguous terms.

16 If the **claim is being conceded in part or not being conceded at all**, the reply should say so in clear and unambiguous terms, and:

(a) where appropriate, contain a new decision, clearly identifying what aspects of the claim are being conceded and what are not, or, give a clear timescale within which the new decision will be issued;

(b) provide a fuller explanation for the decision, if considered appropriate to do so;

(c) address any points of dispute, or explain why they cannot be addressed;

(d) enclose any **relevant** documentation requested by the claimant, or explain why the documents are not being enclosed; and

(e) where appropriate, confirm whether or not they will oppose any application for an interim remedy.

17 The response should be sent to **all interested parties**(<u>7</u>) identified by the claimant and contain details of any other parties who the defendant considers also have an interest.

ANNEX A
LETTER BEFORE CLAIM

SECTION 1. INFORMATION REQUIRED IN A LETTER BEFORE CLAIM

PROPOSED CLAIM FOR JUDICIAL REVIEW

1 **To**

   (Insert the name and address of the proposed defendant—see details in section 2)

2 **The claimant**

   (Insert the title, first and last name and the address of the claimant)

3 **Reference details**

   (When dealing with large organisations it is important to understand that the information relating to any particular individual's previous dealings with it may not be immediately available, therefore it is important to set out the relevant reference numbers for the matter in dispute and/or the identity of those within the public body who have been handling the particular matter in dispute—see details in section 3)

4 **The details of the matter being challenged**

   (Set out clearly the matter being challenged, particularly if there has been more than one decision)

5 **The issue**

   (Set out the date and details of the decision, or act or omission being challenged, a brief summary of the facts and why it is contented to be wrong)

6 **The details of the action that the defendant is expected to take**

   (Set out the details of the remedy sought, including whether a review or any interim remedy are being requested)

7 **The details of the legal advisers, if any, dealing with this claim**

   (Set out the name, address and reference details of any legal advisers dealing with the claim)

8 **The details of any interested parties**

   (Set out the details of any interested parties and confirm that they have been sent a copy of this letter)

9 **The details of any information sought**

   (Set out the details of any information that is sought. This may include a request for a fuller explanation of the reasons for the decision that is being challenged)

10 **The details of any documents that are considered relevant and necessary**

   (Set out the details of any documentation or policy in respect of which the disclosure is sought and explain why these are relevant. If you rely on a statutory duty to disclose, this should be specified)

11 **The address for reply and service of court documents**

   (Insert the address for the reply)

12 **Proposed reply date**

(The precise time will depend upon the circumstances of the individual case. However, although a shorter or longer time may be appropriate in a particular case, 14 days is a reasonable time to allow in most circumstances)

SECTION 2. ADDRESS FOR SENDING THE LETTER BEFORE CLAIM

Public bodies have requested that, for certain types of cases, in order to ensure a prompt response, letters before claim should be sent to specific addresses.

- **Where the claim concerns a decision in an Immigration, Asylum or Nationality case:**

—Judicial Review Unit,
  Immigration and Nationality Directorate,
  St Anne's House
  20–26 Wellesley Road
  Croydon CR9 2RL

- **Where the claim concerns a decision by the Legal Services Commission:**

—The address on the decision letter/notification; and

—Policy and Legal Department
  Legal Services Commission
  85 Gray's Inn Road
  London WC1X 8TX

- **Where the claim concerns a decision by a local authority:**

—The address on the decision letter/notification; and

—Their legal department[8]

- **Where the claim concerns a decision by a dapartment or body for whom Treasury Solicitor acts** *and Treasury Solicitor has already been involved in the case* **a copy should also be sent, quoting the Treasury Solicitor's reference, to:**

—The Treasury Solicitor,
  One Kemble Street,
  London WC2B 4TS

In all other circumstances, the letter should be sent to the address on the letter notifying the decision.

SECTION 3. SPECIFIC REFERENCE DETAILS REQUIRED

Public bodies have requested that the following information should be provided in order to ensure prompt response.

- **Where the claim concerns an Immigration, Asylum or Nationality case, dependent upon the nature of the case:**

—The Home Office reference number
—The Port reference number
—The Asylum and Immigration Tribunal reference number

—The National Asylum Support Service reference number

Or, if these are unavailable:

—The full name, nationality and date of birth of the claimant.

- **Where the claim concerns a decision by the Legal Services Commission:**

  —The certificate reference number.

ANNEX B

RESPONSE TO A LETTER BEFORE CLAIM

INFORMATION REQUIRED IN A RESPONSE TO A LETTER BEFORE CLAIM

PROPOSED CLAIM FOR JUDICIAL REVIEW

1   **The claimant**

(Insert the title, first and last names and the address to which any reply should be sent)

2   **From**

(Insert the name and address of the defendant)

3   **Reference details**

(Set out the relevant reference numbers for the matter in dispute and the identity of those within the public body who have been handling the issue)

4   **The details of the matter being challenged**

(Set out details of the matter being challenged, providing a fuller explanation of the decision, where this is considered appropriate)

5   **Response to the proposed claim**

(Set out whether the issue in question is conceded in part, or in full, or will be contested. Where it is not proposed to disclose any information that has been requested, explain the reason for this. Where an interim reply is being sent and there is a realistic prospect of settlement, details should be included)

6   **Details of any other interested parties**

(Identify any other parties who you consider have an interest who have not already been sent a letter by the claimant)

7   **Address for further correspondence and service of court documents**

(Set out the address for any future correspondence on this matter)

ANNEX C

NOTES ON PUBLIC FUNDING FOR LEGAL COSTS IN JUDICIAL REVIEW

Public funding for legal costs in judicial review is available from legal professionals and advice agencies which have contracts with the Legal Services Commission as part of the Community Legal Service. Funding may be provided for:

- *Legal Help* to provide initial advice and assistance with any legal problem; or

- *Legal Representation* to allow you to be represented in court if you are taking or defending court proceedings. This is available in two forms:

  —*Investigative Help* is limited to funding to investigate the strength of the proposed claim. It includes the issue and conduct of proceedings only so far as is necessary to obtain disclosure of relevant information or to protect the client's position in relation to any urgent hearing or time limit for the issue of proceedings. This includes the work necessary to write a **letter before claim** to the body potentially under challenge, setting out the grounds of challenge, and giving that body a reasonable opportunity, typically 14 days, in which to respond.

  —*Full Representation* is provided to represent you in legal proceedings and includes litigation services, advocacy services, and all such help as is usually given by a person providing representation in proceedings, including steps preliminary or incidental to proceedings, and/or arriving at or giving effect to a compromise to avoid or bring to an end any proceedings. Except in emergency cases, a proper **letter before claim** must be sent and the other side must be given an opportunity to respond before *Full Representation* is granted.

Further information on the type(s) of help available and the criteria for receiving that help may be found in the Legal Service Manual Volume 3: "*The Funding Code*". This may be found on the Legal Services Commission website at:

www.legalservices.gov.uk

A list of contracted firms and Advice Agencies may be found on the Community Legal Services website at:

www.justask.org.uk

64.6 Judicial Review Urgent Cases Procedure

**Annual Statement by the Hon Mr Justice Scott Baker, Lead Judge of the
Administrative Court**

Urgent Cases Procedure

Annex B

The Procedure for Urgent Applications to the Administrative Court

1. In October 2000 CPR Part 54 was introduced which makes no express provision for urgent applications for permission to apply for judicial review to be made orally.
2. The Administrative Court is now issuing the following guidance on the procedure to be applied for urgent applications and for interim injunctions. It is the duty of the advocate to comply with this guidance; and where a manifestly inappropriate application is made, consideration will be given to a wasted costs order.
3. The Administrative Court currently allocates paper applications for judicial review on a daily basis and one Judge also acts as the 'Urgent Judge'.
4. Where a claimant makes an application for the permission application to be heard as a matter of urgency and/or seeks an interim injunction, he must complete a prescribed form which states:

    (a) the need for urgency;
    (b) the timescale sought for the consideration of the permission application, e.g. within 72 hours or sooner if necessary (see paragraph 8 below); and
    (c) the date by which the substantive hearing should take place.

5. Where an interim injunction is sought, a claimant must, in addition, provide:

    (a) a draft order; and
    (b) the grounds for the injunction.

6. The claimant must serve (by FAX and post) the claim form and application for urgency on the defendant and interested parties, advising them of the application and that they may make representations.
7. Where an interim injunction is sought, the claimant must serve (by FAX and post) the draft order and grounds for the application on the defendant and interested parties, advising them of the application and that they may make representations.
8. A Judge will consider the application within the time requested and may make such order as he considers appropriate.
9. If the Judge directs that an oral hearing take place within a specified time the representatives of the parties and the Administrative Court will liaise to fix a permission hearing within the time period directed.

Administrative Court Office Reference Number: CO/

REQUEST FOR URGENT CONSIDERATION

THIS FORM MUST BE COMPLETED BY THE ADVOCATE FOR THE CLAIMANT

THIS FORM AND THE CLAIM FORM MUST BE SERVED BY THE CLAIMANT'S

SOLICITORS, BY FAX AND POST, ON THE DEFENDANT AND INTERESTED PARTIES

NAME OF CLAIMANT:
Name, address and fax number of Solicitor acting for the Claimant
Name of Counsel/Advocate acting for the Claimant

NAME OF DEFENDANT
Date of service of this form and claim form
Fax number served

NAME OF INTERESTED PARTY(IES)
Date of service of this form and claim form
Fax number served

1. REASONS FOR URGENCY
2. PROPOSED TIMETABLE

    (a)   The application for permission should be considered within hours/days

    (b)   Abridgement of time is sought for the lodging of Acknowledgments of Service

    (c)   If permission is granted, a substantive hearing is sought by (date)

3. INTERIM RELIEF
Interim relief is sought in terms of the attached draft order on the following grounds:

SIGNED

ADVOCATE FOR THE CLAIMANT

DATE

NOTE TO THE DEFENDANT AND INTERESTED PARTIES
Representations as to the urgency of the claim may be made to the Administrative Court
Office by fax—0207 947 6802

• A fuller version of this statement, including an amended form of application for urgent consideration, together with a Form 86B (renewal of permission) can be found at [2002] 1 All ER 633.

Scott Baker J
1 February 2002

64.7 Human Rights Act 1998

An Act to give further effect to rights and freedoms guaranteed under the European Convention on Human Rights; to make provision with respect to holders of certain judicial offices who become judges of the European Court of Human Rights; and for connected purposes.

[9th November 1998]

BE IT ENACTED by the Queen's most Excellent Majesty, by and with the advice and consent of the Lords Spiritual and Temporal, and Commons, in this present Parliament assembled, and by the authority of the same, as follows:—

Introduction

1.— (1) In this Act "the Convention rights" means the rights and fundamental freedoms set out in—

(a) Articles 2 to 12 and 14 of the Convention,

(b) Articles 1 to 3 of the First Protocol, and

(c) Articles 1 and 2 of the Sixth Protocol,

as read with Articles 16 to 18 of the Convention.

(2) Those Articles are to have effect for the purposes of this Act subject to any designated derogation or reservation (as to which see sections 14 and 15).

(3) The Articles are set out in Schedule 1.

(4) The Secretary of State may by order make such amendments to this Act as he considers appropriate to reflect the effect, in relation to the United Kingdom, of a protocol.

(5) In subsection (4) "protocol" means a protocol to the Convention—

(a) which the United Kingdom has ratified; or

(b) which the United Kingdom has signed with a view to ratification.

(6) No amendment may be made by an order under subsection (4) so as to come into force before the protocol concerned is in force in relation to the United Kingdom.

Interpretation of Convention rights.

2.— (1) A court or tribunal determining a question which has arisen in connection with a Convention right must take into account any—

(a) judgment, decision, declaration or advisory opinion of the European Court of Human Rights,

(b) opinion of the Commission given in a report adopted under Article 31 of the Convention,

(c) decision of the Commission in connection with Article 26 or 27(2) of the Convention, or

(d) decision of the Committee of Ministers taken under Article 46 of the Convention,

whenever made or given, so far as, in the opinion of the court or tribunal, it is relevant to the proceedings in which that question has arisen.

(2) Evidence of any judgment, decision, declaration or opinion of which account may have to be taken under this section is to be given in proceedings before any court or tribunal in such manner as may be provided by rules.

(3) In this section "rules" means rules of court or, in the case of proceedings before a tribunal, rules made for the purposes of this section—

(a) by the Lord Chancellor or the Secretary of State, in relation to any proceedings outside Scotland;

(b) by the Secretary of State, in relation to proceedings in Scotland; or

(c) by a Northern Ireland department, in relation to proceedings before a tribunal in Northern Ireland—

(i) which deals with transferred matters; and

(ii) for which no rules made under paragraph (a) are in force.

Legislation

3.— (1) So far as it is possible to do so, primary legislation and subordinate legislation must be read and given effect in a way which is compatible with the Convention rights.

(2) This section—

(a) applies to primary legislation and subordinate legislation whenever enacted;

(b) does not affect the validity, continuing operation or enforcement of any incompatible primary legislation; and

(c) does not affect the validity, continuing operation or enforcement of any incompatible subordinate legislation if (disregarding any possibility of revocation) primary legislation prevents removal of the incompatibility.

4.— (1) Subsection (2) applies in any proceedings in which a court determines whether a provision of primary legislation is compatible with a Convention right.

(2) If the court is satisfied that the provision is incompatible with a Convention right, it may make a declaration of that incompatibility.

(3) Subsection (4) applies in any proceedings in which a court determines whether a provision of subordinate legislation, made in the exercise of a power conferred by primary legislation, is compatible with a Convention right.

(4) If the court is satisfied—

(a) that the provision is incompatible with a Convention right, and

(b) that (disregarding any possibility of revocation) the primary legislation concerned prevents removal of the incompatibility,

it may make a declaration of that incompatibility.

(5) In this section "court" means—

(a) the House of Lords;

(b) the Judicial Committee of the Privy Council;

(c) the Courts-Martial Appeal Court;

(d) in Scotland, the High Court of Justiciary sitting otherwise than as a trial court or the Court of Session;

(e) in England and Wales or Northern Ireland, the High Court or the Court of Appeal.

(6) A declaration under this section ("a declaration of incompatibility")—

(a) does not affect the validity, continuing operation or enforcement of the provision in respect of which it is given; and

(b) is not binding on the parties to the proceedings in which it is made.

5.— (1) Where a court is considering whether to make a declaration of incompatibility, the Crown is entitled to notice in accordance with rules of court.

(2) In any case to which subsection (1) applies—

(a) a Minister of the Crown (or a person nominated by him),

(b) a member of the Scottish Executive,

(c) a Northern Ireland Minister,

(d) a Northern Ireland department,

is entitled, on giving notice in accordance with rules of court, to be joined as a party to the proceedings.

(3) Notice under subsection (2) may be given at any time during the proceedings.

(4) A person who has been made a party to criminal proceedings (other than in Scotland) as the result of a notice under subsection (2) may, with leave, appeal to the House of Lords against any declaration of incompatibility made in the proceedings.

(5) In subsection (4)—

"criminal proceedings" includes all proceedings before the Courts-Martial Appeal Court; and

"leave" means leave granted by the court making the declaration of incompatibility or by the House of Lords.

Public authorities

6.— (1) It is unlawful for a public authority to act in a way which is incompatible with a Convention right.

(2) Subsection (1) does not apply to an act if—

(a) as the result of one or more provisions of primary legislation, the authority could not have acted differently; or

(b) in the case of one or more provisions of, or made under, primary legislation which cannot be read or given effect in a way which is compatible with the Convention rights, the authority was acting so as to give effect to or enforce those provisions.

(3) In this section "public authority" includes—

(a) a court or tribunal, and

(b) any person certain of whose functions are functions of a public nature,

but does not include either House of Parliament or a person exercising functions in connection with proceedings in Parliament.

(4) In subsection (3) "Parliament" does not include the House of Lords in its judicial capacity.

(5) In relation to a particular act, a person is not a public authority by virtue only of subsection (3)(b) if the nature of the act is private.

(6) "An act" includes a failure to act but does not include a failure to—

(a) introduce in, or lay before, Parliament a proposal for legislation; or

(b) make any primary legislation or remedial order.

7.— (1) A person who claims that a public authority has acted (or proposes to act) in a way which is made unlawful by section 6(1) may—

(a) bring proceedings against the authority under this Act in the appropriate court or tribunal, or

(b) rely on the Convention right or rights concerned in any legal proceedings,

but only if he is (or would be) a victim of the unlawful act.

(2) In subsection (1)(a) "appropriate court or tribunal" means such court or tribunal as may be determined in accordance with rules; and proceedings against an authority include a counterclaim or similar proceeding.

(3) If the proceedings are brought on an application for judicial review, the applicant is to be taken to have a sufficient interest in relation to the unlawful act only if he is, or would be, a victim of that act.

(4) If the proceedings are made by way of a petition for judicial review in Scotland, the applicant shall be taken to have title and interest to sue in relation to the unlawful act only if he is, or would be, a victim of that act.

(5) Proceedings under subsection (1)(a) must be brought before the end of—

(a) the period of one year beginning with the date on which the act complained of took place; or

(b) such longer period as the court or tribunal considers equitable having regard to all the circumstances,

but that is subject to any rule imposing a stricter time limit in relation to the procedure in question.

(6) In subsection (1)(b) "legal proceedings" includes—

(a) proceedings brought by or at the instigation of a public authority; and

(b) an appeal against the decision of a court or tribunal.

(7) For the purposes of this section, a person is a victim of an unlawful act only if he would be a victim for the purposes of Article 34 of the Convention if proceedings were brought in the European Court of Human Rights in respect of that act.

(8) Nothing in this Act creates a criminal offence.

(9) In this section "rules" means—

(a) in relation to proceedings before a court or tribunal outside Scotland, rules made by the Lord Chancellor or the Secretary of State for the purposes of this section or rules of court,

(b) in relation to proceedings before a court or tribunal in Scotland, rules made by the Secretary of State for those purposes,

(c) in relation to proceedings before a tribunal in Northern Ireland—

(i) which deals with transferred matters; and

(ii) for which no rules made under paragraph (a) are in force,

rules made by a Northern Ireland department for those purposes,

and includes provision made by order under section 1 of the Courts and Legal Services Act 1990.

(10) In making rules, regard must be had to section 9.

(11) The Minister who has power to make rules in relation to a particular tribunal may, to the extent he considers it necessary to ensure that the tribunal can provide an appropriate remedy in relation to an act (or proposed act) of a public authority which is (or would be) unlawful as a result of section 6(1), by order add to—

    (a) the relief or remedies which the tribunal may grant; or

    (b) the grounds on which it may grant any of them.

(12) An order made under subsection (11) may contain such incidental, supplemental, consequential or transitional provision as the Minister making it considers appropriate.

(13) "The Minister" includes the Northern Ireland department concerned.

8.— (1) In relation to any act (or proposed act) of a public authority which the court finds is (or would be) unlawful, it may grant such relief or remedy, or make such order, within its powers as it considers just and appropriate.

(2) But damages may be awarded only by a court which has power to award damages, or to order the payment of compensation, in civil proceedings.

(3) No award of damages is to be made unless, taking account of all the circumstances of the case, including—

    (a) any other relief or remedy granted, or order made, in relation to the act in question (by that or any other court), and

    (b) the consequences of any decision (of that or any other court) in respect of that act,

the court is satisfied that the award is necessary to afford just satisfaction to the person in whose favour it is made.

(4) In determining—

    (a) whether to award damages, or

    (b) the amount of an award,

the court must take into account the principles applied by the European Court of Human Rights in relation to the award of compensation under Article 41 of the Convention.

(5) A public authority against which damages are awarded is to be treated—

    (a) in Scotland, for the purposes of section 3 of the Law Reform (Miscellaneous Provisions) (Scotland) Act 1940 as if the award were made in an action of damages in which the authority has been found liable in respect of loss or damage to the person to whom the award is made;

    (b) for the purposes of the Civil Liability (Contribution) Act 1978 as liable in respect of damage suffered by the person to whom the award is made.

(6) In this section—

"court" includes a tribunal;

"damages" means damages for an unlawful act of a public authority; and

"unlawful" means unlawful under section 6(1).

9.— (1) Proceedings under section 7(1)(a) in respect of a judicial act may be brought only—

    (a) by exercising a right of appeal;

    (b) on an application (in Scotland a petition) for judicial review; or

    (c) in such other forum as may be prescribed by rules.

(2) That does not affect any rule of law which prevents a court from being the subject of judicial review.

(3) In proceedings under this Act in respect of a judicial act done in good faith, damages may not be awarded otherwise than to compensate a person to the extent required by Article 5(5) of the Convention.

(4) An award of damages permitted by subsection (3) is to be made against the Crown; but no award may be made unless the appropriate person, if not a party to the proceedings, is joined.

(5) In this section—

"appropriate person" means the Minister responsible for the court concerned, or a person or government department nominated by him;

"court" includes a tribunal;

"judge" includes a member of a tribunal, a justice of the peace and a clerk or other officer entitled to exercise the jurisdiction of a court;

"judicial act" means a judicial act of a court and includes an act done on the instructions, or on behalf, of a judge; and

"rules" has the same meaning as in section 7(9).

Remedial action

10.—(1) This section applies if—

(a) a provision of legislation has been declared under section 4 to be incompatible with a Convention right and, if an appeal lies—

    (i) all persons who may appeal have stated in writing that they do not intend to do so;

    (ii) the time for bringing an appeal has expired and no appeal has been brought within that time; or

    (iii) an appeal brought within that time has been determined or abandoned; or

(b) it appears to a Minister of the Crown or Her Majesty in Council that, having regard to a finding of the European Court of Human Rights made after the coming into force of this section in proceedings against the United Kingdom, a provision of legislation is incompatible with an obligation of the United Kingdom arising from the Convention.

(2) If a Minister of the Crown considers that there are compelling reasons for proceeding under this section, he may by order make such amendments to the legislation as he considers necessary to remove the incompatibility.

(3) If, in the case of subordinate legislation, a Minister of the Crown considers—

(a) that it is necessary to amend the primary legislation under which the subordinate legislation in question was made, in order to enable the incompatibility to be removed, and

(b) that there are compelling reasons for proceeding under this section,

he may by order make such amendments to the primary legislation as he considers necessary.

(4) This section also applies where the provision in question is in subordinate legislation and has been quashed, or declared invalid, by reason of incompatibility with a Convention right and the Minister proposes to proceed under paragraph 2(b) of Schedule 2.

(5) If the legislation is an Order in Council, the power conferred by subsection (2) or (3) is exercisable by Her Majesty in Council.

(6) In this section "legislation" does not include a Measure of the Church Assembly or of the General Synod of the Church of England.

(7) Schedule 2 makes further provision about remedial orders.

Other rights and proceedings

11. A person's reliance on a Convention right does not restrict—

    (a) any other right or freedom conferred on him by or under any law having effect in any part of the United Kingdom; or

    (b) his right to make any claim or bring any proceedings which he could make or bring apart from sections 7 to 9.

12.—(1) This section applies if a court is considering whether to grant any relief which, if granted, might affect the exercise of the Convention right to freedom of expression.

    (2) If the person against whom the application for relief is made ("the respondent") is neither present nor represented, no such relief is to be granted unless the court is satisfied—

    (a) that the applicant has taken all practicable steps to notify the respondent; or

    (b) that there are compelling reasons why the respondent should not be notified.

    (3) No such relief is to be granted so as to restrain publication before trial unless the court is satisfied that the applicant is likely to establish that publication should not be allowed.

    (4) The court must have particular regard to the importance of the Convention right to freedom of expression and, where the proceedings relate to material which the respondent claims, or which appears to the court, to be journalistic, literary or artistic material (or to conduct connected with such material), to—

    (a) the extent to which—

        (i)   the material has, or is about to, become available to the public; or

        (ii) it is, or would be, in the public interest for the material to be published;

    (b) any relevant privacy code.

    (5) In this section—

"court" includes a tribunal; and

"relief" includes any remedy or order (other than in criminal proceedings).

13.—(1) If a court's determination of any question arising under this Act might affect the exercise by a religious organisation (itself or its members collectively) of the Convention right to freedom of thought, conscience and religion, it must have particular regard to the importance of that right.

    (2) In this section "court" includes a tribunal.

Derogations and reservations

14.—(1) In this Act "designated derogation" means—

    (a) the United Kingdom's derogation from Article 5(3) of the Convention; and

    (b) any derogation by the United Kingdom from an Article of the Convention, or of any protocol to the Convention, which is designated for the purposes of this Act in an order made by the Secretary of State.

    (2) The derogation referred to in subsection (1)(a) is set out in Part I of Schedule 3.

    (3) If a designated derogation is amended or replaced it ceases to be a designated derogation.

    (4) But subsection (3) does not prevent the Secretary of State from exercising his power under subsection (1)(b) to make a fresh designation order in respect of the Article concerned.

(5) The Secretary of State must by order make such amendments to Schedule 3 as he considers appropriate to reflect—

(a) any designation order; or
(b) the effect of subsection (3).

(6) A designation order may be made in anticipation of the making by the United Kingdom of a proposed derogation.

15.—(1) In this Act "designated reservation" means—

(a) the United Kingdom's reservation to Article 2 of the First Protocol to the Convention; and
(b) any other reservation by the United Kingdom to an Article of the Convention, or of any protocol to the Convention, which is designated for the purposes of this Act in an order made by the Secretary of State.

(2) The text of the reservation referred to in subsection (1)(a) is set out in Part II of Schedule 3.
(3) If a designated reservation is withdrawn wholly or in part it ceases to be a designated reservation.
(4) But subsection (3) does not prevent the Secretary of State from exercising his power under subsection (1)(b) to make a fresh designation order in respect of the Article concerned.
(5) The Secretary of State must by order make such amendments to this Act as he considers appropriate to reflect—

(a) any designation order; or
(b) the effect of subsection (3).

16.—(1) If it has not already been withdrawn by the United Kingdom, a designated derogation ceases to have effect for the purposes of this Act—

(a) in the case of the derogation referred to in section 14(1)(a), at the end of the period of five years beginning with the date on which section 1(2) came into force;
(b) in the case of any other derogation, at the end of the period of five years beginning with the date on which the order designating it was made.

(2) At any time before the period—
(a) fixed by subsection (1)(a) or (b), or
(b) extended by an order under this subsection,

comes to an end, the Secretary of State may by order extend it by a further period of five years.
(3) An order under section 14(1)(b) ceases to have effect at the end of the period for consideration, unless a resolution has been passed by each House approving the order.
(4) Subsection (3) does not affect—

(a) anything done in reliance on the order; or
(b) the power to make a fresh order under section 14(1)(b).

(5) In subsection (3) "period for consideration" means the period of forty days beginning with the day on which the order was made.
(6) In calculating the period for consideration, no account is to be taken of any time during which—

    (a) Parliament is dissolved or prorogued; or

    (b) both Houses are adjourned for more than four days.

(7) If a designated derogation is withdrawn by the United Kingdom, the Secretary of State must by order make such amendments to this Act as he considers are required to reflect that withdrawal.

17.—(1) The appropriate Minister must review the designated reservation referred to in section 15(1)(a)—

    (a) before the end of the period of five years beginning with the date on which section 1(2) came into force; and

    (b) if that designation is still in force, before the end of the period of five years beginning with the date on which the last report relating to it was laid under subsection (3).

(2) The appropriate Minister must review each of the other designated reservations (if any)—

    (a) before the end of the period of five years beginning with the date on which the order designating the reservation first came into force; and

    (b) if the designation is still in force, before the end of the period of five years beginning with the date on which the last report relating to it was laid under subsection (3).

(3) The Minister conducting a review under this section must prepare a report on the result of the review and lay a copy of it before each House of Parliament.

Judges of the European Court of Human Rights

18.—(1) In this section "judicial office" means the office of—

    (a) Lord Justice of Appeal, Justice of the High Court or Circuit judge, in England and Wales;

    (b) judge of the Court of Session or sheriff, in Scotland;

    (c) Lord Justice of Appeal, judge of the High Court or county court judge, in Northern Ireland.

(2) The holder of a judicial office may become a judge of the European Court of Human Rights ("the Court") without being required to relinquish his office.

(3) But he is not required to perform the duties of his judicial office while he is a judge of the Court.

(4) In respect of any period during which he is a judge of the Court—

    (a) a Lord Justice of Appeal or Justice of the High Court is not to count as a judge of the relevant court for the purposes of section 2(1) or 4(1) of the Supreme Court Act 1981 (maximum number of judges) nor as a judge of the Supreme Court for the purposes of section 12(1) to (6) of that Act (salaries etc.);

    (b) a judge of the Court of Session is not to count as a judge of that court for the purposes of section 1(1) of the Court of Session Act 1988 (maximum number of judges) or of section 9(1)(c) of the Administration of Justice Act 1973 ("the 1973 Act") (salaries etc.);

    (c) a Lord Justice of Appeal or judge of the High Court in Northern Ireland is not to count as a judge of the relevant court for the purposes of section 2(1) or 3(1) of the Judicature (Northern Ireland) Act 1978 (maximum number of judges) nor as a judge of the Supreme Court of Northern Ireland for the purposes of section 9(1)(d) of the 1973 Act (salaries etc.);

    (d) a Circuit judge is not to count as such for the purposes of section 18 of the Courts Act 1971 (salaries etc.);

    (e) a sheriff is not to count as such for the purposes of section 14 of the Sheriff Courts (Scotland) Act 1907 (salaries etc.);

    (f) a county court judge of Northern Ireland is not to count as such for the purposes of section 106 of the County Courts Act Northern Ireland) 1959 (salaries etc.).

(5) If a sheriff principal is appointed a judge of the Court, section 11(1) of the Sheriff Courts (Scotland) Act 1971 (temporary appointment of sheriff principal) applies, while he holds that appointment, as if his office is vacant.

(6) Schedule 4 makes provision about judicial pensions in relation to the holder of a judicial office who serves as a judge of the Court.

(7) The Lord Chancellor or the Secretary of State may by order make such transitional provision (including, in particular, provision for a temporary increase in the maximum number of judges) as he considers appropriate in relation to any holder of a judicial office who has completed his service as a judge of the Court.

Parliamentary procedure

19.—(1) A Minister of the Crown in charge of a Bill in either House of Parliament must, before Second Reading of the Bill—

    (a) make a statement to the effect that in his view the provisions of the Bill are compatible with the Convention rights ("a statement of compatibility"); or

    (b) make a statement to the effect that although he is unable to make a statement of compatibility the government nevertheless wishes the House to proceed with the Bill.

(2) The statement must be in writing and be published in such manner as the Minister making it considers appropriate.

Supplemental

20.—(1) Any power of a Minister of the Crown to make an order under this Act is exercisable by statutory instrument.

(2) The power of the Lord Chancellor or the Secretary of State to make rules (other than rules of court) under section 2(3) or 7(9) is exercisable by statutory instrument.

(3) Any statutory instrument made under section 14, 15 or 16(7) must be laid before Parliament.

(4) No order may be made by the Lord Chancellor or the Secretary of State under section 1(4), 7(11) or 16(2) unless a draft of the order has been laid before, and approved by, each House of Parliament.

(5) Any statutory instrument made under section 18(7) or Schedule 4, or to which subsection (2) applies, shall be subject to annulment in pursuance of a resolution of either House of Parliament.

(6) The power of a Northern Ireland department to make—

    (a) rules under section 2(3)(c) or 7(9)(c), or

    (b) an order under section 7(11),

is exercisable by statutory rule for the purposes of the Statutory Rules (Northern Ireland) Order 1979.

(7) Any rules made under section 2(3)(c) or 7(9)(c) shall be subject to negative resolution; and section 41(6) of the Interpretation Act Northern Ireland) 1954 (meaning of "subject to

negative resolution") shall apply as if the power to make the rules were conferred by an Act of the Northern Ireland Assembly.

(8) No order may be made by a Northern Ireland department under section 7(11) unless a draft of the order has been laid before, and approved by, the Northern Ireland Assembly.

21.—(1) In this Act—

"amend" includes repeal and apply (with or without modifications);

"the appropriate Minister" means the Minister of the Crown having charge of the appropriate authorised government department (within the meaning of the Crown Proceedings Act 1947);

"the Commission" means the European Commission of Human Rights;

"the Convention" means the Convention for the Protection of Human Rights and Fundamental Freedoms, agreed by the Council of Europe at Rome on 4th November 1950 as it has effect for the time being in relation to the United Kingdom;

"declaration of incompatibility" means a declaration under section 4;

"Minister of the Crown" has the same meaning as in the Ministers of the Crown Act 1975;

"Northern Ireland Minister" includes the First Minister and the deputy First Minister in Northern Ireland;

"primary legislation" means any—

(a) public general Act;
(b) local and personal Act;
(c) private Act;
(d) Measure of the Church Assembly;
(e) Measure of the General Synod of the Church of England;
(f) Order in Council—

    (i) made in exercise of Her Majesty's Royal Prerogative;

    (ii) made under section 38(1)(a) of the Northern Ireland Constitution Act 1973 or the corresponding provision of the Northern Ireland Act 1998; or

    (iii) amending an Act of a kind mentioned in paragraph (a), (b) or (c);

    and includes an order or other instrument made under primary legislation (otherwise than by the National Assembly for Wales, a member of the Scottish Executive, a Northern Ireland Minister or a Northern Ireland department) to the extent to which it operates to bring one or more provisions of that legislation into force or amends any primary legislation;

"the First Protocol" means the protocol to the Convention agreed at Paris on 20th March 1952;

"the Sixth Protocol" means the protocol to the Convention agreed at Strasbourg on 28th April 1983;

"the Eleventh Protocol" means the protocol to the Convention (restructuring the control machinery established by the Convention) agreed at Strasbourg on 11th May 1994;

"remedial order" means an order under section 10;

"subordinate legislation" means any—

(a) Order in Council other than one—

    (i)   made in exercise of Her Majesty's Royal Prerogative;

    (ii) made under section 38(1)(a) of the Northern Ireland Constitution Act 1973 or the corresponding provision of the Northern Ireland Act 1998; or

    (iii) amending an Act of a kind mentioned in the definition of primary legislation;

(b) Act of the Scottish Parliament;

(c) Act of the Parliament of Northern Ireland;

(d) Measure of the Assembly established under section 1 of the Northern Ireland Assembly Act 1973;

(e) Act of the Northern Ireland Assembly;

(f) order, rules, regulations, scheme, warrant, byelaw or other instrument made under primary legislation (except to the extent to which it operates to bring one or more provisions of that legislation into force or amends any primary legislation);

(g) order, rules, regulations, scheme, warrant, byelaw or other instrument made under legislation mentioned in paragraph (b), (c), (d) or (e) or made under an Order in Council applying only to Northern Ireland;

(h) order, rules, regulations, scheme, warrant, byelaw or other instrument made by a member of the Scottish Executive, a Northern Ireland Minister or a Northern Ireland department in exercise of prerogative or other executive functions of Her Majesty which are exercisable by such a person on behalf of Her Majesty;

"transferred matters" has the same meaning as in the Northern Ireland Act 1998; and

"tribunal" means any tribunal in which legal proceedings may be brought.

(2) The references in paragraphs (b) and (c) of section 2(1) to Articles are to Articles of the Convention as they had effect immediately before the coming into force of the Eleventh Protocol.

(3) The reference in paragraph (d) of section 2(1) to Article 46 includes a reference to Articles 32 and 54 of the Convention as they had effect immediately before the coming into force of the Eleventh Protocol.

(4) The references in section 2(1) to a report or decision of the Commission or a decision of the Committee of Ministers include references to a report or decision made as provided by paragraphs 3, 4 and 6 of Article 5 of the Eleventh Protocol (transitional provisions).

(5) Any liability under the Army Act 1955, the Air Force Act 1955 or the Naval Discipline Act 1957 to suffer death for an offence is replaced by a liability to imprisonment for life or any less punishment authorised by those Acts; and those Acts shall accordingly have effect with the necessary modifications.

22.—(1) This Act may be cited as the Human Rights Act 1998.

(2) Sections 18, 20 and 21(5) and this section come into force on the passing of this Act.

(3) The other provisions of this Act come into force on such day as the Secretary of State may by order appoint; and different days may be appointed for different purposes.

(4) Paragraph (b) of subsection (1) of section 7 applies to proceedings brought by or at the instigation of a public authority whenever the act in question took place; but otherwise that subsection does not apply to an act taking place before the coming into force of that section.

(5) This Act binds the Crown.

(6) This Act extends to Northern Ireland.

(7) Section 21(5), so far as it relates to any provision contained in the Army Act 1955, the Air Force Act 1955 or the Naval Discipline Act 1957, extends to any place to which that provision extends.

Schedule 1—The Articles

Part I
The convention
Rights and Freedoms

Article 2

Right to Life

1. Everyone's right to life shall be protected by law. No one shall be deprived of his life intentionally save in the execution of a sentence of a court following his conviction of a crime for which this penalty is provided by law.
2. Deprivation of life shall not be regarded as inflicted in contravention of this Article when it results from the use of force which is no more than absolutely necessary:

   (a) in defence of any person from unlawful violence;
   (b) in order to effect a lawful arrest or to prevent the escape of a person lawfully detained;
   (c) in action lawfully taken for the purpose of quelling a riot or insurrection.

Article 3

Prohibition of Torture

No one shall be subjected to torture or to inhuman or degrading treatment or punishment.

Article 4

Prohibition of slavery and forced labour

1. No one shall be held in slavery or servitude.
2. No one shall be required to perform forced or compulsory labour.
3. For the purpose of this Article the term "forced or compulsory labour" shall not include:

   (a) any work required to be done in the ordinary course of detention imposed according to the provisions of Article 5 of this Convention or during conditional release from such detention;
   (b) any service of a military character or, in case of conscientious objectors in countries where they are recognised, service exacted instead of compulsory military service;
   (c) any service exacted in case of an emergency or calamity threatening the life or well-being of the community;
   (d) any work or service which forms part of normal civic obligations.

Article 5

Right to liberty and security

1. Everyone has the right to liberty and security of person. No one shall be deprived of his liberty save in the following cases and in accordance with a procedure prescribed by law:

   (a) the lawful detention of a person after conviction by a competent court;
   (b) the lawful arrest or detention of a person for non-compliance with the lawful order of a court or in order to secure the fulfilment of any obligation prescribed by law;

(c) the lawful arrest or detention of a person effected for the purpose of bringing him before the competent legal authority on reasonable suspicion of having committed an offence or when it is reasonably considered necessary to prevent his committing an offence or fleeing after having done so;

(d) the detention of a minor by lawful order for the purpose of educational supervision or his lawful detention for the purpose of bringing him before the competent legal authority;

(e) the lawful detention of persons for the prevention of the spreading of infectious diseases, of persons of unsound mind, alcoholics or drug addicts or vagrants;

(f) the lawful arrest or detention of a person to prevent his effecting an unauthorised entry into the country or of a person against whom action is being taken with a view to deportation or extradition.

2. Everyone who is arrested shall be informed promptly, in a language which he understands, of the reasons for his arrest and of any charge against him.

3. Everyone arrested or detained in accordance with the provisions of paragraph 1(c) of this Article shall be brought promptly before a judge or other officer authorised by law to exercise judicial power and shall be entitled to trial within a reasonable time or to release pending trial. Release may be conditioned by guarantees to appear for trial.

4. Everyone who is deprived of his liberty by arrest or detention shall be entitled to take proceedings by which the lawfulness of his detention shall be decided speedily by a court and his release ordered if the detention is not lawful.

5. Everyone who has been the victim of arrest or detention in contravention of the provisions of this Article shall have an enforceable right to compensation.

Article 6

Right to a fair trial

1. In the determination of his civil rights and obligations or of any criminal charge against him, everyone is entitled to a fair and public hearing within a reasonable time by an independent and impartial tribunal established by law. Judgment shall be pronounced publicly but the press and public may be excluded from all or part of the trial in the interest of morals, public order or national security in a democratic society, where the interests of juveniles or the protection of the private life of the parties so require, or to the extent strictly necessary in the opinion of the court in special circumstances where publicity would prejudice the interests of justice.

2. Everyone charged with a criminal offence shall be presumed innocent until proved guilty according to law.

3. Everyone charged with a criminal offence has the following minimum rights:

(a) to be informed promptly, in a language which he understands and in detail, of the nature and cause of the accusation against him;

(b) to have adequate time and facilities for the preparation of his defence;

(c) to defend himself in person or through legal assistance of his own choosing or, if he has not sufficient means to pay for legal assistance, to be given it free when the interests of justice so require;

(d) to examine or have examined witnesses against him and to obtain the attendance and examination of witnesses on his behalf under the same conditions as witnesses against him;

(e) to have the free assistance of an interpreter if he cannot understand or speak the language used in court.

Article 7

No punishment without law

1. No one shall be held guilty of any criminal offence on account of any act or omission which did not constitute a criminal offence under national or international law at the time when it was committed. Nor shall a heavier penalty be imposed than the one that was applicable at the time the criminal offence was committed.
2. This Article shall not prejudice the trial and punishment of any person for any act or omission which, at the time when it was committed, was criminal according to the general principles of law recognised by civilised nations.

Article 8

Right to respect for private and family life

1. Everyone has the right to respect for his private and family life, his home and his correspondence.
2. There shall be no interference by a public authority with the exercise of this right except such as is in accordance with the law and is necessary in a democratic society in the interests of national security, public safety or the economic well-being of the country, for the prevention of disorder or crime, for the protection of health or morals, or for the protection of the rights and freedoms of others.

Article 9

Freedom of thought, conscience and religion

1. Everyone has the right to freedom of thought, conscience and religion; this right includes freedom to change his religion or belief and freedom, either alone or in community with others and in public or private, to manifest his religion or belief, in worship, teaching, practice and observance.
2. Freedom to manifest one's religion or beliefs shall be subject only to such limitations as are prescribed by law and are necessary in a democratic society in the interests of public safety, for the protection of public order, health or morals, or for the protection of the rights and freedoms of others.

Article 10

Freedom of expression

1. Everyone has the right to freedom of expression. This right shall include freedom to hold opinions and to receive and impart information and ideas without interference by public authority and regardless of frontiers. This Article shall not prevent States from requiring the licensing of broadcasting, television or cinema enterprises.
2. The exercise of these freedoms, since it carries with it duties and responsibilities, may be subject to such formalities, conditions, restrictions or penalties as are prescribed by law and are necessary in a democratic society, in the interests of national security, territorial integrity or public safety, for the prevention of disorder or crime, for the protection of health or morals, for the protection of the reputation or rights of others, for preventing the disclosure of information received in confidence, or for maintaining the authority and impartiality of the judiciary.

Article 11

Freedom of assembly and association

1. Everyone has the right to freedom of peaceful assembly and to freedom of association with others, including the right to form and to join trade unions for the protection of his interests.
2. No restrictions shall be placed on the exercise of these rights other than such as are prescribed by law and are necessary in a democratic society in the interests of national security or public safety, for the prevention of disorder or crime, for the protection of health or morals or for the protection of the rights and freedoms of others. This Article shall not prevent the imposition of lawful restrictions on the exercise of these rights by members of the armed forces, of the police or of the administration of the State.

Article 12

Right to marry

Men and women of marriageable age have the right to marry and to found a family, according to the national laws governing the exercise of this right.

Article 14

Prohibition of discrimination

The enjoyment of the rights and freedoms set forth in this Convention shall be secured without discrimination on any ground such as sex, race, colour, language, religion, political or other opinion, national or social origin, association with a national minority, property, birth or other status.

Article 16

Restrictions on political activity of aliens

Nothing in Articles 10, 11 and 14 shall be regarded as preventing the High Contracting Parties from imposing restrictions on the political activity of aliens.

Article 17

Prohibition of abuse of rights

Nothing in this Convention may be interpreted as implying for any State, group or person any right to engage in any activity or perform any act aimed at the destruction of any of the rights and freedoms set forth herein or at their limitation to a greater extent than is provided for in the Convention.

Article 18

Limitation on use of restrictions on rights

The restrictions permitted under this Convention to the said rights and freedoms shall not be applied for any purpose other than those for which they have been prescribed.

Schedule1, Part II

First protocol

Article 1

Protection of property

Every natural or legal person is entitled to the peaceful enjoyment of his possessions. No one shall be deprived of his possessions except in the public interest and subject to the conditions provided for by law and by the general principles of international law.

The preceding provisions shall not, however, in any way impair the right of a State to enforce such laws as it deems necessary to control the use of property in accordance with the general interest or to secure the payment of taxes or other contributions or penalties.

Article 2

Right to education

No person shall be denied the right to education. In the exercise of any functions which it assumes in relation to education and to teaching, the State shall respect the right of parents to ensure such education and teaching in conformity with their own religious and philosophical convictions.

Article 3

Right to free elections

The High Contracting Parties undertake to hold free elections at reasonable intervals by secret ballot, under conditions which will ensure the free expression of the opinion of the people in the choice of the legislature.

Schedule 1, Part III

Sixth protocol

Article 1

Abolition of the death penalty

The death penalty shall be abolished. No one shall be condemned to such penalty or executed.

Article 2

Death penalty in time of war

A State may make provision in its law for the death penalty in respect of acts committed in time of war or of imminent threat of war; such penalty shall be applied only in the instances laid down in the law and in accordance with its provisions. The State shall communicate to the Secretary General of the Council of Europe the relevant provisions of that law.

Schedule 2

Remedial Orders

Orders

1.— (1) A remedial order may—

    (a) contain such incidental, supplemental, consequential or transitional provision as the person making it considers appropriate;

    (b) be made so as to have effect from a date earlier than that on which it is made;

    (c) make provision for the delegation of specific functions;

    (d) make different provision for different cases.

(2) The power conferred by sub-paragraph (1)(a) includes—

    (a) power to amend primary legislation (including primary legislation other than that which contains the incompatible provision); and

    (b) power to amend or revoke subordinate legislation (including subordinate legislation other than that which contains the incompatible provision).

(3) A remedial order may be made so as to have the same extent as the legislation which it affects.

(4) No person is to be guilty of an offence solely as a result of the retrospective effect of a remedial order.

Procedure

2. No remedial order may be made unless—

    (a) a draft of the order has been approved by a resolution of each House of Parliament made after the end of the period of 60 days beginning with the day on which the draft was laid; or

    (b) it is declared in the order that it appears to the person making it that, because of the urgency of the matter, it is necessary to make the order without a draft being so approved.

Orders laid in draft

3.— (1) No draft may be laid under paragraph 2(a) unless—

    (a) the person proposing to make the order has laid before Parliament a document which contains a draft of the proposed order and the required information; and

    (b) the period of 60 days, beginning with the day on which the document required by this sub-paragraph was laid, has ended.

(2) If representations have been made during that period, the draft laid under paragraph 2(a) must be accompanied by a statement containing—

    (a) a summary of the representations; and

    (b) if, as a result of the representations, the proposed order has been changed, details of the changes.

Urgent cases

4.— (1) If a remedial order ("the original order") is made without being approved in draft, the person making it must lay it before Parliament, accompanied by the required information, after it is made.

(2) If representations have been made during the period of 60 days beginning with the day on which the original order was made, the person making it must (after the end of that period) lay before Parliament a statement containing—

(a) a summary of the representations; and

(b) if, as a result of the representations, he considers it appropriate to make changes to the original order, details of the changes.

(3) If sub-paragraph (2)(b) applies, the person making the statement must—

(a) make a further remedial order replacing the original order; and

(b) lay the replacement order before Parliament.

(4) If, at the end of the period of 120 days beginning with the day on which the original order was made, a resolution has not been passed by each House approving the original or replacement order, the order ceases to have effect (but without that affecting anything previously done under either order or the power to make a fresh remedial order).

Definitions

5. In this Schedule—

"representations" means representations about a remedial order (or proposed remedial order) made to the person making (or proposing to make) it and includes any relevant Parliamentary report or resolution; and

"required information" means—

(a) an explanation of the incompatibility which the order (or proposed order) seeks to remove, including particulars of the relevant declaration, finding or order; and

(b) a statement of the reasons for proceeding under section 10 and for making an order in those terms.

Calculating periods

6. In calculating any period for the purposes of this Schedule, no account is to be taken of any time during which—

(a) Parliament is dissolved or prorogued; or

(b) both Houses are adjourned for more than four days.

Schedule 3
Derogation and Reservation

Part I—Derogation

The 1988 notification

The United Kingdom Permanent Representative to the Council of Europe presents his compliments to the Secretary General of the Council, and has the honour to convey the following information in order to ensure compliance with the obligations of Her Majesty's Government in the United Kingdom under Article 15(3) of the Convention for the Protection of Human Rights and Fundamental Freedoms signed at Rome on 4 November 1950.

There have been in the United Kingdom in recent years campaigns of organised terrorism connected with the affairs of Northern Ireland which have manifested themselves in activities which have included repeated murder, attempted murder, maiming, intimidation and violent civil disturbance and in bombing and fire raising which have resulted in death, injury and widespread destruction of property. As a result, a public emergency within the meaning of Article 15(1) of the Convention exists in the United Kingdom.

The Government found it necessary in 1974 to introduce and since then, in cases concerning persons reasonably suspected of involvement in terrorism connected with the affairs of Northern Ireland, or of certain offences under the legislation, who have been detained for 48 hours, to exercise powers enabling further detention without charge, for periods of up to five days, on the authority of the Secretary of State. These powers are at present to be found in Section 12 of the Prevention of Terrorism (Temporary Provisions) Act 1984, Article 9 of the Prevention of Terrorism (Supplemental Temporary Provisions) Order 1984 and Article 10 of the Prevention of Terrorism (Supplemental Temporary Provisions) (Northern Ireland) Order 1984.

Section 12 of the Prevention of Terrorism (Temporary Provisions) Act 1984 provides for a person whom a constable has arrested on reasonable grounds of suspecting him to be guilty of an offence under Section 1, 9 or 10 of the Act, or to be or to have been involved in terrorism connected with the affairs of Northern Ireland, to be detained in right of the arrest for up to 48 hours and thereafter, where the Secretary of State extends the detention period, for up to a further five days. Section 12 substantially re-enacted Section 12 of the Prevention of Terrorism (Temporary Provisions) Act 1976 which, in turn, substantially re-enacted Section 7 of the Prevention of Terrorism (Temporary Provisions) Act 1974.

Article 10 of the Prevention of Terrorism (Supplemental Temporary Provisions) (Northern Ireland) Order 1984 (SI 1984/417) and Article 9 of the Prevention of Terrorism (Supplemental Temporary Provisions) Order 1984 (SI 1984/418) were both made under Sections 13 and 14 of and Schedule 3 to the 1984 Act and substantially re-enacted powers of detention in Orders made under the 1974 and 1976 Acts. A person who is being examined under Article 4 of either Order on his arrival in, or on seeking to leave, Northern Ireland or Great Britain for the purpose of determining whether he is or has been involved in terrorism connected with the affairs of Northern Ireland, or whether there are grounds for suspecting that he has committed an offence under Section 9 of the 1984 Act, may be detained under Article 9 or 10, as appropriate, pending the conclusion of his examination. The period of this examination may exceed 12 hours if an examining officer has reasonable grounds for suspecting him to be or to have been involved in acts of terrorism connected with the affairs of Northern Ireland.

Where such a person is detained under the said Article 9 or 10 he may be detained for up to 48 hours on the authority of an examining officer and thereafter, where the Secretary of State extends the detention period, for up to a further five days.

In its judgment of 29 November 1988 in the Case of *Brogan and Others*, the European Court of Human Rights held that there had been a violation of Article 5(3) in respect of each of the applicants, all of whom had been detained under Section 12 of the 1984 Act. The Court held that even the shortest of the four periods of detention concerned, namely four days and six hours, fell outside the constraints as to time permitted by the first part of Article 5(3). In addition, the Court held that there had been a violation of Article 5(5) in the case of each applicant.

Following this judgment, the Secretary of State for the Home Department informed Parliament on 6 December 1988 that, against the background of the terrorist campaign, and the over-riding need to bring terrorists to justice, the Government did not believe that the maximum period of detention should be reduced. He informed Parliament that the Government were examining the matter with a view to responding to the judgment. On 22 December 1988, the Secretary of State further informed Parliament that it remained the Government's wish, if it could be achieved, to find a judicial process under which extended detention might be reviewed and where appropriate authorised by a judge or other judicial officer. But a further period of reflection and consultation was necessary before the Government could bring forward a firm and final view.

Since the judgment of 29 November 1988 as well as previously, the Government have found it necessary to continue to exercise, in relation to terrorism connected with the affairs of Northern Ireland, the powers described above enabling further detention without charge for periods of up to 5 days, on the authority of the Secretary of State, to the extent strictly required by the exigencies of the situation to enable necessary enquiries and investigations properly to be completed in order to decide whether criminal proceedings should be instituted. To the extent that the exercise of these powers may be inconsistent with the obligations imposed by the Convention the Government has availed itself of the right of derogation conferred by Article 15(1) of the Convention and will continue to do so until further notice.

Dated 23 December 1988.

The 1989 notification

The United Kingdom Permanent Representative to the Council of Europe presents his compliments to the Secretary General of the Council, and has the honour to convey the following information.

In his communication to the Secretary General of 23 December 1988, reference was made to the introduction and exercise of certain powers under section 12 of the Prevention of Terrorism (Temporary Provisions) Act 1984, Article 9 of the Prevention of Terrorism (Supplemental Temporary Provisions) Order 1984 and Article 10 of the Prevention of Terrorism (Supplemental Temporary Provisions) (Northern Ireland) Order 1984.

These provisions have been replaced by section 14 of and paragraph 6 of Schedule 5 to the Prevention of Terrorism (Temporary Provisions) Act 1989, which make comparable provision. They came into force on 22 March 1989. A copy of these provisions is enclosed.

The United Kingdom Permanent Representative avails himself of this opportunity to renew to the Secretary General the assurance of his highest consideration.

23 March 1989.

Schedule 3

Derogation and Reservation

Part 2—Reservation

At the time of signing the present (First) Protocol, I declare that, in view of certain provisions of the Education Acts in the United Kingdom, the principle affirmed in the second sentence of Article 2 is accepted by the United Kingdom only so far as it is compatible with the provision of efficient instruction and training, and the avoidance of unreasonable public expenditure.

Dated 20 March 1952

Made by the United Kingdom Permanent Representative to the Council of Europe.

Schedule 4

Judicial Pensions

Duty to make orders about pensions

1.— (1) The appropriate Minister must by order make provision with respect to pensions payable to or in respect of any holder of a judicial office who serves as an ECHR judge.

(2) A pensions order must include such provision as the Minister making it considers is necessary to secure that—

(a) an ECHR judge who was, immediately before his appointment as an ECHR judge, a member of a judicial pension scheme is entitled to remain as a member of that scheme;

(b) the terms on which he remains a member of the scheme are those which would have been applicable had he not been appointed as an ECHR judge; and

(c) entitlement to benefits payable in accordance with the scheme continues to be determined as if, while serving as an ECHR judge, his salary was that which would (but for section 18(4)) have been payable to him in respect of his continuing service as the holder of his judicial office.

Contributions

2. A pensions order may, in particular, make provision—

(a) for any contributions which are payable by a person who remains a member of a scheme as a result of the order, and which would otherwise be payable by deduction from his salary, to be made otherwise than by deduction from his salary as an ECHR judge; and

(b) for such contributions to be collected in such manner as may be determined by the administrators of the scheme.

Amendments of other enactments

3. A pensions order may amend any provision of, or made under, a pensions Act in such manner and to such extent as the Minister making the order considers necessary or expedient to ensure the proper administration of any scheme to which it relates.

Definitions

4. In this Schedule—

"appropriate Minister" means—

(a) in relation to any judicial office whose jurisdiction is exercisable exclusively in relation to Scotland, the Secretary of State; and

(b) otherwise, the Lord Chancellor;

"ECHR judge" means the holder of a judicial office who is serving as a judge of the Court;

"judicial pension scheme" means a scheme established by and in accordance with a pensions Act;

"pensions Act" means—

(a) the County Courts Act Northern Ireland) 1959;

(b) the Sheriffs' Pensions (Scotland) Act 1961;

(c) the Judicial Pensions Act 1981; or

(d) the Judicial Pensions and Retirement Act 1993; and

"pensions order" means an order made under paragraph 1.

64.8 Form N461

Judicial Review
Claim Form

Notes for guidance are available which explain how to complete the judicial review claim form. Please read them carefully before you complete the form.

For Court use only	
Administrative Court Reference No.	
Date filed	

In the High Court of Justice
Administrative Court

Seal

SECTION 1 Details of the claimant(s) and defendant(s)

Claimant(s) name and address(es)

name

address

Telephone no.

Fax no.

E-mail address

Claimant's or claimant's solicitors' address to which documents should be sent.

name

address

Telephone no.

Fax no.

E-mail address

Claimant's Counsel's details

name

address

Telephone no.

Fax no.

E-mail address

1st Defendant

name

Defendant's or (where known) Defendant's solicitors' address to which documents should be sent.

name

address

Telephone no.

Fax no.

E-mail address

2nd Defendant

name

Defendant's or (where known) Defendant's solicitors' address to which documents should be sent.

name

address

Telephone no.

Fax no.

E-mail address

SECTION 2 Details of other interested parties

Include name and address and, if appropriate, details of DX, telephone or fax numbers and e-mail

name

address

Telephone no.

Fax no.

E-mail address

name

address

Telephone no.

Fax no.

E-mail address

SECTION 3 Details of the decision to be judicially reviewed

Decision:

Date of decision:

Name and address of the court, tribunal, person or body who made the decision to be reviewed.

name

address

SECTION 4 Permission to proceed with a claim for judicial review

I am seeking permission to proceed with my claim for Judicial Review.

Is this application being made under the terms of Section 18 Practice Direction 54 (Challenging removal)? ☐Yes ☐No

Are you making any other applications? If Yes, complete Section 7. ☐Yes ☐No

Is the claimant in receipt of a Community Legal Service Fund (CLSF) certificate? ☐Yes ☐No

Are you claiming exceptional urgency, or do you need this application determined within a certain time scale? If Yes, complete Form N463 and file this with your application. ☐Yes ☐No

Have you complied with the pre-action protocol? If No, give reasons for non-compliance in the space below. ☐Yes ☐No

Does the claim include any issues arising from the Human Rights Act 1998?
If Yes, state the articles which you contend have been breached in the space below.   ☐ Yes   ☐ No

SECTION 5 Detailed statement of grounds

☐ set out below   ☐ attached

SECTION 6 Details of remedy (including any interim remedy) being sought

SECTION 7 Other applications

I wish to make an application for:-

64.8 N461

SECTION 8 Statement of facts relied on

Statement of Truth

I believe (The claimant believes) that the facts stated in this claim form are true.

Full name _____

Name of claimant's solicitor's firm _____

Signed _____ Position or office held _____

    Claimant ('s solicitor)   (if signing on behalf of firm or company)

694

SECTION 9 Supporting documents

If you do not have a document that you intend to use to support your claim, identify it, give the date when you expect it to be available and give reasons why it is not currently available in the box below.

Please tick the papers you are filing with this claim form and any you will be filing later.

☐ Statement of grounds   ☐ included   ☐ attached

☐ Statement of the facts relied on   ☐ included   ☐ attached

☐ Application to extend the time limit for filing the claim form   ☐ included   ☐ attached

☐ Application for directions   ☐ included   ☐ attached

☐ Any written evidence in support of the claim or
application to extend time

☐ Where the claim for judicial review relates to a decision of
a court or tribunal, an approved copy of the reasons for
reaching that decision

☐ Copies of any documents on which the claimant
proposes to rely

☐ A copy of the legal aid or CSLF certificate *(if legally represented)*

☐ Copies of any relevant statutory material

☐ A list of essential documents for advance reading by
the court *(with page references to the passages relied upon)*

If Section 18 Practice Direction 54 applies, please tick the relevant box(es) below to indicate which papers you are filing with this claim form:

☐ a copy of the removal directions and the decision to which   ☐ included   ☐ attached
the application relates

☐ a copy of the documents served with the removal directions
including any documents which contains the Immigration and   ☐ included   ☐ attached
Nationality Directorate's factual summary of the case

☐ a detailed statement of the grounds   ☐ included   ☐ attached

Reasons why you have not supplied a document and date when you expect it to be available:-

Signed _____ Claimant ('s Solicitor)_____

64.9 Form N462

Judicial Review
Acknowledgment of Service

Name and address of person to be served

┌name─────────────────────────────────┐
│   │
└──────────────────────────────────────┘

┌address──────────────────────────────┐
│   │
│   │
│   │
└──────────────────────────────────────┘

In the High Court of Justice Administrative Court	
Claim No.	
Claimant(s) *(including ref.)*	
Defendant(s)	
Interested Parties	

SECTION A

Tick the appropriate box

1. I intend to contest all of the claim ☐

2. I intend to contest part of the claim ☐

　　　} complete sections B, C, D and E

3. I do not intend to contest the claim ☐　complete section E

4. The defendant (interested party) is a court or tribunal and **intends** to make a submission. ☐　complete sections B, C and E

5. The defendant (interested party) is a court or tribunal and **does not intend** to make a submission. ☐　complete sections B and E

Note: If the application seeks to judicially review the decision of a court or tribunal, the court or tribunal need only provide the Administrative Court with as much evidence as it can about the decision to help the Administrative Court perform its judicial function.

SECTION B

Insert the name and address of any person you consider should be added as an interested party.

┌name─────────────────┐　┌name─────────────────┐
│   │　│   │
└─────────────────────┘　└─────────────────────┘

┌address──────────────┐　┌address──────────────┐
│   │　│   │
│   │　│   │
│   │　│   │
└─────────────────────┘　└─────────────────────┘

┌Telephone no.──┐ ┌Fax no.──┐　┌Telephone no.──┐ ┌Fax no.──┐
└───────────────┘ └─────────┘　└───────────────┘ └─────────┘

┌E-mail address───────┐　┌E-mail address───────┐
│   │　│   │
└─────────────────────┘　└─────────────────────┘

SECTION C

Summary of grounds for contesting the claim. If you are contesting only part of the claim, set out which part before you give your grounds for contesting it. If you are a court or tribunal filing a submission, please indicate that this is the case.

SECTION D

Give details of any directions you will be asking the court to make, or tick the box to indicate that a separate application notice is attached.

SECTION E

*delete as appropriate

*(I believe)(The defendant believes) that the facts stated in this form are true.

*I am duly authorised by the defendant to sign this statement.

(if signing on behalf of firm or company, court or tribunal)

Position or office held

(To be signed by you or by your solicitor or litigation friend)

Signed

Date

Give an address to which notices about this case can be sent to you

If you have instructed counsel, please give their name address and contact details below.

name

address

Telephone no.

Fax no.

E-mail address

name

address

Telephone no.

Fax no.

E-mail address

Completed forms, together with a copy, should be lodged with the Administrative Court Office, Room C315, Royal Courts of Justice, Strand, London, WC2A 2LL, within 21 days of service of the claim upon you, and further copies should be served on the Claimant(s), any other Defendant(s) and any interested parties within 7 days of lodgement with the Court.

64.10 Form N463

Judicial Review
Application for urgent consideration

This form must be completed by the Claimant or the Claimant's advocate if exceptional urgency is being claimed and the application needs to be determined within a certain time scale.

The claimant, or the claimant's solicitors must serve this form on the defendant(s) and any interested parties with the N461 Judicial review claim form.

To the Defendant(s) and Interested party(ies) Representations as to the urgency of the claim may be made by defendants or interested parties to the Administrative Court Office by fax - 020 7947 6802

In the High Court of Justice Administrative Court	
Claim No.	
Claimant(s) *(including ref.)*	
Defendant(s)	
Interested Parties	

SECTION 1 Reasons for urgency

SECTION 2 Proposed timetable *(tick the boxes and complete the following statements that apply)*

☐ a) The application for interim relief should be considered within _____ hours/days

☐ b) The N461 application for permission should be considered within _____ hours/days

☐ c) Abridgement of time is sought for the lodging of acknowledgments of service

☐ d) If permission for judicial review is granted, a substantive hearing is sought by _____ (date)

SECTION 3 Interim relief *(state what interim relief is sought and why in the box below)*

A draft order must be attached.

SECTION 4 Service

A copy of this form of application was served on the defendant(s) and interested parties as follows:

Defendant

☐ by fax machine to   time sent
Fax no.   time

☐ by handing it to or leaving it with
name

☐ by e-mail to
e-mail address

Date served
Date

Interested party

☐ by fax machine to   time sent
Fax no.   time

☐ by handing it to or leaving it with
name

☐ by e-mail to
e-mail address

Date served
Date

Name of claimant's advocate
name

Claimant (claimant's advocate)
Signed

64.11 LIST OF ARTICLES

Articles on Judicial Review by Michael Fordham:

Practitioner Standards [1996] JR 1
Applicant's Pre-Leave Checklist [1996] JR 16
Respondent's Pre-Leave Checklist [1996] JR 76
What is "Anxious Scrutiny"? [1996] JR 81
Wednesbury Successes of 1995 [1996] JR 115
Interim Relief and the Cross-Undertaking [1997] JR 136
Delay: The "Good Reason" at the Substantive Hearing [1997] JR 208
Reasons: The Third Dimension [1998] JR 158
Judicial Review Under the CPR: A Five-Minute Guide [1999] JR 93
Fresh Evidence in Judicial Review [2000] JR 18
Anxious Scrutiny, the Principle of Legality and the HRA+ [2000] JR 40
Top 20 Cases of 1999 [2000] JR 134
Convention Case-Law: Judicial Warnings [2000] JR 139
Legitimate Expectation I: Domestic Principles [2000] JR 188
Human Rights Act Escapology [2000] JR 262
Monetary Claims Against Public Authorities Part 1++ [2001] JR 44
Monetary Claims Against Public Authorities Part 2++ [2001] JR 109
Top 20 Cases of 2000 [2001] JR 121
The Human Rights Act So Far: 10 Basic Lessons [2001] JR 205
Legitimate Expectation II: Comparison and Prediction [2001] JR 262
The New Procedure: Is It Working? [2002] JR 14
Top 20 Cases of 2001 [2002] JR 62
Common Law Proportionality [2002] JR 110
Top 20 Cases of 2002 [2003] JR 59
Administrative Law: A Practitioner's Long-Range Forecast [2003] JR 67
Reparation for Maladministration: Public Law's Final Frontier [2003] JR 104
Judicial Review Cheat Sheet [2003] JR 131
Common Law Illegality of Ousting Judicial Review [2004] JR 86
The Judge At Your Shoulder: New Principles of Governmental Accountability [2004] JR 122
Top 20 Cases of 2003 [2004] JR 167
Procedural Pearls [2005] JR 90
How To Make the Administrative Court a Better Place: Some Procedural Suggestions [2006] JR 98
Permission Principles [2006] JR 176
Top 20 Cases of 2004 [2006] JR 266
Top 20 Cases of 2005 [2006] JR 270
Advising in Consultation [2007] JR 187
Disclosure Principles [2007] JR 195
Arguability Principles [2007] JR 219
Wednesbury [2007] JR 266
Judicial Review: The Future [2008] JR 66
Top 20 Cases of 2006 [2008] JR 196
Top 20 Cases of 2007 [2008] JR 200

+   with Thomas de la Mare
++ with Gemma White

TABLE OF CASES

703

775

TABLE OF LEGISLATION

TABLE OF STATUTORY INSTRUMENTS

INDEX